M000106185

John Willis and Ben Hodges

THEATRE WORLD®

Volume 64 / 2007-2008

APPLAUSE
THEATRE AND CINEMA BOOKS
An Imprint of Hal Leonard Corporation
New York

THEATRE WORLD

Volume 64

Published in 2008 by Applause Theatre & Cinema Books
An Imprint of Hal Leonard Corporation
7777 West Bluemound Road
Milwaukee, WI 53213

Trade Book Division Editorial Offices
19 West 21st Street, New York, NY 10010

Printed in the United States of America
Book design by Tony Meisel

ISBN 978–1–55783–742–4
ISSN 1088–4564

www.applausepub.com

Standing, left to right: *Bill Willis, Angie Powell, Sherry Hodges, Al Hodges, Sarah Elizabeth Willis*; seated, left to right: *Ben Hodges, Drew Powell*

Dedication

For my father and stepmother, Robert A. "Al" Hodges Jr. and Sherry Hodges, aunt Sarah Elizabeth Hodges Willis and uncle Bill Willis, dear cousins Angie and Drew Powell, and in memory of my beloved great-grandparents, Sarah Elizabeth "Mama Sara" Greene Hodges Ashman and Chester Moralee "Chet" Ashman, and grandparents, Dorothy Isely Hodges and Robert Alfred "Bobby" Hodges Sr.

Without them in my life, it would have been incomplete–they sacrificed much and showed me generosity, support, and grace which has served to help steer me throughout my entire life. It is my every hope that their lives have been enriched by my presence as much as mine has been by theirs.

Ben Hodges, New York, NY

Left to right: *Mama Sara Ashman, Ben Hodges, Chet Ashman*

Bobby Hodges, Dorothy Hodges

PAST EDITOR: Daniel Blum (1945-1963)

EDITOR EMERITUS: John Willis (1964-present)

EDITOR IN CHIEF: Ben Hodges (1998-present)

ASSOCIATE EDITORS: Scott Denny (2005-present)
Allison Graham (2006-present)

ACKNOWLEDGMENTS:
Staff Photographers: Henry Grossman, Michael Riordan, Laura Viade, Michael Viade, Jack Williams; **Applause Books Staff:** Publisher, Michael Messina

SPECIAL THANKS:
Jed Bernstein and Above the Title Productions; Howard Sherman and the American Theatre Wing; Epitacio Arganza; Rommel "Raj" Autencio, Seth Barrish, Lee Brock, Eric Paeper, and The Barrow Group Theater Company/The Barrow Group School; Fred Barton; Wayne Besen; Nicole Boyd; Ben Feldman, Amy Luce, and Beigelman, Feldman, and Associates PC; Boyd; Helen Guditis and the Broadway Theater Museum; Fred Cantor; Michael Che; Jason Cicci, Monday Morning Productions, and Summer Stage New York; Christopher Cohen; The Commercial Theater Institute; Sue Cosson, Susan Cosson, Robert Dean Davis; Carol and Nick Dawson; Bob and Brenda Denny; Carmen Diaz; Diane Dixon; Craig Dudley; Emily Feldman; David Fritz; Stanley Morton Ackert III and Gersen, Blakeman, and Ackert; Yvonne Ghareeb; the estates of the late Charles J. Grant Jr. and Zan Van Antwerp; Christine and David Grimsby; Brad Hampton; Laura and Tommy Hanson; Esther Harriot; Richard M. Henderson Jr. and Jennifer Henderson; Richard M. Henderson Sr. and Patricia Lynn Henderson; Al and Sherry Hodges; Leonard Jacobs; Gretchen, Aaron, Eli, and Max Kerr; Jane, Lynn, and Kris Kircher; Tim Deak, Kim Spanjol, and The Learning Theatre, Inc.; David Lowry; Cecelia McCarton and the staff of the McCarton Center/The McCarton School; Barry Monush and *Screen World*; Virginia Moraweck; Lucy Nathanson; Jason Bowcutt, Shay Gines, Nick Micozzi, and the staff and respective voting committees of the New York Innovative Theatre Awards; Barbara O'Malley and John Ford; Petie Dodrill, Craig Johnson, Rob Johnson, Dennis Romer, Katie Robbins, Dean Jo Ann VanSant, Ed Vaughan, the late Dr. Charles O. Dodrill and the staff of Otterbein College and Otterbein College Department of Theatre and Dance; PJ Owen; Kathie Packer; Hugo Uys and the staff of Paris Commune and Shag; David Plank; Angie and Drew Powell; Carolyn, David, Glenna and Jonas Rapp; Robert Rems; Ric Wanetik, David Hagans, Steven Gelston, Kim Jackson, and Mollie Levin at Ricochet, LLC; Jeutan Dobbs, Sydney Davalos, Todd Haimes, and Roundabout Theatre Company; Kate Rushing; Bill Schaap; Jason Baruch, Mark Sendroff, and Sendroff LLP; William Jack Sibley, Hannah Richman Slosberg, and Jason Slosberg; Susan Stoller; Jamie deRoy, Patricia Elliott, Peter Filichia, Leigh Giroux, Barry Keating, Tom Lynch, Kati Meister, Erin Oestreich, Matthew Murray, and the board of The Theatre World Awards, Inc; Bob Ost and Theater Resources Unlimited; Harry Haun, Howard Kissel, Frank Scheck, Michael Sommers, Doug Watt, Linda Winer, and the voting committee of The Theatre World Awards, Inc; Theatre Communications Group; Theatre Library Association; Renée Isely Tobin and Bob, Kate, Eric, Laura, Anna, Foster, and Lucky Tobin; Wilson Valentin; Jack Williams, Barbara Dewey, and the staff of the University of Tennessee at Knoxville; Sarah and Bill Willis, Shane and Bill Wolters.

Contents

Michael Cerveris and the Cast of Lincoln Center Theater's Cymbeline. *Opened at the Vivian Beaumont Theater December 2, 2007 (photo by Paul Kolnik)*

Kevin Anderson and S. Epatha Merkerson in Manhattan Theatre Club's Come Back, Little Sheba. *Opened at the Biltmore Theatre January 24, 2008 (photo by Joan Marcus)*

Raúl Esparza, Michael McKean and Ian McShane in The Homecoming. *Opened at the Cort Theatre December 16, 2007 (photo by Scott Landis)*

Robin De Jesus, Karen Olivo, and Lin-Manuel Miranda in In the Heights. *Opened at the Richard Rodgers Theatre March 9, 2008 (photo by Joan Marcus)*

Laura Benanti in Gypsy. *Opened at the St. James Theatre March 27, 2008 (photo by Paul Kolnik)*

Kelli O'Hara in Lincoln Center Theater's South Pacific. *Opened at the Vivian Beaumont Theater April 3, 2008 (photo by Joan Marcus)*

Broadway

June 1, 2007–May 31, 2008

Sierra Boggess in The Little Mermaid. *Opened at the Lunt-Fontanne Theatre January 10, 2008 (photo by Joan Marcus)*

Jefferson Mays and Claire Danes in the Roundabout Theatre Company's Pygmalion. *Opened at the American Airlines Theatre October 18, 2007 (photo by Joan Marcus)*

Laura Osnes, Max Crumm, and the Cast of Grease. *Opened at the Brooks Atkinson Theatre August 19, 2007 (photo by Joan Marcus)*

Li Jun Li and Loretta Ables Sayre in Lincoln Center's South Pacific. *Opened at the Vivian Beaumont Theater April 3, 2008 (photo by Paul Kolnik)*

Kevin Kline and cast in Cyrano de Bergerac. *Opened at the Richard Rodgers Theatre November 1, 2007 (photo by Carol Rosegg)*

Sinead Cusack in Rock 'n' Roll. *Opened at the Bernard B. Jacobs Theatre November 4, 2007 (photo by Joan Marcus)*

Sutton Foster, Christopher Fitzgerald and Roger Bart in Young Frankenstein. *Opened at the Hilton Theatre November 8, 2007 (photo by Paul Kolnik)*

The Cast of Dr. Seuss' How The Grinch Stole Christmas. *Opened at the St. James Theatre November 9, 2007 (photo by Paul Kolnick)*

Jimmi Simpson and Hank Azaria in The Farnsworth Invention. *Opened at the Music Box Theatre December 3, 2007 (photo by Joan Marcus)*

Bottom row, from left: *Anika Larsen, Kenita Miller;* Top row, from left: *Mary Testa, Curtis Holbrook, Kerry Butler, Andre Ward, and Jackie Hoffman in* Xanadu. *Opened at the Helen Hayes Theatre July 10, 2007 (photo by Paul Kolnick)*

The Cast of August: Osage County. *Opened at the Imperial Theatre December 4, 2007; transferred to the Music Box Theatre April 29, 2008 (photo by Joan Marcus)*

Stew in Passing Strange. *Opened at the Belasco Theatre February 28, 2008 (photo by Carol Rosegg)*

Jim Norton, Sean Mahon, Conleth Hill, David Morse and Ciarán Hinds in The Seafarer. *Opened at the Booth Theatre December 6, 2007 (photo by Joan Marcus)*

Boyd Gaines and Patti LuPone in Gypsy. *Opened at the St. James Theatre March 27, 2008 (photo by Paul Kolnik)*

John McMartin and Norbert Leo Butz in Is He Dead? *Opened at the Lyceum Theatre December 9, 2007 (photo by Joan Marcus)*

Nathan Lane and Dylan Baker in November*. Opened at the Barrymore Theatre January 17, 2008 (photo by Scvott Landis)*

Lin-Manuel Miranda and Cast in In The Heights*. Opened at the Richard Rodgers Theatre March 9, 2008 (photo by Joan Marcus)*

Alison Horowitz, Jessica Molaskey, Drew McVety, Brynn O'Malley, Jessica Grove, Daniel Evans, Michael Cumpsty, and Jenna Russell in the Roundabout Theatre Company's Sunday in the Park With George*. Opened at Studio 54 February 21, 2008 (photo by Joan Marcus)*

Cliff Saunders and Charles Edwards in The Roundabout Theatre Company's The 39 Steps. *Opened at the American Airlines Theatre January 15, 2008; transferred to the Cort Theatre and reopened May 8, 2008 (photo by Joan Marcus)*

Laurence Fishburne in Thurgood. *Opened at the Booth Theatre April 30, 2008 (photo by Carol Rosegg)*

Phylicia Rashad and James Earl Jones in Cat on a Hot Tin Roof. *Opened at the Broadhurst Theatre March 6, 2008 (photo by Joan Marcus)*

The Cast of Cry-Baby. *Opened at the Marquis Theatre April 24, 2008 (photo by Joan Marcus)*

Mark Rylance in Boeing-Boeing. *Opened at the Longacre Theatre May 4, 2008 (photo by Joan Marcus)*

Elizabeth Marvel and Marisa Tomei in Manhattan Theatre Club's Top Girls. *Opened at the Biltmore Theatre May 7, 2008 (photo by Joan Marcus)*

Ben Daniels and Laura Linney in the Roundabout Theatre Company's Les Liaisons Dangereuses. *Opened at the American Airlines Theatre May 1, 2008 (photo by Joan Marcus)*

OLD ACQUAINTANCE

American Airlines Theatre; First preview: June 1, 2007; Opening Night: June 28, 2007; Closed August 19, 2007; 31 previews, 61 performances

Written by John Van Druten; Produced by the Roundabout Theatre Company (Todd Haimes, Artistic Director; Harold Wolpert, Managing Director; Julia C. Levy, Executive Director); Director, Michael Wilson; Set, Alexander Dodge; Costumes, David C. Woolard; Lighting, Rui Rita; Original Music/Sound, John Gromada; Hair/Wigs, Paul Huntley; Dialect Coach, Deborah Hecht; Fight Coordinator, Mark Olsen; PSM, Roy Harris; Casting, Jim Carnahan, Mele Nagler; Technical Supervisor, Steve Beers; General Manager, Sydney Beers; Founding Director, Gene Feist; Associate Artistic Director, Scott Ellis; Marketing, David B. Steffen; Development, Jeffory Lawson; Finance, Susan Neiman; Sales, Jim Seggelink; Company Manager, Nichole Jennino; Stage Manager, Denise Yaney; Assistant Directors, Max Williams, Ben West; Dramaturg, Ben West; Associate Set Design, Kevin Judge; Assistant Design: Robin Vest (set), Daniel Baker, David Stephen Baker (sound), Stephen Boulmetis (lighting), Daniele Hollywood (costumes); Assistants: Kenichi Takehashi, Andrew Layton (set designer), Jake DeGroot (lighting designer), Angela Harner (costume designer), Elisa Kuhar (technical supervisor); Fight Coordinator, Mark Olsen; Production Properties, Kathy Fabian; Production: Glenn Merwede (carpenter), Brian Maiuri (electrician), Andrew Forste (running props), Dann Wojnar (sound engineer), Chris Mattingly (flyman), Nelson Vaughn (deck props), Brian Shumway, Jill Anania (deck carpenters), Barb Bartel, Jeff Rowland (deck electricians), Carrie Hash, Carrie Mossman (assistant props), Susan J. Fallon (wardrobe supervisor), Manuela LaPorte (hair/wig supervisor), Victoria Grecki, Julie Hilimire (dressers); Advertising, The Eliran Murphy Group; Press, Boneau/Bryan-Brown: Adrian Bryan-Brown, Matt Polk, Jessica Johnson, Amy Kass

Harriet Harris and Margaret Colin (photos by Joan Marcus)

CAST Katherine Markham **Margaret Colin;** Mildred Watson Drake **Harriet Harris;** Preston Drake **Stephen Bogardus;** Susan **Cynthia Darlow;** Deirdre Drake **Diane Davis;** Karina **Gordana Rashovich;** Rudd Kendall **Corey Stoll**

UNDERSTUDIES Tony Carlin (Preston Drake, Rudd Kendall), Cynthia Darlow (Mildred Watson Drake), Virginia Kull (Deirdre Drake, Karina, Susan), Gordana Rashovich (Katherine Markham)

SETTING New York City, November–December, 1940; Revival of the play presented in two acts. Originally produced in 1940 at the Morosco Theatre, starring Jane Cowl and Peggy Wood and adapted for the screen in 1943 starring Bette Davis and Miriam Hopkins.

Corey Stoll and Diane Davis

SYNOPSIS *Old Acquaintance* is a drawing-room comedy about two childhood friends who have grown into very different adults. Though they are both successful authors, independent Katharine 'Kit' Markham carries on an affair with a younger man while divorcee Mildred 'Millie' Drake refuses to loosen the apron-strings on her teenage daughter, Deidre.

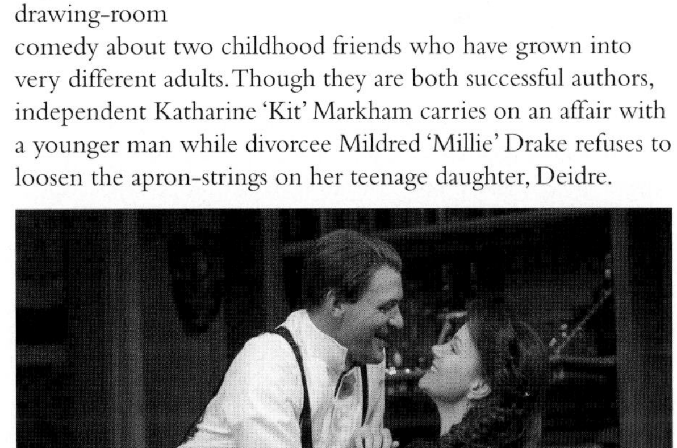

Corey Stoll and Margaret Colin

XANADU

Helen Hayes Theatre; First Preview: May 23, 2007; Opening Night: July 10, 2007; 49 previews, 375 performances as of May 31, 2008

Book by Douglas Carter Beane, music and lyrics by Jeff Lynne & John Farrar, based on the Universal Pictures film screenplay by Richard Danus & Marc Rubel; Produced by Robert Ahrens, Dan Vickery, Sara Murchison/Dale Smith & Tara Smith/B. Swibel; Director, Christopher Ashley; Choreography, Dan Knechtges; Music Direction and Arrangements, Eric Stern; Sets, David Gallo; Lighting, Howell Binkley; Costumes, David Zinn; Sound, T. Richard Fitzgerald, Carl Casella; Projections, Zachary Borovay; Wigs/Hair, Charles LaPointe; Marketing, HHC Marketing; Technical Supervisor, Juniper Street Productions; Music Coordinator, John Miller; Casting, Cindy Tolan; Associate Producers, Allicat Productions, Marc Rubel & Cari Smulyan; PSM, Arturo E. Porazzi; General Manager, Laura Heller; Company Manager, Jolie Gabler; Stage Manager, John M. Atherlay; ASM, Peter Samuel; Associate to Mr. Ahrens, Eric Sanders; Associate Director, Dana Iris Harrel; Associate Choreographer, DJ Gray; Dance Captain, Marty Thomas; Makeup, John Carter; Associate Design: Frank McCullough (set), Ryan O'Gara (lighting), Amelia Dombrowski, Sarah Laux (costumes), Austin Switser (projections); Casting Associate, Adam Caldwell; Assistant Choreographer, Allison Bibicoff; Skating Coach/Dance Assistant, David Tankersley; Skate Trainer/Supplier, Lezly Ziering; Design Studio Assistant, Mary Hamrick; Assistant Lighting, Bradley King; Production: Fred Gallo (carpenter), Joseph Beck (electrician), Peter Sarafin (props supervisor), Doug Purcell (head carpenter), Joseph Maher, Ann Cavanaugh (flymen), Joseph Beck (head electrician), Joseph Redmond (spot), Hillary Knox (automated lights programmer), Scott Silvian (sound engineer), Emile LaFarque (deck sound), Roger Keller (head props), Sabado Lam (wardrobe supervisor), Nicholas Lawson Carbonaro, Cherie Cunningham (assistant wardrobe), Kerry Whigham, Elise Hanley (assistants); Music Copying, Kaye-Houston Music; Synthesizer Programmer, Karl Mansfield; Mr. Miller's Assistant, Charles Butler; Advertising, Eliran Murphy Group; Press, Blue Current Public Relations, Pete Sanders, Andrew Snyder; Cast recording: PS Classics 858

CAST Sonny **Cheyenne Jackson+;** Thalia/Siren/Young Danny/80's Singer/Cyclops **Curtis Holbrook*1;** Euterpe/Siren/40's Singer/Thetis **Anika Larsen*2;** Erato/Siren/40's Singer/Eros/Hera **Kenita Miller*3;** Melpomene/Medusa **Mary Testa;** Calliope/Aphrodite **Jackie Hoffman;** Terpsicore/Siren/80's Singer/Hermes/Centaur **André Ward;** Clio/Kira **Kerry Butler;** Danny Maguire/Zeus **Tony Roberts;** Featured Skater **Marty Thomas+;** Swings **Patti Murin*3, Marty Thomas, Ryan Watkinson, Ken Nelson, Kate Loprest**

Kerry Butler and Cheyenne Jackson (photos by Paul Kolnik)

Kerry Butler and Tony Roberts

UNDERSTUDIES Annie Golden (Calliope/Aphrodite, Melpomene/Medusa), Curtis Holbrook*[1] (Sonny), Anika Larsen*[2] (Calliope/Aphrodite, Clio/Kira, Melpomene/Medusa), Kenita R. Miller*[3] (Clio/Kira), Patti Murin*[4] (Clio/Kira), Peter Samuel*[5] (Danny Maguire, Zeus), Andre Ward (Calliope/Aphrodite, Melpomene/Medusa, Sonny)

Mary Testa and Jackie Hoffman

BAND Eric Stern (Music Director/synthesizers), Karl Mansfield (Associate Music Director/synthesizers), Chris Biesterfeldt (guitar), Eric Halvorson (drums)

MUSICAL NUMBERS I'm Alive, Magic, Evil Woman, Suddenly, Whenever You're Away From Me, Dancin', Strange Magic, All Over the World, Don't Walk Away, Fool, The Fall, Suspended in Time, Have You Never Been Mellow?, Xanadu

2007–2008 AWARDS Drama Desk: Outstanding Book of a Musical; Outer Critics Circle: Outstanding Broadway Musical (tie)

Mary Testa, Jackie Hoffman (center), Anika Larsen, Andre Ward, Curtis Holbrook, Kenita Miller

Mary Testa, Kerry Butler, Jackie Hoffman (standing), Curtis Holbrook, Anika Larsen, Kenita Miller and Andre Ward (kneeling)

Cheyenne Jackson and Kerry Butler

SETTING Time: 1980. Place: Los Angeles and Mount Olympus. World premiere of a new musical presented without intermission.

SYNOPSIS *Xanadu*, based on the 1980 film, tells the story of one of the nine muses of ancient Greece who comes to earth to inspire the greatest of artistic achievements – a roller disco. Along the way she falls in love, bumps into an old acquaintance and for the first time, she feels the desire to create herself.

+Cheyenne Jackson replaced James Carpinello during previews due to injury. Carpinello was unable to return to the production. Ryan Watkinson replaced Marty Thomas temporarily due to injury.

*Succeeded by: 1. Kyle Dean Massey 2. Patti Murin 3. Shannon Antalan, Kenita Miller 4. Kate Loprest 5. Stuart Morland, Peter Samuel

GREASE

Brooks Atkinson Theatre; First Preview: July 24, 2007; Opening Night: August 19, 2007; 31 previews, 305 performances as of May 31, 2008

Book, music and lyrics by Jim Jacobs and Warren Casey; additional songs by Barry Gibb, John Farrar, Louis St. Louis, Scott Simon; Produced by Paul Nicholas and David Ian, Nederlander Presentations Inc., Terry Allen Kramer, by special arrangement with Robert Stigwood; Director/Choreographer, Kathleen Marshall; Music Director, Kimberly Grigsby; Sets, Derek McLane; Costumes, Martin Pakledinaz; Lighting, Kenneth Posner, Sound, Brian Ronan; Wigs/Hair, Paul Huntley; Casting, Jay Binder, Jack Bowdan/Megan Larche; Associate Director, Marc Bruni; Associate Choreographer, Joyce Chittick; Orchestrations, Christopher Jahnke; Music Coordinator, Howard Jones; Production Supervisors, Arthur Siccardi, Patrick Sullivan; PSM, David John O'Brien; Executive Producer, Max Finbow; General Management, Charlotte Wilcox Company; Company Manager, James Lawson; ACM, Megan Trice; Stage Manager, Beverly Jenkins; ASM, Stephen R. Gruse; Dance Captain, Amber Stone; Assistant to Director, Jenny Hogan; Makeup, Joe Dulude II; Associate Design: Ted LeFevre (set), Matthew Pachtman (costumes), Aaron Spivey (lighting), Giovanna Calabretta (wigs and hair); Assistant Design: Anne Allen Goelz, Shoko Kambara (sets); Erica Hemminger, Court Watson (assistants to Mr. McLane), Sarah Sophia Turner (costumes), Tescia Seufferlein (assistant to Mr. Pakledinaz), Kathleen Dobbins (lighting), Michael Creason (sound); Moving Lights, David Arch; Production: James Fedigan, Randall Zaibek (electricians), Gerard Griffin (carpenter), Brian Hutchinson (flyman), Benjamin Horrigan (automation carpenter), Brian GF McGarity (head electrician), Michael Farfalla (sound), TJ McEvoy (deck sound), Christopher Pantuso (props), Lisa Tucci (wardrobe supervisor), John "Jack" Curtin (hair supervisor), Karen L. Eifert (assistant wardrobe); Synthesizer Programmer, Randy Cohen; Advertising, Serino Coyne; Press, Barlow-Hartman, Ryan Ratelle; Cast recording: Masterworks Broadway 88697-16398-2

Lindsay Mendez, Jenny Powers, Robyn Hurder, Kirsten Wyatt (photos by Joan Marcus)

Ryan Patrick Binder and Company

Laura Osnes and Max Crumm

CAST Danny Zuko **Max Crumm;** Sandy Dumbrowski **Laura Osnes;** Kenickie **Matthew Saldívar;** Sonny LaTierri **José Restrepo;** Roger **Daniel Everidge*;** Doody **Ryan Patrick Binder;** Betty Rizzo **Jenny Powers;** Marty **Robyn Hurder;** Jan **Lindsay Mendez;** Frenchy **Kirsten Wyatt;** Patty Simcox **Allison Fischer;** Eugene Florczyk **Jamison Scott;** Miss Lynch **Susan Blommaert;** Vince Fontaine **Jeb Brown;** Cha-Cha DiGregorio **Natalie Hill;** Teen Angel **Stephen R. Buntrock;** Ensemble **Josh Franklin, Cody Green, Natalie Hill, Emily Padgett, Keven Quillon, Brian Sears, Christina Sivrich, Anna Aimee White;** Swings **Matthew Hydzik, Amber Stone, Joe Komara, Lauralynn McClelland**

Kirsten Wyatt, Stephen R. Buntrock and Company

UNDERSTUDIES Josh Franklin (Danny, Vince), Cody Green (Kenickie, Sonny), Natalie Hill (Rizzo, Marty), Matthew Hydzik (Danny, Teen Angel), Emily Padgett (Patty, Sandy), Keven Quillon (Roger, Sonny), Brian Sears (Doody, Eugene), Christina Sivrich (Frenchy, Jan, Miss Lynch), Amber Stone (Cha-Cha, Frenchy, Jan), Anna Aimee White (Marty, Patty, Sandy)

THE *GREASE* BAND Kimberly Grigsby (Conductor/synthesizer); Chris Fenwick (Associate Conductor/synthesizer/piano); John Clancy (drums); Michael Blanco (bass); Michael Aarons, Jim Hershman (guitars); John Scarpulla (tenor sax/woodwinds); Jack Bashkow (woodwinds)

MUSICAL NUMBERS Grease, Summer Nights, Those Magic Changes, Freddy My Love, Greased Lightnin', Rydell Fight Song, Mooning, Look at Me, I'm Sandra Dee, We Go Together, Shakin' at the High School Hop, It's Raining on Prom Night, Born to Hand-Jive, Hopelessly Devoted to You, Beauty School Dropout, Sandy, Rock 'n' Roll Party Queen, There Are Worse Things I Could Do, Look at Me, I'm Sandra Dee (reprise), You're the One That I Want, We Go Together (reprise)

Laura Osnes, Kirsten Wyatt, Lindsay Mendez, Robyn Hurder, Jenny Powers

Jenny Powers and Matthew Saldívar

SETTING 1959, in and around Rydell High School. Revival of the musical presented in thirteen scenes in two acts. Originally produced Off-Broadway at the Eden Theatre February 14, 1972 (see *Theatre World* Volume 28, page 99); transferred to the Broadhurst Theatre June 7, 1972 (see *Theatre World* Volume 29, page 8), running eight years and 3,388 performances. The show was revived at the Eugene O'Neill Theatre on May 11, 1994, running almost four years (see *Theatre World* Volume 50, page 68).

SYNOPSIS The classic 1970's musical about the 1959 Rydell High School gang receives its second major revival, using songs written for the 1978 feature film. Max Crumm and Laura Osnes were cast from the reality television show "*Grease*: You're The One That I Want", a twelve week talent competition airing on NBC in the spring of 2007. After weekly eliminations, America voted Crumm and Osnes as their "Danny" and "Sandy", marking a unique casting method never before used in Broadway history.

*Succeeded by Will Blum

MAURITIUS

Biltmore Theatre; First Preview: September 13, 2007; Opening Night: October 4, 2007; Closed November 25, 2007; 24 previews, 61 performances

Written by Theresa Rebeck; Produced by Manhattan Theatre Club (Lynne Meadow, Artistic Director; Barry Grove, Executive Producer; Daniel Sullivan, 07-08 Acting Artistic Director) and Huntington Theatre Company (Nicholas Martin, Artistic Director; Michael Maso, Managing Director); Director, Doug Hughes; Set, John Lee Beatty; Costumes, Catherine Zuber; Lighting, Paul Gallo; Sound, David Van Tieghem; Fight Director, Rick Sordelet; PSM, Charles Means; Casting, David Caparelliotis; General Manager, Florie Seery; Associate Artistic Director/Programming, Paige Evans; Associate Artistic Director/Production, Mandy Greenfield; Marketing, Debra A. Waxman; Production Manager, Kurt Gardner; Casting, Nancy Piccione; Development, Jill Turner Lloyd; Finance, Jeffrey Bledsoe; Associate GM, Lindsey Brooks Sag; Subscriber Services, Robert Allenberg; Telesales, George Tetlow; Education, David Shookhoff; Company Manager, Seth Shepsle; Production Supervisor, Bridget Markov; Stage Manager, Elizabeth Moloney; Associate Director, Mark Schneider; Research Dramaturg, Ilana M. Brownstein; Makeup/Hair, Randy Houston Mercer; Associate Design: Philip Rosenberg (lighting), Jill BC DuBoff (sound); Assistant Design, Yoshinori Tanokura (set), Holly Cain & Court Watson (costumes), Paul Hackenmueller (lighting), Matthew O'Hare (sound); Production: Patrick Murray (automation), Leomar Susan (flyman), Jane Masterson (light programmer), Tracey Boone (dresser), Andrea L. Beukema (assistant); Lighting/Sound Supervisor, Matthew T. Gross; Prop Supervisor, Scott Laule; Costume Supervisor, Erin Hennessy Dean; Advertising, SpotCo; Press, Boneau/Bryan-Brown, Jim Byk, Aaron Meier, Heath Schwartz, Steven Padla, Christine Olver

The Cast

CAST Jackie **Alison Pill;** Philip **Dylan Baker;** Dennis **Bobby Cannavale;** Sterling **F. Murray Abraham;** Mary **Katie Finneran**

UNDERSTUDIES Rod Brogan (Dennis), Katya Campbell (Jackie/Mary), Robert Emmet Lunney (Philip/Sterling)

New York premiere of a play presented in two acts. World premiere presented at Boston's Huntington Theatre Company in October, 2006.

SYNOPSIS Jackie and Mary are half-sisters whose mother's death leaves them in possession of a rare stamp collection. But which sister actually owns the stamps? Which of three dealers can be trusted with their sale? And where do we choose to live: the present or the past?

F. Murray Abraham and Bobby Cannavale (photos by Joan Marcus)

Alison Pill, Bobby Cannavale

THE RITZ

Studio 54; First Preview: September 14, 2007; Opening Night: October 11, 2007; Closed December 9, 2007; 30 previews, 69 performances

Written by Terrence McNally; Producer, Roundabout Theatre Company (Todd Haimes, Artistic Director; Harold Wolpert, Managing Director; Julia C. Levy, Executive Director); Director, Joe Mantello; Sets, Scott Pask; Costumes, William Ivey Long; Lighting, Jules Fisher & Peggy Eisenhauer; Sound, Tony Meola; Hair/Wigs, Paul Huntley; Choreographer, Christopher Gattelli; PSM, Tripp Phillips; Casting, Jim Carnahan; Technical Supervisor, Steve Beers; General Manager, Sydney Beers; Marketing/Sales, David B. Steffen; Development, Jeffory Lawson; Founding Director, Gene Feist; Associate Artistic Director, Scott Ellis; Education Director, David A. Miller; Finance, Susan Neiman; Telesales, Daniel Weiss;

Kevin Chamberlin, Rosie Perez, Terrence Riordan, Brooks Ashmanskas (photos by Joan Marcus)

Sales Operations, Charlie Garbowski, Jr.; Company Manager, Denise Cooper; Assistant Director, Dave Solomon; ASM, Jason Hindelang; Assistant to the Choreographer, Michael Lee Scott; Googie's Musical Number Arrangements/Dance Captain, Seth Rudetsky; Musical Number Orchestrations, Jesse Vargas; Rehearsal Pianist, Steve Marzullo; Associate Design: Frank McCullough (sets), Tom Beall (costumes); Assistant Design: Lauren Alvarez, Jeff Hinchee (sets), Donald Sanders, Cathy Parrott (costumes), David Leonard (lighting), Adam Rigby, Zach Williamson (sound); Makeup, Angelina Avallone; Assistant Design: Lauren Alvarez, Jeff Hinchee (set), Donald Sanders, Cathy Parrott (costumes), David Leonard (lighting), Zach Williamson (sound); Production: Dan Hoffman (carpenter), Josh Weitzman (electrician), John Wooding (assistant electrician), Peter Sarafin (properties supervisor), Alan Edwards (props assistant), Nadine Hettel (wardrobe supervisor), Vanessa Anderson (hair/wig supervisor), Duane McKee (sound engineer), Lawrence Jennino, Erin Mary Delaney (props), Paul Ashton (automation), Steve Jones (flyman), Richard Tyndall (moving lights), Dan Schultheis (spot), Dorian Fuchs (deck sound); Press, Boneau/Bryan Brown, Matt Polk, Jessica Johnson, Amy Kass

CAST Old Man Vespucci **Teddy Coluca;** Carmine Vespucci **Lenny Venito;** Vivian Proclo **Ashlie Atkinson;** Aunt Vera **Angela Pietropinto;** Abe **Adam Sietz;** Claude Perkins **Patrick Kerr;** Gaetano Proclo **Kevin Chamberlin;** Chris **Brooks Ashmanskas;** Michael Brick **Terrence Riordan;** Googie Gomez **Rosie Perez;** Maurine **Angela Pietropinto;** Tiger **Lucas Near-Verbrugghe;** Duff **David Turner;** The Patrons: Patron in Chaps **Matthew Montelongo;** Crisco Patron **Ryan Idol;** Chuck **Teddy Coluca;** Snooty Patron **Jeffrey Evan Thomas;** Sheldon Farenthold **Seth Rudetsky;** Other Patrons **John Bantay, Josh Breckenridge, Josh Clynes, Andrew R. Cooksey, Mark Leydorf, Billy Magnussen, Nick Mayo, Dillon Porter;** Standby for Googie: **Andréa Burns**

UNDERSTUDIES Teddy Coluca (Abe), Mark Leydorf (Patron, Sheldon Farenthold), Billy Magnussen (Duff, Michael Brick, Tiger), Lucas Near-Verbrugghe (Claude Perkins), Angela Pietropinto (Vivian Proclo), Seth Rudetsky (Chris), Adam Sietz/Kevin Carolan (Carmine Vespucci, Gaetano Proclo), Jeffrey Evan Thomas (Michael Brick)

Rosie Perez

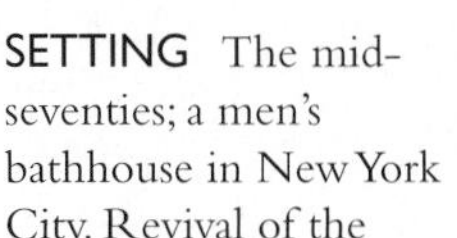

SETTING The mid-seventies; a men's bathhouse in New York City. Revival of the comedy/farce presented in two acts. Originally presented on Broadway at the Longacre Theatre, January 20, 1975, running 398 performances (see *Theatre World* Volume 31, page 37).

SYNOPSIS *The Ritz* is a madcap farce about a man hiding out from a mobster in the titular Turkish bath which is actually a gay bathhouse. He then takes on the guise of a big Broadway producer to avoid being discovered.

PYGMALION

American Airlines Theatre; First Preview: September 21, 2007; Opening Night: October 18, 2007; Closed December 16, 2007; 31 previews, 69 performances

Written by George Bernard Shaw; Producer, Roundabout Theatre Company (Todd Haimes, Artistic Director; Harold Wolpert, Managing Director; Julia C. Levy, Executive Director); Director, David Grindley; Sets/Costumes, Jonathan Fensom; Lighting, Jason Taylor; Sound, Gregory Clarke; Dialect Coach, Majella Hurley; Hair/Wigs, Richard Orton; PSM, Arthur Gaffin; Casting, Jim Carnahan; Technical Supervisor, Steve Beers; General Manager, Sydney Beers; Marketing/Sales, David B. Steffen; Development, Jeffory Lawson; Founding Director, Gene Feist; Associate Artistic Director, Scott Ellis; Properties, Kathy Fabian; Stage Manager, David Sugarman; Education Director, David A. Miller; Finance, Susan Neiman; Telesales, Daniel Weiss; Sales Operations, Charlie Garbowski, Jr.; Company Manager, Nichole Jennino; Fight Coordinator, Tom Schall; Voice Coach, Kate Maré; Associate Properties, Carrie Hash, Carrie Mossman; Assistant Director, Lori Wolter; Associate Design: Chad Owens (set), Patrick Bevilacqua (costumes), Hilary Manners (lighting), David Stephen Baker (sound); Production: Glenn Merwede (carpenter/automation), Brian Maiuri (electrician), Andrew Forste (running props), Dann Wojnar (sound engineer), Chris Mattingly (flyman), Nelson Vaughn (props), Barb Bartel (deck electrician), Susan J. Fallon (wardrobe supervisor); Rain Effects, Jauchem and Meeh; Press, Boneau/Bryan-Brown, Matt Polk, Jessica Johnson, Amy Kass

CAST Miss Clara Eynsford Hill **Kerry Bishé;** Mrs. Eynsford Hill **Sandra Shipley** Bystander/Taxi Driver **Doug Stender;** Freddy Eynsford Hill **Kieran Campion;** Liza Doolittle **Claire Danes** Colonel Pickering **Boyd Gaines** Henry Higgins **Jefferson Mays;** Sarcastic Bystander **Tony Carlin;** Other Bystanders **Jonathan Fielding, Robin Moseley, Jennifer Armour, Brad Heikes, Curtis Shumaker;** Mrs. Pearce **Brenda Wehle;** Alfred Doolittle **Jay O. Sanders;** Mrs. Higgins **Helen Carey;** Parlor Maid **Karen Walsh**

Clare Danes, Jefferson Mays (photos by Joan Marcus)

UNDERSTUDIES Tony Carlin (Colonel Pickering, Henry Higgins), Jonathan Fielding (Bystander, Freddy Eynsford Hill, Sarcastic Bystander, Taxicab Driver), Robin Moseley (Mrs. Eynsford Hill, Mrs. Pearce, Parlor Maid), Sandra Shipley (Mrs. Higgins), Doug Stender (Alfred Doolittle), Karen Walsh (Clara Eynsford Hill, Liza Doolittle)

SETTING London, 1913; Covent Garden, Higgins' laboratory on Wimpole Street, and Mrs. Higgins drawing room in Chelsea embankment. Revival of the comedy presented in five acts with one intermission. Originally presented in New York at the Park Theatre, October 12, 1914, running 74 performances. This production marked the fifth significant New York revival: Guild Theatre, 1926; Maxine Elliot's Theatre, 1938; Barrymore Theatre, December 26, 1945, with Gertrude Lawrence and Raymond Massey (see *Theatre World* Volume 2, page 52); Plymouth Theatre, April 26, 1987 with Amanda Plummer and Peter O'Toole (see *Theatre World* Volume 43, page 44).

Jefferson Mays, Jay O. Sanders, Boyd Gaines

SYNOPSIS When Professor Henry Higgins comes across a poor and uneducated Cockney girl, Higgins makes a bet that he can take her from the gutters of London and pass her off as a society lady, by simply teaching her the right dialect in which to speak.

A BRONX TALE

Walter Kerr Theatre; First Preview: October 4, 2007; Opening Night: October 25, 2007; Closed February 24, 2008; 18 previews, 111 performances

Written by Chazz Palminteri; Produced by Go Productions, John Gaughan/Trent Othick/Matt Othick, Neighborhood Films, in association with Jujamcyn Theaters (Rocco Landesman, President; Paul Lubin, Producing Director; Jack Viertel, Creative Director; Jordan Roth, Vice President); Director, Jerry Zaks; Set, James Noone; Lighting, Paul Gallo; Original Music and Sound, John Gromada; PSM, James Harker; Wardrobe, Isaia; Promotions, HHC Marketing; Production Management, Aurora Productions (Gene O'Donovan, W. Benjamin Heller II, Bethany Weinstein, Melissa Mazdra, John Horsman, Asia Evans); General Management, Stuart Thompson Productions/James Triner, Caroline Prugh; Associate Producers, Robert H. Moretti, Richard Carrigan; Executive Producer, Nicole Kastrinos; Company Manager, Cassidy J. Briggs; Stage Manager, Thea Bradshaw Scott; Design Assistants: Patrick Tennant (set), Michael Jones, Paul Hackenmueller (lighting), Christopher Cronin, Sten Severson (sound); Production Electrician, Dan Coey; Moving Lights, David Arch; Production Sound, Greg Peeler; Wardrobe Supervisor, Christel Murdock; Makeup, Jacqui Phillips; Press, Boneau/Bryan-Brown, Jackie Green, Matt Ross

Chazz Palminteri (photos by Joan Marcus)

CAST Calogero Anello and others **Chazz Palminteri**

SETTING 1960's, 187th and Belmont Ave., Bronx, New York. Revival of a solo performance play presented without intermission. Originally produced Off-Broadway at Playhouse 91, October 10, 1989 (see *Theatre World* Volume 46, page 56). The screen adaptation of the play was released in 1993, starring Palminteri along with Robert DeNiro, who made his directorial debut with the film.

SYNOPSIS A fictionalized story based on a true incident, Chazz Palminteri brings eighteen characters to life in this gripping tale of a rough childhood on the Bronx streets.

Chazz Palminteri

CYRANO DE BERGERAC

Richard Rodgers Theatre; First Preview: October 12, 2007; Opening Night: November 1, 2007; Closed January 6, 2008; 21 previews, 56 performances

Written by Edmond Rostand, translated and adapted by Anthony Burgess; Produced by Susan Bristow LLC, James L. Nederlander, Terry Allen Kramer, Stewart F. Lane, Bonnie Comley, Barbara Manocherian, Stephanie McClelland and Jon B. Platt; Director, David Leveaux; Sets, Tom Pye; Costumes, Gregory Gale; Lighting, Donald Holder; Sound, David Van Tieghem; Hair and Wigs, Tom Watson; Casting, J.V. Mercanti; Technical Supervisor, Hudson Theatrical Associates/ Neil A. Mazzella, Irene Wang; PSM, Marybeth Abel; General Manager, Charlotte Wilcox; Company Manager, Alexandra Gushin; Fight Director, Mark Deklin; Makeup & Prosthetics, Todd Kleitsch; Musical Arrangements/Incidental Music, Lucas Papaelias, Alexander Sovronsky; Additional Arrangements, Fred Rose, Leenya Rideout; Stage Manager, Andrew Neal; Associate Director, Eli Gonda; Management Associate, Abigail Rose Solomon; Vocal/Dialect Coach, Deborah Hecht; Fight Captain, Carman Lacivita; Associate Design: Frank McCullough (sets), Hilary Manners and Michael Jones (lighting), Warren Flynn (moving lights), T.J. McEvoy (sound system); Props, Kathy Fabian, Rose Howard, Elisa Kuhar; Assistant Design: Lauren Alvarez, Robert Jay Braun, Christine Peters (sets), Colleen Kesterson, Sky Switser, Abby Taylor Redmond (costumes), David Stollings (sound); Production: Brian Aman (electrician), Joseph Gracey (automation), Jason Wilkosz (head electrician), Mike Smanko (head props), William Ruger (sound engineer), Robert Guy (wardrobe supervisor), Elisa Acevedo (hair supervisor), Vincent Schicchi (makeup supervisor); Advertising, SpotCo; Press, Barlow-Hartman, Leslie Baden, Kevin Robak

CAST Roxane **Jennifer Garner;** Cyrano de Bergerac **Kevin Kline;** Christian De Neuvillette **Daniel Sunjata;** Ragueneau **Max Baker;** Lingniére/Théophraste Renaudot **Euan Morton;** Compte de Guiche **Chris Sarandon;** La Bret **John Douglas Thompson;** Roxane's Duenna/ Sister Marthe **Concetta Tomei;** Gascony Cadet **Stephen Balantzian;** Montfleury/A Porter/Gascony Cadet **Tom Bloom;** Guard/Poet/Gascony Cadet **Keith Eric Chappelle;** Jodelet/A Capuchin/Gascony Cadet **MacIntyre Dixon;** Theatregoer's Son/Gascony Cadet **David Duffield;** Gascony Cadet **Amefika El-Amin;** Carbon de Castel Jaloux **Peter Jay Fernandez;** Food Seller/Nun **Kate Guyton;** Actress/Sister Claire **Ginifer King;** Vicomte de Valvert/Gascony Cadet **Carmen Lacivita;** Marquis de Brissaille/Gascony Cadet **Piter Marek;** Page/Cook/Cadet/ Guitar Player and Drums **Lucas Papaelias;** Lady/Singer/ Nun **Leenya Rideout;** Poet/Gascony Cadet/Cellist **Fred Rose;** Theatregoer/Poet/Gascony Cadet **Thomas Schall;** Musketeer/Gascony Cadet **Daniel Stewart Sherman;** Page/Cook/Cadet/Violin, Mandolin, Tin Whistle, Fife, Drums **Alexander Sovronsky;** Marquis de Cuigy/Gascony Cadet **Baylen Thomas;** Lise/Mother Marguerite **Nance Williamson**

Jennifer Garner, Daniel Sunjata (far right) and the cast (photo by Carol Rosegg)

UNDERSTUDIES Stephen Balantzian (Comte de Guiche, Le Bret), Keith Eric Chappelle (Carbon de Castel Jaloux, Vicomte de Valvert), Kate Guyton (Lise, Mother Marguerite, Roxane's Duenna, Sister Marthe), Ginifer King (Roxane), Thomas Schall (A Capuchin, Cyrano de Bergerac, Jodelet), Daniel Stewart Sherman (Montfleury, Ragueneau), Baylen Thomas (Christian De Neuvillette)

2007–2008 AWARDS Outer Critics Circle: Outstanding Actor in a Play (Kevin Kline)

SETTING 1640-1655. Paris: Hotel de Bourgogne, Ragueneau's pastry shop, courtyard outside Roxanne's house, battlefield at the siege of Arras, Garden of a convent. Revival of the comedy presented in two acts. Originally produced in New York at the Garden Theatre, October 3, 1898. This production marked the twelfth major New York revival of the play.

SYNOPSIS The classic story of the soulful poet/philosopher and brilliant swordsman Cyrano who falls for the beautiful, strong-willed Roxane, but is too ashamed of his large nose to tell her. When he learns that she loves the handsome Christian de Neuvillette, his dim-witted comrade, he pens poetry and love letters to Roxane on Christian's behalf. After many years, the truth is revealed.

ROCK 'N' ROLL

Bernard B. Jacobs Theatre; First Preview: October 19, 2007; Opening Night: November 4, 2007; Closed March 9, 2008; 16 previews, 123 performances

Written by Tom Stoppard; Originally presented by the Royal Court Theatre; Produced by Bob Boyett & Sonya Friedman Productions, Ostar Productions, Roger Berlind, Tulchin/Bartner, Douglas G. Smith, Dancap Productions, Jam Theatricals, The Weinstein Company, in association with Lincoln Center Theater; Director, Trevor Nunn; Sets, Robert Jones; Costumes, Emma Ryott; Lighting, Howard Harrison; Sound/Projections, Ian Dickinson; Casting, Tara Rubin (US), Lisa Makin (UK); PSM, Rick Steiger; Technical Supervisor, Aurora Productions; Associate Producer for RBT, Tim Levy; US General Management, 101 Productions, Ltd.; UK General Management for SFP, Diane Benjamin & Matthew Gordon; Associate Producer, Carole Shorenstein Hays; Company Manager, Penelope Daulton; Stage Manager, Alexis Shorter; ASM, Timothy Eaker; Assistant Director, Seth Sklar-Heyn; US Hair/Wigs/Makeup, David H. Lawrence; Associate Design: Ted LeFevre (sets), Scott Traugott (costumes), Dan Walker (lighting), Marc Polimeni (moving lights), Chris Cronin (sound); Dialect Coach, Elizabeth Smith; Fight Director, Tom Schall; Production: David Cohen (carpenter), James Maloney, Jr. (electrician), Andy Meeker (props), Kelly Saxon (wardrobe); Advertising, SpotCo; Press, Boneau/Bryan-Brown, Jim Byk, Matt Ross

CAST The Piper/Policeman **Seth Fisher;** Esme (Younger)/ Alice **Alice Eve;** Jan **Rufus Sewell;** Max **Brian Cox;** Eleanor/Esme (Older) **Sinead Cusack;** Gillian/Magda **Mary Bacon;** Interrogator/Nigel **Quentin Maré;** Ferdinand **Stephen Kunken;** Milan/Waiter **Ken Marks;** Lenka **Nicole Ansari;** Stephen **Brian Avers;** Candida **Alexandra Neil;** Pupil **Anna O'Donoghue**

Nicole Ansari, Brian Avers, Alexandra Neil, Quentin Maré, Rufus Sewell, Brian Cox

Alice Eve, Sinead Cusack (photos by Joan Marcus)

UNDERSTUDIES Brian Avers (Jan, The Piper/Policeman), Mary Bacon (Candida, Lenka), Joseph Collins (Ferdinand, Jan, Nigel/Interrogator, Stephen, The Piper/Policeman), Seth Fisher (Ferdinand, Pupil, Stephen), Julie Jesneck (Gilian, Margo, Pupil), Ken Marks (Max), Alexandra Neil (Eleanor/Esme {Older}), Anna O'Donoghue (Esme {Younger}/Alice, Gillian/ Magda), Angela Reed (Candida, Eleanor/Esme {Older}, Gillian/Magda, Lenka, Pupil), Joe Vincent (Max, Milan/Waiter, Nigel/Interrogator)

SETTING Prague and Cambridge from 1968 to 1990. American premiere of a new play presented in two acts. Originally produced in London at the Royal Court Theatre, June 3–July 15, 2006, featuring Mr. Cox, Mr. Sewell, Ms. Eve, Ms. Ansari, and Ms. Cusak. The show transferred to the West End at the Duke of York's Theatre, July 22, 2006–February 25, 2007.

SYNOPSIS *Rock 'n' Roll* spans several years from the double perspective of Prague, Czechoslovakia, where a rock 'n' roll band comes to symbolize resistance to the Communist regime, and of Cambridge, England, where the verities of love and death are shaping the lives of three generations in the family of a Marxist philosopher.

Nicole Ansari and Brian Cox

YOUNG FRANKENSTEIN The New Mel Brooks Musical

Hilton Theatre; First Preview: November 11, 2007; Opening Night: November 8, 2007; 29 previews, 236 performances as of May 31, 2008

Book by Mel Brooks and Thomas Meehan, music and lyrics by Mel Brooks; Based on the story and screenplay by Gene Wilder and Mel Brooks and on the motion picture by special arrangement with Twentieth Century Fox; "Puttin' on the Ritz" music and lyrics by Irving Berlin; Produced by Robert F.X. Sillerman and Mel Brooks, in association with The R/F/B/V Group; Director & Choreography, Susan Stroman; Music Arrangements and Supervision, Glen Kelly; Sets, Robin Wagner, Costumes, William Ivey Long; Lighting, Peter Kaczorowski; Sound, Jonathan Deans; Special Effects, Marc Brickman; Wigs/Hair, Paul Huntley; Makeup, Angelina Avallone; Casting, Tara Rubin; Associate Director/PSM, Steven Zweigbaum; Associate Choreographer, Chris Peterson; Music Direction/Vocal Arrangements, Patrick S. Brady; Orchestrations, Doug Besterman; Music Coordinator, John Miller; General Management, Richard Frankel Productions, Laura Green; Technical Supervisors, Hudson Theatrical Associates/Neil Mazzella, Sam Ellis; Associate Producer, One Viking Productions, Carl Pasbjerg; Company Manager, Kathy Lowe; Associate Company Manager, Bobby Driggers; Stage Manager, Ira Mont; ASMs, Ara Marx, Julia P. Jones; Assistant Director, Scott Bishop; Assistant Choreographer, Jeff Whiting; Dance Captains, James Gray, Courtney Young; Associate Design: David Peterson (set), Scott Traugott (costume), John Viesta (lighting); Animations, Joshua Frankel; Puppet Design, Michael Curry; Prosthetics, John Dods; Production Heads: Todd Frank (carpenter), Mark Diaz, Thomas Sherman (automation), Richard Mortell, Brian Dawson (electrics), Josh Weitzman (moving lights), Thomas Hague (GrandMa/Hippotizer Programmer), Simon Matthew (sound); Supervisors: Laura Koch, Eric Castaldo (props) Douglas Petitjean (wardrobe), Edward J. Wilson (hair/wigs), Juliet White (makeup); Dialect Coach, Deborah Hecht, Additional Orchestrations, Michael Starobin; Synthesizer Programmer, Randy Cohen; Advertising, SpotCo; Press, Barlow-Hartman, Dennis Crowley, Michelle Bergmann; Cast recording: Decca Broadway B0010374-02

CAST Inspector Kemp/Hermit **Fred Applegate;** Dr. Frederick Frankenstein **Roger Bart;** Elizabeth **Megan Mullally;** Igor **Christopher Fitzgerald;** Inga **Sutton Foster;** Frau Blucher **Andrea Martin;** The Monster **Shuler Hensley;** Masha **Heather Ayers;** Ziggy/Shoeshine Man/ Lawrence **Jim Borstelmann;** Herald/Bob/Transylvania Quartet **Paul Castree;** Mr. Hilltop/Transylvania Quartet **Jack Doyle;** Equine/Sasha/Ritz Specialty **Eric Jackson;** Medical Student/The Count **Matthew Labanca;** Medical Student/Victor/Transylvania Quartet **Kevin Ligon;** Tasha **Linda Mugleston;** Basha **Christina Marie Norrup;** Medical Student/Equine **Justin Patterson;** Telegraph Boy/ Transylvania Quartet **Brian Shepard;** Ensemble **Heather Ayers, Jim Borstelmann, Paul Castree, Jennifer Lee Crowl, Jack Doyle, Renée Feder, Amy Heggins, Eric Jackson, Matthew Labanca, Kevin Ligon, Barrett Martin, Linda Mugleston, Christina Marie Norrup, Justin Patterson, Ángie Schworer, Brian Shepard, Sarah Strimel;** Swings **James Gray, Kristin Marie Johnson, Craig Waletzko, Courtney Young**

Megan Mullally and Roger Bart (photos by Paul Kolnik)

UNDERSTUDIES Heather Ayers (Elizabeth, Frau Blucher), Jim Borstelmann (Inspector Kemp/Hermit, The Monster), Paul Castree (Dr. Frederick Frankenstein), Renée Feder (Inga), James Gray (Igor), Matthew Labanca (Dr. Frederick Frankenstein), Kevin Ligon (Inspector Kemp/Hermit,), Linda Mugleston (Elizabeth, Frau Blucher), Christina Marie Norrup (Inga), Justin Patterson (The Monster), Brian Shepard (Igor), John Patrick Walker (Frederick/Igor)

ORCHESTRA Patrick Brady (Conductor/keyboard); Gregory J. Dlugos (Associate Conductor/keyboard 1); David Gursky (Assistant Conductor/keyboard 2); Vincent DellaRocca, Steven J. Greenfield, Charles Pillow, Frank Santagata (woodwinds); Don Downs, Glenn Drewes, Scott Harrell (trumpets); Tim Sessions, Mike Christianson (trombones); Patrick Pridemore, Judy Yin-Chi Lee (French horns); Rick Dolan (Concert Master), Ashley D. Horne, Helen Kim (violins); Maxine Roach, Debra Shufelt-Dine (violas); Laura Bontrager, Chungsun Kim (cello); Bob Renino (bass); Perry Cavari (drums); Charles Descarfino (percussion)

MUSICAL NUMBERS The Happiest Town, The Brain, Please Don't Touch Me, Together Again, Roll in the Hay, Join the Family Business, He Vas My Boyfriend, The Law; Life, Life; Welcome to Transylvania, Transylvania Mania, He's Loose, Listen To Your Heart, Surprise, Please Send Me Someone, Man About Town, Puttin' on the Ritz, Deep Love, Frederick's Soliloquy, Deep Love (reprise), Finale Ultimo

2007–2008 AWARDS Outer Critics Circle: Outstanding Broadway Musical (tie)

SETTING Transylvania and New York City. World premiere of a new musical presented in two acts. Prior to its Broadway engagement, the show had an out-of-town tryout at the Paramount Theatre in Seattle, Washington, August 7–September 1, 2007.

SYNOPSIS Based on the hit 1974 film, *Young Frankenstein* is the wickedly inspired re-imagining of the Mary Shelley classic from the comic genius of Mel Brooks. When Frederick Frankenstein, an esteemed New York brain surgeon and professor, inherits a castle and laboratory in Transylvania from his deranged genius grandfather, he faces a dilemma: does he continue to run from his family's tortured past, or does he stay in Transylvania to carry on his grandfather's mad experiments reanimating the dead and, in the process, fall in love with his sexy lab assistant, Inga?

Roger Bart, Shuler Hensley (above), Andrea Martin, Christopher Fitzgerald, and Sutton Foster

Andrea Martin

Shuler Hensley and Roger Bart

DR. SEUSS' HOW THE GRINCH STOLE CHRISTMAS

St. James Theatre; First Preview: November 1, 2007; Opening Night: November 9, 2007; Closed January 7, 2008; 13 previews, 96 performances

Book and lyrics by Timothy Mason, music by Mel Marvin, based on the book *How the Grinch Stole Christmas* by Dr. Seuss, additional music and lyrics by Albert Hague and Dr. Seuss; Presented by Citi; Produced by Running Subway, EMI Music Publishing, Michael Speyer, Allen Spivak, Janet Pailet, Amy Jen Sharyn, and Maximum Entertainment; Original production conceived and directed by Jack O'Brien; Director, Matt August, Original Choreography, John DeLuca; Co-Choreographer, Bob Richard; Executive Producer, James Sanna; Sets, John Lee Beatty; Lighting, Pat Collins; Costumes, Robert Morgan; Sound, Acme Sound Partners; Puppet Design, Michael Curry; Wigs/Hair/Wardrobe Supervisor, Thomas Augustine; Makeup, Angelina Avallone; Special Effects, Gregory Meeh; Music Direction/Arrangements, Joshua Rosenblum; Orchestrator, Michael Starobin; Dance Arrangements, David Krane; Music Coordinator, Seymour Red Press; Technical Supervisor, Don S. Gilmore; PSM, Daniel S. Rosokoff; Casting, Telsey + Company; Associate Producers, Audrey Geisel, Joshua Rosenblum; General Manager, David Waggett, Kathryn Schwarz; Marketing, Tomm Miller; Company Manager, Heidi Neven; Advertising, Running Subway; ASMs, James D. Latus, Pamela Edington, Nancy Elizabeth Vest; Asst. Company Managers, Erica Ezold, Bruce Perry; Asst. Director, Caitlin Moon; Associate Choreographer, Shane Rhoades; Dance Captain, Kurt Kelly; Projection Consultant, Mark Mongold; Associate Projection Consultant, Michael Zaleski; Music Preparation, Emily Grishman/Katharine Edmonds; Synthesizer Programming, Bruce Samuels; Press, Allison Brod Public Relations, Jodi Hasan, Jen Roche, Annabelle Abouab

The Company (photo by Paul Kolnik)

CAST Old Max **Ed Dixon;** Cindy Lou-Who **Caroline London** or **Athena Ripka;** Papa Who **Aaron Galligan-Stierle;** Mama Who **Tari Kelly;** Grandpa Who **Darin De Paul;** Grandma Who **Jan Neuberger;** Boo Who **Jordan Samuels/Johnny Schaffer;** Annie Who **Katie Micha** or **Sami Gayle;** Danny Who **Sky Flaherty** or **Andy Richardson;** Betty-Lou Who **Janelle Viscomi** or **Jahaan Amin;** Citizens of Whoville **Hunter Bell, Janet Dickinson, Carly Hughes, Josephine Rose Roberts, William Ryall, Jeff Skowron;** Little Whos–Red Cast **Brianna Gentilella, Michael Hoey, Marina Micalizz, Simon Pincus;** Little Whos–White Cast **Juliette Allen Angelo, Caitlin Belcik, Joseph Harrington, Jillian Mueller, Jacob Pincus;** Young Max **Rusty Ross;** The Grinch **Patrick Page;** Swings **Kurt Kelly, Eamon Foley, Amy Griffin, Liesl Jaye, Jess Leprotto, Heather Tepe**

UNDERSTUDIES Juliette Allen Angelo (Cindy Lou Who –White Cast), Hunter Bell (Papa Who, Young Max), Darin DePaul (Old Max), Janet Dickinson (Grandma Who), Carly Hughes (Mama Who), Kurt Kelly (Young Max), William Ryall (Old Max, The Grinch), Jeff Skowron (Grandpa Who, The Grinch), Tianna Jane Stevens (Cindy Lou Who–Red Cast)

MUSICIANS Joshua Rosenblum (Conductor); Sue Anschutz (Associate Conductor/keyboards); Mark Mitchell (Assistant Conductor/keyboards); Steven Kenyon, Robert DeBellis; Terrence Cook, John Winder (woodwinds); Christian Jaudes, Philip Granger, Wayne DuMaine (trumpets); Wayne Goodman, Robert Fournier (trombones); Louis Bruno (bass); Gregory Landes (drums); David Roth (percussion)

MUSICAL NUMBERS Who Likes Christmas?, This Time of Year, I Hate Christmas Eve, Whatchama Who, Welcome Christmas, I Hate Christmas Eve (reprise), It's the Thought That Counts, One of a Kind, Now's the Time, You're a Mean One Mr. Grinch, Santa for a Day, You're a Mean One Mr. Grinch (reprise), Who Likes Christmas? (reprise), One of a Kind (reprise), Welcome Christmas (reprise), Santa for a Day (reprise), Who Likes Christmas? (reprise)

Return engagement of the musical presented without intermission. This production was presented last season at the Hilton Theatre, November 8, 2006-January 7, 2007 (see *Theatre World* Volume 63).

SYNOPSIS The mean and scheming Grinch, whose heart is "two sizes too small" learns that holidays are about togetherness and love, and not about accumulating material things.

CYMBELINE

Vivian Beaumont Theatre; First Preview: November 1, 2007; Opening Night: December 2, 2007; Closed January 8, 2008; 34 previews, 40 performances

Written by William Shakespeare; Produced by Lincoln Center Theater (André Bishop, Artistic Director; Bernard Gersten, Executive Producer); Director, Mark Lamos; Sets, Michael Yeargan; Costumes, Jess Goldstein; Lighting, Brian MacDevitt; Original Music, Mel Marvin; Sound, Tony Smolenski IV & Walter Trarbach; Movement Consultant, Seán Curran; Fight Director, Rick Sordelet; Stage Manager, Michael McGoff; Casting, Daniel Swee; Dramaturg, Anne Cattaneo; Development, Hattie K. Jutagir; Marketing, Linda Mason Ross; General Manager, Adam Siegel; Production Manager, Jeff Hamlin; Finance, David S. Brown; Education, Kati Koerner; ASM, Elizabeth Miller; Company Manager, Matthew Markoff; ACM, Jessica Perlmeter Cochrane; Assistant Director, Jennifer Vellenga; Director's Assistant, Jeff Miller; Wigs/Hair, Charles LaPointe; Makeup, Angelina Avallone; Props, Scott Laule; Associate Composer, Curtis Moore; Fight Captains, Jeff Bender, Michael Rossmy; Associate Design: China Lee (costumes), Michael O'Connor (lighting), Curtis Moore (sound); Production/Supervisors: William Nagle (carpenter), Patrick Merryman (electrics), Karl Rausenberger (props), John Weingart (flyman), Lynn Bowling (wardrobe), Cindy Demand (hair); Vocal Consultant, Elizabeth Smith; Press, Philip Rinaldi, Barbara Carroll

CAST Cymbeline **John Cullum;** Princess Imogen **Martha Plimpton;** Helen/Ghost of Posthumus' mother **Gordana Rashovich;** Queen **Phylicia Rashad;** Lord Cloten **Adam Dannheisser;** Posthumus Leonatus **Michael Cerveris;** Pisanio **John Pankow;** Cornelius/Ghost of Posthumus' father **Herb Foster;** Two Gentlemen **Richard Topol, Daniel Breaker;** Philario/Jupiter **Daniel Oreskes;** Iachimo **Jonathan Cake;** A Frenchman/A Roman Captain **Anthony Cochrane;** A Dutchman **Jeff Woodman;** A Spaniard/ Ghost of Posthumus' brother **Noshir Dalal;** Caius Lucius **Ezra Knight;** Philarmonus **Michael W. Howell;** Belarius **Paul O'Brien;** Guiderius, now called Polydore **David Furr;** Arviragus, now called Cadwal **Gregory Wooddell;** Ghost of Posthumus' second brother **Adam Greer;** Officers, Captains, Soldiers, Lords, Ladies, Messengers, Attendants **Jeffrey M. Bender, Jordan Dean, LeRoy McClain, Nancy Rodriguez, Michael Rossmy**

John Cullum, Michael Cerveris, Martha Plimpton and Company (photos by Paul Kolnik)

UNDERSTUDIES Jeffery M. Bender (Cloten), Anthony Cochrane (Caius Lucius, Jupiter, Philarmonus), Noshir Dalal (The Ghost of Posthumus' brother), Jordan Dean (Guiderius), Herb Foster (Cymbeline), David Furr (Posthumus Leonatus), Adam Greer (Arviragus, Gentleman, The Ghost of Posthumus' brother), Ezra Knight (Pisanio), LeRoy McClain (A Frenchman, A Roman Captain), Daniel Oreskes (Belarius), Gordana Rashovich (Queen), Nancy Rodriguez (Helen, Imogen, The Ghost of Posthumus' mother), Michael Rossmy (A Dutchman, A Spaniard), Gregory Wooddell (Iachimo), Jeff Woodman (Cornelius, Gentleman, Philarmonus, The Ghost of Posthumus' father)

Martha Plimpton and Jonathan Cake

SETTING Britain, Italy and Wales; In and around Cymbeline's palace in Britain in the time of the Roman Empire. Revival of the classic drama presented in two acts. This production marked the first Broadway production of the play since the early 1900's.

SYNOPSIS *Cymbeline* combines comedy, tragedy and history into an epic tale of power and magic– its action sweeping across Britain and Italy, as two warring powers clash until its eventual joyful conclusion.

THE FARNSWORTH INVENTION

Music Box Theatre; First Preview: October 15, 2007; Opening Night: December 3, 2007; Closed March 2, 2008; 34 previews, 104 performances

Written by Aaron Sorkin; Produced by Dodger Properties, Steven Spielberg for Rabbit Ears, LLC, in association with Fred Zollo and Jeffrey Sine, Dancap Productions, Latitude Link/Pelican Group; Director, Des McAnuff; Original Music, Andrew Lippa; Sets, Klara Zieglerova; Costumes, David C. Woolard; Lighting, Howell Binkley; Sound, Walter Trarbach, Tony Smolenski; Hair/Wigs, Mark Adam Rampmeyer; Movement, Lisa Shriver; Fight Direction, Steve Rankin; PSM, Frank Hartenstein; Casting, Tara Rubin (East), Sharon Bialy and Sherry Thomas (West); Technical Supervisor, Peter Fulbright; Company Manager, Jennifer Hindman Kemp; Associate Producer, Lauren Mitchell; Executive Producer, Sally Campbell Morse; Promotions, HHC Marketing; Stage Manager, Kelly A. Martindale; ASM, Stephanie Atlan; Dialects, Stephen Gabis; Music Coordinator, Howard Jones; Associate General Manager, Jennifer F. Vaughan; Assistant General Manager, Dean A. Carpenter; Assistant Director, Daisy Walker; Associate Design: Robert John Andrusko (set), Matthew Patchman (costumes), Mark Simpson (lighting), Ashley Hanson (sound); Production & Supervisors: Erik Hanson (carpenter), Ray Harold (head carpenter); Brian GF McGarity (electrician); Pete Donovan (head electrician), Jim Bay (sound), Emiliano Pares (props), John Paull III (head props), Scott Westervelt (wardrobe), Renee Kelly (hair); Set Model, Tim McMath; Recorded Musicians: Andrew Lippa (Conductor/piano), Matthew Peterson (trumpet), Mark Thrasher (woodwinds), Christian Hebel, Christopher Cardona (violins), Claire Chan (viola), Anja Wood (cello), William Ellison (bass); Advertising, Serino Coyne; Press, Boneau/Bryan-Brown, Susanne Tighe, Heath Schwartz

CAST David Sarnoff **Hank Azaria;** Lizette Sarnoff/Mary Pickford/others **Nadia Bowers;** Pem's Father/Cliff Gardner/others **Kyle Fabel;** Atkins/Walter Gifford/Douglas Fairbanks/others **Maurice Godin;** Young Philo T. Farnsworth/others **Christian M. Johansen;** Wilkins/Analyst/others **Aaron Krohn;** George Everson/Vladimir Zworykin/others **Bruce McKenzie;** Young David Sarnoff/others **Malcolm Morano;** Stan Willis/others **Spencer Moses;** Leslie Gorrell/others **Michael Mulheren;** Justin Tolman/Jim Harbord/Doctor/others **Jim Ortlieb;** Sarnoff's Father/Simms/Lippincott/Houston Control/others **Michael Pemberton;** Betty/others **Katharine Powell;** Harlan Honn/Radio Announcer/Lennox/others **Steve Rosen;** Philo T. Farnsworth **Jimmi Simpson;** Russian Officer/William Crocker/others **James Sutorius;** Sarnoff's Mother/Pem's Mother/Agnes Farnsworth/Mina Edison/others **Margot White;** Pem Farnsworth/others **Alexandra Wilson;** Wachtel/others **William Youmans**

UNDERSTUDIES Aaron Krohn (Atkins/Gifford/Fairbanks, Everson/Zworykin, Honn/Announcer/Lennox), Kate MacCluggage (Betty, Pem, Lizette Sarnoff/Mary Pickford, Agnes Farnsworth/Mina Edison/Pem's Mother/Sarnoff's Mother), Spencer Moses (Pem's Father/Gardner, Philo Farnsworth, Wachtel), Javier Picayo (Willis, Young Sarnoff, Young Farnsworth), Steve Rosen (David Sarnoff), Brian Russell (Wilkins/Analyst, Tolman/Harbord/Doctor, Gorrell, Sarnoff's Father/Simms/Lippincott, Russian Officer/Crocker)

2007–2008 AWARDS **Theatre World Award:** Jimmi Simpson

SETTING 1920-1940's, New York, Idaho, and various places. New York premiere of a new play with music presented in two acts. World premiere presented in the "Page to Stage" Program at La Jolla Playhouse (Christopher Ashley, Artistic Director; Steven Libman Managing Director), La Jolla, California, February 27, 2007 (see *Theatre World* Volume 63).

SYNOPSIS The turning point of the 20th century wasn't on television. It was television. Two ambitious visionaries race against each other to invent a device called "television." Separated by two thousand miles, each knows that if he stops working, even for a moment, the other will gain the edge. Who will unlock the key to the greatest innovation of the 20th century: the ruthless media mogul, or the self-taught Idaho farm boy?

The Company (photo by Joan Marcus)

AUGUST: OSAGE COUNTY

Imperial Theatre+; First Preview: October 30, 2007; Opening Night: December 4, 2007; 18 previews, 199 performances as of May 31, 2008

Written by Tracy Letts; Originally produced by the Steppenwolf Theatre Company (Martha Lavey, Artistic Director; David Hawkanson, Executive Director); Produced by Jeffrey Richards, Jean Doumanian, Steve Traxler, Jerry Frankel, Ostar Productions, Jennifer Manocherian, The Weinstein Company, Debra Black/Daryl Roth, Ronald & Marc Frankel/Barbara Freitag, Rick Steiner/Staton Bell Group; Director, Anna D. Shapiro; Sets, Todd Rosenthal; Costumes, Ana Kuzmanic; Lighting, Ann G. Wrightson; Sound, Richard Woodbury; Original Music, David Singe; Dramaturg, Edward Sobel; Original Casting, Erica Daniels; New York Casting, Stuart Howard, Amy Schecter, Paul Hardt; Fight Choreography, Chuck Coyl; Dialect Coach, Cecilie O'Reilly; PSM, Deb Styer; Production Supervisor, Jane Grey; Technical Supervisor, Theatersmith, Inc./Smitty (Christopher C. Smith); Marketing Services, TMG-The Marketing Group; General Management, Richards/Climan, Inc.; Assistant Producers, Mark Barber, Patrick Daly, Ben West; Company Manager, Mary Miller; Assistant Director, Henry Wishcamper; Design Assistants: Kevin Depinet, Matthew D. Jordan, Martin Andrew Orlowicz, Stephen T. Sorenson (sets), Amelia Dombrowski (costumes), Kathleen Dobbins, Kristina Kloss (lighting), Joanna Lynne Staub (sound), Management Associate, Jeromy Smith; Production: Don Oberpriller (carpenter), Neil McShane (electrician), Neil Rosenberg (props), Valerie Spradling (sound), Walter Bullard (head carpenter), Paul Dean, Jr. (head electrician), Jay Satterwite (head props), Rob Bevenger (wardrobe supervisor); Advertising, SpotCo; Press, Jeffrey Richards Associates, Irene Gandy, Judith Hansen, Noah Himmelstein, Elon Rutberg

Jeff Perry, Amy Morton (photos by Joan Marcus)

CAST Beverly Weston **Dennis Letts***; Violet Weston **Deanna Dunagan**; Barbara Fordham **Amy Morton**; Bill Fordham **Jeff Perry**; Jean Fordham **Madeleine Martin**; Ivy Weston **Sally Murphy**; Karen Weston **Mariann Mayberry**; Mattie Fae Aiken **Rondi Reed**; Charlie Aiken **Francis Guinan**; Little Charles **Ian Barford**; Johnna Monevata **Kimberly Guerrero**; Steve Heidebrecht **Brian Kerwin**; Sheriff Deon Gilbeau **Troy West**

Amy Morton, Sally Murphy, Deanna Dunagan

Sally Murphy, Francis Guinan, Rondi Reed

+ The show temporarily closed April 20, 2008 and transferred to the Music Box Theatre April 29, 2008

*Succeeded by: Munson Hicks, Michael McGuire (Mr. Letts passed away February 22, 2008, after a battle with cancer.) Anne Berkowtiz (Jean), Aaron Serotsky (Little Charles/Sheriff)

UNDERSTUDIES/ STANDBYS*

Munson Hicks (Beverly Weston, Charlie Aiken), Susanne Marley (Mattie Fae Aiken, Violet Weston), Jay Patterson (Bill Fordham, Sheriff Deon Gilbeau, Steve Heidebrecht), Dee Pelletier (Barbara Fordham, Ivy Weston, Karen Weston), Molly Ranson (Jean Fordham), Kristina Valada-Viars (Johnna Monevata), Troy West (Little Charles)

Deanna Dunagan

SETTING A large country home outside Pawhuska, Oklahoma, 60 miles northwest of Tulsa. New York premiere of a new play presented in three acts with two intermissions. World Premiere presented at the Steppenwolf Theatre Company, Chicago, Illinois, June 28, 2007 (see Theatre World Volume 63) with most of this cast.

Amy Morton, Troy West

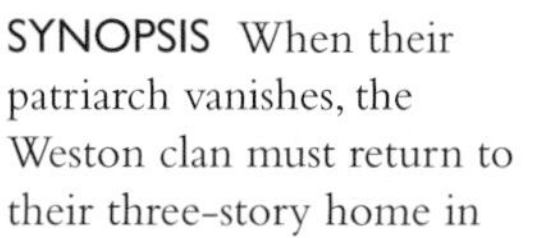

SYNOPSIS When their patriarch vanishes, the Weston clan must return to their three-story home in rural Oklahoma to get to the heart of the matter. With rich insight and brilliant humor, Letts paints a vivid portrait of a Midwestern family at a turning point.

2007–2008 AWARDS Tonys: Best Play, Best Direction of a Play, Best Leading Actress in a Play (Deanna Dunagan), Best Featured Actress in a Play (Rondi Reed), Best Scenic Design of a Play; Drama Desk and Outer Critics Circle: Outstanding Play, Outstanding Actress in a Play (Deanna Dunagan), Outstanding Director of a Play (Anna D. Shapiro); New York Drama Critics' Circle: Best Play; Drama League: Distinguished Production of a Play; Pulitzer Prize for Drama; **Theatre World Award:** Deanna Dunagan

Ian Bradford, Francis Guinan

Brian Kerwin, Madeline Martin (front), Mariann Mayberry

Dennis Letts, Kimberly Guerrero

THE SEAFARER

Booth Theatre; First Preview: October 30, 2007; Opening Night: December 6, 2007; Closed March 30, 2007; 19 previews, 133 performances

Written and directed by Conor McPherson; Originally presented by the National Theatre of Great Britain; Produced by Ostar Productions, Bob Boyett, Roy Furman, Lawrence Horowitz, Jam Theatricals, Bill Rollnick/Nancy Ellison Rollnick, James D'Orta, Thomas S. Murphy, Ralph Guild/Jon Avnet, Philip Geier/Keough Partners, Eric Falkenstein/Max OnStage; Set/Costumes, Rae Smith; Lighting, Neil Austin; Sound, Matthew Smethurst-Evans; Fight Director, Thomas Schall; Casting, Laura Stanczyk & Howie Cherpakov; Marketing, HHC Marketing; General Management, 101 Productions, Ltd.; PSM, Barclay Stiff; Technical Supervisor, David Benken; Production Management, David Benken, Rose Palombo; Stage Manager, Mary Kathryn Flynt; Assistant to the Director, Mark Schneider; Associate Lighting, Aaron Spivey; Assistant Costumes, Barry Doss; Scenic Coordinator, Diane Wilmott; Production: Jon Lawson (electrician), Denise J. Grillo (props), Wayne Smith (sound), Jack Anderson (advance carpenter), Bobby Harrell (lighting programmer), Eileen Miller (wardrobe supervisor), Barry Doss (dresser), Ross Evans and Kyle Gates (production assistants); Associate Producer for Ostar, Rachel Neuburger, Associate Producer for Boyett Theatricals, Tim Levy; Advertising, Serino Coyne; Press, Boneau/Bryan-Brown, Aaron Meier, Christine Olver

Jim Norton, Conleth Hill (photos by Joan Marcus)

CAST Ivan Curry **Conleth Hill;** Mr. Lockhart **Ciarán Hinds;** Nicky Giblin **Sean Mahon;** James 'Sharky' Harkin **David Morse;** Richard Harkin **Jim Norton**

UNDERSTUDIES Peter Rogan (Richard Harkin, Mr. Lockhart), Declan Mooney (James 'Sharky' Harkin, Ivan Curry, Nicky Giblin)

Jim Norton, Sean Mahon, Conleth Hill, David Morse, Ciarán Hinds

2007–2008 AWARDS Tonys: Best Featured Actor in a Play (Jim Norton); Drama Desk: Outstanding Featured Actor in a Play (Conleth Hill)

SETTING A house in Baldoyle, a coastal settlement north of Dublin city, Ireland; Christmas Eve. American premiere of a new play presented in two acts. World premiere at the National Theatre of Great Britain's Cottesloe Theatre (Sir Hayden Phillips, Chairman; Nicholas Hytner, Director; Nick Starr, Executive Director), September 28, 2006–January 30, 2007, featuring Mr. Hill and Mr. Norton.

SYNOPSIS It's Christmas Eve and Sharky has returned to Dublin to look after his irascible, aging brother who's recently gone blind. Old drinking buddies Ivan and Nicky are holed up at the house too, hoping to play some cards. But with the arrival of a stranger from the distant past, the stakes get raised and Sharky finds himself playing for his very soul in this chilling new play about the sea, Ireland, and the power of myth.

David Morse, Ciarán Hinds

IS HE DEAD?

Lyceum Theatre; First Preview: November 8, 2007; Opening Night: December 9, 2007; Closed March 9, 2008; 13 previews, 105 performances

Marylouise Burke, John McMartin, Patricia Conolly, Bridget Regan, Michael McGrath, Norbert Leo Butz, Jenn Gambatese, David Pittu (photos by Joan Marcus)

Written by Mark Twain, adapted by David Ives; Produced by Bob Boyett, Roger Berlind, Daryl Roth, Jane Bergére, E. Morten/P. Robbins; J. O'Boyle-R. Stevens, Roy Miller, Sonia Friedman Productions/Ambassador Theatre Group, Tim Levy, in association with Shelley Fisher Fishkin; Director, Michael Blakemore; Sets, Peter J. Davison; Costumes, Martin Pakledinaz; Lighting, Peter Kaczorowski; Music/Sound, David Van Tieghem; Hair/Wigs, Paul Huntley; Casting, Jay Binder/ Jack Bowdan; Associate Producers, Jacki Barlia Florin, Robert G. Bartner; Marketing, HHC Marketing; Dance Sequences, Pamela Remler; General Management/Executive Producers, 101 Productions, Ltd; Production Supervisor, Steven Beckler; Technical Supervisor, Aurora Productions; Company Manager, Gregg Arst; Makeup, Angelina Avallone; Stage Manager, Alexander Libby; Associate Director, Kim Weild; Associate Design: Bryan Johnson (set), Jill BC DuBoff (sound), TJ McEvoy (sound system); Assistant Costumes, Katie Irish, Tescia A. Seufferlein; London Costume Supervisor, Lynette Mauro; Assistant Lighting, Aaron Sporer, Aaron Spivey; Production: Peter Sarafin (props supervisor), Michael Pitzer (electrician), Adam Braunstein (head carpenter), Reg Vessey (head props), Rebecca Heroff (assistant props), Kevin Greene (head electrician), Tucker Howard (sound), Kay Grunder (wardrobe supervisor), Robin Maginsky Day (hair/makeup supervisor); Advertising, SpotCo; Press, Boneau/Bryan-Brown, Steven Padla, Heath Schwartz

CAST Agamemnon Buckner ("Chicago") **Michael McGrath;** Hans von Bismarck ("Dutchy") **Tom Alan Robbins;** Papa Leroux **John McMartin;** Marie Leroux **Jenn Gambatese;** Cecile Leroux **Bridget Regan;** Jean-François Millet **Norbert Leo Butz;** Bastien André **Byron Jennings;** Madame Bathilde **Patricia Conolly;** Madame Caron **Marylouise Burke;** Phelim O'Shaughnessy **Jeremy Bobb;** Basil Thorpe/Claude Riviére/Charlie/The King of France **David Pittu**

UNDERSTUDIES Sheffield Chastain (Agamemnon Buckner, Basil Thorpe, Jean-François Millet, Phelim O'Shaughnessy), Wilbur Edwin Henry (Bastien André, Hans von Bismarck, Papa Leroux), Liv Rooth (Cecile Leroux, Marie Leroux), Peggy J. Scott (Madame Bathilde, Madame Caron)

SETTING Act 1: Two afternoons in Spring, 1846, at Barbizon, near Paris, Millet's studio. Act 2: Three months later, at the Widow's palatial drawing room in Paris. World premiere of a comedy presented in two acts.

SYNOPSIS In this newly discovered Mark Twain comedy, the original master of American humor dishes out a sly critique of the art world with acerbic wit and social commentary well ahead of his time. *Is He Dead?* is a fast-paced play about a struggling artist who stages his own death to drive up the price of his paintings. As the riotous scheme unfolds, Twain poses daring questions about fame, greed and the value of art, and pokes his signature, mischievous fun at everyone involved. Written in 1898, *Is He Dead?* remained unpublished until it was rediscovered in 2002 by noted Twain scholar Shelley Fisher Fishkin.

Norbert Leo Butz, Jenn Gambatese

THE HOMECOMING

Cort Theatre; First preview: December 4, 2007; Opening Night: December 16, 2007; Closed April 13, 2008; 15 previews, 137 performances

Written by Harold Pinter; Produced by Jeffrey Richards, Jerry Frankel, Jam Theatricals, Ergo Entertainment, Barbara & Buddy Freitag, Michael Gardner, Herbert Goldsmith Productions, Terry E. Schnuck, Harold Thau, Michael Filerman/Lynne Peyser; Ronald Frankel/David Jaroslawicz, in association with Love Bunny Entertainment; Director, Daniel Sullivan; Set, Eugene Lee; Costumes, Jess Goldstein; Lighting, Kenneth Posner; Sound, John Gromada; Casting, Telsey + Company; PSM, Roy Harris; Fight Director, Rick Sordelet; Marketing, HHC Marketing; Special Promotions, TMG; General Management, Albert Poland; Technical Supervision, Hudson Theatrical Associates/Neil A. Mazzella; Props Coordinator, Kathy Fabian; Stage Manager, Denise Yaney; Dialect Coach, Liz Smith; Company Manager, Daniel Kuney; Assistant Producer, Noah Himmelstein; Assistant Director, Joshua Brody; Associate Design: Nick Francone, Edward Pierce (set), Anne Kenney (costume), Aaron Spivey (lighting), Chris Cronin (sound), Carrie Hash (props); Assistant Design: Tristan Jeffers (set), Bridget O'Connor (sound); Associate Technical Supervisor, Sam Ellis; Producer Assistants, Noah Himmelstein, Brandi Preston, Cesar Hawas; Production: Ed Diaz (carpenter), Scott DeVerna (electrician), Lonnie Gaddy & Jens McVoy (props), Penny Davis (wardrobe supervisor), Patricia A. Peek (hair supervisor), Kevin O'Brien, Kimberly Butler, Yvonne Jensen, Laura Totero (dressers); Advertising, Serino Coyne; Press, Jeffrey Richards Associates, Irene Gandy, Judith Hansen, Elon Rutberg

Eve Best, Raúl Esparza (front), James Frain (back) (photos by Scott Landis)

Eve Best

CAST Max **Ian McShane;** Lenny **Raúl Esparza;** Sam **Michael McKean;** Joey **Gareth Saxe;** Teddy **James Frain;** Ruth **Eve Best**

UNDERSTUDIES/STANDBYS Jarlath Conroy (Max, Sam), Francesca Faridany (Ruth), Creighton James (Lenny, Teddy, Joey)

2007–2008 AWARDS Drama Desk: Outstanding Ensemble; Outer Critics Circle: Outstanding Revival of a Play

SETTING Summer. An old house in North London. Revival of a drama presented in two acts. Originally presented on Broadway at the Music Box Theatre, January 5–October 14, 1967 (see *Theatre World* Volume 23, page 42). The Roundabout Theatre Company revived the play at the Criterion Center October 27–December 8, 1991 (see *Theatre World* Volume 48, page 12).

SYNOPSIS *The Homecoming* concerns the ultimate dysfunctional family, presided over by its patriarch, Max. Living under his dilapidated roof are his younger brother Sam, and two of his sons: Lenny, the town pimp, and Joey, a boxer-in-training. Tensions begin to flair with the arrival of Max's eldest son Teddy, who returns home after six years with his new wife Ruth. Seduction, betrayal, and divisiveness ensue, as the family welcomes the homecoming of its estranged brother and vies for the attention of his dangerously alluring wife.

THE LITTLE MERMAID

Lunt-Fontanne Theatre; First Preview: November 3, 2007; Opening Night: January 10, 2008; 50 previews, 164 performances as of May 31, 2008

Music by Alan Menken, lyrics by Howard Ashman and Glenn Slater, book by Doug Wright; based on the Hans Christian Anderson story and the Disney film produced by Howard Ashman & John Musker and written and directed by John Musker & Ron Clements; Produced by Disney Theatrical Productions under the direction of Thomas Schumacher; Director, Francesca Zambello; Produced by Disney Theatricasl Productions under the direction of Thomas Schumacher; Choreography, Stephen Mear; Music Director/Incidental Music/Vocal Arrangements, Michael Kosarin; Orchestrations, Danny Troob; Sets, George Tsypin; Costumes, Tatiana Noginova; Lighting, Natasha Katz; Sound, John Shivers; Hair, David Brian Brown; Makeup, Angelina Avallone; Projections/Video, Sven Ortel; Dance Arrangements, David Chase; Music Coordinator, Michael Keller; Fight Director, Rick Sordelet; Casting, Tara Rubin; Associate Producer, Todd Lacy; Associate Director, Brian Hill; Associate Choreographer, Tara Young; Technical Director, David Benken; PSM/Supervisor, Clifford Schwartz; Aerial Design, Pichón Baldinu; Dialogue/Vocal Coach, Deborah Hecht; Company Manager, Randy Meyer; ACM, Margie Freeswick; Production Associate, Jane Abramson; Stage Manager, Theresa Bailey; ASMs, Kenneth J. McGee, Matthew Aaron Stern, Sarah Tschipke; Dance Captain, Joanne Manning; Fight Captain/Assistant Dance Captain, James Brown III; Associate Design: Peter Eastman (set), Tracy Christensen (costumes), Yael Lubetzky (lighting), David Potridge (sound), Jonathan Carter (hair), Peter Acken, Katy Tucker (projection), Angela Phillips (aerial); Magic/Illusion Design, Joe Eddie Fairchild; Sculptor, Arturs Virtmanis; Automated Lights, Aland Henderson, Joel Shier; Assistant Design: Gaetane Bertol, Larry Brown, Kelly Hanso, Niki Hernandez-Adams, Nathan Heverin, Rachel Short Janocko, Jee an Jung, Mimi Lien, Frank McCullough, Arnulfo Maldonado, Robert Pyzocha, Chisato Uno (set), Brian J. Bustos, Amy Clark (costumes), Craig Stelzenmuller, Richard Swan (lighting), Thomas Augustine (hair/hair supervisor); Production: Stephen Detmer (carpenter), Patrick Eviston (head carpenter), Jeff Zink (fly automation), Michael L. Shepp, Jr. (deck automation), Rick Howard (rigger), Rick Baxter (electrician), Joseph Pearson (head electrician), Damian Caza-Cleypool (assistant electrician), Jesse Hancox (moving lights), Jerry L. Marshall, Steven E. Wood (props), David Partridge (sound engineer), George Huckins (head sound), Scott Anderson (deck sound), Nancy Schaefer (wardrobe supervisor), Gary Arave (assistant hair supervisor), Tiffany Hicks (makeup supervisor), Jorge Vargas (assistant makeup supervisor); Additional Orchestrations, Larry Hochman, Michael Starobin; Electronic Music Design, Andrew Barrett; Music Preparation, Anixter Rice Music Service; Associate to Mr. Menken, Rick Kunis; Advertising, Serino Coyne; Press, Boneau/Bryan-Brown, Aaron Meier, Christine Olver, Susanne Tighe; Cast recording: Walt Disney Records D000108102

Sean Palmer and Sierra Boggess (photos by Joan Marcus)

CAST Pilot **Merwin Foard;** Prince Eric **Sean Palmer;** Grimsby **Jonathan Freeman;** King Triton **Norm Lewis;** Sebastian **Tituss Burgess;** Ariel **Sierra Boggess;** Flounder **Trevor Braun/Brian D'Addario;** Scuttle **Eddie Korbich;** Gulls **Robert Creighton, Tim Federle, Arbender Robinson;** Ursula **Sherie Rene Scott;** Flotsam **Tyler Maynard;** Jetsam **Derrick Baskin;** Carlotta **Heidi Blickenstaff;** Chef Louis **John Treacy Egan;** Ensemble **Adrian Bailey, Cathryn Basile, Heidi Blickenstaff, Robert Creighton, Cicily Daniels, John Treacy Egan, Tim Federle, Merwin Foard, Ben Hartley, Michelle Lookadoo, Alan Mingo, Jr., Zakiya Young Mizen, Arbender Robinson, Bahiyah Sayyed Gaines, Bret Shuford, Chelsea Morgan Stock, Kay Trinidad, Daniel J. Watts;** Swings **Julie Barnes, James Brown III, Meredith Inglesby, Joanne Manning, Betsy Morgan, Jason Snow, Price Waldman**

UNDERSTUDIES Adrian Bailey (King Triton), Derrick Baskin (Sebastian), Heidi Blickenstaff (Ursula), Robert Creighton (Scuttle), Cicily Daniels (Ursula), Tim Federle (Jetsam, Scuttle), Merwin Foard (Grimsby, King Triton), Alan Mingo Jr. (Sebastian), Betsy Morgan (Ariel), Arbender J. Robinson (Prince Eric), Bret Shuford (Flotsam, Prince Eric), Jason Snow (Flotsam), Chelsea Morgan Stock (Ariel), Price Waldman (Flotsam, Grimsby, Jetsam)

ORCHESTRA Michael Kosarin (Conductor); Greg Anthony (Associate Conductor/keyboard 2); Suzanne Ornstein (Concert Master); Mineko Yajima (violin); Roger Shell, Deborah Assael (celli); Nicholas Marchione, Frank Greene (trumpets); Gary Grimaldi (trombone); Jeff Caswell (bass trombone/tuba); Steven Kenyon, David Young, Marc Phaneuf (reeds); Zohar Schondorf (French horn); Aron Accurso (keyboard 1); Andrew Grobengieser (keyboard 3); Richard Sarpola (bass); John Redsecker (drums); Joe Passaro (percussion)

MUSICAL NUMBERS Overture, Fathoms Below, Daughters of Triton, The World Above, Human Stuff, I Want the Good Times Back, Part of Your World, Storm at Sea, Part of Your World (reprise), She's in Love, Her Voice, The World Above (reprise), Under the Sea, Sweet Child, Poor Unfortunate Souls, Entr'acte, Positoovity, Beyond My Wildest Dreams, Les Poissons, Les Poissons (reprise), One Step Closer, I Want the Good Times Back (reprise), Kiss the Girl, Sweet Child (reprise), If Only, The Contest, Poor Unfortunate Souls (reprise), If Only (reprise), Finale

World premiere of a new musical presented in two acts. The show had an out-of-town tryout in Denver, Colorado at the Denver Center, July 26, 2007.

Sierra Boggess and Company

Derrick Baskin, Sierra Boggess, Sherie Rene Scott, Tyler Maynard

SYNOPSIS Based on the 1989 Disney film and the Hans Christian Anderson fairy tale, *The Little Mermaid* is set in a magical kingdom beneath the sea, where a beautiful young mermaid named Ariel longs to leave her ocean home to live in the world above. But first, she'll have to defy her father, the king of the sea, escape the clutches of an evil sea witch and convince a prince that she's the girl with the perfect voice.

Tituss Burgess

BROADWAY – Opened June 1, 2007–May 31, 2008

THE 39 STEPS

American Airlines Theatre; First Preview: January 4, 2008; Opening Night: January 15, 2008; Closed March 29, 2008; 12 previews, 87 performances; transferred to the Cort Theatre; Second Previews: April 29, 2008; Second Opening Night: May 8, 2008; 11 previews, 28 performances as of May 31, 2008

Adapted by Patrick Barlow from the film by Alfred Hitchcock and the book by John Buchan; based on an original concept by Simon Corble and Nobby Dimon; Produced by the Roundabout Theatre Company (Todd Haimes, Artistic Director; Harold Wolpert, Managing Director; Julia C. Levy, Executive Director) in association with Bob Boyett, Harriet Newman Leve/Ron Nicynski, Stewart F. Lane/Bonnie Comley, Manocherian Golden Productions, Olympus Theatricals/Douglas Denoff, Marek J. Cantor/Pat Addiss, and the Huntington Theatre Company (Nicholas Martin, Artistic Director; Michael Maso, Managing Director), and Edward Snape for Fiery Angel Ltd.; Director, Maria Aitken; Set/Costumes, Peter McKintosh; Lighting, Kevin Adams; Sound, Mic Pool; Dialect Coach, Stephen Gabis; Original Movement, Toby Sedgewick; Additional Movement, Christopher Bays; Production Manager, Aurora Productions; PSM, Nevin Hedley; Casting, Jay Binder, Jack Bowdan; General Manager, Rebecca Habel, Roy Gabay; Associate Producer/Roundabout General Manager, Sydney Beers; Marketing/Sales Promotion, David B. Steffen; Development, Jeffory Lawson; Founding Director, Gene Feist; Associate Artistic Director, Scott Ellis; Artistic Development/Casting, Jim Carnahan; Education, David A. Miller; Telesales, Daniel Weiss; Finance, Susan Neiman; Sales Operations, Charlie Garbowski, Jr.; Company Manager, Nichole Jennino; ACM, Carly DiFulvio; Stage Manager, Janet Takami; Wigs, Jason Allen; Assistant Director, Kevin Bigger; Assistant Design: Josh Zangen (set), Aaron Sporer (lighting), Drew Levy (sound); Production: Peter Sarafin (properties), Glenn Merwede (carpenter), Brian Maiuri (electrician), Andrew Forste (running props), Dann Wojnar (sound engineer), Nelson Vaughn, Carmel Sheehan (props), Barb Bartel (deck electrician), Susan J. Fallon (wardrobe supervisor), Manuela LaPorte (hair and wig supervisor), Renee Mariotti, Margaret M. Donovan (dressers), Melissa Crawford (day wardrobe), Rosy Garner (assistant); For commercial transfer: Executive Producer, 101 Productions, Ltd.; Associate Producer, Marek J. Cantor; Company Manager, Daniel Kuney; Crew: Ed Diaz (carpenter), Kevin Diaz (flyman), Rebecca Heroff/Nelson Vaughn/Lonnie Gaddy (properties), Scott DeVerna/Shannon January (electricians), Dann Wojnar (sound), Jesse Galvan (wardrobe), Alice Ramos (hair and wigs); Advertising, Eliran Murphy Group; Press, Boneau/Bryan-Brown: Adrian Bryan-Brown, Matt Polk, Jessica Johnson, Amy Kass

CAST Man #1 **Cliff Saunders;** Man #2 **Arnie Burton;** Richard Hannay **Charles Edwards;** Annabella Schmidt/Pamela/Margaret **Jennifer Ferrin**

UNDERSTUDIES Claire Brownell (Annabella Schmidt/Pamela/Margaret), Cameron Folmar (Man #1/Man #2), Mark Shanahan (Richard Hannay)

2007–2008 AWARDS Tonys: Best Lighting Design of a Play, Best Sound Design of a Play; Drama Desk: Unique Theatrical Experience, Outstanding Lighting Design

SETTING Scotland and London. New York premiere of a new comedy/thriller presented in two acts. Previously presented at the Tricycle Theatre in London in 2006, and at Boston's Huntington Theatre Company, September 14, 2007, prior to this engagement.

SYNOPSIS Four cast members play over 150 roles in this hilarious whodunit, part espionage thriller and part slapstick comedy. The story revolves around an innocent man who learns too much about a dangerous spy ring and is then pursued across Scotland and to London. *The 39 Steps* contains every legendary scene from the award-winning movie—the chase on the Flying Scotsman, the escape on the Forth Bridge, the first theatrical bi-plane crash ever staged, and the sensational death-defying finale in the London Palladium.

Charles Edwards, Arnie Burton, Cliff Saunders and Jennifer Ferrin (photo by Joan Marcus)

NOVEMBER

Barrymore Theatre; First Preview: December 20, 2007; Opening Night: January 17, 2008; 33 previews, 156 performances as of May 31, 2008

Written by David Mamet; Produced by Jeffrey Richards, Jerry Frankel, Jam Theatricals, Bat-Barry Productions, Michael Cohl, Ergo Entertainment, Michael Filerman, Ronald Frankel, Barbara & Buddy Freitag, James Fuld Jr., Roy Furman, JK Productions, Harold A. Thau, Jamie deRoy/Ted Snowdon; Director, Joe Mantello; Set, Scott Pask; Costumes, Laura Bauer; Lighting, Paul Gallo; Casting, Telsey + Company; PSM, Jill Cordle; Technical Supervision, Hudson Theatrical Associates (Neil A. Mazzella, Sam Ellis, Irene Wang); General Management, Richards/Climan, Inc. (David R. Richards, Tamar Haimes, Laura Janik Cronin); Marketing Services, TMG; Company Manager, Bruce Klinger; Associate Producer/Assistant to Mr. Richards, Noah Himmelstein; Stage Manager, Neil Krasnow; Assistant Director, Stephanie Yankwitt; Associate Lighting, Phillip Rosenberg; Consultant, Darron L West; Assistant to Mr. West, Matt Hubbs; Wigs, Paul Huntley, Martial Corneville; Assistant Set, Jeffrey Hinchee, Orit Carroll; Assistant Costumes, Bobby Tilley; General Management Associate, Jeromy Smith; Production: Nathan K. Claus (assistant), Frank Illo (carpenter), Jimmy Maloney (electrician), Denise J. Grillo (props), Kristine Bellerud (wardrobe supervisor), Erin Kennedy Lunsford (hair supervisor), Ken Brown (Mr. Lane's dresser), Rose Marie Cappelluti (dresser); Advertising, Serino Coyne; Press, Jeffrey Richards, Irene Gandy, Elon Rutberg

Laurie Metcalf

Nathan Lane, Ethan Phillips, Dylan Baker (photos by Scott Landis)

CAST Charles Smith **Nathan Lane;** Archer Brown **Dylan Baker;** A Representative of the National Association of Turkey By-Products Manufacturers **Ethan Phillips;** Clarice Bernstein **Laurie Metcalf;** Dwight Grackle **Michael Nichols**

STANDBYS Richard Kline (Charles Smith), Amy Hohn (Clarice Bernstein), Greg Stuhr (Archer Brown, Turkey Guy), Victor Talmadge (Dwight Grackle)

2007–2008 AWARDS Outer Critics Circle: Outstanding Featured Actress in a Play (Laurie Metcalf)

SETTING Morning, night, and morning; an office. World premiere of a new comedy presented in two acts.

SYNOPSIS Set just days before a major presidential election, *November* involves civil marriages, gambling casinos, lesbians, American Indians, presidential libraries, questionable pardons and campaign contributions.

COME BACK, LITTLE SHEBA

Biltmore Theatre; First Preview: January 3, 2008; Opening Night: January 24, 2008; Closed March 16, 2008; 27 previews, 58 performances

Written by William Inge; Produced by Manhattan Theatre Club (Lynne Meadow, Artistic Director; Barry Grove, Executive Producer; Daniel Sullivan, 07-08 Acting Artistic Director); Director, Michael Pressman; Set, James Noone; Costumes, Jennifer von Mayrhauser; Lighting, Jane Cox; Sound, Obadiah Eaves; Original Music, James Golub; Fight Director, J. David Brimmer; PSM, James Fitzsimmons; Casting, David Caparelliotis; General Manager, Florie Seery; Associate Artistic Director/Production, Mandy Greenfield; Marketing, Debra A. Waxman; Production Manager, Kurt Gardner; Casting, Nancy Piccione; Development, Jill Turner Lloyd; Artistic Administration/Assistant to Artistic Director, Amy Gilkes Loe; Literary Manager, Raphael Martin; Musical Development, Clifford Lee Johnson III; Finance, Jeffrey Bledsoe; Associate GM, Lindsey Brooks Sag; Subscriber Services, Robert Allenberg; Telesales, George Tetlow; Education, David Shookhoff; Associate PM, Philip Naudé; Lighting/Sound Supervisor, Matthew T. Gross; Prop Supervisor, Scott Laule; Costume Supervisor, Erin Hennessy Dean; Company Manager, Seth Shepsle; Stage Manager, Bryce McDonald; Assistant Director, Jose Zayas; Associate Design: Joshua Epstein (lighting), Ashley Hanson (sound); Assistant Design: Patrick Tennant (set), Suzanne Chesney (costumes); Ms. Merkerson's wig, Anita Crawford; Hair/Makeup Supervisor, Jon Jordan; Lighting Programmer, Marc Polimeni; Dresser, Tracey Boone; Magic Consultant, Eli Bosnick; Advertising, SpotCo; Press, Boneau/Bryan-Brown, Jim Byk, Aaron Meier, Heath Schwartz, Christine Olver

S. Epatha Merkerson

CAST Doc **Kevin Anderson;** Marie **Zoe Kazan;** Lola **S. Epatha Merkerson;** Turk **Brian J. Smith;** Postman **Lyle Kanouse;** Mrs. Coffman **Brenda Wehle;** Milkman **Matthew J. Williamson;** Messenger **Daniel Damon Joyce;** Bruce **Chad Hoeppner;** Ed **Keith Randolph Smith;** Elmo **Joseph Adams**

UNDERSTUDIES Joseph Adams (Doc), Phillip Clark (Ed, Elmo, Postman), Caroline Stefanie Clay (Lola), Chad Hoeppner (Messenger), Daniel Damon Joyce (Bruce, Milkman, Turk), Darrie Lawrence (Mrs. Coffman)

SETTING An old house in a Midwestern city in the spring of 1950. Revival of a drama presented in two acts. This production was previously presented by Center Theatre Group's Kirk Theatre, Los Angeles, June 17-July 15, 2007, starring Ms. Merkerson (see *Theatre World* Volume 63). Originally produced on Broadway at the Booth Theatre, February 15-July 29, 1950 (see *Theatre World* Volume 6, page 84).

SYNOPSIS Lola is a faded beauty queen trapped in a lonely marriage to Doc, a recovering alcoholic on the brink of relapse. When a pretty young woman becomes a boarder in their cluttered Midwest home, their lives are unsettled as unspoken passions rise to the surface. As the emptiness of their marriage is laid bare, can they find their way back to each other or will they be undone?

Zoe Kazan, S. Epatha Merkerson, Brian J. Smith (photos by Joan Marcus)

SUNDAY IN THE PARK WITH GEORGE

Studio 54; First Preview: January 18, 2008; Opening Night: February 21, 2008; 32 previews, 116 performances as of May 31, 2008

Music and lyrics by Stephen Sondheim, book by James Lapine; Originally presented by The Menier Chocolate Factory; Produced by the Roundabout Theatre Company (Todd Haimes, Artistic Director; Harold Wolpert, Managing Director; Julia C. Levy, Executive Director) in association with Bob Boyett, Debra Black, Jam Theatricals, Stephanie P. McClelland, Stewart F. Lane/Bonnie Comley, Barbara Manocherian/Jennifer Manocherian, and Ostar Productions; Presented in association with Caro Newling for Neal Street Productions and Mark Rubenstein; Director, Sam Buntrock; Musical Staging, Christopher Gattelli; Sets/Costumes, David Farley; Lighting, Ken Billington; Sound, Sebastian Frost; Projections, Timothy Bird & The Knifedge Creative Network; Musical Supervisor, Caroline Humphris; Orchestrations, Jason Carr; Music Coordinator, John Miller; PSM, Peter Hanson; Hair/Wigs, Tom Watson; Dialect Coach, Kate Wilson; Casting, Jim Carnahan; Technical Supervisor, Steve Beers; Executive Producer, Sydney Beers; Marketing/Sales, David B. Steffen; Development, Jeffory Lawson; Founding Director, Gene Feist; Associate Artistic Director, Scott Ellis; Education Director, David A. Miller; Finance, Susan Neiman; Sales Operations, Charlie Garbowski, Jr.; Telesales, Daniel Weiss; Company Manager, Denise Cooper; Company Manager Assistant, Brent McCreary; Stage Manager, Jon Krause; ASM, Rachel Zack; Assistant Director, Dave Solomon; Associate Director/Choreographer (UK), Tara Wilkinson; Assistant to the Choreographer, Lou Castro; Dance Captain, Hayley Podschun; Makeup, Angelina Avallone; Associate Design: Matthew Pachtman (costumes), Paul Toben (lighting), Nick Borisjuk (sound); UK Assistants to Mr. Farley, Julie Bowles, Sarah Cant, Machiko Hombu; Music Coordinator Assistant, Charles Butler; Production: Dan Hoffman (carpenter), Josh Weitzman (electrician), John Wooding (assistant electrician), Sam Hopkins (assistant projection engineer/media programmer), Kathy Fabian/Propstar (production properties), Rose Howard (assistant props), Nadine Hettel (wardrobe supervisor), Barry Ernst (hair/wig supervisor), Joe Goodwin, Victoria Grecki, Mary Ann Oberpiller (dressers), Timothy Miller (hair assistant), Brad Gyorgak (sound engineer), Lawrence Jennino (house props), Erin Mary Delaney (props run crew), Paul Ashton (automation carpenter), Steve Jones (flyman), David Arch (moving light programmer), Jessica Morton (obsession programmer), Larry White (spot), Larry White (deck sound); Music Preparation, Emily Grishman, Katharine Edmonds; Synthesizer Programmer, Bruce Samuels; For Knifedge The Creative Network: Timothy Bird (Creative Director), Sam Hopkins & his Light Studio (Revisualization & Projection Strategy), Nina Wilson (team leader/AFX Animator), Raf Anzovin (rigging), Ciara Fanning (content librarian), Shaun Freeman (character animator), John Keates (animator/technical director), Alex Laurent (matte artist), Andy McNamara (3D animator), Stephen Millingen (animator), Aaron Trinder (AFX animator), Sam Buntrock (additional animation), Amy Di Prima ("Putting It Together" effects Producer), John Chimples ("Putting It Together" effects Videographer), Advertising, SpotCo; Press, Boneau/Bryan-Brown, Matt Polk, Jessica Johnson, Amy Kass; London Cast recording: PS Classics 640

Daniel Evans, Jenna Russell (photos by Joan Marcus)

Allison Horowitz, Jessica Molaskey, Drew McVety, Brynn O'Malley, Jessica Grové, Daniel Evans, Michael Cumpsty, Jenna Russell

2007–2008 AWARDS Drama Desk: Outstanding Orchestrations; Outer Critics Circle: Outstanding Scenic Design, Outstanding Lighting Design; **Theatre World Award:** Jenna Russell

SETTING Act 1: A series of Sundays from 1884-1886 in a park on an island in the Seine just outside of Paris, and George's studio. Act 2: 1984, at an American art museum and on the island. Revival of the musical presented in two acts. This production was previously presented at the Menier Chocolate Factory (David Babani, Artistic Director), London, in 2005, and transferred to the Wyndham's Theatre in the West End on May 23, 2006 starring Mr. Evans and Ms. Russell. The production won five Olivier awards. The show was originally produced at Playwrights Horizons (directed by James Lapine) from November 8, 1983-January 15, 1984; the show transferred to Broadway at the Booth Theatre on May 2, 1984, garnering the Pulitzer Prize, two Tony Awards, and eight Drama Desk Awards (see *Theatre World* Volume 40, pages 39 and 114). A tenth anniversary concert production was produced at the St. James Theatre on May 15, 1994, reuniting most of the original cast members (see *Theatre World* Volume 50, page 70).

CAST George **Daniel Evans;** Dot/Marie **Jenna Russell;** An Old Lady/Blair Daniels **Mary Beth Piel;** Nurse/Mrs./ Harriet Pawling **Anne L. Nathan;** Franz/Lee Randolph **David Turner;** Jules/Bob Greenburg **Michael Cumpsty;** Yvonne/Naomi Eisen **Jessica Molaskey;** A Boatman/ Dennis **Alexander Gemignani;** Celeste #1/Elaine **Brynn O'Malley;** Celeste #2/Photographer **Jessica Grové;** Bather/ Louis/Billy Webster **Drew McVety;** Louise/Bather **Kelsey Fowler** or **Alison Horowitz;** Frieda/Betty **Stacie Morgain Lewis;** Bather/A Soldier/Alex **Santino Fontana;** Mr./ Charles Redmond **Ed Dixon**

UNDERSTUDIES Colleen Fitzpatrick (Yvonne/Naomi Eisen, Old Lady/Blair Daniels, Nurse/Mrs./Harriet Pawling), Santino Fontana (George), Jeff Kready (Soldier/Alex, Louis/Billy, Franz/Lee Randolph), Brynn O'Malley (Dot/Marie), Hayley Podschun (Celeste #1/Elaine, Celeste #2/A Photographer, Frieda/Betty); Standby: Andrew Varela (Mr./Charles Redmond, Boatman/Dennis, Jules/Bob Greenburg)

ORCHESTRA Caroline Humphris (Conductor/piano); Thomas Murray (Associate Conductor/keyboard), Matthew Lehmann (violin/House Contractor), Mairi Dorman-Phaneuf (Cello), Todd Groves (Woodwinds)

MUSICAL NUMBERS Sunday in the Park With George, No Life, Color and Light, Gossip, The Day Off, Everybody Loves Louis, Finishing the Hat, We Do Not Belong Together, Beautiful, Sunday, It's Hot Up Here, Chromolume #7, Putting It Together, Children and Art, Lesson #8, Move On, Sunday

SYNOPSIS The Georges Seurat painting, "A Sunday Afternoon on the Island of La Grande Jatte," is the inspiration for this compelling musical fantasy which celebrates the art of creation and the creation of art. The first half of the show, set in 1884, sees the painting and its rich comic tapestry come to life in a world where, for George, art comes before love, before everything. In the second half, set in the 1980's, we see the great grandson of George and his search for inspiration amongst the unfolding world of contemporary art.

Jenna Russell, Daniel Evans

PASSING STRANGE

Belasco Theatre; First Preview: February 8, 2008; Opening Night: February 28, 2008; 20 previews, 108 performances as of May 31, 2008

Book and lyrics by Stew, music by Stew and Heidi Rodewald; Created in collaboration with Annie Dorsen; Produced by The Shubert Organization, Elizabeth Ireland McCann, Bill Kenwright, Chase Mishkin, Barbara & Buddy Freitag, Broadway Across America, Emily Fisher Landau, Peter May, Boyett Ostar, Ellie Hirschfeld/Jed Bernstein, Wendy Federman/Jacki B. Florin, Spring Sirkin/Ruth Hendel, Vasi Laurence/Pat Flicker Addiss, in association with The Public Theater (Oscar Eustace, Artistic Director; Mara Manus, Executive Director) and The Berkeley Repertory Theatre (Tony Taccone, Artistic Director; Susan Medak, Managing Director); Executive Producer/General Management, Joey Parnes; Director, Annie Dorsen; Choreography, Karole Armitage; Sets, David Korins; Costumes, Elizabeth Hope Clancy; Lighting, Kevin Adams; Sound, Tom Morse; Music Supervision/Orchestrations, Stew & Heidi Rodewald; Music Coordinator, Seymour Red Press; Casting, Jordan Thaler & Heidi Griffiths; PSM, Tripp Phillips; Company Manager, Kim Sellon; Associate Producer, S.D. Wagner; Assistant Producer, John Johnson; Stage Manager, Jason Hindelang; ASM, Cynthia Cahill; Management Associate, Kit Ingui; Assistant Director, Stephen P. Brackett; Assistant Choreographer, William Isaac; Dance Captain, David Ryan Smith; Light Wall Design, Kevin Adams, David Korins; Associate Set Design, Rod Lemmond; Design Assistants: Amanda Stephens, Nathan Koch (set), Aaron Sporer (lighting), Chloe Chapin (costumes), Kevin Brubaker (sound); Vocal Coach, Barbara Maier; Dialect Coach, Elizabeth Smith: Production: Larry Morley (carpenter), Steve Cochrane (electrician), Mike Smanko (prop supervisor), Tucker Howard (sound engineer), Bill Craven (head carpenter), Susan Goulet (head electrician), Dylan Foley (head props), Rich Mortel (moving light programmer), Dave Olin Rogers (wardrobe supervisor), Francine Buryiak, Julienne Shubert-Blechman (dressers), Thelma L. Pollard (hair consultant), John Bantay (assistant); Music Transcription, Matthew Henning; Music Copyist, Emily Grishman, Katharine Edmonds; Literary Manager, Gaydon Phillips; Management Assistant, Matt Farabee; Assistant to Stew, Mike James; Guitar Technician, Mike Fornatale; Guitar Instructor, Steve Bargunet; Advertising, Serino Coyne; Press, Sam Rudy Media Relations, Dale R. Heller, Robert Lasko, Charlie Siedenburg; Cast recording: Sh-K-Boom/Ghostlight Records 84429

CAST Narrator **Stew;** Bass/Vocals **Heidi Rodewald;** Keyboard/Guitar/Backing Vocals **Jon Spurney;** Drums **Christian Cassan;** Guitar/Keyboard/Backing Vocals **Christian Gibbs;** Mother **Eisa Davis;** Youth **Daniel Breaker;** Terry/Christophe/Hugo **Chad Goodridge;** Sherry/Renata/Desi **Rebecca Naomi Jones;** Franklin/Joop/Mr. Venus **Colman Domingo;** Edwina/Marianna/Sudabey **de'Adre Aziza**

Chad Goodridge, Daniel Breaker, Colman Domingo, Stew and Rebecca Naomi Jones (photos by Carol Rosegg)

Stew

Front: Daniel Breaker, and Eisa Davis, Back: Stew

UNDERSTUDIES Billy Eugene Jones (Franklin/Joop/Mr. Venus), Kelly McReary (Edwina Mariana/Sudabey, Sherry/Renata/Desi), Karen Pittman (Mother), David Ryan Smith (Narrator), Lawrence Stallings (Youth, Hugo/Christophe/Terry)

MUSICAL NUMBERS Prologue (We Might Play All Night), Baptist Fashion Show, Blues Revelation/Freight Train, Arlington Hill, Sole Brother, Must've Been High, Mom Song, Merci Beaucoup M. Godard, Amsterdam, Keys, We Just Had Sex, May Day, Surface, Damage, Identity, The Black One, Come Down Now, Work the Wound, Passing Phase, Love Like That

2007–2008 AWARDS Tony: Best Book of a Musical; Drama Desk: Outstanding New Musical, Outstanding Music, Outstanding Lyrics; New York Drama Critics' Circle: Best Musical; **Theatre World Awards:** de'Adre Aziza, Daniel Breaker

SETTING Los Angeles, Amsterdam, Berlin. The present. A new musical presented in two acts. Originally presented by Berkeley Repertory Theatre, California, October 25–December 3, 2006, and The Public Theater, May 14–June 3, 2007 (see *Theatre World* Volume 63).

SYNOPSIS Developed at the Stanford Institute for Creativity the Arts, Berkeley Repertory Theatre, and the Public Theater, *Passing Strange* takes audiences on an international journey from L.A. to Amsterdam, Berlin, and beyond as a young man from California searches for his identity. It features blues, rock and roll, gospel, and pop music written by Stew and Rodewald, who head the band The Negro Problem.

Eisa Davis (background) and de'Adre Aziza

Colman Domingo, Daniel Breaker, Chad Goodridge

CAT ON A HOT TIN ROOF

Broadhurst Theatre; First Preview: February 12, 2008; Opening Night: March 6, 2008; 25 previews, 100 performances as of May 31, 2008

Written by Tennessee Williams; Produced by Front Row Productions and Stephen C. Byrd, in association with Alia M. Jones; Director, Debbie Allen; Set, Ray Klausen; Costumes, Jane Greenwood: Lighting, William H. Grant III; Sound, John Shivers; Hair, Charles LaPointe; Casting, Peter Wise & Associates; Production Supervisor, Theatresmith, Inc.; PSM, Gwendolyn M Gilliam; General Management, Nina Lannan Associates/Devin Keudell; Original Music, Andrew "Tex" Allen; Group Sales/Marketing, Marcia Pendelton/ WTGP; Associate Producers, Clarence J. Chandran, Anthony Lacavera, Norm Nixon, Sheanna Pang, Beatrice L. Rangel, Jovan Vitagliano, Terrie Williams, Al Wilson; ASM, Charles Underhill; Associate Design: Randall Parsons (set), MaryAnn D. Smith (costumes), Temishia Johnson (lighting), David Partridge (sound/sound mixer); Assistant to Ms. Greenwood, Christina Bullard; Dramaturg, Shauneille Perry; Dialects, Barbara Montgomery; Production: Gerry Griffin (carpenter), Jimmy Fedigan (electrician), Peter Donovan (head electrician), Philo Lojo (sound), Emiliano Pares, Laura MacGaritty (props); Kathy Guida (wardrobe supervisor), Michele Rutter (hair/ makeup supervisor); Advertising, SpotCo; Marketing, Walk Tall Girl Productions/Marcia Pendleton; General Management Associate, Carol M. Oune; Saxophone Player, Gerald Hayes; Press, Springer Associates, Gary Springer, Joe Trentacosta, Shane Marshall Brown, D'Arcy Drollinger, Jennifer Blum, Ethnee Lea

CAST Maggie **Anika Noni Rose;** Brick **Terrence Howard*;** Reverend Tooker **Lou Myers;** Doctor Baugh **Count Stovall;** Mae **Lisa Arrindell Anderson;** Sonny **Skye Jasmine Allen-McBean;** Big Mama **Phylicia Rashad;** Gooper **Giancarlo Esposito;** Sookey **Marja Harmon;** Dixie **Heaven Howard*;** Trixie **Marissa Chisolm;** Lacey **Clark Jackson;** Big Daddy **James Earl Jones;** Servants **Bethany Butler, Robert Christopher Riley**

UNDERSTUDIES Count Stovall (Big Daddy), Robert Christopher Riley (Brick, Rev. Tooker, Lacey), Marja Harmon (Maggie, Mae), Bethany Butler (Maggie, Mae), Jane White (Big Mama), Clark Jackson (Gooper, Dr. Baugh, Rev. Tooker)

Terrence Howard and Anika Noni Rose (photos by Joan Marcus)

SETTING A summer evening gathering at the Pollitt family estate in Mississippi. Revival of the drama presented in three acts with two intermissions. Originally presented on Broadway at the Morosco Theatre, March 24, 1955-November 17, 1956, playing 694 performances (see *Theatre World* Volume 11, page 87). The play has seen three major New York revivals prior to this production: ANTA Playhouse, September 24, 1974–February 8, 1975 (see *Theatre World* Volume 31, page 9); Eugene O'Neill Theatre, March 21–August 9, 1990, (see *Theatre World* Volume 46, page 28); Music Box Theatre, November 2, 2003–March 7, 2004 (see *Theatre World* Volume 60, page 36).

SYNOPSIS Winner of the 1955 Pulitzer Prize for Drama, the classic is revived with an Afro-American cast. Will manipulative patriarch Big Daddy leave his plantation to his weasly son Gooper or his handsome alcoholic son Brick? And why doesn't Brick have a son of his own? Hot-blooded wife Maggie does her best to tempt Brick from his brooding and back into her bed.

*Boris Kodjoe replaced Mr. Howard and Alessandra Chisholm replaced Miss Howard from April 15-May 4.

Heaven Howard, Skye Jasmine Allen-McBean, Giancarlo Esposito, Marja Harmon, Marissa Chisolm, Clark Jackson, Bethany Butler, Anika Noni Rose, James Earl Jones, Phylicia Rashad, Lisa Arrindell Anderson

BROADWAY – Opened June 1, 2007–May 31, 2008

IN THE HEIGHTS

Richard Rodgers Theatre; First Preview: February 14, 2008; Opening Night: March 9, 2008; 29 previews, 95 performances as of May 31, 2008

Concept, music and lyrics by Lin-Manuel Miranda, book by Quiara Alegría Hudes; Produced by Kevin McCollum, Jeffrey Seller, Jill Furman, Sander Jacobs, Goodman/Grossman, Peter Fine, Everett/Skipper; Director, Thomas Kail; Choreographer, Andy Blankenbuehler; Music Director, Alex Lacamoire; Sets, Anna Louizos; Costumes, Paul Tazewell; Lighting, Howell Binkley; Sound, Acme Sound Partners; Arrangements and Orchestrations, Alex Lacamoire & Bill Sherman; Music Coordinator, Michael Keller; Casting, Telsey + Company; Marketing, Scott A. Moore; Company Manager, Brig Berney; General Manager, John S. Corker, Lizbeth Cone; Technical Supervisor, Brian Lynch; PSM, J. Philip Bassett; Associate Producers, Ruth Hendel, Harold Newman; Wigs, Charles LaPointe; Assistant Director, Casey Hushion; Assistant Choreographer, Joey Dowling; Fight Director, Ron Piretti; Latin Assistant Choreographer, Luis Salgado; Fight/Dance Captain, Michael Balderrama; Stage Manager, Amber Wedin; ASM, Heather Hogan; Associate Design: Donyale Werle, Todd Potter (set), Michael Zecker (costumes), Mark Simpson (lighting), Sten Severson (sound); Assistant Design: Hilary Noxon, Heather Dunbar (set), Caitlin Hunt (costumes), Greg Bloxham, Ryan O'Gara (lighting); Moving Lights, David Arch; Production: McBrien Dunbar (advance carpenter), Cheyenne Benson (advance flyman), Keith Buchanan (electrician), Dan Robillard (sound), George Wagner (propmaster), Christopher Kurtz (spots), Brandon Rice (sound engineer), Rick Kelly (wardrobe supervisor), Jamie Stewart (hair supervisor), Gray Biangone, Jennifer Hohn, Moira MacGregor-Conrad (dressers); Music Copying, Emily Grishman; Rehearsal Pianist, Zachary Dietz; Keyboard Programming, Randy Cohen; Advertising, SpotCo; Press, Barlow-Harman, Wayne Wolfe, Melissa Bixler; Cast recording: Sh-K-Boom/Ghostlight Records 8-4428

CAST Graffiti Pete **Seth Stewart;** Usnavi **Lin-Manuel Miranda;** Piragua Guy **Eliseo Román;** Abuela Claudia **Olga Merediz;** Carla **Janet Dacal;** Daniela **Andréa Burns;** Kevin **Carlos Gomez;** Camila **Priscilla Lopez;** Sonny **Robin De Jesus;** Benny **Christopher Jackson;** Vanessa **Karen Olivo;** Nina **Mandy Gonzalez;** Ensemble **Tony Chiroldes, Rosie Lani Fiedelman, Joshua Henry, Afra Hines, Nina LaFarga, Doreen Montalvo, Javier Muñoz, Krysta Rodriguez, Eliseo Roman, Luis Salgado, Shaun Taylor-Corbett; Rickey Tripp;** Swings **Michael Balderrama, Blanca Camacho, Rogelio Douglas Jr., Stephanie Klemons**

Andrea Burns, Janet Dacal, Eliseo Roman (photos by Joan Marcus)

UNDERSTUDIES Michael Balderrama (Graffiti Pete, Piragua Guy), Blanca Camacho (Abuela Claudia, Camila, Daniela), Tony Chiroldes (Kevin), Janet Dacal (Vanessa, Nina), Rogelio Douglas Jr. (Benny), Joshua Henry (Benny), Stephanie Klemons (Carla), Nina LaFarga (Nina), Doreen Montalvo (Abuela Claudia, Camila, Daniela), Javier Muñoz (Usnavi/ Sonny/Graffiti Pete), Krysta Rodriguez (Nina, Carla, Vanessa), Eliseo Román (Kevin), Shaun Taylor-Corbett (Usnavi, Sonny), Rickey Tripp (Benny)

ORCHESTRA Alex Lacamoire (Conductor/keyboard 1); Zachary Dietz (Associate Conductor/keyboard 2); Raul Agraz (lead trumpet); Trevor Neumann (trumpet); Joe Fiedler, Ryan Keberle (trombones); Dave Richards, Kristy Norter (reeds); Andres Forero (drums); Doug Hinrichs, Wilson Torres (percussion); Irio O'Farrill (bass); Manny Moreira (guitars)

MUSICAL NUMBERS In the Heights, Breathe, Benny's Dispatch, It Won't Be Long Now, Inútil (Useless), No Me Diga, 96,000, Paciencia Y Fe (Patience and Faith), When You're Home, Piragua, Siempre (Always), The Club/Fireworks, Sunrise, Hundreds of Stories, Enough, Carnaval del Barrio, Atencíon, Alabanza, Everything I Know, No Me Diga (reprise), Champagne, When the Sun Goes Down, Finale

Olga Merediz and Mandy Gonzalez

Mandy Gonzalez and Christopher Jackson

2007–2008 AWARDS Tonys: Best Musical, Best Original Score, Best Orchestrations, Best Choreography

SETTING Washington Heights, Manhattan. Fourth of July weekend, the present. A new musical presented in two acts. Previously presented Off-Broadway at 37 Arts, February 8–July 15, 2007 (see *Theatre World* Volume 63). The Off-Broadway Production garnered two Drama Desk Awards for choreography and outstanding ensemble, two Outer Critics Circle Awards for best Off-Broadway musical and best choreography, two Lucille Lortel Awards for outstanding musical and choreography, and the Theatre World Award and Clarence Derwent Award for Lin-Manuel Miranda. Originally developed at The Eugene O'Neill Theater Center in 2005; initially developed by Back House Productions.

The Cast

SYNOPSIS *In the Heights* follows two days in Washington Heights, a vibrant immigrant neighborhood at the top of Manhattan. From the vantage point of Usnavi's corner bodega, we experience the joys, heartbreaks and bonds of a Latino community struggling to redefine home. This original musical features a mix of hip-hop, salsa and meringue music.

GYPSY

St. James Theatre; First Preview: March 3, 2008; Opening Night: March 27, 2008; 27 previews, 76 performances as of May 31, 2008

Book by Arthur Laurents, music by Jule Styne, lyrics by Stephen Sondheim; suggested by the memoirs of Gypsy Rose Lee; Produced by Roger Berlind, The Routh · Frankel · Baruch · Viertel Group, Roy Furman, Debra Black, Ted Hartley, Roger Horchow, David Ian, Scott Rudin, Jack Viertel; based on the City Center *Encores! Summer Stars 2007* production; Director, Arthur Laurents; Choreography, Jerome Robbins, reproduced by Bonnie Walker; Music Director, Patrick Vaccariello; Sets, James Youmans; Costumes, Martin Pakledinaz; Lighting, Howell Binkley; Sound, Dan Moses Schreier; Casting, Jay Binder; Wigs/Hair, Paul Huntley; Makeup, Angelina Avallone; PSM, Craig Jacobs; Orchestrations, Sid Ramin, Robert Ginzler; Dance Arrangements, John Kander; Music Coordinator, Seymour Red Press; General Management, Richard Frankel Productions, Laura Green; Technical Supervision, Juniper Street Productions; Company Manager, Sammy Ledbetter; Associate Company Manager, Townsend Teague; Stage Manager, Gary Mickelson; ASMs, Nancy Elizabeth Vest, Isaac Klein; Assistant Choreographer, Roger Preston Smith; Dance Captain, Bill Bateman; Associate Design: Jerome Martin (set), Martha Bromelmeier (costumes), Ryan O'Gara (lighting), David Bullard (sound), Giovanna Calabretta (wigs); Assistant Design: Adrienne Kapalko (set), Amanda Zieve (lighting), David Stollings (sound); Costumes Assistants, Sarah Cubbage, Tescia Seufferlein; Production: Jack Anderson (carpenter), John Paull (head carpenter), Mark Hallisey (assistant carpenter), Dan Coey (electrician), Sandy Paradise (assistant electrician), Tim Rogers (moving lights), David Gotwald (sound engineer), Tim Abel (prop master), J. Marvin Crosland (head props), Robert Guy (wardrobe supervisor), Kimberly Baird (assistant wardrobe supervisor), Nathaniel A. Hathaway (hair & wig supervisor), Carmel Vargyas (assistant hair & wig supervisor), Pat White (Ms. LuPone's dresser); Special Keyboard Arrangements, Danny Troob, Nathan Kelly; Synthesizer Programmer, Randy Cohen; Music Preparation; Anixter Rice Music Services; Advertising, Serino Coyne; Press, Barlow-Hartman, Ryan Ratelle, Melissa Bixler

CAST Uncle Jocko/Pastey **Jim Bracchitta;** Georgie/Mr. Goldstone/Bougeron-Cochon **Bill Bateman;** Vladimir/Rich Boy **Kyrian Friedenberg;** Balloon Girl **Katie Micha;** Baby June **Sami Gayle;** Baby Louise **Emma Rowley;** Charlie/Tap Dancer **Matthew Lobenhofer;** Hopalong **Rider Quentin Stanton;** Rose **Patti LuPone;** Pop/Cigar **Bill Raymond;** Boy Scout **Andy Richardson;** Weber/Phil **Brian Reddy;** Herbie **Boyd Gaines;** Dainty June **Leigh Ann Larkin;** Louise **Laura Benanti;** Yonkers/Driver **Pearce Wegener;** L.A. **Steve Konopelski;** Tulsa **Tony Yazbeck;** Kansas **John Scacchetti;** Little Rock **Geo Seery;** East St. Louis **Matty Price;** Waitress/Renée **Jessica Rush;** Miss Cratchitt/Mazeppa **Lenora Nemitz;** Agnes **Nicole Mangi;** Marjorie May **Alicia Sable;** Geraldine **Mindy Dougherty;** Edna Mae **Nancy Renée Braun;** Carol Ann **Sarah Marie Hicks;** Betsy Ann **Beckley Andrews;** Tessie Tura **Alison Fraser**; Electra **Marilyn Caskey**

Patti LuPone (photos by Joan Marcus)

STANDBYS Lenora Nemitz (Rose), Jim Bracchitta (Herbie), Jessica Rush (Louise, Miss Cratchitt), Mindy Dougherty (Dainty June), Pearce Wegener (Tulsa, Pastey), Dorothy Stanley (Miss Cratchitt, Tessie Tura, Mazeppa, Electra), Matt Gibson (Georgie, Pastey), John Scacchetti (Bougeron-Cochon), Andrew Boyer (Uncle Jocko, Cigar), Katie Micha (Baby Louise, Baby June), Alicia Sable (Balloon Girl, Agnes), Kyrian Friedenberg (Military Boys), Rider Quentin Stanton (Newsboys), Matty Price (Yonkers, L.A., Kansas), Lisa Rohinsky (Renée, Waitress)

ORCHESTRA Patrick Vaccariello (Conductor); Jeffrey Harris (Associate Conductor-Musical Director/keyboard); Marilyn Reynolds, Fritz Krakowski Eric DeGioia, Dana Ianculovici (violins); Crystal Garner, Sally Shumway (violas); Peter Prosser, Vivian Israel (cello); Brian Cassier (bass); Edward Salkin, Adam Kolker, Dennis Anderson, Ralph Olsen, John Winder (woodwinds); Tony Kadleck, James Delagarza, Kamau Adilifu (trumpets); Bruce Eidem, Wayne Goodman, Robert Fournier (trombones); Nancy Billman (French horn); Susan Jolles (harp); Paul Pizzuti (drums); Thad Wheeler (percussion)

Laura Benanti, Patti LuPone, Boyd Gaines

MUSICAL NUMBERS Overture, May We Entertain You, Some People, Some People (reprise), Small World, Baby June and Her Newsboys, Mr. Goldstone, Little Lamb, You'll Never Get Away From Me, Dainty June and Her Farmboys, If Momma Was Married, All I Need Is the Girl, Everything's Coming Up Roses; Madame Rose's Toreadorables, Together Wherever We Go, You Gotta Get a Gimmick, The Strip, Rose's Turn

2007–2008 AWARDS Tonys: Best Leading Actress in a Musical (Patti LuPone), Best Featured Actor in a Musical (Boyd Gaines), Best Featured Actress in a Musical (Laura Benanti); Drama Desk: Outstanding Actress in a Musical (Patti LuPone), Outstanding Featured Actor in a Musical (Boyd Gaines), Outstanding Featured Actress in a Musical (Laura Benanti); Outer Critics Circle: Outstanding Actress in a Musical (Patti LuPone), Outstanding Featured Actress in a Musical (Laura Benanti); Drama League: Distinguished Performance (Patti LuPone)

SETTING Various cities throughout the U.S., 1920's–1930's. Revival of the musical presented in two acts. Originally produced at the Broadway Theatre starring Ethel Merman on May 21, 1959, transferred to the Imperial Theatre and closed March 25, 1961 after 702 performances (see *Theatre World* Volume 15, page 116). This production marked the fourth major revival: Winter Garden Theatre, starring Angela Lansbury, September 23, 1974–January 4, 1975 (see *Theatre World* Volume 31, page 8); St. James/Marquis Theatre starring Tyne Daly and subsequently Linda Lavin, October 27, 1989–July 28, 1991, 476 performances (see *Theatre World* Volume 46, page 20); Shubert Theatre, starring Bernadette Peters, March 31, 2003–May 30, 2004, 451 performances (see *Theatre World* Volume 59, page 58).

Lenora Nemitz, Alison Fraser and Marilyn Caskey

SYNOPSIS This new production is based on the acclaimed City Center *Encores!* production which had a triumphant three-week engagement in July, 2007 (see Off-Broadway Company Series in this volume). The musical fable, suggested by the memoirs of Gypsy Rose Lee, tells of the quintessential stage mother, Rose, as she embarks her daughters Louise and June across the vaudeville circuit in search of fame and success for them, only to find it in the halls of burlesque.

SOUTH PACIFIC

Vivian Beaumont Theatre; First Preview: March 1, 2008; Opening Night: April 3, 2008; 37 previews, 68 performances as of May 31, 2008

Music by Richard Rodgers, lyrics and book by Oscar Hammerstein II, book and original staging by Joshua Logan, adapted from the novel "Tales of the South Pacific" by James A. Michener; Produced by Lincoln Center Theater (André Bishop, Artistic Director; Bernard Gersten, Executive Producer) in association with Bob Boyett; Director, Bartlett Sher; Musical Staging, Christopher Gattelli; Music Director, Ted Sperling; Sets, Michael Yeargan; Costumes, Catherine Zuber; Lighting, Donald Holder; Sound, Scott Lehrer; Orchestrations, Robert Russell Bennett; Dance & Incidental Music Arrangements, Trude Rittmann; Casting, Telsey + Company; PSM, Michael Brunner; Musical Theatre Associate Producer, Ira Weitzman; General Manager, Adam Siegel; Production Manager, Jeff Hamlin; Development, Hattie K. Jutagir; Marketing, Linda Mason Ross; Finance, David S. Brown; Education, Kati Koerner; Dramaturg, Anne Cattaneo; Vocal Coach, Deborah Hecht; Company Manager, Matthew Markoff; ACM, Jessica Perlmeter Cochrane; ASMs, David Sugarman, Samantha Greene; Dance Captain, Wendy Bergamini; Assistant Dance Captain, Grady McLeod Bowman; Assistant Director, Sarna Lapine; Associate Choreographer, Joe Langworth; Associate Design: Lawrence King (sets), Karen Spahn (lighting), Leon Rothenberg (sound); Assistant Design: Mikiko Suzuki (sets), Holly Cain, David Newell, Court Watson (costumes), Caroline Chao (lighting); Rehearsal Pianist, Jonathan Rose; Wigs and Hair, Tom Watson; Makeup, Cookie Jordan; Properties Coordinator, Kathy Fabian; Music Coordinator, David Lai; Production: William Nagle (carpenter), Patrick Merryman (electrician), Karl Rausenberger (props), John Weingart (flyman), Lynn Bowling (wardrobe supervisor), Cindy Demand (hair supervisor); Mark Caine, David Caudle, Mark Klein, Tammi Kopko, Patti Luther, Linda McAllister, James Nadeaux, Leo Namba, Stacia Williams (dressers), Carrie Rohm (hair assistant), Brandon Kahn (assistant); Press, Philip Rinaldi, Barbara Carroll; Cast recording: Sony BMG – Masterworks Broadway 88697-30457-2

Paulo Szot and Kelli O'Hara (photos by Paul Kolnik)

CAST Ensign Nellie Forbush **Kelli O'Hara;** Emile de Becque **Paulo Szot;** Ngana **Laurissa Romain;** Jerome **Luka Kain;** Henry **Helmar Augustus Cooper;** Bloody Mary **Loretta Ables Sayre;** Liat **Li Jun Li;** Bloody Mary's Assistants **Mary Ann Hu, Emily Morales, Kimber Monroe;** Luther Billis **Danny Burstein;** Stewpot **Victor Hawks;** Professor **Noah Weisberg;** Lt. Joseph Cable, USMC **Matthew Morrison;** Capt. George Bracket, USN **Skipp Sudduth;** Cmdr. William Harbison, USN **Sean Cullen;** Lt. Buzz Adams **George Merrick;** Yeoman Herbert Quale **Christian Delcroix;** Radio Operator Bob McCaffrey **Matt Caplan;** Seabee Morton Wise **Genson Blimline;** Seabee Richard West **Nick Mayo;** Seabee Johnny Noonan **Jeremy Davis;** Seabee Billy Whitmore **Robert Lenzi;** Sailor Tom O'Brien **Mike Evariste;** Sailor James Hayes **Jerold E. Solomon;** Sailor Kenneth Johnson **Christian Carter;** Petty Officer Hamilton Steeves **Charlie Brady;** Seaman Thomas Hassinger **Zachary James;** Shore Patrolman Lt. Eustis Carmichael **Andrew Samonsky;** Lead nurse Lt. Genevieve Marshall **Lisa Howard;** Ensign Dinah Murphy **Laura Marie Duncan;** Ensign Janet MacGregor **Laura Griffith;** Ensign Connie Walewska **Margot de la Barre;** Ensign Sue Yeager **Garrett Long;** Ensign Cora MacRae **Becca Ayers;** Islanders, Sailors, Seabees, Party Guests: **Becca Ayers, Genson Blimline, Charlie Brady, Matt Caplan, Christian Carter, Helmar Augustus Cooper, Jeremy Davis, Margot de la Barre, Mike Evariste, Laura Griffith, Lisa Howard, Maryann Hu, Zachary James, Robert Lenzi, Garrett Long, Nick Mayo, George Merrick, Kimber Monroe,**

Danny Burstein and the Company

Emily Morales, Andrew Samonsky, Jerold E. Solomon; Swings **Wendi Bergamini, Grady McLeod Bowman, Darius Nichols, George Psomas**

UNDERSTUDIES Wendi Bergamini (Liat), Genson Blimline (Stewpot, Capt. Brackett), Grady McLeod Bowman (McCaffery, Quale), Charlie Brady (Lt. Carmichael, Buzz Adams), Matt Caplan (Professor), Christian Carter (Henry), Jeremy Davis (Stewpot), Laura Marie Duncan (Nellie), Mike Evariste (Henry), Laura Griffith (Dinah Murphy), Victor Hawks (Luther Billis, Capt. Brackett), Lisa Howard (Bloody Mary), Maryann Hu (Bloody Mary), Robert Lenzi (Cable), Garrett Long (Nellie), George Merrick (Professor, Cmdr. Harbison), William Michals (Emile), Kimber Monroe (Ngana and Jerome), Emily Morales (Liat), Nick Mayo (Luther Billis, Lt. Carmichael, Buzz Adams), George Psomas (McCaffery, Quale), Andrew Samonsky (Cable, Cmdr. Harbison)

ORCHESTRA Ted Sperling (Conductor); Fred Lassen (Associate Conductor); Belinda Whitney (concertmistress), Antoine Silverman, Karl Kawahara, Katherine Livolsi-Landau, Lisa Matricardi, Jim Tsao, Michael Nicholas, Rena Isbin (violins); David Blinn, David Creswell (violas); Peter Sachon, Caryl Paisner (celli); Charles du Chateau (Assistant Conductor/cello); Lisa Stokes-Chin (bass); Liz Mann (flute/piccolo); Todd Palmer, Shari Hoffman (clarinet); Matt Dine (oboe/English horn); Damian Primis (bassoon): Robert Carlisle, Chris Komer, Shelagh Abate (French horns); Dominic Derasse, Gareth Flowers, Wayne Dumaine (trumpets); Mark Patterson, Mike Boschen (trombones); Marcus Rojas (tuba); Grace Paradise (harp); Bill Lanham (drums/percussion)

MUSICAL NUMBERS Overture, Dites-Moi, A Cockeyed Optimist, Twin Soliloquies, Some Enchanted Evening, Dites-Moi (reprise), Bloody Mary, There Is Nothin' Like a Dame, Bali Ha'i, My Girl Back Home, I'm Gonna Wash That Man Right Outa My Hair, Some Enchanted Evening (reprise), A Wonderful Guy, Bali Ha'i (reprise), Younger Than Springtime, Finale Act I, Entr'acte, Happy Talk, Honey Bun, You've Got to Be Carefully Taught; This Nearly Was Mine, Some Enchanted Evening (reprise), Finale Ultimo

2007–2008 AWARDS Tonys: Best Revival of a Musical, Best Director of a Musical, Best Leading Actor in a Musical (Paulo Szot), Best Scenic Design of a Musical, Best Lighting Design of a Musical, Best Costume Design of a Musical, Best Sound Design of a Musical; Drama Desk: Outstanding Revival of a Musical, Outstanding Actor in a Musical (Paulo Szot), Outstanding Director of a Musical, Outstanding Set Design of a Musical, Outstanding Sound Design; Outer Critics Circle: Outstanding Revival of a Musical, Outstanding Director of a Musical, Outstanding Actor in a Musical (Paulo Szot), Outstanding Featured Actor in a Musical (Danny Burstein); Drama League: Distinguished Revival of a Musical, Julia Hansen Award for Excellence in Directing; **Theatre World Awards:** Loretta Ables Sayre, Paulo Szot

SETTING The action takes place on two islands in the South Pacific during World War II. Revival of a musical presented in two acts. The original production opened at the Majestic Theatre April 7, 1949, transferring later to the Broadway Theatre, and ran until January 16, 1954, playing 1,925 performances (see *Theatre World* Volume 5, page 109). The show won the 1950 Pulitzer Prize for Drama and nine Tony Awards.

SYNOPSIS Rodgers and Hammerstein's classic receives its first major New York revival, almost 60 years after its debut. The story centers on the romance between a southern nurse and a French planter who find love on a small tropical island amidst a backdrop of war and racism.

Matthew Morrison and Li Jun Li

MACBETH

Lyceum Theatre; First Preview: March 29, 2008; Opening Night: April 8, 2008; Closed May 24, 2008; 11 previews, 52 performances

Patrick Stewart (photos by Manuel Harlan)

Written by William Shakespeare; Produced by Triumph Entertainment, Ltd. (Duncan C. Weldon & Paul Elliott, Directors), Jeffrey Archer, Bill Ballard, Terri & Timothy Childs, Rodger Hess, David Mirvish, Adriana Mnuchin and Emanuel Azenberg, in association with Brooklyn Academy of Music and the Chichester Festival Theatre (The Rt. Hon. Lord Young of Graffham DL, Chairman; Jonathan Church, Artistic Director; Alan Finch, Executive Director); Director, Rupert Goold; Design, Anthony Ward; Lighting, Howard Harrison; Composer & Sound, Adam Cork; Video & Projections, Lorna Heavey; Associate Director, Steve Marmion; Movement Director, Georgina Lamb; Fight Director, Terry King; UK Production Manager, Dan Watkins/The Production Desk; Technical Supervisor, Neil A. Mazzella; General Manager, Abbie M. Strassler; PSM, Jane Pole; Company Manager, John E. Gendron; Stage Manager, Lorna Seymour; ASMs, Laura Levis, Sarah Coates; Production Stage Engineer, Paul Miller; Associate Technical Supervisor, Sam Ellis; Assistant Lighting, Paul Miller; Video Engineer, Gareth Jeanne; Production: Adam Braunstein (carpenter), Frank Illo (advance carpenter), Kevin Barry (electrician), Wallace Flores (sound engineer), Reg Vessey (properties), Augie Mericola (assistant properties), Terri Purcell (wardrobe supervisor), Joby Horrigan (assistant wardrobe), Zinda Williams (Mr. Stewart's dresser), Shana Dunbar, Frances Myer, Pat Sullivan (dressers), Gina Leon (makeup); Management Assistant, Michael Salonia; Additional Casting, Jay Binder, Jack Bowdan; For Triumph Entertainment: David Bownes (General Manager), Dinesh Khanderia (Finance Director), Beth Eden (Production Administrator); Advertising, Serino Coyne; Press, Barlow-Hartman, Tom D'Ambrosio, Michelle Bergmann

CAST Duncan, King of Scotland/A Scottish Doctor **Byron Jennings;** Malcolm **Scott Handy;** Bloody Sergeant/Murderer **Hywel John;** Donalbain/Young Seyward **Ben Carpenter;** Witch **Sophie Hunter;** Witch/Gentlewoman **Polly Frame;** Witch **Niamh McGrady;** Macbeth **Patrick Stewart;** Banquo **Martin Turner;** Lennox **Mark Rawlings;** Ross **Tim Treloar;** Angus **Bill Nash;** Lady Macbeth **Kate Fleetwood;** Lady Macbeth's Servant **Oliver Birch;** Fleance **Christopher Patrick Nolan;** Seyton, a Porter **Michael Feast;** Macduff **Rachel Ticotin;** Macduff Children **Gabrielle Piacentile, Jacob Rosenbaum, Phoebe Keeling VanDusen;** Old Seyward/Murderer **Christopher Knott**

UNDERSTUDIES Oliver Birch (Ross/2nd Murderer), Ben Carpenter (Malcolm/Bloody Sergeant/1st Murderer/Angus), Polly Frame (Lady Macbeth/Witch/Servant), Henry Hodges (Macduff Children), Sophie Hunter (Witches), Rachel Ticotin (Witches), Hywel John (Seyton/Young Seyward), Christopher Knott (Duncan/Doctor/Servant), Niamh McGrady (Lady Macduff/Witch/Gentlewoman), Bill Nash (Banquo/Old Seyward), Christopher Patrick Nolan (Lennox), Mark Rawlings (Macduff), Tim Treloar (Macbeth)

2007–2008 AWARDS Drama League: Distinguished Revival of a Play

SETTING A subterranean kitchen that serves as a military hospital in a timeless and nameless country. Revival of the play presented in two acts. This production was previously presented at the Chichester Festival Theatre, England, on May 25, 2007. Transferred to the Gielgud Theatre in London on September 21, 2007, and played a limited engagement at Brooklyn Academy of Music February 12–March 22, 2008 (see Off-Broadway Company Series in this volume).

Kate Fleetwood and Patrick Stewart

SYNOPSIS Shakespeare's bloody tragedy about a murderous general's ascent to the throne with the aid of his plotting wife returns to Broadway in this Olivier nominated production.

A CATERED AFFAIR

Walter Kerr Theatre; First Preview: March 25, 2008; Opening Night: April 17, 2008; 27 previews, 51 performances as of May 31, 2008

Book by Harvey Fierstein, music and lyrics by John Bucchino; based on the Turner Entertainment motion picture distributed by Warner Brothers and written by Gore Vidal, and the original teleplay by Paddy Chayefsky; Produced by Jujamcyn Theatres, Jordan Roth, Harvey Entertainment/Ron Fierstein, Richie Jackson, Daryl Roth, John O'Boyle/Ricky Stevens/Davis-Tolentino, Barbara Russell/Ron Sharpe, in association with Frankel · Baruch · Viertel · Routh Group, Broadway Across America, True Love Productions, Rick Steiner/Mayerson-Bell-Stanton-Osher Group, and Jan Kallish; Director, John Doyle; Sets, David Gallo; Costumes, Ann Hould-Ward; Lighting, Brian MacDevitt; Sound, Dan Moses Schreier; Projections, Zachary Borovay; Hair, David Lawrence; Casting, Telsey + Company; Associate Director, Adam John Hunter; Music Director/ Arrangements, Constantine Kitsopoulos; Orchestrations, Jonathan Tunick; Music Coordinator, John Miller; Associate Producers, Stacey Mindich, Rhoda Mayerson; Marketing, Type A Marketing; Production Management, Juniper Street Productions; General Management, Alan Wasser, Allan Williams; Makeup, Angelina Avallone; Dialects/Vocal Coach, Deborah Hecht; PSM, Adam John Hunter; Company Manager, Penelope Daulton; Stage Manager, Claudia Lynch; ASM, Heather J. Weiss; Associate General Manager, Aaron Lustbader; Assistant General Manager, Jake Hirzel; ACM, Ashley Berman; Associate Design: Josh Zangen (sets), Sidney Shannon (costumes), Jennifer Schriever (lighting); David Bullard (sound), Austin Switser (projections); Assistant Design: Peter Hoerburger (lighting), Jeannette Harrington (hair); Automated Lighting, Timothy F. Rogers; Production: Tony Menditto (carpenter), Jack Anderson (head carpenter), Geoff Vaughn (automation), Michael S. LoBue (electrician), Drayton Allison (head electrician), Chris Pantuso (props supervisor), Eric Smith (assistant props supervisor), Penny Davis (wardrobe supervisor), Kevin O'Brien, Keith Shaw, Lolly Totero (dressers); Music Preparation, Kaye-Houston Music; Music Transcription, Mario Vaz De Mello; Advertising, Serino Coyne; Press, O & M Company, Rick Miramontez, Jon Dimond, Molly Barnett, Jaron Caldwell; Cast recording: PS Classics 864

CAST Winston **Harvey Fierstein;** Dolores/Caterer **Heather Mac Rae;** Myra/Wedding Dress Saleswoman **Kristine Zbornik;** Pasha/Mrs. Halloran **Lori Wilner;** Janey **Leslie Kritzer;** Ralph **Matt Cavenaugh;** Sam/Mr. Halloran **Philip Hoffman;** Tom **Tom Wopat;** Aggie **Faith Prince;** Alice/Army Sergeant **Katie Klaus;** Swings **Jennifer Allen, Britta Ollmann**

Matt Cavenaugh, Leslie Kritzer, Lori Wilner, Harvey Fierstein, Philip Hoffman, Tom Wopat and Faith Prince (photo by Jim Cox)

UNDERSTUDIES Jennifer Allen (Aggie), Philip Hoffman (Tom), Katie Klaus (Janey), Britta Ollmann (Janey), Matthew Scott (Ralph), Lori Willner (Aggie), Mark Zimmerman (Winston, Sam/Mr. Halloran)

MUSICIANS Constantine Kitsopoulos (Conductor); Ethyl Will (Associate Conductor/piano); Dale Stuckenbruck (Concert Master); Liz Lim-Dutton (violin); Ken Burward-Hoy (viola); Susannah Chapman (cello); John Arbo (bass); Jim Ercole, Don McGeen (woodwinds); Neil Balm (trumpet/ flugel); Dean Witten (percussion)

MUSICAL NUMBERS Partners, Ralph and Me, Married, Women Chatter, No Fuss, Your Children's Happiness, Immediate Family, Our Only Daughter, Women Chatter 2, One White Dress, Vision, Don't Ever Stop Saying 'I Love You', I Stayed, Married (reprise), Coney Island, Don't Ever Stop Saying 'I Love You' (reprise), Coney Island (reprise)

2007–2008 AWARDS Drama League: Distinguished Production of a Musical

SETTING The Bronx, New York, the morning after Memorial Day and onward, 1953. A new musical presented without intermission. World premiere presented at the Old Globe Theatre, San Diego, California (Louis G. Spisto, Executive Producer) September 20–November 11, 2007.

SYNOPSIS *A Catered Affair* reveals relationships strained to their limits when a couple must decide whether to spend their life savings on a family business or to launch their only daughter's marriage with a lavish catered affair.

CRY-BABY

Marquis Theatre; First Preview: March 15, 2008; Opening Night: April 24, 2008; 45 previews, 43 performances as of May 31, 2008

Book by Mark O'Donnell & Thomas Meehan, songs by David Javerbaum & Adam Schlesinger; based on the 1990 Universal Pictures film written and directed by John Waters; Produced by Adam Epstein, Allan S. Gordon, Élan V. McAllister, Brian Grazer, James P. MacGilvray, Universal Pictures Stage Productions, Anne Caruso, Adam S. Gordon, Latitude Link, The Pelican Group, in association with Philip Morgaman, Andrew Faber/Richard Mishaan; Director, Mark Brokaw; Choreography, Rob Ashford; Incidental Music/Arrangements/ Music Director, Lynne Shankel; Creative Consultant, John Waters; Sets, Scott Pask; Costumes, Catherine Zuber; Lighting, Howell Binkley; Sound, Peter Hylenski; Hair, Tom Watson; Makeup, Randy Houston Mercer; Fight Director, Rick Sordelet; Orchestrator, Christopher Jahnke; Dance Arrangements, David Chase; Music Producer, Steven M. Gold; Music Coordinator, John Miller; Production Manager, Juniper Street Productions; PSM, Rolt Smith; Associate Choreographer, Joey Pizzi; Marketing, HHC Marketing; Casting, Telsey + Company; General Management, Alan Wasser, Allan Williams; Company Manager, Kimberly Kelley; Associate Company Manager, Christopher D'Angelo; Stage Manager, Andrea O. Saraffian; ASM, Jenny Slattery; Associate Director, Moritz von Stuelpnagel; Assistant Choreography/Dance Captain, Spencer Liff; Assistant Choreographer, Christopher Bailey; Assistant Dance Captain, Andrew C. Call; Baton Sequences, Pamela Remler; Associate Design: Orit Jacoby Carroll (set), Holly Cain (costumes), Ryan O'Gara (lighting), Keith Caggiano (sound), Assistant Design: Jeffrey A. Hinchee (set), Lynn Bowling, Court Watson (costumes), Carrie J. Wood (lighting); Production: Fred Gallo (carpenter), Matthew Lynch (head carpenter), Andrew D. Elman (flyman), Hugh Hardyman (automation), David Fulton (assistant carpenter), Randall Zaibek (electrician), Michael Cornell (head electrician), Eric Norris (automated lights), Joseph Harris, Jr. (props supervisor), David Bornstein (head props), David Dignazio (sound engineer), Jesse Stevens (assistant sound), Patrick Bevilacqua (wardrobe supervisor), Tom Bertsch (assistant wardrobe supervisor), Katie Beatty (hair supervisor); Music Preparation, Kaye-Houston Music; Synthesizer Programmer, Randy Cohen; Advertising, Serino Coyne; Press; Richard Kornberg, Don Summa

CAST* Mrs. Vernon-Williams **Harriet Harris;** Baldwin **Christopher J. Hanke;** Allison **Elizabeth Stanley;** Skippy Wagstaff **Ryan Silverman;** Pepper **Carly Jibson;** Wanda **Lacey Kohl;** Mona **Courtney Balan;** Dupree **Chester Gregory II;** Cry-Baby **James Snyder;** Lenora **Alli**

Harriet Harris and the Cast (photos by Joan Marcus)

Mauzey; Judge Stone **Richard Poe;** Ensemble **Cameron Adams, Ashley Amber, Nick Blaemire, Michael Buchanan, Eric L. Christian, Colin Cunliffe, Stacey Todd Holt, Laura Jordan, Marty Lawson, Spencer Liff, Mayumi Miguel, Tory Ross; Eric Sciotto, Ryan Silverman, Peter Matthew Smith, Allison Spratt, Charlie Sutton;** Swings **Lisa Gajda, Michael D. Jablonski, Brendan King, Courtney Laine Mazza**

UNDERSTUDIES Cameron Adams (Allison), Ashley Amber (Wanda), Michael Buchanan (Dupree), Eric L. Christian (Dupree), Colin Cunliffe (Baldwin), Lisa Gajda (Pepper, Mona), Stacey Todd Holt (Judge Stone), Laura Jordan (Mrs. Vernon-Williams), Courtney Laine Mazza (Wanda, Lenora), Tory Ross (Mrs. Vernon-Williams, Pepper, Mona), Eric Sciotto (Cry-Baby), Ryan Silverman (Cry-Baby), Peter Matthew Smith (Judge Stone, Baldwin), Allison Spratt (Allison, Lenora)

***CRY-BABY* MUSICIANS** Lynn Shankel (Conductor/keyboard 1); Henry Aronson (Associate Conductor/keyboard 2); John Benthal, Chris Biesterfeldt (guitars); Cenovia Cummins, Maxim Moston (violin/mandolin); Orlando Wells (violin/viola); Sarah Seiver (cello); Steve Count (bass); Frank Pagano (drums); Scott Kreitzer, Cliff Lyons, Roger Rosenberg (reeds); Brian O'Flaherty (trumpet); Dan Levine (trombone); Joe Mowatt (percussion)

Lacey Kohl, Courtney Balan & Carly Jibson

MUSICAL NUMBERS* The Anti-Polio Picnic; Watch Your Ass; I'm Infected; Squeaky Clean; Nobody Gets Me; Nobody Gets Me (reprise); Jukebox Jamboree; Screw Loose; Baby Baby Baby Baby Baby (Baby Baby); Girl, Can I Kiss You...?; I'm Infected (reprise), You Can't Beat the System; Misery, Agony, Helplessness, Hopelessness, Heartache and Woe; All in My Head; Jailyard Jubilee; A Little Upset; I Did Something Wrong...Once; Thanks for the Nifty Country!; This Amazing Offer; Do That Again; Nothing Bad's Ever Gonna Happen Again

2007–2008 AWARDS Drama Desk: Outstanding Choreography; **Theatre World Award:** Alli Mauzey

James Snyder and Elizabeth Stanley

SETTING Baltimore, 1954. New York premiere of a new musical presented in two acts. World premiere at La Jolla Playhouse (Christopher Ashley, Artistic Director; Steven B. Libman, Managing Director), November 6–December 16, 2007 (see Regional Theatre listings in this volume).

SYNOPSIS
Everyone likes Ike, nobody likes communism, and Wade "Cry-Baby" Walker is the coolest boy in town. He's a bad boy with a good cause – truth, justice, and the pursuit of rock 'n roll – and when he falls for a good girl who wants to be bad, her charm school world of bobby sox and barbershop quartets will never be the same. Wayward youth, juvenile delinquents, sexual repression, cool music, dirty lyrics, bizarre rejects...finally, the 50's come to life – for real this time!

James Snyder, Alli Mauzey, Christopher J. Hanke, & Elizabeth Stanley

*During previews, the cast included Andrew C. Call (Ensemble) who left the show when *Glory Days* was announced for Broadway (incidentally written by *Cry-Baby* ensemble member Nick Blaemire). He was succeeded by Ryan Silverman. Two songs were cut during previews: "Let's Get Some Air" and "Class Dismissed"

THE COUNTRY GIRL

Bernard B. Jacobs Theatre; First Preview: April 3, 2008 Opening Night: April 27, 2008; 25 previews, 40 performances as of May 31, 2008

Written by Clifford Odets; Produced by Ostar Productions, Bob Boyett, The Shubert Organization, Eric Falkenstein, Roy Furman, Lawrence Horowitz, Jam Theatricals, Stephanie P. McClelland, Bill Rollnick/Nancy Ellison Rollnick, Daryl Roth/Debra Black, in association with Jon Avnet/Ralph Guild, Michael Coppel, Jamie deRoy/Michael Filerman, Philip Geier/Donald Keough, Max OnStage, Mary Lu Roffe; Director, Mike Nichols; Set, Tim Hatley; Costumes, Albert Wolsky; Lighting, Natasha Katz; Sound, Acme Sound Partners; Hair, David Brian Brown; Casting, Tara Rubin; Production Manager, Aurora Productions; PSM, Barclay Stiff; General Management, 101 Productions Ltd; Associate Director, B.T. McNicholl; Company Management, Barbara Crompton, Steven Lukens; Stage Manager, Alexis Shorter; Makeup, Angelina Avallone; Mr. Nichols' Assistants, Colleen O'Donnell, Daniel Murray; Associate Design: Ted LeFevre (set), MaryAnn D. Smith (costumes), Yael Lubetzky (lighting), Jeffrey Yoshi Lee (sound); Assistant Costumes (L.A.), Susan Kowarsh Hall; Assistant to Mr. Wolsky, Marnie Russell; Production: David M. Cohen (carpenter), James Sturek (assistant carpenter), Michael Pitzer (electrician), Daryl Kral (sound), Peter Sarafin (props), Alan Edward (prop assistant), Andrew Meeker (head props), Kelly A. Saxon (wardrobe supervisor), Richard Orton (hair supervisor), Mickey Abbate, Sandy Binion, Franc Weinperl (dressers), Kyle Gates, Libby Unsworth (production assistants); Associate Producers, Rachel Neuburger (for Ostar), Tim Levy (for Boyett); Music Consultant, Suzana Peri ; Advertising, Serino Coyne; Press, Boneau/Bryan-Brown, Jackie Green, Matt Ross

Joe Roland, Morgan Freeman, Peter Gallagher and Frances McDormand

CAST Bernie Dodd **Peter Gallagher;** Larry **Lucas Caleb Rooney;** Phil Cook **Chip Zien;** Nancy Stoddard **Anna Camp;** Paul Unger **Remy Auberjonois;** Frank Elgin **Morgan Freeman;** Georgie Elgin **Frances McDormand;** Ralph **Joe Roland**

UNDERSTUDIES Joe Roland (Bernie, Larry), Amanda Leigh Cobb (Nancy), Peter Ratray (Frank), Angela Reed (Georgie)

SETTING 1950. The stage of a New York theatre, Frank's apartment, a dressing room in a Boston theatre, and a dressing room of a New York theatre. Revival of a play presented in eight scenes in two acts. Originally presented at the Lyceum Theatre starring Paul Kelly, Uta Hagen, and Steven Hill, November 10, 1950–June 2, 1951, (see *Theatre World* Volume 12, page 42), running 236 performances. Revived at the Billy Rose Theatre (now the Nederlander) starring Jason Robards, Maureen Stapleton, and George Grizzard, March 15–May 6, 1972 (see *Theatre World* Volume 28, page 39), running 62 performances.

SYNOPSIS *The Country Girl* is a classic backstage story. The title character, Georgie is married to actor Frank Elgin, once a great theatre star, now down on his luck. When Frank is offered a major role by hotshot director Bernie Dodd, he has the chance to make a major comeback.

Frances McDormand, Morgan Freeman and Peter Gallagher (photos by Brigitte Lacombe)

THURGOOD

Booth Theatre; First Preview: April 12, 2008; Opening Night: April 30, 2008; 19 previews, 37 performances as of May 31, 2008

Written by George Stevens, Jr.; Produced by Vernon Jordan, The Shubert Organization, Bill Rollnick/Nancy Ellison Rollnick; Matt Murphy, Daryl Roth/Debra Black, Roy Furman, Jam Theatricals, Lawrence Horowitz, Eric Falkenstein, Max Onstage, James D'Orta, Jamie deRoy, Amy Nederlander, in association with Ostar Productions and The Westport Country Playhouse; Director, Leonard Foglia; Set, Allen Moyer; Costumes, Jane Greenwood; Lighting, Brian Nason; Projections, Elaine McCarthy; Sound, Ryan Rumery; PSM, Marti McIntosh; Production Manager, Juniper Street Productions; General Management, Alan Wasser, Allan Williams; Company Manager, Dwayne Mann; Stage Manager, Bernita Robinson; Assistant Director, Cat Williams; Associate Set, Warren Karp; Associate Sound, Chris Cronin; Assistant Design: Christina Bullard (costumes), Michael Barczys (lighting), Shawn E. Boyle (projections); Dialect Coach, Suzanne Celeste Brown; Production: Ken McDonough (carpenter), Jon K. Lawson (electrician), Ronnie Burns (house electrician), Drew Scott (moving lights programmer), Randolph S. Briggs (projection programmer), Richard S. Briggs (projection research), Vita Tzykun (projection digital artist); Pete Sarafin (props), James Keane (house props), Bill Lewis (production sound), Valer Gladstone (wardrobe supervisor); Associate Producer, Rachel Neuburger for Ostar Enterprises; Assistant to Mr. Stevens, Dottie McCarthy; Research, Julie Goetz; Marketing, Type A Marketing; Assistant to Mr. Fishburne, Justin Cox; Press, Pete Sanders/Fifteen Minutes Public Relations

Laurence Fishburne (photos by Carol Rosegg)

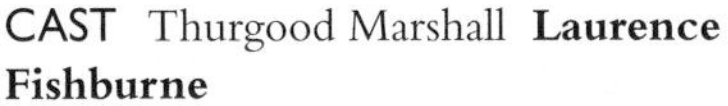

CAST Thurgood Marshall **Laurence Fishburne**

2007–2008 AWARDS Drama Desk and Outer Critics Circle: Outstanding Solo Performance

New York premiere of a new play presented without intermission. World premiere at Westport Country Playhouse in 2006 starring James Earl Jones.

SYNOPSIS *Thurgood* is a biographical portrait of Thurgood Marshall, which includes his childhood in Baltimore and his service as chief counsel of the NAACP, for which he argued the landmark Brown vs. Board of Education desegregation case in 1954. Marshall was appointed to the Supreme Court in 1967 and died in 1993

LES LIAISONS DANGEREUSES

American Airlines Theatre; First Preview: April 12, 2008; Opening Night: May 1, 2008; 22 previews, 36 performances as of May 31, 2008

Written by Christopher Hampton, based on the novel by Choderlos de Laclos; Produced by the Roundabout Theatre Company (Todd Haimes, Artistic Director; Harold Wolpert, Managing Director; Julia C. Levy, Executive Director); Director, Rufus Norris; Sets, Scott Pask; Costumes, Katrina Lindsay; Lighting, Donald Holder; Sound, Paul Arditti; Hair/Wigs, Paul Huntley; Voice & Speech Coach, Deborah Hecht; Fight Director, Rick Sordelet; Properties Coordinator, Kathy Fabian/Propstar; PSM, Arthur Gaffin; Stage Manager, Jamie Greathouse; Casting, Jim Carnahan; General Manager, Sydney Beers; Technical Supervisor, Steve Beers; Marketing/Sales, David B. Steffen; Development, Jeffory Lawson; Founding Director, Gene Feist; Associate Artistic Director, Scott Ellis; Education Director, David A. Miller; Finance, Susan Neiman; Telesales, Daniel Weiss; Sales Operations, Charlie Garbowski, Jr.; Company Manager, Nichole Jennino; Assistant Director, Wes Grantom; ACM, Carly DiFulvio; Associate Design: Jeff Hinchee (set), Mitchell Bloom (costumes), Caroline Chao (lighting), David Stephen Baker (sound); Assistant to Costume Designer, Daryl Stone; Production: Glenn Merwede (carpenter/automation), Brian Maiuri (electrician), Barb Bartel (deck electrician), Andrew Forste & Carmel Sheehan (properties), Chris Mattingly (flyman), Jill Anania (sound op), Susan J. Fallon (wardrobe supervisor); Brittany Jones-Pugh, Susan Kroeter, Luana Michaels (dressers); Rehearsal Pianist, Chris Fenwick; Press, Boneau/Bryan-Brown, Matt Polk, Jessica Johnson, Amy Kass

Ben Daniels and Mamie Gummer (photos by Joan Marcus)

Ben Daniels and Laura Linney

CAST La Marquise de Merteuil **Laura Linney;** Madame de Volanges **Kristine Nielsen;** Cécile Volanges **Mamie Gummer;** Major-domo **Tim McGeever;** La Vicomte de Valmont **Ben Daniels;** Azolan **Derek Cecil;** Madame de Rosemonde **Siân Phillips;** La Présidente de Tourvel **Jessica Collins;** Émilie **Rosie Benton;** Le Chevalier Danceny **Benjamin Walker;** Footman/Tenor **Kevin Duda;** Maid/Soprano **Jane Pfitsch;** Servants **Delphi Harrington, Nicole Orth-Pallavicini**

UNDERSTUDIES Nicole Orth-Pallavicini (Merteuil, Mme. de Volanges), Jane Pfitsch (Cécile, Émilie), Kevin Duda (Major-domo, Danceny), Tim McGeever (Valmont, Azolan), Delphi Harrington (Mme. de Rosemonde), Rosie Benton (Tourvel)

2007–2008 AWARDS Tonys: Best Costume Design of a Play, Drama Desk: Outstanding Set Design of a Play, Outstanding Costume Design of a Play; Outer Critics Circle: Costume Design; **Theatre World Award:** Ben Daniels

SETTING Various salons and bedrooms in a number of houses and châteaux in and around Paris, and in the Bois de Vincennes, one autumn and winter in the 1780's. Revival of a play presented in 18 scenes in two acts. Previously presented on Broadway at the Music Box Theatre April 30-September 6, 1987, playing 149 performances (see *Theatre World* Volume 43, page 45).

SYNOPSIS The battle of the sexes springs to life in this modern classic Olivier-winning play. For long-time friends and occasional lovers Vicomte de Valmont and Marquise de Merteuil love is simply a game of chess. But in a few false moves, they're about to find themselves locked in the ultimate checkmate. Filled with seduction, betrayal, and plenty of illicit passion, this dark comedy paints the pre-Revolutionary French aristocracy in all its cynicism and decadence.

BOEING-BOEING

Longacre Theatre; First Preview: April 19, 2008; Opening Night: May 4, 2008; 17 previews, 32 performances as of May 31, 2008

Christine Baranski and Mary McCormack (photos by Joan Marcus)

Written by Marc Camoletti, translated by Beverley Cross & Francis Evans; Produced by Sonia Friedman Productions, Bob Boyett, ACT Productions, Matthew Byam Shaw, Robert G. Bartner, The Weinstein Company, Susan Gallin/Mary Lu Roffe, Broadway Across America, Tulchin/Jenkins/DSM, and The Araca Group; Director, Matthew Warchus; Set and Costumes, Rob Howell; Lighting, Hugh Vanstone; Original Music, Claire Van Kampen; Sound, Simon Baker; PSM, William Joseph Barnes; Curtain Call Choreography, Kathleen Marshall; US Casting, Jim Carnahan; Dialect Coach, Deborah Hecht; Sales and Marketing, On the Rialto; Production Management, Aurora Productions (Gene O'Donovan, W. Benjamin Heller II, Bethany Weinstein, Melissa Mazdra, John Horsman, Asia Evans); Associate Producer for Boyett Theatricals, Tim Levy; UK General Management for Sonia Friedman, Diane Benjamin, Matthew Gordon; General Management, Stuart Thompson Productions (Caroline Prugh, James Triner, David Turner); Associate Producers, Jill Lenhart, Douglas G. Smith; Stage Manager, Robert Witherow; Associate Director, Mark Schneider; Hair, Larry R. Boyette; Company Manager, Cassidy J. Briggs; Literal Translation, Chris Campbell; Associate Design: Ted LeFevre (set), Brian Russman (costumes), Anthony Pearson (lighting), Christopher Cronin (sound); Production: Dan Coey (electrician), Wayne Smith (sound operator), Peter Sarafin (production props), Alan C. Edwards (props assistant), Kay Grunder (wardrobe supervisor), Elisa Acevedo (hair supervisor), Barry Doss, Kim Prentice (dressers), Caroline Anderson (production assistant); Casting Associate, Kate Schwabe; UK Costume Supervisor, Irene Bohan; Advertising, SpotCo; Press, Barlow-Hartman, Dennis Crowley, Michelle Bergmann

CAST Gloria **Kathryn Hahn;** Bernard **Bradley Whitford;** Berthe **Christine Baranski;** Robert **Mark Rylance;** Gabriella **Gina Gershon;** Gretchen **Mary McCormack**

UNDERSTUDIES Ray Virta (Bernard), Pippa Pearthree (Berthe), Roxanna Hope (Gabriella, Gretchen, Gloria)

2007–2008 AWARDS Tonys: Best Leading Actor in a Play (Mark Rylance), Best Revival of a Play; Drama Desk: Outstanding Revival of a Play, Outstanding Actor in a Play (Mark Rylance); **Theatre World Award:** Mark Rylance

SETTING Bernard's apartment in Paris, one Saturday in April; early 1960's. Revival of a play presented in two acts. Originally produced in London in 1962 (playing over 2,000 performances), the show premiered on Broadway at the Cort Theatre February 1-20, 1965, running only 23 performances (see *Theatre World* Volume 21, page 71). Matthew Warchus directed an Olivier nominated West End revival, featuring Mr. Rylance, which opened February 15, 2007 and is still running.

SYNOPSIS Bernard is an English playboy in Paris with three girlfriends, who are all flight attendants. With the help of his housekeeper, Berthe, Bernard has organized a schedule to allow his three loves to each spend a night at his apartment whenever they are in Paris. This all works perfectly until the new double-speed Super Boeing arrives and changes the flight schedules.

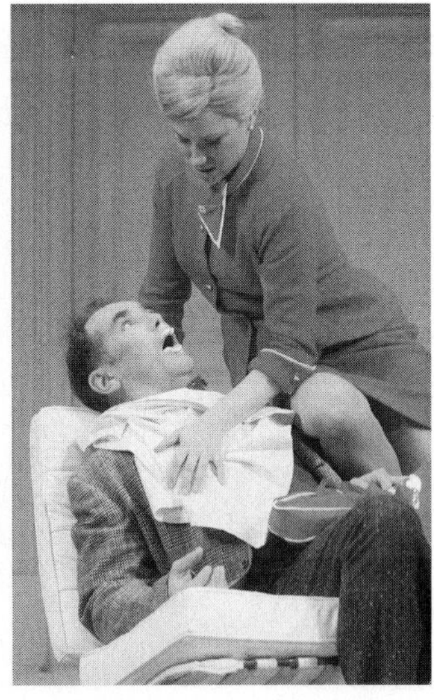

Mark Rylance and Kathryn Hahn

GLORY DAYS

Circle in the Square; First Preview: April 22, 2008 Opening and Closing Night: May 6, 2008; 17 previews, 1 performance

Music and lyrics by Nick Blaemire, book by James Gardiner; Produced by John O'Boyle, Ricky Stevens, Richard E. Leopold, Lizzie Leopold, Max Productions, and Broadway Across America, in association with the Signature Theatre; Director, Eric Schaeffer; Set, Jim Kronzer; Costumes, Sasha Ludwig-Siegel; Lighting, Mark Lanks; Sound, Peter Hylenski; Musical Director, Ethan Popp; Vocal Arrangements, Nick Blaemire & Jesse Vargas; Music Supervision/Arrangements & Orchestrations, Jesse Vargas; Casting, Tara Rubin; Marketing, Marcia Pendleton/WTGP; PSM, Gregg Kirsopp; Production Management, Juniper Street Productions; Inc. (Hilary Blanken, Guy Kwan, Kevin Broomell, Ana-Rose Greene); General Management, Carl D. White, Ricky Stevens; Company Manager, Lauren P. Yates; Stage Manager, Jess. W. Speaker III; Assistant Director, Matt Gardiner; Associate Sound, Keith Caggiano; Assistant Design: Larry Brown (set), Nick Houfek (lighting), Jeremy Foil (assistant to set designer); Production: Ryan Rossetto (wardrobe supervisor), Robert Gordon (head carpenter), Stewart Wagner (head electrician), Owen Pamele (head props), J. Jason Daunter (assistant); Music Department Coordinator, Michael Keller; Music Copying, Kaye Houston Music; Advertising, Serino Coyne; General Management Associates, Scott DelaCruz, Steven DeLuca; Press, Boneau/Bryan-Brown, Jim Byk, Adriana Douzos, Matt Ross

CAST Will **Steven Booth;** Andy **Andrew C. Call;** Skip **Adam Halpin;** Jack **Jesse JP Johnson**

Jesse JP Johnson, Steven Booth, Andrew C. Call, and Adam Halpin

UNDERSTUDIES Alex Brightman (Will, Jack), Jeremy Woodard (Andy, Skip)

ORCHESTRA Ethan Popp (Conductor/keyboards), Alec Berlin (Associate Conductor/electric guitar), Damien Bassman (drums), Gary Bristol (bass)

MUSICAL NUMBERS My Three Best Friends, Are You Ready for Tonight?, We've Got Girls, Right Here, Open Road, Things Are Different, Generation Apathy, After All, The Good Old Glory Type Days, The Thing About Andy, Forget About It, Other Human Beings, My Turn, Boys, My Next Story

SETTING A high school football field in May; the present. New York premiere of a new musical presented without intermission. Originally produced at the Signature Theatre (Arlington, Virginia) January 15–February 17, 2008 with this company.

SYNOPSIS A poignant, coming-of-age story, *Glory Days* tells the story of four high school friends who reunite one year after graduation to discover how dramatically their lives have grown apart. While they attempt to reconnect and understand each other's differences, nothing can compare to the glory days of high school when life was simpler and all appeared right with the world.

Andrew C. Call, Jesse JP Johnson, Adam Halpin, and Steven Booth (photos by Scott Suchman)

TOP GIRLS

Ana Reeder, Jennifer Ikeda, Elizabeth Marvel, Marisa Tomei, Mary Catherine Garrison, Mary Beth Hurt, and Martha Plimpton (photos by Joan Marcus)

Biltmore Theatre; First Preview: April 12, 2007 Opening Night: May 3, 2007; 24 previews, 29 performances as of May 31, 2008

Written by Caryl Churchill; Produced by Manhattan Theatre Club (Lynne Meadow, Artistic Director; Barry Grove, Executive Producer; Daniel Sullivan, 07-08 Acting Artistic Director); Director, James Macdonald; Set, Tom Pye; Costumes, Laura Bauer; Lighting, Christopher Akerlind; Sound, Darron L West; Original Music, Matthew Herbert; Hair & Wigs, Paul Huntley; Dialect Consultant, Elizabeth Smith; PSM, Martha Donaldson; General Manager, Florie Seery; Associate Artistic Director/Production, Mandy Greenfield; Marketing, Debra A. Waxman; Production Manager, Kurt Gardner; Casting, Nancy Piccione; Development, Jill Turner Lloyd; Artistic Administration/Assistant to Artistic Director, Amy Gilkes Loe; Literary Manager, Raphael Martin; Musical Development, Clifford Lee Johnson III; Finance, Jeffrey Bledsoe; Associate GM, Lindsey Brooks Sag; Subscriber Services, Robert Allenberg; Telesales, George Tetlow; Education, David Shookhoff; Associate PM, Philip Naudé; Lighting/Sound Supervisor, Matthew T. Gross; Prop Supervisor, Scott Laule; Costume Supervisor, Erin Hennessy Dean; Company Manager, Seth Shepsle; Stage Manager, Amy McCraney; Assistant Director, Gaye Taylor Upchruch; Associate Design: Frank McCullough (set), Bobby F. Tillery (costumes), Ben Krall (lighting), Matthew Hubbs (sound); Assistant Design: Bray Poor (sound); Hair/Makeup Supervisor, Jon Jordan; Assistant Hair/Makeup, La Sonya Gunter; Flymen, Patrick Murray, Leomar Susana; Assistant Propertyman, Sue Poulin; Lighting Programmer, Marc Polimeni; Dressers, Janet Anderson, Jackeva Hill; Production Assistant, Christina Elefante; Advertising, SpotCo; Press, Boneau/Bryan-Brown, Jim Byk, Aaron Meier, Heath Schwartz, Christine Olver

CAST Patient Griselda/Kit/Jeanine/Shona **Mary Catherine Garrison;** Waitress/Louise **Mary Beth Hurt;** Lady Nijo/Win **Jennifer Ikeda;** Marlene **Elizabeth Marvel;** Pope Joan/Angie **Martha Plimpton;** Dull Gret/Nell **Ana Reeder;** Isabella Bird/Joyce/Mrs. Kidd **Marisa Tomei**

UNDERSTUDIES Tina Benko (Marlene, Pope Joan/Angie), Angela Lin (Patient Griselda/Kit/Jeanine/Shona, Lady Nijo/Win), Anne Torsiglieri (Waitress/Louise, Dull Gret/Nell, Isabella Bird/Joyce/Mrs. Kidd)

SETTING Early 1980's; a restaurant in London, Joyce's back yard and kitchen in Suffolk, and Top Girls Employment Agency, London. Broadway premiere of a play presented in three acts with one intermission. Originally produced Off-Broadway at the Public Theater with a British cast December 28, 1982–January 30, 1983, playing 40 performances; reopened with an American cast February 24–May 29, 1983, playing 89 performances (see *Theatre World* Volume 39, page 116).

SYNOPSIS Marlene has just been appointed head of the Top Girls Employment Agency. To celebrate, she throws a 'Mad Hatter' type dinner party for a fanciful array of mythical and historical women, including a Victorian-era Scottish traveler, a Japanese courtesan turned Buddhist nun, Pope Joan and Chaucer's Patient Griselda. Crossing cultures, generations and politics, the sparkling dinner conversation reveals the sacrifices made as well as the joys experienced by these extraordinary women. This bold, ingenious work offers an honest portrait of what it means to be a woman in the modern world.

Mary Catherine Garrison and Martha Plimpton

110 IN THE SHADE

Studio 54; First Preview: April 13, 2007; Opening Night: May 9, 2007; Closed July 29, 2007; 27 previews, 94 performances

Book by N. Richard Nash (based on his play *The Rainmaker*), music by Harvey Schmidt, lyrics by Tom Jones; Produced by the Roundabout Theatre Company (Todd Haimes, Artistic Director; Harold Wolpert, Managing Director; Julia C. Levy, Executive Director); Director, Lonny Price; Choreography, Dan Knechtges; Music Director, Paul Gemignani; Orchestrations, Jonathan Tunick; Set/Costumes, Santo Loquasto; Lighting, Christopher Akerlind; Sound, Dan Moses Schreier; Hair/Wigs, Tom Watson; Dance Arrangements, David Krane; Dialect Coach, Stephen Gabis; PSM, Peter Hanson; Fight Director, Rick Sordelet; Casting, Jim Carnahan; Makeup, Angelina Avallone; Technical Supervisor, Steve Beers; General Manager, Sydney Beers; Founding Director, Gene Feist; Associate Artistic Director, Scott Ellis; Marketing/Sales Promotions, David B. Steffen; Development, Jeffory Lawson; Company Manager, Nancy Mulliner; ASM, Dan da Silva; ACM, Dave Solomon; Assistant Director, Matt Cowart; Director's Assistant, Will Nunziata; Dance Captain, Matt Wall; Assistant Choreographer, Caitlin Carter; Assistant Technical Supervisor, Elisa Kuhar; Associate Design: Jenny Sawyers (set), Matthew Pachtman (costumes), Ben Krall (lighting), Phillip Scott Peglow (sound); Synthesizer Programmer, Bruce Samuels; Music Associate, Paul Ford; Music Copying, Emily Grishman Music Preparation; Properties Coordinator, Kathy Fabian/Propstar Inc.; Moving Lights, Victor Seastore; Conventional Lights, Jessica Morton; Production: Dan Hoffman (carpenter), Josh Weitzman (electrician), John Wooding (assistant electrician), Nadine Hettel (wardrobe supervisor), Carrie Mossman, Carrie Hash (assistant props), Daryl Terry (hair and wig supervisor), Kat Ventura (stylist), David Gotwald (sound), Paul Ashton (automation), Dorian Fuchs, Dan Schultheis (spots), Steve Jones (flyman), Larry White (deck sound), Al Talbot (deck electrician); Rain Equipment, Jauchem & Meeh; Advertising, The Eliran Murphy Group; Press, Boneau/Bryan-Brown, Matt Polk, Jessica Johnson, Amy Kass; Cast recording: PS Classics 754

CAST File **Christopher Innvar;** H.C. Curry **John Cullum;** Noah Curry **Chris Butler;** Jimmy Curry **Bobby Steggert;** Lizzie Curry **Audra McDonald;** Snookie **Carla Duren;** Starbuck **Steve Kazee;** Little Girl **Valisia Lekae Little;** Clarence **Darius Nichols;** Townspeople: Odetta Clark **Colleen Fitzpatrick;** Vivian Lorraine Taylor **Valisia Lekae Little;** Clarence J. Taylor **Darius Nichols;** Curjith (Curt) McGlaughlin **Devin Richards;** Reverend Clark **Michael Scott;** Cody Bridger **Will Swenson;** Lily Ann Beasley **Elisa Van Duyne;** Katheryn Brawner **Betsy Wolfe;** Swings **Matt Wall, Mamie Parris**

Audra McDonald, John Cullum (photo by Joan Marcus)

UNDERSTUDIES Colleen Fitzpatrick (Lizzie), Will Swenson (Starbuck), Michael Scott (H.C., File), Devin Richards (Noah), Darius Nichols (Jimmy), Valisia Lekae Little (Snookie)

ORCHESTRA Paul Gemignani (Conductor); Mark Mitchell (Associate Conductor/keyboard); Sylvia D'Avanzo, Sean Carney (violins); Joe Gottsman (viola); Roger Shell (cello); Susan Rothoiz (flute/piccolo); Rick Heckman, Eric Weidman, Don McGeen (woodwinds); Dominic Derasse, Mike Ponella (trumpets); Bruce Ediem (trombone); Jennifer Hoult (harp); John Beal (bass); Paul Pizutti (drums/percussion)

MUSICAL NUMBERS Another Hot Day, Lizzie's Coming Home, Love, Don't Turn Away, Poker Polka, Hungry Men, The Rain Song, You're Not Foolin' Me, Raunchy, A Man and a Woman, Old Maid, Evenin' Star, Everything Beautiful, Melisande, Simple Little Things, Little Red Hat, Is It Really Me?, Wonderful Music, The Rain Song (reprise)

SETTING July 4, 1936, the Texas Panhandle. Revival of a musical presented in two acts. Original Broadway production at the Broadhurst Theatre October 24, 1963–August 9, 1964, 330 performances (see *Theatre World* Volume 20, page 42).

SYNOPSIS In the middle of a heat wave when everyone is longing for rain, Lizzie Curry is on the verge of becoming an old maid. Even the town sheriff, for whom she harbors a secret yen, won't take a chance. When a charismatic rainmaker named Starbuck enters the town, Lizzie's world is turned upside down.

The 25TH ANNUAL PUTNAM COUNTY SPELLING BEE

Circle in the Square; First Preview: April 15, 2005; Opening Night: May 2, 2005; Closed January 20, 2008; 21 previews, 1,136 performances

Music and lyrics by William Finn, book by Rachel Sheinkin, conceived by Rebecca Feldman, additional material by Jay Reiss; based on "C-R-E-P-U-S-C-U-L-E," an original play by The Farm; Produced by David Stone, James L. Nederlander, Barbara Whitman, Patrick Catullo, Barrington Stage Company and Second Stage Theatre (Carole Rothman, Artistic Director; Timothy J. McClimon, Executive Director). Director, James Lapine, Choreography, Dan Knechtges; Set /Lobby Design, Beowulf Boritt; Costumes, Jennifer Caprio; Lighting, Natasha Katz; Sound, Dan Moses Schreier; Orchestrations, Michael Starobin; Music Director, Vadim Feichtner; Vocal Arrangements, Carmel Dean; Music Coordinator, Michael Keller; Casting, Tara Rubin; PSM, Andrea "Spook" Testani; Production Manager, Kai Brothers; General Management, 321 Theatrical Management (Nancy Nagel Gibbs, Nina Essman, Marcia Goldberg); Marketing, The Araca Group; Company Manager, David Turner; Resident Director, Darren Katz; Stage Manager, Kelly Hance; ASM, Carly Hughes/Angelica-Lee Aspiras; Dance Captain, Jacqui Polk; Assistant Choreographer, DJ Gray; Hair and Wigs, Marty Kapulsky; Associate Design: Philip Rosenberg (lighting), David Bullard (sound); Associate Production Manager, Jason Block; Music Preparation, Emily Grishman; Advertising, Serino Coyne; Press, Barlow-Hartman, John Barlow, Michael Hartman, Tom D'Ambrosio, Michelle Bergmann; Cast recording: Sh-K-Boom/Ghostlight Records 7915584407-2

CAST Chip Tolentino **Aaron Albano;** Leaf Coneybear **Stanley Bahorek**; Olive Ostrovsky **Jenni Barber;** William Barfee **Jared Gertner;** Mitch Mahoney **James Monroe Iglehart;** Logainne Schwartzandgrubenierre **Sarah Inbar**; Marcy Park **Greta Lee;** Douglas Panch **Mo Rocca**[*1]**;** Rona Lisa Peretti **Jennifer Simard**

UNDERSTUDIES Brian Gonzales (Douglas/Leaf/William), Carly Hughes[*2] (Marcy/Rona Lisa), Jacqui Polk (Logainne/Marcy/Olive) Maurice Murphy (Chip/Mitch/Douglas/Leaf)

ORCHESTRA Vadim Feichtner (Conductor/piano); Carmel Dean (Associate Conductor/synthesizer); Rick Heckman (reeds); Amy Ralske (cello); Glenn Rhian (drums/percussion)

MUSICAL NUMBERS The 25th Annual Putnam County Spelling Bee, The Spelling Bee Rules/My Favorite Moment Of The Bee 1, My Friend, The Dictionary, The First Goodbye, Pandemonium, I'm Not That Smart, The Second Goodbye, Magic Foot, Pandemonium Reprise/My Favorite Moment Of The Bee 2, Prayer Of The Comfort Counselor, My Unfortunate Erection (Chip's Lament), Woe Is Me, I'm Not That Smart (reprise), I Speak Six Languages, The I Love You Song, Woe Is Me (reprise), My Favorite Moment Of The Bee 3/Second, Finale, The Last Goodbye

SETTING Now. The Putnam County Junior High School Gymnasium. A musical presented without intermission. Originally produced Off-Broadway at Second Stage, January, 2005, and at the Barrington Stage Company, Sheffield, Massachusetts, July, 2004. For original production credits see *Theatre World* Volume 61, page 80.

SYNOPSIS Four audience participants and six young people experience the anxiety and pressure of a regional spelling bee. The six kids in the throes of puberty, overseen by grown-ups who barely managed to escape childhood themselves, learn that winning isn't everything and that losing doesn't necessarily make you a loser.

*Succeeded by: 1. Darrell Hammond (6/10/07), Daniel Pearce (7/20/07) 2. Angelica-Lee Aspiras

Greta Lee (front), Sarah Inbar, Aaron Albano, Jared Gertner, Stanley Bahorek, and Jenni Barber (photo by Joan Marcus)

AVENUE Q

Golden Theatre; First Preview: July 10, 2003; Opening Night: July 31, 2003; 22 previews, 1,996 performances as of May 31, 2008

Mary Faber and Lucy the Slut (photos by Nick Reuchel)

Music and lyrics by Robert Lopez and Jeff Marx, book by Jeff Whitty; Produced by Kevin McCollum, Robyn Goodman, Jeffrey Seller, Vineyard Theatre & The New Group; Director, Jason Moore; Choreography, Ken Roberson; Music Supervision/ Orchestrations/ Arrangements, Stephen Oremus; Puppets Conception/Design, Rick Lyon; Set, Anna Louizos; Costumes, Mirena Rada; Lighting, Howell Binkley; Sound, Acme Sound Partners; Animation, Robert Lopez; Music Director/Incidental Music, Gary Adler; Music Coordinator, Michael Keller; General Manager, John Corker; Technical Supervisor, Brian Lynch; PSM, Robert Witherow; Casting, Cindy Tolan; Marketing, TMG-The Marketing Group; Associate Producers, Sonny Everett, Walter Grossman, Mort Swinsky; Stage Manager, Christine M. Daly; Company Manager, Nick Lugo; Resident Director, Evan Ensign; Associate Conductor, Mark Hartman; Assistant Director, Jen Bender; ASM/Dance Captain, Aymee Garcia; Associate Design: Todd Potter (set), Timothy F. Rogers (lighting); Music Copying, Emily Grishman and Alex Lacamoire; Animation and Video Production, Noodle Soup Production, Jeremy Rosenberg; Sound and Video Design Effects, Brett Jarvis; Advertising, SpotCo; Press, Sam Rudy Media Relations; Cast recording: RCA 82876-55923-2

CAST Princeton/Rod **Howie Michael Smith;** Brian **Evan Harrington**[*1]**;** Kate Monster/Lucy the Slut **Mary Faber**[*2]**;** Nicky/Trekkie Monster/Bad Idea Bear **Christian Anderson**[*3]**;** Christmas Eve **Sala Iwamatsu**[*4]**;** Gary Coleman **Haneefah Wood**[*5]**;** Mrs. T./Bad Idea Bear/ Others **Jennifer Barnhart;** Ensemble **Jonathan Root, Matt Schreiber;** Swings **Carmen Ruby Floyd, Aymee Garcia, Hazel Anne Raymundo, Heather Hawkins, Leo Daignault, Jasmin Walker**

UNDERSTUDIES Jennifer Barnhart (Kate Monster/Lucy), Carmen Ruby Floyd (Gary Coleman, Mrs. T./Bear), Aymee Garcia (Kate Monster/Lucy, Mrs. T./Bear, Christmas Eve), Sala Iwamatsu (Christmas Eve, Mrs. T/Bear), Jonathan Root (Princeton/Rod, Brian, Nicky/Trekkie/Bear), Matt Schreiber (Brian, Nicky/Trekkie/Bear, Princeton/Rod)

ORCHESTRA Gary Adler (Conductor/keyboard); Mark Hartman (Associate Conductor/keyboard); Maryann McSweeney (bass); Brian Koonin (guitar); Patience Higgins (reeds); Michael Croiter (drums)

MUSICAL NUMBERS Avenue Q Theme, What Do You Do With a BA in English?/It Sucks to be Me, If You Were Gay, Purpose, Everyone's a Little Bit Racist, The Internet Is for Porn, Mix Tape, I'm Not Wearing Underwear Today, Special, You Can Be as Loud as the Hell You Want (When You're Making Love), Fantasies Come True, My Girlfriend, Who Lives in Canada, There's a Fine, Fine Line, There Is Life Outside Your Apartment, The More You Ruv Someone, Schadenfreude, I Wish I Could Go Back to College, The Money Song, For Now

SETTING The present, an outer borough of New York City. A musical presented in two acts. For original production credits see *Theatre World* Volume 60, page 25.

SYNOPSIS *Avenue Q* is about real life: finding a job, losing a job, learning about racism, getting an apartment, getting kicked out of your apartment, being different, falling in love, promiscuity, avoiding commitment, and internet porn. Twenty and thirty-something puppets and humans survive life in the big city and search for their purpose in this naughty but timely musical that features "full puppet nudity!"

*Succeeded by: 1 Nicholas Kohn (4/10/08) 2. Sarah Stiles (11/30/07) 3. David Benoit (6/18/07), Christian Anderson (10/8/07) 4. Ann Sanders 5. Rashidra Scott (12/17/07)

Evan Harrington, Ann Sanders

BEAUTY AND THE BEAST

Lunt-Fontanne Theatre; First Preview: March 9, 1994; Opened: April 18, 1994; Closed: July 29, 2007; 46 previews, 5,464 performances

Music by Alan Menken, lyrics by Howard Ashman, Tim Rice, book by Linda Woolverton; Produced by Walt Disney Theatre Productions; Associate Producer, Donald Frantz; Director, Robert Jess Roth; Orchestrations, Danny Troob; Musical Supervision/Vocal Arrangements, David Friedman; Musical Director/Incidental Arrangements, Michael Kosarin; Choreography, Matt West; Scenery, Stan Meyer; Costumes, Ann Hould-Ward; Lighting, Natasha Katz; Sound, T. Richard Fitzgerald; Hair, David H. Lawrence; Illusions, Jim Steinmeyer, John Gaughan; Prosthetics, John Dods; Fight Director, Rick Sordelet; General Manager, Dodger Productions; Production Supervisor, Jeremiah J. Harris; Company Manager, Kim Sellon; Stage Managers, James Harker, John M. Atherlay, Pat Sosnow, Kim Vernace; Dance Captain, Daria Lynn Scatton; Press, Boneau/Bryan-Brown, Jim Byk, Juliana Hannett; Cast recording: Walt Disney 60861

CAST Enchantress **Elizabeth Polito;** Young Prince/ Doormat **Connor Gallagher;** Beast **Steve Blanchard;** Belle **Anneliese van der Pol;** Lefou **Aldrin Gonzalez;** Gaston **Steven Buntrock*1;** Three Silly Girls **Tracy Generalovich*2, Jennifer Marcum*3, Tia Maria Zorne;** Maurice **Jamie Ross;** Wolves **Ana Maria Andricain, Connor Gallagher, Elizabeth Polito, Bret Shuford*4;** Cogsworth **Glenn Rainey;** Lumiere **David deVries;** Babette **Ann Mandrella;** Mrs. Potts **Jeanne Lehman;** Chip **Trevor Braun** or **Marlon Sherman;** Salt and Pepper **Bret Shuford*4, Garrett Miller;** Cheesegrater **Rod Roberts;** Madame de la Grande Bouche **Mary Stout;** Bookseller/ Monsieur D'Arque **Billy Vitelli;** Prologue Narrator **David Ogden Stiers;** Townspeople/Enchanted Objects: **Ana Maria Andricain, Gina Carlette Statile, Keith Fortner, Connor Gallagher, Tracy Generalovich*2, David E. Liddell, Stephanie Lynge*5, Jennifer Marcum*3, Garrett Miller, Bill Nabel, James Patterson, Elizabeth Polito, Rod Roberts, Daria Lynn Scatton, Jennifer Shrader, Bret Shuford*4, David Spangenthal, Ann Van Cleave, Billy Vitelli, Tia Maria Zorne;** Swings: **Keith Fortner, Alisa Klein, David E. Liddell, Daria Lynn Scatton, Gina Carlette Statile**

*Succeeded by: 1. Chris Hoch (6/25/07) Donny Osmond (closing night) 2. Alisa Klein 3. Tracy Rae Wilson 4. Christopher DeAngelis 5. Marguerite Wilbanks

Chris Hoch (photo by Joan Marcus)

UNDERSTUDIES Ana Maria Andricain (Belle), Gina Carlette Statile (Enchantress, Silly Girls, Wolves), Keith Fortner (Young Prince, Bookseller, Lefou, Wolves, Salt and Pepper, Doormat, Cheesegrater), Connor Gallagher (Lefou), Tracy Generalovich (Babette), Alisa Klein (Enchantress, Silly Girls, Wolves, Babette), David E. Liddell (Young Prince, Bookseller, Wolves, Salt and Pepper, Doormat, Cheesegrater), Stephanie Lynge (Mrs. Potts, Madame de la Grande Bouche), Bill Nabel (Maurice, Cogsworth, Lumiere, Monsieur D'Arque), James Patterson (Beast, Gaston), Daria Lynn Scatton (Enchantress, Silly Girls, Wolves), Jennifer Shrader (Belle), Bret Shuford*4, (Lumiere), David Spangenthal (Beast, Gaston, Monsieur D'Arque), Ann Van Cleave (Mrs. Potts, Madame de la Grande Bouche), Billy Vitelli (Maurice, Cogsworth)

MUSICAL NUMBERS Overture, Prologue (Enchantress), Belle, No Matter What, Me, Home, Gaston, How Long Must This Go On?, Be Our Guest, If I Can't Love Her, Entr'acte/Wolf Chase, Something There, Human Again, Maison des Lunes, Beauty and the Beast, Mob Song, The Battle, Transformation, Finale

A musical presented in two acts. For original production credits see *Theatre World* Volume 50, page 55. At closing, Disney's first ever theatrical venture is the sixth longest running show in Broadway history. The show opened at the Palace Theatre where it played for five years before transferring to the Lunt-Fontanne Theatre on November 11, 1999. Over 250 actors performed in the show on Broadway. Original ensemble member Bill Nabel remained in the show during its entire 13 year run. *Beauty and the Beast* has played in 13 countries and over 115 cities around the world, as well as spawning two North American tours playing combined 137 engagements in 90 cities in 36 states, Washington, DC, and Canada from November 1993 to August 2003, playing a total of 2,893 performances.

SYNOPSIS A stage adaptation of the animated Walt Disney film about a strong-willed young woman who breaks the spell that turned a handsome prince into a monstrous beast. Trying to save her beloved father from the Beast's clutches, Belle agrees to become his prisoner forever. But once she is inside the Beast's enchanted castle, the members of his court, who have been transformed into household objects like clocks and candlesticks, decide to play matchmakers. As the Beast begins to fall in love with Belle, he becomes progressively less beastly. But the spell can be broken only if the Beast can get her to love him in return.

Jeanne Lehman (photo by Craig Schwartz)

Anneliese van der Pol (photo by George Holz)

More than 125 former cast, creative and crew members reunite to celebrate Beauty and the Beast's 13th year on Broadway. (Photo by Lyn Hughes)

CHICAGO

Ambassador Theatre; First Preview: October 23, 1996; Opening Night: November 14, 1996; 25 previews, 4,786 performances as of May 31, 2008

Lyrics by Fred Ebb, music by John Kander, book by Fred Ebb and Bob Fosse; based on the play by Maurine Dallas Watkins; Production based on the 1996 City Center *Encores!* production; Original production directed and choreographed by Bob Fosse; Produced by Barry & Fran Weissler/Kardana/Hart Sharp Productions, in association with Live Nation; Director, Walter Bobbie; Choreography, Ann Reinking in the style of Bob Fosse; Supervising Music Director, Rob Fisher; Music Director, Leslie Stifelman; Set, John Lee Beatty; Costumes, William Ivey Long; Lighting, Ken Billington; Sound, Scott Lehrer; Orchestrations, Ralph Burns; Dance Arrangements, Peter Howard; Adaptation, David Thompson; Musical Coordinator, Seymour Red Press; Hair/Wigs, David Brian Brown; Casting, James Calleri/Duncan Stewart (current), Jay Binder (original); Technical Supervisor, Arthur P. Siccardi; Dance Supervisor, Gary Chryst; PSM, David Hyslop; Associate Producer, Alecia Parker; General Manager, B.J. Holt; Company Manager, Jean Haring; Stage Managers, Terrence J. Witter, Mindy Farbrother; Assistant Choreographer, Debra McWaters; Dance Captains, Gregory Butler, Bernard Dotson, Gabriela Garcia; Press, The Publicity Office, Jeremy Shaffer; Cast recording: RCA 68727-2

CAST Velma Kelly **Brenda Braxton**[*1]; Roxie Hart **Bianca Marroquin**[*2]; Amos Hart **Rob Bartlett**[*3]; Matron "Mama" Morton **Roz Ryan**[*4]; Billy Flynn **Joey Lawrence**[*5]; Mary Sunshine **R. Lowe**[*6]; Fred Casely **Gregory Butler**[*7]; Sergeant Fogarty **Adam Zotovitch;** Liz **Michelle Marie Robinson**[*8]; Annie **Solange Sandy**[*9]; June **Donna Marie Asbury;** Hunyak **Emily Fletcher**[*10]; Mona **Angel Reda**[*11]; Go-To-Hell-Kitty **Melissa Rae Mahon**[*12]; Harry/The Jury **Shawn Emanjomeh**; Aaron **Eric Jordan Young;** Doctor/Judge **Bernard Dotson;** Martin Harrison/Doctor **Michael Cusumano;** Bailiff/Court Clerk **Denny Paschall**[*13]

UNDERSTUDIES Melissa Rae Mahon (Roxie/Velma), Michelle Potterf (Roxie), Donna Marie Asbury (Velma, "Mama" Morton), Bernard Dotson (Billy), Eric Jordan Young (Billy, Amos), Adam Zotovich (Amos), Michelle M. Robinson ("Mama" Morton), David Kent/Denny Paschall/Brian Spitulnik (Fred Casely, "Me and My Baby"), J. Loeffelholtz (Mary Sunshine); Mark Anthony Taylor (Amos, Fred), Julio Augustin (Sergeant Fogarty) Josh Rhodes (Doctor, Judge), Gabriela Garcia, David Kent, Sharon Moore, Brian Spitulnik, Jennifer West (All other roles)

ORCHESTRA Leslie Stifelman (Conductor); Scott Cady (Associate Conductor/piano); Seymour Red Press, Jack Stuckey, Richard Centalonza (woodwinds); John Frosk, Darryl Shaw (trumpets); Dave Bargeron, Bruce Bonvissuto (trombones); John Johnson (piano/accordion); Jay Berliner (banjo); Ronald Raffio (bass/tuba); Marshall Coid (violin); Ronald Zito (drums/percussion)

Lisa Rinna and Harry Hamlin (photo by Joan Marcus)

SETTING Chicago, Illinois. The late 1920's. A musical vaudeville presented in two acts. This production originally opened at the Richard Rodgers Theatre; transferred to the Shubert on February 12, 1997; and transferred to the Ambassador on January 29, 2003. For original production credits see *Theatre World* Volume 53, page 14.

SYNOPSIS Murder, media circus, vaudeville, and celebrity meet in this 1920's tale of two of the Windy City's most celebrated felons and their rise to fame amidst a razzle dazzle trial.

*Succeeded by: 1. Terra C. MacLeod (2/21/08), Brenda Braxton (3/7/08), Nicole Bridgewater (5/12/08), Nancy Lemenager (5/19/08) 2. Lisa Rinna (6/19/07), Michelle DeJean (8/7/07), Tracy Shane (9/4/07), Michelle DeJean (9/11/07), Bianca Marroquin (1/14/08) 3. Vincent Pastore (11/29/07), Rob Bartlett (1/14/08), Ron Orbach (1/28/08), Ray Bokhour (4/28/08) 4. Adriane Lenox (8/7/07), Aida Turturro (11/29/07), Roz Ryan (1/14/08), Kecia Lewis-Evans (3/18/08) 5. Harry Hamlin (6/19/07), Tom Wopat (8/7/07), George Hamilton (9/10/07), Brian McNight (10/8/07), Maxwell Caulfield (11/29/07), Jeff McCarthy (12/7/07), John Schneider (1/14/08), Jeff McCarthy (3/18/08) 6. D. Sabella-Mills (8/28/07), R. Lowe (9/11/07), D. Micciche (4/28/08) 7. Dan LoBuono, Gregory Butler 8. Nichole Bridgewater 9. Kelly Crandall, Nicole Bridgewater, Kelly Crandall, Dylis Croman 10. Kate Dunn, Jill Nicklaus, Kate Dunn, Nili Bassman, Jill Nicklaus 11. Robyn Hurder, Melissa Rae Mahon, Michelle DeJean 12. Michelle Potterf, Melissa Rae Mahon 13. Eddie Bennett, Dan LoBuono

A CHORUS LINE

Gerald Schoenfeld Theatre; First Preview: September 18, 2006; Opening Night: October 5, 2006; 18 previews, 670 performances as of May 31, 2008

Conceived and originally choreographed and directed by Michael Bennett, book by James Kirkwood and Nicholas Dante, music by Marvin Hamlisch, lyrics by Edward Kleban; Originally co-choreographed by Bob Avian; Produced by Vienna Waits; Director, Bob Avian; Choreography restaged by Baayork Lee; Set, Robin Wagner; Costumes, Theoni V. Aldredge; Lighting, Tharon Musser, adapted by Natasha Katz; Sound, Acme Sound Partners; Music Direction and Supervision, Patrick Vaccariello; Orchestrations, Jonathan Tunick, Billy Byers, and Hershy Kay; Vocal Arrangements, Don Pippin; General Management, Alan Wasser Associates; Casting, Jay Binder; Production Manager, Arthur Siccardi; PSM, William Joseph Barnes; Marketing, Apel; Company Manager, Susan Bell; Associate CM Adam J. Miller/Michael Altbaum; Stage Manager, Laurie Goldfeder; ASM, Timothy Semon; Assistant Choreographer/Dance Captain, Michael Gorman; Assistant Dance Captain, Lyndy Franklin; Assistant Director, Peter Pileski; Music Coordinator, Michael Keller; Synthesizer Programming, Bruce Samuels; Music Copying, Emily Grishman/Katharine Edmonds; Advertising, Serino Coyne; Marketing, TMG; Press, Barlow-Hartman; Wayne Wolfe; Cast recording: Sony BMG Music/Masterworks Broadway 82876-89785-2

CAST Bobby **Ken Alan***[1]; Don **Brad Anderson***[2]; Tricia **Michelle Aravena;** Roy **David Baum;** Zach **Michael Berresse***[3]; Tom **Mike Cannon;** Butch **E. Clayton Cornelious;** Diana **Natalie Cortez;** Cassie **Charlotte d'Amboise**+; Maggie **Mary Davi***[4]; Val **Jessica Lee Goldyn;** Sheila **Deidre Goodwin;** Larry **Tyler Hanes***[5]; Lois **Nadine Isenegger;** Richie **James T. Lane;** Vicki **Pamela Fabello***[6]; Mark **Paul McGill;** Judy **Heather Parcells;** Greg **Michael Paternostro***[7]; Bebe **Alisan Porter***[8]; Mike **Jeffrey Schecter;** Connie **Lisa Ho***[9]; Paul **Jason Tam***[10]; Frank **Grant Turner;** Kristine **Chryssie Whitehead***[11]; Al **Tony Yazbeck***[12]; Swings*[13] **Joey Dudding, Lyndy Franklin**

ORCHESTRA Patrick Vaccariello (Conductor); Jim Laev (Associate Conductor/keyboard 2); Ted Nash, Lino Gomez, David Young, Jacqueline Henderson (woodwinds); John Chudoba, Trevor Neumann, Scott Wenholt (trumpets); Michael Seltzer, Ben Herrington, Jack Schatz (trombones); Bill Sloat (bass); Greg Anthony/Ann Gerschefski (keyboard 1); Maggie Torre (Assistant Conductor/keyboard 3); Dan McMillan (percussion); Brian Brake (drums)

MUSICAL NUMBERS I Hope I Get It, I Can Do That, And, At the Ballet, Sing!; Hello Twelve, Hello Thirteen, Hello Love; Nothing, Dance: Ten; Looks: Three, The Music and the Mirror, One, The Tap Combination, What I Did for Love, One: Reprise

SETTING An Audition. Time: 1975. Place: A Broadway Theatre. Revival of the musical presented without intermission. For original production credits see *Theatre World* Volume 63. Originally produced by the Public Theater in association with Plum Productions on May 21–July 13, 1975 (see *Theatre World* Volume 31, page 132) for 101 performances; transferred to Broadway at the Shubert Theatre October 17, 1975 (see *Theatre World* Volume 32, page 14) and ran for 6,137 performances.

SYNOPSIS Broadway gypsies lay their talents–and hearts–on the line at a unique chorus call audition for a Broadway musical. "This show is dedicated to anyone who has ever danced in a chorus or marched in step…anywhere."—Michael Bennett.

*Succeeded by: 1. Will Taylor (7/24/07) 2. Jason Patrick Sands (7/24/07) 3. Mario Lopez (4/15/08) 4. Melissa Lone (7/24/07) 5. Nick Adams (7/24/07) 6. Pamela Jordan, Kim Shriver, Jennifer Foote, Emily Fletcher 7. Michael Gruber (7/24/07), Tommy Berklund 8. Krysta Rodriguez, Dena DiGiacinto 9. J. Elaine Marcos (7/24/07) 10. Bryan Knowlton (7/24/07) 11. Katherine Tokarz (7/24/07) 12. Kevin B. Worley (7/3/07) 13. Additional and/or replacement: Aaron J. Albano, Jessica Lea Patty, Josh Walden, Dena DiGiacinto, Courtney Laine Mazza, Eric Sciotto, Denis Lambert, Deone Zanotto, Deanna Aguinaga, Todd Anderson, Kurt Domoney, Eric Dysart, Kimberly Dawn Neumann

The Cast (photo by Paul Kolnik)

BROADWAY – Played Through / Closed This Season

THE COLOR PURPLE

Broadway Theatre; First Preview: November 1, 2005; Opening Night: December 1, 2005; Closed February 24, 2008; 30 previews, 910 performances

Book by Marsha Norman, music and lyrics by Brenda Russell, Allee Willis, Stephen Bray; based on Alice Walker's novel and the Warner Brothers/Amblin Entertainment 1986 film directed by Steven Spielberg; Produced by Oprah Winfrey, Scott Sanders, Roy Furman, Quincy Jones, Creative Battery, Anna Fantaci & Cheryl Lachowicz, Independent Presenters Network, David Lowy, Stephanie P. McClelland, Gary Winnick, Jan Kallish, Nederlander Presentations, Inc., Bob & Harvey Weinstein, Andrew Asnes & Adam Zotovich, Todd Johnson; Director, Gary Griffin, Sets, John Lee Beatty, Costumes, Paul Tazewell; Lighting, Brian MacDevitt; Sound, Jon Weston; Choreography, Donald Byrd, Music Supervisor/Incidental Music, Kevin Stites; Music Director, Linda Twine; Arrangements, Daryl Waters, Joseph Joubert; Music Coordinator, Seymour Red Press; Orchestrations, Jonathan Tunick; Casting, Bernard Telsey; Hair, Charles LaPointe; Production Managers, Arthur Siccardi, Patrick Sullivan; PSM, Kristen Harris; General Management, Amy Jacobs; Marketing, TMG; Company Manager, Kimberly Kelly; Associate Director, Nona Lloyd; Stage Manager, Lisa Dawn Cave; ASM, Neveen Mahmoud; Fight Director, J. Steven White; Fight Captain, James Brown III; Dialects, Deborah Hecht; Makeup, Angelina Avallone; Dance Captain, Stephanie Guiland-Brown; Press, Barlow-Hartman; Cast recording: Angel/EMI 0946 3 42954 2 0

CAST Young Nettie/Mister Daughter **Chantylla Johnson*1**; Young Celie/Mister Daughter/Young Olivia/Henrietta **Zipporah G. Gatling*2**; Church Soloist **Carol Dennis*3**; Church Lady (Doris) **Charlotte Crossley*4**; Church Lady (Darlene) **Rosena M. Hill*5**; Church Lady (Jarenne)/Daisy **Mai Nkenge Wilson*6**; Preacher, Prison Guard **Doug Eskew**; Pa/Grady **JC Montgomery**; Nettie **Darlesia Cearcy*7**; Celie **Fantasia*8**; Mister **Alton Fitzgerald White**; Young Harpo/Young Adam **Ricky Smith**; Harpo **Chaz Lamar Shepherd*9**; Sofia **NaTasha Yvette Williams*10**; Squeak **Krisha Marcano**; Shug Avery **Elisabeth Withers Mendes*11**; Ol' Mister **Larry Marshall**; Buster/Chief **Gavin Gregory**; Bobby **James Brown III*12**; Older Olivia **Bahiyah Sayyed Gaines*13**; Older Adam **Grasan Kingsberry*14**; Ensemble **James Brown III*12, Leilani N. Bryant, LaTrisa A. Coleman, Charlotte Crossley*4, Carol Dennis*3, Doug Eskew, Anika Ellis, Doug Eskew, Bahiyah Sayyed Gaines*13, Zipporah G. Gatiling*2, Charles Gray, Gavin Gregory, James Harkness, Francesca Harper, Rosena M. Hill*5, Chantylla Johnson*1, Grassan Kingsberry*14, Kenya Unique Massey, JC Montgomery, Lou Myers, Angela Robinson, Ricky Smith, Nathaniel Stampley, Jamal Story, Marion Willis III, Mai Nkenge Wilson*6**; Swings **Tmothy George Anderson, Jordan D. Bratton, Shelby Braxton-Brooks, Deidra H. Brooks, Eric L. Christian, Darius Crenshaw, Bobby Daye, Stephanie Guiland-Brown, Kemba Shannon, LaVon Fisher-Wilson, Guy Fortt, Chauncey Jenkins, Ashley Renée Jordan**

ORCHESTRA Linda Twine (Conductor); Joseph Joubert, (Associate Conductor); Barry Danielian, Brian O'Flaherty, Kamau Adilifu; Larry Farrell, Jason Jackson; Les Scott, Lawrence Feldman, Jay Brandford; Joseph Joubert, Shelton Becton; Buddy Williams, Damien Bassman, Steve Bargonetti, Ben Brown, Paul Woodiel, Mineko Yajima, David Creswell, Clay C. Ruede

SETTING Georgia, 1909-1949. A musical presented in two acts. For original production credits see *Theatre World* Volume 62, page 39.

SYNOPSIS An inspiring story of a woman, who, through love, finds the strength to triumph over adversity and discover her unique voice in the world.

*Succeeded by 1. Ruby E. Crawford 2. Jenny Mollet 3. Kitra Williams, LaKisha Jones 4. Yolanda Wyns 5. Teresa Stanley 6. Leilani N. Bryant 7. Montego Glover 8. Zonya Love (1/9//08) 9. BeBe Winans (1/9/08) 10. Chaka Khan (1/9/08) 11. Angela Robinson (2/1/08) 12. Todrick D. Hall 13. Marla McReynolds 14. Levensky Smith

Fantasia and NaTasha Yvette Williams (photo by Paul Kolnik)

COMPANY

Barrymore Theatre; First Preview: October 30, 2006; Opening Night: November 29, 2007; Closed July 1, 2007; 34 previews, 247 performances

Music and lyrics by Stephen Sondheim, book by George Furth; Produced by Marc Routh, Richard Frankel, Steven Baruch, Ambassador Theatre Group, Tulchin/Bartner Productions, Darren Bagert, and Cincinnati Playhouse in the Park (Edward Stern, Producing Artistic Director; Buzz Ward, Executive Director); Director and Musical Staging, John Doyle; Musical Supervision/Orchestrations, Mary-Mitchell Campbell; Set, David Gallo; Costumes, Ann Hould-Ward; Lighting, Thomas C. Hase; Sound, Andrew Keister; Hair/Wigs, David Lawrence; Makeup, Angelina Avallone; Casting, Telsey + Company; Associate Director, Adam John Hunter; PSM, Gary Mickelson; Music Supervisor, Lynne Shankel; General Manager, Richard Frankel Productions, Jo Porter; Production Management, Juniper Street Productions, Hilary Blanken, Guy Kwan, Kevin Broomell, Ana Rose Greene, Elana Soderblom; Company Manager, Sammy Ledbetter; Associate Company Manager, Jason Pelusio; Stage Manager/Dance Captain, Newton Cole; ASM, Claudia Lynch; Action Arrangement, Drew Fracher; Associate Design: Mary Hamrick (set), Sidney Shannon (costumes), Paul Miller (lighting); Set Model, Frank McCullough; Design Assistants, Josh Zangen (set), Bradley Clements (lighting), Michael Bogden (sound); Advertising, Serino Coyne; Music Copying, Kaye-Houston; Press, Barlow-Hartman, Leslie Baden; Cast recording: Nonesuch 79635

CAST Robert – *Percussion* **Raúl Esparza;** Joanne – *Orchestra Bells, Percussion* **Barbara Walsh;** Harry – *Trumpet, Trombone* **Keith Buterbaugh;** Peter – *Piano/keyboards, Double Bass* **Matt Castle;** Paul – *Trumpet, Drums* **Robert Cunningham;** Marta – *Keyboard, Violin, Alto Sax* **Angel Desai;** Kathy – *Flute, Alto Sax* **Kelly Jeanne Grant;** Sarah – *Flute, Alto Sax, Piccolo* **Kristin Huffman;** Susan – *Piano/keyboards, Orchestra Bells* **Amy Justman;** Amy – *French Horn, Trumpet, Flute* **Heather Laws;** Jenny – *Violin, Guitar, Double Bass* **Leenya Rideout;** David – *Cello, Alto Sax, Tenor Sax* **Fred Rose;** Larry – *Clarinet, Drums* **Bruce Sabath;** April – *Oboe, Tuba, Alto Sax* **Elizabeth Stanley**

STANDBYS Fred Rose (Robert), Renée Bang Allen (Sarah, Joanne), Brandon Ellis (David, Paul), David Garry (Harry, Larry, Paul), Jason Ostrowski (Peter), Jessica Wright (Amy, Jenny, Susan), Katrina Yaukey (Marta, Kathy, April)

MUSICAL NUMBERS Company, The Little Things You Do Together, Sorry-Grateful, You Could Drive a Person Crazy, Have I Got a Girl for You, Someone is Waiting, Another Hundred People, Getting Married Today, Marry Me a Little, Side by Side by Side, What Would We Do Without You?, Poor Baby, Barcelona, The Ladies Who Lunch, Being Alive

Elizabeth Stanley, Kelly Jeanne Grant, Angel Desai (front), Raúl Esparza (back) (photo by Paul Kolnik)

SETTING New York City. Now. Revival of the musical presented in two acts. This production was previously produced at Cincinnati Playhouse in the Park, March 14-April 14, 2006 (see *Theatre World* Volume 62, page 276). Originally produced on Broadway at the Alvin Theatre on April 26, 1970 (see *Theatre World* Volume 26, page 57). Revived by the Roundabout Theatre Company at the Criterion Center on August 30, 1995 (see *Theatre World* Volume 52, page 12).

SYNOPSIS A revolutionary, unconventional look at love and commitment in a complex modern world, *Company* is a remarkably honest and sophisticated portrayal of five married couples as seen through the eyes of their mutual friend Robert, a bachelor weighing the pros and cons of wedded life. The show explores not only fear and longing but also the simple joys of being alive. Doyle's production is a bold reinvention of the show in which the actors play all of the musical instruments.

CURTAINS

Al Hirschfeld Theatre; First Preview: February 27, 2007; Opening Night: March 22, 2007; 26 previews, 478 performances as of May 31, 2008

Book and additional lyrics by Rupert Holmes, music & additional lyrics by John Kander, lyrics by Fred Ebb, original book & concept by Peter Stone; Produced by Roger Berlind, Roger Horchow, Daryl Roth, Jane Bergére, Ted Hartley, Center Theatre Group; Director, Scott Ellis; Choreography, Rob Ashford; Music Director/Vocal Arrangements, David Loud; Orchestrations, William David Brohn; Sets, Anna Louizos; Costumes, William Ivey Long; Lighting, Peter Kaczorowski; Sound, Brian Ronan; Hair/Wigs, Paul Huntley; Dance Arrangements, David Chase; Fight Director, Rick Sordelet; Aerial Effects, Paul Rubin; Makeup, Angelina Avallone; Associate Choreographer, Joann M. Hunter; Casting, Jim Carnahan; Production Supervisor, Beverly Randolph; Technical Supervisor, Peter Fulbright; Music Coordinator, John Monaco; General Management, 101 Productions, Ltd.; Marketing Services, TMG; Associate Producers, Barbara & Peter Fodor; Company Manager, Bruce Klinger; Stage Manager, Scott Taylor Rollison; ASM, Kevin Bertolacci, Jerome Vivona; Associate Company Manager, Beverly Edwards/Kevin Beebee; Dance Captain, David Eggers; Assistant Dance Captain, Ashley Amber; Assistant Director, Dave Solomon; Music Copying, Larry H. Abel, Music Preparation International; Advertising, Serino Coyne; Press, Boneau/Bryan-Brown, Jim Byk, Juliana Hannett, Matt Ross; Cast recording: Manhattan Records/EMI Broadway Angel 92212 2

CAST Jessica Cranshaw/Connie Subbotin **Patty Goble;** Randy Dexter **Jim Newman*[1];** Niki Harris **Jill Paice*[2];** Bambi Bernét **Megan Sikora;** Bobby Pepper **Noah Racey;** Johnny Harmon **Michael X. Martin;** Georgia Hendricks **Karen Ziemba;** Aaron Fox **Jason Danieley;** Carmen Bernstein **Debra Monk;** Oscar Shapiro **Michael McCormick;** Christopher Belling **Edward Hibbert;** Lieutenant Frank Cioffi **David Hyde Pierce;** Mona Page **Mary Ann Lamb*[3];** Harv Fremont **Matt Farnsworth*[4];** Roberta Wooster **Darcie Roberts*[5];** Sidney Bernstein **Ernie Sabella*[6];** Detective O'Farrell/Roy Stetson **Kevin Bernard;** Daryl Grady **John Bolton;** Sasha Iljinsky **David Loud;** Marjorie Cook **Paula Leggett Chase*[7];** Arlene Barruca **Nili Bassman;** Brick Hawvermale **Ward Billeisen;** Jan Setler **Jennifer Dunne;** Peg Prentice **Brittany Marcin;** Ronnie Driscoll **Joe Aaron Reid*[8];** Russ Cochran **Christopher Spaulding;** Swings **Ashley Amber*[9], David Eggers, J. Austin Eyer, Allison Spratt*[10], Jerome Vivona**

ORCHESTRA David Loud (Conductor); Sam Davis (Associate Music Director/piano-synthesizer); Steven Kenyon, Al Hunt, Owen Kotler, Mark Thrasher (woodwinds); R.J. Kelley, Angela Cordell (French horns); Don Downs, Matthew Peterson; Charles Gordon (House Contractor, trombone); Jennifer Wharton (bass trombone/tuba); Gregory Landes (percussion); Bruce Doctor (drums): Greg Utzig (guitars/banjo); Robert Renino (bass)

MUSICAL NUMBERS Wide Open Spaces, What Kind of Man?, Thinking of Him, The Woman's Dead, Show People, Coffee Shop Nights, In the Same Boat 1, I Miss the Music, Thataway!, He Did It, It's a Business, Kansasland, In the Same Boat 2, Thinking of Him (reprise), A Tough Act to Follow, In the Same Boat 3, A Tough Act to Follow (reprise)

SETTING 1959. Boston's Colonial Theatre during the out-of-town tryout of the new musical, *Robbin' Hood!*. A new musical presented in two acts. American premiere produced at the Ahmanson Theatre by Center Theatre Group in Los Angeles, August–September, 2006.

SYNOPSIS When the hapless, talent-free star of a potential Broadway hit trying out in Boston dies on opening night during her curtain call, Lieutenant Frank Cioffi arrives on the scene to conduct an investigation. But the lure of the theatre proves irresistible. After an unexpected romance blooms for the stage-struck detective, he finds himself just as drawn toward making the show a hit, as he is in solving the murder.

*Succeeded by: 1. John McInnis, Matt Wall 2. Erin Davie (2/15/08) 3. Shannon Lewis (12/18/07) 4. Aaron Ramey (12/26/07) 5. Bridget Berger (10/16/07), Julie Tolivar (4/8/08) 6. Gerry Vichi (1/8/08) 7. Jennifer Frankel 8. Sean Samuels, Joe Aaron Reid 9. Lorin Latarro 10. Stephanie Youell; Temporary replacements: Sean McKnight (Brick), David Elder (Bobby, Randy), Shannon Lewis (Jan), Sean Martin Hingston (Bobby: 5/13-25), Callie Carter (Arlene)

Erin Davie and David Hyde Pierce (photo by Joan Marcus)

DEUCE

Music Box Theatre; First Preview: April 11, 2007; Opening Night: May 6, 2007; Closed August 19, 2007; 27 previews, 121 performances

Written by Terrence McNally; Producers, Scott Rudin, Stuart Thompson, Maberry Theatricals, The Shubert Organization, Roger Berlind, Debra Black, Bob Boyett, Susan Dietz, Daryl Roth; Director, Michael Blakemore; Set, Peter J. Davison; Costumes, Ann Roth; Lighting, Mark Henderson; Video/ Projections, Sven Ortel; Sound, Paul Charlier; Casting, Telsey + Company; PSM, Steven Beckler; Production Management, Aurora Productions; Company Manager, Brig Berney; General Management, Stuart Thompson Productions, James Triner, Caroline Prugh; Stage Manager, Mary MacLeod; Associate Design: Michelle Matland (costumes), Daniel Walker (lighting), Walter Trarbach, Tony Smolenski IV (sound); Makeup Consultant, Angelina Avallone; Production: Brian GF McGarity (electrician), Paul Delcioppo (sound operator), David Cohen (projections operator), Kristin Gardner (wardrobe supervisor), Maeve Fiona Butler (Ms. Lansbury's dresser), Anna Hoffman (hair supervisor); Production Assistant, John Bantay; Dramaturg, Tessa LaNeve; Assistant Director, Kim Weild; Tennis Consultant, Tom Santopietro; Producer Assistants: Diana Short, Jeffrey Hillock, Ana Pilar Camacho, Greg Raby, Diane Murphy, Angela Sidlow; Advertising, SpotCo; Marketing, Leanne Schanzer Promotions; Press, Boneau/Bryan-Brown, Chris Boneau, Jim Byk, Danielle Crinnion

CAST An Admirer **Michael Mulheren;** Midge Barker **Marian Seldes;** Leona Mullen **Angela Lansbury;** Ryan Becker **Brian Haley;** Kelly Short **Joanna P. Adler**

STANDBYS Jennifer Harmon (Midge), Diane Kagan (Leona), Linda Marie Larson (Kelly), Robert Emmet Lunney (Ryan/ An Admirer)

SETTING US Grand Slam Tennis tournament, now. World premiere of a new play presented without intermission.

SYNOPSIS In the winter of their lives, two former doubles tennis legends reunite to watch a championship match, and try to make sense of the partnership that took them to the top of their game.

Angela Lansbury (photos by Joan Marcus)

Marian Seldes, Angela Lansbury

THE DROWSY CHAPERONE

Marquis Theatre; First Preview: April 3, 2006; Opening Night: May 1, 2006; Closed December 30, 2007; 32 previews, 674 performances

Music and lyrics by Lisa Lambert and Greg Morrison, book by Bob Martin and Don McKellar, by special arrangement with Paul Mack; Produced by Kevin McCollum, Roy Miller, Boyett Ostar Productions, Stephanie McClelland, Barbara Freitag, Jill Furman; Director/Choreography, Casey Nicholaw; Sets, David Gallo; Costumes, Gregg Barnes; Lighting, Ken Billington, Brian Monahan; Sound, Acme Sound Partners; Casting, Bernard Telsey; Hair, Josh Marquette; Makeup, Justen M. Brosnan; Orchestrations, Larry Blank; Dance/Incidental Arrangements, Glen Kelly; Music Director/Vocal Arrangements, Phil Reno; Music Coordinator, John Miller; Production Supervisors, Brian Lynch, Chris Kluth; PSM, Karen Moore; Associate Producers; Sonny Everett, Mariano Tolentino, Jr.; Marketing, TMG; General Management, Charlotte Wilcox Company; Company Manager, Bruce Kagel; ACM, Robert E. Jones; Stage Manager, Josh Halperin; ASM, Rachel S. McCutchen; Assistant Director, Josh Rhodes; Dance Captain, Angela Pupello; Props, George Wagner; Music Preparation, Hotstave, Ltd.; Press, Boneau/Bryan Brown; Cast Recording: Sh-K-Boom Records/Ghostlight 7915584411-2

CAST Man in Chair **John Glover**[*1]; Mrs. Tottendale **Joanne Worley**[*2]; Underling **Peter Bartlett;** Robert Martin **Troy Britton Johnson;** George **Patrick Wetzel;** Feldzieg **Lenny Wolpe**[*3]; Kitty **Jennifer Smith;** Gangster #1 **Jason Kravits;** Gangster #2 **Garth Kravits;** Aldolpho **Danny Burstein;** Janet Van De Graaff **Janine LaManna**[*4]; The Drowsy Chaperone **Beth Leavel;** Trix **Kecia Lewis-Evans;** Ensemble **Linda Gabler, Dale Hensley, Joey Sorge**[*5], **Joanna Young;** Swings **Jay Douglas, Stacia Fernandez, Kilty Reidy, Tripp Hanson, Brian J. Marcum, Mamie Parris, Stacy Dodd Holt, Kate Loprest, Andrea Chamberlin**

UNDERSTUDIES Jay Douglas (Robert, Aldolpho, Man in Chair, Feldzieg), Joanna Young (Janet, Kitty), Mamie Parris (Janet, Kitty, Chaperone), Joey Sorge (Robert, Aldolpho, Gangster 1 & 2), Linda Gabler (Kitty, Mrs. Tottendale, Trix), Stacia Fernandez (Chaperone, Mrs. Tottendale, Trix), Kilty Reidy (Underling, George, Gangster 1 & 2), Dale Hensley (Adolpho, Feldzieg, Gangster 1 & 2), Matt Wall (George, Robert, Gangster 1 & 2), Tripp Hanson (Gangster 1 & 2, Underling)

ORCHESTRA Phil Reno (Conductor); Lawrence Goldberg (Associate Conductor/keyboards); Matt Perri (keyboards); Edward Joffe, Tom Murray, Tom Christensen, Ron Jannelli (reeds); Dave Stahl, Glenn Drewes, Jeremy Miloszewicz (trumpet); Steve Armour, Jeff Nelson (trombone); Ed Hamilton (guitar); Michael Keunnen (bass); Perry Cavari (drums); Bill Hayes (percussion)

Janine LaManna and the company (photo by Joan Marcus)

MUSICAL NUMBERS Overture, Fancy Dress, Cold Feets, Show Off, As We Stumble Along, I Am Aldolpho, Accident Waiting Happen, Toledo Surprise; Message From a Nightingale, Bride's Lament, Love Is Always Lovely, I Do I Do in the Sky, As We Stumble Along (reprise)

SETTING The New York apartment and in the mind of Man in Chair, now. A musical presented without intermission. For original production credits see *Theatre World* Volume 62, page 60.

SYNOPSIS To chase his blues, a musical theatre addict drops the needle on his favorite LP – the 1928 musical comedy *The Drowsy Chaperone*. From the crackle of his hi-fi, the musical magically bursts to life, telling the tale of a pampered Broadway starlet who wants to give up show business to get married. Enter her producer who sets out to sabotage the nuptials, the "drowsy" chaperone, the debonair groom, a dizzy chorine, a Latin lover, a couple of gangsters and ruses are played, hi-jinks occur and the plot spins completely out of control.

*Succeeded by: 1. Jonathan Crombie (8/21/07), Bob Saget (10/19/07) 2. Sally Struthers (12/9/07) 3. Gerry Vichi (6/5/07) 4. Mara Davi (7/31/07) 5. Matt Wall, Joey Sorge

FROST/NIXON

Bernard B. Jacobs Theatre; First Preview: March 31, 2007; Opening Night: April 22, 2007; Closed August 19, 2007; 23 previews, 137 performances

Written by Peter Morgan; Originally presented by The Donmar Warehouse (Michael Grandage, Artistic Director; Lucy Davies, Executive Producer; James Bierman, General Manager); Produced by Arielle Tepper Madover, Matthew Byam Shaw, Robert Fox, Act Productions, David Binder, Debra Black, Annette Niemitzow/Harlene Freezer, The Weinstein Company; Director, Michael Grandage; Set and Costumes, Christopher Oram; Lighting, Neil Austin; Composer and Sound, Adam Cork; Video, Jon Driscoll; Hair and Wigs, Richard Mawbey; Casting, Daniel Swee (US), Anne McNulty (UK); Marketing, Eric Schnall; General Management, 101 Productions, Ltd.; PSM, Rick Steiger; Technical Supervisor, Aurora Productions (US), Patrick Molony (UK); Company Manager, Alexandra Gushin; Stage Manager, Lisa Buxbauk; Assistant Director, Seth Sklar-Heyn; Associate Design: Scott Traugott (costumes), Daniel Walker (lighting), Victoria Smerdon (moving light programmer), Chris Cronin (sound); Screen Technician, Colin Barnes; Makeup, Angelina Avallone; Production: Michael Van Praagh (carpenter), Edward Ruggerio (flyman), Jon Lawson, Herbert Messing (electricians), Christopher Kurtz (video), Dave Fulton (props supervisor), Alfred Ricci (house props), John Alban, Daniel Carpio (props), Kelly A. Saxon (wardrobe supervisor), Patrick Bevilacqua, Lyle Jones, Philip Heckman (dressers), Joel Mendenhall (hair supervisor), Timothy Eaker, Brian Maschka, Holly Ferguson (assistants); Advertising, SpotCo; Press, Boneau/Bryan-Brown, Adrian Bryan-Brown, Steven Padla, Heath Schwartz

Michael Sheen and Frank Langella

Remy Auberjonois, Michael Sheen, Armand Schultz, Stephen Kunken (photos by Joan Marcus)

CAST Richard Nixon **Frank Langella;** Jim Reston **Stephen Kunken;** David Frost **Michael Sheen;** Jack Brennan **Corey Johnson;** Evonne Goolagong **Shira Gregory;** John Birt **Remy Auberjonois;** Manolo Sanchez **Triney Sandoval;** Swifty Lazar/Mike Wallace **Stephen Rowe;** Caroline Cushing **Sonya Walger;** Bob Zelnick **Armand Schultz;** Ensemble **Dennis Cockrum, Antony Hagopian, Roxanna Hope**

UNDERSTUDIES Bob Ari (Richard Nixon), Remy Auberjonois (David Frost), Dennis Cockrum (Swifty Lazar, Bob Zelnick, Manolo Sanchez), Anthony Hagopian (John Birt, Jack Brennan, Manolo Sanchez), Roxanna Hope (Evonne Goolagong, Caroline Cushing), Triney Sandoval (Jim Reston)

SETTING England, Australia, and the U.S., 1977. American premiere of a new play presented without intermission. Originally presented at the Donmar Warehouse, London, August 15, 2006, and transferred to the Gielgud Theatre, November 16, 2006.

SYNOPSIS A dramatization of the events surrounding David Frost's 1977 television interviews with Richard Nixon, *Frost/Nixon* tackles the question: How did David Frost, a famous British talk-show host with a playboy reputation, elicit the apology that the rest of the world was waiting to hear from former President Richard Nixon? The fast-paced new play shows the determination, conviction and cunning of two men as they square off in one of the most monumental political interviews of all time.

GREY GARDENS

Walter Kerr Theatre; First Preview: October 3, 2006; Opening Night: November 2, 2006; Closed July 29, 2007; 22 previews, 307 performances

Book by Doug Wright, music by Scott Frankel, lyrics by Michael Korie; based on the documentary film *Grey Gardens* by David Maysles, Albert Maysles, Ellen Hovde, Muffie Meyer, and Susan Froemke; Produced by East of Doheny, Staunch Entertainment, Randall L. Wreghitt/Mort Swinsky; Michael Alden, Edwin W. Schloss, in association with Playwrights Horizons; Director, Michael Greif; Musical Staging, Jeff Calhoun; Sets, Allen Moyer; Costumes, William Ivey Long; Lighting, Peter Kaczorowski; Sound, Brian Ronan; Projections, Wendall K. Harrington; Hair/Wigs, Paul Huntley; Orchestrations, Bruce Coughlin; Music Director, Lawrence Yurman; Music Coordinator, John Miller; Executive Producer, Beth Williams; General Management, Alan Wasser, Allan Williams; PSM, Judith Schoenfeld; Management, Juniper Street Productions; Marketing, TMG; Casting, Telsey + Company; Original Casting, Alan Filderman, Alaine Alldaffer, James Calleri; Company Manager, Mark Shacket; Stage Manager, J. Philip Bassett; ASM, Stephen R. Gruse; Associate Director, Johanna McKeon; ACM, Carrie Sherriff; Associate Choreographer, Jodi Moccia; Dance Captain, Megan Lewis; Dialect Coach, Deborah Hecht; Advertising, Serino Coyne; Music Copying, Emily Grishman/Katharine Edmonds; Synthesizer Programmer, Randy Cohen; Press, The Publicity Office; Cast Recording: PS Classics 642

CAST *Prologue (1973):* Edith Bouvier Beale **Mary Louise Wilson;** "Little" Edie Beale **Christine Ebersole;** *Act One (1941):* Edith Bouvier Beale **Christine Ebersole;** Young "Little" Edie Beale **Erin Davie;** George Gould Strong **Bob Stillman;** Brooks, Sr. **Michael Potts;** Jacqueline "Jackie" Bouvier **Sarah Hyland;** Lee Bouvier **Kelsey Fowler;** Joseph Patrick Kennedy, Jr. **Matt Cavenaugh;** J.V. "Major" Bouvier **John McMartin;** *Act Two (1973):* Edith Bouvier Beale **Mary Louise Wilson;** "Little" Edie Beale **Christine Ebersole;** Brooks, Jr. **Michael Potts;** Jerry **Matt Cavenaugh;** Norman Vincent Peale **John McMartin**

STANDBYS Maureen Moore (for Christine Ebersole), Dale Soules (for Mary Louise Wilson), Abigail Ferenczy (for Sarah Hyland, Kelsey Fowler), Donald Grody (for John McMartin), Michael W. Howell (for Michael Potts), Megan Lewis (for Erin Davie), Asa Somers (for Matt Cavenaugh, Bob Stillman)

MUSICIANS Lawrence Yurman (Conductor); Paul Staroba (Associate Conductor/keyboards); Eric DeGioia (violin); Anik Oulianine (cello); Ken Hitchcock, Todd Groves (reeds); Daniel Urness (trumpet/flugelhorn); Patrick Pridemore (French horn); Brian Cassier (acoustic bass); Tim McLafferty (percussion/drums)

Erin Davie, John McMartin (photo by Paul Kolnik)

MUSICAL NUMBERS The Girl Who Has Everything, The Five-Fifteen, Mother Darling, Goin' Places, Marry Well, Hominy Grits, Peas in a Pod, Drift Away, The Five-Fifteen (reprise), Daddy's Girl, The Telegram, Will You?, The Revolutionary Costume for Today, The Cake I Had, Entering Grey Gardens, The House We Live In, Jerry Likes My Corn, Around the World, Will You? (reprise), Choose to Be Happy, Around the World (reprise), Another Winter in a Summer Town, The Girl Who Has Everything (reprise)

SETTING Grey Gardens, East Hampton, Long Island, New York 1941 and 1973; Transfer of the Off-Broadway musical presented in two acts. Originally presented at Playwrights Horizons February 10–April 30, 2006 (see *Theatre World* Volume 62, page 165).

SYNOPSIS Once among the brightest names in the pre-Camelot social register, the deliciously eccentric aunt and cousin of Jacqueline Kennedy Onassis are now East Hampton's most notorious recluses. Facing an uncertain future, Edith Bouvier Beale and her adult daughter, 'Little' Edie, are forced to revisit their storied past and come to terms with it – for better, and for worse.

HAIRSPRAY

Neil Simon Theatre; First Preview: July 18, 2002; Opening Night: August 15, 2002; 31 previews, 2,393 performances as of May 31, 2008

Book by Mark O'Donnell and Thomas Meehan, music by Marc Shaiman, lyrics by Marc Shaiman and Scott Wittman; based on the 1988 film written and directed by John Waters; Produced by Margo Lion, Adam Epstein, The Baruch-Viertel-Routh-Frankel Group, James D. Stern/Douglas L. Meyer, Rick Steiner/Frederic H. Mayerson, SEL & GFO, New Line Cinema, in association with Live Nation, Allan S. Gordon, Elan V. McAllister, Dede Harris, Morton Swinsky, John and Bonnie Osher; Director, Jack O'Brien, Choreography, Jerry Mitchell; Sets, David Rockwell; Costumes, William Ivey Long; Lighting, Kenneth Posner; Sound, Steve C. Kennedy; Casting, Telsey + Company; Wigs/Hair, Paul Huntley; PSM, Lois L. Griffing; Associate Director, Matt Lenz; Associate Choreographer, Michele Lynch; Orchestrations, Harold Wheeler, Music Director, Lon Hoyt, Arrangements, Marc Shaiman; Music Coordinator, John Miller, General Management, Richard Frankel, Laura Green; Technical Supervisor, Tech Production Services, Inc./Peter Fulbright; Associate Producers, Rhoda Mayerson, the Aspen Group, Daniel C. Staton; Company Managers, Bruce Kagel, Tracy Geltman; Stage Managers, Marisha Ploski, Thomas J. Gates; Makeup, Randy Houston Mercer; Music Copying, Emily Grishman, Katharine Edmonds; Dance Captains, Brooke Leigh Engen, Robbie Roby; Press, Richard Kornberg, Don Summa, Alyssa Hart; Cast recording: Sony SK 87708

CAST Tracy Turnblad **Shannon Durig**[*1]; Corny Collins **Jonathan Dokuchitz**[*2]; Amber Von Tussle **Brynn O'Malley**[*3]; Brad **Michael Cunio**[*4]; Tammy **Hayley Podschun**[*5]; Fender **Daniel Robinson;** Brenda **Leslie Goddard;** Sketch **Bryan West**[*6]; Shelley **Lori Eve Marinacci;** IQ **Todd Michel Smith;** Lou Ann **Leslie McDonel**[*7]; Link Larkin **Ashley Parker Angel+;** Prudy Pingleton/Gym Teacher/Matron **Susan Mosher;** Edna Turnblad **Paul Vogt**[*8]; Penny Pingleton **Alexa Vega**[*9]; Velma Von Tussle **Isabel Keating**[*10]; Harriman F. Spritzer/Principal/Mr. Pinky/Guard **Blake Hammond**[*11]; Wilbur Turnblad **Jere Burns**[*12]; Seaweed J. Stubbs **Tevin Campbell;** Duane **Tyrick Wiltez Jones**[*13]; Gilbert **Arbender J. Robinson**[*14]; Lorraine **Terita R. Redd;** Thad **Dwayne Cooper;** The Dynamites **Carla Jay Hargrove, Judine Richard Somerville, Iris Burruss;** Little Inez **Naturi Naughton**[*15]; Motormouth Maybelle **Darlene Love**[*16]; Denizens of Baltimore **Iris Burruss, Dwayne Cooper, Michael Cunio**[*3]**, Hayley Podschun**[*5]**, Daniel Robinson, Leslie Goddard, Blake Hammond**[*11]**, Carla Jay Hargrove, Lori Eve Marinacci, Leslie McDonal**[*7]**, Susan Mosher, Arbender J. Robinson**[*14]**, Terita R. Redd, Todd Michel Smith; Judine Richard Somerville, Bryan West**[*6]**, Tyrick Wiltez Jones;** Swings **Cameron Adams, Abdul Latif, Peter Matthew Smith, Lauren Kling, Tracee Beazer, Ryan Christopher Chotto, Jason Snow, Willis White, Nicole Powell, Gretchen Bieber**[*17]**, Matthew S. Morgan, Brooke Leigh Engen, Jacqui Polk, Robbie Roby, Scott Davidson**

Ashley Parker Angel and Cast (photo by Paul Kolnik)

UNDERSTUDIES Ed Romanoff (Edna, Wilbur, Male Authority Figure), Michelle Dowdy/Annie Fuuke (Tracy)

ORCHESTRA Lon Hoyt, Keith Cotton, Seth Farber, David Spinozza, Peter Calo, Francisco Centeno, Clint de Ganon, Walter "Wally" Usiatynski, David Mann, Dave Rickenberg, Bob Milliken, Birch Johnson, Rob Shaw, Carol Pool, Sarah Hewitt Roth,

SETTING Time: 1962. Place: Baltimore. A musical presented in two acts. For original production credits see *Theatre World* Volume 59, page 25.

SYNOPSIS *Hairspray* is the story of Tracy Turnblad, who is going to do whatever it takes to dance her way onto TV's most popular show. Can a big girl with big dreams—and even bigger hair—turn the whole town around?

*Succeeded by: 1. Marissa Perry (4/15/08) 2. Lance Bass (8/14/07), Clarke Thorell (1/8/08) 3. Ashley Spencer (7/24/07) 4. Kasey Marino 5. Brooke Leigh Engen 6. Van Hughes, Curt Hansen 7. Kirsten Bracken 8. George Wendt (10/23/07) 9. Niki Scalera (8/7/07) 10. Michelle Pawk (8/21/07), Mary Birdsong (1/29/08), Karen Mason (4/8/08) 11. Kevin Meany 12. Jerry Mathers (6/5/07), Jim J. Bullock (9/18/07), Tom Rooney, Ken Marks 13. Travis Robertson 14. Steven Cutts 15. Carla Duren 16. Jenifer Lewis (4/22/08) 17. Leslie McDonel
+Aaron Tveit temporarily replaced Mr. Angel in April due to medical leave.

INHERIT THE WIND

Lyceum Theatre; First Preview: March 19, 2007; Opening Night: April 12, 2007; Closed July 8, 2007; 26 previews, 100 performances

Written by Jerome Lawrence and Robert E. Lee; Produced by Boyett Ostar Productions, The Shubert Organization, Lawrence Horowitz, Jon Avnet/Ralph Guild, Roy Furman, Debra Black/Daryl Roth, Bill Rollnick/Nancy Ellison Rollnick, Stephanie McClelland; Director, Doug Hughes; Set/Costumes, Santo Loquasto; Lighting, Brian MacDevitt; Original Music/Sound, David Van Tieghem; Hair/Wigs, Paul Huntley; Casting, Jay Binder/Jack Bowdan; PSM, Michael Brunner; Technical Supervisor, Peter Fulbright; Marketing, HHC Marketing; General Management, 101 Productions; Associate Producer, Judith Resnick; Company Manager, Gregg Arst; Stage Manager, Barclay Stiff; Associate Director, Mark Schneider; Music Supervisor, David M. Lutken; Associate Design: Jenny B. Sawyers (set), Matthew Pachtman (costume), Michael O'Connor (lighting), Jill BC DuBoff (sound); Design Assistants, Tobin Ost, Kanae Heike (set), Sarah Sophia Turner (costumes); Production: Charley P. Mann (carpenter), Abraham Morrison (props supervisor), Brian GF McGarity (electrician), Brien Brannigan (sound supervisor), John Paull III (head props), William Rowland II (head electrician), Marc Polimeni (lighting programmer), Dave Olin Rogers (wardrobe supervisor), Robin Maginsky Day (hair supervisor); Press, Boneau/Bryan-Brown, Adrian Bryan-Brown, Jackie Green, Danielle Crinnion

CAST Howard **Conor Donovan;** Melinda **Amanda Sprecher;** Rachel **Maggie Lacey;** Mr. Meeker **Scott Sowers;** Bert Cates **Benjamin Walker;** Mr. Goodfellow **Henry Stram;** Mrs. Krebs **Charlotte Maier;** Reverend Jeremiah Brown **Byron Jennings;** Sillers **Andrew Weems;** Dunlap **Jay Patterson;** Bannister **Bill Buell;** Mrs. Loomis **Anne Bowles;** Mrs. Blair **Pippa Pearthree;** Vendor **Bill Christ;** Elijah **Lanny Flaherty;** Timmy **Matthew Nardozzi;** E.K. Hornbeck **Denis O'Hare;** Monkey Man **Kevin C. Loomis;** Matthew Harrison Brady **Brian Dennehy;** Mrs. Brady **Beth Fowler;** Mayor **Jeff Steitzer;** Judge **Terry Beaver;** Tom Davenport **Jordan Lage;** Photographer **Randall Newsome;** Henry Drummond **Christopher Plummer;** Reuters Reporter/Esterbrook **Erik Steele;** Gospel Quartet **Carson Church, Katie Klaus, Mary Kate Law, David M. Lutken;** Townspeople **Anne Bowles, Steve Brady, Bill Christ, Kit Flanagan, Sherman Howard, Philip LeStrange, Kevin C. Loomis, Charlotte Maier, Matthew Nardozzi, Randall Newsome, Jay Patterson, Pippa Pearthree, Erick Steele, Andrew Weems**

UNDERSTUDIES Anne Bowles (Rachel Brown), Steve Brady (Dunlap, Elijah, Sillers), Bill Christ (Mr. Goodfellow, Rev. Jeremiah Brown), Kit Flanagan (Mrs. Blair, Mrs. Brady, Mrs. Krebs), Sherman Howard (Henry Drummond, Monkey Man), Jordan Lage (E. K. Hornbeck), Philip LeStrange (Judge, Mayor, Mr. Bannister), Kevin Loomis (Meeker, Reuter's Man), Matthew Nardozzi (Howard, Melinda), Erik Steele (Bertram Cates, Photographer), Jeff Steitzer (Matthew Harrison Brady)

SETTING A small town; Summer, not too long ago. Revival of a courtroom drama presented in two acts. Originally presented at the National Theatre April 21, 1955–June 22, 1957, 806 performances (see *Theatre World* Volume 12, page 130). A previous revival played the Royale Theatre April 3–May 12, 1996 (see *Theatre World* Volume 52, page 46).

SYNOPSIS *Inherit the Wind* is a fictionalized retelling of the famous 1925 "Monkey Trial" in which science teacher John Scopes was tried and convicted for teaching Darwin's theory of evolution, violating a Tennessee law that forbade teaching any theory that conflicted with the Biblical conception of Divine Creation. Matthew Harrison Brady is based on William Jennings Bryan and Henry Drummond is based on Clarence Darrow.

Christopher Plummer and Brian Dennehy (photo by Joan Marcus)

JERSEY BOYS

August Wilson Theatre; First Preview: October 4, 2005; Opening Night: November 6, 2005; 38 previews, 1,050 performances as of May 31, 2008

Book by Marshall Brickman and Rick Elice, music by Bob Gaudio, lyrics by Bob Crewe; Produced by Dodger Theatricals (Michael David, Edward Strong, Rocco Landesman, Des McAnuff), Joseph J. Grano, Pelican Group, Tamara Kinsella and Kevin Kinsella, in association with Latitude Link, Rick Steiner and Osher/Staton/Bell/Mayerson Group; Director, Des McAnuff; Choreography, Sergio Trujillo; Musical Director, Vocal Arrangements/Incidental Music, Ron Melrose; Sets, Klara Zieglerova; Costumes, Jess Goldstein; Lighting, Howell Binkley; Sound, Steve Canyon Kennedy; Projections, Michael Clark; Hair/Wigs, Charles LaPointe; Fight Director, Steve Rankin; PSM, Richard Hester; Orchestrations, Steve Orich; Music Coordinator, John Miller; Technical Supervisor, Peter Fulbright; Casting, Tara Rubin (East), Sharon Bialy, Sherry Thomas (West); Company Manager, Sandra Carlson; Associate Producers, Lauren Mitchell and Rhoda Mayerson; Executive Producer, Sally Campbell Morse; Promotions, HHC Marketing; Stage Manager, Michelle Bosch; ASM, Michael T. Clarkston; Dialect Coach, Stephen Gabis; Dance Captain, Peter Gregus; Fight Captain, Peter Gregus; Music Technical Design, Deborah Hurwitz; Associate General Manager, Jennifer F. Vaughan; Marketing, Dodger Marketing; Advertising, Serino Coyne; Press, Boneau/Bryan-Brown, Susanne Tighe, Heath Schwartz; Cast recording: Rhino R2 73271

CAST French Rap Star/Detective #1/Hal Miller/Barry Belson/Police Officer/Davis **Kris Coleman;** Stanley/Hank Majewski/Crewe's PA/Joe Long **Colin Donnell***1**;** Bob Crewe/others **Peter Gregus;** Tommy DeVito **Christian Hoff;** Nick DeVito/Stosh/Billy Dixon/Norman Waxman/ Charlie Calello/others **Donnie Kehr;** Joey/Recording Studio Engineer/others **Michael Longoria***2**;** Gyp De Carlo/others **Mark Lotito;** Mary Delgado/Angel/others **Jennifer Naimo***3**;** Church Lady/Miss Frankie Nolan/ Bob's Party Girl/Angel/Lorraine/others **Erica Piccininni;** Bob Gaudio **Daniel Reichard***4**;** Frankie's Mother/Nick's Date/Angel/Francine/others **Sara Schmidt;** Nick Massi **J. Robert Spencer;** Frankie Valli **John Lloyd Young***5 (evenings)/ **Michael Longoria***6 (matinees); Thugs **Ken Dow, Joe Payne;** Swings **Heather Ferguson, John Leone, Dominic Nolfi, Matthew Scott, Eric Schneider, Rebecca Kupka, Graham Fenton, Jonathan Hadley**

UNDERSTUDIES*7 Colin Donnell (Gaudio, Massi), Donnie Kehr (Gyp, DeVito), John Leone (Gyp, Massi, DeVito, Crewe), Michael Longoria (Valli), Dominic Nolfi (Gaudio, Valli, Joey), Matthew Scott (DeVito, Valli, Gaudio)

MUSICIANS Ron Melrose (Conductor/keyboards); Deborah Hurwitz (Associate Conductor/keyboards); Stephen "Hoops" Snyder (keyboards); Joe Payne (guitars); Ken Dow (bass); Kevin Dow (drums); Matt Hong, Ben Kono (reeds); David Spier (trumpet)

MUSICAL NUMBERS Ces Soirées-La (Oh What a Night), Silhouettes, You're the Apple of My Eye, I Can't Give You Anything But Love, Earth Angel, Sunday Kind of Love, My Mother's Eyes, I Go Ape, (Who Wears) Short Shorts, I'm in the Mood for Love/Moody's Mood for Love, Cry for Me, An Angel Cried, I Still Care, Trance, Sherry, Big Girls Don't Cry, Walk Like a Man, December, 1963 (Oh What a Night), My Boyfriend's Back, My Eyes Adored You, Dawn (Go Away), Walk Like a Man (reprise), Big Man in Town, Beggin', Stay, Let's Hang On (To What We've Got), Opus 17 (Don't You Worry 'Bout Me), Bye Bye Baby, C'mon Marianne, Can't Take My Eyes Off of You, Working My Way Back to You, Fallen Angel, Rag Doll, Who Loves You

SETTING New Jersey, New York, and across the U.S., 1950's–now. A new musical presented in two acts. For original production credits see *Theatre World* Volume 62, page 34. World Premiere produced by La Jolla Playhouse, October 5, 2004.

SYNOPSIS "How did four blue-collar kids become one of the greatest successes in pop music history? You ask four guys, you get four different answers." *Jersey Boys* is the story of the legendary Four Seasons, blue-collar boys who formed a singing group and reached the heights of rock 'n' roll stardom.

*Succeeded by: 1. Eric Gutman (12/15/07) 2. Travis Cloer 3. Bridget Berger (4/8/08) 4. Sebastian Arcelus (1/10/08) 5. Michael Longoria (11/29/07) 6. Cory Grant 7. Additional: Eric Schneider (Valli, Joey), Travis Cloer (Valli, Joey), Graham Fenton (DeVito), Eric Gutman (Gaudio, Massi)

Sebastian Arcelus, Michael Longoria, Christian Hoff, J. Robert Spencer (photo by Joan Marcus)

JOURNEY'S END

Belasco Theatre; First Preview: February 8, 2007; Opening Night: February 22, 2007; Closed June 10, 2007; 15 previews, 125 performances

Written by R.C. Sherriff; Produced by Boyett Ostar Productions, Stephanie P. McClelland, Bill Rollnick, James D'Orta, Philip Geier; Director, David Grindley; Sets and Costumes, Jonathan Fensom; Lighting, Jason Taylor; Sound, Gregory Lake; Casting, Jay Binder, Jack Bowdan; PSM, Arthur Gaffin; Technical Supervisor, Larry Morley; Marketing, HHC Marketing; General Management, Alan Wasser, Allan Williams; Company Manager, Penelope Daulton; UK Technical Supervisor, The Production Desk, Ltd., Paul Hennessy; Stage Manager, David Sugarman; Dialect Coach, Majella Hurley; Fight Director, Thomas Schall; Fight Captain, John Behlmann; Scenic Artist, James Rowse; Scenic Drop Artwork, Alasdair Oliver; Production Props, Eric J. Castaldo; Production: George Dummitt (carpenter), Joe Mortitz (flyman), Susan Goulet (electrician), Neil McShane (Electrician), Heidi Brown (props), Tucker Howard (sound), Brien Brannigan (sound), Kay Grunder (wardrobe supervisor), Jeff McGovney (dresser); UK Wardrobe Consultant, Charlotte Bird; US Wardrobe Consultant, Patrick Bevilacqua; UK Props Supervisor, Fahmida Bakht; Press, Pete Sanders, Glenna Freedman

CAST Captain Hardy/Sergeant Major **John Curless;** Lieutenant Osborne **Boyd Gaines;** Private Mason **Jefferson Mays;** 2nd Lieutenant Raleigh **Stark Sands;** Captain Stanhope **Hugh Dancy;** 2nd Lieutenant Trotter **John Ahlin;** Private Albert Brown **John Behlmann;** 2nd Lieutenant Hibbert **Justin Blanchard;** Colonel **Richard Poe;** German Soldier **Kieran Campion;** Lance Corporal Broughton **Nick Berg Barnes**

John Ahlin, Jefferson Mays, Boyd Gaines (photos by Paul Kolnik)

Hugh Dancy and Justin Blanchard

UNDERSTUDIES John Behlmann (Stanhope, German Soldier, Broughton), Richard Poe (Osborne), John Curless (Mason, Colonel), Kieran Campion (Raleigh, Hibbert, Albert, Broughton), Nick Berg Barnes (Hardy, Sergeant Major, Trotter)

SETTING A dugout in the British trenches near St. Quentin, France; Act I–Evening on Monday March 18, 1918, Act II–Tuesday morning and afternoon, Act III–Wednesday afternoon, night, and Thursday, toward dawn. Revival of a play presented in six scenes in three acts with one intermission. Originally produced on Broadway at Henry Miller's Theatre, March 22, 1929–May, 1930; revived at the Empire Theatre, September 18–30, 1939.

SYNOPSIS Based on Sherriff's own experiences in the First World War, *Journey's End* is about a group of British soldiers living together in a cramped trench in France while fighting the last great German offensive in March 1918. This production was based on Mr. Grindley's successful London production which opened at the Comedy Theatre in 2004, toured the UK, and had runs at three West End Theatres before closing in January, 2006.

LEGALLY BLONDE

Palace Theatre; First Preview: April 3, 2007; Opening Night: April 29, 2007; 30 previews, 433 performances as of May 31, 2008

Music and lyrics by Laurence O'Keefe and Nell Benjamin, book by Heather Hatch; based on the novel by Amanda Brown and the MGM motion picture; Produced by Hal Luftig, Fox Theatricals, Dori Berinstein, James L. Nederlander, Independent Presenters Network, Roy Furman, Amanda Lipitz, Broadway Asia, Barbara Whitman, FWPM Group, Ruth Hendel/Cheryl Wiesenfeld, Hal Golberg/David Binder, James D. Stern/Douglas L. Meyer, Robert Bartner-Michael A. Jenkins/Albert Nocciolino, Warner Trepp, in association with MGM ON STAGE, Darcie Denkert, Dean Stobler; Director/Choreographer, Jerry Mitchell; Music Director/Conductor, James Sampliner; Orchestrations, Christopher Jahnke; Arrangements, Laurence O'Keefe & James Sampliner; Music Coordinator, Michael Keller; Sets, David Rockwell; Costumes, Gregg Barnes; Lighting, Kenneth Posner & Paul Miller; Sound, Acme Sound Partners; Casting, Telsey + Company; Hair, David Brian Brown; Associate Director, Marc Bruni; Associate Choreographer, Denis Jones; Technical Supervisor, Theatresmith, Inc.; Animal Trainer, William Berloni; PSM, Bonnie L. Becker; General Management, NLA/Maggie Brohn; Marketing, TMG; Associate Producers, PMC Productions, Yasuhiro Kawana, Andrew Asnes/Adam Zotovich; Company Managers, Kimberly Kelley, Nathan Gehan; Stage Manager, Kimberly Russell; ASM, Scott Rowen; Dance Captains, Rusty Mowery, Michelle Kittrell; Dialect Coach, Stephen Gabis; Fight Director, Thomas Schall; Makeup, Justen M. Brosnan; Additional Arrangements, Alex Lacamoire; Music Copyist, Emily Grishman; Synthesizer Programmer, Leland Music Company; Advertising, Serino Coyne; Press, Barlow-Hartman, Carol Fineman, Kevin Robak; Cast Recording: Sh-K-Boom/Ghostlight Records 84423

CAST Elle Woods **Laura Bell Bundy;** Warner Huntington III **Richard H. Blake;** Vivienne Kensington **Kate Shindle;** Emmett Forrest **Christian Borle;** Professor Callahan **Michael Rupert;** Paulette **Orfeh;** Serena **Leslie Kritzer**[*1]; Margot **Annaleigh Ashford**[*2]; Pilar **DeQuina Moore**[*3]; Shandi/Brooke Wyndam **Nikki Snelson**[*4]; Kate/Chutney **Kate Wetherhead**[*5]; Leilani **Becky Gulsvig;** Cece **Michelle Kittrell;** Kristine **April Berry;** Gabby **Beth Curry;** Veronica/Enid **Natalie Joy Johnson;** Judge **Amber Efé;** Mom/Whitney **Gaelen Gilliland;** Grandmaster Chad/Dewey/Kyle **Andy Karl;** Dad/Winthrop **Kevin Pariseau;** Carlos/Lowell **Matthew Risch;** Padamadan/Nikos **Manuel Herrera;** Aaron/Guard **Noah Weisberg**[*6]; Pforzhiemer **Jason Gillman**; Bruiser **Chico;** Rufus **Chloe;** Harvard

Kate Shindle, Richard H. Blake, Laura Bell Bundy, Michael Rupert and Cast (photo by Paul Kolnik)

Students, Marching Band, Cheerleaders, Inmates, Salespeople **April Berry, Paul Canaan, Beth Curry, Amber Efé, Gaelen Gilliland, Jason Gillman, Becky Gulsvig, Manuel Herrera, Natalie Joy Johnson, Andy Karl, Nick Kenkel, Michelle Kittrell, Kevin Pariseau, Matthew Risch, Jason Patrick Sands**[*7]**; Noah Weisberg**[*6]**; Kate Wetherhead**[*5]; Swings **Lindsay Nicole Chambers, Tracy Jai Edwards**[*8], **Rusty Mowery, Rod Harrelson**

ORCHESTRA James Sampliner (Conductor/keyboard 1); Jason DeBord (Associate Conductor/keyboard 2); Antoine Silverman (violin/Concert Master); Jonathan Dinklage (viola); Peter Sachon (cello); Dave Trigg; Bud Burridge (trumpets); Keith O'Quinn (trombone); Vincent DellaRocca, Dan Willis, Chad Smith (reeds); Roger Wendt (French horn); Greg Joseph (drums); Mark Vanderpoel (bass); Matt Gallagher (keyboard 3); John Putnam, Kenny Brescia (guitars); Pablo Rieppi (percussion)

SETTING The Delta Nu house in Southern California and Harvard Law campus in Cambridge, Massachusetts. New York premiere of a new musical presented in two acts.

SYNOPSIS Sorority star Elle Woods doesn't take "no" for an answer. So when her boyfriend dumps her for someone more "serious," Elle puts down the credit card, hits the books and sets out to go where no Delta Nu has gone before: Harvard Law. Along the way, Elle proves that being true to herself never goes out of style.

*Succeeded by: 1. Tracy Jai Edwards 2. Haven Burton, Kate Rockwell (5/14/08) 3. Asmeret Ghebremichael 4. Nicolette Hart (5/7/08) 5. Stephanie Fittro 6. Bryce Ryness 7. Nathan Balser 8. Cara Cooper, Tracy Jai Edwards, Tiffany Engen; Vacation Swings: Dani Spieler, Casey Leigh Thompson

LES MISÉRABLES

Broadhurst Theatre; First Preview: October 24, 2006; Opening Night: November 9, 2006; Closed January 6, 2008; 17 previews, 463 performances

Book by Alain Boublil and Claude-Michel Schönberg, based on the novel by Victor Hugo; Music by Claude-Michel Schönberg; Lyrics by Herbert Kretzmer; Original French text by Alain Boublil and Jean-Marc Natel; Additional material by James Fenton; Produced by Cameron Mackintosh; Directed and Adapted by John Caird and Trevor Nunn; Design, John Napier; Lighting, David Hershey; Original Sound, Andrew Bruce; Costumes, Adreane Neofitou; Associate Director, Shaun Kerrison; New Orchestrations, Christopher Jahnke; Co-Orchestrator, Stephen Metcalfe; Original Orchestrations, John Cameron; Orchestral Adaptation/Musical Supervision, Stephen Brooker; Music Director, Kevin Stites; Sound, Jon Weston; Executive Producers, Nicholas Allott, Matthew Dalco, Fred Hanson; Casting, Tara Rubin, General Management, Alan Wasser; Production Manager, Jake Bell; Company Managers, Abra Stanley Leonard, Steve Greer; PSM, Michael J. Passaro; Stage Managers, Charles Underhill, Jim Athens; Dance Captain, Matt Clemens; Music Coordinator, John Miller; Press, The Publicity Office

CAST Jean Valjean **Alexander Gemignani***1; Javert **Ben Davis***2; Farmer **Doug Kreeger**; Innkeeper **Drew Sarich***3; Innkeeper's Wife **Soara-Joye Ross***4; Laborer **JD Goldblatt***5; The Bishop of Digne **James Chip Leonard**; Constables **Nehal Joshi***6, **Jeff Kready**; Factory Foreman **Ben Crawford***7; Fantine **Lea Salonga***8; Factory Girl **Haviland Stillwell**; Factory Workers **Becca Ayers, Daniel Bogart, Nikki Renée Daniels***9, **Blake Ginther***10, **JD Goldblatt***5, **Marya Grandy***11, **Victor Hawks***12, **Nehal Joshi***6, **Jeff Kready, Doug Kreeger, James Chip Leonard, Megan McGinnis***13, **Soara-Joye Ross***4, **Drew Sarich***3, **Lucia Spina, Kevin David Thomas, Idara Victor**; Sailors **Victor Hawks***7, **Nehal Joshi***6, **Kevin David Thomas**; Pimp **JD Goldblatt***5; Madame **Lucia Spina**; Whores **Becca Ayers, Mandy Bruno***14, **Nikki Renée Daniels***9, **Ali Ewoldt***15, **Megan McGinnis***13, **Haviland Stilwell, Idara Victor**; Old Woman **Soara-Joye Ross***4; Crone **Marya Grandy***11; Bamatabois **Daniel Bogart;** Fauchelevant **Jeff Kready;** Champmathieu **Ben Crawford***7; Young Cosette **Kaylie Rubinaccio** or **Kylie Liya Goldstein** or **Carly Rose Sonenclar;** Thénardier **Gary Beach***16; Madame Thénardier **Ann Harada***17; Young Eponine **Kaylie Rubinaccio** or **Kylie Liya Goldstein** or **Carly Rose Sonenclar;** Old Beggar Woman **Soara-Joye Ross***4; Madeleine **Nikki Renée Daniels***8; Gavroche **Brian D'Addario***18 or **Zach Rand**; Eponine **Mandy Bruno***14; Cosette **Ali Ewoldt***15; Major Domo **Kevin David Thomas;** *Thénardier's Gang:* Montparnasse **JD Goldblatt***5; Babet **Jeff Kready;** Brujon **Victor Hawks***12; Claquesous **James Chip Leonard;** *Students:* Enjolras **Max von Essen;** Marius **Adam Jacobs;** Combeferre **Daniel Bogart;** Feuilly **Blake Ginther***9; Courfeyrac **Ben Crawford***7; Joly **Kevin David Thomas;** Grantaire **Drew Sarich***3**;** Lesgles **Nehal Joshi***6; Jean Prouvaire **Doug Kreeger;** Swings **Matt Clemens, Marissa McGowan, Q. Smith, Stephen Trafton***19

Alexander Gemignani and the Company (photo by Michael Le Poer Trench)

MUSICIANS Kevin Stites (Conductor); Paul Raiman (Associate Conductor/keyboards); Annbritt duChateau (Assistant Conductor/keyboards); Bob Bush, Laura Wallis, Jonathan Levine (woodwinds); Timothy Schadt (trumpet/flugel); Chris Olness (trombone/tuba); Brad Gemeinhardt, Sara Cyrus (French horn); Martin Agee; Debra Shufelt-Dine, Clay C. Ruede, Dave Phillips (strings); Charles Descarfino (percussion)

SETTING Paris and surrounding areas, 1815–1832. Revival of a musical presented in two acts. Original American production opened at the Broadway Theatre on March 12, 1987 (see *Theatre World* Volume 43, page 32), subsequently transferred to the Imperial, and closed May 18, 2003, playing 6,680 performances.

SYNOPSIS Jean Valjean, a man in search of personal redemption, is pursued by Inspector Javert. Both find themselves in the middle of a revolution, the aftermath of which will determine all their fates.

*Succeeded by: 1. Drew Sarich (7/23/07), John Owen-Jones (9/5/07) 2. Robert Hunt (7/6/07) 3. Michael Minarik, Don Brewer 4. Karen Elliott 5. Mike Evariste 6. Anderson Davis 7. Don Brewer, Stephen Trafton 8. Judy Kuhn (10/23/07) 9. Rona Figueroa 10. Carlos Encinias 11. Kristy Reese 11. Christy Faber 12. Ben Crawford 13. Cortney Wolfson 14. Megan McGinnis 15. Leah Horowitz 16. Chip Zien, Gary Beach 17. Jenny Galloway 18. Sean Gilbert 19. Jeremy Hayes

THE LION KING

Minskoff Theatre; First Preview: October 15, 1997; Opening Night: November 13, 1997; 33 previews, 4,371 performances as of May 31, 2008

Music by Elton John, lyrics by Tim Rice, additional music and lyrics by Lebo M, Mark Mancina, Jay Rifkin, Julie Taymor, Hans Zimmer; book by Roger Allers and Irene Mecchi, adapted from screenplay by Ms. Mecchi, Jonathan Roberts and Linda Woolverton; Produced by Walt Disney Theatrical Productions (Peter Schneider, President; Thomas Schumacher, Executive VP); Director, Julie Taymor; Choreography, Garth Fagan; Orchestrations, Robert Elhai, David Metzger, Bruce Fowler; Music Director, Joseph Church; Sets, Richard Hudson; Costumes/Masks/Puppets, Julie Taymor; Lighting, Donald Holder; Masks/Puppets, Michael Curry; Sound, Tony Meola/Steve Canyon Kennedy; Hair/Makeup, Michael Ward; Projections, Geoff Puckett; Technical Director, David Benken; General Manager, Alan Levey; Project Manager, Nina Essman; PSM, Ron Vodicka; Stage Manager, Antonia Gianino; ASMs, Victoria A. Epstein, Arabella Powell; Associate Director, Jeff Lee; Music Director/Supervisor, Colin Welford; Resident Director, Jen Bender; Resident Dance Supervisor, Ruthlyn Salomons; Associate Conductor, Karl Jurman; Executive Music Producer, Chris Montan; Vocal Arrangements, Lebo M; Company Manager, Steven Chaikelson; Associate Producer, Donald B. Frantz; Casting, Jay Binder; Press, Boneau/Bryan-Brown; Cast recording: Walt Disney 60802-7

CAST Rafiki **Tshidi Manye;** Mufasa **Nathaniel Stampley;** Sarabi **Jean Michelle Grier;** Zazu **Tony Freeman***[1]; Scar **Patrick Page***[2]; Young Simba **Guy V. Barfield II** or **Shavar McIntosh;** Young Nala **Halle Vargas Sullivan** or **NicKayla Tucker;** Shenzi **Bonita J. Hamilton;** Banzai **James Brown-Orleans;** Ed **Enrique Segura;** Timon **Danny Rutigliano;** Pumbaa **Tom Alan Robbins***[3]; Simba **Josh Tower***[4]; Nala **Kissy Simmons;** Ensemble*[5] Singers: **Alvin Crawford, Bongi Duma, Jean Michelle Grier, Michael Alexander Henry, Meena T. Jahi, Joel Karie, Ron Kunene, S'bu Ngema, Selloane Albertina Nkhela, L. Steven Taylor, Rema Webb, Kyle Wrentz, Kenny Redell Williams;** Dancers: **Kristina Michelle Bethel, Camille M. Brown, Michelle Aguilar Camaya, Gabriel Croom, Alicia Fisher, Nicole Adell Johnson, Gregory A. King, Lisa Lewis, Brandon Louis Matthieus, Sheryl McCallum, Ray Mercer, Brandon Christopher O'Neal, Robin Payne, Natalie Ridley, Phillip W. Turner;** Swings **Sean Bradford, Garland Days, Angelica Edwards, Ian Yuri Gardner, Tony James, Cornelius Jones, Jr.,Dennis Johnston, Jennifer Harrison Newman, C. Ross Edwards, Sophia N. Stephens, Lisa Nicole Wilkerson, Torya** Standbys **Jim Ferris***[6] (Timon, Pumbaa), **Jack Koenig** (Scar, Pumbaa)

MUSICAL NUMBERS Circle of Life, Morning Report, I Just Can't Wait to Be King, Chow Down, They Live in You, Be Prepared, Hakuna Matata, One by One, Madness of King Scar, Shadowland, Endless Night, Can You Feel the Love Tonight, King of Pride Rock/Finale

A musical presented in two acts. For original production credits see *Theatre World* Volume 54, page 20. Originally opened at the New Amsterdam Theatre; transferred to the Minskoff Theatre June 13, 2006. *The Lion King* celebrated its tenth anniversary during this season.

SYNOPSIS Based on the 1994 Disney animated feature film, *The Lion King* tells the story of the adventures of Simba, a young lion cub, as he struggles to accept the responsibilities of adulthood and his destined role as king.

*Succeeded by: 1. Jeff Binder 2. Dan Donohue, Derek Smith 3. Blake Hammond, Jim Ferris 4. Wallace Smith, Dashaun Young, Wallace Smith 5. Mucuy Bolles, Michelle Brugal, Willa-Noel Montague, Theresa Nguyen, Mpume Sikakane, Ryan Brooke Taylor, Kylin Brady, Lindiwe Dlamini, Lisa, Nicole Wilkerson 6. John E. Brady

The Company (photo by Joan Marcus)

LOVEMUSIK

Biltmore Theatre; First Preview: April 12, 2007; Opening Night: May 3, 2007; Closed June 24, 2007; 24 previews, 60 performances

Book by Alfred Uhry, music by Kurt Weill, lyrics by Maxwell Anderson, Bertolt Brecht, Howard Dietz, Roger Fernay, Ira Gershwin, Oscar Hammerstein II, Langston Hughes, Alan Jay Lerner, Maurice Magre, Ogden Nash, Elmer Rice, Kurt Weill; suggested by the letters of Kurt Weill and Lotte Lenya; Produced by Manhattan Theatre Club (Lynne Meadow, Artistic Director; Barry Grove, Executive Producer) in special arrangement with Marty Bell, Aldo Scrofani, Boyett Ostar Productions, Tracy Aron, Roger Berlind/Debra Black, Chase Mishkin, Ted Snowdon; Director, Harold Prince, Musical Staging, Patricia Birch; Sets, Beowulf Boritt; Costumes, Judith Dolan; Lighting, Howell Binley; Sound, Duncan Robert Edwards; Wigs, Paul Huntley; Makeup, Angelina Avallone; PSM, Joshua Halperin; Casting, Mark Simon; Orchestrations, Jonathan Tunick; Musical Supervisor, Kristen Blodgette; Music Coordinator, Seymour Red Press; Additional Vocal Arrangements, Milton Granger; Director of Artistic Operations, Mandy Greenfield; Production Manager, Ryan McMahon; Development, Jill Turner Lloyd; Marketing, Debra A. Waxman; General Manager, Florie Seery; Artistic Development, Paige Evans; Artistic Consultant, Daniel Sullivan; Artistic Administration/Assistant to the Artistic Director, Amy Gilkes Loe; Finance, Jeffrey Bledsoe; Associate General Manager, Lindsey Brooks Sag; Company Manager, Seth Shepsle; Production Manager, Bridget Markov; Stage Manager, Jason Brouillard; Assistant to Mr. Prince, Daniel Kutner; Assistant Choreographer, Deanna Dys; Dance Captain, Ann Morrison; Associate Design: Jo Winiarski (set), Ryan O'Gara (lighting); Dialect Consultant, Stephen Gabis; Advertising, SpotCo; Press, Boneau/Bryan-Brown; Cast recording: Sh-K-Boom/ Ghostlight Records 84424

CAST Kurt Weill **Michael Cerveris;** Lotte Lenya **Donna Murphy;** Bertolt Brecht **David Pittu;** George Davis **John Scherer;** Woman on the Stairs/Brecht Woman **Judith Blazer;** Magistrate/Judge/Auditioners **Herndon Lackey;** Court Secretary/Brecht Woman/Auditioners **Rachel Ulanet;** Brecht Woman/Photographer **Ann Morrison,** Interviewer/ Handyman **Erik Liberman;** Otto/Allen Lake **Graham Rowat;** Swings **Edwin Cahill, Jessica Wright**

UNDERSTUDIES Edwin Cahill (Brecht, Weill), Erik Liberman (Brecht), Ann Morrison (Lenya), Graham Rowat (Davis)

Rachel Ulanet, David Pittu, Ann Morrison, Judith Blazer (photo by Carol Rosegg)

ORCHESTRA Nicholas Archer (Conductor/piano); Stan Tucker (Associate Conductor); Katherine Livolsi-Landau, Suzy Perelman (violin); David Blinn (viola); Mairi Dorman (cello); James Ercole, John Winder (woodwinds); Christian Jaudes (trumpet); Jeff Cooper (bass); Billy Miller (drums/percussion)

MUSICAL NUMBERS Speak Low, Nanna's Lied, Kiddush, Songs of the Rhineland, Klops Lied (Meatball Song), Berlin Im Licht, Wooden Wedding, Tango Ballad, Alabama Song, Girl of the Moment, Moritat, Schickelgruber, Come to Paris, I Don't Love You, Wouldn't You Like to Be on Broadway, Alabama Song (reprise), How Can You Tell an American, Very, Very, Very, It's Never Too Late to Mendelssohn, Surabaya Johnny, Youkali, Buddy on the Night Shift, That's Him, Hosannah Rockefeller, I Don't Love You (Reprise), The Illusion Wedding Show, It Never Was You, A Bird of Passage, September Song

SETTING Europe and America, 1920's–1940's. World premiere of a new musical presented in two acts.

SYNOPSIS An epic romance set in Berlin, Paris, Broadway and Hollywood, *LoveMusik* follows the lives of the unlikeliest of lovers—the brilliant, intellectual German composer Kurt Weill and a lusty girl from the streets of Vienna who became his muse and star, Lotte Lenya. The show spans 25 years in the lives of this complicated couple.

MAMMA MIA!

Winter Garden Theatre; First Preview: October 5, 2001: Opening Night: October 18, 2001; 14 previews, 2,734 performances as of May 31, 2008

Book by Catherine Johnson, music, lyrics, and orchestrations by Benny Andersson, Björn Ulvaeus, some songs with Stig Anderson; Produced by Judy Craymer, Richard East and Björn Ulvaeus for Littlestar Services Limited, in association with Universal; Director, Phyllida Lloyd; Scenery and Costumes, Mark Thompson; Lighting, Howard Harrison; Sound, Andrew Bruce & Bobby Aitken; Wigs, Paul Huntley; Choreography, Anthony Van Laast; Musical Supervision/Orchestrations, Martin Koch; Associate Musical Director, David Holcenberg; Musical Coordination, Michael Keller; Associate Director, Robert McQueen; Associate Choreographer, Nichola Treherne; Technical Supervisor, Arthur Siccardi; General Manager, Nina Lannan; Associate General Manager/Company Manager, Rina L. Saltzman; PSM, Andrew Fenton; Stage Managers, Sherry Cohen, Dean R. Greer; Dance Captain, Janet Rothermel; Resident Director, Martha Banta; Casting, Tara Rubin; Music Coordinator, Michael Keller; Synthesizer Programmer, Nicholas Gilpin; Press, Boneau/Bryan-Brown; London Cast recording: Polydor 543 115 2

CAST Sophie Sheridan **Carey Anderson;** Ali **Veronica J. Kuehn;** Lisa **Samantha Eggers;** Tanya **Judy McLane**[*1]**;** Rosie **Gina Ferrall;** Donna Sheridan **Carolee Carmello;** Sky **Andy Kelso;** Pepper **Ben Gettinger;** Eddie **Raymond J. Lee;** Harry Bright **Michael Mastro**[*2]**;** Bill Austin **Pearce Bunting;** Sam Carmicheal **David McDonald**[*3]**;** Father Alexandrios **Bryan Scott Johnson;** Ensemble[*4] **Brent Black, Timothy Booth, Isaac Calpito, Allyson Carr, Meghann Dreyfuss, Lori Haley Fox, Frankie James Grande, Bryan Scott Johnson, Monica Kapoor, Steve Morgan, Courtney Reed, Amina Robinson, Sandy Rosenberg, Gerard Salvador, Laurie Wells, Leah Zepel;** Swings **Lanene Charters, Matthew Farver, Ryan Sander, Collette Simmons, Jon-Erik Goldberg**

UNDERSTUDIES Brent Black (Bill, Sam, Father Alexandrios), Timothy Booth (Harry, Bill, Sam), Jen Burleigh-Bentz (Donna), Isaac Calpito (Pepper), Lanene Charters (Lisa), Meghann Dreyfuss (Sophie), Samantha Eggers(Sophie), Matthew Farver (Eddie, Father Alexandrios), Lori Haley Fox (Tanya, Rosie, Donna), Frankie James Grande (Eddie), Bryan Scott Johnson (Harry, Bill), Monica Kapoor (Lisa), Veronica J. Kuehn (Sophie), Steve Morgan (Sky), Courtney Reed (Ali), Amina Robinson (Ali), Sandy Rosenberg (Rosie), Ryan Sander (Sky, Eddie), Gerard Salvador (Pepper), Laurie Wells (Tanya, Donna), Leah Zepel (Ali)

Judy McLane, Carolee Carmello, Gina Ferrall (photo by Joan Marcus)

ORCHESTRA Wendy Bobbitt Cavett (Conductor/keyboard); Rob Preuss (Associate Conductor/keyboard 3); Steve Marzullo (keyboard 2); Myles Chase (keyboard 4); Doug Quinn, Jeff Campbell (guitars); Paul Adamy (bass); Gary Tillman (drums); David Nyberg (percussion)

MUSICAL NUMBERS Chiquitita; Dancing Queen; Does Your Mother Know?; Gimme! Gimmie! Gimmie!; Honey, Honey; I Do, I Do, I Do, I Do; I Have a Dream; Knowing Me Knowing You; Lay All Your Love on Me; Mamma Mia; Money Money Money; One of Us; Our Last Summer; Slipping Through My Fingers; S.O.S.; Super Trouper; Take a Chance on Me; Thank You For the Music; The Name of the Game; The Winner Takes All; Under Attack; Voulez-Vous

SETTING Time: A wedding weekend. Place: A tiny Greek island. A musical presented in two acts. For original production credits see *Theatre World* Volume 58, Page 27.

SYNOPSIS Songs of the 1970s group ABBA are strung together in a story of baby boomer wistfulness and a girl's search for her unknown father.

*Succeeded by: 1. Joan Hess, Judy McLane (9/26/07) 2. Ben Livingston (9/26/07) 3. Christopher Shyer (9/26/07) 4. Jen Burleigh Bentz, Christopher Carl, Shakiem Evans, Heidi Godt, Lori Hammel, Robin Levine, Corinne Melançon, Joi Danielle Price

MARY POPPINS

New Amsterdam Theatre; First Preview: October 14, 2006; Opening Night: November 16, 2006; 30 previews, 643 performances as of May 31, 2008

Music and lyrics by Richard M. Sherman and Robert B. Sherman, book by Julian Fellowes, new songs and additional music/lyrics by George Stiles and Anthony Drewe; based on the stories of P.L. Travers and the 1964 Walt Disney Film; Produced and co-created by Cameron Mackintosh; Produced for Disney Theatrical Productions by Thomas Schumacher; Director, Richard Eyre; Co-Direction/Choreography, Matthew Bourne; Sets/Costumes, Bob Crowley; Lighting, Howard Harrison; Co-choreographer, Stephen Mear; Music Supervisor, David Caddick; Music Director, Brad Haak; Orchestrations, William David Brohn; Sound, Steve Canyon Kennedy; Dance/Vocal Arrangements, George Stiles; Associates: Anthony Lyn (director), Geoffrey Garratt (choreography) James Thane (producer); Makeup, Naomi Donne; Casting, Tara Rubin; Technical Director, David Benken; PSM, Tom Capps; Resident Choreographer, Tom Kosis; Company Manager, Dave Ehle; Associate GM, Alan Wasser; Stage Management, Mark Dobrow, Valerie Lau-Kee Lai, Jason Trubitt, Michael Wilhoite; Dance Captain, Rommy Sandhu, Dialect/Vocal Coach, Deborah Hecht; Wigs, Angela Cobbin; Illusions, Jim Steinmeyer; Technical Director, David Benken; Production Supervisor, Patrick Eviston; Flying, Raymond King; Automation, Steve Stackle, David Helk; Properties, Victor Amerling, Tim Abel, Joe Bivone, John Saye; Keyboard Programming, Stuart Andrews; Music Contractor, David Lai; Advertising, Serino Coyne; Music Copyist, Emily Grishman Music Preparation; Press, Boneau/Bryan-Brown; London cast recording: Disney Theatricals 61391-7

CAST Bert **Gavin Lee;** George Banks **Daniel Jenkins;** Winifred Banks **Rebecca Luker;** Jane Banks **Nichole Bocchi** or **Kathryn Faughnan**[*1] or **Devynn Pedell**[*2]; Michael Banks **Matthew Gumley** or **Henry Hodges**[*3] or **Jacob Levine;** Katie Nanna/Annie **Megan Osterhaus;** Policeman **James Hindman**[*4]; Miss Lark **Ann Arvia;** Admiral Boom/Bank Chairman **Michael McCarty**[*5]; Mrs. Brill **Jane Carr;** Robertson Ay **Mark Price;** Mary Poppins **Ashley Brown;** Park Keeper **Nick Corley**[*6]; Neleus **Brian Letendre;** Queen Victoria/Miss Smythe/Miss Andrew **Ruth Gottschall;** Von Hussler **Sean McCourt;** Northbrook **Matt Loehr;** Bird Woman **Cass Morgan;** Mrs. Corry **Janelle Anne Robinson;** Fannie **Vasthy E. Mompoint;** Valentine **Mark Ledbetter**[*7]; William **Eric B. Anthony**[*8]; Mr. Punch **James Hindman;** Glamorous Doll **Catherine Walker;** Ensemble[*9] **Eric B. Anthony, Ann Arvia, Kristin Carbone, Nick Corley, Case Dillard, Ruth Gottschall, James Hindman, Mark Ledbetter, Brian Letendre, Matt Loehr, Melissa Lone, Michelle Lookadoo, Tony Mankser, Michael McCarty, Sean McCourt, Vasthy E. Mompoint, Jesse Nager, Kathleen Nanni, Megan Osterhaus, Dominic Roberts, Janelle Anne Robinson, Shekitra Starke, Catherine Walker, Kevin Samual Yee;** Swings **Pam Bradley, Brian Collier**[*10]**, Nicholas Dromard, Suzanne Hylenski, Stephanie Kurtzuba, Rommy Sandhu, Regan Kays**[*11]**, Jeff Metzler**

MUSICIANS Brad Haak (Conductor); Kristen Blodgette (Associate Conductor/2nd keyboard); Milton Granger (Piano); Peter Donovan (bass); Dave Ratajczak (drums); Daniel Haskins (percussion), Nate Brown (guitar/banjo/E-Bow); Russ Rizner, Larry DiBello (horns); Jon Sheppard, Louis Hanzlik (trumpets); Marc Donatelle (trombone/euphonium); Randy Andos (bass trombone/tuba); Paul Garment (clarinet); Alexandra Knoll (oboe/English horn); Brian Miller (flutes); Stephanie Cummins (cello)

SETTING In and around the Banks' household somewhere in London at the turn of the last century. American premiere of a new musical presented in two acts. Originally opened in London at the Prince Edward Theatre on December 15, 2004.

SYNOPSIS *Mary Poppins* is the story of the Banks family and how their lives change after the arrival of nanny Mary Poppins at their home at 17 Cherry Tree Lane in London.

*Succeeded by: 1. Alexandra Berro 2. Lila Coogan 3. Daniel Marconi 4. Corey Skaggs 5. Jeff Steitzer 6. James Hindman 7. Dominic Roberts 8. T. Oliver Reid 9. Eric Hatch, Jeff Metzler, Jayne Paterson, Dominic Roberts, T. Oliver Reid, Nick Sanchez, Laura Shutter 10. Chad Seib 11. Sarah Solie

Ashley Brown (photo by Joan Marcus)

MONTY PYTHON'S SPAMALOT

Shubert Theatre; First Preview: February 14, 2004; Opening Night: March 17, 2005; 35 previews, 1,317 performances as of May 31, 2008

Book and lyrics by Eric Idle, music by John DuPrez and Eric Idle; based on the screenplay of the motion picture *Monty Python and the Holy Grail* by Eric Idle, John Cleese, Terry Gilliam, Terry Jones, Michael Palin and Graham Chapman; Produced by Boyett Ostar Productions, The Shubert Organization, Arielle Tepper, Stephanie McClelland, Lawrence Horowitz, Élan V. McAllister, Allan S. Gordon, Independent Presenters Network, Roy Furman, GRS Associates, Jam Theatricals, TGA Entertainment, Ltd., Clear Channel Entertainment; Associate Producer, Randi Grossman, Tisch/Avnet Financial; Director, Mike Nichols; Choreography, Casey Nicholaw; Sets and Costumes, Tim Hatley; Lighting, Hugh Vanstone; Sound, Acme Sound Partners; Hair/Wigs, David Brian Brown; Special Effects, Gregory Meeh; Projections, Elaine J. McCarthy; Music Director/Vocal Arrangements, Todd Ellison; Orchestrations, Larry Hochman; Music Arrangements, Glen Kelly; Music Coordinator, Michael Keller; Casting, Tara Rubin; Associate Director, Peter Lawrence; PSM, Mahlon Kruse; Associate Choreography, Darlene Wilson; General Management, 101 Productions, Ltd. Marketing, HHC Marketing; Company Management, Elie Landau, Steven Lukens; Production Management, Aurora Productions/Gene O'Donovan; Fight Director, David DeBesse; Makeup, Joseph A. Campayno; Stage Management, Jim Woolley, Sheri K. Turner, Chad Lewis; Dance Captain, Pamela Remler, Scott Taylor/Lee Wilkins; Fight Captain, Greg Reuter; Vocal Coach, Kate Wilson; Magic Consultant, Marshall Magoon; Puppetry Consultant, Michael Curry; Music Copying, Emily Grishman; Advertising, Serino Coyne; Press, Boneau/Bryan-Brown; Cast recording: Decca Broadway, B0004265-02

CAST Historian/Not Dead Fred/French Guard,/Minstrel/Prince Herbert **Tom Deckman;** Mayor/Patsy/Guard 2 **Michael McGrath***[1]; King Arthur **Jonathan Hadary;** Sir Robin/Guard 1/Brother Maynard **Martin Moran***[2]; Sir Lancelot/The French Taunter/Knight of Ni/Tim the Enchanter **Rick Holmes;** Sir Dennis Galahad/The Black Knight/Prince Herbert's Father **Christopher Sieber***[3]; Dennis' Mother/Sir Bedevere/Concorde **Jeffrey Kuhn***[4]; The Lady of the Lake **Marin Mazzie***[5]; Sir Not Appearing/Monk **Kevin Covert***[6]; Nun **Brian Shepard***[7]; God **John Cleese;** French Guards **Thomas Cannizzaro***[8], **Greg Reuter;** Minstrels **Brad Bradley***[9], **Emily Hsu, Greg Reuter;** Sir Bors **Brad Bradley***[9]; Ensemble **Brad Bradley***[9], **Thomas Cannizzaro***[8], **Kevin Covert***[6], **Jennifer Frankel***[10], **Amy Heggins***[11], **Jenny Hill, Emily Hsu, Ariel Reid, Greg Reuter, Brian Shepard***[7], **Vanessa Sonon, Scott Taylor***[12]; Standbys **James Ludwig***[13], **Napiera Groves, Chris Hoch***[14]; Swings*[15] **Beth Johnson, Pamela Remler, Rick Spaans, Lee A. Wilkins**

ORCHESTRA Todd Ellison (Conductor); Ethyl Will (Associate Conductor/keyboard); Ann Labin (Concertmaster); Maura Giannini, Ming Yeh (violins); Richard Brice (viola); Diane Barere (cello); Ken Dybisz, Alden Banta (reeds); John Chudoba, Anthony Gorruso (trumpets); Mark Patterson (trombone); Zohar Schondorf (French horn); Antony Geralis (keyboard 2); Scott Kuney (guitars); Dave Kuhn (bass); Sean McDaniel (drums); Dave Mancuso (percussion)

MUSICAL NUMBERS Fisch Schlapping Song, King Arthur's Song, I Am Not Dead Yet, Come With Me, The Song That Goes Like This, All for One, Knights of the Round Table, The Song That Goes Like This (reprise), Find Your Grail, Run Away, Always Look on the Bright Side of Life, Brave Sir Robin, You Won't Succeed on Broadway, The Diva's Lament, Where Are You?, Here Are You, His Name Is Lancelot, I'm All Alone, The Song That Goes Like This (reprise), The Holy Grail, Find Your Grail Finale – Medley

A new musical presented in two acts. For original production credits see *Theatre World* Volume 61, page 55.

SYNOPSIS Telling the legendary tale of King Arthur and the Knights of the Round Table, and their quest for the Holy Grail, *Monty Python's Spamalot* features a chorus line of dancing divas and knights, flatulent Frenchmen, killer rabbits and one legless knight.

Clay Aiken (photo by Joan Marcus)

*Succeeded by: 1. David Hibbard 2. Clay Aiken (1/18/08), Robert Petkoff (5/6/08) 3. Lewis Cleale, Christopher Sieber, Bradley Dean (3/25/08) 4. Brad Oscar (12/18/07), Steve Rosen (4/29/08) 5. Hannah Waddingham 6. Gavin Lodge, Kevin Covert 7. Matthew Crowle 8. Jonathan Brody 9. Brian J. Marcum 10. Abby O'Brien 11. Brandi Wooten 12. Brian J. Marcum, Andrew Fitch 13. Anthony Holds 14. Michael O'Donnell 15. Additional: Kristie Kerwin, Callie Carter)

A MOON FOR THE MISBEGOTTEN

Brooks Atkinson Theatre; First Preview: March 29, 2007; Opening Night: April 9, 2007; Closed June 10, 2007; 13 previews, 71 performances

Written by Eugene O'Neill; Produced by Elliot Martin, Max Cooper, Ben Sprecher, Nica Burns, Max Weitzenhoffer, The Old Vic, Spring Sirkin, Wendy Federman, Louise Forlenza, Ian Osborne, Thomas Steven Perakos, James L. Nederlander; Director, Howard Davies; Set, Bob Crowley; Costumes, Lynette Mauro; Lighting, Mark Henderson; Sound, Christopher Shutt; Sound System Design, T. Richard Fitzgerald and Carl Casella; Original Music, Dominic Muldowney; Casting, Maggie Lunn (UK), Stuart Howard Associates (US); Production Manager, Brian Lynch; PSM, Bruce A. Hoover; General Manager, Peter Bogye; Company Manager, Mary Miller; Original London Lighting, Paule Constable; Stage Manager, Bernita Robinson; Production Assistant, Cyrille Blackburn; Assistant Director, Nathan Curry; Associate Design: Paul Atkinson, Alistair Turner (UK set), Bryan Johnson (US set), Colin Pink (US sound); Assistant Lighting, Daniel Walker; Production: Thomas A. LaVaia (carpenter), Manuel Becker (electrician), Joseph DePaulo (props), Wallace Flores (sound), Kathleen Gallaher (wardrobe supervisor); Advertising, SpotCo; Press, Barlow-Hartman, Dennis Crowley, Ryan Ratelle, Michelle Bergmann

Eve Best and Colm Meaney (photos by Simon Annand)

CAST Josie Hogan **Eve Best;** Mike Hogan **Eugene O'Hare;** Phil Hogan **Colm Meaney;** Jim Tyrone **Kevin Spacey;** T. Stedman Harder **Billy Carter**

UNDERSTUDIES Kati Brazda (Josie), Billy Carter (Phil Hogan), Nick Westrate (Mike, T. Stedman Harder)

SETTING Connecticut, September, 1923. Revival of a play presented in two acts. This production was presented at London's Old Vic Theatre Company (Sally Greene, Chief Executive; Kevin Spacey, Artistic Director), September 15–December 23, 2006, with Mr. Spacey, Mr. Meaney, and Ms. Best. Originally produced on Broadway at the Bijou Theatre May 2, 1957 (see *Theatre World* Volume 13, page 114). The play has had three revivals prior to this production: Morosco Theatre, December 29, 1973–November 17, 1974 (see *Theatre World* Volume 30, page 34); Cort Theatre, May 1–June 9, 1984 (see *Theatre World* Volume 40, page 38); Walter Kerr Theatre, March 10–July 2, 2000 (see *Theatre World* Volume 56, page 29).

SYNOPSIS *A Moon for the Misbegotten* explores the tormented and alcoholic James Tyrone, who finds solace one moonlit night in the healing arms of the shy, virginal Josie Hogan. Possessed by the memory of his dead mother and guilt ridden by his own blasphemous behavior, the doomed Tyrone is the only man Josie will ever really know.

Colm Meaney and Kevin Spacey

THE PHANTOM OF THE OPERA

Majestic Theatre; First Preview: January 9, 1988. Opening Night: January 26, 1988; 16 previews, 8,463 performances as of May 31, 2008

Music and book by Andrew Lloyd Webber, lyrics by Charles Hart; additional lyrics and book by Richard Stilgoe; based on the novel by Gaston Leroux; Produced by Cameron Mackintosh and The Really Useful Theatre Company; Director, Harold Prince; Musical Staging/Choreography, Gillian Lynne; Orchestrations, David Cullen, Mr. Lloyd Webber; Design, Maria Björnson; Lighting, Andrew Bridge; Sound, Martin Levan; Original Musical Director and Supervisor, David Caddick; Musical Director, David Lai; Production Supervisor, Peter von Mayrhauser; Casting, Tara Rubin; Original Casting, Johnson-Liff Associates; General Manager, Alan Wasser; Production Dance Supervisor, Denny Berry; Associate Musical Supervisor, Kristen Blodgette; Associate General Manager, Allan Williams; Technical Production Managers, John H. Paull III, Jake Bell; Company Manager, Steve Greer; Stage Managers, Craig Jacobs, Bethe Ward, Brendan Smith; Assistant Company Manager, Cathy Kwon; Press, The Publicity Office, Marc Thibodeau, Michael S. Borowski, Jeremy Shaffer; London Cast recording: Polydor 831273.

CAST The Phantom of the Opera **Howard McGillin***1; Christine Daae **Jennifer Hope Wills;** Christine Daae (alt.) **Susan Owen***2; Raoul, Vicomte de Chagny **Michael Shawn Lewis***3; Carlotta Giudicelli **Patricia Phillips***4; Monsieur Andre **George Lee Andrews;** Monsieur Firmin **David Cryer;** Madame Giry **Marilyn Caskey***5; Ubaldo Piangi **Roland Rusinek***6; Meg Giry **Heather McFadden;** Monsieur Reyer/Hairdresser **Geoff Packard;** Auctioneer **Jason Mills***7; Jeweler (Il Muto) **Frank Mastrone***8; Monsieur Lefevre/Firechief **Kenneth Kantor;** Joseph Buquet **Richard Poole;** Don Attilio **Gregory Emanuel Rahming***9; Passarino **Jason Mills***10; Slave Master **Daniel Rychlec;** Solo Dancer/Flunky/Stagehand **Jack Hayes;** Page **Kris Koop;** Porter/Fireman **John Wasiniak***11; Spanish Lady **Sally Williams;** Wardrobe Mistress/Confidante **Katie Banks;** Princess **Sara Jean Ford***12; Madame Firmin **Melody Rubie***13; Innkeeper's Wife **Wren Marie Harrington;** Marksman **Paul A. Schaefer;** Ballet Chorus of the Opera Populaire*14 **Emily Adonna, Polly Baird, Julianne Cavendish, Kara Klein, Gianna Loungway, Mabel Modrono, Jessica Radetsky, Carly Blake Sebouhian, Dianna Warren;** Ballet Swing **Harriet Clark;** Swings **Dara Adler, Michael Babin, Scott Mikita, James Romick, Fred Rose, Janet Saia, Julie Schmidt, Jim Weitzer**

Patricia Phillips and Wayne Hobbs (photo by Joan Marcus)

MUSICAL NUMBERS Think of Me, Angel of Music, Little Lotte/The Mirror, Phantom of the Opera, Music of the Night, I Remember/Stranger Than You Dreamt It, Magical Lasso, Notes/Prima Donna, Poor Fool He Makes Me Laugh, Why Have You Brought Me Here?/Raoul I've Been There, All I Ask of You, Masquerade/Why So Silent?, Twisted Every Way, Wishing You Were Somehow Here Again, Wandering Child/Bravo Bravo, Point of No Return, Down Once More/Track Down This Murderer, Finale

ORCHESTRA David Caddick, Kristen Blodgette, David Lai, Tim Stella, Norman Weiss (Conductors); Joyce Hammann (Concert Master), Alvin E. Rogers, Gayle Dixon, Kurt Coble, Jan Mullen, Karen Milne (violins); Stephanie Fricker, Veronica Salas (violas); Ted Ackerman, Karl Bennion (cellos); Melissa Slocum (bass); Henry Fanelli (harp); Sheryl Henze, Ed Matthew, Melanie Feld, Matthew Goodman, Atsuko Sato (woodwinds); Lowell Hershey, Francis Bonny (trumpets); William Whitaker (trombone); Daniel Culpepper, Peter Reit, David Smith (French horn); Eric Cohen, Jan Hagiwara (percussion); Tim Stella, Norman Weiss (keyboards)

SETTING In and around the Paris Opera House, 1881–1911. A musical presented in two acts with nineteen scenes and a prologue. For original production credits see *Theatre World* Volume 44, page 20. The show became the longest running show in Broadway history on January 9, 2006, and this season celebrated its 20th anniversary.

SYNOPSIS A disfigured musical genius haunts the catacombs beneath the Paris Opera and exerts strange control over a lovely young soprano.

*Succeeded by: 1. John Cudia (5/22/08) 2. Julie Hanson, Elizabeth Loyacano (12/8/07) 3. Tim Martin Gleason 4. Kim Stengel (3/27/08) 5. Rebecca Judd, Marilyn Caskey, Rebecca Judd 6. Jimmy Smagula, Wayne Hobbs, David Gashen, Evan Harrington (4/10/08) 7. John Kuether 8. Jim Weitzer 9. Wayne Hobbs, John Kuether 10. Jeremy Stolle 11. Chris Bohannon 12. Susan Owen, Marni Raab 13. Kristie Dale Sanders 14. Amanda Edge, Janice Niggeling

THE PIRATE QUEEN

Hilton Theatre; First Preview: March 6, 2007; Opening Night: April 5, 2007; Closed June 17, 2007; 32 previews, 85 performances

Book by Alain Boublil, Claude-Michel Schönberg and Richard Maltby, Jr., music by Claude-Michel Schönberg; lyrics by Alain Boublil, Richard Maltby, Jr. and John Dempsey; based upon the novel, "Grania– She King of the Irish Seas" by Morgan Llywelyn; Produced by Riverdream, Moya Doherty and John McColgan; Director, Frank Galati; Musical Staging, Graciela Daniele; Orchestrations/Vocal Arrangements/Musical Supervision and Direction, Julian Kelly; Artistic Director, John McColgan; Irish Dance Choreographer, Carol Leavy Joyce; Sets, Eugene Lee; Costumes, Martin Pakledinaz; Lighting, Kenneth Posner; Sound, Jonathan Deans; Hair, Paul Huntley; Special Effects, Gregory Meeh; Aerial Sequence, Paul Rubin; Makeup, Angelina Avallone; Fight Director, J. Steven White; Associates: Tara Young (director), Rachel Bress (choreographer), Brian Connor (music director); Casting, Tara Rubin; Production Manager, Peter W. Lamb; PSM, C. Randall White; Music Coordinator, Sam Lutfiyya, Music Services International; Marketing, TMG; Associate Producer, Dancap Productions, Inc.; Executive Producers, Ronan Smith (development), Edgar Dobie; General Manager, Theatre Production Group; Company Management, Jim Brandeberry, Elizabeth M. Talmadge; Stage Management, Kathleen E. Purvis, Sandra M. Franck, Charlene Speyerer, Michael Wilhoite; Additional Choreography, Mark Dendy; Dance Captains, Rachel Bress, Padraic Moyles; Fight Captain/Assistant Fight Director/Dance Captain, Timothy W. Bish; Electronic Music, Brett Alan Sommer, Jim Harp; Music Copying/Preparation, Mark Cumberland for Hotstave, Ltd., Anixter Rice; Irish Music Consultant, David Downes; Advertising, SpotCo; Press, Boneau/Bryan-Brown, Adrian Bryan-Brown; Cast Recording: Sony/BMG Masterworks Broadway 7118102

CAST Grace (Grania) O'Malley **Stephanie J. Block;** Tiernan **Hadley Fraser;** Dubhdara **Jeff McCarthy;** Evleen **Áine Uí Cheallaigh;** Queen Elizabeth I **Linda Balgord;** Sir Richard Bingham **William Youmans;** Donal O'Flaherty **Marcus Chait;** Chieftain O'Flaherty **Joseph Mahowald;** Majella **Brooke Elliot;** Eoin **Christopher Grey Misa** or **Steven Barath**; Ensemble **Nick Adams, Richard Todd Adams, Caitlin Allen, Sean Beglan, Jerad Bortz, Troy Edward Bowles, Grady McLeod Bowman, Alexis Ann Carra, Noelle Curran, Bobbie Ann Dunn, Brooke Elliott, Christopher Garbrecht, Eric Hatch, Cristin J. Hubbard, David Koch, Timothy Kochka, Jamie LaVerdiere, Joseph Mahowald, Tokiko Masuda, Padraic Moyles, Brian O'Brien, Kyle James O'Connor, Michael James Scott, Greg Stone, Katie Erin Tomlinson, Daniel Torres, Jennifer Waiser, Briana Yacavone;** Swings **Timothy W. Bish, Rachel Bress, Don Brewer, Kimilee Bryant;** Standby for Grace: **Kathy Voytko**

ORCHESTRA Julian Kelly (Conductor); Brian Connor (Associate Conductor/keyboard 1); Joshua Rosenblum (Assistant Conductor/keyboard II); Liz Knowles (fiddle/violin); Kieran O'Hare (Uilleann pipes/whistles); Kenneth Edge (Sax/Clarinet); Jeff Nelsen (horn); Kristen Agresta (harp/Gaelic harp); Steve Roberts (guitars/banjo); Michael Pearce (electric bass); Dave Roth (percussion); Frank Pagano (drums/Bodhran)

MUSICAL NUMBERS Prologue, The Pirate Queen, Woman, The Storm, My Grace, Here on This Night, The Waking of the Queen, Rah-Rah, Tip-Top; The Choice Is Mine, The Bride's Song, Boys'll Be Boys, The Wedding, I'll Be There, Boys'll Be Boys (reprise), Trouble at Rockfleet, A Day Beyond Belclare, Go Serve Your Queen, Dubhdara's Farewell, Sail to the Stars; Entr'acte, It's a boy, Enemy at Port Side, I Dismiss You, If I Said I Loved You, The Role of the Queen, The Christening, Let a Father Stand By His Son, Surrender, She Who Has All, Lament, The Sea of Life, Terra Marique Potens, Woman to Woman, Behind the Screen, Grace's Exit, Finale

SETTING Ireland and England, the Sixteenth Century; New York premiere of a new musical presented in two acts. The show had out-of-town tryouts at the Cadillac Palace Theatre, Chicago, October 3–November 26, 2006.

SYNOPSIS *The Pirate Queen* combines classic storytelling with a sweeping score and joyous dancing to celebrate the real-life story of legendary Irish chieftain Grace O'Malley: a compelling, inspiring heroine who led an extraordinary life as a pirate, chieftain, lover and mother in 16th-century Ireland.

Stephanie J. Block, Jeff McCarthy, Marcus Chait (photo by Joan Marcus)

RADIO GOLF

Cort Theatre; First Preview: April 20, 2007; Opening Night: May 8, 2007; Closed July 1, 2007; 17 previews, 64 performances

Written by August Wilson; Produced by Jujamcyn Theatres (Rocco Landesman, President; Paul Libin, Producing Director; Jack Viertel, Creative Director; Jordan Roth, Vice President), Margo Lion, Jeffrey Richards, Jerry Frankel, Tamara Tunie, Wendell Pierce, Fran Kirmser, The Bunting Management Group, Georgia Frontiere, Open Pictures, Lauren Doll, Steven Greil, The August Wilson Group, Wonder City, Inc, Townsend Teague, in association with Jack Viertel and Gordon Davidson; Director, Kenny Leon; Set, David Gallo; Costumes, Susan Hilferty; Lighting, Donald Holder; Original Music/Sound, Dan Moses Schreier; Dramaturg, Todd Kreidler; Casting, Stanczyk/Cherpakov; Production Management, Aurora Productions; PSM, Narda Alcorn; Executive Producer, Nicole Kastrinos; General Manager, 101 Productions, Ltd.; Marketing, TMG; Company Manager, Chris Morey; Additional Marketing, Images USA, Walker International Communications Group, Brothers and Sisters Marketing, Situation Marketing; Original Casting, Harriet Bass; Assistant Director, Derrick Sanders; Stage Manager, Marion Friedman; Vocal Coach, Erin Annarella; Associate Design: Charlie Smith (set), Maiko Matsushima (costume), Hilary Manners (lighting), David Bullard (sound); Production: Ed Diaz (carpenter), Dylan Foley (props supervisor), Scott DeVerna (electrician), Jens McVoy (sound supervisor), Philip Lojo (head sound), Lonnie Gaddy (head props), Eileen Miller (wardrobe supervisor), David Rubie (dresser), Barbara Roman (hair supervisor); Advertising, SpotCo; Press, Barlow-Hartman, John Barlow, Michael Hartman, Dennis Crowley, Michelle Bergmann

Anthony Chisholm and Harry Lennix (photos by Carol Rosegg)

John Earl Jelks and Anthony Chisholm

CAST Hammond Wilks **Harry Lennix;** Mame Wilks **Tonya Pinkins;** Roosevelt Hicks **James A. Williams;** Sterling Johnson **John Earl Jelks;** Elder Joseph Barlow **Anthony Chisholm**

STANDBYS Rosalyn Coleman (Mame Wilks), Billy Eugene Jones (Hammond Wilks, Roosevelt Hicks), Cedric Young (Elder Joseph Barlow, Sterling Johnson)

SETTING The Hill District, Pittsburg, Pennsylvania, 1997; the office of Bedford Hills Redevelopment, Inc., in a storefront on Centre Avenue. New York premiere of a new play presented in two acts. Originally produced at Yale Repertory Theatre (James Bundy, Artistic Director; Victoria Nolan, Managing Director) in New Haven, Connecticut, April 2005.

SYNOPSIS *Radio Golf* is the story of a successful entrepreneur who aspires to become the city's first black mayor. But when the past begins to catch up with him, secrets get revealed that could be his undoing. *Radio Golf* is the final installment in August Wilson's ten play, decade by decade, cycle chronicling the African-American experience in the twentieth century. Wilson passed away October 16, 2005.

RENT

Nederlander Theatre; First Preview: April 16, 1996; Opening Night: April 29, 1996; 16 previews, 5,009 performances as of May 31, 2008

Book, music, and lyrics by Jonathan Larson; Produced by Jeffrey Seller, Kevin McCollum, Allan S. Gordon, and New York Theatre Workshop; Director, Michael Greif; Arrangements, Steve Skinner; Musical Supervision/Additional Arrangements, Tim Weill; Choreography, Marlies Yearby; Original Concept/Additional Lyrics, Billy Aronson; Scenery, Paul Clay; Costumes, Angela Wendt; Lighting, Blake Burba; Sound, Kurt Fischer; Wigs/Hair/Makeup, David Santana; Film, Tony Gerber; General Management, Emanuel Azenberg, John Corker; Company Manager, Nick Kaledin; PSM, John Vivian; Stage Manager, Crystal Huntington; Dramaturg, Lynn M. Thompson, Production Coordinator, Susan White; Technical Supervision, Unitech Productions, Inc; Advertising, SpotCo; Press, Richard Kornberg, Don Summa; Cast recording: Dreamworks 50003

The Cast (photo by Joan Marcus)

CAST Roger Davis **Tim Howar*1**; Mark Cohen **Christopher J. Hanke*2**; Tom Collins **Troy Horne*3**; Benjamin Coffin III **D'Monroe*4**; Joanne Jefferson **Tonya Dixon*5**; Angel Schunard **Justin Johnson;** Mimi Marquez **Tamyra Gray;** Maureen Johnson **Nicolette Hart*6**; Mark's Mom/Alison/Others **Haven Burton*7**; Christmas Caroler/ Mr. Jefferson/Pastor/Others **Marcus Paul James;** Mrs. Jefferson/Woman with Bags/Others **Maia Nkenge Wilson;** Gordon/The Man/Mr. Grey/Others **Luther Creek*8**; Steve/ Man with Squeegee/Waiter/Others **Telly Leung;** Paul/ Cop/Others **Shaun Earl;** Alexi Darling/Roger's Mom/ Others **Mayumi Ando*9**; Swings: **Karmine Alers, Owen Johnston II, Crystal Monée Hall, Antonique Smith*10, Philip Dorian McAdoo, Moeisha McGill, John Eric Parker, Todd E. Pettiford, Kyle Post;** Standby for Mark: **Matt Caplan*11**

UNDERSTUDIES Haven Burton (Maureen), Luther Creek (Mark, Roger), Crystal Monée Hall (Joanne), Marcus Paul James (Bennie, Tom), Trisha Jeffrey (Joanne, Mimi), Owen Johnston II (Angel, Roger), Telly Leung (Angel), Philip Dorian McAdoo (Bennie, Tom), Kyle Post (Mark, Roger), Antonique Smith (Maureen, Mimi), Maia Nkenge Wilson (Joanne Jefferson), Dana Dawson (Ensemble)

MUSICIANS Tim Weil (Conductor/keyboards), Steve Mack (bass), Kenny Brescia (guitar), Daniel A. Weiss (Associate Conductor/guitar), Jeffrey Potter (drums)

MUSICAL NUMBERS Tune Up, Voice Mail (#1–#5), Rent, You Okay Honey?, One Song Glory, Light My Candle, Today 4 U, You'll See, Tango: Maureen, Life Support, Out Tonight, Another Day, Will I?, On the Street, Santa Fe, We're Okay, I'll Cover You, Christmas Bells, Over the Moon, La Vie Boheme/I Should Tell You, Seasons of Love, Happy New Year, Take Me or Leave Me, Without You, Contact, Halloween, Goodbye Love, What You Own, Finale/Your Eyes

SETTING Time and place: New York City's East Village, 1990. A musical presented in two acts. For original production credits see *Theatre World* Volume 52, Page 58. Originally presented Off-Broadway at the New York Theatre Workshop on February 13, 1996.

SYNOPSIS Based on Puccini's opera *La Boheme*, the musical centers on a group of impoverished young artists and musicians struggling to survive and create in New York's Alphabet City in the early 1990s, under the shadow of AIDS. Tragedy occurred when the 35-year-old author Jonathan Larson died of an aortic aneurysm after watching the final dress rehearsal of his show on January 24, 1996.

*Succeeded by: 1. Adam Pascal (7/30/07), Declan Bennett (10/8/07), Will Chase (5/5/08) 2. Anthony Rapp (7/30/07), Harley Jay (10/8/07), Adam Kantor (3/24/08) 3. Michael McElroy 4. Rodney Hicks (9/13/07) 5. Kenna J. Ramsey, Merle Dandridge 6. Caren Lyn Manuel, Eden Espinoza (5/30/08) 7. Caren Lyn Manuel, Tracy McDowell 8. Matt Caplan, Jay Wilkison 9. Andrea Goss 10. Trisha Jeffrey 11. Jay Wilkison

SPRING AWAKENING

Eugene O'Neill Theatre; First Preview: November 16, 2006; Opening Night: December 10, 2006; 28 previews, 593 performances as of May 31, 2008

Book and lyrics by Steven Sater, music by Duncan Sheik, based on the play *The Awakening of Spring* by Frank Wedekind; Produced by Ira Pittelman, Tom Hulce, Jeffrey Richards, Jerry Frankel, Atlantic Theater Company, Jeffrey Sine, Freddy DeMann, Max Cooper, Mort Swinsky, Cindy & Jay Gutterman, Joe McGinnis, Judith Ann Abrams, ZenDog Productions, CarJac Productions, Aron Bergson Productions, Jennifer Manocherian, Ted Snowdon, Harold Thau, Terry Schnuck, Cold Spring Productions, Amanda Dubois, Elizabeth Eynon Wetherell, Jennifer Maloney, Tamara Tunie, Joe Cilibrasi, StyleFour Productions; Director, Michael Mayer; Choreography, Bill T. Jones; Musical Director, Kimberly Grigsby; Set, Christine Jones; Costumes, Susan Hilferty; Lighting, Kevin Adams; Sound, Brian Ronan; Orchestrations, Duncan Sheik; Arrangements, AnnMarie Milazzo, Simon Hale; Music Coordinator, Michael Keller; Casting, Jim Carnahan, Carrie Gardner; Fight Director, J. David Brimmer; PSM, Heather Cousens; Associate Producers, Joan Cullman Productions, Patricia Flicker Addiss; Technical Supervision, Neil A. Mazzella, Sam Ellis; General Management, Abbie M. Strassler, Iron Mountain Productions; Company Manager, John E. Gendron; Marketing/Promotions, Situation Marketing, Damian Bazadona, Steve Tate; Stage Manager, Rick Steiger; ASM, Bethany Russell, Assistant Company Manager, Scott Turowsky; Dance Captain, Lauren Pritchard; Fight Captain, Brian Charles Johnson; Consultants, Susan Blond, Simone Smalls, Liza Bychkov; Rubenstein Communications, Inc., Amy Jacobs, Andy Shearer, Alice McGillion; Assistant Director, Beatrice Terry; Assistant Choreographer, Miguel Anaya, Jr.; Associate Musical Director, Deborah Abramson; Music Copyist, Steven M. Alper; Press, Jeffrey Richards, Irene Gandy; Cast recording: Decca Broadway B0008020-02

CAST Wendla **Lea Michelle*[1]**; The Adult Women **Christine Estabrook*[2]**; Martha **Lilli Cooper**; Ilse **Lauren Pritchard*[3]**; Anna **Phoebe Strole**; Thea **Remy Zaken**; The Adult Men **Stephen Spinella*[4]**; Otto **Brian Charles Johnson**; Hanschen **Jonathan B. Wright*[5]**; Ernst **Gideon Glick*[6]**; Georg **Skylar Astin**; Moritz **John Gallagher, Jr.*[7]**; Melchior **Jonathan Groff*[8]**; Ensemble **Gerard Canonico, Jennifer Damiano*[9], Robert Hager*[10]**; **Krysta Rodriguez*[11]** Swings: **Rob Devaney*[12], Frances Mercanti-Anthony, Tony Carln**

THE BAND Kimberly Grigsby (Conductor/keyboards); Thad DeBrock (guitars); George Farmer (bass); Trey Files (Associate Conductor/drums); Benjamin Kalb (cello); Oliver Manchon (violin/guitar); Hiroko Taguchi (violin)

Skylar Astin and The Company (photo by Doug Hamilton)

MUSICAL NUMBERS Mama Who Bore Me, Mama Who Bore Me (reprise), All That's Known, The Bitch of Living, My Junk, Touch Me, The Word of Your Body, The Dark I Know Well, And Then There Were None, The Mirror-Blue Night, I Believe, The Guilty Ones, Don't Do Sadness, Blue Wind, Left Behind, Totally Fucked, The Word of Your Body (reprise), Whispering, Those You've Known, The Song of Purple Summer

SETTING A provincial German town in the 1890's. Transfer of the Off-Broadway musical presented in two acts. Originally produced at the Atlantic Theatre Company May 19-August 5, 2006 (see *Theatre World* Volume 62, page 151.).

SYNOPSIS *Spring Awakening* is the contemporary musical adaptation of one of literature's most controversial plays. The musical boldly depicts a dozen young people and how they make their way through the complicated, confusing, and mysterious time of their sexual awakening. The story centers around a brilliant young student named Melchior, his troubled friend Moritz, and Wendla, a beautiful young girl on the verge of womanhood. Sheik and Sater's score features songs that illuminate the urgency of adolescent self-discovery, the burning intensity of teen friendships and the innate suspicion of the uncomprehending adult world.

*Succeeded by: 1. Alexandra Socha (5/20/08) 2. Kate Burton (12/21/07), Kristine Nielson (3/3/08), Christine Estabrook 3. Emma Hunton (2/18/08) 4. Ken Marks, Glenn Fleshler 5. Drew Tyler Bell, Matt Doyle 6. Blake Daniel 7. Blake Bashoff (12/18/07) 8. Kyle Riabko (5/20/08) 9. Eryn Murman 10. Matt Doyle, Matt Shingledecker 11. Alexandra Socha, Alice Lee 12. Jesse Swenson; Added Swing: Jenna Ushkowitz

TALK RADIO

Longacre Theatre; First Preview: February 15, 2007; Opening Night: March 11, 2007; Closed June 24, 2007; 29 previews, 121 performances

Written and created for the stage by Eric Bogosian, original idea and created for the stage by Ted Savinar; Produced by Jeffrey Richards, Jerry Frankel, Jam Theatricals, Francis Finlay, Ronald Frankel, James Fuld, Jr., Steve Green, Judith Hansen, Patty Ann Lacrete, James Riley, Mary Lu Roffe/Mort Swinsky, Sheldon Stein, Terri & Timothy Childs/StyleFour Productions, Irving Welzer/Herb Boldgett, in association with the Atlantic Theater Company; Director, Robert Falls; Set, Mark Wendland; Costumes, Laura Bauer; Lighting, Christopher Akerlind; Sound, Richard Woodbury; Casting, Telsey + Company; PSM, Jane Grey; General Management, Albert Poland, Technical Supervisor, Neil A. Mazzella; Company Manager, Daniel Kuney; Stage Manager, Matthew Farrell; Assistant Director, José Zayas; Associate Design: Bobby Tilley (costumes), Jeremy Lee (sound); Design Assistants: Rachel Nemec (sets), Ben Krall (lighting); Props, Kathy Fabian, Carrie Hash, Carrie Mossman, Melanie Mulder; Furniture, Jason Gandy/Aardvark Interiors; Radio Equipment, Richard Fitzgerald/Sound Associates; Production Assistant, Ben West; Associate Technical Supervisor, Sam Ellis; Production: Ed Diaz (carpenter), James Maloney (electrician), Brad Robertson (head electrician), John Lofgren (props), Valerie Spradling (sound), Kristine Bellerud (wardrobe supervisor); Dialect Coach, Kate Maré; Advertising, Serino Coyne; Press, Jeffrey Richards, Irene Gandy

Liev Schreiber

Stephanie March and Michael Laurence (photos by Joan Marcus)

CAST Sid Greenberg **Adam Sietz;** Bernie **Cornell Womack;** Spike **Kit Williamson;** Stu Noonan **Michael Laurence;** Linda MacArthur **Stephanie March;** Vince Farber **Marc Thompson;** Barry Champlain **Liev Schreiber;** Dan Woodruff **Peter Hermann;** Jordan Grant **Christy Pusz;** Kent **Sebastian Stan;** Dr. Susan Fleming **Barbara Rosenblat;** Rachael **Christine Pedi;** Caller's Voices **Christine Pedi, Christy Pusz, Barbara Rosenblat, Adam Sietz, Marc Thompson, Cornell Womack**

UNDERSTUDIES/STANDBYS Michael Laurence (Barry, Dan), Lee Sellars (Dan, Stu, Spike), Cornell Womack (Stu, Male Callers), Christy Pusz (Linda Mac Arthur, Rachael, Female Callers), Kit Williamson (Kent), Oliver Vaquer (Sid Greenberg, Bernie, Vince Farber, Male Callers), Christine Pedi (Dr. Susan Fleming, Female Callers), Adam Sietz, March Thompson (Male Callers)

SETTING Spring 1987. Studio B of radio station WTLK in Cleveland, Ohio. Revival of a play presented without intermission. Originally produced Off-Broadway at the Public Theater May 12, 1987 (see *Theatre World* Volume 43, page 124).

SYNOPSIS *Talk Radio* follows one night in the career an acid-tongued, late-night talk-show host, whose program is about to be picked up for national syndication. Barry Champlain, whose specialty is insulting the pathetic souls who call in the middle of the night to sound off, upsets the sponsors, juggles his love life, and drowns his pain in an alcoholic stupor as he rages his sharp opinions into the airwaves.

TARZAN

Richard Rodgers Theatre; First Preview: March 24, 2006; Opening Night: May 10, 2006; Closed July 8, 2007; 35 previews, 486 performances

Music and lyrics by Phil Collins, book by David Henry Hwang; Produced by Disney Theatrical Productions and Thomas Schumacher; based on the 1999 Disney animated feature film (screenplay by Tab Murphy, Bob Tzudiker and Noni White; directed by Kevin Lima & Chris Buck) and the story "Tarzan of the Apes" by Edgar Rice Burroughs; Director/Scenery/Costumes, Bob Crowley; Choreography, Meryl Tankard; Musical Production/Vocal Arrangements, Paul Bogaev; Aerial Design, Pichón Baldinu; Lighting, Natasha Katz; Sound, John Shivers; Hair, David Brian Brown; Makeup, Naomi Donne; Soundscape, Lon Bender; Special Creatures; Ivo Coveney; Fight Director, Rick Sordelet; Music Director/Dance Arrangements, Jim Abbott; Orchestrations, Doug Besterman; Music Coordinator, Michael Keller; Casting, Bernard Telsey; Production Supervisor, Clifford Schwartz; Technical Supervisor, Tom Shane Bussey; Associate Director, Jeff Lee; Associate Producer, Marshall B. Purdy; Company Management, Randy Meyer, Eduardo Castro; Animated Sequence, Little Airplane Productions; Stage Manager, Frank Lombardi; ASM, Julia P. Jones, Tanya Gillette, Robert Armitage; Dance Captain, Marlyn Ortiz; Fight Captain/ADC, Stefan Raulston; Dialogue/Vocal Coach, Deborah Hecht, Advertising, Serino Coyne; Press, Boneau/Bryan-Brown; Cast recording: Disney Records 61541-7

CAST Kerchak **Rob Evan;** Kala **Merle Dandridge;** Young Tarzan **Dylan Riley Snyder/Alex Rutherford;** Terk **Chester Gregory II;** Tarzan **Josh Strickland;** Jane Porter **Jenn Gambatese;** Professor Porter **Tim Jerome;** Mr. Clayton **Donnie Keshawarz;** Snipes/Lead Song of Man Vocals **Horace V. Rogers;** Waterfall Ribbon Dancer **Kara Madrid;** Moth **Andy Pellick;** Ensemble **Marcus Bellamy, Celina Carvajal, Dwayne Clark, Kearran Giovann, Michael Hollick, Kara Madrid, Kevin Massey, Anastacia McCleskey, Rika Okamoto, Marlyn Ortiz, John Elliott Oyzon, Andy Pellick, Stefan Raulston, Horace V. Rogers, Sean Samuels, Niki Scalera;** Ensemble Replacements **Veronica deSoyza, Andrea Dora, Nicholas Rodriguez;** Swings **Veronica deSoyza, Joshua Kobak, Whitney Osentoski, Angela Phillips, Nick Sanchez, Natalie Silverlieb, JD Aubrey Smith, Rachel Stern;** Replacement Swings **Alayna Gallo, Jeslyn Kelly, Allison Thomas, Marilyn Ortiz, Michael James Scott;** Standby for Kerchak/Porter **Christopher Carl**

ORCHESTRA Jim Abbott (Conductor/keyboard 1); Ethan Popp (Associate Conductor/keyboard 2); Andrew Barrett (synthesizer programmer); Martyn Axe (keyboard 3); Gary Seligson (drums); Roger Squitero, Javier Diaz (percussion); Hugh Mason (bass); JJ McGeehan (guitar); Leanne LeBlanc (cello); Anders Boström (flutes); Charles Pillow (reeds); Anthony Kadleck (trumpet); Bruce Eidem (trombone); Theresa MacDonnell (French horn)

MUSICAL NUMBERS Two Worlds, You'll Be in My Heart, Jungle Funk, Who Better Than Me, No Other Way, I Need to Know, Son of Man, Son of Man (reprise), Sure As Sun Turns to Moon, Waiting for This Moment, Different, Trashin' the Camp, Like No Man I've Ever Seen, Strangers Like Me, Who Better Than Me (reprise), Everything That I Am, You'll Be in My Heart (reprise), Sure As Sun Turns to Moon (reprise), Two Worlds (Finale)

SETTING The Coast of Africa, early 1900's. World premiere of a musical presented in two acts. For original production credits, see *Theatre World* Volume 62, page 66.

SYNOPSIS Tarzan, a shipwrecked baby who was raised in an African jungle by apes, has his first encounter with humans (including the beautiful Jane) and must choose where he belongs– the "civilized" human world or the "wild" one that nurtured him.

Jenn Gambatese and Josh Strickland (photo by Joan Marcus)

WICKED

Gershwin Theatre; First Preview: October 8, 2003; Opening Night: October 30, 2003; 25 previews, 1,893 performances as of May 31, 2008

Book by Winnie Holzman, music and lyrics by Stephen Schwartz; based on the novel by Gregory Maguire; Produced by Marc Platt, Universal Pictures, The Araca Group, Jon B. Platt and David Stone; Director, Joe Mantello; Musical Staging, Wayne Cilento; Music Supervisor, Stephen Oremus; Orchestrations, William David Brohn; Scenery, Eugene Lee; Costumes, Susan Hilferty; Lighting, Kenneth Posner; Sound, Tony Meola; Projections, Elanie J. McCarthy; Wigs/Hair, Tom Watson; Technical Supervisor, Jake Bell; Arrangements, Alex Lacamoire, Stephen Oremus; Dance Arrangements, James Lynn Abbott; Music Coordinator, Michael Keller; Special Effects, Chic Silber; Production Supervisor, Thom Widmann; Dance Supervisor, Mark Myars; Associate Director, Lisa Leguillou; Casting, Bernard Telsey; PSM, Chris Jamros; General Management, 321 Theatrical Management; Executive Producers, Marcia Goldberg and Nina Essman; Company Management, Susan Sampliner, Robert Brinkerhoff; Stage Management, Jennifer Marik, Christy Ney, Chris Zaccardi; Fight Director, Tom Schall; Flying, Paul Rubin/ZFX Inc.; Dressing/Properties, Kristie Thompson; Makeup, Joe Dulude II; Assistant Choreography, Corinne McFadden-Herrera; Music Preparation, Peter R. Miller; Synthesizer Programming, Andrew Barrett; Advertising, Serino Coyne; Press, Barlow-Hartman; Cast recording: Decca B 0001 682-02

CAST Glinda **Kendra Kassebaum**[*1]**;** Witch's Father/Ozian Official **Michael DeVries;** Witch's Mother **Katie Webber;** Midwife **Jan Neuberger**[*2]**;** Elphaba **Julia Murney**[*3]**;** Nessarose **Cristy Candler;** Boq **Logan Lipton**[*4]**;** Madame Morrible **Jayne Houdyshell**[*5]**;** Doctor Dillamond **Steven Skybell;** Fiyero **Sebastian Arcelus**[*6]**;** The Wonderful Wizard of Oz **David Garrison**[*7]**;** Chistery **Jonathan Warren**[*8]**;** Ensemble[*9] **Ioana Alfonso, Sonshine Allen, Brad Bass, Kathy Deitch, Michael DeVries, Lori Ann Ferreri, Todd Hanebrink, Kenway Hon Wai K. Kua, Caissie Levy, Jan Neuberger, Lindsay K. Northen, Brandon Christopher O'Neal, Eddie Pendergraft, Alexander Quiroga, Noah Rivera, Michael Seelbach, Brian Slaman, Heather Spore, Charlie Sutton, Jonathan Warren, Katie Webber, Samantha Zack;** Standbys **Lisa Brescia**[*10] (Elphaba), **Alli Mauzey**[*11] (Glinda); Swings[*12] **Clyde Alves, Kevin Aubin, Kristina Fernandez, Anthony Galde, Tiffany Haas, Allison Leo, Ryan Weiss**

ORCHESTRA Stephen Oremus/Dominick Amendum (Conductor); David Evans (Associate Conductor/keyboards); Ben Cohn (Assistant Conductor/keyboards); Christian Hebel (Concertmaster); Victor Schultz (violin); Kevin Roy (viola); Dan Miller (cello); Konrad Adderly (bass); Greg Skaff (guitar); John Moses, John Campo, Tuck Lee, Helen Campo (woodwinds); Jon Owens, Tom Hoyt (trumpets); Dale Kirkland, Douglas Purviance (trombones); Theo Primis, Kelly Dent (French horn); Paul Loesel (keyboards); Ric Molina, Greg Skaff (guitars); Andy Jones (percussion); Matt VanderEnde (drums); Laura Sherman (harp)

SETTING The Land of Oz. A musical presented in two acts. For original production credits see *Theatre World* Volume 60, page 34.

SYNOPSIS *Wicked* explores the early life of the witches of Oz, Glinda and Elphaba, who meet at Shiz University. After an initial period of mutual loathing, the roommates begin to learn something about each other. Their lives paths continue to intersect, and eventually their choices and convictions take them on widely different paths.

*Succeeded by: 1. Annaleigh Ashford (10/9/07), Kendra Kassebaum (5/17/08) 2. Kathie Santen 3. Stephanie J. Block (10/9/07) 4. Ben Liebert (2/8/08) 5. Carole Shelley (8/28/07), Miriam Margolyes (1/22/08) 6. Derrick Williams (12/18/07), David Burnham (1/8/08) 7. Lenny Wolpe (7/10/07) 8. Brendan King, Jonathan Warren, Sam Kahn 9. Jerad Bortz, Jason Davies, Lauren Gibbs, Reed Kelly, Ryan Patrick Kelly, Chelsea Krombach, CJ Tyson, Jennifer Waldman 10. Julie Reiber (5/13/08) 11. Katie Adams (10/9/07) 12. Additional or replacement: Stephen Lee Anderson, Kristen Leigh Gorski, Lauren Haughton, Lindsay Janisse, Brian Munn, Robert Pendilla, Adam Perry, Carson Reide, Adam Sanford, Jonathan Richard Sandler, Lorna Ventura, Briana Yacavone

Annaleigh Ashford and Stephanie J. Block (photo by Joan Marcus)

THE YEAR OF MAGICAL THINKING

Booth Theatre; First Preview: March 6, 2007; Opening Night: March 29, 2007; Closed August 25, 2007; 23 previews, 144 performances

Written by Joan Didion, based on her memoir; Produced by Scott Rudin, Roger Berlind, Debra Black, Daryl Roth, The Shubert Organization (Chairman, Gerald Schoenfeld; President, Philip J. Smith; Executive Vice President, Robert E. Wankel); Executive Producers, Stuart Thompson and John Barlow; Director, David Hare; Set, Bob Crowley; Costumes, Ann Roth; Lighting, Jean Kalman; Sound, Paul Arditti; PSM, Karen Armstrong; Associate Director, B.T. McNicholl; Marketing, Eric Schnall; Production Manager, Aurora Productions; General Manager, Stuart Thompson Productions/ James Triner; Company Manager, Cassidy J. Briggs; Casting, Daniel Swee; Hair & Makeup, Naomi Donne; Dialect Coach, Deborah Hecht; Stage Manager, Martha Donaldson; Associate Design: Bryan Johnson, Jeffrey Hinchee (set), Michelle Matland (costumes), Bobby Harrell (lighting), Walter Trarbach & Tony Smolenski, IV (sound); Production: Michael Pitzer (electrician), Ronald Fogel (head electrician), Bill Lewis (sound operator), Laura Beattie (wardrobe supervisor), Aleksandra Nesterchuk (hairdresser), Kenneth McDonough (carpenter), Ed White (assistant carpenter), Jimmy Keane (props), Ronnie Burns, Sr. (house electrician), Craig Grigg (prop fabrication); Assistant to Ms. Redgrave, Eamonn Burke; Advertising: SpotCo, Press, Boneau/Bryan-Brown, Chris Boneau, Steven Padla, Heath Schwartz

Vanessa Redgrave (photos by Brigitte Lacombe)

CAST Joan Didion **Vanessa Redgrave**

STANDBY Maureen Anderman

World premiere of a new solo performance play presented without intermission.

SYNOPSIS In the one-woman play, Redgrave plays Didion, reliving a shocking period in the famed author's life. One night, as Didion's daughter Quintana lay in a coma, her husband of 40 years, the writer John Gregory Dunne, died suddenly of a massive coronary as the two of them sat down to dinner in their New York apartment. Redgrave, as Didion, recounts the events of that night, Didion's memories of her marriage, the grieving period and the treatment of her daughter, who subsequently passed away as well.

Off-Broadway

June 1, 2007–May 31, 2008

ROSEBUD: THE LIVES OF ORSON WELLES

59E59 Theater C; First Preview: May 29, 2007; Opening Night: June 1, 2007; Closed June 10, 2007; 3 previews, 13 performances

Written by Mark Jenkins; Presented by Atomic80 Productions as part of the Brits Off Broadway 2007; Director, Josh Richards; Company Manager, Emily McKay; Stage Manager, Jessie Ksanznak; Press, Karen Greco

CAST Orson Welles **Christian McKay**

U.S. premiere of a solo performance play presented without intermission.

SYNOPSIS *Rosebud: The Lives of Orson Welles* chronicles the meteoric rise and even more spectacular fall of one of the greatest directors of the 20th century, exploding the Faustian myth that surrounded him.

THE RULES OF CHARITY

Lion Theatre on Theatre Row; First Preview: May 26, 2007; Opening Night: June 3, 2007; Closed June 24, 2007; 27 performances

Written by John Belluso; Produced by Theatre By The Blind (George Ashiotis and Ike Schambelan, Artistic Directors); Director, Ike Schambelan; Set and Lighting, Bert Scott; Costumes, Renee Mariotti; Fight Director, J. David Brimmer; Sound, Nicholas Viselli; Stage Manager, Ann Marie Morelli; ASM, Francis Eric Montesa; Production Manager, Nicholas Lazzaro; Assistant Production Manager, David Chontos; Marketing, Michelle Brandon; Outreach, Matt Stuart; Graphics, Jane O'Wyatt; Press, Shirley Herz Associates, Daniel Demello

CAST Narrator **Gregg Mozgala;** Loretta **Pamela Sabaugh;** Monty **Christopher Hurt;** L.H./Mr. Millicent **Nicholas Viselli;** Horace **Brian Bielawski;** Paz/Joyce **Hollis Hamilton**

New York premiere of a play presented without intermission.

SYNOPSIS Monty, a man with cerebral palsy and confined to his wheelchair, must rely upon his daughter Loretta to care for him. When a young man sparks the idea of romance in Loretta's life, she wants to move out of Monty's home and conflicts escalate. *The Rules of Charity* suggests that the power love holds over us is contrary and contradictory—a combination of love and hate, cruelty and goodness.

IF WISHES WERE HORSES

Altered Stages; First Preview: June 7, 2007; Opening Night: June 9, 2007; Closed June 30, 2007; 2 previews, 24 performances

Written by Kari Floren; Produced by Right Down Broadway Productions; Director, Julia Gibson; Set/Technical Director, Elisha Schaefer; Costumes, Dana Murdock; Lighting, Michael Salvas; Original Music, Roger Murdock; Sound, Zach Moore; PSM, Emileena Pedigo; Casting, Stephanie Klapper; Master Carpenter, Brian Smallwood; Press, Timothy Haskell/Publicity Outfitters

CAST Karen **Suzanne Grodner;** Doug **Michael McKenzie;** Bill **Robertson Carricart**

SETTING A suburban home in New Jersey, August 2006. World premiere of a new play presented in two acts.

SYNOPSIS Doug, a downsized exec needs a job. His wife Karen has been supporting him for a year. Doug unravels after Karen's father has to move in with them. Using pro-golfer Phil Mickelson's tortured odyssey to the pinnacle of stardom as inspiration, Doug pulls himself up by the bootstraps and starts creating new business opportunities for himself that no one supports. Can these three people get out of the rough and on with their lives without killing each other?

RABBIT

59E59 Theater B; First Preview: June 5, 2007; Opening Night: June 10, 2007; Closed July 1, 2007; 7 previews, 25 performances

Written and directed by Nina Raine; Produced by 59E59 Theaters (Elysabeth Kleinhans, Artistic Director; Peter Tear, Executive Producer); Presented by Joanna Morgan Productions as part of the Brits Off Broadway 2007; Design, Jaime Todd; Lighting, Colin Grenfell; Sound, Fergus O'Hare; Production Manager, Gary Beestone for Giraffe Production; PSM, Jennifer Maire Russo; Press, Karen Greco

CAST Bella **Charlotte Randle;** Father **Hilton McRae;** Emily **Ruth Everett;** Tom **Alan Westaway;** Richard **Adam James;** Sandy **Susannah Wise**

SETTING A London restaurant, the present. U.S. premiere of a new play presented in two acts. World premiere at the Old Red Lion Theatre, London, May 16, 2006, and subsequently transferred to Trafalgar Studios in the West End on September 5, 2006.

SYNOPSIS Friends and former lovers meet for a drink to celebrate Bella's 29th birthday. But as the Bloody Marys flow, the bar soon becomes a battlefield in an uncivil and hilarious war between the sexes.

SESSIONS

Peter J. Sharp Theatre; First Preview: May 30, 2007; Opening Night: June 10, 2007; Closed August 25, 2007; 12 previews, 77 performances

Book, music and lyrics by Albert Tapper, Produced by Algonquin Theater Productions and Ten Grand Productions, Inc.; Director/Choreographer, Steven Petrillo; Set/Costumes, Peter Barbieri, Jr.; Lighting, Deborah Constantine; Sound, Wallace J. Flores; Arrangement/Orchestrations/Music Supervisor, Steven Gross; Assistant Director/Choreographer, Cheryl Swift; Production Manager, B.D. White; Casting, Cyndi Rush; Music Director, Fran Minarik; PSM, Brad Gore; ASM, Max Daniel Weinstein; Props, Chris Johnson; Executive Producers, Tony Sportiello & Jason Hewitt; General Manager, Sharon Osowski, Joan Pelzer; Assistant Director, Cheryl Swift; Dance Captain, Natalie Buster; Technical Director, Joseph Reddington; Keyboard Programmer, James Mironchik; Music Preparation, Brett Macias; Marketing, Leanne Schanzer; Advertising, Hofstetter + Partners/Agency 212; Press, The Publicity Office/Jeremy Shaffer; Cast recording: Original Cast Records 6220

CAST Mrs. Murphy **Bertilla Baker;** Leila **Amy Bodnar;** Baxter **Al Bundonis;** Dylan **David Patrick Ford;** George Preston **Scott Richard Foster;** Mr. Murphy **Jim Madden;** Sunshine **Kelli Maguire;** Mary **Trisha Rapier;** Peterson **Matthew Shepard;** Voice **Ed Reynolds Young;** Understudies: **Natalie Buster** (Leila, Mary, Sunshine, Mrs. Murphy), **Al Bundonis** (Peterson), **Joseph Kolinski** (Mr. Murphy, Baxter, Voice), **David Reiser** (Dylan, Preston)

MUSICIANS Fran Minarik (Conductor/keyboard), Sam Sadigursky (reed), Lisa Pike (horn), Peter Prosser (cello), Jonathan Gleich (percussion)

MUSICAL NUMBERS I'm Only Human, It's All on the Record, Wendy, Above the Clouds, I'm an Average Guy, Feels Like Home, Breathe, The Murphy's Squabble, If I Could Just Be Like Pete, I Saw the Rest of My Life, You Should Dance, This Is One River I Can't Cross, Living Out a Lie, I Never Spent Time with My Dad, Suddenly Somehow/Human (reprise), I Just Want to Hold You for a While/There Should Be Love, The Sun Shines In, This Is One River I Can't Cross (reprise), I Will Never Find Another You, Finale: You Should Dance/Human (reprise)

SETTING Present. In Dr. Peterson's office and waiting room, and various locales in New York City. World premiere of a new musical presented in two acts.

SYNOPSIS Dr. Peter Peterson listens, advises and tests his patients. *Sessions* offers a humorous, poignant and relatable look into the familiar worlds of self-help, personal growth and those long hours that many have spent on a therapist's couch.

Valerie Fagan (as Sandy from Grease*), Janet Dickinson (as Meryl Streep in* Mamma Mia!*) and Jared Bradshaw (as Cheyenne Jackson in* Xanadu*) in* Forbidden Broadway - Rude Awakening *(photo by Carol Rosegg)*

FORBIDDEN BROADWAY

The Roast of Utopia–Special Summer Edition
Rude Awakening–25th Anniversary Edition

47th Street Theatre; *The Roast of Utopia:* Opening Night: June 13, 2007; Closed August 29, 2007; 96 performances; *Rude Awakening:* First Preview: August 31, 2007; Opening Night: October 2, 2007; 232 performances as of May 31, 2008+

Created and written by Gerard Alessandrini; Produced by John Freedson, Harriet Yellin & Jon B. Platt in association with Gary Hoffman, Jerry Kravat, Masakazu Shibaoka; Directors, Gerard Alessandrini and Phillip George; Costumes, Alvin Colt; Set, Megan K. Halpern; Lighting, Marc Janowitz; Music Director, David Caldwell; Production Consultant, Pete Blue; PSM, Jim Griffith; General Manager, Ellen Rusconi; Company Manager,

Adam Levi; Group Sales/Marketing, SRO Marketing, Meri Krassner/Chris Presley; Advertising, Eliran Murphy Group; Assistant Costumes, David Moyer; Wardrobe Supervisor, Kayla Greeley; Wigs/Hair, Carol Sherry; Sound, Sound Associates; Press, Keith Sherman & Associates, Glenna Freedman, DJ Martin, Brett Oberman, Scott Klein; Cast recording: DRG Records 12632

CAST *The Roast of Utopia:* **Jared Bradshaw, Erin Crosby, Janet Dickinson, James Donegan; Pianist: David Caldwell;** *Rude Awakening:* **Jared Bradshaw, Janet Dickinson**[*1]**, Valerie Fagan, Michael West**[*2]**;** Pianist: **David Caldwell**[*3]**;** Understudies: **Gina Kreiezmar, William Selby**

A musical revue presented in two acts.

SYNOPSIS Off-Broadway's longest continuing revue which parodies the current crop of Broadway shows and stars continues with a special summer edition and a new 25th Anniversary edition. This season's spoofs included: *Xanadu, Jersey Boys, The Drowsy Chaperone, Curtains, A Chorus Line, Grease, Legally Blonde, Spamalot, Mary Poppins, Company, Grey Gardens,* and last years mega-hit, *Spring Awakening.* Broadway stars such as Ethyl Merman, Harvey Fierstein, Michael Crawford, David Hyde Pierce and Christine Ebersole are lovingly skewered by the genius pen of Alessandrini.

*Temporary replacements: 1. Megan Lewis 2. James Donegan 3. Steve Saari

+ The show went on temporary hiatus March 21-June 27 per contract with the 47th Street Theatre to allow its resident company The Puerto Rican Traveling to perform.

INTIMATE EXCHANGES

59E59 Theater A; First Preview: May 31, 2007; Opening Night: June 14, 2007; Closed July 1, 2007; 36 performances

Written by Alan Ayckbourn; Produced by 59E59 Theaters (Elysabeth Kleinhans, Artistic Director; Peter Tear, Executive Producer); Presented The Stephen Joseph Theatre, Scarborough, UK as part of the Brits Off Broadway 2007; Directors, Alan Ayckbourn and Tim Luscombe; Design, Michael Holt; Lighting, Ben Vickers; Assistant Director, Joe Douglas; Company Stage Manager, Emily Vickers; Deputy Stage Manager, Andy Hall; ASM, Lisa Mellor; PSM, Misha Siegel-Rivers; Sound Operator, Scott Earley; Touring & Programming Director, Amanda Saunders; Production Manager, Adrian Sweeney; Carpenter, Frank Matthews; Press, Karen Greco

CAST Celia Teasdale/Sylvie Bell/Rowena Coombes/Irene/Josephine **Claudia Elmhirst;** Toby Teasdale/Miles Coombes/Lionel Hepplewick/Reg/Joe **Bill Champion**

A cycle of eight plays presented in tandem, each performed in two acts. The plays and number of performances for each included: *Affairs in a Tent* (5), *Events on a Hotel Terrace* (5), *A Garden Fête* (4), *A Pageant* (4), *A Cricket Match* (5), *A Game of Golf* (4), A *One Man Protest* (5), and *Love in the Mist* (4).

SYNOPSIS *Intimate Exchanges* is a unique theatrical event in which two actors portray 10 different characters in eight different full length plays. One character's dilemma--to smoke or not smoke--kicks off each play, and each of the eight plays has two different endings. *Intimate Exchanges* follows the fortunes of headmaster Toby Teasdale and his long-suffering wife Celia, whose marriage is going through a bit of a sticky patch to say the least. With suicidal friends, busybody neighbors, sexy school caretakers, pushy fathers and mad mothers-in-law to add to their troubles, will they ever be able to sort things out? It all depends on which ending you want to see!

THE FABULOUS LIFE OF A SIZE ZERO

DR2; First Preview: June 14, 2007; Opening Night: June 17, 2007; Closed July 1, 2007; 3 previews, 13 performances

Written and produced by Marissa Kamin; Produced by Isaac Robert Hurwitz and Métropole Ink (JP Sarni and Amanda Ward) in association with Jossip.com; Director/Producer, Ben Rimalower; Set, Wilson Chin; Costumes, David Kaley; Lighting, Ben Stanton; Sound, Zach Williamson; Projections, Ruth Lacera; Casting, Erica Jensen; Dramaturg, Christie Evangelisto; Choreography, Josh Walden; Music Supervisor, DJ Brenda Black; PSM, Andrea Jess Berkey; Press, Springer Associates, Shane Marshall Brown

CAST Girl Chorus **Anna Chlumsky;** Girl **Gillian Jacobs;** Superstar **Kate Reinders;** Entourage 1 **Brian J. Smith;** Entourage 2 **Christopher Sloan**

Claudia Elmhirst and Bill Champion in A Game of Golf, *one of the plays in* Intimate Exchanges *(photo by Tony Bartholomew)*

New York premiere of a new play presented without intermission. Workshopped at Barestage Productions, UC Berkeley, March 2007.

SYNOPSIS *The Fabulous Life of a Size Zero* follows a girl in her senior year of high school as she attempts to achieve the ultimate: effortless perfection. Feeling the pressure of the forces around her, she shrinks to a size zero and descends into a filthy/gorgeous world of booze, beauty and boyfriends all while attempting to get into the Ivy League school of her choice. Utilizing the tabloids, headlines, and real blogs, the play proposes, "How can a girl find herself if she is lost being someone else?"

RADIO

59E59 Theater C; First Preview: June 12, 2007; Opening Night: June 17, 2007; Closed July 1, 2007; 7 previews, 17 performances

Written by Al Smith; Produced by 59E59 Theaters (Elysabeth Kleinhans, Artistic Director; Peter Tear, Executive Producer); Presented by Kandinsky Theatre Company (Oscar Mathew, Producer) as part of the Brits Off Broadway 2007; Director, James Yeatman; Lighting, Neil E. Hobbs; PSM, Jessie Ksanznak; Press, Karen Greco, Oscar Mathew, Kelly Davis

CAST Charlie Fairbanks **Tom Ferguson**

SETTING Lebanon, Kansas, 1950-1969. American premiere of a solo performance play presented without intermission. Originally premiered at the 2006 Edinburgh Fringe Festival and subsequently transferred to London's Soho Theatre in the West End.

SYNOPSIS *Radio* is about a farmer-turned-flag maker's son who shoots for the moon. A play about memory, love and spaceships, it parallels a young man's coming of age with the birth and death of the Apollo Space Program, and explores the consequences of our losing sight of the Earth.

theAtrainplays vol. XXII

New World Stages – Stage 4; June 20, 2007; 1 performance

Produced by Lawrence Feeney, Valley Theatre League and The Off-Broadway Brainstormers; Production Supervisor, Andrea "Spook" Testani; PSM, Melanie T. Morgan; Technical Supervisor, Rocky Noel; Set, Andrew Donovan; Librettists: Erica Silberman, Michael Lazan, Stephen O'Rourke, P. Seth Bauer; Playwrights: Shawn Nacol, Barbara Hammond; Composers/Lyricists, Gaby Alter, Brian J. Nash, Brandon Patton, Joe Iconis; Directors/Choreographers: Mark Lonergan, Wendy Seyb, Carol Schulberg, Stas' Kmiec', Tony Stevens, David Brind, Michael Duling, Edie Cowan, David Hilder; Music Director, Alec Berlin

CAST Musicals **Natalie Douglas, Ryan Duncan, Tim Johnson, Tracie Thoms, Stephanie D'Abruzzo, Emy Baysic, Thom Sesma, Blythe Gruda, Robin Skye, Darius de Haas, Adam Fleming, Darcie Siciliano, Cristin Hubbard, Lawrence Feeney, Donovan Patton;** Plays **Eric Michael Gillett, Cady Huffman, Melanie Vaughan, Kevin Daniels, Lisa Barnes;** Band **Alec Berlin, Jordan Perlson, Rick Hip Flores, Tony Ormond**

An evening of short plays and musicals presented without intermission. Originally presented at the Neighborhood Playhouse in 2002. This was the twenty-second edition of the series.

SYNOPSIS *theAtrainplays* are a celebration of New York, created by six teams while traveling the entire route of the A train, from 207th Street & Broadway to Far Rockaway and back. Blind drawings are done to connect librettist with composers and lyricists, directors and choreographers, and cast members. The plays, all set on the A train, are created, rehearsed and presented in a 24-hour period, creating a unique and raw performance experience.

ELVIS PEOPLE

New World Stages – Stage 1; First Preview: June 6, 2007; Opening Night: June 21, 2001; Closed June 23, 2007; 20 previews, 4 performances

Written by Doug Grissom; Produced by E.P. Productions, Robert A. Rush, Emilee MacDonald; Associate Producer, Emilee MacDonald; Director, Henry Wishcamper; Set, Cameron Anderson; Costumes, Theresa Squire; Lighting, Robert P. Robins; Sound, Graham Johnson; Video/Projections, Maya Ciarrocchi; Properties, Lorelei Esser; Wigs/Hair/Makeup, Erin Lunsford Kennedy; Casting, Stephanie Klapper; Production Manager, Joshua Helman; PSM, Eric Tysinger; General Management, Martian Entertainment; Marketing, The Keleen Company, Leanne Schanzer Promotions; Company Manager, Lauren P. Yates; ASM, Alex Jepson; Press, David Gersten & Associates

CAST John L/Col. Parker/Art/Elvis (asleep)/ Townsperson/ Guy Plagett **Jordan Gelber;** Susie/Marsha/Young Carol/ Hannah/Seraphina/Townsperson/Linda/Dalia **Jenny Maguire;** Stuart/Keith/Officer Fallon/Townsperson/Doc/ Winston **David McCann;** Eddie/Vick/Young Keith/Boy/ LD/Brad/Elvis Impersonator **Nick Newell;** Mom/Carol/ Louise/Nettie **Nell Page;** Dad/Godwin/Townsperson/ Publisher/Hank **Ed Sala;** Understudies: **Kristen Bedard, Ned Noyes**

Off-Broadway premiere of a new play presented in twelve scenes in two acts. Originally presented at Mill Mountain Playhouse (Roanoke, Virginia) in 2006.

SYNOPSIS No performer before or since has had the impact of Elvis Presley, from the first groundbreaking appearance on Ed Sullivan Show, to Las Vegas and Graceland. Eighty-four percent of all Americans say their lives have been touched by Elvis in some way. In *Elvis People,* you meet some of the funny and touching characters whose lives were forever changed by "The King."

GONE MISSING

Barrow Street Theatre; Previews: June 14, 2007; Opening Night: June 24, 2007; Closed January 6, 2008; 194 performances

Created by The Civilians, directed and written by Steve Cosson from interviews by the company (Damian Bladet, Trey Lyford, Jennifer R. Morris, Brian Sgambati, Alison Weller, Colleen Werthmann with additional material from Quincy Bernstine, Matthew Francis, Winter Miller, and Charlie Schroeder); Music and Lyrics, Michael Friedman; "Interview with Dr. Palinurus" by Peter Morris & "Teri's Theme" composed by Andy Boroson; Presented by Scott Morfee and Tom Wirtshafter in association with The Civilians; Set, Takeshi Kata, Lighting, Thomas Dunn; Sound, Ken Travis; Choreography, Jim Augustine; Costumes, Sarah Beers; Music Director, Andy Boroson; General Management, The Company, Cris Buchner, Kate Mott; Production Manager, Jason Reuter; PSM, Robert Signom III; ASM, Matt Dellapina; Advertising, Eliran Murphy Group; Press, O+M Co., Rick Miramontez, Jon Dimond; Cast recording: Sh-K-Boom/Ghostlight Records 8-4426

CAST **Emily Ackerman**[*1], **Damian Baldet, Jennifer R. Morris, Stephen Plunkett, Robbie Collier Sublett, Colleen Werthmann;** Voice of Teri **Nina Hellman;** Voice of Dr. Palinurus **T. Ryder Smith;** Understudies: **Matt Dellapina**[*2], **Caitlin Miller**[*3]; Musicians **Andy Boroson** (piano), **David Purcell** (drums); **Steve Gilewski** (bass)

MUSICAL NUMBERS Gone Missing, The Only Thing Missing Is You, La Bodega, Hide & Seek, I Gave It Away, Ich Traumt Du Kamst An Mich, Lost Horizon, Etch a Sketch, Stars

Off-Broadway premiere of a new musical presented without intermission. Originally presented at Joe's Pub, Galapagos Art Space, and the Belt Theatre in 2003.

SYNOPSIS Devised by the Civilians from interviews with real-life New Yorkers, *Gone Missing* is a wry and whimsical documentary musical about things that go missing—keys, personal identification, a Gucci pump...or one's mind. The show is a collection of very personal accounts of things lost and found, creating a unique tapestry of the ways in which we deal with and relate to loss in our lives.

Emily Ackerman, Stephen Plunkett, Colleen Werthmann, Jennifer R. Morris, Robbie Collier Sublett and Damian Baldet in Gone Missing *(photo by Sheldon Noland)*

*Succeeded by: 1. Alison Weller 2. Michael Page 3. Lexy Fridell

AT WAR: AMERICAN PLAYWRIGHTS RESPOND TO IRAQ

National Arts Club: June 25, 2007; Theatres at 45 Bleecker: January 21, 28, February 4, 2008

Presented by The Fire Dept; (June 25 – presented in association with The National Arts Club); Collaged by Jessica Blank, Erica Gould, Audrey Rosenberg; Director, Audrey Rosenberg; Associate Producer, Erin McCann; Graphic Design, Hart/Larsson; Press, Keith Sherman and Associates

CAST June 25: **Jason Antoon, Jessica Blank, David Calvitto, Michael Cerveris, Judith Hawking, Laura Heisler, Sal Inzerillo, Erik Jensen, Ty Jones, Haskell King, Aasif Mandvi, Heather Raffo, Audrey Rosenberg, Peter Sarsgaard, Jonathan Schaefer, Jeremy Schwartz, Paul Sparks, David Strathairn, Mather Zickel;** Guest speakers **Paul Reickhoff, Mark Crispin Miller, Marla Bertagnolli.** January 21–February 4: Featured Guests (rotating): **Bebe Neuwirth, Bobby Cannavale, Josh Hamilton, Daniel Sunjata; Janeane Garofolo, Denis O'Hare, Gloria Reuben, David Strathairn;** Core Cast **Jennifer Albano, Jessica Blank, Judith Hawking, Korey Jackson, Erik Jensen, Amanda Marikar, Steven Rattazzi, Jake Robards, Audrey Rosenberg, Jonathan Schaefer, Jeremy Schwartz, Michael Warner, Jeremy Webb**

An evening of staged readings of excerpts of new plays, and guest speakers. Plays included: *Back From the Front* by Lyn Rosen, *Phosphorescence* by Cory Hinkle, *Abu Ghraib Tryptich* by Peter Maloney, *A Bengal Tiger in the Baghdad Zoo* by Rajiv Joseph, *The Professor* by Jessica Blank & Erik Jensen, *Rendition* by Ryan Kelly, *Gas* by Jose Rivera, *Two Soldiers* by Bathsheba Doran, *Zahra* by Jessica Blank with Jennifer Abrahamson, *Fubar* by Jonathan Schaefer.

SYNOPSIS Presented as the Fire Dept's Salon Series inaugural event in June at the National Arts Club, the evening was expanded and presented for 3 more performances at 45 Bleecker six months later.

LA VIE

Spiegeltent at South Street Seaport; Opening Night: July 2, 2007; Closed September 30, 2007; 103 performances

Created, written and directed by Les 7 Doigts de la Main (The 7 Fingers), Montreal, Canada (Shana Carrol, Isabelle Chassé, Patrick Léonard, Fain Shane, Gypsy Snider, Sébastien Soldevila, Samuel Tétreault); Presented by Spiegelworld, Ross Mollison, and Vallejo Gantner; Additional Texts, Jon Carroll; Sound, Art Williams; Lighting, John Grenay; Rigging, Peter Wellington; Stage Manager, Max Engler; Press, Richard Kornberg & Associates

CAST Emcee **Sébastien Soldevila;** Patrick **Patrick Léonard;** Chain Aerialist **Faon Shane;** Vamp **Emilie Bonnavaud;** Wheelchair Balancer **Samuel Tétreault;** Disc Jockey **DJ Pocket;** Emcee Assistant/Singer/Stewardess **Shana Carroll;** Insane Girl **Isabelle Chassé;** Swing **Marjorie Nantel**

New York premiere of a theatrical circus/acrobatic performance spectacle presented in two acts.

SYNOPSIS *La Vie* is a cabaret... on the outskirts of life. Before exiting either upstage or downstage, the players are literally dying to prove themselves. Flying high above the audience, the MC cajoles the players to act out unfulfilled fantasies, reveal hidden taboos and indulge unrequited passions. The final judgment is up to you. Remember, someone's hell is another's heaven. *La Vie* dares you to explore all of life's extremes.

ABSINTHE

Spiegeltent at South Street Seaport; Opening Night: July 3, 2007; Closed September 30, 2007; 104 performances

Created and Produced by Spiegelworld, Ross Mollison, and Vallejo Gantner; Director, Wayne Harrison; Lighting Design, Martin Kinnane; Production Stage Manager, Niluka Samaseker; Lighting, Chris Coyle; Sound, Art Williams, Rigger, Daryl Johns; Press, Richard Kornberg and Associates

CAST **Raphaelle Boitel, Olaf Triebel, Marieve Hemond, Annie-Kim Dery, Adil Rida, Paul Capsis, Julie Atlas Muz, Voki Kalfayan, Anais Thomassian, Nate Cooper, Wanda Poissonnet, Jean-Pierre Poissonnet**

An expanded version of the cabaret/circus/variety-burlesque show presented in two acts. Previously presented August 3–October 1, 2006 at the South Street Seaport.

SYNOPSIS Combining the traditions of vaudeville and music hall with Berliner Kabarett, *ABSINTHE – Les Artistes de La Clique* is a variety show on acid, a late-night saunter through the sultriest, strangest circus in town. Fairground attraction collides with sideshow burlesque to transform the elegant, sumptuous confines of the Spiegeltent into something just a little ... below the belt.

Jean-Pierre and Wanda Poissonnet as "The Willers" in Absinthe *(photo by Jean Marcus)*

GUILTY

Acorn Theatre at Theatre Row; First Preview: July 1, 2007; Opening Night: July 5, 2007; Closed July 30, 2007; 3 previews, 21 performances

Written by Nancy Manocherian; Produced by The Cell Theatre Company; Director, Kira Simring; Set, Tim McMath; Costumes, Jason A. Bishop; Lighting, Ben Zamora; Sound/Composer, Ken Hypes; Stage Manager, Mandy Berry; ASM, Amy Kaskeski; Production Manager, Travis Walker; Marketing, Wren Longo; Managing Director, Matt Lillo; Press, Springer Associates, Shane Marshall Brown

CAST Lindsey **Tracee Chimo;** Marcie **Mary Ann Conk;** Dori **Glory Gallo;** Laura **Heather Kenzie;** Jake **Ned Massey;** Adam **Darnell Williams**

World premiere of a new play presented without intermission.

SYNOPSIS Sex, Lies... and Botox. White-collar crime never looked so good. *Guilty* follows the unraveling of a group of friends in the top echelon of New York society enjoying their lives of plenty. But as the characters' indiscretions culminate, linings of corruption and deceit are stripped away to reveal universal frailty underneath the facade of the social elite.

THE LAST YEAR IN THE LIFE OF THE REVEREND DR. MARTIN LUTHER KING JR. As Devised by Waterwell: A Rock Operetta

Barrow Street Theatre; First Preview: June 21, 2007; Opening Night: July 7, 2007; Closed August 11, 2007; 18 performances

Written, created and produced by Waterwell; Director, Tom Ridgely; Composer, Lauren Cregor; Choreography, Lynn Peterson; Set, Dave Lombard; Costumes, Elizabeth Payne; Lighting, Stacey Boggs; Associate Lighting, Zack Brown; Sound, Jeff Devine; Graphics, Brian McMullen; Stage Manager, Taylor James; Press, O+M Co., Rick Miramontez, Jon Dimond

CAST **Hanna Cheek, Rodney Gardiner, Arian Moayed, Tom Ridgely, Kevin Townley;** Musicians **Lauren Cregor, Jeremy Daigle, Gunter Gruner, Joe Morse**

A theatrical event with music presented without intermission.

SYNOPSIS Featuring an exuberant score of hard-edged rock, blues and funk, *The King/Operetta* draws on speeches, writings and interviews to give a blistering account of Martin Luther King as he barnstorms the country squaring off against the most powerful forces in politics and commerce. Facing criticism on all sides and even doubts from his closest advisors, he speaks his mind fearlessly and fights to the end against war, poverty and his own government.

ANGRY YOUNG WOMEN IN LOW RISE JEANS WITH HIGH CLASS ISSUES

Players Theatre; Opening Night: July 12, 2007; Closed October 20, 2007; 58 performances (Thursdays-Saturdays)

Written and directed by Matt Morillo; Starring the KADM Players; Produced by Matt Morillo, Jessica Durdock, Richard Barbadillo; Set, Jana Mattioli; Lighting, Amith A. Chandrashaker; Stage Manager, Mei Acevedo; Press, Jonathan Slaff & Associates

CAST Part 1–*My Last Thong:* Soleil **Devon Pipars*1;** Part 2–*Playtime in the Park:* Rebecca **Angelique Letizia;** Ronnie **Martin Friedrichs*2;** Sarah **Jessica Durdock;** Part 3–*Unprotected Sex:* Brian **Nicholas J. Coleman;** Joe **Thomas J. Pilutik;** Rachel **Rachel Nau;** Part 4–*The Miseduction of Elissa:* Elissa **Angelique Letizia*3;** Part 5–*The Nude Scene:* Jennifer **Devon Pipars*4;** Spencer **Thomas J. Pilutik;** Kristoff **Nicholas J. Coleman;** Katy **Rachel Nau*5;** Barry **Martin Friedrichs*2;** Understudy: **Jason Dumright*6**

Transfer of the Off-Off-Broadway comedy presented in five parts without intermission. Previously presented at the Duo Theatre, January 19–February 25, 2006, and Theater for the New City, January 4–February 24, 2007.

SYNOPSIS A light-to-serious look at the psychology of nervous urban goddesses, the show examines a series of foxy, witty and anxious women as they bear the expectations of the world like an itchy muffler. These coffee-driven, sensitive, wired, misunderstood girls are fuming with awkward issues and frustrated with the perceptions men have of them.

*Succeeded by 1. Rachel Nau 2. John Driscoll 3. Jennifer Missoni 4. Angelique Letizia 5. Jessica Durdock 6. Zachary Harrison (Ronnie/Barry)

SURFACE TO AIR

Symphony Space; First Preview: July 11, 2007; Opening Night: July 18, 2007; Closed August 5, 2007; 7 previews, 18 performances

Written by David Epstein; Presented by Symphony Space (Isaiah Sheffer, Artistic Director; Cynthia Elliott, Executive Director); Producers, Darren Critz & Lisa Dozier; Director, James Naughton; Set, James Noone; Costumes, Laurie Churba; Lighting, Clifton Taylor; Sound, Ray Schilke; Casting, Deborah Brown; Stage Manager, Diane DiVita; ASM, Megan Smith; Production Manager, Matthew Cecchini; Technical Director, Denis Heron; Props, Yana Babaev; Projections, William Moser; Fight Choreographer, B.H. Barry; Assistant Design, Patrick Kenna (set), Christian Kohn (costume), Kate Ashton (lighting); Press, Helene Davis

CAST Andrew **Bruce Altman;** Hank **Larry Bryggman;** Eddie **James Colby;** Airman **Brian Delate;** Magdalena **Marisa Echeverria;** Terri **Cady Huffman;** Princess **Lois Smith;** Rob **Mark J. Sullivan**

World premiere of a new play presented without intermission.

SYNOPSIS *Surface to Air* is the story of a family forced to confront long-repressed issues and current realities when the remains of their son, a Vietnam veteran, are returned to them 30 years after his plane was shot down over Vietnam. The unresolved passions and long-lasting effects of the Vietnam War seem especially timely in light of the issues of today.

33 TO NOTHING

The Wild Project; First Preview: July 19, 2007; Opening Night: July 25, 2007; Closed October 13, 2007; 5 previews, 57 performances

Book, music, and lyrics by Grant James Varjas, music by John Good, Preston Clarke; Produced by The Wild Project; Director, Randal Myler; Music Supervisor/Arrangements, Keith Levenson; Additional Music, John Good, Preston Clarke; Set, Paul Smithyman; Lighting, Brian Nason; Sound, Eric Stahlhammer; PSM, Ana Mari de Quesada; ASM, Kristin Mueller; Assistant Set, Jack Robinson; Assistant Sound, Sam Mallery; Graphics, Michael Robinson; Program, Bryan Wizemann; Marketing, Art Meets Commerce; Press, Timothy Haskell

CAST Bri **Preston Clarke;** Barry **Ken Forman;** Tyler **John Good;** Alex **Amanda Gruss;** Gray **Grant James Varjas**

MUSICAL NUMBERS Happy Moral Suicide, Low to the Ground, Now That Its Over, Less Than Nothing, 33 to Nothing, Lost to Me, The Same Old Song, 28 Bars

Transfer of the Off-Off Broadway play with music presented without intermission. Previously produced at the Wild Project (formerly The Bottle Factory) March 8, 2006.

SYNOPSIS Taking place during one alcohol laced rehearsal, *33 to Nothing* rocks hard and breaks hearts. This downtown NYC garage band is on the edge of breaking-up as the lead singer and his boyfriend (also in the band) are breaking-up. With each year that passes that they aren't rock stars the incessant pull of adulthood becomes harder to ignore.

MY FIRST TIME

New World Stages – Stage 5; First Preview: July 12, 2007; Opening Night: July 28, 2008; 114 performances as of May 31, 2008 (Friday and Saturday evenings)

Written by Ken Davenport and Real People Just Like You; Inspired by the website www.MyFirstTime.com created by Peter Foldy and Craig Stuart; Produced and directed by Ken Davenport; Production Design, Matthew A. Smith; Marketing, HHC Marketing; Casting, Daryl Eisenberg; Associate Producer/Press, David J. Gersten; General Management, DTE, Inc.; PSM, Kathryn Galloway; Associate General Manager, Matt Kovich; Associate to the Producer, Nicole Brodeur; Crew, Allison Hersh; Davenport Theatrical Enterprises: Jamie Lynn Ballard, Amanda Butcher, Matt Kovich

CAST **Bill Dawes**[*1]**, Josh Heine**[*2]**, Kathy Searle**[*3]**, Cyndee Welburn**[*3]

World premiere of a new play presented without intermission.

SYNOPSIS *My First Time* is a new play in the style of *The Vagina Monologues,* featuring hysterical and heartbreaking stories about first sexual experiences written by real people, just like you. Four actors bring to life confessional monologues about the silly, sweet, absurd, funny, heterosexual, homosexual, awkward, shy, sexy and everything-in-between stories of first times submitted to the website. *My First Time:* I'll tell you mine if, you tell me yours.

*Succeeded by: 1. Dana Watkins 2. Marcel Simoneau 3. Temporary replacement: Emily McNamara

Bill Dawes, Cydnee Welburn, Josh Heine, and Katy Searle in My First Time *(photo by Drew Geraci)*

MASKED

DR2; First Preview: July 20, 2007; Opening Night: August 2, 2007; Closed December 30, 2007; 10 previews, 171 performances

Written by Ilan Hatsor, translated by Michael Taub; Produced by Maya Productions, The Splinter Group, Highbrow Entertainment; Director, Ami Dayan; Set, Wilson Chin & Ola Maslik; Costumes, Jennifer Caprio; Lighting, Thom Weaver; Sound, Joachim Horsely; Original Music, Omri Hason; Fight Director, Christian Kelly-Sordelet; Fight Consultant, Rick Sordelet; Advertising, Hofstetter & Partners, Agency 212; Marketing, Leanne Schanzer Promotions; Casting, Stuart Howard, Amy Schecter, Paul Hardt; General Manager, The Splinter Group; Management Associate, Carly DiFulvio; Associate Producers, Steve Klein, Janet Pailet/Sharon Carr; PSM, Jana Llyn; Assistant Director, Lisa Brailoff; Press, Keith Sherman & Associates

CAST Na'im **Arian Moayed**[*1]**;** Daoud **Daoud Heidami**[*2]**;** Khalid **Sanjit De Silva**[*3]**;** Understudies: **Rajesh Bose** (Daoud/Na'im), **Rafi Silver** (Khalid/Na'im)

SETTING Fall 1990, evening to dawn in a large Arab village in the West Bank. A play presented without intermission.

SYNOPSIS *Masked,* an explosive drama about three Palestinian bothers, tackles the cultural divide at the heart of the Middle East conflict. The play depicts the tragedy of one family torn between obligations, kinship, principles and survival, and is the first play by an Israeli playwright about the Intifada (Palestinian uprising).

*Succeeded by: 1. Sanjit De Silva 2. Waleed Zuaiter 3. Rafi Silver

Arian Moayed, Sanjit DeSilva and Daoud Heidami in Masked *(photo by Aaron Epstein)*

IDOL: THE MUSICAL

45th Street Theatre; First Preview: July 5, 2007; Opening and Closing Night: August 12, 2007; 47 previews, 1 performance

Music and lyrics by Jon Balcourt, book and lyrics by Bill Boland, concept and additional book and lyrics by Todd Ellis; Produced by Todd Ellis and BiPolar Productions; Director, Dan Tursi; Set, Brian Howard; Costumes, Keith Axton; Lighting, Charles Shatzkin; Sound, Brady Dombroske; Music Director/ Orchestrations, Jon Balcourt; Office Manager, Wendy Shuron; Assoicate Choreography, Joe Walker

CAST* Connor **Philip Deyesso;** Duncan **Saum Eskandani;** Alex **Jillian Giacchi;** Midge **Dawn Barry;** Cicada **Kaitlin Rose Mercurio**; Adrienne **Katy Reinsel;** Kodi **Shadeae Smith;** Emily **Stephanie Robinson;** Cass **Kierstyn Sharrow;** JD **Joe Walker;** Understudies **Kenneth D'Elia** (Duncan & Kodi), **Jennifer Margulis** (Cicaida, Cass & Alex), **Shannon O'Keefe** (Adrienne & Emily)

MUSICAL NUMBERS Opening: Idolize, The Meeting, Small Town Blues, Fifteen Minutes, Discipline, I Could Have Been a Contender, Chip & Dale Days, Prima Donna Fabulous, Quakin' for Aiken, Prima Donna Fabulous (reprise), Burnin' Hunk of Clay, Simon Says, Distance, Family of Misfits, Finale, Fifteen Minutes (reprise)

SETTING In and around Steubenville, Ohio; the present. New York premiere of a new musical presented in two acts. Originally presented at the Syracuse Civic Theatre (Syracuse, New York) June 2007.

SYNOPSIS In this satirical musical comedy, nine misfit students who worship Clay Aiken ("Claymates') are determined to drag themselves out of the dregs of their middle-of-nowhere home town. When the mid-America leg of the "Idol Tour" starring Aiken is announced to play their hometown, the group dreams of winning a spot as the opening act in Clay's new tour and prepares a routine to audition for him.

*These cast members (except for Joe Walker) replaced the original cast during previews. The preview cast included: Jon Balcourt (Connor), Courtney Ellis (Cicada), Roy George (Kodi), Nikita Richards (Cass), Babs Rubenstein (Adrienne), Joella Burt (Emily), Jennie Riverso (Alex), Ryan Sprague (Duncan)

THE ALL-AMERICAN SPORT OF BIPARTISAN BASHING

New World Stages – Stage 5; First Preview: August 6, 2007; Opening Night: August 15, 2007; Closed October 14, 2007; 49 performances

Created by Will Durst; Produced by Hanging Chad Production, Jennifer Sachs and Allen Spivak; Director, Eric Krebs; Production Design Consultant, Peter Feuchtwanger; General Manager, EKTM, Inc., Jonathan Shulman; Production Coordinators, Jason Quinn, Brian Westmoreland; Company Manager, Rebecca Sherman; Press, Keith Sherman & Associates, Brett Oberman

Performed by **Will Durst**

A solo performance of political comedy and satire presented without intermission.

SYNOPSIS San Francisco-based commentator and political pundit Will Durst takes on the current sad state of politics, offending both sides of aisle. A five-time Emmy nominee, he has made more than 400 television appearances in his more-than-30-year career,

NEVA SMALL: NOT QUITE AN INGENUE

The Actors Temple; First Preview: August 16, 2007; Opening Night: August 23, 2007; Closed September 30, 2007; 11 performances (Thursdays and Saturdays)

Written by Neva Small; Produced by Edmund Gaynes, Pamela Hall and Louis S. Salamone; Director, Pamela Hall; Music Director, Don Rebic; Musical Supervisor, Jay Kerr; Associate Producer, Letty Simon; Stage Manager, Kimberly Jade Parker; Electrician, Jeff Thom; General Manager, Jessimeg Productions; Projections, Ron Spivak; Graphics, JCJohnsonDesign.com; Technical Director, Josh Iacovelli; Featuring songs by Joseph Stein, Jerry Bock, Sheldon Harnick, Stephen Schwartz, Leonard Bernstein, Marilyn and Alan Bergman, Bob Merrill, Kurt Weill; Press, Brett Singer & Associates

Performed by **Neva Small;** Pianist **Steven Silverstein;** Bass **Mark Wade, Daniel Stein**

A solo performance musical revue presented without intermission.

SYNOPSIS Neva Small, best known as "Chava" in the film version of *Fiddler on the Roof,* whimsically traces the highlights of her life through the music that has carried and nurtured her professionally and personally.

David Rhodes in Rites of Privacy *(photo by Tom Contrino)*

RITES OF PRIVACY

Urban Stages; First Preview: August 16, 2007; Opening Night: August 30, 2007; Closed September 30, 2007; 36 performances

Written, produced, and costumes by David Rhodes; Produced by Moving Parts Theatre, Michael T. Cohen; Produced, directed and sound by Charles Lofredo; Set/Projections, Greg Emetaz; Lighting, Charles Cameron; Choreography, Eric Chan, Corey Hill & David Rhodes; PSM, Tara Nachtigall; Music Accompaniment/Arrangements/Performed by Eric Chan; Projection and Sound Operation, Christopher Cass; Press, Sam Rudy Media Relations

Performed by **David Rhodes**

Off-Broadway premiere of a solo performance play presented without intermission.

SYNOPSIS Actor and author David Rhodes explores the impact of secrets and the people who keep them as he shifts gears and costumes to portray an array of characters with dark secrets: a fading Southern pageant queen, an aging refugee from Nazi Germany, a fish-out-of-water Jew in New Hampshire, a suburban doctor in a predicament, and a Euro club-kid with and unsavory edge. Throughout, Rhodes alternates these characters with candid stories from his own creative and personal life.

WALMARTOPIA

Minetta Lane Theatre; First Preview: August 23, 2007; Opening Night: September 3, 2007; Closed December 30, 2007; 10 previews, 136 performances

Book, music & lyrics by Catherine Capellaro & Andrew Rohn; Produced by WMTopia, LLC; Director, Daniel Goldstein; Choreography, Wendy Seyb; Music Direction/Orchestrations & Arrangements, August Eriksmoen; Set, David Korins; Costumes, Miranda Hoffman; Lighting, Ben Stanton; Sound, Tony Smolenski IV/Walter Trarbach; Projections, Leah Gelpe; Hair/Wigs/Makeup, Erin Kennedy Lunsford; Casting, Alaine Alldaffer; Production Manager, Peter Dean; General Manager; Roy Gabay; PSM, Bess Marie Glorioso; Dance Captain, Brennen Leath; Company Manager, Jennifer Pluff; Associate Production Manager, Thomas Goehring; Stage Manager, Ana M. Garcia; Assistant Director, Kate Marks; P.A., Sarah Michele Penland; Assistant Choreographer, Cody D. Smith; Press, O+M Co., Rick Miramontez, Philip Carrubba; Cast recording: Outside the Big Box LLC

CAST Jamie/Guard/etc **Sarah Bolt;** Miguel/Zeb/etc **Bradley Dean;** Dr. Normal/Otis/etc **Stephen DeRosa;** Vicki Latrell **Cheryl Freeman;** Maia Latrell **Nikki M. James;** Scott "Scooter" Smiley/etc **John Jellison;** Darin/Alan/etc **Brennen Leath*;** Pearson/Lawrence/etc **Andrew Polk;** Xu Fu/Counselor James/etc **Pearl Sun;** Sam Walton/etc **Scotty Watson;** Hooters Girl/Daphne/etc **Heléne Yorke**

UNDERSTUDIES Charl Brown (Darin/Pearson/Zeb), Jessica Cope (Maia/Dapne/Guard), Tanesha Gary (Vicki/Counselor James), Neal Mayer (Sam Walton/Scott Smiley/Dr. Normal)

MUSICIANS August Eriksmoen (Conductor/keyboards), Matt Beck (guitar/banjo), David Richards (saxophone/clarinet/bass clarinet), Cary Potts (bass), Steve Bartosik (drums/percussion)

MUSICAL NUMBERS A New Age Has Begun, American Dream, March of the Executives, Baby Girl, The Future is Ours, A Woman's Place, Flash Them Bootstraps, Heave-Ho, Walmartopia, American Dream (reprise), One-Stop Salvation, The Future is Ours (reprise), These Bullets Are Freedom, Consume and American Dream (reprise), What Kind of Mother, Outside the Big Box

SETTING Act One: Madison, Wisconsin, the present; Act Two: Bentonville, Arkansas, 30 years later. Off-Broadway debut of a new musical presented in two acts. Previously played the New York International Fringe Festival in 2006.

SYNOPSIS It's Mom vs. Mart! *Walmartopia* tells the hilarious and timely tale of Vicki Latrell, a single mom and Wal-Mart employee who speaks out against her company's working conditions and finds herself and her young daughter jettisoned to 2036, into a future where Wal-Mart dominates the entire world. Yes, the musical features the singing head of Wal-Mart founder Sam Walton.

*Brennan Leath tragically passed away due to complications from diabetes on September 22, 2008. He was succeeded by DeMond B. Nason on October 10, 2008

AMERICA LoveSexDeath

Flea Theater; First Preview: August 23, 2007; Opening Night: September 6, 2007; Closed September 30, 2008; 43 performances

Created and directed by Billy the Mime; Produced by the Flea Theater (Jim Simpson, Artistic Director; Carol Ostrow, Producing Director); Set, Kyle Chepulis; Lighting, Brian Aldous; Costumes, Eleni J. Christou; Sound, Josh Higgason; Music; Additional Music, Gary Stockdale; PSM, Yvonne Perez; Graphics, David Prittie; Production Assistant, Bobby Moreno; Press, David Gersten

Performed by **Billy the Mime**

A play presented in mime without intermission

SYNOPSIS Billy the Mime has rejuvenated an art form that has been justly ridiculed due to untrained and amateur practitioners, and he has restored its ability to entertain, amuse, shock, and move an audience. *America LoveSexDeath* tackles controversial subject matter with such routines as "JFK JR. We Hardly Knew Ye," "Thomas & Sally: A Night at Monticello," "The Priest and The Altar Boy," "Terry Schiavo, Adieu," "A Day Called 9/11," "Love & Death: OJ and Nicole," "A Night with Jeffrey Dahmer, " "Virginia Tech 4/16/07" and many more.

Bradley Dean, Nikki M. James and Cheryl Freeman in Walmartopia (photo by Carol Rosegg)

EDGE

ArcLight Theatre+; First Preview: September 4, 2007; Opening Night: September 9, 2007; Closed December 16, 2007; 6 previews, 56 performances

Written and directed by Paul Alexander; Produced by The Artists Group and Torn Page Productions; Associate Producer, Lucky Penny Productions (Penny Landau); Set & Lighting, William St. John; PSM, Samantha Tella; Assistant to the Producer, Glenn Grieves; ASM, Matt Everett; House, Maya Flock; Press, Maya Public Relations, Penny Landau

CAST Sylvia Plath **Angelica Torn**

SETTING London, February 11, 1963. A solo performance play presented in two acts. Originally produced at The Actors Studio on February 11, 2003, ran a brief engagement at DR2, as well as touring the U.S., England, New Zealand and Australia with Ms. Torn.

SYNOPSIS Set on the last day of her life, Plath reflects on her life, including her early years in Massachusetts, her time at Smith College, and her 1953 suicide attempt—the subject of her autobiographical novel "The Bell Jar." *Edge* also focuses on her two children, her love/hate relationship with poet Ted Hughes and the events that led to her early death at 30.

+Closed October 9 and transferred to the Theatres at 45 Bleecker beginning October 18.

ROCK DOVES

Donaghy Theatre at the Irish Arts Center; First Preview: September 6, 2007; Opening Night: September 16, 2007; Closed October 28, 2007; 49 performances

Written by Marie Jones; Presented by the Irish Arts Center in association with Georganne Aldrich Heller and Anita Waxman; Director, Ian McElhinney; Sets, Charlie Corcoran; Lighting, Daniel Meeker; Costumes, Chris Rumery; Sound, Drew Levey; Music, Salvatore Carolei; Casting, Stanczyk/Cherpakov Casting; Fight Choreography, Curtis Billings; Dialect Coach, Stephen Gabis; Marketing, Art Meets Commerce; PSM, Nicole Press; Stage Manager, Jenny Deady; Managing Director, Brídín Murphy Mitchell; Executive Producer, Aidan Connolly; Associate Producer, Pauline Turley

CAST The Boy **Johnny Hopkins;** Knacker **Marty Maguire;** Bella **Natalie Brown;** Lillian **Tim Ruddy**

SETTING A derelict house on the fringes of a Protestant estate in inner-city Belfast, Ireland; the present, mid-July. World premiere of a new play presented in five scenes in two acts.

SYNOPSIS *Rock Doves* is the story of four colorful misfits —a knacker, an aging prostitute, a transvestite and a teenager — who rely on each other and the worlds they have created for themselves as they navigate the strange new forces of 'post-war' Northern Ireland.

THE LADY SWIMS TODAY

TADA! Theatre; First Preview: September 13, 2007; Opening Night: September 23, 2007; Closed October 21, 2007; 11 previews, 29 performances

Written by H.G. Brown; Produced by WBISI Productions; Director, Stephen Sunderlin; Set, Joseph Spirito; Costumes, Vanessa Leuck; Lighting, Brett Maughan; PSM, Joanna Leigh Jacobsen; ASM, Connie Baker; Assistant Director, Avriel Hillman; Fight Choreographer, Jim Bender; General Manager, Tom Smedes; Photographer, Roger Gaess; Web & Print Design, Keith Paul; Press, Jim Randolph

CAST George Santos **Gordon Silva;** Eddie Hajazi **Robert Funaro;** Harley Davis **Jack Rodgerson;** Mal Peters **Rob Sheridan;** Beverly Sharon Peters **Vivenne Leheny;** Joyce Stevens **Kate Udall;** Alice Bender **Kelli K Barnett**

SETTING A Tuesday and Wednesday in August, 1994. The barroom of the Carney Hook Marina Motel, on the Eastern Shore of the Chesapeake Bay. Off-Broadway premiere of a mystery/thriller presented in two acts. Previously presented at the Richmond Shepard Theatre February 7–18, 2007.

SYNOPSIS Four would-be criminals are cooking up the heist of a lifetime. Eddie has a plan to steal two million dollars off a boat in the Chesapeake Bay—now he just needs a crew to pull it off. But when these schemers and dreamers collide with three tough and sultry broads, the course to a fortune is threatened by more than bad weather.

Marty Maguire and Johnny Hopkins in Rock Doves *(photo by Jaisen Crockett)*

LOVE LETTERS

New World Stages; September 24, 2007; 1 performance

Written by A.R. Gurney; Produced by Opening Act (Julia Kamin, Founder and Executive Director; Suzy Myers, Creative and Development Director; Meg McInerney, Creative and Development Associate); Director, Michael Mastro; Associate Director, Joe Danisi; Stage Manager, Allison Sommer; Miss Peter's Assistant, Patty Saccente; Production Associates, Nancy Ann Chatty, Dena Douglas, Jared Gertner, Ben Gettinger, Britt Shubow, Matt Walters; Mentoring Artists, Andrew McCarthy, Kristen Bell; Press, Judy Katz Public Relations

CAST Melissa Gardner **Bernadette Peters;** Andrew Makepeace Ladd III **John Dossett**

A staged reading of the play presented without intermission.

SYNOPSIS *Love Letters* chronicles a relationship solely through the written correspondence of two people, whose poignantly funny friendship and ill-fated romance takes them from second grade through adolescence and then into maturity and middle age. This one-night-only event was a benefit for Opening Act, an innovative nonprofit that provides free after-school theater programming to New York City's most under-served public high schools.

CELIA: The Life and Music of Celia Cruz

New World Stages – Stage 2; First Preview: August 8, 2007; Opening Night: September 26, 2007; Closed May 25, 2008; 25 previews, 269 performances

Book by Carmen Rivera & Candido Tirado; Produced by Henry Cardenas & David Maldonado; Director, Jaime Azpilicueta; Choreography/Production Supervisor, Maria

Xiomara Laugart in Celia (photo by Erica Rojas)

Torres; Orchestrations/Arrangements/Music Director, Isidro Infante; Set, Narelle Sissons; Lighting, Sarah Sidman; Costumes Haydée Morales; Projections, Jan Hartley; Sound, Bernard Fox; Hair/Makeup, Ruth Sanchez; PSM, Elis C. Arroyo; Casting, Orpheus Group; Production Manager/Creative Consultant, Peter Dean; Associate Producer, Gerry Fojo; Executive Producer, Daddy Yankee; Company Manager, Michael Heitzler; General Manager, Cesa Entertainment; Stage Manager, Ben Folstein; Associate Production Manager, Monica Moore; Associate Director, Daniel Garcia Chávez; Technical Director, Adam Lang; Props, Andrea Steiner; Translations, Cándido Tirado, Carmen Rivera; Press, O+M Co., Rick Miramontez, Richard Hillman

CAST Celia Cruz **Xiomara Laugart;** Pedro Knight **Modesto Lacén;** Nurse **Pedro Capó;** Woman **Selenis Leyva;** Ollita/Assitant **Annissa Gathers;** Simon/Rogelio Martinez/Ralph Mercado/others **Elvis Nolasco;** Announcer/Theatre-Club Manager/Friend-Amigo/Tito Puente/Johnny Pacheco/others **Wilson Mendieta;** Ensemble **Sunilda Caraballo, Sekou McMiller;** Swings: **Grizel "Chachi" Del Vallee, Sekou McMiller**

UNDERSTUDIES Annisa Gathers (Celia, Woman), Sunilda Caraballo (Woman), Elvis Nolasco (Pedro Knight), Wilson Mendieta (Nurse), Sonja Perryman (all female roles)

CELIA'S BAND Isidro Infante (Music Director/piano), Diomedes Matos (bass), Anderson Quintero (Timbal and percussion), Carlos Padron (Congas and percussion), Nelson González (Trés and Bongos), Nelson Jaime (trumpet/keyboards), Julie Acosta (trumpet)

MUSICAL NUMBERS Toro Mata, Drume Negrita/Canto Lucumi, Cumbachero, Caramelos, Burundanga/El Yerbero Moderno/Que Bueno Baila Usted, Mexico Lindo, Cao Cao Maní Picao, Tu Voz, Drume Negrita, La Guarachera, Bemba Colorá, Isadora Duncan/Encantigo/Guantanamera, Usted Abusó, Las Caras Lindas, Quimbara, Cúcala, Canto a la Habana, Dos Jueyes, Cuba, Soy Antillana/La Dicha Mia/Cuando Volverás, Celi's Oye Como Va, El Guabá, La Negra Tiene Tumbao, Yo Viviré, No Habra-Final, La Vida es un Carnaval

World premiere of a new musical presented in two acts.

SYNOPSIS *Celia* is a biographical musical about the life of the Latin music icon Celia Cruz (featuring her music) as seen through the eyes of her husband, Pedro Knight. From her humble beginnings in Santo Suarez, Cuba to international stardom, Celia lived a mythic life full of triumphs and tribulations, and overcame great obstacles with courage and grace.

THREE MO' TENORS

Little Shubert Theatre; First Preview: September 12, 2007; Opening Night: September 27, 2007; Closed January 27, 2008; 126 performances

Conceived, directed and choreographed by Marion J. Caffey; Produced by Willette Murphy Klausner; Music Director, Keith Burton; Sets, Michael Carnahan; Lighting, Richard Winkler; Costumes, Gail Cooper-Hecht; Sound, Domonic Sack; Musical Supervision/Arranger/Orchestrations, Joseph Joubert; Additional Arrangements, Danny Holgate, Michael McElroy; Music Director, Keith Burton; Casting, Barry Moss and Bob Kale; Production Manager, Wanza A&E Management/Curtis V. Hodge; Audience Development, Walker International Communications Group, Inc.; Marketing, Leanne Schanzer Promotions; PSM, Roumel Reaux; ASM, Catherine Peoples; General Management, Maria Productions/Maria Di Dia; Associate General Manager/Tour General Management, Bryan K.L. Byrd, III; Opera Consultant, Michael Recchiuti; Press,

Keith Sherman & Associates, Scott Klein, DJ Martin, Glenna Freedman, Brett Oberman

CAST (cast A) **James N. Berger Jr., Duane A. Moody, Victor Robertson**; (cast 1) **Kenneth D. Alston Jr., Ramone Diggs, Phumzile Sojola;** Standby **Sean Miller**

MUSICIANS Keith Burton (Conductor/piano), Emi Yabuno (keyboard 1), Etienne Lytle (keyboard 2), Carl Carter (bass), Steve Williams (drums)

MUSICAL NUMBERS La donna è mobile, Questa o quella, De miei bollenti spiriti, Ombra mai fû, I Hear an Army, Le Rêve, Ah mes amis, The Three Mo' Way, Let the Good Times Roll, Bring Him Home, Make Them Hear You, I've Gotta Be Me, Being Alive, Who Can I Turn To, Azure Te, This Is the Moment, Rain, South African Medley: Circle of Life/Dali Wam, Minnie the Moocher, Queen Medley: Bohemian Rhapsody/I Want It All/We Are the Champions/We Will Rock You, To Ray, With Love: Don't Set Me Free/Hit the Road Jack/Georgia on My Mind, Today I Sing the Blues, Azure Te, Spain, I Believe in You and Me, Superstar/Let's Get It On, Soul Medley: Love Train/My Girl/Stop Look Listen/Midnight Train to Georgia/Heaven Must Be Missing an Angel, New School Medley: Yeah/If I Ain't Got You/Ordinary People/Yeah, Spiritual Medley: Lord How Come Me Here/Hush Somebody's Calling My Name/Guide My Feet, Noways Tired, Glorious, How Sweet It Is to Be Loved by You, Make Them Hear You (reprise)

New York premiere of a theatrical concert presented in two acts.

SYNOPSIS Marion J. Caffey's *Three Mo' Tenors*, is an exciting staged concert featuring three amazingly versatile African American tenors. These tenors bring the house down with thrilling performances of Opera, Broadway, Jazz, Gospel, Soul, Spirituals, and the Blues. The program begins with Verdi, but soon the music of Motown, Ray Charles and Usher has the tenors grooving on the stage and the audience dancing in the aisles.

NIGHT OVER TAOS

Theater for the New City; First Preview: September 20, 2007; Opening Night: October 1, 2007; Closed October 20, 2007; 29 performances

Written by Maxwell Anderson; Produced by INTAR Theatre (Eduardo Machado, Artistic Director; John McCormack, Executive Director; Alina Troyano, Associate Artistic Director); Director, Estelle Parsons; Set, Peter Larkin; Costumes, Michael Krass; Original Music, Yukio Tsuji; Lighting, Howard Thies; Sound, Erich Bechtel; Props, Stephanie Tucci; Production Manager, Kryssy Wright; Company Manager, Michael Alifanz; Marketing, Walker International Communications; Casting, Judy Bowman; PSM, Alan Fox; ASM Hannah Woodward; Vocals, Alfonso Cid; Assistant to the Director, Mike Roche; Technical Director, Sam Ryan; Press, Richard Kornberg & Associates

James N. Berger Jr., Victor Robertson, Duane A. Moody in Three Mo' Tenors *(photo by Aaron Epstein)*

CAST Maria **Veronica Reyes;** Nuna **Maria Helan;** Conchita **Yaremis Felix;** Raquel **Sibyl Santiago;** Carlotta **Irma-Estel LaGuerre;** Cristina **Sarah Nina Hayon;** Graso/Mateo **Emilio Delgado;** Dona Veri **Miriam Colon Valle;** Valeria **Hortencia Colorado;** Dona Josefa **Mercedes Herrero;** Father Martinez **Shawn Elliott;** Diana **Cheryl Lynn Bowers;** Diego **Ricardo Valdez;** Federico **Bryant Mason;** Narciso **David Anzuelo;** Captain Molyneaux **James Gale;** Don Hermano **Liam Torres;** Don Miguel **Juan Luis Acevedo;** Felipe **Mickey Solis;** Pablo Montoya **Jack Landron;** Andros **Ron Moreno;** Don Fernanado **Marshall Factora;** 2nd American **Mike Roche;** 3rd American **Michael Frederic**

SETTING The Great Hall of the Montoya Hacienda in Taos, New Mexico, 1847. Revival of the play in three acts presented with two intermissions. Originally produced on Broadway at the 48th Street Theatre by The Group Theatre, March 9, 1932.

SYNOPSIS During the US-Mexican War, Mexico lost nearly half of its territory, including what is now the state of New Mexico. *Night Over Taos* is the true story about a Mexican freedom fighter, Pablo Montoya, who in 1847 led a bloody and ultimately futile siege to protect New Mexico from being ceded to the United States.

THE CHILDREN OF VONDERLY

East 13th Street Theater; First Preview: September 22, 2007; Opening Night: October 4, 2007; Closed October 21, 2007; 34 performances

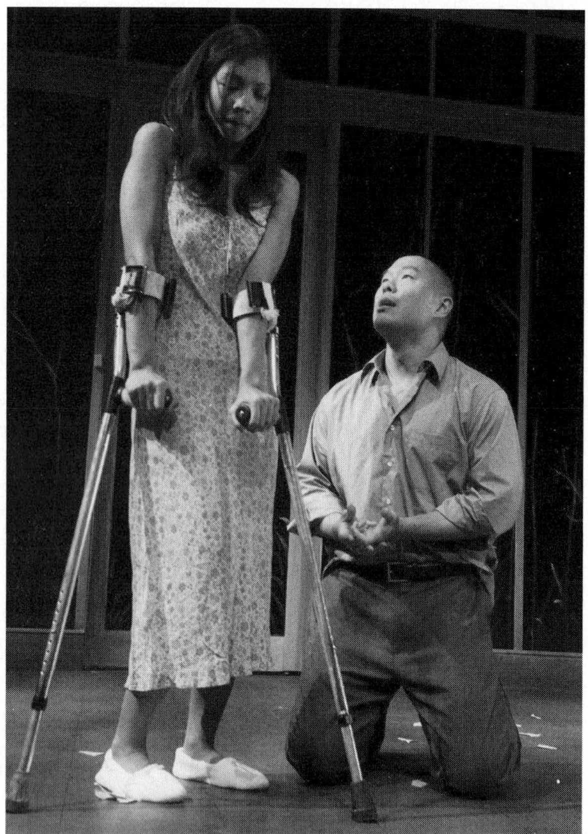

Maureen Sebastian and Hoon Lee in The Children of Vonderly *(photo by Matt Zugale)*

Written by Lloyd Suh; Produced by the Ma-Yi Theater Company (Jorge Z. Ortoll, Executive Director; Ralph B. Peña, Artistic Director) and Suzette Porte; Director, Ralph B. Peña; Set, Sarah Lambert; Costumes, Maiko Matsushima; Lighting, Josh Bradford; Sound, Fabian Obispo; PSM, Mary Leach; ASM, Jessica Percharsky; Production Manager, Gregg Bellón/ Productions Consolidated; Fight Consultant, Qui Nguyen; Assistant Tech Director/Carpenter, Kevin Bartlett; Associate Sound, Bill Grady; Props, Sarah Bird; Press, Sam Rudy Media Relations

CAST Sasha Vonderly **Jackie Chung;** Norma Vonderly **Lynn Cohen;** Jerry Vonderly **William Jackson Harper;** Noah Vonderly **Hoon Lee;** Benjamin Vonderly **Stephen Jutras;** Abraham Vonderly **Shawn Randall**; Georgia Vonderly **Maureen Sebastian**; Chuck Halberstreith **Paco Tolson;** Understudy **Jane Strauss**

SETTING A cloistered mansion estate in Indianapolis, Indiana, the present. World premiere of a new drama presented in two acts.

SYNOPSIS There's never a dull moment in the Vonderly household. Led by a headstrong Jewish matriarch, this unconventional multi-ethnic family of adopted and disabled children band together after a crisis threatens to rip them apart. Bound by his wheelchair and burdened by family obligations, oldest brother Jerry looks for ways to balance his mother's outlandish expectations and his own dreams of a 'normal' life outside the family's anything-but-traditional home.

GREETINGS FROM YORKVILLE

SoHo Playhouse; First Preview: September 25, 2007; Opening Night: October 4, 2007; Closed November 4, 2007; 48 performances

Music and lyrics by Robert Grusecki, lyrics and book by Anya Turner; Produced by Who Knows Productions and SoHo Playhouse (Darren Lee Cole and Faith Mulvihill); Director, Thommie Walsh★; Set, Jesse Poleshuck; Costumes, Dona Granata; Lighting, Natasha Katz; Sound, David Stollings; Illustrator, Robert Risko; Stage Manager, Jillian Zeman; General Manager, Brent Peek Productions; Company Manager, Shaun Garrett; Hair and Makeup, Nathan Johnson; Press Shirley Herz & Associates, Dan Demello

Performed by **Anya Turner** and **Robert Grusecki**

MUSICAL NUMBERS Greetings From Yorkville, Secret Song, Ordinary People, Robert's Song, Showcases, It's Called a Piano, The Farmer and His Wife, Showcases (reprise), So You're Not From New York, What a Lovely Thing, Destiny, Clara Drum, Musical Comedy Dream, I Know You Too Well, Not As I Was/ All Out of Tune, Happy, Just Lucky I Guess, The Road, Hole-in-the-Head Blues, Handle Me With Care, Iowa Summer, Greetings From Yorkville (reprise), Life Is Good

SETTING The present and everything leading up to it; an apartment in a Yorkville, a television studio in New Jersey, an NYC Cabaret on Restaurant Row, and a supper club in Peoria, Illinois. Off-Broadway premiere of a new musical presented in two acts. A one-act version of the musical was initially presented at the Woodstock Fringe Festival in September 2004 and workshopped as a two-act musical at the 78th Street Theatre Lab in June 2005. In 2007 the show received a developmental reading at the York Theatre.

SYNOPSIS Lovers, collaborators, partners in all things, a couple of songwriters from the Midwest arrive in the Big City. From their fifth-floor walkup in Yorkville, they set out to navigate the turbulent waters of show business. Whether it's writing special material, recording CD's, or creating full-length musicals, the pair constantly strives to find new ways to get their songs out there.

*Thommie Walsh, who had directed the initial two versions of the show, was slated to direct this production but passed away in June of 2007. He asked his longtime friend and associate Baayork Lee to fulfill his vision for this run of the show.

THE RISE OF DOROTHY HALE

Theatre at St. Luke's; First Preview: September 9, 2007; Opening Night: October 4, 2007; Closed January 27, 2008; 12 previews, 147 performances

Written by Myra Bairstow; Produced by Edmund Gaynes and Aridyne Productions LLC; Director, Pamela Hall+; Set, Josh Iacovelli; Lighting, Graham Kindred; Costumes, Rebecca J. Bernstein; PSM, C.J. Thom (succeeded by Jana Lynn); Casting, Judy Henderson; ASM, Richard T. Lester (succeeded by Nicholas Martin-Smith); Video and Sound Production, Caltana Productions; Hair/Makeup, J. Jared Janas & Rob Greene; General Management, Jessimeg Productions; Associate General Manager, Julia Beardsley; Advertising, Eliran Murphy Group; Press, David Gersten & Associates

Michael Badalucco, Sarah Wynter, and Sarita Choudhury in The Rise of Dorothy Hale *(photo by Carol Rosegg)*

CAST Frida Kahlo **Sarita Choudhury**[*1]; Mitch Davenport **Patrick Boll;** Clare Boothe Luce **Sarah Wynter**[*2]; Dorothy Hale **Laura Koffman;** Frank Deluca **Michael Badalucco**[*3]; Harry Hopkins **Mark La Mura**[*4]

SETTING Fall 1938; a political rally and Dorothy Hale's apartment at the Hampshire House in New York City. Off-Broadway premiere of a new mystery play presented in two acts.

SYNOPSIS On October 21, 1938, Dorothy Hale, the 33-year old widow of muralist Gardner Hale, plunged to her death sixteen stories from her apartment window at the Hampshire House on Central Park South. Ruled a suicide, the story of Dorothy Hale has never really been thoroughly examined. Until now. *The Rise Of Dorothy Hale* explores her life and death through the creative process of Frida Kahlo and enables the contradictions in history to stand face to face. Was Dorothy Hale's death a suicide or a murder made to look like a suicide?

*Succeeded by: 1. Purva Bedi 2. Dina Ann Comolli 3. Matthew Cowles, Stuart Marshall 4. Larry Sharp

+ Pamela Hall replaced Penny Templeton as the director during previews.

THE SENSUOUS WOMAN

The Zipper Factory; First Preview: September 26, 2007; Opening Night: October 6, 2007; Closed November 17, 2007; 45 performances

Written by Margaret Cho; Presented by Westbeth Entertainment, Arnold Engelman and Chris Petrelli; Director, Randall Rapstine; Choreography, Kitty McNamee; Set, Steven Capone; Lighting, Josh Monroe; Tech Director, Production Consolidated/Gregg Bellon; Stage Manager, Jessie Boemper; Production Supervisor/Electrician, Ian Grunes

CAST Star and Host **Margaret Cho,** Los Angeles Belly Dancer and Burlesque Sensation **Princess Farhana,** Transgendered Comic **Ian Harvie,** Internationally Acclaimed Dancer and Choreographer **Ryan Heffington,** Comic actor **Liam Sullivan** (as "Kelly"), Burlesque Performer **Selene Luna,** New York Downtown Favorite **Miss Dirty Martini,** and Sketch Comedians of the Gay Mafia Comedy Troupe of West Hollywood **Diana Yanez & Kurt Hall**

Off-Broadway premiere of a stand-up, sketch comedy and burlesque variety show with dance and music performed without intermission. Previously played engagements in Los Angeles, San Francisco and Chicago.

SYNOPSIS *The Sensuous Woman* is a burlesque-style show that celebrates women's bodies. Created by and starring Margaret Cho the evening features an impressive line-up of the country's most renowned burlesque performers, along with hilarious comedy all presided over by the incomparable Margaret Cho.

THE VEILED MONOLOGUES & IS.MAN

St. Ann's Warehouse; Opening Nights: October 5 (*The Veiled Monologues*) & October 6 (*Is.Man*), 2007; Closed October 14, 2007; 7 performances each

Two plays written and directed by Adelheid Roosen; Produced

Margaret Cho and the cast of The Sensuous Woman *(photo by Carol Rosegg)*

by St. Ann's Warehouse (Susan Feldman, Artistic Director) in association with the Female Economy Foundation; Dramaturgy, Dirkje Houtman; Lighting, Geldof, Verhaart & Den Ottolander; *The Veiled Monolgues:* Set, Adelheid Roosen, Mijke de Jong; Muisc, Adelheid Roosen, Serval Okyay; Video, Titus Tiel Groenestege; English Translation, Discordia Translations; U.S. Acting Coach, Elizabeth Ingram; Research, Liesbeth Maas; *Is.Man:* Set, Harry de Dood; Composition, Boudewijn Tarenskeen; Adaptation, PARKSTUDIO Bakker/Haworth; Music, Nalin Musiki; Video, Joanneke Meester; Business Manager, Mieke Baars; Casting, Kemna Casting; Research, Emine Igdi, Ahmet Olgun, Nayat Elmarsse; Production, Janneke den Engelsen; Translation, Hans Dowit; Acting Coaches, Macteld Hauer, Annemarie Broekhuizen; Language Coaches, Dennis Krausnick, Dave Demke; Press, Blake Zidell

CAST *The Veiled Monologues*: **Oya Capelle, Nazmiye Oral, Meral Polat;** Musician: **Sercan Engin**; *Is.Man*: The Musician, The grandfather **Brader Musiki;** The Father, Cabbar **Ya ar Üstüner;** The Son, Furkan **Youssef Sjoerd Idibli;** The Dervish dancer **Oruç Sürücü**

English Language and American premieres of two plays performed in repertory, both without intermission.

SYNOPSIS *The Veiled Monologues* explores Muslim women's attitudes towards sex and sexuality from non-Muslims. *Is.Man* unveils the secretive world and complex motivations that underlie the tradition of honor killings in some Muslim societies.

JUMP

Union Square Theatre; First Preview: September 25, 2007; Opening Night: October 7, 2007; Closed July 20, 2008; 15 previews, 329 performances

Created by Yeagam Inc.; Produced by Cami Ventures LLC in association with Yegam Inc., Amuse Inc., New York Networks, Inc., and Hobijisu, LLC; Director, Chul-Ki Choi; Composer, Dong-Joon Lee; Choreography, Young-Sub Jin; Set, Tae-young Kim; Costumes, Dolsilnai Inc.; Original Lighting, Sung-Bin Lim; New York Lighting, Benjamin Pearcy; Sound, Soo-Yong Lee; Makeup, Pan Company; Comedy Director, Won-Kil Paek; Consulting Director, Jim Millan; Resident Director, Min-Seob Kim; Assistant Director, Jong-Ho Lee; General Manager, One Viking Productions/Carl Pasbjerg; International Supervision, Kyung-Ah Han; Technical Director, John H. Paull; Marketing, TMG–The Marketing Gourp; Korean Marketing, New York Networks Inc.; Executive Producer, Mark S. Maluso; Executive Producer/CEO, Yegam Inc., Kyung-Hun Kim; Martial Arts Choreography, Gye-Hwan Park; Production Supervisor, Matt Marholin; Music Consultant, Josh Heineman; Wigs and Makeup, Anna Hoffman; Stage Manager, Adam Norris; Associate Technical Director, Ron Nilson; Press, O+M Co, Rick Miramontez, Molly Barnett

CAST Old Man **Woon-Yong Lee** or **Joo-Sun Kim** or **Dong-Kyung Kim;** Grandfather **Cheol-Ho Lim** or **Han-Chang Lim** or **Sun-Gi Jung;** Father **Cheol-Ho Lim** or **Joo-Sun Kim;** Mother **Kyung-Ae Hong** or **Yeon-Jeong Park** or **Mi-Hwa Sung;** Uncle **Han-Chang Lim** or **Young-Jo Choi;** Daughter **Hee-Jeong Hwang** or **Kyung-Ae Hong** or **Yeon-Jeong Gong;** Son-in-Law **Hun-Young Jo** or **Dong-Kyun Kim;** Burglar 1 **Yun-Gab Hong** or **Hun-Young Jo** or **Young-Jo Choi;** Burglar 2 **Seung-Youl Lee** or **Tae-Sung Kim**

American premiere of a theatrical performance piece performed without intermission.

SYNOPSIS *Jump*, the high flying, internationally acclaimed new martial arts theater event, comes to New York following wildly successful engagements all around the world. The nonverbal Korean extravaganza brings the combination of slapstick comedy, acrobatics and martial arts to the stage, for the first time ever in live performance, in a highly unique theater spectacle that has been described as "Jackie Chan meets Charlie Chaplin."

WHEN THE MESSENGER IS HOT

59E59 Theater B; First Preview: October 3, 2007; Opening Night: October 7, 2007; Closed October 28, 2007; 31 performances

Written by Laura Eason, adapted from the book by Elizabeth Crane; Presented by the Steppenwolf Theatre Company (Martha Lavey, Artistic Director; David Hawkanson, Executive

Cheol-Ho Lim (in air) and Young-Jo Choi in Jump *(photo by Carol Rosegg)*

Director); Director, Jessica Thebus; Set, Marcus Stephens; Lighting, J.R. Lederle; Costumes, Debbie Baer; Sound, Gregor Mortis; Stage Manager, Jenny Deady; ASM, Terri Kohler; Casting, Erica Daniels; Press, Karen Greco

CAST Josie 1 **Kate Arrington;** Josie 2 **Lauren Katz;** Josie 3 **Amy Warren;** Mom **Molly Regan;** Man **Coburn Goss**

World premiere of a new play presented without intermission. Presented as part of the Go Chicago! Festival at 59E59. Developed at Steppenwolf as part of the First Look Repertory of New Work Series.

SYNOPSIS Three years after Josie's mother died, no one expects her to telephone from a bus station in North Dakota. This smart and slyly comic study of love and letting go is an insightful look at the disparity between what you expect and what is delivered.

VENGEANCE

Cherry Lane Studio Theatre; First Preview: October 4, 2007; Opening Night: October 9, 2007; Closed December 1, 2007; 4 previews, 40 performances

Five short plays: *Squalor* by Gina Gionfriddo; *Skin & Bones* by Julian Sheppard, *Giftbox* by Francine Volpe; *Rats* by Ron Fitzgerald; *Specter* by Neena Beber; Produced by the stageFARM Theatre Company (Carrie Shaltz, Founder and Executive Director; Alex Kilgore, Artistic Director); Directors, Ari Edelson & Alex Kilgore; Set, John McDermott; Lighting, Nicole Pearce; Sound, John Kilgore; PSM, Jillian Oliver; ASM, Steve Henry; Production Coordinator, Christine Renee Miller; Casting, Calleri Casting; Press, O+M Co, Philip Carrubba

CAST *Squalor*: Pete **David Wilson Barnes;** Marnie **Rebecca Henderson;** Mike **David Ross;** *Giftbox*: A **Lisa Joyce;** C **Rebecca Henderson;** *Skin & Bones*: Alex **Michael Mosley;** Jesse **Lisa Joyce;** *Rats*: Tom **Michael Mosley;** Ray **David Ross;** *Specter*: Lana **Lisa Joyce;** Phil **David Wilson Barnes**

World premiere of five one-act plays presented without intermission.

SYNOPSIS The plays in *Vengeance* explore mankind's current cycle of retribution.

ELECTRA

New York City Center; Opening Night: October 10, 2007; Closed October 14, 2007; 6 performances

National Theatre of Greece (Yannis Houvardas, Artistic Director) production of the play by Sophocles, translated by Minos Volanakis; Director, Peter Stein; Set and Costumes, Dionissis Fotopoulos; Lighting, Jady Weideman; Music Director/Composer, Alessando Nidi; Choreography, Lisa Tsolaki; Text/Translation Editor, Petros Markaris; Stage Text Editing, Peter Stein and the cast; Press, Richard Kornberg and Associates

CAST Electra **Stefania Goulioti;** Orestes **Apostolis Totskias;** Clytemnestra **Karyofylia Karabeti;** Aegisthus **Lazaros Georgakopoulos;** Pylades **Miltos Sotiriadis;** Tutor **Yannis Fertis;** Chrysothemis **Kora Karvouni;** Chorus **Margarita Amarantidi, Errika Bigiou, Katerina Daskalaki, Kika Georgiou, Ioanna Zoi Karavasili, Irini Kirmizaki, Christina Maxouri, Lida Maniatiatakou, Marili Milia, Yota Militsi, Georgina Palaiothodorou, Maria Saltiri, Pinelopi Sergounioti, Mara Vlachak**

Revival of the classic drama presented in modern Greek with English subtitles without intermission.

SYNOPSIS The National Theatre of Greece marks its sixth U.S. engagement in the last twelve years with this production of the classic and quintessential revenge drama. Electra is frenzied to avenge her father's death, which not only reveals her character, but serves as a metaphor for the enormous breadth of pain that the human heart can withstand.

NONE OF THE ABOVE

Lion Theatre on Theatre Row; First Preview: September 25, 2007; Opening Night: October 10, 2007; Closed November 25, 2007; 16 previews, 54 performances

Halley Feiffer and Adam Green in None of the Above *(photo by Carol Rosegg)*

Written by Jenny Lyn Bader; Premiere production of the South Ark Stage Company (Rhoda Herrick, Producing/ Artistic Director); Director, Julie Kramer; Set, Lauren Helpern; Lighting, Graham Kindred; Costumes, Melissa Schlactmeyer; Sound, Joshua Higgason; PSM, Sarah Butke; Casting, Stephanie Klapper; General Management, Martian Entertainment/Carl D. White; Company Manager, Scott DelaCruz; Voice Over, Amy Wilson; Advertising, Eliran Murphy Group; Press, Sam Rudy Media Relations, Dale Heller

CAST Jamie **Halley Feiffer;** Clark **Adam Green**

SETTING The Upper East Side, November-May. Off-Broadway premiere of a play presented in eight scenes in two acts.

SYNOPSIS *None of the Above* is a comedy about privilege, addiction, transcending stereotypes…and getting into Princeton. What happens when a high-priced SAT tutor is hired to coach a spoiled Upper East Side girl? When both of their futures depend on her success, will she surprise everyone and rise to the occasion or will she fail to make the grade?

THE HG WELLS SCIENCE FICTION FESTIVAL

59E59 Theater C; Opening Night: October 11, 2007; Closed November 4, 2007; 34 performances

Written by H.G. Wells, adapted and directed by Dan Bianchi; Presented by RadioTheatre (Dan Bianchi, Creator; Cynthia Bianchi, Executive Producer); Composer/Sound Design, Dan Bianchi; Stage Manager/Lighting, Lauren Parrish; Sound Engineer, Wes Shippee; Press, Karen Greco.

CAST **Elizabeth Burke, Peter Iasillo, Tom Lacey, Jerry Lazar, Patrick O'Connor, Sarah Stephens, Cash Tilton, Nicholas Warren-Gray, Frank Zilinyi**

Four Radio dramas presented in repertory without intermission.

SYNOPSIS For the first time in American theatre, RadioTheatre presents all 4 Sci-Fi classics in repertory adapted and directed for the stage by Dan Bianchi from H.G. Wells' prophetic novels *The Time Machine*, *The Invisible Man*, *The War Of The Worlds* and *The Island Of Dr. Moreau*. On Halloween weekend all four dramas were presented in an all-day marathon format.

Cash Tilton, Patrick Alberty and Sarah Stephens in The HG Wells Science Fiction Festival *(photo by Peter Iasillo)*

A GLANCE AT NEW YORK

Axis Theatre; Opening Night: October 12, 2007; Closed November 17, 2008; 13 performances (Fridays and Saturdays)

Written by Benjamin Baker; Conceived and produced by Axis Company (Randy Sharp, Artistic Director; Jeffrey Resnick, Executive Producer); Director, Randy Sharp; Lighting, David Zeffren; Sound/Music Production and Arrangements, Steve Fontaine; Costumes, Lee Harper, Matthew Simonelli; Stage Manager, Edward Terhune; ASM, Marc Palmieri; Assistant Lighting, Amy Harper; Sound Operator, David Balutanski; Graphics, Ethan Crenson; Producing Director, Brian Barnhart; Production Manager, Ian Tooley; Press, Spin Cycle/Ron Lasko

CAST Jake **Brian Barnhart;** Mary **Marlene Berner;** Mike (alternate) **Regina Betancourt;** Mike **David Crabb;** Harry Gordon **George Demas;** Lize **Britt Genelin;** Jane **Laurie Kilmartin;** Mr. & Mrs. Morton/Major Gates **Edgar Oliver;** Mose (alternate) **Marc Palmieri;** Mose **Jim Sterling;** George Parsells **Ian Tooley**

Regina Betancourt, Laurie Kilmartin, Edgar Oliver, Jim Sterling, Britt Genelin and Ian Tooley in A Glance at New York *(photo by Dixie Sheridan)*

SETTING 1848, New York City. Off-Broadway premiere of a revival of a melodrama/vaudeville play presented without intermission. Originally produced in 1848. This version was workshopped in 2003 and played the Edinburgh Fringe Festival in 2007.

SYNOPSIS *A Glance at New York* is set during a dangerous and raw period in New York City history. The play is an unmitigated conglomeration of vulgarity and illiteracy following a burly firefighter named Big Mose. Known4 as the toughest man in the nation's toughest city, Mose spends much of his time beating whoever is in his path before rushing off to rescue a screaming innocent from a burning tenement.

MINIMUM WAGE

Theatres at 45 Bleecker – The Green Room; First Preview: September 28, 2007; Opening Night: October 20, 2007; Closed December 15, 2007; 13 previews, 30 performances

Written by Charlie and Jeff LaGreca, music by Sean Altman, Charlie and Jeff LaGreca, additional material by Mike Gribbin and Rob Utesh; Produced by the LaGrecca Brothers; Director, Guy Stroman; Musical Director, Will Bryan; Movement, Scott Rinc; Set and Lighting, Ian Grunes; Costumes, Daniel James; Sound, Marty Gasper; Arrangements, Warren Bloom; PSM, John Michael Crotty; Press, The Karpel Group

CAST Bradbury **Bill Caleo;** Hux **Jeff Lagreca;** Orewell **Charlie LaGreca;** Piercy **Elena Meulener;** Titus **Tony Daussat**

SETTING The Happy Burger Training College. A musical presented without intermission.

SYNOPSIS *Minimum Wage* is an inventive, insane and delightful blend of a cappella, sketch comedy and improv musical in which five hapless staffers of a Big Brother-type fast food chain attempt to initiate new trainees (the audience) into the wonders of Hamburgerology. Working their way from the bottom all the way to the middle, these underachieving fast-food employees spend their days experiencing psychopathic French fry hallucinations and the occasional sci-fi spatula battle.

DIE MOMMIE DIE!

New World Stages – Stage 1; First Preview: October 9, 2007; Opening Night: October 21, 2007; Closed January 13, 2008; 12 previews, 97 performances

Written by Charles Busch; Produced by Daryl Roth and Bob Boyett; Director, Carl Andress; Original Music, Lewis Flinn; Charles Bush's Costumes, Michael Bottari and Ronald Case; Set, Michael Anania; Lighting, Ben Stanton; Costumes, Jessica Jahn; Sound System, Ken Hypes; Wigs, Katherine Carr; Projections, Chris Kateff; Graphics, B.T. Whitehill; Marketing, The Karpel Group; Casting, Mark Simon; Associate Producers, Elyse Pasquale, Tim Levy; General Manager, Adam Hess; PSM, Donald William Myers; Production Manager, Travis Walker; Assistant Director, Brian Swasey; Fight Coordinator, Jedediah Schultz; ASM, Andrew Haver; Fight Captain, Van Hansis; Props, Amelia Freeman-Lynde; Press, The Publicity Office, Jeremy Shaffer, Marc Thibodeau, Michael Borowski, Matt Fasano

CAST Bootsie Carp **Kristine Nielsen;** Edith Sussman **Ashley Morris;** Tony Parker **Chris Hoch;** Angela Arden **Charles Busch;** Sol Sussman **Bob Ari;** Lance Sussman **Van Hansis;** Standby: **Melinda Helfrich** (Bootsie/Edith)

Van Hansis, Charles Busch, Chris Hoch, Bob Ari and Kristine Nielsen in Die Mommie Die! *(photo by Carol Rosegg)*

SETTING 1967, Beverly Hills, California. Off-Broadway premiere of a new comedy noir presented without intermission. Originally presented in Los Angeles in 1999, and subsequently a film in 2003 starring Busch, Jason Priestly, Natasha Lyonne, Frances Conroy, and Philip Baker Hall. A staged reading benefit for The Actors Fund was performed at the Hudson Theatre June 19, 2006.

SYNOPSIS Angela Arden, a fallen pop diva trapped in a hateful marriage to film producer Sol Sussman, is desperate to find happiness with her younger lover, Tony Parker. Angela gruesomely murders her husband with the aid of a poisoned suppository. In a plot that reflects Greek tragedy as well as Hollywood kitsch, Angela's manipulative daughter, Edith, convinces her 'emotionally disturbed' brother, Lance, that together they must avenge their father's death by killing their mother.

FUERZABRUTA

Daryl Roth Theatre; First Preview: October 11, 2007; Opening Night: October 24, 2007; 14 previews, 254 performances as of May 31, 2008

Created and directed by Diqui James; Produced by Live Nation Artists Events Group, Fuerzabruta, Ozono, and David Binder; Composer/Musical Director, Gaby Kerpel; Lighting, Edi Pampin; Sound, Hernan Nupieri; Costumes, Andrea Mattio; Automation, Alberto Figueiras; General Coordinator, Fabio D'Aquila; Production, Agustina James; Technical Director, Alejandro Garcia; Marketing, Eric Schnall; Casting, James Calleri; Set-up Technical Supervisor, Bradley Thompson; General Manager, Laura Kirspel; PSM, Jeff Benish; Production Coordinator/ASM, E. Cameron Holsinger; Special Effects, Rick Sordelet; Press, The Karpel Group, Bridget Klapinski

CAST **Freddy Bosche, Hallie Bulleit, Daniel Case, Michael Hollick, John Hartzell, Joshua Kobak, Gwyneth Larsen, Tamara Levinson, Rose Mallare, Brooke Miyasaki, Jon Morris, Jason Novak, Marlyn Ortiz, Kepani Salgado-Ramos**

U.S. premiere of a theatrical experience piece with music presented without intermission. Originally presented in Buenos Aries, and subsequently in Lisbon, London, and Bogata.

SYNOPSIS The creators of the long running hit *De La Guarda* push the boundaries of theatrical creativity, motivation and innovation in their new work featuring a non-stop collision of dynamic music, visceral emotion, and kinetic aerial imagery. *Fuerzabruta* breaks free from the confines of spoken language and theatrical convention as both performers and audience are immersed in an environment that floods the senses, evoking pure visceral emotion in a place where individual imagination soars.

BLACK WATCH

St. Ann's Warehouse; First Preview: October 20, 2007; Opening Night: October 26, 2007; Closed November 11, 2007; 5 previews, 18 performances

Written by Gregory Burke; Presented by the National Theatre of Scotland (Vicky Featherstone, Artistic Director) and St. Ann's Warehouse (Susan Feldman, Artistic Director) in association with Affinity Company Theater; Director, John Tiffany; Associate Directors, Steven Hoggett (movement), Davey Anderson (music); Sets, Laura Hopkins; Costumes, Jessica Brettle; Lighting, Colin Grenfell; Video, Leo Warner and Mark Grimmer for Fifty Nine Prods.; Company Stage Manager, Carrie Hutcheon; Deputy Stage Manager, Sarah Alford-Smith; ASM, Fiona Kennedy; Casting, Anne Henderson; For St. Ann's: Finance, Alex Berg; External Affairs, Marilynn Donini; Marketing, Bill Updegraff; Development, Inga J. Glodowski; Production Manager, Owen Hughes; Company Manager, Keren-Or Reiss; Technical Director, Bill Kennedy; Production Coordinator, Aaron Rosenblum; Master Electrician, Christopher Heilman; Press, Blake Zidell & Associates

CAST Macca **David Colvin**; Stewarty **Ali Craig**; Fraz **Emun Elliott**; Kenzie **Ryan Fletcher**; Officer **Jack Fortune**; Writer/Sergeant **Paul Higgins**; Rossco **Henry Pettigrew**; Nabsy **Nabil Stuart;** Cammy **Paul Rattray**; Granty **Jordan Young**

The cast of the National Theatre of Scotland's Black Watch *(photo by PA)*

New York premiere of a new play presented without intermission.

SYNOPSIS *Black Watch* follows the disassembling of Scotland's most esteemed regiment over the course of its final tour in Iraq, written from the personal testimonies of ten men on the ground. *Black Watch* reveals what it really means to be part of the War on Terror and what it means to make the journey home again. Lyrical and loaded with testosterone, the production makes powerful and inventive use of movement, music and song to create a visceral, complex and urgent piece of theater.

CHUCKLEBALL: JAILHOUSE JOCKS

Snapple Theater Center; First Preview: October 24, 2007; Opening Night: October 26, 2007; Closed December 30, 2007; 44 performances

Co-written/directed and produced by Jason Goldstein, co-written/directed by Ian Nemser; Music Director/Pianist, Meg Zervoulis; Production & Stage Manager, Brad Resnick; Company Manager, Mike Poreda; Wigs, Erika Smith; Production Consultant, Kenny Goldstein; Comedy Consultant, Aly Friedman; Production Assistants, Chris Baron, Arielle Brettler, Lisa Smith, Rachel Wolkowitz; Press, Evan Ross Associates (theatrical), Marty Appel Public Relations (sports)

CAST **Katey Daniel, Noah DeBiase, Mike Mitchell Jr., Justin Senense**

New York premiere of a sports comedy/musical review presented without intermission.

SYNOPSIS In the style of *Forbidden Broadway* and *The Capital Steps, Chuckleball* lampoons the foibles, fumbles and felonies of today's sports headlines: O.J. Simpson's sports memorabilia caper, Michael Vick's dog-fighting fiasco and Isaiah Thomas' sexual harassment hullabaloo are just a few of the stories that receive a parody pounding in this face-paced romp from the locker room to the court room.

CROSSING BROOKLYN

Connelly Theatre; First Preview: October 19, 2007; Opening Night: October 28, 2007; Closed November 18, 2007; 9 previews, 22 performances

Music by Jenny Giering, book and lyrics by Laura Harrington; Presented by Transport Group (Jack Cummings III, Artistic Director); Director, Jack Cummings III; Set, Sandra Goldmark; Costumes, Shana Albery; Lighting, R. Lee Kennedy; Sound, Michael Rasbury; Choreography, Scott Rink; Orchestrations, Mary-Mitchell Campbell; Music Director, Brian J. Nash; Casting, Nora Brennan; Dramaturgy, Adam Perlaman; PSM, Wendy Patten; Press, Richard Kornberg & Associates

CAST Kevin **J. Bradley Bowers**; Des **Jenny Fellner**, Madeline **Blythe Gruda;** Olive **Susan Lehman**; AJ **Bryce Ryness**; Travis **Clayton Dean Smith;** Jimmy **Ken Triwush**; Beryl **Kate Weiman;** Bobby **Jason F. Williams**

MUSICIANS Brian J. Nash (Conductor/piano), Summer Boggess (cello), Arnold F. Gottlieb (bass), Charles Kiger (percussion), Laurent Medelgi (guitar)

MUSICAL NUMBERS Opening; Every Day a New Day; Everything's Gonna Be All Right; Over the Edge/Can't Breathe; I Think About It All the Time; Off the Map/The Wrong Guy; Turn to Me; If I Could Escape; Weed, Weed, Weed; Imagine That; Over the Edge/Scraps of Paper; Everybody Says; Turn to Me (reprise); Common Little Catechism; Don't Let Me Go; AJ on the Subway; What If?; Scraps of Paper (reprise); Everybody Says (reprise); First Grade; If I'm Honest With You; Four Square Blocks/Find Me; Talk to Me; Brooklyn Bridge/First Step

SETTING New York City. World premiere of a new musical presented without intermission.

SYNOPSIS *Crossing Brooklyn,* a modern musical that deals with the emotional aftermath of September 11 in New York, tells the story of Des and AJ, a young, idealistic couple—both public school teachers bent on changing the world, one kid at a time. Life is full of promise and endless possibility until Des begins to unravel under the weight of her fears, ignited from that fateful September day. Splitting apart from the pressure, they struggle to find their way back to each other.

LUCY

Ensemble Studio Theatre; First Preview: October 24, 2007; Opening Night: October 29, 2007; Closed November 19, 2007; 6 previews, 21 performances

Written by Damien Atkins; Presented by The Ensemble Studio Theatre (William Carden, Artistic Director; Paul A. Slee, Executive Director) and The Alfred P. Sloan Foundation; Director, William Carden; Producer, James Carter; Associate Producer, Jessi D. Hill; Set, Ryan Elliot Kravetz; Lighting, Chris Dallos; Costumes, Suzanne Chesney; Sound, David Margolin Lawson; Props, Troy Campbell; Set provided by No Time For Love, LLC; PSM, Jeffrey Davolt; ASM, Michal V. Mendelson; Science Advisor, Darcey Kelley; Casting, Janet Foster; Alfred P. Sloan Foundation Program Director, Doron Weber; E.S.T/Sloan Project Co-Directors, Carlos Armesto and Graeme Gillis; Press, David Gersten & Associates

CAST Lucy **Lucy DeVito;** Vivian **Lisa Emery;** Gavin **Scott Sowers;** Julia **Keira Naughton;** Morris **Christopher Duva**

Lisa Emery, Lucy DeVito, and Scott Sowers in Lucy *(photo by Carol Rosegg)*

American premiere of a new play presented in two acts. Originally produced by the Canadian Stage Company on March 8, 2007 at the Berkeley Street Theatre.

SYNOPSIS Vivian is an anthropologist at the top of her field. She craves solitude—motherhood was never an option. But when forced to care for her estranged teenage daughter, Lucy, her life is turned upside down. Lucy is autistic...and might be the next step in Vivian's evolution.

1001

Baruch Performing Arts Center – Rose Nagelberg Theatre; First Preview: October 22, 2007; Opening Night: October 31, 2007; Closed November 17, 2007; 9 previews, 18 performances

Written by Jason Grote; Produced by Page 73 Productions (Liz Jones & Asher Richelli, Executive Directors) in association with Doug Nevin, Caroline Prugh & Erica Lynn Schwartz; Director, Ethan Sweeny; Set/Projections, Rachel Hauck; Costumes, Murell Horton; Lighting, Tyler Micoleau; Sound, Lindsay Jones; Original Music, DJ Arisa Sound; PSM, Bonnie Brady; Line Producer, R. Erin Craig/La Vie Productions; Production Management, Vadim Malinskiy & Aurora Productions; Casting, Jack Doulin; Company Manager, Beth Reisman; ASM, Tiffany Tabatchnik; Assistant Director, Anthony Luciano; Press, Richard Kornberg & Associates

CAST Virgin Bride/Dunyazade/Princess Maridah/Juml/Kuchuk Hanem/Lubna **Mia Barron**; Yahya Al-Husayni/Asser/Gustave Flaubert/Orthodox Jewish Student/Voice of Moderator/Eunuch **Drew Cortese**; Scheherazade/Dahna **Roxanna Hope**; The One-Eyed Arab/Juml's Master, Mostafa/Slave/Sinbad/Voice of Alan Dershowitz/Djinn **Jonathan Hova**; Shahriyar/Alan **Matthew Rauch**; Jorge Luis Borges/Emir Ghassan/Horrible Monster/Osama Bin Laden/Wazir **John Livingstone Rolle**

New York premiere of a new play presented without intermission. World premiere at the Denver Center Theatre Company (Ken Thompson, Artistic Director) February 2007.

SYNOPSIS Mixing the wordplay of Jorge Louis Borges, the ideas of Edward Said, and the comedy of Monty Python, *1001* hyperlinks Scheherazade's "A Thousand and One Arabian Nights" to contemporary Manhattan. Reality is fractured and reconstructed in a world inhabited by characters whose identity shifts unpredictably and deliriously. Using rollicking storytelling, magic realism, and trip-hop music, *1001* defaces and energizes to guide us through precarious world of the 21st century.

FRANKENSTEIN

37 Arts Theatre A; First Preview: October 10, 2007; Opening Night: November 1, 2007; Closed December 9, 2007; 25 previews, 45 performances

Music by Mark Baron, book and lyrics by Jeffrey Jackson, original story adapted from Mary Shelley's novel by Gary P. Cohen; Produced by Douglas C. Evans, Gerald Goehring, Michael F. Mitri, David S. Stone, in association with Barbara & Emery Olcott; Director, Bill Fennelly; Music Director, Stephen Purdy; Choreography, Kelly Devine; Sets, Kevin Judge; Costumes, Emily Pepper; Lighting, Thom Weaver; Sound, Dominic Sack & Carl Cassella; Projections, Michael Clark; Orchestrations, Richard DeRosa & Mark Baron; PSM, Joshua Pilote; ASM, Karen Parlato; General Manager, William Repicci; Production Manager, Gregg Bellon, Kevin Bartlett; Music Coordinator, Alan Cohen; Company Manager, Eddie Marrero; Line Producer, Bill Repiccci; Advertising/Marketing, Agency 212; Marketing/Promotions, Leanne Schanzer Promotions; Casting, Stephanie Klapper; Assistant Director, Richard J. Hinds; Dance Captain, Nick Cartell; Wigs, Leah Loukas; Props, Elizabeth Katchen; Video Programmer, Paul Vershbow; Press, Keith Sherman & Associates; Cast recording: Friends of Ghostlight

CAST Cpt. Robert Walton/A Blind Man **Aaron Serotsky;** Victor Frankenstein **Hunter Foster;** Alphonse Frankenstein, *Victor's father* **Eric Michael Gillett;** Caroline Frankenstein, *Victor's Mother* **Becky Barta;** William, *Victor's young brother* **Struan Erlenborn;** Justine Moritz, *William's Governess* **Mandy Bruno;** Henry Clerval **Jim Stanek;** Elizabeth Lavenza **Christiane Noll;** A Condemned Man/the "Creature" **Steve Blanchard;** Agatha, *the blind man's daughter* **Casey Erin Clark;** Various other characters **Nick Cartell, Leslie Henstock, Patrick Mellen;** Understudies: Nick Cartell (Henry/Victor/University Official), Casey Erin

Clark (Elizabeth/Mother), Leslie Henstock (Agatha/William/Young Victor/Justine); Patrick Mellen (Walton/Blind Man/Magistrate), Aaron Serotsky (The "Creature"/Alphonse), Jim Stanek (Victor)

MUSICIANS Stephen Purdy (Conductor/keyboard); John Bowen (keyboard); Martyn Axe (keyboard); Greg Giannascoli/Keith Crupi (drums/percussion); Christine MacDonald (oboe/English horn/flute/clarinet); Alan Cohen (guitar); Hugh Mason (bass)

Hunter Foster and Mandy Bruno in Frankenstein *(photo by Carol Rosegg)*

MUSICAL NUMBERS Prelude, A Golden Age, Amen, Birth to My Creation, Dear Victor, The Hands of Time, Your Father's Eyes, The Creature's Tale, The Waking Nightmare, The Music of Love, Why?, The Proposition, A Happier Day, The Modern Prometheus, The Hands of Time (reprise), The Workings of the Heart, An Angel's Embrace, The Workings of the Heart (reprise), Your Father's Eyes (reprise), These Hands, The Chase, The Coming of the Dawn; Amen (reprise)

SETTING The late 18th century, Geneva, Switzerland; Ingolstadt, Germany; and various locales throughout Europe and the Arctic. World premiere of a new musical presented in two acts.

SYNOPSIS *Frankenstein* is the story of a rebel scientist who challenges the laws of nature and morality when he breathes life into his inanimate creature. Faced with intolerance and adversity, the scientist's creation rebels against the world around him, destroying the very man who gave him life.

HOODOO LOVE

Cherry Lane Theatre; First Preview: October 16, 2007; Opening Night: November 1, 2007; Closed December 8, 2007; 43 performances

Written by Katori Hall; Produced by the Cherry Lane Theatre (Angelina Fiordellisi, Artistic Director; James King, Managing Director); Director, Lucie Tiberghien; Mentor, Lynn Nottage; Set, Robin Vest; Costumes, Rebecca Bernstein; Lighting, Pat Dignan; Sound/Original Music, Daniel Baker and the Broken Chord Collective; Fight Director, David Debesse; Production Manager, Janio Marrero; PSM, Paige van den Burg; ASM, Joan H. Capello; Development, Emilay Raabe, Joanna Gottlieb; Administrative Assistant, Angela Scott; Business Manager, Friedman & LaRosa, Inc., Joyce Friedman; Company Coordinator, Alexander Orbovich; Technical Director, Ian Grunes; Properties, Christina Lind; Hair, J. Jared Janas; Casting, Hopkins, Smith & Parden, Pamela Pernell; Marketing, Walker International Communications Group; Advertising, Eliran Murphy Group; Press, Art Meets Commerce, Timothy Haskell

CAST Jib **Keith Davis**; Candy Lady **Marjorie Johnson;** Toulou **Angela Lewis;** Ace of Spades **Kevin Mambo**

SETTING Memphis, 1933. Off-Broadway premiere of a new play with music presented in two acts. Previously presented as part of the Cherry Lane's 2006 Mentor Project.

SYNOPSIS In a southern tale of love, magic, jealousy and secrets, Toulou escapes from the Mississippi Delta cotton fields to pursue her dream of singing the blues in Memphis. When she meets a rambling blues man, the notorious Ace of Spades, this dream is realized in a way she could never have imagined.

ACTS OF LOVE

Kirk Theatre at Theatre Row+; First Preview: November 1, 2007; Opening Night: November 6, 2007; Closed January 6, 2008; 40 performances

Written by Kathryn Chetkovich; Produced by Dangerous Arrangement, Inc., Stephen Morfesis; Director, Marc Geller; Set, Aaron Mastin; Costumes, Dennis Ballard; Lighting, Frank DenDanto III; Original Music, Daniel T. Denver; Stage Manager, Bernita Robinson; Production Assistant, Cristina Knutson; Original song "September Man" written and performed by Meg Flather; Technical Director, Lance Harkins, Associate Lighting, Janice Olsson; Press, KPM Associates/Kevin P. McAnarney

CAST Ed **Andrew Dawson;** Sheila **Diana Tyler;** Tom **Andrew Rein;** Annie **Abby Royle;** Understudy **Tracey Gilbert** (Sheila and Annie)

Angela Lewis and Kevin Mambo in Hoodoo Love *(photo by Jaisen Crockett)*

SETTING The present, a summer cottage by a lake. World premiere of a new play presented in five scenes in one act without intermission.

SYNOPSIS *Acts of Love* is about the things we never get over, the things we do for love and the damage we do to others in the process. Tom brings his new girlfriend home to meet his parents, who have been happily married for 20 years. The door the family has managed to keep closed for 20 years is finally forced open. Every happy family has its secrets—those we keep from each other and those we keep from ourselves; and sometimes we get the chance to make the same mistakes twice.

+Due to popular demand, the show played through November 18, then transferred to the Lion Theatre at Theatre Row, resuming performances on November 26 for the extension. Tracey Gilbert succeeded Diana Tyler during the extension.

CRIME AND PUNISHMENT

59E59 Theater B; First Preview: November 1, 2007; Opening Night: November 7, 2007; Closed December 2; 38 performances

Written by Fyodor Dostoevsky, adapted by Marilyn Campbell and Curt Columbus; Presented by Writers' Theatre, Chicago (Michael Halberstam, Artistic Director; Kathryn M. Lipuma, Executive Director); Director, Michael Halberstam; Set, Eugene Lee; Costumes, Theresa Squire; Lighting, Keith Parham; Sound, Josh Schmidt; Props, Matt Hodges; Production Supervisor, PRF Productions; PSM, Samone B. Weissman; ASM, Kate DeCoste; Assistant Director, Michael Rau; Press, Karen Greco

CAST Raskolnikov **Scott Parkinson;** Porfiry Petrovich **John Judd;** Sonia **Susan Bennett**

New York premiere of a new play presented without intermission. Presented as part of the Go Chicago! Festival at 59E59.

SYNOPSIS A poor student commits a brutal murder in order to prove a theory. Relentlessly pursued by a wily policeman, he seeks refuge with his only confidant who is a young woman forced into prostitution by desperate circumstances. Slowly, his theory begins to crumble and he must choose whether or not to face the horror of his crime.

Susan Bennett, Scott Parkinson, and John Judd in Crime and Punishment *(photo by Carol Rosegg)*

THE SCREWTAPE LETTERS

Theatre at St. Clements; First Preview: October 18, 2007; Opening Night: November 8, 2007; Closed January 6, 2007; 15 previews, 50 performances

Written by C.S. Lewis, adapted for the stage by Jeffrey Fiske and Max McLean; Produced by Fellowship for the Performing Arts, Sir Thomas Moore, Walt & Anne Waldie, William & Bridget Coughran, Ron & Rene Joelson, and Fleet & Katie Maddox; Director, Jeffrey Fiske; Set, Cameron Anderson; Costumes, Michael Bevins; Lighting, Tyler Micoleau; Sound, Bart Fasbender; General Management, Aruba Productions, Ken Denison & Carol Fishman; Production Supervisor, Vincent DeMarco, Pam Traynor (assistant); Advertising, Eliran Murphy Group; PSM, Alaina J. Taylor; ASM, Jared Abram DeBacker; Dramaturg, Aaron Leichter; Vocal Coach, Katie Bull, Daniel Sergio (assistant); Props, Tim McMath; Makeup, Karen E.

Wight, David Winthrow (consultant); Technical Director, Jack Brady; Press, Springer Associates, Joe Trentacosta

CAST His Abysmal Sublimity Screwtape **Max McLean;** Toadpipe, Screwtape's personal secretary **Karen Eleanor Wight**

SETTING A Dining Hall in Hell–The Graduation Banquet at Tempters' Training College for Young Devils, and Screwtape's Office in Hell. Off-Off-Broadway transfer of a play presented without intermission. Previously presented at Theater 315 January 26-April 10, 2006 (see *Theatre World* Volume 62, page 210).

SYNOPSIS C.S. Lewis' brilliant and amusing portrait of spiritual warfare from a demon's point of view returns to the stage. The story unfolds through a series of letters written by Screwtape to a young tempter-in-training known as Wormwood. Together, they plot to compromise the salvation of an unwitting soul—not through spectacular sins, but through daily temptations that can ultimately destroy any hope of living a life of virtue.

BINGO WITH THE INDIANS

Flea Theatre; First Preview: October 25, 2007; Opening Night: November 9, 2007; Closed December 22, 2007; 11 previews, 36 performances

Written and directed by Adam Rapp; Produced by The Flea Theater (Jim Simpson, Artistic Director; Carol Ostrow, Producing Director); Sets, John McDermott; Lighting, Miranda Hardy; Costumes, Daphne Javitch; Sound, Brandon Wolcott; PSM, Rachel Sterner; Graphics, Elizabeth Kandel; Equipment and Support, Technical Artistry; Assistant Director, Jessica Fitch; General Manager, Beth Dembrow; Technical Director, Zack Tinkelman; Literary Manager, Gary Winter; Audience Development/Marketing, Sherri Kronfeld; Press, Spin Cycle, Ron Lasko

CAST Stash **Cooper Daniels;** Dee **Jessica Pohly;** Wilson **Rob Yang;** Steve **Evan Enderle;** Mrs. Wood **Missel Leddington;** Jackson **Corinne Donly;** The Indian **Ben Horner**

SETTING A small New England town. World premiere of a new play presented without intermission.

SYNOPSIS A disgruntled East Village theater company descends upon a small New England town with a plan to pay for their next production—heist the local bingo game.

BAD JAZZ

Ohio Theatre; First Preview: November 4, 2007; Opening Night: November 11, 2007; Closed November 25, 2007; 22 performances

Written by Robert Farquhar; Produced by the Play Company (Kate Loewald, Co-founder and Producer; Lauren Weigel, Managing Producer); Director, Trip Cullman; Set and Costumes, Dane Laffrey; Lighting, Ben Stanton; Sound, Bart Fasbender; PSM, Marion Friedman; Production Manager, Neal Wilkinson; Casting, Judy Henderson; Associate Producer, Linda Bartholomai; ASM, Lauren Kurinskas; Props, Mary Robinette Kowal; Dialect Coach, Samara Bay; Literary Associate/Company Manager, Melissa Hardy; Assistant Design, Hallie Stern; Assistant Sound, David Sanderson; Technical Director, Joshua Higgason; Press, The Karpel Group, Bridget Klapinski, Darren Molovinsky, Beth Sorrell

CAST Natasha **Marin Ireland;** Ben **Darren Goldstein**; Danny **Ryan O'Nan**; Gavin **Rob Campbell**; Hannah/Danielle/Props Mistress **Susie Pourfar;** Ewan **Colby Chambers**

U.S. premiere of a new play presented without intermission. Originally performed at the Drum Theatre (Plymouth, England) February 22, 2007.

SYNOPSIS *Bad Jazz* chronicles the lives of young artists in pursuit of a shared dream, as an actress takes a role that puts her sanity at risk, an actor struggles to remain true to his artistic ideals, and a director drives his company past the point of reason. When the reality and performance begin to blur, relationships are tested and this group is forced to ask themselves how far they're prepared to go for art's sake.

Jessica Pohly, Rob Yang and Cooper Daniels in Bingo with the Indians *(photo by Joan Marcus)*

A HARD HEART

Clurman Theatre at Theatre Row; First Preview: October 30, 2007; Opening Night: November 11, 2007; Closed December 2, 2007; 42 performances

Written by Howard Barker; Produced by Epic Theatre Ensemble (Producing Artists: Zak Berkman, Melissa Friedman, Ron Russell, Godfrey L. Simmons Jr., James Wallert, Sarah Winkler); Director, Will Pomerantz; Set, Narelle Sissons; Costumes, Chris Rumery; Lighting, Lenore Doxsee; Sound, Mutt Huang; PSM, Kate Hefel; ASM, Andrea Hayward; Production Manager, Jeff Wild/Robert Mahon; Assistant Director, Ben Kahn; Casting, Paul Davis/Calleri Casting; Props, Yana Babaev; Assistant Lighting, Natalie Robin; Press, O+M Co., Rick Miramontez, Jon Dimond, Molly Barnett

CAST Riddler **Kathleen Chalfant;** Praxis **Melissa Friedman;** Plevna **Dion Graham;** Sentry **Alex Organ;** Seemore **Thom Sesma;** Attila **James Wallert;** Woman **Sarah Winkler**

New York premiere of a 1992 play presented without intermission. Originally broadcast on BBC Radio and premiered at the Almeida Theatre in London.

SYNOPSIS *A Hard Heart* is a prescient and electrifying play exploring the ways we protect our political and human borders. Barker's prophetic drama imagines a country facing invasion. 'Praxis' the Queen enlists the Genius 'Riddler' to devise a strategy to protect their threatened culture, but is the sacrifice too much?

MAKE ME A SONG: THE MUSIC OF WILLIAM FINN

New World Stages – Stage 5; First Preview: October 30, 2007; Opening Night: November 12, 2007; Closed December 30, 2007; 14 previews, 55 performances

Conceived and directed by Rob Ruggiero; Presented by Junkyard Dog Productions (Randy Adams, Sue Frost, Kenny Alhadeff), Larry Hirschhorn, Jayson Raitt, Stacey Mindich, Jamie deRoy/Eric Falkenstein, in association with Nick Demos/Francine Bizar, Bob Eckert, Impresario's Choice on Broadway, Eileen T'Kaye, Barbara Manocherian/Remmel T. Dickinson; Set, Luke Hegel-Cantarella; Costumes, Alejo Vietti; Lighting, John Lasiter; Sound, Zachary Williamson; Musical Supervisor, Michael Morris; Music Director, Darren R. Cohen; Casting, Stuart Howard, Amy Schecter, & Paul Hardt; Marketing, HHC Marketing; PSM, Cambra Overend; Production Supervisor, Craig Caccamise; General Management, Snug Harbor Productions, Steven Chaikelson & Brannon Wiles; ASM, Fred Hemminger; Assistant Director, Nick Eilerman; Associate General Manager, Kendra Bator; Advertising, Eliran Murphy Group; Additional Vocal Arrangements, Jason Robert Brown, Vadim Feichtner, Darren Cohen, Carmel Dean, Michael Starobin, Michael Morris, Press, Pete Sanders/Blue Current Public Relations; Cast recording: Sh-K-Boom/Ghostlight Records 84427

CAST **Sandy Binion, D.B. Bonds, Adam Heller, Sally Wilfert;** Piano **Darren R. Cohen;** Understudies **Jason Dula, Alysha Umphress**

MUSICAL NUMBERS Make Me a Song, Heart and Music, Hitchhiking Across America, Billy's Law of Genetics, Passover, Republicans Part 1, Only One, I'd Rather Be Sailing/Set Those Sails; Republicans Part 2, Change, I Have Found, Republicans Part 3, You're Even Better Than You Think You Are, Falsettos Suite (Four Jews in a Room Bitching/A Tight-Knit Family/Love is Blind/My Father Is a Homo/Trina's Song/March of the Falsettos/The Year of the Child/The Baseball Game/Unlikely Loves/Falsettoland), All Fall Down, Republicans Part 4, Stupid Things I Won't Do, That's Enough For Me, I Went Fishing With My Dad, When the Earth Stopped Turning, Anytime (I Am There), Song of Innocence and Experience, Finale

New York premiere of a new musical revue presented without intermission. Originally produced at Theatreworks in Hartford, Connecticut.

SYNOPSIS *Make Me a Song: The Music of William Finn* showcases the songs of one of the most acclaimed composer-lyricists of our time. A two-time Tony Award winner for the groundbreaking musical *Falsettos,* Finn is currently represented on Broadway with *The 25th Annual Putnam County Spelling Bee*. Featuring classics from these shows juxtaposed with rarely-heard selections from *Romance in Hard Times, Elegies* and the

Tim Simons, Denice Sally Wilfert, Darren R. Cohen (at the piano), Adam Heller, Sandy Binion, and D.B. Bonds in Make Me a Song: The Music of William Finn *(photo by Carol Rosegg)*

yet to be produced *The Royal Family*, *Make Me a Song* is big, boisterous and life-loving, like Finn himself.

THE 4th GRADERS PRESENT AN UNNAMED LOVE-SUICIDE

59E59 Theater C; First Preview November 8, 2007; Opening Night: November 14, 2007; Closed December 2, 2007; 24 performances

Written by Sean Craney; Presented by The Hypocrites (Sean Craney, Artistic Director; Heather Clark, Executive Director); Costumes, Alison Siple; Lighting, Jared Moore; Composer/Sound, Kevin O'Donnell; Set, Sean Craney and Devin Brain; Stage Manager, Mike Ooi; Press, Karen Greco

CAST Johnny **Joseph Binder;** Rachel **Jennifer Grace;** Sally **Stacy Stoltz;** Brenda **Samantha Gleisten;** Mike Rice **Tim Simons;** Lucy Law **Denice Lee;** The Singer **Lydia Benecke**

New York premiere of a play presented without intermission. Presented as part of the Go Chicago! Festival at 59E59. Originally produced in collaboration with Jimmy McDermott and The Side Project, Chicago, September 2004.

SYNOPSIS *The 4th Graders Present an Unnamed Love-Suicide* mixes tragedy and comedy while exploring a world of adolescent turmoil including bullies, eating disorders, and alienation when one classmate commits suicide and leaves a play behind as his suicide note.

GROWING UP 70s

HA! Comedy Club Theatre; Opening Night: November 15, 2007; Closed: December 30, 2007

Created by Anthony Dinapoli & Chuck Nice, written by Jason Summers & Jim Mendrinos, original music and lyrics by Ronnie Dee; Presented by The Theatre at HA! and G-LUC Productions; Produced by Anthony Dinapoli and Barry Williams Enterprises in association with Mayuri Breen; Director, Jason Summers; Musical Director, Joe Valeri; Choreography, Leland Morrow; Lighting, Michael L. Kimmel; Costumes, Doreen Breen; Set, Kyle Dixon; PSM, Lisa Weinshrott; ASM, Jill Zakrzewski; Company Manager, Victoria Dinapoli; Sales, Biagio Tripodi; General Manager/Press, Mayuri Breen

CAST Narrator/Father **Barry Williams;** Catherine **Leslie E. Hughes;** Jason **Paul Wyatt;** Jessica **Sara Jayne Blackmore;** Luther **Kenney M. Green;** Patrick **Trevor Braun;** Shelly **Lauren Marcus;** Ensemble **Candace Reyes Newton, Chris Alderete;** Understudies: **Candace Reyes Newton** (Catherine, Shelly, Jessica), **Joe Perce** (Narrator)

MUSICAL NUMBERS Growing Up 70s, I Love Greg Brady, The Real Greg Brady, "Carter Clan" Theme, I Married Rock and Roll, (Going to) 54, Disco Inferno, Lava Lamps and Mood Rings, Whatever Happened to the 50s, Disco Medley, Listen to the Music, Heartbeat, Bubblegum Medley, Drift Away, Rock and Roll Medley

World premiere of a new musical revue presented in two acts.

SYNOPSIS Barry Williams, best known as "Greg Brady" on the classic TV sitcom "The Brady Bunch," produces and stars in this new revue which takes audiences on an interactive journey filled with colorful characters, disco, bell-bottoms, mood-rings, and unforgettable music.

Barry Williams (center) and the cast of Growing Up 70s *(photo courtesy of Ha! Comedy Club)*

SECRET ORDER

59E59 Theater A; First Preview: November 9, 2007; Opening Night: November 15, 2007; Closed December 9, 2007; 33 performances

Written by Bob Clyman; Produced by Merrimack Repertory Theatre (Charles Towers, Artistic Director; Tom Parrish, Executive Director) in association with Nancy and Richard Donahue, Daniel and Mary Frantz, Adam Richard Wagfors, Lincoln and Peg Pinsky; Director, Charles Towers; Set, Bill Clarke; Costumes, Martha Hally; Lighting, Dan Kotlowitz; Assistant Lighting, Juliet Chia; Sound, Jamie Whoolery; PSM, Jon William Goldman; Casting, Harriet Bass, Eileen Duffy; Production Assistants, Kathleen Munroe, Lisa Mei Ling Fong; Wardrobe, Deidre Higgins; Electrician, Tom Dyer; Light/Sound Operator, Mia Parise; For Merrimack: Edgar Cyrus (General Manager), Adam C. Scarano (Artistic Administrator); Press, Karen Greco

CAST William Shumway **Dan Colman;** Robert Brock **Larry Pine;** Alice Curiton **Jessi Campbell;** Saul Roth **Kenneth Tigar**

SETTING Champaign-Urbana, Illinois and New York City. Now. Off-Broadway premiere of a play presented in two acts. This production was presented at Merrimac Repertory Theatre in 2006–2007; world premiere at Ensemble Studio Theatre/ Alfred P. Sloan Foundation Project on April 8, 2002.

SYNOPSIS This biomedical drama is about a brilliant young research biologist who works in an obscure university lab and discovers a possible cure for cancer. When the dynamic director of New York's leading cancer institute becomes his mentor, he is set on a path of acclaim and prestige that could lead to the Nobel Prize. However the halls of science twist and turn, and the doctor is thrust into the high-stakes world of medicine, money and power.

DAI (enough)

47th Street Theatre; First Preview: November 12, 2007; Opening Night: November 19, 2007; Closed March 2, 2008; 7 previews, 83 performances

Written by Iris Bahr; Produced by Bernie Kukoff, Jonathan Pollard, Jon Cutler, Highbrow Entertainment; Director/ Set/Lighting, Marc Janowitz; Sound, Frank Gaeta; Associate Sound, David Roy; PSM, Stephanie McFarland; General Manager, Jonathan Pollard; Advertising, Eliran Murphy Group; Marketing, SRO Theatrical/Meri Krassner, Chris Presley; Technical Supervisor, Wilburn Bonnell; Management Assistant, Brian Bender; Press, Keith Sherman & Associates, Patrick Paris

Performed by **Iris Bahr**

Limited return engagement of the Off-Broadway solo performance play presented without intermission. Previously presented at the Culture Project last season. The production shared the theatre with *Forbidden Broadway.*

SYNOPSIS *Dai* transports us into the fast-paced world of a bustling Tel Aviv café, just moments before a suicide bomber enters. Brought to life through Iris Bahr's razor sharp characterizations, members of all strata of Israeli society, as well as its observers and critics, are captured in what are to be their final moments. Bahr finds humor and humanity in the most dire and tragic circumstances as we come to know these eccentric, lost, troubled souls, and peer into their hilarious lives, quirks and neuroses

I KNOCK AT THE DOOR & PICTURES IN THE HALLWAY

Theatre Three (Mint Theatre Space); Opening Night: November 24, 2007; Closed December 23, 2007; 13 & 14 performances

Written by Paul Shyre, adapted from the works of Sean O'Casey; Produced by The New Globe Theatre, Inc.; Director and Producer, Stuart Vaughan; Set/Lighting, Bart Healy; PSM, Kimothy Cruse; Associate Producers, Anne Thompson Vaughan and Vincent Curcio; Press, O+M Co., Philip Carrubba, Rick Miramontez

CAST Mr. Cassidy/Various roles **Salome Jens;** Sean O'Casey/Narrator **Gil Rogers;** Various roles **John FitzGibbon;** Johnny **Grant Kretchik;** Various roles **Nancy McNulty;** Various roles **Craig Rising**

50th Anniversary revivals of two plays performed in rotating repertory, both in two acts.

SYNOPSIS Six accomplished actors, on six stools, in a fully-rehearsed staged concert presentation of Sean O'Casey's acclaimed autobiographies, bring the Dublin of the great wordsmith's youth alive —a vivid gallery of rogues, patriots, saints, and hypocrites. With perspective and wit, we meet a young O'Casey who surmounts poverty, and illness, fighting with spunky humor to swim upstream in a society divided by nationality, class, religion, and ignorance.

KLEYNKUNST! Warsaw's Brave and Brilliant Yiddish Cabaret

Goldman-Sonnenfeldt Auditorium at the JCC; First Preview: November 8, 2007; Opening Night: November 29, 2007; Closed December 30, 2007; 29 performances

Written, researched and originally produced by Rebecca Joy Fletcher; Presented by National Yiddish Theatre – Folksbiene (Motl Didner, Artistic Director; Georgia Buchanan, Managing Director); Director, Michael Montel; Music Director/ Arrangements/Pianist, Bob Goldstone; English Lyrics, Jeremy Lawrence; Additional English Lyrics, Stephen Mo Hanan; Set & Lighting, Brian Nason; Costumes, Gail-Cooper Hecht; Sound, Don Jacobs; Choreography, Ananda Bena-Weber; Props, Kathy Fabian/Propstar; Stage Manager, Marci Skolnick; ASM, Penny Ayn Maas; Supertitles, Matt Temkin; Production Manager, Production Consolidated; Russian Supertitles Translator, Anna Plotkina; Press, Beck Lee Media Blitz

CAST **Rebecca Joy Fletcher, Stephen Mo Hanan**

Musical Numbers and Sketches: Mack the Knife, The Ararat Hymn, I Steal the Night, How Hard and Bitter, Krochmalna Street, Come Leybke–dance!, The World to Come, Whiskey!, The Necklace of Beads, Oy, Madagaskar!, The Last Jew in Poland, Mues (Money), Moments of Believing, The Song of our Time

SETTING 1921-1941, Warsaw, Poland. Off-Broadway

premiere of a cabaret theatre spectacle presented in English and Yiddish without intermission. World premiere in the Kabarett Fête in January, 2007.

SYNOPSIS During pre-WWII, secular, passionate Jews frequented kleynkunst theaters —Yiddish cabarets. These hipsters soaked up satiric music, laughed at anti-Semitism, drank whiskey, and danced the Charleston. They were riding the wave of Polish independence, fighting for a freer world. *Kleynkunst!* reveals the courage, brilliance and bite of a lost era.

OH, THE HUMANITY
and other good exclamations

Flea Theater; First Preview: November 3, 2007; Opening Night: November 29, 2007; Closed February 2, 2008; 18 previews, 56 performances

Short plays written by Will Eno: *Behold The Coach, in a Blazer, Uninsured; Ladies and Gentlemen: The Rain; Enter the Spokeswoman, Gently; The Bully Composition* and *Oh, the Humanity*; Presented by The Flea Theater (Jim Simpson, Artistic Director; Carol Ostrow, Producing Director); Director, Jim Simpson; Set, Kyle Chepulis; Lighting, Brian Aldous; Costumes, Claudia Brown; Sound, Jill BC DuBoff; Video/Projections, Dustin O'Neill; Casting, Calleri Casting; Stage Manager, Lindsay Stares; Assistant to the Director, Jeremy Bloom; Bat Back-up, Catherine Gowl; Graphics, David Prittie; General Manager, Beth Dembrow; Technical Director, Zack Tinkelman; Development/Marketing Manager, Sherri Kronfeld; Literary Manager, Gary Winter; Press, Spin Cycle/Ron Lasko

CAST The Coach/Gentleman/Photographer/Man **Brian Hutchison;** Lady/Spokeswoman/Assistant/Woman **Marisa Tomei;** Man #2 **Drew Hildebrand**

World premiere of five short plays presented without intermission.

SYNOPSIS *Oh the Humanity and other good exclamations* is five short plays about people like you, facing lives like yours. About life, in a word.

PIED-À-TERRE

Kirk Theatre on Theatre Row; First Preview: November 26, 2007; Opening Night: December 1, 2007; Closed January 5, 2008; 36 performances

Written by John Anastasi; Produced by Stageplays Theatre Company (Tom Ferriter, Artistic Director); Director/General Manager, Tom Ferriter; Set/Technical Director, Randall Parsons; Costumes, Brad L. Scoggins; Lighting, Jeffrey Koger; Sound, Chris Rummel; Original Music, Michael Valenti; Choreography, Ron De Jesús; Hair/Wigs/Makeup, Wendy Parson; Casting, Laura Dragomir; PSM, Cheryl D. Olszowka; ASM, Danielle Teague-Daniels; Artistic Associate/Marketing, Michael Citriniti; Studio Musicians, Michael Valenti (piano), Meg Okura (violin), Chip M. Fabrizi (percussion); Press, Blue Current Public Relations/Pete Sanders

CAST Julia **Robin Riker**; Katie **Jessica McKee;** Jack **John Howard Swain**

SETTING New York City, the present, six months ago, four months ago, two months ago. World premiere of a new play presented in nine scenes in two acts.

SYNOPSIS Julia, a TV journalist, discovers a penthouse owned by her husband, Jack. As Julia explores the apartment, she is interrupted by Katie, a young woman, who seems to know Jack a little too well. As the two women face off and secrets unfold revealing the burdens each has been carrying, the two women learn they have more in common than either thought possible.

Robin Riker, John Swain in Pied-á-Terre *(photo by Gerry Goodstein)*

HARVEST

Beckett Theatre at Theatre Row; First Preview: November 30, 2007; Opening Night: December 4, 2007; Closed December 23, 2007; 5 previews, 23 performances

Written by David Wright Crawford; Produced by The Alchemy Theatre Company of Manhattan, Inc. (Robert

Saxner, Producing Artistic Director); Directors, Judson Jones and Benard Cummings; Set, Terry Gipson/Gipson Design; Costumes, Ben Taylor Ridgeway; Lighting, Jessica M. Burgess; Sound/Original Music, Scott O'Brien; PSM, Joseph Mitchell Parks; Voice/Dialect Coach, Christa Kimlicko Jones & Kohil Calhoun; Casting, Laura Maxwell-Scott; Technical Director, Amber Estes; Press, Kevin P. McAnarney

CAST Act 1–Spring 1966: Rick Childress **Judson Jones;** Toni Childress **Christa Kimlicko Jones;** Copeland **Doug Sheppard;** Act 2–Summer 1981: Rick Childress **Jeremy Stuart;** Rafael Lamas **Morgan Baker;** Aggy Taylor **Shorey Walker;** Act 3–Fall, present: Rick Childress **Richard Mawe;** Maggie Falls **Kymberlie Stansell;** Toni Childress **Kathleen Huber**

SETTING West Texas; 1966, 1981, and the present. Off-Broadway premiere of a new play presented in three acts.

SYNOPSIS *Harvest* is a tender and poignant story spanning 45 years about a Texas farmer who battles to keep his farm and his family while struggling against inevitable change. In the spirit of Chekhov, with the surroundings of Horton Foote, this timely account of what could be the last generation of an American family farm asks the questions, "How would you choose to live your life?" and "At the end of your life…where do you want to die?"

RUNT OF THE LITTER

37 Arts Theatre A; First Preview: November 30, 2007; Opening Night: December 9, 2007; Closed February 24, 2008; 8 previews, 76 performances

Written by Bo Eason; Produced by Tom Quinn, Larry Safir, Alonzo Cantu, Dawn Eason & Peter Fitzgerald; Director, Larry Moss; Set, James Dardenne; Lighting, David Gipson; Sound, Peter Fitzgerald; Costumes, Sports Robe; PSM, Joe Gladstone; Sports Public Relations, Chip Namais; General Manager, Joey Franco; Executive Producer, Forbes Candlish; Movement Specialist, Jean-Louise Rodrigue; Production Supervisor, Peter R. Feuchtwanger; Advertising, Eliran Murphy Group; Carpenter, John Martinez; Electrician, Tom Dyer; Audio, David Arnold; Light Programmer, Anjeanette Stokes; Press, Sam Rudy Media Relations, Charlie Siedenburg, Robert Lasko, Dale Heller

CAST Jack Henry **Bo Eason**

SETTING A locker room just before the Super Bowl. Revival of a solo performance play presented without intermission. Previously presented at MCC Theatre in 2002 with Mr. Eason (see *Theatre World* Volume 58, page 158).

SYNOPSIS A semi-autobiographical play, *Runt of the Litter* opens in the final hour of Jack Henry's lifelong dream —to win the Super Bowl, but only one thing stands in his way — his brother. The play looks at what happens to two brothers in a family of over-achievers: when their parents assure their oldest son he is destined for football superstardom, and tell their youngest son he is too small to compete, a line in the family sand is drawn that colors the rest of their lives.

Bo Eason in Runt of the Litter *(photo by Joan Marcus)*

THE CITY THAT CRIED WOLF

59E59 Theater C; First Preview: December 5, 2007; Opening Night: December 11, 2007; Closed December 30; 29 performances

Written by Brooks Reeves; Presented by State of the Play Theatre–Inaugural Production (Chloe Demrovsky & Rebecca Jones, Executive Producers); Directors, Dan Barnes & Leta Tremblay; Set, Joshua Higgason; Lighting, Jarrod Jahoda; Costumes, Chloe Demrovsky; Sound Mat Bussler; Props, Tom Dudley and Chris Zinn; Stage Manager, Jessica Suter; Original Music, Brendan Barr; Assistant Composers, Christopher Coughlin & Sam Jones; Choreography, Alberto Peart; Fight Consultant, David Debesse; Fight Captain, Rebecca Jones; Dance Captain, Michelle Concha; Press, Karen Greco; Musicians: Ethan Braun (piano), Krystyana Chelminski (violin), Christopher Coughlin (percussion/accordion), Douglas Mosher (saxophone), Matthew Verzola (trumpet)

CAST Jack B. Nimble **Adam La Faci;** Little Bo Peep **Chloe Demrovsky;** Mother Goose **Michelle Concha;** Humpty Dumpty/Jacob/Radio & Runway Announcers/Frog/Hansel/BB/Bunny Foo Foo **Loren Vandegrift;** Newsie/Cat with Fiddle/Cabbie/Radio Princess/Owl/Gretel/Crone/Jill/Mary Mary/Beauty/Granny **Rebecca Jones;** Peter/

Dog Comedian/Wilhelm/Reporter/King Cole/Butler/Plucky Lucky **Mat Bussler;** Miss Muffett/Goldilocks/Radio Princess/Fox/Leprechaun/Cinderella/Turkey Lurkey/Mary **Jyll Marie Mihlek**

A new play with music presented without intermission. World premiere at Hampshire College in 2006. New York premiere at the 2006 New York International Fringe Festival produced by The Present Company.

SYNOPSIS *The City That Cried Wolf* is a noir style detective story with a contemporary and satirical political edge starring nursery rhyme and fairytale characters. Little Bo Peep is a sultry singer who seeks her sheep. Jack B. Nimble is the Private Eye hot on her tail as he tries to crack Rhyme Town's stickiest murder–Councilman Humpty Dumpty. With three little pigs in satin, bears in teddies, and rub-a-dub-dub three men in a tub, this not your average fairytale.

CUT TO THE CHASE

59E59 Theater B; First Preview: December 6, 2007; Opening Night: December 12, 2007; Closed December 30, 2007; 30 performances

Written and conceived by Joel Jeske, developed and presented by Parallel Exit; Director, Mark Lonergan; Choreography, Ryan Kasprzak and Derek Roland; Sets, Anna Kiraly; Lighting, Eric J. Kwak; Costumes, Juliet Jeske; Stage Manager, Olivia O'Brien; Logo, Dance Art FX; Load-In, Anh Dang and Shana Robbins; Press, Karen Greco

CAST Dilly **Laura Dillman;** Dobson **Mike Dobson;** The Great Jeske **Joel Jeske;** Julietta Massina **Juliet Jeske;** Kaspar **Ryan Kasprzak;** Little Angela **Andrea Kehler;** Roland Derek **Derek Roland**

World premiere of a family vaudeville revue with magic, music, slapstick, and physical comedy presented without intermission.

SYNOPSIS A troupe of madcap performers attempt to put on the biggest wee show in town, creating a backstage adventure filled with comic chaos and fast-paced action. Incorporating music, magic, tap and slapstick, *Cut to the Chase* is a rollicking speed-of-light comedy for the whole family.

EDWARD THE SECOND

Peter Jay Sharp Theatre; First Preview: December 9, 2007; Opening Night: December 15, 2007; Closed January 27, 2008; 44 performances

Written by Christopher Marlowe, adaptation by Garland Wright; Produced by the Red Bull Theater (Jesse Berger, Artistic Director; Amanda Brandes, Business Manager); Director, Jesse Berger; Set, John Arnone; Costumes, Clint Ramos; Lighting, Peter West; Composer/Sound, Scott Killian; Fight Director, Rick Sordelet; Movement Consultant, Tracy Bersley; Vocal Coach, Shane Ann Younts; Wigs/Makeup, Erin Kennedy Lunsford; Props, Sean McArdle; Aerial Effects, Paul Rubin; PSM, Kat West; Production Manager, Shannon Case; General Manager, Sandra Garner; Casting, Stuart Howard; Associate Producer, Amanda Brandes; ASM, Mary Leach; Assistants to the Director, Dailya Bros, Damon Krometis, Louisa Proske; Press, David Gersten & Associates

CAST Edward II **Marc Vietor**; Isabella **Claire Lautier**; Prince Edward **Raum-Aron**; Kent **Lucas Hall**; Gaveston **Kenajuan Bentley;** Spencer **Randy Harrison;** Mortimer **Matthew Rauch**; Lancaster **Davis Hall**; Warwick **Joseph Costa**; Bishop of Coventry **Arthur Bartow**; Archbishop of Canterbury **Raphael Nash Thompson;** Herald/Lightborn **Rob Breckenridge;** Monk **Arthur Bartow;** Gurney **Wesley Broulik;** Ensemble Players **Wesley Broulk, William DeMerritt, Garth Wells McCardle, Derrick Lemont Sanders, Patrick Vaill**

Kenajuan Bentley and Marc Victor in Edward the Second *(photo by Brian Dolg)*

UNDERSTUDIES Arthur Bartow (Canterbury), Rob Breckenridge (Mortimer), Weslye Broulik (Warwick), William DeMeritt (Gaveston, Lightborn), Patrick McAndrew

(Ensemble), Garth Wells McCardle (Lancaster, Bishop, Monk), Lydia Perez-Carpenter (Isabella), Derrick LeMont Sanders (Spencer, Gurney), Patrick Vaill (Kent, Herald)

World premiere of a new adaptation of the classic presented in two acts. The play has not had a major New York production in over thirty years.

SYNOPSIS *Edward the Second* is a timely examination of the struggle for personal human rights amidst a powerful public need for political expediency. England's only openly gay monarch, who ruled from 1307-1327, asserts his right to have the private life he desires, only to have his love, his life and his kingdom destroyed. Do those in power have the right to a personal life? Should personal needs be sacrificed for "the greater good?"

"Illuminating the Divine Land" performed by Ying Tang Lion and Dragon Troupe, one of the musical numbers in Holiday Wonders *(photo courtesy of New Tang Dynasty TV)*

HOLIDAY WONDERS & CHINESE NEW YEAR SPLENDOR

Holiday Wonders – Beacon Theatre; December 18–26, 2007; 10 performances; *Chinese New Year Splendor* – Radio City Music Hall; January 31–February 9, 2008; 15 performances

Presented by New Tang Dynasty TV and Divine Performing Arts; Conductor, Rutang Chen; Choreography, Yung Yung Tsuai, Vina Lee, Michelle Ren, Guan Guimin

CAST **Xiaochun Qi, Vina Lee, Michelle Ren, Guimin Guan, Xuejun Wang, Jason Shi, Cecilia Xiong, Alina Wang, Peijong Hsieh, Ying Han, Rutang Chen, Chia-Chi Lin**

Two theatrical spectaculars presented with intermission.

SYNOPSIS Combining an exciting selection of dance, music and song, and featuring over 200 dancers and musicians, *Holiday Wonders* is a vibrant and inspiring event that fuses the classical Eastern and Western cultures of the Holidays. *Chinese New Year Splendor* is inspired by over 5000 years of history and tradition and creates stunning experiences on stage featuring traditional dances, songs and symphony.

STRIKING 12

The Zipper Factory; December 27–31, 2007; 4 performances

Book, music and lyrics by Brendan Millburn, Valerie Vigoda, and Rachel Sheinkin; Director, Ted Spurling; Press, Bill Coyle; Cast recording: PS Classics 526

CAST The Man Who's Had Enough **Brendan Milburn;** SAD Light Seller and Others **Valerie Vigoda;** Party Host and others **Gene Lewin**

MUSICAL NUMBERS Snow Song (It's Coming Down), Last Day of the Year, Resolution, The Sales Pitch, Red and Green (And I'm Feeling Blue), Matches for Sale, Say What? Hey La La/Fine Fine Fine, Can't Go Home, Wonderful, Give the Drummer Some, Picture This, Caution to the Wind, It's Not All Right, Wonderful (reprise), Picture This/Snow Song (reprise), Closing

Limited return engagement of a musical performed without intermission. Originally presented by the Prince Music Theater, Philadelphia, and subsequently at The Old Globe, San Diego and Ars Nova in New York; Off-Broadway premiere at the Daryl Roth Theatre November 6–December 31, 2006.

SYNOPSIS *Striking 12* is the story of a Grumpy Guy who decides to avoid the hectic, loveless world on New Year's Eve, until he's visited by an incandescent salesgirl with the promise to chase away his winter doldrums. Combining pop-rock, musical comedy and old-fashioned uplift with a healthy dose of 21st-century skepticism, this festive tale, performed by the members of the indie pop-rock band Groovelily, ignites the holiday spirit and connects lush musical textures and soaring vocals to make a new music that's all their own.

DEEP TRANCE BEHAVIOR IN POTATOLAND (A Richard Foreman Theater Machine)

Ontological Theater at St. Marks; Opening Night: January 22, 2008; Closed April 27, 2008; 71 performances

Written, directed, designed and score by Richard Foreman; Presented by The Ontological-Hysteric Theater (Richard

Foreman, Artistic Director; Shannon Sindelar, Managing Director); Technical Director, Peter Ksander; Stage Manager, Brendan Regimbal; Sound, Travis Just; Props and Costumes, Meghan Buchanan and Nellie Fleischner; Engineers, Miranda Hardy, Eduardo Band; Graphics, Elka Krajewska; Construction, Adela Keuhnn; Development, Arwen Lowbridge and Alice Reagan; Press, Manny Igrejas

CAST Man in Striped Suit **Joel Israel**; Girl in Sailor Hat **Caitlin McDonough-Thayer**, Girl With Black Hair **Fulya Peker**; Girl With the Golden Dress **Caitlin Rucker**; Girl With the Tiara **Sarah Dahlen;** Voices on Tape: **Richard Foreman, Kate Manheim, André Malraux**

An experimental theatre piece presented without intermission

SYNOPSIS Plunging deeper into ravishing abstract theater, Foreman's latest production uses digital material filmed in Japan and England and takes place on a stage in New York in which everything is askew—the windows, the walls, the projection screens, the furniture, which includes two pianos. Within this setting, the mind is asked to jump from world to world, Japan to England, filmed world to live stage world. Foreman evokes the atmosphere of a séance, combining the tableaus filmed in Japan and England with five live New York actors who navigate a sinking grand piano.

SLAUGHTERHOUSE-FIVE, or: The Children's Crusade

59E59 Theater C; First Preview: January 11, 2008; Opening Night: January 22, 2008; Closed February 17. 2008; 44 performances

Written by Kurt Vonnegut, adapted by Eric Simonson; Presented by Godlight Theatre Company (Joe Tantalo, Artistic Director); Director, Joe Tantalo; Design, Maruti Evans; Original Music and Sound, Andrew Recinos; Movement Director/Choreographer, Hachi Yu; Fight Choreographer, Josh Renfree; Music Supervisor, Rob Maitner; Electricians, Wilburn Bonnell, Todd Nonn, Carrie Cheek; Stage Managers, Nick Tochelli, Amy Vonvett; Press, Karen Greco

CAST Man **Ashton Crosby;** Boy Billy Pilgrim **Darren Curley;** Billy Pilgrim **Gregory Koknow;** Young Billy Pilgrim **Dustin Olson;** Ensemble **David Bartlett, Deanna McGovern, Nick Paglino, Aaron Paternoster, Michael Shimkin, Michael Tranzeilli**

New York premiere of a play presented without intermission.

SYNOPSIS Billy Pilgrim is a man who becomes unstuck in time after he is abducted by aliens from the planet Tralfamadore. In a plot-scrambling display of virtuosity, we follow Pilgrim simultaneously through all phases of his life, concentrating on his (and Vonnegut's) shattering experience as an American prisoner of war who witnesses the firebombing of Dresden. *Slaughterhouse-Five* boasts the same imagination, humanity, and gleeful appreciation of the absurd found in Vonnegut's other works, but the play's basis in rock-hard, tragic fact gives it a unique poignancy—and humor.

Mike Shimkin, Ashton Crosby and Dustin Olson in Slaughterhouse-Five, or: The Children's Crusade *(photo by Danata Zanotti)*

WANDA'S WORLD

45th Street Theatre; First Preview: January 16, 2008; Opening Night: January 23, 2008; Closed February 10, 2008; 6 previews, 28 performances

Book and story by Eric H. Weinberger, music, lyrics and story by Beth Falcone; Presented by Amas Musical Theatre (Donna Trinkoff, Producing Artistic Director) in association with Terry Schnuck; Director and Choreography, Lynne Taylor-Corbett; Music Director, Doug Oberhamer; Set, Beowulf Boritt; Costumes, Jennifer Caprio; Lighting, Aaron Spivey; Sound, Brett Jarvis; Projections, Matthew Myrhum; PSM, Brian Westmoreland; Production Supervisor, Ian Grunes; Casting, Carol Hanzel; Company Manager, Christopher Scott; Marketing, HHC Marketing; ASM, Karen Parlato; Assistant to the Director, Shaun Taylor-Corbett, Christa Capone; Dance Captain, Heather Jane Rolff; Props, Sheila Blanc; Makeup, Matt Thomas; Press, Springer Associates, Joe Trentacosta

CAST Spangles/Mr. Lemmings **Chris Vettel;** Corey/Caller #1 **Christine Scharf;** Meghan/Caller #2 **Lakisha Anne Bowen;** Alison Carmichael/Caller #3 **Heather Jane Rolff;** Wanda Butternut **Sandie Rosa;** Ty Belvedere **James Royce Edwards;** Jake **Devin Ilaw;** Ethan **Michael Dexter;** P.J. Dunbar **Leo Ash Evens;** Jenny Hightower **Jennifer Bowles;** Ms. Dinglederry/Mrs. Butternut **Valerie Wright**

THE BAND Doug Oberhamer (Conductor/keyboard), David Anthony (percussion), Scott Thornton (bass), Sean Harkness (guitar)

MUSICAL NUMBERS Wanda's World, Now One Can Know, She's So Last Week, Cheese Valley Cheer, What's Not to Like? Operation Shutdown, Don't Mess With Me, Blow Them Away, Not Everyone Eats Cheese, Not Everyone Eats Cheese (reprise), Diva Latina, Not a Routine Halloween, A Face Like Mine, What's Not to Like (reprise), Wanda's World Finale

SETTING The present. Cheese Valley, USA. World premiere of a new musical presented without intermission.

SYNOPSIS Wanda is the popular host of the hit TV talk show, *Wanda's World*, where kids call in and she helps them solve their problems. She is beautiful, confident and always knows what to say...in her fantasy. In real life, Wanda Butternut has a unique problem of her own and is dreading her first day of school in a new town. With hip music and a warm message of inclusiveness and acceptance *Wanda's World* will win your heart.

STRAIGHT UP WITH A TWIST

Players Theatre; First Preview: January 17, 2008; Opening Night: January 24, 2008; Closed May 4, 2008; 6 previews, 85 performances

Written by Paul Stroili; Produced by Millrock (David and Hyra George); Director, Bill Penton; Design, David George; Costumes, Crystal Thompson; Lighting, Christopher Ryan; Sound and Original Music, Christopher Ryan & Chris Caspar; Assistant Lighting, Matthew Piercy & Ariel Benjamin; Production Manager, C.J. Thom; General Manager, Louis Salmone; Advertising, Ark PR and Marketing; Press, Keith Sherman & Associates; Original Press, Penny Landau/Maya Public Relations

Performed by **Paul Stroili**

New York premiere of a solo performance play presented without intermission. Originally produced at Grove Theatre Center, Garden Grove, California. An earlier version of the play (originally entitled *Renaissance Geek)* had its world premiere at The Gascon Center Theater in Los Angeles.

SYNOPSIS Inspired by Stroili's life, *Straight Up with a Twist* challenges our conventions on what it means to be straight, gay and everything in between. The show takes a look at one family trying to figure out a straight son who loves to vacuum, knows how to fold a fitted sheet, and can quantify the difference between egg-shell and ecru. Stroili portrays a host of characters and uses his experience to tell audiences about that straight guy you've always wondered about.

THREE TRAVELERS

Theatre at St. Clements; First Preview: January 15, 2008; Opening Night: January 24, 2008; Closed February 17, 2008; 8 previews, 22 performances

Written by Richard Abrons; Presented by Woody King's New Federal Theater; Director, Jay Broad; Set, Don Llewellyn; Costumes, Karen Perry; Lighting, David Segal; Sound, Sean O'Halloran; Casting, Stephanie Klapper; Stage Manager, Jacqui Casto; Press, Shirley Herz & Associates

CAST Mavis **Judith Lightfoot Clarke**; Travis **Stephen Schnetzer**; Lydia **Kathleen McNenny**; Munishree **Kenneth Maharaj**

SETTING India. New York premiere of a play presented without intermission. New Federal Theater previously co-produced the show in March 2005 with the Odyssey Theater Ensemble, Los Angeles.

SYNOPSIS Three jaded western tourists (a corporate whiz, his uptight wife and their free-spirited British friend) search for answers to their discontent by seeking wisdom in India from a world-famous, deceptively irreverent Guru.

JERRY SPRINGER – THE OPERA: In Concert

Carnegie Hall Stern Auditorium; January 29-30, 2008; 2 performances

Music by Richard Thomas, book and lyrics by Stewart Lee and Richard Thomas; Produced by David J. Foster, Jared Geller, Avalon Promotions in association with Ruth Hendel and Jonathan Reinis; Director, Jason Moore. Music Director, Stephen Oremus; Choreography, Josh Prince; Set, David Korins; Costumes, Ilona Somogyi; Lighting, Jeff Croiter; Sound, Brian Ronan; Video, Aaron Rhyne; Wits, Charles LaPointe; Hair and Makeup, Erin Kennedy Lunsford; Orchestrations and Programming, Martin Koch, Nick Gilpin; Music Coordinator, Michael Keller; Technical Supervisor, Aurora Productions; PSM, Evan Ensign; Casting, Teley + Company; General Manager, Foster Entertainment/Jennie Connery; Stage Manager, Jim Wooley; Associate Music Director, Ben Cohn; Assistant to the Director, Stephen Sposito; Press, Barlow-Hartman, Ryan Ratelle, Melissa Bixler

CAST Steve **Sam Kitchin;** Warm Up Man/Satan **David Bedella;** Jerry Springer **Harvey Keitel;** Dwight/God **Luke Grooms;** Peaches **Patricia Phillips;** Zandra/Irene/Mary **Linda Balgord;** Valkyrie **Patty Goble;** Tremont/Angel Gabriel **Max von Essen;** Montel/Jesus **Lawrence Clayton;** Andrea/Archangel Michael **Emily Skinner;** Baby Jane **Laura Shoop;** Shawntel/Eve **Katrina Rose**

Luke Grooms, Harvey Keitel, Patricia Phillips and Linda Balgord in Jerry Springer – The Opera: In Concert *(photo by Walter McBride)*

Dideriksen; Chucky/Adam **Sean Jenness;** Ensemble **Katie Banks, Kristy Cates, Patty Goble, Chris Gunn, Celisse Henderson, Robert Hunt, John Eric Parker, Kate Pazakis, Eddie Pendergraft, Richard Poole, Soara-Joye Ross, Tory Ross, Roland Rusinek, John Schiappa, Michael James Scott, Dennis Stowe, Edwin Vega, Sasha Weiss, Jim Weitzer, Betsy Werbel, Lauren Worsham**

MUSICIANS Stephen Oremus (Conductor), Ben Cohen (Associate Conductor/keyboard 1), Ethan Popp (keyboard 2), Brian Koonin (guitars), Sean McDaniel (drums/percussion), Nicholas Marchione (trumpet), Chad Yarbrough (French horn), Ed Salkin (reeds), John Moses (reeds)

MUSICAL NUMBERS Overtly-ture, Audience Very Plainsong, Ladies & Gentlemen, Have Yourselves A Good Time, Bigger Than Oprah Winfrey, Foursome Guests, I've Been Seeing Someone Else, Chick With A Dick, Talk To The Hand, Adverts 1, Intro To Diaper Man, Diaper Man, Montel Cums Dirty, This Is My Jerry Springer Moment, Mama Gimmee Smack On The Asshole, I Wanna Sing Something Beautiful, Adverts II, First Time I Saw Jerry, Backstage Scene, Poledancer, I Just Wanna Dance, It Has No Name, Some Are Descended From Angels, Jerrycam, Klan Entrance/End Of Act One, Gloomy Nurses, Purgatory Dawning, Eat Excrete, Haunting, Him Am The Devil, Every Last Mother Fucker Should Go Down, Grilled & Roasted, Transition Music, Once In Happy Realms Of Light, Fuck You Talk, Satan & Jesus Spat, Adam & Eve & Mary, Where Were You?, Behold God, Marriage Of Heaven & Hell, This Is My Cheesey, Jerry It Is Finished, Jerry Eleison, Please Don't Die, Take Care, Martin's Richard-Esque Finale De Grand Fromage, Play Out

SETTING The set of the Jerry Springer Show and Hell. New York premiere of a concert version of a musical presented in two acts.

SYNOPSIS The smash London musical *Jerry Springer – The Opera* is inspired by America's most lurid TV talk show host who brought worldwide television audiences episodes including "Pregnant by a Transsexual," "Here Come the Hookers" and "I Refuse to Wear Clothes." The first half of the musical takes the usual format of a Springer Show with guests making their bizarre revelations whilst being verbally abused by the audience. The second half takes place in hell in which God, Jesus, Mary and other figures from Christianity are forced to make confessions and are treated with the same disdain as any other guest.

DEATHBED

McGinn/Cazale Theatre; First Preview: January 23, 2008; Opening Night: January 31, 2008; Closed March 1, 2008; 8 previews, 26 performances

Written by Mark Schultz; Produced by Apparition Productions (David McMahon & Emily Donahoe, Founders & Producers); Director, Wendy C. Goldberg; Sets, Alexander Dodge; Costumes, Anne Kennedy; Lighting, Josh Epstein; Original Music and Sound, Ryan Rumery; PSM, Stephanie Gatton; ASM, Rachel Motz; Production Manager, Peter Dean; General Manager, The Splinter Group, Seth A. Goldstein, Chelsea Kaczmarek, Heather Schings, Demos Tsilikoudis, Laura A. Wright; Casting Consultant, Harriet Bass, Meredith McDonough; Marketing, CHMajor Group; Press, Springer Associates, Shane Marshall Brown

CAST Thomas **Ross Bickell;** Jane **Charlotte Booker;** Susan **Emily Donahoe;** Ian **Clifton Guterman;** Martin **Ryan King;** Steven **Brandon Miller;** Betty **Patricia Randell;** Martha **Christa Scott-Reed;** Danny **Jonathan Walker**

A new play presented without intermission.

SYNOPSIS *Deathbed* paints a landscape of longing and desperation as its characters struggle to come to terms with loss and suffering and explore the boundaries of human compassion. Martha has cancer and demands attention; Danny doesn't want to deal; Thomas would rather forget; Steven loves too much; Susan feels betrayed; Martin is confused and Ian wants to know what death is really like.

BRIAN DYKSTRA: THE JESUS FACTOR

Barrow Street Theatre; First Preview: February 2, 2008; Opening Night: February 7, 2008; Closed March 15, 2008; 21 performances

Written by Brian Dykstra; Presented by Fresh Ice Productions, Inc. & Jack W. Batman; Director, Margarett Perry; Lighting, Solomon Weisbard; Producer, Lou Viola; Assistant Producer, Ashley T. Mowry; Press, O+M Co

Performed by **Brian Dykstra**

A solo performance play presented without intermission. Previously presented at the Barrow Street Fortnight January 19–21, 2008

SYNOPSIS Brian Dykstra's rage ignites in *The Jesus Factor,* his latest uncensored and outrageously funny one-man tour-de-force about religious hypocrisy and power. If dissent is a hallmark of the American tradition, Brian Dykstra stands in the forefront of a new generation of America's greatest patriots.

CLAYMONT

Baruch Performing Arts Center – Rose Nagelberg Theatre; First Preview: February 5, 2008; Opening Night: February 9, 2008; Closed March 2, 2008; 2 previews, 15 performances

Written by Kevin Brofsky; Produced by Emerging Artists Theatre (Paul Adams, Founder & Artistic Director); Director, Derek Jamison; Set, Tim Mcmath; Lighting, Joyce Liao; Costumes, Meredith Neal; Sound, Ned Thorne; Stage Manager, Jennifer Granrud; Props, Stephanie Wiesner; Technical Director, Patrick T. Cecala II; Prop Intern, Ellys R. Abrams; Crew, Tara Vetter, Alison Carroll, Jin Hamano; Production Manager, Tzipora Kaplan; Voice Actors: Ron Bopst, Laura Dillman, Ned Thorne; Press/Marketing, Katie Rosin

CAST Sharon Letts **Aimee Howard;** Shayna **Glory Gallo;** Neil **Jason Hare;** Grandma **Rebecca Hoodwin;** Mr. Ramsey **Ron Bopst;** Dallas Hitchens **Stephen Sherman;** Dolores **Wynne Anders**

Christopher Sloan, Wayne Henry, Christopher Borg, and Chad Austin in The Play About the Naked Guy *(photo by Erica Parise)*

SETTING Claymont, Delaware; Summer 1969. Off-Broadway premiere of a new play presented in two acts. Presented as part of Emerging Artists Theatre's TRIPLE THREAT in repertory with *Sisters' Dance* and *The Play About the Naked Guy.* Previously produced at EAT at the Intar Theatre, February 2004.

SYNOPSIS Neil lives with his mother and grandmother in the small town of Claymont. To make ends meet, his mother decides to take in a tenant in the basement by the name of Dallas. Neil falls quietly but passionately in love and is inspired by the rebellious Dallas to follow his own dreams of becoming an artist. When Neil learns that Dallas has been drafted to go to Vietnam, he takes his own steps toward manhood by deciding to go to California against his mother's wishes.

THE PLAY ABOUT THE NAKED GUY

Baruch Performing Arts Center – Rose Nagelberg Theatre; First Preview: February 4, 2008; Opening Night: February 9, 2008; Closed March 2, 2008; 2 previews, 15 performances

Written by David Bell; Produced by Emerging Artists Theatre (Paul Adams, Founder & Artistic Director); Director, Tom Wojtunik; Set, Michael P. Kramer; Lighting, Travis Walker; Costumes, David Withrow; Composition Sound, Ryan Homsey; Choreographer, Ryan Kasprzak; Stage Manager, Jennifer Marie Russo; Crew, Jamie Phelps, Terra Vetter, Julie Feltman, Kevin Wilder; Props, Ellys R. Abrams; Sound Supervisor, Aaron Blank; Production Manager, Tziproa Kaplan; Assistant Choreographer, Derek Roland; Press/Marketing, Katie Rosin

CAST Eddie Russini **Christopher Borg;** T. Scott **Christopher Sloan;** Kit **Dan Amboyer;** Mrs. Anderson **Ellen Reilly;** Dan **Jason Schuchman;** Amanda **Stacy Mayer;** Harold **Wayne Henry;** Adonis **Chad Austin**

SETTING A New York City theatre, the present. Off-Broadway premiere of a play presented without intermission. Presented as part of Emerging Artists Theatre's TRIPLE THREAT in repertory with *Sisters' Dance* and *Claymont.* Previously presented at EAT in 2004

SYNOPSIS In *The Play About the Naked Guy*, the Integrity Players, an Off-Off Broadway theater company dedicated to faithfully presenting the "lesser known" classics, is on the brink of shuttering. When a trio of artistically questionable though financially successful impresarios, responsible for such stage hits as "Naked Boys Running Around Naked" and "Drunk Frat Boys Making Porn," offer to help save their company, an epic and hilarious battle between commercialism and artistic allegiance ensues.

SISTERS' DANCE

Baruch Performing Arts Center – Rose Nagelberg Theatre; First Preview: February 6, 2008; Opening Night: February 9, 2008; Closed March 2, 2008; 2 previews, 15 performances

Written by Sarah Hollister; Produced by Emerging Artists Theatre (Paul Adams, Founder & Artistic Director); Director, Paul Adams; Original Music, Lewis Flinn; Set, Brian Garber; Costumes, Melanie Blythe; Lighting, G. Benjamin Swope; Sound, Kristyn R. Smith; Stage Manager, Amanda Schulze; Props, Stephanie Wiesner; Production Manager, Tzipora Kaplan; Fight Choreographer, Al Pagano; Crew, Julie Feltman, Alison Carroll, Kevin Wilder; Press & Marketing, Katie Rosin

CAST Mother **Blanche Cholet;** Duncan **Chuck Saculla;** Fleur **Janice Mann;** Alice **Laura Fois;** Roy Rune **Nick Ruggeri**

SETTING 1981, a farm in Michigan. Off-Broadway premiere of a play presented in two acts. Presented as part of Emerging Artists Theatre's TRIPLE THREAT in repertory with *Claymont* and *The Play About the Naked Guy.* Previously presented in 1995 at the Judith Anderson Theatre.

SYNOPSIS *Sisters' Dance* is about two estranged sisters, Fleur and Alice, who reunite on the family farm after the death of their mother. Long held resentment simmers to the surface when they realize their mother's will is still forcing them to cooperate. When Alice's husband and Fleur's hustler boyfriend enter the picture the sisters' dance becomes one of betrayal and seduction. Fleur and Alice will be forever changed in this searing drama about sisterhood, forgiveness, and a mother's love.

VITA & VIRGINIA

The Zipper Factory; First Preview: February 18, 1994; Opening Night: February 27, 1994; 12 performances (Monday evenings only)

Written by Eileen Atkins, adapted from the correspondence between Virginia Woolf and Vita Sackville-West; Produced by the no frills company (Caryl Young, Executive Producer; Sue Brady, Creative Director); Director, Pamela Berlin; Stage Manager, Susan D. Lange; General Manager, Peter Bogyo; Design Consultant, Andromache Chalfant; Legal, Kathleen Williamson; Press, Susan L. Schulman

CAST Vita Sackville-West **Patricia Elliott;** Virginia Woolf **Kathleen Chalfant***

SETTING The 1920's through the early years of World War II. Revival of the play presented in two acts. Originally produced Off-Broadway in 1994 with Ms. Atkins and Vanessa Redgrave.

Kathleen Chalfant and Patricia Elliott in Vita and Virginia *(photo by Carol Rosegg)*

SYNOPSIS Actress and author Eileen Adkins' *Vita & Virginia* deftly weaves the letters and diaries of Virginia Woolf and Vita Sackville-West into the story of the friendship — improbable, briefly physical and emotionally enduring — between the aloof literary genius Virginia and the aristocratic yet middle-brow novelist and poet Vita.

*Frances Sternhagen replaced Ms. Chalfant on March 17 & 31.

THE JAZZ AGE

59E59 Theater B; First Preview: February 8, 2008; Opening Night: February 14, 2008; Closed March 2, 2008; 26 performances

Written by Allan Knee, inspired by "A Moveable Feast" by Ernest Hemingway; Produced by The Lost Generation; Director, Christopher McElroen; Set, Troy Hourie; Costumes, Kimberly Glennon; Lighting, Colin D. Young; PSM, Anita Ross; Technical Supervisor, Vadim Malinskiy; Music Director/ Arrangements, Kelvyn Bell; Casting, Geoff Josselson; General Manager, R. Erin Craig/La Vie Productions; Executive Producer, Jana Robbins; Production Assistant, Melissa Mae Gregus; Press, Karen Greco

CAST Zelda Sayre **Amy Rutberg;** Ernest Hemingway **PJ Sosko;** F. Scott Fitzgerald **Dana Watkins;** Musicians **Kelvyn Bell** (guitar)**, Kim Davis** (bass)**, Shayshahn Macpherson** (drums/viola)

SETTING The 1920's, Paris. World premiere of a new play presented in two acts.

SYNOPSIS *The Jazz Age* travels through the artistically vibrant 1920s, examining the complex and stormy relationship between three compelling figures of the literary elite–Scott Fitzgerald, Zelda Sayre and Ernest Hemingway —who set out to invent a new world —and almost did.

GRAY AREA

The Barrow Group Theatre; First Preview: February 13, 2008; Opening Night: February 18, 2008; Closed March 16, 2008; 33 performances

Written by John Ahlin; Produced by The Barrow Group (Eric Paeper, Executive Director; Seth Barrish & Lee Brock, Artistic Directors); Director, Seth Barrish; Set and Costumes, Markas Henry; Lighting, Aaron Copp & Lauren Parish; Sound, Stefano Zazzera; PSM, Cassie Kivnick; Assistant Director, Alex Steel; Props, Kimberly Lorenz; Associate Producer, Porter Pickard; ASM, Joe Williamson; Assistant Lighting, Lauren Parish; Fight Director, Ron Piretti; Technical Director, Tyler Hall; Graphics, Dan Via; Press, Shirley Herz & Associates, Dan Demello

CAST Farregut **Keith Jochim;** Keith **John Ahlin**; Horse **Aaron Goodwin;** Randall **Taylor Ruckle**

Off-Broadway premiere of a new play presented in two acts. World premiere at The Virtual Theatre Project, Los Angeles, in April 2005.

SYNOPSIS *Gray Area* is a hilarious and moving war . . . between the states, as New York's leading drama and social critic decides to call it quits. He spends his final radio broadcast firing salvos at a variety of targets, saving a savage barrage against Civil War re-enactors for last. Three hardcore re-enactors take profound offense against him and stage a "redress for the ages," ensuing in a full out black-white, blue-gray, blue-red raging debate by characters who are, ironically, the most colorful because they come from the opposite ends of the spectrum.

ADDING MACHINE

Minetta Lane Theatre; First Preview: February 7, 2008; Opening Night: February 25, 2008; Closed July 20, 2008; 16 previews, 149 performances

Original music by Joshua Schmidt, libretto by Jason Loewith & Joshua Schmidt, based on the play *The Adding Machine* by Elmer Rice; Produced by Scott Morfee, Tom Wirtshafter, Margaret Cotter; Director, David Cromer; Set, Takeshi Kata; Lighting, Keith Parham; Sound, Tony Smolenski IV; Costumes, Kristine Knanishu; Video, Peter Flaherty; Properties, Michele Spardaro; Music Director, J. Oconer Navarro; PSM, Richard A. Hodge; Production Management, Aurora Productions; Casting, Pat McCorkle/Joe Lopick; General Management, Two Step Productions; Advertising, Eliran Murphy Group; Company Manager, Kate Mott; ASM, Kate McDaniel; Assistant Director, Jessica Redish; Associate Sound, Drew Levy; Video Associate/Programmer, Dustin O'Neill; Original Sound, Jeff Dublinske & Josh Schmidt; Original Set, Matthew York; Recordings, Dan Gnader; Press, O&M Co., Rick Miramontez, Jon Dimond; Cast recording: PS Classics 865

Roger E. DeWitt, Joel Hatch, Adinah Alexander, Niffer Clarke and Amy Warren in Adding Machine *(photo by Carol Rosegg)*

CAST Mrs. Zero **Cyrilla Baer;** Mr. Zero **Joel Hatch;** Daisy **Amy Warren;** Mr. One **Daniel Marcus;** Mrs. One **Niffer Clarke;** Mr. Two **Roger E. DeWitt;** Mrs. Two **Adinah Alexander;** Boss **Jeff Still;** Shrdlu **Joe Farrell**

UNDERSTUDIES Adinah Alexander (Daisy), Randy Blair (Mr One/Mr. Two/Shrdlu), Niffer Clarke (Mrs. Zero), Roger E. DeWitt (Boss), Daniel Marcus (Mr. Zero), Ariela Morgenstern (Mrs. One, Mrs. Two)

MUSICIANS J. Oconer Navarro (Musical Director), Andy Boroson (piano/Assistant Music Director), Brad "Gorilla" Carbone (percussion), Timothy Splain (synthesizer/assistant to the Composer)

MUSICAL NUMBERS In Numbers, Office Reverie, In Numbers (reprise), I'd Rather Watch You, The Party, Zero's Confession, Once More, Ham and Eggs!, Didn't We?, The Gospel According to Shrdlu, Shrdlu's Blues, Daisy's Confession, I'd Rather Watch You (reprise), Freedom!, In Numbers (reprise), Freedom! (reprise), The Music of The Machine

SETTING Here and the afterlife, an American city in the 1920's. New York premiere of a new musical presented without intermission. Developed and world premiere at Chicago's Next Theatre Company (Jason Loewith, Artistic Director) on February 5, 2007.

SYNOPSIS Based on Rice's 1923 incendiary play, *Adding Machine* tells the story of Mr. Zero, a nameless cog in American business. After 25 years of exemplary work, he finds that his pencil and paper efforts have been replaced by a mechanical adding machine. In a vengeful rage, Mr. Zero murders his boss. He journeys through life, death and an afterlife in the Elysian Fields, where he is met with one last chance for romance and redemption.

ARTFUCKERS

DR2; First Preview: February 9, 2008; Opening Night: February 26, 2008; Closed March 16, 2008; 14 previews, 22 performances

Written by Michael Domitrovich; Produced by Diane Passage and Victor Syrmis; Director, Eduardo Machado; Set and Lighting, Maruti Evans; Costumes, Margaret Moy; Sound, Ken Hypes, Projections, Chris Kateff; Marketing, Jim Glaub/New Media Marketing; Casting, Billy Hopkins; General Manager, Adam Hess; PSM, Michael Alifanz; Line Producer, Megan Smith; Production Manager, Alex Senchak; Props, Jeena Soon; Original Music, DJ Jon S, Moody Mammoth/Stefano Zazzera & Ken Hypes; Makeup/Hair, Danielle Fonseca; Press, Richard Kornberg & Associates

CAST Bella **Nicole Laliberte;** Owen **Will Janowitz;** Trevor **Asher Grodman;** Maggie **Jessica Kaye;** Max **Tuomas Hiltunen;** Understudies **J.J. Kandel, Emily Tremaine**

Transfer of the Off-Off Broadway play presented in two acts. Previously presented at Theater for the New City, February 15–March 4, 2007.

SYNOPSIS *ArtFuckers* follows a group of young, hot, creative twentysomethings standing at the top of the Celebrity Art World, who are collaborating on their friend's debut showing at New York Fashion week.

FABULOUS DIVAS OF BROADWAY

Theatre at St. Luke's; First Preview: February 13, 2008; Opening Night: February 27, 2008; Closed April 20, 2008; 17 previews, 66 performances

Written and directed by Alan Palmer; Produced by Berlique, Inc. in association with Edmund Gaynes; Set, Jessa Orr; Costumes, C. Buckey; Lighting, Peter Ray; Marketing, HHC Marketing; Production Manager, Kimberly Jade Tompkins; Musical Director, Curtis Jerome; General Manager, Jessimeg Productions, Edmund Gaynes and Julia Beardsley; Wigs, Ingrid Bakis; Makeup, Aimee Scarpino; Dresser, Sandy Sardar; Logo, Justin Robertson; Web, Jim Orr; Graphics, Scott Fowler; Production Photography, Thomas McTeer; Press, Technical Director, Josh Iacovelli; The Publicity Office, Michael S. Borowski, Marc Thibodeau, Jeremy Shaffer

Performed by **Alan Palmer**

New York premiere of a solo performance musical presented without intermission. Originally produced at Open Stage West, Los Angeles, California.

Alan Palmer in Fabulous Divas of Broadway *(photo by Josef Reiter)*

SYNOPSIS In rapid succession — and a non-stop turnover of gorgeous costumes — Alan Palmer brings to life eighteen divas including Merman, Channing, Minnelli, Lansbury, Garland, Andrews, and Rivera, and stars of today as Christine Ebersole, Patti LuPone, Sutton Foster, Kristin Chenoweth and Beth Leavel. Performing 25 songs in each lady's style, he weaves together reminiscences of growing up in Utah obsessed with cast albums, auditioning for shows in New York, onstage and backstage mishaps, raising his young son, and interacting with many of the ladies represented in the show.

LOWER NINTH

Flea Theater; First Preview: February 14, 2007; Opening Night: February 28, 2007; Closed Apirl 5, 2008; 13 previews, 34 performances

Written by Beau Willimon; Produced by The Flea Theater (Jim Simpson, Artistic Director; Carol Ostrow, Producing Director); Director, Daniel Goldstein; Set, Donyale Werle; Lighting, Ben Stanton; Costumes, Heather Dunbar; Sound, Jill BC DuBoff; Original Music, Aaron Meicht; Stage Manager, Jess Johnston; Set Assistant/Scenic Artist, Hannah Davis; Costume Assistant, Chris Rummery; Bat Back-ups, W. Tré Davis, Ronald Washington; Graphics, David Prittie; Casting, Erica Jensen/Calleri Casting; Assistant Director, Andrew K. Russell; Equipment and Support, Technical Artistry; Marketing Consultant, Marcia Pendelton/Walk Tall Girl Productions; General Manager, Beth Dembrow; Technical Director, Zack Tinkelman; Development/Marketing Manager, Sherri Kronfeld; Literary Manager, Gary Winter; Press, Spin Cycle/Ron Lasko

CAST Malcolm **James McDaniel;** E-Z **Gaius Charles**; Lowboy **Gvenga Akinnagbe**

SETTING A rooftop in the lower Ninth District of New

Orleans after Hurricane Katrina, August 2005. World premiere of a new play presented without intermission.

SYNOPSIS *Lower Ninth* is about two men stranded on a roof after a terrible storm. As Malcom and E-Z struggle to survive, they must battle heat, hunger and their pasts. Ultimately, their only hope for salvation rests with each other.

U.S. DRAG

Beckett Theatre on Theatre Row; First Preview: February 23, 2008; Opening Night: March 1, 2008;Closed March 16, 2008; 23 performances

Written by Gina Gionfriddo; Produced by the stageFARM Theatre Company (Carrie Shaltz, Founder and Executive Director; Alex Kilgore, Artistic Director); Director, Trip Cullman; Sets, Sandra Goldmark; Costumes, Emily Rebholz; Lighting, Nicole Pearce; Sound, Bart Fasbender; Choreography, Jacquie Dumas; Props, John McDaniel; Stage Manager, Emily Ellen Roberts; ASM, Amy Kaskeski; Assistants: Aimee Dombo (set), Denise Maroney (costumes), Tess James and Michael Jarret (lighting); Casting, Calleri Casting; Marketing, Kate Laughlin; Christine Renee Miller, Production Coordinator; Press, O + M Company, Philip Carrubba

Tanya Fischer, Lucas Papaelias, Logan Marshall Green, and Lisa Joyce in U.S. Drag *(photo by Richard Termine)*

CAST Allison **Tanya Fischer;** Angela **Lisa Joyce;** James **James Martinez;** Ned **Matthew Stadelmann;** Evan **Lucas Papaelias;** Mary **Audrey Lynn Weston;** Christopher **Logan Marshall-Green;** Manager/Janice/Bartender/ Christian **Rebecca Henderson**

SETTING New York City. Off-Broadway premiere of a play presented without intermission.

SYNOPSIS *U.S. Drag* is a dark comedy/satire about a sensationalizing celebrity culture where even murder can be turned into entertainment. In the play, two recent college grads who find that making a living in New York City isn't so easy go on the hunt for love, money, meaning, and Ed —New York's most elusive serial attacker.

JAMAICA, FAREWELL

SoHo Playhouse; First Preview: February 22, 2008; Opening Night: March 3, 2008; Closed April 20, 2008; 5 previews, 42 performances

Written by Debra Ehrhardt; Produced by The SoHo Playhouse (Darren Lee Cole, Producing Director; Faith A. Mulvihill, Executive Director); Director, Wallace Norman; Design, Richard Currie; Sound, Danny Ehrhardt; Stage Manager, Jenny Reagan; Scenic Artists, Loretta Argo, Anastasios "Taso" Megaris; Graphics, Stephanie Layton; Press, Keith Sherman & Associates, Glenna Freedman, Brett Oberman, Scott Klein, DJ Martin, Patrick Paris

Performed by **Debra Ehrhardt**

Off-Broadway debut of a solo performance play presented without intermission. Previously presented in the 2007 Fringe Festival, and the show has been performed in Los Angeles, Santa Barbara, Atlanta, Tampa, Ft. Lauderdale, and Toronto

SYNOPSIS *Jamaica, Farewell* tells the story of Debra Ehrhardt's journey in which she escapes revolution-torn Jamaica in the 1970's. Left to her own devices, she risked prison time, and even death in an attempt to pull off a daring and dangerous caper with the unwitting help of an infatuated American CIA agent to fulfill her lifelong dream of starting over in America.

BEEBO BRINKER CHRONICLES

37 Arts Theatre B; First Preview: February 19, 2008; Opening Night: March 5, 2008; Closed April 27, 2008; 17 previews, 63 performances

Written by Kate Moira Ryan & Linda S. Chapman, based on the books *I am a Woman, Woman in the Shadows* and *Journey to a Woman* by Ann Bannon; Presented by the Hourglass Group; Produced by Lily Tomlin and Jane Wagner, Harriet Newman Leve, Elyse Singer, Jamie deRoy, Pam Laudenslager and Douglas Denoff, Double Play Connection; Director, Leigh Silverman; Set, Rachel Hauck; Costumes, Theresa Squire; Lighting, Nicole Pearce; Sound, Jill BC DuBoff; Wigs/Hair/ Makeup, J. Jared Janas/Rob Greene; Casting, Jack Doulin; Marketing, Blue Streak Consulting; Production Manager, Bradley Thompson; PSM, Pamela Edington; General Manager, Roy Gabay; Associate Producers, Ric Wanetik, Jennifer Isaacson, Greg Hall; Company Manager, Chris Aniello;

Technical Director, Christine Parker; Assistant Director, Michele Pace; ASM, Sunneva Stapleton; Props, Meghan Bachanan; Fight Choreography, Marin Ireland; Press, Spin Cycle, Ron Lasko

CAST Marcie/Lili/Nina **Carolyn Baeumler;** Beebo Brinker **Jenn Colella;** Charlie/Burr **Bill Dawes;** Beth **Autumn Dornfeld;** Laura **Marin Ireland*;** Jack **David Greenspan;** Understudies: **Bronwyn Coleman, Nick Basta**

SETTING 1952–1960, California and New York City. Transfer of the Off-Off-Broadway play presented without intermission. Originally presented by the Hourglass Group at the 4th Street Theatre (New York Theatre Workshop) September 27–October 20, 2007.

SYNOPSIS *Beebo Brinker Chronicles* follows the lives and loves of four friends in pre-Stonewall Greenwich Village. Beth and Laura, secret lovers in college, still pine for each other. Before they can reunite, they find themselves entangled in a web spun by Beebo Brinker, a butch denizen of the underground bar scene, and Jack, a flamboyant fop with caustic wit.

*Succeeded by Xanthe Elbrick (3/25/08)

Carolyn Baeumler & Marin Ireland in Beebo Brinker Chronicles *(photo by Dixie Sheridan)*

SECRETS OF A SOCCER MOM

Snapple Theatre Center – 3rd Floor; First Preview: February 9, 2007; Opening Night: March 5, 2008; Closed May 4, 2008; 17 previews, 69 performances

Written by Kathleen Clark; Produced by A-Frame Productions; Director, Judith Ivey; Set, Lex Liang; Costumes, Elizabeth Flauto; Lighting, Jeff Croiter; Sound, Zachary Williamson; Casting, Tara Rubin; Associate Director, Holly-Anne Ruggiero; PSM, Scott Pegg; General Manager, Richard Frankel Productions/Leslie Ledbetter; Technical Supervisor, Smitty/Theatresmith, Inc.; Assistant Lighting, Grant Yeager; Assistant Sound, Adam Rigby; Wardrobe Supervisor, Ryan Rossetto; Props, Brandon Giles; Marketing, Christina Papagijika; Advertising, Serino Coyne; Press, Barlow-Hartman, Leslie Baden, Kevin Robak

CAST Nancy **Nancy Ringham;** Lynn **Deborah Sonnenberg;** Alison **Caralyn Kozlowski;** Standbys: **Elyse Knight, Renée Bang Allen**

SETTING A soccer field on a Sunday. New York premiere of a new play presented without intermission. World premiere at Fleetwood Stage, Westchester, New York.

SYNOPSIS Three women leave their traditional spot on the sidelines to play in the annual mother-son soccer game. This ordinary day becomes extraordinary as the competition ignites their fierce desire to recapture their spirit, humor and passion. *Secrets of a Soccer Mom* speaks to everyone, no matter age or gender, in attempting to answer that age old question: how in the world did I wind up here?

TIM MINCHIN

New World Stages – Stage 5; First Preview: March 3, 2008; Opening Night: March 5, 2008; Closed April 12, 2008; 2 previews, 34 performances

Produced by Phil McIntyre Entertainment; Lighting, Paul Jones; Sound, Zane Birdwell; Production Manager, Jason Adams; Marketing, HHC Marketing; Advertising, Sold Out (UK); Lighting Operator, Vivan Tong; Press, PMK HBH

Performed by **Tim Minchin**

A solo performance comedy show presented without intermission.

SYNOPSIS Tim Minchin, winner of the 2007 "Best Alternative Comedian" Award at the Aspen Comedy Festival, performs his dark, piano driven, pop-comedic cabaret. Australian-born Minchin launched onto the world comedy scene in 2005 with *Darkside*, which won the Perrier Comedy Award for Best Newcomer at the Edinburgh Fringe Festival. His second show *So Rock*, earned both the Most Outstanding Show and the Festival Directors Award at the Melbourne International Comedy Festival.

THE SCARIEST

Theatres at 45 Bleecker – Green Room; First Preview: March 2, 2007; Opening Night: March 6, 2007; Closed March 30, 2007; 3 previews, 22 performances

Written by Kristin Newborn, Laura Schellhardt, Mark Schultz and Gary Sunshine with additional material by Dan Dietz, Ann Marie Healy, Liz Duffy Adams and Victoria Stewart; Based on stories by WW Jacobs, Nathaniel Hawthorne, Hans Christian Anderson, and the Book of Revelations; Produced by The Exchange; Directors, Ari Edelson and Meredith McDonough; Set, Clint Ramos; Costumes, Emily Pepper; Lighting, Christopher Studley; Sound, Lindsay Jones; Stage/Production Manager, Jared DeBacker; ASM, Alex Jepson; Assistant Director, Lileana Blain-Cruz; Line Producer, Jaimie Mayer; Casting, Vince Liebhart; Set and Props Fabrication, Joseph Cairo; Press, Spin Cycle/Ron Lasko

CAST **Rebecca Brooksher, Angel Desai, Andy Groteluschen, Jesse Hooker, Mandy Siegfried, Joaquin Torres**

Five one-act plays, and four short stories/monologues presented in two acts. Pieces included: *Delightful, Finally, The Names of Foods, Night Games, The Apothecary's Daughter, The Uses of Fear, Third Wish, Lobster Boy,* and *Revelations.*

SYNOPSIS No matter where in the world, no matter what culture, people know that there is something lurking around the shadows, creeping under the bed. For *The Scariest*, the Exchange commissioned four of New York's most exciting playwrights to remix some of the greatest classics of the horror genre. These modern stage interpretations have all been recast into contemporary settings and to confront modern-day terrors with humor and a bit of the macabre.

ROMEO AND JULIET

Kirk Theatre on Theatre Row; First Preview: March 5, 2008; Opening Night: March 16, 2008; Closed April 6, 2008; 34 performances

Written by William Shakespeare; Produced by Theatre Breaking Through Barriers (formerly Theatre By The Blind – George Ashiotis and Ike Schambelan, Artistic Directors); Director, Ike Schambelan; Set and Lighting, Bert Scott; Costumes, Chloe Chapin; Fight Director, J. David Brimmer; Sound, Nicholas Viselli; Stage Manager, Kimothy Cruse; ASM, Nathan K. Claus; Production Managers, David Chontos, Nicholas Lazzaro; Marketing, Michelle Brandon; Fight Assistants, James Hutchinson, Corey Pierno, Mike Yahn; Press, Shirley Herz Associates, Daniel Demello

Gregg Mozgala & Emily Young in Romeo and Juliet *(photo by Carol Rosegg)*

CAST Friar/Nurse/Apothecary/Tybalt/Montague/Gregory/Old Capulet/Capulet Servant/Paris's Page/Musician/Watchman/Citizen/Chorus **George Ashiotis;** Romeo/Lady Capulet/Abraham/Servant/Musician/Watchman/Citizen/Chorus **Greg Mozgala;** Capulet/Benvolio/Sampson/Balthazar/Capulet Servant/Musician/Watchman/Citizen/Chorus **Nicholas Viselli;** Juliet/Mercutio/Paris/Prince/Peter/Potpan/Lady Montague/Friar John/Abraham's Friend/Citizen/Chorus **Emily Young**

SETTING July 15–19, 2007; New York City. Revival of the play presented without intermission.

SYNOPSIS TBTB tackles *Romeo and Juliet* with four actors playing all of the roles, without cutting a single scene, character or entrance. Set in modern Upper East Side, the Capulets are nouveau riche and the Montagues are old money. In TBTB's production, the time progression stays true to Shakespeare's precision of five days in mid-July.

JACKIE MASON – THE ULTIMATE JEW

New World Stages – Stage 1; Opening Night: March 18, 2008; Closed July 20, 2008; 120 performances

Written and directed by Jackie Mason; Produced by Jyll Rosenfeld, IAG & Allen Spivak/Adam Spivak/Larry Magrid; Set, Brian Webb; Lighting, Paul Miller; Sound, Ryan Powers; General Management, Theatre Production Group LLC; Associate Producers, Mickey Shapiro, Archie Gianunzio; PSM, Steve Sabaugh; Marketing, Keith Hurd; Technical Supervision, production glue, llc; Advertising, Endeavour; Assistant General Manager, Tegan Meyer; Personal Assistant, Melissa Flores; Technical Supervisor, Richard Cocchiara; Electrician, Michael Barczys; Master Electrician, John Paul Nardecchia; Production Sound, Joshua Redfearn; Press, David Gersten & Associates, Kevin P. McAnarney/James Lopez

Performed by **Jackie Mason**

A solo performance comedy show presented without intermission.

SYNOPSIS No election year would be complete without the irascible, irreplaceable and incomparable Jackie Mason, who brings his 8th and final one-man comedy tour de force, *Jackie Mason – The Ultimate Jew*, to New World Stages. Long passionate about politics, Mason is well known for his tough and outspoken position on a variety of issues. An elder statesman of the stand-up comedy world, he combines pungent political satire, insightful observations on the foibles of modern life, and impeccable timing to create material that leaves audiences laughing until they cry show after show.

RAINBOW KISS

59E59 Theater B; First Preview: March 12, 2008; Opening Night: March 22, 2008; Closed April 13, 2008; 34 performances

Written by Simon Farquhar; Presented by The Play Company (Kate Loewald, Founding Producer; Lauren Weigel, Managing Producer); Director, Will Frears; Set, Thomas Lynch; Costumes, Sarah Beers; Lighting, Tyler Micoleau; Sound, Drew Levy; PSM, Rachel E. Miller; Production Manager, R. Erin Craig/ La Vie Productions; Casting, Judy Henderson; Dialect Coach, Stephen Gabis; Fight Director, Rick Sordelet; Literary Associate/Company Manager, Melissa Hardy; Associate Producer, Linda Bartholomai; Properties, Mary Robinette Kowal; Associate Set, Charlie Corcoran; Associate Fight Director, Christian Kelly-Sordelet; Assistant Director, Hondo Weiss-Richmond; ASM, Erica E. Conrad; Technical Supervisor, Vadim Malinskiy; Graphics, Noah Scalin; For The Play Company: Trip Cullman (Associate Artist), Phillip Guttman (Development/Communications Consultant); Press, The Karpel Group/Bridget Klapinski, Beth Sorell

CAST Shazza **Charlotte Parry;** Keith **Peter Scanavino;** Murdo **Robert Hogan;** Scobie **Michael Cates**

SETTING Keith's flat in Aberdeen, Scotland. U.S. Premiere of a new play presented in two acts. Originally produced at The Royal Court Jerwood Theatre Upstairs, Sloane Square, London on April 5, 2006.

SYNOPSIS *Rainbow Kiss* starts with a kiss and ends in blood. Keith, raising his infant son alone while holding down a dead-end job, stakes his future on a one-night stand with Shazza, an upwardly mobile beautician he meets at a club. She has a master plan and he doesn't belong. Yet she keeps coming back for more.

DI KSUBE (The Marriage Contract)

Goldman-Sonnenfeldt Auditorium at the JCC; First Preview: March 16, 2008; Opening Night: March 23, 2008; Closed April 6, 2008; 7 preview, 16 performances

Written by Epraim Kison, translated by Israel Beker, music by Shimon Cohen, lyrics by Moshe Sacher; Presented by National Yiddish Theatre – Folksbiene (Motl Didner, Artistic Director; Georgia Buchanan, Managing Director); Director, Mioti Didner; Music Director, Zalmen Mlotek; Choreography/ASM, Penny Ayn Maas; Set, Joseph Spirito; Costumes, Gail Cooper-Hecht; Lighting, Dan Scully; Sound, Don Jacobs; Supertitle, Matt Temkin; Stage Manager, Marci Skolnick; Production Manager, Production Consolidated of NY; Russian Tranlation, Anna Plotkina; English Translation, Goldie Adler Gold; Voiceover, Robert Paul Abelson; Press, Beck Lee Media Blitz

CAST Yafa Birnboym **Mena Levit;** Shifre Borozovski **Suzanne Toren;** Ayala Borozovski **Dani Marcus;** Elimeylekh Borozovski **Itzy Firestone;** Robert Knal **Eyal Sherf;** Buki Vays **Ilan Kwittken;** Musicians: Patrick Farrell (accordion), Stephen Borsuk (piano)

MUSICAL NUMBERS Enough Already, What Have I Gotten Myself Into?, I Remember, Oy Is This a Dance, Take Me to the Symphony, I'll Be a Bachelor Again, Epilogue

Dani Marcus, Suzanne Toren, and I.W. "Itzy" Firestone in Di Ksube (The Marriage Contract) *(photo by Scott Wynn)*

SETTING The apartment of the Borozokvski's in Tel Aviv, Israel, 1974. Revival of a musical comedy presented in Yiddish with English and Russian titles in four scenes in two acts. Originally produced by Folksbiene in 1982 and 1991.

SYNOPSIS In this 1953 musical, a long running hit on the Israeli stage, Eli and Shifre's 25-year marriage is questioned when their daughter's future in-laws insist on checking their wedding contract to insure that their son is marrying a legitimate young lady. When the contract is not readily produced (it may or may not exist since the Borozovskis were married on a kibbutz), the family is thrown into chaos. Shifre uses the occasion to get back at her chauvinist husband, but the attentions of a flirtatious upstairs neighbor and the appearance of a young kibbutznik put uproarious strain on the parents, their daughter and her intended.

THE AMERICAN DREAM & THE SANDBOX

Cherry Lane Theatre; First Preview: March 11, 2008; Opening Night: March 25, 2008; Closed May 3, 2008; 45 performances

Written and directed by Edward Albee; Set, Neil Patel; Costumes, Carrie Robbins; Lighting, Nicole Pearce; Sound, Arielle Edwards; PSM, Paige van den Burg; Casting, Hopkins, Smith & Barden; Marketing, Walker International Communications Group; Advertising, Eliran Murphy Group; Facility Manager, Janio Marrero; Development, Joanna Gottlieb; Administrative Assistant, Angela Scott; Business Management, Friedman & LaRosa, Inc., Joyce Friedman; Company Coordinator, Alexander Orbovich; Production Manager, Peter Dean; ASM, Tiffany Tabatchnick; Wigs, Paul Huntley; Associate Production Manager/Tech Director, Jeffrey Duer; Press, Art Meets Commerce, Timothy Haskell, Jim Galub

CAST *The American Dream*: Mommy **Judith Ivey*;** Daddy **George Bartenieff**; Grandma **Lois Markle;** Mrs Barker **Kathleen Butler;** Young Man **Harmon Walsh;** *The Sandbox*: The Young Man **Jesse Williams;** Mommy **Judith Ivey*;** Daddy **George Bartenieff;** The Musician **Daniel Shelvin;** Grandma **Lois Markle;** Understudy: **Noshir Dalal** (The Young Man – *The Sandbox*)

Revival of two one-act plays presented with intermission. *The Sandbox* was originally presented at Jazz Gallery in a series called *4 in 1* on May 15, 1960 (see *Theatre World* Volume 16, page 174). *The American Dream* premiered at the Cherry Lane on a bill with Samuel Beckett's *Happy Days* and Albee's *The Death of Bessie Smith* on September 17, 1961; both plays were included in a series entitled *Theatre of the Absurd* featuring the works of Albee, Genet, Ionesco, Beckett, Jack Richardson, and Fernando Arrabal at the Cherry Lane on February 11, 1962 (see *Theatre World* Volume 18, pages 127 & 149).

SYNOPSIS *The Sandbox* introduces one of America's most dysfunctional families, a grasping, materialistic married couple who stage a perverse seaside idyll destined to end in the demise of the wife's aged mother. *The American Dream* is a ferocious attack on the substitution of artificial for real values, a startling tale of murder and morality that rocks middle-class ethics to their complacent foundations. Albee explores the hollowness of the American dream, as well as the fallacy of the ideal American family

*Succeeded by Kate Mulgrew (4/22-5/3)

ALMOST AN EVENING

Theatres at 45 Bleecker – Bleecker Street Theatre; First Preview: March 20, 2008; Opening Night: April 2, 2008; Closed June 1, 2008; 86 performances

Written by Ethan Coen; Produced by Atlantic Theater Company and Art Meets Commerce (Chip Meyrelles, Executive Director; Ken Greiner, Producing Director) and Carole Shorenstein Hays; Director, Neil Pepe; Sets, Riccardo Hernandez; Costumes, Ilona Somogyi; Lighting, Donald Holder; Sound, Eric Shim; Fight Director, J. David Brimmer; Casting, Telsey + Company; PSM, Marion Friedman/Alison Desantis; Stage Manager, Rebecca Goldstein-Glaze; Production Manager, Michael Wade; Advertising/Marketing, Jim Glaub, Laurie Connor, Jodi Sheeler; Associate General Manager, Catharine Guiher, Sumeet Bharati; Associate Artistic Director, Christian Parker; General Manager, Jamie Tyrol; Executive Producers, Andrew D. Hamingson, Chip Meyrelles, Kenneth Greiner; Wigs, Charles LaPointe; Press, Boneau/Bryan-Brown

CAST *Waiting*: Nelson **Joey Slotnick**; Receptionist **Mary McCann*1**; Mr. Sabatacheck **Jordan Lage**; McMartin **Mark Linn-Baker**, Polhemus **Del Pentecost;** *Four Benches*: One **Tim Hopper;** Earl **Del Pentecost;** Mr. Boodrum

F. Murray Abraham and Mark-Linn Baker in Almost an Evening *(photo by Doug Hamilton)*

J.R. Horne; Control **F. Murray Abraham***2; Woman with Pram **Johanna Day;** Texan **Jordan Lage**; *Debate:* God Who Judges **F. Murray Abraham***2; God Who Loves **Mark Linn-Baker;** Angel 1 **Del Pentecost**; Angel 2/Understudy **J.R. Horne**; Young Woman **Mary McCann***1; Young Man **Jordan Lage;** Maître D' **Tim Hopper;** Waiter **Joey Slotnick**; Lady Friend **Johanna Day**

Commercial extension of three new short plays presented without intermission. Previously presented at Atlantic Stage 2 January 9-February 10 with most of this cast (Mr. Hopper replaced Jonathan Cake, Ms. Day replaced Elizabeth Marvel). See "Company Series" listings in this volume.

SYNOPSIS Three short plays unsuccessfully tackle important questions. In *Waiting*, someone waits somewhere for quite some time. In *Four Benches*, a voyage to self-discovery takes a British intelligence agent to steam baths in New York and Texas, and to park benches in the U.S. and U.K. In *Debate*, cosmic questions are taken up. Not much is learned.

*Succeeded by: 1. Kate Blumberg (5/13/08) 2. Peter Maloney (5/13/08)

AMERICAN GIRLS

45th Street Theatre; First Preview: April 3, 2008; Opening Night: April 6, 2008; Closed April 27, 2008; 4 previews, 19 performances

Written by Hilary Bettis; Presented by Dog Run Rep (A.J. Hirsch, Producer) and Pat Blake; Director, Jeff Cohen; Set, Ryan Elliot Kravetz; Costumes, Gail Cooper-Hecht; Lighting, Evan Purcell; Video, Gray M. Winslow; PSM, Michal V. Mendelson; ASM, Mara Kassin; Technical Director, Brian Smallwood; Electrician, Wilburn Bonnell; Graphics, Sydney Cohen; Development, Amy Fleischer; Press, David Gersten

CAST Amanda **Hilary Bettis;** Katie **Kira Sternbach**

RECORDED CAST Scott Johnson (Opal Banks Announcer), Adam Hirsch (Mr. Branbalt), Mark Chin (Classy Mirage DJ), Sydney Cohen (Angry Stripper), Maxwell Zener (Frank Miller), Traci Hovel (Dr. Opal Banks)

SETTING In and around a small town in Iowa. A new play presented without intermission.

SYNOPSIS *American Girls* is the story of two 14-year old Midwestern girls who are on a collision course with faith-based culture and the sex industry.

MARCY IN THE GALAXY

Connelly Theatre; First Preview: March 28, 2007; Opening Night: April 6, 2008; Closed April 20, 2008; 10 preview, 13 performances

Book, music and lyrics by Nancy Shayne, based on a story by Nancy Shayne and Michael Patrick King; Presented by The Transport Group (Jack Cummings III, Artistic Director; Lori Fineman, Executive Director), Paula & Jeff Davis, Jamie deRoy, Ted Snowdon & Jerry Wade, in association with Sarah Ackerman, Steven Ernst, Joanne & Ron Falcon, Victoria & Ben Feder, Debbie & Lawrence Freitag, Lila & Richard Holl, Yael & Nick Jekogian, Louis Kunsch, Claire Labine, Joanna & Josh Lipman, Lin-Manuel Miranda, Christine & Philip Werner; Director, Jack Cummings III; Music Director/Orchestrations & Arrangements, Mark Berman; Set, Sandra Goldmark; Costumes, Kathryn Rohe; Lighting, R. Lee Kennedy; Sound, Michael Rasbury; Hair and Wigs, Paul Huntley; PSM, Wendy Patten; Stage Manager, Theresa Flanagan; ASM, Jenn Hedges; Associate Director, Gregg Wiggans; Dramaturg, Adam R. Perlman; Music Preparation FireFly Music Service; General Manager, Michael Coglan; Casting, Nora Brennan; Production Manager, Travis Walker; Technical Director, Stewart Metcalf; Press, Richard Kornberg & Associates

CAST Marcy **Donna Lynne Champlin;** The Waiter **Jonathan Hammond;** Dorothea **Janet Carroll;** Joyce **Mary-Pat Green;** Sharon **Jenny Fellner;** Peppy **Teri Ralston**

ORCHESTRA Mark Berman (Conductor/piano), Garo Yellin (cello), David Gold (viola), Rick Kriska (clarinet/flute)

MUSICAL NUMBERS Overture, January First, Not a Consideration, Keep Me Away, Twenty-One, Conversations With My Mother, Complex-Simple, The Marcy Show, Amazing Destinations, Not a Consideration (reprise), One Room Mansion, Who Gets to Shine, Justin, Michigan By Monday, I Will Blaze, Hang In There, The Tide, Who Gets to Shine (reprise)

SETTING The Galaxy Diner, New York City, January 1. World premiere of a new musical presented without intermission.

SYNOPSIS *Marcy in the Galaxy* is a humorous and poignant musical glimpse at what happens when dreams of being a New York artist take longer to come true than planned. At mid-life, Marcy finds herself alone in the Galaxy Diner—out of money and almost out of hope—in this darkly comic romp through dreams, disappointment, family, first love, and absolutely delicious diner desserts.

CANDIDE

New York State Theatre; Opening Night: April 8, 2008; Closed April 20, 2008; 14 performances

Music, orchestrations and additional lyrics by Leonard Bernstein, book adapted from Voltaire by Hugh Wheeler, lyrics by Richard Wilbur, additional lyrics by John LaTouche & Stephen Sondheim; Produced by New York City Opera (Gerard Mortier, General Manager; Jane M. Gullong, Executive Director; Robin Thompson, Producing Artistic Director); Conductor/NYCO Music Director, George Manahan; Orchestrations, Hershy Kay & John Mauceri; Production, Harold Prince; Stage Director, Arthur Masella; Choreographer, Patricia Birch; Set, Clarke Dunham; Costumes, Judith Dolan; Lighting, Ken Billington; Sound, Abe Jacob; Associate Choreographer, Deanna L. Dys; Casting, Mark Simon; Supertitles, Celeste Montemarano; Chorus Master, Charles F. Prestinari; Associate Conductor, Braden Toan; Stage Managers, Cindy Knight, Anne Dechêne, Peggy Imbire, Lisa Jean Lewis, Chad Zodrow; Diction, Kathryn LaBouf; Assistants: Anthony Piccolo, Mozart de Oliveira (chorus), Lynn Baker, Steven Mosteller, Marijo Newman (conductors), Cynthia Edwards, Andrew Chown, Albert Sherman (directors); Publicity, Corinne J. Zadik

Daniel Reichard, Jessica Wright, Richard Kind, Kyle Pfortmiller and Lauren Worsham in New York City Opera's Candide *(photo by Carol Rosegg)*

CAST Voltaire/Dr. Pangloss/Businessman/Governor/Police Chief/Sage **Richard Kind;** Candide **Daniel Reichard;** Cunegonde **Lauren Worsham** or **Lielle Berman;** Paquette **Jessica Wright;** Maximilian **Kyle Pfortmiller;** Old Lady **Judith Blazer;** Baron/Inquisitor/Slave Driver/Pasha-Prefect **Robert Ousley**; Baroness/Calliope Player **Sandy Rosenberg;** Huntsman/Soldier/Don **Peter Samuel;** Servant of Maximilian/Soldier/Don Issachar/Judge/Father Bernard/Judge/Gambler **Eric Michael Gillett;** Soldier/Judge/Don/Pirate **William Ledbetter;** Heresy Agent/Don **John Paul Almon;** Lion **Christopher Jackson;** Pink Sheep **Sarah Moulton, Deborah Lew;** Ensemble **Trey Gillen, Travis Kelly, Robin Masella, Francis Toumbakaris; William Ward, Carolyn Doherty, Tyler Ingram, Matt Rivera, Noah Amberlin, Dennis O'Bannion, John Henry Thomas, Richard Almanshofer, Tom Myers;** Chorus: New York City Opera Chorus and Dancers

MUSICAL NUMBERS Overture; Life Is Happiness Indeed; The Best of All Possible Worlds; Oh, Happy We; It Must Be So; Fanfare, Chorale and Battle; Glitter and Be Gay, Auto da Fé; Candide's Lament; You Were Dead, You Know; I Am Easily Assimilated; Finale; Entr'acte and Ballad: To the New World; My Love; The Old Lady's Tale (Barcarolle); Alleluia; Sheep Song; Governor's Waltz; Bon Voyage; Quiet; The Best of All Possible Worlds (reprise); What's the Use; You Were Dead, You Know (reprise); Finale: Make Our Garden Grow

Revival of the Opera House version of the musical presented in two acts. This version was originally produced at NYCO in October 1982–1984; revived in November 1986, and again in March 2005. The original Broadway production opened December 1, 1956 at the Martin Beck playing 73 performances (see *Theatre World* Volume 13, page 56); a new revised version (upon which the Opera version is based) played at the Broadway Theatre March 10, 1974–January 4, 1976, running 740 performances (see *Theatre World* Volume 30, page 42). The musical was revived at the Gershwin Theatre April 29–July 27, 1997, running 104 performances (see *Theatre World* Volume 53, page 48).

SYNOPSIS *Candide* tells the story of a young man who is determined to follow his instructor's creed of mindless optimism. Even after being banished from his homeland, captured by Bulgarians, beaten by the Spanish Inquisition, robbed of everything he owns, and torn repeatedly from the woman he loves, Candide still clings to the philosophy that everything is for the best in this, "the best of all possible worlds."

OUR DAD IS IN ATLANTIS

Theatres at 45 Bleecker – Lafayette Street Theatre; First Preview: April 4, 2008; Opening Night: April 8, 2008; Closed April 20, 2008; 17 performances

Written by Javier Malpica, translated into English by Jorge Ignacio Cortiñas; Produced by Working Theater (Mark Plesent, Producing Director; Connie Grappo, Artistic Director) and Queens Theatre in the Park; Director, Debbie Saivetz; Set, Mikiko Suzuki MacAdams; Lighting, Jack Mehler; Sound, Bray Poor; Costumes, Jessica Gaffney; Casting, Stephanie Klapper; Production Manager, Josh Iacovelli; PSM, Elyzabeth Gorman;

ASM, Shea Elmore; Financial Support, David Schwartz Foundation; Assistant Set/Props, Kina Park; Props, Jana Mattioli; Press, Sam Rudy Media Relations

CAST Little Brother **Sergio Ferreira;** Big Brother **Steven D. Garcia**

SETTING Mexico, the present. Off-Broadway premiere of a new play presented without intermission.

SYNOPSIS *Our Dad Is in Atlantis* concerns two Mexican brothers, ages 8 and 11, who are left with their grandmother in a rural village while their father goes to the United States to look for work. Motherless, missing their father, and left in the care of relatives they scarcely know, the boys rely on one another for emotional support they are unequipped to provide, and for physical support in a naive and desperate attempt to reach their father in "Atlantis."

MARK TWAIN'S BLUES

DR2; First Preview: April 2, 2008; Opening Night: April 13, 2008; Closed May 10, 2008; 13 previews, 27 performances

Book by Walt Stepp, music and lyrics by Walt Stepp and Mark Twain; Produced by Cinna Productions; Director, Tom Herman; Set, Jen Varblalow; Costumes, Cathy Small; Lighting, Charles Forster; Sound, Peter Carpenter; Music Director/Vocal Arrangements, David Wolfson; Choreographer, James Beaudry; PSM, Michael Palmer; ASM, Malachy Orozco; Production Management, Peter & Julie Sylvester; Technical Director, John Sisson; Casting, Tom Stanton; Press, Mark Cannistraro/ Empower PR

CAST Mark Twain **Bill Tatum;** Actress/Mark Twain's Mother/Aunt Sally/Clara/Emmeline **Bonne Kramer;** Huck Finn **Lance Olds;** Jim **Barry Phillips**

SONGS I Got De Raff, Mother, I Am Not a Christian, Nothing Left But Me, Everlasting Aphorisms, Every Day's and Invention Youth, I Couldn't Let You Go, Old Son, I'll Be Gone Forever, First Thing I Do When I Gets to Cayro, What's the Use of Learnin' to Do Right?, The Belle of New York, Stephen Dowling Botts, I Always Knew It Was You, Boiler Factory, Dat Truck Dah Is Trash Huck, Dey Calls You White Trash, One Sweet Chile, Kind of Lazy and Jolly, I Got De Raff (reprise)

SETTING The turn of the 20th century, Mark Twain's imagination, a dressing room in a Southern theatre just before one of his famous lectures. Transfer of the Off-Off Broadway play with songs presented in two acts. The show previously played Altered Stages February 15–March 8, 2008

SYNOPSIS As the 65-year-old Mark Twain is preparing for another of his frequent humorous lectures, he is surprised by a voice from the audience: it's Huckleberry Finn, now 20 years older than he was in Twain's book. He's soon joined by escaped slave Jim, now 50 years old—and together the two accuse their creator of betraying the truth of their lives in order to boost book sales. Determined to set the record straight once and for all, Huck and Jim re-enact some of the scenes in Twain's book...but this time, the way they should have happened.

SETH'S BROADWAY 101

New World Stages – Stage 3; April 14, 2008; 2 performances

Conceived and written by Seth Rudetsky; Produced by Tim Pinckney; Presented by The Actors Fund; Director, Peter Flynn; Choreography, Devanand Janki; Music Director, Steve Marzullo; Set Consultant, Paul Wimer & Josh Zangen; Lighting Consultant, Jeff Croiter; Costume Supervisor, Michael Growler; Sound, Scott Stauffer; Event Marketing, Adam Jay; PSM, Jeff Davolt; Orchestrations, Jesse Vargas; Line Producer, Patrick Weaver; Program, Tina Royero; Assistant Director, Larry Adelman; Assistant Choreographers, Nandita Shenoy/ Robert Tatad; Projections, Leo Daignault; Stage Manager, Samuel-Moses Jones; Assistant Stage Managers, Zac Chandler, Ruth Kramer; Assistant Musical Director, Ben Cohen & Brent-Alan Huffman; Music Preparation, Julie Danielson; Music Contractor, Charles Gordon; Sound/Video, Pete McElligott; Assistants, Jeff Carnevale, Gabriel Kirshner

CAST **Seth Rudetsky, Andréa Burns, Jen Cody, Jonathan Groff, Norm Lewis, Andrea McArdle, Julia Murney, Pamela Myers, Lillias White;** Dancers **Mathias Anderson, Nancy Braun, Isaac Calpito, Allyson Carr, Joshua Eckblom, Frankie Grande, Emily Lockhart, Naomi Naughton, Kat Nejat, Luis Salgado, Nandita Shenoy, Rickey Tripp;** Singers **Kate Chapman, Christina Conners, Brian Golub, Val Moranto, Jesse Nager, Kate Pazakis, Jason Veasey, Chris Zelno**

MUSICIANS Steve Marzullo (conductor); Rick Dolan, Kiku Enomoto, Blair Lawhead, Irina Karlin, Julia Koo, Bryony Stroud-Watson (violins); Todd Sullivan, Lara Lynne Hicks (viola/violin); Steve Greenfield, Marc Phaneuf, Greg Thymius, Julie Ferrara, Mark Thrasher (woodwinds); Don Downs, Ron Buttacavoli, Scott Harrell (trumpets); Eric Davis (French horn); Charles Gordon, Joel Shelton (trombones); Ben Cohn, Paul Loesel (keyboards); Kevin Kuhn (guitar); Marc Schmied (bass); Sean McDaniel (drums); Kerry Meads (percussion)

A master class in belting, divas and hostile opinions presented without intermission. A benefit for the Actors Fund.

SYNOPSIS The Actors Fund presents this endlessly entertaining event for the second year in a row. Using a full orchestra, audio/visual aids and the talents of some "a-mah-zing" Broadway guest stars, the always hilarious Seth Rudetsky, a leading authority and completely obsessive master of all things Broadway, shows you—up close and personal—what is brilliant about Broadway, how the whole thing works and why it can sometimes be a splitting headache!

UMBRELLA

Kirk Theatre on Theatre Row; First Preview: April 11, 2008; Opening Night: April 15, 2008; Closed May 4, 2008; 5 previews, 18 performances

Written by L. Pontius; Produced by the Alchemy Theatre Company of Manhattan (Robert Saxner, Producing Artistic Director); Director, Padraic Lillis; Set & Costumes, Lea Umberger; Lighting, Sarah Sidman; Sound, Jill BC DuBoff; PSM, Jessica J. Felix; Props, Ashley Gagner; Vocal Coach, Kohli Calhoun; Assistant Director, James David Jackson; Fight Choreographer, Judson Jones; Technical Director, Vadim Malinskiy; Production Consultant, La Vie Productions, R. Erin Craig; Press, Kevin P. McAnarney

CAST Helen **Christa Kimlicko Jones;** Frank **Judson Jones**

SETTING The rooftop of an apartment building in a large city, late summer. New York premiere of a new play presented without intermission.

SYNOPSIS *Umbrella* is a mix of tragedy and comedy about the loneliness and despair of living in a big city and the choices we make to relieve the pressure. Two strangers on a rooftop, one a peeping Tom, the other a cutter, try to find common ground but it all changes as taboos and secrets are revealed and dreams fall apart. What began as an act of kindness turns into a war of wills.

THE WALWORTH FARCE

St. Ann's Warehouse; First Preview: April 15, 2007; Opening Night: April 17, 2008; Closed May 4, 2008; 2 previews, 19 performances

Written by Enda Walsh; Produced by St. Ann's Warehouse (Susan Feldman, Artistic Director) in association with Piece by Piece Productions and Jean Stein; Presented by Druid Theater Company (Galway, Ireland); Director, Mikel Murfi; Set and Costumes, Sabine Dargent; Lighting, Paul Keogan; Production Manager, Eamonn Fox; Stage Manager, Tim Smith; Stage Director, Sarah Lynch; Casting, Maureen Hughes; Technical Manager, Barry O'Brien; Costume Supervisor, Doreen McKenna; Press, Blake Zidell & Associates

Garrett Lombard, Denis Conway, Tadhg Murphy in The Walworth Farce *(photo by PA)*

CAST Dinny **Denis Conway;** Sean **Tadhg Murphy;** Blake **Garrett Lombard;** Hayley **Mercy Ojelade**

SETTING A council flat on the Walworth Road, off the Elephant and Castle in South London. American premiere of a new farce presented in two acts. Originally produced at the Town Hall Theatre, Galway in March 2006, The Everyman Palace Theatre (Cork) March 28, 2006, The Helix (Dublin) April 4, 2006. The show also played at Scotland's Edinburgh Fringe Festival at the Traverse Theatre August 5, 2007.

SYNOPSIS *The Walworth Farce* is a play disguised as an old-fashioned high farce, complete with rapid costume changes, cross-dressing, and mistaken identity. Dinny, a mad father who has written a farce, forces his family to act out endless encore performances of his delusions in his play within the play. Combining hilarious moments with shocking realism, *The Walworth Farce* delivers an achingly tender insight into what happens when we become stuck in the stories we tell ourselves about our lives.

THE FIASCOES

Baruch Performing Arts Center – Rose Nagelberg Theatre; Opening Night: April 16, 2008; Closed April 26, 2008; 11 performances

Two one act comedies – *A Fake Fiasco* & *A Friendly Fiasco* – by Frederick Timm; Presented by New Heights Productions in association with Dramatic Endeavors; Director, Paula J. Riley; Set/Graphics, Steve J. Hill; Costumes, Peter Mussared; Lighting, Lance A. Michael; Stage Manager, Marisa Merrigan; Press, Penny Landau

CAST *A Fake Fiasco:* Henry **Philip Bartolf;** Gwenyth **Christine Laydon**; George **Hank Offinger;** David **Gregory Singleton;** *A Friendly Fiasco:* Ken **Philip Bartolf;**

Sandy **Paul Fiteni;** Nancy **Linda S. Nelson;** Greg **Hank Offinger**

SETTING *A Fake Fiasco:* An upscale Manhattan Apartment, present day; *A Friendly Fiasco:* The fun room in a Hamptons beach home, present day. World premiere of two one-act plays on a double bill presented with intermission. *A Fake Fiasco* was previously presented at NY Artists Unlimited Bad Plays Festival, September 2007.

SYNOPSIS *The Fiascoes* is an amusing, yet profound look at contemporary relationships, which centers upon the deconstruction of the lives of four couples.

THE CASTLE

New World Stages – Stage 5; First Preview: March 30, 2008; Opening Night: April 27, 2008; 8 previews, 9 performances as of May 31, 2008 (Saturdays and Sundays)

Conceived and directed by David Rothenberg, written in collaboration with the cast and Kenneth Harrigan; Produced by Eric Krebs and Chase Mishkin by arrangement with the Fortune Society; Press, O+M Co., Richard Hillman, Philip Carrubba

CAST **Vilma Ortiz Donovan, Angel Ramos, Kenneth Harrington, Casimiro Torres**

Off-Broadway premiere of a unique theatrical event presented without intermission.

SYNOPSIS Four formerly imprisoned New Yorkers with a total of 70 years of incarceration relate their journeys of crime, privation, and redemption.

YELLOW MOON The Ballad of Leila and Lee

59E59 Theater C; First Preview: April 23, 2008; Opening Night: April 29, 2008; Closed May 18, 2008; 7 previews, 24 performances

Written by David Greig; Music by Nigel Dunn; Produced by 59E59 Theaters (Elysabeth Kleinhans, Artistic Director; Peter Tear, Executive Producer); Presented by TAG Theatre Company/Citizens' Theatre of Glasgow, Scotland, as part of the Brits Off Broadway 2008; Director, Guy Hollands; Production Manager, Andrew Coulton; Stage Manager, Raynelle Wright; Press, Karen Greco

CAST Leila Sulieiman **Nalini Chetty;** Billy Logan/Drunk Frank **Keith Macpherson;** Jenni Macalinden/Holly Malone **Beth Marshall;** Stag Lee Macalinden **Andrew Scott-Ramsay**

American premiere of a new play presented without intermission.

SYNOPSIS *Yellow Moon* is a fast-paced modern Bonnie and Clyde tale of two teenagers on the run in the highlands of Scotland. Silent Leila is an introverted girl who has a passion for celebrity magazines. Stag Lee Macalinden is the deadest of dead end kids in a dead end town. They never meant to get mixed up in murder.

Nalini Chetty, Andrew Scott-Ramsay, and Keith Macpherson in Yellow Moon *(photo by Tim Morozzo)*

THE SET UP

ArcLight Theatre; First Preview: April 25, 2008; Opening Night: April 30, 2008; Closed May 22, 2008; 3 previews, 17 performances

Written and directed by James Lindenberg; Produced by Son of Thunder Productions and Alternative Advertising; Set, Josh Starr; Costumes, Laura Catignani; Lighting, Dan Hansell; Sound, Jose Conde; Stage & Production Manager, Jeremiah Peay; House/Sound/Technical Director, Daniel Koehler; ASM, Harmony Ingraham; Original Music, Jose Conde, Tamela D'Amico, Rico King, Sali B, Monsterline Entertainment; Press, David Gersten

CAST Carolyn **Tara Westwood;** Robert **James Lindenberg**; Doris **Jennifer Danielle;** Bill **Scott Cunningham**; Nina **Tracy Weiler**; Mike/Tony/Ted **Major Dodge**

SETTING New York City and Greenwich, CT, three months ago and then the present day. World premiere of a new play presented without intermission.

SYNOPSIS Terminally single thirty-somethings experience a train wreck of a blind date that suddenly derails their matchmaker/friends' marriage. Even an auspicious second encounter leaves cupid stymied, so the matchmakers must reunite for one last 'set up.'

SUBSTITUTION

SoHo Playhouse; First Preview: April 26, 2008; Opening Night: May 4, 2008; Closed May 17, 2008; 8 previews, 14 performances

Written by Anton Dudley; Produced by The Playwrights Realm – Inaugural Production (John Dias and Katherine Kovner, Co-Artistic Directors); Director, Katherine Kovner; Set, Tom Gleeson; Lighting, Jeff Croiter; Costumes, Theresa Squire; Sound, Jill BC DuBoff; PSM, James FitzSimmons; Casting, David Caparelliotis; Production Manager, Peter Dean; General Manager, Seth Shepsle; ASM, Joshua Pilote; Props, Arianna Zindler; Technical Director, Jesse Wilson; Producing Consultant, Judy Mauer; Marketing Consultant, Wiley Hausam; Development Consultant, Diane Morrison; Press, Spin Cycle/ Ron Lasko

CAST Calvin's Mom **Jan Maxwell;** Paul **Kieran Campion;** Jule **Shana Dowdeswell;** Dax **Brandon Espinoza**

World premiere of a new play presented without intermission. Originally developed at the Lark Play Development Center.

SYNOPSIS When a tragedy occurs, the choices we make about how we live, and how we love, can bring about endless surprises. Calvin's Mom is coping with the death of her teenage son as best as she can. When a substitute teacher challenges everything she thinks she knows about her child, their volatile bond creates a complex unfolding of revelations. *Substitution* takes us to a place where sadness, solace, hope and laughter intermingle, forging unexpected connections against a chasm of loss and grief.

ALL EYES AND EARS

Lion Theatre at Theatre Row; First Preview: April 30, 2008; Opening Night: May 5, 2008; Closed May 22, 2008; 5 previews, 12 performances

Written by Rogelio Martinez; Produced by INTAR Theatre (Eduardo Machado, Artistic Director; John McCormack, Executive Director; Alina Troyano, Associate Artistic Director); Director, Eduardo Machado; Set and Lighting, Maruti Evans; Costumes, Michael Bevins; Sound, Elizabeth Rhodes; Hair & Makeup, Brenda Bush; Casting, Billy Hopkins; Production Manager, Stephanie Madona; Assistant Director, Meiyin Wang; PSM, Michael Alifanz; Stage Manager, Hannah Woodward; Props, Aaron Paternoster; Press, David Gersten & Associates

CAST Carmen **Terumi Matthews;** Yolanda **Christina Pumariega;** Emilio **Martín Solá;** Alvaro **Liam Torres;** Stepan **Ed Vassallo;** Maria **Maria Helan**

Christina Pumariega, Ed Vassallo and Maria Helan in All Eyes and Ears (photo by Carol Rosegg)

SETTING Cuba, 1961, shortly after the Bay of Pigs and before the Missile Crisis. World premiere of a new play presented in two acts.

SYNOPSIS A seamstress is catapulted into a new life, new house, and new government job. But good fortunes quickly change when her new position attracts unexpected guests and reveals more secrets about herself than of political conspiracies.

MOBY DICK REHEARSED

Baruch Performing Arts Center – Rose Nagelberg Theatre; Opening Night: May 6, 2008; Closed May 17, 2008; 8 performances

Adapted by Orson Welles from the novel by Herman Melville; Presented by The Acting Company (Margot Harley, Producing Artistic Director); Director, Casey Biggs; Set, Neil Patel; Costumes, Jared Aswegan; Lighting, Michael Chybowski; Sound and Music Fitz Patton; Movement, Felix Ivanov; Voice Coach, Deborah Hecht; Staff Repertory Director, Jessi D. Hill; Casting, Liz Woodman; Production Manager, Steve Lorick; PSM, Janice M. Brandine; ASM, Marisa Levy; Company Manager, Gretchen Margaroli; Technical Director, Joel Howell; Props, Scott Brodsky; Text Preparations, Dakin Matthews; Voice and Text Consultant, Elizabeth Smith; Crew Supervisors, David Phyfe, Brie Fuches, Andrew Ruiz; Press, Judy Katz

CAST Young Actor/Ishmael **Timothy Sekk;** Young Actress/Pip **Kelley Curran;** Stage Manager/Tashtego/Voice of "The Rachel" **Luis Curran;** Middle-Aged Actor/Elijah/ Flask **David Foubert;** Serious Actor/Starbuck **Michael**

Stewart Allen; Old Pro/Peleg/Voice of "The Bachelor" **Christopher Oden;** Cynical Actor/Daggoo/Carpenter **Victoire Charles;** Actor with Newspaper/Stubb **Robb Martinez;** Governor/Father Mapple/Ahab **Seth Duerr;** Actor/Queequeg **Peter Macklin;** Actor/Masthead **Jay Leibowitz**

SETTING An empty theatre. Revival of the play presented in two acts.

SYNOPSIS A troupe of actors abandon their rehearsal of a play about one unforgiving, vengeance obsessed man, King Lear, to recreate another of the same emotional stripe, Captain Ahab. Set in an empty theater, a tyrannical actor-manager leads his crew and transports audiences to Captain Ahab's fateful voyage across the open seas aboard the Pequod in search of the great white whale, Moby Dick.

CAMELOT

Avery Fisher Hall; Opening Night: May 7, 2008; Closed May 10, 2008; 5 performances

Book and lyrics by Alan Jay Lerner, music by Frederick Loewe, based on T.H. White's novel *The Once and Future King*; Produced by the New York Philharmonic and Thomas Z. Shepard; Executive Producer, Matías Tarnopolsky; Director and Book Adaptation, Lonny Price; Music Director/Conductor, Paul Gemignani; Choreography, Josh Prince; Associate Director, Matt Cowart; PSM, Peter Hanson; Set, James Noone; Costumes, Tracy Christensen; Lighting, Paul Miller; Sound, Peter Fitzgerald; Fight Director, Rick Sordelet; Casting, Jim Carnahan; Dialects, Stephen Gabis; Wigs, David Lawrence; Makeup, Angelina Avallone; Production Manager, Alex Johnston; Assistant Director, Kitt Lavoie; Associate Choreography, Nancy Lemenager; ASM, Jeffrey Rodriguez; Props, Mike Pilipski; Production Mixer, Ty Lacky; Rehearsal Pianists, Paul Ford, Nick Archer

CAST Merlyn **Stacey Keach;** King Arthur **Gabriel Byrne;** Guenevere **Marin Mazzie;** Sir Dinadan **Christopher Sieber;** Sir Lionel **Marc Kudisch;** Sir Sagamore **Will Swenson;** Nimue **Erin Morley;** Page **Justin Stein;** Lancelot **Nathan Gunn;** Squire Dap **Weston Wells Olson;** Pellinore **Christopher Lloyd;** Lady Anne **Jane Brockman;** Mordred **Bobby Steggert;** Morgan Le Fey **Fran Drescher;** Tom of Warwick **Rishi Mutalik;** Ensemble **Joel Abels, Derin Altay, Terence Archie, Maxime de Toldeo, Ryan Thomas Dunn, Ivan Hernandez, Sydney James, Catherine Cheng Jones, Catherine LaValle, Valisia Lekae, Amy Mahoney, Frank Mastrone, Raymond Jaramillo McLeod, Paolo Montalban, Devin Richards, Brian Charles Rooney, Idara Victor, Alison Walla, Betsy Wolfe**; Dancers **Kristine Bendul, Kathryn Eleni Fraggos, Nick Kepley, Sabra Lewis, Michael Mindlin, Denny Paschall, Jermaine Rembert, Krista Saab, Michael Scirrotto, Alison Soloman**

MUSICAL NUMBERS I Wonder What the King is Doing Tonight, The Simple Joys of Maidenhood, Camelot, Guenevere's Welcome, Camelot (reprise), Follow Me, C'est Moi, The Lusty Month of May, Then You May Take Me to the Fair, How to Handle a Woman, The Jousts, Entr'acte, Before I Gaze at You Again, If Ever I Would Leave You, The Seven Deadly Virtues, What Do the Simple Folk Do? I Loved You Once in Silence, Guenevere; Farewell, Finale Ultimo

A semi-staged concert of the musical presented in two acts. Originally produced at the Majestic Theatre December 3, 1960–January 5, 1963, running 873 performances (see *Theatre World* Volume 17, page 48). The show has had three brief revivals on Broadway in 1980, 1981, and 1983.

SYNOPSIS Idealistic King Arthur longs to create a perfectly principled kingdom, but sees his dream undone by a tragic love triangle involving Queen Guenevere and his best friend Lancelot.

Gabriel Byrne and Company in Camelot (photo by Chris Lee for the New York Philharmonic)

THE UNCONQUERED

59E59 Theater C; First Preview: May 1, 2008; Opening Night: May 7, 2008; Closed May 18; 7 previews, 15 performances

Written by Torben Betts; Produced by 59E59 Theaters (Elysabeth Kleinhans, Artistic Director; Peter Tear, Executive Producer); Presented by the Stellar Quines Theatre Company (Edinburgh, Scotland) as part of the Brits Off Broadway 2008; Artistic Director/Director, Muriel Romanes; Co-Director, James Dacre; Visual Artist/Design, Keith McIntyre; Lighting, Jeanine Davies; Costumes, Catriona Maddocks; Sound, Peter Vilk; Voice Coach, Linda Wise; Production Manager, Fiona Fraser; Technical Stage Manager, Lee Davis; AEA Stage

Manager, Jared Abram DeBacker; Press, Karen Greco

CAST Mother **Alexandra Mathie;** Father **Neil McKinven;** Girl **Nicola Harrison;** Soldier **Neal Barry**

American premiere of a new play presented without intermission. Originally produced at the Byre Theatre of St. Andrews (Edinburgh, Scotland) February–March 2007. This cast toured the production in the UK prior to its New York debut.

SYNOPSIS *The Unconquered* is a hard-hitting and enthralling story about a fiercely intelligent young girl and her relentless refusal of the establishment. When a people's revolution breaks out and a mercenary soldier intrudes the family home, the conflict between the regime and the unconquered girl is revealed

THE TEMPEST

Baruch Performing Arts Center – Rose Nagelberg Theatre; Opening Night: May 8, 2008; Closed May 12, 2008; 5 performances

Written by William Shakespeare; Presented by The Acting Company (Margot Harley, Producing Artistic Director); Director, Davis McCallum; Set, Neil Patel; Costumes, Clint Ramos; Lighting, Michael Chybowski; Music, Thomas Shaw; Sound, Fitz Patton; Movement, Tracy Bersley; Puppets, Emily DeCola; Voice and Text Coach, Elizabeth Smith; Staff Repertory Director, Jessi D. Hill; Casting, Liz Woodman; Production Manager, Steve Lorick; PSM, Janice M. Brandine; ASM, Marisa Levy; Company Manager, Gretchen Margaroli; Technical Director, Joel Howell; Props, Scott Brodsky; Text Preparations, Dakin Matthews; Crew Supervisors, David Phyfe, Brie Fuches, Andrew Ruiz; Press, Judy Katz

Christoper Oden and Kelley Curran in The Tempest *(photo by James Culp)*

CAST Prospero **Christopher Oden;** Alonso **Luis Moreno;** Antonio **Seth Duerr;** Gonzalo **Jay Leibowitz;** Sebastain **Robb Martinez;** Ferdinand **Timothy Sekk;** Miranda **Kelley Curran;** Ariel **Victoire Charles;** Caliban **Michael Stewart Allen;** Trinculo **Peter Macklin;** Stephano **David Foubert**

Revival of the play presented in two acts.

SYNOPSIS Shakespeare's magical last play, his poignant farewell to the stage, has love, tragedy and comedy combined in equal measure. The usurped wizard, Prospero, draws his enemies to his enchanted island to exact revenge yet, ultimately, finds peace and the ability to forgive. Hailed as a stunning climax to the career of England's favorite dramatist, *The Tempest* is a play praising the glories of reconciliation and forgiveness.

DAMASCUS

59E59 Theater A; First Preview: May 8, 2008; Opening Night: May 14, 2008; Closed June 1, 2008; 5 previews, 25 performances

Written by David Greig; Produced by 59E59 Theaters (Elysabeth Kleinhans, Artistic Director; Peter Tear, Executive Producer); Presented by the Traverse Theatre (Edinburgh, Scotland) as part of the Brits Off Broadway 2008; Director, Philip Howard; Sets/Costumes, Anthony MacIlwaine; Lighting, Chahine Yavoyan; Sound, Graham Sutherland; Composer and Arrangements, Jon Beales; Dialects, Ros Steen; AEA Stage Manager, Amy Kaskeski; Press, Karen Greco

CAST Paul **Ewen Bremner**; Muna **Nathalie Armin;** Wasim **Alex Elliott;** Elena **Dolya Gavanski;** Zakaria **Khalid Laith**

SETTING An airport in Damascus, Syria; the present. American premiere of a new play presented in two acts.

SYNOPSIS Paul travels to Damascus to sell English language textbooks. It's Valentine's Day and he'd rather be at home with his wife. A brief encounter in a Syrian hotel finds him grappling with language and love, meanings and misunderstandings. As his flight home is delayed by a bomb at Beirut Airport, he begins to wonder—will he ever leave?

THE BULLY PULPIT

Beckett Theatre on Theatre Row; First Preview: April 29, 2008; Opening Night: May 14, 2008; Closed June 29, 2008; 15 previews, 48 performances

Written by Michael O. Smith; Produced by South Ark Stage (Rhoda Herrick, Producing Artistic Director); Director, Byam Stevens; Set, Charlie Corcoran; Lighting, Jill Nagle; Sound, Tom Shread; Props, Mary Robinette Kowal; PSM, April Ann Kline; Production Supervisor, Peter R. Feuchtwanger/PRF Productions; Advertising, Eliran Murphy Group; Associate Producing/Artistic Director, Adam Fitzgerald; Production Assistant, Susan Manikas; Crew: John Martinez (carpenter), Caroline Abella (lighting programmer), George Faya (production audio); Press, Keith Sherman and Associates, DJ Martin

CAST Theodore Roosevelt **Michael O. Smith**

SETTING 1918. Sagamore Hill, New York. Off-Broadway premiere of a solo performance play presented without in two acts. World premiere at Florida Studio Theatre in 2004.

SYNOPSIS On his 60th birthday and ten years out of the Oval Office, Teddy Roosevelt is coming to grips with his legacy. Surrounded by mementos of his adventures as a rancher, Rough Rider, naturalist and President, Roosevelt re-examines the events of his colorful life with a humorous and blunt perspective. *The Bully Pulpit* takes audiences on a passionate journey behind Roosevelt's gruff exterior into the complex persona of a true American legend.

Michael O. Smith in The Bully Pulpit *(photo by Rick Tellers)*

DINNER FOR TWO (CENA PARA DOS)

47th Street Theatre; First Preview: May 8, 2008; Opening Night: May 15, 2008; Closed June 1, 2008; 7 previews, 20 performances

Written by Santiago Moncada; Produced by the Puerto Rican Traveling Theater (Miriam Colón Valle, Artistic Director); Director, Tony Mata; Traslator, Charles Philip Thomas; Set, Christina Gould; Lighting/Technical Director/Production Manager, Scott Cally; Costumes, Summer Lee Jack; Dramaturg, David Varquez; PSM, Alan Fox; Graphic Designer, Paul Xavier Cordero; Props and Costumier, Adolfo Vázquez; Development, Tom Scharff; Press, Jonathan Slaff

CAST Berta **Jezabel Montero;** Emi **Angelica Ayala;** Pedro **Fred Valle**

SETTING New York City on the Upper West Side. New York premiere of a new play presented in Spanish or in English in two acts; world premiere of the English language version.

SYNOPSIS Emi, a 40-ish, attractive, introverted widow who is a bit shy and hopelessly romantic, is coached out of her shell by Berta, her extroverted and lively friend of who revels in the pursuit of men. Berta plans a bait-and-switch date in order to match up Emi with Pedro, a suave, wealthy and eligible widower in his early sixties. What follows is a comedy of errors with embarrassments, sudden reversals, surprising twists and ultimately, a happy ending.

THE GREAT AMERICAN ALL-STAR TRAVELING WAR MACHINE

Theater for the New City; Opening Night: May 16, 2008; Closed June 15, 2008; 21 performances

Inspired by Lapham's Quarterly "States of War" Issue; Presented by the Irondale Theatre Project (Jim Niesen, Artistic Director); Director, Jim Niesen; Set, Ken Rothchild; Lighitng, Paul Hackenmueller; Costumes, Liz Prince; Choreography, Thea Brooks; Graphics, Sam Ferri; Music Director, Michael David Gordon; Acting Coach, Barbara MacKenzie Wood; Stage Manager, Maria Knapp; Press, Timothy Haskell/Art Meets Commerce

CAST **Thea Brooks, Michael-David Gordon, Nolan Kennedy, Patrena Murray, Scarlet Rivera, Damen Scranton, Welland Hardwick, Lindsay Vrab**

World premiere of a cabaret with sketches and songs presented without intermission.

SYNOPSIS *The Great American All-Star Traveling War Machine* is a cabaret combining songs from the Revolutionary War, War of

1812, Civil War, Spanish American War, both World Wars, Viet Nam, and the Iraq War with scenes, sketches and monologues taken from Lewis Lapham's "States of War" which contains first hand accounts, speeches, poetry, songs and more related to the machinations of war and the people who perpetuate, or try to stop them.

Mike Daisey in How Theater Failed America *(photo by Peter Dylan O'Connor)*

HOW THEATER FAILED AMERICA

Barrow Street Theatre; Opening Night: May 16, 2008; Closed June 22, 2008; 18 performances

Written by Mike Daisey; Produced by AJ Epstein and An Ethereal Mutt Productions; Director, Jean-Michele Gregory; Lighting, AJ Epstein; General Management, Two Step Productions, Cris Buchner and Kate Mott; Stage Manager, Jason Reuter; Company Manager, Heather Levine; Graphic Design, Osiris Indriya; Theatre Managing Director, Scott Morfee; Theatre Executive Director, Tom Wirshafter; Theatre General Manager, Anne Johnson; Press, The Karpel Group, Bridget Klapinski, Meg Owen

Performed by **Mike Daisey**

Off-Broadway transfer of a solo performance play presented without intermission. Previously presented at Joe's Pub on Sunday evenings, April 14–May 11, 2008.

SYNOPSIS From gorgeous new theatres standing empty as cathedrals, to 'successful' working actors traveling like migrant farmhands, to an arts culture unwilling to speak or listen to its own nation, Daisey takes stock of the dystopian state of theatre in America: a shrinking world with smaller audiences every year. Fearlessly implicating himself and the system he works within, Daisey seeks answers to essential and dangerous questions about the art we're making, the legacy we leave the future, and who it is we believe we're speaking to.

PAMELA'S FIRST MUSICAL

Town Hall; May 18, 2008; 1 performance

Music by Cy Coleman, lyrics by David Zippel, book by Wendy Wasserstein, based on the children's book by Wendy Wasserstein; Produced by Broadway Cares/Equity Fights AIDS; Director, Graciela Daniele; Music Director, Kevin Stites; Orchestrations, Don Sebesky; Stage Design, Nathan Hurlin; Sound, Matthew Maloney, Michael Pistone; Lighting, Tony Marques; PSM, Arturo Porazzi; Production Manager, Nathan Hurlin; Music Coordinator, John Miller; Press, Boneau/Bryan-Brown

CAST Pamela **Lila Coogan;** Aunt Louise/Tony Punero **Donna Murphy;** Kevin/Nathan Hines-Klines **Gregg Edelman;** Daniel/Jules Gels **Matthew Gumley;** Thomas/Billy Ivey Zippers **Malcolm Morano;** Lyndell/Mary Ethel Bernadette **Carolee Carmello;** Jessica/Heidi Lee Lee **Audrey Twitchell;** Nick **Ben Crawford;** Robert/Harrison **Christian Borle;** Bernie S. Gerry **David S. Garrison;** As themselves: **Sandy Duncan, Christine Ebersole, Kathie Lee Gifford, Joel Grey, Donna McKechnie, Tommy Tune, Lillias White;** Simon Crankley **Michael Riedel;** Hal Hitner **Christopher Sieber;** Betty Songheim **Lynn Ahrens;** Cy Songheim **Stephen Flaherty;** Man in Uniform **Kevin Stites;** Gladys **Kathie Lee Gifford;** Ensemble **Cathryn Basile, Dan Bogart, Ben Crawford, Adam Jacobs, Jay Jaski, Deborah Lew, Marissa McGowan, Carrie Manolakos, Jayne Patterson, Dan Petrotta, Devin Richards, Maia Nkenge Wilson**

MUSICIANS Kevin Stites (Conductor); Nicholas Archer (synthesizer/piano); John Miller (bass); Ray Marchica (drums); Charlie Descarfino (percussion); Don Downs, Glen Drewes (trumpets); Larry Farrell (trombone); Will DeVos (French horn); Chuck Wilson, Tom Christensen, Walt Weiskopf, Mark Thrasher (reeds); Rick Dolan, Sylvia D'Avanzo (violins); Deborah Shufelt-Dine (viola), Charles duChateau (cello)

MUSICAL NUMBERS The Broadway Song, Where All the Pieces Fit, Where All the Pieces Fit (reprise), The Tony Punero Show, Perfection, Anything That You Do, Manhattan Moves Me, Reinvent Yourself, Welcome to Sardi's, The Critic's Song, Behind the Scenes, Overture, Feet Don't Fail Me Now, Except You, The Broadway Song, It Started With a Dream, You Make Me Proud, It Started with a Dream (reprise)

World premiere benefit concert performance of a new musical presented without intermission.

SYNOPSIS *Pamela's First Musical* tells the story of a young girl from the suburbs who spends an unforgettable birthday with her eccentric, sophisticated Aunt Louise attending a lavish Broadway production and meeting all the glamorous, creative people who made it possible.

Donna Murphy, Lila Coogan, and Christian Borle in Pamela's First Musical *(photo by Jay Brady)*

BLINK

59E59 Theater C; First Preview: May 21, 2008; Opening Night: May 25, 2008; Closed May 18; 6 previews, 17 performances

Written by Ian Rowlands; Produced by 59E59 Theaters (Elysabeth Kleinhans, Artistic Director; Peter Tear, Executive Producer); Presented by the F.A.B. Theatre (Cardiff, Wales) as part of the Brits Off Broadway 2008; Director, Stephen Fisher; Design, Rhys Jarman; Lighting, Trevor Turton; Sound, Gareth Potter; Producer, Emma Goad; Production Manager, Sarah Cole; Company Stage Manager, Stephen Hawkins; AEA Stage Manager, Raynelle Wright; Set Construction, Square Leg Productions; Scenic Artist, Sam Holland; Press, Karen Greco

CAST Kay **Rhian Blythe;** Mam **Lisa Palfrey;** Si **Sion Pritchard**

SETTING Cardiff, Wales, the present and seven years ago. American premiere of a new play presented in two acts.

SYNOPSIS The initial inspiration for *Blink* was the events surrounding the Clywch enquiry—a report into the systematic abuse of children at a Welsh language school. *Blink* is an edgy examination of the close-knit lives and lies of small south Wales communities, whose secrets start with the rudey club and end with '12 words that ruined a life.'

ARTEFACTS

59E59 Theater B; First Preview: May 21, 2008; Opening Night: May 25,2008; Closed June 8, 2008; 6 previews, 17 performances

Written by Mike Bartlett; Produced by 59E59 Theaters (Elysabeth Kleinhans, Artistic Director; Peter Tear, Executive Producer); Presented by nabokov (James Grieve and George Perrin, Artistic Directors) in association with The American Associates of the Old Vic as part of the Brits Off Broadway 2008; Director, James Grieve; Design, Lucy Osborne; Lighting, Hartley T.A. Kemp; Composer, Arthur Darvill; Assistant Director, Tara Wilkinson; General/Production Manager, Ric Moutjoy; Producer, Emma Brunjes; AEA Stage Manager, Jared Abram DeBacker; Administrator, Sally Christopher; Press, Karen Greco

CAST Kelly **Lizzy Watts;** Susan **Karen Ascoe;** Ibrahim **Peter Polycarpou;** Faiza **Mouna Albakry;** Raya **Amy Hamdoon**

SETTING London, the present. American premiere of a new play presented without intermission.

SYNOPSIS 16-year-old Kelly is having a normal Saturday when her unknown father, who is Iraqi, turns up out of the blue. He's smuggled a priceless antique from the Baghdad Museum and wants Kelly to look after it. He's got a plane to catch, but Kelly threatens to smash it unless he stays and gets to know her, launching an epic journey of discovery in a tender and provocative play about family, identity and the clash of cultures.

Rhian Blythe and Sion Pritchard in Blink *(photo courtesy of F.A.B. Theatre)*

ALTAR BOYZ

New World Stages – Stage 4; First Preview: February 15, 2005; Opening Night: March 1, 2005; 1,358 performances as of May 31, 2008

Book by Kevin Del Aguila, music, lyrics, and vocal arrangements by Gary Adler and Michael Patrick Walker, conceived by Marc Kessler and Ken Davenport; Produced by Ken Davenport and Robyn Goodman, in association with Walt Grossman, Ruth Hendel, Sharon Karmazin, Matt Murphy, and Mark Shacket; Director, Stafford Arima; Choreography, Christopher Gattelli; Musical Director/Dance Music and Additional Arrangements, Lynne Shankel; Set, Anna Louizos; Costumes, Gail Brassard; Lighting, Natasha Katz; Sound, Simon Matthews; Orchestrations, Doug Katsaros, Lynne Shankel; Casting, David Caparelliotis; PSM, Sara Jaramillo; Hair, Josh Marquette; Production Manager, Andrew Cappelli; Associate Producer, Stephen Kocis; Press; David Gersten and Associates; General Manager, Martian Entertainment; Company Manager, Ryan Lympus; ASM, Alyssa Stone; Casting, David Petro; Associate Choreographer, Tammy Colucci; Cast recording: Sh-K-Boom Records 86050

Landon Beard, Ryan J. Ratliff, Chad Doreck, Jay Garcia, and Ryan Strand in Altar Boyz *(photo by Carol Rosegg)*

CAST Matthew **Matthew Buckner***1; Mark **Ryan J Ratliff;** Luke **Landon Beard***2; Juan **Jay Garcia;** Abraham **Ryan Strand;** Voice of GOD **Shadoe Stevens;** Understudies **Jim Daly***3, **Joey Khoury**

ALTAR BOYZ BAND Jason Loffredo (Conductor/keyboard), Danny Percefull (keyboard), David Matos (guitar), Clayton Craddock (drums), Doug Katsaros (music programmer)

MUSICAL NUMBERS We Are the Altar Boyz, Rhythm in Me, Church Rulz, The Calling, The Miracle Song, Everybody Fits, Something About You, Body Mind & Soul, La Vida Eternal, Epiphany, Number 918, Finale: I Believe

SETTING Here and Now. A musical presented without intermission. Originally produced at the New York Musical Theatre Festival, September, 2004. For original production credits see *Theatre World* Volume 61, page 142.

SYNOPSIS A struggling Christian boy band (with one nice Jewish boy), trying to save the world one screaming fan at a time, perform their last tour date at the New World Stages. Their pious pop act worked wonders on the home state Ohio bingo-hall-and-pancake breakfast circuit, but will temptation for solo record deals threaten to split the Boyz as take a bite out of the forbidden Big Apple?

*Succeeded by: 1. Chad Doreck (9/3/07), Matthew Kaden Craig (3/31/08) 2. Andrew C. Call (9/21/07), Austin Lesch (12/17/07), Jesse JP Johnson (2/22/08), Neil Haskell (4/22/08) 3. Austin Lesch (2/22/08)

THE AWESOME 80'S PROM

Webster Hall; First Performance: July 23, 2004 (Friday evenings only); Opening Night: September 10, 2004 (Fridays and Saturdays); 211 performances as of May 31, 2008 (Saturday evening performances only)

Written and produced by Ken Davenport; Co-Authored by The Class of '89 (Sheila Berzan, Alex Black, Adam Bloom, Anne Bobby, Courtney Balan, Mary Faber, Emily McNamara, Troy Metcalf, Jenna Pace, Amanda Ryan Paige, Mark Shunock, Josh Walden, Noah Weisberg, Brandon Williams, Simon Wong and Fletcher Young); Director, Ken Davenport; Choreography, Drew Geraci; Costumes, Randall E. Klein; Lighting, Martin Postma; Production Stage Manger, Carlos Maisonet; Associate Producers, Amanda Dubois, Jennifer Manocherian; Company Manager, Matt Kovich; Assistant Stage Manager, Kathryn Galloway; Casting, Daryl Eisenberg; Press, David Gersten & Associates

CAST Johnny Hughes (The DJ) **Scott Sussman***1; Lloyd Parker (The Photographer) **Craig Jorczak***2; Dickie Harrington (The Drama Queen) **Bennett Leak;** Michael Jay (The Class President) **Jake Mosser***3; Mr. Snelgrove (The Principal) **Fletcher Young***4; Molly Parker (The Freshman) **Lauren Schafler;** Inga Swanson (The Swedish Exchange Student) **Emily McNamara;** Joshua "Beef" Beefarowski (A Football Player) **David Surkin***5; Whitley Whitiker (The Head Cheerleader) **Jessica West Regan;** Nick Fender (The Rebel) **Sean Attebury***6; Heather #1 (A Cheerleader) **Tiffany Engen***7; Heather #2 (The Other Cheerleader) **Kate Wood Riley;** Kerrie Kowalski (The Spaz) **Kathy Searle***8; Melissa Ann Martin (Head of the Prom Committee) **Brooke Engen***9; Louis Fensterpock (The Nerd) **Nick Austin;** Blake Williams (Captain of the Football Team) **Major Dodge;** Mrs. Lascalzo (The Drama Teacher) **Jennifer Miller***10; Feung Schwey (The Asian Exchange Student) **Anderson Lim;** The Mystery Guest **CP Lacey**

SETTING Wanaget High's Senior Prom, 1989. An interactive theatrical experience presented without intermission

SYNOPSIS The Captain of the Football Team, the Asian Exchange Student, the Geek, the Head Cheerleader are all competing for Prom King and Queen. The audience decides who wins while moonwalking to retro hits from the decade.

*Succeeded by: 1. Dillon Porter 2. Daryl Embry 3. Craig Jorczak 4. Thomas Poarch 5. Michael Barra 6. Michael Maloney 7. Allison Carter Thomas 8. Courtney Ell 9. Angie Blocher 10. Andrea Biggs

BLUE MAN GROUP

Astor Place Theatre; Opening Night: November 7, 1991; 8,589 performances as of May 31, 2008

Created and written by Matt Goldman, Phil Stanton, Chris Wink; Produced by Blue Man Productions; Director, Marlene Swartz and Blue Man Group; Artistic Directors, Caryl Glaab, Michael Quinn; Artistic/Musical Collaborators, Larry Heinemann, Ian Pai; Set, Kevin Joseph Roach; Costumes, Lydia Tanji, Patricia Murphy; Lighting, Brian Aldous, Matthew McCarthy; Sound, Raymond Schilke, Jon Weston; Computer Graphics, Kurisu-Chan; Video, Caryl Glaab, Dennis Diamond; PSM, Patti McCabe; Company Manager, Akia Squitieri; Stage Managers, Bernadette Castro, Jenny Lynch; Resident General Manager, Leslie Witthohn; General Manager of North American Productions, Alison Schwartz; Performing Director, Chris Bowen; Performing Directors, Chris Bowen, Michael Dahlen, Randall Jaynes, Jeffrey Doornbos, Brian Scott; Original Executive Producer, Maria Di Dia; Casting, Deb Burton; Press, Laura Camien

Blue Man Group, *Off-Broadway's longest running theatrical experience (photo by David Hawe)*

CAST (rotating) **Shaneca Adams, Kalen Allmandinger, Gideon Banner, Wes Day, Josh Elrod, Isaac Gardner, Matt Goldman, John Hartzell, Colin Hurd, Michael Rahhal, Matt Ramsey, Pete Simpson, Phil Stanton, Steve White, Chris Wink**

MUSICIANS (rotating) Tom Shad, Geoff Gersh, Clem Waldmann, Dan Dobson, Dan Dobson, Jeff Lipstein, Byron Estep, Matt Hankle, Tommy Kessler, Jerry Kops, Josh Matthews, Jordan Perlson, Dave Corter

An evening of performance art presented without intermission. For original production credits see *Theatre World* Volume 48, Page 90.

SYNOPSIS The three-man new-vaudeville Blue Man Group combines comedy, music, art, and multimedia to produce a unique form of entertainment.

THE FANTASTICKS

Snapple Theater Center; First Preview: July 28, 2006; Opening Night: August 23, 2006; Temporarily Closed February 24, 2008[+]; 27 previews, 678 performances

Book and lyrics by Tom Jones, music by Harvey Schmidt, suggested by the play *Les Romanesques* by Edmond Rostand; Produced by Steven Baruch, Marc Routh, Richard Frankel, Thomas Viertel; Director, Tom Jones; Original Production Staged by Word Baker; Sets and Costumes, Ed Wittstein; Lighting, Mary Jo Dondlinger; Sound, Dominic Sack; Casting, Telsey + Company; Musical Director, Dorothy Martin; Production Stage Manager, Gregory R. Covert; Stage Manager/Dance Captain, Kim Moore; Production Management, Aduro Productions; Production Supervisor, Dan Shaheen; General Management, Richard Frankel Productions, Ed Kaats; Musical Staging, Janet Watson; Company Manager, Leslie Anne Pinney; Press, Barlow-Hartman, Andrew Snyder; Cast recording: Sh-K-Boom/Ghostlight 84415

CAST The Narrator **Burke Moses;** The Boy (Matt) **Anthony Federov[*1];** The Girl (Luisa) **Betsy Morgan[*2];** The Boy's Father (Hucklebee) **John Deyle;** The Girl's Father (Bellomy) **Martin Vidnovic;** The Old Actor (Henry) **Thomas Bruce;** The Man Who Dies (Mortimer) **Robert R. Oliver[*3];** The Mute **Nick Spangler[*4];** At the Piano **Robert Felstein;** At the Harp **Erin Hill**

STANDBYS Tom Flagg (Hucklebee/Henry/Mortimer), Stuart Marland (El Gallo/Hucklebee/Bellomy), Julie Craig[*5] (The Mute/Luisa), Nick Spangler[*4] (Matt)

MUSICAL NUMBERS Overture, Try to Remember, Much More, Metaphor, Never Say No, It Depends on What You Pay,

John Deyle, Burke Moses, and Martin Vidnovic in The Fantasticks *(photo by Joan Marcus)*

Soon It's Gonna Rain, Abduction Ballet, Happy Ending, This Plum is Too Ripe, I Can See It, Plant a Radish, Round and Round, They Were You, Try to Remember (reprise)

Revival of the musical presented in two acts. *The Fantasticks* is the world's longest running musical and the longest running Off-Broadway production ever. The original production opened at the Sullivan Street Playhouse on May 3, 1960 and closed January 13, 2002 playing over 17,000 performances (see *Theatre World* Volume 16 page 167 for original credits). For this production, Tom Jones, author and lyricist, (using the pseudonym 'Thomas Bruce') recreates the role of "Henry."

SYNOPSIS *The Fantasticks* tells the story of a young boy and girl who fall madly in love at the hands of their meddling fathers, but soon grow restless and stray from one another. Will their separation provide a deeper appreciation for the love they once shared or create a permanent gulf between them?

*Succeeded by: 1. Nick Spangler 2. Julie Craig 3. Tom Flagg 4. Jordan Nichols 5. Liz Holtan

+The show was slated to resume performances June 16, 2008.

THE GAZILLION BUBBLE SHOW

New World Stages – Stage 3; Previews: January 17–23, 2007; Opening Night: February 15, 2007; 637 performances as of May 31, 2008

Created and staged by Fan Yang; Produced and Set Design by Fan Yang and Neodus Company, Ltd.; Artistic Director, Jamie Jan; Show Director, Steve Lee; Lighting, Jin Ho Kim; Sound, Joon Lee; Gazilllion Bubbles FX, Special Effects, Alex Cheung; Theatrical Special Effects, CITC/Gary and Stephanie Crawford; Original Music, Workspace Co, Ltd.; Laser Design, Abhilash George; Lumalaser, Tim Ziegenbein; Lighting Effects, David Lau; Special Effects Inventor, Dragan Maricic; Production Stage Manager, Yeung Jin Son; Stage Manager, Min Song; Technical Director, Alan Kho; Production Manager, Vanes D'Andrea; General Management, The Splinter Group; Marketing, HHC Marketing; Marketing Director, Chermaine Cho; Press, Springer Associates, Joe Trentacosta, Gary Springer

Performed by **Fan Yang, Ana Yang,** or **Jano Yang**

New York premiere of an interactive theatrical event presented without intermission. Fan Yang opened the Las Vegas production on February 2, 2008 and his wife and brother performed the show in New York.

SYNOPSIS The first interactive stage production of its kind, complete with fantastic light effects and lasers, Fan Yang blends art and science to dazzle audiences with his jaw-dropping masterpieces of bubble artistry that defy gravity and logic as we know it.

I LOVE YOU, YOU'RE PERFECT, NOW CHANGE

Westside Theatre/Upstairs; First Preview: July 15, 1996; Opening Night: August 1, 1996; 4,937 performances as of May 31, 2008

Music and Arrangements by Jimmy Roberts; lyrics and book, by Joe DiPietro; Produced by James Hammerstein, Bernie Kukoff, Jonathan Pollard; Director, Joel Bishoff; Musical Director, Kim Douglas Steiner; Set & Lighting, Neil Peter Jampolis; Costumes, Pamela Scofield; Original Costumes, Candice Donnelly; Sound, Duncan Edwards; Production Supervisor, Matthew G. Marholin; Stage Manager, William H. Lang; General Management, 321 Theatrical Management: Nancy Nagel Gibbs, Marcia Goldberg, Nina Essman; Associate Producer, Matt Garfield; Company Manager, Eric Cornell; Assistant Director/ASM, Wendy Loomis; Casting, Stuart Howard, Amy Schecter & Paul Hardt; Marketing, SRO Marketing; Press, Jim Randolph; Cast recording, Varese Sarabande VSD-5771

CAST **Jim Stanek**[*1], **Bryan McElroy**[*2], **Courtney Balan**[*3], **Anne Bobby;** Standbys **Will Erat, Karyn Quackenbush;** MUSICIANS **Kim Douglas Steiner** (Piano), **Patti Ditzel** (Violinist)

MUSICAL NUMBERS Cantata for a First Date, Stud and a Babe, Single Man Drought, Why? 'Cause I'm a Guy, Tear Jerk, I Will Be Loved Tonight, Hey There Single Guy/Gal, He Called Me, Wedding Vows, Always a Bridesmaid, Baby Song, Marriage Tango, On the Highway of Love, Waiting Trio, Shouldn't I Be Less in Love with You?, I Can Live with That, I Love You You're Perfect Now Change

Amy White, Anne Bobby, Jim Stanek, and Bryan McElroy in I Love You, You're Perfect, Now Change *(photo by Carol Rosegg)*

A musical revue presented in two acts. For original production credits see *Theatre World* Volume 53, page 116.

SYNOPSIS A musical comedy with everything you ever secretly thought about dating, romance, marriage, lovers, husbands, wives and in-laws, but were afraid to admit.

*Succeeded by: 1. Frank Vlastnik (10/1/07) 2. Jonathan Rayson (10/26/07) 3. Amy White (6/4/07), Christy Faber (1/14/08)

The J.A.P. SHOW Jewish American Princesses of Comedy

The Actors Temple Theatre; First Preview: April 7, 2007; Opening Night: April 18, 2007; Closed September 30, 2007; 110 performances

Created by Cory Kahaney; Produced by Foster Entertainment, Maximum Entertainment, Avalon Entertainment, and Judith Marinoff, Director, Dan Fields; Sets, Jo Winiarski; Projections, Aaron Rhyne; Lighting, Jeff Croiter; Assistant Video Design, Linsey Bostwick; Associate Producer, Victoria Winkelman; Press, Richard Kornberg and Associates, Laura Kaplow-Goldman, Billy Zavelson

CAST (rotating) **Cory Kahaney, Cathy Ladman, Jessica Kirson, Sherry Davey, Julie Goldman, Betsy Salkind; Adrianne Tolsch**

World premiere of a stand-up comedy theatrical experience presented without intermission.

SYNOPSIS A rotating cast of four comics demonstrate how the Jewish female comics of yore are treasured pioneers without whom they would not exist.

MY MOTHER'S ITALIAN, MY FATHER'S JEWISH & I'M IN THERAPY

Westside Theatre (Downstairs); First Preview: November 3, 2006; Opening Night: December 8, 2006; 651 performances as of May 31, 2008

Written by Steve Solomon; Produced by Rodger Hess, Abby Koffler, Howard Rapp & Arnold Graham, Leah & Ed Frankel; Director, John Bowab; Sets, Ray Klausen; Lighting, Brian Nason; Sound, Carl Casella; Production Stage Manager, Jamie Rog; Production Management, Aurora Productions; General Manager, Richards/Climan Inc; Associate Producer, Carol & Andy Caviar; Marketing, Leanne Schanzer Promotions; Press, Keith Sherman & Associates

Performed by **Steve Solomon***

New York premiere of a new solo performance play presented without intermission. Originally opened at Little Shubert Theatre starring Mr. Solomon; transferred to the Westside Theatre May 4, 2007.

SYNOPSIS In his biographical show, *Italian + Jewish = Therapy*, Steve Solomon combines comic voices, sound effects and astounding characters to bring alive a myriad of people from all walks of life. Billed as "one part lasagna, one part kreplach and two parts prozac," the show relates to the wacky side of the human condition.

*Succeeded by Paul Kreppel while Mr. Solomon took the show on tour in the fall of 2007. Solomon returned to the show from April 18-25, 2007 during Mr. Kreppel's vacation.

NAKED BOYS SINGING!

New World Stages – Stage 4; First Preview: July 2, 1999; Opening Night: July 22, 1999; 2,690 performances as of May 31, 2008 (Weekends only)

Written by Stephen Bates, Marie Cain, Perry Hart, Shelly Markham, Jim Morgan, David Pevsner, Rayme Sciaroni, Mark Savage, Ben Schaechter, Robert Schrock, Trance Thompson, Bruce Vilanch, Mark Winkler; Conceived and directed by Robert Schrock; Produced by Jamie Cesa, Carl D. White, Hugh Hayes, Tom Smedes, Jennifer Dumas; Choreography, Jeffry Denman; Music Director, Jeffrey Biering; Original Musical Director and Arrangements, Stephen Bates; Set/Costumes, Carl D. White; Lighting, Aaron Copp; Production Stage Manager, Heather Weiss/Scott DelaCruz; Assistant Stage Manager, Mike Kirsch/Dave August; Dance Captain, Craig Lowry; Press, David Gersten; Original Press, Peter Cromarty; L.A. Cast recording: Café Pacific Records

The Cast of Naked Boys Singing *(photo by Joan Marcus)*

CAST Naked Maid **Michael Chapman***1; Radio **Eric Dean Davis;** Robert Mitchum **Frank Galgano***2; Entertainer **Brian M. Golub***3; Bris **Matthew Kilgore***4; Porn Star **George Livengood;** Muscle Addiction **Craig Lowry***5; Window **Timothy John Mandala;** Swings: **Phil Simmons***6, **Mike Kirsch***7; Piano: **Jeffrey Biering**

MUSICAL NUMBERS Gratuitous Nudity, Naked Maid, The Bliss of a Bris, Window to Window, Fight the Urge, Robert Mitchum, Jack's Song, Members Only, Perky Little Porn Star, Kris Look What You've Missed, Muscle Addiction, Nothin' But the Radio On, The Entertainer, Window to the Soul, Finale/ Naked Boys Singing!

A musical revue presented in two acts. For original production credits see *Theatre World* Volume 56, page 114. Originally opened at The Actors' Playhouse; transferred to Theatre Four March 17, 2004; transferred to the John Houseman Theater September 17, 2004; transferred to the 47th Street Theatre November 12, 2004; transferred to the Julia Miles Theatre May 6, 2005; transferred to New World Stages October 14, 2005.

SYNOPSIS The title says it all! Caution and costumes are thrown to the wind in this all-new musical revue featuring an original score and a handful of hunks displaying their special charms as they celebrate the splendors of male nudity in comedy, song and dance.

*Succeeded by: 1. Trevor Southworth, Stephen Carrasco, Ronald Hornsby, Gregory Stockbridge 2. Marc Ginsburg 3. Eric Potter 4. Spencer Gates, Chris Layton 5. Scott McLean Harrison, Craig Lowry 6. Spencer Gates 7. Dave August

PERFECT CRIME

Snapple Theatre Center – 4th Floor; Opening Night: April 18, 1987; 8,618 performances as of May 31, 2008

Written by Warren Manzi; Presented by The Actors Collective in association with the Methuen Company; Director, Jeffrey Hyatt; Set, Jay Stone, Mr. Manzi; Costumes, Nancy Bush; Lighting, Jeff Fontaine; Sound, David Lawson; Stage Manager, Michael Danek; Press, Debenham Smythe/Michelle Vincents, Paul Lewis, Jeffrey Clarke

CAST Margaret Thorne Brent **Catherine Russell;** Inspector James Ascher **Richard Shoberg;** W. Harrison Brent **David Butler***1; Lionel McAuley **Philip Hoffman***2; David Breuer **Patrick Robustelli**

SETTING Windsor Locks, Connecticut. A mystery presented in two acts. For original production credits see *Theatre World* Volume 43, page 96. Catherine Russell has only missed four performances since the show opened in 1987. Originally opened at the Courtyard Playhouse then transferred to the Second Stage, 47th St. Playhouse, Intar 53 Theater, Harold Clurman Theatre, Theatre Four, The Duffy Theatre, and currently the Snapple Theatre Center.

SYNOPSIS *Perfect Crime* is a murder mystery about a psychiatrist who is accused of killing her husband by a detective who can't quite pin the murder on her. The complication is that the psychiatrist and the detective are in love.

*Succeeded by: 1. Patrick Ryan Sullivan 2. Michael Brian Dunn

THE QUANTUM EYE: MAGIC DECPTIONS

Soho Playhouse –The Huron Club+; First Preview: September 27, 2007; Opening Night: February 9, 2007 (Friday nights); 103 performances as of May 31, 2008

Created by Sam Eaton; Produced and directed by Samuel Rosenthal; Original Music, Scott O'Brien; Art Design, Fearless Design; Assistant Producer, Janet Oldenbrook; Artwork, Glenn Hidalago; House Manger, Janet Oldenbrook; Wardrobe, Larry the Tailer; Press, Timothy Haskell

Performed by **Sam Eato**

A mentalist/magic show presented without intermission.

SYNOPSIS The spirit of Harry Houdini, and Victorian era New York are alive and none of your secrets are safe from *The Quantum Eye*.... Eaton takes audiences to the outer limits of human perception. His masterful use of prediction, supernormal mentalism, memorization and calculation will amaze and entertain audiences. It is an extraordinary blend of 21st Century mentalism and Victorian-era mystery. *The Quantum Eye* is proof that there is still magic in the air.

+Transferred to the Snapple Theater Center – Duffy Theater on November 24, 2007, performing on Saturday twilights.

STOMP

Orpheum Theatre; First Preview: February 18, 1994; Opening Night: February 27, 1994; 6,009 performances as of May 31, 2008

Created/Directed by Luke Cresswell and Steve McNicholas; Produced by Columbia Artists Management, Harriet Newman Leve, James D. Stern, Morton Wolkowitz, Schuster/Maxwell, Galin/Sandler, and Markley/Manocherian; Lighting, Mr. McNicholas, Neil Tiplady; Casting, Vince Liebhart/Scot Willingham; Executive Producers, Richard Frankel Productions/Marc Routh; Associate Producer, Fred Bracken; General Manager, Richard Frankel Productions/Joe Watson; PSM, Paul Botchis; ASM, Elizabeth Grunewald; Technical Director, Joseph Robinson; Company Manager, Tim Grassel; Assistant Company Manager, Maia Watson; Press, Chris Boneau/Adrian Bryan-Brown, Jackie Green, Joe Perrotta

CAST (rotating): **Camille Armstrong, Alan Asuncion, Michelle Dorrance, Sean Edwards, Fritzlyn Hector, Brad Holland, Patrick Lovejoy, Stephanie Marshall, Keith Middleton, Jason Mills, Yako Miyamoto, Raymond Poitier, Joeseph Russomano, Marivaldo Dos Santos, Carlos Thomas, Jeremy Tracy, Dan Weiner, Nicholas V. Young, Elec Simon, Fiona Wilkes**

A percussive performance art piece presented with an intermission. For original production credits see *Theatre World* Volume 50, Page 113.

SYNOPSIS Stomp is a high-energy, percussive symphony, coupled with dance, played entirely on non-traditional instruments, such as garbage can lids, buckets, brooms and sticks.

TONY 'n' TINAS WEDDING

Vinnie Black's Coliseum at Edison Hotel; Opening Night: February 6, 1988; 5,702 performances as of May 31, 2008 (Friday and Saturday evenings only)

Written by Artificial Intelligence; Conceived by Nancy Cassaro; Originally created by Thomas Allen, James Altuner, Mark Campbell, Nancy Cassaro, Patricia Cregan, Elizabeth Dennehy, Chris Fracchiolla, Jack Fris, Kevin Alexander, Mark Nassar, Larry Pellegrini, Susan Varon, Moira Wilson); Produced by Big Apple Entertainment, Raphael Berko, Jeff Gitlin; Director, Larry Pelligrini; Choreography, Hal Simons; Costumes/Hair/Makeup, Juan DeArmas; Stage Manager, Christy Benanti; ASM, Ryan Delorge; Wardrobe and Hair, Rebecca Gaston; Senior Production Coordinator, Drew Seltzer; Production Coordinator, Evan Weinstein; Marketing, Gary Shaffer; Promotions, DeMarcus Reed

CAST Valentina Lynne Vitale Nunzio **Joli Tribuzio**; Anthony Angelo Nunzio Jr. **Craig Thomas Rivela;** Connie Mocogni **Dina Rizzo**i; Barry Wheeler **Scott Voloshin;** Donna Marsala **Jessica Aquino**; Dominick Fabrizzi **Anthony Augello;** Marina Gulino **Dawn Luebbe**; Johnny Nunzio **Deno Vourderis**; Josephine Vitale **Anita Salvate**; Joseph Vitale **Rhett Kalman;** Sister Albert Maria **Daniela Genoble**; Anthony Angelo Nunzio, Sr. **Mark Nasser**; Madeline Monore **Alison Leigh Mills;** Michael Just **Matthew Knowland;** Father Mark **James J. Hendricks;** Vinnie Black **Alan Tulin**; Loretta Black **Cindi Kostello;** Sal Antonucci **John DiBenedetto;** Donny Dolce **Johnny Tammaro;** Celeste Romano **Lynn Portas**; Carlo Cannoli **Anthony Ventura**; Rocco Caruso **Ray Grappone**

SETTING Tony and Tina's wedding and reception. An interactive environmental theatre production. For original production credits see *Theatre World* Volume 44, page 63. Originally played at Washington Square Church and Carmelita's; transferred to St. John's Church (wedding ceremony) and Vinnie Black's Coliseum (reception) until August, 1988; transferred to St. Luke's Church and Vinnie Black's Vegas Room Coliseum in the Edison Hotel. The production closed May 18, 2003, then reopened on October 3, 2003. It closed again May 1, 2004, reopened under new co-producers (Raphael Berko and Jeff Gitlin) on May 15th, 2004.

SYNOPSIS Tony and Tina are getting hitched. Audience members become part of the exuberant Italian family—attending the ceremony, mingling with relatives and friends, eating, drinking and dancing to the band.

Stephanie Marshall of Stomp *(photo by Steve McNicholas)*

David Beach, Richard Topol, Douglas Rees and Michael Laurence in Primary Stages' Opus *(photo by James Leynse)*

Sarah Paulson, Jennifer Dundas and Lily Rabe in Roundabout Theatre Company's Crimes of the Heart *(photo by Joan Marcus)*

Mary-Louise Parker in Playwrights Horizons' Dead Man's Cell Phone *(photo by Joan Marcus)*

Richard Easton and Jeremy Strong in Classic Stage Company's New Jerusalem *(photo by Joan Marcus)*

Waleed F. Zuaiter, Jeremy Beck and Sevan Greene in The Culture Project's Betrayed *(photo by Carol Rosegg)*

Mercedes Ruehl and Larry Bryggman in Signature Theatre Company's Edward Albee's Occupant *(photo by Carol Rosegg)*

Abingdon Theatre Company

Fifteenth Season

Artistic Director, Jan Buttram; Managing Director, Samuel Bellinger; Associate Artistic Director/Literary Manager, Kim T. Sharp; Marketing, Doug DeVita; Play Development Advisor, Pamela Paul; Rental/Facilities Manager, Stephen Squibb; Development, Edward J. McKearney, Elliot J. Cohen; Business/Box Office Manager, James Holland; Casting, William Schill; Dramaturg, Julie Hegner; Playwright Group Coordinator, Frank Tangredi; Production Manager, Ian Grunes; Press, Shirley Herz, Dan Demello

THE GOLDMAN PROJECT by Staci Swedeen; Presented in association with Penguin Repertory Company (Joe Brancato, Artistic Director; Andrew M. Horn, Executive Director); Director, Joe Brancato; Sets, Ken Larson; Lighting, Matthew McCarthy; Costumes, Patricia E. Doherty; Original Sound, Dimitri Tisseyre; Sound Recreation, Matt O'Hare; PSM, Jack D. McDowell; Original Casting, Judy Henderson; Assistant to the Director, Jennifer Hunt; ASMs, Chandra Jean Ahr, Sheila Blanc; Assistant Production Manager, Shawn Duan; Props/Set Décor, Joseph J. Egan; Hair, Jon Jordan; Cast: Anita Keal (Naomi Goldman), Sam Guncler (Tony Marks), Bernadette Quigley (Aviva)

Setting: Naomi's apartment in Inwood, New York City, 1994. New York premiere of a new play presented in two acts; June Havoc Theatre; September 28–October 28, 2007 (Opened October 3); 32 performances. Originally presented at the Penguin Repertory Company (Stony Point, NY) October 6–November 5, 2006.

CRY HAVOC by Tom Coash; Director, Kim T. Sharp; Sets, Blair Mielnik; Costumes, Deborah J. Caney; Lighting, Anthony Kudner; Sound, Ken Feldman; Scenic Paint, James DeWoody; PSM, Genevieve Ortiz; Assistant to the Director, Max Schulman; ASM, Yuriy Nayer; Cast: Sameer Sheikh (Mohammed El-Qahira), Keith Merrill (Nicholas Field), Pamela Paul (Ms. Nevers)

Setting: Mohammed's small flat in Cairo, Egypt; the present. New York premiere of a play presented in two acts; Dorothy Strelsin Theatre; October 20–November 11, 2007 (Opened October 28); 23 performances.

RUM & COKE by Carmen Peláez; Director, Carl Andress; Sets, Ken Larson; Costumes, Jessica Jahn; Lighting, Matthew McCarthy; Projections, Chris Kateff; Sound, Matt O'Hare; PSM, Genevieve Ortiz; Assistant Production Manager, Andy Waters; Assistant Costumes, Kelli Haase; Cast: Carmen Peláez (Camila and others)

Setting: New York, Miami, and Cuba. Off-Broadway premiere of a new solo performance play presented without intermission; June Havoc Theatre; February 1–March 2, 2008 (Opened February 13); 32 performances. Previously presented by The Present Company at the 2006 New York Fringe Festival.

Carmen Pelaez in Rum & Coke *(photo by Kim T. Sharp)*

ANOTHER VERMEER by Bruce Robinson; Director, Kelly Morgan; Sets, Jeff Pajer; Costumes, Deborah Caney; Lighting, Tony Kudner; Sound, Kevin Lloyd; PSM, Yuriy Nayer; Cast: Austin Pendleton (Han Van Meegeren), Justin Grace (Bram Van Ter Horst), Dan Cordle (Jan Vermeer/Bartus Korteling), Christian Pedersen (Lt. Thomas Keller), Thom Christopher (Dr. Abraham Bredius)

New York premiere of a play presented without intermission; Dorothy Strelsin Theatre; March 29–April 20, 2008 (Opened April 6); 23 performances.

Atlantic Theater Company

Twenty-Second Season

Artistic Director, Neil Pepe; Executive Director, Andrew D. Hamingson; School Executive Director, Mary McCann; General Manager, Jamie Tyrol; Associate Artistic Director, Christian Parker; Development, Roni Ferretti; Production Manager, New Medium (Lester Grant, Jee Han); Marketing, Jodi Sheeler; Business Associate/Audience Services, Sara Montgomery; Operations, Anthony Francavilla; Company Manager, Juan Carlos Salinas; School Associate Directors, Steven Hawley, Kate Blumberg; Education, Frances Tarr; School Artistic Director, Geoff Berman; School Production Manager, Gabriel Evansohn; Casting, Telsey + Company; Press, Boneau/Bryan-Brown, Joe Perotta

SCARCITY by Lucy Thurber; Director, Jackson Gay; Sets, Walt Spangler; Costumes, Ilona Somogyi; Lighting, Jason Lyons; Sound, Daniel Baker; Original Music, Jason Mills; Fight Directors, Kathryn Ekblad, J. David Brimmer; PSM, Marion Friedman; ASM, Alison DeSantis; Technical Director, Mike Giordano; Cast: Meredith Brandt (Rachel), Kristen Johnston (Martha), Todd Weeks (Louie), Michael T. Weiss (Herb), Jesse Eisenberg (Billy), Maggie Kiley (Ellen), Miriam Shor (Gloria); Understudies: Brandon Espinoza (Billy), Susan Finch (Gloria)

Time/Place: The Present/The Hill Towns, Western Massachusetts. World premiere of a new play presented in two acts; Linda Gross Theater; August 29–October 21, 2007 (Opened September 20); 22 previews, 33 performances.

Meredith Brandt, Kristen Johnston, Jesse Eisenberg, Michael T. Weiss in Scarcity *(photo by Doug Hamilton)*

TRUMPERY by Peter Parnell; Director, David Esbjornson; Sets, Santo Loquasto; Costumes, Jane Greenwood; Lighting, James Ingalls; Sound, Obadiah Eaves; Dialect Coach, Deborah Hecht; PSM, Matthew Silver; ASM, Jillian M. Oliver; Assistant Director, Joanie Shultz; Technical Director, Adam Shive; Cast: Michael Cristofer (Darwin), Jack Tartaglia (George/Horace), Bianca Amato (Emma), Timothy Deenihan (Vicar/Protester), Michael Countryman (Hooker), Paris Rose Yates (Annie Darwin/Girl), Neal Huff (Huxley), Peter Maloney (Owen/Williams), Manoel Felciano (Wallace)

Setting: Down House, England; a weekend in June 1958, and October, three years later. World premiere of a new play presented in two acts; Linda Gross Theater; November 1–December 30, 2007 (Opened December 5); 21 previews, 27 performances.

ALMOST AN EVENING Three short plays by Ethan Coen; Presented in association with Art Meets Commerce (Chip Meyrelles, Executive Director; Ken Greiner, Producing Director); Director, Neil Pepe; Sets, Riccardo Hernandez; Costumes, Ilona Somogyi; Lighting, Donald Holder; Sound, Eric Shim; Fight Director, J. David Brimmer; PSM, Marion Friedman; Production Manager, Gabriel Evansohn; Assistant Director, Jaime Castaneda; Cast: *Waiting*: Joey Slotnick (Nelson), Mary McCann (Receptionist), Jordan Lage (Mr. Sabatacheck), Mark Linn-Baker (McMartin), Del Pentecost (Polhemus); *Four Benches*: Jonathan Cake (One), Del Pentecost (Earl), J.R. Horne (Mr. Boodrum), F. Murray Abraham (Control), Elizabeth Marvel (Woman with Pram), Jordan Lage (Texan); *Debate*: F. Murray Abraham (God Who Judges), Mark Linn-Baker (God Who Loves), Del Pentecost (Angel 1), J.R. Horne (Angel 2/Understudy), Mary McCann (Young Woman), Jordan Lage (Young Man), Jonathan Cake (Maître D'), Joey Slotnick (Waiter), Elizabeth Marvel (Lady Friend)

World premiere of three new short plays presented without intermission; Atlantic Stage 2; January 9–February 10, 2007 (Opened January 22); 14 previews, 24 performances. Transferred to The Theatres at 45 Bleecker on March 20 for a limited commercial run (see page 142 in this volume).

PARLOUR SONG by Jez Butterworth; Director, Neil Pepe; Sets, Robert Brill; Costumes, Sarah Edwards; Lighting, Kenneth Posner; Sound, Obadiah Eaves; Projections, Dustin O'Neil; Dialect Coach, Stephen Gabis; PSM, Freda Farrell; ASM, Rebecca Spinac; Associate Director, Jaime Castaneda; Associate Production Manager, Austin Tidwell; Technical Director, Brant Underwood; Cast: Jonathan Cake (Dale), Chris Bauer (Ned), Emily Mortimer (Joy)

Setting: England, in the late Summer, Autumn. In and around the small suburban new-built home of Ned and Joy. World premiere of a new play presented without intermission; Linda Gross Theater; February 15–April 6, 2007 (Opened March 5); 19 previews, 53 performances.

PORT AUTHORITY by Conor McPherson; Director, Henry Wishcamper; Sets, Takeshi Kata; Costumes, Jenny Mannis; Lighting, Matthew Richards; Sound, Bart Fasbender; Dialects, Stephen Gabis; PSM, Mary Kathryn Flynt; Production Manager, Michael Wade; ASM, Deanna Weiner; Assistant Director, Portia Krieger; Cast: John Gallagher, Jr. (Kevin), Brian d'Arcy James (Dermot), Jim Norton (Joe)

Setting: Dublin, the present. New York premiere of a new play presented without intermission; Linda Gross Theater; April 30–June 22, 2008, 2007 (Opened May 21); 21 previews, 34 performances.

BODY AWARENESS by Annie Baker; Director, Karen Kohlhaas; Set, Walt Spangler; Costumes, Bobby Frederick Tilley II; Lighting, Jason Lyons; Sound, Anthony Gabriele; Casting, MelCap Casting; PSM, Jillian M. Oliver; ASM, John Randolph Ferry; Assistant Director, Marcie Grambeau; Properties, Lauren Barbara; Technical Director, Mike Szeles; Cast: Mary McCann

(Phyllis), JoBeth Williams (Joyce), Jonathan Clem (Jared), Peter Friedman (Frank Bonitatibus)

World premiere of a new play presented without intermission; Atlantic Stage 2; May 28–June 22, 2008 (Opened June 4); 7 previews, 20 performances.

Brooklyn Academy of Music

Founded in 1861

Alan H. Fishman, Chairman of the Board; Karen Brooks Hopkins, President; William I. Campbell, Vice Chairman of the Board; Joseph V. Melillo, Executive Producer

ROYAL SHAKESPEARE COMPANY'S *KING LEAR* AND *THE SEAGULL* Director, Trevor Nunn; Sets, Christopher Oram; Lighting, Neil Austin; Music, Steve Edis; Sound, Fergus O'Hare; Fights, Malcolm Ranson; US Stage Manager, Jane Pole; Assistant Director, Gemma Fairlie; Music Director, Jeff Moore; Associate Design, Morgan Large; Dialects, Penny Dyer; Company Voice Work, Morgan Large; Casting, Sam Jones; Production Manager, Simon Ash; Costume Supervisor, Stephanie Arditti/Janet Bench; Company Manager, Richard Clayton; Stage Manager, Ben Delfont; Deputy Stage Manager, Klare Roger; ASM, Harry Niland/Rhiannon Harper; Musicians: Adam Cross (clarinet), Simon Lenton (trumpet/keyboard), John Gibson (percussion/keyboard), Jeff Moore (keyboard/violin/accordion)

KING LEAR by William Shakespeare; Cast: Ian McKellen (Lear), Frances Barber (Goneril), Monica Dolan (Regan), Romola Garai (Cordelia), Julian Harries (Duke of Albany), Guy Williams (Duke of Cornwall), Ben Addis (King of France), Peter Hinton (Duke of Burgundy/A Captain), Jonathan Hyde (Earl of Kent), William Gaunt (Earl of Gloucester), Ben Meyjes (Edgar), Philip Winchester (Edmund), Sylvester McCoy (Fool), John Heffernan (Oswald), Seymour Matthews (Curran), David Weston (Gentleman), Adam Booth (Knight/Servant of Cornwall), Richard Goulding (Knight/Messenger), Zoe Boyle (Lady in Waiting to Goneril), Russell Byrne (1st Gloucester Servant/A Doctor), Melanie Jessop (2nd Gloucester Servant), Gerald Kyd (A Soldier), Naomi Capron (A Maid)

Revival of the play presented in two acts; presented in repertory with *The Seagull*; Harvey Theater; September 6–30, 2007 (Opened September 11); 3 previews, 12 performances.

THE SEAGULL by Anton Chekhov, translation by Noah Birksted-Breen; Cast: Frances Barber (Arkadina), Richard Goulding (Konstantin), Ian McKellen or William Gaunt (Sorin), Romola Garai (Nina), Guy Williams (Shamrayev), Melanie Jessop (Polina), Monica Dolan (Masha), Gerald Kyd (Trigorin), Jonathan Hyde (Dr. Dorn), Ben Meyjes (Medvedenko), Peter Hinton (Yakov), Zoe Boyle (Arkadina's Maid), Naomi Capron (Cook), David Weston (Butler), Seymour Matthews, Ben Addis & Russell Byrne (Servants), Adam Booth, Julian Harries, John Herrernan and Philip Winchester (Estate Workers)

Revival of the play presented in two acts; presented in repertory with *King Lear*; Harvey Theater; September 7–29, 2007 (Opened September 12); 2 previews, 9 performances.

2007 Next Wave Festival – 25th Annual – Theatre Events

HOTEL CASSIOPEIA Written by Charles Mee, created and performed by SITI Company; Director, Anne Bogart; Set, Neil Patel; Costumes, James Schuette; Lighting, Brian H. Scott; Sound, Darron L West; Projections, Greg King; Assistant Sound, Matthew Hubbs; Props, Mark Walston; Company Stage Manager, Elizabeth Moreau; ASM, Justin Donham; Dramaturg, Adrien Hansel; Managing Director, Megan Wanlass Szalla; Associate Managing Director, Brad Carlin; Cast: Barney O'Hanlon (Joseph), Michi Barall (Waitress), Stephen Webber (Astronomer), Leon Ingulsrud (Herbalist), J. Ed Araiza (Pharmacist), Ellen Lauren (Ballerina), Akiko Aizawa (Mother)

New York premier of a new play presented in without intermission; Harvey Theatre; October 9–13, 2006; 6 performances.

Ellen Lauren and the cast of SITI Company's Hotel Cassiopeia *(photo by Richard Termine)*

KRUM by Hanoch Levin; Presented by TR Warszawa of Poland (Grezegorz Jarzyna, Artistic Director), Co-produced by Stary Teatr (Cracow); Director, Krzysztof Warlikowski; Set/Costumes, Marłgorzata Szczaniak; Lighting, Felice Ross; Sound, Paweł Mykietyn; Film, Paweł Łoziaski; Cast: Jacek Poniedziałek (Krum), Malgorzata Rolniatowska (Krum's Mother), Magdalena Cielecka (Truda), Małgorzata Hajewska-Krzysztofik (Dupa), Anna Radwan-Gancarczyk (Felicia), Danuta Stenka (Cica), Redbad Klijnstra (Tugati), Marek Kalita (Takhtikh),

Zygmunt Malanowicz (Dulce), Adam Nawojczyk (Bertolda), Miron Hakenbeck (Dr. Shiboigen/Nurse/Photographer/Barber/Undertaker), Paweł Kruszelnicki (Shkita)

American premiere of a new play presented in Polish with English subtitles without intermission; Harvey Theater; October 17–20, 2007; 4 performances.

LULU by Frank Wedekind; Presented by Thalia Theater of Hamburg, Germany; Director, Michael Thalheimer; Set, Olaf Altmann; Costumes, Barbara Drosihn; Music, Bert Wrede; Video, Alexander du Prel; Lighting, Stefan Bolliger; Dramaturgy, Sonja Anders; Stage Manager, Corinna Fussbach; Production Manager, Thoralf Kunze; Makeup, Julia Wilms; Technical Director, Andreas Dietz; Technical Management, Uwe Barkhahn, Oliver Canis; Cast: Fritzi Haberlandt (Lulu), Norman Hacker (Dr. Franz Schöning), Felix Knopp (Alwa Schöning), Christoph Bantzer (Dr. Goll), Markus Graf (Schigolch), Hans Löw (Eduard Schwarz), Maren Eggert (Gräfin von Geschwitz), Peter Moltzen (Rodrigo Quast), Helmut Mooshammer (Casti-Piani), Christoph Bantzer (Mr. Hopkins), Andreas Döhler (Kungu-Poti), Harald Weiler (Dr. Hilti), Michael Benthin (Jack)

U.S. premiere of a play performed in German with English subtitles without intermission; Harvey Theater; November 27–December 1, 2007; 4 performances

Spring Season

HAPPY DAYS by Samuel Beckett; Presented by the National Theatre of Great Britain; Producer, Karl Sydow; Director, Deborah Warner; Set, Tom Pye; Lighting, Jean Kalman; Sound Score, Mel Mercier; Sound, Christopher Shutt; Costume Consultant, Luca Costigliolo; U.S. Stage Manager, Jane Pole; Production Manager, Katrina Gilroy; Company Manager, Sarah Ford; General Manager, Nick Salmon, Imogen Kinchin; Cast: Fiona Shaw (Winnie), Tim Potter (Willie)

Revival of the play presented in two acts; Harvey Theater; January 8–February 2, 2008; 27 performances

MACBETH by William Shakespeare; Presented by Chichester Festival Theatre; Producers, Duncan C. Weldon & Paul Elliott; Director, Rupert Goold; Design, Anthony Ward; Lighting, Howard Harrison; Composer and Sound, Adam Cork; Video/Projections, Lorna Heavey; Movement, Georgina Lamb; Fight Director, Terry King; U.S. Stage Manager, Jane Pole; Assistant Director, Christopher Haydon; Production Manager, Dan Wilkins; Cast: Paul Shelley (Duncan/A Scottish Doctor), Scott Handy (Malcolm), Ben Carpenter (Donalbain/Young Seyward), Patrick Stewart (Macbeth), Martin Turner (Banquo), Michael Feast (Macduff), Mark Rawlings (Lennox), Tim Treloar (Ross), Bill Nash (Angus), Emmett White (Fleance), Christopher Knott (Old Seyward/Murderer), Christopher

Fiona Shaw in The National Theatre's Happy Days *(photo by Neil Libbert)*

Patrick Nolan (Seyton), Hywel John (Bloody Sergeant), Kate Fleetwood (Lady Macbeth), Suzanne Burden (Lady Macduff), Niamh McGrady & Sophie Hunter (Witches), Polly Frame (Witch/Gentlewoman), Oliver Birch (Lady Macbeth's servant), Gabrielle Piacentile, Jacob Rosenbaum, Phoebe Keeling VanDusen (Macduff Children)

Revival of the play presented in two acts; Harvey Theater; February 12–March 22, 2008; 48 performances. This production transferred to Broadway for a limited engagement from March 29–May 24, 2008 (see page 52 in this volume).

SIZWE BANZI IS DEAD by Athol Fugard, John Kani, and Winston Ntshona; Presented by Baxter Theatre Centre and the National Arts Festival (Grahamstown, South Africa); Director, Aubrey Sekhabi; Lighting, Mannie Manim; American Stage Manager, Mary Susan Gregon; Cast: John Kani (Buntu), Winston Ntshona (Sizwe Bannzi)

Setting: South Africa, 1972. Revival of the play presented without intermission; Harvey Theater; April 8–13, 2008; 10 performances.

ENDGAME by Samuel Beckett; Director, Andrei Belgrader; Set, Anita Stewart; Costumes, Candice Donnelly; Lighting, Michael Chybowski; PSM, James Latus; ASM, Tom Taylor; Casting, Nancy Piccione; Props, Jung K. Griffith; Cast: Max Casella (Clov), John Turturro (Hamm), Alvin Epstein (Nagg), Elaine Stritch (Nell); Understudies: Patrick Kerr (Clov, Ham, Nagg), Kathryn Grody (Nell)

Revival of the play presented without intermission; Harvey Theater; April 25–May 18, 2008; 24 performances.

City Center Encores!

Artistic Director, Jack Viertel; Music Director, Rob Berman; President/CEO, City Center, Arlene Shuler; Senior Vice President/Managing Director, Mark Litvin; Scenic Consultant, John Lee Beatty; Concert Adaptation, David Ives; Music Coordinator, Seymour Red Press; Company Manager, Michael Zande; Casting; Jay Binder, Jack Bowdan; Press, Helene Davis; Encores Artistic Associates: John Lee Beatty, Jay Binder, Walter Bobbie, David Ives, Kathleen Marshall

2007 Encores! Summer Stars (Premiere Season)

GYPSY Book and direction by Arthur Laurents, music by Jule Styne, lyrics by Stephen Sondheim; suggested by the Memoirs of Gypsy Rose Lee; original production directed and choreographed by Jerome Robbins, and produced by David Merrick & Leland Hayward; Music Director, Patrick Vaccariello; Mr. Robbins' choreography reproduction, Bonnie Walker; Sets, James Youmans, Costumes, Martin Pakledinaz; Lighting, Howell Binkley; Sound, Dan Moses Schreier; Casting, Jay Binder; Wigs/Hair, Paul Huntley; PSM, Craig Jacobs; Orchestrations, Sid Ramin & Robert Ginzler; Dance Arrangements, John Kander; General Management Associate, Stephanie Overton; Stage Manager, Tom Capps, ASM, Adam John Hunter; Associate Music Director, Ethyl Will; Additional Dance Music, Betty Walberg; Dance Captain, Bill Bateman; Cast: Jim Bracchitta (Uncle Jocko/Pastey), Bill Bateman (Georgie/Mr. Goldstone/Bougeron-Cochon), Kyrian Friedenberg (Vladimir/Rich Boy), Katie Micha (Balloon Girl), Emma Rowley (Baby Louise), Sami Gayle (Baby June), Patti LuPone (Rose), Bill Raymond (Pop/Cigar), Pearce Wegener (Driver/Yonkers), Matthew Lobenhofer (Tap Dancer/Julius), Andy Richardson (Boy Scout/Charlie), Brian Reddy (Weber/Phil), Boyd Gaines (Herbie), Rider Quentin Stanton (Hopalong), Leigh Ann Larkin (Dainty June), Laura Benanti (Louise), Steve Konopelski (L.A), Tony Yazbeck (Tulsa), John Scacchetti (Kansas), Geo Seery (Little Rock), Matty Price (East St. Louis), Jessica Rush (Waitress/Renée), Nancy Opel (Miss Cratchitt/Mazeppa), Nicole Mangi (Agnes), Alicia Sable (Marjorie May), Mindy Dougherty (Geraldine), Nancy Renée Braun (Edna Mae), Sarah Marie Hicks (Carol Ann), Beckley Andrews (Betsy Ann), Alison Fraser (Tessie Tura), Marilyn Caskey (Electra)

Musical Numbers: Overture, Let Me Entertain You, Some People, Some People (reprise), Small World, Baby June and Her Newsboys, Mr. Goldstone, Little Lamb, You'll Never Get Away From Me, Dainty June and Her Farmboys, If Momma Was Married, All I Need Is the Girl, Everything's Coming Up Roses, Entr'acte, Madame Rose's Toreadorables, Together, You Gotta Get a Gimmick, The Strip, Rose's Turn

Concert version of the musical presented in two acts; July 9–29, 2007 (Opened July 14); 7 previews, 15 performances. This production transferred to Broadway later in the season (see page 48 in this volume).

Christine Ebersole and Michael Park in Applause *(photo by Joan Marcus)*

Spring Series (Fifteenth Season)

APPLAUSE Book by Betty Comden and Adolph Green, music by Charles Strouse, lyrics by Lee Adams; Director and Choreography, Kathleen Marshall; Costume Consultant, Martin Pakledinaz; Lighting, Kenneth Posner; Sound, Peter Hylenski; PSM, Karen Moore; Original Orchestrations, Philip J. Lang; Associate Director, Marc Bruni; New Arrangements, David Chase; New Orchestrations, Larry Blank; Associate Music Director, David Gursky; Music Associate, Joshua Clayton; Associate Choreographer, Rommy Sandhu; Stage Manager, Jeffrey Rodriguez; General Management Associate, Stephanie Overton; Cast: Christine Ebersole (Margo Channing), Erin Davie (Eve Harrington), Bob Gaynor (Tony Awards Announcer/Peter), Tom Hewitt (Howard Benedict), David Studwell (Bert), Chip Zien (Buzz Richards), Michael Park (Bill Sampson), Mario Cantone (Duane Fox), Kate Burton (Karen Richards), Gregg Goodbrod (Bartender), Tony Freeman (Stan Harding), Megan Sikora (Bonnie), James Harkness (Waiter), Steven Sofia (Waiter), J.D. Webster (TV Director), Ensemble: Cole Burden, John Carroll, Paula Leggett Chase, Susan Derry, Sarah Jane Everman, Tony Freeman, Lisa Gajda, Bob Gaynor, Gregg Goodbrod, Justin Greer, James Harkness, Joe Komara, Raymond J. Lee, Monica L. Patton, Manuel Santos, Jennifer Savelli, Chauntee´ Schuler, Steven Sofia, David Studwell, Kevin Vortmann, J.D. Webster, Kristen Beth Williams

Musical Numbers: Overture, Backstage Babble, Think How It's Gonna Be, But Alive, The Best Night of My Life; Who's That Girl?, Applause, Hurry Back, Fasten Your Seat Belts, Welcome to the Theatre; Inner Thoughts, Good Friends, The Best Night of My Life (reprise), She's No Longer a Gypsy, One of a Kind, One Hallowe'en, Something Greater

Setting: The action takes place in and around New York, 1970–1972. Concert version of the musical presented in two acts; February 7–10, 2008; 5 performances. The original production opened at the Palace Theatre on March 30, 1970 and played 896 performances (see *Theatre World* Volume 26, page 50).

JUNO Book by Joseph Stein, music and lyrics by Marc Blitzstein, based on the play *Juno and the Paycock* by Sean O'Casey; Director, Garry Hynes; Costume Consultant, Toni-Leslie James; Lighting, Ken Billington; Sound, Scott Lehrer; PSM, Karen Moore; Original Orchestrations, Robert Russell Bennett, Marc Blitzstein and Hershy Kay; Choreography, Warren Carlyle; Guest Music Director, Eric Stern; Associate Musical Director, Lawrence Yurman; Music Associate, Joshua Clayton; Cast: Timothy Shew (Sullivan), Rosaleen Linehan (Mrs. Maisie Madigan), Kay Walbye (Mrs. Coyne), Louisa Flaningam (Mrs. Brady), Jennifer Smith (Miss Quinn), Kurt Froman (Robbie Tancred), Annie McGreevey (Mrs. Tancred), Celia Keenan-Bolger (Mary Boyle), Tyler Hanes (Johnny Boyle), Victoria Clark (Juno Boyle), Michael Arden (Jerry Devine), Clarke Thorell (Charlie Bentham), Greg Stone (Foley), Conrad John Schuck ("Captain" Jack Boyle), Dermot Crowley ("Joxer" Daly), Kevin Vortmann (First IRA Man), Patrick Wetzel (Second IRA Man), J. Maxwell Miller (Irish Tenor), Jay Lustek (Policeman); Ensemble: Timothy W. Bish, Troy Edward Bowles, Pamela Brumley, Callie Carter, Leah Edwards, Ryan Jackson, Jay Lusteck, Mary MacLeod, Melissa Rae Mahon, J. Maxwell Miller, Pamela Otterson, John Selya, Timothy Shew, Greg Stone, Megan Thomas, Kevin Vortmann, Alan M-L Wagner, Patrick Wetzel

Musical Numbers: Overture, We're Alive, I Wish It So, Song of the Ma, We Can Be Proud, Daarlin' Man, One Kind Word, Old Sayin's, What Is the Stars?, Old Sayin's (reprise), Poor Thing, My True Heart, On A Day Like This, Entr'acte, Bird Upon the Tree, Music in the House, It's Not Irish, The Liffey Waltz, Hymm, Ballet: The Ballad of Johnny Boyle, Poor Thing (reprise), Farewell Me Butty, For Love, One Kind Word (reprise), I Wish It So (reprise), Lament, Bird Upon the Tree (reprise), Finale Act II

Setting: Dublin, 1921. Concert version of the musical presented in two acts; March 27-30, 2008; 5 performances. The original production opened at the Winter Garden Theatre on March 9, 1959 and played 16 performances (see *Theatre World* Volume 15, page 98).

NO, NO, NANETTE Book by Otto Harbach and Frank Mandel, lyrics by Irving Caesar and Otto Harbach, music by Vincent Youmans; Originally adapted and directed by Bert Shevelove; Director, Walter Bobbie; Guest Music Director, Rob Fisher; Choreography, Randy Skinner; Costume Consultant, Gregg Barnes; Lighting, Ken Billington; Sound, Scott Lehrer; Original Orchestrations, Ralph Burns & Luther Henderson; PSM, Karen Moore; Stage Manager, Rachel S. McCutchen; Associate Director, Marc Bruni; Associate Choreographer, Kelli Barclay; Assistant Choreographer, Mary Giattino; Associate Music Director, Mark Mitchell; Music Associate, Joshua Clayton; Pianists, Joseph Thalken & Todd Ellison; General Management Associate, Stephanie Overton; Cast: Rosie O'Donnell (Pauline), Beth Leavel (Lucille Early), Sandy Duncan (Sue Smith), Charles Kimbrough (Jimmy Smith), Michael Berresse (Billy Early), Shonn Wiley (Tom Trainor), Mara Davi (Nanette), Angel Reda (Flora Latham), Jennifer Cody (Betty Brown), Nancy Anderson (Winnie Winslow); Ensemble: David Baum, Jacob ben Widmar, Brandon Davidson, Lean Edwards, Sara Edwards, Zak Edwards, Mary Giattino, Luke Hawkins, Matthew J. Kilgore, Cara Kjellman, Todd Lattimore, Deborah Lew, Ryan Malyar, Brent McBeth, Alessa Neeck, Carolann M. Sanita, Kiira Schmidt, Chad Seib, Kelly Sheehan, Anna Aimee White

Mary Davi and Company in No, No, Nanette

Musical Numbers: Overture, Too Many Rings Around Rosie, I've Confessed to the Breeze, The Call of the Sea, I Want to Be Happy, No, No, Nanette, Finaletto Act I, Opening Act II – Peach on the Beach; The Three Happies, Tea for Two, You Can Dance With Any Girl, Finaletto Act II; Entr'acte, Telephone Girlie, The "Where-Has-My-Hubby-Gone" Blues, Waiting for You, Take a Little One-Step, Finale

Setting: A weekend in early summer, 1925; the home of James Smith in NYC, and the Chickadee Cottage in Atlantic City. Concert version of the musical presented in three acts; May 8–12, 2008; 6 performances. The original production opened at the Globe (Lunt-Fontanne) Theatre September 16, 1925 and played 321 performances. The show was revived/revised January 19, 1971 at the 46th Street (Richard Rodgers) Theatre, playing 861 performances (see *Theatre World* Volume 27, page 30). The *Encores* production was based on the 1971 version of the show.

Classic Stage Company

Fortieth Season

Artistic Director, Brian Kulick; Executive Director, Jessica R. Jenen; General Manager, Lisa Barnes; Development, Natalie Johnsonius; Associate Artistic Director, Jeff Janisheski; Marketing, Leanne Schanzer Promotions; Audience Services, Christopher Walters; Management Associate, Jen McArdle; Development Associate, Jody Christopherson; Production Manager, B.D. White; Casting, James Calleri; Press, The Publicity Office, Michael Borowski, Marc Thibodeau

RICHARD III by William Shakespeare; Directors, Brian Kulick and Michael Cumpsty; Sets, Mark Wendland; Costumes, Oana Botez-Ban; Lighting, Brian H. Scott; Sound, Jorge Muelle; Music, Mark Bennett; PSM, Sid King; ASM, Freda Farrell; Original Music, Mark Bennett; Fight Director, Adam Rihacek; Technical Director, Joseph Reddington; Assistant Director, Tony Speciale; Props, Jeremy Lydic; Cast: Craig Baldwin (Lord Hastings/Sir James Tyrrell), Steven Boyer (Marquis of Dorset/ Murderer/Bishop of Ely), Michael Cumpsty (Richard Duke of Gloucester), Philip Goodwin (King Edward IV/Lord Mayor/ Lord Stanley), Chad Hoeppner (Brackenbury/Sir William Catesby), Paul Lazar (Earl Rivers/Murderer/Scrivener), Roberta Maxwell (Queen Margaret), KK Moggie (Mistress Shore/Lady Anne/Young Prince Richard of York), Andy Phelan (Young Prince Edward/Messenger), Michael Potts (Duke of Buckingham), Judith Roberts (Duchess of York), Maria Tucci (Queen Elizabeth), Graham Winton (George Duke of Clarence/Henry Earl of Richmond)

Revival of the play presented in two acts; East 13th Street Theatre; November 1–December 9, 2007 (Opened November 13); 12 previews, 28 performances.

NEW JERUSALEM (The Interrogation, Excommunication and Expulsion of Baruch de Spinoza at Talmud Torah Congregation: Amsterdam, July 27, 1656) by David Ives; Presented by special arrangement with Bob Boyett; Director, Walter Bobbie; Set, John Lee Beatty; Lighting, Ken Billington; Costumes, Anita Yavich; Sound, Acme Sound Partners; PSM, Robyn Henry; ASM, Nicole Bouclier; Technical Director, Joseph Reddington; Assistant Director, Lauren Keating; Cast: David Garrison (Abraham van Valkenburgh), Richard Easton (Saul Levi Mortera), Fyvush FInkel (Gaspar Rodrigues Ben Israel), Jeremy Strong (Baruch de Spinoza), Michael Izquierdo (Simon de Vries), Natalia Payne (Clara Van den Enden), Jenn Harris (Rebekah de Spinoza)

Setting: Temple Talmud Torah, Amsterdam. July 27, 1656. World premiere of a new play presented in two acts; East 13th Street Theatre; December 28, 2007–February 10, 2008 (Opened January 13); 17 previews, 28 performances.

THE SEAGULL by Anton Chekhov, translated by Paul Schmidt; Production Support, Carole Shorenstein Hays; Director, Viacheslav Dolgache; Set, Santo Loquasto; Costumes, Suzy Benzinger; Lighting, Brian MacDevitt; Sound; Jorge Muelle; Hair, Paul Huntley; PSM, Michaella K. McCoy; ASM, Annette Adamska; Assistant Directors, Ellen Orenstein, Marta Rainer; Props, Sarah Bird; Cast: Greg Keller (Semyón Semyónovich Medvedénko), Marjan Neshat (Masha), John Christopher Jones (Pyótr Nikoláyevich Sórin), Ryan O'Nan (Konstantín Gavrílovich Tréplev), Ryan Homchick (Yákov), Kelli Garner (Nína Mikháilovna Zaréchnaya), Annette O'Toole (Paulina Andréyevna), David Rasche (Yevgény Sergéyevich Dorn), Bill Christ (Ilya Shamrávev), Diane Wiest (Irína Nikoláyevna Arkádina), Alan Cumming (Borís Alexéyevich Trigórin)

Setting: Sórin's farm. Between Acts Three and Four, two years go by. Revival of the play presented in four acts with one intermission; East 13th Street Theatre; February 20–April 13, 2008 (Opened March 13); 22 previews, 33 performances.

Alan Cumming, Dianne Wiest and Company in The Seagull *(photo by Joan Marcus)*

OLD COMEDY AFTER ARISTOPHANES' FROGS by David Greenspan, original music by Thomas Cabaniss; Presented by the Target Margin Theater (David Herskovits, Artistic Director); Director, David Herskovits; Set, David Evans Morris; Lighting, Lenore Doxsee; Costumes, Meredith Palin; Associate Set, Carolyn Mraz; Sound, Kate Marvin; David Herskovits, Alex Hawthorn; PSM, Ryan C. Durham; Production Manager, Jason Adams; ASM, Mary E. Leach; Music Director, David Rosenmeyer; TMT General Manager, Michael Levinton; Producer, Stacey Cooper McMath; Cast: Purva Bedi (Euripedes/others), Davina Cohen (Tantalus/Bazoomba/ others), Charlie Hudson III (Corpse/Phynichus/others), Michael Levinton (Herakles/others), Derek Lucci (Xanthias), Pedro Pascal (Dionysus), Tina Shepard (Charon/Aeacus/ others), Anthony Mark Stockard (Aeschylus/others); Musicians: Kate Marvin (Sound Demon), Mike Dobson (Percussionist); Understudy: Curt Hostetter

Setting: Go Figure. Time: You must be kidding. World premiere of a new play based on a classic presented in two acts; East 13th Street Theatre; May 7-31, 2008 (Opened May 11); 5 previews, 21 performances.

Additional Events

MONDAY NIGHT MACBETH Open rehearsal series of the play by William Shakespeare; November 12: Directed by Brian Kulick, featuring Steven Skybell; November 19: Directed by Barry Edelstein, featuring Elizabeth Marvel and Ruben Santiago-Hudson; November 26: Directed by Michael Sexton, featuring Frances McDormand and David Strathairn; December 3: Directed by Anne Bogart, featuring SITI Company

THE YOUNG COMPANY: THE TAMING OF THE SHREW by William Shakespeare & **THE TAMER TAMED** by John Fletcher; Presented by the Graduate Acting Program of the Columbia University School for the Arts; Director, Tony Speciale; January 28–February 10, 2008; 6 performances.

FIRST LOOK FESTIVAL: THE ORESTEIA One night only staged reading and workshop productions; Translated by Anne Carson; March 17: *Agamemnon* by Aeschylus, directed by Michael Cumpsty, with Michael Cumpsty and Kate Mulgrew; March 24: *Electra* by Sophocles, directed by Brian Kulick, featuring Elizabeth Marvel; March 31: *Orestes* by Euripides, directed by Paul Lazar & Annie-B Parson, featuring Michael Stuhlbarg; April 7: *Agamemnon* with Steven Skybell, directed by Javierantonio Gonzalez; and *Electra* with Annika Boras, directed by Brian Kulick; April 14: *Orestes* with Jeremy Strong, directed by Paul Lazar & Annie-B Parson

MANDY PATINKIN ON BROADWAY Benefit concert to celebrate the 40th Anniversary of CSC; Music Director, Paul Ford; Gerald Schoenfeld Theatre; May 19, 2008

Classical Theatre of Harlem

Ninth Season

Co-Founder/Artistic Director Alfred Preisser; Co-Founder/Executive Producer, Christopher McElroen; Producing/Development Associate, Jaime Carrillo; Producing Director, Susan Jonas; Artistic Associate, Karan Kendrick; Production Supervisor, Vincent J. DeMarco/Kelvin Productions, LLC; Press, Brett Singer and Associates

ROMEO AND JULIET by William Shakespeare; Co-Produced by City Parks Foundation; Director, Alfred Preisser; Costumes, Kimberly Glennon; Choreography, Tracy Jack; PSM, Kevin M.S. Brophy; Fight Director, Alexander Sovronsky; Cast: Andrea Cosley (Nurse), Carlton Byrd (Balthasar), Daniel Morgan Shelley (Mercutio/Cop), Duane Allen (Romeo), Willie E. Teacher (Lord Capulet), Jamyl Dobson (Lord Montague/Apothecary), Keith Jamal Downing (Tybalt), Kimberly Dalton Mitchell (Sampson), Libya Pugh (Lady Capulet), Mo Brown (Rosaline), Robin LeMon (Juliet), Alexander Sovronsky (Escalus/Paris), Taharaqa Patterson (Cop), Tracy Jack (Benvolio), Troy Scarborough (Friar/Cop), Alphonso Walker (Peter); Jack McKeane (Servant/Altar Boy)

Setting: Harlem, in the near future. New adaptation of the play presented without intermission; Von King Park/Marcus Garvey Park/Tompkins Square Park; July 27–August 10, 2008; 6 performances. The production toured during the fall of 2007 in repertory with *Ain't Supposed to Die a Natural Death* to Florida, North Carolina, Pennsylvania, and Westchester, New York, playing an additional 24 performances.

Lizan Mitchell & Kiat Sing Teo in Trojan Women *(photo by Ruth Sovronsky)*

BLACK NATIVITY by Langston Hughes; Presented with The New 42nd Street; Director, Alfred Preisser, Sets, Troy Hourie; Costumes, Kimberly Glennon; Lighting, Aaron Black; Musical Director, Kelvyn Bell; Fight Director, Denise Hurd, Choreography, Tracy Jack; Cast: André De Shields (Narrator/Pastor), Tracy Jack (Mary), Enrique Cruz DeJesus (Joseph); Chorus: Melvin Bell III, Laiona Michelle, Nikki Stephenson, Tryphena Wade, Rejinald Woods, Phyre Hawkins, Alexander Elisa, Ebony Blake, The Shangilia Youth Choir

Setting: Times Square, 1973. Revival of a play presented without intermission; Duke on 42nd Street; November 30–December 30, 2007 (Opened December 2); 2 previews, 37 performances. Originally produced at the 41st Street Theatre, December 11, 1962 (see *Theatre World* Volume 18, page 140).

TROJAN WOMEN Adapted and directed by Alfred Preisser, based on the play by Euripides; Produced in association with Harlem Stage; Original Score/Music Director, Kelvyn Bell; Choreography, Tracy Jack; Sets, Troy Hourie; Lighting, Aaron Black; Costumes, Kimberly Glennon; Stage Manager, Jessica

Pecharsky; Cast: Zenzelé Cooper (Ramatu), Michael Early (Talthybius), Christel Halliburton (Agnes), Zainab Jah (Helen), Ty Jones (Meleleus), Linda Kurlioff (Andromache), Amanda Marie (Samretta), Lizan Mitchell (Hecuba), Sipiwe Moyo (Hawa), Alexander Mulzac (Soldier), Angela Polite (Choral Leader), Brandi Rhonme (Lucia), Sui-Lin Robinson (Finda), Kiat-Sing Teo (Polyxenes), Nabil Vinas (Soldier), Tryphena Wade (Cassandra)

Revival of a new adaptation of the play presented without intermission; Harlem Stage Gatehouse; January 10–February 10, 2008 (Opened January 17); 5 previews, 23 performances. Previously presented by CTH April 1, 2004.

EMANCIPATION by Ty Jones; Presented in association with The Malcolm X. & Dr. Betty Shabazz Memorial and Educational Center; Director, Christopher McElroen; Costumes, Kimberly Glennon; Sets, Troy Hourie; Lighting, Aaron Black; Stage Manager, Jessica Pecharsky; Musical Supervisor, Lelund Durond Thompson; Projections, Aaron Rhyne; Technical Director, Pam Traynor; Production Assistants, Jeffrey Glaser, Jeff Barnes; Cast: Happy Anderson (Buchanan/Helms/Stevens), Jenny Bennett (Mary/Elisabeth), Gisela Chípe (Christina), Michael Cummings (Young Nat Turner/Goop), Ty Jones (Nat Turner), Jaymes Jorsling (Nelson), Jack McKeane (Young John Clarke), Stephen Conrad Moore (Henry), Jason Podplesky (Ferguson/Ben Turner/York), Angela Polite (Bessie), Wayne Pyle (John Clarke/Travis/Mann/Silas' Master), Sean Patrick Reilly (Thomas Gray), James E. Singletary (Hark), Lelund Durond Thompson (Sam)

World premiere of a new play presented without intermission; Shabazz Center at the Audubon Ballroom; April 10–May 10, 2008 (Opened April 17); 5 previews, 19 performances.

The Culture Project

Artistic Director, Allan Buchman; General Manager, Dave Friedman; Business Manager, Casey Cordon; Women Center Stage, Olivia Greer; Associate Producer, Julianne Hoffenberg; Box Office Manager, Becky White; Technical Director, Garin Marschall; Resident Director, Will Pomerantz; Education Associate, Simnia Singer-Sayada; Press, O&M Co., Rick Miramontez, Jon Dimond, Molly Barnett

TINGS DEY HAPPEN Written and performed by Dan Hoyle; Directed and co-developed by Charlie Varon; Sound, David Hines; Lighting, Garin Marschall; PSM, Molly Eustis; Technician, Marion Hurt; Culture Project Design, Brian Thomas, *Tings* Design, Lyra Harris

New York premiere of a new solo performance play presented without intermission; 55 Mercer; July 26–December 22, 2007 (Opened August 7); 108 performances. Premiered in San Francisco at The Marsh (Stephanie Weisman, Artistic Director), January 6, 2007.

TILL THE BREAK OF DAWN Written and directed by Danny Hoch; Presented in association with Hip-Hop Theater Festival (Sekka Scher & Clyde Valentin); Sets, Andromache Chalfant; Costumes, Valerie Marcus Ramshur; Lighting, Garin Marschall; Sound, Jill BC DuBoff; Props, Nicole Frankel; PSM, Leanne L. Long; Assistant Director, Jerry Ruiz; Cast: Bambadjan Bamba (Toulouse), Dominic Colon (Big Miff), Matthew-Lee Erlbach (Adam), Flaco Navaja (Hector), pattydukes (Nancy), Gwendolen Hardwick (Dana), Jimmie James (Bobby), Jaymes Jorsling (Gibran), Maribel Lizardo (Rebeca), Johnny Sánchez (Robert), Luis Vega (Felito)

Setting: New York; Summer, 2001. World premiere of a new play presented in two acts; Abrons Arts Center; September 4–October 21, 2007 (Opened September 13); 48 performances.

Johnny Sanchez, Jaymes Jorsling, Luis Vega, pattydukes, Flaco Navaja, Dominic Colon in Till the Break of Dawn *(photo by Carol Rosegg)*

REBEL VOICES Adapted by Rob Urbinati with Howard Zinn and Anthony Arnove (from their book "Voices of a People's History of the United States"); Directors, Will Pomerantz and Rob Urbinati; Lighting, Garin Marschall; Projections, Gisele Parson; Image Research, Jessie Kindig; PSM, Molly Minor Eustis; ASM, Erin Maureen Koster; Cast: Opal Alladin, Tim Cain, Morgan Hallett, Lenelle Moïse, Allison Moorer, Thom Rivera; Special Guests: Staceyann Chin, Steve Earle, Danny Glover, Lili Taylor, Wallace Shawn, Rich Robinson, Larry Pine, Harris Yulin, Patti Smith, Ally Sheedy, Eve Ensler, David Strathairn

A collection of songs, speeches, monologues and writings presented without intermission; 55 Mercer; November 10–December 16, 2007 (Opened November 18); 22 performances.

A QUESTION OF IMPEACHMENT: TRIAL BY THEATER Scripting Director, Darrell Larson; Coordinating Producers,

Olivia Greer, Julianne Hoffenberg; Assistant Producer, Manda Martin; Production Supervisors, Marlon Hunt, David Roy, Projections, Gisele Parson; Videography, Emily and Sarah Kunstler; Performers: Gerry Bamman, Frank Bidart, Tom Bower, Jackson Browne, Bobby Cannavale, Kathleen Chalfant, Staceyann Chin, Scott Cohen, Eisa Davis, Rinde Eckert, Ned Eisenberg, Courtney Esser, Willie Garson, Josh Hamilton, Holly Hunter, Mary Lee Kortes, Aasif Mandvi, Jodie Markell, Michael Mastro, Chris McKinney, Angela McCluskey, Nana Mensah, Jack Moran, Denis O'Hare, Alix Olson, Sarah-Doe Osborne, Maulik Pancholy, Steven Sater, Annabella Sciorra, Duncan Sheik, Phoebe Snow, Tracie Thoms, Callie Thorne, Bradley White, Grace Zandarski, and special appearances by Vanessa, Lynn, Corin and Jemma Redgrave; Participants: Alec Baldwin, Judith Browne-Dianis, Marjorie Cohn, Cynthia L. Cooper, Elizabeth de la Vega, Jonathan Demme, Joshua L. Dratel, Larry Everest, Marc Falkoff, Bruce Fein, Charles Ferguson, Laura Flanders, Tiffany Gardner, Carol Gilligan, Amy Goodman, Jonathan Hafetz, Hendrik Hertzberg, Elizabeth Holtzman, Scott Horton, Erica Hunt, Aziz Huq, Sam Jackson, Shayana Kadidal, Lewis Lapham, David Lindorff, Ray McGovern, Tara McKelvey, Denis Moynihan, John Nichols, Michael Ratner, David Swanson, Richard Valeriani, Vincent Warren, Naomi Wolf, Colonel (Ret.) Ann Wright

A discussion series presented with theatre, film, music, and art debating the presidency of George W. Bush and Vice President Dick Cheney; 55 Mercer; Sundays & Mondays November 18–December 16, 2007; 7 performances.

BETRAYED by George Packer; Director/Dramaturg, Pippin Parker; Sets/Lighting, Garin Marschall; Costumes, Rabiah Troncelliti; Sound, Eric Shim; PSM, Leanne L. Long; Assistant Director, Erika Christensen; ASM, Jennifer Noterman; Props, Michael Guagno; Cast: Jeremy Beck (Soldier/Regional Security Officer), Aadya Bedi (Intisar), Mike Doyle (Prescott), Ramsey Faragallah (Cursing Man/Old Man/Dishdasha Man/Eggplant Face/Ambassador), Sevan Greene (Laith), Waleed F. Zuaiter (Adnan); Understudy: Ramiz Monsef

World premiere of a new play presented without intermission; 55 Mercer; January 25–June 16, 2008 (Opened February 5); 137 performances.

THE ATHEIST by Ronan Noone; Director, Justin Waldman; Cast: Campbell Scott (Augustine Early)

Benefit performance of a solo performance play presented without intermission; May 20, 2008

Irish Repertory Theatre

Twentieth Season

Artistic Director, Charlotte Moore; Producing Director, Ciarán O'Reilly; Managing Director, Patrick A. Kelsey; Development, Terry Diamond; Literary Manager, Kara Manning; Box Office Manager, Jeffrey Wingfield; Audience Services, Jared Dawson; Groups, Jen Nelson; Dialect Coach, Stephen Gabis; Production Coordinator, Mac Smith; Casting, Laura Maxwell-Scott/Deborah Brown; Press, Shirley Herz Associates, Dan Demello

SIVE by John B. Keane; Director, Ciarán O'Reilly; Sets, Charles Corcoran; Costumes, Martha Hally; Lighting, Jason Lyons; Hair/Wigs, Robert-Charles Vallance; PSM, April Ann Kline; Stage Manager, Janice M. Brandine; Props, Rene Becker; Assistant to the Director, Helena Gleissner; Fiddle Player, Diane Montalbine; Cast: James Barry (Carthalawn), Donie Carroll (Pats Bocock), Terry Donnelly (Nanna), Patrick Fitzgerald (Thomasheen Sean Rua), Christopher Joseph Jones (Sean Dota), Aidan Redmond (Mike), Wrenn Schmidt (Sive), Mark Thornton (Liam), Fiana Toibin (Mena)

Setting: The kitchen of the Galvin home, County Kerry, Ireland, March, 1957. New York premiere of the 1959 play presented in two acts; Mainstage; September 20–November 25, 2007 (Opened September 27); 7 previews, 60 performances.

THE DEVIL'S DISCIPLE by George Bernard Shaw; Director and Design, Tony Walton; Co-Costumes, Rebecca Lustig; Lighting, Brian Nason; Sound, Zachary Williamson; Associate Set Design, Heather Wolensky; Hair/Wigs, Robert-Charles Vallance; Fight Director, Rick Sordelet; PSM, Christine Lemme; Stage Manager, Jonathan Donahue; Cast: Darcy Pulliam (Mrs. Dudgeon), Cristin Milioti (Essie), Craig Pattison (Christy Dudgeon/Executioner), Curzon Dobell (Anthony Anderson), Jenny Fellner (Judith Anderson), Richard B. Watson (Lawyer Hawkins/The Sergeant), Robert Sedgwick (Major Swindon/Uncle Titus Dudgeon), Lorenzo Pisoni (Dick Dudgeon), Sean Gormley (Guard), Jonathan Donahue (Guard), John Windsor-Cunningham (General Burgoyne)

Setting: 1777, Websterbridge, New Hampshire. Revival of the play presented in four acts with one intermission; Mainstage; December 6, 2007–February 10, 2008 (Opened December 13); 7 previews, 61 performances. Originally produced at the Fifth Avenue Theatre, October 4, 1897.

A CHILD'S CHRISTMAS IN WALES by Dylan Thomas & **'TWAS THE NIGHT BEFORE CHRISTMAS** by Clement Clark Moore; Adapted, designed and directed by Charlotte Moore; Music Director, John Bell; Costumes, David Toser; Lighting, Mac Smith; Original Music, Ken Darby; PSM, Rhonda Picou; Cast: Kerry Conte, Bonnie Fraser, Justin Packard, Joshua Park, Ashley Robinson

Two one act plays presented without intermission; W. Scott McLucas Studio Theatre; December 6–30, 2007 (Opened December 13); 7 previews, 19 performances.

TAKE ME ALONG Music and lyrics by Bob Merrill, book by Joseph Stein & Robert Russell, based on the play *Ah, Wilderness!* by Eugene O'Neill; Director, Charlotte Moore; Music Director, Mark Hartman; Choreography, Barry McNabb; Sets, James Morgan; Costumes, Linda Fisher; Lighting, Mary Jo Dondlinger; Sound, Zachary Williamson; Hair/Wigs, Robert-Charles Vallance; PSM, Ronda Picou; Stage Manager, Arthur Atkinson; Cast: William Parry (Nat Miller), Donna Bullock (Essie Miller), Dewey Caddell (Art Miller), Teddy Eck (Richard Miller), Noah Ruff (Tommy Miller), Don Stephenson (Sid Davis), Beth Glover (Lily Miller), Emily Skeggs (Muriel McComber), Gordon Stanley (Dave McComber), Justin Packard (Wint), Anastasia Barzee (Belle); Orchestra: Mark Hartman (piano), Steve Gilewski (bass), Nicholas DiFabbio (banjo/guitar), Jeremy Clayon (woodwinds)

Musical Numbers: Overture; Opening; Oh, Please; Oh, Please (reprise); I Would Die; Sid, Ol' Kid; Staying Young; I Get Embarrassed; We're Home; Take Me Along; Take Me Along/The Only Pair I've Got; Pleasant Beach House, The Hurt They Write About; The Hurt They Write About/I Would Die; Entr'acte; If Jesus Don't Love You; Oh, Please (reprise 2); Promise Me a Rose; Staying Young (reprise); Little Green Snake; Nine O'Clock; Nine O'Clock (reprise); But Yours, But Yours (tag); I Would Die (reprise 2), Finale

Setting: Centerville, Connecticut, July 4, 1920. Revival of the musical presented in two acts, Mainstage; February 20–May 4, 2008 (Opened February 28); 7 previews, 68 performances. Originally produced on Broadway at the Shubert Theatre October 22, 1959–December 17, 1960, starring Jackie Gleason, Walter Pigeon, and Eileen Herlie, 448 performances (see *Theatre World* Volume 16, page 20). Following a run at the Goodspeed Opera House in 1984, the show was revived at the Martin Beck April 14, 1985 and closed on opening night after 7 previews and 1 performance (see *Theatre World* Volume 41, pages 35 & 161).

PRISONER OF THE CROWN by Robert F. Stockton; Director, Ciarán O'Reilly; Sets, Charles Corcoran; Costumes, David Toser; Lighting, Brian Nason; Sound, Zachary Williamson; Movement Consultant, Barry McNabb; Hair and Wigs, Robert-Charles Vallance; Fight Director, Rick Sordelet; Aerial Effects, Paul Rubin; Assistant Director, Helena Gleissner; PSM, Elis C. Arroyo; Stage Manager, Leslie Grisdale; Cast: Patrick Fitzgerald (Chorus/Welsh Sentry/Parchment Guard/German Guard/Press Reporter/Juror), Philip Goodwin (Sir Roger Casement/Juror), John C. Vennema (Judge Reading/Sergeant Hearn/Captain Reginald Hall/Executioner/Juror), Peter Cormican (Bailiff/Military Police Officer/Richard Morton/Mr. Allen/Professor Morgan/Sir Edward Grey/Juror), John Windsor-Cunningham (Constable Riley/Sir Frederick Smith/Neill/Juror), Ian Stuart (Inspector Quinn/Sir Ernley Blackwell/Robinson/Mr. Shorter/Juror), Emma O'Donnell (Gertrude Bannister/Father Ryan/Tower of London Guard/Artemus Jones/Juror), Tim Ruddy (Basil Thompson/Tower of London Guard/Sergeant Sullivan/Juror)

Phillip Goodwin & Emma O'Donnell in Prisoner of the Crown (photo by Carol Rosegg)

Setting: 1916. London, Germany, and County Kerry, Ireland. New York premiere of a play presented in two acts; Mainstage Theatre; May 14–July 6, 2008 (Opened May 22); 9 previews, 47 performances.

The Keen Company

Ninth Season

Artistic Director, Carl Forsman; Executive Director, Wayne Kelton; Production Manager, Josh Bradford; Artistic Associate, Blake Lawrence; Audience Development Associate, Amanda Brandes; Season Designers, Theresa Squire (Costumes), Josh Bradford (Lighting), Daniel Baker (Sound); Casting, Kelly Gillespie, McCorkle Casting; Press, Karen Greco

THE DINING ROOM by A.R. Gurney; Director, Jonathan Silverstein; Set, Dana Moran Williams; PSM, Erin Greiner; ASM, Amanda Cynkin, Krysta Piccoli; Technical Director, Brant Underwood; Original Music, The Broken Chord Collective; Props, Lisa Mei Ling Fong; Cast: Dan Daily (Man 1), Claire Lautier (Woman 2), Mark J. Sullivan (Man 3), Samantha Soule (Woman 3), Anne McDonough (Woman 1), Timothy McCracken (Man 2)

Setting: The 20th Century; the dining room. Revival of the

play presented in two acts; Clurman Theatre at Theatre Row; September 7–October 20, 2007 (Opened September 16); 8 preview, 27 performances. Originally produced at Playwrights Horizons, February 11, 1982, where it transferred to Astor Place Theatre April 27, 1982–July 17, 1983, running 607 performances (see *Theatre World* Volume 38, page 94; Volume 39, page 72).

THE MADDENING TRUTH by David Hay; Co-Producer, Neal Weisman; Director, Carl Forsman; Sets, Beowulf Boritt; Stage Manager, Emily Arnold; Dramaturg, Jonathan Shandell; Dialect Coach, Samara Bay; ASM, Jackie Prats; Assistant Director, Lexie Pregosin; Technical Director, Josh Higgason; Props, Lisa Mei Ling Fong; Cast: William Connell (Peter Wilkinson), Lisa Emery (Martha Gellhorn), Richard Bekins (Laurence Rockefeller), Peter Benson (James Hastings), Terry Layman (Ernest Hemingway/Geoffrey Brooks/"Joshua")

World premiere of a play presented in two acts; Clurman Theatre at Theatre Row; January 15–February 23, 2008 (Opened January 30); 12 previews, 24 performances.

DB Woodside and John Cullum in The Conscientious Objector *(photo by Theresa Squire)*

THE CONSCIENTIOUS OBJECTOR by Michael Murphy; Director, Carl Forsman; Set, Beowulf Borritt; Stage Manager, Dave Polato; Dramaturg, Melissa Hardy; Assistant Stage Manager, Jackie Prats; Technical Director, Josh Higgason; Dialect Coach, Meagan Prahl; Cast: DB Woodside (Martin Luther King), Rachel Leslie (Coretta Scott King), John Cullum (Lyndon Baines Johnson), Jonathan Hogan (Journalist/Senator Thomas Dodd/J. Edgar Hoover/Panelist), Geddeth Smith (Ambassador Goldberg/Representative John Ashbrook/Panelist), Harold Surratt (Whitney Young), Bryan Hicks (Ralph Abernathy), Steve Routman (Stanley Levison), James Miles (Andrew Young), Jimonn Cole (James Bevel) Chad Carstarphen (Bernard Lee/Stokely Carmichael)

Setting: February 1965–April 1968, Washington D.C, Jamaica, New York, and Atlanta. World premiere of a new play presented in two acts; Clurman Theatre at Theatre Row; March 4–April 19, 2007 (Opened March 18); 12 previews, 30 performances.

Lincoln Center Theater

Twenty-Third Season

Artistic Director, André Bishop; Executive Producer, Bernard Gersten; General Manager, Adam Siegel; Production Manager, Jeff Hamlin; Development, Hattie K. Jutagir; Finance, David S. Brown; Marketing, Linda Mason Ross; Education, Kati Koerner; Musical Theatre Associate Producer, Ira Weitzman; Dramaturg/LCT Directors Lab, Anne Cattaneo; Associate Directors, Graciela Danielle, Nicholas Hytner, Jack O'Brien, Susan Stroman, Daniel Sullivan; Casting, Daniel Swee; Press, Philip Rinaldi, Barbara Carroll

THE GLORIOUS ONES Book and lyrics by Lynn Ahrens, music by Stephen Flaherty, based on the novel by Francine Prose; Director/Choreographer, Graciela Daniele; Sets, Dan Ostling; Costumes, Mara Blumenfeld; Lighting, Stephen Strawbridge; Sound, Scott Stauffer; Orchestrations, Michael Starobin; Music Director, David Holcenberg; Vocal Arrangements, Stephen Flaherty; Casting, Stanczyk/Cherpakov Casting; Associate Director/Choreographer, Madeleine Ehlert-Kelly; Stage Manager, Michael Brunner; ASM, Brandon Kahn; Company Manager, Matthew Markoff; Assistant Company Manager, Jessica Perlmeter Cochrane; Dance Captain, Ana Maria Andricain, Music Coordinator, John Miller; Cast: Marc Kudisch (Flaminio Scala), David Patrick Kelly (Pantalone), Natalie Venetia Belcon (Columbina), Julyana Soelistyo (Armanda Ragusa), John Kassir (Dottore), Erin Davie (Isabella Andreini/Young Boy Actor), Jeremy Webb (Francesco Andreini/Comic Servant); Understudies: Ana Maria Andricain (Columbina, Isabella), Scott Robertson (Dottore, Pantalone), Neal Benari (Flaminio), Nitya Vidyasagar (Armanda), Chris Peluso (Francesco, Dottore); Orchestra: David Holcenberg (Conductor/piano), Deborah Abramson (Associate Conductor/keyboard 2), Cenovia Cummins (violin/mandolin), Katie Schlaikjer (cello), Scott Shachter (reeds), Will De Vos (French horn), Marc Schmied (bass), Norbert Goldberg (percussion), David Patrick Kelly (Cuatro); Cast recording: Jay Records

Musical Numbers: Prologue: The Glorious Ones, Making Love, Pantalone Alone, The Comedy of Love, Scenario: The Madness of Columbina, The Comedy of Love (reprise), The Glorious Ones (reprise), Madness to Act, Absalom, The Invitation to France, Flaminio Scala's Historical Journey to France, Two Lazzi, Armanda's Tarantella, Improvisation, The World She Writes, Opposite You, My Body Wasn't Why, Scenario: The Madness of Isabella, Flaminio Scala's Ominous Dream, The World She Writes (reprise), Rise and Fall, The Moon Woman-A Play, The Glorious Ones (reprise), I Was Here, Armanda's Sack, Finale

Setting: The Late 1500's and beyond; the streets of Italy.

New York premiere of a new musical presented without intermission; Mitzi E. Newhouse Theatre; October 11, 2007–January 6, 2008 (Opened November 5); 30 previews, 48 performances. World premiere produced by Pittsburgh Public Theatre (Ted Pappas, Producing Artistic Director), April 19, 2007.

THE NEW CENTURY by Paul Rudnick; Director, Nicholas Martin; Sets, Allen Moyer; Costumes, William Ivey Long; Lighting, Kenneth Posner; Original Music and Sound, Mark Bennett; Stage Manager, Stephen M. Kaus; ASM, Kelly Beaulieu; Company Manager, Matthew Markoff; Assistant Director, Erick Herrscher; Wigs/Hair, Paul Huntley; Makeup, Angelina Avallone; Movement Consultant, Brooks Ashmanskas; Props, Susan Barras; Cast: Peter Bartlett (Mr. Charles), Mike Doyle (David Nadler/Shane), Jayne Houdyshell (Barbara Ellen Diggs), Linda Lavin (Helene Nadler), Christy Pusz (Joann Milderry); Jordan Dean (Announcer); Understudies: Maggie Burke (Helene, Barbara), Jordan Dean (David/Shane), Jay Rogers (Mr. Charles), Robyn J. Kramer (Joann)

Linda Lavin, Jayne Houdyshell and Peter Bartlett in The New Century *(photo by T. Charles Erickson)*

Setting: *Pride and Joy:* A small auditorium on Long Island; *Mr. Charles, Currently of Palm Beach:* A bare-bones public access television studio in Florida; *Crafty:* A conference room in a municipal building in Decatur, Illinois; *The New Century*: The maternity ward in a Manhattan hospital. Four short plays interwoven into one, presented in two acts; Mitzi E. Newhouse Theatre; March 20–June 8, 2008 (Opened April 14); 28 previews, 64 performances.

JOHN LITHGOW: STORIES BY HEART Written and performed by John Lithgow; Director, Jack O'Brien; Stage Manager, Brandon Kahn; ASM, Zoe Chapin; Company Manager, Matthew Markoff; Assistant Company Manager, Jessica Perlmeter Cochrane; Lighting Operator, Josh Rich; Set, Allen Moyer; Lighting, Kenneth Posner

A solo performance show presented without intermission; Mitzi E. Newhouse Theatre; Sunday and Monday evenings April 20–June 2, 2008 (Opened May 12); 7 previews, 7 performances.

MCC Theater (Manhattan Class Company)

Twenty-Second Season

Artistic Directors, Robert LuPone & Bernard Telsey; Associate Artistic Director, William Cantler; Executive Director, Blake West; General Manager, Ted Rounsaville; Assistant General Manager, Lauren Levitt; Literary Manager/Dramaturg, Stephen Willems; Literary Associate, Jamie Green; Development, Mara Richards; Development Associate, Nicole Cardamone; Marketing, Ian Allen; Marketing Assistant/Audience Services, Isabel Sinistore; Education/Outreach, John DiResta; Youth Company, Stephen DiMenna; Production Manager, B.D. White; Resident Director, Doug Hughes; Resident Playwright, Neil LaBute; Technical Director, James Reddington; Casting, Bernard Telsey; Press, O&M Co., Jon Dimond

SPAIN by Jim Knable; Director, Jeremy Dobrish; Sets, Beowulf Boritt; Costumes, Jenny Mannis; Lighting, Michael Gottlieb; Sound, Jill BC DuBoff; Fight Director, Rick Sordelet; Choreography, Elizabeth Roxas; PSM, Alexis R. Prussack; Assistant Director, Sharon Lennon; ASM, Jonathan Donahue; Cast: Michael Aranov (Conquistador), Veanne Cox (Diversion), Erik Jensen (John), Lisa Kron (Ancient), Annabella Sciorra (Barbara)

A play presented in two acts; Lucille Lortel Theatre; October 10–November 17, 2007 (Opened October 30); 40 performances. Previously presented at the 2006 Summer Play Festival and at the Woolly Mammoth Theatre.

GRACE by Mick Gordon and AC Grayling; Director, Joseph Hardy; Sets, Tobin Ost; Costumes, Alejo Vietti; Lighting, Matthew Richards; Original Music and Sound, Fabian Obispo; PSM, Robert Bennett; ASM, Shanna Spinello; Dialects, Patricia Fletcher; Assistant to Director, Gerrie Gillin; Properties, Jeremy Chernick; Technical Director, Joseph Reddington; Cast: Philip Goodwin (Tony), Oscar Isaac (Tom), Robert Emmett Lunney (Voice of Dr. Michael Persinger), K.K. Moggie (Ruth), Lynn Redgrave (Grace)

Setting: Oxford and London. American premiere of a new play presented without intermission; Lucille Lortel Theatre; January 23–March 8, 2007 (Opened February 11); 47 performances.

reasons to be pretty by Neil LaBute; Director, Terry Kinney; Set, David Gallo; Costumes, Sarah J. Holden; Lighting, David

Weiner; Music & Sound, Rob Milburn & Michael Bodeen; Fight Director, Manny Siverio; PSM, Christine Lemme; Assistant Director, Ilana Becker; ASM, Jonathan Donahue; Properties, Jeremy Chernick; Cast: Piper Perabo (Carly), Alison Pill (Steph), Thomas Sadoski (Greg), Pablo Schreiber (Kent)

Setting: The outlying suburbs, not long ago. World premiere of a new play presented in two acts; Lucille Lortel Theatre; May 14–July 5, 2007 (Opened June 2); 55 performances.

Manhattan Theatre Club

Thirty-Sixth Season

Artistic Director Lynne Meadow; Executive Producer, Barry Grove; Acting Artistic Director 07-08, Daniel Sullivan; General Manager, Florie Seery; Associate Artistic Director/Production, Mandy Greenfield; Casting, Nancy Piccione; Literary Manager, Emily Shooltz; Director of Musical Theatre, Clifford Lee Johnson III; Development, Jill Turner Lloyd; Marketing, Debra A. Waxman; Finance, Jeffrey Bledsoe; Associate General Manager, Lindsey Brooks Sag; Subscriber Services, Robert Allenberg; Company Manager, Erin Moeller; Production Manager, Kurt Gardner; Lights/Sound Supervisor, Matthew T. Gross; Properties Supervisor, Scott Laule; Costume Supervisor, Erin Hennessy Dean; Press, Boneau/Bryan-Brown, Jim Byk, Aaron Meier, Heath Schwartz, Christine Olver

THE RECEPTIONIST by Adam Bock; Director, Joe Mantello; Set, David Korins; Costumes, Jane Greenwood; Lighting, Brian MacDevitt; Sound, Darron L West; PSM, Martha Donaldson; Stage Manager, Amy McCraney; Cast: Josh Charles (Mr. Dart), Robert Foxworth (Mr. Raymond), Jayne Houdyshell (Beverly Wilkins), Kendra Kassebaum (Lorraine Taylor); Understudies: Tom Hammond (Mr. Dart, Mr. Raymond), Danielle Skraastad (Lorraine Taylor)

Setting: A busy office in the Northeast, the present. World premiere of a play presented without intermission; City Center Stage I; October 12, 2006–December 30, 2007 (Opening Night October 30); 20 previews, 72 performances.

PUMPGIRL by Abbie Spallen; Director, Carolyn Cantor; Set, David Korins; Costumes, Mimi O'Donnell; Lighting, David Weiner; Original Music & Sound, Robert Kaplowitz; Dialect Coach, Deborah Hecht; PSM, Rachel E. Miller; Stage Manager, Kasey Ostopchuck; Cast: Hannah Cabell (Pumpgirl), Geraldine Hughes (Sinead), Paul Sparks (Hammy); Understudies: Jane Pfitsch (Pumpgirl, Sinead), Tim Ruddy (Hammy)

Setting: A border town in Northern Ireland, roundabout now. American Premiere of a play presented in two acts; City Center Stage II; November 8, 2007–January 13, 2008 (Opened December 4); 29 previews, 48 performances.

THE FOUR OF US by Itamar Moses; Director, Pam MacKinnon; Set and Costumes, David Zinn; Lighting, Russell H. Champa; Sound, David Baker; PSM, Robyn Henry; Stage Manager, Nicole Bouclier; Cast: Gideon Banner (Benjamin), Michael Esper (David); Understudy: Eli James

New York premiere of a play presented in two acts; City Center Stage II; March 6–May 18, 2008 (Opened March 25); 21 previews, 65 performances. World premiere at The Old Globe, San Diego, and workshopped at American Conservatory Theater, San Francisco.

FROM UP HERE by Liz Flahive; Produced in association with Ars Nova; Director, Leigh Silverman; Set, Allen Moyer; Costumes, Mattie Ullrich; Lighting, Pat Collins; Sound, Jill BC DuBoff; Original Music, Tom Kitt; PSM, David H. Lurie; Stage Manager, Steve Henry; Makeup Consultant, Angelina Avallone; Cast: Jenni Barber (Kate), Arija Bareikis (Caroline), Aya Cash (Lauren Barrett), Brian Hutchison (Daniel Warren), Will Rogers (Charlie), Tobias Segal (Kenny Barrett), Joel Van Liew (Mr. Goldberger/Stevens) Julie White (Grace Warren); Understudies: Ben Hollandsworth (Charlie, Kenny), Amelia Jean (Kate, Lauren), Colleen Quinlan (Caroline, Grace), Baylen Thomas (Daniel, Mr. Goldberger/Stevens)

Setting: Now, The Suburban Midwest. World premiere of a play presented without intermission; City Center Stage I; March 27–June 8, 2008 (Opened April 16); 22 previews, 63 performances. Originally developed and workshopped at Ars Nova.

Mint Theater Company

Sixteenth Season

Artistic Director, Jonathan Bank; General Manager, Sherri Kotimsky; Box Office Manager, Colleen T. Sullivan; Casting, Stuart Howard, Amy Schecter & Paul Hardt; Assistant to the Artistic Director, Hunter Kaczorowski; Development Consultant, Ellen Mittenthal; Press, David Gersten & Associates

THE POWER OF DARKNESS by Leo Tolstoy; Translated and directed by Martin Platt; Sets, Bill Clarke; Costumes, Holly Poe Durbin; Lighting, Jeff Nellis; Original Music, Ellen Mandel; Props, Scott Brodsky; PSM, Allison Deutsch; ASM, Lyndsey Goode; Graphics, Jude Dvorak; Assistant Design: Jessica Paz (sound), Ben Krall (lighting); Fight Choreographer Michael Chin; Cast: Peter Bretz (Pyotr Ignatich/A Police Officer), Angela Reed (Anisya), Annie Letscher (Akulina), Jennifer Bissell (Anyutka), Goldie Zwiebel (Marfa/Anna), Jeff Steitzer (Mitritch), Mark Alhadeff (Nikita), Steve Brady (Akim), Randy Danson (Matryona), Letitia Lange (Marina), Alok Tewari

(Marina), Lisa Altomare (Marva), Matthew A. J. Gregory (Pavlovich), Peter Levine (Ivan)

Setting: The village of Tula, Russia, in 1886–87. Revival of a play presented in two acts; September 6–November 4, 2007 (Opened September 24); 53 performances. Originally presented in 1888 in Paris. A Yiddish translation premiered in New York in 1904, and the Theatre Guild presented an English-language premiere of the play on Broadway in 1920.

THE FIFTH COLUMN by Ernest Hemingway; Director, Jonathan Bank; Set, Vicki R. Davis; Costumes, Clint Ramos; Lighting, Jeff Nellis; Sound, Jane Shaw; Properties, Scott Brodsky; Hair/Makeup, Erin Kennedy Lunsford; Dramaturgy, Juan Salas; Dialect Coach, Amy Stoller; Assistant Director, Jerry Ruiz; Stage Manager, Linda Harris; ASM, Allison Deutsch; Assistant Design: Lara Fabian (set), Hunter Kaczorowski (costume), Ben Krall (lighting), Enrico Wey (sound); Illustration, Stefano Imbert; Graphics, Hunter Kaczorowski; Assistant Director, Jerry Ruiz; Assistant Production Manager, Kelly Moore; Cast: John Patrick Hayden (International Brigade Soldier/Aide), Maria Parra (Girl/Maid), Heidi Armbruster (Dorothy Bridges), Joe Hickey (Robert Preston/General), Carlos Lopez (Manager), Kelly AuCoin (Philip Rawlings), Ryan Duncan (Electrician/Assault Guard/Killer/Waiter/Civilian), Nicole Shalhoub (Anita), Ned Noyes (International Brigade Soldier/Sentry), Teresa Yenque (Petra), Joe Rayome (Wilkinson/Signaller), James Andreassi (Antonio), Ronald Guttman (Max)

Setting: In and around Madrid in the fall of 1937. World premiere of a play presented in three acts; February 26–May 18, 2008 (Opened March 27); 85 performances. The play was published in 1938, and a diluted adaptation of the original script was presented on Broadway by the Theatre Guild in 1940, directed by Lee Strasberg, running 87 performances.

The New Group

Twelfth Season

Artistic Director, Scott Elliott; Executive Director, Geoffrey Rich; Managing Producer, Barrack Evans; Managing Director/Development, Oliver Dow; Associate Artistic Director, Ian Morgan; Marketing, Phillip Gutlman; Company Manager, Tim McCann; Business Manager, Elisabeth Bayer; Individual Giving, Barbara Toy/Kristina Hoge; Production Supervisor, Peter R. Feuchtwanger/PRF Productions; Casting, Judy Henderson; Press, The Karpel Group, Bridget Klapinski, Meg Owen

THINGS WE WANT by Jonathan Marc Sherman; Presented in association with Janice Montana; Director, Ethan Hawke; Sets, Derek McLane; Costumes, Mattie Ullrich; Lighting, Jeff Croiter; Sound, Daniel Baker; PSM, Valerie A. Paterson; Assistant Director, Azar Kazemi; ASM, Fran Rubenstein; Props, Gella Zefira; Cast: Paul Dano (Charles), Peter Dinklage (Sty), Josh Hamilton (Teddy), Zoe Kazan (Stella)

Teresa Yenque & Heidi Armbruster in The Fifth Column *(photo by Richard Termine)*

Setting: New York, the present. World premiere of a new play presented in two acts; Acorn Theatre at Theatre Row; October 22–December 30, 2007 (Opened November 7); 62 performances.

TWO THOUSAND YEARS by Mike Leigh; Director, Scott Elliott; Sets, Derek McLane; Costumes, Mimi O'Donnell; Lighting, Jason Lyons; Sound, Ken Travis; Original Music, The Klezmatics; PSM, Valerie A. Peterson; Assistant Director, Marie Masters; Dialect Coach, Stephen Gabis; ASM, Fran Rubenstein; Cast: Yuval Boim (Tzachi), David Cale (Jonathan), Laura Esterman (Rachel), Jordan Gelber (Josh), Merwin Goldsmith (Dave), Cindy Katz (Michelle), Natasha Lyonne (Tammy), Richard Masur (Danny)

Setting: Cricklewood, North London, July 2004–September 2005. American premiere of a play presented in two acts; Acorn Theatre at Theatre Row; January 15–March 22, 2008 (Opened February 7); 69 performances.

RAFTA, RAFTA by Ayub Khan-Din, based on the play *All in Good Time* by Bill Naughton; Director, Scott Elliott; Sets, Derek McLane; Costumes, Theresa Squire; Lighting, Jason Lyons; Sound, Shane Rettig; Original Music, DJ Rekha; Dialects, Stephen Gabis; PSM, Valerie A. Peterson; Assistant Director, Marie Masters; ASM, Fran Rubenstein; Properties, Jeremy Lydic & Matt Hodges; Fight Choreographer, David Anzuelo; Original Music Composer, Qasim Naqvi; Cast: Utkarsh Ambudkar (Etash Tailor), Satya Bhabha (Jai Dutt), Sarita Choudhury (Lata Patel), Ranjit Chowdhry (Eeshwar Dutt), Manish Dayal (Atul Dutt), Skina Jaffrey (Lopa Dutt), Sean T. Krishnan (Jivaj Bhatt), Reshma Shetty (Vina Patel), Alok Tewari (Laxman Patel), Alison Wright (Molly Bhatt)

American premiere of a play presented in two acts; Acorn Theatre at Theatre Row; April 16–June 28, 2008 (Opened May 8); 75 performances. Originally presented at the National Theatre in London, April 26, 2007.

Sarita Choudhury, Reshma Shetty, Sakina Jaffrey & Alison Wright in Rafta, Rafta *(photo by Carol Rosegg)*

New Victory Theater

Twelfth Season

President, Cora Cahan, SVP, Lisa Lawer Post; VP Operations, Joe Rooney; VP Finance, Judy Leventhal; Marketing, Thomas Cott; SVP Development, Cheryl Kohn; Education, Edie Demas; Marketing/PR, Laura Kaplow-Goldman, Allison Mui; Duke/42nd Street Studios Operations, Alma Malabnan-McGrath; Production, David Jensen; New Vic Technical Director, Joe O'Dea; New Vic Production Coordinator, Coleen Davis; Programming, Mary Rose Lloyd; Ticketing, Robin Leeds

COMET IN MOOMINLAND Based on the book by Tove Jansson, adapted and created by Graham Whitehead; Co-created by William Chesney and Leslee Silverman; Presented by Manitoba Theatre for Young People; Director, Kim Selody; Original Direction, Graham Whitehead; Set/Puppet/Environment Design, William Chesney; Original Music, Cathy Nosaty; Lighting, Bill Williams; Stage Manager, Carolyn T. Kutchyera; Puppet Builder, Shawn Kettner; Cast: Jennifer Lyon, David Warburton

A puppet show presented without intermission; Duke on 42nd Street; September 28–October 14, 2007; 15 performances.

THE WOLVES IN THE WALLS Based on the book by Neil Gaiman and Dave McKean; Presented by National Theatre of Scotland in collaboration with Improbable theater company of London; Conceived and developed for the stage by Vicky Featherstone, Julian Crouch, Nick Powell; Director, Vicky Featherston; Design, Julian Crouch; Music/Sound/Arrangements, Nick Powell; Additional lyrics, Neil Gaiman; Lighting, Natasha Chivers; Stage Manager, Mary-Susan Gregson; Music Director/Arrangements, Robert Melling; Movement, Steven Hoggett; Company Stage Manager, Helen Maguire; Deputy Stage Manager, Emma Skaer; Technical Stage Manager, Colin Bell; Casting, Anne Henderson; Cast: Helen Mallon (Lucy), Anita Vettesse (Mum), George Drennan (Dad), Paul James Corrigan (Brother), Ewan Hunter, Neil McNulty, Sharon Smith, Jessica Tomchak (Wolves); Musicians: Andrew Brown, Robert Melling, Brian Molley, Robert Owen

A musical pandemonium presented without intermission; October 5–21, 2007; 16 performances.

MAYHEM POETS Created by Kyle Sutton, Scott Raven Tarazevits, Mason Granger, Diane Roy, Kristin Mingoia; Cast: Mason Granger, Kyle Sutton, Scott Raven Tarazevits

A performance of hip-hop and slam poetry presented without intermission; October 26–November 4, 2007; 11 performances.

TAPEIRE Written, directed, choreographed and performed by James Devine; Produced by Devine Dance Company of Ireland; Music, Tapeire Band; Co-Choreography, Jimmy Tate; Visual Design, Tim Redfern; Lighting/Tour Manager/Technical Director, Brett Maughan; Sound/Veejay, Tom Cassetta; Photography, Helen McLennan, John Savage, Risteard Macaodha, Bill Lynch; US Tour Producer, Thomas O. Kriegsmann/Arktype; Musicians: Ashley MacIsaac (fiddle), Paul Jennings (percussion), Phamie Gow (harp)

A Celtic tap dance show with music presented without intermission; November 9–25, 2007; 18 performances.

THE NEW SHANGHAI CIRCUS Art Director, Xu Ying; Producing Artistic Director, Lizhi Zhao; Company Manager, Ziqian Tan; Assistant Company Manager, Xiaojun Kong; Tour Representation, Gurtman And Murtha Associates; Lighting and PSM, Chris Dunlop; Cast: Ma Aili, Li Rong, Wang Pandi, Liu Yang, Song Yubin, Song Ying, Liu Yang, Zhai Yanan, Zhai Junnan, Lu Wei, Bai Yang, Li Jiqing, Zhou Guan, Wang Xinyi, Cai Yong

A Chinese circus presented in two acts; November 30, 2007–January 6, 2008; 39 performances.

JOHN LITHGOW'S THE SUNNY SIDE OF THE STREET Director and conductor, J.C. Hopkins; Set, Josh Zangen; Lighting, Alan Adelman; Sound, Simon Nathan; Starring: John Lithgow; Musicians: (The Sunny Side Strutters): Danny Lipton, J. Walter Hawkes, Doug Weiselman, Doug Largent, Kevin Dorn, Amanda Monaco, Jon-Erik "Amazin" Kelso, Marcus Rojas

The Cast of Aeros *(Photo by Luca Missoni)*

A concert with songs and stories from his recent album for kids performed without intermission; January 18–20, 2008; 5 performances.

LUNA NEGRA DANCE THEATER Founder and Artistic Director, Eduardo Vilaro; Pieces included: *Sonetos de Amor* (Choreography by Pedro Ruiz, inspired by the words of Pablo Neruda), *Sugar in the Raw* (Choreography by Michelle Manzanales, composed by Gustavo Santaolalla), and *Quinceañera* (Choreography by Eduardo Vilaro, composed by Ana Lara); Rehearsal Director, Michelle Manzanales; Lighting, Clifton Taylor; Technical Director, Josh Preston; PSM, Kay Lea Meyers; Wardrobe Supervisor, Diana Ruettiger; Ballet Mistress, Graca Salas; Cast: Jonathan Alsberry, Kimberly Bleich, Dustin Crumbaugh, Ricardo J. Garcia, Alejandra González, Veronica Guadalupe, Dario Mejia, Anthony Peyla, Kirsten Shelton, JP Tenuta, Jorge Quinter Troetsch, Vanessa Valecillos, Jessica Alejandra Wyatt

Three dance pieces presented without in two acts; January 25–February 3, 2008; 10 performances.

TRACES Directed and choreographed by Shana Carroll and Gypsy Snider; Presented by 7 Fingers (Nassib Samir El-Husseini, Executive Director), Montreal; Co-Produced by National Arts Centre, Ottawa; Coaching/Acrobat Research, Sebastien Soldevila; Original Music, Francisco Cruz; Lighting, Nol van Genuchten; Sets, Flavia Hevia; Costumes, Manon Desmarais; Production Manager, Gregg Parks; Video, Paul Ahad; Technical Director, Yves Touchette; Cast and Conception: Héloïse Bourgeois, Francisco Cruz, Raphael Cruz, Brad Henderson, Will Underwood

Circus Theater with dance, music, acrobats, and skateboarding presented without intermission; February 8–March 2, 2008; 22 performances.

RAPUNZEL by Annie Siddons; Presented by Kneehigh Theatre (Cornwall UK) and Battersea Arts Center; Director/Adaptation, Emma Rice; Set/Costumes, Michael Vale; Original Music, Stu Barker; Lighting, Alex Wardle; Sound, Dom Bilkey; Stage Manager, Mary-Susan Gregson; Musical Director, Alex Vann; Producers, Paul Crewes (Kneehigh), Alex Wardle (BAC); Company Stage Manager, Amy Griffin; Technical Stage Manager, Geraldine Ramsay; Prop/Puppets, Laura MacKenzie; Cast: Paul Hunter (Umberto/Pierluigi Ambrosi), Pieter Lawman (Patrizio), Charlie Barnecut (Mother Gothel/Paulo), Edith Tankus (Rapunzel), James Traherne (The Duke of Tuscany/Shark Fantini), Kate Hewitt (Prezzemolina), Alex Vann (Musician)

A play with physical theater, puppetry, animation, live music and comedy presented without intermission; March 7–23, 2008; 14 performances.

PIGS, BEARS AND BILLY GOATS GRUFF Adapted and directed by Dave Brown; Presented by Patch Theatre Company (Adelaide, Australia); Set/Costumes, Dean Hills; Lighting, Dave Green; Choreography, Jenn Havelberg; Production/Stage Manager, Bob Weatherly; Music Director, Stuart Day; Cast: Eileen Darley, Stuart Day, Jacqy Phillips, Stephen Sheehan

A play presented without intermission; March 28–April 6, 2008; 10 performances.

AEROS Directed and choreographed by Daniel Ezralow, David Parsons, Moses Pendleton, in collaboration with Luke Cresswell and Steve McNicholas; Based on an idea by Antonio Gnecchi Ruscone; Movement Coordinator, Maria Fumea; Costumes, Luca Missoni; Original Music/Arrangements, TTG Music Lab; Lighting, Giancarlo Toscani; General Manager, Ianthe Demos; Company Manager, Tyler Penfield; Production Manager, John H. Finen III; Stage Manager, Kevin Brophy; Gymnastics Coach, Mariana Mezel; Cast: Members of the Romanina Gymanstics Federation (Bucharest) – Lucian Alexa, Mariana Mezei, Raluca Balaban, Alexandru Bors, Madalina Cioveie, Laura Cristache, Andrei Damsa, Denisa Ganea, Oana Ganea, Ana Georgescu, Ioana Gheorghiu, Cristina Marin, Teodora Nasta, Florin Nebunu, Sebastian Petrut, Lucian Raducanu, Madalina Susan

A gymnastics and dance performance piece presented without intermission; April 11–27, 2008; 18 performances.

ONE OF A KIND by Yossi Vassa & Shai Ben Attar, translated by Howard Rypp; Presented by Nephesh Theatre (Tel Aviv, Israel); Director, Shai Ben Attar; Music, Idan Zilbershtein; Sound, Oded Weinstock; Animation, Adi Katz; Set, Alexander Sasha Lesansky; Costumes, Sky Gete; Choreography, Iddi Saaka; Lighting, Meir Alon; Stage Manager, Mary Susan Gregson; Dialects, Prina Joy Isseroff & Linda Lovitch; Cast: Yossi Vassa (AndArgay), Tehitina Assefa (Grandmother), Mahareta Baruch

(Masi), Shai Fredo (Asmamo), Benny Gatahon (The Teacher/ Case Pakudu), Sky Gete (Yeshitu), Roy Zaddok (Isaac)

A play presented without intermission; May 2–11, 2008; 10 performances.

PAST HALF REMEMBERED Created and presented by New International Encounter (Czech Republic-Norway-United Kingdom-France); Director, Alex Byrne; Set and Costumes, Katerina Houskova; Musical Director, David Pagan; Movement Director, Kasia Zaremba; Production Manager, Elke Laleman; Production Coordinator, Kathleen Connor; Stage Manager, Robert I. Cohen; Cast: Aude Henry, Anna Healey, Tomáš Mechácek, Iva Moberg, Kjell Moberg, David Pagan

American premiere of a play with music presented without intermission; Duke on 42nd Street; May 8–25, 2008; 10 performances.

IJK Created by Olivier Alenda, Aurélien Bory, Christian Coumin, Thierry Dussout, Stéphanie Ley, Katja Wehrlin; Conceived by Aurélien Bory; Presented by Compagnie 111 (Toulouse, France); Artistic Consultant, Phil Soltanoff; Original Direction, Christian Coumin; Costumes, Sylvie Marcucci; Lighting, Arno Veyrat; Sound, Stéphanie Ley; Administration/ Production/Distribution, Florence Meurisse, Delphine Justumus; Cast: Olivier Alenda, Aurélien Bory, Anne De Buck

A wordless physical theatre piece with jugging and circus art presented without intermission; May 16–June 1, 2008; 15 performances.

New York Gilbert & Sullivan Players

Thirty-Fourth Season

Artistic Director & General Manager, Albert Bergeret; Sales/ Assistant General Manager, David Wannen; Assistant Music Director, Andrea Stryker-Rodda; Technical Director/PSM, David Sigafoose; Press, Peter Cromarty; Librettos by Sir William S. Gilbert; Music by Sir Arthur Sullivan; Lighting, Sally Small; Costumes, Gail Wofford; ASM, Suzy Hailey Ungar/ Annette Dieli

PRINCESS IDA Director/Conductor, Albert Bergeret; Choreography, Janis Ansley Unger; Set, Albere; Co-Costumes, Stivanello Costume Company (original design by Jean Brookman); Cast: Keith Jurosko (King Hildebrand), Colm Fitzmaurice (Hilarion), Patrick Hogan (Cyril), William Whitefield (Florian), Stephen Quint (King Gama), David Wannen (Arac), David Auxier (Guron), Louis Dall'Ava (Scynthius), Kimilee Bryant (Princess Ida), Dianna Dollman (Lady Blanche), Shana Farr (Lady Psyche), Melissa Attebury (Melissa), Megan Loomis (Sacharissa), Rebecca O'Sullivan (Chloe), Victoria Devany (Ada); Ensemble: Meredith Borden, Joshua Bouchard, Ted Bouton, Susan Case, Derrick Cobey, Michael Connolly, Michael Galante, Matthew Harrison, Katie Hall, Amy Helfer, Alan Hill, David Macaluso, Robin Mahon, Nick Mannix, Lance Olds, Marcie Passley, Monique Pelletier, Paul Sigrist, Angela Smith, Chris-Ian Sanchez, Amber Smoke

Setting: The Pavilion of King Hildebrand's Palace, and the Garden and Courtyard of Castle Adamant. An operetta presented in three acts with one intermission; City Center; January 4, 6, 12, 2008; 3 performances.

THE PIRATES OF PENZANCE Director/Conductor, Albert Bergeret; Choreography, Bill Fabris; Co-Conductor, Jeffrey Kresky; Set, Lou Anne Gilleland; Cast: Stephen Quint (Major-General Stanley), David Wannen (The Pirate King), David Macaluso (Samuel), Colm Fitzmaurice (Frederic), Keith Jurosko/David Auxier (Sergeant of Police), Laurelyn Watson Chase/Sarah Caldwell Smith (Mabel), Erika Person (Edith), Melissa Attebury/Amy Helfer (Kate), Robin Mahon/Meredith Borden (Isabel), Angela Smith (Ruth); Ensemble: Ashley Adler, David Auxier, Meredith Borden, Cáitlín Burke, Derrick Cobey, Michael Connolly, Louis Dall'Ava, Dianna Dollman, Katie Hall, Matthew Harrison, Amy Helfer, Alan Hill, Lynelle Johnson, Robin Mahon, James Mills, Jenny Millsap, Lance Olds, Rebecca O'Sullivan, Natalie Ross, Paul Sigrist, Sarah Caldwell Smith, Chris-Ian Sanchez, Kathy Tarello, Eric Werner, William Whitefield; Summer Ensemble: Ashley Adler, Kimberly Deana Bennett, Cáitlín Burke, Derrick Cobey, Louis Dall'Ava, Victoria Devany; Michael Galante, Katie Hall, Betina Hershey, Alan Hill, Lynelle Johnson, Michael Levesque, Daniel Lockwood, Jenny Millsap, Lance Olds, Natalie Ross, Rebecca O'Sullivan, Paul Sigrist, Chris-Ian Sanchez, Eric Werner, William Whitefield; Swings: Megan Loomis, Michael Galante

Setting: A Rocky Seashore on the Coast of Cornwall; A ruined Chapel by Moonlight. An operetta presented in two acts, City Center; January 5, 11, 13; June 7, 13, 2008; 5 performances.

TRIAL BY JURY and **G&S Á LA CARTE** Director/Conductor Albert Bergeret; Choreography, Robin Mahon; Book for *G&S a la Carte*, David Auxier; Cast (*Trial by Jury*): Stephen Quint (The Learned Judge), Richard Holmes (Counsel for the Plaintiff), Patrick Hogan(The Defendant Edwin), Ted Bouton (Foreman of the Jury), David Wannen (Usher), Laurelyn Watson Chase (The Plaintiff Angelina); Ensemble: David Auixer, Meredith Borden, Susan Case, Michael Connelly, Louis Dall'Ava, Victoria Devany; Dianna Dollman, Michael Galante, Katie Hall, Alan Hill, Lynelle Johnson, Keith Jurosko, Daniel Lockwood, Megan Loomis, David Macaluso, Robin Mahon, Jenny Millsap, Lance Olds, Monique Pelletier, Erika Person, Edward Prostak, Chris-Ian Sanchez, Paul Sigrist,

Willliam Whitefield, Colm Firzmaurice, Patrick Hogan and Kimilee Bryant (seated) in Princess Ida *(photo by Pien Nagy)*

Angela Smith, Michael J. Strone, William Whitefield; (*G&S a la Carte*): Richard Alan Holmes (Richard D'Oyly Carte), Erika Person (Helen Lenoir), Stephen Quint (Arthur Sullivan), Keith Jurosko (W.S. Gilbert)

Setting: Act 1–A Courtroom, 1935; Act 2–A Cast Party following the opening of *Trial by Jury.* An operetta in one act followed by the world premiere of a topsy-turvy historically inaccurate musical soirée presented with intermission; City Center; January 10, 2008; 1 performance.

THE MIKADO Director/Conductor, Albert Bergeret; Set, Albere; Co-Costumes, Kayko Nakamura; Cast: Keith Jurosko/ David Wannen (The Mikado of Japan), Daniel Lockwood (Nanki-Poo), David Macaluso (Ko-Ko), Louis Dall'Ava (Pooh-Bah), Edward Prostak (Pish-Tush), Laurelyn Watson Chase (Yum-Yum), Melissa Attebury (Pitti-Sing), Robin Mahon/ Lauren Wenegrat (Peep-Bo), Dianna Dollman (Katisha); Ensemble: David Auxier, Susan Case, Derrick Cobey, Michael Connolly, Michael Galante, Robert Garner, Katie Hall, Alan Hill, Lynelle Johnson, Jenny Millsap, Lance Olds, Rebecca O'Sullivan, Monique Pelletier, Paul Sigrist, Chris-Ian Sanchez, Angela Smith, Kathy Glauber Tarello, William Whitefield; Summer Ensemble: David Auxier, Kimberly Deana Bennett, Susan Case, Derrick Cobey, Michael J. Connolly, Victoria Devany, Michael Galante, Katie Hall, Alan Hill, Lynelle Johnson, Michael Levesque, Jenny Millsap, Rebecca O'Sullivan, Lance Olds, Erika Person, Natalie Ross, Chris-Ian Sanchez, Paul Sigrist, Angela Smith, William Whitefield; Understudy: Chris-Ian Sanchez (Nanki-Poo)

Setting: A Japanese Garden. An operetta presented in two acts; City Center; January 12; June 7, 14, 2008; 3 performances.

H.M.S. PINAFORE Director/Music Director/Conductor, Albert Bergeret; Choreography, Bill Fabris; Co-Conductor, Stephen Quint; Set, Albére; Cast: Stephen Quint/David Macaluso (The Rt. Hon. Sir Joseph Porter, K.C.B.), Richard Alan Holmes (Captain Corcoran), Colm Fitzmaurice (Ralph Rackstraw), Louis Dall'Ava (Dick Deadeye), William Whitefield (Bill Bobstay), David Wannen (Bob Becket), Laurelyn Watson Chase/Elizabeth Hillebrand (Josephine), Victoria Devany (Cousin Hebe), Angela Smith (Little Buttercup), Paul Sigrist (Sergeant of Marines); Ensemble: Ashley Adler, Cáitlín Burke, David Auxier, Kimberly Deana Bennett, Meredith Borden, Susan Case, Derrick Cobey, Michael J. Connolly, Michael Galante, Katie Hall, Amy Helfer, Alan Hill, Lynelle Johnson, Michael Levesque, Michele McConnell, James Mills, Rebecca OíSullivan, Lance Olds, Erika Person, Chris-Ian Sanchez, Sarah Caldwell Smith, Matthew Wages, Lauren Wenegrat

Setting: Quarterdeck of H.M.S. Pinafore. An operetta presented in two acts; City Center; June 6, 8, 10, 11, 2008; 4 performances.

THE GONDOLIERS Director/Conductor, Albert Bergeret; Assistant Director, Robin Mahon; Choreography, Bill Fabris; Set, Jack Garver; Costumes, Jan Holland; Cast: Stephen Quint (The Duke of Plaza-Toro), Matt Nelson (Luiz), Richard Alan Holmes (Don Alhambra Del Bolero), William Whitefield (Giuseppe Palmieri), Colm Fitzmaurice (Marco Palmieri), Lance Olds (Antonio), Michael Galante (Francesco), David Auxier (Giorgio), Michael J. Connolly (Annibale), Angela Smith (The Duchess of Plaza Toro), Michele McConnell (Casilda), Laurelyn Watson Chase (Gianetta), Erika Person (Tessa), Meredith Borden (Fiametta), Kimberly Deana Bennett (Vittoria), Rebecca O'Sullivan (Giulia), Victoria Devany (Inez), Joshua Strone (Young Gondolier/Drummer Boy); Ensemble: Ashley Adler, Kimberly Deana Bennett, Caítlín Burke, Louis Dall'Ava, Katie Hall, Amy Helfer, Betina Hershey, Alan Hill, Lynelle Johnson, Michael Levesque, David Macaluso, James Mills, Chris-Ian Sanchez, Paul Sigrist, Sarah Caldwell Smith, David Wannen, Lauren Wenegrat; Understudies: David Macaluso (Giuseppe), Lance Olds (Luiz), Chris-Ian Sanchez (Marco), Sarah Caldwell Smith (Gianetta), Amy Helfer(Tessa), Katie Hall (Vittoria), Lauren Wenegrat (Fiametta)

Setting: Venice: The Piazetta and Pavillion in the Palace of Barataria. An operetta presented in two acts; City Center; June 12, 14, 15, 2008; 3 performances.

New York Theatre Workshop

Twenty-Fifth Season

Artistic Director, James C. Nicola; Managing Director, Lynn Moffat/Fred Walker; Associate Artistic Director, Linda S.

Chapman; Casting, Jack Doulin; Planning and Development, Carl M. Sylvestre; Finance and Administration, George Cochran; General Manager, Harry J. McFadden; Education, Jen Zoble; Marketing, Robert Marlin/Cathy Popowytsch; Literary Associate, Geoffrey Scott; Artistic Associates, Michael Greif, Michael Friedman, Ruben Polendo; Production Manager, Michael Casselli; Press, Richard Kornberg, Don Summa

HORIZON Created, written and composed by Rinde Eckert; Director, David Schweizer; Sets & Lighting, Alexander V. Nichols; Sound, Gregory T. Kuhn; Costumes, David Zinn; Recording composition and performance, Rinde Eckert; Choreography, David Barlow; PSM, Chad Brown; NYTW Stage Management, Odessa "Niki" Spruill, Richard A. Hodge; Executive Producer, Susan Endrizzi; Cast: Rinde Eckert (Reinhart Poole), David Barlow (Mason #1/Reinhart's Wife/ Reinhart's Brother), Howard Swain (Mason #2/Reinhart's Mother/Reinhart's Father)

A new play presented without intermission; June 1–July 1, 2008 (Opened June 6); 37 performances.

THE BLACK EYED by Betty Shamieh; Director, Sam Gold; Sets, Paul Steinberg; Costumes, Gabriel Berry; Lighting, Jane Cox; Sound, Darron L West; PSM, Rachel Zak; ASM, Terri K. Kohler; Assistant Director, Tracy C. Francis; Voice/Dialect Coach, Beth McGuire; Hair/Makeup, Cookie Jordan; Cast: Aysan Celik (Aiesha), Lameece Issaq (Tamam), Jeanine Serralles (The Architect), Emily Swallow (Delilah)

A new play presented without intermission; July 17–August 19, 2007 (Opened July 31); 39 performances.

THE MISANTHROPE by Moliére, translated by Tony Harrison; Director, Ivo van Hove; Production Design, Jan Versweyveld; Costumes, Emilio Sosa; Sound, Raul Vincent Enriquez; Video, Tal Yarden; Dramaturg, Bart Van den Eynde; PSM, Larry K. Ash; ASM, Tom Dooley; Assistant Director, Kirk Jackson; Vocal Coach, Kate Maré; Hair/Makeup, Martha Melendez; Cast: Quincy Tyler Bernstine (Eliante), Jason C. Brown (Clitandre), Bill Camp (Alceste), Amelia Campbell (Arsinoé), Joan MacIntosh (Acaste), Alfredo Narciso (Oronte), Thomas Jay Ryan (Philinte), Jeanine Serralles (Célimène)

World premiere of a new adaptation of the classic play presented without intermission; September 14–November 11, 2007 (Opened September 24); 67 performances.

BECKETT SHORTS by Samuel Beckett; Director, JoAnne Akalaitis; Original Music, Philip Glass; Sets, Alexander Brodsky; Costumes, Kaye Voyce; Lighting, Jennifer Tipton; Sound, Darron L West; Video, Mirit Tal; PSM, Anthony Cerrato; ASM, Odessa "Niki" Spruill; Assistant Director, Maureen Towey; Cast: *Act Without Words 1:* Mikhail Baryshnikov (Man); *Act Without Words II:* Mikhail Baryshnikov (A), Bill Camp (B); *Rough For Theatre I:* Mikhail Baryshnikov (A), David Neumann (B); *Eh Joe:* Mikhail Baryshnikov (Joe), Karen Kandel (Woman)

Four one-act plays presented without intermission; December 5, 2007–January 20, 2008 (Opened December 18); 53 performances.

LIBERTY CITY by Jessica Blank and April Yvette Thompson; Director, Jessica Blank; Sets, Antje Ellermann; Costume Consultant, Mattie Ullrich; Lighting, David Lander; Sound, Jane Shaw; Video, Tal Yarden; Associate Video, Keith Skretch; PSM, Larry K. Ash; Assistant Director/Dramaturgical Support, Gwenyth Reitz; Cast: April Yvette Thompson

A solo performance play presented without intermission; February 15–March 16, 2008 (Opened March 4); 35 performances.

THE SOUND AND THE FURY *(April Seventh, 1928)* Created and presented by Elevator Repair Service (John Collins, Artistic Director), based on Part 1 of William Faulkner's novel; Director, John Collins; Set, David Zinn; Costumes, Colleen Werthmann; Lighting, Mark Barton; Sound, Matt Tierney; Stage Manager, Sarah C. Hughes; Assistant Director, Rachel Chavkin; Technical Director, Ben Williams; Company Manager, Ariana Smart Truman; Producing Director ERS, Tory Vazquez; Production Manager, B.D. White; Cast: Mike Iveson, Vin Knight, Aaron Landsman, April Matthis, Annie McNamara, Randolph Curtis Rand, Greig Sargeant, Kate Scelsa, Kaneza Schaal, Susie Sokol, Tory Vazquez, Ben Williams

Setting: Seventeen separate days between a funeral in 1898 and the day before Easter in 1928. World premiere of a new play presented in two acts; April 15–June 1, 2008 (Opened April 29); 47 performances.

Joan MacIntosh, Jeanine Serralles, Thomas Jay Ryan, Jason C. Brown, Quincy Tyler Bernstine in The Misanthrope *(photo by Carol Rosegg)*

Pan Asian Repertory Theatre

Thirty-First Season

Artistic Producing Director, Tisa Chang; Artistic Associate, Ron Nakahar; General Manager, Fran Smyth; Producing Assistant, Abby Felder; Marketing/Education Associate, Steven Osborn; Workshop Instructor, Ernest Abuba; Fight Coordinator, Michael G. Chin; Bookkeeper, Rosemary Khan; Marketing Consultant, Reva Cooper; Crew Chief, Jared Welch; Master Electrician, Paul Jones; Photo Archivist, Corky Lee; Administrative Assistant, Shiegeko Suga; Press, Keith Sherman and Associates

THE JOY LUCK CLUB by Susan Kim, adapted from the novel by Amy Tan; Director and Musical Staging, Tisa Chang; Sets, Kaori Akazawa; Costumes, Carol Pelletier; Lighting, Victor En Yu Tan; Sound, Peter Griggs; Additional Sound, Ty Sanders; PSM, James W. Carringer; ASM, Leslie A. Grisdale; Cast: Dian Kobayashi (Suyuan Woo/2nd wife of Wu Tsing), Wai Ching Ho (An Mei Hsu), ,Virginia Wing (Lindo Jong), Lydia Gaston (Ying-Ying St. Clair), Han Nah Kim (Jing Mei Woo), Rosanne Ma (Rose Hsu Jordan), Sacha Iskra (Lena St. Clair), Tina Chilip (Waverly Jong), Ming Lee (Canning Woo/Wu Tsing/Moon Lady), Scott Klavan (Clifford/Harold/Rich/Ted), Les J. N. Mau (Tin Jong/Tyan Yu/Archer), Tom Matsusaka (Mr. Chong/Lau Po/Drunk), Carol A. Honda (Huang TaiTai/PoPo/Amah/Yan Chang), Kathleen Kwan (Mother of An-Mei/Matchmaker/ Chuwun-Yu), Tran T. Thuc Hanh (An-Mei's Aunt/Servant/ Chwun-Hwa)

Setting: San Francisco, the 1980's and China, 1918–1980's. Revival of the new play presented in two acts; Julia Miles Theater; October 28–December 1, 2007 (Opened November 8); 36 performances. World premiere presented in 1993 by Shanghai People's Art Theatre and The Long Wharf Theatre. Pan Asian Rep produced the New York premiere in 1999.

THE MISSING WOMAN Written and directed by Nguyen Thi Minh Ngoc; Presented in association with the Institute for Vietnamese Culture & Education, with help from Music Fans Company; Sets, Kim B; Music, Tran Vuong Thach & Hai Phuong; Lighting, Joyce Lial; Production Coordinator, Elis C. Arroyo; Choreographers, Tan Loc, Huynh Mai; Cast: Thanh Loc Lang-Husband/Ho Nguyet Co-Fox Woman / Poet's Husband), Hai Phuong (Gian Nhan-Wife), My Hang (Kieu Nguyet Nga-Woman from Painting/Child), Ngoc Dang (Trung Trac-Lady General/Tiet Giao-Fox Woman's Lover), Thuc Hanh (Poet/Trung Nhi-Lady General's Sister/Chorus), Nguyen Thi Minh Ngoc (Mother/The Spirit of Ho Xuan Hong's Poetry/Chorus), Leon Le (Father/Thi Sach-Lady General's Husband/Chorus)

New York premiere of a folk parable with music and dance presented in Vietnamese with English narration; West End Theatre; April 2-12, 2008 (Opened April 7); 12 performances.

Readings/Workshops

December Staged Reading Series at the Bruce Mitchell Room: *The Secret of O Sono* by Elsa Okon Rael; Director, Ron Nakahara; Improvised Music, Jason Hwang; Cast: John Baray, Paul Keoni Chun, Chris Doi, Emi Fujinami Jones, Wai Ching Ho, Carol Honda, David Ige, Shigeko Suga, Henry Yuk; December 5, 2007; *Dumpling* by Wesley Du; Director, Nelson T. Eusebio III; Cast: Claro Austria, Louis Changchien, Chris Doi, Glenn Kubota, Ron Nakahara, Bea Soon; December 12, 2007; Scenes from *The Missing Woman* written and directed by Nguyen Thi Minh Ngoc; Cast: Tiffany Rothman, Hanh T. Thuc Tran; Nguyen Thi Minh Ngoc, Giovanni Sferrazza, John Nguyen

Winter Actors/Solo Performance/Playwrights Workshop November 5, 2007–January 14, 2008; Workshop Presentation January 16, 2008, included: *The Seagull* by Anton Chekhov, featuring Paul Keoni Chun and Shelley Molad; *Carry the Tiger to the Mountain* by Cherlene Lee, with Nancy Eng; *A Day in the Life of a Hindu God: Sati Woke Me Up* written and performed by David Elyha; *"grits are good for you"* written and performed by Sarah-Zane Moore; *Iris* written and performed by Jen Yip; *Jesus Hopped the A Train* by Stephen Adly Guirgis, with Una Osato; *Beast on the Moon* by Richard Kalinoski, with Shelley Molad and Paul Keoni Chun; *Opposite Day* written and performed by Sean Tarjoto; *The Cherry Orchard* by Anton Chekhov, with Anne Miyamoto, David Elyha, and Paul Keoni

Sacha Iskra and Rosanne Ma in The Joy Luck Club *(photo by Corky Lee)*

Chun; *Curse* by Nancy Eng, with Anne Miyamoto and Paul Keoni Chun; *Mango Tree* by Anne Miyamoto, with Paul Keoni Chun, Una Osato, Shelley Molad, Jen Yip, and Ron Nakahara

2+3 Nights Only A Series of Readings; Program A (March 19–20, 2008): *Five Movements Toward Freedom: A Choreopoem* written and performed by Dawn Crandell; *Opposite Day* written and performed by Sean Tarjoto with soundscape and didgeridoo by Baba Israel; *Recess* written and performed by Una Aya Osato; Program B (March 21–22): *Iris* written and performed by Jen Yip; *Goy Vey! Adventures of a Dim Sun in Search of His Wanton Father* written and performed by Richard Chang; *Finding Ways to Prove You're Not an Al-Qaeda* written and performed by Snehal Desai; Program C (March 24–26, 2008): *Merica* by John Quincy Lee; Director, Ernest Abuba; Cast: Ariel Estrada, Anne Miyamoto Timmins, Ruth Zhang; Program D (March 27–29, 2008): *Mango Tree* by Anne Miyamoto Timmons; Director, Kaipo Schwab; Cast: Tina Chilip, Nancy Eng, Sacha Iskra, Han Nah Kim, Paul Keoni Chun, Ron Nakahara and Una Aya Osato

Pearl Theatre Company

Twenty-Fourth Season

Artistic Director, Shepard Sobel; Managing Director, Shira Beckerman; Associate Director, Joanne Camp; Development Director, Jim Farrell; Marketing/Press Director, Michael Page; Production and Facilities Manager, Gary Levinson; Casting/Project Manager, Craig Evans; Dramaturg, Kate Farrington; Marketing Manager, Colin McKenna; Grants, Jesica Avellone; Audience Services Manager Christian Clayton; Education, Carol Schultz; Costume Shop Manager, Katy Conover; Speech/Text Coach, Robert Neff Williams; Season Designers: Harry Feiner (set), Stephen Petrilli (lighting); Technical Director, Gary Levinson

HAMLET by William Shakespeare; Director, Shepard Sobel; Costumes, Devon Painter; Sound, Sara Bader; Stage Manager, Lisa Ledwich; Props, Mary Houston; Fight Director, Felix Ivanov; Cast: Jolly Abraham (Ophelia), Robin Leslie Brown (Gertrude), Bradford Cover (Horatio), Dominic Cuskern (Polonius), Jimmy Davis (Reynaldo/Osric/Francisco/Player Queen), TJ Edwards (Claudius), R.J. Foster (Bernardo/Norwegian Captain), Robert Hock (Apparition/Player King/Gravedigger), Regi Huc (Cornelius/Fortinbras/Lucianus), Kenneth Lee (Guildenstern), Sean McNall (Hamlet), Eduardo Placer (Rosencrantz), David Sedgwick (Voltemand/Prologue), Christopher Thornton (Marcellus/A Priest/English Ambassador), David L. Townsend (Laertes)

Setting: In and around Elsinore Castle, Denmark. Revival of the play presented in two acts; 80 St Marks Place; September 11–October 28, 2007 (Opened September 23); 15 previews, 34 performances.

THE CONSTANT COUPLE by George Farquhar; Director, Jean Randich; Costumes, Liz Covey; Sound, Jane Shaw; Stage Manager, Dale Smallwood; Props, Mary Houston; Fight Director, Felix Ivanov; Choreography, Alice Teirstein; Cast: Jolly Abraham (Angelica/Tom Errand's Wife), Rachel Botchan (Lady Lurewell), Robin Leslie Brown (Parly), Joanne Camp (Lady Darling), Bradford Cover (Sir Harry Wildair), Dominic Cuskern (Smuggler), Meg McCrossen (Musician/Servant/Mob), Sean McNall (Clincher Jr.), Orville Mendoza (Tom Errand/Constable/Butler/Newgate Gaoler/Musician), Jack Moran (Footman/Servant/Musician/Mob), John Pasha (Colonel Standard), Eduardo Placer (Clincher Sr.), Caleb Rupp (Dicky/Musician/Mob), David L. Townsend (Vizard)

Setting: 18th Century London. Revival of a play presented in two acts; 80 St. Marks Place; November 13–December 23, 2007 (Opened November 28); 13 previews, 28 performances.

THE MANDRAKE by Niccolo Machiavelli, translated by Peter Constantine; Director, Jim Calder; Costumes, Barbara A. Bell; Sound/Original Music, Jane Shaw; PSM, Richard Morrison; Props, Mary Houston; Fight Director, Felix Ivanov; Cast: Rachel Botchan (Lucrezi), Bradford Cover (Ligurio), Dominic Cuskern (Messer Nicia), TJ Edwards (Friar Timoteo), Edward Seamon (Sir), Carol Schultz (Sostrata), Erik Steele (Callimaco), Rocelyn Halili (A Servant Woman)

Setting: A piazza in Florence, Italy. Early 1500's. Revival of a play in three acts presented with one intermission; 80 St. Marks Place; January 8–February 10, 2008 (Opening Night January 20); 15 previews, 21 performances.

GHOSTS by Henrik Ibsen, translated by Peter Watts; Director, Regge Life; Costumes, Sam Fleming; Sound, Mark Huang; Stage Manager, Lisa Ledwich; Props, Stephanie Tucci; Cast: Joanne Camp (Mrs. Alving), TJ Edwards (Engstrand), John Behlmann (Osvald Alving), Tom Galantich (Pastor Manders), Keiana Richàrd (Regina Engstrand)

Setting: Mrs. Alving's country house by a large fjord in Western Norway. Revival of a play presented in two acts; 80 St. Marks Place; February 26–March 30, 2008 (Opened March 9); 15 previews, 21 performances.

THE IMPORTANCE OF BEING EARNEST by Oscar Wilde; Director, J.R. Sullivan; Costumes, Devon Painter; Sound, Mark Huang; Stage Manager, Dale Smallwood; Properties, Stephanie Tucci; Assistant Director, Patrick McNulty; Cast: Dominic Cuskern (Lane/Merriman), Sean McNall (Algernon Moncrieff), Bradford Cover (John Worthing), Carol Schultz (Lady Bracknell), Joanne Camp (Miss Prism), Rachel Botchan (Gwendolen Fairfax), Ali Ahn (Cecily Cardew), TJ Edwards (Rev. Canon Chasuble)

Setting: Algernon's flat in Half-Moon Street, London; the garden and drawing room/library of Worthing's Manor House in Woolton, Hertfordshire. Revival of a play presented in three acts with two intermissions; 80 St. Marks Place; April 15–June 8, 2008 (Opened April 27); 15 previews, 42 performances.

Sean McNall, Ali Ahn, Bradford Cover (front), Joanne Camp and TJ Edwards (back) in The Importance of Being Earnest *(photo by Gregory Costanzo)*

Playwrights Horizons

Thirty-Seventh Season

Artistic Director, Tim Sanford; Managing Director, Leslie Marcus; General Manager, William Russo;

Director of Musical Theatre, Christie Evangelisto; Literary Manager, Adam Greenfield; Casting, Alaine Alldaffer; Production Managers, Christopher Boll, Shannon Nicole Case; Development, Jill Garland; Controller, Anne Heibach; Marketing, Eric Winick; Director of Ticket Central, Emily Wilbur; School Director, Helen R. Cook; Company Manager, Caroline Aquino; Associate Production Manager, Shannon Nicole Case; Technical Director, Brian Coleman; Press, The Publicity Office, Marc Thibodeau, Michael S. Borowski

100 SAINTS YOU SHOULD KNOW by Kate Fodor; Director, Ethan McSweeny; Sets, Rachel Hauck; Costumes, Mimi O'Donnell; Lighting, Jane Cox; Sound, Matt Hubbs; PSM, Michaella K. McCoy, ASM, Brian Maschka; Vocal Coach, Wendy Waterman; Cast: Janel Moloney (Theresa), Jeremy Shamos (Matthew), Zoe Kazan (Abby), Lois Smith (Colleen), Will Rogers (Garrett)

World premiere of a new play presented in two acts; Mainstage Theater; August 24–September 30, 2007 (Opened September 18); 43 performances. Developed by Steppenwolf Theatre Company and originally workshopped at the Chautauqua Theater Company.

A FEMININE ENDING by Sarah Treem; Director, Blair Brown; Set, Cameron Anderson; Costumes, Michael Krass; Lighting, Ben Stanton; Original Music/Sound, Obadiah Eaves; PSM, Robyn Henry; ASM, Nicole Bouclier; Dramaturg, Christie Evangelisto; Cast: Gillian Jacobs (Amanda), Alec Beard (Jack), Marsha Mason (Kim), Richard Masur (David), Joe Paulik (Billy)

Setting: Brooklyn, NY and New Hampshire, the present. World premiere of a new play presented without intermission; Peter Jay Sharp Theater; October 4–November 11, 2007 (Opened October 17); 43 performances. Originally developed at JAW: A Playwrights Festival, Portland Center Stage, 2006.

DORIS TO DARLENE, A CAUTIONARY VALENTINE by Jordan Harrison; Director, Les Waters; Set, Takeshi Kata; Costumes, Christal Weatherly; Lighting, Jane Cox; Soundscape, Darron L West; Original Music, Kirsten Childs; Music Arrangement/Production, Victor Zupanc; PSM, Elizabeth Moreau; ASM, Marla K. Shaffer; Cast: de'Adre Aziza (Doris), Michael Crane (Vic Watts), Laura Heisler (King Ludwig II), David Chandler (Richard Wagner), Tobias Segal (Young Man), Tom Nelis (Mr. Campani)

World premiere of a new play with music presented in two acts; Mainstage Theatre; November 16–December 23, 2007 (Opened December 11); 44 performances.

DEAD MAN'S CELL PHONE by Sarah Ruhl; Director, Anne Bogart; Set/Costumes, G.W. Mercier; Lighting, Brian Scott; Soundscape, Darron L West; PSM, Elizabeth Moreau; ASM, Danielle Monica Long; Fight Director, Joseph Travers; Dialect Coach, Stephen Gabis; Cast:, Mary-Louise Parker (Jean), T. Ryder Smith (Gordon), Kathleen Chalfant (Mrs. Gottlieb), Carla Harting (The Other Woman), Kelly Maurer (Hermia), David Aaron Baker (Dwight)

New York premiere of a new play presented in two acts; Mainstage Theater; February 8–March 30, 2008 (Opened March 4); 56 performances. Originally produced by Woolly Mammoth Theatre Company, Washington, DC.

THE DRUNKEN CITY by Adam Bock; Director, Trip Cullman; Set, David Korins; Costumes, Jenny Mannis; Lighting, Matthew Richards, Sound, Bart Fasbender; Original Music, Michael Friedman; Choreography, John Carrafa; PSM, Bess Marie Glorioso; ASM, Ana M. Garcia; Cast: Maria Dizzia (Melissa), Cassie Beck (Marnie), Sue Jean Kim (Linda), Barrett Foa (Eddie), Mike Colter (Frank), Alfredo Narciso (Bob)

New York premiere of a new play presented without intermission; Peter Jay Sharp Theater; March 15–April 27, 2008 (Opened March 28); 45 performances. Commissioned by and originally premiered in July 2005 at Kitchen Theatre Company, Ithaca, NY (Rachel Lampert, Artistic Director), and subsequently revised during a developmental workshop with TheatreWorks of Palo Alto, California (Robert Kelly, Artistic Director). *2008 Theatre World Award:* Cassie Beck.

SAVED Music and lyrics by Michael Friedman, book and lyrics by John Dempsey and Rinne Groff; Based on the 2004 MGM motion picture with screenplay by Brian Dannelly and Michael Urban, directed by Mr. Dannelly; Director, Gary Griffin; Choreography, Sergio Trujillo; Set, Scott Pask; Costumes, Jess Goldstein; Lighting, Donald Holder; Sound, Brian Ronan; Music Director/Arrangements, Jesse Vargas; Orchestrations, Curtis Moore; Music Coordinator, John Miller; PSM, Judith Schoenfeld; Stage Manager, Michael McGoff; Assistant Director, David F. Chapman; Music Copying, Emily Grishman/Katharine Edmonds; Synthesizer Programmer, Randy Cohen; Cast: Celia Keenan-Bolger (Mary), John Dossett (Pastor Skip), Mary Faber (Hilary Faye), Juliana Ashley Hansen (Lana), Curtis Holbrook (Roland), Emily Walton (Tia), Aaron Tveit (Dean), Josh Breckenridge (Shane), Jason Michael Snow (Zac), Morgan Weed (Cassandra), Daniel Zaitchik (Jesus/Nurse/Mitch), Julia Murney (Lillian), Van Hughes (Patrick); Musicians: Jesse Vargas (Conductor/keyboards), Paul Staroba (Associate Conductor/keyboards), Jake Schwartz (guitars), Steve Gilewski (bass), Brad Carbone (drums)

Musical Numbers: In the Light of God, I'm Not That Kind of Girl, Orlando, I Can't Help It (The Love Song), What's Wrong With Me?, Make It True, Saved, What Am I Missing?, Prayers, Something Wrong, Changing, Heaven, The Pastor's Son, I'm Not The Man I Thought I'd Be, Prayers (reprise), How To, Prom, Corinthians

World premiere of a new musical presented in two acts; Mainstage Theater; May 9–June 22, 2008 (Opened June 3); 55 performances.

Primary Stages

Twenty-Third Season

Founder and Executive Producer, Casey Childs; Artistic Director, Andrew Leynse; Managing Director, Elliot Fox; Associate Artistic Director, Michelle Bossy; Literary Manager, Tessa LaNeve; Development, Erica Raven; Marketing, Louis Bavaro/Steven Box/Shanta Mali; Business Manager, Reuben Saunders; Production Supervisor, Peter R. Feuchtwanger; Casting, Stephanie Klapper; Press, O&M Co., Rick Miramontez, Philip Carrubba

OPUS by Michael Hollinger; Produced in association with Jamie deRoy; Director, Terrence J. Nolen; Set, James Kronzer; Costumes, Anne Kennedy; Lighting, Justin Townsend; Sound, Jorge Cousineau; PSM, Fred Hemminger; Assistant Director, Tessa LaNeve; ASM, Cambra Overend; Props, Stephanie Wiesner; Quartet Music, The Vertigo String Quartet (Jose Maria Blumenschein, Johannes Dickbauer, Lily Francis, Nicholas Canellakis; Cast: Douglas Rees (Carl), Richard Topol (Alan), David Beach (Elliot), Michael Laurence (Dorian), Mahira Kakkar (Grace)

Setting: Now, and a few years ago; various interiors in New York, Pittsburgh, and Washington, D.C. New York premiere of a new play presented without intermission; 59E59 Theater A; July 24–September 1, 2007 (Opened August 7); 14 previews, 28 performances. Originally produced in January, 2006 at Philadelphia's Arden Theatre and in March, 2006 at Pittsburgh's City Theatre Company.

DIVIDING THE ESTATE by Horton Foote; Produced in association with Jamie deRoy; Director, Michael Wilson; Set, Jeff Cowie; Costumes, David C. Woolard; Lighting, Rui Rita; Original Music and Sound, John Gromada; Wigs, Paul Huntley; Fight Director, B.H. Barry; PSM, Cole Bonenberger; Associate Director, Max Williams; ASM, Marisa Levy; Props, Matthew Hodges; Cast: Devon Abner (Son), Elizabeth Ashley (Stella), Penny Fuller (Lucille), Lynda Gravátt (Mildred), Arthur French (Doug), Gerald McRaney (Lewis), Keiana Richard (Cathleen), Maggie Lacey (Pauline), Hallie Foote (Mary Jo), Jenny Dare Paulin (Emily), Nicole Lowrance (Sissie), James Demarse (Bob), Virginia Kull (Irene); Replacement: Pat Bowie (Mildred)

Setting: 1987; Harrison, Texas. New York premiere of a new play presented in two acts; 59E59 Theater A; September 18–October 28, 2007 (Opened September 27); 9 previews, 33 performances. An earlier version of the play was produced in 1989 at the McCarter Theatre (Princeton, New Jersey).

Penny Fuller, Hallie Foote and Elizabeth Ashley in Dividing the Estate *(photo by James Leynse)*

HUNTING AND GATHERING by Brooke Berman; Director, Leigh Silverman; Set, David Korins; Costumes, Miranda Hoffman; Lighting, Ben Stanton, Original Music & Sound,

Robert Kaplowitz; PSM, Kate Hefel; ASM, Andrea Hayward; Cast: Keira Naughton (Ruth), Michael Chernus (Astor), Jeremy Shamos (Jesse), Mamie Gummer (Bess)

Setting: The present, New York City. World premiere of a new play presented without intermission; 59E59 Theater A; January 22–March 1, 2008 (Opened February 3); 14 previews, 28 performances.

SOMETHING YOU DID by Willy Holtzman; Director, Carolyn Cantor; Set, Eugene Lee; Costumes, Jenny Mannis; Lighting, Jeff Croiter; Original Music and Sound, Lindsay Jones; PSM, Samone B. Weissman; ASM, Lyndsey Goode; Assistant Director, Christopher Czyz; Props, Meghan Buchanan; Cast: Portia (Uneeq), Joanna Gleason (Alison), Jordan Charney (Arthur), Victor Slezak (Gene), Adriane Lenox (Lenora)

New York premiere of a new play presented without intermission; 59E59 Theater A; March 18–April 26, 2008 (Opened April 1); 14 previews, 27 performances. Originally produced October 2006 by People's Light & Theatre Company, Malvern, Pennsylvania (Abigail Adams, Artistic Director; Grace E. Grillet, Managing Director).

The Public Theater

Fifty-Second Season

Artistic Director, Oskar Eustis; Executive Director, Mara Manus; General Manager, Nicki Genovese; Associate Producers, Peter Dubois, Mandy Hackett, Jenny Gersten; Casting, Jordan Thaler, Heidi Griffiths; Director of Production, Ruth E. Sternberg; Marketing, Ilene Rosen; Communications, Candi Adams; Development, Casey Reitz; IT, Russell Richardson; Finance, Jack Feher; Ticket Services, Jimmy Goodsey; Press, Sam Neuman

365 DAYS/365 PLAYS by Suzan-Lori Parks; November 13, 2006–November 12, 2007; *365 Days/365 Plays* National Festival presented the work simultaneously across the country, creating the largest collaboration in the history of American theater. The Public Theater spearheads the New York festival. Over the course of the year, over 60 selected theater companies—curated by The Public and the *365 Days/365 Plays* National Festival—perform these brief, brilliant plays. Participants: Week 30 (June 4–10): Hip-Hop Theater Festival; Week 31 (June 11–17): Despina and Company; Week 32 (June 18-24): Alec Duffy; Week 33 (June 25–July 1): duende arts; Week 34 (July 2–8): Boomerang Theatre Company, Dixon Place, Delacorte Theater, Shakespeare Lab at the Public, The Tank; Week 35 (July 9-15): Partial Comfort Productions, RAACA's Seaport Salon, Robot Vs. Dinosaur, Untitled Theater Company #61, Collaboration Town, Gansfeld Theatre Company, Vortex Theater Company; Week 37 (July 23-29): Genesius Theatre Group, The Faux-Real Theatre Company, SLANT Theatre Project, Temporary Theatre Company; Week 38 (July 30–August 5): 3-d, Engine 37, Lucid Theatre, The TEAM; Week 39 (August 6–12): Ma Yi Theatre Company; Week 40 (August 13–19): TADA! Youth Theater; Week 41 (August 20–26): Classical Theatre of Harlem; Week 42 (August 27–September 2): MUD/BONE; Week 43 (September 3–9): The H.A.D.L.E.Y. Players; Week 44 (September 10–16): LAByrinth Theater; Week 45 (September 17–23): The Brick Theater; Week 46 (September 24–30): viBe Theater Experience; Week 47 (October 1–7): Rising Phoenix Repertory; Week 48 (October 8–14): Universes; Week 49 (October 15–21): Rebel Theater Company; Week 50 (October 22–28): HERE Arts Center; Week 51 (October 29–November 4); Pig Iron Theatre Company; Week 52 (November 5-12): The Public Theater

ROMEO AND JULIET by William Shakespeare; Director, Michael Greif; Sets, Mark Wendland; Costumes, Emilio Sosa; Lighting, Donald Holder; Composer, Michael Friedman; Sound, Acme Sound Partners; Fight Director, Rick Sordelet; Choreographer, Sergio Trujillo; PSM, Michael McGoff; Cast: Opal Alladin (Lady Capulet), Lauren Ambrose (Juliet), George Bartenieff (Lord Montague/Apothecary/ Cousin Capulet), Dan Colman (Paris), Michael Cristofer (Lord Capulet), (Ensemble), Saidah Arrika Ekulona (Lady Montague), Brian Tyree Henry (Tybalt), Oscar Isaac (Romeo), Camryn Manheim (Nurse), Owiso Odera (Benvolio), Austin Pendleton (Friar Laurence), Timothy D. Stickney (Prince Escalus), Christopher Evan Welch (Mercutio); Ensemble/Understudies: Ari Brand, Anthony Carrigan, Tiffany Danielle, Seth Duerr, Quincy Dunn-Baker, Christian Felix, Susan Hyon, Orville Mendoza, Jeffrey Omura, Lucas Papaelias, Alex Podulke, Mary Rasmussen, Cornelius Smith, Jr., Alexander Sovronsky

Revival of the play presented in two acts; Delacorte Theater; June 6–July 8, 2007 (Opened June 24); 16 previews, 13 performances.

A MIDSUMMER NIGHT'S DREAM by William Shakespeare; Director, Daniel Sullivan; Sets, Eugene Lee; Costumes, Ann Hould-Ward; Lighting, Michael Chybowski; Composer, Dan Moses Schreier; Sound, Acme Sound Partners; Choreographer, David Neumann; PSM, James Latus; Stage Manager, Buzz Cohen; Dramaturg, Silvana Tropea; Fight Director, Thomas Schall; Magic Consultant, Mark Mitton; Voice and Speech, Claudia Hill-Sparks; Music Director, Steven Malone; Orchestrations, Jonathan Tunick; Assistant Director, Lauren Keating; Cast: Opal Alladin (Hippolyta), Jason Antoon (Tom Snout), Chelsea Bacon (First Fairy), Ken Cheeseman (Robin Starveling), Keith David (Oberon), Mireille Enos (Hermia), Jesse Tyler Ferguson (Francis Flute), Herb Foster (Philostrate),

Simon Garratt (Fairy), Jon Michael Hill (Puck/Robin Goodfellow), Erica Huang (Fairy), Cassady Leonard (Fairy), Austin Lysy (Lysander), Lily Maketansky (Fairy), George Morfogen (Egeus), Tim Blake Nelson (Peter Quince), Daniel Oreskes (Theseus), Martha Plimpton (Helena), Laila Robins (Titania), Lina Silver (Fairy), Jay O. Sanders (Nick Bottom), Keith Randolph Smith (Snug), Jack Tartaglia (Fairy), Elliot Villar (Demetrius); Ensemble/Understudies: Christine Corpuz, Ben Huber, Mallory Portnoy

Revival of the play with original music presented in two acts; Delacorte Theater; August 8–September 9, 2007 (Opened August 23); 13 previews, 16 performances.

Keith David, Laila Robins, and Jay O. Sanders in A Midsummer Night's Dream *(photo by James Leynse)*

HAIR Book and lyrics by James Rado and Gerome Ragni, music by Galt MacDermot; Director, Diane Paulus; Scenic Consultant, Scott Pask; Costumes, Michael McDonald; Lighting, Michael Chybowski; Sound, Acme Sound Partners; Movement Coordinator, Karole Armitage; Music Director, Rob Fisher; Cast: Allison Case (Crissy), Jonathan Groff (Claude), Andrew Kober (Father/Margaret Mead), Megan Lawrence (Mother), Patina Miller (Dionne), Darius Nichols (Hud), Karen Olivo (Sheila), Bryce Ryness (Woof), Kacie Sheik (Jeanie), Will Swenson (Berger), Nicole Lewis, Saycon Sengbloh (White Boys Trio/Tribe); Alisan Porter, Megan Reinking (Black Boys Trio/Tribe); Tribe: Ato Blankson-Wood, Steel Burkhardt, Lauren Elder, Allison Guinn, Anthony Hollock, Kaitlin Kiyan, John Moauro, Brandon Pearson, Paris Remillard, Maya Sharpe, Theo Stockman, Tommar Wilson

40th Anniversary concert version of the musical presented as part of Joe's Pub in the Park; Delacorte Theater; September 22–24, 2007; 3 performances. *Hair* was the first off-Broadway musical to transfer to Broadway and was the show that officially opened The Public Theater's long-time home on Lafayette Street. The original production premiered October 17, 1967 and ran for six weeks; transferred on April 29, 1968 running 1,873 performances (see *Theatre World* Volume 24, pages 59, 111).

THE WOOSTER GROUP'S *HAMLET* by William Shakespeare; Presented in association with St. Ann's Warehouse and special arrangement with Paul Brownstein; Director, Elizabeth LeCompte; Sets, Ruud van den Akker; Lighting, Jennifer Tipton and Gabe Maxson; Sound, Geoff Abbas, Joby Emmons & Matt Schloss; Video, Reid Farrington; Video Operator, Andrew Schneider; Costumes, Claudia Hill; Production Manager, Bozkurt Karasu; Assistant to the Director, Teresa Hartmann; Technical Director/Video Operator, Aron Deyo; Fight Coach, Felix Ivanov; Movement Coach, Natalie Thomas; Songs, Fischerspooner; Additional Music, Warren Fischer; PSM, Buzz Cohen; Stage Manager, Ruth E. Sternberg; Cast: Scott Shepherd (Hamlet), Ari Fliakos (Claudius/Marcellus/Ghost/Gravedigger), Kate Valk (Gertrude/Ophelia), Bill Raymond (Polonius), Casey Spooner (Laertes/Rosencrantz/Guildenstern/Player King), Judson Williams (Horatio), Dominique Bousquet (Nurse), Alessandro Magania (Attendant/Soldier/Banister), Daniel Pettrow (Bernardo/Rosencrantz/Guildenstern/Player Queen/Osric)

Revival of a an experimental theatrical piece presented in two acts; Anspacher Theater; October 9–December 2, 2007 (Opened October 31); 19 previews, 29 performances. Previously presented at St. Ann's Warehouse last season (see *Theatre World* Volume 63).

THE BROTHERS SIZE by Tarell Alvin McCraney; Produced in association with the Foundry Theatre; Director, Tea Alagic; Set, Peter Ksander, Douglas Stein; Costumes, Zane Pihlstrom; Lighting, Burke Brown; Original Composition, Vincent Olivieri; Percussion/Additional Composition, Jonathan M. Pratt; PSM, Barbara Reo; Stage Manager, Katrina Lynn Olson; Assistant Director, Awoye Timpo; Dialects, Charlotte Fleck; Cast: Gilbert Owuor (Ogun), Brian Tyree Henry (Oshoosi), Elliot Villar (Elegba)

Setting: San Pere, Louisiana near the Bayou in the distant present. World premiere of a new play presented without intermission; Shiva Theater; October 23–December 23, 2007 (Opened November 6); 15 previews, 56 performances.

YELLOW FACE by David Henry Hwang; Co-produced by Center Theatre Group; Director, Leigh Silverman; Sets, David Korins; Costumes, Myung Hee Cho; Lighting, Donald Holder; Soundscape, Darron L West; PSM, Cole P. Bonenberger; Rebecca Goldstein-Glaze; Assistant Director, Emily Campbell; Consultant, Lisa Shriver; Cast: Noah Bean (Marcus), Francis Jue (HYH and others), Julienne Hanzelka Kim (Leah and others), Kathryn A. Layng (Jane Miles and others), Hoon Lee (DHH), Lucas Caleb Rooney (Stuart, Rocco and others), Anthony Torn (Announcer and [Name Withheld on Advice of Counsel])

Hoon Lee and Noah Bean in Yellow Face *(photo by Joan Marcus)*

Setting: 1988-The Present. New York, Los Angeles, Washington D.C, San Francisco, Boston, and Guizhou Province, China. World premiere of a play with songs presented in two acts; Martinson Theater; February 9–March 25, 2007 (Opened March 7); 23 previews, 39 performances. Previously played at the Mark Taper Forum May 10–July 1, 2007. *2008 Theatre World Award:* Hoon Lee

CONVERSATIONS IN TUSCULUM Written and directed by Richard Nelson; Sets, Thomas Lynch; Costumes, Susan Hilferty; Lighting, Jennifer Tipton; Original Music and Sound, John Gromada; PSM, Matthew L. Silver; Stage Manager, Jillian M. Oliver; Assistant Director, Niegel Smith; Cast: Aidan Quinn (Brutus), Gloria Reuben (Porcia), David Strathairn (Cassius), Maria Tucci (Servilia), Brian Dennehy (Cicero), Joe Grifasi (Syrus)

Setting: May–September, 45 B.C. Villas and hillsides in Tusculum, Italy. World premiere of a new play presented in two acts; Anspacher Theater; February 19–March 30, 2008 (Opened March 11); 23 previews, 15 performances.

DRUNK ENOUGH TO SAY I LOVE YOU? by Caryl Churchill; Co-presented with The Royal Court Theatre; Director, James MacDonald; Sets, Eugene Lee; Costumes, Susan Hilferty; Lighting, Peter Mumford; Sound, Daniel Erdberg; Music, Matthew Herbert; PSM, Michael McGoff; Stage Manager, Elizabeth Miller; Assistant Director, Awoye Timpo; Assistant Director/Dramaturg, Lyndsey Turner; Original Sound, Ian Dickinson; Cast: Samuel West (Guy), Scott Cohen (Sam)

American premiere of a new play presented without intermission; Newman Theater; March 5–April 6, 2008 (Opened March 16); 12 previews, 35 performances. World premiere at the Royal Court Theatre, London, November 10–December 22, 2006.

KICKING A DEAD HORSE Written and directed by Sam Shepard; Co-produced by the Abbey Theatre (Director, Flach Mac Conghail); Set, Brien Vahey; Lighting, John Comiskey; Costumes, Joan Bergin; Sound, Dan Moses Schreier; PSM, Barbara Reo; Cast: Stephen Rea (Hobart Struther), Elissa Piszel (Young Woman)

American premiere of a new play presented without intermission; Martinson Hall; June 25–August 10, 2008 (Opened July 14); 24 previews, 32 performances.

LAByrinth Theater

In residence at The Public Theater

Sixteenth Season

Artistic Directors, John Ortiz, Philip Seymour Hoffman; Co-Artistic Director/Executive Director, John Gould Rubin; Associate Producer, Marieke Gaboury; Associate Artistic Director, Florencia Lozano; Marketing, Trevor Brown; Development, Veronica R. Bainbridge; Company Manager, Kristina Poe; Production Manager, Peter Dean; Literary Manager, Andrea Ciannavei; Marketing/Development Associate, Lyssa Mandel; Technical Director, Charles Romaine; Office Manager, Nikki Hughes; Press, O&M Co., Rick Miramontez, Philip Carrubba

A VIEW FROM 151ST STREET by Bob Glaudini; Director, Peter DuBois; Set, David Korins; Costumes, Mimi O'Donnell; Lighting; Japhy Weideman; Sound, Bart Fasbender; Composer, Michael Cain; Musical Director, Paul J. Thompson; Conductor, Bryan Noll; Musicians: Andrew Emer (band leader), Nir Felder, and Q; PSM, Nicola Rossini; ASM, Libby Steiner; Projections, luckydave; Assistant Director, Damon Arrington; Props, Jeremy Chernick; Vocal Coach, Andrea Haring; Fight Choreographer, Qui Nguyen; Cast: Gbenga Akinnagbe (Dwight), Liza Colón-Zayas (Lena), Craig "muMs" Grant (Delroy), Juan Carlos Hernandez (Daniel), Russell G. Jones (Monroe), Marisa Malone (Mara), Elizabeth Rodriguez (Irene), Andre Royo (Ray)

Setting: New York City; the present. World premiere new play with music presented in two acts; LuEsther Hall; October 10–November 5, 2006 (Opened October 22); 11 previews, 22 performances. Previously read in the 2006 Barn Series.

UNCONDITIONAL by Brett C. Leonard; Director, Mark Wing-Davey; Set, Mark Wendland; Costumes, Mimi O'Donnell; Lighting, Japhy Weideman; Sound, Bart Fasbender; PSM, Libby Steiner; ASM, Libby Unsworth; Additional Casting, Judy Bowman; Special Effects/Props, Jeremy Chernick; Fight Choreographer, Qui Nguyen; Assistant

Saidah Arrika Ekulona and Kevin Geer in Unconditional (photo by Monique Carboni)

Director, Scott Illingworth; Cast: Chris Chalk (Spike), Anna Chlumsky (Missy), John Doman (Keith), Saidah Arrika Ekulona (Lotty), Kevin Geer (Gary), Trevor Long (Daniel), Elizabeth Rodriguez (Jessica), Yolanda Ross (Tracie), Iaiah Whitlock, Jr. (Newton)

Setting: New York City. World premiere of a new play performed in two acts; LuEsther Hall; February 7–March 2. 2008 (Opened February 18); 9 previews, 24 performances.

LITTLE FLOWER OF EAST ORANGE by Stephen Adly Guirgis; Joint Production with the Public Theater; Director, Philip Seymour Hoffman; Set, Narelle Sissons; Costumes, Mimi O'Donnell; Lighting, Japhy Weideman; Composer/Sound, David Van Tieghem; Choreography, Barry McNabb; Casting, Jordan Thaler/Heidi Griffiths; PSM, Monica Moore; ASM, Kat West; Production Manager, Peter Dean; Props, Jeremy Lydic; Assistant Director, Brian Roff; Hair/Makeup Consultant, Randy Houston Mercer; Vocal Coach, Andrea Haring; Speech Coach, Louis Coliaianni; Video, Charles Grantham, Pauly Burke; Sign Interpreter, Mary Carter; Cast: Ellen Burstyn (Therese Marie), Elizabeth Canavan (Aunt Margaret/Justina/Nurse 2), Liza Colón-Zayas (Magnolia/Nurse 1/Pope John XXIII), Arthur French (Detective Baker/Jimmy Stewart/Father Lander/Orderly), Gillian Jacobs (Nadine/Cathleen); Ajay Naidu (Dr. Shankar), Howie Seago (Francis James), Michael Shannon (Danny), Sidney Williams (David Halzig/Plainclothes Detective/Surgeon 1/Bobby Kennedy/Uncle Barney), David Zayas (Espinosa/Surgeon 2)

Setting: New York City. The present and the past. World premiere of a new play performed in two acts; Martinson Hall; March 18–May 4, 2008 (Opened April 6); 22 previews, 17 performances.

Rattlestick Playwrights Theater

Thirteenth Season

Co-Founder/Artistic Director, David Van Asselt; Managing Director, Sandra Coudert; Associate Artistic Director, Lou Moreno; Production Manager, Kathryn Pierroz; Literary Associate, Christine Rydeck; Box Office Manager, Ira Lopez; Casting, Jodi Collins; Press, O&M Co.

AMERICAN SLIGO Written and directed by Adam Rapp; Set, John McDermott; Costumes, Daphne Javitch, Lighting, Ben Stanton; Sound, Eric Shim; Fight Choreographer, Rick Sordelet; PSM, Jess Johnston; ASM, Zac Chandler; Assistant Director, Dominic D'Andrea; Cast: Guy Boyd (Art Sligo), Marylouise Burke (Aunt Bobbie), Michael Chernus (Kyle Sligo), Emily Cass McDonnell (Lucy), Megan Mostyn-Brown (Cammie), Paul Sparks (Victor Sligo), Matthew Stadelmann (Bobby Bibby)

World premiere of a new play presented without intermission; Theatre 224 Waverly; September 12–October 14, 2007 (Opened September 24); 28 performances.

RAG AND BONE by Noah Haidle; Director, Sam Gold; Sets, Dane Laffrey; Costumes, Oana Botez-Ban; Lighting, Ben Stanton; Sound, Eric Shim; Fight Choreography, David Anzuelo; Stage Manager, Christina Lowe; ASM, Heather Davidson; Assistant Director, D. Wambui Richardson; Props, Brandon Giles; Cast: Michael Chernus (George), Kevin Jackson (Pimp), Deirdre O'Connell (Hooker), Matthew Stadelmann (Jeff), Henry Stram (Poet), Audrey Lynn Weston (Customer/Waiter), David Wohl (Millionaire)

New York premiere of a new play presented in two acts; Theatre 224 Waverly; November 14–December 16, 2007 (Opened November 20); 26 performances.

WAR by Lars Norén; Director, Anders Cato; Translator, Marita Lindholm Gochman; Sets, Van Santvoord; Costumes, Meghan E. Healey; Lighting, Ed McCarthy; Composer/Sound, Eric Shim; Dramaturg, Ulrika Josephsson; Stage Manager, Kyle Gates; ASM, Molly Eustis; Assistant Director, Zoe Aja Moore; Technical Director, Brian MacInnis Smallwood; Cast: Ngozi Anyanwu (Beenina), Rosalyn Coleman (Mother), Flora Diaz (Semira), Laith Nakli (Father), Alok Tewari (Uncle Ivan)

American premiere of a new play presented without intermission; Theatre 224 Waverly; January 31–March 2, 2008 (Opened February 11); 28 performances.

STEVE & IDI by David Grimm; Director, Eleanor Holdridge; Set, Kris Stone; Costumes, Jessica Ford; Lighting, Les Dickert; Sound, Scott Killian; Composer/Sound Design, Scott Killian; Props, Mary Robinette Kowal; Dialects, Doug Honorof; Stage Manager, Emily M. Arnold; ASM, Jacqueline Prats; Fight

Choreography, Michael Rossi; Cast: David Grimm (Steve), Evan Parke (Idi Amin), Michael Busillo (Brad), Greg Keller (Ralph), Zachary Knower (Max)

Setting: Brooklyn, NY, the present. World premiere of a new play presented in two acts; Theatre 224 Waverly; April 23–May 24, 2008 (Opened May 8); 26 performances.

Henry Stram and Deirdre O'Connell in Rag and Bone *(photo by Sandra Coudert)*

Roundabout Theatre Company

Forty-Second Season

Artistic Director, Todd Haimes; Managing Director, Harold Wolpert; Executive Director, Julia C. Levy; Associate Artistic Director, Scott Ellis; Founding Director, Gene Feist; Artistic Development/Casting, Jim Carnahan; Education, David A. Miller; General Manager, Sydney Beers; General Manager Steinberg Center, Rebecca Habel; Finance, Susan Neiman; Marketing/Sales Promotion, David B. Steffen; Development, Jeffory Lawson; Sales, Charlie Garbowski, Jr.; Production Manager, Kai Brothers; Company Manager, Nicholas Caccavo; Casting, Mele Nagler; Press, Boneau/Bryan-Brown, Jessica Johnson

Laura Pels Theatre

THE OVERWHELMING by J.T. Rogers; Director, Max Stafford-Clark; Set, Tim Shortall; Costumes, Tobin Ost; Lighting, David Weiner; Sound, Gareth Fry; Hair/Makeup, Justen M. Brosnan; Dialects, Beth McGuire; Fight Director, Rick Sordelet; PSM, Pat Sosnow; Casting, Carrie Gardner; Stage Manager, Gregori T. Livoti; Associate Production Manager, Michael Wade; Cast: Mark Blum (Charles Woolsey/British Doctor), Chris Chalk (Gérard), Ron Cephas Jones (Joseph Gasana), Tisola Logan (Emiritha), Boris McGiver (Jean-Claude Buisson/Jan Verbeek), Owiso Odera (Rwandan Man/Policeman/UN Major), Charles Parnell (Samuel Mizinga), Linda Powell (Linda White-Keeler), Sam Robards (Jack Exley), Michael Stahl-David (Geoffrey Exley), Sharon Washington (Rwandan Doctor/Elise Kayitesi); Understudies: Christopher Abbott (Geoffrey), Peter Bradbury (Exley), Chinasa Ogbuagu (White-Keeler, Elise/Rwandan Doctor, Emirtha), Maduka Steady (Gérard, Rwandan Man/Policeman/UN Major), Daniel Stewart (Woolsey/British Doctor, Buisson/Verbeek), Andrew Stewart-Jones (Mizinga, Gasana)

Setting: Kigali, Rwanda, early 1994. American premiere of a new play presented in two acts; September 28–December 23, 2007 (Opened October 23); 29 previews, 72 performances. World premiere presented at the National Theatre of Great Britain's Cottesloe Theatre, Theatre, in association with Out of Joint, in May 2006.

CRIMES OF THE HEART by Beth Henley; Director, Kathleen Turner; Sets, Anna Louizos; Costumes, David Murin; Lighting, Natasha Katz; Original Music/Sound, John Gromada; Wigs, Paul Huntley; Dialects, Deborah Hecht; PSM, Charles Means; Casting, Tara Rubin; Stage Manager, Elizabeth Moloney; Assistant Director, Jacob Murphy; Associate Production Manager, Mike Wade; Cast: Jennifer Dundas (Lenny Magrath), Jessica Stone (Chick Boyle), Patch Darragh (Doc Porter), Sarah Paulson (Meg Magrath), Lily Rabe (Babe Botrelle), Chandler Williams (Barnette Lloyd); Understudies: Jessica Cummings (Babe, Chick), Mycah Hogan (Doc, Lloyd), Kelly Mares (Meg, Lenny)

Setting: The Magrath sisters' house in Hazlehurst, Mississippi, fall of 1974. Revival of the play in three acts presented with one intermission; January 16–April 20, 2008 (Opened February 14); 31 previews, 77 performances. Originally produced at Actors Theatre of Louisville. New York premiere at Manhattan Theatre Club, December 9, 1980–January 11, 1981 (see *Theatre World* Volume 37, page 125); opened on Broadway at the Golden Theatre November 4, 1981 (see *Theatre World* Volume 38, page 13).

THE MARRIAGE OF BETTE AND BOO by Christopher Durang; Director, Walter Bobbie; Set, David Korins; Costumes, Susan Hilferty; Lighting, Donald Holder; Sound, Acme Sound Partners; PSM, Robyn Henry; Stage Manager, Bryce McDonald; Casting, Carrie Gardner; Assistant Director, David Ruttura; Associate Production Manager, Michael Wade; Properties, Julia Sandy; Cast: Kate Jennings Grant (Bette Brennan), Victoria Clark (Margaret Brennan), Adam Lefevre (Paul Brennan), Zoe Lister-Jones (Joan Brennan), Heather Burns (Emily Brennan), Christopher Evan Welch (Boo Hudlocke), John Glover (Karl Hudlocke), Julie Hagerty (Soot Hudlocke), Terry Beaver (Father Donnally/Doctor), Charles

Socarides (Matt); Understudies: Jessie Austrian (Bette, Emily, Joan), Ian Blackman (Karl, Paul), Ben Hollandsworth (Matt), Lizbeth Mackay (Soot, Margaret), Michael Warner (Boo, Father Donnally/Doctor)

Revival of the play presented in two acts; June 12–September 7, 2008 (Opened July 13); 34 previews, 69 performances. Originally produced by the Public Theater May 16–July 28, 1985 (see *Theatre World* Volume 41, page 114).

Heather Burns, Zoe Lister-Jones, Adam LeFevre, Victoria Clark, Kate Jennings Grant, Christopher Evan Welch, Julie Hagerty, John Glover in The Marriage of Bette and Boo *(photo by Joan Marcus)*

Roundabout Underground – Black Box Theatre – Premiere Production

SPEECH AND DEBATE by Stephen Karam; Director, Jason Moore; Set, Anna Louizos; Costumes, Heather Dunbar; Lighting, Justin Townsend; Choreography, Boo Killebrew; PSM, James FitzSimmons; Production Manager, Michael Wade; Sound/Projections, Brett Jarvis; Cast: Susan Blackwell (Teacher/Reporter), Jason Fuchs (Solomon), Gideon Glick (Howie), Sarah Steele (Diwata)

Setting: A classroom at North Salem High School in Salem, Oregon the present. World premiere of a comedy presented without intermission; October 5, 2007–February 24, 2008 (Opened October 29); 29 previews, 130 performances.

Second Stage Theatre

Twenty-Ninth Season

Artistic Director, Carole Rothman; Executive Director, Ellen Richard; Associate Artistic Director, Christopher Burney; Production Manager, Jeff Wild; Finance, Janice B. Cwill; Management, Don-Scott Cooper; Development, Sarah Bordy; Sales, Jeff Collins; Marketing, Robert Marlin; Ticket Services Manager, Greg Turner; Technical Director, Robert G. Mahon III; Literary Manager, Sara Bagley; Casting, Tara Rubin; Press, Barlow-Hartman, Tom D'Ambrosio, Ryan Ratelle

EDWARD ALBEE'S *PETER AND JERRY* Act One: *Homelife;* Act Two: *The Zoo Story;* Director, Pam MacKinnon; Set, Neil Patel; Costumes, Theresa Squire; Lighting, Kevin Adams; PSM, C.A. Clark; Stage Manager, Annette Verga-Lagier; Fight Director, Brent Langdon; Props, Susan Barras; Cast: Johanna Day (Ann), Bill Pullman (Peter), Dallas Roberts (Jerry)

Setting: Act One: Peter and Ann's living room, East 70's, New York City. Act 2: Central Park. New York premiere and revival of a play presented in two acts; October 19–December 9, 2007 (Opened November 11); 28 previews, 57 performances. *The Zoo Story* premiered in at Provincetown Playhouse on January 14, 1960 in a double bill with Samuel Becket's *Krapp's Last Tape* (see *Theatre World* Volume 16, page 140). *Homelife,* written as a prequel to the *The Zoo Story,* premiered in 2004 at Hartford Stage.

NEXT TO NORMAL Music by Tom Kitt, book and lyrics by Brian Yorkey; Director, Michael Greif; Musical Staging, Sergio Trujillo; Set, Mark Wendland; Costumes, Jeff Mahshie; Lighting, Kevin Adams; Sound, Brian Ronan; Musical Director, Mary-Mitchell Campbell; Orchestrations, Michael Starobin, Tom Kitt; Vocal Arrangements, AnnMarie Milazzo; Music Coordinator, Michael Keller; Casting, Telsey + Company; PSM, Judith Schoenfeld; Stage Manager, Lori Ann Zepp; Assistant Director, Anthony Rapp; Assistant Musical Director, Julie McBride; Van Lier Assistant Director, Jade King Carroll; Assistant Choreographer, Dontee Kiehn; Music Copying, Emily Grishman; Creative Assistant, Laura Pietropinto; Cast: Adam Chanler-Berat (Henry), Jennifer Damiano (Natalie), Brian d'Arcy James (Dan), Alice Ripley (Diana), Asa Somers (Dr. Madden/Dr. Fine), Aaron Tveit (Gabe); Understudies: Corey Boardman (Henry, Gabe), Kevin Kern (Dan, Dr. Madden/Dr. Fine), Jessica Phillips (Diana), Morgan Weed (Natalie); Musicians: Mary Mitchell-Campbell (Conductor/piano), Michael Aarons (guitar/additional arrangements), Damien Bassman (drums/percussion/additional arrangements), Christian Hebel (violin/keyboard), Randy Landau (bass), Ted Mook (cello)

A new musical presented in two acts; January 16–March 16, 2008 (Opened February 13); 33 previews, 37 performances. Developed at Village Theatre, Issaquah, Washington (Robb Hunt, Executive Producer; Steve Tompkins, Artistic Director). An earlier version (entitled *Feeling Electric*) was presented in the 2005 Musical Theatre Festival.

GOOD BOYS AND TRUE by Roberto Aguirre-Sacasa; Director, Scott Ellis; Set, Derek McLane; Costumes, Tom Broecker; Lighting, Kenneth Posner; Original Music, Lewis Flinn; PSM, Diane DiVita; Stage Manager, Megan Smith; Casting, Mele Nagler; Assistant Director, Kareem Fahmy; Props,

Bill Pullman and Dallas Roberts in Peter and Jerry *(photo by Joan Marcus)*

Susan Barras; Cast: Christopher Abbott (Justin Simmons), Betty Gilpin (Cheryl Moody), Kellie Overbey (Maddy Emerson), Brian J. Smith (Brandon Hardy), J. Smith-Cameron (Elizabeth Hardy), Lee Tergesen (Coach Russell Shea)

New York premiere of a new play presented without intermission; April 23–June 1, 2008 (Opened May 19); 31 previews, 16 performances. World premiere at Chicago's Steppenwolf Theatre, December, 2007

SOME AMERICANS ABROAD by Richard Nelson; Director, Gordon Edelstein; Set, Michael Yeargan; Costumes, Jennifer von Mayrhauser; Lighting, Donald Holder; Original Music/Sound, John Gromada; PSM, Charles M. Turner III; Stage Manager, Courtney James; Cast: Tom Cavanagh (Joe Taylor), Corey Stoll (Philip Brown), Anthony Rapp (Henry McNeil), Emily Bergl (Betty McNeill), Enid Graham (Frankie Lewis), Cristin Milioti (Katie Taylor), Pamela Peyton-Wright (Harriet Baldwin), John Cunningham (Orson Baldwin), Halley Feiffer (Joanne Smith), Todd Weeks (An American), Fiona Dourif (Donna Silliman)

Setting: 1989; various locations in England. Revival of a play presented in two acts; June 26–August 3, 2008 (Opened July 24); 33 previews, 13 performances. Originally performed at the The Pit, London, July 19, 1989. Originally produced on Broadway at the Vivian Beaumont May 2–June 17, 1990 (see *Theatre World* Volume 46, page 81).

Second Stage Uptown Series

LEN, ASLEEP IN VINYL by Carly Mensch; Director, Jackson Gay; Set, Wilson Chin; Costumes, Jessica Ford; Lighting, Matthew Richards; Sound, Mark Huang; PSM, Lori Ann Zepp; Stage Manager, Stephanie Gatton; Cast: Michael Cullen (Len), Megan Ferguson (Zoe), Daniel Eric Gold (Max), Leslie Lyles (Isabelle), Dan McCabe (William)

World premiere of a new play presented without intermission; McGinn/Cazale Theater; May 13–June 22, 2008 (Opened June 2); 22 previews, 22 performances.

ANIMALS OUT OF PAPER by Rajiv Joseph; Director, Giovanna Sardelli; Set, Beowulf Boritt; Costumes, Amy Clark; Lighting, Josh Bradford; Sound, Bart Fasbender; PSM, Lori Ann Zepp; Cast: Utkarsh Ambudkar (Suresh), Kellie Overbey (Ilana), Jeremy Shamos (Andy)

World premiere of a new play presented; McGinn/Cazale Theater; July 15–August 24, 2008 (Opened August 4); 22 previews, 23 performances.

Signature Theatre Company

Seventeenth Season

Founding Artistic Director, James Houghton; Executive Director, Erika Mallin; Associate Artistic Director, Beth Whitaker; Theatre Advancement, Jennie Greer; Development, Katherine Jaeger; General Manager, Adam Bernstein; Production Manager, Paul Ziemer; Marketing Manager, Nella Vera; Literary Associate/Dramaturg, Kirsten Bowen; Box Office Manager, Chris Fuller; Casting, Bernard Telsey; Press, The Publicity Office (first show) & Boneau/Bryan-Brown, Juliana Hannett, Matt Ross

Playwright in residence: Charles Mee

IPHIGENIA 2.0 Based on *Iphigenia at Aulus* by Euripides; Director, Tina Landau; Set, Blythe R.D. Quinlan; Lighting, Scott Zielinski; Costumes, Anita Yavich; Sound, Jill BC DuBoff; PSM, Winnie Y. Lok; ASM, Chandra LaViolette; Assistant Director, Kim Weild; Props, Susan Barras; Cast: Angelo Niakas (Greek Man), JD Goldblatt (Soldier 1), Will Fowler (Soldier 2), Jimonn Cole (Soldier 3), Jesse Hooker (Soldier 4), Rocco Sisto (Menelaus), Seth Numrich (Achilles), Louisa Krause (Iphigenia), Emily Kinney (Bridesmaid 1), Chasten Harmon (Bridesmaid 2), Kate Mulgrew (Clytemnestra), Tom Nelis (Agamemnon)

New York premiere of a reinvention of the classic play presented without intermission; Peter Norton Space; August 7–October 7, 2007 (Opened August 23); 21 previews, 46 performances.

QUEENS BOULEVARD (the musical) Inspired by the Katha-Kali play *The Flower of Good Fortune* by Kottayan Tampuran; Songs by Shoukichi Kina, Anu Malik & Craig Pruess, Benny Andersson, Björn Ulvaeus & Stig Anderson, Rizwan-Mauzzam Qawwali, Akhénaton, Maya Arulpragasam & Richard X, Jaitin Lalit; Director, Davis McCallum; Choreography, Peter Pucci; Music Supervisor/Arrangements, Michael Friedman; Music Director, Matt Castle; Set, Mimi Lien; Costumes, Christal

Weatherly; Lighting, Marcus Doshi; Sound, Ken Travis; Video, Joseph Spirito; Dialects, Stephen Gabis; PSM, Winnie Y. Lok; Assistant Director, Gaye Taylor Upchurch; ASM, Chandra LaViolette; Song Translator/Assistant Choreographer, Waka Flores; Wigs/Hair, Leah Loukas; Props, Susan Barras; ASL Coach, Kim Weild; Cast: Amir Arison (Vijay), Michi Barall (Shizuko), Satya Bhabha (The DJ), Marsha Stephanie Blake (Doctor 3/Esther), Bill Buell (Patrick/Bartender/Bather 1/Bob/Detective), Demosthenes Chrysan (Doctor 1/Cabbie 2/Bather 3/Giorgio/Rabbi/Criminal 3), Geeta Citygirl (Vivian/Doctor 5), Emily Donahoe (Katya/Colleen), William Jackson Harper (Flower Seller/Doctor 2/Cabbie 1/Criminal 1), Jodi Lin (Mimi), Arian Moayed (Abdi), Debargo Sanyal (Paan Beedi Guy/Bather 2/Doctor 4/Criminal 2/Dance Captain), Jon Norman Schneider (Aly/Cabbie 3), Ruth Zhang (Min/Jenny)

World premiere of a musical presented without intermission; Peter Norton Space; November 6, 2007–January 6, 2008 (Opened December 2); 29 previews, 37 performances.

Amir Arison and Michi Barall in Queens Boulevard *(the musical) (photo by Carol Rosegg)*

PARADISE PARK Presented in association with True Love Productions (Jeanne Donovan Fisher and Laurie Williams Gilmore); Director, Daniel Fish; Choreography, Peter Pucci; Music Director & Arrangements, Bill Schimmel; Set, David Zinn; Costumes, Kaye Voyce; Lighting, Mark Barton; Sound, Elizabeth Rhodes; Video, Joshua Thorson; PSM, Winnie Y. Lok; ASM, Chandra LaViollette; Assistant Director, Ásta Bennie Hostetter; Assistant Choreographer, Yoav Kaddar; Props, Susan Barras; Magic Consultant, Peter Samelson; Dialects, Gillian Lane-Plescia; Vocal Coach, Dev Lepidus; Cast: Vanessa Aspillaga (Darling), Satya Bhabha (Vikram), Veanne Cox (Nancy), Gian Murray Gianino (Bob), William Jackson Harper (Benny/Dance Captain), Christopher McCann (Morton), Paul Mullins (Jorge), Alan Semok (Edgar/Mortimer), Laurie Williams (Ella), Bill Schimmel (Accordion Player)

World premiere of a play with music presented without intermission; Peter Norton Space; February 12–April 6, 2008 (Opened March 2); 18 previews, 26 performances.

Legacy Production

EDWARDS ALBEE'S *OCCUPANT* Director, Pam McKinnon; Set, Christine Jones; Costumes, Jane Greenwood; Lighting, David Lander; Makeup, Angelina Avallone; PSM, Lloyd Davis, Jr.; ASM, Chandra LaViolette; Assistant Director, Andrew Russell; Cast: Mercedes Ruehl (Louise Nevelson), Larry Bryggman (The Man)

Revival of a play presented in two acts; Peter Norton Space; May 6–July 13, 2008 (Opened June 5); 30 previews, 43 performances. Originally produced by the Signature in 2002.

Soho Rep

Thirty-Second Season*

Artistic Director, Sarah Benson; Executive Director, Alexandra Conley; Development, Holly Golden; Producer, Rob Marcato; Technical Director, Mark Stiko; Press, Sam Rudy Media Relations, Dale Heller

PHILOKTETES Written, directed, and designed by John Jesurun; based on the play by Sophocles; Costumes, Ruth Pongstaphone; Lighting, Jeff Nash; PSM, Andrea Jess Berkey; Assistant Director, Rafael Gallegos; Technical Director, Ray Roy; Casting, Calleri Casting; Assistants: Miranda Hardy (lighting), Sarah Hoit & Lorelei Ignas (costumes), Crisman Cooley (technical), Dan Moyer (video); Marketing Consultant, Melissa Ross; Cast: Will Badgett (Odysseus), Louis Cancelmi (Philoktetes), Jason Lew (Neoptolemus)

American premiere of a new play presented without intermission; Soho Rep at 46 Walker; October 13–28, 2007 (Opened October 17): 4 previews, 10 performances.

NO DICE Created and presented by the Nature Theater of Oklahoma; Conceived and directed by Pavol Liska and Kelly Copper; Design, Peter Nigrini; Music, Lumberob and Kristin Worrall; Production Manager, Kell Condon; Marketing Consultant, Melissa Ross; Graphics, An Art Service; Cast: Anne Gridley, Thomas Hummel, Robert M. Johanson, Zachary Oberzan, Kristin Worrall

Premiere full staging of a theatrical experience presented without intermission; 66 White Street; December 6, 2007–January 4, 2008 (Opened December 8); 2 previews, 16 performances. Commissioned by Soho Rep in 2006; previously workshopped at the Under-the-Radar Festival, January, 2007.

Readings and Workshops

Soho Rep Studio *Macbeth* by William Shakespeare, adapted by The Theatre of the Two-headed Calf; Cast: Jess Barbagallo, Mike Mikos, Heidi Schreck; September 20, 2007; *Caligula* by David Adjmi; Director, Brian Mertes; Cast: Reed Birney, Matt Lawler, Clancy O'Connor, Jesse J. Perez; September 26, 2007; *born bad* by Debbie Tucker Green; Director, Leah C. Gardiner; Cast: Teagle F. Bougere, Sandra Daley, Mike Hodge, Patrice Johnson, Lizan Mitchell, Heather Alicia Simms; October 1, 2007; *Crime or Emergency* by Sibyl Kempson; Director, John Collins; Dramaturg, Andi Stover; Performed by Mike Iveson and Sibyl Kempson; January 11–13, 2008

Writer/Director Lab Reading Series Co-Chaired by Maria Goyanes and Daniel Manley; Included: *The Moon is a Dead World* by Mike Daisey; Director, Maria Goyanes; April 7; *The Past is Not a Foreign Country – (Very Personal) Maps of Seattle* by Mallery Avidon; Director, Jose Zayas; April 14; *Mr. Apocope* by Amber Reed; Director, Alec Duffy; April 20; *Precious Little* by Madeleine George; Director, Miriam Weiner; April 28; *In the Labyrinth – A Spectacle With Stories* by Dan LeFranc; Director, Linsay Firman; May 5; *Putting the Daisies to Bed* by Deron Bos; Director, Jimena Duca; May 11

*This is the first season Soho Rep moved from and Off-Off-Broadway company to a full-fledged Off-Broadway company.

Thomas Sadoski and Jordan Gelber in The Joke *(photo by George H. McLaughlin)*

Studio Dante

Fourth Season

Co-Founders and Artistic Directors, Victoria and Michael Imperioli; Executive Directors, Raisa and Ryczard Chlebowski; Director of Play Development, Francine Volpe; Managing Director, Toni Marie Davis; Development, Serafina Lawrence; Co-producers, Tina Thor, Howard Axel; Intern, Mike Micalizzi; Press, The Karpel Group, Bridget Klapinski, Beth Sorrell, David Ford

THE JOKE by Sam Marks; Director, Sam Gold; Set and Costumes, Victoria Imperioli; Lighting, Tony Giovannetti; Sound, David Margolin Lawson; Consultant, Jerry Grayson; Carpenter, Ryczard Chlebowski; Stage Manager, Darren Rosen; Assistant Stage Manager, Devon Butler; Dramaturg, Francine Volpe; Artwork, Nathanial Kilcer; Casting, Jack Doulin, Jenn Haltman; Cast: Jordan Gelber (Doug), Thomas Sadoski (Ed)

Setting: The Catskills, 1965-1973. World premiere of a new play presented without intermission; October 17–November 10, 2007 (Opened October 21); 17 performances.

SISTERS, SUCH DEVOTED SISTERS by Russell Barr; Director, Michael Imperioli; Set & Costumes, Victoria Imperioli; Lighting, Tony Giovannetti; Sound, David M. Lawson; Stage Manager, Annette Verga-Lagier; Carpenter, Ryczard Chlebowski; Cast: Russell Barr (Bernice)

Revival of a solo performance play presented without intermission; January 23–February 16, 2008 (Opened January 26, 2007); 17 performances. Previously presented in the 2005 Brits off Broadway at 59E59.

SAFE by Ron Fitzgerald; Director, Zetna Fuentes; Set and Costumes, Victoria Imperioli; Lighting, Tony Giovannetti; Sound, David Margolin Lawson; Dramaturge/Casting, Francine Volpe; Stage Manager, Annette Verga-Lagier; ASM, Keleigh Eisen; Projections, Johnny Moreno; Master Carpenter, Ryczard Chlebowski; Artwork, Nathanial Kilcer; Casting Consultant, Jack Doulin; Cast: Alfredo Narciso (Muzzy), Patch Darragh (Van), Jess Weixler (Ginger)

Setting: Now and Then. Here and now. World premiere of a new play presented without intermission; June 10–29, 2008 (Opened June 14); 15 performances.

Theatre for a New Audience

Twenty-Ninth Season

Artistic Director, Jeffrey Horowitz; Managing Director, Dorothy Ryan; General Manager, Theresa von Klug; Development, Ernest A. Hood; Education, Joseph Giardina; Finance, Lisa J. Weir; Capital Campaign, Rachel Lovett; Associate Artistic Director, Arin Arbus; Associate General Manager, Sarah Elkashef; Casting, Deborah Brown; Production Manager, Ken Larson; Technical Director, John Martinez; Press, The Bruce Cohen Group

OHIO STATE MURDERS by Adrienne Kennedy; Director, Evan Yionoulis; Sets, Neil Patel; Costumes, Emilio Sosa; Lighting, Christopher Akerlind; Original Music & Sound, Mike Yionoulis/Sarah Pickett; Projections, Leah Gelpe; PSM, Linda Marvel; ASM, Melissa M. Spengler; Dramaturgs,

Micahel Feingold, Ben Nadler; Wigs/Makeup, J. Jared Janas, Rob Greene; Props, Tessa Dunning; Cast: LisaGay Hamilton (Suzanne Alexander, present), Saxon Palmer (Robert Hampshire), Cherise Boothe (Suzanne Alexander, 1949–1952), Julia Pace Mitchell (Iris Ann), Aleta Mitchell (Aunt Louise), Kobi Libii (David Alexander/Val)

Setting: Ohio State University, the present. Revival of a drama presented without intermission; Duke on 42nd Street; October 27–November 18, 2007; 9 previews, 16 performances. World premiere at Great Lakes Theatre Festival, March 1992. New York premiere at Signature Theatre Company in 1995.

OROONOKO by Aphra Behn, adapted from his 1688 novella by Biyi Bandele; Director, Kate Whoriskey; Music, Juwon Ogungbe; Choreography, Warren Adams; Sets, John Arnone; Costumes, Emilio Sosa; Lighting, Donald Holder; Sound, Fabian Obispo; Voice/Text Consultant, Jane Gooderham; Fight Director, Rick Sordelet; PSM, Renee Lutz; ASM, Lara Terrell; Properties, Tessa Dunning; Wigs/Makeup, J. Jared Janas, Rob Greene, Aina Lee; Cast: Ezra Knight (Akogun), Albert Jones (Oroonoko), LeRoy McClain (Aboan), Jordan C. Haynes (Laye), John Douglas Thompson (Orombo), Christen Simon (Lady Onola), Ira Hawkins (Kabiyesi), Toi Perkins (Omoinda), Gregory Derelian (Captain Stanmore), David Barlow (Trefry), Graeme Malcolm (Byam), Che Ayende (Otman); Musicians: Mar Gueye, David Barlow, Greogry Derelian, Jordan C. Haynes, Ira Hawkins, Graeme Malcom

Setting: The mid-1600s, The West African kingdom of Coramantien, and the British West Indies colony of Surinam; American premiere of a play presented in two acts; Duke on 42nd Street; February 2–March 9, 2008 (Opened February 10); 9 previews, 30 performances. Originally presented by the Royal Shakespeare Company in 1999.

ANTONY AND CLEOPATRA by William Shakespeare; Director, Darko Tresnjak; Set, Alexander Dodge; Costumes, Linda Cho; Lighting, York Kennedy; Sound, Jane Shaw; Voice/Text Consultants, Robert Neff Williams, Cicely Beery; Choreography, Peggy Hickey; Fight Director, Rick Sordelet; Production Stage Manager, Renee Lutz; ASM, Jamie Rose Thoma; Dramaturg, Michael Feingold; Properties, Tessa Dunning; Wigs, Charles LaPointe; Makeup; Dave Bova; Cast: Marton Csokas (Antony), Jeffrey Carlson (Octavius Caesar), George Morfogen (Lepidus/Old Soldier), John Douglas Thompson (Enobarbus), Randy Harrison (Eros), Matthew Schneck (Dercetas/Menecrates), Gregory Derelian (Canidius/Dolabella/Varrius), James Knight (Scarus/Pompey), Grant Goodman (Agrippa), Nathan Blew (Maecenas), Christian Rummel (Thidias/Menas), Lisa Velten Smith (Octavia), Laila Robins (Cleopatra), Michael Rogers (Alexas/Clown), Christen Simon (Charmian/Dancer), Christine Corpuz (Iris/Dancer),

Laila Robins and Marton Csokas in Antony and Cleopatra *(photo by Gerry Goodstein)*

Ryan Quinn (Diomedes/Dancer), Erik Singer (Soothsayer/Mardian/Euphronius)

Setting: Alexandria, Rome, Misenum, Athens, and Actium. 1884. Revival of the play presented in two acts; Duke on 42nd Street; March 22–May 2, 2008 (Opened April 3); 12 previews, 26 performances.

TheatreWorks USA – New York

Forty-Sixth Season

Artistic Director, Barbara Pasternack; Managing Director, Ken Arthur; Chief Development, Patrick Key; Marketing, Barbara Sandek, Steve Cochran; Education, Beth Prater; Planning, Steven A. Lattanzi; Production Manager, Bob Daley; Company Manager, Teresa L. Hagar; Casting, Robin D. Carus; Associate Artistic Director, David Coolidge; Marketing Associate, Paula Marchiel; Business Manager, Alyssa Seiden; Business Associate, Justin Zell; Associate Development, Sammi Sicinski; Institutional Giving, Liz S. Alsina; Marketing Coordinator, Patrick Dwyer; Associate to Managing Director, Kirk A. Curtis; Technical Coordinator, B.D. White; Press, The Publicity Office, Jeremy Shaffer

SEUSSICAL Music and book by Stephen Flaherty, lyrics and book by Lynn Ahrens; based on the works of Dr. Seuss, conceived by Ms. Ahrens, Mr. Flaherty and Eric Idle; Director/ Choreography, Marcia Milgrom Dodge; Music Director, W. Brent Sawyer; Set, Narelle Sissons; Costumes, Tracy Christensen; Lighting, Matthew Richards; Sound, Eric Shim; Puppets, Eric Wright; Associate Director/Choreographer, Josh Walden; Stage Manager, Timothy P. Debo; ASM, Amanda-Mae Goodridge; Tech Director, Joseph Reddington; Cast: Kelly Felthous (Mayzie La Bird), Brian Michael Hoffman (Horton the Elephant), Nikka Graff Lanzarone (Bird Girl), Willie Lee-Williams (Wickersham Brother), Ebony Marshall-Oliver (Sour Kangaroo/Young Kangaroo), Amelia Morgan-Rothschild (Bird Girl/Mrs. Mayor), Ben Tostado (Wickersham Brother), Josh Walden (Mayor of Who/Wickersham Brother), Shorey Walker (The Cat In The Hat), Michael Wartella (JoJo), Karen Weinberg (Gertrude McFuzz), Ellen Zolezzi (Bird Girl); Understudies: Kennan Butler (Wickersham Brothers), Mallory Hawk (Bird Girls), Krista Kurtzberg (Cat, Gertrude, Mayzie, Sour Kangaroo, JoJo), Josh Walden (Horton)

Musical Numbers: Overture, Oh the Thinks You Can Think!, Horton Hears a Who, Biggest Blame Fool, How to Raise a Child, Oh the Thinks You Can Think (reprise), It's Possible, Alone in the Universe, The One Feather Tale of Miss Gertrude McFuzz/Amayzing Mayzie, Amayzing Gertrude, Monkey Around/Chasing the Whos, Notice Me Horton, How Lucky You Are, Mayzie's Exit/Horton Sits on the Egg/Dilemma/ Hunters, Egg Nest and Tree, Mayzie in Palm Beach, Alone in the Universe, Solla Sollew, All for You, The People vs. Horton the Elephant, Oh the Thinks You Can Think (finale), Green Eggs & Ham

Revised version of the musical presented without intermission; Lucille Lortel Theatre; July 16–August 17, 2007 (Opened July 19); 57 performances. Previously presented on Broadway at the Richard Rodgers Theatre November 30, 2000 (see *Theatre World* Volume 57, page 24).

MAX AND RUBY Music and lyrics by Carol Hall, book by Glen Berger, based on the stories by Rosemary Wells; Director, Randy White; Choreography, Tracy Bersley; Music Director/Additional Arrangements, Jana Zielonka; Set, Louisa Thompson; Costumes, Junghyun Georgia Lee; Lighting, Tyler Micoleau; Sound, Eric Shim; Orchestrations, Dave Hab; PSM, Jeff Davolt; Tech Director, Joseph Reddington; Cast: Kelly Felthous (Ruby), Lee Markham (Max), Karla Mosely (Louise/Glow-in-the-Dark Eel), Amelia Morgan-Rothschild (Valerie/Sally-Swims-A-Lot), Jonathan Monk (Gracie/Alien Green Gorilla), Nancy Slusser (Grandma/Lobster Balladeer); Understudies: Michelle Czepyha (Ruby, Louise/Eel/, Valerie/ Sally), Ren Casey (Max, Gracie/Gorilla), Amelia Morgan-Rothschild (Grandma/Lobster Balladeer)

Shorey Walker and Company in Seussical *(photo by Joan Marcus)*

Musical Numbers: Looking for Max; Bunny Scout Anthem; Cowboy; Treasure; Teeny Weeny; Blue Tarantula; Happily Ever, Then What?; The Story; Finale

A musical for young audiences presented without intermission; Lucille Lortel Theatre; December 7, 2007–January 13, 2008 (Opened December 9); 44 performances.

JUNIE B. JONES Book and lyrics by Marcy Heisler and music by Zina Goldrich, based on the books by Barbara Park; Director, Peter Flynn; Music Director, W. Brent Sawyer; Choreography, Devanand Janki; Set, Luke Hegel-Cantarella; Costumes, Lora LaVon; Lighting, Jeff Croiter; Sound, Eric Shim; PSM, Jeff Davolt; Orchestrations, Scott Davenport Richards; Associate Choreographer, Robert Tatad; Assistant Director, Alexis Jacknow; Assistant to the Choreographer, Rachel Frankenthal; Marketing, Aria Arts Consulting, Erin Pauahi Auerbach; Cast: Jennifer Cody (Junie B. Jones), John Scherer (Mr. Scary & others), Sarah Saltzberg (May & others), Shannon Antalan (Lucille & others), Blake Ginther (Herb & others), Randy Aaron (Sheldon & others); Understudies: Carole J. Bufford (Junie/May/Lucille), Jonathan Monk (Mr. Scary/ Herb/Sheldon)

Musical Numbers: Top Secret Personal Beeswax; Lucille, Camille, Chenille; You Can Be My Friend; Time to Make a Drawing; Now I See; Lunch Box; Gladys Gutzman; Kickball Tournament; Sheldon Potts' Halftime Show; When Life Gives You Lemons; Kickball Tournament (reprise); When Life Gives You Lemons (reprise); Writing Down the Story of My Life

Second revival of a musical for young audiences presented without intermission; Lucille Lortel Theatre; March 20–May 4 (Opened March 22); 47 performances. Previously presented at the Lortel on July 21, 2004 and revived November 4, 2005 (see *Theatre World* Volume 61, page 118; Volume 62, page 108).

Urban Stages

Twenty-Fourth Season

Artistic Director; Frances Hill; Managing Director, Sonia Kozlova; Program Director,, Lori Ann Laster; Casting, Stephanie Klapper, Jennifer Pardilla; Graphics, Sondra Graff; Marketing, Michelle Brandon; Master Electrician, Christina Watanabe; Press, Brett Singer & Associates

THE OXFORD CLIMBER'S REBELLION by Stephen Massicotte; Director, Roger Danforth; Set, Roman Tatarowicz; Costumes, David Toser; Lighting, Josh Bradford; Sound, Daniel Baker & David Thomas; Video, Alex Koch; Dialects, Amy Stoller; Stage Manager, Dan Zittel; Props, Joe Osheroff;; ASM, Christopher Bonnell; Assistant Director, Alicia Becker; Scenery, No Time for Love Productions; Cast: Dylan Chalfy (T.E. Lawrence), Stafford Clark-Price (Robert Graves), Tom Cleary (Jack), Erin Moon (Nancy Nicholson), George Morfogen (Lord Curzon)

Setting: 1920, Oxford, England. American premiere of a play presented without intermission; October 13–November 18, 2007 (Opened October 18); 32 performances.

THE BLUE BIRD by Stanton Wood & Lori Laster, based on the classic by Maurice Maeterlinck; Director, Heath Cullens; Set & Costumes, Andrey Bartenev; Original Music & Sound, Colm Clark; Video, Alex Koch; Sound, David Thomas; Lighting, Josh Bradford; Associate Lighting, Raquel Davis; PSM, Carol Sullivan; ASM, Christopher Bonnell, Derek Goddard; Props, Lisa Mei Ling Fong; Cast: Ronit Aranoff (Martha), Drew Battles (Mr. Luxury/Time/Father), Rachel Evans (Maggie/Blue Girl), Jenny Gammello (Leah/Mrs. Luxury/Night), Francis Mateo (Mingus/Blue Boy), Maureen Silliman (Mother/Fairy)

Musical Numbers: Turn the Diamond, The Luxury Song, Martha and the Ghosts, Just Click Reset, Lullabye

World premiere of a new play presented without intermission; December 14, 2007–January 13, 2008; 34 performances.

27 RUE DE FLEURUS Book and lyrics by Ted Sod, music and lyrics by Lisa Koch; Director, Frances Hill; Music Director/Pianist, John Bell; Choreography, Jessica Hayden; Set, Roman Tatarowicz; Costumes, Carrie Robbins; Lighting, Raquel Davis; Video, Alex Koch; Sound, David Margolin Lawson; PSM, Carol A. Sullivan; ASM, Patrice Walker; Technical Director, Daniel ZS. Jagendorf; Associate Choreographer/Dance Captain, Susan Haefner; Cast: Cheryl Stern (Alice B. Toklas), Emily Zacharias (Leo Stein/Sylvia Beach/Violet Startyo), Sarah Chalfy (Pablo Picasso/Mabel Dodge/Jean Harlow), Susan Haefner (Marian Walker/F. Scott Fitzgerald/May Bookstaver), Barbara Rosenblat (Gertrude Stein)

Musical Numbers: Salon (Let's Talk); Genius; Place on the Wall; I Taught You Everything; Be My Wife; Role Play; Violette (Destiny); Salon (Let's Talk) Reprise #1; Hemingway/Wives; I Am Your Muse; Don't, Pussy, Don't; Violette (Destiny) Reprise #1, 2, & 3; Salon (Let's Talk) Reprise #2; Don't, Lovey, Don't; Alone; Salon Finale

Setting: 1910 and beyond; the mind and imagination of Alice B. Toklas. A new musical presented without intermission; March 1–April 16, 2008 (Opened March 6); 36 performances.

Susan Haefner, Barbara Rosenblat, Cheryl Stern in 27 rue de Fleurus (photo courtesy of Urban Stages)

Vineyard Theatre

Twenty-Seventh Season

Artistic Director, Douglas Aibel; Executive Director, Jennifer Garvey-Blackwell; General Manager, Reed Ridgley; Associate Artistic Director, Sarah Stern; External Affairs, Amy Fiore; Development, Scott Pyne; Education, Gad Guterman; Production Manager, Ben Morris; Marketing Associate, Jonathan Waller; Company Manager, Rachel E. Ayers; Box Office, Dennis Hruska; Casting, Cindy Tolan; Press, Sam Rudy, Bob Lasko, Dale Heller

THE PIANO TEACHER by Julia Cho; Director, Kate Whoriskey; Set, Derek McLane; Costumes, Ilona Somogyi; Lighting, David Weiner; Original Music & Sound, Obadiah Eaves; Wigs, Charles LaPointe; PSM, Bryce McDonald; ASM, Talia Krispel; Technical Director, David Nelson; Dialect Coach, Deborah Hecht; Assistant Director, Devorah Bondarin; Properties, Jay Duckworth; Music Consultant, Brent Frederick; Cast: Elizabeth Franz (Mrs. K), Carmen M. Herlihy (Mary Fields), John Boyd (Michael)

A new play presented without intermission; Gertrude and Irving Dimson Theatre; October 30–December 23, 2007 (Opened November 18); 48 performances.

THE SLUG BEARERS OF KAYROL ISLAND ***(or, The Friends of Dr. Rushower)*** Libretto & drawings by Ben Katchor, music by Mark Mulcahy; Director, Bob McGrath; Choreography, John Carrafa; Set/Projections, Jim Findlay & Jeff Sugg; Costumes, Mattie Ullrich; Lighting, Russell H. Champa; Sound, David Arnold & Brett Jarvis; Musical Director, Erik James; Music Supervisor, Randall Eng; PSM, Megan Smith; Dramaturg, Daniel Zippi; Music Transcription/Preparation, Randal Eng; Hair/Wigs, Gerrard Kelly; ASM, Ryan C. Durham; Properties, Jay Duckworth; Cast: Tom Riis Farrell (Butler/Pilot), Will Swenson (Psychiatrist/Dry Cleaner), Stephen Lee Anderson (George Klatter), Matt Pearson (Samson), Jody Flader (GinGin), Bobby Steggert (Immanuel Lubang), Peter Friedman (Dr. Rushower); Band: Erik James (piano), Stew Cutler (guitar), Paul Ossola (bass), Denny McDermott (drums)

Musical Numbers: Hi, It's Me/The Doctor's Explanation, GinGin's Song, The Birth of Immanuel Lubang, Last Christmas/The Mating Behavior of Gulls, Your Coat Will Be Ready at 9, Lumin Rushower Is My Name, Is There Something I Should Know About?, Can Someone Get the Phone?/In Bed Early Tonight, The Psychiatrist's House Call, The Friends of Dr. Rushower, They're Not Like You and I, An Ice Cream In A Root-Beer Float, George Klatter Was Right/ Stay On The Path, The Story of Samson Layaway/Kayrol Cola (and the Bubbles), The Tent Meeting, Where Were You All Night? You Say She's Happy, Shhh! We're Trying to Listen

Setting: New York City and Kayrol Island, present day. A new musical presented in two acts; Gertrude and Irving Dimson Theatre; January 25–March 16, 2008 (Opened February 12); 51 performances. Originally presented at The Kitchen in March, 2004.

GOD'S EAR by Jenny Schwartz; Presented in association with New Georges (Susan Bernfield, Artistic Director; Sarah Cameron Sunde, Associate Director); Director, Anne Kauffman; Songs, Michael Friedman; Additional Lyrics, Jenny Schwartz; Set, Kris Stone; Costumes, Olivera Gajic; Lighting, Tyler Micoleau; Sound, Leah Gelpe; PSM, Megan Schwarz; Casting, Paul Davis/Calleri Casting; Music Supervisor, Kris Kukul; ASM, Danielle Teague-Daniels; Props, Jay Duckworth; Assistant Director, Reshmi Hazra; Cast: Christina Kirk (Mel), Gibson Frazier (Ted), Monique Vukovic (Lanie), Judith Greentree (Tooth Fairy), Rebecca Wisocky (Lenora), Matthew Montelongo (Flight Attendant/G.I. Joe), Raymond McAnally (Guy)

Off-Broadway debut of a new play with original songs presented in two acts; Gertrude and Irving Dimson Theatre; April 9–May 18, 2008 (Opened April 17); 41 performances. World premiere produced Off-Off Broadway by New Georges at East 13th Street Theater, May 2–June 2, 2007.

Anniversary Reading Series

GOBLIN MARKET by Polly Pen and Peggy Harmon, adapted from the poem by Christina Rosetti; Director, Evan Yionoulis; Music Director, Lawrence Yurman; Cast: Terri Klausner, Ann Morrison; November 11–12, 2007

Monique Vukovic and Judith Greentree in God's Ear *(photo by Carol Rosegg)*

RAISED IN CAPTIVITY by Nicky Silver; Director, David Warren; Cast: Leslie Ayvazian, Patricia Clarkson, Peter Frechette, Brian Kerwin, Anthony Rapp; Laura Pels Theatre; December 3, 2007

Women's Project

Thirtieth Season

Producing Artistic Director, Julie Crosby, PhD.; Artistic Advisor, Liz Diamond; Artistic Associate & Dramaturg, Megan E. Carter; Associate Producer, Allison Prouty; Marketing, Jessica Roberts; Grants, R. Justin Hunt; Business Manager, Lauren White; Production Manager, Aduro Productions (Carolyn Kelson & Jason Janicki); Education, Fran Tarr, Rebecca Hochman Masback; Casting, Alaine Alldaffer; Consultants, Kat Williams, Bruce Cohen; Financial Services, Patricia Taylor; Press, Bruce Cohen

WAPATO by Peggy Stafford; Director, Rebecca Patterson; Set, Marion Williams; Jenny C. Fulton; Lighting, Dawn Chiang; Sound, Jane Shaw; Fight Director, Kathryn Ekblad; PSM, Jack Gianino; Stage Manager, Gian-Murray Gianino; Assistant Director, Kim Bartling; Cast: Kathleen Butler (Bonnie), Nancy Franklin (Mary Lou), Lucy Martin (Janice), Dale Soules (Bev), Kaipo Schwab (Rascal Lev/Crazy Horse)

World premiere of a new play presented in two acts; Julia Miles Theatre; December 7–22, 2007; 6 performances. Inaugural production for the new "HotHouse" play development series for new works by Lab artists.

SAND by Trista Baldwin; Director, Daniella Topol; Set, Anita Fuchs; Costumes, Clint Ramos; Lighting, Traci Klainer; Sound, Daniel Baker; Original Music, Broken Chord Collective; Fight Director, J. David Brimmer; Dramaturg, Megan E. Carter; PSM, Jack Gianino; Dialect/Cultural Consultant, Mike Mosallam; Stage Manager, Zac Chandler; Assistant Director, Michele Pace; Cast: Alec Beard (Justin), Angela Lewis (Keisha), Pedro Pascal (Armando/Ahmed)

World premiere of a new play presented without intermission; Julia Miles Theatre; February 1–March 2, 2008 (Opened February 10); 31 performances.

crooked by Catherine Treischmann; Director, Liz Diamond; Set, Jennifer Moeller; Costumes, Ilona Somogyi; Lighting, S. Ryan Schmidt; Original Music & Sound, Jane Shaw; PSM, Jack Gianino; Stage Manager, Zac Chandler; Dialects, Deborah Hecht; Alexander Technique, Belinda Mello; Assistant Director, Jennifer Chambers; Technical Director, Gest Scenic Creations; Props, Ashley Gagner; Assistant Design: Deb O. (set), Alex Hawthorn (sound), Maria Nebritoff (lighting); Casting Associate, Lisa Donadio; Cast: Carmen M. Herlihy (Maribel), Cristin Milioti (Laney), Betsy Aidem (Elise)

Alec Beard and Pedro Pascal in Sand *(photo by Carol Rosegg)*

New York premiere of a play presented without intermission; Julia Miles Theatre; April 11 –May 10, 2008; (Opened April 20); 31 performances.

CORPORATE CARNIVAL Conceived and created by Megan E. Carter, Julie Crosby, Jyana S. Gregory and the cast, text by Andy Paris; Presented with Arts World Financial Center and Debra Simon; Director, Jyana S. Gregory; Set and Costumes, Junghyun Georgia Lee; Original Music & Sound, Fitz Patton; Dramaturge, Megan E. Carter; PSM, Howard Klein; Stage Manager, Amanda Schulze; Assistant Director, Nicole A. Watson; Cast: David Anzuelo (Marco, the Market Tamer), Karen Grenke (Svetlana, the Sultress of Spin), Andrew Grusetskie (Simon, the Scourge of Stagflation), Andy Paris (Talker Tipper McGee), Richard Saudek (The Marvelous Herman Wilkins), Meghan Williams (Ultra Equilibrium Yvette); The Temps: Lisa Rafaela Clair, Prudence Heyert, Megan Raye Manzi, Austin Sanders, Jeff Willis

A collection of new short plays presented without intermission; various locations throughout the World Financial Center; May 16–May 19, 2007; 9 performances.

York Theatre Company

Thirty-Ninth Season

Artistic Director, James Morgan,; Chairman of the Board, David McCoy, Founding Director F. Janet Hayes Walker; Associate Artistic Director, Brian Blythe; General Manager, Elisa Spencer; Development, Nancy P. Barry; Company Administrator, Alyssa Seiden; Company Manager, Scott DelaCruz; Production Manager, Chris Robinson; Communications, Alana Karpoff/John Kenrick; Audience Services Manager, Jessie Blum/Bryan Guffey; Developmental Reading Series Coordinator, Jeff Landsman; Casting, Norman Meranus/ Geoff Josselson; Press, David Gersten

A KID'S LIFE! Book by Cynthia Riddle & Peter Hunziker, music and lyrics byCorey Leland; Producer and Director, Keith Markinson; Choreography/Assistant Director, Ellie Mooney; Design, Bradley Kaye; Lighting, Jeff Porter; Stage Manager, Emily During; Deck Manager/Wardrobe, Ali Psiuk; Tech, Chris Robinson; Music Director, Mike Borth; Musical Supervisor, Laura Bergquist; Press, Springer Associates, Joe Trentacosta; Cast: Carlos Avilas (Zack), Ashley Wallace (Zoe), Mark Borum (Mr. Sullivan), Yoav Levin (Starsky the Dog), Jessica Blyweiss (Old Ben the Clock), Joshua Greenwood (Bart the Tree), Kaitlin Becker (Bells the Owl), William Broyles (Young Boy/ Swing)

Musical Numbers: A Kid's Life!, Start My Day, Shoes and Socks, Will You Be My Friend, Things Your Dog Might Say, Animals Have Feelings Too, I Like Juice, Have You Ever Hugged a Tree, I Love My New Town, It's About Time, I Believe in Me, Thank You, When I Group Up I Wanna Be Happy!

Setting: Zack's hometown, the present. A new youth musical presented without intermission; Theatre at St. Peter's Church; December 8, 2007–January 13, 2008 (Opened December 16); 24 performances.

Musicals In Mufti – Musical Theatre Gems in Staged Concert Performances

Twenty First Series

IT'S A BIRD…IT'S A PLANE…IT'S SUPERMAN Book by David Newman & Robert Benton, music by Charles Strouse, lyrics by Lee Adams; based on the comic strip "Superman"; Director/Concert Adaptation, Stuart Ross; Music Director, Torquil Munro; Lighting, Chris Robinson; PSM, Sarah Butke; ASM, Pamela Brusoski; Cast: David Rasche (Max Mencken), Jean Louisa Kelly (Lois Lane), Cheyenne Jackson (Superman), Shoshana Bean (Sydney), Stan Chandler (Jim Morgan), Lea DeLaria (Dr. Abner Sedgwick), Michael Winther (Le Tete/Newsman), Amy Ryder (Mayor), Rachel Jones (Miss Metropolis/Narrator), Scot Fedderly (Superman Wanna Be), Katherine Von Till (Guide), Rodney Peck (Henderson); Musicians: Torquil Munro (piano), Larry Lelli (drums)

A musical presented in two acts; June 15–17, 2007; 5 performances.

I AND ALBERT Book by Jay Presson Allen, music by Charles Strouse, lyrics by Lee Adams; Director, Michael Montel; Music Director, James Bassi; Lighting, Chris Robinson, Casting, Mark Simon; PSM, Sarah Butke; ASM, Elise Hanley; Cast: Nancy Anderson (Victoria), Brooke Sunny Moriber (Duchess/Vicky/Ensemble), Nick Wyman (Pamerston/Gladstone), Stephen Mo Hanan (Disraeli/Melbourne), Lorinda Lasitza (Daisy/Ensemble), Edwin Cahill (Bertie/Ensemble), Sasha Weiss (Lady Caro/Ensemble), Ken Krugman (Bishop/Billings/Brown/Ensemble), Roger DeWitt (Brown/Archbishop/Ensemble), Nick Galbraith (Guard/Cockney Man), Mackenzie Thomas (Nurse/Alice/Ensemble), Adam Riegler (Ensemble), Gabriella Malek (Ensemble), Gerritt VanderMeer (Albert); Musicians: James Bassi (piano), Jay Mack (percussion)

American premiere of musical presented in two acts; June 29–July 1, 2007; 5 performances.

BAJOUR Book by Ernest Kinoy, music and lyrics by Walter Marks; Director, Stuart Ross; Music Director, Mark Hartman; Lighting, Chris Robinson; Casting, Cindi Rush; PSM, Sarah Butke; ASM, Elise Hanley; Cast: Teri Ralston (Momma), Nancy McCall (Realtor/Mitya/Ensemble), Thom Christopher (Johnny Dembo), Erick Devine (Vanno/Cop/Ensemble), Nicholas Rodriguez (Steve), Laura Kenyon (Loopa/Ensemble), Talia Barzilay (Rosa/Ensemble), Michael Iannucci (Frank/Cop/Ensemble), Don Mayo (Newark), Lee Rosen (Lou), Angel Desai (Emily), Deone Zanotto (Anyanka); Musicians: Mark Hartman (piano), Paul Davis (percussion)

A musical presented in two acts; July 13–15, 2008; 5 performances.

THE DAY BEFORE SPRING Book and lyrics, Alan Jay Lerner, music by Frederick Loewe; Director, David Glenn Armstrong; Arrangements/Score Restoration/Music Director, Aaron Gandy; Lighting, Chris Robinson; Casting, DFK Casting; Associate Director, Daniel Haley; PSM, Sarah Butke; ASM, Elise Hanley; Associate Music Director/Pianist/Arrangements, Mark York; Cast: Amanda Watkins (Katherine Townsend), Richard Todd Adams (Peter Townsend), Tia Speros (May Tompkins), Mark York (Bill Tompkins), Ed Watts (Alex Maitland), Summer Broyhill (Leonore), Janine DiVita (Susan), Ashlee Fife (Marie), Lindsay Packard (Lucille), Hunter Bell (Gerald Barker), David Abeles (Eddie Warren/Freud), Daniel C. Levine (Joe McDonald/Voltaire), Orville Mendoza (Harry Scott/Plato), Robyn Kramer (Christopher Randolph)

Musical Numbers: The Day Before Spring, The Invitation, Bill, Peter & May, God's Green World, You Haven't Changed At All, Katherine & Alex, My Love Is A Married Man, The Day Before Spring (reprise), Katherine, What Are You Gonna Do?, Katherine Receives Advice, Act One Finale, Friends To The End, A Jug Of Wine, Peter Reads The Book, Come To The Bower Of Love, Happy, Happy, I Love You This Morning, Where's My Wife?, This Is My Holiday, Finale Ultimo

A musical presented in two acts; July 27–29, 2007; 5 performances.

The cast of A Kid's Life!

Twenty-Second Series

ZORBA Book and lyrics by Joseph Stein, music by John Kander, lyrics by Fred Ebb, adapted from the novel by Nikos Kazantzakis; Director, Steven Yuhasz; Music Director, Patrick Vaccariello; Lighting, Chris Robinson, PSM, Andrea Jo Martin; ASM, Jose Docen; Cast: Emily Skinner (The Leader), Ken McMullen (Maurodani), Vincent D'Elia (Manolakas), Tina Stafford (Marika), Jane Brockman (Sophia), Denis Lambert (The Turk/Yorgie), Raymond Bokhour (Father Zahoria), Robin de Jesus (Mikiko), Joseph Cullinane (Pauli), Deone Zanotto (Katina), Jeff McCarthy (Zorba), Aaron Ramey (Nikos), Crista Moore (The Widow), Beth Fowler (Hortense); Musicians: Jim Laev (piano), Peter Margolis (Bouzouki)

Musical Numbers: Life Is, The First Time, The Top of the Hill, No Boom Boom, Viva La Difference, The Butterfly, Goodbye Canavaro, Grandpapa, Only Love, The Bend in the Road, Only Love (reprise), Y'ssou, Why Can't I Speak?/That's A Beginning, The Crow, Happy Birthday, I Am Free, Life Is (reprise)

A musical presented in two acts; September 14–16, 2007; 5 performances.

ENTER LAUGHING (previously titled *So Long 174th Street*) Book by Joseph Stein, music and lyrics by Stan Daniels, based on the play *Enter Laughing* by Joseph Stein from the novel by Carl Reiner; Director, Stuart Ross; Music Director/Piano, Matt Castle; Lighting, Chris Robinson; PSM, Andrea Jo Martin/ Zoya Kachadurian, ASM, Jose A. Docen; Cast: Matt Castle (Roger), Josh Grisetti (David Kolowitz), Bruce Adler (Mr. Foreman), Jill Eikenberry (Mother), Michael Tucker (Father), Emily Shoolin (Wanda), Robb Sapp (Marvin), Paul Binotto (Don 1), Erick Devine (Pike), Kaitlin Hopkins (Angela), George S. Irving (Marlowe), Wayne Pretlow (Don 2), Trisha Rapier (Female Ensemble), Kelly Sullivan (Miss B); Encore replacements: Richard Kind (Marlowe), Michael Winther (Pike), Michael Iannucci (Don 2)

Musical Numbers: David Kolowitz, the Actor; Its Like, I'm Undressing Girls With My Eyes; You; The Man I Can Love; Say The Words; Whoever You Are; My Son, the Druggist; He Touched Her; Men; Hot Cha Cha; Boy, Oh Boy; The Butlers Song; Being With You; If You Want To Break Your Mothers Heart; So Long, 174th Street

Setting: New York, 1936. A musical presented in two acts; September 28–30, 2007; 5 performances; Encored from December 13–15, 2007; 4 performances.

THE BODY BEAUTIFUL Book by Joseph Stein with Will Glickman, music by Jerry Bock, lyrics by Sheldon Harnick; Director, David Glenn Armstrong; Music Director, John Bell; Lighting, Chris Robinson; PSM, Andrea Jo Martin; ASM, Jose A. Docen; Associate Music Director, Amanda Morton; Associate Director, Daniel Haley; Cast: Brad Oscar (Dave Coleman), Stephen Bienskie (Richie/Pete), Jonathan Kay (Eddie/Artie), Ryan Duncan (Dominic/Frank), Jim Sorensen (Jimm/George/Campbell), Patrick Richwood (Albert), Laura Marie Duncan (Ann), Mike McGowan (Bob Stockton), Cady Huffman (Florence Colman), John Eric Parker (Harry Marsh), Capathia Jenkins (Marge Marsh), Angie Schworer (Jane Coleman/Camper/College Girl), Amy Goldberger (Kathy/ Camper/College Girl), Megan Lawrence (Gloria); Musicians: John Bell (piano), Allan Molnar (percussion); Cast recording: Jay Records

Musical Numbers: Where Are They?, The Body Beautiful, Fair Warning, Leave Well Enough Alone, Blonde Blues, Uh-Huh Oh Yea, Hidden In My Heart, Nobility, All of These and More, The Body Beautiful (reprise), Summer Is, The Honeymoon Is Over, Just My Luck, Art of Conversation, Gloria, A Relatively Simple Affair, Uh-Huh Oh Yea – Finale

A musical presented in two acts; October 12–14, 2007; 5 performances.

THE BAKER'S WIFE Book by Joseph Stein, music and lyrics by Stephen Schwartz; Director, Gordon Greenberg; Music Director, Mark Hartman; Lighting, Chris Robinson; Sound, Randy Hansen; PSM, Andrea Jo Martin; ASM, Jose A. Docen; Cast: Mitchell Greenberg (Teacher), Richard Pruitt (Claude), Gay Marshall (Denise), Clint Zugel (Philippe), Joy Franz (Therese), Richard Crom (Pierre), John O'Creagh (Domergue), David Rossmer (Antoine), Maureen Silliman (Hortense), Michael Medieros (Barnaby), Kevin Cahoon (Priest), Laurent Giroux (Marquis), Jacque Carnahan (Nicole), Betsy DeLellio (Simone), Wendi Bergamini (Inez), Lenny Wolpe (Aimable), Renée Elise Goldsberry (Genevieve), Max von Essen (Dominique); Musicians: Mark Hartman (piano), Paul Masse (accordion/keyboard)

Musical Numbers: Chanson, If It Wasn't For You, Merci Madame, Bread, Gifts of Love, Proud Lady, If It Wasn't For Her, Serenade, Meadowlark, Any Day Now, Chanson (reprise), The World's Luckiest Man, Feminine Companionship, If It Wasn't For You (reprise), If I Have to Live Alone, Romance, Where Is the Warmth, Finale

A musical presented in two acts; October 26–28, 2007; 5 performances.

Special Events

NEO3 A benefit concert celebrating new, emerging, outstanding music theatre writers; Produced by Brian Blythe; Director, Annette Jolles; Music Director, Matt Castle; Hosts, Bobby Lopez & Ann Harada; Writers: Kristen Anderson-Lopez/Lisa DeSpain, Leslie Arden, Stephen Cole/David Krane, Jim Colleran, Rick Crom, Miriam Daly, Jeremy Desmon/

Vadim Feichtner, Harris Doran/Arthur Lafrentz Bacon, Michelle Elliott/Danny Larsen, Adam Gwon, Tim Huang, Tom Kenaston, Paul Libman/Dave Hudson, Benj Pasek/Justin Paul, Kyle Rosen, Laurence Holzman/Felicia Needleman, Joy Son/Steve Routman, Robby Stamper/Arianna Rose; Performers: Judith Blazer, Tituss Burgess, Edwin Cahill, Matt Cavenaugh, Robyn S. Clark, Adam Heller, Shaun Taylor-Corbett, Ana Gasteyer, Tom Gualtieri, Jaclyn Huberman, Doug Kreeger, Megan Lawrence, Jeanne Lehman, Jenny Powers, Michele Ragusa, Kate Reinders, Seth Rudetsky, Will Swenson, Yuka Takara, Jim Weitzer, Lynne Wintersteller, Chip Zien; June 11, 2007

TRIUMPHANT BABY Music by Joe Iconis, lyrics by Robert Maddock; Director, Brad Oscar; Musicians, Matt Hinkley, Matt Wigton, Joe Iconis; Cast: Lorinda Lisitza with Liz Lark Brown and Tanya Holt; August 13, 20, 27, September 10, 2007; 4 performances.

JOHN KENRICK'S CONVERSATIONS A lecture/talkback series: MGM Freed Unit: The Musical Makers (March 4, 2008); The Wizard of Oz: Production #1060 (March 18, 2008); In Person With Marge Champion (April 1, 2008)

NEO SPOTLIGHT CONCERT SERIES *Reach for the Sky: Songs by Adam Gwon* Music and lyrics by Adam Gwon, Music Director, Vadim Feichtner; Cast: Jill Abramovitz, Jared Gertner, Michael Hunsaker, Natalie Weiss; March 3, 2008; *Short Story Long: The Songs of Timothy Huang* Music and lyrics by Timothy Huang; Music Director, Doug Oberhamer; Cast: Marie France Arcilla, Orville Mendoza, Lauren Lebowitz, Shonn Wiley. Musicians: Dave Anthony (percussion), Scott Thornton (bass); March 3, 2008; *Does This Song Make My Ass Look Fat? An Evening of Elegant Lyrics by Amanda Green* Lyrics by Amanda Green; Music by John Bucchino, Amanda Green, Larry Grossman, Skip Kennon, Tom Kitt, Sam Lorber, Curtis Moore; Music Director, Matt Gallagher; Cast: Randy Blair, Jenn Colella, Jennifer Foote, Brad Oscar, Amy Spanger, Max Von Essen; Musicians: Damien Bassman (drums); March 21, 2008; *The Songs of Joe Iconis* Director, John Simpkins, Sound, Craig Kaufman; Stage Manager, Brian Blythe; Lighting, Chris Robinson; Cast: Katrina Rose Dideriksen, Matt Hinkley, Ian Kagey, Krysta Rodriguez, Lance Rubin, Chandra Lee Schwartz, Brent Stranathan, Jason Williams; April 21, 2008; *Sailing Against the Current: The Songs of Robert Bartley & Danny Whitman* Director, Robert Bartley, Music Director/Pianist, Chris Tilley; Percussionist, Raphael Torn; Lighting, Chris Robinson; Stage Manager, Brian Blythe; Cast: Jenn Colella, Beth Curry, Tony Yazbeck, Judith Moore, Tituss Burgess, Kristen Wyatt; May 12, 2008

THE PEOPLE VS. MONA Concert staging of the musical with book by Patricia Miller, book, music and lyrics by Jim Wann; Director, Annette Jones; Music Director, Rob Miluski; PSM, Scott DelaCruz; Cast: Marci Henderson (Tish Thomas/"Blind Willy" Carter); Marc Kudisch (Jim Summerford), Christiane Noll (Mavis Frye), Ron Raines (Officer Bell/Katt's Kitten), Omri Schein (Baliff/Katt's Kitten/Dr. Theo Bloodweather/Euple R. Pugh/Rafsanjani Pate), Natalie Toro (Ramona Maria "Mona Mae" Katt), Lillias White (Judge Ella Jordan/Reverend Rosetta Purify); Musicians: Bob Gustafson (Piano/Nat McGnatt), Ritt Henn (bass guitar/Mack McGnatt), Dan Weiss (guitar/Mike McGnatt); March 30, 2008

PENN STATE AT THE YORK Two new one-acts developed by PSU students; program conceived by Raymond Sage and Dr. Susan Russell of Penn State, and James Morgan and Brian Blythe. *Ordinary Days,* a musical by Adam Gwon; Director, Matthew Kaylor Toronto; Music Director, Dan Riddle; Stage Manager, Rachel Harpham; Cast: Gina Duci (Deb), Nathan Gardner (Jason), Morgan Faulkner (Claire), Nathan Lucrezio (Warren); *The Aperture,* a play by Sean Christopher Lewis; Director, Dan Carter; Stage Manager, Lauren Williams; PSM, Matt Richards; Cast: Anna Elwood (Alex), Delius Doherty (Okello John); April 5-6, 2008; 3 performances.

4@15 Four fifteen-minute mini-musicals by University of California, Irvine writers: Jim Colleran, Miriam Daly, Sophia Chapadjiev & Allison Leyton-Brown, Robby Stamper & Arianna Rose; Director, Brian Blythe; Music Director, Tammy Holder; April 18–19, 2008

NEO4 A benefit concert celebrating new, emerging, outstanding music theatre writers; Produced by Brian Blythe; Songs by Brad Alexander & Adam Mathias, Varick Bacon & Powers McElhone, Maggie-Kate Coleman & Daniel Maté, Dan Collins & Julianne Wick Davis, Ryan Cunningham & Joshua Salzman, Brian Feinstein & Amanda Yesnowitz, Peter Hilliard & Matt Boresi, Rick Hip-Flores, James-Allen Ford & Sara Wordsworth, Noel Katz, John Mercurio, Thomas Mizer & Curtis Moore, Andy Monroe, Scott Murphy & Nathan Christensen, Ryan Scott Oliver, David Zellnik & Joe Zellnik; Director, Annette Jolles; Musical Director, Matt Castle; Lighting, Chris Robinson; PSM, Sarah Butke; Hosts, Amanda Green and Sammy Buck; Cast: Nancy Anderson, Michael Arden, Bobby Belfry, Barbara Brussell, Deborah S. Craig, Kevin Duda, Ivan Hernandez, Curtis Holbrook, Jaclyn Huberman, Ramona Keller, Emily Murphy, Pamela Myers, Christiane Noll, Laura Osnes, Eric Petersen, Aaron Ramey, Anthony Rapp, Bob Ross Juice Box, Madison Rozynek, Robb Sapp, Tally Sessions, Bobby Steggert, Kelly Sullivan, Aaron Tveit, Jason Williams; May 19, 2008

Kendra Kassebaum, Jayne Houdyshell, Josh Charles & Robert Foxworth in Manhattan Theatre Club's The Receptionist *(photo by Joan Marcus)*

Pablo Schreiber and Thomas Sadoski in Manhattan Class Company's reasons to be pretty *(photo by Joan Marcus)*

Van Hughes and the Company of Playwrights Horizons' Saved *(photo by Joan Marcus)*

Asa Somers, Alice Ripley, and Brian d'Arcy James in Second Stage's Next to Normal *(photo by Joan Marcus)*

Conrad John Schuck, Victoria Clark and Company in Encores!'s Juno *(photo by Joan Marcus)*

Julyana Soelistyo, John Kassir, Jeremy Webb, Marc Kudisch, and David Patrick Kelly in Lincoln Center Theater's The Glorious Ones *(photo by Joan Marcus)*

Off-Off-Broadway

June 1, 2007–May 31, 2008

Judith Malina and Pat Russell in The Living Theatre's Maudie and Jane *(photo by Chante Cherisse Lucier)*

Allan Mirchin, Steve Sterner and Susan Greenhill in The Peccadillo Theatre Company's Morning Star *(photo by Dick Larson)*

Valerie Stack Dodge (seated), Craig Dudley, Greg Lauterbach (background), Susan Case in Out of the Box's production of The Miser *(photo by Lisa Allen)*

Sheila Dabney (front), Harry Mann, Jasper McGruder and Yukio Tsuji in Conjur Woman *at La MaMa E.T.C. (photo by Brian Dilg)*

Karen Murphy and Shonn Wiley in the New York Musical Theatre Festival production of Mud Donahue *(photo by Carol Rosegg)*

Jason Cicci and Danielle Ferland in Monday Morning Productions' Hate Mail

13th Street Repertory

Edith O'Hara, Artistic Director/Founder

LINE by Israel Horovitz; Director, Edith O'Hara; 34th year Off-Off-Broadway; Open run

LEGENDS OF LAUGHTER Created and performed by Spatz Donovan; Opened January 4, 2004; Closed January 29, 2008

ADVENTURES OF THE HEART Created and performed by the 2007 Interns: Alicia Steinmetz, Akilah Jeffers, Becky Sweren, Buddy Pease, Cameron Stuckey, Denise Sillman, Erica Stratton, Jessica Thanki, Joanna Zelman, Katie Nelson-Croner, Krsnaa Fitch, Melissa Koval, Norah Scheinman, Ouida Maedel, Philip Rademeyer, Suzanne Reed; July 18–27, 2007

ORPHANS by Joel Shatzky; Director, Mark Bloom; September 14–November 3, 2007

BENT by Martin Sherman; Produced with Blue Asphalt Productions & Counting Squares Theatre; Director, Joshua Gold; Cast: Ryan Nicholoff, Ed Davis, Jim Halloran, Chris Worley, Ronald Hornsby, Chris Layton, Richard Kirkwood; October 17–November 29, 2007

A CHRISTMAS CAROL by Charles Dickens, adapted by Sandra Nordgren; Director Craig Anthony Bannister; December 7, 2007–January 6, 2008

NUNCHUCK NINJA NUNS by Lauren M. Cavanaugh; Director, Michael Flanagan; AD/Stage Manager, Melanie Beck; Cast: Kalina Dalton, Katie Nelson-Croner, Errol W. Greaves, Danielle Newell, Ari Jacobson, Grace M. Trull, Lindsey Johnston, Franck Juste; March 6–April 26, 2008

ANY1MAN Written and performed by George A. Peters and Brandon F. Johnson; March 24–27, 2008

A MUSE IN MANHATTAN Written and directed by Terence Patrick Hughes; April 28–May 18, 2008

East 13th Street Theater (CSC space)

DJ: A REMIX OF MOLIERE'S DON JUAN Adapted and directed by Javierantonio Gonzalez; Set, Jian Jung; Lighting, Dans Maree Sheehan; Costumes, Amanda Bujak; Cast: Tania Molina, James Ryan Caldwell, Billy Fenderson, Stephanie Shipp, Meiyin Wang, Ricardo Hinoa, Anna Marshall; June 19–July 1, 2007

UNCLE VANYA Adapted and directed by Rachel Chavkin; Set, Ace Eure; Lighting, Brad King; Sound, Ryan Maeker; Cast: Gillian Chadsey, Libby King, Marjo-Riikka Makela, Rebecca Lingafelter, Luis Moreno, Rachel Benbow Murdy, Janet Prince, Ryan West; June 20–30, 2007

14th Street Theater

COUNT TO TEN Book and lyrics by Michael Blevins & Beth Clary, music by Michael Blevins, Scott Knipe, Bruce Sacks & David Wollenberger; Produced by The Group Theatre Too; Diretor/Chroeographer, Michael Blevins; Musical Director, Christine Riley; Lighting, Paul Carbone; PSM, Cristina Marie; Associate Producers, Mary Ann Penzero, Denise Brysett, Doug Francisco, Kenny Wiener; Cast: Brian Merker, Justin Boccitto, Jennifer Avila, Lexie Spiers, Heather Lightcap, Jacob Burlas, Hunter Gross, Dylan Bush, Chris Kinsey, Doug Francisco, Jenna Black, Michael Breslin, Elissa Dauria, Eddy Francisco, Ricky Jones, T.J Lark, Josiah Marcarelli, Katelyn Morgan, Samantha Pearlman, Tyler Rai, Brandon Wiener; June 22–July 1, 2007; Encored at the Connelly Theatre February 29–March 16, 2008

QUICK CURTAINS One-acts produced by The Group Theatre Too; Director, Michael Blevins; Included: *The Stronger* by August Strinberg, *Aftermath* by Alexander D. Rulin, *Six Who Pass While the Lentils Boil* by Stuart Waker, and *A Pairl of Lunatics* by W.R. Walkes; June 26–30, 2007

THE QUICK-CHANGE ROOM: SCENES FROM A REVOLUTION by Nagle Jackson; Produced by RJeneration in association with The York Shakespeare Company and the 14th Street Y; Director, Seth Duerr; Cast: Victoria Levin, Michelle Sims, Seth Duerr, Michael De Nola, Robin Madel, Tarek Khan, John Dalmon, Elizabeth Kelly, Marina Klochan; July 11–15, 2007

HAVE YOU SEEN STEVE STEVEN? by Ann Marie Healy; Presented by 13P; Executive Producer, Maria Goyanes; Director, Anne Kauffman; Set, Sue Rees; Costumes, Emily Rebholz; Lighting, Garin Marschall; Sound, Jeremy J. Lee; PSM, Megan Schwarz; Producer, Sandra Garner; Cast: Frank Deal, Tom Riis Farrell, Alissa Ford, Kate Hampton, Jocelyn Kuritsky, Matt Maher, Carol Rosenfeld, Stephanie Wright Thompson; September 15–October 6, 2007

THE "M" GAME Adapted and directed by Julianne Just; Presented by Mir Productions; Choreography, Joyce Trotta; Fight Choreography, Carlo Riviecco; Design, Marisa Champoonote, Hunter Kacsorowski, Erinina Marie Ness, E. I. Read and Elisha Shaefer; Stage Managers, Andi Cohen & Elizabeth Nielsen; Cast: Naomi Finkelstein, Genevieve Gearhart, Miebaka Johannes, Jarett Karlsberg, Jeff Kissam, Miriam Lind, Clinton Lowe, Scott MacKenzie, Cynthia Osuji, Christina Shipp, Lindsay Strachan, Mattie Whipple, Joyce Wu; October 11–20, 2007

EDWARD II by Christopher Marlow; Produced by (Re:) Directions Theatre Company (Founding Artists: Tom Berger, Alisyn Brock, Martha Goode, Michael Littner, Blair Mielnik, Ben Rathbun, Chrissie Love Santiago, Erin Smiley, Kasey Williams, David Withrow); Director, Tom Berger; Sets, Blair Mielnik; Lighting, Kevin Hardy; Costumes, David Withrow; Sound, Martha Goode; Stage Manager, Courtney Ferrell; Projections, David Bengali; Cast: Josh Brechner, John Bronston,

Nick Fondulis, Cary Hite, Jarred Kjack, Anaïs Koivisto, Kathryn Elisabeth Lawson, Michael Littner, Ralph Petrarca, Jason Summers, J.T. Michael Tayor, Miriam Tobin, Kasey Williams, Ciara Wong; November 29–December 16, 2007

CELEBRATION Book and lyrics by Tom Jones, music by Harvey Schmidt; Produced by (Re:)Directions Theatre Company; Director, Erin Smiley; Choreography, Jessica Redish, Sets, Blair Mielnik; Costumes, David Withrow; Lighting, Tim Kaufman; Cast: Kristen Alberda, Tom Berger, Nathan Bovos, George Croom, Joshuah Robinson, Ben Griessmeyer, Liz Kimball, Kristian Lazzaro, Stefanie O'Connell, Kasey Williams; December 27, 2007–January 6, 2008

BORDERTOWN by Steve Ives; Produced by (Re:)Directions Theatre Company; Director, Tom Berger; Sound, Henry Akona, Costumes, David Withrow; Lighting, Tim Kaufman; Stage Manager, Courtney Ferrell; Cast: Michael Bertollini, Carlo de los Reyes, Nick Fondulis, Cary Hite, Michael Kingsbaker, Marta Kuersten, TD White, Andrew Schecter, Kasey Williams; April 24–May 11, 2008

29th Street Rep (Altered Stages)

Artistic Director, David Mogentale

THE CONVERSATION by Francis Ford Coppola, adapted by Kate Harris; Director, Leo Farley; Set, Mark Symczak; Costumes, Rebecca Ming; Lighting, Stewart Wagner; Sound, Joseph Fosco; PSM, Sabrina Morabito; Cast: David Mogentale, Tim Corcoran, Amber Gallery, James E. Smith, Thomas Wehrle, Julianne Carpenter, Jack Dillon, Leigh Feldpausch, Craig Butta; April 3–May 4, 2008

Non-resident Productions

FRIJOLES COLORADOS by Cristina Rebull Pradas; Produced by Retablo Theater; Director, Gabriel Gorces; Set & Costumes, Orlando Gonzalez; Sound, Michael Rodriguez; Stage Manager, Sara Valle; Cast: Teresa Yenque, Gabriel Gorces; July 26–29, 2007

TRUE GENIUS by David Holstein; Produced by Small Pond Entertainment; Director, Jill Sierchio; Design, Graham T. Posner; Cast: Perry Tiberio, Nancy Evans, Regina Myers, Ken Scudder, Tyler S. Guilizio; September 23–October 7, 2008

I'VE BEEN DRUNK FOR THREE WEEKS AND I HAVE A GUN Written and directed by Jim Farmer; Produced by Susanne Columbia; Set, Victoria Imperioli; Costumes, Astrid Bruckner; Lighting, David Zeffren; PSM, Emileena Pedigo; Cast: Samantha Buck, Alex Hurt, Leslie Lyles, Jon Levenson, Peter Stoll, Sara Surrey; October 13–November 3, 2007

ARCHIPELAGO Short solo performance plays presented by Intentional Theatre Group in association with Small Pond Entertainment; Director, Emerie Snyder; Set, Michael Kerns; Lighting, Eileen Goddard; Costumes, Elisabeth Vastola; Sound, Peter Wood; Props, Ashley Gagner; Stage Manager, Melissa Figueroa; Press, Emily Owens; Included: *Scarface* by Davy Rothbart, *Hold This* by Sheila Callaghan, *Cranberry* by Brian Patrick Leahy, *The Cat's Fault* by Sarah Carbiener, *The Way Down* by Richard Strand, *Up Here/In Here* by Anton Dudley, *Orbit* by Erica Rosbe, *Act Without Words 1* by Samuel Beckett, *(A Diptych)* by Joyce Carol Oates, *Yes* by Stephen Belber; Cast: Therese Barbato, Sarah Carbiener, Daniel Owen Dungan, Nick Lewis, Lethia Nall, Gavin-Keith Umeh, Dan Via; November 8–18, 2007

HE'S HAVING A BABY Written and performed by Andrew Kaplan; Produced by VBAC Productions; Director, Cosmin Chivu; Set & Lighting, Evan O'Brient; December 5–23, 2007

2.5 MINUTE RIDE by Lisa Kron; Produced by Electric Pear Productions; Director, Matt M. Morrow; Set, Mark Erbaugh; Lighting, Gina Scherr; Sound, Amy Altadonna; Cast: Nicole Golden; January 18–February 9, 2008

MARK TWAIN'S BLUES by Walt Stepp; February 15–March 8, 2008 (This production transferred Off-Broadway to the DR2; see production credits on page 145).

3Graces Theater Co.

Executive Director, Chelsea Silverman; Artistic Directors, Elizabeth Bunnell and Annie McGovern; Managing Director, Kelli Lynn Harrison

A GOOD FARMER by Sharyn Rothstein; Director, Matthew Arbour; Set, Michael Kramer; Lighting, Greg Mitchell; Costumes, Courtney McClain; Sound, John D. Ivy; Music, Chip Barrow; Dramaturgy, Margot Avery and Patrick T. Cecalla II; Stage Manager, Christy Thede; ASM, Jimmy Whitacre; Cast: Eliabeth Bunnell, Annie McGovern, Chelsea Silverman, Gerald McCullouch, Jacqueline Duprey, Borden Hallowes, Anfew Giarolo, Sharon Eisman; Musicians: Chip Barry, John D. Ivy; Bank Street Theatre; September 25–October 20, 2007

YOUR BASIC AMERICAN MONDAY Monologues by L.E. McCullough; Director, Kathleen Bishop; Cast: Dacyl Acevedo, Margot Avery, Kally Duling, Anita Hollander, Kate Kearney-Patch, Krystal Marshall, Joan Preston, Deborah Jean Templin; Bank Street Theatre; September 29–October 16, 2007

SPRING SHORTS 2 Eight short plays; included: *Good Morning, Lady* by Steve Wisniewski, *What Price?* by Craig Pospisil, *Blood Sisters* by Robin Rice Lichtig, *Bang Day* by Rich Espey, *Big Girl* by Andrew Biss, *Yog Sothoth* by Lia Romeo, *Falutin'* by C.S. Hanson, *Sally Sees the Light* by Barbara Lindsay; Directors, Margot Avery, Tracy Bersley, Kathleen Bishop, Elizabeth Bunnell, Chris Dolman, Jim Elliott, Joanna Strange; Cast: Dorothy Abrahams, Dacyl Acevedo, Suzanne Barbetta, Kathleen Bishop, Elizabeth Bunnell, George Diehl, Uys DuBoisson, Andrew Giaolo, Jenny Greer, Daniel Halden, Kelli Lynn Harrison, Suzanne Johnson, Shevy Katan, Kate Kearney-Patch, Rock Kohli, Brian McFadden, Annie McGovern, Chelsea Silverman, Lucy Walters; Turtle Shell Theatre; April 3–13, 2008

3LD Art & Technology Center

DOPPELGÄNGER by Simon Heath; Presented by Feed the Herd Theatre Company; Director, Manny Bocchieri; June 30–July 21, 2007

LOOP DIVER Created and choreographed by Dawn Stoppiello; Presented by Troika Ranch; Dramaturg, Peter C. von Salis; Lighting, David Tirosh, Jennifer Sherburn; Music/Media, Mark Coniglio; Cast: Robert Clark Jen (JJ) Kovacevich, Johanna Levy, Daniel Suominen, Lucia Tong, Benjamin Wegman; September 5–23, 2007

MILK 'N' HONEY by Madeleine George; Presented by LightBox and The Food Theater Project; Director, Ellen Beckerman; Set, Narelle Sissons; Sound, Bray Poor; Lighting, Justin Townsend; Costumes, Meghan Healey; Video, Nicole Betancourt and C. Andrew Bauer; Producing Director, Nicole Betancourt; Cast: Aysan Celik and Shawn Fagan, Brian D. Coats, Vaneik Echeverria, Signe V. Harriday, Adam Rihacek; October 21–November 18, 2007

FIRE ISLAND by Charles Mee; Presented by 3LD; Director, Kevin Cunningham; Set, Paul DePietro; Costumes, Nellie Fleishcner; Sound, John Plenge; Lighting, David Tirosh; Video, Jeff Morey; Live Cast: Allison Keating, Catherine Yeager, David Tirosh, Gautham Prasad, Jenny Lee Mitchell, Jon Okabayashi, Joshua Koehn, Kate Moran, Kiku Collins, Livia de Paolis, Stephen Payne, Tina Alexis Allen, and Victor Weinstock; Live Musicians: Albert Kuvezin, Aldo Perez, Matthew Talmage; April 10–May 3, 2008

45th Street Theatre

THE SECOND TOSCA by Tom Rowan; Produced by Sorrel Tomlinson; Director, Kevin Newbury; Sets, Charlie Corcoran; Costumes, Joanne M. Haas; Lighting, D.M. Wood; Sound, Jill BC DuBoff; PSM, Mary Kathryn Blazek; ASM, Kathleen Stakenas; Cast: Rachel de Benedet, Vivian Reed, Jeremy Beck, Tug Coker, Eve Gigliotti, Mark Light-Orr, Melissa Picarello, Carrington Vilmont, Christian Whelan; June 8–July 1, 2007

BILLIONAIRES FOREVER by Melody Bates and David Bennett; Presented by Heart of Gold Productions, Billionaires for Bush, and James Simon; Director, Melody Bates; Choreography, DJ McDonald; Original Music, Clifford J. Tasner; Music Director, Joseph Reina; Lighting, Kate Greenburg; Cast: Kellie Aiken, Dave Bennett, Dave Case, Melissa Collom, Yvonne Willrich-Teague, Alex Mitchell, Brandi Rhome; September 4–9, 2007

LOVE OF A PIG by Leslie Caveny; Presented by The Cardinal Group, Jeffrey Schulman, Richard Pepenella; Director, D.H. Johnson; Supervising Directorr, Daniel Kutner; Set, Maiko Chii; Lighting, Cat Tate; Costumes, Melanie Swersey; Sound, Garrett Montgomery; Stage Manager, Brianne Muelle; Cast: Steven Strobel, Marie C. Anderson, Michael Ferrell, Jenny Greer, David Nelson, Ginny Lee, Aaron Davis, Dana Brooke; October 12–28, 2007

MRS. BARRY'S MARRIAGE Written and performed by Bronwen Coleman; Presented by the Cardinal Group, Jeffrey Schulman, and Richard Pepenella; Director, Anna Jones; October 14–23, 2007

ARPEGGIO by David Stallings, music by Alec Bridges; Presented by MTWorks Theatre Company, Jillian Zeman; Director, Cristina Alicea; Music Director, Sarah Chaney; Set, Craig Napoliello; Cotumes, Angela Curcuru; Lighting, Ian Crawford; Choreography, Carolina Almont; Associate Producer, Julie Griffith; Cast: Andy Travis, Allison Ikin, Kristina Kohl, Marino Antonio Minino, Jonathan Scott Albert; Band: Chris Conly, David Moore; November 1–18, 2007

MUD by Maria Irene Fornes; Director, Josh Hoglund; Set, Syaka Nagata; Costumes, Felix Ciprian; Lighting, Christine Shallenberg; Stage Manager, Liz Giorgis; Cast: Mireya Lucio, Dylan Dawson, Eric Clem, Nick Cregor, Ava Jarden; November 8–11, 2007

MISS WHITE HOUSE by Ira Shapiro; Director, Harland Meltzer; Cast: Kaitlin Stillwell; November 20–December 9, 2007

THE REV. BILL AND BETTY HOLLANDS' INTERFAITH CHRISTMAS SHOW Created by Marty Hill; Presented by Punch 59 Sketch Comedy; Music, Sudden Death; Cast: Mindy Raf, Marty Hill; December 6–22, 2007

JANE EYRE Adapted and directed by N.G. McClernan from the novel by Charlote Brontë; Produced by Mergatroyd Productions; Costumes, Viviane Galloway; Lighting, Keith Traux; Media, Charles Jeffreys; Stage Manager, Amanda Elaan; Dialects, Annalisa Loeffler; Choreography, Reagan Wilson; Cast: Mary Murphy, Greg Oliver Bodine, Alice Connorton, Nat Cassidy, Bruce Barton, Annalisa Loeffler; February 14–March 2, 2008

MY LIFE ON THE CRAIGSLIST Written and performed by Jeffrey Self, Developed and directed by Ryan J. Davis; Presented by Solomon Weisbard and Chris Ryan; Music, DJ Drew G. Montalvo; February 15–29, 2008 (Friday late-nites only; previously presented one night only at New World Stages on November 1, 2007.)

FUGITIVE SONGS Music by Chris Miller, lyrics by Nathan Tysen; Produced by Dreamlight Theatre Company; Director, Joe Calarco; Set, Brian Prather; Costumes, Jennifer Caprio; Cast: D.B. Bonds, Halle Petro, Todd E. Pettiford, Ben Roseberry, Lucia Spina; March 8–30, 2008

59E59

EAST TO EDINBURG FESTIVAL July 10–29, 2007; Theaters B and C; Included: *Rash* written and performed by Jenni Wolfson, directed by Jen Nails; *Grasmere* by Kristina Leach, directed by Noel Neeb; *Stinky Flowers and the Bad Banana* written and performed by Croft Vaught, directed by Adam Goldstein, presented by Wasted Theatre Education and Drawing Board Arts Project; *Inside Private Lives* conceived by Kristin Stone, directed by Lee Michael Cohn, presented by Kristin Stone Entertainment; Cast: Leonora Gershman, Maddisen Krown, Adam LeBow, Mary MacDonald, Eileen O'Connell, Paul Ryan, Bryan Safi, David Shofner, Kristin Stone, Sheila Wolf, Yee Yee Lee; *A Thousand Cranes* by Kathryn Shultz Miller, directed by Masha Obolensky, presented by PSFilms and Productions; *The Boys Next Door* by Tom Griffin, directed by Christian Galpin and Benjy Schrim, presented by PSFilms and Productions; Cast: Mike Pfaff, Elizabeth Olson, Christopher Mack, Tom Wilson, Renee Miller, Ed Sorrell, Holly Payne-Strange; *An Age of Angels* written and performed by Mark Soper, directed by Ines Wurth; Presented by IMC Productions; *MOD* book by Paul Andrew Perez, music & lyrics by George Griggs, directed by Chantel Pascente, presented by Infinity Repertory Company; Cast: Alexa Bonaros, Lucy Braid, Andre Catrini, Mike Greco, Jasmine Schwab, Sarah Shankman, Craig Sogel, Susannah Genty-Waksberg, Rachel Warren, Lizzie Campolongo, Christine Barnwell, Amy Secunda; *tender* by Shapour Benard, directed by Julie Baber, presented by BrownElyse Productions and 20% Theatre Company; Cast: Kellie McCants, Kelly Dwyer, Andrea Dionne, Amber Gray; *La Femme Est Morte or Why I Should Not F%!# My Son* written and directed by Shoshona Currier, presented by The Shalimar; Cast: Laura Lee Anderson, Joe Curnutte, Kim Gainer, Marissa Lupp, Craig Peugh, Atticus Rowe, Jen Taher, Joey Williamson; *The Nina Variations* by Steven Dietz, directed by Douglas "Chip" Rome, presented by Rams2Scotland; Cast: Hannah Blechman, Josh Berrent, Kathleen Burnard, Sammi Grozbean, Nazzi Haririnia, Andy Hirsch, Lindsay Ferris, Mimi Lynch, Seph Normandy, Ella Robertson, Sarah Russell, Katy Summerlin, Sam Wharton, Liz Venz; *Miralcle in Rwanda* based on the true story of Immaculée Ilibagiza, written and performed by Edward Vilga, directed by Schele Williams, presented by Broadveiw Phoenix

SUMMER SHORTS August 2–30, 2007; Theater B; Presented by John McCormack & J.J. Kandel in association with The Open Book; included: Series A: *Afternoon Tea* Book and lyrics by Eduardo Machado, music by Skip Kennon; *Rain, Heavy at Times* by Leslie Lyes; *Amici, Ascoltat* by Warren Leight; *Real World Experience* by Michael Domitrovich; Series B: *The PA* by Tom O'Brien; *Merwins Lane* by Keith Reddin; *Windowshire* by Randee Smith; *Father's Day* by John Augustine; *Skin Deep* by Tina Howe

THE HANGING OF RAZOR BROWN by Le Wilhelm; Presented by Rage Against Time and Love Creek Productions; Director, Merry Beamer; Cast: Nick Giello, John Mervini, Tracy Newirth, Jon Oak, Lynn Osborn, Erin Singleton, Jaclyn Sokol, Kenya Wilson; Theater C; August 2–26, 2007

THE SHATTERING OF THE GOLDEN PANE by Le Wilhelm; Presented by Rage Against Time and Love Creek Productions; Director, Gregg David Shore; Cast: Kristin Carter, Kevin Perri, Kirsten Walsh; Theater C; August 16–September 2, 2007

THE SHAPE OF METAL by Thomas Kilroy; Presented by Origin Theatre Company in association with The Sullivan Project; Director, Brian Murray; Set, Lex Liang; Costumes, Elizabeth Flauto; Lighting, Phil Monat; Sound, Zachary Williamson; Dialects; Amy Stoller; Cast: Roberta Maxwell, Julia Gibson, Molly Ward; Theater B; September 7–30, 2007

FLAGS by Jane Martin; Presented by Firefly Theatre in association with Dog Run Repertory Theatre Company; Director, Henry Wishcamper; Set, Kelly Hanson; Costumes, Anne Keeney; Lighting, Miriam Nilofa Crowe; Sound, Graham Johnson; Video, Aaron Rhyne; Cast: Chris Mulkey, Karen Landry, Ryan Johnston, Stephen Mendillo, Steven Klein, Ian Beford, Kyle Johnston, Yvans Jourdain, Quonta Beasley; Theater C; September 12–30, 2007

WIDOWS by Ariel Dorman; Presented by Reverie Productions; Director, Hal Brooks; Set, Wilson Chin; Artistic Director/Lighting, Colin D. Young; Costumes, Kimberly Glennon; Sound/Composer, Matt O'Hare; Casting, Judy Bowman; Associate Producer, Layna Fisher; Associate Director, Johanna Gruenhut; PSM, Samone B. Weissman; ASM, Laureen McArthur; Cast: Josh Alexander, Mark Alhadeff, Veronica Cruz, Sam Dingman, Sarah Nina Hayon, Mercedes Herrero, Guiesseppe Jones, Ana Cruz Kayne, Ephraim Lopez, Melissa Miller, Sean J. Moran, Gita Reddy, James Saba, Anca Suiu, Joaquín Torres, Ching Valdes-Aran, Audrey Lynn Weston, Yan Xi; Theater B; January 10–February 3, 2008

LIFE IN A MARITAL INSTITUTION (20 Years of Monogomy in One Terrifying Hour) Written and performed by James Braly; Presented by The Deep End Productions and Little Johnny Koerber; Director, Hal Brooks; Producers, Anna Becker, Joel Bassin; Stage Manager, Lauren McArthur; Set, Michael V. Moore; Lighting, Colin D. Young; Theater C; February 19–March 16, 2008

MISSIVES by Garret Jon Groenveld; Presented by Animated Theaterworks Inc., Theater Resourses Unlimited and Playground; Director, Elysabeth Kleinhans; Set/Lighting, Maruti Evans; Sound, Scott O'Brien; Video, Kevin R. Frech; Costumes/Projections, Barbara Iams Korein; Cast: Shamika Cotton, Richard Gallagher, Peter Kleinhans, Jay Randall, Ashely West; Theater C; March 20–April 6, 2008

78th Street Theatre Lab

BOTANICAL GARDENS by Todd Logan; Director, Rob Urbinati; Set, Sarah Pearline; Cast: Anne Carney, Malachy Cleary; August 31–September 30, 2007

ALL THE HELP YOU NEED, The Adventures of a Hollywood Handyman Written and performed by Tim Ryan; September 27–October 27, 2007

ROMEO AND JULIET by William Shakespeare; Director, Kevin Connell; September 21–23, 2007

THE BLOOD BROTHERS PRESENT: PULP by James Comtois, Qui Nguyen, Mac Rogers; Directors, Pete Boisvert, Rebecca Comtois, Matt Johnston, Patrick Shearer and Stephanie

Williams; Presented by Nosedive Productions; Lighting, Phil Shearer; Sound, Patrick Shearer; Music, Larry Lees; Fights, Qui Nguyen; Production Manager, Stephanie Cox-Williams; Stage Manager, Jessica Lazar; Cast: Pete Boisvert, Patrick Shearer, Stephanie Cox-Williams, Jessi Gotta, Gyda Arber, Anna Kull, Michael Criscuolo, Brian Silliman, Marc Landers; 2nd Floor Lab; October 11–27, 2007

THE EXONERATED by Jessica Blank and Erik Jensen; Presented by the Red Fern Theatre Company; Director, Melanie Moyer Williams; Set, Adreinne Kapalko; Lighting, Jessica Greenberg; Stage Manager, Laura Luciano; Cast: Jeffery Belford, Steven Bennett, Kim Carlson, Alexandra Cremer, Reg Ferguson, Karen Gayle, Scott Shaw Matthews, Emilie Elizabeth Miller, David Pringle, Lorenzo Scott, Brad Thomason; November 1–11, 2007

STAGE THIS! AN EVENING OF F----N FABULOUS TEN-MINUTE PLAYS Written by David-Matthew Barnes, Alex Broun, Bill Cosgriff, Wendy-Marie Foerster, J. Michael Harper, La'Chris Jordan, Jeffrey James Keyes, Steven Korbar, John Tyler Owens, Evelyn J. Pine, Lowell Press, Greg Tito and Cara Vander Wiel; Produced by FN Productions; Directors: Frank Blocker, Murray Scott Changar, Mark Finley, Iftiaz Haroon, Jon Michael Murphy, Sydney Stone, Halina Ujda, Cara Vander Wiel; Stage Manager, Yan Wu; Cast: Eric C. Bailey, Moti Margolin, Frank Blocker, Sydney Stone, Charnele Crick, Chima Chikazunga, Emile Byron, Brian Distance, Stacie Theon, Heather Koren, Bobby Abid, Chris von Hoffmann; 3rd Floor Lab; December 6–22, 2007

CEMETERY GOLF Written and performed by Jim Loucks; Producer, Deb Loucks; Director, Carol Rusoff; 2nd Floor Lab; February 1–10, 2008

SHEL'S SHORTS by Shel Silverstein; Presented by Project: Theatre; Directors, James Barry, Tara Franlin, Joe Jung, Andrew McLeod; Stage Manager, Jacob Seelbach; Lighting, Jane McKillery; Sets, J.J. Bernard & Francois Portier; Sound, James Barry & Joe Jung; Cast: Michael Andrew Baker, Amanda Byron, Brian Frank, Tara Franklin, John Hashop, Amy Hattemer, Joe Jung, Christine Piche, Ben Rosenblatt, Jenny Schutzman, Brian Sell, Joe Therrien; 3rd Floor Lab; February 7–23, 2008

OUR COUNTRY'S GOOD by Timbelake Wertenbaker; Produced by Folding Chair Classical Theatre; Director, Marcus Geduld; Cast: Lisa Blankenship, Gowan Campbell, Francine Margolis, Jessika Hardy, James Arden, Jordan Barbour, Paul Edward Hope, Ian Gould, Brad Makarowski, Karen Ogle; February 28–March 22, 2008

HANNAH AND THE HOLLOW CHALLAH by Alice Eve Cohen; Presented by Practical Cats Theatre; Director, Elizabeth Margid; Puppets, Emily DeCola; Set, Mary Robinette Kowal; Sound, Gerard McConville; Lighting, Eric Nightengale; Cast: Maria McConville, Michael Orth; March 15–April 6, 2008

COLORFUL WORLD by Jame Comtois; Produced by Nosedive Productions; Director, Pete Boisvert; Lighting, Phil Shearer; Sound, Patrick Shearer; Dramaturg, Rebecca Comtois; Cast: Abe Goldfarb, Jessi Gotta, Marc Landers, Zack Calhoon, Mac Rogers, Patrick Shearer, Ben VandenBoom, Christopher Yustin; May 8–31, 2008

A PIECE OF MY HEART by Shirley Lauro, based on the book by Keith Walker; Produced by the Red Fern Theatre Company; Director, Melanie Moyer Williams; Set, Adreinne Kapalko; Costumes, Summer Lee Jack; Lighting, Jessica Greenberg; Stage Manager, Laura Luciano; Cast: Christopher Clawson, Siho Ellsmore, Elizabeth Flax, Catherine Gowl, Emilie Elizabeth Miller, Kendall Rileigh, Phoenix Vaughn; May 1–11, 2008

BEEF by Lawrence Dial; Produced by Slant Theatre Project; Director, Adam Knight; Lighting, Lauren Duffie; Sound, Wes Grantom; Stage Managers, Amy Windle, Amanda Kay McDonald; Dramaturg, Sarah Slight; Fights, Adam Rihacek; Cast: Nick Mills, Robert Karma Robinson, Kristin Friedlander, Jacob Ming-Trent; May 17–June 1, 2008

Abingdon Theatre Complex

June Havoc Theatre

THE HUNT FOR TREASURE by Adam Risbridger & Byron Laviolette; Presented by English Rose Productions; Director, Fritz Brekeller; Set, Justin Haskell; Lighting, Robin A. Paterson; Costumes, Jim P. Hammer; Fight Director, Vince Cupone; Cast: John Calvin Kelley, Avery Pearson; June 26–July 8, 2007

THE PEOPLE VS. MONA by Jim Wann and Patricia Miller; Presented by Ground UP Productions; Director, Kate Middleton; Musical Director, Robert K. Mikulski; Choreography, Jill Gorrie; Set/Lighting, Travis McHale; Costumes, Elisa R. Richards; Sound, Duane McKee; Assistant Musical Director, Ritt Henn; Stage Manager, Devan Hibbard; ASM, Elizabeth Doyle; Technical Directors, Jeff Besselman & Dan Wheeless; Press, Sam Rudy Media Relations; Casting, Amy Heiddt, Guy Olivieri; Cast: Richard Binder, Mariand Torres, Karen Culp, Natalie Douglas, Omri Schein, David Jon Wilson, Marcie Henderson, Ritt Henn, Jason Chimonides, Dan Bailey; July 12–August 4, 2007

THE SEAGULL by Anton Chekhov, translated by Carol Rocamora; Presented by Hesterhouse Productions; Director, Lisette Hazan; Original Music, Paul DiRito; Cast: Jon Cantor, John D'Arcangelo, Sean M. Grady, Rosemary Howard, Jessica Hester, Michael Lichtstein, Peter Lillo, Tommee May, Hamilton Meadows, Lori Russo; September 5–16, 2007

THE OPTIMIST by Jason Chimonides; Produced by Ground UP Productions, Kate Middleton and Matt Olin; Director, Jace Alexander; Set/Lighting, Travis McHale; Costumes, Elisa Richards; Fight Choreography, Ron Piretti; Stage Manager, Devan Elise Hibbard; ASM, Kate August; Press, Sam Rudy, Lanie Zipoy and Avec Productions; Cast: Matt Burns, Caitlin FitzGerald, Chris Thorn, Ryland Blackington,; March 20–April 12, 2008

THE LONE WOLF SERIES Four solo performance shows presented by Coyote Rep; Producer, Michael Dean Morgan; Set, Gran Van Zevern; Lighting, Jason Teague; Stage Manager, Lyndsey Goode; Included: *the cowboy is dying* written and performed by Isaac Byrne, directed by Donnetta Lavinia Grays; *Stella by Starlight* written and performed by Heidi Tokheim, directed by Donnetta Lavinia Grays; *Spoiled Bea* written and performed by Jeanne LaSala with Brian Homer, directed and designed by Mitch Greenhill; *You got questions? I got answers!* written and performed by Andrea Caban, directed by Caitlin Moon; May 15–25, 2008

Dorothy Strelsin Theatre

PROFESSIONAL SKEPTICISM by James Rasheed; Produced by Zootopia Theatre Company; Director, Kareem Fahmy; Set, Andrew Lu; Costumes, Anne K. Wood; Lighting, Scott Bolman; Sound, Andrew Papadeas; PSM, Nilous Safinya; Cast: Britney Burgess, Steve French, Matthew J. Nichols, Wesley Allen Thornton; June 28–July 15, 2007

SIN by Wendy MacLeod; Presented by Bohemian Archeology; Director, Jordana Kritzer; Set, Roberta Berman; Lighting, Ethan Kaplan; Costumes, Allison Choi Braun; Cast: Megan Hill, Collin MacKenzie Smith, Carter Roy, Kelly Miller, Amy Broder, Henry Caplan, Christopher Armond, Douglas Scott Sorenson; July 18–July 29, 2007

AMERICAN STORY PROJECT SUMMER FESTIVAL Productions included: *Daguerreotype* by Stephen Aubrey; Director, Jess Chayes; *Lunch Box Sketch Comedy*; Developmental Readings: *The Death of the Ball Turret Gunner* by Anna Moench, *Bury My Heart* by Bob McClure, *The Architect Ages* by David Haan, *L'elue* by Kevin Anthony Kautzman, *Percy & Shell* by Chris Kaminstein; *The American Musical Project: New Voices in NY Musical Theatre*; August 2–11, 2007

THE CASCADE FALLS Written and directed by Adam Michael Cohen; Produced by Bat Country; Director, Ryan Hemphill; Set/Costume Consultant, David Henderson; Lighting, Oscar Mendoza; Fight Choreography, Ian Merrigan; Cast: Lucas Beck, Kristen Scoles, Samuel Whitten; August 23–September 1, 2007

DIRECTORFEST 2007 Four one-acts: *Sugar Mouth Sam Don't Dance No More* by Don Evans, directed by D. Wambui Richardson; *The 100 Most Beautiful Names of Todd* by Julia Cho, directed by Dan Rigazzi; *Autophagy* by Sean Graney, directed by Joanie Schultz; *Fit for Feet* by Jordan Harrison, directed by Gaye Taylor Upchurch; December 6–9, 2007

'TIL SUNDAY Written and performed by Nairoby Otera; Director, Presented by Loeber Productions; Michelle Tattenbaum; February 22–March 9, 2008

SYMPATHETIC DIVISION by Gia Marotta; Presented by Sweeter Theater Productions; Director, Maura Farver; Stage Manager, Colin Miller; Costumes, Summer Lee Jack; Lighting, Andrew Fritsch; Cast: Colleen Allen, Robyn Frank, Charlotte Patton, Ron Stetson; May 15–18, 2008

THIS IS A COWBOY POEM MY DADDY TAUGHT ME by Katie Bender; Produced by Rockstead Productions & The Cardinal Group, Carly J. Price, DH Johnson and Richard Pepenella; Stage Manager, Kayla Shriner; Press, Katie Adams; Director, Stephanie Yankwitt; Set, Stephanie Tucci; Costumes, Jennifer L. Adams; Light, John Wolf; Sound: Eric C. Dente; Cast: Stephen Payne, Katie Bender, Jesse Presler, Mary Guiteras; May 22–June 15, 2008

Access Theater

WOMEN OF MANHATTAN by John Patrick Shanley; Presented by Madair Productions; Director, Antonio Merneda; Lighting, Lauren Parrish; Cast: Cory Gibson, Caroline Hearns, Vina Less, Carly Miller, Werner Pauliks; July 17–22, 2007

THE DANISH MEDIATIONS/SLOTS by Sergei Burbank; Presented by A2K Productions; Director, Adam Karsten; Lighting, Kate Ashton; Set, Kathryn Singer; Costumes, Daonne Huff; Fights, Corey Richmond Skaggs; Stage Manager, Susan J. Sunday; Dramaturg, Aditi Saxton; Cast: Jason Altman, Noelle Holly, Anna Kull, Gary Patent, Fayna Sanchez, Jason Updike; August 16–September 9, 2007

THE BALTIMORE WALTZ by Paula Vogel; Presented by Inch Mile Entertainment; Director, Kristen Dreger; Producer/ Set, Luke Hancock; Cast: Jennie Kilcullen, Joe Lattanzi, Luke Hancock; August 23–September 1, 2007

LILITH by Alexandra Devin; Presented by Core Theatre Company; Director, John Hurley; Cast: Lisa Bruno, Tom Cleary, Gil Bar-Sela; Alisha Campbell, Craig Zisel; September 7–23, 2007

THE ROAD TO NOWHERE Created and presented by Overturn Theatre Ensemble; Director, Kristy Dodson; Cast: Lawrence St. Victor, Shanna Sharp, David Brown, Alex Pierce, Joshua Levine, Erin Renee Smith; September 13–22, 2007

PROJECT PLAYWRIGHT III New works by Robert Charles Gompers, Richard Martin Hirsch, Brett Hursey, Steve Koppman, and Craig McNulty; Presented by Madair Productions; Directors, Melani Adair, Robert Charles Gompers, Antonio Merenda, and Guil Parreiras; Cast: Toni Christopher, Heather Edwards, Jeff Feller, Chris Flynn, Kevin Gay, Evan Joiner, Abe Koogler, Kate Murrin, Kristine Pregot, Doug Rossi, Ina Smith; September 25–30, 2007

DEPARTURES by Kristen Palmer; Presented by Blue Coyote Theater Group; Director, Kyle Ancowitz; Cast: Keira Keeley, Travis York; October 7–28, 2007

STRAIGHT CHASER Written, directed and produced by Dave Tianga; Presented by Subterranean Theater Ensemble; Executive Producer, Alexis Suarez; Set/Lighting, Patrick Mahaney; Stage Manager, Nataliya Vasilyeva; Cast: Vanessa Hidray, Alex Lozano, Jessica Philbin, Nathanael Reimer, Reza Salazar, Alexis Suarez, Stefanie Walmsley; October 4–13, 2007

SHIRLEY AT THE TROPICANA Written and performed by Amanda Ronconi; Director, Joan Evans; Films, Jeff Wiens; Presented by Natasha Corbie and Sonja Pzepski in association with Interaction Arts Foundation; October 19–November 18, 2007

LOCAL STORY by Kristen Palmer; Presented by Overlap Productions, Tania Inessa Kirkman; Director, Susanna L. Harris; Set, Kina Park; Lighting, Ben Kato; Sound, Amy Altadonna; Costumes, Jessica Gaffney; Stage Manager, Susan Sunday; Technical Director, Rick LeBrenz; Press, Karen Greco; Cast: Travis York, Mark David Watson, Keira Keeley, Havilah Brewster, Ben Scaccia, Mariella Heller, Sarah Kate Jackson; November 27–December 30, 2007

BUSINESS AS USUAL by Mark Souza; Presented by Prophecy Productions; Director, Edwin Hansen-Nelson; Cast: Michael Mraz, Corey Ann Haydu, Steven Todd Smith; Gallery Space; December 6–17, 2007

LYSISTRATA or Lay Don't Slay based on the play by Aristophanes; Presented by Ashberry Productions; Director, Daniel Waldron; Stage Manager, Sarah Magno; Design, Juan Rivera, Rob Heller, Deborah Waldron, Stacey Maltin; Cast: Amanda Berry, Liz Alderfer, Stacey Maltin, Lindsay Tanner, Lily Blau, Lauren Michaels, Sarah Hansel, Sarah Todes, Brittany Scott, Eric Eastman, Brandon McCluskey, Rocco Chierichella, Mike Rudez, Jay DeYonker, Paul Howell, Michael Lister, and Marty Glyer; January 17–26, 2008

BLUE COYOTE'S HAPPY ENDINGS Works by Blair Fell, Matthew Freeman, David Foley, Brian Fuqua, David Johnston, Boo Killebrew, Stan Richardson, Christine Whitley, and John Yearley; Presented by Blue Coyote Theatre Group; Directors, Kyle Ancowitz, Robert Buckwalter, Gary Shrader, Stephen Speights; February 12–March 1, 2008

EUPHORIC TENDENCIES by Tanya Marten; Director, Johnathan Marten; Producing Director, Susan Biderman Montez; Set, Elisha Schaefer; Lighting, Duane Pagano; Costumes, Crystal Fergusson; Cast: Katherine Barron, Nandita Chandra, Lizzie Czerner, Nicole Godino, Dona Elena Hatcher, Jonny Blaze Leavitt, Jonathan Marten, Tanya Marten, Gary Mink, Carol Padiernos, Stephanie Sellars, Dayle Pivetta, Bella Vendramini; March 6–22, 2008

HOW TO BE A DOLL Created and directed by Genevieve Gearhart, text by Alissa Riccardelli; Presented by Mir Productions; March 13–23, 2008

THE WENDY COMPLEX Written and directed by Jeremy Bloom; Produced by Vagabond Theatre Ensemble; Set, Stephanie Tucci; Lighting, Brian Tovar; Costumes, Erin B. Schultz; Music, Renee Dunway/Jetsetter; Cast: Kara Peters, Sarah Billington Stevens, Jordan Cohen, Sarah Ann Masse, Kevin Reed, Paige Dana; April 3–6, 2008

WHEN IS A CLOCK by Matthew Freeman; Presented by Blue Coyote Theater Group; Director, Kyle Ancowitz; Set, Robert Monaco; Lighting, Daniel Meeker; Sound, Brandon Wolcott; Graphics, Bruce Goldstone; Press Karen Greco; Stage Manager, Susan Sunday; Cast: Beau Allulli, David Del Grosso, Laura Desmond, Tracey Gilbert, Ian Gould, Tom Staggs, Matthew Trumbull, Megan Tusing; April 15–May 10, 2008

THE MARY TRILOGY by Adreienne Dawes; Presented by Mir Productions; Director, Julianne Just; Cast: Deborah Anderson, Carissa Cordes, Jason Cutler, Elizabeth Fraatz, Genevieve Gearhart, Cindy N. Kawasaki, Michael Cooke Kendrick, Anthony C. E. Nelson, Lindsay Strachan; May 15–25, 2008

STANDING CLEAR Written, produced, and featuring Ishah Janssen-Faith & Jack McGowan; Created in collaboration and featuring Melinda Ferraraccio, Becca Hackett, Ben Holbrook; Presented by the Coffee Cup Theatre Company; Director, Barbara Karger; Set/Props, Kina Park; Lighting, Peter Hoerburger; Costumes, Young-Yoon Kim; Sound, Ryan Maeker; PSM, Jaimie Van Dyke; Press, David Gibbs; May 29–June 21, 2008

Ace of Clubs

FITZ AND WALLOUGHS GET IT IN THE END! Playwright/Director, Paul Hagen; Lyricist/Performer, Micah Bucey; Composer/Accompanist, Andrew Edwards; June 3–July 8, 2007

BEN, OR THE FUCK'D UP STORY OF MY BRO RO AND HIS CUNT JULES Adapted and directed by J. Marshall Denuskek; Cast: Chris Schultz, Brian Kimmet, Jennie Sheffield, Shayna Ferm, Rob Adler, S. Quincy Beard, Joseph Langham, Nate Dushku, Mike Rushton, Avery Pearson, Mick Mellamphy, Senna McCandless; August 21–September 6, 2007

SEMI-PERMANENT Written and performed by Rick Gradone; Director, Johanna McKeon; Set, Lara Fabian; Video, Adam Larsen; Lighting, Joel Silver; Sound, Stefano Zazzera; Stage Manager, Megan Schwarz; Press, Ron Lasko; February 3–March 23, 2008; previously presented at the 2007 New York International Fringe Festival

The Alternate Theatre

Founder/Artistic Director, Kareem Fahmy

DON JUAN DOES NEW JERSEY Adapted from Molière, conceived and directed by Kareem Fahmy; Co-presented by Prospect Theatre Company's Dark Night Series; Choreography, Nicole Holst; Set, Jeffery Eisenmann; Costumes, Anne K. Wood; Sound/Music, Andrew Papadeas; Cast: Julio Vincent Gambuto, Catherine Gowl, Heather Hollingsworth, Dana Jacks, Arthur Lazalde, Christina Pumariega, Zak Risinger, Doug Roland; Hudson Guild Theatre; October 6–9, 2007

Amas Musical Theatre

Producing Director, Donna Trinkoff

MAMA I WANT TO SING Book and lyrics by Vy Higginsen & Ken Wydo, original music by Rudolph V. Hawkins, Pat

Holley, Steven Taylor, and Doris Troy; Director, Rejendra Ramoon Maharaj; Musical Director, David Alan Bunn; Choreography, James Harkness, Michael Susko; Production Supervisor, Peter Feuchtwanger; Sound, Ray Shilke; Press, Joe Trentacosta, Springer Associates; PSM, Brian Westmoreland; Stage Manager, Karen Parlato; Cast: Chuck Cooper, Ahmaya Knoelle Higginson, Capathia Jenkins, Ted Louis Levy, Brandi Chavonne Massey, Chaundra Cameron, Danielle Chambers, Ryan Duncan, Jessica Fields, Carmen Ruby Floyd, Robert H. Fowler, McKenzie Frye, Jené Hernandez, Jonathan Lee Iverson, Vanessa A. Jones, Ano Okera, John Eric Parker, Antyon Smith, Christopher Zelno; Students of the Rosetta LeNoire Musical Theatre Academy; Special Guests: Maurice Hines, Melba Moore; Honorees: Phylicia Rashad, Pricewaterhouse Coopers; Blast from the Past Benefit; New World Stages; March 31, 2008

STREET DREAMS – THE INNER CITY MUSICAL Book and lyrics by Eve Merriam, music by Helen Miller; Director, Christopher Scott; Set, Andrew Farrugia; Lighting, Ben Hagen; Costumes, Cheryl A. McCarron; Music Director, Marshall Keating; Choreography, Monica Johnson; Production Supervisor, Ian Grunes; Rosetta LeNoire Musical Theatre Academy Production; American Theatre of Actors; May 9–18, 2008

Amas Six O'Clock Musical Theatre Lab

BURLY-Q! A GAY BURLESQUE by Phillip George, Peter Charles Morris, Ernie Lijoi and Tom Orr; Songs by Brad Ellis, Ethan Fein, Matt Eisenstein, Fred Barton, Matt Ward, Dick Gallagher; Players Theatre Loft; October 16–18, 2008

LORENZO Music and book by Judd Woldin, lyrics and book by Richard Engquist; Co-presented by Eric Krebs; Director, Christopher Scott; Music Director, John Baxindine; Cast: Joel Blum, Kathy Calahan, Bradley Dean, Kimberly Reid Dunbar, Vanessa Jones, Don Mayo, Trish Rapier, Steve Sterner, Chris Zelno; Players Theatre; November 13–15, 2007

American Globe Theatre

Producing Artistic Director, John Basil

THE WINTER'S TALE by William Shakespeare; Director, John Basil; Set, Kevin Lee Allen; Costumes, Jim Parks; Lighting, Mark Hankla; Choreography, Alisa Claire; Cast: Geoffrey Barnes, Diedre Da Silva, Rick Fay, Robert Lerardi, David Katchen, Rebecca McDougall, Mary Riley, Mat Sanders, Christina Shipp, Jefferson Slinkard, Daniel Smith, Joseph Small, Robert Lee Taylor, Jacob Troy, Micah James Watterson, Jillian Welsh; March 13–April 5, 2008

14TH ANNUAL 15 MINUTE PLAY FESTIVAL Presented in association with Turnip Theatre Company; April 15–27, 2008

American Theatre of Actors

Courtyard Theatre

ASTERISK* by Tom Diriwachter; Producer Dean Negri; and March Forth Productions in Association with Tower Athletics; Director, Jason Grant; Publicity, Emily Owens PR; Graphic Design, Jeff Gordon; Cast: Jon Coats, Jeff Gordon, Ned Lynch, Lou Mastantouno, Dean Negri, John Sollitto, Artie Ray; Courtyard Theatre; June 6–24, 2007

Chernuchin Theatre

32ND ANNUAL SAMUEL FRENCH ORIGINAL SHORT PLAY FESTIVAL June 5–17, 2007

YOU SHOULDN'T HAVE TOLD by Anne L. Thompson-Scretching; Director, Tippi; Cast: Jai Howard, John Myers, Susaye Lawson, Nick Dorvil, Denise Collins, Kelli Kinchelow, Rory Clarke, Jeannie Rae Kempa, Ivan Moore; July 12–22, 2007

STRAWBERRY ONE-ACT FESTIVAL Presented by the Riant Theatre; August 2–19, 2007 and February 15–25, 2008

LYRICAL ARTS Witten and produced by Rashawn Strife; Director, Davin McLeod; Cast: Rashawn Strife; Bonnie Jones, Kofi Nshafoah, Helen Tong, Cherish Duke, Albert Williams, Emmanuel Brown, Emil Mequita, Tamarra Scott, Davin McLeod, Zay Pierre-Louis, To-Tam Ton-Nu, Jennifer Reagan, Holmes Lindsay IV, Leroy Hankins; October 3–21, 2007

SAVE THE WORLD by Chris Kipiniak; Director, Michael Barakiva; Producer, Joshua P. Weiss; Set, Shoko Kambara; Costumes, Ona Botez-Ban; Lighting, Nick Francone; Stage Manager, Danielle Teague-Daniels; Cast: Craig Bridger, Charissa Chamorro, Christine Corpuz, Noshir Dalal, Kelly Hutchinson, Danielle Skraastad, Stephen Bel Davies; January 18–February 9, 2008

Sargent Theatre

TAPE by Stephen Belber; Cast: Wade Dunham, Scott Brocious, Sarah Kostulias; August 10–12, 2007

THE POSSIBILITIES by Howard Barker; Presented by Collective Productions in association with Inner Circle Theater Company; Director, Albert Aeed; Set, Obadiah Savage; Costumes, Brad L. Scoggins; Lighting, Chris Cotone; Sound, Jewels Eubanks; Movement, Tracy Bersley; Fights, Dan Zisson; PSM, Tatiana Gelfand; Cast: Michael Benjamin, Jeremy Brena, Marilyn Duryea, Lori Feiler, Ramesh Ganeshram, Rodney Hakim, Charles Hendricks, Angus Hepburn, Malina Linkas, Alison Ostergaard, Maureen Mooney, Carly Robins, Fred Rueck, Molly Rydzel, John Stagnari, Reema Zaman; September 27–October 13, 2007

DEALER'S CHOICE by Patrick Marber; Presented by Axiom Theatre Company; Director, Matthew Hancock; Cast: James T. Cernero, Aaron Eisenberg, Ethan Frank, Korey Jackson, Nick Merritt, Gregory Porter Miller; February 7–16, 2008

DINNER WITH AHMED by Paul Rawlings; Presented by Blume Media Group Ltd.; Director, Danielle Campbell; PSM, TaShwan Jackson; Cast: Michael Jaye, Joseph Callari, Ray Durand, Rory Wheeler, Amir Darvish, Scott Glascock, Lauren Milberger, Sue Mathys, Alex Herrald, Corinne Palermo, Ross Anthony Evans; February 28–March 9, 2008

KINGDOM COME by Allan Farbman; Director, Jeremy Wechter; Cast: Bill Growney, Dean Negri; March 12–16, 2008

OUT OF IGNORANCE by Peter F. Langmen; Director, Laurie Rae Waugh; April 17–20, 2008

Beckmann Theatre

OLD KID COD by Lawrence Dial; Director, Adam Knight; Cast: Elan Moss-Bachrach, Lindsey Broad; June 21–July 7, 2007

RICHARD III by William Shakespeare; Presented by Foolish Mortals Theatre Company; Adaptation and Director, Michael Hagins; March 13–22, 2008

GHOSTS by Henrick Ibsen; Presented by Phare Play; Director, Kymm Zuckert; Cast: Jean Walker, Yury Lomakin, Sarah Schmidt, Laurence Waltman, Alan Altschuler; March 26–April 6, 2008

OFFICE HOURS by Norm Foster; Presented by Phare Play; Director, Christine Vinh; Cast: Beth Adler, Blake Bradford, Christopher James Cramer, Nicholas Masson, Katie McConaghy, Edward Monterosso, Nora Vetter, Michael Weems; March 30–April 6, 2008

BURN THIS by Lanford Wilson; Presented by Benchmark Artists and Dick DeBain Productions; Director, Sarah Kostulias; Cast: Christina Christman, Chad Ackerman, Scott Brocious, Wade Dunham; April 29–May 4, 2008

ARCADIA by Tom Stoppard; Presented by Phare Play; Directors, Blake Bradford, Kymm Zuckert; Cast: Christopher Burris, Tamara Cacchione, Robert Carroll, Carrie Colden, Sarah Hankins, Matt Klan, Peggy Queener, Eddie Rodriguez, Nicholas Santasier, Christopher Simon, Aref Syed, Ellis J. Wells; May 8–11, 2008

Andhow! Theater Company

Artistic Director, Jessica Davis-Irons; Producing Director, Andrew Irons

AREA OF RESCUE by Laura Eason; Director, Jessica David-Irons; Set, Neal Wilkinson; Costumes, Becky Lasky; Video, Dustin O'Neill; Sound, Jill BC DuBoff; Lighting, Owen Hughes; Production Manager, Andrew Irons; Stage Manager, Kelly Anne Shaffer; Associate Producer, Danya Haber; Cast: Kiki Hernandez, Abby Royle, Jackie Chung, Arthur Aulisi, Hazel G. Medina, Maria Cellario, Omar Evans, Joe Woolfson, Marta Garcia; Connelly Theatre; June 7–30, 2007

LINUS & ALORA by Andrew Irons; Workshop production; Flea Theater; May 4, 2008

ArcLight Theatre

IF TRUTH BE KNOWN by Judi Komaki; Presented by Blue Heron Theatre; Director, Christine Simpson; Set, Czerton Lim; Costumes, Deborah J. Caney; Lighting, Alan Kanevsky; Sound, David M. Lawson; PSM, Sarah Ford; Cast: Lydia Gaston, James Patrick Earley, Constance Boardman, Bea Soong; June 4–24, 2007

THE BOYCOTT Written, produced and performed by Kathryn Blume; Director, Jason Jacobs; General Manager/Stage Manager, Melissa Thompson; Set/Costume Consultant, Jenny C. Fulton; Lighting, Charles Foster; ASM, Debra Eileen Lewis; Composer, Arthur Blume; Dramaturg, Mark Nash; Press, Brett Singer; October 11–November 11, 2007

THE PUPPETMASTER OF LODZ by Gilles Segal, translated by Sara O'Conner; Presented by Blue Heron Theatre and Mirth, A Theatre Company; Director, Bruce Levitt; Puppets, Ralph Lee; Lighting, Paul Bartlett; Sound, Chuck Hatcher; Set, Roman Tatarowicz; Costumes, Elizabeth Flauto; PSM, Sarah Ford; Producing Artistic Director, Ardelle Striker; Dialect Coach, Krista Scott; Cast: Robert Zuckerman, Daniel Damiano, Herbert Rubens, Suzanne Toren; November 30–December 23, 2007

THE CRUCIBLE by Arthur Miller; Produced by The Schoolhouse Theater and Mare Nostrum; Director, Pamela Moller Kareman; Lighting, David Pentz; Costumes, Kimberly Matela; Sound, Matt Stine; Stage Manager, James Kalinski; ASM, Kari Geddes; Choreography, Walita; Vocal Coach, Deborah Thomas; Tech Director, Ken Larson; Cast: Bob Jones, Lauren Currie Lewis, Keith Barber, Walita, Sherry Stegack, Cheryl Orisini, Bruce Smolanoff, Jennifer Hildner, Simon MacLean, Terry Ashe-Croft, John Tyrell, Kevin Albert, Sarah Bennett, James S. Smith, George Kareman, David Rigo, Tyne Formin, David Licht, Virginia Linden; February 6–March 2, 2008

ECHO LAKE Created and performed by Patrick Hogan and Robert O'Neill; Director, Rosemary Quinn; March 6–16, 2008

MY DEAD MOTHER IS FUNNIER THAN YOU by Katherine Williams; Produced by Jaye Maynard and Katherine Williams; Set, Sarah Phykitt; Lighting, Tim Walsh; Sound, Mark Sutton and Rob Carpenter; Stage Manager, Rome Brown; Cast: Franklin Abrams, Dan Almekinder, Makenzie Caine, Joseph Callari, Todd Conner, Jaye Maynard, Gabriel Silva, Jeff Stevens, Michael Scott King, Katherine Williams; April 3–13, 2008

Arthur Seelen Theatre at the Drama Book Shop

THE STRIKING VIKING STORY PIRATES Presented by Benjamin Salka, Lee Overtree, and Drew Callander; All stories written by elementary school children, adapted by the Story

Pirates; Composer/Musical Director, Eli Bolin; Piano, Brendan O'Grady, Brad Whitley; Managing Director, Jessie Salka; Stage Manger, Nicki Scandiffio, Assistant, Nicole Brodeur, Production Manager, Erin Watts; Production Associate, Jeremy Basescu; Production Assistant, Amy Gargan; Pirates Ensemble: Drew Callander, Lee Overtree, Jacob Rossmer, Laura Hernandez, Liz Bangs, Jess Lacher, Chris Ferry, Nick Kanellis, Duke Doyle, Peter McNerney, Joanna Simmons, Micaela Blei, Chris Tuttle, Peter Russo, Darcy Fowler, Heather Robb, Marcy Jarreau, Elana Fishbein, Louie Pearlman, Karsten Cross, Megan Campisi, Jo Kroger, Ron Dizon, Lisa Barker, Beth Cartier; Weekly on Saturdays

THREE KINGS AND THEIR DEAD by Kat Chamberlin; Presented by Are the Fish Happy? Theatre in association with The Personal Theatre Project; Cast: Daniel Abse, Tom Hedlund, Effie Hortis, Wael Omar, Julio C. Peña, Nick Roesler; May 30–June 16, 2007

Artistic New Directions

Artistic Co-Directors, Janice Goldberg, Kristine Niven

AN ECLECTIC EVENING OF SHORT WORKS Series included: *Storm on Storm* by Gary Garrison; Director, Maggie Lally; *If There's A Cure For This, I Don't Want It, I Don't Want It* by Roland Tec; Director, Mark Robinson, Choreography, Wendy Seyb; *Look Me In The Eyes* by Margo Hammond; Director, Kathryn Long; *Sneaks* by Jeffrey Sweet; Director, John Monteith; *El Magnifico* by Hilary Chaplain & David Arden Engel; Directorial Consultant, Bob Berky; *The River Jordan Lamp* by Carol Hall; Director, Janice Goldberg; *Frontier* by Kia Corthron; Director Tlaloc Rivas; *Wash and Dry* by Kristine Niven; Director, Michael Rock; 78th Street Theatre, March 27–30, 2008

Plays-in-Progress Workshop Series

Cut and Run by Kristine Niven; Director Janice Goldberg, October 21, 2007; *The Art of War* by Tom Shergalis; Director, Janice Goldberg; December 19, 2007; *Some of These Days: A Jewish Woman's Journey Through Chutzpah, Passion and Pastry with Sophie Tucker* by Carol Fox Prescott; Musical Director, Edward Strauss; February 11, 2008; *That Dorothy Parker* by Carol Lempert; Director, Janice Goldberg; March 16, 2008

The Ateh Theater Group

Artistic Director, Bridgette Dunlap

MR. A'S AMAZING MAZE PLAYS by Alan Ayckbourn; Director, Carlton Ward; Cast: Charley Layton, Madeleine Maby, Sara Montgomery, Elizabeth Neptune, Ben Wood; chashama 217; May 25 –October 19, 2007

LONG DISTANCE Adapted and directed by Bridgette Dunlap from the stories of Judy Budnitz; Co-director, Alexis Grausz; Set, Emily French; Lighting, Natalie Robin; Costumes, Amy VanMullekom; Stage Manager, Hannah Miller; Cast: Dianna Lynne Drew, Kathryn Ekblad, Charley Layton, Madeleine Maby, Sara Montgomery, Elizabeth Neptune, Hugh Scully, Jake Thomas, Jesse Wilson; chashama 217; August 9–September 1, 2007

THE GIRL DETECTIVE Adapted by Bridgette Dunlap from the story by Kelly Link; Director, Bridgette Dunlap; Original Choreography, Whitney Stock; Additional Choreography, Alexis Grausz and Anthony Palenscar; Set, Emily French; Costumes, Amy VanMullekom; Lighting, James Bedell; Sound, Chris Rummel; Assistant Director, Hannah Miller; Cast: Stephen Agosto, Kathryn Ekblad, Glory Gallo, Alexis Grausz, Charley Layton, Madeleine Maby, Sara Montgomery, Javier Muños, Elizabeth Neptune, Anthony Palenscar, Hugh Scully, Danielle Thorpe, Marie Weller, Ben Wood; Abron Arts Center, Henry Du Jur Playhouse (presented as part of the Crown Point Festival); October 26–November 17, 2007

Atlantic Theater Company

Artistic Director, Neil Pepe; Executive Director, Andrew D. Hamingson

THE 24 HOUR PLAYS: OLD VIC NEW VOICES Hosted by Kevin Spacey; Produced by Kelcie Beene, Jaime Green, Rachel Helson and Carly Hugo; Writers: Bekah Brunstetter, Laura Jacqmin, Josh Koenigsberg, Mike Lew, Olivia Mandelbaum and Harrison Rivers; Directors: Sherri Barber, James Dacre, Alli Maxwell, Colette Robert, David Ruttura and Laura Savia; Cast: Zoe Anastassiou, Satya Bhabha, Stefanie Estes, Julia Grob, Matthew Hadley, Lauren Hines, Melissa Joyner, Jamie Klassel, Rory Lipede, Bobby Moreno, Devin Norik, Zoe Perry, Mary Quick, Sarah Ries, Krysten Ritter, Zack Robidas, Will Rogers, Roarke Satava, Brandon Scott, Chris Smith, Nick Spangler, Federico Trigo and Kit Williamson; Linda Gross Theater; July 2, 2007

Atlantic for Kids

THE REVENGE OF THE SPACE PANDAS OR BINKY RUDICH AND THE TWO-SPEED CLOCK by David Mamet; Director, Paul Urcioli; Costumes, Katja Andreiev; Fights, John Hayden; Graphics, Matthew Hadley; Assistant Director, Lauren Smerkanictch; Cast: Ted Caine, Rick Dacey, Renee Delio, Lindsay Dombrowski, Sarah Hartley, Lauren Hines, Natalie Kuhn, Hannah Miller, Cassie Newman, Nicole Pacent, Mike Piazza, Dave Toomey, Chris Wendelken, Chloé Wepper, Kelly Wilson; September 29–October 14, 2007

REALLY ROSIE Book & lyrics by Maurice Sendak, music by Carole King; Based on the book by Maurice Sendak; Director/Choreography, Alison Beatty; Cast: Janet Passanante, Michael Guagno, Kari Floberg, Marta Kuersten, Thomas Matthews, Andy Schneeflock; March 8–April 13, 2008

Non-resident Productions

POLITICS OF PASSION Three plays by Anthony Minghella: *Truly, Madly, Deeply; Hang Up; Cigarettes and Chocolate*; Director,

Cheryl Faraone; Presented by Potomac Theatre Project; Set, Aaron Gensler; Costumes, Frances Bohar; Lighting, Hallie Zieselman; Sound, Matt Nielsen and Lucas Kavner; Cast: Cassidy Freeman, Tara Giordano, James Matthew Ryan, Laura C. Harris, Willie Orbison, David Barlow, Michael Wrynn Doyle, Julia Proctor, Jessie Hooker, MacLeod Andrews, Lauren Turner Kiel, Michael Doyle, Colby DiSarro; Atlantic Stage 2; June 20–July 14, 2007

NO END OF BLAME by Howard Barker; Director, Richard Romagnoli; Presented by Potomac Theatre Project; Set, Aaron Gensler; Costumes, Catherine Vigne; Lighting, Hallie Zieselman; Sound, Matt Nielsen and Lucas Kavner; Cast: Megan Byrne, Christopher Duva, Julia Proctor, Peter Schmitz, Alex Cranmer, Bill Army, Alex Draper, MacLeod Andrews, Caitlin Dennis, Lucas Kavner, Jeanne LeSala, Sally Swallow, Alec Strum; Atlantic Stage 2; June 23–July 13, 2007

Axis Company

Executive Producer, Jeffrey Resnick

SEVEN IN ONE BLOW, OR THE BRAVE LITTLE KID Written, directed and music by Randy Sharp; Stage Manager, Edward Terhune; Lighting, David Zeffren; Sound/Music Production, Steve Fontaine; Set and Costumes, Kate Aronsson-Brown; Costumes 2007, Matthew Simonelli, Lee Harper; Film, Dan Hersey; Editor, Mike Huetz; Set Graphics, Lynn Mancinelli; Cast: Marc Palmieri, David Crabb, Abigail Savage, Jim Sterling, Brian Barnhart, George Demas, Lynn Mancinelli, Sue Ann Molinell, Edgar Oliver, Laurie Kilmartin, Marlene Berner; 6th Annual Production at the Axis Theatre; December 7–22, 2007

Non-resident productions

CONFIDENCE, WOMEN! Written and directed by Robert Cucuzza; Presented by ACME Acting Lab; Cast: Kelsey Bacon, Regina Betancourt, Ella Bole, Britt Genelin, Gina Guarnieri, Hagar Moor, Kelly Sharp; March 1–17, 2008

CARPENTERS GOLD Written and directed by Robert Cucuzza; Presented by ACME Acting Lab; Cast: Ella Bole, Gina Guarnieri, Patrick Long, Rebecca Lukens, Hagar Moor, Cori-Ann Roublick, Josh Wolinsky; March 13–29, 2008

Babel Theatre Project

Artistic Director, Geordie Broadwater; Producing Director, Jeremy Blocker

YOU MAY GO NOW by Bekah Brunstetter; Director, Geordie Broadwater; Set, Tristan Jeffers; Costumes, Candice Thompson; Lighting, Tim Cryan; Sound, Anthony Gabriele; Props, KathrynAnn Pierroz; Production Stage Manager, Paige Williams; Cast: Justin Blanchard, Ginger Eckert, Melinda Helfrich, Ben Vershbow; 45th Street Theatre Upstairs; September 6–29, 2007

STOMP AND SHOUT (AN' WORK IT ALL OUT) by James Carmichael; Director, Geordie Broadwater; Set, Tristan Jeffers; Costumes, Becky Lasky; Lighting, Eric Southern; Sound, Matt Hubbs; Cast: Geraldine Bartlett, Brian D. Coats, Katrina Foy, William Jackson Harper, Carolyn McCandlish, Cary McClelland, Joe Mullen, Frank Rodriguez, Christopher Rubin, Jeremy Schwartz, Joseph C. Sullivan, Andrew Zimmerman; Upstairs at the 45th Street Theatre; May 29–June 21, 2008

Workshops/Readings

STOMP AND SHOUT (AN' WORK IT ALL OUT) by James Carmichael; Director, Molly Kramer; December 3–9, 2007

PUNKPLAY by Greg Moss; Director, Geordie Broadwater; February 18–24, 2008

BACKYARD by Dan LeFranc; Director, Geordie Broadwater; March 24–26, 2008

GROUNDWORKS: READINGS FESTIVAL; January 26–27, 2008; Series Included: *Le Fou* by Bekah Brunstetter; Director, Geordie Broadwater; *Smart Cookie* by Julia Brownell; Director, Molly Kramer; *The Home Maker* by Thomas Higgins; Director, Molly Kramer; *Sadgirrl113* by Corey Hinkle; Director, Geordie Broadwater; *A Great Place to Be From* by Norman Lasca; Director, Molly Kramer; *Melena Brown* by Emily Young; Director, Geordie Broadwater

Bank Street Theatre

MORNING STAR by Sylvia Regan; Presented by the Peccadillo Theater Company; Director, Dan Wackerman; Set, Joseph Spirito; Costumes, Gail Cooper-Hecht; Lighting, Jeffrey E. Salzberg; Sound, Owen O'Malley; PSM, D.C. Rosenberg; Cast: Susan Greenhill, Darcy Yellin, Caroline Tamas, Steve Sterner, Michael Tommer, Matthew DeCapua, Lena Kaminsky, Josh Philip Weinstein, Peter J. Coriaty, Allan Mirchin, David Lavine, Geany Masai; June 28–July 28, 2007

THE MISER by Moliere; Presented by Out of the Box Theatre Company; Director, Scott Robinson; Production Manager, John Montgomery; Assistant Director, Marge Linney; Set, John Scheffler; Music/Sound, Bettina Covo, Brian Taylor, Heady Stuff Productions; Stage Manager, Maureen McCluskey; Costumes, Kathryn Squitieri, Lisa Allen; Lighting, Karen Sweeney; Makeup/Hair, Chima Chikazunga; Technical Director, Tony Zimbardi; Dramaturge, Mike Goldman; Press, Sam Hoyt; Cast: Lawrence Merritt, Lorraine Serabian, Craig Dudley, Valerie Stack Dodge, Larry Gutman, Nona Pipes, Arthur Pellman, Daryl Brown, Peter J. Coriaty, Dudley Stone, Paul DeLuca, Robert Oliver, Oscar Salazar, Susan Case, Gregg Lauterbach, Lin Snider; August 15–26, 2007

THE TURN OF THE SCREW Adapted by Jeffrey Hatcher from the story by Henry James; Produced by Wake Up, Marconi! Theater Company; Director, Don K. Williams; Set, Mark Delancy; Costumes, Marion Talan; Lighting, Karl Chmielewski; Assistant Director, Grace Riley; Stage Manager, Audrey

Marshall; Press, David Gibbs; Cast: Melissa Pinsly, Steve Cook; October 31–November 17, 2007

THE MOONLIGHT ROOM by Tristine Skyler; Presented by Larrikin Productions; Director, Nicole Kempskie; Set, Carl Tallent; Lighting and Sound, David Higham; Cast: Jeffrey Farber, Denise Hugerford, Mara Kassin, Leo Kin, Matthew Murumba; February 7–17, 2008

TEA by Velina Hasu Houston; Presented by E Phoenix Idealis Theater Inc.; Directors, Ben Combe and Ben Fabrizi; Cast: Jan Mizushima, Hiroko Tanaka, Yuki Akashi, Maylin Murphy, Yoko Hyun; April 16–20, 2008; also presented at the Poppenhusen Institute April 4–5, 2008

The Barrow Group (TBG Theatre)

SHORT STUFF IV: THE WAR AT HOME Five short plays: *40 Stat. 76* by Arlene Hutton; *The Knife* by K. Lorrel Manning and Julia Ryan; *Source of Information* by Dee Ann Newkirk; *Here to Serve You* by Barbara Lindsay; *Happy New Year* by K. Lorrel Manning; June 15–July 2, 2007

ALMOST, MAINE by John Cariani; Director, Alix Steel; Set, Bret Haines, Costumes, Meredith Mosley-Bennett; Lighting, Shaun Suchan; Sound, Mat Bussler; Cast: Lyndsay Becker, Jamey Isenor, Allyson Morgan, Reggie Oldham; Studio Theatre; September 14–24, 2007

Non-resident Productions

THE INTERGALACTIC NEMESIS by Jason Neulander and Chad Nichols; Presented by Salvage Vanguard Theater; Director, Jason Neulander; Sound, Buzz Moran; Music, Graham Reynolds; July 5–14, 2007

PURGATORIO by Ariel Dorfman; Presented by The Spare in NY Productions; Directors, Stephen Singer, Alix Steel; Lighting, Marshall Coles; Cast: Sarah Babb, Daniel Aho; July 13–21, 2007

THE LEOPARD & THE FOX Adapted by Rajiv Joseph from the novel by Tariq Ali; Presented by Alter Ego Productions; Director, Giovnna Sardelli; Set, David Newell; Lighting, Nick Francone; Costumes, Leon Dobkowski; Sound/Music, Mitun Sinha; Stage Manager, Matthew Enhoffer; Cast: Ramiz Monsef, Andrew Guilarte, Gita Reddy, Sanjiv Jhaveri, Rock Kohli, Michael Crane, David Sajadi; October 17–November 3, 2007

A CHRISTMAS CAROL by Charles Dickens, adapted and directed by Stephen Wargo; Presented by Personal Space Theatrics; Arrangements, Dianne Adams McDowell; Musical Director/Conductor, Jamie Reed, Choreographer Kate Vallee; Set, Taline Alexander; Lighting, Timothy Swiss; Costumes, Kathleen Leary; Sound, Chris Rummel; Props, Casey Smith; Cast: Robert Ian Mackenzie, Paul Aguirre, Frank Anderson, Antonio Copeland, Stephanie Ferro, Kelly Francis, Nathan Freeman, Justin Hall, Carol Hickey, Kathleen Hinders, Andrea McCullough, Adair Moran, Nicholas Alexiy Moran, John McCarthy Moriarty, Allyson Pace, Shelley Rae Phetteplace, Justin Randolph, Daniel Scott Richards, Steven Douglas Stewart, Caitlin Thurnauer, Michael Turay, Ryan Wagner, Emily Wright, Katie Zaffrann; December 8–22, 2007

SHAPESHIFTER by Jonathan Wallace; Presented by Howling Moon Cab Company; Director, Glory Bowen; Set, Stephanie Tucci; Lighting, Ryan Metzler; Costumes, David Thompson; Fights, Ian Marshal; Stage Managers, Amanda Adili and Amber Gallery; Cast: Jennifer Boehm, V. Orion Delwaterman, Shane Jerome, Yvonne Roen, Shelley Virginia; Studio Theatre; March 9–29, 2008

TORRENTS by Robert Attenweiler; Presented by The Barracuda Theatre Club; Director, Taibi Magar; Cast: Daniel Aho, Lyndsay Becker, Allyson Morgan, Reggie Oldham, Jesse Wilson; April 4–14, 2008

GAYFEST NYC 2008 Second Annual; Produced by Bruce Robert Harris and Jack W. Batman; Associates: Marvin Kahan, Jeffrey Schulman, Robert A. Sherrill, Jerry Wade, Adam Weinstock; Mainstage: *Edward the King* by David Brendan Hopes, directed by Sidney J. Burgoyne; *Spill the Wine* by Brian Dykstra, directed by Margarett Perry; *Jumping Blind* by Philip Gerson, directed by David Hilder; Studio Theatre: *The Wrath of Aphrodite* by Tim O'Leary, directed by Martin Cassella; *Steve Hayes' Hollywood Reunion* by Steve Hayes, directed by Vincent J. Cardinal; May 14–June 15, 2008

Barrow Street Theatre

TJ & DAVE with TJ Jagodowski and Dave Pasquesi; December 14–16, 2007 and March 28–30, 2008

FORTNIGHT January 9–20, 2008; Included: *What? And Give Up Show Biz?* created and presented by Asylum Street Spankers: Christina Marrs, Wammo, Stanley Smith, Nevada Newman, Korey Simeone, Scott Marcus, Josh Hoag, Charlie King; *Masquerade: Calypso and Home* written and performed by Roger Bonair-Agard; *Two Men Talking* created and performed by Paul Browde and Murray Nossel; Director, Dan Milne (extended to May 3, 2008); *Yellow Shoes* created and performed by Lisa Biales; *FreeLoveFourm* with Jeremy Beiler, Paul Dorfman, Jared Gramstrup, Gabe Gronli, Anne Johnson, Dieter Klipstein; *Way to Go!* written and performed by Caitlin Miller, directed by Michael Page; *Music From Almost Yesterday* featuring Loop 243, Tim Splain, Steve Gilewski and works by Josh Schmidt and John Cage; *Pugilist: The Staged Reading!; The Jesus Factor* written and performed by Brian Dykstra

FLOATING Written and performed by Hugh Hughes and Sioned Rowlands; Presented by HoiPolloi with Paul Lucas Producitons; February 28–March 3, 2008

Billie Holiday Theatre

SASSY MAMAS by Celeste Bedford Walker; Director, Marjorie Moon; Cast: Yaa Asantewa, Buena Batiste, Lauren Davis, Kaci

M. Fannin, D.C. Lewis, Cameron Miller, Jahi-Kassa Taquara; October 27–December 23, 2007

'TWAS THE NIGHT BEFORE KWANZAA by Carl Clay; Director, Passion; Cast: Fulton Hodges, Marcha Tracey Amanda Kenny, Romell Sermons, Christine Gaines, Jamilah Mahdi, Katrell Clay, Damani Young; December 28–30, 2007

LOSING THE LIGHT by John Shévin Foster; Director, Jackie Alexander; Cast: Leopold Lowe, Alexander Mulzac, M. Neko Parham, C.J. Walker; February 28–March 30, 2008

BIRTHRIGHT Written and directed by Jackie Alexander; Cast: Victor Dickerson, Suzette-Azariah Gunn, Stephen Hill, Nedra McClyde, Jaime Lincoln Smith, Susan Spain; April 25–June 29, 2008

Boomerang Theatre Company

Artistic Director, Tim Errickson

ALL'S WELL THAT ENDS WELL by William Shakespeare; Director, John Hurley; Costumes, Carolyn Pallister; Fight Director, Carrie Brewer; PSM, Angela Allen; Cast: Karen Sternberg, Aaron Michael Zook, Christopher Illing, Mary Round, Timothy Flynn, Tom Knutson, Benjamin Ellis Fine, Chris Harcum, Alex Pappas, David Berent, Alisha Spielmann, Felicia J. Hudson, Robert Grossman, Cassandra Kassell; Central Park; June 23–July 22, 2007

365 DAYS/365 PLAYS by Suzan-Lori Parks; Directors, Tim Errickson, Jack Halpin, Amy Henault, and Francis Kuzler; Cast: Claire Alpern, Preston Ellis, Philip Emeott, Carlo Fiorletta, Christine Goodman, Justin R.G. Holcomb, Beth Anne Leone; Central Park, NYC; July 5–7, 2007

STOPPARD GOES ELECTRIC by Tom Stoppard; Directors, Tim Errickson (*Teeth*), Christopher Thomasson (*Another Moon Called Earth*), and Rachel Wood (*A Separate Peace*); Set, Joe Powell; Costumes, Cheryl McCarron; Lighting, Melanie Smock; Sound, Amy Altadonna; Dialect Coach, Amy Stoller; Production Manager, Brian MacInnis Smallwood; PSM, Angela Allen; Cast: Mac Brydon, Sara Thigpen, Christopher Yeatts, Richard Brundage, Kate Ross, Bill Green, Shauna Kelly; Center Stage NY; September 6–22, 2007

DANGEROUS CORNER by J.B. Priestley; Director, Philip Emeott; Set, Joe Powell; Costumes, Cheryl McCarron; Lighting, Melanie Smock; Sound, Amy Altadonna; Dialect Coach, Amy Stoller; Production Manager, Brian MacInnis Smallwood; PSM, Trisha Benson; Cast: Chris Thorn, Karen Sternberg, Jaime West, David Nelson, Anthony Bertram, Catherine McNelis, Barbara Drum Sullivan; Center Stage NY; September 8–29, 2007

THE HEART HAS A MIND OF ITS OWN by Larry Kirwan; Director, Cailin Heffernan; Set, Joe Powell; Costumes, Cheryl McCarron; Lighting, Melanie Smock; Sound, Amy Altadonna; Dialect Coach, Amy Stoller; Production Manager, Brian MacInnis Smallwood; PSM, Theresa Flanagan; Cast: Aurora Nessly, Kevin Collins, Doc Dougherty, Connie Barron; Center Stage NY; September 12–30, 2007

MADONNA & CHILD by John Pielmeier; Director, Tim Errickson; May 12, 2008

The Brick

THE PRETENTIOUS FESTIVAL June 1–July 29, 2007; Included: *Between the Legs of God* written and directed by Art Wallace; Cast: Trav S.D., Heath Kelts, Ursala Cataan, Mike Rutkoski, Joseph Cacace, Devon Hawkes Ludlow; *The Children of Truffaut* written and directed by Eric Bland; *The Cole Kazdin Amnesia Project* written and performed by Cole Kazdin; *Commedia dell'Artemisia* by Kiran Rikhye, directed by Jon Stancato, presented by Horse Trade Theatre's Stolen Chair Theatre Company; Cast: David Bengali, Layna Fisher, Cameron J. Oro, Liza Wade White; *Dinner at Precisely Eight-Thirteen* book and lyrics by Lisa Ferber, music by Paul Nelson, directed by Elizabeth London; *Evangeline* directed by Sarah Ashford Hart; *Every Play Ever Written: A distillation of the essence of theatre* conceived, cultivated, written, directed and presented by Robert Honeywell in collaboration with Numerous Playwrights Throughout History and Lynn Berg, Audrey Crabtree and Moira Stone; *Hamlet* by William Shakespeare, directed and designed by Ian W. Hill, presented by Gemini Collision Works; *The Impending Theatrical Blogging Event* curated by Michael Gardner; *Interview With the Author* written and performed by Matthew Freeman, directed by Kyle Ancowitz; *Ivory Tower or Sagan?* created and performed by Adrian Jevicki, Rebecca Ketchum, Elodie Escarmelle, Nathan Kosla, Gabriel Forestieri; *Macbeth Without Words* directed by Jeff Lewonczyk, presented by Piper McKenzie, created with and performed by Fred Backus, Katie Brack, Hope Cartelli, Bryan Enk, Stacia French, Robert Pinnock, Robin Reed, Iracel Rivero; *Soundscape* by Ryan Holsopple; *The Mercury Menifesto* created by John Del Signore; *Mother Is Looking So Well Today: A Grand Opera in 1 Page* music by Craig Lenzi, book and lyrics by Ed Valentine, co-created with Robin Reed; presented by Cardium Mechanicum; *Nihils* written and performed by Trav S.D.; *Nothing* created by Michael Gardner; *Project 365* written and performed by Miriam Daly; *Q1: The Bad Hamlet* by William Shakespeare, directed by Cynthia Dillon, presented by Dillon/Liebman/Schafer in association with New World Theatre Company; *Rockberry: The Last One Man Show (a play)* by Nick Jones, directed by Peter J. Cook, presented by Jollyship the Whiz-Bang; *The Sophisticates* by John DeVore, directed by RJ Tolan; *This Is the New American Theatre* written and performed by Danny Bowes and Tom X. Chao, directed by Danny Bowes; *Three Angels Dancing on a Needle* by Assurbanipal Babilla, directed by Michael Yawney; *Tunnel Vision* written and performed by C. Stangenberg, directed by Mercedes Murphy, videos and images, Katurah Hutcheson; *Yudkoswki Returns! (The Rise and Fall and Rise Again of Dr. Eliezer Yudkowski)* written and directed by Bob Saietta

GEMINI COLLISIONWORKS August 4–25, 2007

NEW YORK CLOWN THEATRE FESTIVAL October 5–28, 2007

SECRETS HISTORY REMEMBERS Written, directed, designed and performed by Tanya Khordoc and Barry Weil; Presented by Evolve Company; Music and Sounds, Josh McLane; Lighting, Solomon Weisbard; Stage Manger, Berit Johnson; November 14–18, 2007

THE THOUGHT ABOUT RAYA by Hannah Bos and Paul Thureen; Presented by the Debate Society; Director, Oliver Butler; November 8–10, 2007

PENNY DREADFUL Episodes 1–6; A serialized horror suspense adventure written, directed, produced and featuring Matt Gray and Bryan Enk; Presented by Third Lows Productions; Co-directors, Danny Bowes, Cristiaan Koop, Adam Swiderski, Ian W. Hill, Michael Gardner; Cast: Fred Backus, Danny Bowes, Hope Cartelli, Dina Rose Rivera, Jeff Lewonczyk, Clive Dobbs, Sarah Brodsky, Jessica Savage, Aaron Baker, Clay Drinko, Jerod Hobbs, Kent Meister, Josh Mertz, Becky Byers, Cristiaan Koop, Mateo Moreno, Trawets Sivart, Dan Maccarone, Maggie Cin, Joseph Ryan, Randall Middleton, Bob Laine, Tom Reid, Roger Nasser, Cyrus Pierce, Ian W. Hill; November 17, 2007–April 20, 2008

THE BABY JESUS ONE-ACT JUBILEE December 6–22, 2007

BITCH MACBETH Written, directed and designed by Frank Cwiklik; Cast: Adam Swiderski, Samantha Mason, Becky Byers, David Mills Boynton, Bob Lane, Fred Backus, Bryan Enk, Matthew Gray, Michele Schlossberg, Kevin Myers, Alexandra Cohen-Spiegler, Emma Peele, Sarah E. Jacobs, Jess Beveridge, Sarah Bordsky, Mercedes Emelina, Patrick Pizzolorusso, Candace Yoshioka; January 4–27, 2008

NOTES FROM UNDERGROUND Adapted and directed by Michael Garnder; Cast: Robert Honeywell, Heath Kelts, Mick O'Brien, Alyssa Simon; Moira Stone; February 15–March 22, 2008

BABYLON BABYLON Written and directed by Jeff Lewonczyk; Presented by Piper McKenzie; Cast: Gyda Arber, Fred Backus, Aaron Baker, Ali Skye Bennet, Eric Bland, Danny Bowes, Katie Brack, Lily Burd, Michele Carlo, Hope Cartelli, Maggie Cino, Michael Criscuolo, V. Orion Delwaterman, Siobhan Doherty, Marguerite French, Melina Gac-Artigas, Adrian Jevicki, Gavin Starr Kendall, Kamran Khan, Angela Lewonczyk, Jeff Lewonczyk, Toya Lillard, Marisa Marquez, Roger Nasser, Robert Pinnock, Robin Reed, Iracel Rivero, Heather Lee Rogers, Alexis Sottile, Adam Swiderski, Elizabeth Hope Williams, Rasha Zamamiri; April 18–May 10, 2008

The Bridge Theatre Company

Artistic Directors, Esther Barlow and Dustin Olson

DUSA, FISH, STAS & VI by Pam Gems; Directors, Joya Scott and Christie Tufano; Stage Manager, Estie Sarvasy; Cast: Pia Elisabeth Weber, Jessica Woodrow, Liz Markey, Erika Helen Smith; Shetler Theatre 54; August 24–September 2, 2007

HUMANS ANONYMOUS by Kate Hewlett; Director, Robin A. Paterson; Cast: Esther Barlow, Philip Graeme, Kate Hewlett, Dustin Olson, Jennifer Laine Williams; Shetler Theatre 54; November 3–18, 2007

Broadway By The Year

Creator/Writer and Host, Scott Siegal; Advisor; Barbara Siegel, Musical Director/Arranger, Ross Patterson, Consultant, Michael Lavine

THE BROADWAY MUSICALS OF 1947 Director and Choreography, Jeffry Denman; Cast: Howard McGillin, Marc Kudisch, Eddie Korbich, Noah Racey, Donna Lynne Champlin, Meredith Patterson, Kerry O'Malley, Kendrick Jones, Alexander Gemignani, Christiane Noll, Jeffry Denman, Kristen Beth Williams, Erin Crouch. Christine Pedi; Town Hall, March 3, 2008

THE BROADWAY MUSICALS OF 1954 Director, Scott Coulter, Chroeography, Josh Rhodes; Cast: Sierra Boggess, Sean Palmer, Cheyenne Jackson, Emily Skinner, Noah Racey, Kendrick Jones, Melinda Sullivan, Scott Coulter, Debbie Gravitte, Mark Price, Natalie Venetia Belcon, Jen Cody, Harvey Evans, Paul Schoeffler, Don Percassie, Bert Michaels; Town Hall; April 7, 2008

THE BROADWAY MUSICALS OF 1965 Director, Marc Kudisch; Choreography, Lorin Lattaro and David Eggers; Cast: Brian d'Arcy James, Marc Kudisch, Gregg Edelman, Julia Murney, Kendrick Jones, Shannon Lewis, Melinda Sullivan, Julie Reyburn, Brandon Cutrell, Lorin Latarro; Town Hall May 12, 2008

THE BROADWAY MUSICALS OF 1979 Director, Emily Skinner; Choreography, Noah Racey; Cast: Chuck Cooper, Scott Coulter, Jason Graae, Terri Klausner, Lorin Latarro, Jeff McCarthy, Noah Racey, Emily Skinner, Melinda Sullivan, Sarah Uriarte Berry, Max Von Essen; Town Hall; June 16, 2008

Center Stage NY

NEVER THE SINNER by John Logan; Presented by Convergent Theatre Company; Director, Matt Greer; Technical Director, John Martinez; AD, Josh Vasquez; Cast: Jack Walker-Pearson, Anthony Wofford, Sam Antar, Mark Konrad Stokes, Bethany Heinrich, Sam Man, John Martinez, Patrick Brian Scherrer, Zoe Tucker-Winters, Jimmy Walker Pearson; August 15–25, 2007

SPLATTER by Charles Cissel; Director, Terese Hayden; Cast: John Bale, Jacqueline Brookes, Charles Cissel, Terese Hayden, Roger Kovary, Robin Long, Jacqueline Jacobus, Roberta MacIvor, Ayanna Siveris, James Stevenson; October 9–14, 2007

DREAMS OF HOME by Migdalia Cruz; Presented by Monarch Theatre Company; Director, Jennifer Ortega; Set,

Eliza Brown; Costumes, David Withrow; Lighting, Christopher Brown; Sound, Curtis Curtis; Cast: Stacey Jensen, Juan F. Villa, Elisa Bocanegra, Jeremy Beck, Tyler Hollinger, Heidi Azaro; October 24–November 11, 2007

THE LESSON by Euguene Ionesco; Presented by The Collective; Director, Jessica Forsythe; Set, Zachary Michael Lawson; Sound, Samuel Doerr; Lighting, Randy Harmon; Cast: Robert Z. Grant, Rachelle Wintzen, Elizabeth Steinhart; November 15–December 2, 2007

WONDER WOMAN WEEK FESTIVAL Presented by Groove MaMa Ink; December 11–16, 2007

WHO WILL CARRY THE WORD? by Charlotte Delbo; Director, Melanie Moyer Williams; Produced by the Red Fern Theatre Company; Set, Adrienne Kapalko; Costumes, Summer Lee Jack; Lighting, Jessica Greenberg; Stage Manager, Kimberly J. Weston; Cast: Lindsey Andersen, Laura Anderson, Julia Arazi, Jarusha Ariel, Ilana Becker, Kirsten Benjamin, Alexandra Cremer, Storm Garner, Nicole Grillos, Anaïs Koivisto, Kasey W. Lockwood, Mariya King, Laura Luciano, Sierra Marcks, Paige McDonnell, Emilie Elizabeth Miller, Adair Moran, Dot Portella, Kendall Rileigh, Emily Riordan, Jacquelyn Schultz, Alicia St. Louis, Christine Wolff; February 21–March 2, 2008

WITH THE CURRENT by Sholem Asch; Presented by New Worlds Theatre Project; Director, Marc Geller; Cast: Alice Cannon-Perkins, Chandler Frantz, Jesse Liebman, David Little, Sarah Stockton; May 1–18, 2008

ZEN AND THE ART OF DOING NOTHING Written and directed by Michael Wallach; **GERALD'S METHOD** Written and directed by Daniel Gallant; Two one-acts; Cast: Allen Warnock, Kira Sternbach, Brad Russell, Robert Fitzpatrick, Elya Ottenberg, Daniel Zen, Bethany Libeson, Susana Kraglievich, Charles Roby, Kam Metcalf; May 28–June 8, 2008

chashama

Founder, Anita Durst

WHAT TIME IS THIS PLACE Curated by Hope Hilton; June 6–23, 2007

TRIFECTA: A FESTIVAL OF NEW WORK Produced by Jennifer Shipp; Included: *Dead Letter Office* conceived and directed by Meiyen Wang, devised by Performance Lab 115; *W.M.D (just the low points)* directed by Kevin Doyle; *Puppet Kafka* by B. Walker Sampson, directed by Gretchen Van Lente; June 7–10, 2007

DARK OF THE MOON by Howard Richardson and William Berney; Presented by Thirsty Turtle Productions; Director, Ian R. Crawford; Set, Emily French; Lighting, James Bedell; Costumes, Layla Sogut; Sound, Duncan Cutler; PSM, Jillian Zeman; Cast: Adelgiza Chemountd, Renee Delto, Sarah Hayes Donnell, Noah J. Dunham, Adam K. Fujita, Matthew Hadley, Russell Harder, Jessica Howell, Chris Masullo, Brendan Norton, Katey Parker, Amanda Peck, Minna Richardson, Jake Thomas, Dennis Tseng; June 15–July 7, 2007

THE CHALK BOY Written and directed by Joshua Conkel; Presented by The Management Company; Stage Manager, Marguerite French; Producer, Amy Patrice Golden; Cast: Mallery Avidon, Mary Catherine Donnelly, Jennifer Harder, Courtney Sale; July 18–29, 2007

ORPHEUS & ERUYDICE Adapted and directed by Kelly Hanson; Set, Heather Wolensky; Costumes, Cristal Weatherly; Lighting, Jay Scott; Cast: Beth Bradford, Alison Taylor Chesseman, Todd d'Amour, Tom Delpizzo, Jason Dietz Marchant; August 2–5, 2007

BECCA & HEIDI by Sharon Eberhart; Director, Blake Lawrence; Lighting, Daniel Ordower; Sound, Joanna Lynne Staub; Set, Erica Hemminger; Stage Manager, Samanthe Turvill; Cast: Lindsay Anderson; August 12–22, 2007

THE AUSTRALIA PROJECT II: AUSTRALIA STRIKES BACK! Presented by The Production Company; Sets, Erica Beck Hemminger; Lighting, Stacey Boggs; Costumes, Amy Lyn VanMullekom, Emily K. French, Jessica Gaffney; Sound, Ann Warren; Fights, Bethany Burgess-Smith; Production Manager, Mary E. Leach; Stage Managers, Lily Perlmutter, Nicole Brodeur; Associate Producer, Matt Wolf; Press, Katie Rosin; Included: *Pinter's Explanation* by Ross Mueller, directed by Mark Armstrong; Cast: Mary Cross, Michael Szeles; *The Melancholy Keeper of the Deep, Deep Green* by Anthony Crowley, directed by Bridgette Dunlap; Cast: Andrew Lawton, Kevin O'Donnell, Eleanor Handley, Simon Trevorrov; *Goodbye New York, Goodbye Heart* by Lally Katz, directed by Kara-Lynn Vaeni; Cast: Nicolle Bradford, Ryan King, Megan McQuillan, Joe Menino, Kathy Danzer; *967 Tuna* by Brendan Cowell, directed by Mark Armstrong; Cast: Nick Flint, Michael Gnat, Sarah Eliana Bisman; *The Beekeeper* by Emma Vuletic, directed by Patrick McNulty; Cast: Chandler Vinton, Lethia Nall; *Syphon* by Tommy Murphy, directed by Shana Gold; Cast: Todd D'Amour, Steven Pilkerton, Erin Krakow, Chad Kessler; *The Will of the Cockroach* by Alexandra Collier, directed by May Adrales; Cast: Mary Jane Gibson, Tim Major; *All This Beautiful Life* by Veronica Gleeson, directed by Alexis Poledouris; Cast: Mary Cross, Sean Williams; *Beneath Us* by Ben Ellis, directed by Mark Armstrong; Cast: Joe Menino, Ilene Bergelson, Tim McGeever; *Continuing Occupation* by Van Badham, directed by Jordana Williams; Cast: Erin Maya Darke, Michael Poignand, Mac Rogers, Nancy Sirianni; September 13–30, 2007

HELLO IN THERE Written and performed by Daniel Reinisch; October 8–10, 2007

MUSINGS OF A MAN–BIRD RECLUSE by Andrew Gilchrist and Ramsey Prather; Director, Julie Rossman; Cast: Andrew Gilchrist; November 12–16, 2007

Cherry Lane Theatre

Founder/Artistic Director, Angelina Fiordellisi; Managing Director, James King

Mentor Project 2008 – Studio Theatre

THE WOODPECKER by Samuel Brett Williams; Mentor, Charles Fuller; Director, Drew Decorleto; Cast: Stephanie Cannon, Dan Moran, Cosmo Pfeil, Debargo Sanyal, Matt Unger; March 26–April 5, 2008

THE YOUNG LEFT by Greg Keller; Mentor, Gretchen Cryer; Director, Kip Fagan; Cast: Mark Alhadeff, Diane Davis, Michael Crane; Keira Keeley, Joe Tippet; April 15–26, 2008

JAILBAIT by Deirdre O'Connor; Mentor, Michael Weller; Director, Suzanne Agins; Cast: Flora Diaz, Natalia Payne, Peter O'Connor, David Wilson Barnes; May 6–17, 2008

Cherry Pit Late Nite

IT IS THE SEEING Written and performed by Renita Martin; Presented in conjunction with Aporia Repertory Company; November 16–17, 2007

BEST OF FUCT Sketch comedy and songs by the comedy troupe FUCT: Sarah Bell, Jon Crane, Joe Galan, Tommy Galan, Brian Gillespie, Ian Sinclair Lassiter, Janio Marrero, Graham Skipper; Band: Van Hughe, Matt Accardo, Red Guy; December 15, 2007

VAN DRIVER Presented by The Operating Theater; With: Dr. Schüler, Kourtney Rutherford, Tim Donovan Jr., Megan Stevenson, Eben Moore, Alison Folland, Dori Ann Scagnelli, David Michael Holmes, Elizabeth Stine, Helene Montagna, Harry Meat Bahl; May 9–June 7, 2008

Non-resident Productions

THE QUEST (or what really happened on the quest for the Golden Fleece as told by Orpheus the Musician) by Mrinalini Kamath; Director, Jesse Jou; Produced by Fluid Motion Theater & Film; Studio Theatre; June 21–23, 2007

GETTING TOM by Kevin Coyle; Presented by Marmot Theatre Company; Cast: Mia Price, Rob Yang, Kevin Coyle, Thomas Poarch; September 19–24, 2007

HARRY THE HUNK IS ON HIS WAY OUT by Warren G. Bodow; Presented by Joan and Richard Firestone; Director, Melanie Sutherland; Set/Lighting, Maruti Evans; Cast: Gerry Butler, Anne Carney, John Dalton Hill, Michelle Maxson, Paul Pryce, Peter Reznikoff, Andy Schneeflock; October 26–November 10, 2007

THE PAST IS STILL AHEAD by Oded Be'eri, adapted by Sophia Romma; Directors, François Rochaix and Sophia Romma; Cast: Yelena Romanova, Alexander Rapoport, Inna Leytush, Charles Sprinkle, Queen Bee, Yulia Frenkel, Helen Fousteris, Veronica Mitina; December 6–15, 2007

KILLING THE BOSS by Catherine Filloux; Presented by Theaproductions; Producer, Morgan Allen; Associate Producer, Erin Levendorf; Director, Jean Randich; Set, Sandra Goldmark; Lighting, Matthew E. Adelson; Costumes, Camille Assaf; Sound, Jane Shaw; Fights/Movement, Flelix Ivanov; Stage Manager, Leta Tremblay; Cast: Alexis Camins, Sue Cremin, John Daggett, Edward Hajj, Mercedes Herrero, Orville Mendoza, Dale Soules; February 6–28, 2008

Chocolate Factory Theater

OLD TRICKS Created by Red Metal Mailbox; Lighting, Chloe Z. Brown; Music, Sarah Gancher; Set, Brad Kisicki; Costumes, Mary McKenzie; Cast: Sarah Gancher, Alison Harmer, Sarah Maxfield, Rachel Tiemann; June 14–July 5, 2007

WASHING MACHINE by Jason Stuart; Director, Michael Chamberlin; Movement, Brendan Mccall; Lighting, Ben Kato; Sound, Betsy Rhodes; Set, Akiko Kosaka; Costumes, Amanda Bujak; Stage Manager, Laine Goerner; Cast: Dana Berger; June 22–July 7, 2007

WELCOME TO NOWHERE (BULLET HOLE ROAD) Written, directed, sets and lighting by Kenneth Collins; Presented by Temporary Distortion; Video, William Cusick; Sound/Music, John Sullivan; Costumes, TaraFawn Marek; Cast: Ben Beckley, Stacey Collins, Brian Greer, Lorraine Mattox, Jessica Pagan, Stephanie Silver; October 12–27, 2007

KO'OLAU (A TRUE STORY OF KAUA'I) Created, directed, animation and puppets by Tom Lee; Music, Yukio Tsuji and Bill Ruyle; Costumes, Kanako Hiyama; Cast: Matt Acheson, Marina Celander, Frankie Cordero, Miranda Hardy, Yoko Myoi, Nao Otaka; November 8–17, 2007

THE BLUE PUPPIES CYCLE Written and directed by David Vining; Produced by Cagey Productions; Sets, Susan Barras; Costumes, Asta Bennie Hostetter; Sound, Ann Warren; Lighting, Jeanette Yew; Stage Manager, Leta Tremblay; ASM, Nikki Calcado; Cast: Karen Grenke, Andrew Hurley, Christina Nicosia, Brad Aldous, John Grace, Kevin Lapin, Josh Matthews, Randy Harmon, Valerie McCann; November 29–December 8, 2007

WELLSPRING by Ruth Margraff, music by Nikos Brisco; Presented by The Hourglass Group; Director, Elyse Singer; Musical Director, Jill Brunelle; Cast: Jennifer Gibbs, Stephen Bel Davies, Tony Naumovski; December 13–15, 2007

DON JUAN by Moliére, adapted by James P. Stanley and Normandy Raven Sherwood; Presented by the National Theatre of the USA; Director, Jonathan Jacobs; PSM, David Stadler; Cast: James Stanley, Yehuda Deuenyas, Jesse Hawley, Aimee McCormick Ford, Matt Kalman, Ryan Bronz, Ean Shehe, Normandy Raven Sherwood, Ilan Bachrach; February 6–March 1, 2008

KICKED OUT OF DEATH Created and performed by Peter Jacobs and MKS Volcofsky; April 24–May 3, 2008

THE SWAN CATCHERS by Aaron Siegel, Bryan Markovitz, and the Flux Quartet; Cast: Aaron Siegel Bryan Markovitz, Ryan Dahoney, Kate Soper, Tom Chiu, Conrad Harris, Max Mandel, Ha-Yang Kim; April 24–26, 2008

Clemente Soto Vélez Cultural Center

ALBIZU: TODO O NADA by Viviana Torres; Presented by Teatro La Tea; Director, Luis Oliva; Cast: Moncho Conde; June 14–23, 2007

2007 ONE FESTIVAL WINNERS *Sleep Tight Mick* by Halley Bondy, directed by Robert Dominguez; *Delivery Boy* by Eduardo Leanez, directed by Merceds Ilarraza; Presented by Teatro La Tea & Caicedo Productions; June 27–July 1, 2007

NEVER THE SINNER by John Logan; Conceived and presented by Woodshed Collective; Director, Gabriel Hainer Evansohn; Set, Eric Southern; Lighting, Carl Faber; Costumes, Jessica Pabst; Sound, Joshua Higgason; Props, Lauren DiGuilio; Cast: Teddy Bergman, Chris Cole, Dan Cozzens, Meredith Holzman, E.C. Kelly, Keith Lubeley, Derek Manson, Stephen Squibb, Hugh Sinclair; Flamboyan Theatre; July 13–28, 2007

MASTERING SEX & TORTILLAS Written and performed by Adelina Anthony; Presented by Teatro La Tea & Caicedo Productions; September 5–29, 2007

NIGHTMARE: GHOST STORIES Created by the Psycho Clan; Creator/Director/Sound, Timothy Haskell; Executive Producer, Chip Meyrelles; Set, Paul Smithyman; Lighting, Garin Marschall; Special Effects, David Andora; Props, Aaron Haskell; Gore Design, Justin Haskell; Costumes, Wendy Yang; Flamboyan Theatre; September 28–November 3, 2007

SEW & SING (COSER Y CANTAR) by Dolores Prida; Director, Mario F. Robles; Presented by the Latin American Theatre Ensemble and Teatro La Tea; Cast: Silvia Tovar, Chala Savino; Flamboyan Theatre; October 5–21, 2007

C'EST DUCKIE Performed and presented by London performance troup Duckie; Produced by PS 122; December 20, 2007–January 19, 2008

IPHEGENIA AT AULIS by Euripides; Presented by Highwire Theatre; Director, Jill Landaker; Music, Kendall Jane Meade; Set, David Newell; Costumes, David Withrow; Lighting, KJ Hardy; Music Director, Evan Greene; Dramaturg, Jessica Corn; Cast: Sarah Brill, Julia Davis, Tommy Dickie, David Douglas, Jason Griffith, Eli James, David Ian Lee, Michelle O'Connor, Thomas Poarch, Ninon Rogers, Gillian Visco; Milagro Theatre; December 6–16, 2007

CLOSER by Patrick Marber; Presented by Teatro La Tea; Director, Veronica Caicedo; Cast: Ricardo Hinoa, Carissa Jocett Toro, Sol Marina Crespo, Antonio Aponte; January 16–February 2, 2007

THE TWO LIVES OF NAPOLEON BEAZLEY by John Fleming from a concept by Dana Nau; Presented by the Incumbo Theatre Company; Director, Alexandra Farkas; Cast: Richard D. Busser, Carlton Byrd Jr., Ethan Cadoff, Gina Daniels, Christian Felix, Rita Marchelya, William C. McGee, Rob Sheridan; Flamboyan Theatre; February 21–March 16, 2008

JULIUS CAESAR by William Shakespeare; Presented by Coyote Laboratory, Inc.; Director, Turner Smtih; Cast: Steve Boyle, Seth Andrew Bridges, Marian Brock, Alex Coppola, Kyle Kate Dudley, Doug Harvey, Whit Leyenberger, Shannon Pritchard, Harry John Shephard, Elizabeth Spano, Kimberly Wong; March 1–15, 2008

THE JUDAS TREE by Mary Fengar Gail; Presented by MultiStages; Director, Lorca Peress; Music, Anika Paris; Lyrics, James Schevill; Choreography, Jennifer Chin; Cast: Roseanne Medina, John Haggerty, Jose Febus, Daniel Hicks, Lily Mercer, Tanya Perez, Colleen Cosgrove; Flamboyan Theatre; April 24–May 11, 2008

THE ACCIDENTAL PATRIOT: The Lamentable Tragedy of the Pirate Desmond Connelly, Irish by Birth, English by Blood, and American by Inclination by Kiran Rikhye, conceived and directed by Jon Stancato; Presented by The Stolen Chair Theatre Company; Dramaturg/Music Director, Emily Otto; Fights, Barbara Charlene; Set/Lights, David Bengali; Costumes, Julie B. Schworm with Chris McCardell; Arrangements, Raphael Biran; Stage Manager, Aviva Meyer; Cast: David Bengali, David Berent, Tommy Dickie, Cameron J. Oro, Sarah Stephens, Liza Wade White, Alec Barbour, Raphael Biran, Stanley Brode, Rainbow Dickerson, Jessica Geguzis, Chris Hale, Cat Johnson, Will LeVasseur, Jared R. Pike, Noah Schultz, Turner Smith, and Sean-Michael Wilkinson; Milagro Theater; April 25–May 17, 2008

Collective: Unconscious

THE MOXIE SHOW Weekly variety show hosted by Trav S.D., ongoing

UNDERGROUNDZERO FESTIVAL Included: *It Came From New York: The Battle of New York* curated by Michelle Carlo; Cast: Julie Booth, Big Mike, Andy Christie, Peter Lubell, Marie Mundaca, Nanci Richards; *Broken Dog Legs* written and performed by Emily Conbere; Director, Rachel Rayment; *Jamal Lullabies* by Emily Conbere; Director, Paul Bargetto; Cast: Bekah Coulter, Larissa Lury, Allison Jill Posner, Nicole Stefonek; *Bottoms Over Broadway: Burlesque Goes Legit* Hosted by Johnny Porkpie and Nasty Canasta; *The Ted Haggard Monologues* written and perfomed by Michael Yates Crowley; *The Sistahs* and *Let Us Go then You and I* by Harrison Rivers; Directors, Matt Torney, James Dacre; Cast: Eliza Bell, Erin Layton, Becky Flaum; *The Moxie Show* hosted by Trav S.D.; *Why He Drinks Coffee* by Josh Koenigsberg; Director, Matt Torney; Cast: Allison Weisgall, Adam Radford, Josh Sauerman; *Celine's Journey to the End of the Night* by Jason Linder; Director, Joshua Carlebach; Cast: Richard Crawford; *Commedia dell' Artemisia* by Kiran Rikhye; Director, Jon Stancato; Cast: David Bengali, Cameron J. Oro, Layna Fisher, Liza Wade White; *Go!* written and performed by Gillian Chadsey and Michelle Talgarow; Director, Kara Tyler; *SICK: Sick of it All* written and directed by Caleb Hammond; Cast: Dan Cozzens, Aimee Phelan-Deconinck, Kim Carpenter, Jorge Rubio, Jordan Harrison, Jeff Clarke, Eric Dean Scott, Marion Wood; *I Was On*

The Right by Leah Gelpe; *Verizon Monologues* by Nora Woolley; July 19–August 5, 2007

TUCKER IN A BOX by Edward P. Clapp; Director, Rebecca V. Nellis; The Tank; August 9–12, 2007

THE PLAY ABOUT THE COACH Written and performed by Paden Fallis; The Tank; September 20–22; Subsequently played The People's Improv Theatre October 4–25, 2007

THINGS ARE GOING TO CHANGE, I CAN FEEL IT by Michael Smart; Presented by Immedite Medium, Inc,; Director, JJ Lind; Set, Jared Lawton; Choreography, Liz Vacco; Cast: Max Dana, Brady Jenkins, Ainna Manapat, Robert Ramirez, Liz Vacco, Mai Ushihroku; The Tank; November 2–December 2, 2007

DOUBLE PENDULUM AND OTHER PLAYS by John William Schiffbauer; Director, Michael Flanagan; Co-director/Lighting, Alexandria Celeste Muniz; Co-director/Set, John William Schiffbauer; Costumes, Elisabeth Vastola; Sound, Mat Bussler; Cast: Leslie Boles, Elizabeth Boyle, Mat Bussler, Connor Carew, Paige Dana, Courtney D. Ellis, William Gozdziewski, Kyle Knauf, Bruce Lemon, Loren Vandegrift, Halleluyah Walcott; January 16–18, 2008

THE TED HAGGARD MONOLOGUES Written and performed by Michael Yates Crowley; Presented by The Fort Awesome Theater Fund; Director, Michael Rau; January 19–February 9, 2008

FLOATING BROTHEL Created and performed by Megan Campisi, Loren Fenton, Kevin Lapin, Liz Vacco, Ben Vershbow; April 9–25, 2008

SHERRI ZAHAD AND HER ARABIAN KNIGHTS Created by Laboratory Theater; Director, Yvan Greenberg; Cast: Corey Dargel, Sheila Donovan, Oleg Dubson, and Andrew Gilchrist; The Tank; April 13–30, 2008

TELL by Julia Holeman; Presented by The Subjective Theatre Company; Director, Jeffrey Whitted; Music, Lucas Cantor; Stage Manager, Audrey Neddermann; Costumes, Mary McKenzie; Lighting, Charlie Forster; Fights, Lisa Kopitsky; Cast: Dyalekt, Valerie Feingold, Nathan Francis, Zach Griffiths, Heidi Jackson, Angela Lombardo , Elena McGhee, Matthew McIver, Timothy Meadows, Lucy Owen, Stephanie Vella, Joanna Walchuk, Andy Waldschmidt; May 16–June 1, 2008

Connelly Theater

THE MAGNIFICENT CUCKOLD by Fernand Crommelynck, adapted by Ben Sonnenberg and Amiel Melnick; Director, Paul Bargetto; Sets, Mimi Lien; Costumes, Amanda Bujak; Composer, Nico Muhly; Lighting, Tim Cryan; Cast: Troy Lavallee, Morgan Lynch, Tuomas Hiltunen, Reet Roos Varnik, Jeffrey Woodard, Jorge Rubio, Eric Dean Scott, Laura Wickens, Meredith Napolitano, Joe Sevier, Dan Cozzens, Max Woertendyke, Jessica Bates, Ishah Janssen-Faith, Ashley Avis and Kayla Lian; September 14–October 6, 2007

GRAVITY Conceived and directed by Steven Pearson, text by Robyn Hunt; Presented by Pacific Performance Project/East; Choreography, Peter Kyle; Cast: Christina Amendolia, Felicia Bertch, Eric Bultman, Lee Fitzpatrick, Ichiho Hayashi, Robyn Hunt, Peter Kyle, Shanga Parker; December 6–16, 2007

C.E.O. & CINDERELLA Written and performed by Angela Madden; Presented by Phoenix Theatre Ensemble; Director, Barbara Bosch; AD/Video Coordinator, Alexis Powell; Dramagturg, Dodja Zupanc Lotker; Lighting, Tony Mulanix; Sound, Brian Hurley; Technical Assistant, Jessica V. Urtecho; January 24–February 19, 2008

THE LIFEBLOOD by Glyn Maxwell; Presented by Phoenix Theatre Ensemble; Director, Robert Hupp; Set, George Xenos; Costumes, Peggy McKowen and Nicole Frachiseur; Lighting, Izzy Einsidler; Sound, Betsy Rhodes; Composer, Ellen Mandel; Cast: Elise Stone, Craig Smith, Joseph J. Menino, Jason O'Connell, Mark Waterman, Douglas McKeown, Brian Costello, Jolie Garrett; February 1–23, 2008

LITTLE RED Music and lyrics by Ellen Mandel, written and directed by Kathy Menino; February 16–23, 2008

SEESAW Book by Michael Bennett, music by Cy Coleman, lyrics by Dorothy Fields; Produced by The Group Theatre Too; Director/Choreography, Michael Blevins; Music Director, Christine Riley; Lighting Designer, Paul Gregorio; PSM, Kelly Varley; Cast: Paul Aguirre, Sara Andreas, Crystal Chapman, Brian Duryea, Ann Ehnes, Tim Falter, Ryan Gregorio, Kevin B. Johnson, Stephanie Long, Cristina Marie, Geoffrey Mergele, Janelle Neal, Emily Knox Peterson, Jennifer Sanchez, Alisa Schiff, Stacey Sipowicz, Sidney Erik Wright; March 9–15, 2008

The Culture Project

WOMEN CENTER STAGE '07 Festival Director, Olivia Greer; Theatre events: *St. Joan of the Stockyards* directed by Lear de Bessonnet (in conjunction with P.S. 122); *Becoming Natasha* presented by Isadora Productions; *A Write to Heal* with Lisa Regina; *The Scarlet Letter* by Nathaniel Hawthorne, adapted by Carol Gilligan, directed by Leigh Silverman, featuring Marisa Tomei and David Strathairn; *We Got Issues!* founded by Rha Goddess and JLove Calderon; *Womb-Words, Thirsting* created by Lenelle Moïse; *An evening with Stacyann Chin;* Comedy events: *Julie Godman: Premptive Strike;* Liz Swados's *Political Subversities; Ladies Laugh Last,* featuring Lizz Winstead, Julie Goldman, Negin Farsad, Katie Halper, Desiree Burch; 55 Mercer/The Knitting Factory/P.S. 122; June 25–July 17, 2007

THE CAT WHO WENT TO HEAVEN Music and lyrics by Nancy Harrow, based on the book by Elizabeth Coatsworth; Director, Will Pomerantz; Puppets, Jane Catherine Shaw, Amanda Maddock; Set, Joseph Silovsky; Cast: Grady Tate, Daryl Sherman, Anton Krukowski, Nancy Harrow; Puppeteers: Matt Brooks, Melissa Creighton, Ulysses Jones, Amanda Maddock, Megan McNerney, Sarah Provost, Anna Sobel; March 25–May 18, 2008

WOMEN CENTER STAGE '08 Festival Director, Olivia Greer; Theatre events: *Expatriate* Music and lyrics by Lanelle Moïse, Director, Tamilla Woodard; *Seven* by Marina Pisklakova-Parker (Russia), Mukhtar Mai (Pakistan), Hafsat Abiola (Nigeria), Inez McCormack (Northern Ireland), Farida Azizi (Afghanistan), Annabella De Leon (Guatemala), and Sochua Mu (Cambodia); Director, Evan Yianoulis; *I Have Been to Hiroshima Mon Amour* by Chiori Miyagawa; Presented by Voice and Vision; Director, Jean Wagner, Music, Du Yun; *Vibesolos* Presented by ViBe Theater Experience; *The Last Days of Desmond Nani Reese: A Stripper's History of the World* by Heather Woodbury; *The Magic Show: The Story of the Barefoot Angels* Written and performed by Abigail Nessen; *Warriors Don't Cry* Written and performed by Eisa Davis; *Suk Aur Duk Ki Kahani: A Journey of Love, Risk, and Loss* Created by Andolan Theater Project; Events at 55 Mercer/ The Puffin Room/Great Hall at Cooper Union/The Living Room; April 8–27, 2008

Dixon Place

PETER NEOFOTIS: CONCORD, VIRGINIA June 18, 2007

HOT! 16TH ANNUAL NYC CLEBRATION OF QUEER CULTURE July 2–August 25, 2007

THE FURTHER MIS-ADVENTURES OF THE MYSTIC RENALDO THE Director, Victor Weinstock; Set/Technical Director, Paul DiPietro; Production Manager/Lighting, David Tirosh; Costumes, Allison Keating; Video, Jeff Morey; Sound, Nick Parker; Stage Manager, Erin Delperdang; Cast: Aldo Perez, Richard Ginnoccio, Jennifer Mitchell, Nick Parker, Patrick Klein, Psycho the Clown; September 8–22, 2007

DEEP FEELINGS Written and performed by Jibz Cameron as Dynasty Handbag; September 14–29, 2007

O YES I WILL (I Will Remember the Spirit and Texture of this Conversation) Written and performed by Deb Margolin; September 27–October 7, 2007

FLUID Written and perfomed by Erika Kate MacDonald; Presented by Pack of Others; Director, Sophie Nimmannit; October 12–13, 2007

PUPPET BLOK Curated by Leslie Strongwater with works by Great Small Works, Kevin Augustine and Jennifer Ortega; November 2–3, 2007

ASSHOLE DIFFERENTIAL by Moira Cutler; Cast: Yvette King, Jennifer Boutell, Ian Gould, Katherine Sanderlin, Patricia Drozda, Catron Booker, Phoenix, Zoe Anastassiou; November 10–17, 2007

WHITE ELEPHANT Created and performed by Lake Simons and John Dyer; February 15–23, 2008

DJM Productions

Artistic Director, Dave McCracken

ONE SUMMER NIGHT An evening of music and comedy; Cast: Dave McCracken, Karen Case Cook, Dale Church, Doug Spagnola, Bernadette Hoke, Charlie Schmid, Set Okrend; L'il Peach Theatre; August 18, 2007

FEVER Written and directed by Dave McCracken, based on *Philoctetes* by Sophocles; Design, DJM Productions; Cast: Miguel Belmonte, Rick Lattimer, Gregory Thornsbury; L'il Peach Theatre; May 21–July 5, 2008

DR2 & The D- Lounge

PICKING UP by Jacey Powers; Director, Emma Poltrack; Producer, Megan Walker; Associate Producer, Alison Isicoff; Composer, Evan Newman; Set, Zach Matusow; Costumes, Bridget Waterhouse; Lighting, Reece Nunez; Sound, Shawn Duan; Stage Manager, Brittany Gischner; Cast: Jacey Powers, Steven Todd Smith, Christopher Norwood, Asher Bailey, Ian Campbell Dunn; July 5–15, 2007

A DOLPHIN UP A TREE by Kimberly Foster and John Fleming; Produced by Daryl Roth; Director, Paul Urcioli; Cast: Zack Friedman, Dan Ajl Kitrosser, Stephanie Acevedo, Evan Greene; Daniel Kitrosser; Weekend afternoons, September 29, 2007–April 13, 2008

The Drilling CompaNY

Hamilton Clancy, Producing Artistic Director; Karen Kitz, Associate Producer

ROMEO AND JULIET by William Shakespeare, Director, Tom Demenkoff; Design, Hannah Sharfran; Fights, Peter Ruvolo; Cast: Brad Coolidge, Emilie Stark-Maneg, David Marantz, Keith Fasciani, Ron Dreyer, Don Carter, Laura Johnston, Harlan Work, Alex Herrald, Iriemimen Oniha, Brandt Adams, Colleen Cosgrove; Shakespeare in the Parking Lot at Ludlow and Broome; July 12–28, 2007

MUCH ADO ABOUT NOTHING by William Shakespeare; Director, Kathy Curtiss; Costumes, Shari Kfare; Cast: Mike Still, Jonathan Cantor, Samuel Perwin, Ray Wortel, James Beneduce, Jane Guyer, Dana Slamp, Carolyn Stone, Melissa Condren, Adam Fujita, Robert Matye, Will Schneider, Bill Green, Jennifer Alfaro; Shakespeare in the Parking Lot at Ludlow and Broome; August 2–18, 2007

ATOMIC FARMGIRL by C. Denby Swanson, based on the novel by Teri Hein; Co-developed, conceived and directed by Brooke Brod; Set, Rebecca Lord; Costumes, Lisa Renee Jordan; Lighting, Miriam Crowe; Sound, Chris Rummel; Cast: Hamilton Clancy, Melissa Condren, Brad Coolidge, Dawn Evans, Dennis Gagomiros, Jane Guyer, Karen Kitz, David Marantz, Maria McConville, Kathleen O'Grady; 78th Street Theatre Lab; November 14–December 1, 2007

HERO One act plays by Justin Boyd, Colleen Cosgrove, Brian Dykstra, Sheri Graubert, David Miller, Andrea Moon, Neil Olson, Eric Sanders, C. Denby Swanson, Brian Christopher

Williams; Directors, Stephen Bittrick, Hamilton Clancy, Sheri Graubert, David Marantz, Desmond Mosley, Bradford Olson, Dan Teachout, Gail Winar; Cast: David Adams, Brigitte Barnett, Veronica Cruz, Rebecca Darke, Kwaku Driskell, Tom Demenkoff, Adam Fujita, Michael Gnat, Jane Guyer, Karla Hendrick, Serena Hui, Alvin Keith, Iriemimen Oniha, Greg Skura, Daniel Smith, Dan Teachout, Sam Underwood, Amber Voliles, Harlan Works; 78th Street Theatre Lab; April 11–27, 2008

Duo Theatre

Executive/Artistic Director, Michael Alasa

KENNEDY'S CHILDREN by Robert Patrick; Presented by Duo Theatre's A Different Light program; Director, Michelangelo Alasá; Cast: Sol Marina Crespo, Robert Gonzalez Jr., Tristan Laurence, Alba Ponce de Leon, Indira Obregon; June 11–20, 2007

SAVAGE IN LIMBO by John Patrick Shanley; Presented by The Process Group; Director, Bryan Close; Set/Lighting, David Bengali; Costumes, Katherine Brown; Cast: Jenny Grace, Rebecca Whitehurst, Robert Bray, Brooke Delaney, Henry Zebrowski; October 18–November 4, 2007

DOGS by Norman Lasca; Presented by the Grid Theater Company; Producer, Brittany O'Neill; Director, Justin Ball; Set, Grady Barker; Lighting, Christina Watanabe; Sound, Joshua William Gelb; Cast: Joshua Leonard, Ross Partridge, Jeffiner Lafleur; December 6–22, 2007

MAN OF LA MANCHA Book by Dale Wasserman, music by Mitch Leigh, lyrics by Joe Darion; Co-presented with Room 5001 Theatre; March 20–30, 2008

The Duplex

MONDAY NIGHT NEW VOICES Created and presented by Scott Alan; Third Mondays, monthly series

MOSTLY SONDHEIM Hosted by Kate Pazakis, Brian Nash, and Todd Buonopane; Guest hosts, Marty Thomas, Emily McNamara; Friday late-night, weekly series

WHOOP UP Music by Moose Charlap, lyrics by Norman Gimbel, book by Cy Feuer, Ernest H. Martin & Dan Cushman; Presented by Opening Doors Theatre Company (Suzanne Adams, Artistic and Managing Director; Hector Coris, Associate Artistic Director and Marketing; Eric Martin, Production Manager); Producer, Hector Coris; Musical Director, Ray Bailey; Choreography, Dawn Trautman; Stage Manager, Brian Busby; Cast: Matt David, David Demato, Christopher deProphetis, Alison Renee Foster, Nicole Hilliger, Dan Joiner, Gretchen Reinhagen, Michelle Solomon, Rachel Louise Thomas, Brian Walker, John Weigand; July 10–12, 2007

OVERHEARD by Russell Dobular; Director, Greg Cicchino; Produced by End Times Productions; Assistant Director: Jeremy Pape; Cast: Matthew Watkins, Martha Lee, Bennett Harrell, Kat Garson, Byron Beane, Jessica Ko, Luke Tudball, Robert Yang, Ashley Gray; Saturdays, June 30–July 21

BRIEF CONFESSIONS by Anthony Fusco; Cast: Damion Fitz, Anthony Fusco, Joe DiGregorio, Jacob Liddell, Jeese McDowell, David Montalvo, Roy War; August 2–4, 2007

ON THE ROCKS WITH DANNY LEARY Variety show hosted and produced by Danny Leary; Piano, Ben Rauch; Thursdays, September 13, 2007–May 29, 2008

MEL & EL: THIS SHOW RHYMES Written and performed by Melanie Adelman and Ellie Dvorkin; October 10, 2007–June 21, 2008

GASHOLE: HOLE-O-MATIC Written and performed by Michael Holland and Karen Mack; Intern, Michael Anderson; Technical Director, Lisa Moss; Saturdays, Opened October 20, 2007, Saturday evenings, weekly series

NEW YORK THEATRE BARN MONTHLY CABARET Produced by David Rigler and Joe Barros; Opened January 14, 2007; Mondays, monthly series

THE STUDY OF LIVING THINGS Two one-act plays: *English Made Simple* by David Ives, directed by Kate August; *Home Free!* by Lanford Wilson, directed by David Newer; Stage Manager, Kate August; Presented by An Everyday Production; Music, Desmond Ivey; Cast: Joseph Kathrein, Michelle David, Michael Barra; Tuesdays, January 22–February 5, 2008

FLORA THE RED MENACE Music by John Kander, lyrics by Fred Ebb, book by David Thompson; Presented by Opening Doors Theatre Company; (Suzanne Adams, Artistic and Managing Director; Hector Coris, Associate Artistic Director and Marketing; Eric Martin, Production Manager); Director/Staging, Suzanne Adams; Producer, Holli Leggett; Assistant Director, Eric Martin; Music Director, Ray Bailey; Choreography, Christine Schwalenberg; Cast: Desireè Davar, Alison Renee Foster, Francis Kelly, Andrew Lebon, Kevin Michael Murphy, Jillian Prefach, Buzz Roddy, Kevin C. Wanzor, Erin West; February 24–March 3, 2008

Emerging Artists Theatre Company

Artistic Director, Paul Adams; Associate Artistic Director, Derek Jamison

EATFEST FALL 2007 Series A: *The List* by Kristyn Leigh Robinson, directed by Molly Marinik; *Water and Discarded Hair* by Jessamyn Fiore, directed by Kel Haney; *National Treasure* by Jon Spano, directed by Derek Jamison; *Tom Cruise, Get Off the Couch* by Kevin Brofsky, directed by Aimee Howard; *Emily Breathes* by Matt Casarino, directed by Ryan Hilliard; *Stray by* Corey Rieger, directed by Robert Cambeiro; Series B: *Clothes Encounter* by David Almeida and Stephen J. Miller directed by Nick Micozzi; *Den of Iniquity* by Patrick Gabridge, directed by Ian Streicher; *Layout* by Richard Ploetz, directed by Paul Adams; *Lucky Day* by Mark Lambeck directed by Jonathan

Warman; *UnEmbalmed* by Joe Byers, directed by Carter Inskeep; *Is That a Gun in Your Pocket* by Carol Mullen, directed by Ned Thorne; Series C: *The Adventures Of* by Kathleen Warnock, directed by Deb Guston; *For the Good of the Nation* by Jeff Hollman, directed by Eric Chase; *The Gipper* by Peter Levine, directed by Deb Guston; *Martin, Are You Mad At Me?* by Colette Herbstman, directed by Samantha Manas; *Safe* by D.W. Gregory, directed by Ian Streicher; *Pithy* by Chris Widney, directed by Melissa Attebery; Producer's Club Grand Theatre; October 16–November 4, 2007

A QUEER CAROL by Joe Godfrey; Director, Melissa Attebery; Cast: Ron Bopst, Brett Douglas, Jason Alan Griffin, Hunter Gilmore, Jason Hare, Ryan Hillard, Stephen Hauck, Yvonne Roen, Karen Stanion; Producer's Club; December 19, 2007

EATfest Spring 2008 Series A: *The Food Monologues* by Kerri Kochanski, directed by Deb Guston; Series B: *Islands of Repair* by Leslie Bramm, directed by Melissa Attebery; *Love, Me (Margaret)* by Jennie Contuzzi, directed by Kevin Brofsky; *The Letter by Chuck Rose*, directed by Rasa Allan Kazlas; *Onions* by FJ Hartland, directed by Daniel Allan Dinero; Series C: *Antiques* by Stan Lachow, directed by James Jaworski; *Break* by J. Stephen Brantley, directed by Jonathan Warman; *Undercurrents* by Marc Castle, directed by Roberto Cambeiro; *Fast Light and Brilliant* by Richard Martin Hirsch, directed by Ian Streicher; *George & Bill are Friends* by Susan West Chamberlin, directed by Molly Marinik; Roy Arias Theatre Center; April 15–May 4, 2008

EAT Developmental Series 2008 at the Roy Arias Theatre Center

ONE WOMAN STANDING A developmental series for one-woman shows, curated by Stacy Mayer; May 12–18, 2008

ONE MAN TALKING A developmental series for one-man shows; May 20–25, 2008

LAUGH OUT LOUD Curated by Jenny Lee Mitchell, Honey Goodenough, Carol Lee Sirugo; May 27–June 1, 2008

CATCH A CABARET Curated by Jonathan Warman and Damon Boggess; June 2–7, 2008

NOTES FROM A PAGE New Ensemble Musicals, curated by Derek Jamison; June 10–14, 2008

Ensemble Studio Theatre

Artistic Director, William Carden; Executive Director, Paul Alexander Slee; Youngblood Artistic Directors, Graeme Gillis and R.J. Tolan

ON THE WAY TO TIMBUKTU Written and Performed by Petronia Paley; Director, Talvin Wilks; Music composed and performed by Min Xiao-Fen; Set/Lighting, Maruti Evans; Costumes, Suzanne Chesney; Projections, Maya Ciarrocchi December 6–21, 2007

GOING TO THE RIVER 2007 A gala festival of staged readings by African-American women playwrights; Elizabeth van Dyke, Producing Artistic Director; September 21–30, 2007; Series included: *A Song for Coretta* by Pearl Cleage; *Sweet Maladies* by Zakiyyah Alexander; *Floating Under Water* by France-Luce Benson; Director, Matt Morrow; *River Poetry Slam Jam* with Hasna Muhammad, Maria Chisolm, Melissa Maxwell & Bridgette Wimberley; *Puberty Rites* by Elaine Jackson; Director, Woodie King, Jr.; *Uncle* by Eleanor Herman; Director, Henry Miller; *When January Feels Like Summer* by Cori Thomas; Director, Chuck Patterson; *The Ressurrection of Alice* by Perri Gaffney; Director, Talvin Wilks; *The Irrersistible Death Club* by Kathleen McGhee-Anderson; Director, Charles Randolph Wright; *Roscoe and the Devil* by Ruby Dee, adapted from "How John Boscoe Outsung the Devil" by Arthur P. Davis; Director, Elizabeth Van Dyke; Choreography, Dyane Harvey; Music, Gregg Payne and DK Dyson

FIRST LIGHT 2008 Presented by EST/Alfred P. Sloan Foundation Science & Technology Project; Tenth Annual; April 8–May 3, 2008; Program Directors, Carlos Armesto and Graeme Gillis; Workshops: *Pure* by Rey Pamatmat, directed by Carlos Armesto; *Case Study* by Amy Fox, directed by William Carden; *Ada* Music by Kim Sherman, book & lyrics by Margaret Vandenburg, directed by Lisa Rothe; *The Flower Hunter* by Romulus Linney, directed by Jamie Richards; Special Events: *Cabaret Scientifique,* an evening of music, comedy and prizes; A concert reading of *The Physicists* by Frederich Durrenmatt, directed by Mary Robinson, featuring Laurence Luckinbill, James Rebhorn, and Peter Maloney; Satellite Productions: *Untitled Mars* written and directed by Jay Scheib; Presented in association with P.S. 122 at P.S. 122

EST Marathon 2008 – 30th Annual Festival of New One-Act Plays

Series A (May 8–31, 2008): *An Upset* by David Auburn; Director, Harris Yulin; Cast: Matt Lauria, Darren Goldstein; *Christmas Present* by Amy Herzog; Director, R.J. Tolan; Cast: Julie Fitzpatrick, Jake Hoffman; *A Little Soul-Searching* by Willie Reale, music by Patrick Barnes; Director, Evan Cabnet; Cast: Michael Potts, Karen Trott; *Tostitos* by Michael John Garcés; Director, Mae Adrales; Cast: Andres Munar, Jenny Gomez, Berrett Doss, Howard Overshown; *Wedding Pictures* by Quincy Long; Director, Kathleen Dimmick; Cast: Petronia Paley, Autumn Dornfield, Eric Gilde, Jacob Hawkins

Series B (May 23–June 20, 2008): *The Great War* by Neil LaBute; Director, Andrew McCarthy; Cast: Grant Shaud, Laila Robins; *Okay* by Taylor Mac; Director, Jose Zayas; Cast: Jessica Jade Andres, Kether Donohue, Susannah Flood, Danny Fernandez, Travis Hsieh, Olivia Mandell, Johnny Pruit; *Happy Birthday William Abernathy* by Lloyd Suh; Director, Deborah Hedwall; Cast: Joe Paneseki, Peter Kim; *Ideogram* by David Zellnik; Director, Abigail Zealy Bess; Cast: Pun Bandhu, Bryan Fenkart, Siho Ellsmore; *October/November* by Anne Washburn; Director, Ken Rus Schmoll; Cast: Gioi Perez, Amelia McLai

Series C (June 6–28, 2008): *In Between Songs* by Lewis Black; Director, Joe Grifasi and Rebecca Nelson; Cast: Jack Gilpin, David Wohl, CC deWolf; *Japanoir* by Michael Feingold; Director, Richard Hamburger; Cast: Alexis Camins, Jackie Chung, Karen Lee, Glenn Kuboto, Jo Mei, Raj Bose, Steven Eng, John Haggerty, Leslie Ayvazian; *Piscary* by Frank D. Gilroy; Director, Janet Zarish; Cast: Diane Davis Mark Alhadeff; *Flowers* by José Rivera; Director, Linsay Firman; Cast: Raul Castillo, Flora Diaz; *A Very Very Short Play* by Jacquelyn Reingold; Director, Jonathan Bernstein; Cast: Julie Fitzpatrick, Adam Dannheisser

Youngblood Company

ASKING FOR TROUBLE Short plays by Delaney Britt Brewer, Jihan Crowther, Justin Deable, Amy Herzog, Courtney Booke Lauria, Michael Lew, Daria Polatin, Sharyn Rothstein, Matt Schatz, Michael Sendrow, Emily Chadick Weiss; Directors, Mark Armstrong, Christine Farrell, Neal Freeman, Heidi Handelsman, Jessi Hill, Marlo Hunter, Nate Lemone, Alexis Poledouris, Alexa Polmer, Moritz Von Steulpnagel, Abigail Zealey-Bess; Cast: Denny Bess, Jamie Bonelli, Steve Boyer, Matthew Conlon, Dana Eskelson, Dawn Evans, Julie Fitzpatrick, Nancy Franklin, Fiona Gallagher, Kristen Harlow, David Gelles Hurwitz, Ryan Karels, Julie Lake, Florencia Lozano, Erin Mallon, Melanie Maras, Gregg Mozgala, Jeffrey Nauman, Melanie Nicolls-King, Peter O'Connor, Annie O'Sullivan, Joel Rooks, Steve Sanpietro, Debargo Sanyal, Victor Slezak, Amy Staats, Paco Tolson, Beth Wittig; September 6–8, 2007

THICKER THAN WATER Series of seven new plays and musicals by EST ensemble of emerging playwrights; Series included: *508* by Amy Herzog; Director, Mario Hunter; Cast: Julie Fitzpatrick and Miguel Govea; *La Fête* by Daria Polatin; Director, RJ Tolan; Cast: Geneva Carr, Lucy DeVito, Grant Shaud; *For Candy* by Michael Sendrow; Director, Marlo Hunter; Cast: David Gelles-Hurwitz, Grant Shaud; *Red Blue and Purple* by Justin Deabler; Director, Michael Goldfried; Cast: Miguel Govea, Kelli Lynn Harrison; *I'll Soon Be Here* by Delaney Britt Brewer, music by Eric Kuehnemann; Director, Abigail Zealey Bess; Cast: Jenny Greer, Debbie Lee Jones, Lance Rubin; *Co-op* Book by Courtney Brooke Lauria, music and lyrics by Matt Schatz; Director, Jordan Young; Cast: Julie Fitzpatrick, Thomas Lyons, Steve Boyer; *Both* by Emily Chadick Weiss; Director, Alexa Polmer; Cast: Steve Boyer, David Gelles-Hurwitz, Jenny Greer, Lance Rubin, Maureen Sebastian; February 3–March 1, 2008

YOUNGBLOOD UNFILTERD WORKSHOPS Studio Workshops of two full-length plays: *The Curious Distance Between Who I Should Be Fucking and Who I Let Fuck Me* by Jihan Crowther; Director, May Adrales; *A Better Babylon* by Michael Lew; Director, Linsay Firman; February 18–27, 2008

BLOODWORKS 2008 New full length plays; Series included: *Nodding Off* by Emily Chadick Weiss, directed by R.J. Tolan; *Guidance* by Daria Polatin, directed by Moritz von Stuelpnagel; *Almost Suck* by Steven Levenson, directed by Evan Cabnet; *Easybake* by Lucy Alibar, directed by Kara-Lynn Vaeni; *Princes of Waco* by Robert Askins, directed by Dylan McCullough; *Thus Have I Heard: : Tales of the Last Bodhisattva* by Jesse Cameron Alick, directed by Andrew Russell; *Bridges and Boundaries* by Courtney Brooke Lauria, directed by Jordan Young; *The Gated Community of Anhedonia Finds Joy* by Michael Sendrow, directed by R.J. Tolan; *A Fine Line* by Delaney Britt Brewer, directed by Jordan Young; *The Silence Next Door* by Jihan Crowther, directed by Dominic D'Andrea; *Plan Z* by Justin Deabler, directed by Giovanna Sardelli; *Neanderthal Love* by Michael Lew; *Hearing Things* a new musical by Matt Schatz, directed by Carlos Armesto; Cast: Polly Adams, Leslie Ayvasian, Jeremy Beck, Jeff Biehl, Bill Bowers, Steve Boyer, Geneva Carr, Chris Ceraso, Cindy Cheung, Michael Crane, Michael Cyril Creighton, Lucy DeVito, Jenny Greer, Kristin Griffith, Chad Hoeppner, Lian-Maria Holmes, David Hurwitz, Haskell King, Courtney Lauria, Norman Lee, Adam MacLean, Meg McQuillan, Anne O'Sullivan, Maya Parra, John Pirie, Shawn Randall, James Rebhorn, Monica Raymund, Debargo Sanyal, Ted Schneider, Heidi Schreck, Grant Shaud, Howard Sherman, Victor Slezak, Liam Torres, Candice Thompson, Colleen Werthman, Audrey Lynn Weston; Landmark Tavern; May 21–June 28, 2008

The Flea Theater

Artistic Director, Jim Simpson; Producing Director, Carol Ostrow

Downstairs @ The Flea

SEATING ARRANGEMENTS Created and performed by The Bats, inspired by "Babette's Feast" by Isak Dinesen; Presented in association with Pold Worm Jensen (Denmark); Director, Erik Pold; Cast: Donal Brophy, Jane Elliot, Ben Horner, Max Jenkins, Jocelyn Kuritsky, Nana Mensah, Sylvia Mincewicz, Bobby Moreno; October 10–27, 2007

OFFENDING THE AUDIENCE By Peter Handke; Director, Jim Simpson; Lights, Zack Tinkelman. Cast: Raniah Al-Sayed, Ivory Aquino, Felipe Bonilla, Jon Cage, Jaime Robert Carrillo, Young-I Chang, Dan Cozzens, Erwin Falcon, Drew Hildebrand, Emily Hyberger, Alexis Macnab, Bobby Moreno, Chance Mullen, Lisa Pettersson, Rachel Richman, Erin Roth, John Russo, Sarah Sakaan, Annie Scott, Sarah Silk, Ronald Washington, Jeff Worden; January 21–February 23, 2008

THE BREAK-UP by Tommy Smith and **THE HAPPY SAD** by Ken Urban; Director, Sherri Kronfeld; Set, John McDermott; Lights, Ben Kato; Costumes, Erin Elizabeth Murphy; Sound, Brandon Walcott. Cast: Felipe Bonilla, Havilah Brewster, Jane Elliott, Pete Forester, Tom Lipinski, Stephen O'Reilly, John Russo, Annie Scott Ronald Washington; March 6–April 26, 2008

Non-resident productions

DES MOINES by Denis Johnson; Presented by Evenstar Films; Director, Will Patton; Cast: LaTonya Borsay, Emily McDonnell, Deirdre O'Connell, Will Paton; February 26–March 1, 2008

Gallery Players

Artistic Director/Board Vice-President, Heather Siobhan Curran; Director of Production, Cathy Bencivenga

SIX DEGREES OF SEPARATION by John Guare; Producer, Cathy Bencivenga; Director, Tom Wojtunik; Set, Tim McMath; Lighting, Travis I. Walker; Sound, Todd Hendricks; Casting Scott Wojcik; PSM, Dan Boulos; Cast: Tommy Buck, Jonathan Gregg, Mark Hattan, Laura Heidinger, Justin Herfel, Craig Jessup, Kevin Kelleher, Joe Moretti, Musto Pelinkovicci, Richard Prioleau, Ben Roberts, Kelly Scanlon, Ben Schnickel, Robert Schorr, Jacqueline van Biene, Jamee Vance, Richard Vernon; September 15–30, 2007

YANK! A NEW MUSICAL Book and lyrics by David Zellnik, music by Joseph Zellnik; Producer, Matt Schicker; Director, Igor Goldin; Choreography, Jeffry Denman; Music Director, Daniel Feyer; Set, Ray Klausen; Lighting, Ken Lapham; Costumes, Tricia Barsamian; Casting, Kerry Watterson; Orchestrations, Joe Zellnik, Daniel Feyer, Josh Clayton, Rob Berman; PSM, Kathleen Munroe; ASM, Kayla Shriner-Cahn, Kati Foy; Cast: Nancy Anderson, Chris Carfizzi, Jonathan Day, Maxime de Toledo, Jeffry Denman, Todd Faulkner, Chad Harlow, Tyson Kaup, Matthew Marks, Brian Mulay, Daniel Shevlin, Bobby Steggert, James Stover; October 20–November 4, 2007

THE SANTALAND DIARIES by David Sedaris, adapted by Joe Mantello; Producer, Ben Tostado; Director, Jason Podplesky; Set/Costumes, Michael Wilson Morgan; Lighting, Marnie Cumings; Sound, Neal J. Freeman; PSM, Abigail Wesley; Cast: B. Brian Argotsinger; December 1–16, 2007

THE WILD PARTY Book, music, lyrics by Andrew Lippa; Producer, Heather Siobhan Curran; Director, Neal Freeman; Musical Director, Jeffrey Campos; Choreography, Brian Swasey; Set, Hannah Shafran; Costumes, Summer Lee Jack; Lighting, John Eckert; PSM, Emily Ballou; Associate Producer, Becca Goland-Van Ryn; Cast: Justin Birdsong, Julie Cardia, Rebecca Cox, Zak Edwards, Matthew Gray, Jonathan Hack, Tauren Hagans, Justin Herfel, Michael Jones, KC Leiber, Matthew Oaks, Jeremy Ritz, Julia Royter, Allie Schulz, Ashley Speigel, Nicole Sterling, Theis Weckesser, Jennifer Wren; February 2–24, 2008

LYSISTRATA by Aristophanes, translated by Drue Robinson Hagen; Producer, Jen Rogers; Director, Alexa Polmer; Set, Stephanie Tucci; Costumes, Crystal Fergusson; Lighting, Christina Wantanable; Associate Producer, Angela Astle; Sound, Jason Thomas Spencer; PSM, Stephanie Sottile; Cast: Meagan Prahl, Melissa D'Amico, Shannon Noecker, Maya Parra, Meg Loftus, Loren Fenton, D. Zhonzinsky, Joseph Raik, Allen Arthur, Victor Bell, Amanda Bruton, Jeff Bush, Gabriel Grant; March 15–30, 2008

MAN OF LA MANCHA Book by Dale Wasserman, music by Mitch Leigh, lyrics by Joe Darion; Producer, Seth Soloway; Director, Tom Wojtunik; Music Director, Chris Tilley; Choreography, Ryan Kasprzak; Associate Producer, Brian Michael Flanagan; Set, Martin Andrew; Lighting, Tony Galaska; Costumes, David Withrow; Sound, Kristyn Smith; Stage Manager, Lara Tarrell; Cast: Jan-Peter Pedross, Jennifer McCabe, Robert Anthony Jones, Justin Herfel, James Andrew Walsh, Jonathan Gregg, Alex Pearlman, Chris Kind, Rob Langeder, Tim Shelton, Todd Metzker, Mark Kirschenbaum, Dawn Derow, Jenn Zarine Habeck, Patricia Levin, Andrew Boyd, Dennis Michael Keefe, Luke Tudball, Aaron Thomsen, Joe DiGennaro, Angela Dirksen; April 26–May 18, 2008

2008 BLACK BOX NEW PLAY FESTIVAL Co-produced with Engine 37; Producers, Neal J. Freeman & Anna Olivia Moore; Set, Hannah Shafran; Costumes, Ana Marie A. Salamat; Lighting, John Eckert; Festival Stage Manager, Emily Ballou; Stage Manager, G. Zhang; Associate Producer, Angela Astle; Assistant Director/ASM, Emily Johnson; Series included: *The Reckoning of Kit & Little Boots* by Nat Cassidy, directed by Neal J. Freeman; Cast: Nat Cassidy, David Ian Lee, Alex Herrald, Keith Foster, Lara Stoby, Anna Olivia Moore, Andrew Firda; *Hope's Arbor* by Rich Espey, directed by Heather Siobhan Curran; Cast: Lauren Marcus, Justine Campbell-Elliott, Justin Herfel, James Holloway, Emily Hagburg, Jessica Ko; *The Resurrection of Disman & Gastas* by Jacob M. Appel, directed by Angela Astle; Cast: Thomas DelPizzo, Allison Whittinghill, Hanna Hayes, Russell Feder, Dominique Leavitt; Gallery Players and Manhattan Theatre Source; June 6–21, 2008

Gene Frankel Theatre

THE SCARLET LETTER Adapted by Stuart Vaughan from the novel by Nathaniel Hawthorne; Presented by The New Globe Theatre; Director, Marie Kreutziger; Cast: Jana Mestecky, Bridget Riley, Craig Rising, William Shust; June 3–17, 2007

PURPLE HEARTS by Burgess Clark; Presented by Invisible City Theatre Company; Director, David Epstein; Set, Elisha Schaefer; Lighting, Joe W. Novak; Costumes, Jennifer Raskopf; Sound, Peter Wood; Cast: Ryan Serhant, Dan Patrick Brady, Anneka Fagundes, Rebecca White, Cecilla Frontero, Kevin T. Collins; September 8–22, 2007

OEDIPUS REX by Sophocles; Presented by Mortals Theater; Director, Tom Keener; Producer, Lilith Beitchman; Costumes, Michele Bidault; Set, John Scheffler; Lighting, Victoria Kiely; Sound, Brendan Connolly; Stage Manager, Judy Merrick; Cast: Omar Abdali, Doug Barron, Robert F. Cole, Petra Kipke, Elizabeth Lord, Billy McCue, Thomas S. Nielsen, Paul Pricer, Remy Selma, Dan Snow, Luanne Surace, John Tobias; October 17–28, 2007

THE PIED PIPER OF THE LOWER EAST SIDE Written and directed by Derek Ahonen; Producer, James Kautz; Presented by the Amoralists; Stage Manager, Judy Merrick; Lighting, Linda Burstyn; Set, Matthew Pilieci; Sound, Bart Lucas; Cast: Tom Bain, Sarah Fraunfelder, James Kautz, Nick Lawson, Helena Lee, Matthew Pilieci; November 2–25, 2007

THE GOLDFISH DIARIES by Amy E. Witting; Presented by aWe Creative Group; Director, Bruce Ornstein; Cast: Wayne Brusseau, Michael Lengyel, Amy E. Witting, Kerry Fitzgibbons, Billy Weimer; November 2–December 2, 2007

JOURNEY TO THE END OF THE NIGHT Adapted by Jason Lindner from the novel by Louis-Ferdinand Celine; Presented by The Flying Machine; Director, Joshua Carlebach; Set, Anna Kiraly; Costumes, Olivera Gajic; Lighting, Anjeanette Stokes; Sound, Zach Williamson; Cast: Richard Crawford; January 8–26, 2008

ON THE VERGE, OR THE GEOGRAPHY OF YEARNING by Eric Overmeyer; Presented by Fool's Pearls Productions; Director, John Grabowski; Cast: Helen Kim, Joey Schaljoand, Madeline Virbasius-Walsh, Casey McClellan; January 30–February 10, 2008

DOES ANYONE KNOW SARAH PAISNER? by Jennifer Lane; Presented by Intravenous Theatre, Inc.; Directory, Elyzabeth Gorman; Cast: Kathryn Merry, Alana Jackler, Jason Odell Williams, Maggie Benedict, Keenan Caldwell, Yvette King, Sadrina Johnson, David Beukema, Justin Herfel, Andy Travis, Nathaniel P. Claridad, David Stallings; February 16–March 2, 2008

MUCH ADO ABOUT NOTHING by William Shakespeare; Presented by Wide Eyed Productions; Director, Kristin Skye Hoffmann; Cast: Lea McKenna-Garcia, Brian Floyd, Justin Ness, Lauren Bahlman, Trevor Dallier, Sky Seals, Andrew Harriss, Scott Voloshin, Sage Seals, Danny Gardner, Vanessa Gibens, Jerrod Bogard, Paul Basile, Kym Smith, Brianne Mai, Anthony Reimer, Nick Basile, Devin Moriarty, Melissa Johnson; Underground Theatre; February 21–March 16, 2008

FINOKIO: THE LYIN' QUEEN OR THE SOUND OF CRICKETS Written and performed by TABBOO!; March 7–16, 2008

CROSSTOWN PLAYWRIGHTS SPRING FORWARD Presented by Ignited States; Included: Evening A– *Doctor Ravish: A Roach in a Rodent's Clothes* by Philip Wilson, directed by Chris Czyz; Cast: Angel Wuellner, Kelly Allen, Colin Fisher, Tony Wolf, Joe Beuerlein, Philip Wilson; *Sex and Money and Money and Sex* by Jack Karp, directed by Javierantonio Gonzalez; Cast: Richard Kass, Deborah Radloff; *Sad, Brutal, and Short* by Shalini Tripathi, directed by Rebecca Bass; Cast: Jennifer Lucas, Eric Rice; *One Little Duck* by Michael Niederman, directed by Javierantonio Gonzalez; Cast: Amanda Boekelheidee, Ted Schneider, Shawn Kathryn Kane; Evening B– *The Trouble with Day Care* by Josh McIlvain, directed by Deborah Wolfson; Cast: Nicola Barber, Thomas DeMarcus, Kevin Lyons; *Tom Comes Home* by Bronwyn Clark, directed by Cristina Alicea; Cast: Nick Fondulis, Dennis Wit, Lynn Ross; *Lola Got Bite* by Siobhon Antonioli, directed by Melissa Fendell; Cast: Mark Cisneros, Shayna Padovano, Katy Rubin, Cary Hite; *Eli and Cheryl Jump* by Daniel McCoy, directed by Nicole A. Watson; Cast: Charles Linshaw, Maria Silverman; Underground; March 20–30, 2008

CHAMBER MUSIC and **THE DAY THE WHORES CAME OUT TO PLAY TENNIS** One-acts by Arthur Kopit; Presented by Mortals Theatre and Graylady Entertainment; Directors, Robert F. Cole, John Scheffler; Cast: Omar Abdali, Victoria Boomsma, Margie Catov, Petra Kipke, Judy Merrick, Julianne Nelson, Dan Snow, Laura Spaeth, Luanne Surace, Kim Vasquez. Robert F. Cole, Bill Krakauer, Thomas S. Nielsen, Paul Pricer, Jonathan Pereira, Zachary Zito; April 9–27, 2008

THE HEY YOU MONSTER A two part play by Derek Ahonen; Presented by The Amoralists Theatre Company; Part One: *Pokin the Bears in a Zoo* directed by Derek Ahonen; Assistant Director, Selene Beretta; Cast: James Kautz, Rochelle Mikulich, Craig Peugh, Matthew Pilieci, George Walsh; Part Two: *Bring Us the Head of Your Daughter* directed by David Levy-Horton; Cast: Deshja Driggs-Hall, Duane Chvon Ferguson, Jennifer Fouche, Helena Lee; April 25–May 31, 2008

Gingold Theatrical Group: Project Shaw

Founder and Artistic Director, David Staller

Monthly public readings of the complete works of George Bernard Shaw at The Players Club, Grammercy Park South; produced and directed by David Staller; Associate Producers, Jerry Wade, Theresa Diamond, Anita Jaffe, Kate Ross

VILLAGE WOOING and **HOW HE LIED TO HER HUSBAND** Host, Michael Feingold; Narrator, Clover Lalehzar; Cast: Karen Ziemba, Brian Murray, Matt Cavanaugh; June 18, 2007

THE MILLIONAIRESS Host, Howard Kissel; Narrator, Roma Torre; Cast: Jonathan Hadary, Tyne Daly, Daniel Jenkins, Rebecca Luker, Simon Jones, John McMartin, John Martello, Charlotte Moore, Adam Feldman; July 23, 2007

MAN AND SUPERMAN Host, Jeremy McCarter; Narrator, Michael Riedel; Cast: George S. Irving, Euan Morton, Michael Cerveris, Kerry Butler, Jackie Hoffman, KT Sullivan, Elena Shaddow, Matthew Arkin, Noah Racey, Marc Kudisch, Nick Wyman; September 17, 2007

PRESS CUTTINGS and **PASSION, POISON AND PETRIFICATION** Host, Howard Kissel; Cast: Jayne Houdyshell, Annie Golden, Brian Murray, Euan Morton, Charlotte Moore, Matthew Arkin, October 22, 2007

WIDOWERS HOUSES Host, Jeremy McCarter; Narrator, Adam Feldman; Cast: Jeremy Webb, Barrett Foa, Fritz Weaver, Kathy Brier, Sarah Moon, Lenny Wolpe; November 19, 2007

PYGMALION Host, David Cote; Narrator, Michael Riedel; Cast: Jennifer Smith, Liz Morton, Allen McCullough, Matt Cavenaugh, Hannah Cabell, Daniel Jenkins, David Staller, Beth Fowler, Brian Murray, Marian Seldes; December 17, 2007

GENEVA Host, Michael Feingold; Narrator, Adam Feldman; Cast: Bridget Regan, Simon Kendall, Bill Kux, Carole Shelley, Michael Riedel, Howard Kissel, George S. Irving, Peter Flynn,

Simon Jones, Lorenzo Pisoni, Boyd Gaines, Victor Slezak, John Bolton, John Martello, Charlotte Moore; January 21, 2008

TOO GOOD TO BE TRUE Host, Howard Kissel; Narrator, Eric Grode; Cast: Michael Feingold, Kathy Brier, Marylouise Burke, Eric Grode, Charles Busch, Marc Kudisch, John Windsor-Cunningham, John Scherer, Nick Wyman, Louis Zorich; February 11, 2008

IN GOOD KING CHARLES'S GOLDEN DAYS Host, Michael Riedel; Narrator, Sarah Moon; Cast: Pam Paul, Ed Dixon, Graham Rowat, Daniel Jenkins, Liz Morton, Jenn Thompson, Hannah Cabell, Jack Koenig, Bill Kux, Mary Bacon, Sarah Moon; March 17, 2008

THE FASCINATING FOUNDLING AND FARFETCHED FABLES Host, David Cote; Narrator, Charlotte Moore; Cast: Kate Mulgrew, Victor Slezak, Lenny Wolpe, Simon Jones; April 21, 2008

DEVIL'S DISCIPLE Host, Howard Kissel; Narrator, Charlotte Moore; Cast: Mary Beth Peil, Dan Truman, Emily Young, Charles Edwards, Howard Kissel, John Martello, John Bolton, Euan Morton, Larry Gleason, Edward Hibbert; May 19, 2008

Harlem Repertory Theatre

Artistic Director, Keith Lee Grant

FINIAN'S RAINBOW Music by Burton Lane, book and lyrics by E.Y. Harburg, book by Fred Saidy; Aaron Davis Hall; July 20–September 6, 2007

TAMBOURINES TO GLORY by Langston Hughes; Aaron Davis Hall; August 10–September 28, October 26–27, 2007

Horse Trade Theater Group

Managing Director, Erez Ziv; Associate Producer, Morgan Lindsey Tachco

Kraine Theater

TOO MUCH LIGHT MAKES THE BABY GO BLIND Created by Greg Allen; Presented by the Neo-Futurists; 30 Plays in 60 minutes; Cast: Joe Basile, Christopher Borg, Jeffrey Cranor, Kevin R. Free, Ryan Good, Eevin Hartsough, Jacquelyn Landgraf, Sarah Levy, Erica Livingston, Rob Neill, Joey Rizzolo, Justin Tolley, Jenny Williams; Friday and Saturday evenings, open run

ACCIDENTAL DEATH OF AN ANARCHIST by Dario Fo; Presented by My Fair Heathen; Director, Janet Bobcean; Set, Katrina Alix and Matt McAdon; Lighting, Justin Townsend; Sound, Keller McGuiness; Costumes, Frances McSherry; Stage Manager, Anne Marie Chouinard; Cast: Megan O'Leary, Dan Doohan, Michael Satow, Matthew Wanders, Del Lewis, Gretchen Knapp; June 28–July 22, 2007

THE MAGIC OF MRS. CROWLING by Brian Silliman; Director, Abe Goldfarb; Presented by The Royal Circus; Score, Larry Lees; Design, Robin Mates; Stage Manager, Stephanie Williams; Cast: Dennis Hurley, Ronica V. Reddick, Patrick Shearer, Paul Wyatt, Shelly Smith, Brian Silliman, Collin McConnell; July 10–August 5, 2007

THE CHILD DREAMS by Hanoch Levin; Director, Keith Dixon; August 25–September 9, 2007

WHITE PAPER by Christie Perfetti; Director, Todd Rycynski; Cast: Rachel Feldman, Christopher Lueck, Roxanne Kapitsa, Matt W. Cody, Hugh Martin, Vikki Massulli, Laurel Reese, John Carey; September 6–9, 2007

MELODRAMA AND MAYHEM ON MAIN STREET Short plays by Louise Bryant, Alice Gerstenberg, and Susan Glaspell; Presented by Women Seeking…; Directors/Costumes/Lighting, Christine Mosere and Dan Jacoby; Set, Heidi B. Anderson and Marcia Gilbert; Sound, Katharina Tapp; Included: *The Game, Patient Griselda,* and *From Paris to Main Street* by Bryant; *Overtones* and *Fourteen* by Gerstenberg; *Trifles* by Glaspell; Cast: Dan Jacoby, Vivian Meisner, Matthew Russell, Anna Malinoski, Jase Draper, Kira Blaskovich, Ann Parker, Susan Atwood, Hannah Ingram, Rhonda Ayers, Keith Maxwell, Ann Parker; September 5–29, 2007

MERCY THIEVES by Mark Kilmurry; Presented by the Outhouse Theatre Company; Director, Craig Baldwin; Cast: Nick Stevenson, Jeremy Waters, Paul Swinnerton, Nico Evers-Swindell, Emma Jackson, Victoria Roberts; October 12–27, 2007

MY DINNER WITH ANTOSHA: NOTES FROM THE COUNTRY DOCTOR by Anton Chekhov; Presented by Studio Six of the Moscow Art Theater; December 12–22, 2007

BOY'S LIFE by Howard Korder; Presented by Counting Squares Theatre; Director, Dena Kology; Set/Co-Artistic Director, Joshua Chase Gold; Costumes, Claire Magruder; Lighting, Jessica Burgess; Sound, James E. Cleveland; Cast: Ryan Nicholoff (Co-Artistic Director), Ed Davis, Sarah Matthay, Chris Worley, Dena Kology, Abigail Flynn, Kendra Holton; Previously presented at the Spoon Theatre; January 22–February 13, 2008

NEW YORK FRIGID FESTIVAL February 27–March 9, 2008; Productions at the Kraine included: *American Badass, American Cake, Antonin…mon Artaud, Clinical Depression (The Funny Kind), Diversey Harbor, Great Hymm of Thanksgiving/Conversation Storm, Speedo & the Straight Man, Sporknotes, Stuck! Telegrams from the New Canadian Cinema*

ATTORNEY FOR THE DAMNED by Denis Woychuk, music and music direction by Rob McCulloch; Director, Stephen Vincent Brennan; Design, Lance Harkins; Costumes, Jeaho Lee; Cast: Allison Johnson, Ray Fisher, Denny Blake, Brian Ferrari, Patrick Mattingly, Vadim Newquist, Maria Dalbotten, Juliana Smith, Teddy Williams, Norma Gomez, Amanda Ochoa, Boksim Jean, Lee Goffin-Bonnenfant; Band: Rob McCulloch,

Teddy Williams, Jamie Morris, Adam Lippman, Jesse Lynn, Baksim Jeon; March 13–June 11, 2008

HOSTAGE SONG Music and lyrics by Kyle Jarrow, stories and book by Clay McLeod Chapman; Director, Oliver Butler; Set, Amanda Rehbein; Costumes, Sean Tribble; Lighting, Mike Riggs; Cast: Paul Thureen, Hanna Cheek, Hannah Bos, Abe Goldfarb, Clay McLeod Chapman; Band: Kyle Jarrow, Drew. St. Aubin, Paul Bates, Jonathan Sherrill; April 4–26, 2008

F*CK ME, B*AT ME, L*VE ME by Kevin Podgorski; Presented by Orange Hanky Productions; Director, Brian Olsen; Set, Arnulfo Maldonado; Lighting, Benjamin C. Tevelow; Costumes, Benjamin Taylor Ridgway; Sound, Michael Allen; Cast: Felipe Forero, Jeff Godfisher, Jim Halloran, Jason Romas; May 1–24, 2008

UNDER St. Marks

UNACCESSORIZED Written and performed by Rich Kiamco; June 5–26, 2007

for colored girls who have considered suicide/when the rainbow is enuf by Ntozake Shange; Director, Alycya Miller; June 7–9, 2007

I GOOGLE MYSELF by Jason Schafer; Director, Jason Jacobs; June 14–July 14, 2007

TYRANNOS REX by Joshua Pangorn; Presented by The Living Room Theatre; July 19–August 5, 2007

DECADEENCE by P. William Pinto; Presented by Rising Sun; Director, Akia; AD, Matthew Kreiner; Lighting, Jessica Greenberg; Costumes, Dara Fargotstein; Sound, Roman Battaglia; Stage Manager, Jenna Dempesy; Cast: Adam Purvis, Lindsey Smith, Elizabeth Burke, Michelle Robinson, Nicolette Callaway, Ray Oliver Bune, Patrick J. Egan, Reginald V. Ferguson, Tommy Farrell, Robert Richardson, Crystal Franceshini, Mimi Jefferson, Kathleen Schlemmer, Julie Bain; July 11–August 25, 2007

...and we all wore leather pants by Robert Attenweiler; Presented by Horse Trade in association with Disgraced Productions; Director, John Patrick Hayden; Cast: Becky Benhayon, Adam Groves, Ariana Shore, Joe Stipek; September 6–29, 2007

CHOSEN Written and directed by Rick Vorndran; Presented by the Dysfunctional Theatre Company and Horse Trade Theatre; Cast: Robert Brown, Danaher Dempsey, Allison Sell, Amy Oppenheim, Theresa Unfried, Alex Warner; September 17–26, 2007

HARM'S WAY by Mac Wellman; Presented by Horse Trade in association with newfangled theatReR; Director, jonmichael rossi; Set/Props, Niluka Hotaling; Costumes, Howard S. Klein; Lighting, Justin Sturges; Sound, Jason F. Williams; Cast: Ashleigh Beyer, Esra Cizmeci, Megan Raye Manzi, Seth Reich, Niluka Hotaling, Justin Sturges, Jason F. Williams; October 2–30, 2007

KINDERSPIEL by Kiran Rikhye; Presented by Horse Trade Theatre in association with Stolen Chair Theatre Company; Director, Jon Stancato; Set/Lighting, David Bengali; Costumes, Mary Elbaz; Dramaturg/Music, Emily Otto; Stage Manager/Props, Aviva Meyer; Cast: Sam Dingman, Lanya Fisher, Cameron J. Oro, Alexia Vernon, Lisa Wade White; October 4–27, 2007

GLASS HOUSES Written and directed by Harrison Williams; Presented by The Beggars Group in association with Horse Trade; Cast: Randy Anderson, Stephanie Farnell-Wilson, DR Mann Hanson, Brian Morgan; November 1–17, 2007

ALREADY IN PROGRESS by Jeff Sproul and Jeremy Mather with Dana Rossi, Lindsey Moore and Jesse Jones; Presented by No Tea Productions; Director, Lindsey Moore; Stage Manager, D. Robert Wolcheck; Video, Nicholas Gray, Lisa Nussbaum; Cast: Vonia Arslanian, Alicia Barnatchez, Jesse Jones, Jeremy Mather, Lindsey Moore, Matt Sears, Jeff Sproul; November 29–December 8, 2007

THE SWINGIN 60'S OFFICE CHRISTMAS PARTY Written and directed by P. William Pinto; Presented by Rising Sun Performance Company and Horse Trade Theatre; Music Director, Jovier Sanchez; Accompanist, Jonathan Tuzman; Choreography, Rachel Klein; Cast: Brandon Drea, Mimi Jefferson, Nicolette Callaway, Anjali Abraham, Michelle Robinson, Keith C. Bevins, Geoff Parrish; December 16–18, 2007

NEW YORK FRIGID FESTIVAL February 27–March 9, 2008; Productions at UNDER St. Marks included: *Boom, Chosen, ExcesSecret Circus: "Guess What 'It's' About?", Giant Invisible Robot, Modern Medival, Subway Series, Thanks for the Scabies, Jerkface!, Two In the uBush, Whence Came Ye Scarlett O'Hara O'Hanranhan?, XY(T)*

MASTIPHICUS MEGLODON by Daniel B. Keleher; Presented by Native Aliens Theatre Collective; Director, Peter Schuyler; Stage Manager, Katie McGrath; Cast: Jesse Lawrence, Jason Unfried, Joe Carusone, Tarik Davis, Justin Plowman, Amanda Sisk, Patrick J. Egan, David Stadler, Nate Steinwach; March 13–29, 2008

DIRT by Robert Schneider, translated by Paul Dvorak; Presented by Dreck Productions and the Austrian Cultural Forum; Director, David Robinson; Design, Greg Brostrom, Rebecka Domig, Gabriel Garza; Stage Manager, Kate Neff; Cast: Christopher Domig; April 2–26, 2008

ARMOR OF WILLS Written and directed by Randy Anderson; Presented by The Beggars Group; Music, Patricia Ju; Cast: Scott Rad Brown, Kristi Funk; Jennifer Harder, Brian Morgan, Josh Krebs, Harrison Williams; May 1–17, 2008

RETROGRADE Created and presented by ALL BALLS OUT Ensemble: Danny Gibel, Danielle McGovern, Jessica Ryan, Sydney de los Reyes, Jennifer Stephens, Dave Sturm, Tim W.; May 5–16, 2008

Red Room

STEINESE TAKEOUT Plays by Gertrude Stein; June 14–16, 2007

MUD by Maria Irene Fornes; Presented by AthroughZ Productions; Director, Catlin S. Hart; Stage Manager, Nora Coughlin; Set, Noah Wilson; Dramaturg, Karen Walcott; Lighting, Harry John Shephard; Sound, Jessie Askinazi; Costumes, Desiree Eckert; Cast: Alia Williamson, Evan Heird, Frederic Heringes, July 19–21, 2007

SAY YOUR PRAYERS, MUG! Todd Michael; Presented by Horse Trade in association with Grayce Productions; Cast: Jimmy Blackman; Sarah Bunker, Thom Brown, III, Walter J. Hoffman, Lawrence Lesher, Patrick McColley, Todd Michael, Ryan Stadler, Jill Yablon, October 4–27, 2007

EPIONE Created and performed by Tragic Improv; Director, John Montague; Cast: Helen Abell, Gil Browdy, Darnell Holguin, Alexa Kryzaniwsky, Thomas Poarch, Kelly Reeves, Cathy Simpson, Brendan Wahlers, Chriss Williams; October 20–27, 2007

DOCTOR FAUSTUS by Christopher Marlowe; Presented by Haberdasher Theatre; Director, Tyler D. Hall; Stage Manager, Amanda Ochoa; TD, Nick Allen; Production Manager, Hollie Klem; Cast: Ivory Aquino, Ryan Gorton, Joseph Dale Harris, Krista Hoffman, Christen Madrazo, Will Ramirez, Kerry-Jo Rizzo, Neill Robertson, Evan Storey, Keri Taylor, George K. Wells, Adam Wier; November 1–10, 2007

A'SPRESS by Adam Purvis; Presented by Rising Sun Performance Compnay in association with Horse Trade; Director, Akia; Stage Manager, Matthew Kreiner; Lighting, P. William Pinto; Sound, Di Drago; Set, Eli E. Kaplan-Wildmann; Cast: Patrick J. Egan, Adam Purvis, Julie Bain, Marguerite Desir, Robert Richardson, Nicolette Callaway, Brian Drea, Mimi Jefferson; November 4–14, 2007

THE EIGHT: REINDEER MONOLOGUES by Jeff Goode; Presented by Horse Trade and the Dysfuntional Theatre Company; 3rd Annual presentation; Director, Rob Brown; Set and Lighting, Jason Unfried; Sound, Justin Plowman; Cast: Geoffrey Warren Barnes III, Rob Brown, Jennifer Gill, Rachel Grundy, Amy Overman, Peter Schuyler, Jason Unfried, Theresa Unfried; November 29–December 21, 2007

A VERY NOSEDIVE CHRISTMAS CAROL by James Comtois; Presented by Nosedive Productions; Director, Pete Boisvert; Set, Lauren DiGiulio; Stage Manager, Jessical Lazar; Cast: Rebecca Comtois, Stephanie Cox-Williams, Jessi Gotta, Matt Johnston, Marc Landers, Marsha Martinez, Patrick Shearer, Brian Silliman, Ben Trawick-Smith, Ben VandenBoom, Scott Lee Williams; December 6–15, 2007

THE HAND THAT FEEDS YOU by Greg Turner; Presented by Horse Trade and Do Not Disturb Theatre; Director, Sara Sahin; Cast: Nathan Dame, Ellen Lanese, David Levin, Michael Judson Pace, Patrick Stafford; February 7–23, 2008

NEW YORK FRIGID FESTIVAL February 27–March 9, 2008; Productions at Red Room included: *Diary of a Mad Fashionista, Fool for a Client, Hap Scotch, Her Majesty, Korean Badass, Leaving Normal, parts is parts, Preparation Hex, Rebel Without a Niche, Working it Out*

HOUSE and **MONSTER** by Daniel Mac Ivor; Presented by English Rose Productions; Directors, Fritz Brekeller, Steve Cook; Cast: John Calvin Kelly, Avery Pearson; April 23–26, 2008

NAKED Presented by The Wreckio Ensemble; Director, Kimberlea Kressa; Included: *The Corner* by Michelle Diaz, *The Ladies Aide Society Invites You to a Poverty Party to Benefit the Foundation for Ethical Art and Culture* by the Ensemble, *Rooftops* by Karly Maurer; Cast: Randi Berry, Mike Bradley, Dechelle Damien, Lauren Turner Keil, Katherine Huth, Karly Maurer, Mika Porro, Benjamin Spradley; May 1–17, 2008

THE WILD, WILD WOMEN OF WAKKI-NUNU! Written, designed, produced and directed by Frank Cwiklik; Presented by Horse Trade Theater and Do What Now Media; Choreography, Sarah E. Jacobs; Cast: Patrick Pizzolorusso, Becky Byers, Samantha Mason, Kevin Myers, Sarah E. Jacobs, Douglas Mackrell, Kelly Ainsworth, Jess Beveridge, Sarah Brodsky, Leah Dietrich, Celestine Rae, Candace Yoshioka, Haley Zane, Frank Cwiklik; May 11–June 3, 2008

Hudson Guild Theatre

DON QUIXOTE by Miguel Cervantes; Director, Jim Furlong; June 28–30, 2007

LOVE, LIFE & REDEMPTION Written and directed by Setor Attipoe; Produced by Lamb to a Lion Productions; July 30–August 5, 2007

THE COLORED MUSEUM by George C. Wolfe; Director, Jason Summers; Stage Manager, Dave Harper; Cast: James Becton, Suzanne Harvin, Be Rivers, Marlana Marie, Erica Young; January 10–20, 2008

ALICE IN WONDERLAND by Lewis Carroll, adapted by Andre Gregory; Presented by Hudson Guild Theatre Company; Director, Jim Furlong; February 15–24, 2008

Henry Street Settlement –
Abrons Arts Center and Harry de Jur Playhouse

TO THE DEATH OF MY OWN FAMILY by David L. Meth; Director, Peter Ratray; Cast: Farah Bala; September 27–October 13, 2007

CROWN POINT FESTIVAL Theatre productions included: *At the Seashore* by Libby Emmons, directed by Peter Sanfilippo; Cast: Eric Yellin, Alex Goode, Emily Season; *Beef* by Lawrence Dial, directed by Jason Podplesky; Cast: Elan Moss-Bachrach, Brandon Jones, Kira Steinback; *The Trailers* by David L. Williams, directed by Lauren Keating; Cast: Michelle Pruett,

Jack Perry; *Hostages Stories* by Clay McLeod Chapman, music and lyrics by Kyle Jarrow, directed by Oliver Butler; Cast: Hanna Cheek, Paul Thureen, Abe Goldfarb, Hannah Bos; *The Persians: A Comedy about War with Five Songs* adapted by and featuring members of Waterwell, directed by Kevin Townley; Cast: Tom Ridgeley, Hanna Cheek, Rodney Gardiner, Arian Moayed; *Like I said, my name is Shells* created by Nick Chase and Roslyn Hart, with Rosalyn Hart; *IXOMIA* by Eric Sanders directed by Stephen Brackett; Cast: Jared Culverhouse, Danny Defarri, Orion Taraban, Philip Taratula, Sarah Turner, Cole Wimpee; *The Girl Detective* (see listing in this section under Ateh Theater Group); October 27–November 17, 2007

JOSH & SATCHEL Two one-acts presented by the New Federal Theater and the Castillo Theatre; *Satchel: A Requiem for Racism* by Fred Newman; *Josh: The Black Babe Ruth* by Michael Jones; January 31–February 24, 2008

SWEET MAMA STRINGBEAN by Beth Turner; Presented by the New Federal Theater; Director, Elizabeth Van Dyke; Music Director, Gregg Payne; Choreography, Mickey Davidson; Sets, Ademola Olugebefola; Costumes, Carolyn Adams; Lighting, Shirley Prendergast; Sound, Sean O'Halloran; Cast: Sandra Reaves-Phillips, Marishka Shanice Phillips, Cjay Hardy Philip, Gary E. Vincent, Darryl Jovan Williams; April 3–27, 2008

HERE Arts Center

REMOVABLE PARTS by Corey Dargel; Director, Emma Griffin; Lighting, Raquel Davis; Choreographer, Yvan Greenberg; Cast: Corey Dargel; Kathleen Supové; September 6–15, 2007

curioser and curioser Written, designed, directed and adapted by Gretchen Van Lente from Lewis Carroll's novels; Presented by Drama of Works; Music, Jonathan Portera; Lighting, Jeanette Yew; Cast: Amy Carrigan, Taluara Harms, Adam Sullivan, Ben Sulzbach, Megahan Williams; September 19–October 5, 2007

THE YOUNG LADIES OF Written and performed by Taylor Mac; Director Tracy Trevett; September 26–October 19, 2007

400 YEARS IN MANHATTAN Written and performed by Noah Diamond; Presented by Nero Fiddled; Director, Amanda Sisk; October 1–9, 2007

DRUM OF THE WAVES OF HORIKAWA by Monzaemon Chikamatsu; Adaptation by The Theatre of a Two-Headed Calf; Translation by Donald Keene; Director, Brooke O'Harra; Composer, Brendan Connelly; Sets/Costumes/Lights, Peter Ksander, Emily Rebholz, Justin Townsend; Dramaturg, Roger Babb; Performed by Jess Barbagallo, David Brooks, Laryssa Husiak, Mike Mikos, Tatiana Pavela, Heidi Schreck, Laura Stinger; Music performed by The Weirding Way, Ian Antonio, Russell Greenberg, Tony Gedrich, Brendan Connelly; October 24–November 17, 2007

10 PLATES Created and performed by by Ex.Pgirl: Suzi Takahashi, Bertie Ferdman, Kiyoko Kashiwagi, Paula Salomon; October 24–28, 2007

MAN IS MAN by Bertolt Brecht; Presented by The Elephant Brigade and Rebecca Keren Eisenstadt; Director, Paul Binnerts; Set, Amy Charlotte Rubin; Costumes, Caleb Hammons; Lighting, Bradley King and Kevin Guzewich; Sound, Richard Kamerman; Video, Marilys Ernst; Cast: Lauren Blumenfeld, Tristin Daley, Eric Eastman, Brandon Kyle Goodman, Natalie Kuhn, Justin Lauro, Sarah Wood; December 5–22, 2007

NEW AMSTERDAMES by Ellen K. Anderson; Produced by Flying Fig Theater in association with Middle Tennessee State University; Director, Heather Ondersma; Set/Lighting, Scott Boyd; Costumes/Masks, Alisha Engle & Mark D. Spain; Music, Ryan M. Brown; Stage Manager, Alexandra Biss; Dramaturg and Dance Choreographer, Michaela Goldhaber; Fight Choreographer, Judi Lewis Ockler; Cast: Andrea Caban, Arlene Chico-Lugo, Ian Christiansen, Nathaniel P. Claridad, Jeannie Dalton, Lucille Duncan, Lori Gardner, Michaela Goldhaber, Tina Lee, Abigail Ramsay; December 3–17, 2007; Additional performances at Queen's Theatre in the Park, December 18–19, 2007

CULTUREMART 2008 Work-in-progress stagings; included: *The Lily's Revenge* created by Taylor Mac; January 4–5; *Ego* created by David Michael Friend; *Miranda 5x* created by Kamala Sankaram; *Water* created by Sheila Callaghan, William Cusick, Daniella Topol; *The Gospel According to Jack Vitrolo* created by The South Wing; *MOSHEH – a videOpera* created by Yoav Gal; *Paris Syndrome* created by Ex.Pgirl; *837 Venice Boulevard* created by Faye Driscoll; *Foodstable* created by Richard Toth; *What Comes After Happy* created by Alexandra Beller; *Red Fly/Blue Bottle* created by Christina Campanella, Stephanie Fleischmann; January 4–21, 2008

FRANKENSTEIN: MORTAL TOYS written by Eric Ehn; Based on the novel by Mary Shelley; Project of Automata; Director/Designer, Janie Geiser, Susan Simpson; Music by Severin Behnen; January 8–19, 2008

(RUS)H Text and video by James Scruggs; Director Kristin Marting; Lighting, Christopher Brown; Media Effects, Hal Eagar; Environment, Michael O' Reilley; Music, Steve Adorno; Choreographer, Anabella Lenzu; Fight Choreographer, Qui Nguyen; Sound Designer, Matthew Tennie; Costume Designer, Chris Rumery; Stage Manager, Stacey Haggin; Cast: Marc Bovino, Chandra Thomas, Dax Valdes, Juis Vega, Lathrop Walker; February 27–March 22, 2008

Impact Theater

A MIDSUMMER NIGHT'S DREAM by William Shakespeare, adapted and directed by Michael Hagins; Presented by Tuckaberry Productions; Cast: Joshua Sloyer, Brian T. Wilson, John Forkner, Matt Bernhard, Sarah Amandes, Rebecca Overholt, Joe Kurtz, Ziad Ghanem, Brandi Rhome, Jonathan Craig, Lawrence Lesher, Jennifer Lauren Brown, Lorinne Lampert, Corey Pajka, Cat Johnson; December 6–15, 2007

AESOP'S FOIBLES Written and composed by Aaron Michael Zook; Presented by Tuckaberry Productions; Cast: Adam Baritot, Joshua Triplett, Sarah Amandes, Jessann Smith; Leah Carrell; March 29–April 12, 2008

Impetuous Theater Group

Artistic Director, James David Jackson; Managing Director, Josh Sherman

SWIM SHORTS 3: ARE YOU IN? Short Plays; Executive Producer, Joe Cecala; Included: *Joe the Lifeguard* by CL Weatherstone, directed by Holli Harms; Cast: Tyler Hollinger, Christine Verleny, CL Weatherstone; *Forgiveness* by Janet Zarecor, directed by Sarah Ali; Cast: Kira Blaskovich, Chad Meador, Mark Souza; *Jettison* by Brendan Bradley, directed by Brian P. Leahy; Cast: Bryce Gill, Clayton Dean Smith, Steve T. Smith; *A Proverbial Affair* written and directed by Roi Escudero; Cast: Andy Chmelko, Jennifer Loryn, Eddy Rimada; *Der Eisbar* by Joe Mathers & Brian MacInnis Smallwood, directed by John Hurley; Cast: Felicia Hudson, Alex Pappas, Jason Paradine, Taylor Shann, Gus Schulenburg, Lindsay Wolf; *Practice* by Josh Sherman, directed by Michele Renee Pace; Cast: Candler Budd, Mike Eisenstein; *Twins* by Seth Kramer, directed by Paula D'Alessandris; Cast: Callin McDonald, CL Weatherstone; *A Simple Prop* by Jesse Cervantes, directed by Morgan Doninger; Cast: Nina Camp, Jesse Cervantes, Joy Shatz, Rolfe Winkler; *Crash Landing* by Joe Powell, directed by Rachel Gordon, Cast: Chris Bell, Edward Campbell Jr., Rebeka Pinon-Cassidy; *The Pitch* by Eric Walton, directed by Michael Kimmel; Cast: Jessica Jolly, Meg McCrossen, Eric Walton; Holiday Inn Rooftop Pool at West 57th Street; July 18–August 12, 2007

12TH NIGHT OF THE LIVING DEAD by Brian Macinnis Smallwood and William Shakespeare; Director, John Hurley; Set, Rachel Gordon; Costumes, Lilli Rhiger; Lighting/Sound, Lily Fossner; Makeup/Effects, Allison Getz & Janet Zarecor; Sound, Ryan Down; Puppets, Joe Powell; Fights, Carrie Brewer & Maggie Macdonald; Stage Manager, Sarah Locke; Cast: Aaron Zook, Shashannah Newman, Lindsay Wolf, Reyna De Courcy, Timothy J. Cox, Ben Fine, Erin Jerozal, Larry Giantonio, Tom Knutson, Will Schminke, Neimah Djourachi, Alex Pappas, Joe Mathers, Jason Paradine, CL Weathersone; Teatro La Tea at CSV Cultural Center; October 25–November 10, 2007

The Independent Theater

HATE MAIL by Bill Corbett and Kira Obolensky; Produced by Monday Morning Productions; Director, Catherine Zambri; Set, Maruti Evans; Costumes, Chelsea White; Lighting, Chris Dallos; Sound, Andrew Bellware; PSM, Mel McCue; Cast: Jason Cicci, Danielle Ferland; May 18–June 3, 2007

THE SESSIONS by Nisha Beech; Director, Khary Wilson; Stage Manager, Allison May; Cast: Aaron Oetting, Carolyn Messina, Darien Clark, David Bodenschatz, Doug Barron, Ian Eaton, Melvin Huffnagle, Michelle Lally; June 6–10, 2007

BEAUTIFUL BODIES by Laura Shaine Cunningham; Presented by NativeAliens Theatre Collective; Director, Jodi Smith; Set/Costumes, Scott Smith, Yasmine Jahanmir; Lighting, Peter Schuyler; Lighting/Sound, Nancy Rogers; AD, Liza Ramirez; Cast: Christine Anderson, Jennifer Ankenbrand, Marcia Hopson, Molly Pope, Susan Quinn, Kat Truitt; October 16–20, 2007

Interborough Repertory Theater

TRYING TO GET TO THE MOON Written and directed by Jordan Schacter; Produced by IceWater Pictures; September 7–29, 2007

BOSOMS AND NEGLECT by John Guare; Director, David Epstein; Costumes, Sari Zoe; Lighting, Joe Novak; Set, Kara M. Tyler; Stage Manager, Charles C. Casano; Cast: Nate Dushku, Sarah Mack, Charlotte Hampden; November 29–December 23, 2007

Interart Annex

SNAKEBIT by David Marshall Grant; Produced by Improbabl Fiction; Director, Kal Haney; Stage Manager, Jessie Barr; Cast: Paul Downs Colaizzo, Todd Courson, Quinn Michael Mattfeld, Erin Roberts; July 26–August 5, 2007

ILLUMINATION ROUNDS by Josh Liveright; Director, Paul Smithyman; Set, Anita Fuchs; Lighting, Lucrecia Briceno; Sound, David M. Lawson; Video, William Cusick, Alex Koch; Costumes, Tarafawn Marek; Fights, Judi Lewis-Ocker; Stage Manager, Julie Griffith; Cast: Mark Schulte, Freya Fox; October 4–15, 2007

T HOLD: THE JAMES WILDE PROJECT by Matthew Opatrny; Produced by Blessed Unrest; Director, Damen Scranton; Choreographer, Kelly Hayes; Stage Manager, Amy E. VonVett; Lighting, Benjamin C. Tevelow; Costumes, Sarah Lafferty; Painting Coach, Ian Robertson Duncan; Cast: Jessica Burr, Zenzelé Cooper, Dave Edson, Jason Griffin, Anna Kepe, Eunjee Lee, Celli Pitt, Matthew Sincell, Darrell Stokes, Laura Wickens; October 27–November 12, 2007

YOU PEOPLE: SHORT PLAYS ABOUT THOSE PEOPLE Presented by The Shalimar, Kim Gainer and Shoshona Currier; Original Musical Numbers by Tommy Smith and Davide Beradi, directed by Shoshona Currier and Joey Williamson; Lighting, Lucas Benjamin Krech; Sound, Ien DeNiro; Costumes, Ariella Beth Bowden; Fights, Lisa Kopitsky; Music Director, Joey Williamson; Stage Manager, Shani Colleen Murfin; Plays included: *Blanco* by Hilly Hicks Jr., directed by Sam Buggeln; *Deseret Desire* by Josh Liveright, directed by Camilo Fontecilla; *Miss Morely's Revenge* by Sharyn Rothstein, directed by R.J. Tolan; *Splinter* by Nastaran Ahmadi, directed by Jessi D. Hill; *Tostitos* by Michael John Garcés, directed by May Adrales; Cast: Matt Bridges, Chip Brookes, Blaire Brooks, Devin Dunne Cannon, Barrett Doss, Dawn Evans, Nina Freeman, Edwin Lee Gibson, Jenny Gomez, Kelli Lynn Harrison, Heather Lamb, Lizzie Moore, Andres Munar, Laurie Naughton, Justin Okin, Allison Jill Posner, Charles Semine, Jen Taher; November 30–December 16, 2007

Jaradoa Theater Company

Co-Founder/Managing Artistic Director, April Nickell; Co-Founder/Associate Artistic Director, Anika Larsen

SERENADE Book, lyrics and story by Rachel Sheinkin, music and story by Nils Olaf Dolven; Premiere production; Produced in association with Ben Bartolone and Robert E. Schneider; Director, April Nickell; Choreography, Luis Salgado; Musical Director, Jared Stein; Set, Tobin Ost; Costumes, Andrea Varga; Lighting, Herrick Goldman; Sound, Mike Farfalla; Stage Manager, Adam Grosswirth; ASM, Sunneva Stapleton; Assistant Producer, Telly Leung; Production Manager, John Martinez; Press, Jim Randolph; Cast: Sara Andreas, Ron Bagden, Anton Briones, Joe Donohoe, Mindy Dougherty, Michael Fielder, Chris Harbur, Joshua Henry, Amanda Hunt, Adam Kaokept, Anika Larsen, Nicole Lewis, Mario Martinez, Kelly McCreary, Eileen Rivera, Robb Sapp, Cara Samantha Scherker, Alison Solomon; Teatro La Tea/Clemente Soto Vélez Cultural Center; December 1–15, 2007

THE SMALL OF HER BACK by Russell Leigh Sharman; Director, April Nickell; Set, Brandon Giles; Costumes, Andrea Varga; Lighting, Zack Tinkelman; Sound, Pea-Jae Stasuk; Production Manager, John Martinez; Producer, Robert E. Schneider; Cast: Eileen Rivera, Jeremy O'Grady; Times Square Arts Center–411 Theater; May 9–19, 2008

Joria Productions

DICK 2 (A.K.A. RICHARD II) by William Shakespeare; Presented by Theatre of the Expandable; Director, Jesse Edward Rosbrow; Lighting, Alison Cherry; Technical Director, Christopher Hardy; Dramaturgs, Marc Etlin and Geoffrey Roecker; Press, Stephanie Rose; Cast: Gregory Engbrecht, John Forkner, Mim Granahan, Christopher Hardy, Jennifer Lagasse, Caitlin McColl, Alan McNaney, Jacob Ming-Trent, Andrew Nisinson, Geoffrey Roecker, Raushanah Simmons, Alisha Soper, Alexander Yakovleff, Morgan Anne Zipf; June 21–July 8, 2007

Judith Shakespeare Company NYC

Joanne Zipay, Artistic Director and Producer

CORIOLANUS by William Shakespeare ("Shakespeare Unplugged" Concert Performance); Director/Dramaturg, Joanne Zipay; Stage Manager, Brady Amoon; Assistant Director/Assistant Stage Manager, Alice Alcala; Movement Coach, Elizabeth Mozer; Voice Coach, Donna Germain; Fight Choreographer, Dan O'Driscoll; Composer/Percussionist, Brady Miller; Cast: David Huber, Jane Titus, Richard Lear, Rachael Hip-Flores, Jan-Peter Pedross, Mariah Hernandez, Oliver Conant, Laurie Bannister-Colón, Natasha Yannacañedo, Elizabeth Flax, Amar Srivastava, Mary Hodges, Alvin Chan, Gwenyth Reitz, Carlos Ponton, Amy Driesler, Tyrone Davis, Sheila Joon; Spoon Theatre; December 17–19, 2007

LAByrith Theater

Artistic Directors, John Ortiz, Philip Seymour Hoffman; Co-Artistic Director/Executive Director, John Gould Rubin

Developmental Productions/Readings

THE BARN 2007 Eighth Annual Reading Series Festival; Shiva Theatre; November 27–December 15, 2007,; Included *Knives and Other Sharp Objects* by Raul Castillo; Director, Felix Solis; *Philip Roth in Khartoum* by David Bar Katz; Director, John Gould Rubin; *A Sinister Man* by Gian DiDonna; Director, Paula Pizzi; *The Long Red Road* by Brett C. Leonard; Director, Philip Seymour Hoffman; *Ruined* by Lynn Nottage; Director, Kate Whoriskey; *Fault Lines* by Stephen Belber; Director, Lucie Tibergheien; *For Dear Life* by Melissa Ross; Director, Mimi O'Donnell; *Switzerland* by Rebecca Cohen; Director, John Gould Rubin; *Lady Luck* by Elizabeth Canavan & Salvatore Inzerillo; Director, Mimi O'Donnell; *Dead Letters* by Kohl Sudduth; Director, Padraic Lillis

LIVE NUDE PLAYS December 16–17, 2007; Included *Guaranteed Second Base* by Michael Puzzo; Director, David Bar Katz; *The Killing Play* by David Anzuelo; Director, Cristian Amigo; *Six Minutes* by Eisa Davis; Director, Sarah Sidman; *Able Man* by Ron Cephas Jones; Director, Salvatore Inzerillo

BITTER HONEY A collection of monologues written and performed by Eric Bogosian; Benfit for LAByrinth Theatre Company; May 21–22, 2008

Public Lab (Innaugural Year)

Vital New Plays in Bare-Bones Productions Presented in Association with the Public Theater

PENALTIES & INTERESTS by Rebecca Cohen; Director, John Gould Rubin; Set, Chris Barreca; Costumes, Oana Botez-Ban; Lighting, Nichole Pearce; Sound, Betsy Rhodes; Dramaturg, Paula Pizza; Cast: Julian Acosta, Elizabeth Canavan, Yetta Gottesman, Craig "muMs" Grant, Michael Puzzo; Shiva Theater; June 10–28, 2008

SWEET STORM by Scott Hudson; Director, Padraic Lillis; Set, Martin Andrew; Costumes, Lee Umberger; Lighting, Sarah Sidman; Cast: Jamie Dunn, Eric T. Miller; Shiva Theater; June 29–June 30

La MaMa Experimental Theatre Club (ETC)

FORTY-SIXTH SEASON

Founder and Director, Ellen Stewart

First Floor Theatre

CARAVAGGIO CHIAROSCURO Conceived, libretto and set by Gian Marco Lo Forte; Presented in association with Magis Theatre and Pioneers go East Theatre Company; Director, George Drance; Composer, Duane Boutte; Costumes, Denise Greber; Lighting, Federico Restrepo; Music Director, Jason Sagebiel; Scenic Artist, Mark Tambella; Cast: Duane Boutte, Matt Nasser, Jeffrey Glaser, Dana Cote, Ralph Martin, Graham Skipper, Kat Yew, Sara Galashini, Silvia Giampaola, Elizabeth Mutton, Erika Iverson; September 27–October 14, 2007

EXPERIMENTA A Festival of Plays; Director, George Ferencz; Costumes, Sally Lesser; Lighting, Federico Restrepo; Sound, Tim Schellenbaum; Production Manager, Julie Rosier; Press, Jonathan Slaff; Program A: *Waiting for Mert* by Michael Zettler; Music, Bob Jeweett; Cast: Alexander Alioto, Peter McCabe; *Plains* by Stacia Saint Owens; Music, Tim Schellenbaum; Cast: Nick Denning, Juliet O'Brien, Julie Rosier; Program B: *The Warzone in My Bed* by Yasmine Beverly Rana; Music, Gengi Ito; Cast: Alexander Alioto, Sheila Dabney, Jason Howard, John-Andrew Morrison, Candace Reid, Jenne Vath; Program C: *Tentagatnet* by Peter Dizozza; Cast: Leslie Ann Hendricks, John Andrew Morrison, Sonja Perryman, Chris Zorker, Sarah Ford, Ulrich Flada; *Schrodinger's Cat* by Stan Kaplan; Cast: Timothy Doyler; Program D: *Auditioning Angels* by Pieter-Dirk Uys; Cast: Sheila Dabney, Peter McCabe, Sonja Perryman, Will Rhys, Jenne Vath; October 18–November 4, 2007

MINA by Leslie Lee; Director, Cyndy A. Marion; Inspired by the work of Mina Loy; Set, Andis Gjoni; Music Director, James David Jacobs; Lighitng, Russel Phillip Drpakin; Choreography, Rosalie Purvis; Costumes, Kylie Ward; Production Manager, Sarah Ford; Stage Manager, Elliott Lanes; Cast: Heather Massie, Laurence Cantor, Bern Cohen, Bridget Gethins, Christopher Johnson; Pamela Monroe, Matthew J. Nichols, Juliet O'Brien, Heather Lee Rogers, Josh Silverman; November 8–25, 2007

WEST BANK, UK Written and directed by Oren Safdi; Music and lyrics by Ronnie Cohen; Presented in association with Malibu Stage Company; Set, Michael V. Moore; Lighting, Matt Berman; Costumes, Greco; Music Director, Scott Baldyga; Choreography, Wendy Seyb; Casting, Stephanie Klapper; Press, Sam Rudy; Cast: Jeremy Cohen, Mike Mosallam, Anthony Patellis, Michelle Soloman; November 29–December 16, 2007

DAYS OF ANTONIO Writen and directed by Dario D'Ambosi; Presented by Pathological Theater; Set, Sonia Peng; Lighting, Danilo Facco; Costumes, Giada Esposito; Cast: Celeste Moratti, David R. Duenias, Gerry Sheridan, Ira Lopez; December 20–30, 2007

MORNING, AFTERNOON AND GOOD NIGHT Three one-act playces directed by Oleg Barude; Set, Alex Polyakov; Sound, Tim Schellenbaum; Series included: *A Corner of a Morning* by Michael Locascio, *Talk to Me Like the Rain and Let Me Listen* by Tennessee Williams, and *Good Night, and I Love You* by William H. Hoffman; Cast: Melissa Schoenberg, Scott Douglas Cunningham, Emma Decorsey, Shea Elmore, Alicia Henry, Guy Chachkes; Voices: Eamon & Ambrose Doster-Schellenbaum; January 4–13, 2008

NEWLAND Written and performed by Sasha Painter; January 17–21, 2008

THE JACK OF TARTS Book and lyrics by Chris Tanner and Eric Wallach, music and lyrics by Paul Johnson; Director/Choreographer, Erich Wallach; Set, Garry Hayes; Costumes, Becky Hubbert; Lighting, Paul Jebson; Stage Managers, Gonzalo Cosmelli & Mariana Santos; Cast: Chris Tanner, Julie Atlas Muz, Lance Cruce, Michael Lynch, Flloyd, Agosto Machado, Richard Spore; January 31–February 17, 2008

THE CHERRY ORCHARD SEQUEL Written and directed by Nic Ularu; Presented by UniArt; Set, Carl Hamilton and Craig Vetter; Costumes, Kimi Maeda; Lighting, James Hunter; Sound, Walter Clissen; PSM, K. Dale White; Cast: Robyn Hunt, Robert Hungerford, Richard Jennings, Paul Kaufman, John Patrick Driscoll, Zach Hanks, Steven Pearson, Patrick Kelly; February 21–March 9, 2008

SEVEN DAYS by Shlomi Moskovitz, translated by Anthony Berris; Director, Geula Jeffet Attar & Victor Attar; Movement, Neta Pulvermacher; Music, Yuval Mesner; Design, Robert Eggers, Lighting, Watoku Ueno; Cast: Victor Attar, Udi Razzin, Deborah Carlson, Ofrit Shiran Peres; March 13–30, 2008

AFTER THE RAIN Created and directed by Watoku Ueno with the Yara Arts Group, inspired by three short stories by Ryunosuke Akutagawa including *Rashomon*; Music composed and performed by Kato Hideki; Set/Lighting, Watoku Ueno, Costumes, Luba Kierkosz; Shadow Image Design, Watoku Ueno and Makoto Takeuchi; Stage Manager, Shuhei Kinoshita; Projections, Rashid Mamun; Produced by Yara Arts Group; Cast: Hana A. Kalinski, Rex Marin, Stephanie Silver, Kazue Tani; Puppeteers: Megan Talley, Alan Barnes Nethertona, Yuji Mianjo; April 4–20, 2008

ALICE: END OF DAZE Conceived and directed by Beth Skinner; Conceived and composed by Edward Herbst; Masks/Puppets, WindRose Morris; Set, Jun Maeda, Lighting, Paul Clay; Video, Paul Clay and Nico Herbst; Cast: Mari Andrejco, Sara Bragdon, Emma Dweck, Edward Herbst, WindRose Morris, Chang-Jin Lee; April 24–May 11, 2008

MISS AMERICA Written and performed by Peggy Shaw and Lois Weaver; Music/Sound, Vivian Stoll; Lighiting, Jan Bell; Movement, Stormy Brandenberger; June 12–29, 2008

The Annex

DELTA Concept, Direction, Choreography and Music by Satores (Peter Todorov and Gregor Kamnikar); Presented by Pro Rodopi Art Center and Satores & Arepo Group (Bosnia/Bulgaria); September 20–30, 2007

DEADLY CONFESSION Based on a novel by Tatiana Niculescu Bran; Presented by Andrei Serban Traveling Academy (Romania); Cast: Csilla Albert, Richard Balint, Ionut Caras, Ramona Dumitrean, Cristian Grosu, Catalin Herlo, Cristina Holtzli, Silvius Iorga, Nora Labancz, Mara Opris, Florentina Tilea, and Andrea Tokai; October 1, 2007

IPHIGENIA AT AULIS Presented by Centre for Theatre Practices Gardzienice (Poland), in association with Polish Cultural Institute; Director, Wlodzimierz Staniewski; Cast: Mariusz Golaj, Joanna Holcgreber, Maniucha Bikont, Charlie Cattrall, Karolina Cicha, Anna Dabrowska, Benedict Hotchins, Justyna Jary, Tanushka Marah, Agnieszka Mendel, Marcin Mrowca, Jacek Timingeriu, Barbara Wesolowska; October 4–21, 2007

BIG BROTHER Presented by HT. Dance Company; November 9–18, 2007

TRASH (MONEZZA) Text by Pier Pasolini; Presented in association with the Fondazione Aido Teatro Stabile di Innovazione Verona; Editor, Simone Azzoni; Director, Andrea Mancini; November 29–December 1, 2007

THE HONOR AND GLORY OF WHALING Written and directed by Mike Gorman; Presented by The Forty Hour Club; Co-director, David Bennett; Score, Tonya Ridgely; Set, Marguerite White; Costumes, Sarah Boyden; Lighting, Carla Bosnjak; Sound, Tim Schellenbaum; Cast: David Bennett, David Branch, Ruth Coughlin, J.P. Guimont, Al Joyce, Michael Kimball, Anita Menotti; December 28, 2007–January 6, 2008

PINOCCHIO AND BIANCANEVE (SNOW WHITE) Adapted and directed by Maria Grazi Cipriani; Presented by Teatro Del Carretto; Design, Graziano Gregori; Sound, Hubert Westkemper; Lighting, Angelo Linzalata; Cast: *Pinocchio:* Giandomencio Cupaiulo, Elsa Bossi, Elena Nene Barini, Nicolo Belliti, Carlo Gambaro, Giacomo Pecchia, Giacomo Vennzani, Johnathan Bertolai; *Biancaneve:* Elsa Bossi, Elena Nene Barini, Johnathan Bertolai, Giacomo Pecchia, Giacomo Vezzani; January 10–27, 2008

CONJUR WOMAN by Beatrice Manley; Director, George Ferencz; Featuring Shela Dabney; Set, Jun Maeda; Lighting, Jeff Tapper; Music, Ellen Stewart, Sheila Dabney, Harry Mann, Jasper McGruder, Yukio Tsuji; January 31–February 10, 2008

IMMINENCE Written and directed by Paul Zimet; Music, Peter Gordon and Ellen Maddow; Video, Kit Fitzgerald; Choreography, Hilary Easton; Cast: William Badgett, David Brooks, Kim Gambino, Lula Graves, Kristine Lee, Ellen Maddow, Greg Manley, Steven Rattazzi, Tina Shepard, Amelia Campbell; February 15–March 2, 2008

TEMPTATION by Vaclav Havel, translated by Marie Winn; Director/Design, Zishan Ugurlu; Composer, Stefania de Kennessey; Featuring students of Eugene Lang College and The New School for Liberal Arts; March 6–9, 2008

MEDEA Adapted, designed and directed by Theodora Skipitares; Music, Tim Shellenbaum; Puppets, Cecilia Schiller; Lighting, Pat Dignan; Video, Kay Hines; March 13–30, 2008

B-ALIVE Created and performed by Gorilla Crew (Korea); April 3–6, 2008

SEJNY CHRONICLES Written and directed by Bozena Szroeder, translated by Danuta Borchardt; Presented in association with the Borderland Foundation and the Polish Cultural Institute; Collaboration: Malgorzata Sporek-Czyzewska, Urszula Wasilewska, Jerzy Czyzynski, Wieslaw Szuminski; Cast: Aleksandra Tomal, Edyta Rogucka, Dominika Turowicz, Aleksandra Kotarska, Katarzyna Ostrowska, Dagmara Nieszczerzewska, Ula Kapp, Aleksandra Szruba, Jakub Ostrowski, Artur Mazewski, Robert Ogurkis, Patryk Zubowicz, Piotr Szroeder, Michal Pawlowski; April 10–20, 2008

BROTHERS Created and directed by Andrea Paciotto, inspired by a poem by Ellen Stewart, based on the Old Testament; Presented in association with City Theatre Jazavac (Bosnia) and Offucina Eclectic Arts (Italy); Score/Video, Jan. H. Klug; April 24–May 11, 2008

THE G-WORD: FOR THOSE BORN LATER Written and directed by L.D. Napier; April 27–30, 2008

ELECTIONS & ERECTIONS Written and performed by Pieter-Dirk Uys; May 5–7, 2008

THE RAVEN by Carlo Gozzi, adapted, composed and directed by Ellen Stewart; Presented and performed by the Great Jones Repertory Company; Additional Music, Michael Sirotta, Heather Paauwe, Yukio Tsuji, Cao Bao An; Choreography, Lu Yu, Ying Tank, Juliana Lau, Rob Laqui, Sinan Kajtazi; Lighting, Filippo de Capitani; Video, Jeffrey Isaac, Jan Klug, Andrea Paciotto; Puppets, Federico Restrepo; Masks, Gretchen Green; Costumes, Lu Yu and Ellen Stewart; June 12–29, 2008

The Club

A GLOBAL DIONYSUS IN NAPOLI by Giuliana Ciancio, Nicola Ciancio, and Paolo Favero; Presented by OPS association, Italy; DJ and performer, Marco Messina; September 21–30, 2007

THE OSIANDER PREFACE by Geoffrey Paul Gordon and David Morgan; Director, Zishan Ugurlu; Composer, Ivan Raykoff; October 8, 2007

OXYGEN by Carl Djerassi and Roald Hoffmann; Director, Zishan Ugurlu; Music, Ivan Raykoff; October 9, 2007

TOWNVILLE Created and Performed by Collabortion Town (Jessica Avellone, Geoffrey Decas, Terri Gabriel, Matthew Hopkins, Boo Killebrew, Jordan Seavey, TJ Witham); October 6–21, 2007

THE USUAL FREAK SHOW Written and performed by Jeffrey Essmann, with Michael John LaChiusa; November 2–18, 2007

SEVEN DAYS by Shlomi Moskovitz, translated by Antony Berris; Directors, Geula and Victor Attar; November 14, 2007

A BRIEF LOOK @ EVERYTHING AND NOTHING by Laraine Goodman; Cast: Laraine Goodman, Anke Frohlich, Rachelle Garniez, Chikako Iwahori, Hank Smith, Michela Lerman, Traci Mann, Megan Haungs, Toes Tiranoff, Jane Goldberg, Rashida Bumbray, Noah Damer, Michael Arian, Staphane Larriere, Scott Lyons, Bernice Brooks, Debbie Kennedy, Ayako Shirasaki, Heather Paauwe; November 20–21, 2007

THE TWO GENTLEMEN OF VERONA by William Shakespeare; Director, Artemis Preeshi; Presented in association with Artemis and the Wild Things; Cast: Joost de Muinck Keizer, Laura Rikard, Sage Suppa, Sarah Tucker, Baris Tuncer, Fredric Villano, Rob Welsh; November 26, 2007

WIN WIN POWER AUCTION Performed by Uwe Mengel; December 3, 2007

IT'S A WONDERFUL LIFE IN NICKYLAND Curated by Nicky Paraiso; Performances: Micah Bucey, Ellen Fisher, Jeffrey Marsh with Rick Sorkin, Kris Olness, Benjamin Marcantoni, Heather Christian, Mitch Bucey, Matt Nasser, Ryan Doyle, Brooke O'Harra, Joseph Keckler, Julia Frodahl, Jeffrey Essmann, Meredith Monk; December 7–9, 2007

THE BABY JANES Created and perfumed by The Imaginaerialists (Kristin Olness, Michelle Dortignac, Laura Witwer, Angela Jones); Special Guests, Terry Beeman, Sara Moore, and live music by Rob Scheps and the Baby Jane–ettes; December 14–23, 2007

FOUNTAIN OF YOUTH by Akim Funk Buddhaf; January 4–13, 2008

ROOM FOR CREAM by Jess Barbagallo; Presented by The Dyke Division of Theatre of the Two-Headed Calf; Director, Brooke O'Harra; Cast: Elizabeth Reddin, Kate Benson, Tina Shepard, Nehassaiu deGannes, Brooke O'Harra, Jess Barbagallo, Laryssa Husiak, Becca Blackwell, Amber Valentine, Nina Hoffmann, Daphne Fitzpatrick, Kevin J. Gay, Ben Forester, Brendan Connelly, Jill Guidera; January 5–June 7, 2008

NORTH Written and performed by Heather Christian and the Arbornauts; January 18–February 2, 2008

JEFFREY & RICK Written and performed by Jeffrey Marsh, Rick Sorkin and Jefferson Kidd, with special guest Clay McLeod Chapman; January 28 & February 15–17, 2008

LAST LAUGH Written and performed by Eric Lockley; Director, Jonathan McCrory; Lighting, Ben McCardell; Sound, Ellie Famutimi; Set, Jaun Grafton; February 22–24, 2008

JOHN MORAN AND HIS NEIGHBOR SAORI and CAT LADY Double bill written and performed by John Moran, Saori Tsukada, and John Keckler; February 25, 2008

NO STRANGERS HERE TODAY Written and directed by Susan Banyas; Composer, David Ornette Cherry; Performed by Susan Banyas and David Ornette Cherry; February 29–March 2, 2008

CRENZA IN A WOBBLY Two new plays: *The Finest Bovine Coming Down the Pike* Written and directed by Joel Hanson; *Al's Donuts* Written and directed by Ernest Curci; March 7–16, 2008

RAILROAD BACKWARD Written and directed by Kestutis Nakas; Cast: Nicky Paraiso, Edgar Oliver, Kestutis Nakas, Chris Amos, Kent Brown, Kevin Crowley, Samantha Grisafe, John David Hall, Frederick Harris; March 21–23, 2008

LOLY N STICK Created and performed by Julia and Chad Bantner; March 24, 2008

DOTTIE HOPE Written and performed by Laurie Sanderson; Directors, Anastasia Barzee and Andrew Asnes; Set/Lighting, Brian Nason; Sound, Bart Fasbender; March 28–April 6, 2008

THE HOLE IN THE WALL An evening with Haim Isaacs; March 31, 2008

CLOWNS BY DEAD RECKONING Created and directed by Kendall Cornell; Cast: Amanda Barron, Christine Bodwitch, Kendall Cornell, Melinda Ferraraccio, Kathie Horejsi, Ishah Janssen-Faith, Mona Le Roy, Judi Lewis Ockler, Julie Plumettaz, Gina Samardge, Maria Smushkovich, Virginia Venk; Special guests: Fiona Landers, Rod Ferrone, Alfonso Cid, Kevin Draine, Sean Ryan; April 11–13, 2008

THE BRAIN Written and directed by Alissa Mello; Puppet/Sets/Puppeteer, Michael Kelly; Puppeteer Cast:–Michael Parducci, Brian Snapp; Film/Video, Blaine Hicklin; April 18–27, 2008

Linhart Theater at 440 Studios

TALL TALES OF TRUE STORIES An evening of short plays by Jonathan Todd Ross: *Morning Breath, I Was a Man, Halftime, Comfortable Pants, Closure, Force of Habit*; Presented by Propinquity Productions; Directors, Steve Bebout, Courtney Phelps, Helena Prezio, Jeff Tabnick, Joseph Ward; Cast: Ari Butler, Brian J. Carter, Nick Cearley, Daniel Cohen, Emily Haggurg, Birch Harms, Shannon Kirk, Rachel Martsolf, Talia Rubel, Matty D. Stuar; August 1–4, 2007

THE PRIVATE LIVES OF ESKIMOS by Ken Urban; Presented by The Committee Theatre; Director, Dylan McCullough; Set, Lee Savage; Lighting, Thom Weaver; Sound, Elizabeth Rhodes; Costumes, Emily Rebholz; Cast: Michael Tisdale, Carol Monda, Melissa Miller, Andrew Breving; September 8–October 1, 2007

Lincoln Center Festival 2007 – Theatre Events

Director, Nigel Redden

FABLES DE LA FONTAINE Direction, Set, Lighting by Robert Wilson, original music by Michael Galasso; Presented by the Comédie-Française; Costumes, Moidele Bickel; Dramaturgy, Ellen Hammer; Cast: Christine Fersen, Gérard Giroudon, Cécile Brune, Christian Blanc, Coraly Zahonero, Françoise Gillard, Céline Samie, Laurent Stocker, Laurent Natrella, Nicolas Lormeau, Madeleine Marion, Muriel Mayette, Bakary Sangaré, Léonie Simaga, Grégory Gadebois, Charles Chemin; Gerald W. Lynch Theater; July 10–15, 2007

GEMELOS Adapted and directed by Laura Pizarro and Juan Carlos Zagal from the novel "The Notebook" by Agota Kristof; Co-adapted by Jaime Lorca; Presented by Compaña Teatro Cinema (Chile); Original Music, Mr. Zagal; Lighting, Juan Cristóbal Castillo; Sets/Artifacts/Props, Rodrigo Bazaes, Eduardo Jiménez, Ms. Pizarro, Mr. Zagal and Mr. Lorca; Costumes/Masks, Mr. Bazaes, Mr. Jiménez, Ms. Pizarro, Mr. Zagal and Mr. Lorca; Cast: Laura Pizarro, Juan Carlos Zagal, Diego Fontecilla; Pope Auditorium at Fordham; July 10–14, 2007

RENJISHI by Kawatake Mokuami, from the Noh play *Shakkyo*; Presented by Heisei Nakamura-za (Japan); Director, Nakamua Kanzaburo XVIII; Cast: Nakamura Kanzaburo XVIII, Kataro II, Shichinosuke II; Avery Fisher Hall; July 16, 2007

HOKAIBO by Nakawa Shimesuke; Presented by Heisei Nakamura-za; Produced by Aramaki Daishiro, Seki Ichiro, Nakano Masao and Hashimoto Yoshitaka; Director, Kushida Kazuyoshi; Choreography, Fujima Kanjuro; Dialogue produced and translated by Linda Hoaglund, read by Paul Lazar; Technical Director, Kanai Yuichiro; Costumes, Arai Kumiko, Hiruta Noritaka and Kurosaki Atsuhiro; Lighting, Saito Shigeo; Stage Manager, Takeshiba Tokutaro; Cast: Nakamura Kanzaburo, Nakamura Senjaku, Nakamura Hashinosuke, Bando Yajuro, Nakamura Kantaro, Nakamura Shichinosuke, Kataoka Kamezo, Sasano Takashi; Avery Fisher Hall; July 17–22, 2007

UN HOMBRE QUE SE AHOGA Adapted from Chekhov's *The Three Sisters*; Presented by Proyecto Chjov (Argentina); Director/Sets/Lighting, Daniel Veronese; Lighting, Gonzalo Cordova; Cast: Claudio Da Passano, Adriana Ferrer, Gabriela Ferrero, Malena Figó, María Figueras, Fernando Llosa, Marta Lubos, Pablo Messiez, Elvira Onetto, Silvina Sabater, Luciano Suardi, Claudio Tolcachir; Mitzi E. Newhouse Theater; July 17–19, 2007

DE MONSTRUOS Y PRODIGIOS: LA HISTORIA DE LOS CASTRATI by Jorge Kuri and Claudio Valdés Kuri, inspired by "The World of the Castriti: The History of an Extraordinary Operatic Phenomenon" by Patrick Barbier; Presented by Teatro de Ciertos Habitantes (Mexico); Director, Claudio Valdés Kuri; Cast: Raúl Román, Gastón Yanes, Javier Medina, Kaveh Parmas, Edwin Calderón, Miguel Angel López, Luis Fernando Villegas; Gerald W. Lynch Theater; July 20–22, 2007

DIVINAS PALABRAS by Ramón María del Valle-Inclán, adapted by Juan Mayorga; Director, Gerardo Vera; Presented by Centro Dramático Nacional (Spain); Set, Ricardo Sanchez Cuerda and Gerardo Vera; Costumes, Alejandro Andújar; Lighting, Juan Gómez-Cornjo; Music, Luis Delgado; Video, Avalr Luna; Cast: Fidel Almansa, Ester Bellver, Sonsoles Benedicto, Míriam Cano, Paco Dénize, Charo Gallego, Gabriel Garbisu, Carlota Gaviño, Emilio Gavira, Elisabet Gelabert, Elena González, Alicia Hermida, Daniel Holguín, Javier Lara, Jesús Noguero, Pietro Olivera, Idoia Ruiz de Lara, Sergio Sánchez, Fernando Sansegundo, Julieta Serrano, Julia Trujillo, Pablo Vásquez, and Abel Vitón; Rose Theater; July 26–28, 2007

The Living Theatre

Founder, Judith Malina

MYSTERIES... AND SMALLER PIECES Created and directed by Judith Malina and Gary Brackett; Performed by members of the company; October 11–November 11, 2007

MAUDIE & JANE by Luciano Nattino, based on *The Diary of Jane Somers* by Doris Lessing; Director, Hanon Rezinkov; Assistant Director, Brad Burgess; Set/Lighting, Gary Brackett; Music, Patrick Grant; Cast: Judith Malina, Pat Russell; Replacement: Monika Hunken; December 7, 2007–March 9, 2008

FLYING HIGH and **VOICES** by Shaneca Adams and Philip Hamilton; Two one-acts; Director/Choreography, Brooke Notary; Co-Director/Co-Writer, Brian Osborne; Set, Bret Haines; Lighting, Greg Balla; Sound, John Oyzon; Cast: Philip Hamilton, Kenny Muhammed, Shaneca Adams, Veronica deSoyza, John Hartzell, Luke Notary, Collin Couvillion; March 27–31, 2008

Looking Glass Theatre

Artistic Director, Justine Lambert; Managing Director, Jenn Boehm

THE THREE SILLIES by Joseph Jacobs, adapted and directed by Aliza Shane with Shira Danan; Stage Manager, Shira Danan; Set, Jana Mattioli; Lighting, Alison May; Costumes, Brent Barkhouse; Cast: Ayelet Blumberg, Christine Burnett, Mark DeFrancis, Michelle Foytek, Catherine Gasta, Kyle Minshew, Matthew Rini, Miranda Shields; October 6–November 18, 2007

LESBIAN BATHHOUSE by Helen Eisenbach; Director, Rose Ginsberg; Stage Manager, Naima Moffet-Warden; Lighting, Ryan Metzler; Costumes, Elizabeth Vastola; Cast: Colleen Benedict, Daryl Ray Carliles, Elena Chang, Claudia Debs, Kate Murrin, Ashley Omadevuae, Ina Marie Smith, JessAnn Smith; October 12–November 17, 2007

WINTER 2007 WRITER/DIRECTOR FORUM Assistant Directors/Stage Managers: Margot Fitzsimmons, Laura Neuhau, Jennifer Browne, Becca Hutton, Laura Pestronk; Included: *Chicken with Stars* by Lila Rose Kaplan, directed by Marie Darden; *Paradise* by Yasmine Rana, directed by Jacquelyn Honeybourne; *Ice Floes* by Kate McLeod, directed by Krystal Osborne; *The Ancient Curse of the Druid* by Ruth Tyndall Baker, directed by Norah Turnham; *All in My Head* by Terri

McKinstry, directed by Chanda Calentine; *Losing It* by Judith Pratt, directed by Leigh Hile; *A Buthman Family Dinner* by Stephanie Timm, directed by Carly Hirschberg; *The Inquisition* by Robin Reese, directed by Holly Nañes; *Cardboard Box* by Celia McBride, directed by Toby Bercovici; *Damnation* by Jean K. Hedgecock, directed by Natalie Golonka; *Zachary Zwillinger Eats People* by Lauren D.Yee, directed by Audrey Neddermann; *Spirits!* by Karin Diann Wiliams, directed by Erin Winebark; Casts: Melisa Annis, Regina Bartkoff, Jenifer Borntrager, Marie Buck, J. Dolan Byrnes, Joane Cajuste, Joe Cappelli, Leigh Ellen Caudill, Cassandra Cruz, Aneesah Dambreville, Amy Dellagiarino, Griffin Dubois, Russell Feder, Meg Flaherty, Candice Fortin, Dee Frazier, Charles Graytok, Tom Hedlund, Elliot Hill, Dennis Hruska, Beth Jastroch, Ben Harrison, Lucas Kavner, Meagan Kenney, Kristen Kittel, Barrie Kreinik, Amanda Marino, Helen McTernan, Hank Offinger, Craig O'Brien, Erin Blair O'Malley, Cheri Paige, Daphne Peterson-VanKanegan, Michael Rachlis, Maya Ray, Julia Rousseau, JD Scalzo, Alec Scott, Dana Shaw, Zarina Shea, Sarah Billington Stevens, Julia Susman, Rebecca Tello, Jamie Lea Thompson, Rachael Villacis; November 29–December 16, 2007

THE BUTTONHOLE BANDIT - An Intergalactic Musical Fantasy Book and lyrics by Mary Fengar Gail, music by Michael Silversher; Director, Emily Plumb; Set, Jacquelyn D. Marolt; Costumes, Lynn Wheeler; Lighting, Ryan Metzler; AD/Stage Managers, Cristina Knutson and Kayla Shriner-Cahn; Music Director, Ahmed Alabaca; Puppets, Margot Fitzsimmons; Cast: Rick Benson, Angela Donovan, Griffin DuBois, Brooke Lyn Hetrick, Nidia Medina, Michael Reyna, Jordan Ungerer, Elizabeth Yocam, Emily Clare Zempel, Melissa Zimmerman; February 23–April 6, 2008

EVERYMAN by Anonymous; Director, Shari Johnson; Set, Wheeler Kincaid; Costumes, Mark Richard Caswell; Lighting, Rachelle Beckerman; Sound, Juan Aboites; Stage Manager, Amanda Thompson, Shannon Ward; Cast: Celeste Arias, Phillip Chavira, Jonah Dill-D'Ascoli, Megan Gaffney, Anne Gill, Madeleine Pramik, Charlotte Purser, Kimberlee Walker, Christopher Williams; May 8–June 1, 2008

SPRING 2008 WRITER/DIRECTOR FORUM Assistant Directors/Stage Managers: Jessica Lazar Rebecca Lewis-Whitson, Melody Erfani, Sarah Wansley; Included: *Sketch* by Carolyn Kras, directed by Jen Browne; *American Infidelity*, by Isabella Russell-Ides, directed by Shira Danan; *Surfacing* written and directed by Julia Martin; *Moving Parts* by Judith Pratt, directed by Caroline Lakin; *Baby Boom* by Lia Romeo, directed by Krystal Osborne; *Gentle Girl* by Gail Bennington, directed by Rose Ginsberg; *HolyMarriage.com* by Kate McLeod, directed by Cristina Knutson; *Whatever and Delicately* by Pia Wilson, directed by Naima Moffet-Warden; *The Untitled Pregnancy* by Michelle Bradley, directed by Nikki Rothenberg; *No More Therapy* by Lyralen Kaye and Amy West, directed by Katrina Foy; *Intimate Things* by Laylage Courie, directed by Toby Bercovici; *Phaedra* by Jean-Baptiste Racine, translated by R.B. Boswell, adapted and directed by Jacquelyn Honeybourne; Casts: Afreen Akhter, TJ Black, Jeanette Bonner, Joe Carusone, Lizzie Chazen, Lena Diechle, Jamie Farrell, Meghan Flaherty, Megan Gaffney, Danny Gibel, Hannah Ginsberg, Jocelyn Greene, Jenna Harder, Nic Heppe, Katie Hyde, Adam Hyland, Emily Marro, Leslie Marseglia, Blake Merriman, Katie Nelson-Croner, Chelsea O'Conner, Jessica Palmer, Jill Pettigrew, Sarah Pullman, Leah Reddy, Ryan Russell, Sana Sepehri, Zdenko Slobodnik, Daniel Smith, Ryan Sprague, Jared Stern, Katherine Stults, Jowan Thomas, Alice Wiesner, Chris Wild, Elizabeth Yocam; June 5–29, 2008

Non-resident Productions

THE BROKEN JUMP by King Talent; Presented by Baby Hippopotamus Productions; Director, J.B. Lawrence; Cast: King Talent, Melissa Jo Talent, Matt 'Mo' Talent, Tony King, Caitlin Mehner, Greg Hormison, Dan Hernandez, Jack Boice; Heldover from the Midtown International Theatre Festival; August 17–26, 2007

SOFTLY SARA FALLS by Jay Hanagan; Presented by Wizard Oil Productions; Director, Amanda Kate Joshi; AD, Ahmed Tigani; SM, Jaimie Van Dyke; Set, Cynthia Jankowski; Lighting, David Edri; Producer, Demi Williams; Associate Producer, Patrice Miller; Graphics, Arthur Kosmider; Sound, Adam Sontag; Fight Captain, Nikolas Priest; Cast: Saida Cooper, Cecil Powell, Jonathan Ledoux, Michael Mattie, Ellery Schaar, Natasha Gilgen; November 7–18, 2007

A MIDSUMMER NIGHT'S DREAM by William Shakespeare; Presented by the invisible company; Director, Darragh Martin; Cast: Peter Mende-Siedlecki, Katherine Atwill, Siobhán Gilbert, Elizabeth Richardson, Chas Carey, Ameneh Bordi, Tim Dudek, Jane Bacon, Lakshmi Sundaram, Fergus Scully, Lydia Brunner, Shawn Carrié, Courtney D. Ellis, Tom Slot, Michael Molina, Pardis Dabashi, Nora Weber, Rosie DuPont; February 27–March 1, 2008

THE INFERNO PROJECT Created and directed by Lauren Reinhard, based on "Dante's Inferno;" Presented by The Rapscallion Theatre Collective; Cast: Christopher Speziale, Harlan Short, Laura Gale, Michelle Burns, Meredith Dillard, Jessica Newton, Rachel Martsolf, Michelle Francesa Thomas, Sarah Burns, Nicki Miller, Kenneth Naanep, Jess White, Tom Rothacker, Adam Law, Reynold Malcom Hewitt; March 6–16, 2008

Manhattan Theatre Source

IN THE ROOM WITH MOLLY BLOOM Excerpts from "Ulysses" by James Joyce; Presented by the Joyce Society; Cast: Kate Mueth; June 25–26, 2007

UNIVERSAL ROBOTS Written and directed by Mac Rogers;Cast: Esther Barlow, Jason Howard, David Ian Lee, Michelle O'Connor, Ridley Parson, Nancy Sirianni, Tarantino Smith, Ben Sulzbach, Jennifer Gordon Thomas, and James Wetzel; July 9–19, 2007

THE GREENWICH VILLAGE FOLLIES Created by Andrew

Frank and Doug Silver, based on a concept by Fran Kirmser; Director, Andrew Frank; Cast: Patti Goetticher, John-Andrew Morrison; Guy Oliveri, Charlie Parker; July 5–28, 2007

POE, TIMES TWO Written and performed by Greg Oliver Bodine; Director, Amber Estes; Costumes, Jeanette Aultz Look; Dramaturg, DeLisa M. White; July 23–26, 2007

GULL(ABILITY) An evening of works inspired by "Jonathan Livingston Seagull" by Richard Bach; Presnted by Melissa Riker and the Kinesis Project Dance Theater; July 30–August 2, 2007

MEASURE FOR MEASURE: Provide Your Blood and Axe by William Shakespeare, adapted by Doug Silver; Co-presented by A Frank Productions; Director, Andrew Frank; Design, Stephen Arnold; Stage Manager, Laura Schlactmeyer; Cast: Ato Essandoh, Lex Woutas, Meghan Reily, Fiona Jones, John-Andrew Morrison, Ridley Parson, James Edward Becton, Jon Ecklund, Dave Koenig; August 3–25, 2007

OH, HAPPY THREE Three original one-acts; PSM, Lauren Arneson; Series included: *Judge, Yuri and Executioner* by Ed Malin, with Mac Rogers; *I Shall Not Be Suede* by Ed Malin, directed by John Di Benedetto; Cast: Irene Antoniazzi, Jordan Auslander, Mike Bordwell, Robert Glasser, Alan Haley, Vincent Ianuzzi, Amil Levi; *Hermaphroditism Through the Ages* by Peter Dizozza, Ed Malin and Maria Micheles, directed by Sarah Mack; Cast: James Edward Becton, Peter Dizozza, Mike Allen Hill, Jeff House, Jocelyn O'Neill, Lydia Ooghe, Emily Riordan, Stefania Diana Schramm, Adam Michael Tilford, Anthony Tsambouki, Toni Wickstrom; August 6–16, 2007

PORTRAIT OF THE ARTIST AS A DUMB BLONDE Written and directed by Sharon Fogarty; Cast: Pete Aguero, Karen Christie-Ward, Sharon Fogarty, Marnee Hollis, Bonnie Lee, Rachel McPhee, Denise Demirjian, Matthew Porter, Thomas Rainey, Debra Wassum; August 19–23, 2007

BRITBITS An evening of plays by Deborah Grimberg, Dan Remmes, Glyn Cannon, Elliot Joseph, Nancy Harris, Lucy Kirwood, and Catherine Donavon; Presented by Mind the Gap Theatre; Directors, Paula D'Alessandris and Joel H. Jones; Cast: Paula Burton, Stephen Donovan, Martin Ewens, Elizabeth Jasicki, Elliot Joseph, Ruth Kavanagh, Jassim Lone, Cailin McDonald, Mia Moreland, Maria Pastel, Dan Remmes, Gwenfair Vaughan, Robin Goldsmith, Ria Ulleri; August 30–September 1, 2007

TWO GENTLEMEN OF VERONA by William Shakespeare; Presented by Four O'Clock Productions; Director, Erik Lurz; Set, Carla Cruz; Costumes, Nicole Quinones & Christina Hernandez; Music/Music Director, Nicholas Isles; Lights/Sound, Vadim Ledvin & Shawn Duan; Cast: Katherine Emily Mills, Zack Zimbler, Kelly Rosenblatt, John Buxton, Adam Reich, Caroyln Demisch, Isaiah Tanenbaum, Michael Dulev, T.J. Fix, Max Hambleton, Chris Beier, Andrews Landsman; September 6–15, 2007

LIBERTY AND JOE DIMAGGIO by David Ian Lee & L. Jay Meyer; Presented by Small Pond Entertainment; Director, Nat Cassidy; Cast: Nat Cassidy, John-Patrick Driscoll, David Ian Lee; September 10–11, 2007

ESTROGENIUS FESTIVAL 2007 Included: *A Cure for Panacea* by Laura Schlactmeyer, directed by Regina Robbins; *After People* by Fiona Jones, directed by Mhari Sandoval; *Wedding (Re)Gift* by Jennifer Thatcher, directed by Devon Highy; *The End* by Shoshonna Currier, directed by Michelle Salerno; *Swan Song* by Anton Chekhov, adapted and directed by Andrew Frank, co-adapted by Doug Silver; *The Curse of the Horned Baby* by Lisa Dillman, directed by Heidi Handelsman; *I Have It* by Bekah Brunstetter, directed by Irene Carroll; *Parents of Typical Children* by Michele Markarian, directed by Leah Bonvissuto; *Kid Sister* by Carrie Louise Nutt, directed by Lanie Zipoy; *Saguaro* by Philip Dawkins, directed by Shannon Ward; *Please Remove This Stuffed Animal From My Head* by Crystal Jackson, directed by Dev Bondarin; *Rumple Schmumple* by Megan Gogerty, directed by Megan Demarest; *Crossing Over* by Natalie Naman, directed by Mary Hodges; *In Dog Years* by TD Mitchell, directed by Rosalie Purvis; *The Body Water* by Rosemary Frisino Toohey, directed by Zoya Kachadurian; *Family Time* by Pamela Danforth Yaco, directed by Leslie Cloninger; *Fetus Envy* by Melissa Maxwell, directed by Kathleen O'Neill; *For Want of a Shoe* by Kristine McGovern, directed by Ester Neff; *Rainbow Sprinkles* by Stacey Lane, directed by Tegan Meyer; *Red Carpet* by Kristina Romero, directed by Maura Kelley; September 18–October 13, 2007

WICKED TAVERN TALES by Greg Oliver Bodine; Director, Amber Estes; Stage Manager, Mozz Mendez; Set, Gregg Bellon; Sound, Andy Cohen; Lighting, Keith Truax; Cast: Libby Collins, Kevin G. Shinnick, Ridley Parson, Nancy Sirianni, Brianna Hansen; October 17–November 3, 2007

OUR MAN IN CHOCOLATE Written and directed by Frank John Verderame; Presented by Teatro Oscuro; Cast: Tod Engle, Mike Hill, Cheri Wicks, Jasmine Spiess; October 21–23, 2007

FOLLOWING ANNIE by Todd Pate; Presented by Broken Blade Theatre; Director, Daniel Stageman; October 28–31, 2007

BABY WITH THE BATHWATER by Christopher Durang; Presented by Ground UP Productions; Director, Kevin Connell; Cast: Karen Culp, Anna Fitzwater, Andy Phelan, Gina Retani, Victor Verhaeghe; November 7–17, 2007

BREAKROOM by Nadia Owusu; Presented by Where's My Waitress; Director, Rachel Egenes; Producer, Shlomit Zebersky; Cast: Ryan Andes, Ajay Bhai, Michael Galyon, Kristin Howard, Jessica Knutson, Matt Laspata, Nathan Lippy, Scotty Morgan, Kwasi Osei, Nadia Owusu, Susan Quinn, Kareem Savinon, Sheldon Shaw, Antwan Tate; November 11–13, 2007

NOTE TO SELF Written and directed by Vincent Marano; Cast: Jerry Ferris, Christina Romanello; November 18–20, 2007; Encored February 27–March 15, 2008

MULATTOS DILEMMA by Juliette Fairley; Presented by Diana Richards and Quenton Hunt; Director, Jake S. Witlen; Cast: Juliette Fairley, Susan Neuffer, Sakinah Garrett Benjamin, Herman Eppert, David Emani, William Sudan Mason; November 23–24, 2007

CHEKHOV'S CHICKS Adapted by Elizabeth Rosengren; Presented by Inner Circle Theatre; Director, Jewels Eubanks; Cast: Carolinne Messihi, Chris Cotone, Elizabeth Rosengren, Kate Geller, Maria Hurdle, Diana Buirski, Taryn DeVito, Alexandra Seal, Prudence Heyert, Stu Richel, Ramesh Ganeshram; November 29–December 15, 2007

SAVAGE IN LIMBO by John Patrick Shanley; Presented by Bow and Arrow Productions; Director, Lexie Pregosin; Cast: Teddy Alvaro, Eve Danzeisen, Jocelyn O'Neil, Brian Patacca, Amanda Peters; December 2–4, 2007

PRAYER Written and produced by Jonathan Kravets; Director, Damon Krometis; Cast: James Edward Becton, Daniel Owen Dungan, Marisa Merrigan, Kevin G. Shinnick, Tobias Squier-Roper, Joe Tippett; December 9–11, 2007

A CHRISTMAS CAROL Written and performed by Greg Oliver Bodine; Director, Shana Solomon; Stage Manager, Matt Quint; December 17–18, 2007

HI-FI CHRISTMAS Conceived by Julie Perkins; Cast: Julie Perkins, Nancy Sirianni, Erin Muroski, Allen Wamock, Brian Longwell; December 19–28, 2007

WITCH CHRISTMAS Written and directed by Sharon Fogarty; Cast: Kyrian Friedenberg, Alyssa Heinemann, Allison Snyder, Krysten Wagner, Peter Auero, Sharon Fogarty, Sara Peters, Susan Secunda, John Windsor-Cunningham, Sasha Friedenberg, Dmitri Friedenberg; December 21–30, 2007

LA RONDE by Arthur Schnitzler, translated and directed by Akiva Daube; Cast: Chelsea Morgan Hoffman, Naftali Ungar-Sargon, Nadine Zygaj, Eric Wdowiak, Jessica Scott, Mike Gomez, Shannon Davies, Adam Reich, Elizabeth Jamison, Jon Risk; January 4–26, 2008

ME AND MY CHAKRAS Written and performed by Cindy D. Hanson; Director, Michael Schiralli; Design, Gina Reimann; January 13–15, 2008

BRIT BITS 2 Presented by Mind The Gap Theatre; included: *Lazy Stalker* by Jason Grossman, *Sunday in the Park with Frank* by Matthew Wilkie, *A Castle in a Meadow* by Rachel Barnett, *Things We Leave Behind* by Dan Remmes, *Mr. Blue Sky* by Ian Kershaw, *Sorry Mr. Walsingham* by Steve Thompson, *Another Sunda Afternoon* by Paula D'Alessandris; Directors, Paula Burton, Paula D'Alessandris, Joel H. Jones, Elliot Joseph, Janet Prince; Cast: Nick Berg Barnes, Paula Buton, Stephen Donovan, Michael Graves, Hollis Hamilton, Emily Harvey, Elliot Joseph, Richard T. Lester, Cailin McDonald, Mia Moreland, Maria Pastel, Vinnie Penna, Amanda Plant, Janet Prince, Dan Remmes, Gwenfair Vaughan, Lauretta Vaughn; January 20–22, 2008

THOROUGHLY STUPID THINGS by Montserrat Mendez; Presented by Whirled Peas Productions; Director, Megan Demerest; Cast: Jennifer Semrick, Amy Forney, Darrell Glasgow, Stephen Laferriere, Justin McKenna, Stephanie Lovell, Synge Maher, John Buxton, Dean Jones; January 30–February 9, 2008

MOVING VEHICLES Written and performed by Paul Ricciardi; February 4–5, 2008

PLAY WITH JACKIE Created by Jackie Martling, Nancy Sirianni, Ed McNamee, Rob Perna & Ian Karr; Presented by: JokeLand in association with Spinning Plates and Stand & Deliver Productions; Director, Rob Perna; Producer, Nancy Sirianni; Design, Ed McNamee; Lighting, Chris Cotone; Sound, Tony DiMito; Set, David Palieri; Costumes, Isabella Marlej; Stage Manager, Ben Sulzbach; Starring Jackie Martling; February 13–16, 2008

YOU HAPPY NOW? SOMEBODY JUST LOST AN EYE! by Jason Grossman and Julie Perkins; Produced by J& Productions; Director, Chip Phillips; Lighting, Ben Sulzbach; Stage Manager Laura Imperatu; Publicity, Lanie Zipoy; Cast: Karen Christie-Ward, Ryan Stadler, Allen Warnock, Amy Lynne Darling, Julie Perkins, Jason Grossman; February 20–23, 2008

FROM HARLEM TO THE BRONX: Two Plays by Israel Horovitz *The Indian Wants the Bronx* and *Rats*; Director, Doug Schneider; Fights, Michael G. Chin; Set, Stanley Czarnecki & Diane Corrado; Lighting, Kevin B. Ploth; Cast: Himad Beg, Monisha Shiva, Roy DeVito, Josh Farhadi, Delanie Shawn Murray, Doug Schneider; March 19–29, 2008

KITTY & LINA by Manuel Igrejas; Director, Lory Henning; Cast: Jennifer Boutell, Marilyn Bernard; April 3–26, 2008

THE STORY OF HERR RATH by Paul J. Schrag; Presented by BOO Productions; Director, Kathleen O'Neill; Cast: Steven Hauck, E.C. Kelly, Rick Lohman, Maurice Neuhaus, Jaye Restivo, Stephanie Schmiderer; April 6–8, 2008

SKITZ & GIGGLES by Evan Farber & T.R. Hayes; Director, Greg Schaefer; Cast: Paige Allen, Francis Badia, Lexi Cullen-Baker, James Brown, Cameron Cole, Evan Farber, Helene Galek, TR Hayes, Lauren Johnson, Liza Mulvenna, Greg Schaefer; April 13–15, 2008

A BODY WITHOUT A HEAD Written and directed by George R. Carr; Presented by Veritas Productions; Cast: Courtney Allen, James Edward Becton, Sarah Doudna, Matt Drago, Olivia Julien, Brian Karim, Catherine Kjome, Terrence Michael McCrossan, Barbara Mundy, John Van Ness Philip, Brandon Ruckdashel, Stephen Seidel; April 28–May 2, 2008

TWELVE ANGRY WOMEN by Reginald Wise; Presented by BOO Productions; Director, Kathleen O'Neill; Cast: Amy Dickenson, Sheila Joon, Crystina Wyler, Stephanie Schmiderer, Rana Kay, Cindy Keiter, Dyanne Court, Campbell Echols, Reet Roos Varnik, Michelle Goltzman, Mami Kimura, Nancy Georgini, Dana Monagan; May 7–31, 2008

TURTLE HUNTING by Paul Jordan; Director, Paul Sado; Cast: Colleen Bachman, Paul Jordan, Evan Neumann; May 12–13, 2008

JANEY MILLER'S WORLD TOUR by John Cassel; Director, Heidi Handelsman; Stage Manager, Jennifer Thatcher; Cast: Andrew Glaszek, Mikki Jordan, Blake Kubena, Erica Miller; May 18–20, 2008

The Medicine Show Theatre Ensemble

Artistic Director, Barbara Vann

THE THEORY OF COLOR by Lella Heins; Director, Alexander Harrington; Set/Lighting, Tony Penna; Projections, Caterina Bertolotto; Cast: Geoff Wigdor, James Nugent, Celeste Moratti, Charlotte Patton, Alexandra Devin, Kathryn Savannah; July 12–29, 2007

FRANK & STEIN AND FRIENDS An evening of short verse plays featuring the world premiere of "The Houses At Falling Hanging" by Frank O' Hara, and plays by Gertrude Stein, Edna St. Vincent Millay and others; Director, Barbara Vann; June 14–30, 2007

THE SHEIK Written and directed by Deloss Brown; Co-produced by Cressid Theater Company; Set/Lighting, Geoffrey Sherman; Cast: Jacqueline Herbach, Marc Palmieri, Lisa Peart, Jack Perry, Amber Voiles; September 8–22, 2007

ON THE BORDER by Howard Pflanzer; Director, Barbara Vann; Sets/Lighting, Joseph T. Barna; Costumes, Uta Bekaia; Choreography, Dieter Riesle; Cast: Elaine Evans, Felix Gardan, Mike Lesser, Lauren LoGiudice, Monica Lynch, Vince Phillip, Charles J. Roby, Lutin Tanner, Alok Tewari; November 15–December 2, 2007

HOORAY FOR WHAT! Music and lyrics by Harold Arlen and E.Y. Harburg, book by Howard Lindsay and Russell Crouse; Director, Barbara Vann; Set, Joel Handorff; Costumes, Uta Bekaia; Musical Director, Jake Lloyd; Choreography, Dieter Riesle; Cast: Josh Bishop, Danielle Carter, Mark Dempsey, James Eden, Sarah Engelke, Ilona Farkas, Mark Gering, Beth Griffith, Rachel Grundy, Adrienne Hurd, Richard Keyser, Mike Lesser, Vince Phillip, Constantine Montana, Lynda Rodolitz; March 13–April 6, 2008

Non-resident Productions

ONE NATION UNDER by Adrea Lepcio; Presented by At Hand Theatre Company; Director, Tye Blue; Costumes, Michelle Andre; Set, Nathan Elsener; Sound, Nathan Leigh; Lighting, Josh Starr; Stage Manager, Sarah Ripper; Production Manager, Marty Strenczewilk; Press, Daniel Horrigan, Stephen Sunderlin; Cast: Adrienne Hurd, Peter Reznikoff, Toks Olagundoye, Christopher Abbott, J'nelle Bobb-Semple, Chrystal Stone; August 9–26, 2007

CLOSER by Patrick Marber; Presented by Hesterhouse Productions; Director, David Epstein; Cast: Jessica Hester, Michael Lichtstein, Sean Grady, Tommee May; February 1–10, 2008

ROMEO AND JULIET by William Shakespeare; Presented by the TheatreRats; Director, Alexis M. Hadsall; Cast: Walter Brandes, Eric Chase, Michael Kevin Darnall, Caitlin Davies, Greg Engbrecht, Rachel Grundy, Cedric Jones, Brendon Katon-Donegal, Joe Kurtz, Francis Mateo, Rachel McPhee, Elia Monte-Brown, Brandi Rhome, Reza Salazar, Peter Schuyler, John Triana, Yanni Walker; April 24–May 3, 2008

Metropolitan Playhouse

Artistic Director, Alex Roe; Associate Artistic Director, Michael Bloom

ALPHABET CITY IV Solo performance plays based on real residents of Alphabet City; Director, Derek Jamison; Stage Manager, Aryana Law; Residents interviewed: Theresa Byrnes, Bill DiPaola, Tamara Hey, Evelyn Milan, Mary Lee Kortes, Blake, David Ores, Jim Power, Miguel Algarin; Cast: Todd Woodard, Guenevere Donahue, Katherine Renee Cortez, Amber Godfrey, Chris Harcum, Todd Lawson, Jane O'Leary, Keri Setaro, Abraham Sparrow; August 8–19, 2007

MARGARET FLEMING by James A. Herne; Director, Alex Roe; Stage Manager, Livia Hill; Lighting, Christopher Studley; Production Manager, Alexander Senchak; Cast: Sidney Fortner, Peter Judd, Teresa Kelsey, Margaret Loesser Robinson, Marshall Sharer, Scott Sortman, Todd Woodard; September 21–October 21, 2008

THE PIONEER Five one-acts by Eugene O'Neill: *The Web, The Movie Man, Ile, Before Breakfast,* and *The Last Will and Testament of Silverdene Emblem O'Neill*; Director, Mark Harborth; Cast: Ron Dreyer, Andrew Firda, David Patrick Ford, Sidney Fortner, Michael Hardart, Keri Setaro, Alex Roe; November 9–December 9, 2007

HAWTHORNUCOPIA Seven series of plays and musicals inspired from the works of Nathaniel Hawthorne; Included: *Tetherfop* Book, lyrics and music by Michael Kosch; *The Scarlet Whale* by Dan Evan; *The Birthmark* by Scott Barrow; *A Pearl of Great Price* by Laura Livingston; *Misty Phantoms* by Anthony P. Pennino; *Rappcini's Daughter* and *The Future Mrs. Bullfrog* by Robert Kornfeld; *The House of Celestial Experiments* by Jeremy X. Halpern and Irving Gregory; *Making Light: The Found Letters of Hester Prynne* by Michael Bettencourt; *The Master's Black Veil or Deacon Turnip: A Tragedy* by Amber Reed; *Little Edie and The Marble Faun* by David Lally; *MerryMount* by Travos S.D; *A Twice Told Romance* by Laura Livingston; January 14–27, 2008

MORTAL DECISIONS: A Diary of the Donner Party Written and performed by Stu Richel; February 8–16, 2008

YEAR ONE OF THE EMPIRE by Elinor Fuchs and Joyce Antler; Director, Alex Roe; Stage Manager, Livia Hill; Costumes, Megan Ann Richardson; Sound/Music, Ryan Homsey; Cast: Michael Durkin, Jeanmarie Esposito, David

Patrick Ford, Sam Gordon, Michael Hardart, Gregory Jones, Mikel Sarah Lambert, Oliva Lawrence, J. M. McDonough, Brian Richardson, John Tobias; February 29–March 30, 2008

THE DEVIL AND TOM WALKER Conceived and directed by Yvonne Conybeare, adapted by Anthony P. Pennio from Washington Irving's Tale; Music, Rob Kendt; Costumes, Melissa Estro; Lighting, Anthony Galaska; Cast: Michael Durkin, Justin Flagg, Eric Gratton, Rebecca Hart, Sarah Hund, Michael Jerome Johnson; April 18–May 18, 2008

EAST VILLAGE CHRONICLES VOLUME 5 Eight new plays; Evening A – Directed by Melissa Maxwell: *Famine Church* by Michael Bettencourt and Elfin Vogel; *M21/Bellevue* by George Holets; *South Delancey* by David Parr; *The Pickle Lady* by Sharyn Rothstein; Evening B – Directed by Michael Hardart: *McGurk's "Suicide Hall" Saloon* by Dan Evan; *Tracking Gerturde Tredwell* by Jackob G. Hofmann; *East Sixth Street, between First and Second* by Debargo Sanyal; *All Good Cretins Go to Heaven* by Kathleen Warnock; Lighting, Maryvel Bergen; Stage Manager, Brian Taylor; Cast: Lyndsay Becker, William Cefalo, David Eiduks, Amy Fulgham, Scott Glascock, Chris Harcum, Paul Hufker, Carrie Heitman, Jenny Greeman, Bill Mootos, Joel Nagle, Anita Sabherwal, Brian Seibert; June 5–22, 2008

Michael Weller Theatre

LIFE IS A DREAM by Pedro Calderón de la Barca, translated by John Clifford; Presented by Flux Theatre Ensemble; Director, Kelly O'Donnell; Cast: Jake Alexander, David Crommett, Michael Davis, Scout Durwood, Tatiana Gomberg, Katie Hartke, Joe Medina, Lawrence Merritt, Christina Shipp, Isaiah Tanenbaum; June 7–24, 2007

TWO THIRDS HOME by Padraic Lillis; Presented by the Broken Watch Theatre Company (Drew DeCorleto); Director, Giovanna Sardelli; Set, Laura Jellinek; Costumes, Rebecca Lustig; Lighting and Sound, Joshua Rose; Stage Manager, Jessica Felix; Casting, Stephanie Klapper; Press, Springer Associates; ASM/Props, Aleysha Anderson; Assistant Director, Brianna Roth; Graphics, Jito Lee; Cast: Peggy Scott, Aaron Roman Weiner, Ryan Woodle; Michael Weller Theatre; July 21–August 12, 2007

ALFRED KINSEY: A LOVE STORY by Mike Folie; Presented by the New York Theatre Collective; Director, Craig J. George; Set, Sarah Lambert; Costumes, Irma Escobar; Lighting, Richard Tatum; Projections, Shaun Fillion; Sound, Mark Goodloe; Stage Manager, Eileen Arnold; AD, Jennifer Hunt; Cast: Jessica Dickey, Wayne Maugans, Carter Roy, Melinda Wade; September 5–23, 2007

A YORKSHIRE FAIRIE TALE by Thomas H. Diggs; Presented by On The Leesh Productions; Director, Nancy Robillard; Set, Diana Whitten; Costumes, Jessica Jahn; Lighting, Chris Conti; Sound, Craig Lenti; Cast: Jessica Arinella, Peter Russo, Susan Wands, Matt Rashdid, Paul de Cordova; September 27–October 14, 2007

WAR UNCENSORED and **THE DERSHOWITZ PROTOCOL** One-acts by Andrew Carrol and Robert Fothergill; Presented by I Got Da Beat Productions; Directors, Diana Basmajian, Anthony Frisina; Stage Manager David Ricklick; Score, Steve Landis; Set, Hilary Noxon; Lighting, Christopher Chambers; Costumes, Samuel Ellingson; Sound, Steve McIntosh; Cast: Marinda Thea Anderson, Joseph Ditmyer, Megan Hart, Mark Emerson, Derrence Washington, Kate Geller, Kevin Guadin, Ken Maharaj, Jason Tomarken; November 8–18, 2007

MOLLY'S DELICIOUS by Craig Wright; November 29–December 2, 2007

TENDER by Abi Morgan; Presented by Thirteenth Night Theatre; Director, Kevin O'Rourke; Set, Kevin Judge; Costumes, Alixandra Gage Englund; Lighting, Lilly Fossner; Sound, Arielle Edwards; Cast: Betsey Aidem, Noel Joseph Allain, Torsten Hillhouse, Alysia Reiner, John Rothman, Sarah Megan Thomas, Jeffrey Woodard; January 19–February 9, 2008

SUNDAY ON THE ROCKS by Theresa Rebeck; Presented by Ampersand Theatre Company; Director, Bryn Boice; Cast: Lauren Bauer, Leslie Dock, Kelly Howe, Melissa Menzie; February 14–24, 2008

BURNING MY DREAMS TO THE GROUND Written and performed by Gregory Marcel; Presented by Art Jock Productions with A Chip and a Chair; Director, Nicholas Gray; Stage Manager, Robert Funk; March 26–30, 2008

WE CALL HER BENNY Written and directed by Suzanne Bachner; Presented by the John Montgomery Theatre Company; Choreography, Julie Rosier; Stage Manager/TD, Douglas Shearer; Lighting, John Tees III; Costumes, Nadia Volvic; Music, Jessica Owen; Bob Brader, Anna Bridgforth, Bob Celli, Nathan Faudree, Einar Gunn, Judy Krause, Candice Owens, Tim Smallwood, Morgan Lindsey Tachco, Danny Wiseman; April 7–28, 2008

Midtown International Theatre Festival

Founder and Executive Producer, John Chatterton

Eighth Annual; July 16–August 5, 2007; Venues included the WorkShop Theatre Mainstage and Jewel Box; Where Eagles Dare Theatre and Studio

ADDICTED TO CHRISTMAS by David Patrick Stearn; Director, Shari Johnson

ALL THE KING'S WOMEN by Luigi Jannuzzi; Director, Branan Whitehead

AS LONG A TIME AS A LONG TIME IS IN LONG TIME LAND by Todd Pate; Director, Barbara Suter

BLOODY LIES by Greg Machlin; Director, Samantha Schectman

THE BROKEN JUMP by King Talent; Director, J.B. Lawrence

CAT-HER-IN-E Written and performed by Amy Staats; Director, Jorelle Aronovitch

THE CHOLMONDELEY CHRONICLES by Michael Rudez; Director, Michael Roderick

THE CONJUGALITY TEST by Michael Lazan; Director, David Gautschy

DupleX by Scott Brooks; Director, Sam Viverito

THE EXECUTIONER by Jon Kern; Director, Pedro Salazar

EXHIBIT THIS!–THE MUSEUM COMEDIES by Luigi Jannuzzi; Director, Elizabeth Rothan

FIVE BY THREE Written and directed by Nicole Greevy, Uma Incorocci, Eric Jensen

FIX-IT Written and performed by Megan Griswold

four unfold: a story with song by Katie Lemos and TJ Moss; Director, Katie Lemos

THE HAND AND THE HEN by Fernando Josseau, translated by Adolfo Perez Alvarez, co-translation and directed by Oscar A. Mendoza

THE HOUSE OF BLUE LEAVES by John Guare; Director, Emily Plumb

I am not a chimpanzee by Michael Stockman; Director, Douglas S. Hall

I'M IN LOVE WITH YOUR WIFE by Alex Goldberg; Director, Tom Wojtunik

THE LAST ONE LEFT by John Pizzarello

A LINE IN THE SAND Written and performed by Adina Taubman; Director, Padraic Lillis

LOVE AND ISRAEL Written and produced by Sissy Block and Ilana Lipski; Director, Ilana Lipski

NOSFERATU: THE MORNING OF MY DEATH Adapted by Stanton Wood; Director, Edward Elefterion

OUT OF THE FLAMES by David Marken; Director, Natasha Matallana

OUTROVERTED Written and performed by Susan Rankus, Simona Berman, Richie McCall, Craig Durante, Brian Bielawski; Directors, Cheryl King, Diana Basmajian, Matt Hoverman

PAPA'S WILL Written and directed by Rob Egginton

PATRIOT ACTS by Marshall Jones III; Director, Rico Rosetti

THE PURPOSE OF MATTER IN THE UNIVERSE Written and performed by Joe Hucheson; Director, DB Levin

SECRETS WOMEN SHARE by Meri Wallce; Director, Leah Bonvissuto

THE SHADOW PIER by Jonathan Wallce; Director, James E. Duff

SONS OF MOLLY MAGUIRE John Kearn; Director, Candace O'Neil Cihocki

STORIA Written and performed by Troy Diana; Director, Jennifer Ortega

THE SPEED QUEEN by Stewart O'Nan, adapted and performed by Anne Stockton; Director, Austin Pendleton

STRAY DOG HEARTS by Padraic O'Reilly; Director, Jennifer Gelfer

THE STREET Book by Ronnie Cohen with support from Jane Beale, music and lyrics by Ronnie Cohen; Director/Choreography, Heidi Lauren Duke; Music Director, Daniel Cataneo

STUCK by Jessica Goldberg; Director, Daniel Waldron

TAKE ME AMERICA Music by, Bob Christianson, book, lyrics and direction by Bill Nabel

TO THE CONTRARY by Craig Jacobs; Director, James Valletti

TRANSIT Written and performed by Mary Jane Wells; Director, Ben Sander

TWIST Book, lyrics, additional music and direction by Gila Sand, music by Paul Leschen, additional music by Garrit Guadan

WEBEIME Written and directed by Layon Gray

WILL SUCCESS SPOIL ROCK HUNTER? by Goerge Axelrod; Director, Holly-Anne Ruggiero

Milk Can Theatre Company

Artistic Director, Julie Fei-Fan Balzer; Managing Director, Bethany Larsen

BY OSCAR MICHEAUX by Cheryl L. Davis; Director, Julie Fei-Fan Balzer; Set, Ann Bartek, Lighting, Christopher Edwards; Original Music, Elise Morris; Recording and Design, Rene Migliaccio; PSM, John Simmons; Stage Manager, Colleen Darnell; Cast: Garret Hendricks, Becky Lake, April McCants, Vladimi Versailles, Amelia Workman, Justin Zimmerman; in repertory with *P.O.V.*; Michael Weller Theatre; October 20–November 4, 2007

P.O.V. by Sharon E. Cooper, Cheryl L. Davis, ML Kinney, & Bethany Larsen; Director, Riv Massey; Set, Ann Bartek, Lighting, Christopher Edwards; Original Music, Elise Morris; Fight Choreographer, Ryan Bartruff; Dramaturg, Julie Fei-Fan Balzer; Stage Managers, Elizabeth Irwin, Nikki Rothenberg; Cast: Maria Teresa Creasey, Kwaku Driskell, Jodi Epstein, Elliot Hill, Michael Saenz; in repertory with *By Oscar Micheaux;*

Michael Weller Theatre; October 20–November 4, 2007

RUNNING by Sharon E. Cooper; Director, Pat Diamond; Set, Ann Bartek; Costumes, Deb O.; Lighting, Christopher Edwards; Sound, Daniel Kluger; Michael Weller Theatre; Cast: Ryan Clardy, Katherine Alt Keener, Lance R. Marshall, Willie Mullins; in repertory with *The 5 Borough Plays;* Micheael Weller Theatre; May 2–17, 2008

THE 5 BOROUGH PLAYS Five short plays; Set, Ann Bartek; Costumes, Deb O.; Lighting, Christopher Edwards; Sound, Daniel Kluger; Series included: *1600 Feet* by Colleen Darnell and Julie Fei-Fan Balzer; Director, Colleen Darnell; Cast: Ashley Griffin, Caley Rose, Mike Steinmetz, Robert Tann, Natalie Weaver, and Chris Yonan; *A Visit to the Bronx* by Sharon E. Cooper; Director, Julie Fei-Fan Balzer; Cast: Nnamudi Amobi, Sarah Brill, Lian-Marie Holmes, Michael McGuirk; *Stan and Illy Await the Coming* Written and directed by ML Kinney; Cast: Zak Kostro, Brad Makarowski, Aaron Sparks, Jonathan Zipper; *Peace Through Understading* by Cheryl L. Davis; Director, Julie Fei-Fan Balzer; Cast: Brad Makarowski, Deanna Gibson; *Greater and Greater Things* by Bethany Larsen; Director and Cast: Katie Northlich; in repertory with *Running;* Michael Weller Theatre; May 3–18, 2008

Scene Herd Uddered: Workshop Series

LIFE AMONG THE NATIVES by ML Kinney; Director, Julie Fei-Fan Balzer; Cast: Maria Teresa Creasey, Adam Law, Amir Levi, Geoffrey Parrish, Kristen Rozanski, Miranda Shields, Adia Tucker, and Amy Windle; September 9, 2007

HEFERTZ by Hannoch Levin; Director, Riv Massey; Cast: Satomi Blair, Maria Teresa Creasey, and Chris Kloko, Zak Kostro, Adam Law, Amir Levi, Cynthia Rice, and Jonathan Zipper; December 18, 2007

CONSEQUENCES by ML Kinney; Director, Riv Massey; Cast: Zak Kostro, Daren Taylor, Jack Wallace and Justin Zimmerman; May 5, 2008

COMMON SENSE by Bethany Larsen; Director, Ryan Ratelle; Cast: Satomi Blair, Benjamin J. Roberts, Lesley Miller, Topher Mikels; May 18, 2008

Moose Hall Theatre Company/Inwood Shakespeare Festival

Producing Artistic, Director Ted Minos

JULIUS CAESAR by William Shakespeare; Director, Ted Minos; Fights, Ray A. Rodriguez; Technical Director/Costumes, Catherine Bruce; Music, Luke St. Francis; PSM, Polly Solomon. General Manager, Frank Zilinyi; Cast: E. Calvin Ahn, Florence Annequin, Craig Clary, Katherine Renée Cortez, Sarah Ecton-Luttrell, Joey Elrose, Melanie Gretchen, Michael Hagins, David Lamb, Marca Leigh, Kristin Price, Kendall Rileigh, Ray A. Rodriguez, Kevin G. Shinnick, Josh Silverman, Aaron Simms, Polly Solomon; Inwood Park; June 6–23, 2007

SPARTACUS Adapted and directed by Ted Minos; Fights, Ray A. Rodriguez; Costumes, Marie Gallas-Suissa and Catherine Bruce; Music, Luke St. Francis; Technical Director, Catherine Bruce; Choreography/PSM, Polly Solomon; General Manager, Frank Zilinyi; Cast: E. Calvin Ahn, Angelo Angrisani, Lauren Balmer, Barbara Charlene, Alex Coelho, Andrew Danish, Dinh Q. Doan, Sarah Ecton-Luttrell, Joey Elrose, Ian Everett, Justin Herfel, Marca Leigh, Galway McCullough, David M. Mead, Catherine Povinelli, Kristin Price, Kendall Rileigh, Nicole Elysse Schalmo, Aaron Simms, Scott Smith, Polly Solomon, Tom Steinbach; Inwood Park; July 18–August 4, 2007

Musicals Tonight

Producer and Artistic Director, Mel Miller

THE BOY FRIEND Book, music and lyrics by Sandy Wilson; Director, Thomas Sabella-Mills; Music Director, David Bishop; Cast: Kathryn Holtkamp, Esther David, Jeremy Michael, Lauren Ruff, Marnie Buckner, Alice Ann Robinson, Sarah Sawyer, Stephen Stubbins, Ian Laskowski, Drew Pournelle, Stefen Basti, Dan Debenport, John O'Creagh, SuEllen Estey, Jacque Carnahan; McGinn/Cazale Theatre; September 25–October 7, 2007

NAUGHTY MARIETTA Music by Victor Herbert, book and lyrics by Rida Johnson Young; Director/Choreographer, Thomas Sabella-Mills; Music Director, David Bishop; Cast: Colin Liander, Tony Barton, Allen Lewis Rickman, Lisa Villamaria, Maegan McConnell, Robert Anthony Jones, Wendy Bergamini, Rolfe Winkler, Michael Jennings Maloney, Adam Levinskas, Brent Heuser, Andrea Schmidt, Natalie Rado, Christine LaDuca; McGinn/Cazale Theatre; October 9–21, 2007

ROBERTA Music by Jerome Kern, book and lyrics by Otto Harbach; Director, Thomas Sabella-Mills; Music Director, James Stenborg; Cast: Heath Calvert, James Donegan, Jenny Neale, Diane J. Findlay, Marni Raab, Patti Perkins, Jaclyn Huberman, William McCauley, James Zannelli, Dawn Cantwell, Aaron Galligan-Stierle, Emma Lorraine Giffen, Aaron Lenhart, Elena Mindlina, Chris Pinnella, Robert Teasdale, Erika Zabelle; McGinn/Cazale Theatre; March 4–16, 2008

HALF A SIXPENCE Music and lyrics by David Heneker, book by Beverley Cross, based on the novel "Kipps" by H.G. Wells; Director, Thomas Sabella-Mills; Music Director, James Stenborg; Cast: Jon Peterson, Robert Lydiard, Amy Griffin, Doug Shapiro, Deborah Jean Templin, Kathryn Holtkamp, Danny Beiruti, Patti Perkins, Roger Rifkin, Sean Bell, Jenna Coker-Jennings, Michael Jennings Mahoney, Sara Sawyer, Christine Walker, Erika Zabelle, Anthony Zillmer; McGinn/Cazale Theatre; April 1–13, 2008

PARIS Music and lyrics by Cole Porter, book by Martin Brown, additional songs by E. Ray Goetz, Walter Kollo, and Louis Alter; Director/Choreographer, Thomas Sabella-Mills; Music Director, Rick Hip-Flores; Cast: Kevin Kraft, Jennifer

Evans, Mary Van Arsdel, David Edwards, Robyne Parrish, John Alban Coughlan, Gina Milo, Selby Brown, Stefan Basti, Sean Bell; McGinn/Cazale Theatre; April 15–27, 2008

National Asian-American Theatre Company (NAATCO)

Founder/Artistic Producing Director, Mia Katigbak; Co-Founder, Richard Eng

THE HOUSE OF BERNARDA ALBA by Federico Garcia Lorca; Adapted and directed by Chay Yew; Set, Mikiko Suzuki, MacAdams (original design by Sarah Lambert); Lighting, Stephen Petrilli; Costumes, Clint Ramos; Original Music, Fabian Obisppo; Choreography, Mildred Ruiz; Stage Manager, Kat Stroot; Musical Director, Dax Valdes; AMS/Props, Shannon Sexton; Fights, Michael G. Chin; Technical Director, Brian Coleman; Press, Sam Rudy; Cast: Mia Katigbak, Kati Kuroda, Sophia Skiles, Jeanne Sakata, Ching Valdes-Aran, Ali Ahn, Natsuko Ohama, Sue Jean Kim, Carmen M. Herlihy, Maile Holck, Jeanne Sakata; Chorus: Nikki Calonge, Ann Chow, Miyoko Conley, Keiko Green, Allison Hiroto, Loresa Lanceta, Juni Ng, Indika Senanayake, Kiat Sing Teo, Kristin Villanueva, Simmone Yu, Rochelle Zimmerman; Baruch Performing Arts Center – Rose Nagelberg Theatre; June 4–23, 2007; Presented as part of the National Asian American Theater Festival

FALSETTOLAND by William Finn and James Lapine, music and lyrics by William Finn; Director, Alan Muraoka; Music Director, W. Brent Sawyer; Set, Sarah Lambert; Lighting, Stephen Petrilli; Costumes, Ron Glow; PSM, Bruce Johnson; AMS/Understudy, Dana Corral; Cast: Francis Ju, Jason Ma, Manu Narayan, Ben Wu, Ann Sanders, Christine Toy Johnson, Maryann Hu; Dimson Theatre; June 14–July 1, 2007; Presented as part of the National Asian American Theater Festival

BLIND MOUTH SINGING by Jorge Ignacio Cortinas; Director, Ruben Polendo; Set, Zachary Zirlin; Lighting, Kate Ashton; Costumes, Candida K. Nichols; Sound, Jane Shaw; Stage Manager, Hilary Austin; ASM, Leta Tremblay; Fight Consultant, Scott Spahr; Foley Artist/Musician, Adam Cochran; Press, Sam Rudy Media Relations; Cast: Alexis Camins, Mia Katigbak, Sue Jean Kim, Orville Mendoza, Jon Norman Schneider; Baruch Performing Arts Center – Rose Nagelberg Theatre; September 14–October 6, 2007

National Black Theatre

TELL-IT, SING-IT, SHOUT-IT! Written and directed by Hazel Rosetta Smith; Executive Producer, Dr. Barbara Ann Teer; Lighting, Christophe Pierre; Producing Associates, Debra Ann Byrd & Roz D. Fox; Associate Producers, Nabii Faison & Jackie Jeffries; Stage Manager, Norman A. Small; Cast Hazel Rosetta Smith, Lillian Allen,, Alicia Flakes-Cuffee, Phyllis Renee Credle, Anita Wells, Tanyayette Willoughby, Lorraine Moore, Martin Christie, Isaiah Johnson, Tyrone Lewis; September 28–October 14, 2007

BLACK MAN RISING by James Chapmyn; Director, Patricia R. Floyd; Lighting, Christopher Pierre; Choreography, Juson Williams; Costumes, Patrick Cupid; Executive Producer, Barbara Ann Teer; Associate Producers, Nabii Faison, Jackie Jeffreies, Andre Dell, Roz D. Fox; Stage Manager, Debra Ann Byrd; Cast: Nell Dawson, Larry Floyd, Lawrence Saint-Victor, Melvin Shambray, Jr., Juson Williams; October 17–28, 2007

MEDEA by Eruipides, translated by Nicholas Rudall; Presented by Take Wing and Soar; Director, Petronia Paley; Cast: Trezana Beverley, Ian Stuart, Renauld White, Dathan B. Williams, Sharita Hunt, Natasha Yannacanedo, Beverley Prentice, Marishka Phillips, Mary E. Hodges, Ma'at Zachary, Bryan Webster, David Heron, and David D. Wright; February 15–March 2, 2008

Neighborhood Playhouse

THE HOUSE OF YES by Wendy McLeod; Presented by Sweeter Theater Productions; Director/Producer, Maura Farver; Producers, Robyn Frank, Colleen Allen; Set, Adrienne Kapalko; Costumes, Anna Grady; Lighting, Andrew Fritsch; Sound, Greg Hennigan; Stage Mananger, Angela Allen; Cast: Colleen Allen, Robyn Frank, Margret Avery, John Buxton, James Hutchison; June 8–10, 2007

GOD HAVE MERCY ON THE JUNE BUG by Louis Phillips; Presented by the Viking Theater Company; June 21, 2007

FOLLOWING THE YELLOW BRICK ROAD…DOWN THE RABBIT HOLE Written and performed by Terri Campion; Executive Producer, Jeremy Handelman; Director, Elowyn Castle; Stage Manager/Design, TaShawn "Pope" Jackson; July 17–18, 2007

New Georges

Artistic Director, Susan Bernfield,; Associate Director, Sarah Cameron Sunde

GOOD HEIF by Maggie Smith; Director, Sarah Cameron Sunde; Set, Lauren Helpern; Costumes, Olivera Gajic; Lighting, Juliet Chia; Sound, Katie Down; PSM, Pamela Salling; Press, Jim Baldassare; Cast: Paul Klementowicz, April Matthis, John McAdams, Barbara Pitts, Yves Rene, Christopher Ryan Richards; Ohio Theatre; October 6–27, 2007

STRETCH (A FANTASIA) by Susan Bernfield; Music, Rachel Peters; Director, Emma Griffin; Set, Jo Winiarski; Costumes, Jessica Trejos; Lighting, Raquel Davis; Sound, Jessica Paz; PSM, Sarah Burke; Press, Jim Baldassare; Cast: Kristin Griffith; The Living Theatre; May 2–26, 2008

New Stage Theatre Company

Founder/Artistic Director, Ildiko Nemeth

THE ROUND OF PLEASURE by Werner Schwab; Translated

by Michael Mitchell; Director, Ildiko Nemeth; Set/Costumes/Art Directors, Ildiko Nemeth & Jessica Sofia Mitrani; Choreography, Julie Atlas Muz; Lighting, Federico Restrepo; Co-Costumes, Marguerite Lochard; Co-Sets, Joel Grossman; Original Music, ldiko Nemeth & Paul Radelat; General Manager, Fabiyan Pemble-Belkin; Press, Jonathan Slaff; Cast: Kaylin Lee Clinton, Catherine Correa, Charles Finney, Nicole Hafner, Markus Hirnigel, Sarah Lemp, Galway McCullough, John Rosania, Peter Schmitz, Jeanne Lauren Smith; The Flamboyan Theater at Clemente Soto Vélez; November 10–December 16, 2007

New York Musical Theatre Festival (NYMF)

Kris Stewart, Founder and Executive Director; Isaac Robert Hurwitz, Producing Director; Geoff Cohen, Executive Producer

September 17–October 7, 2007; Venues included: The Sage Theater, Julia Miles Theater, 45th Street Theater, Acorn Theater, TBG Theatre, Theatre at St. Clements, Ars Nova, Stitch, Atlantic Stage 2, Times Square Arts Center, Comix, The Paley Center, Hudson Guild, The Times Center, Waltz-Astoria, Philip Coltoff Centre

Next Link Productions

The Angle of the Sun Book and lyrics by Rachel Lampert, music by Larry Pressgrove; Director, Karen Azenberg; *Austentatious* Music and lyrics by Matt Board and Joe Slabe, book by Matt Board, Jane Caplow, Kate Gavlin, Luisa Hinchliff, and Joe Slabe; Director, Mary Catherine Burke; *Back Home Book* by Ronald Sproat, lyrics by Frank Evans, music by Christopher Berg; Director, Bick Goss; *The Boy in the Bathroom* Book and lyrics by Michael Lluberes, music by Joe Maloney; Director, Michael Lluberes; *Emma* Book, lyrics and music by Joel Adlen; Director, Terry Berliner; *The Family Fiorelli* Book and lyrics by Fred Anthony Marco, music by Alastair William King; Director, Robert Bartley; *Gemini the Musical* Book by Albert Innaurato from his play *Gemini*, music and lyrics by Charles Gilbert; Director, Mark Lonergan; *Going Down Swingin'* Book and lyrics by Matt Boresi, music by Peter Hillard; Director, Jenny Lord; *Little Egypt* Book by Lynn Siefert, music and lyrics by Gregg Lee Henry; Director, Lisa James; *Look What A Wonder Jesus Has Done* Book, lyrics and music by Walter Robinson; Director, Hilary Adams; *Love Sucks* Book and lyrics by Stephen O'Rourke and Brandon Patton, music by Brandon Patton; Director, Andy Goldberg; *Mud Donahue & Son* Book by Jeff Hochhauser, based on Jack Donahue's *Letters of a Hoofer to His Ma*, lyrics by Jeff Hochhauser and Bob Johnston, music by Bob Johnston; Director, Lynne Taylor-Cobett; *Petite Rouge: A Cajun Red Riding Hood* Adapted from the book by Mike Artell, Book, music and lyrics by Joan Cushing; *Sherlock Holmes (The Early Years)* Book by Kate Ferguson with Robert Hudson, lyrics by Susannah Pearse, music by Jared M. Dembowski; Director, Nona Lloyd; *Such Good Friends* Book, lyrics, and music by Noel Katz; Director, Marc Bruni; *Sympathy Jones* Book by Brooke Pierce, music and lyrics by Masi Asare; Director, Sarah Gurfield; *Tully (in no particular order)* Book by Joshua William Gelb, music and lyrics by Stephanie Johnstone; Director, Joshua William Gelb; *Yellow Wood* Book and lyrics by Michelle Elliott, music and lyrics by Danny Larsen; Director, BD Wong

Invited Productions

The Beastly Bombing Book and lyrics by Julien Nitzberg, music by Roger Neill; Director, Julien Nitzberg; *Bernice Bobs Her Mullet* Book, lyrics, and music by Joe Major; Director, Andy Sandburg; *The Brain from Planet X* Book by David Wechter and Bruce Kimmel, music and lyrics by Bruce Kimmel; Director, Bruce Kimmel; *The Good Fight* Book and lyrics by Nick Enright, music by David King; Director, Crispin Taylor; *I See London I See France (The Underwear Musical)* Book and lyrics by Vid Guerrerio, music and lyrics by Jeremy Desmon; Director, Jeremy Dobrish; *The Kids Left. The Dog Died. Now What?* Book, lyrics, and music by Carole Lonner; Director, Hilary Adams; *The Last Starfighter* Music and lyrics by Skip Kennon, book by Fred Landdau, based on the screenplay by Jonathan Betuel; Director, Elizabeth Lucas; *Like Love* Book and lyrics by Barry Jay Kaplan, music by Lewis Flynn; *Love Kills* Book, lyrics, and music by Kyle Jarrow; Director, Jason Southerland; *Maccabeat!... The Hanukkah Musical* Songs by Harvey Shield and Richard Jarboe, book, additional lyrics and music by Chayim ben Ze'ev; Director, Jessica Redish; *The Piper* Book, lyrics and music by Marcus Hummon; Director, Michael Bush; *Platforms* Conceived by Holly-Anne Ruggiero and Delaney Britt Brewer, book by Delaney Britt Brewer, music by Brent Lord; Director, Holly-Anne Ruggerio; *Roller Derby* Book and lyrics by Barry Arnold, music by Harold Wheeler; Director, Donald McKayle; *Unlock'd* Book and lyrics by Sam Carner, music by Derek Gregor; Director, Igor Goldin; *Virtuosa* Book by Diane Seymour, featuring the music of Frederic Chopin, Robert and Clara Schumann, and Johannes Brahms; Director, Bruce Roach; *With Glee* Book, lyrics and music by John Gregor; Director, Ryan MeKenian

Special Events

Die Hard the Puppet Musical Book and Lyrics by John Ardolino; Music by James Walton; *Freshly Tossed* Curated by Wendy Seyb and Mark Lonergan; *Intervention – A Teen Musical Comedy* Book by Jill Jaysen, book, music and lyrics by Matt Corriel; *The Seven Year B★tch* Music by Daniel S. Acquisto, words by Sammy Buck; Director, Carlos Armesto; *Step* Book by Harrison Rivers, music by Wayne Lyle; *Suddenly Summer!* Book, lyrics and music by Dan Cohen

Developmental Reading Series

The Cousins Grimm Book by Ted Sod, lyrics by Michael Biello, music by Dan Martin; Director, Michael Bush; *Cutman – A Boxing Musical* Book by Jared Coseglia, music and lyrics by Drew Brody, story by Jared Coseglia and Cory Grant; Director, Jared Coseglia; *JC2K* Book, music and lyrics by Brian Fountain; Director, Evan Cabnet; *Naughty! The Musical World of*

Emmet Taylor Farkas Book, lyrics, and music by Leo Schwartz; Director, Fred Hanson; *Top of the Heap* Music by Jeffrey Lodin, book and lyrics by William Squier; Director, Karen Carpenter; *Warsaw* Book and lyrics by John Atkins, music by William Wade; Director, Jamibeth Margolis

ARS NOVA Concert Series

Chopsticks Larry: A Tribute The songs of Larry Mendelbaum performed by Eli Bolin and Sam Forman; *Clear Blue Tuesday* Concert of songs from the upcoming movie musical directed by Elizabeth Lucas; *Paul Scott Goodman: Songs, Stories, Friends* Director, Scott Schwartz; Music Director, Jesse Vargas; *Hearken to a Piehole* Music by Joe Iconis, lyrics by Robert Maddock; Director, John Simpkins; *Junk in the Trunk: Some Songs by Lin-Manuel Miranda; Mel & El: This Show Rhymes* Created and performed by Melanie Adelman and Ellie Dvorkin, music by Patrick Spencer Bodd, Evan Toth, Kimberly Stern, Noah Diamond, Amanda Sisk; *Daniel Reichard: Kegger '07; Jeremy Schonfeld: New York Storybook; Todd Almond Loves You; Without Skin or Hair: The Music of Nick Jones and Benjamin Ickies*

NYMF@Nite!

Broadway Idol 2007 Celebrity Judges: Manoel Felciano, Stephanie D'Abruzzo, Lonnie Price; Winner: George Psomas; Finalists: Isabel Santiago, Auri Marcus

Partner Productions

Antonin by Roi "Bubi: Escudero; *APAC: A New Generation of Song: The Future of Musical Theatre* Up and coming songwriters showcast: *Girl Gang* Music & lyrics by David G. Smith, book & direction by Mark W. Knowles; *Jungle Queen Debutante* Book by Sean O'Donnell, lyrics and music by Thomas Tierney; *Live Wire* Music and comedy show; *Magic to Do: An Evening With Stephen Schwartz* Hosted by Sean Hartley, featuring Debbie Gravitte, Liz Callaway, Marni Nixon; *Musicals on Television: West Side Story, The Best of Broadway: Panama Hattie, Applause, Hallmark Hall of Fame: You're a Good Man Charlie Brown, Hallmark Hall of Fame: The Fantasticks; The Rockae* Lyrics, music and adaptation by Peter Mills, adaptation and direction by Cara Reichel

Nicu's Spoon

Founder and Artistic Director, Stephanie Barton-Farcas

RICHARD III by William Shakespeare; Director, Heidi Lauren Duke; Set, Victoria Roxo, Costumes, Nicu's Spoon; Lighting, Steven Wolf; Sound, Sarah Gromko; PSM, Julia Berman; Cast: Amber Allison, Wynee Anders, Rebecca Challis, Haley Channing, Andrew Hutcheson, Henry Holden, Jason Loughlin, Timothy McDonough, Scott Nogi, Christopher Thompson, Jim Williams; July 11–July 29, 2007

KOSHER HARRY by Nick Grosso; Director, Stephanie Barton-Farcas and Aaron Kubey; Set & Costumes, Nicu's Spoon & NY Deaf Theatre; Lighting, Stephen Halouvas; Cast: Andrew Hutcheson, Michael DiMartino, Wynne Anders, Shira Grabelsky, Alvaro Sena, Darren Fudenske, Sherrie Morgan, Jennifer Giroux; October 10–October 28, 2007

ELIZABETH REX by Timothy Findley; Director, Joanne Zipay; Set, John Trevellini, Costumes, Rien Schlecht; Lighting, Steven Wolf; Cast: Melanie Horton, Stephanie Barton-Farcas, Rebecca Challis, Oliver Conant, Michael DiGoia, Bill Galarno, Andrew Hutcheson, Merle Louise, Sammy Mena, Scott Nogi, Tim Romero, Alvaro Sena, David Tully; April 2–April 19, 2008

Non-resident Productions

BOY'S LIFE by Howard Korder; Presented by Counting Squares Theatre; Director, Dena Kology; Set/Co-Artistic Director, Joshua Chase Gold; Costumes, Claire Magruder; Lighting, Jessica Burgess; Sound, James E. Cleveland; Cast: Ryan Nicholoff (Co-Artistic Director), Ed Davis, Sarah Matthay, Chris Worley, Dena Kology, Abigail Flynn, Kendra Holton; August 27–September 3, 2007

THEY WALK AMONG US by Nicholas O'Neill; Presented by Rene's Project/My Own Delirium; Producer, Rene Bionat; Director/Choreography, Merete Muenter; Playwright Representative, Christian O'Neill; PSM, Catherine Lynch; Cast: Gabriel Bly, Jullian Coneys, Lisa Fiebert, Lincoln L. Hayes, Jimmy Joe McGurl, Kelsey Schelling, Anthony Martinez, Anne Schroeder, Lori Spada, Valoneecia Tolbert, Courtni Wilson; March 2–9, 2008

NY Artists Unlimited

Artistic Director, Melba LaRose

VOICES OF THE TOWN - A VAUDEVILLE SALUTE! Written & directed by Melba LaRose, Musical Director, Robert Felstein, choreography by Francis J. Roach; Touring various venues in the city

EBONY BLACK Written & directed by Melba LaRose, inspired by *Snow White;* Composer & Musical Director, Rachel Kaufman, Choreography, Francis J. Roach; Touring various venues in the city

INTERNATIONAL CRINGE FESTIVAL Including the Bad Plays Festival and Bad Musicals Festival; Players Theatre; September 10-30, 2007; Schedule included: Carmen Miranda Opening Benefit honoring Tom O'Horgan (September 10); *Sex, Thugs & Rock 'n' Roll: Revenge is Best Served Cold* by Samuel Toll; Director Thomas Amici; *God's Pants Too Huge* by George Holets; Director, Kenny Wade Marshall; Artist Vs. Landlord by Doron Braunshtein a/k/a Apollo Braun; Director, Melba LaRose; *Sexual Perversity in Connecticut* by Mike Folie; Director, Mary Lee Kellerman; *The Age Game* by Joan Blake & Tia Maria; Director, Karen Raphaeli; September 10, 20, 24; *Something to Offend Everyone: Hollywood Saves Africa* by K. Knapp; Director, Maria Benedek; *The Mexican Cleaning Lady or How I Almost Offended the Dalai Lama* by Leslie Bramm; Director, Kristofer Holz; *The Hootens of Hollerville* by Michael Paul Girard; Director, Court Sweeting; *The Jewish Roaches* by

Richard Ravits; Director, Court Sweeting; September 11, 21, 25); *Is That a Gun in Your Pocket?: Aphrodite's Night* by Frank O'Donnell; Director, David Sheppard Jr.; *Berry Season* by Rosemary Frisino Toohey; Director, Mary Lee Kellerman; *Down Goes Rocky* by Reid MacCluggage; Director, Jason Weis; *The Devil and His Sunglasses* by Csaba Teglas; Director, Jason Weis; *Time Went By But Slowly* by J. Boyer; Director, Catherine Lamm; September 12, 22, 26; *Little Boxes Made of Ticky-Tacky: Going Postal* by George Holets; Director, Elyzabeth Gorman; *The Greatest in the Whole Wide World* by David Kosh; Director, Thomas Amici; *A Fake Fiasco* by Frederick Timm; Director, Paula J Riley; *The Canary* by Don Chan Mark; Director, Kelly Campbell; *Perfect Pitch* by Patricia Lee Stotter; September 13, 17, 27; *Poking at Sacred Cows (a faux classical romp): The Moor's Pastiche* by Jean Hart; Director, Robyne Parrish; *Come Again?* by Richard J. Budin; Director, Robyne Parrish; *The Queen's Privy* by Michael Paul Girard; Director, Melba LaRose; September 14, 18, 28; Swingtime for Hitler (& Friends): *Goebbels! One Night Only! Live from Hell!* by Scott Munson; Director, Kenny Wade Marshall; *Better than Hitler* by Jon Brooks; Director, Will Nunziata; *God Bless America* by William Morton; Director, Charles Majo; September 15, 19, 29; Ebony Black September 15, 22, 29; Best in Fest September 16, 23, 30

Brown Bag Lunch Series – Staged Readings

Long Night's Journey Into Day by Stuart Boyce; Director, Robyne Parrish; *An Acute Triangle* by Rosemary Martino; Director, David Sheppard; Jr.; *Chunnel* by Paavo Tom Tammi; Director, Mary Lee Kellerman; *Don't Wait/'Til It's Too Late* by Lenore Blumenfeld; Director, Elyzabeth Gorman; *60 Guilders' Worth* by Anthony P. Pennino; Director, Court Sweeting; *Woman-Bomb/de Sade* by Allan Graubard & Caroline McGee; Director, Jason Weiss; *Vilification* by Laura K. Emack; Director, Paul Nicholas; Red November; *Charlie December* by Penelope Prentice; Director, Robyne Parrish; September 12, 19, 26, 2007

Ohio Theatre

SUMMERWORKS 2007 Presented by Clubbed Thumb; Series included; Special opening nightevent: *The Fifty States: A Pageant of the Americas* Fifty one-minute playlettes about every state of the union; May 30; *Greedy* by Karl Gajdusek, directed by Drew Barr; June 3–9; *Amazons and Their Men* by Jordan Harrison, directed by Ken Rus Schmoll; June 10–16; *One Think I Like to Say Is* by Amy Fox; June 16–23

ICE FACTORY '07 14th Annual presented by Soho Think Tank; July 4–August 18, 2007; Included: *No More Pretending (aka The Return of Indiebot)* by Kir Wood Bromley, directed by Howard Thoresen, presented by Inverse Theatre; *Johnny Applef$%&er* by Rachel Shukert, directed by Stephen Brackett, music by Jerm Pollett, presented by The Bushwich Hotel; *STRETCH: a fantasia* by Susan Bernfield, music by Rachel Peters, directed by Emma Griffin, presented by New Georges; *The Lacy Project* by Alena Smith, directed by Susanna Gellert, produced by Shira Beckerman; *80% of Love* choreographed by Elke Rindfleisch, music by Chris Woltmann and Ryan Tracy, presented by Rindfleish; *Vampire University* by John Kaplan, directed by Desmond Mosley, produced by Meghan May Hart; *The7 Battles TheBest* written and directed by Eamonn Farrell, music by Jim Isleman III

PORNOGRAPHIC ANGEL by Nelson Rodriquez, translated by Alex Ladd; Presented by The Lord Strange Company and Tantrum Theater; Director, Cláudia Tatinge Nascimento; Set/Video/Art, Marcela Oteíza; Sound, Veronika Vorel; Lighting, Ji-Youn Chang; Props, Nick Bencerraf; Cast: Sara Bremen, Jeff Morrison, Cláudia Tatinge Nascimento, Tom Rabstenek, Paul de Sousa, Perri Yaniv; September 2–30, 2007

HOMESICK Conceived and directed by Deborah Wallace; Presented by Saga Theater; Created and performed by Beau Allulli, Sophie Amieva Zina Anaplioti, TChristie, John Dalmon, Lily Feinn, George Frye, Meghan May Hart, Harold Kennedy German, Maranda Kosten, Mark Jaynes, Seth Miller, Lakshmi Picazo, Pablo Ribot, Pedro Rodriguez; Design, Brian Scott; Music, Andy Gillis; Dramaturgy, Suzana Berger; November 29–December 22, 2007

AMAZONS AND THEIR MEN by Jordan Harrison; Presented by Clubbed Thumb; Director, Ken Rus Schmoll; Set., Sue Rees; Costumes, Kirche Leigh Zeile; Sound, Leah Gelpe; Cast: Gio Perez, Heidi Schreck, Brian Sgambati, Rebecca Wisocky; January 5–26, 2008

THE CENCI by Antonin Artaud, translated by Richar Sieburth, adapted and directed by John Jahnke; Presented by The Hotel Savant; Set, Peter Ksander; Sound, Kristin Worrall; Lighting, Miranda Hardy; Costumes, Ramona Ponce, Carlos Soto; Choreography, Benjamin Asriel; Stage Manager, Karen Oughtred; ASM, Melissa Jernigan; Production Manager, Nina Kulmala; Cast: Anthony Torn, Lauren Blumenfeld, Anna Fitzwater, Kobi Libii, Alexander Nifoong, Todd D'amour, Mauricio Salgado, Joshua Seidner, Tanisha Thompson, Alexander Lane; February 3–27, 2008

MAN-MADE Written and directed by Susan Masakowski; Presented by Creation Production Company; Set, Michael Casselli; Costumes, Dorothy Fennell; Lighting, Pat Dignan; Sound, Timothy Anderson; Cast: Kate Hall, James Himelsbach, Bryant Bradshaw, Michael Kevin Ryan, Eva Patton, Richard Prioleua, Amelia Workman; February 29–March 22, 2008

SILVER BULLET TRAILER by Julie Shaver; Presented by Black Rocking Chair; Director, Dan O'Brien; Set, Kevin Bartlett; Composer, Phil Carluzzo; Lighting, Laura Mroczkowski; Costumes, Alisha Silver; Film, Ian Savage; Stage Manager, Libby Emmons; Film Design, Ian Savage: Cast: Kate Albarelli, Gina Bonati, Cate Bottiglione, Sean-Michael Bowles, Benjamin Ellis Fine, Michael Hannon, Chris Hury, Moti Margolin, Chris O'Brien, Brent Popolizio, Julie Shavers, Ashley Ward, Ryan Woodle, Lilli Zaunner; March 28–April 19, 2008

ME Book and lyrics by Kirk Wood Bromley, music by John Gideon; Presented by Inverse Theater; Director, Alec Duffy;

Choreography, Jill Guidera; Set, Jane Stein; Lighting, Jeff Nash; Costumes, Karen Flood; Stage Manager, Casey McLain; Production Manager, Ruthie Conde; Dramaturg, Joe Pindelski; Cast: Arthur Aulisi, Lora Chio, Drew Cortese, Sarah Engelke, Josh Hartung, Bob Laine, Dan Renkin, Annie Scott, Erwin Thomas, Paula Wilson, Brenda Withers, Marshall York; May 3–24, 2008

Ontological-Hysteric Theater

Founder and Artistic Director, Richard Foreman;, Managing Director, Shannon Sindelar

FAMOUS ACTORS Written and directed by Kara Feely; Presented in association with Object Collection; Music/Sound, Travis Just; Design, Hannah Dougherty; Lighting, Miranda Hardy; Cast: Ross Beschler, Avi Glickstein, Annie Kunjappy, Daniel Allen Nelson, Jessica Grace Pagan, Zuzanna Szadkowski; June 14–23, 2007

ART OF MEMORY Conceived by Tanya Calamoneri; Dramtrugy, Kenn Watt; Music/Sound, Allen Willner; Cast: Tanya Calamoneri, Cassie Terman, Heather Harpham; July 12–21, 2007

JOURNEYPATH: An Experiment in Rightness Presented with Title:Point Productions; Director/Costumes, Theresa Buchheister; Set/Production Manager, Samara Naeymi; Lighting, Jennifer Luck; Executive Producer, Shannon Sindelar; Stage Manager, Brendan Regimbal; Cast: Justin Anselmi, Morgan Pecelli, Averyn Mackey, Tom Picasso; July 25–28, 2007

DYSPHORIA Written and directed by Alec Duffy; Presented with Hoi Polloi Company; Set, Justin Townsend, Costumes, Jessica Pabst; Lighting, Miranda Hardy; Sound, Dave Malloy; Cast: David Frank, Amy Laird Webb, Masayasu Nakanishi, Nisi Sturgis, Marshall York; August 2–11, 2007

WHEN DAY BECOMES NIGHT Curated and performed by Leigh Evans; Sound, Benjamin Robison; August 15–18, 2007

BUILDING A HOUSE OUT OF FEATHERS Developed and directed by James Peterson; Presented by The Paper Industry; Composers, Robert Jonas, Adam Lerman, Carter Matscullat, Kosuke Kasza, Chris Dauray; Cast: Adam Lerman, Ashley LaFond, Haley Greenstein; August 22–25, 2007

iph.then Written and directed by Peter Campbell; Cast: Amanda Boekelheide, David Gordon, Senami D'Almeida, James Schaffner, Ramona Thomasius; August 29–September 1, 2007

THE MYSTERIES OF PARIS by Normandy Raven Sherwood, adpted from Eugene Sue's novel; Director, Dylan Latimer; Cast: Jenny Seastone Stern, Edgar Oliver, Alex Colwell; September 6–8, 2007

Non-resident Productions

UNIVERSAL ROBOTS by Ryan Holsopple and Shannon Sindelar, based on the writings of Karel Capek; Presented by 31 Down Radio Theater; Director, Shannon Sindelar; Video, Mirit Tal; Set, Thom Sibbitt; Lighting, Jon Luton; Costumes, Tara Fawn; Sound/Music, Ryan Holsopple with Mike Rodesta, Benjamin Brown; Cast: Justin Tolley, Thom Sibbitt, Kelly Tuohy, Ryan Holsopple, Shauna Kelly, Jonathan Valuckas, DJ Mendel; June 28–July 7, 2007

Paradise Factory

DOWN THE ROAD by Lee Blessing; Debut Production of the Cheap & Easy Theatre Company (Co-Artistic Directors/Founders: David Ballog, Chesare' Hardy, Heather McAllister, Thatcher Stevens); Director/Set/Sound, Heather McAllister; Lighting, Jerry McAllister; Assistant to the Director, Alex Covington; Cast: David Ballog, Chesare' Hardy, Thatcher Stevens, Liz Eggers, Heather McAllister, Sarah Mollo-Christensen, Jackie Smythe; September 20–October 6, 2007

MADNESS OF DAY by Maurice Blanchot; Presented by Dangerous Ground Productions; Director, Doris Mirescu; March 7–22, 2008

Peculiar Works Project

Co-Artistic Directors, Ralph Lewis, Catherine Porter, Barry Rowell

OFF STAGE: THE EAST VILLAGE FRAGMENTS Series included: *Introduction* by Ralph Lewis, Catherine Porter & Barry Rowell, Director, Jim Fritzler; *Hair* by Jerome Ragni & James Rado; Director, Robert Bartley; *The Indian Wants the Bronx* by Israel Horovitz; Director, Jonathan Solari; *The Foreigners* by Michael McGrinder; Director Jim Fritzler; *Five Spot Jazz* written and directed by Spencer Katzman; *Monuments* by Diane di Prima; Director, Lauren Keating; *18 Happenings in 6 Parts (tribute)* by Allan Kaprow; Director, Leslie Strongwater; *The Maids* by Jean Genét; Director, Leslie Strongwater; *Birdbath* by Leonard Melfi; Director, Kay Mitchell; *Murder Cake* by Diane di Prima; Director, Lauren Keating; *The Hawk* by Murray Mednick & Anthony Barsha; Director, David Vining; *The Rock Garden* by Sam Shepard; Director, Bryn Manion; *Hurrah for the Bridge* by Paul Foster; Director, Helena Gleissner; *A Corner of a Morning* by Michael Locascio; Director, Belinda Mello; *Balls* by Paul Foster; Director, Helena Gleissner; *America Hurrah: Interview* by Jean-Claude van Itallie; Director, Jeff Janisheski; *Why Tuesday Never Has a Blue Monday* by Robert Heide; Director, Elaine Molinaro; *The Mulberry Bush* by Phoebe Wray; Director, Casey McLain; *Futz* by Rochelle Owens; Director, Jose Zayas; *That's How the Rent Gets Paid* by Jeff Weiss; Director, Jon Michael Murphy; *Why Hanna's Skirt Won't Stay Down* by Tom Eyen; Director, Mark Finley; *XXXXXXs* by William M. Hoffman; Director, Jon Michael Murphy; *Camera Obscura* by Robert Patrick; Director,

Tim Cusack; *The Bundle Man* by Ilsa Gilbert; Director, Casey McLain; *Lullaby for a Dying Man* by Ruth LandshoffYorck; Director, Halina Ujda; *Conquest of the Universe* by Charles Ludlam; Directors, Gabriel Shanks & Christopher Mirto; *Viet Rock* by Megan Terry & Marianne de Pury; Director, Anna McHugh; *Epilogue* by Ralph Lewis, Catherine Porter & Barry Rowell, Director, Jim Fritzler; Streets of the East Village of Manhattan; June 14–30, 2007

Performance Space 122 (P.S. 122)

Artistic Director, Anne Dennin

THE DEVIL ON ALL SIDES by Fabrice Melquiot, adapted and directed by Ben Yalom; Presented by foolsFury; Cast: Debórah Eliezer, Stephen Jacob, Brian Livingston, Ryan O'Donnell, Nora El Samahy, Joseph William; June 13–July 1, 2007

VERSION 2.0 Presented by Readymade Dance Theater Company; Director/Choreography, Zsolt Palcza; July 12–15, 2007

medEia Presented by Dood Paard (Amsterdam), based on the play by Euripides; September 26–30, 2007

THE INTERNATIONAL SHOW: A Panikk Transatlantique Written and directed by Young Jean Lee; Featuring Marie Nerland, Alexander Gerner, Young Jean Lee, and Iver Findley; September 27–29, 2007

FRANCEOFF! Curated by Terry Dean Bartlett and Katie Workum; October 3, 2007

AVANT-GARDE-ARAMA GOES CLUBBING October 6–7, 2007

START UP by Rolad Schimmelpfennig; Presented by GTA Road Theater USA; October 7–14, 2007

A BOWL OF SUMMER Presented by Semnichimae Blue Sky Dance Club; October 18–21, 2007

WHAT IF SAORI HAD A PARTY Created by John Moran with Saori Tsukada, Katherine Brook and Joseph Keckler; Director, John Moran; October 21–November 4, 2007; encore January 9–13, 2008 as part of the Coil Festival

BEETHOVEN LIVE Lhotáková & Soukup Company; October 28–November 3, 2007; encore January 9–12, 2008 as part of the Coil Festival

GLORIA by Maria Hassabi; November 7–10, 2007; encore January 11–12, 2008 as part of the Coil Festival

THE ARCHER CONTEST, a Radio Play Written and directed by John Jahnke; Presented by the Hotel Savant; Soundscape, Kristin Worrall; Sound, Andrew Schneider; November 8–10, 2007

(3-D) DINOSAUR DEATH DANCE by Japanther; November 15–19, 2007

C.L.U.E. Choreographed by robbinschilds; December 5–8, 2007

500 CLOWN: Frankenstien and 500 CLOWN: Christmas December 12–31, 2007

CATCH 27 Curated by Andrew Dinwiddie and Jeff Larson; December 13–22, 2007

COIL FESTIVAL 2008 Series included: *Between the Devil and the Deep Blue Sea* by Suzanne Andrade, presented by 1927 (London); Animation, Paul Barritt; Music, Lillian Henley; Costumes, Esme Appleton Cast: Suzanne Andrade, Esme Appleton, Lillian Henley; *Iodine [YOD]* Created by Deganit Shemy and Company (encored February 5–10); *Particularly in the Heartland* by The TEAM; *The Fall and Rise of the Rising Fallen* by Banana Bag & Bodice (Peter Blomquist, Mallory Catlett, Jennifer Wright Cook, Jason Craig, G Lucas Crane, Miranda Hardy, Rod Hipskind, Peter Ksander, Jessica Jelliffe, Casey Opstad, Morgan von Prelle Pecelli, Heather Peroni, Jamie McElhinney, Morgan Murphey); *Screen Test* conceived and directed by Rob Roth with Theo Kogan, text by Romy Ashby and Rob Roth; Costumes, Todd Thomas; Music Direcotr, Sean Pierce; Choreography, Vangeline; Dancers: Coco Koyama and Mandy Caughney; January 9–15, 2008

WELCOME TO NOWHERE Written, directed, sets and lighting by Kenneth Collins; Presented by Temporary Distortion; Video, William Cusick; Sound/Music, John Sullivan; Costumes, TaraFawn Marek; Cast: Ben Beckley, Stacey Collins, Brian Greer, Lorraine Mattox, Jessica Pagan, Stephanie Silver; February 20–23, 2008

LUSTRE: A MIDWINTER TRANS-FEST With Justin Bond, Our Lady J, Glenn Marla, Nathan Carrera, The Pixie Harlots; Taylor Mac, M. Lamar; Music Director, Jonah Spidel; February 20–March 9, 2008

HELLO FAILURE Written and performed by Kristen Kosmas; Director, Ken Rus Schmoll; Featuring: Michael Chick, Benjamin Forster, Janna Gjesdal, Megan Hart, Joan Jubett, Matthew Maher, Aimee Phelan-Deconinck, Tricia Rodley, Maria Striar; March 2–22, 2008

BRIDE Written and performed by Kevin Augustine; Music, Andrea La Rose; March 17–30, 2008

DEMOCRACY IN AMERICA by Annie Dorsen; Video, Kate Howard; Lighting, Sarah Sidmon; Sound, Bart Fasbender; Dramaturg, Katherine Profeta; Cast; Okwui Okpokwasili, Philippa Kaye, Anthony Torn; March 30–April 20, 2008

UNTITLED MARS (this title may change) Conceived and Directed by Jay Scheib; Set, Peter Ksander; Lighting, Miranda Hardy; Costumes, Oana Botez-Ban; Sound, Catherine McCurry; Video, Balázs Vajna and Miklos Buk; Dramaturg/Hungarian Project Manager, Anna Lengyel; Cast: Karl Allen, Dorka Gryllus, Caleb Hammond, László Keszég, Catherine McCurry, Tanya Selvaratnam, April Sweeney, Natalie, Thomas, Balázs Vajna; On-camera appearances by Waris Ahluwalia,

Phillip Cunio, Kofi Hope-Gund, Henrik Hargitai, Zahra Khan, Dr. Robert Zubrin; Presented in conjunction with the EST/Sloan Foundation; April 8–27, 2008

VENGEANCE CAN WAIT by Yukiko Motoya; Presented in association with the Immediate Theatre Company and Queens Theatre in the Park; Director, Jose Zayas; Translation, Kyoko Yoshida and Andy Bragen; Stage Manager, Mark Karafin; Set, Ryan Elliot Dravetz; Lighting, Evan Purcell; Sound, Matthew Tennie; Costumes, Carla Bellisio; Cast: Becky Yamamoto, Jennifer Lim, Pun Bandhu, Paul H. Juhn; April 25–May 4, 2008

BLACK HOLES Performed by Will Calhoun; With: Louis Reyes Rivera; May 1–4, 2008

REMEMBER THIS MOMENT Created and performed by Gabri Christa and Niles Ford; Video, Marilys Ernst; Music, Ted Graves; May 1–4, 2008

MAYIM RABIM/GREAT WATERS Composed and performed by Ayelet Rose Gottlieb; Director, Franny Silverman; Video, Renate Aller; Musicians: Michael Gottlieb, Deanna Neil, Tammy Scheffe (vocals), Michael Winograd (clarinet), Anat Fort (piano), Greg Heffernan (cello), Ronen Itzik (Drums); May 8–10, 2008

AVANT-GARDE-ARAMA KEEPS HOPE ALIVE Hosted by Yehuda Duenyas, Normandy Sherwood and Jonathan Jacobs; May 9–10, 2008

LA FEMME EST MORTE OR WHY I SHOULD NOT F!%# MY SON Written and directed by Shoshana Currier; Presented by The Shalimar; May 14–24, 2008

OEDIPUS LOVES YOU by Gavin Quinn and Simon Doyle; Presented by Dublin's Pan Pan Company; Director, Gavin Quinn; Music, Gordon Is a Mime; Set, Andrew Clancy; Costumes, Helen McCusker; Lighting, Aedin Cosgrove; Sound, Jimmie Eadie; PSM, Rob Usher; Cast: Aoife Duffin, Dylan Tighe, Ned Dennehy, Gina Moxley, Bush Moukarzel; May 21–June 1, 2008

THE EUTHANASIST by Liza Lentini; Presented by New York Salon; Director, Alan Miller; Set, Adam Dugas; Lighting, Diana Kesselschmidt; Music, Paul Cantelon; Cast: Monika Schneider; May 29–June 8, 2008

Players Theatre

RADIOTHEATRE PRESENTS KING KONG Adapted and directedby Dan Bianchi; Music,/Sound,/Set/Art, Dan Bianchi; Sound Engineer, Wes Shippee; Lighting, Matt Everett; Produced by Cynthia Bianchi; Cast: Mike Borak, Jerry Lazar, Zach Lombardo, Serrah McCall, Cash Tilton, Frank Zilinyi; Players Theatre; May 27–July 29, 2007

SHORTENED ATTENTION SPAN ONE-ACT FESTIVAL First Annual; Included: *Theatre Ghost* by Mim Granahan; *Life in E Sharp* by Jonathan G. Galvez; *Girl Hates Cabs* by Warren Schultz; *Feed Me What I Drink* by Ian Grody; *Yes Before Goodbye* by Dan Chen; *The Titanic Trivia Game* by Lisa Haeber; *Looking for Love* by J. Boyer; *The Solution* by Stewart Rudy and Julia Susman; *Tenacity* by Scott T. Barsotti; *Death and Deception* by Catherine Lamm; *Sunday Kind of Love* by Concetta Rose Rella; *The Café* by Kyle Bradstreet; *Rich On Skins* by Joe Lauinger; *Penguins Are Mad Scary* by Michael Tester; *Plays for the Sunni Triangle Parts 1 and 2* by Jerrod Bogard; *Plays for the Sunni Triangle Part 3* by Jerrod Bogard; *Little Squirrel* by Caroline McGraw; *Sirloins in Space* by Joel Hanson; *Beer and the Meaning of Life* by Carlo Rivieccio; The Loft; June 14–July 8, 2007

BLACK MAN RISING by J. Chapmyn; Presented by StageFace Productions in association with Obsidian Media Group; Director, Patricia R. Floyd; Choreography, Juson Williams; Stage Manager, Bayo; Cast: Neil Dawson, Larry Floyd, Lawrence Saint-Victor, Melvin Shambry, Juson Williams; July 12–28, 2007

CORN BREAD AND FETA CHEESE: GROWING UP FAT AND ALBANIAN Written and performed by Elza Zagreda; Director, Vincent Marano; September 12–November 24, 2007

THEFT OF IMAGINATIONS by David Negrin; Presented by Are the Fish Happy? Theatre Company; Director, Kat Chamberlain and David Negrin; Cast: Max Hambleton, Kit Redding, Christopher Hurt, Angus Hepburn, Brad Russell; November 8–December 9, 2007

FETISH by Joyce Wu; Presented by Mir Productions; Director, Julianne Just; Cast: LeVon Fickling, Michael Lutton, Jacob Troy, Joyce Wu; The Loft; January 10–20, 2008

RHODA HEARTBREAK Written and directed by E. Dale Smith; Presented by Engage Theater Company; Cast: Melanie Blythe, Timothy Dietrich, Glenn Fleary, John Squires; The Loft; January 31–February 29, 2008

STORIA Written and performed by Troy Diana; Presented by Monarch Theater Company; Director, Jennifer Ortega; Composer, Jason Diana; Costumes, David Withrow; The Loft, May 15–June 1, 2008

INTERIM Written, directed and performed by Julie Troost and Scott Troost; Presented by Monarch Theater Company in association with Anima Productions; Score, Griffin Richardson and Cosgrove Watt; Set/Lighting, Shaun Fillion; Costumes, Adele Hunt; The Loft; May 15–June 1, 2008

The Producer's Club

FIVE TWELFTHS by William Shakespeare; Presented by Dramatic Stuff; Cast: Anastasios Filactou, Ashley Martinsen, Chris Braca, Kevin Lapin, Sharla Meese; June 13–17, 2007

A DEAD MAN'S APARTMENT/FACE DIVIDED/SISTER WITH INTENSE MONOLOGUES Three plays by Edward Allan Baker and Steven William; Presented by Quad Boro Entertainment; Director, Bill Barry; Cast: Amy Boeding, Bill Barry, Val Balaj, Kristin Keim, Homa Hynes, Debbie Workman, Charles Hendricks; Tiandra Gayle; June 20–24, 2007

A PIRATE'S LULLABYE by Jessica Litwak; Presented by the Runaway Theater Company; Director, George Domenick; Cast: Traci Timmons, Sydia Cedeno-Lucchese, Monica Nordeen, Heather Steinberg, Elliott G. Robinson, Roger Dykeman; Crowne Theatre; June 21–July 1, 2007

A HANDFUL OF DUST by Mary Jane; Presented by Crystal Studios; Director, Neil Ajodah; Cast: Mary Jane, John Wyatt, Maria Vermeulen, Shawthel Stephenson, Karen Berzanski, Alexa Rose Burger; August 24–26, 2007

MEDEA by Euripides; Presented by Mainspring Collective; Concept/Director, Hilary Krishnan; Cast: Maria Alegre, Hannah Smith, Paul Herbig, Laine Bonstein, John Olson, Alain Laforest, Jenna Weinberg, Kacie Leblong, Melissa Carlile, Jennifer Sessions, Patrick McGhee; August 21–26, 2007

TWO TABLESPOONS OF CRAZY by Julian Rojas; Presented by Test Tube Productions; Director, Shaun S. Orbin; Cast: Paige Fockler, Adam Feingold, Kahlil Gonzalez-Garcia, Jason Cutler, Sarah Shaefer, Adam Wofle, Eric Cole, Julian Rojas; October 4–7, 2007

HELEN by Ellen McLaughlin, based on Euripdes' *Helen of Troy;* Presented by Extant Arts Company; November 8–18, 2007

KINDERGARTEN CONFIDENTIAL Book by Debbie Goodstein with Leslie Wolfowitz, lyrics and direction by Debbie Goodstein and Jahidah Diaab; Presented by Morning Glory Productions; Stage Manager, Oveta Clinton; Cast: Heidi Azaro, Basil Rodericks, Brian Schneider, Christophe Nayel, Mara Gilbert, Kathleen O'Brien, Allison Johnson, Kim Chinh, Pamela Carden, Sophier Campbell, Renee Barnett, Stacey Lightman, Kimberly Folkes, Christopher Sayotovich, Jeffrey Dickinson, Audrey Amey, Joey Oso, Kymoura Kennedy; November 14–18, 2007

MRS. SCROOGE Adapted by Peter Mac; Cast: Lara Parker, Leon Hall, Aaron Lee Battle, Robert H. Fowler, Marla Green, Frantz Hall, Jean Ann Kump, Noelle Pasatieri, Jay Rogers; December 15–16, 2007

MONKEY TRICK Written and directed by Brad Saville; Presented by Eastwind Theatre Company; Cast: Penny Bittone, Anne Fidler, David Marcus; Sonnet Theater; February 28–March 29, 2008

BORSTAL BOY by Brendan Behan; Presented by Elaine Greeley; Director, David Johnson; Grand Theatre; March 17–22, 2008

BOXED IN: TWO NEW PLAYS *Cornered* by Kellie Arens and *Transit* by Jonathan Albert; Presented by Project Oriented Productions; Directors, Debbie Slevin, Cristina Alicea; Royale Theatre; May 1–18, 2008

LEGENDS, MYTHS AND HIEROGLYPHS by Demetrius Wren; Presented by The Mainspring Collective; Director, Hilary Krishnan; Sonnet Theatre; May 9–13, 2008

beTwixt, beTween & beTwain Composed and musical directed by Danny Ashkenasi; Producer, Edward Elder; Director, Tracy Bersley; Stage Manager, Kelly Aliano; Cast: Danny Ashkenasi, Aaron DiPiazza; Jennifer Eden, Alexander Gonzales, Rachel Green, Andrea Pinyan, Michael Satow; Crowne Theatre; May 16–June 8, 2008

Prospect Theater Company

Artistic Director, Cara Reichel; Managing Director, Melissa Huber

THE ROCKAE Music, lyrics, and co-adaptated by Peter Mills; Co-adapted and directed by Cara Reichel; Choreographer, Marlo Hunter; Music Director, Kevin Haden; Stage Manager, Bailie Slevin; Set, Sarah Pearline; Costumes, David Withrow; Lighting,, Lily Fossner; Sound, Daniel Erdberg; Production Manager, Mary E. Leach; Cast: Nancy Reneé Braun, Michael Cunio, Matt DeAngelis, Victoria Huston-Elem, Mitchell Jarvis, Jillian Laub, Stephanie Lo, Jaygee Macapugay, Meghan McGeary, Venita McLemore, Andrew Miramontes, Tracey Petrillo, Michelle Pruiett, Rashidra Scott, Gordon Stanley, Laura Beth Wells, Erin Wilson, Simone Zamore; Hudson Guild Theatre (presented in conjunction with NYMF); September 15–October 14, 2007

THE BLUE FLOWER Music, lyrics, script & videography by Jim Bauer; artwork, story & videography by Ruth Bauer; Director/Choreographer Will Pomerantz; Music Director, Mark Rubinstein; Stage Manager, Marcie A. Friedman; Environmental Artist, Bert Esenherz; Set, Nick Francone; Costumes, Sidney Shannon; Lighting, Cory Pattak; Sound, Jeffrey Yoshi Lee; Props, John P. Sundling; Production Manager, Mary E. Leach; Cast: Nancy Anderson, Jason Collins, Jamie LaVerdiere, Meghan McGeary, Marcus Neville, Robert Petkoff, Eric Starker; West End Theatre; February 2–March 2, 2008

HONOR Music, lyrics, and book by Peter Mills, book and direction by Cara Reichel; Stage Manager, Marcie A. Friedman; ASM, Christine Fisichella; Set, Erika Beck Hemminger; Costumes, Sidney Shannon; Lighting, Evan Purcell; Sound, Ryan Meaker; Cast: Alan Ariano, Caitlin Burke, Eymard Meneses Cabling, Ariel Estrada, Ali Ewoldt, Steven Eng, Christine Toy Johnson, Brian Jose, Ming Lee, Whitney Lee, Jaygee Macapugay, Doan MacKenzie, Mel Maghuyop, Allan Mangaser, Diane V. Phelan, Romney Piamonte, Vincent Rodriguez, David Shih, Toshiji Takeshima, Robert Torigoe; Hudson Guild Theatre; April 19–May 18, 2008

Dark Nights Series

LAST CALL Written and directed by Michael John Garces; West End Theatre; February 18–25, 2008

MUSEUM PIECES Conceived and curated by Donald Butchko and Cara Reichel; Producer, Dev Bondarin; Featuring works by Deborah Abramson & Amanda Yesnowitz, Joshua H. Cohen & Marisa Michelson, Michael L. Cooper & Hyeyoung Kim, Drew Fornarola & Marshall Pailet, Carol Hall, John Herin & Frederick Alden Terry, Kait Kerrigan & Brian Lowdermilk, Michael Mitnick; Directors, Dev Bondarin, Marlo Hinter,

Christine O'Grady, Cara Reichel, Stefanie Sertich; Cast: David Andrew Anderson, Erica Aubrey, Sarah Corey, Alexander Elisa, Karla Mosley, Doug Shapiro, Tina Stafford, Alexandra de Suze, Blake Whyte, Michael Winther; West End Theatre; February 23–26, 2008

ONE ACTS ABOUT DEAD PEOPLE Included: *Fishing* by Jeff Hoffman, *The Ride* by Crystall Skillman, and *The High Cost of Living* by Greg Polin; Directors, Corinne Neal, Lauren Keatin, Shannon Fillion; Hudson Guild Theatre; April 26–29, 2008

Public Theater

Artistic Director, Oskar Eustis; Managing Director, Mara Manus

NATIVE THEATER FESTIVAL December 5–9, 2007; Included: *In a World Created by a Drunken God* by Drew Hayden Taylor, directed by Kennetch Charlette; *Salvage* by Diane Glancy, directed by Sheila Tousey; *A Stray Dog* by William S. Yellow Robe, Jr., directed by Gary Farmer; *Wings of Night Sky, Wings of Morning Light* by Joy Harjo, directed by Lisa Peterson; *Tales of Urban Indian* written and performed by Darrell Dennis

UNDER THE RADAR 2008 January 9–20, 2008; Included: *Church* written and directed by Young Jean Lee, presented by his theatre company; *Disinformation* written and performed by Reggie Watts, directed by Tommy Smith; *Generation Jeans* written and performed by Belarus Free Theatre; *How Theater Failed America* created and performed by Mike Daisey, directed by Jean-Michele Gregory; *In Spite of Everything* by The Suicide Kings, directed by Marc Barmuthi Joseph; Low: *Meditations Trilogy Part 1* conceived, written and performed by Rha Goddess, directed and developed by Chay Yew; *Poetics: A Ballet Brut* conceived and directed by Kelly Copper and Pavol Liska, created and performed by Nature Theater of Oklahoma; *Regurgitophagy* conceived, written and performed by Michel Melamed, directed by Alessandra Colasanti, Marco Abujamra, Michael Melamed; *Stoop Stories* written and performed by Dael Orlandersmith; *Terminus* written and directed by Mark O'Rowe; *The Place is a Desert* conceived and directed by Jay Scheib in collaboration with Leah Gelpe; Partner Events: *Of All the People in All the World* at World Financial Center; *small metal objects* at Whitehall Ferry Terminal; *Big, 3rd Episode* at The Kitchen; *Between the Devil and the Deep Blue Sea* at PS 122; *Etiquette* presented by The Roundry Theatre and Rotozaza at Veselka; Classical Theatre of Harlem's *Trojan Women* adapted and directed by Alfred Preisser at Harlem Stage

Public Lab (Inaugural Year)

Vital New Plays in Bare-Bones Productions Presented in Association with the LAByrinth Theatre

MOM, HOW DID YOU MEET THE BEATLES? by Adam P. Kennedy and Adrienne Kennedy; Director, Peter Dubois; Cast: William Demeritt, Brenda Pressley; Shiva Theater, February 4–23, 2008

THE POOR ITCH by John Belluso; Director, Lisa Peterson; Set, Rachel Hauck; Costumes, Gabriel Berry; Lighting, Ben Stanton; Music and Sound, Robert Kaplowitz; Cast: Michael Chernus, Alicia Goranson, Marc Damon Johnson, Piter Marek, Deidre O'Connell, John Ottavino, Susan Pourfar, Renaldy Smith and Christopher Thornton; Shiva Theater; March 7–23, 2008

THE CIVILIANS' PARIS COMMUNE by Steve Cosson and Michael Friedman; Director, Steve Cosson; Cast: Kate Buddeke, Aysan Celik, Nina Hellman, Dan Lipton, Jeanine Serralles, Brian Sgambati, Jeremy Shamos, IVA, Sam Breslin Wright; Shiva Theater; April 4–20, 2008

THE FEVER CHART: Three Visions of the Middle East by Naomi Wallace; Director, Jo Bonney; Set, Rachel Hauck; Costumes, Ilona Somogyi,; Lighting, Lap Chi Chu; Sound, Christian Frederickson; Cast: Natalie Gold, Lameece Issaq, Omar Metwally, Arian Moayed, Waleed F. Zuaiter, Shiva Theater; April 25–May 11, 2008

THE GOOD NEGRO by Tracey Scott Wilson; Director, Liesl Tommy; Shiva Theater; Cast: Joniece Abbott-Pratt, Francois Battiste, J. Bernard Calloway, Lizzy Cooper Davis, Quincy Dunn-Baker, Anthony Mackie, LeRoy McClain, Brian Wallace, Myk Watford; May 16–June 1, 2008

Joe's Pub

SKINDIVER: A Rock Musical by Nora Hendryx and Charles Randolph-Wright; Cast: Lola Diaz, Peter Jay Fernandez, Anastasia Barzee, Andy Señor, Jr., Skie Ocasio, Marie-France Arcilla, Kiki Hawkins, Keith Anthony Fluitt; October 1, 2007

MIKE DAISEY: THE GREAT AND SECRET SHOWS Written and performed by Mike Daisey; November 5–26, 2007

Red Bull Theatre Company

Artistic Director, Jesse Berger

Revelation Readings at the Playwrights Horizons Peter Jay Sharp Theatre

Desdemona by Paula Vogel, directed by Jesse Berger. Starring Mamie Gummer, Jessica Hecht and Jennifer Ikeda; Benefit Host: Marisa Tomei; Playwrights Horizons Mainstage; October 1, 2007; *The Changeling* by Thomas Middleton and William Rowley, directed by Karin Coonrod. Featuring John Douglas Thompson, Kevin Massey, Griffin Matthews, Tony Torn, Molly Ward, David Patrick Kelly, Juliana Francis, Matthew Rauch; October 8, 2007; *Tallgrass Gothic* by Melanie Marnich, directed by Leigh Silverman, featuring Michael Cerveris and Michael Chernus; October 22, 2007; *The Just* by Albert Camus, adapted by Anthony Clarvoe, directed by Ethan McSweeny, featuring Michael Stuhlbarg and Ellen McLaughlin; Sharp Theatre; October 29, 2007; *The Rover* by Aphra Behn, directed by Eleanor Holdridge, featuring Daniel Breaker and Carla Harting; November 12, 2007; *The Lady's Not for Burning* by Christopher Fry, directed by Joseph Hardy, featuring Lynn

Redgrave and Richard Easton; November 26, 2007; *Edward II* by Bertolt Brecht, directed by Michael Sexton, featuring members from Red Bull Theater's cast of the play; January 7, 2008; *Don't Fuck With Love* by Kay Matschullat, directed by Lear deBessonet; January 14, 2008; *The Cardinal* by James Shirley, directed by Carl Forsman, starring Roger Rees and Philip Goodwin; January 21, 2008

Repertorio Español

NOWHERE ON THE BORDER by Carlos Lacámara; Director, José Zayas; Design, Robert Weber Federico; Production Manager, Fernando Then; Sound, Alfonso Rey; Cast: Ernesto De Villa Bejjani, Gabirel Gutiérrez, Frank Robles, Elka Rodríguez, Ed Trucco, Carlos Valencia; September 13–November 9, 2007

BOXCAR by Silvia González; Director, René Buch; September 16, 2007–January 17, 2008

EL QUIJOTE by Miguel de Cervantes, adapted by Santiago García; Director, Jorge Alí Triana; September 30, 2007–March 25, 2008

THE FEAST OF THE GOAT by Mario Vargas Llosa; Director, Jorge Alí Triana; October 6, 2007–May 3, 2008

CHRONICLE OF A DEATH FORETOLD by Gabriel García Márquez; Director, Jorge Alí Triana; October 7, 2007–May 13, 2008

LA GRINGA by Carmen Rivera; Director, René Buch; October 24, 2007–June 12, 2008

ANNA IN THE TROPICS by Nilo Cruz; Director, René Buch; November 23, 2007–January 28, 2008

TANGO INTIMO Choreographed by Valeria Solomonoff; Cast: Max Pollak, Adriana Salgado, Orlando Reyes, Diego Escobar, Angelina Staudinger; November 15, 2007–February 18, 2008

LAS QUIEROA LAS DOS (I Love Them Both) by Ricardo Talesnik; Director, René Buch; Cast: Francisco Gattorno, Mimí Lazo, Jennifer Díaz; October 25–November 25, 2007

THE HOUSE OF BERNADA ALBA by Federico Garcia Lorca; Director, René Buch; October 31, 2007–March 27, 2008

ESCRITO Y SEELADO (Signed and Sealed) by Isaac Chocrón; Director, René Buch; Cast: Francisco Gattorno, Tatiana Vecino, Zulema Clares, Pedro Serka, Iván Camilo; January 11–March 21, 2008

DOÑA FLORA Y SUS DOS MARIDOS (Doña Flora and her Two Husbands) by Jorge Amado; Director, Jorge Alí Triana; February 22–March 23, 2008

BLOOD WEDDING by Federico Garcia Lorca; Director, René Buch; March 6–May 6, 2008

The Reprise Room at Dillons

27 Heaven by Ian Halperin and Todd Shapiro; Director, Adam Roebuk; June 1 & 3, 2007

WHEN WE COME HOME Written and performed by Kenny Carnes; Producer, Symphony Solutions; Director, Bob Jaffe; Stage Manager, Christine Snyder; Tech Director, Scott Barbarino; January 12–14, 2008

WHAT'S THE POINT?! Music by Alan Cancelino, lyrics by Hector Coris; Director, Collette Black, Choreography, Susan Haefner; Music Director, Joe Regan; Cast: Hector Coris, Patrick Garrigan, Eadie Scott; February 18–March 31, 2008

RENDEZVOUS: An Evening with Piaf, Brel, Aznavour & Friends April 2–10, 2008

DAVID AUXIER: It's a Family Affair Songs by David Auxier, Hector Coris, Mark York, David Wells; Producer, Corinne Rubicco; Music Director, Mark York; Performed by David Auxier, Steve Cancel, Hector Coris, Darlene Majewski, Suzanne Scott, David Wells; April 3–9, 2008

KISS & TELL: THE MUSICAL Written and performed by Camille Savitz; Director, Linda Amiel Burns; Music Director, Paul Chamlin; April 6 & 13, 2008

BACK IN PICTURES Music Director/Arrangements, Lance Horne; Director, Michael Duling; Producer, Tom D'Angora; Cast: Noel Cody, Nicole Johndrown, Dennis Moench, Jennifer Neuland, Vincent D'Elia); April 7–June 30, 2008

ZIEGFELD'S MIDNIGHT FROLIC Producer, Mark York & Suzanne Scott; Music Director/Pianist, Mark York; Choreography, David Auxier; Cast: David Auxier, Dick Barclay, Scott Gofta, Helen Klass, Adrian LiDonni, Amy Montgomery, Sagan Rose, Suzanne Scott, Lexi Windsor; April 12–27, 2008

THE WAR OF THE MAMA ROSES Written by Michael Ferreri; Directorr, Rick Skye; Cast: Steven Brinberg, Rick Skye, Chuck Sweeney, Maggie Graham, Scott Nevins; May 10–June 27, 2008

Retro Productions

Producing Artistic Director, Heather E. Cunningham

WHAT I DID LAST SUMMER by A. R. Gurney; Director, Ric Sechrest; Set, Jack and Rebecca Cunningham; Costumes, Rebecca Cunningham; Lighting, Esther Palmer; Sound, Jesse Flower-Ambroch; PSM, Dana Rossi; Cast: Lauren Coppola, Heather E. Cunningham, Lauren Kelston, Tim Romero, Ben Schnickel, Aubrie Therrien; The Spoon Theatre; November 7–November 24, 2007

MILL FIRE by Sally Nemeth; Director, Angela Astle; Set, Jack and Rebecca Cunningham; Costumes, Kathryn Squitieri; Lighting, Kerrie Lovercheck; Sound, Amy Altadonna; PSM, Larry Pease; Cast: Mark Armstrong, Heather E. Cunningham,

Cliff Jéan, Lauren Kelston, Jim Kilkenny, Mike Mihm, Aimiende Negbenebor, Elise Rovinsky, Kristen Vaughan; Spoon Theatre; May 7–May 24, 2008

Richmond Shepard Theatre

THE BEST PARTY EVER Written, directed and produced by Annie Ward; Opened July 5, 2006; still running as of May 31, 2008 (Saturday evenings)

NO EXIT by Sartre, adapted by Nicholas Wolfson and Richmond Shepard; Director, Richmond Shepard; Lighting, Brett Maugham; Cast: Joe Correa, Micaela Leon, Christele Cervelle, Nicholas Wolfson; Presented with *Paris Café,* a new evening of songs featuring Micaela Leon; June 12–24, 2007

TWO ROOMS IN DAVIS Written, directed and produced by Brad Saville; Producer, Penny Bittone; Assistant Director, Anne Fidler; Press, Penny Landau; Cast: Penny Bittone, Jennifer Dees, Anne Fidler, Tim Scott; September 5–30, 2007

BJ LANG PRESENTS "CYRANO" by Yabo Yablonsky; Director/Producer, Richmond Shepard; Cast: Richmond Shepard, Terri Durso; October 19–November 4, 2007

THE MEDEA by Euripides; Presented by Wide Eyed Productions; Director, Kristin Skye Hoffmann; Cast: Amy Lee Pearsall, Sky Seals, Liz White, Justin Ness, Andrew Hariss, Trevor Dallier, Melissa Johnson, Sage Seals, Sarah Flanagan, Ben Newman; November 6–18, 2007

WHO DO YOU LOVE? Written and directed by Shunda Erikka; Lighting, David Sexton; Set, Gary Wissmann; Choreography, Steven Strickland; Stage Manager, Yvonne Facey; Cast: Murray Adams, Ron Bruce, John Burton, Jr., Joy R. Curry, Ms. Kathy Hazzard, Emily King, Charles Maceo, Okema Moore, Dawn Richardson, Carol Sims, Steven Strickland, Shenelle Wallace, Laneya Wiles; Opened December 18, 2007, still running as of May 31, 2008 (Sunday evenings)

THE PENELOPE PROJECT Written and directed by Christine Simpson; Produced by Fluid Motion Theater & Film and Michelle Chen; Assistant Director, Corinne Neal; Cast: Siho Ellsmore, Brian Nishii, Jose Joaquin Perez, Elizabeth Ruelas, Sara Thigpen, Jane Titus; February 21–23, 2008

THE CREAM OF THE CROP Five one-acts; Included: *The Dentist* by Dave Sweeney, directed by Michael Peterson; *After the Curtain* written and directed by Mim Granahan; *The Seduction* by Tamar Kummel, directed by Stefanie Sertich; *The Games Men Play* by Williard Manus, directed by Richmond Shepard; *Blind Date* by David Lefkowitz, directed by Heather Rush; March 21–29, 2008

Rising Phoenix Repertory

Artistic Director, Daniel Talbott

THE REACHING by Crystal Skillman; Director, Daniel Talbott; Cast: Spencer Aste, Samantha Soule, Elizabeth West; Jimmy's No. 43; June 4–26, 2007

FALL FORWARD by Daniel Reitz; Director, Daniel Talbott; Cast: Dean Imperial, Joel Johnsonte, Julie Kline, Jan Leslie-Harding; John Street Church; June 18–July 30, 2007

WHAT HAPPENED WHEN by Daniel Talbott; Director, Brian Roff; Cast: Jimmy Davis, Jacob Fishel; HERE Arts Center; July 5–16, 2007

365 DAYS/365 PLAYS (Week 47) by Suzan-Lori Parks; Director, Kirsten Kelly; Cast: Kalen Allmandinger, Denis Butkus, Meg Gibson, Kathryn Kates, Julie Kline, Aaron Lisman, Sevrin Anne Mason, Patrick McNulty, Jonathan Pereira, Melle Powers, Julie Rapoport, Keith Reddin, Wayne Alon Scott, Ruby Trujillo; Jimmy's No. 43 and The Public Theater; October 1–7, 2007

Roy Arias Theatre Center – Times Square Arts Center

A NIGHT OF ONE ACTS Produced by Granite Theater Company; Directors, Harry O'Reilly and Jim Burke; June 6–July 1, 2007

GAUGUIN/SAVAGE LIGHT Written and performed by George Fischoff; Mini Theatre; June 12–July 8, 2007

BARRY WHITE: Guided by Destiny Written, designed and directed by Emmitt Thrower; Presented by Wabi Sabi Productions; Music Director, Lanar; Cast: Emmitt Thrower, Lanar, Gezele Portwood, Venus Adore, Pamela Cornelius, Jessica Opong, Karen Amatrading, Valentine Aprile, Eddy Privitizer, Leonard Cornish, Henry Grant, Robert Powell, Michael Robinson; June 14–24, 2007

THE LAST CLOUD Written and directed by Blake Bradford; Presented by Etcetera Theatre Company and Love Creek Productions; Cast: Christine Vinh, Lizzie Ann Schwarz, Michael Weems, Tim Kondrat, Tamara Cacchione, Nick May, Michael Weems; June 20–July 1, 2007

THE LUNCH by Alex DeWitt; Director, Judith Kenny; Cast: Caitlin Cannon, Leanne Barrineau, Chris Frederick, Randi Martire; June 21–30, 2007

DIVERSITY PLAYERS OF HARLEM – THREE PLAYS *A Marriage Proposal* by Anton Chekhov, *He Said, She Said* by Shawn Luckey, *The Red Lamp* by Hilliard Booth; July 25–29, 2007

SHAKESPEARE'S SONNETS ON TAP Presented by Novisi Productions; Director, Awoye Timpo; Cast: Varín Ayala, Francois Battiste, Stephen Bel Davies, Robert Michael Bray, Ayodele Casel, Frank Harts, Ray Hesselink, Di Johnston, Stephanie Larrière, Amanda McCroskery, Christina Moore, Parallel Exit (Derek Roland and Ryan Kasprzak), Max Pollak, Claudia Rahardjanoto, David Rider, Ivy Risser, Dolores Sanchez, Kristyn Smith, David Sochet, and Elisa Van Duyne; August 23–25, 2007

JUNGLE QUEEN DEBUTANTE Book by Sean O'Donnell, music and lyrics by Thomas Tierney; Director, Gwen Arment; PSM, Fred CL Mann III, Music Supervisor, Jack Lee; Music Director, Paul Staroba; Cast: Amy McAlexander, Heather Parcells, Johnny Orenberg, Donna English, Deborah Tranelli, Paul Amodeo, James Walsh, Kristen Bedard, Ian August; Partner Production of the NYMF 2007; September 26–October 6, 2007

THE HOUSE OF YES by Wendy McLeod; Presented by Samsara Theatre Company; Director, Jason Kane; Set, Lindsey Vandevier; Costumes, Michael Plosky; Cast: Anne Ackerman, Matt LaSpata, Jonathan Patton, Marie-Rose Pike, Alicia St. Louis; Payan Theatre; October 3–21, 2007

MATT AND BEN by Brenda Withers and Mindy Kaling; Presented by Samsara Theatre Company; Payan Theatre; October 5–13, 2007

INTIMATE APPAREL by Lynn Nottage; Presented by 'Tis Production Company; Director, Sheila Simmons; Cast: Shelia Simmons, Kevin Sibley, Lisa Landino, Michael Aleff, Schieffle Wilson, Milissa Sellers; October 10–22, 2007

A DREAM PLAY by August Strinberg; Presented by Dalliance Theater; Director, Andy Ottoson; Costumes, Jameson Eaton; Lighting, Matt Garrett; Choreography, Jennifer J. Hopkins; Music, Evan Lewsi; Stage Manager, Aaron Heflich Shapiro; Cast: Ben Diskant, Matt Timme, Lara Stoby Josh Meier Jo Kroger, Michael Morrow Hammack; November 1–10, 2007

BURIED CHILD by Sam Shepard; Director, Heather Arnson; Producer, Tiandra Gayle; Stage Manager, Andrea Perry; Cast: Darryl Brown, Goldie Zwiebel, Bill Barry, Jai Catalano, Collin Smith, Kat Garson; November 7–18, 2007

DIE LAUGHING by Marq Overton; Director/Producer, Ali Williams; Co-Producer, Shawn Luckey; Cast: Gil Charleston, Russel Jordan, Okema T. More, Danielle Renee, Kristen Ivy Haynes, Christina A. Berry, Tiandra Gayle; November 10–18, 2007

REWRITING HER LIFE by Barbara Sutton Masry; Director, Trezana Beverley; Lighting, Ken Davis; Sets, Raisy Derzie; Costumes, Ali Turns; Cast: Rob Alicea, Sandra Bauleo, Jeff Burchfield, James M. Farrell, Joanna Rhinehart, Maja Wampuszyc, Anne Yorke; November 28–December 9, 2007

THE TRIACCA CODE ENCORE Conceived and directed by David Shurman; Presented by Groundworks Theatre Productions; Cast: Mike Borak, Michelle Cox, Craig Fisher, Ethel Fisher, Michael Gentile, Kaitlin Elizabeth Goslee, Noelle Lynch, Ruby Mercado, Kent Sutton and Shauntay Williams; Payan Theatre; December 10–14, 2007

VICTIMS OF THE ZEITGEIST Written and directed by Ellwoodson Williams; January 18–27, 2007

KNOCK 'EM DEAD by Tom Oldendick and Will Roberson; Presented by International Sudio Theatre; Cast: Robert Axel, Hal Brown, Steve Copps, Christine de Frece, Jennifer Gelber, Paul Grawemeyer, Michael C. Harmon, Jamie Taylor Harper, Brittany Shaw, and Cameron Wareham; February 13–24, 2008

PROVIDENCE by Cody Daigle; Presented by Maieutic Theatre Works; Director, Ian Crawford; Cast: Anthony Crep, Kathryn Ekblad, Douglas Scott Sorenson, Aly Wirth; Studio Theatre; February 7–24, 2008

SUNRISE AT THE QUARRY by Nick Sanzo and members of the Black Door Theatre Company; Director, Sara Laudonia; Stage Manager, Lore Davis; Cast: Kristin Cappon, Gina dos Santos, Gina LeMoine, Brandon McCluskey, Josh Marcantel; Payan Theatre; April 24–May 11, 2008

NO MAN CAN SERVE TWO MASTERS by Michael Levesque; Presented by Third Eye Theatre Company; Director, Andrew Glant-Linden; Sets, Darya Gerasimenko; Costumes, Adam Coffia; Lighting, John Eckert; Cast: Devon Young, David Gurland, Susanna Guzman, Verna Pierce, Christopher Regan, Maureen Van Trease, Rob Ventre, Max Woertendyke; Studio Theatre; May 1–10, 2008

WHITE WIDOW, A SICILIAN MUSICAL PASSION Adaptation, music and lyrics by Paul Dick, from Mario Fratti's *Mafia;* Presented by Passajj Productions; Director, Elizabeth Falk; Choreography, Melinda O'Brien; Set, Brandon Giles; Costumes, Dixie Crawford-Rich; Lighting, Tony Mulanix; Cast: Dave Adamick, Elizabeth Daniels, Christopher deProphetis, Claybourne Elder, Phil Franzese, Nick Gaswirth, Chris Gleim, Emilio Magnotta, Katherine Malak, Erin Mosher, Phil Olejack, Michael Padgett, Jeremy Pasha, Thomas Rainey, Tim Realbuto, Jacob Reilly, Kristin Katherine Shields, Amy Elaine Warner, Cassie Wooley, Michael Yeshoin; May 9–25, 2008

Ryan Repertory Company

A THING OF BEAUTY by Maurice Berger; Director/Costumes, Misti B. Wills; Set, Michael Pasternack; Lighting, Barbara Parisi; Cast: Davonne Bacchus, Johnny O'Connell, Geri McKeon, Ephraim Stanfield, Tim Sheehan, Amanda Vick; Harry Warren Theatre; September 27–October 14, 2007

THISTLE BLOSSOMS by Roseanna Beth Whitlow; Director, Misti B. Wills; Cast: Jae Kramisen, Erin Layton; Harry Warren Theatre; April 4–19, 2008

BEN by Bernard Meyer; Director, Barbara Parisi; May 10–18, 2008

KONG Written, directed and performed by Pamela Sneed, co-directed by Barbara Parisi; June 12–29, 2008

The Sackett Group

Artistic Director, Robert J. Weinstein; Producing Director, Dov Lebowitz-Nowak; Managing Director, Dan Haft

NO PLACE TO BE SOMEBODY by Charles Gordone; Director, Woodie King Jr.; Cast: Marcus Naylor, Ralph

McCain, Monrico Ward, Rob O'Hare; Megan Messmer, Brooklyn Music School Playhouse; September 15–October 7, 2007

THE COMPLETE WORKS OF WILLIAM SHAKESPEARE (ABRIDGED) Adam Long, Daniel Singer, and Jess Winfield; Director, Corrine J. Slagle; Set, John C. Scheffler; Costumes, Claire Aquila; Cast: Nicholas Cober, Dov Lebowitz-Nowak, Glenn De Kler; April 25–May 11, 2008

Sage Theater

CHARACTER DOGVILLE: A Theatrical Comedy with Imporvised Dialogue; Presented by the Manhattan Comedy Collective; Opened April 6, 2007; open run (Friday nights)

DON'T TOUCH THE FOOT Stand-up Comedy; Opened June 14, 2007, open run (Thursday nights)

BIGGER FISH TO FRY by Gena Ross and Robert Stone; Director, Dara Centonze; Music Director, David Fletcher; Cast: Sherz Aletaha, Melissa Blatherwick, Noah DeBiase, Kelly Dynan, Zachary Einstein, Kevin Faraci, Jeremy Johnson, Cassiopia Piper; July 13–21, 2007

YELLOW BRICK MONOLOGUES Written, directed and produced by Casey Jones; Aug 3–11

SAVED BY THE PARODY: A Musical Parody of Saved by the Bell by Ren Casey; Presented by Cabin Eleven Productions; Cast: Kelsey Robinson, David Everett Strickler, Ren Casey, Dan Zimmerman, Kimberlee Walker, Jessica Johnson; October 13–November 17, 2007

POE IN PERSON Written and perfomed by David Keltz; October 28, 2007

THE CHRIS BETZ SHOW Comedy and improve hosted by Chris Betz and Laurn Hunter; Choreography, Jennifer L. Mudge; Music Director, Lilli Wosk; Cast: Kerry Flanagan, Mary Kelley, Matty Price, Zoey Rutherford; December 10–11, 2007

NOW THAT YOU'VE SEEN ME NAKED Sketch comedy by Cleo's Comedy Players; February 15–March 22, 2008

CHUCK AND GINGER: Thawed for Your Pleasure by Melissa Cruz, Michael Davis, and Michael Leedy; Director, Michael Davis; Music Director, Aya Kato; Cast: Chuck Babcock, Ginger Babcock, Chie Mizuno; April 11–13, 2008

A POLITICAL PARTY Weekly comedy presented by Spangled LLC; Producers, David Ingber, Zoe Samuel; Director, Robert Ross Parker; Music Director, Steven McCasland; Design, Jen Raskopf; Assistant Director, David Alpert; Graphics, Lydia Nichols; Cast: Lauren Adams, David Ingber, Nick Kanellis, Ben Sinclair, Amy Zelcer; May 28–July 30, 2008 (Wednesday nights)

Sanford Meisner Theatre

GREEN SEA FESTIVAL Presented by Green Sea Theatre; Director, Jimmy Smith; Set & Costumes, Adrian Linford; Lighting, Sebastian Adamo; Costumes, Doug Reker; Video, Shane DeBlasio; Sound, Daniel Schuy; Press, Christine Bastoni; Associate Director, Jessica Forsythe; Choreography, Jimena Paz, Kara Tatelbaum; Cast: Maddalena Maresca, Randy Harmon, Walter Hoffman, Niae Knight, Robert Eigen, Monica Risi, Adele Berne, Kate Duyn, Christina Johnson, Colin Raybin, Jimena Paz; July 24–29, 2007

THE MAIDS by Jean Genet; Presented by Green Sea Theatre; Director, Jimmy Smith; Set & Costumes, Adrian Linford; Lighting, Randy Harmon; Choreography, Abigail Levine, Pei-chun Wang; Associate Director, Jessical Forsythe; Press, Daniel Thaler; Cast: Mia Moreland, Stephanie Staes, Mirand Jonté, Abigail Levine, Pei-chun Wang; October 11–21, 2007

CHERUBINA by Paul Cohen; Produced by Rebecca Lingafelter; Director, Alexis Poledouris; Set/Lighting, Gina Sherr; Costumes, Zane Pihlstrom; Sound, Mark Valadez; Dramaturg, Julie Rossman; Stage Manager, Leslie Ribovisch; Cast: Amanda Fulks, Teddy Bergman, Jimmy Owens; February 4–23, 2008

THE GAY BARBERS APARTMENT by Larry Traiger; Presented by Half Assiduity Arts; Director, Alex Hurt; Set, Chuck Pukanecz; Lighting, Joseph Aniska; Sound, David Beare; Stage Manager, Marina Steinberg; Music, Joe Calluori; Cast: Joseph Aniska, J. Stephen Brantley, Alex Hurt, Jeff Pucillo, Carolina Mesarina, Ashlee Hoffmann, Raul S. Julia, Gillian Amalia; March 5–22, 2008

THE SECRET RAPTURE by David Hare; Produced by Invisible, LLC; Director, Jessica Forstythe; Lighting and Sound, Randy Harmon; Assistant Director, Stephanie Staes; Cast: Elizabeth Steinhart, Mia Moreland, Jacob Grigolia, Miranda Jonté, Zachary Fletcher, Christian Sineath; April 3–27, 2008

BRITBITS 3 Short plays presented by Mind the Gap Theatre; Included: *Pealing Figs* by Bronwen Denton-Davis; *Girl in a Bath* by Nancy Harris; *Boat for Sale Careful Lady Owner* by Denise O'Leary; *Death of a Small Independent Retailer* by Glyn Cannon; *Many Happy Returns* by Paula D'Alessandris; *Modern Life* by Philip Gawthorne; *Minsk* by Declan Feenman; Directors, Paula D'Alessandris, Stephen Donovan, Joel Jones; Cast: Tom Bain, Paula Burton, Stephen Donovan, Martin Ewens, Holly Hamilton, Elliot Joseph, Joel Jones, Polly Lee, Richard T. Lester, Camilla Maxwell, Mia Moreland, Maria Pastel, Stephen Pilkington, Jenny Sterlin, Gwenfair Vaughan, Christine Rendel, Stephanie Stone; April 14–23, 2008

THE GHOST DANCERS by Adam Hunault; Presented by Stone Soup Theatre, Leigh Goldenberg; Director, Nadine Friedman; Set, Chris Johnson & Ramona Albert; Costumes, David Moyer; Lighting, Sean Linehan; Fights, Galway McCullough; Stage Manager, Nat Cauldwell; Choreography, Chris Wild; Cast: Alton Alburo, Jenn Boehm, Seiko Carter,

Dylan Carusona, Justin Dilley, Alejandro Garcia, DR Mann Hanson, Marsha Martinez, Galway McCullough, Banaue Miclat, Maysie Mills, Al Patrick Jo, Sam Joseph, Teresa Jusino, Maria Schirmer; May 8–24, 2008

ShakespeareNYC

Board of Directors: Beverly Bullock, Geoffrey Dawe, Marcus Dean Fuller, Douglas Johnson, Vanessa Vozar

KING JOHN Director/Costumes, Beverly Bullock; Fight Director/Captain, Al Foote III; Sets, Lex Liang; Lighting, James Bedell; Text Coach, Denise Cormier; PSM, Zac Chambers; ASM, Steve Barrett; Assistant Director, Johnny Salinas; Cast: Nicholas Stannard, Libby Hughes, Patrick Knighton, Gretchen Howe, Al Foote III, Peter Herrick, Brian Morvant, Joseph Small, Jim Jack, Jonathan R. Thornsberry, Donna Stearns, Marc Silberschatz, Sam Chase, Miriam Lipner, Vanessa Elder, Bob Armstrong, Christian Roulleau, Steven Eng; Clurman Theatre on Theatre Row; June 9–30, 2007

RICHARD II Director/Costumes, Beverly Bullock; Fight Director, Al Foote III; Set, Lex Liang; Lighting, James Bedell; Text Coach, Denise Cormier; PSM, Zac Chambers; ASM, Steve Barrett; Assistant Director, Johnny Salinas; Fight Captain, Brian Morvant; Cast: Bob Armstrong, Sam Chase, Steven Eng, Peter Herrick, Gretchen Howe, Libby Hughes, Jim Jack, Patrick Knighton, Miriam Lipner, Brian Morvant, Brian Nocella, Christian Roulleau, Marc Silberschatz, Joseph Small, Nicholas Stannard, Donna Stearns, Jonathan R. Thornsberry; Clurman Theatre on Theatre Row; June 9–30, 2007

MACBETH Director/Costumes, Beverly Bullock; Fight Director, Al Foote III; Set, Brandon Giles; Lighting, James Bedell; Sound and Original Music, John D. Ivy; Masks, Jim Jack; Text Coach, Steven Eng; PSM, Steve Barrett; Fight Captain, Paul Edward Hope; Scenic Consultant, Lex Liang; Cast: James Beaman, Andrea Coleman, Daren Dubner, Vanessa Elder, Ian Gould, Susanna Harris, Peter Herrick, Paul Edward Hope, Jim Jack, Miriam Lipner, Patricia McNamara, Peter Richards, Nicholas Stannard, Joseph Small, Jonathan R. Thornsberry, Esther Williamson; Beckett Theatre on Theatre Row; September 7–22, 2007

Shetler Theatre 54 and Shetler Annex

A NEW TELEVISION ARRIVES, FINALLY by Kevin Mandel; Presented by Live From Planet Earth Produtions; Director, Kevin Kittle; Producer, Peter Gordon; Stage Manager, Sara J. Grady; Set/Sound, Chad Brinkman; Lighting, Robin A. Paterson; Costumes, Rebecca Lustig; Press, David Gibbs; Cast: Tom Pelphrey, Victor Villar-Hauser, Kate Russell, Bryan Fenkart; Understudy: Ari Vigoda; Theatre 54, September 6–30, 2007

PIZZA MAN by Dalene Caviotto; Director, Austin Pendleton; Cast: Lyndsey Anderson, Micha Lazare, Kyle Wood; Theatre 54; September 21–October 7, 2007

SECOND HAND SMOKE by Renee Flemings; Director, Kate Place; Produced by Triad Arts Ensemble, Mark Gorman, and Renee Flemings; Cast: Joe Capozzi, Josh Casaubon, Renee Flemings, Michael Jones & Scott Venters; Theatre 54; October 4–21, 2007

DUET Two one-acts: *Sunrise* by Tommy Smith, directed by Portia Krieger; *The Good Thing* by Terry Diamond, directed by Maggie Burkle; Set, Jake France; Lighting, Todd Nonn; Sound, Eben Lillie; Costumes, Jessica Pabst; PSM, Andrea Dionne; ASM, Chuck Heery; Cast: Sunrise: Ben Beckley, Teddy Bergman, Jocelyn Kuritsky; *The Good Thing* Michael Bernstein, Brenda Crawley, Scott Nath, Tammy Tunyavongs; November 30–December 8, 2007

WARNING: ADULT CONTENT by Joseph Gallo; Presented by Shetler Sudios TDG in association with Bridge Theatre Company; Director, Robin A. Paterson; Cast: Christopher Halladay, Julie Tolivar, Eric Michael Gillett, Marnie Klar, Joseph Barbarino, John Calvin Kelly, Jennifer Laine Williams; February 19–March 9, 2008

Six Figures Theatre Company

Artistic Directors, Kimberly Kefgen and Cris Buchner

TRAUMNOVELA Created by Juan Borona, Cris Buchner, Bettina Sheppard; concept by Juan Borona, inspired by *Dream Story* by Arthur Schnitzler; Director, Cris Buchner; Choreography, Juan Borona; Music Director, Bettina Sheppard; Costumes, Tiffany Vollmer; Lighting, Jason Reuter; Stage Managers, Kate Mott, Handri Gunawan; Cast: Damian Norfleet, Brittany Mayer, Jason Garcia Ignacio, Becca Blackwell, Meg Benfield Bettina Sheppard, Evan Edwards, Anna Kepe, Shelly Ley Danilo Barbieri, Steven W. Nielsen, Lauren Rodriguez, Heather White Mayumi Asada, Anthony Castellanos; Musicians: John Blaylock, Mario Gullo, Chieko Honda, Hisako Ishii, Brynlyn Loomis, Motoko Miyama Kristi Roosmaa, Jonathon Winn; Barrow Street Theatre; September 22–October 14, 2007

TIME IS THE MERCY OF ETERNITY by Deb Morgolin; Co-presented with Purple Man Theater Company; Director, Marc Stuart Weitz; Set, Kerry Lee Chipman; Lighting, Anjaeanette Stokes; Costumes, Elizabeth B. Carlin; Sound/Music, Geo Wyeth; Video/Graphics, Zach Sultan; Cast: Curzon Dobell, Lisa Kron, Khris Lewin, Claire Siebers; West End Theatre; April 21–May 10, 2008

ARTISTS OF TOMORROW 2008 Series included: *Martha Mitchell* by Rosanna Yamagiwa Alfaro, music by Jean Ives Ducornet, Marie Buigues, Joan Faber; Director, June Lewin; Cast: Geralyn Horton; *School/unschooled* Director, Ester Neff; Music, Brian McCorkle; Cast: Mary Sheridan, Rachel Handshaw, Anika Solvieg, Michael Connely, Chris Allen; *Detritus* Conceived and developed by: Lynn Berg, Audrey Crabtree, Larissa Lury, Jeff Seal, Anne Sorce & Liza Zapol; Director, Larissa Lury; Music, Dave Edson; Cast: Lynn Berg,

Audrey Crabtree, Jeff Seal, Anne Sorce, Liza Zapol; *waiting... a play in three phases* by Gia Marotta; Director, Chloe Bass; Lighting/Stage Manager, CJ Holm; Sound, Geo Wyeth; Graphics, Adda Birnir; Cast: Summer Hagen, Alexandria LaPorte, Abigail Ziaja, Jamie Klassel, Jamie Burrell; *please don't play it again* Choreographed by Maria Sessa; Dancers: Alan Forbes, Christina Morrissey, Elisa Schreiber, Margherita Tisato; *Lizzie Borden Live* Written and performed by Jill Dalton; Director, Jack McCullough; Music, Larry Hochman; *Shooting Medea* by Valentina Fratti; Director, Mark Schneider; Cast: Hanna Cheedk, Andy Gershenzen, David Rackoff; *In the Crossing* Written and performed by Leila Buck; Director/Development, Shoshana Gold; Dramaturg, Liz Frankel; Design, Adam Abel; *Truth Values* Written and performed by Gioia De Cari; Director, Matt Hoverman; Costumes, Natalia Danilova; West End Theatre; April 19–May 10, 2008

SoHo Playhouse

THE TOAD POEMS by Gerald Locklin, adapted by George Carroll; Director, Ian Morgan; Cast: John Wojda, Marina Squerciati, Barbara Pitts, June 15–July 9, 2007

FLANAGAN'S WAKE Conceived by Jack Bronis, inspired by Joe Liss, created by Amy Binns-Calvey, Geoff Binns-Calvey, Jimmy Binns, Jack Bronis, Phil Lusardi, Pat Musker, Bonnie Shadrake; Opened October 6, 2007; open run

PIAF: LOVE CONQUERS ALL by Roger Peace; Directed, designed and performed by Naomi Emmerson; Piano, Carmelo Sinco; Associate Director, Adam Blanshay; December 8, 2007–February 10, 2008

EVERY GIRL GETS HER MAN by Emma Sheanshang; Presented by Jouissance Theater Company; Director, Michael Melamedoff; Cast: Danny Bernardy, Cass Buggé, Amy Flanagan, Anna Margaret Hollyman, Chloe Whiteford, Sarah Wilson; Huron Club; March 3–30, 2008

St. Bart's Players

1776 Music and lyrics by Sherman Edwards, book by Peter Stone; Director, Brian Feehan; Music Director, Brenna Sage; Set, Brian Howard; Lighting, Jay Scott; Costumes, Anne Lommel; PSM, Jodi Witherell; Producers, Elizabeth Gravitt, Lana Krasnyansky; Cast: Brien Milesi, Jack Molyneaux, Michael Blake, Kevin Kiniry, Jim Mullins, Ken Altman, Joe Hunt, Robert Martz, Bob Oliver, Michael Weems, David Pasteelnick, Mitch Shapiro, Bradford Harlan, Bill McEnaney, Kelvin Ortega, David Salyers, Jason Burrow, Dan Grinko, Miles Lott, Brian Haggerty, Amy Jane Finnerty, Reanna Muskovitz, Rich Berens, Joe Gambino, Michael Vannoni, Jack Barnett; November 8–18, 2007

A CHRISTMAS CAROL Based on the story by Charles Dickens; Director, Brian Feehan; Producers, Bob Berger, Hope Landry; Cast: Maryjane Baer, Robert Berger, Barbara Blomberg, Daniel Burke, Renee DePietro, Faith Elliot, Kevin Kiniry, Hope Landry, Kelvin Ortega, Veronica Shea, Victor Van Etten; December 10–12, 2007

TWELVE ANGRY MEN by Reginald Rose, adapeted by Sherman Sergel; Director, Matt Schicker; Set, Carl Tallent; Lighting, Mike Gugliotti; Costumes, Meredith Neal; PSM, Ellen Marks; Producer, Daniel Burke; Cast: Joe Gambino, Danielle Giorgetti, Neal Jones, Leslie Engel, Jonah Rosen, Jill Conklin, Ulises Giberga, Ken Altman, Brian Haggerty, Penny Robb, Leni Tabb, Max Cohen; February 15–24, 2008

CABARET³- A MUSICAL FUNDRASIER Cast: David Pasteelnick, Chazmond Peacock, Michael Vannoni; February 29–March 1, 2008

FOLLIES Music and lyrics by Stephen Sondheim, book by James Goldman; Director/Choreography, Norb Joerder; Music Director, Jason Wynn; Set, Anne Lommel; Lighting, Michael Megliola; Costumes, Kurt Alger; PSM, Brian Busby; Producers, Elizabeth Gravitt, Brian Haggerty; Cast: Merrill Vaughn, Brien Milesi, Lesley Berry, Kevin Kiniry, Barbara Blomberg, Marielena Logsdon, Michael Vannoni, Kristin Savarese, Carlos Jacinto, Erich Werner, Chazmond Peacock, Melissa Broder, Joe Gambino, Robyn Macey, John Taylor, Hope Landry, Jill Conklin, Vikki Willoughby, Gayle Artino, Lana Krasnyansky, Jed Danforth, Bonnie Berens, Kate Chamuris, Samantha Dworken, Trent Henry, Susan Oettle, Jim Roumeles, Patrick Santos, Jessica Swersey, Jonathan Cody White, Anthony Zillmer; Wings Theatre; April 26–May 4, 2008

The Storm Theatre

THE KAROL WOJTYLA FESTIVAL Two plays by Karol Wojtyla translated by Boleslaw Taborski; Set, Ken Larson, Lighting, Danielle Schembre, Lighting, Michael Abrams; Sound, Scott O'Brien; Producing Director, Chance Michaels; Included: *Job* Director, John Regis; Stage Manager, Matt Marholin; Cast: Adam Couperthwaite, Nina Covalesky, Ross DeGraw, Brooke Evans, Michelle Kafel, Timothy Smallwood, Joseph P. Sullivan, Elizabeth Swearingen, Josh Thelin; October 9–November 11, 2007; *Jeremiah* Director, Peter Dobbins; Stage Manager, Michael Mele; Cast: Nate Begle, Dan Berkey, Robert Carroll, Brian Farish, Daniela Mastropietro, Rebecca MacDougall; October 26–November 16, 2007

THE SHAUGHRAUN by Dion Boucecault; Director, Peter Dobbins; Cast: Clodagh Bowye, Laura Bozzone, Robert Carroll, Holly Davatz, Ross DeGraw, Mark DeYoung, Michelle Kafel, Chris Keveney, Kris Kling, Daniela Mastropietro, Jessica Palmer, Mia Perry, Glenn Peters, Joseph M. Ryan, Tim Seib, Joe Sullivan; January 4–February 2, 2008

Summer Play Festival (SPF)

Founder and Executive Producer, Arielle Tepper

Fourth Annual; July 10–August 5, 2007; Theatre Row Theatres (Lion, Clurman, Beckett, Kirk, Acorn)

ALICE IN WAR by Steven Bogart; Director, Alice Reagan; Cast: Megan Byrne, Lisa Joyce, Jodi Lin, Karl Miller, Jonah Mitropolous, Glenn Peters, Luis Vega, Stephanie Weeks

BLUEPRINT by Bixby Elliot; Director, Jonathan Silverstein; Cast: Nicole Lowrance, Patrick McNulty, Peter Strauss, Amirah Vann

CIPHER by Cory Hinkle; Director, Kip Fagan; Cast: Alyssa Bresnahan, Adam Driver, Haskell King, Mandy Siegfried

DEVIL LAND by Desi Moreno-Penson; Director, Jose Zayas; Cast: Bryant Mason, Vanessa Aspillaga, Jenny Seastone Stern

FLESH AND THE DESERT by Carson Kreitzer; Director, Beth Milles; Cast: Sarah Chalmers, Abigail Gampel, Stan Lachow, Alex Podulke, Anna Camp, Lynne Cohen, Jim Iorio, Jeff Still

THE GABRIELS by Van Badham; Director, Rebecca Patterson; Cast: Danton Stone, Anthony Newfield, Phyllis Johnson, Helen Coxe, Keith Eric Chappelle, Christen Simon, Karen Berthel

HALF OF PLENTY by Lisa Dillman; Director, Meredith McDonough; Cast: Bill Buell, Ian Brennan, Elizabeth Canavan, Alexis McGuinness, Sidney Williams

LOWER NINTH by Beau Willimon; Director, Daniel Goldstein; Cast: James McDaniel, Amari Cheatom, Jamie Hector

minor gods by Charles Forbes; Director, Gaye Taylor Upchurch; Cast: Barnaby Carpenter, Chad Lindsey

MISSING CELIA ROSE by Ian August; Director, Adam Immerwahr; Cast: Andy Phelan, Cheryl Freeman, Kendall Ridgeway, Nancy McDoniel, Charles Borland, Tinashe Kajese, Ron Simons, Willi Burke, Sharon Hope

MY WANDERING BOY by Julie Marie Myatt; Director, John Gould Rubin; Cast: Thomas Jefferson Byrd, Amelia Campbell, J; Chambers, Mia Dillon, Salome M. Krell, Christopher McCann, Brian Smiar

THE NIGHTSHADE FAMILY by Ruth McKee; Director, Shelley Butler; Cast: Julie Jesneck, Creighton James, Laura Heisler, Rodney Hicks

NOT WAVING by Ellen Melaver; Director, Douglas Mercer; Cast: Mary Stout, Jacob Fishel, Kevin O'Donnell, Aya Cash, Brandon Espinoza; Director, Linsay Firman; Cast: Alfredo Narciso, Natalie Gold, Heidi Schreck, Denis Butkus

NOVEL by Anna Ziegler; Director, Michael Goldfried; Cast: Annie McNamara, Jeff Biehl, Chris Henry Coffey, Natalia Payne, Randall Newsome, Keith Perry, Rebecca Schull, Jay Russell, Dan McCabe

UNFOLD ME by Joy Tomasko; Director, Linsay Firman; Cast: Alfredo Narciso, Natalie Gold, Heidi Schreck, Denis Butkus

VROOOMMM! A NASCOMEDY by Janet Allard; Director, David Lee; Cast: Sarah Agnew, Devon Berkshire, Meg Brogan, Laura Jordan, Greer Goodman, Denise Lute

Target Margin Theater

Founder and Artistic Director, David Herskovits

THE ARISTOPHANIC LABORATORY Three week festival of plays by based on the works of Aristophanes; Week 1: *Knights* Adapted by Rob Handel, directed by Alice Reagan; Set/Costumes, Mehang E. Healey; Dramaturg, Ramona Thomasius; Lighting, Chris Brown; Sound, Mark Valadez; Stage Manager, Amara Watkin-Anson; Cast: Peter Judd, Karl Miller, Margaret Loesser Robinson, Indika Senanayake, Luis Vega; *Wasps, or Buzz Buzz in Your Eardrum* by Ken Urban, directed by Jose Zayas; Sets, Ryan Kravetz,; Costumes by Carla Bellisio; Lighting, Chris Brown; Sound, Katie Down; Cast: Nicole Becker, Kate Benson, Joseph Carusone, Ursula Cataan, Siho Ellsmore, Robb Hurst, Sadrina Johnson, Jason Romas, Hugh Sinclair; *Meze* Shorts plays by William Burke, Glennis McMurray, Kathleen Kennedy Tobin, Diana Konopka, Matthew McAlpin, Sherrine Azab, Judith M. Smith and Keith Larson; Director, Kristin Marting; Cast: Paul Boocock, Richard Toth, Ann Carr, Katina Corrao, Matthew McCarthy; Week 2: *Are You a Bird or a Dodo?* Director, Jessica Brater; Stage Manager, Lucia Peters; Set/Costumes, Peiyi Wong; Lighting, Natalie Robin; Cast: Chanelle Benz, Danielle Davenport, Samantha Debicki; Elaine O'Brien; Indiki Senanayake, Lindsay Strachan, Stephen Squibb, Nathash Warener; *Balabustas* by the Company; Director, Michael Levinton; Composer, Joy Nirenstein; Choreography, Aaron Mattocks; Lighting, Tlaloc Lopez-Waterman; Cast: Tonya Canada, Michael Levinton, Aaron Mattocks, Joy Nirenstein, Laura Von Hold, Jessica Joy, Eva Salina Primack, Sarah Small; Week 3: *The Name Means Public Spirited* by Mallery Avidon; Director, Jane Hooker; Choreography, Chris Giarmo; Music, Brian Lawlor & Beck Henderer-Pena; Sets, Carolyn Mraz; Costumes, Asta Bennie Hostetter; Lights, Tlaloc Lopez-Waterman; Stage Manager, Kate Marvin; Cast: Noel Allain, Eliza Bent, Olmo Cefa, Ka-Ling Cheung, Deanna Companion, Nnadi Harriott, Diana Konopka, Julia Sirna-Frest, Stephanie Weeks; *Duo* A Double Header Event – *Fuck! War!* by F. Wolf Moltich, directed by Sherrine Azab; Cast: Amanda Capobianco, Joshua Conkel, Joe Gregori, J.J. Shebesta; *Peace* by Rachel Chavkin & Taylor Mac, directed by Rachel Chavkin; Set, Nick Vaughan; Lighting, Al Roundtree; Stage Manager, Rebecca Spinac; Cast: Christopher Illing, John Lavelle, Nila Leigh, Taylor Mac, Kari Nicole Washington; HERE Arts Center; October 31–November 17, 2007

THE ARGUMENT and **THE DINNER PARTY** Director, David Herskovits; Set, Darah Edkins; Costumes, Asta Bennie Hostetter; Sound, Jane Shaw; Props/Assistant Set, Carolyn Mraz; Associate Lighting, Natalie Robin; Stage Manager, Olivia O'Brien; ASM, Shannon L. Sexton; Production Manager, Brenna St. George Jones; Assistant Director, Sherrine Azab; Dramaturg, Kathleen Kennedy Tobin; Technical Director, Gabriel Evansohn; *The Argument* Written and performed by David Greenspan; *The Dinner Party* Adapted by David Herskovits; Cast: Han Nah Kim, Diana Konopka, Mary Neufeld, Steven Rattazzi, Greig Sargeant, Stephanie Weeks,

Ian Wen; The Kitchen: June 16–30; Theatre Three (Mint Space): January 11–14, 2008

AS YET THOU ART YOUNG AND RASH Adapted and directed by David Herskovits; Set, Susan Barras; Costumes, Meredith Palin; Lighting, Juliet Chia; Original Sound, Jane Shaw; Text Advisor, Madelyn Kent; Original Music, David Rosenmeyer; Dramaturg, Kathleen Kennedy Tobin; Stage Manager, Olivia O'Brien; ASM, Shannon L. Sexton; Production Manager, Brenna St. George Jones; Cast: Satya Bhabha, Mia Katigbok, Mary Neufeld, Tina Shepard, Stephanie Weeks, Kate Marvin; Theatre Three (Mint Space); January 11–14, 2008

Teatro IATI

ON INSOMNIA AND MIDNIGHT by Edgar Chías; Director, Berioska Ipinza; Cast: Pietro Gonzalez, Sonia Portugal; November 1–18, 2007

HOMELESS Written and directed by Lorenzo Parro; Produced by Bordinni Brothers Productions; Cast: Lorenzo Parro, Maria Fajardo, Juan Carlos Parro, Miguel Rosales and Gerardo Gudiño; March 24–April 6, 2008

THE BLACK CONTINENT by Marco Antonio de la Parra; Director, Martin Balmaceda; Set, Yanko Bakulic; Lighting, Jason Sturm; Cast: Patricia Becker, Winston Estevez, Inma Herdia, Fabian González, Laura Spalding; Theater 64 on East 4th Street; April 17–May 4, 2008

Ten Grand Productions, Inc.

Managing Director, Jason Hewitt

SAME TRAIN by Levy Lee Simon; Music & Lyrics by Mark Bruckner; Director, Mary Beth Easley; Set. Jorge Dieppa; Costumes, Ali Turns; Lighting, Deborah E. Constantine; Production Stage Manager, Andrea Jess Berkey; Cast: Cedric Turner, Levy Lee Simon, Eddie Goines, Harrison Lee, Ayeje Feamster, Kami Percinthe; Algonquin Theater: February 11–March 8, 2008

A YEAR IN THE LIFE OF 25 STRANGERS LIVING IN A CITY BY THE LAKE by Matthew Fotis; Director, Shaun Colledge; Costumes, Emelie, Jayne Hanson; Cast: Jessica Vera, Brian Waters, Sabrina Gibber, Stephanis Bush, Gus Ferrari, Edward Chin-Lyn; Eric Orive, Dan Faraguna, Justin Hoch, Taylor Baugh, David Stadler, Michele Rafic, Adam Ferguson, Cory Shoemake, Ben Rosenblatt, Jennifer Bishop, Natalie Whatley, Amy Lynne Darling, Myles Jordan, Walker Hare, Matthew Murumba, Chloe Cahill, Josh Hurley; The Parker Theater/Algonquin Theater; May 2–18, 2008

Theatres at 45 Bleecker

FRINGENYC ENCORE SERIES 2007 Included *Lights Rise on Grace* by Chad Beckim; Presented by 61 Academy Association with Partial Comfort Productions; Director, Robert O'Hara; *A Beautiful Child* by Truman Capote; Produced by the Courthouse Theater Company; Director, Linda Powell; ... *Double Vision* by Barbara Blumenthal-Ehrlich; Produced by Don't Say Miami and Joshua P. Weiss; Director, Ari Laura Kreith; *Hillary Agonistes* by Nick Slamone; Presented by Playwrights' Arena and Frantic Redhead Productions; Director, Jon Lawrence Rivera; Cast: Priscilla Barnes; *Mary Brigit Poppleton is Writing a Memoir* by Madeline Walter; *As Far as We Know* Created by The Torture Project Ensemble in collaboration with Christina Gorman; Director, Laurie Sales; *I Dig Doug* written and performed by Karen DiConcetto and Rochelle Zimmerman; Director, Bert V. Royal; August 30–September 16, 2007

THE HOLIDAY COCKTAIL LOUNGE by Jason Hoey; September 23, 2007

WAKE UP! Written and performed by Karen Finley; Lighting, Josh Iacovelli; The Green Room; October 7–November 4, 2007

THE TURN OF THE SCREW by Henry James, adapted by Jeffrey Hatcher; Presented by Twenty Feet Productions; Director, Marc Silberschatz; October 19–November 3, 2007

WELCOME TO FUNLAND by Magin Schantz; The Green Room; April 17–May 1, 2008

THE CAUCASIAN CHALK CIRCLE by Bertolt Brecht; Presented by Hipgnosis Theater Company; Director, Margot Newkirk; Cast: Rachel Tiemann, John Kevin Jones, John Castro, Ayanna Siverls Simon, Douglas Scott Streater, Demetrios Bonaros, Hal Fickett, Colleen Kennedy, Matthew Kinney, Elizabeth Mirarchi, Dennis J. Paton, Pharah Jean-Philippe, Richard Ugino; April 26–May 11, 2008

BABYLOVE Written and performed by Christen Clifford; Presented by The Hourglass Group and 45 Bleecker; Directed and developed by Julie Kramer; The Green Room; May 4–July 27, 2008

EIGHTBALLS, A COCAINE COMEDY by CJ Thom; Presented by Gadfly Productions; Director, Michael LoPorto; Cast: Frankie Ferrara, Josh Iacovelli, Casey Kruger, CJ Thom; The Green Room; May 15–31, 2008

Theater For The New City

Executive Director, Crystal Field

EMERGENCY CONTRACEPTION!: The Musical Book and direction by Sara Cooper, music by Chris Shimojima; Presented by Talentless Hack Entertainment; Music Director, Marc Giosi; Stage Manager, Michelle Gaidos; Cast: Hannah Kim, Noah DeBiase, Elysia Segal, Teresa Jusino, Brian Griffin, Michael Rehse; September 13–30, 2007

GLOBESITY FESTIVAL: Hunger Strike Theatre Created and produced by Robert Mac and Penny Arcade; Associate

Director, Michael Premo; October 22–28, 2007

RYUJI SAWA: The Return Created by Ryuji Sawa; November 6–11, 2007

A TIMELESS KAIDAN Choreographed and directed by Ximena Garnica and Garnica Acts Lab; Produced by CAVE New York Butoh Festival; November 6–8, 2007

THE SORDID PERILS OF ACTUAL EXISTENCE by Tom Gladwell and Andy Reynolds; Director, Tom Gladwell; Set, Donald L. Brooks; Costumes, Carol Sherry; Stage Manager, Meagan Walker; Cast: Crystal Field, Dick Morrill, Andy Reynolds, Laura Wickens; November 23–December 8, 2007

THE DIVINE REALITY COMEDY and **THE DIVINE REALITY COMEDY CIRCUS** Adaptations of Dante's *Divine Comedy;* Presented by Bread and Puppet Theater Company; Director, Peter Schumann; Cast: Danny McNamara, Maura Gahan, Noah Harrell, Justin Lander, Rose Friedman, Jason Hicks, Federica Collina, Alicia Gerstein, Samantha Wilson; November 29–December 16, 2007

NUTCRACKER: Rated R Produced by Angela Harriell/David F. Slone; Direction, choreography and costumes by Angela Harriell; Musical Remixes, The Hack (a.k.a., David F. Slone, Esq.); Sound: Richard Reta; Lighting, Mark Marcante; Stage Managers/Assistant Lighting Designers, Jason Bogdan/Lezane Trapani; Video Sequences. Jan Luc Van Damme; Photography/Graphics, Jorge Colombo; Cast: Jesús Chapa-Malacara, Sarah Conrad, Gregory Dubin, Christopher Dunston, Angela Harriell, Christina Johnson, Kimberly Lantz, Michael MacLaren, Adam Pellegrine, Joseph Schles, David F. Slone, Esq., Juliana Smith, Emma Stein, Clare Tobin, Jaime Waliczek; November 29–December 23, 2007

VOICE 4 VISION PUPPET FESTIVAL Fourth Annual; Series included: *Tin Lighining* by Chris Green, Lisa Gonzales, Erin Orr; *Tiger Plus: An Evening of Overhead Projection* by Chinese Theater Works, Kuang-Yu Fong and Stephen Kaplin; *Night Shade* by Carrionettes, Liz Adele Allen, Sarah Frechette, Jason Thibodeaux, Alain Z; *The Jester of Tonga* by Joseph Silovsky; November 29–December 9, 2007

TARANTELLA! SPIDER DANCE Created and directed by Alessandra Belloni; December 21–23, 2007

ALL ABOARD THE MARRIAGE HEARSE Written and directed by Matt Morillo; Produced by Jessica Durdock and Matt Morillo; Lighting, Amith A. Chandrashaker; Set, Mark Marcante; Stage Manager, Mei Acevedo; Press, Jonathan Slaff; Cast: Nicholas J. Coleman, Jessica Durdock; January 3–February 9, 2008

AMERINDIANS: the return A Cross-Cultural Performance Exhibition of Dance, Spoken Word, Body Art and a Sound/Video Installation; Host, Cristina Cortes; Artistic Director/Media Concept/Choreographer, Prem Neerajan Totem; Body and Object Design, Tiokasin Ghosthorse (Lakota/Sioux); Spoken Word and Music, Lance White Magpie (Oglala/Lakota/Sioux); Traditional Choreographer Adviser, Elaine Benavides (Apache); Lighting/Costumes/Stage Design/Sound/Video, Dan Goldman, Charlie Buckland, Remy Francis, Kleoni Manoussakis and Alejo Gordillo; Music, Trudell, Robertson, Ghosthorse, Blackfire, Aztlan Underground and Cherokee opera singer Barbara Mcaliste; January 17–20, 2008

LOOKING UP: A Romance with Trapeze by Carla Cantrelle; Presented by Traveling Light Productions; Director, Giovanna Sardelli; Set and Lighting, Nathan Elsener; Sound, Christopher A. Granger; Stage Manager, Emily Glinick; Cast: Carla Cantrelle, Bryant Mason; February 21–March 2, 2008

THE FURTHER ADVENTURES OF UNCLE WIGGILY: Windblown Visitors Book and lyrics by Laurel Hessing, music by Arthur Abrams; Director, Crystal Field; Set, Donald L. Brooks; Costumes, Myrna Duarte; Lighting, Jason Sturm; Sound, Joy Linscheid and Walter Gurbo; Music Director, A.J. Mantas; Puppets, Morgan Eckert, Momo Felix, Spica Wobbe; Choreography, Lisa Giobbi Movement Theater; February 28–March 23, 2008

THE MAN WHO APPEARED** Created by Gary Brackett, Martin Reckhaus, Jessica Slote; Set, Gary Brackett; Cast: Sheila Dabney, John Kohan, Martin Reckhaus, Jessica Slote, Asoka Esuruosa; February 28–March 9, 2008

SEX! DRUGS! & UKULELES! Book and lyrics by Uke Jackson, music by Terry Waldo; Director, Victor Maog; Choreography, Celia Rowlson-Hall; Set, Mark Marcante; Sound, Richard Reta; Costumes, Susan Gittens; Lighting, Michael Jarett; PSM, David Alpert; Production Supervisor, Nancy Vitale; Cast: Meg Cavanaugh, Lindsay Foreman, John Forkner, Andrew Guilarte, Mia Breaux, Tammy Carrasco, Jenna Fakhoury, Kristen Lewis, Guy Lockard, Dustin Flores; March 13–April 6, 2008

NEW YORK UKE FEST 2008 Emcees: J. Walter Hawkes, Ali Lexa, Spats White, Heather Lev; Performers: Uncle Zac, Dreamboat, Hal Brolund, Evy Mayer and Triboro, Des O'Connor, The Ukulady, J Walter Hawkes Trio, Lil' Rev, The Kennedys, Les Chauds Lapins, Gerald Ross, Elvira Bira, Moth Wranglers, LD Beghtol & Chris Xefos, Jim and Liz Beloff, Rose Turtle Erthler, New York Ukulele Ensemble, John King, Melvern Taylor and the Meltones, Agent 99, Ali Lexa, bedroom community, Sweet Soubrette, Ron Gordon and the Hokum Hotshots, Tim Sweeney, Jen Kwok, Bosko and Honey; April 3–6, 2008

COLLAPSING UNIVERSE Written, composed, directed and musical directed by Michael Vasques; April 10–27, 2008

THE SYSTEM OF DOCTOR TARR AND PROFESSOR FETHER by Edgar Allan Poe, adapted for the stage by Candice Burridge and David Zen Mansley, music by Jon Vomit/Strange Walls; Shadow Puppets/Masks, Candice Burridge; Hand Puppets/Assistant Director, David Zen Mansley; Production Manager, Adrian Gallard; Set, Mark Marcante; Lighting, Jason Sturm; Costumes, Susan Gittens; Sound, Roy Chang; Cast: Dan Drogyny, David Zen Mansley, Ilana Landecker, Michael Sanders, Lissa Moira, Charles Battersby, Ellen Steier, T. Scott

Lilly, William Abbott; April 10–27, 2008

ON NAKED SOIL – Imagining Anna Akhmatova by Rebecca Schull; Director, Susan Einhorn; Set, Ursula Belden; Costumes, Mimi Maxmen; Lighting, Victor en yu Tan; Video, Aaron Ryne; Sound, Megan Henninger; Cast: Rebecca Schull (Anna Akhmatova), Sue Cremin (Lydia Chukovskaya), Lenore Loveman (Nadezhda Mandelstam); April 12–May 4, 2008

PHALLIC FABLES: A Rabelaisian Epic by Walter Corwin; Composer, Arthur Abrams; Director, Jonathan Weber; May 1–18, 2008

WHISTLE ME HIGHER – Imaginary Dances From Bingo Palace Created by Laura Ward; Score, Fa Ventilato and Frank Heer; May 1–4, 2008

STIRRING RHYTHMS Presented by Kinding Sindaw Dance Company; May 14–18, 2008

13TH ANNUAL LOWER EAST SIDE FESTIVAL OF THE ARTS May 23–25, 2008

GOD LOVES TINY TIM A one-man odyssey by and starring Spats White; May 31–June 31, 2008

CROTHER SPYGLASS by Timothy Dowd, and **THE RESISTIBLE RISE OF FATLINDA** by Marcy Wallabout; Double bill directed by Leah Bonvissuto; Presented by Serenitas Media and Extrabold Productions; June 11–15, 2008

FORBIDDEN CITY WEST Book, lyrics and direction by Joanna Chan, music by Gregory Frederick; Presented by Yangtze Repertory Theater Company; Choreography, David Chien Hui Shen; Set, Martin Andrew Orlowicz; Costumes, Xu HouJian; Lighting, Kathleen Dobbins; Vocal Coach, Richard Malone; Arrangements, Tom Berger; Cast: Debbie Wong, Ji Wang, Richard Anthony, DeShen Cao, Kyle Cheng, Rachel Filsoof, Ron Flores, Daneile Gonzalez, Aki Goto, Carl Hsu, Gloria Lai, Ashley Liang, Rachel Lin, Sean Lin, Satomi Makida, Ruri Saito, Annie Qian, HaoWen Wang, Lei Zhou; June 13–July 1, 2008

BRUNCH AT THE LUTHERS Written and directed by Misha Shulman; Cast: Mort Kroos, Joanie Fritz Zosike, Robert Hieger, Be Laroe, Priscilla Lopes; June 19–July 6, 2008

MAKE IT SO by Ed Miller; Presented by Making Light Productions and the Little Rascals Theater Company; Director, Sharon Fogarty; Costumes, Michael Bevin; Set, Mark Marcante; Lighting, Alexander Bartenieff; Cast: Beverly Bonner, Althea Alexis, Leonard Dozier, Brian Karim, Monica Russell, Milan Conner, Georgia Southern-Penn, Adam R. Deremer; June 19–July 13, 2008

Theatre Row Theatres

Acorn Theatre

HAIR by James Rado and Gerome Ragni; Presented by The Real Theatre Company; Director, Maggie Levin; Choreography, Wilhelmina Frankfurt; Music Director, Peter Saxe; Music August 31–September 9, 2007

Beckett Theatre

BEAUTIFUL SOULS by Sven Swenson; Presented by Springboard Theatre Company; Director, Jeremy Dobrish; Cast: Jake Robards, Emma Dean, Luke Wrights; June 27–30, 2007

SNAPSHOTS Three one-act plays about women presented by Diverse City Theatre; Director, Gregory Simmons; Set and Lighting, Maruti Evans; Sound, Elizabeth Rhodes; Costumes, Arnulfo Maldonado; PSM, Amy Kaskeski; Associate Producer/ASM, Phil Guiterrez; Plays included: *Colleen Ireland* by Stuart Harris; *The "A" Word* by Linda Faigo-Hall, and *The End of Civilization as We Know It* by Lydia Stryk; August 16–September 1, 2007

THE COFFEE TREES by Arthur Giron, inspired by *The Cherry Orchard* by Anton Chekhov; Presented by Resonance Ensemble; Director, Marion Castleberry; Set, Dustin O'Neill; Costumes, Sidney Shannon; Lighting, Bobby Bradley; Sound, Nick Moore; PSM, Stew Awalt; Production Manager, Joe Doran; Press, Sam Rudy; Cast: Teddy Canez, Chris Ceraso, Elizabeth A. Davis, Dan Domingues, Christine Farrell, Annie Henk, Veronica Matta, Steven Pounders, Victor Truro; Presented in repertory with *The Cherry Orchard;* October 3–21, 2007

THE CHERRY ORCHARD by Anton Chekhov; Presented by Resonance Ensemble; Adapted and directed by Eric Parness; Set, Dustin O'Neill; Costumes, Sidney Shannon; Lighting, Bobby Bradley; Sound, Nick Moore; PSM, Stew Awalt; Production Manager, Joe Doran; Press, Sam Rudy; Cast: Alberto Bonilla, Chris Ceraso, Brian D. Coats, Elizabeth A. Davis, Bill Fairbairn, Susan Ferrara, Sacha Iskra, Ben Masur, Jessica Myhr, James Ware, Kari Nicole Washington, Evan Zes; Cast: Presented in repertory with *The Coffee Trees;* October 4–21, 2007

APARTMENT 3A by Jeff Daniels; Produced by The Clockwork Theatre (Jay Rohloff, Artistic Director; Owen M. Smith, Producing Director; Harrison Harvey, Executive Director); Director, Owen M. Smith; Set, Olga Mill; Lighting, Joshua Windhausen & Taryn Kennedy; Costumes, Jocelyn Melechinsky; Sound, R. Canterberry Hall & Iæden Hovorka; PSM, Stephanie Cali; Music, Iæden Hovorka, Angelo Miliano & Jillian Russo; Cast: Marianna McClellan, Philip J. Cutrone, Doug Nyman, Jay Rohloff, Vincent Vigilante; January 26–February 16, 2008

FIRECRACKER Adapted and directed by Jessica Lanius; Presented by Theatre Lila; Set/Lighting, Michael Reese; Costumes, Ellen Stockbridge; Composer/Sound, Bill Barclay; Stage Manager, Kelly Shaffer; Cast: Alexis Slade, Gregory D. Manley, James Patrick Flynn, David Randolph Irving, Eunice Ha, Francile Albright, Liam Joynt, Paul L. Coffey, Richard Waddingham, Scott Giguere, Jennifer Donlin; March 21–April 19, 2008

WONDER:lust Conceived and directed by Andy Arden Reese; Presented by Theatre Lila; Set/Lighting, Michael Reese; Costumes, Niki Hernandez-Adams; Composer/Sound, Bill Barclay; Stage Manager, Lindsay Stares; Cast: Emily Mitchell, Jessica Pohly, John Mulcahy, Kate Russell, Shadae Smith, Stanley Brode, Susan Schuld, Vanessa Morosco; March 26–April 19, 2008

Clurman Theatre

FRESHPLAY FESTIVAL Four one-acts by New York teens; Presented by MCC Theatre: *The Fishes Dream in January* by Jennifer Goris, directed by Jackson Gay; *Caught Up by Delilah Rivera,* directed by Lou Moreno; *Man with Trench Coat* by Kyle-Steven Porter, directed by Michael Barakiva; *Them* by the MCC Youth Company and Lucy Thurber, directed by Michael Barakiva; August 15–18, 2007

Kirk Theatre

RECONSTRUCTING MAMA Book, lyrics and direction by Stephen Svoboda, music, lyrics and musical direction by N. David Williams; Presented by Fresco; Choreography, Randall Pollard: Set/Lighting, Tim Brown; Costumes and Puppets, Michiko Kitayama; PSM, Laura Marsh; Cast: Jonathan White, Ariana Shore, Lauren Connolly, Danny Marr, Chris Teutsch; August 12–19, 2007

ALWAYS FAMILY by Jeremy Lum and Simmone Yu; Produced by Small Pond Entertainment, Simmone Yu, Michael Roderick in association with Jeremy Lum, Alexa Casciari, Hana Maori Taylor; Director, Glory Sims Bowen; Assistant Director/ Stage Manager, Allison R. Smith; Set, Jessie Moore; Costumes, David Withrow; Lighting, Ryan Metzler; Composer, Kenny Wood; Sound, Gennaro Marletta III; Choreography, Christine Bokhour; Fights, Michael G. Chin; Marketing/Press, Sidnei Beall III, Matt Siccoli; Cast: Simmone Yu, Christopher Larkin, Jennifer Boehm, Kenneth L. Naanep, Jeanie Tse, V. Orion Delwaterman; October 12–27, 2007

SHERLOCK SOLO Written and performed by Victor L. Cahn; Presented by Resonance Ensemble; Director, Eric Parness; January 10–February 2, 2008

ANCHORS by Tony Zertuche; Presented by Living Image Arts; Director, Eliza Beckwith; Set, Elisha Schaefer; Lighting, Wilburn O. Bonnell; Costumes, Kim Walker; Sound, Geoffrey Roecker; Stage Manager Jay Koepke; Producer/Artistic Director, Peter Marsh; Production Supervisor/Executive Director, Mia Vaculik; Associate Producers, Kendra Dolton, Tyler Penfield; Cast: Bryan Close, Helen Coxe, Andrew Eisenman, Laura Hall, Kyle Masteller, Banaue Miclat, Raushanah Simmons, Renaldy Smith, Kristin Villanueva; February 7–23, 2008

Lion Theatre

FAIR GAME by Karl Gajdusek; Presented by Genesius Theatre Group (Dana I. Harrel, March Parees) and South Ark Stage; Director, Andrew Volkoff; Set, Brian Prather; Lighting, Jim Milkey; Sound, Matt O'Hare; Costumes, Matthew Hemesath; Stage Manager, Barbara Kielhofer; ASM, Carly Hirschberg, Jeremy Stamps; Associate Producer, Johanna Gruenhut; Cast: Joy Franz, Caralyn Kozlowski, Chris Henry Coffey, Sarah-Doe Osborne, Ray McDavitt; August 17–September 7, 2007

THE MAIN(E) PLAY by Chad Beckim; Presented by Partial Comfort Productions; Director, Robert O'Hara; Set, Caleb Levengood; Lighting, Jason Jeunnette; Costumes, Whitney Locher; Sound, Daniel Odham; Cast: Michael Gladis, Alexander Alioto, Susan Dahl, Curran Connor, Allyson Morgan; January 23–February 9, 2008

AFFLUENZA! by James Sherman; Presented by Heiress Productions; Director, Maura Farver; Cast; Nancy Evans, Paul Herbig, Philipe D. Preston, Michael Saenz, Stephen Squibb, Mary Willis White; March 13–April 6, 2008

COMING HOME Three one-acts: *Sparrow* by Linda Faigao-Hall, directed by Ian Morgan; *Counting* by Maria Gabriele, directed by Christine Farrell; *Last Call on Bourbon Street* by William K. Powers, directed by Alexa Polmer; Presented by Living Image Arts; Sets, Sarah B. Brown; Lighting, Scott Hay; Costumes, Sara James; Sound, Keith Rubenstein; PSM, Treasa O'Neill; Producers, Peter Marsh, Mia Vaculik; Cast: Amanda Bruton, Tyler Bunch, Todd Davis, Andrew Eisenman, Maria Gabriele, Luz Lor, Banaue Miclat, Stu Richel, Maria Elizabeth Ryan, Raushanah Simmons; May 29–June 14, 2008

Studio Theatre

NATE & BETTE by Julio Tumbaco and Jim Gibson; Presented by JJ Entertainment; Director, Dee Spencer; Stage Manager, Blaze Kelly Coyle; Cast: David King, Debbie Klaar; August 2–26, 2007

DAMNÉE MANON, SACRÉE SANDRA by Michael Tremblay, translated by John Van Burek; Presented by Beyond the Wall Productions; Director, Danya Nardi; Cast: Elise Link, Carlton Tanis; January 18–February 1, 2008

LOVE LETTERS by A.R. Gurney; Presented by Eastcheap Rep; Director, Chris Chaberski; Cast: Luke Rose & Sally Jackson or Peter Chenot & Megan Keith; February 7–9, 2008

NEW YORK FAIRYTALE FESTIVAL Adapted and directed by Johannes Galli; February 12–17, 2008

CINEPHILIA by Leslye Headland; Presented by PossEble Theater Company; Director, Michael Silverstone; Cast: Katie Cappiello, Christian Durso, Nila K. Leigh; May 31–June 15, 2008

Theater Ten Ten

Producing Artistic Director, Judith Jarosz

INNOCENT DIVERSIONS Written and directed by Lynn Marie Macy; Set, David Fuller; Costumes, Deborah Wright Houston; Lighting, Hajera Dehqanzada; PSM, Shauna

Horn; Assistant Director, Aaron Diehl; ASM, Malizsha Then; Dialects, Annalisa Loeffler; Cast: Denise Alessandria Hurd, Karen Eterovich, Judith Jarosz, Christiana L. Kuczma, Vanessa Morosco, Eyal Sherf, Chelsea Jo Pattison, David Arthur Bachrach, Esther David, Annalisa Loeffler, Christopher Michael Todd, Talaura Harms; November 16–December 16, 2007

THE IMPORTANCE OF BEING EARNEST by Oscar Wilde; Director, Judith Jarosz; Set. David Fuller; Costumes, Lydia Gladstone and Kristin Yungkurth Raphael; Lighting, Hajera Dehqanzada; Sound, Shauna Horn; Stage Manager, Lauren Ameson; ASM, Cesar Malantic and Sarah Marck; Cast: David Jacks, David Fuller, Christopher Michael Todd, Christiane Young, Vanessa Morosco, Sheila Joon, Talaura Harms, Greg Horton; February 8–March 9, 2008

A GRAND NIGHT FOR SINGING Music by Richard Rodgers, lyrics by Oscar Hammerstein II, conceived by Walter Bobbie; Music Arrangements, Fred Wells; Orchestrations, Jonathan Tunick and Michael Gibson; Director, David Fuller; Music Director, Michael Harren; PSM, Jaime Phelps; Assistant Director, Aaron Diehl; Stage Managers, Adam Blondin, Emily Glasser, Greg Loproto; Set/Lighting, Giles Hogya; Costumes, Viviane Galloway; Choreography, Brittney Jensen; Cast: Jessica Greeley, David Tillistrand, Judith Jarosz, Mishi Schueller, Kerry Conte; April 25–May 25, 2008

Theatre Three (Mint Theatre Space)

MAFIA ON PROZAC and THE SEVENTEENTH OF JUNE Two dark comedies by Edward Allen Baker; Presented by IAAM Productions (Lisa Weisglass, Executive Producer); Director, Doug MacHugh; Casting, Amy Gossels; Cast: Tom Cappadona, Jake Myers, Joe WIssler, Suzanne DiDonna, Hannah Snyder-Beck, Wayne Stills, Darlene Violette; July 25–29, 2007

UNDER MILK WOOD by Dylan Thomas; Presented by Intimation Theatre Company (Founders: Elise Corey, Michelle Dean, Jesse R. Tendler, and Jennifer Weedon); Director, Michelle Dean, Composer/Musical Director/Sound, Arvi Sreenivasan; Lighting, Guy Chachkes and Ilya Dubelsky; Projections, Chris Kateff; Stage Manager, Elliot Lanes; Cast: Lyle Blaker, Elizabeth Bove, Betsy Head, Deidre Ann Johnson, Chris Kateff, John Mervini, Robert Moreira, Owen Panettieri, Amanda Kay Schill, Melissa Schoenberg, Jesse R. Tendler, Jennifer Weedon; January 23–February 10, 2008

The Actors Company Theatre (TACT)

Co-Artistic Directors, Scott Alan Evans, Cynthia Harris, and Simon Jones; General Manager, Cathy Bencivenga

THE RUNNER STUMBLES by Milan Stitt; Director, Scott Alan Evans; Sets, Dana Moran-Williams; Lighting, Mary Louise Geiger; Costumes, David Toser; Sound, Daryl Bornstein; Original Music, Josephe Trapanese; Props, Esther Neff; PSM, Dawn Dunlop; ASM, Mel McCue; Assistant Director, Barry Satchwell Smtih; Press, Joe Trentacosta; Cast: Mark L. Montgomery, Ashley West, Cynthia Darlow, Chirs Hietikko, James Murtaugh, Julie Jesneck, Jamie Bennett, Christopher Halladay, Christina Bennett Lind; Beckett Theatre at Theatre Row; October 28–November 24, 2007

THE ECCENTRICITIES OF A NIGHTINGALE by Tennessee Williams; Director, Jenn Thompson; Costumes, David Toser; Set, Bill Clarke; Lighting, Lucrecia Briceno; Sound, Daryl Bornstein; Original Music, Jonathan Faiman; PSM, Mel McCue; ASM, Syche Hamilton; Assistant Director, Jay Cohen; Props, Jennifer Blazek; Press, Joe Trentacosta; Cast: Larry Keith, Mary Bacon, Nora Chester, Todd Gearheart, Darrie Lawrence, Scott Schafer, James Prendergast, Cynthia Darlow, Francesca Di Mauro, John Plumpis; Clurman Theatre at Theatre Row; April 27–May 24, 2008; 24 perforamances

Salon Series at TACT Studio

A Shot in the Dark by Marcel Archard, adapted by Harry Kurnitz; Director, Drew Barr; September 30–October 1, 2007; *My Three Angels* by Sam & Bella Spewack; Director, Jenn Thompson; December 8–10, 2007; *Witness for the Procsecution* by Agatha Christie; Director, Harris Yulin; January 12–14, 2008; *The Andersonville Trial* by Saul Leveitt; Director, Henry Wishcamper; February 9–11, 2008; *Dock Brief* by John Mortimer & *If Men Played Cards as Women Do* by George S. Kaufman; Director, Simon Jones; March 8–10, 2008

T. Schreiber Studio

Terry Schreiber, Founder

SISTER CITIES by Colette Freedman; Director, Cat Parker; Stage Manager, Eliza Jane Bowman; Set, George Allison; Lighting, Andrea Boccanfuso; Costumes, Karen Ann Ledger; Sound, Christopher Rummel; Cast: Judith Scarpone, Ellen Reilly; Maeve Yore, Emberli Edwards, Jaime Neumann; October 18–November 18, 2007

THE NIGHT OF THE IGUANA by Tennesee Williams; Director, Terry Schreiber; Cast: Peter Aguero, Bruce Colbert, Ian Campbell Dunn, Loren Dunn, Denise Fiore, Peter Judd, Alecia Medley, Armando Merlo, Pat Patterson, Derek Roché, Janet Saia, Jenny Strassburg; February 21–March 30, 2008

THE ACTOR'S NIGHTMARE and THE REAL INSPECTOR HOUND Two one-acts by Christopher Durang and Tom Stoppard; Director, Peter Jensen; Lighting, Andrea Boccanfuso; Sound, Chris Rummel; Costumes, Anne Wingate; Stage Manager, Jaclyn Bouton; Cast: Michael Black, Therese Tucker, Nan Wray, Oliver Burns, Shawn Wilson, Julian Elfer, Rick Forstmann, Shane Colt, Jenny Strassburg, Maggie Dashiell, Ben Prayz, Michael Horan; May 8–June 15, 2008

Triad Theatre

LAST JEW IN EUROPE Written and originally directed by Tuvia Tenenbom; Produced by The Jewish Theater of

New York; Director, Leya Adler; Set/Scene Paintings, Mark Symczak; Costumes, Elgie C. Johnson; General Manager, Isi Tenenbom; Cantorial Music, Cantor Israel Singer; Cast: Maria Leigh Feldpausch*[1]; Dr. Kweczke Igor Litwinowicz*[2]; Jozef RJ Lewis*[3]; Zbrodzka Martina Mank*[4]; John Jay Smith Michael Rachlis*[5]; Papa Jocka Stewart Schneck*[6]; Understudy: Christine Seisler (Zbrodzka); Opened October 14, 2007; still running as of May 31, 2008. (*Succeeded by: 1. Meghan Powe 2. Dennis Brito 3. Zal Owen 4. Andrea Prendamano 5. Eric Noone 6. Christopher Ryan Renni)

POLITICAL IDOL by Robert Yarnall, with additional lyrics by Marc Emory and Rob Seitelman; Presented by The Freedom Toast; Director, Julie Blanciak; Music Director, Chris Haberl; Costumes/Wigs, Kat Martin; Stage Manager, Liza Baron; Drums, Mike Dobson; General Manager, Olson Rohdes; Press, Peter Cromarty; Cast: Lara Buck, Enga Davis, Joe DiSalle, Robert Yarnall; October 30–December 18, 2007; Encored March 16–April 27, 2008

WINE LOVERS Conceived and co-written by Michael Green, book by Travis Kramer and Gary Negbauer, music/lyrics and musical direction by Gary Negbauer; Director, Holly-Anne Ruggiero; Choreography, Holly Cruz; Stage Manager, Andrea Wales; Design, Anne Allen Goelz; Projections, Chris Kateff; Costumes, Maria Zamansky; Cast: Tuck Milligan, Eric Rubbe, Jessica Phillips; December 1–10, 2007

CELEBRITY AUTOBIOGRAPHY: In Their Own Words Created by Eugene Pack; Guest Casts included: Fred Armisen, Joy Behar, Matthew Broderick, Bobby Cannavale, Alan Cumming, Rachel Dratch, Cheyenne Jackson, Kristen Johnston, Carson Kressley, Richard Kind, Michael McKean, Donna Murphy, Eugene Pack, Jack Plotnick, Dayle Reyfel, Seth Rudetsky, Claudia Shear, Sherri Shepherd, Jason Sudeikis, Kristen Wiig, Karen Ziemba; January 28–May 12, 2008

WHEN THE LIGHTS GO ON AGAIN Conceived, written and directed by Bill Daugherty; Produced by Thoroughbred Records and Max Weintraub; Musical Director, Doyle Newmyer; Musical Staging, Lori Leshner; Lighting and Sound, Tonya Pierre; Makeup/Hair, Jimmy Cortes; Press, Peter Cromary; Cast: Bill Daugherty, Eli Schneider, Christina Morrell, Connie Pachl; Musicians: Doyle Newmyer (Musical Director/piano), Jim Conant (guitar), John Loehrke (bass), Chip Fabrizi (drums); March 7–May 24, 2008

Turtle Shell Productions

Artistic Director, John W. Cooper

FRITZ AND FROYIM Book and lyrics by Norman Beim, music by Mark Barkan and Rolf Barnes; based on material from "The Dance of Genghis Cohn" by Roamin Gary; Producer/Director, John W. Cooper; Music Director, Tracy Stark, Choreography, Cheryl Cutlip; General Manager, Jeremy Handelman; Set, Ryan Scott; Costumes, Christina Gianini; Lighting, Eric Larson; Sound, Scott Sexton; Stage Manager, Sarah-Dakotah Farney; Cast: Joan Barber, Erin Cronican, Matthew Hardy, Dennis Holland, T.J. Mannix, Tracy Stark, Richard B. Watson; June 1–June 16, 2007

JEWEL THIEVES! Written and directed by Norman Beim; Produced by John W. Cooper; Set, Ryan Scott; Costumes, Christina Giannini; Lighting, Lisa Weinshrott & Michael L. Kimmel; Stage Manager, Kelly Lincoln; Cast: Davis Hall, Marnie Klar, Gerrianne Raphael, Adam Raynen; September 19–October 24, 2007

SCAPIN by Moliére, new adaptation by Scott McCrea; Produced by John W. Cooper; Director, Shawn Rosza; Set, Kevin Lock; Lighting, Eric Larson; Sound, David Roy, Adam Zorn; Costumes, Christina Giannini; Stage Manager, Neal Kowalsky; Cast: Spencer Aste, Christie Booker, Jonathan M. Castro, Nico Evers-Swindell, John Freimann, Roger Grunwald, Matt Luceno, Emile Nebbia, Jay Painter, Maya Rosewood, Catherine Wronowski; December 5–22, 2007

A MARRIAGE OF CONVENIENCE Written and directed by Norman Beim; Produced by John W. Cooper; Sets, Ryan Scott; Costumes, Whitney Locher; Lighting/Sound, David Roy; Cast: January 16–February 2, 2008

8-MINUTE MADNESS PLAYWRIGHT FESTIVAL OF 2008 Three-week competive short play festival; Winners: Best Playwright: Aoise Stratford for *Our Lady of the Sea;* Best Production: *I Understand Your Frustration* by Steven Korbar, directed by David Leduox, with Patrick Cann and Pia Ambardar; Best Performances: Justin Morck, Pia Ambardar; February 26–March 16, 2008

THE ASPERN PAPERS Adapted by Martin M. Zuckerman from the novella by Henry James; Produced by John W. Cooper; Director, Shawn Rozsa; Set, Kyle Dixon; Costumes, A. Christina Giannini; Lighting, Shaun Suchan; Sound, Patrick Grant; Press/Production Manager, Jeremy Handelman; Cast: Kelly King, Carol Lambert, Elisabeth Grace Rothan; Understudies: Susan McCallum, Dara O'Brien; April 30–May 24, 2008

Non resident productions

HURT SO GOOD by Johnny Blaze Leavitt; Presented by Point of You Productions; Director, Marc Adam Smith; Lighting/ Stage Manager, Jeff Love; Cast: Johnny Blaze Leavitt, Chris Keating, Melanie Kuchinski Rodriguez, Leslie Marseglia, Alyssa Mann, Gerard J. Savoy, Tina Trimble, Melissa Garde, Jessie J. Fahay, Lee Solomon, Curt Dixon, Paul Weissman, Cedric Jones, Kitty Hendrix, Lizzie Czerner, Melodye Brant, Keri Ann Peterson, Dawne Garrett, Meghan Dickerson; October 11–27, 2007

Urban Stages Theatre

JUMP/ROPE by John Kuntz; Presented by Square Peg Productions; Director, Doug Mercer; Set, Arnulfo Maldonado; Costumes, Valerie Marcus Ramshur; Lighting, Paul

Hackenmueller; Sound, Michael Bogden; Cast: John Kuntz, Bill Mootos, Nathan Flower; June 9–24, 2007

THE MYSTERY OF IRMA VEP by Charles Ludlam; Presented by MadCaP Productions; Director, Tony Caselli; Cast: Paul Pecorino, Chris Dell'Armo; July 3–21, 2007

FABRIK Written, directed, designed and presented and performed by Wakka Wakka (David Arkema, Gabrielle Brechner, Kirjan Waage, Gwendolyn Warnock); Co-Produced with The Nordland Visual Theater; Sound/Music, Lars Peter Hagen, Directing Consultant, Danny Goldstein; Puppets, Kirjan Waage; January 17–February 17, 2008

7 STORIES by Nicholas J. Peterka; Presented by The B.E. Company; Director, Ethan Matthews; Design, Michael McKenna, Mike Piscitelli, Charles Leisenring; Stage Manager, Amanda Moore; Cast: Dionne Audain, Jurt Bardele, Philipp Christopher, David H. Hamilton, Paty Lombard, Rebecca Lovett, Kathleen Turco-Lyon, Chris Wendelken; April 25–May 4, 2008

Vampire Cowboys Theatre Company

Artistic Directors, Qui Nguyen and Robert Ross Parker; Managing Director, Abby Marcus

LIVING DEAD IN DENMARK by Qui Nguyen; Presented as part of the National Asian American Theater Festival; Director, Robert Ross Parker; Fight Director, Marius Hanford; Set/Lighting, Nick Francone; Costumes, Jessica Wegener; Masks/Gore Effects, Chuck Varga; Puppets, David Valentine; Composer, Dan Deming; Stage Managers, Florencio Palomo, Sharon Walsh; Cast: Carlo Alban, Alexis Black, Jason Liebman, Maggie Macdonald, Tom Myers, Melissa Paladino, Jason Schumacher, Andrea Marie Smith, Temar Underwood, Amy Kim Waschke; Beckett Theatre at Theatre Row; June 12–15, 2007

FIGHT GIRL BATTLE WORLD Co-created and fights by Qui Nguyen, Co-created and direction by Robert Ross Parker; Set/Lighting, Nick Francone; Costumes, Jessica Wegener; Puppets, David Valentine; Sound, Patrick Shearer; Cast: Melissa Paladino, Elena Chang, Noshir Dalal, Jon Hoche, Kelley Rae O'Donnell, Maureen Sebastian, Andrea Marie Smith, Paco Tolson, Temar Underwood; Center Stage NY; March 6–30, 2008

Vital Theatre Company

Producing Artistic Director, Stephen Sunderlin; Director of Vital Children's Theatre Suzu McConnell-Wood; General Manager, Cynthia Thomas

VITAL SIGNS: New Works Festival Three Week festival of new short plays; November 29–December 16, 2007; Series 1: *The Dysinformationist* by Ross Maxwell, directed by Michael Page; *Dead Lucy* by Suzanne Bradbeer, directed by Charles Maryan *A Contribution to Domestic Architecture* by Robert Shaffron, directed by Tlaloc Rivas; *LA 8 AM* by Mark Harvey Levine, directed by David Ledoux; Series Two: *Evict This* Book and lyrics by Sonya Sobieski, music by Jana Zielonka, directed by Beatrice Terry; *Kiss & Tell* by Steve Yockey, directed by Bob Cline; *Lost in the Supermarket* by Laura Eason, directed by Awoye Timpo; *Class Behavior* by Catherine Allen, directed by Gwenyth Reitz; *Meeting* by Jason Salmon, directed by Jack Reiling; Series 3: *Senor Jay's Tango Palace* by Sharyn Rothstein, directed by Marlo Hunter; *Ayravana Flies or a Pretty Dish* by Sheila Callaghan, directed by David A. Miller; *It's Our Town, Too* by Susan Miller, directed by Holli Harms; *The Lock* by Cheri Magid, directed by Blake Lawrence

THE LITTLEST LIGHT ON THE CHRISTMAS TREE Book by Jim Hindman and Cheryl Stern, music by Peter Lewis, lyrics by Tommy Marolda and Larry Hoelcffener, based on the animated film; Produced in association with Little Light Live LP; Director, Steven Harris, based on original direction and choreography by Luis Perez; Orchestrations, Ethan Deppe; Music Director, Justin Stoney; Set, Michael Lasswell; Costumes, Brenda Phelps; Lighting, Rebecca R.M. Makus; Original Lighting, Aimee Hanyzewski; Additional Choreography, Jeremy Benton; Assistant Choreography, Jamie Grayson; Stage Manager, Sharon Gregory; Cast: Erin Wegner Brooks, William Nash Broyles Thom Caska, Reid Kendall, Adam Mosebach, Katherine Rose Riley, Justin Stoney, Linsie Van Winkle, Jon Vertuno, Amy Zelcer; McGinn/Cazale Theatre; December 8, 2007–January 6, 2008

Vital Children's Theatre

EXTRAORDINARY! Book and lyrics by Dante Russo, music by David F.M. Vaughn; Director, Teresa Pond; Choreography, Derek Roland; Music Director, Jad Bernardo; Set, Elisha Schaeffer; Lighting, Jason Teague; Costumes, Hunter Kaczorowski; PSM, Kara Teolis; Cast: Kristi McCarson, Harrison M. Ford, Alan Houser, Heather Lynn Milnes, Michael Maricondi, Grace Sumner; Understudies: John Magalhaes, Susan Maris, Clifford Berry, Jodi Vaccarro, Megan Stern, Joshua Adam Ramos; McGinn/Cazale Theatre; September 15–October 21, 2007

WELCOME TO NEW JERSEY Book and lyrics by J. Holtham, music by Kwame Brandt-Pierce; Director, Tzipora Kaplan; Choreography, Dax Valdes; Music Director, Justin Stoney; Set, Jaquelyn Marolt; Lighting, Rebecca M.K. Makus; Costumes, Hunter Kaczorowski; PSM, Kara Teolis; Cast: Monique Beasley, Adam Cerny, Marc Ginsburg, Jason Jacoby, Cara Maltz, Michael Maricondi, Kristina Teschner; McGinn/Cazale Theatre; November 3–December 2, 2007

PINKALICIOUS, THE MUSICAL Book and lyrics by Elizabeth Kann & Victoria Kann, music, orchestrations and lyrics by John Gregor; Director, Teresa K. Pond; Sets, Mary Hamrick & Jesse Poleshuck; Costumes, Colleen Kesterson & Randi Fowler; Props/Additional Sets, Kerry McGuire & Dan Jagendorf; Choreography, Dax Valdes; Musical Director, Jad Bernardo; Original Direction, Suzu McConnell-Wood; PSM, Kara Teolis; Stage Manager, Annalee Fannan, Susan Manikas; Cast: Meg

Phillips, Greg Barresi, Molly Gilman, Matthew Pelliccia, Erin Wegner Brooks; Replacements: Courtney Elise Brown, Jeffrey Maggs, Lindsie Van Winkle; New World Stages – Stage 5; Weekends, January 12–May 25, 2008 (Previously played at the McGinn/Cazale and SoHo Playhouse last season)

A (TOOTH) FAIRY TALE Book by Ben Winters, music and lyrics by Rick Hip-Flores; Director, Linda Ames Key; Choreography, Dax Valdes; Music Director, Justin Scott Fischer; Set, Jaquelyn Marolt; Lighting, Rebecca M.K. Makus; Costumes, Hunter Kaczorowski; PSM, Kara Teolis; Stage Manager, Sallyann Turnbull; Cast: Jarusha Ariel, Chris Braca, Holly Buczek, Alan Houser, John Magalhaes, Abigail Taylor, Kristina Teschner; McGinn/Cazale Theatre; January 19–March 24, 2008; Transferred to SoHo Playhouse March 15–April 20, 2008

THE TOP JOB Music by Brian Feinstein, book and lyrics by Robin Moyer Chung; Director, Tamara Fisch; Choreography, Sabrina Jacob; Music Director, Jad Bernardo; Set, Jesse Poleshuck; Lighting, Christina Watanabe; Costumes, Brittany Jones-Pugh; Stage Manager, Shani Murfin; Cast: Natalie Bird, Julie Goldin, Roderick Justice, Andy Lindberg, Mychal Phillips, Rob Morrison, Tommy Waltz; McGinn/Cazale Theatre; March 8–April 27, 2008

Vortex Theatre Company

Artistic Director, Joshua Randall; Managing Director, Allison Glenzer

KISS OF THE SPIDER WOMAN Music by John Kander, lyrics by Fred Ebb, book by Terrence McNally, based on Manuel Puig's novel; Originally directed by Harold Prince; Director, Gisela Cardenas; Music Director, Milica Paranosic; Producer/ Choreography, Joshua Randall; Set, Jian Jung; Lighting, Lucrecia Briceno; Sound, Marcelo Añez; Video, Melina Leon; Assistant Director, Cara Scarmack; Assistant Producer, Julianna Slaten; Cast: Liza Baron, Michael Beatty, Gabe Belyeu, Damien DeShaun Smith, Max Ferguson, Marc Ginsburg, Harold Lewter, David Macaluso, Kim Shipley, Nikki Van Cassele, Rolfe Winkler, Michael Jared Yeshion); Sanford Meisner Theater; September 13–October 6, 2007

A CHRISTMAS CAROL – A New Musical Music and adaptation by Joel Bravo; Director, Kris Thor; Costumes, Kylie Ward; Stage Manager Carter Edwards; Producer, Joshua Randall; Cast: Mikey Barringer, Kelly Eubanks, Libby King, Deborah Knox, Julie LaMendola, Michael Martin, Joe Ornstein, Tracy Weller, Isaac Woofter, Jason Trachtenburg; Musicians: Ian Everall, Dan Gower; Sanford Meisner Theater; November 29–December 22, 2007

WalkerSpace (Soho Rep Theatre)

BABYFACE by Ashlin Halfnight; Presented by Electric Pear Productions; Director, Alexis Poledouris; Set, Jesse Poleshuck; Costumes, Sarah Laux; Lighting, Gina Scherr; Sound, Mark Valadez; Cast: Rebecca Henderson, Jordan Kaplan, Michael McGregor Mahoney, Carolyn Popp; June 7–23, 2007

I KREON Adapted by Aole T. Miller from *Antigone* by Sophocles; Presented by New Moon Rep and Roust Theatre Company; Cast: Claire Siebers, James Luse, Maggie Surovell, Max Arnaud, David Beck, Ian Eaton, Rebecca Hackett, Paul Harkins, Rafael Jordan and Ian Lowe; November 8–December 1, 2007

CAT'S CRADLE Adapted and directed by Edward Einhorn; based on the novel by Kurt Vonnegut; Presented by Untitled Theater Company #61; Director, Edward Einhorn; Musical Director, Henry Akona; Puppets, Tanya Khordoc and Barry Weil (Evolve Company); Set, Amy Davis; Costumes, Carla Gant; Lighting, Jeff Nash; Properties, Berit Johnson; Production Coordinator Alex Senchak; Dramaturg Karen Lee Ott; Choreographer Tom Berger; Stage Manager, Amanda Anderson; ASM, Spencer R. Soloway; Press, Emily Owens PR: Cast: Sean Allison, Michael Bertolini, John Blaylock, Katherine Boynton, Jerome Brooks, Daryl Brown, Rosalynd Darling, Sarah Engelke, Andrew Haserlat, Sheila Johnson, Jenny McClintock, Martin J Mitchell, Paul Pricer, Michelle Rabbani, Timothy McCown Reynolds, Horace V. Rogers, Phoebe Silva, Josh Silverman, Darius Stone, Barry Weil, Sandy York; February 22–March 15, 2008

HIROSHIMA: CRUCIBLE OF LIGHT Text by Robert Laswon; Presented by Untitled Theater Company #61; Director/ Composer, Henry Akona; Set, Amy Davis; Costumes, Isabelle Fields; Lighting, Jeff Nash, Solomon Weisbard; Properties, Berit Johnson; Puppets, Tanya Khordoc and Barry Weil (Evolve Company); Production Coordinator, Alex Senchak; Technical Consultant, Obadiah Savage; Dramaturg Karen Lee Ott; Video, Ian W. Hill, Daniel McKlienfeld; Fight Director, Dan Zisson; Stage Manager, Carmen Chen; AD/ASM, Elizabeth Irwin; Press, Emily Owens PR; Cast: Peter Bean, Dmitri Friedendberg, Joe Gately, Saysha Heinzman, Kris Lundberg, Jared Mezzochi, Shelley Ray, Timothy Roselle, Yvonne Roen, Sandy York; February 27–March 15, 2008

BRAINS AND PUPPETS by Edward Einhorn; Presented by Untitled Theater Company #61 and Evolve Company; Directed, designed and performed by Tanya Khordoc and Barry Well; Lighting, Solomon Weisbard; Stage Manager, Jennifer Spinello; Sound, Henry Akona; Press, Emily Owens PR; March 1–15, 2008

THE SITE by Al Schnupp; Director, Mark Sitko; Cast: Marty Brown, Rebecca Lingafelter, Sarah Claspell, Bobby Hodgson, Ian Merrigan, Jenny Seastone Stern, Aimeé Phelan-Deconinck; May 18–June 7, 2008

West End Theatre

HELL'S BELLES Book and lyrics by Bryan D. Leys, music by Steve Liebman; Director, John Znidarsic; Set, Craig M. Napoliello; Lighting, Anjeanette Stokes; Costumes, Gail

Cooper-Hecht; Music Director, Elaina Cope; Cast: Laura Daniel, Deborah Radloff, Alicia Sable, Omri Schein; January 16–27, 2008

THE WITLINGS by Frances Burney; Presented by Magis Theatre Company; Director, Deborah Philips; Set, Gian Marco Lo Forte; Costumes, Deb O; Lighting, Jeffrey Salzberg; Sound, Martha Goode; Cast: George Drance, Casey Groves, Erika Iverson, Wendy Mapes, Frank Mihelich, Rachel Benbow Murdy, Elizabeth Mutton, Gabriel Portuondo, Margi Sharp, Graham Skipper; May 16–June 1, 2008

Where Eagles Dare Theatre

MOTHERGUN by Christine Evan; Presented by Emergency Theater Project; Director, Joya Scott; Lighting, Eileen Goddard, Set/Costumes, Hannah Rose; Sound, Peter Wood; Cast: Danelle Eliav, Claro de los Reyes, David Roberts, Michael R. Rosete; June 4–27, 2007

NOSFERATU: The Morning of My Death Adapted by Stanton Wood from the film by F.W. Murnau and Bram Stoker's novel "Dracula"; Presented by Rabbit Hole Ensemble; Director/Lighting, Edward Elefterion; Stage Manager, Kelly Aliano; Cast: Jenna Kalinowski, Matthew Cody, Paul Daily, Emily Hartford, David Miceli, Danny Ashkenasi; July 17–August 5, 2007

DORM STORIES by Sarah-Violet Bliss; Presented by 4th Meal Productions; Director, Paul Moser; August 10–18, 2007

THE GREATEST STORY NEVER TOLD Written and directed by Michael Licwinko; Stage Manager, Marissa Bea; Cast: Janelle Mims, Billy Mitchell, Simcha Borenstein, Breanna Lee, Michael Licwinko; October 10–November 4, 2007

GUNS, SHACKLES & WINTER COATS Written, designed and directed by M. Stefan Strozier; Produced by La Muse Venale; Stage Manager, Sean Manning; Cast: Chris McGuire, Abigail Ziaja, Jeff Lyons, Evelyn Voura, Alfredo Diaz, Richard Essig, Robbie Rescigno, Sean Manning; October 25–November 18, 2007

ANIMALS R US Presented by The Playwrights/Actors Contemporary; November 6–15, 2007

BARCINDA FOREST by Janeen Stevens; Director, Barry Gomolka; Set, Hoyt Charles; Lighting, Hillery Makatura; Costumes, Georgien; Cast: James A. Clark, Sean Demers, Johnny Ferro, Erin Fogel, Ashley Noel Jones, Manny Llyes, Elda Luisi, Jorge Tapia, Mary Trotter; April 16–May 3, 2008

The Wild Project

ACTORS ARE F*@#ING STUPID by Ian McWethy; Presented by Push Productions; Director, Michael Kimmel; Set/Lighting, Ban Kato; Costumes, Jessical Gaffney; Cast: Tom Escovar, Josh LaCasse, Roger Lirtsman, Susan Maris, Carrie McCrossen, Heidi Niedermeyer; February 15–March 22, 2008

THE CREDITORS by August Strinburg; Presented by Miscreant Theatre; Sets, Lee Savage; Cast: Jacob Knoll, Tracy Liz Miller, Jeff Barry; March 26–April 6, 2008

Wings Theatre Company

Artistic Director, Jeffrey Corrick; Managing Director, Robert Mooney

AUNTIE MAYHEM by David Pumo; Co-produced by Gato Flaco Productions; Director, Donna Jean Fogel; Set, Florencio Flores Palomo; Songs, Lisa Gold; Lighting, Michael Megliola; Fight Choreographer, Kymberli Morris; PSM, Shuhei Sho; Cast: Moe Bertran, Ivan Davila, Mark Finley, Carl Ka-Ho Li, Jason Luna Flores, André Darnell Myers; September 6–29, 2007

DIMAGGIO – The Man Behind the Myth Book, music and lyrics by Robert Mitchell; Director/Choreography, Don Johnason; Costumes, Marietta Clark; Lighting, Robert Weinstein; Cast: Christopher Vettel, Michael Basile, Pamela Brumley, John Moss, Alissa Alter, Peter Carrier, Andrew Claus, Joe Cummings, Anna Hanson, Robert Kalman, Stephanie Martinez, Matthew Naclerio, Stephen Nichols; November 29–December 22, 2007

CAROL CHANNING IN CONCERT Created and performed by Richard Skipper; Director, Miles Phillips; Music Director/Pianist, Paul L. Johnson; Musicians: Chris Clement (percussion), Brian Grochowski (bass); Choreography, Tracy Wilson; Set/Lighting, Wheeler Kincaid; Vocalists: Rocco Larrico, Michael Hopewell, Kristopher Monroe; January 19–February 16, 2008

QUESTA by Victor Bumbalo; Director, Jeffrey Corrick; Sets, Elisha Schaefer; Lighting, Anthony Galaska; Costumes, Laura Kleeman; Cast: Krista Amigone, Dana Benningfield, Jason Alan Griffin, John Haggerty, Jeremiah Maestas, G. Alverez Reid, Danny Wildman; February 23–March 22, 2008

DUTCH COURAGE Music and lyrics by Sean Peter, book by Barry Lowe; Director/Choreography, Fred C.L. Mann III; Cast: Kenny Wade Marshall, Daryl Brown, Frank Galgano, Jared Joplin, Matthew Napoli, Matthew Burton, Dustin Tyler Moore, Daniel Moser, Ben Strothmann; May 23–June 21, 2008

Partner Productions

PIOUS POETIC PIE by Yubelky Rodriguez; Produced by Fluid Motion Theater & Film; Director, Christine Simpson; AD/Stage Manager, Sarah Ford; Producer, Michelle Chen; Cast: Darian Dauchan, Erinina Marie Ness, Jose Joacquin Perez, Celli Pitt, Yubelky Rodriguez, Carolyn Michelle Smith, Rick Younger; April 18–19, 2008

THE RAREST OF BIRDS Written and directed by John Lisbon Wood; Presented by The Gallery Players & Engine 37; Based on the life and works of Montgomery Clift; Music and lyrics by Howard Goodall; Stage Manager, Stefanie Tara; Cast: Omar Prince; June 1–July 4, 2008

DANCE AT BATAAN Written and directed by Blake Bradford; Presented in association with Phare Play Productions; Assistant Director, Brooklyn Scalzo; Stage Manager, Bridget Halloran; ASMs, Mary Brown & Taylor Fee; Costumes, Carrie Colden; Lighting, Mike Megliola; Sound, Kymm Zuckert; Fight Choreography, Matt Klan; Cast: Tamara Cacchione, Sarah Hankins, Jim Heaphy, Patrick McGhee, Annie Pesch, Jade Rothman, Christopher Simon, Christine Vinh, Michael Weems; June 28–July 26, 2008

Non-resident Productions

ENGAGEMENT Written and produced by Carolyn M. Brown, written and directed by Denise E. Womack; Presented by All in Black and White Productions; Lighting, Vanessa Wendt; Tech Director, Trisha Henson; Cast: Shanell Sapp, Lashambi Britton, Lorraine Mattox, Celiné Justice, Kianné Muschett, Candice A. Hassell, Jamil A. C. Mangan, Tyrone Saulsbury, Tim Romero, Stephanie Gilchrist; June 15–July 22, 2007

FALL SHORTS Presented by Phare Play; Included: *The War on Halloween* by Jonathan Joy, directed by Robyn; *The Spell that Always Works* written and directed by Kymm Zuckert; *The Boys at the IHOP* by Carl L. Williams, directed by Caitlin Davies; *Poisoned* by Kristyn Leigh Robinson, directed by Gregori Liosi; *Don't Eat the Neighbors* by Jennifer Spragg, directed by Kathryn Hnatio; *Deceased-o-logues* by Blake Bradford, Kymm Zuckert, Peggy Queener, Emily Cohen, Bekah Brunstetter; directed by Blake Bradford; October 13–17, 2007

ME, MYSELF, I AND THE OTHERS by Dachelle Damien; Presented by Wreckio Ensemble; Directors, Kimberlea Kressal and Dechelle Damien; October 22–November 4, 2007

FINDING THE DOORBELL Written and performed by Cindy Pierce; November 7–10, 2007

THE TEMPEST by William Shakespeare; Presented by Phare Play; Director, Blake Bradford; Cast: John Darling, Kerry Shear, Kendall Rileigh, Dolores Kenan, Marly Yost, Beth Adler, Kim Carlson, Susanne Gottesman-Traub, Kymm Zuckert, Dianna Lora, Sara Strasser, Sarah Hankins, Alexandra Devin, Carrie Colden, Amanda Knox, Elizabeth English; December 28, 2007– January 12, 2008

FAT KIDS ON FIRE by Bekah Brunstetter; Presented by Phare Play; Director, Karen M. Dabney; Cast: Noelle Fair, Matt Farabee, Mark Garkusha, Maggie Hamilton, Kayla Kuzbel, Rachel Lin, Erin McCarson, Faye Rex and Ryan Serhant; January 26–February 6, 2008

Working Man's Clothes Productions

Co-Founder and Artistic Director, Isaac Byrne; Co-Founder and Executive Director, Jared Culverhouse

PENETRATOR by Anthony Nielsen; Director, Jeremy Torres; Score/Sound, Adam Smith; Dramaturg, Bekah Brunstetter; Set, Ace Eure; Costumes, Candace Thompson; Lighting, Jake Platt; Cast: Cole Wimpee, Jared Culverhouse, Michael Mason; American Place Theater; June 2–23, 2007

SECOND ANNUAL BINGE FESTIVAL Writers: Paul John DeSena, Jennie Berman Eng, Elizabeth Emmons, Kyle Jarrow, Eric Sanders, Casey Wimpee. Directors: Tom Bonner, Matthew Hancock, Karen Dabney, Kara Ayn Napolitano, Julie Rossman, Gia Forakis; Special Guests: Carla Rhodes, Greg Walloch, Natasha Schull, Vanessa Sparling, Steven Gillenwater, Clay McLeod Chapman, Ronald Pelican, Burlesque Dancers Lil Miss Lixx and Scarlet O'Gasm, the girls of CUDZOO, Stumblebum Brass Band; Jimmy's Number 43, September 7–15, 2007

I USED TO WRITE ON WALLS by Bekah Brunstetter; Directors, Isaac Byrne and Diana Basmanjian; Producer, Jared Culverhouse; Production Manager, Will Neuman; Set, April Bartlett; Costumes, Candice Thompson; Music, Randy Garcia; Cast: Maggie Hamilton, Darcie Champagne, Levita Shaurice, Jeff Berg, Chelsey Shannon, Rachel Dorman, Mary Round, Ellen David; Gene Frankel Theatre; October 11–27, 2007

THIRTY–SEVEN STONES (or the Man Who Was a Quarry) by Mark Charney; Director, Will Neuman; Set, Jessica Parks; Sound, David Ogle; Cast: Steven Strobel, Mary Round, Emily B. Murray, Ellen David, Dane Peterson; Looking Glass Theater; April 12–26, 2008

WorkShop Theatre

Artistic Director, Timothy Scott Harris; Executive Director, David Pincus

ONLY KIDDING! by Jim Geoghan; Director, Timothy Scott Harris; Stage Manager, Elliot Lanes; Cast: Trey Albright, Nelson Lugo, Bob Manus, Sean Singer; September 12–22, 2007

THE GIFTS OF THE MAGI & THE BLUE CARBUNCLE WITH SHERLOCK HOLMES Two one-acts adapted by Andrew Joffe from the stories by O. Henry and Sir Arthur Conan Doyle; Presented in association with JB Theatricals; Director, Kathleen Brant; Music Director, Jeffrey Buchsbaum; Set/Props, Sefani Nicole Oxman; Lighting, Lauren Duffie; Costumes, Anna Gerdes; Stage Manager, Michael Palmer; Press, Jonathan Slaff & Associates; Cast: *The Gift of the Magi:* Richard Kent Green, Jodie Bentley, Tyler Hollinger, Kate Andres, Jon Lonoff, Ken Linsk, Tom DelPizzo; *The Blue Carbuncle with Sherlock Holmes:* Todd Butera, Ken Linsk, Tyler Hollinger, Michael Gnat, Jodie Bentley, Bruce Barton, Kate Andres, Paul Singleton, Richard Kent Green, Jon Lonoff, Kelly Campbell; December 6–22, 2007

THE GUEST AT CENTRAL PARK WEST by Levy Lee Simon; Director, Thomas Cote; Set, Craig Napoliello; Lighting, Evan Purcell; Cotumes, Joanie Schumacher; Stage Manager, Michael Palmer; ASM, Malachy Orozco; Cast: Harvy Vlanks, Curt Bouril, Jed Dickson, Erinn Holmes, John Marshall Jones, Trish McCall, Tracy Newirth; February 20–March 15, 2008

Plays in Process

FRENCH KISSES 2007 Four short plays: *American Thighs* by Gary Giovannetti, directed by Manfred Bormann; *Cassiopeia* by Scott C. Sickles, directed by Timothy Scott Harris; *The Organist's Daughter* by William C. Kovacsik, directed by Tom Herman; *What I really Want to Say* by Alex Lewin, directed by David Gautschy; Cast: Alexandra Devin, Lori Faiella, Jeremy Feldman, Charles E. Gerber, John Jimerson, Riley Jones-Cohen, Cam Kornman, Jonathan Pereira, Linda Segal, Ben Sumrall, Jess Cassidy White; November 7–17, 2007

THE SIMPLE STORIES Adapted from the stories of Langston Hughes by Sandy Moore; Director/Conceiver, Charles E. Gerber; Cast: Sandy Moore; February 6–16, 2008

A BRUSH WITH GEORGIA O'KEEFE by Natlie Mosco; Director, Robert Kalfin; Producer, Briana Seferian; Stage Manager, Emily B. Compton; Composer/Sound, Margaret Pine; Set, Kevin Judge; Costumes, Gail Cooper-Hecht; Lighting, Paul Hudson; Projections, Marilys Ernst; Cast: Natalie Mosco, Virginia Roncetti, David Lloyd Walters; March 20–April 5, 2008

Non-resident Productions

THE NIGHT OF NOSFERATU by Stanton Wood, adapted from Bram Stoker; Presented by Rabbit Hole Ensemble; Director, Edward Elefterion; Lighting, Kevin Hardy; Makeup, Courtney Daily; PSM, Kelly Alliano; ASM, Cassie Dykes; Cast: Danny Ashkenasi, Matt W. Cody, Paul Daily, Tatiana Gomberg, Emily Hartford, Ned Massey; September 28–October 13, 2007

STRANGE SNOW by Stephen Metcalfe; Presented by the Eos Theater Company; Director, Jeff Cureton; October 27–November 4, 2007

BECAUSE OF BETH by Elana Gartner; Presented by Small Pond Entertainment; Director, Clara Barton Green; Set, Sean Tribble; Lighting, Solomon Weisbard; Stage Manager, Amanda Cynkin; Cast: Hyosun Choi, David Douglas, Susan Graham, George Raboni, Elizabeth Ruelas; January 9–20, 2008

DOMINO COURTS by William Hauptman; Director, Michael Mislove; Cast: Michele Ammon, Elizabeth Irene, Curtis Nielsen, Shade Vaughn; Main Stage; March 20–29, 2008

STILL LIVES by Paul Hancock; Presented by SP Theatre Productions; Director, Jocelyn Sawyer; Cast: Jerzy Gwiazdowski, Bridget Barkan, Candace Thaxton, Jeff Berg, Ashley Davis, Alixandra Liiv, Tim Intravia; April 4–19, 2008

CHERRY DOCS Written and directed by David Gow; Presented by Theatre of the Expendable; Set, Caleb Levengood; Lighting, Ryan Metzler; Costumes, Elizabeth Hammett; Stage Manager, Alexander Yakovleff; Press, Emily Owens; Cast: Mark Zeisler, Maximilian Osinski; April 24–May 18, 2008

Zipper Factory Theatre

CELEBRITY AUTOBIOGRAPHY: In Their Own Words Created by Eugene Pack; Cast: Jackie Hoffman, Cheyenne Jackson, Tony Roberts, Mary Testa, Kristen Johnston, Karen Ziemba, Richard Kind, Seth Rudetsky, Jack Plotnick, Dayle Reyfel, Eugene Pack; September 10 and October 15, 2007, March 3, 2008

DON'T QUIT YOUR NIGHT JOB Created and performed by Dan Lipton, Steve Rosen, David Rossmer, and Sarah Saltzberg, with special Broadway guests; Monthly, Opened November 15, 2007

BINDLESTIFF FAMILY CIRKUS WINTER CABARET Co-founded and starring Philomena and Kinko the Clown; March 2–30, 2008

INNER VOICES: Solo Musicals Three one-act solo performance musicals; included: *Tres Niñas* by Ellen Fitzhugh and Michael John LaChiusa; Director, Jonathan Butterell; Music Director, Todd Almond; Cast: Victoria Clark; *Alice Unwrapped* by Laura Harrington and Jenny Giering; Director, Jeremy Dobrish; Music Director, Julie McBride; Cast: Jennifer Damiano; *A Thousand Words Come to Mind* by Michele Lowe and Scott Davenport; Director, Jack Cummings III; Music Director, Jon DiPinto; Cast: Barbara Walsh; May 12–30, 2008

Additional Off-Off Broadway Productions

MURDERED BY THE MOB by Joni Pacie; Anro Ristorante Dinner Theater; Opened January 1, 1996; open run

MONDAY NIGHT MAGIC Presented by Magical Nights, Inc.; Theatre at St. Clements, transferred to Bleecker Street Theatre; Opened June, 1997; open run

BIRDIE'S BACHELORETTE PARTY by Mark Nassar, Denise Fennel and Suzanna Melendez; Culture Club; Opened July 19, 2002; open run

CHAMBER MAGIC With Steve Cohen; Waldorf Towers; Opened March 4, 2005; open run

ACCOMPLICE: The Village Written and produced by Tom and Betsy Salamon; Cast: Lauren Potter, Sarah Glendening, Joseph Luongo, John Cannatella, Joseph Tomasini, Brendan Irving, Sean Allison, Paolo Andino, Jeremy Banks, Kevin Lind; Mystery locations; Opened February 3, 2007; open run

ACCOMPLICE: New York Written and produced by Tom and Betsy Salamon; April 7–October 28, 2007

MADAME BOVARY Adaptation, music and lyrics by Paul Dick from the novel by Gustave Flaubert; Presented by PASSAJJ Productions; Director, Elizabeth Falk; Set, Brian Garber; Costumes, Noah Marin; Lighting, Tony Mulanix; Music Director, Russell Stern; Choreography, Melinda O'Brien; Stage Manager, Angela Theresa Collins; ASM, Mei Ling Acevedo;

Press, Eskay Public Relations; Cast: Meghann Babo, Tony Barton, Kyle Fichtman, Lauren Hauser, Steven Magnuson, Sarah McCullough, Nicholas Mongiardo-Cooper, Steven Patterson, Christopher Vettel; Theatre 5; June 1–17, 2007

SCARAB TALE by Sita Mani; Developed with Fay Simpson; Presented by Center for Remembering and Sharing and Dharma Road; Performed by Sita Mani and Sarita Chowdhury; CRS Theatre; June 8–16, 2007

BADGE by Matthew Schneck; Presented by BeaconNY Productions; Director, Jenn Thompson; Set, Brian Prather; Lighting, Bryan Keller; Sound, Stephen Kunken; Cast: Greg McFadden, Glynis Bell, Tara Falk, Darrell James; Rattlestick Theatre; June 15–July 1, 2007

ADVENTURES IN MATING Written by Joseph Scrimshaw; Director, Bree O'Connor; Cast (rotating): Steve W. Chappell (Jeffrey), Cesa Kobe-Smith (Miranda), Tom Lacey (The Waiter), Bree O'Connor (The Waiter), Sarah Paige (Miranda), Ben Perry (Jeffrey/The Waiter); Jimmy's No. 43; June 21, 2007–February 14, 2008

BEHIND THE LID by Lee Nagrin and Basil Twist; Silver Whale Gallery; June 3–28, 2007

THE LITTLE TRAGEDIES by Alexander Puskin, translated by Nancy K. Anderson; Director, Slava Stepnov; Choreography/Costumes, Katya Zhdanova; Set, Victor Pushkin; Cast: Tyree Giroux, Michael McKeogh, Robert Pivec, Giverny Petitmermet, John Nahigian, Jennifer Lee Snowden, Douglas Allen and Joy Lynn Andersen; Philip Coltoff Center; June 14–23, 2007

VOICES IN CONFLICT Created and performed by Sarah Anderson, Nick Basile, Erin Clancy, Afton Fleming, Devon Fontaine, Seth Koproski, Chris Kozlowski, Natalie Kropf, Nick Lanza, Cameron Scott Nadler, Jimmy Presson, Allie Rizzo, Tara Ross, Dagan Rossini, Taylor Telyan, Mike Ward; Vineyard Theatre; July 11–13, 2007

TIMES SQUARE THE MUSICAL Written and directed by John Dentanto; Presented by Jondee Productions; Co-director, Carlos Morales; Cast: Alison Bacewicz, Adam Pellegrine, Joan Vayda, Mark Unger, Izzy Durakovic, Coleen Guikoff, Preston Handy, Henry Lampert, Robert Mitchell, John Weigand; Sofia's Restaurant Downstairs Theatre; August 1–September 17, 2007

SEAPORT SUMMER THEATRE FESTIVAL Presented by Jeff Cohen; Included: Twelfth Night by William Shakespeare; Snapshots '07 One-acts presented by the Worth Street Theater Company; Late–Night Comedy featuring various performers; South Street Seaport August 2–26, 2007

BUCKLE MY SHOE, OR TERROR FIRMA Written and directed by Crystal Field; Coposer, Joseph Vernon Banks; various venues

JOHANNES DOKCHTOR FAUST by Vít Horejš; Presented by Czechoslovak-American Marionette Theatre; Cast: Deorah Beshaw, Michelle Beshaw, Jonathan Cross, Vít Horejš, JTheresa Linnihan; Bohemian National Hall; August 23–September 9, 2007

TENGO UN ARMA Written and performed by Alberto Sosa; Director, Adriana Millán; Marilyn Monroe Theatre; August 30–31, 2007

SONG FOR NEW YORK: What Women Do While Men Sit Knitting Texts by Migdalia Cruz, Maggie Dubris, Patricia Spears Jones, Karen Kandel, Imelda O'Reilly; Presented by Mabou Mines; Director, Ruth Maleczech; Music, Lisa Gutkin; Various locations on the East River; August 31–September 9, 2007

CYMBELINE by William Shakespeare; Presented by the New York Neo-Classical Ensemble; Director, Michael Bartelle; Set, Jesse Sideman; Costumes, Campbell Ringel; Cast: Teddy Alvaro, Jessica Jade Andres, Matthew roi Berger, Kimberly DiPersia, Richard Douglas, Cale Krise, Beth Lopes, Matthew Meixler, Steven Smith, Stephen Stout, Randy Thompson, Gillian Wiggin; 37 Arts; September 5–9, 2007

ONE MILLION FORGOTTEN Presented by The National Theater of the United States; 38 Park Row; September 11–16, 2007

PEACE by Aristophanes; Presented by the Mettawee River Theatre Company; Director/Design, Ralph Lee; Cast: Angela DiVeglia, Kim Gambino, Kevin Lawler, Jan-Peter Pedross, Tom Marion, Clea Rivera; Musicians: Ian Antonio, Sam Kulik; Garden at Cathedral of St. John the Divine; September 7–16, 2007

GAUGUIN/SAVAGE LIGHT Written and performed by George Fischoff; Studio 353; September 26, 2007–July 27, 2008

THE BEEBO BRINKER CHRONICLES by Moria Ryan and Linda S. Chapman; Presented by The Hourglass Group (Elyse Singer, Carolyn Baeumler, Nina Hellman); Director, Leigh Silverman; Set, Rachel Hauck; Lighting, Nicole Pearce; Costumes, Theresa Squire; Sound, Jill BC DuBoff; Props, Tessa Dunning; Cast: David Greenspan, Carolyn Baeumeler, Autumn Dornfeld, Marin Ireland, Anna Foss Wilson, Bill Dawes; October 1–28, 2007 (subsequently transferred Off-Broadway to 37 Arts)

THE "LADIES" OF AVIGNON by Jaime Salom, translated by Charles Philip Thomas; Director/Design/Producer, Angel Gil Orrios; Associate Director, Hector Luis Rivera; Masks, Jane Stein; Cast: Soledad Lopez, Kathy Tejada, Coco Nuñez, Ivette Oliveras, Angela Perez, Lorena Jorge; Raul Julia; Thalia Spanish Theater; October 5–November 11, 2007

THE CHAOS THEORIES Written and co-directed by Alexander Dinelaris; Presented by Shotgun Productions in association with The Resistance Theatre Company and MILJam Productions; Co-Director, Stewart M. Schulman; Assistant Director, Mariel Goddu; Set, Tema L. Staig; Lighting, David A. Griffith; Costumes, Bobby Pearce; Casting, Jaon Lynn;

Stage Manager, Carol A. Sullivan; TD, Quinn K. Stone; Cast: Richard Bekins, Max Darwin, Alison Fraser, Ted Koch, Amanda Mantovani, Todd Gearhart, Darcie Siciliano, Maryann Towne; McGinn/Cazale Theatre; October 25–November 17, 2007

THE TRICKY PART Written and performed by Martin Moran; Gerald Lynch Theater at John Jay College; October 26, 2007

CARL THE SECOND by Marc Palmieri; Presented by Phare Play; Director, Christine Viny; Cast: Scott Morales, Tamara Cacchione, Steve Nelson, Amber Ford, Alex Moshofsky, Christopher Simon, Adam Souza; The Independent Theatre; November 1–11, 2008

BEYOND BRECHT by Ed Malin, Les Hunter, Felipe Ossa, Maria Micheles, Chris Force, Marcy Wallabout, Jerry Polner, and Will Cordeiro; Presented by Brooklyn Playwrights Collective; Cast: Richard West, Lissa Moira, Peter Dizozza, Joe Bendik, Johnathan Zalben, Jason Ellis, Margot Lee Sherman, Lauren O'Brien, Amelia June; November 1–17, 2007

CIRQUE DU SOLEIL: Wintuk Theatre at Madison Square Garden; November 1–January 6, 2008

ODE TO THE MAN WHO KNEELS Written and directed by Richard Maxwell; Presented by New York City Players and Piece by Piece Productions; Sets/Lighting, Sascha Van Riel; Costumes, Troy Vazquez; Dramaturge, Tom King; Cast: Jim Fletcher, Anna Kohler, Emily Cass McDonnell, Greg Mehrten, Brian Mendes; Wooster Group's Performing Garage; November 1–December 2, 2007

HAMLET, PRINCE OF DENMARK by William Shakespeare; Presented by the Czechoslovakian-American Marionette Theatre; Director, Vit Horejs, Pavel Dobrusky; Costumes, Magdelana Vavakova, Theresa Linnihan; Set and Lighting, Pavel Dobrusky; Cast: Josh Adler, Nat Cassidy, Deborah Beshaw, Vit Horejs, Theresa Linnihan; Jane's Carousel in DUMBO; November 1–26, 2007

4.48 PSYCHOSIS by Sarah Kane; Director, Christine Vartoughian; Presented by An Awkward Society; Sound, Andrew Armstrong; Cast: Christine Vartoughian, Marian Brock, Maria Oppedisano; Instrument Corporation of Brooklyn, November 2–12, 2007

BOTTOMLESS by Kellie Ahrens; Director, Denyse Owens; Presented by RVLP Productions; Bowery Poetry Club; November 3–24, 2007

URGE Translated by Hans Moennig from Der Drang Franz Xaver Kroetz; Presented by Spring Theatreworks; Director, Jeffrey Horne; Cast: Tony Naumovski, Karen Forte, Jonathan Stemmler, Erin Treadway; November 28–December 8, 2007

THE BUDDHA: In His Own Words Written and performed by Evan Brenner; December 12, 2007–June 28, 2008

LOS NUTCRACKERS: A Christmas Carajo by Charles Rice-Gonzalez; Director, Jorge Merced; Cast: Jonathan Cedano, Gabriel Morales, Orlando Rios, Cisco Perez, Carlos Valencia, Appolonia Cruz; Bronx Academy of Arts and Dance; December 6–15, 2007

JAMES BALDWIN: Down from the Mountain Top Written and performed by Calvin Levels; Schomburg Center for Research in Black Culture; December 7–9, 2007

OF ALL THE PEOPLE IN THE WORLD: USA Presented by Stan's Café (UK); Cast: Alison Carney, Amanda Hadingue, Jake Oldershaw, Karen Stafford, Craig Stephens, James Yarker, Natasha Giliberti, Adam Walck; World Financial Center; January 9–20, 2008

AT THE HAND OF MY MOTHER Conceived and written by Wendy Ward; Presented by Ward Studio Company; Cast: Roni Yaniv, Merel Smitt, Megan Barno, Gina Galliano; January 12–April 5, 2008

GLIMPSES OF THE MOON Book and lyrics by Tajlei Levis, music by John Mercurio, based on the novel by Edith Wharton; Director, Marc Bruni; Choreography, Denis Jones; Set, Ted LeFevre; Costumes, Lisa Zinni; Lighting, Jim Milkey; Press, Katie Rosin; PSM, Carlos Maisonet; Cast: Beth Glover, Laura Jordan, Daren Kelly, Michael Minarik, Patti Murin, Glenn Peters; Guest Stars, Liz Larsen, KT Sullivan, Jana Robbins, Jane Summerhays, Susan Lucci, Joyce DeWitt; The Oak Room at the Algonquin; Mondays, January 21–March 10, 2008

THE GREAT NEBULA IN ORION Music by Kenneth Fuchs, based on a play by Lanford Wilson; Director, Wallace Norman; Musical Director, Michael Conley; Cast: Lynelle Johnson, Watson Heintz; Judson Memorial Church; January 25–February 2, 2007

THE BUTTERFLY by Charles Greenberg and Barbara Zinn Krieger, based on the book by Patricia Polacco; Presented by Making Books Sing; Director, David Schechter; Cast: Alyssa May Gold, Victoria Huston-Elem, Alexa Hozberger, Al Pagano, Gordon Stanely; January 28–February 15, 2008

THE ACTOR'S RAP! by J. Kyle Manzy; Cast: J. Kyle Manzy, Shaun Cruz, Vanessa Simmons, Michael Shawn, Ann Tripp, Deja Vu, Carmen Gill, Glenn Gordon, Willie Teacher, Lawrence Ballard, Melle Powers, Danny Camiel, Nina Daniels, Jordan Mahome; Engleman Recital Hall at Baruch PAC; January 31–March 1, 2008

3800 ELIZABETH by Aaron Baker and Frank Padellaro; Presented by The Welding Club; Cast: Michael Criscuolo, Peter Handy, Iracel River; Special Guests, Gyda Arber, Alexis Black, Becky Byers, Hope Cartelli, Bryan Enk, Ian W Hill, Heath Kelts, Christiaan Koop; The Battle Ranch; February 3–March 16, 2008

OPEN HOUSE by Aaron Landsman; Presented by The Foundary Theatre; Director, Melanie Joseph; Various living rooms in New York City; Cast: Heidi Schreck, Paul Willis, Raul Castillo; February 7–March 16, 2008

IN CIRCLES by Al Carmines and Gertrude Stein; Director/Design, John Sowle; Choreography, Jack Dyville; Cast: Paul

Boesing, Sarah Ferro, Meghan Hales, Michael Lazar, Paul Lincoln, Robin Manning, Noelle McGrath, Steven Patterson, Maureen Taylor, Anthony Wills Jr.; Judson Memorial Church; February 12–22, 2008

LADIES & GENTS Written and directed by Paul Walker; Presented by Irish Arts Center in association with Georganne Aldrich Heller and Semper Fi (Ireland); Cast: Sean Gormley, John Keating, David McDonald, Paul Nugent, John O'Callaghan, Laoisa Sexton; Central Park's Bethesda Fountain Toilets; March 17–29, 2008

STREET LIMBO BLUES Created and presented by Cruel Theatre; Director, Taurie Zalman Kinoshita; Café Pick Me Up; Cast: Nancy Randall, Erick Daniels, Samuel Burr, Josh Hunt, Jeremy Pippin, Chris Doi, Ebru Yonak, Scott Troost, Juan Carlos Rodriguez, Catherine Gasta, Vanessa Hardy, Sara Gaddis, Anthony Marks, Michael Auwusie, Jason Natale; March 27–May 18, 2008

SYNESTHESIA Presented by Electric Pear Productions; Participants: Gregory Stuart Edwards, Damian Lanigan, Peter Hapak, Nathan Phillips, Joe Schiappa, Brian Whiteley, Shanelle Gabriel, Clay McLeod Chapman, Jo-anne Lee, Leah Siegel, JayCeeOh, Avriel Hillman, Zac Lasher; Judson Memorial Church; April 2–6, 2008

Joshua Henry and Anika Larsen in Jaradoa Theater Company's Serenade *(photo by Ben Strothmann)*

THREE CALLA LILLIES by Abniel Marat; Presented by the Puerto Rican Traveling Theatre; Director, Josean Ortiz; Translation, Charles Philip Thomas; Set, Ann Bartek, Lighting, Wilburn Bonnell; Cast: Dalia Davi, Crystal Espinal, Elvira Franco, Gabriela Lugo, Sophia Angelica Nitkin, Susan Rybin; 47th Street Theatre; April 9–May 4, 2007

DARGELOS Written and performed by John Kelly; Bar 13; May 4–18, 2008

APPEARANCE – A Suspense in Being Created and directed by Carlo Altomare and Orietta Crispino; Presented by Theaterlab; Music, Carlo Altomare and Joerg Burger; Film, Jeanne Liotta; Cast: Liza Cassidy, Joy Lynn Anderson, Orietta Crispino, Jeanine T. Abraham; May 6–17, 2008

[EXTINGUISH] Written and performed by Ezra LeBank; Presented by Lynx Co; EJ Studio Theatre; May 9–24, 2008

DON'T WORRY, BE JEWISH Concept, book and direction by Mark Kleyner, music and lyrics by Alexander Butov and Brian Starr, translation by Julie Burke; Promise Theatre; Presented by Children's Talent Development Fund; Cast: Lawrence Benin, Kristina Biddle, Alexa Burger, Lauren Dennis, Justin Hall, Tyler Hall, Natalya Khmaryuk, Nathan Kay, Elina Raklin, Elan Kvitko, Simona Meynekhdrun, Jasmine Petraru, Kailand Novak, Mitchell Sapoff; May 10–June 4, 2008

Maggie Hamilton in Working Man's Clothes Productions' I Used to Write on Walls *at the Gene Frankel Theatre (photo by Cole Wimpee)*

Illinois Theatre Center: *Howie Hohnson, Mark Stegman, Bernard Rice, Tucker Curtis, Peter Robel in* That Championship Season *(photo by Warren Skalski)*

Paper Mill Playhouse: *Charlotte Booker, Kelly Bishop, Monique Fowler, Beth Fowler, Kelly Sullivan, and Kate Wetherhead in* Steel Magnolias *(photo by Gerry Goodstein)*

Laguna Playhouse: *Myk Watford, Mark Baczynski, Regan Southard, Van Zeiler, and Stephen G. Anthony in* Hank Williams: Lost Highway *(photo by Ed Krieger)*

The Old Globe: *Leslie Kritzer, Matt Cavenaugh, Lori Wilner, Harvey Fierstein, Tom Wopat, and Philip Hoffman in the World Premiere of* A Catered Affair *(photo by Craig Schwartz)*

Goodspeed Musicals: *Stephen Bienskie and the Cast of* High Button Shoes *(photo by Diane Sobolewski)*

Guthrie Theater: *Mark Rylance and Miriam Silverman with Jonas Goslow, Jim Lichtscheidl and Richard Ooms in* Peer Gynt *(photo by Michal Daniel)*

Professional Regional Companies

Arena Stage: *Tijuana T. Ricks, Terry Burrell, Cheryl Alexander, Shelley Thomas, Tina Fabrique and Marva Hicks in* The Women of Brewster Place *(photo by Scott Suchman)*

The Cleveland Playhouse: *Rachel Warren, Philip Hernández, and Jamie LaVerdiere in* Man of La Mancha *(photo by Roger Masteoianni)*

Goodman Theatre: *Meghan Andrews and Lois Smith in* The Trip to Bountiful *(photo by Michael Brosilow)*

McCarter Theatre Center: *Tyne Daly and Brian Murray in the world premiere of Edward Albee's* Me, Myself & I *(photo by T. Charles Erickson)*

Repertory Theatre of St. Louis: *Darryl Reuben Hall and the Company of* Kiss Me, Kate *(photo by Jerry Naunheim, Jr.)*

Theatre Under the Stars: *The Touring Cast of* The 25th Annual Putnam County Spelling Bee *(photo by Joan Marcus)*

ACT – A Contemporary Theatre

Seattle, Washington

FORTY-THIRD SEASON

Artistic Director, Kurt Beattie

THE CLEAN HOUSE by Sarah Ruhl; Director, Allison Narver; Set, Matthew Smucker; Costumes, Frances Kenny; Lighting, Michael Wellborn; Sound/Composer, Eric Chappelle; Choreographer, Wade Madsen; Dialects, Judith Shahn; SM, Jeffrey K. Hanson; ASM, Nora Menkin; Cast: Anne Allgood (Virginia), Suzanne Bouchard (Lane), Christine Calfas (Matilde), Allen Fitzpatrick (Charles/Man), Priscilla Hake Lauris (Ana/Woman); Allen Theatre; March 30–April 29, 2007

SOUVENIR by Stephen Temperley; Director, R. Hamilton Wright; Set, Edie Whitsett; Costumes, Marcia Dixcy Jory; Lighting, Rick Paulsen; Sound, Ron Geier; Musical Director, D.J. Gommels; SM, JR Welden; Production Assistant, Jaime Soulé; Assistant Lighting, Lynne Ellis; Cast: Mark Anders (Cosme McMoon), Patti Cohenour (Florence Foster Jenkins); Falls Theatre; May 11–June 10, 2007

STUFF HAPPENS by David Hare; Director, Victor Pappas; Set, Robert A. Dahlstrom; Costumes, Catherine Hunt; Lighting, Mary Louise Geiger; Sound, Dominic Cody Kramers; Dialects, Alyssa Keene; SM, Jeffrey K. Hanson; ASM, JR Welden; Cast: Mathew Ahrens (Alastair Campbell/Jeremy Greenstock/ Ensemble), Julie Briskman (Palestinian Academic/Brit in New York/Ensemble), Mark Chamberlin (Tony Blair), Frank Corrado (Donald Rumsfeld), Peter Crook (David Manning/ Angry Journalist/Michael Gerson/Ensemble), Charles Dumas (Colin Powell), John Farrage (John Negroponte/Iraqi Exile/ Ensemble), Tim Gouran (Jonathan Powell/Jean-David Levitte/ Ensemble), Tracy Michelle Hughes (Condoleezza Rice), Mark Jenkins (Hans Blix/Jack Straw/Ensemble), Marianne Owen (Laura Bush/New Labour Politician/Ensemble), Larry Paulsen (Paul Wolfowitz/Sir Richard Dearlove/Ensemble), David Pichette (Dominique de Villepin/Jeremy Paxman/Ensemble), Michael Winters (Dick Cheney), R. Hamilton Wright (George W. Bush), Richard Ziman (George Tenet/John McCain/ Ensemble); Allen Theatre; June 22–July 22, 2007

FIRST CLASS by David Wagoner; Director, Kurt Beattie; Set, Carey Wong; Costumes, Deb Trout; Lighting, Rick Paulsen; Sound, Eric Chappelle; SM, Michael B. Paul; Production Assistant, Jaime Soulé; Assistant Director, Christine Sumption; Assistant Lighting, Ashley Born; Cast: John Aylward (Theodore Roethke); Falls Theatre; July 27–August 26, 2007

THE MOJO AND THE SAYSO by Aishah Rahman; Director, Valerie Curtis-Newton; Set, Jennifer Zeyl; Costumes, Melanie Taylor Burgess; Lighting, Michael Wellborn; Sound, Chris R. Walker; SM, JR Welden; ASM, Nora Menkin; Assistant Lighting, Lynne Ellis; Cast: Tracy Michelle Hughes (Awilda), Lindsay Smiling (Acts), Jose A. Rufino (Blood), Timothy McCuen Piggee (Pastor); Allen Theatre; August 31–September 30, 2007

THE WOMEN by Clare Boothe Luce; Director, Warner Shook; Set, Matthew Smucker; Costumes, David Zinn; Lighting, Mary Louise Geiger; Original Music, Michael Roth; SM, Jeffrey K. Hanson; Cast: Anne Allgood (Edith Potter), Suzanne Bouchard (Mary Haines), Julie Briskman (Sylvia Fowler), Emily Cedergreen (Peggy Day), Deborah Fialkow (Miriam Aarons), Peggy Gannon (Ensemble), Elizabeth Huddle (Mrs. Morehead), Elise Hunt (Jane), Suzy Hunt (Countess de Lage), Anne Kennedy (Ensemble), Laura Kenny (Lucy), Jennifer Lyon (Crystal Allen), Marianne Owen (Maggie), Megan Schutzler (Little Mary), Annette Toutonghi (Olga), Susanna Wilson (Nancy Blake); Falls Theatre; October 5–December 16, 2007

A CHRISTMAS CAROL by Charles Dickens; adapted by Gregory A. Falls; Director, R. Hamilton Wright; Set, Shelley Henze Schermer; Costumes, Deb Trout; Lighting, Michael Wellborn; Sound/Music Director, Eric Chappelle; Original Sound, Steven M. Klein; Choreographer, Wade Madsen; Dialects, Alyssa Keene; SM, JR Welden; ASM, Nora Menkin; Cast: Mark Chamberlin or David Pichette (Scrooge), Ian Bell (Gentleman #1/Mr. Fezziwig/Grocer/Topper/Businessman #1), Amelia Rose Brummel (Belinda Cratchit/Fan), Lisa Carswell (Mrs. Cratchit/Dancer), Brandon Engman (Charles Cratchit/Master Fezziwig), Lindsay Evans (Belle/Niece), Allen Fitzpatrick (Marley/Poor Man/Old Joe), Erika Godwin (Spirit #1/Party Guest/Charwoman), Madison Avery Gordon (Martha Cratchit/Dancer), Analiese Guettinger (Tiny Tim/ Want), Leslie Law (Mrs. Dilber/Mrs. Fezziwig/Sugar Plum Seller/Sister), Izabel Mar Elizabeth Cratchit/Lil Fezziwig/ Ignorance), George Mount (Middle Scrooge/Robin Crusoe/ Beggar/Party Guest/Businessman #2), Galen Joseph Osier (Bob Cratchit/Dancer), Nick Robinson (Singing Thief/ Undertaker's Assistant/Turkey Boy), MJ Sieber (Fred/Dick Wilkins/Bread Lady/Spirit #3), Jeremy Weizenbaum (Peter Cratchit/Young Scrooge), Richard Ziman (Gentleman #2/ Spirit #2/Ragpicker); Allen Theatre; November 23–December 24, 2007

Actors Theatre of Louisville

Louisville, Kentucky

FORTY-FOURTH SEASON

Artistic Director, Marc Masterson; Managing Director, Jennifer Bielstein

Pamela Brown Auditorium

FIRE ON THE MOUNTAIN by Randal Myler and Dan Wheetman; Director, Randal Myer; Set, Vicki Smith; Costumes, Marcia Dixcy Jory; Lighting, Don Darnutzer; Sound, Matt Calllahan; Props, Jolene Oberlin; Musical Director, Dan Wheetman; Cast: Molly Andrews, Mark Baczynski, "Mississippi" Charles Bevel, Margaret Bowman, Jason Edwards, A.J. Glaser, Lee Morgan, Mike Regan, Ed Snodderly; August 28–September 23, 2007

THE UNDERPANTS Adapted by Steve Martin from the play by Carl Sternheim; Director, BJ Jones; Set, Paul Owen; Costumes, Lorraine Venberg; Lighting, Brian J. Lilienthal; Sound, Benjamin Marcum; Props, Mark Watson; Cast: Triney Sandoval (Theo Maske), Bethany Caputo (Louise Maske), Brandy Zarle (Gertrude Duter), Jonathan Hammond (Frank Versati), Tony Hoty (Klinglehoff), Michael Keyloun (Benjamin Cohen), Anthony R. Haigh (A Friend); October 2–27, 2007

A CHRISTMAS CAROL by Charles Dickens, adapted by Barbara Field; Director, Sean Daniels; Sets, Paul Owen; Costumes, Lorraine Venberg; Lighting, Deb Sullivan; Sound, Matt Callahan; Properties, Doc Manning and Mark Walston; Cast: William McNulty (Scrooge), Mark J. Stringham (Bob Cratchit), Max Gordon Moore (Fred), David Hansbury (Marley/Young Marley/Grasper), Ann Hodapp (Mrs. Grigsby/Cook), Dara Jade Tiller (Ghost of Christmas Past/ Mrs. Blakely), Isaac J. Kresse (Boy Scrooge/Simon), Fred Major (Schoolmaster/Undertaker), Nathan Gregory (Young Ebenezer/Snarkers), Sarah Nealis (Belle/Mrs. Fred), Lelund Durond Thompson (Dick Wilkens/Topper), Immanuel Guest (Caroler/2nd Man/Pallbearer), Emily Scott (Fan/Martha Cratchit), Mark Sawyer-Dailey (Mr. Fezziwig/Old Joe), Katie Blackerby (Mrs. Fezziwig/Mrs. Dilber), Elizabeth Gilbert (Petunia Fezziwig/Dorothea), Teresa Wentzel (Marigold Fezziwig/Sophia), Chris Gaynor (Basil Fezziwig/Jeremiah/ Tom Cratchit), Jessica Lauren Howell (Belinda Cratchit/ Marjoram, Want), Christopher Scheer (Fezziwig Guest/Ghost of Christmas Future/1st Man), David Ryan Smith (Ghost of Christmas Present/Forrest), Sarah Grace Wilson (Mrs. Cratchit), Samuel Blackerby Weible (Tiny Tim/Ignorance), Bing Putney (Peter Cratchit/Billy/Fezziwig Child); Ensemble: Grey Alston, Danielle Gay, Jesimiel R. Jenkins, Andy Lutz, Yuko Takeda, Jose Urbino; November 21–December 23, 2007

THE CLEAN HOUSE by Sarah Ruhl; Director, Jon Jory; Set, Neil Patel; Costumes, Lorraine Venberg; Lighting, Brian J. Lilienthal; Sound, Matt Callahan; Props, Mark Walston; Cast: Felicity LaFortune (Lane), Alexandra Tavares (Matilde), Kate Goehring (Virginia), Bernard Burak Sheredy (Charles), Rae C. Wright (Ana); January 29–February 23, 2008

DOUBT by John Patrick Shanley; Director, Wendy C. Goldberg; Set, Todd Rosenthal; Costumes, Gordon DeVinney; Lighting, Josh Epstein; Sound/Original Music, Ryan Rumery; Props, Mark Walston; Cast: Ted Deasy (Father Brendan Flynn), Joy C. Hooper (Mrs. Muller), Caitlin O'Connell (Sister Aloysius), Makela Speilman (Sister James); April 16–May 11, 2008

MENOPAUSE THE MUSICAL Book and lyrics by Jeanie Linders, music by various; Director, Kathyn Conte; Choreography, Patty Bender; Set, Bud Clark; Lighting, Ryan Partridge and Jean-Yves Tessier; Sound, Gary Faller; Musical Director, Alan Plado; Cast: Laura Lee O'Connell/Ingrid Cole (Earth Mother), Marsha Waterbury/Laura Lee O'Connell (Iowa Housewife), Kathy St. George (Soap Star), Cynthia Jones (Professional Woman), Alex Ryer (Understudy); May 30–July 27, 2008

Bingham Theatre

Dracula by Hamilton Deane and John L. Balderston from Bram Stoker's novel, new adaptation and direction by William McNulty; Set, Paul Owen; Costumes, Lorraine Venberg; Lighting, Tony Penna; Sound, Benjamin Marcum; Props, Doc Manning, William Griffith; Video, Jason Czaja; Cast: David Ian Lee (Jonathan Harker), Jonathan Kells Phillips (Dr. Seward), William McNulty (Van Helsing), Marc Bovino (Renfield), Sarah Sexton (Ms. Sullivan), Nathan Gregory (Mr. Briggs), Sandra Struthers (Lucy), Misha Kuznetsov (Count Dracula), Undead Ensemble: Elizabeth Gilbert, Sophie C. Hill, Genisis Oliver, Dara Tiller; September 21–October 31, 2007

SPUNK Three tales by Zora Neale Hurston, adapted by George C. Wolfe; Music, Chic Street Man; Director, Seret Scott; Set, Paul Owen; Costumes, Lorraine Venberg; Lighting, Brian J. Lilienthal; Sound, Matt Callahan; Props, Doc Manning; Cast: Angela Karol Grovey (Blues Speak Woman), Keith Johnston (Guitar Man), Tracey Conyer Lee (Delia/Girl/Missie May), Avery Glymph (Jelly/Man on Joe Clark's porch), Billy Eugene Jones (Joe/Slang Talk Man/Man on Joe Clark's porch), Derric Harris (Sykes/Sweet Back); November 13–December 15, 2007

THE TEMPEST by William Shakespeare; Director, Marc Masterson; Original Music, Christian Frederickson, Gregory King, Jason Noble; Set, Paul Owen; Costumes, Lorraine Venberg; Lighting, Brian J. Lilienthal; Sound, Matt Callahan; Props, Mark Walston; Cast: Henry Woronicz (Prospero), Eric Bondoc (Ariel), Avery Glymph (Ferdinand), William McNulty (Antonio), Graham Smith (Gonzolo), David Alan Anderson (Sebastian), Ernest Perry, Jr. (Alonso), Jose Urbino (Boatswain), Jesimiel Jenkins (Master), Virginia Kull (Miranda), Jeffery V. Thompson (Caliban), Casey Greig (Trinculo), Aaron Munoz (Stephano), Christian Frederickson (Bracken), Gregory King (Thorn), Jason Noble (Tangle); January 2–February 2, 2008

Victor Jory Theatre

HEDWIG AND THE ANGRY INCH Text by John Cameron Mitchell, music and lyrics by Stephen Trask; Director, Sean Daniles; Sets, Michael B. Raiford; Costumes, Lorraine Venberg; Lighting, Brian J. Lilienthal; Sound, Matt Callahan; Props, Mark Walston; Musical Director, Jon Spurney; Puppets, Dan Kerr-Hobart, Bernie McGovern; Cast: David Hansbury (Hedwig/ Tommy Gnosis), Angela Motter (Yitzhak/Bass), Scott Anthony (Schlatko/Lead Guitar), Jeff McAllister (Jacek/Drums), Jon Spurney (Skszp); September 11–30, 2007

THE SANTALAND DIARIES by David Sedaris, adapted by Joe Mantello; Director, Sean Daniels; Set, Paul Owen; Costumes, Susan Neason; Lighting, Tony Penna; Sound, Benjamin Marcum; Props, Joe Cunningham; Cast: Oliver Wadsworth (David); October 31–December 30, 2007

A TUNA CHRISTMAS by Jaston Williams, Joe Sears and Ed Howard; Director, Russell Treyz; Sets, Paul Owen; Costumes, John P. White; Lighting, Tony Penna; Sound, Benjamin

Marcum; Properties, Joe Cunningham; SM, Kathy Preher; Cast: Jody Cook (Thurston Wheelis et al.), Diane Wasnak (Arles Struvie et al.); November 22, 2007–January 2, 2008

TOPDOG/UNDERDOG by Suzan-Lori Parks; Director, Will MacAdams; Set, Mikiko Suzuki MacAdams; Costumes, Lorraine Venberg; Lighting, Brian J. Lilienthal; Sound, Benjamin Marcum; Props, Doc Manning; Cast: Stephen Tyrone Williams (Booth), Don Guillory (Lincoln); January 17–February 3, 2008

32nd Annual Humana Festival of New American Plays – February 24–March 30, 2008

GREAT FALLS by Lee Blessing; Director, Lucie Tiberghien; Set, Paul Owen; Costumes, Lorraine Venberg; Lighting, Brian J. Lilienthal; Sound, Matt Callahan; Props, Doc Manning; Cast: Tom Nelis (Monkey Man), Halley Wegryn Gross (Bitch); Bingham Theatre

BECKY SHAW by Gina Gionfriddo; Director, Peter DuBois; Set, Paul Owen; Costumes, Jessica Ford; Lighting, Brian J. Lilienthal; Sound, Benjamin Marcum; Props, Mark Walston; Cast: Mia Barron (Suzanna Slater), David Wilson Barnes (Max Garrett), Janis Dardaris (Susan Slater), Davis Duffield (Andrew Porter), Annie Parisse (Becky Shaw); Bingham Theatre

THIS BEAUTIFUL CITY by Steven Cosson and Jim Lewis, music and lyrics by Michael Friedman, from interviews by The Civilians; Director, Steven Cosson; Choreography, Chase Brock; Set/Video, Debra Booth; Costumes, Lorraine Venberg; Lighting, Deb Sullivan; Sound, Matt Callahan; Props, Adriane Binky Donley; Cast: Marsha Stephanie Blake, Dori Legg, Brad Herberlee, Stephen Plunkett, Emily Ackerman, Ian Brennan; Ensemble: Elizabeth Gilbert, Katie Gould, Andy Lutz, Bing Putney, Ashley Robinson, Matthew Sa; Pamela Brown Auditorium

the break/s by Marc Bamuthi Joseph; Director, Michael John Garcés; Set, Michael B. Raiford; Costumes, Jessica Ford; Lighting, Brian J. Lilienthal; Original Music, Ajayi Jackson; Props, Doc Manning; Video, David Szalsa; Cast: Marc Bamuthi Joseph, DJ Excess, Tommy Shepherd aka Soulati; Bingham Theatre

ALL HAIL HURRICANE GORDO by Carly Mensch; Director, Sean Daniels; Set, Paul Owen; Costumes, Lorraine Venberg; Lighting, Deb Sullivan; Sound, Matt Callahan; Props, Mark Walston; Cast: Matthew Dellapina (Chaz), Patrick James Lynch (Gordo), Tracee Chimo (India), William McNulty (Oscar); Victory Jory Theatre

NEIGHBORHOOD 3: Requisition of Doom by Jennifer Haley; Director, Kip Fagan; Set, Michael B. Raiford; Costumes, Jessica Ford; Lighting, Brian J. Lilienthal; Sound, Benjamin Marcum; Props, Doc Manning; Cast: John Leonard Thompson (steve/doug/tobias), Kate Hampton (leslie/vicki/barbara/joy), Robin Lord Taylor (trevor/ryan/jared/zombiekllr14/blake), Reyna DeCourcy (makaela/kaitlyn/madison/chelsea), William McNulty (walkthroughs); Victor Jory Theatre

Bill of Four Ten Minute Plays: *Tongue Tied* by M. Thomas Cooper; *Dead Right* by Elaine Jarvik; *In Paris You Will Find Many Baguettes but Only One True Love* by Michael Lew; *One Short Sleepe* by Naomi Wallace; Pamela Brown Auditorium

GAME ON by Zakiyyah Alexander, Rolin Jones, Alice Tuan, Daryl Watson, Marisa Wegryzn, Ken Weitzman, music and lyrics by Jon Spurney; Director, Will MacAdams; Bingham Theatre

Alabama Shakespeare Festival

Montgomery, Alabama

THIRTY-SIXTH SEASON

Producing Artistic Director, Geoffrey Sherman

MENOPAUSE THE MUSICAL Book and lyrics by Jeanie Linders; Director, Kathryn Conte; Choreographer, Patty Bender; Set, Bud Clark; Lighting, Ryan Patridge; Sound, Gary Faller; Musical Director, Alan Plado; SM, Ellen Jones; Production Assistant, Michele Fugate; Cast: Nyree Martinez (Soap Opera Star), Paula Estess (Iowa Housewife), Judy Dery (Earth Mother), Fredena Williams/Monique Whittington (Professional Woman), Lisa Harris (Understudy); Festival Stage; Summer 2007

CROWNS by Regina Taylor; adapted from the book by Michael Cunningham and Craig Marberry; Director, Janet Cleveland; Costumes, Susan Branch; Lighting, Anne Marie Duggan; Sound, Brett Rominger; Musical Director, Bill Sims Jr.; SM, Tanya J. Searle: Cast, Margo Moorer (Jeanette), Jenelle Lynn Randall (Velma), Afton Williamson (Yolanda), Fredena J. Williams (Mabel), James Bowen (Man), Laiona Michelle (Wanda), Linda Boston (Mother Shaw); Octagon Stage; October 12–November 11, 2007

PETER PAN Based on the play by James M. Barrie, lyrics by Carolyn Leigh, music by Mark Charlap, additional music by Julie Styne, additional lyrics by Betty Comden and Adolph Green; Director, Geoffrey Sherman; Choreographer, Peggy Hickey; Costumes, Patrick Holt; Lighting, Phil Monat; Sound, Richelle Thompson; SM, Sara Lee Howell; Cast: Liz Pearce (Peter Pan), Rodney Clark (Mr. Darling/Captain Hook), Chevy Anz (Mrs. Darling), Meredith Hagner (Wendy), Reed Chisenhall, Cameron Morgan (John), Crispin South/Matthew Sailors (Michael), Sarah Thornton (Older Wendy/Mermaid) Lillian Wilson (Liza), Kraig Swartz (Smee), Olivia Policicchio (Tiger Lily), Anthony Napoletano (Slightly), Erin Webley (Tootles), Megan Grubel (Curly), Tara Siesener (Twin 1), Alison Frederick (Twin 2), Nick Lawson (Nana/Crocodile), Roger Preston Smith (Mullins/Indian), Ben Franklin (Starkey/ Indian), Adam Cates (Noodler/Indian), Roy Lightner (Jukes/ Indian), Timothy George Anderson (Raul/Indian), Cassie Abate (Indian/Mermaid), Sandy Draper/Laura McDaniel (Jane), David Dortch, Nathan Lange (Indians), Jerry Ferraccio,

Greg Foro (Pirates); Festival Stage; November 9-Decemeber 30, 2007

WINNIE THE POOH Adapted from the stories of A.A Milne, dramatized by le Clanche' du Rand; music by Allan J. Friedman; lyrics by A.A Milne and Kristen Sergel; additional lyrics by le Clanche' du Rand; Director, Nancy Rominger; Costumes, Rosa Lazaro; Lighting, Curtis Hodge; Sound, Richelle Thompson; Musical Director, Brett Rominger; SM, Kerrie Riber; Cast: Jarrod Yuskauskus (Pooh), Gregory Spradlin (Christopher Robbin), Matt Renskers (Rabbit), Chris Roe (Piglet), Corey Coleman (Roo), Graham Allen (Owl), Patrick Vest (Eeyore), Lauren Martin (Kanga); Octagon Stage; January 12–February 24, 2008

OVER THE TAVERN by Tom Dudzick; Director, Gavin Cameron-Webb; Costumes, Beth Novak; Lighting, Tom Rodman; Sound, Richelle Thompson; Dramaturg, Susan Willis; SM, Mark Leslie; Cast: Thomas Borrillo (Chet Pazinski), Greta Lambert (Ellen Pazinski), Seth Meriwether (Rudy), Trey Christopher (Georgie), Jeremy Rishe (Eddie), Elizabeth Bemis (Annie), Celia Howard (Sister Clarissa); Octagon Stage; March 7–April 6, 2008

ROMEO AND JULIET by William Shakespeare; Directors, Geoffrey Sherman and Diana Van Fossen, Set, Robert Wolin; Costumes, Beth Novak; Lighting, Lonnie Alcaraz, Sound, Richelle Thompson; SM, Tanya J. Searle; Cast: Larry Bull (Escalus), Anthony Marble (Mercutio), Christopher T. VanDijk (Paris), Jerry Ferraccio (Montague), Hollis McCarthy (Lady Montague/Masquer), Avery Clark (Romeo), Nathan Lange (Benvolio), David Dortch (Abram/an Apothecary/Member of the watch/Masquer), Sarah Walker Thornton (Beatrice/Masquer), Matt D'Amico (Capulet), Sarah Dandridge (Lady Capulet), Paul Nicholas (Tybalt), Chet Carlin (Capulet's cousin/Citizen of Verona), Annie-Marie Cusson (Nurse), Nick Lawson (Peter), Greg Foro (Sampson/Watch,/Servant), Afton Williamson (Regan/Watch/Masquer/Servant), Rodney Clark (Friar Laurence), Anthony Marble (Bodyguard to the Prince); Festival Stage; April 11–June 28, 2008

ROCKET CITY by Mark Saltzman; Director, David Ellenstien; Set, Michael Schweikardt; Costumes, Susan Branch; Lighting, Mike Post; Sound, Richelle Thompson; SM, Sara Lee Howell; Cast: Lori Prince (Amy Lubin), Fletcher McTaggart (Major Hamilton Pike Jr.), Daniel Cameron Talbott (Jed Kessler), Matthew Sullivan (Wehrner Von Braun), Kevin Mambo (Israel Watkins), Paul Hopper (Harry S. Truman/Benjy/Lemuel Decatur), Allen Rickman (General Barklee/Heinz Klauber/Rabbi), Greta Lambert (Susanna Pruitt/Sarah), Susanna Hay (Bertina Dupray/Euvella/Polly/Baroness Von Braun); Octagon Stage; April 18–May 18, 2008

CYMBELINE by William Shakespeare; Director, Geoffrey Sherman; Set, Robert Wolin; Costumes, Beth Novak; Sound, Richelle Thompson; Composer, James Conely; Movement, Denise Gabriel; Fight Director, Jason Armit; SM, Tanya J. Searle; Cast: Rodney Clark (Cymbeline), David Dortch (Cloten), Anthony Marble (Posthumus Leonatus), Avery Clark (Guiderius), Nathan Lange (Arviragus), Christopher T. VanDijk (Philario/Roman Captain), Matt D'Amico (Iachimo), J. Paul Nicholas (Caius Lucius), Larry Bull (Pisanio), Chet Carlin (Cornelius), Diana Van Fossen (Queen), Sarah Dandrige (Imogen), Sarah Walker Thorton (Helen), Annie-Marie Cusson (First Lady), Adriana Gaviria (Second Lady), Afton Williamson (Soothsayer), Greg Foro (British Captain 1/Lord 1), Matt Renskers (British Captain 2), Nick Lawson (Lord 2/Briton Lord), Chris Roe (Gaoler/Solider), Patrick Vest (Jupiter), Jerry Ferraccio (Sicilius/Attendant), Alison Frederick (Mother); Ensemble: Corey Coleman, Lauren Martin, Jarrod Yuskauskas, Greg Spradlin, Matt Renskers; Festival Stage; April 25–June 28, 2008

Alley Theatre

Houston, Texas

SIXTY-FIRST SEASON

Artistic Director, Gregory Boyd; Managing Director, Dean Gladden

DEATH ON THE NILE by Agatha Christie; Director, James Black; Set and Lighting, Kevin Rigdon, Costumes, Alejo Vietti; Sound, Ryan Rumery; Cast: Paul Hope (1st Bead Seller/Egyptian Police Official), James Belcher (2nd Bead Seller/McNaught), David Rainey (Steward), Annalee Jeffries (Miss Ffoliot-Ffoulkes), Elizabeth Heflin (Christina Grant), Todd Waite (Smith), Melissa Pritchett (Louise), Jeffrey Bean (Dr. Bessner), Christian Corp (Kay Mostyn), Chris Hutchison (Simon Mostyn), John Tyson (Canon Pennefather), Elizabeth Bunch (Jacqueline De Severac), James Belcher (McNaught); Hubbard Stage; July 6–29, 2007

DOUBT by John Patrick Shanley; Director, James Black; Set, Hugh Landwehr; Costumes, David Murin; Lighting, Clifton Taylor; Sound, Joe Pino; Cast: Elizabeth Heflin (Sister Aloysius), Jeffrey Bean (Father Flynn), Elizabeth Bunch (Sister James), Alice M. Gatling (Mrs. Muller); Hubbard Stage; August 31–September 23, 2007

ARSENIC AND OLD LACE by Joseph Kesselring; Director, Gregory Boyd; Set, Hugh Landwehr; Costumes, Judith Dolan; Lighting, Pat Collins; Sound, Joe Pino; Dialects, Jim Johnson; Cast: Dixie Carter (Abby Brewster), Charles Krohn (Reverend Harper/Lieutenant Rooney), James Belcher (Teddy Brewster), David Rainey (Officer Brophy), Chris Hutchison (Officer Klein), Mia Dillon (Martha Brewster), Elizabeth Heflin (Elaine Harper), Todd Waite (Mortimer Brewster), Colin McPhillamy (Mr. Gibbs/Mr. Witherspoon), James Black (Jonathan Brewster), John Tyson (Dr. Einstein), Paul Hope (Officer O'Hara); Hubbard Stage; October 5–November 4, 2007

THE SCENE by Theresa Rebeck; Director, Jeremy B. Cohen; Set and Lighting, Kevin Rigdon; Costumes, Alejo Vietti;

Original Composition & Sound, Paul James Prendergast; Cast: Elizabeth Bunch (Clea), Liam Craig (Lewis), Jeffrey Bean (Charlie), Elizabeth Rich (Stella); Neuhaus Stage; October 25–November 25, 2007

LOVE, JANIS Conceived, adapted and directed by Randal Myler; inspired by the book "Love, Janis" by Laura Joplin; Set, Norm Schwab; Costumes, Lorraine Venberg; Lighting, Don Darnutzer; Sound, Eric Stahlhammer; Projection, Jeffrey Cady; Music Director, Sam Andrew; Music Supervisor, Eric Massimino; Cast: Katrina Chester (Janis Joplin -singing), Mary Bridget Davies (Janis Joplin –singing), Marisa Ryan (Janis Joplin – speaking), Paul Hope (Interviewer), Eric Massimino (bass guitar), Ben Nieves (lead guitar), Jim Wall (percussion), Stephan Badreau (rhythm guitar), Duane Massey (keyboards), Steven Brown (trumpet), Sylvester LeBlanc (saxophone); Hubbard Stage; January 11–February 10, 2008

THE LIEUTENANT OF INISHMORE by Martin McDonagh; Director, Gregory Boyd; Set and Lighting, Kevin Rigdon; Costumes, Judith Dolan; Sound, Garth Hemphill; Fight Director, Steve Rankin; Special Effects/Fire Arms Safety, Waldo Warshaw; Dialect/Voice/Text Coach, Pamela Prather; Cast: John Tyson (Donny), Brandon Hearnsberger (Davey), Chris Hutchison (Padraic), Justin Doran (James), Elizabeth Bunch (Mairead), Todd Waite (Christy), Jeffrey Bean (Brendan), John Paul Green (Joey); Neuhaus Stage; January 25–February 24, 2008

OTHELLO by William Shakespeare; Director, Scott Schwartz; Set, Walt Spangler; Costumes, Alejo Vietti; Lighting, David Lander; Sound, Jill BC Du Boff; Original Music, Michael Holland; Fight Director, Brian Byrnes; Voice amd Text Coach, Pamela Prather; Dramaturg, Robert Shimko; Cast: David Rainey (Othello), James Black (Iago), Elizabeth Bunch (Desdemona), Elizabeth Heflin (Emilia), Todd Waite (Roderigo), Brandon Hearnsberger (Cassio), James Belcher (Brabantio/Ensemble), Paul Hope (Duke of Venice/Ensemble), Chris Hutchison (Montano/Ensemble), Melissa Pritchett (Bianca/Ensemble), Jeffrey Bean (Lodovico), Charles Krohn (Gratiano/Ensemble), Luis Galindo (Ensemble), Josh Kenny Cruz (Ensemble), Dan J. Gordon (Ensemble), Andrew J. Love (Ensemble), Matt Redden (Ensemble); Hubbard Stage; March 7–30, 2008

UNDERNEATH THE LINTEL by Glen Berger; Director, Alex Harvey; Set and Lighting, Kevin Rigdon; Cast: John Tyson (The Librarian); Neuhaus Stage; March 21–April 20, 2008

THE GERSHWINS' *AN AMERICAN IN PARIS* Words and music by George Gershwin and Ira Gershwin, book by Ken Ludwig; Director, Gregory Boyd; Choreographer, Randy Skinner; Set, Douglas W. Schmidt; Costumes, Carrie F. Robbins; Lighting, Paul Gallo; Musical Supervisor, Rod Berman; Orchestrations, Doug Berman; Cast: Harry Groener (Michel Gerard), Erin Dilly (Rebecca Klem), Felicia Finley (Hermia Chase), Jeffry Denman (Preston), Meredith Patteron (Yvette), Stephen DeRosa (Hamish), Alix Korey (Hilda); Hubbard Stage; April 29–June 1, 2008

Alliance Theatre

Atlanta, Georgia

THIRTY-NINTH SEASON

Artistic Director, Susan V. Booth; Managing Director, Thomas Pechar; Associate Artistic Director, Kent Gash; Sally G. Tomlinson Artistic Director of Theatre for Youth, Rosemary Newcott

Alliance Stage

THE WOMEN OF BREWSTER PLACE Book, music, lyrics, orchestrations and vocal arrangements by Tim Acito; based on the novel by Gloria Naylor; Director, Molly Smith; Choreographer, Kenneth L. Roberson; Set, Anne Patterson; Costumes, Paul Tazewell; Lighting, Darren W. McCroom; Sound, Garth Hemphill; Music Director/Orchestrations, William Foster McDaniel; Projections, Adam Larsen; PSM, Susan R. White; Dramaturg, Celise Kalke; Casting, Jody Feldman, Eli Dawson; ASM, R. Lamar Williams; Assistant Set, Andrew Lu; Cast: Cheryl Alexander (Sophie/Ensemble), Terry Burrell (Mrs. Browne/Ensemble), Suzzanne Douglas (Tee/Ensemble), Tina Fabrique (Mattie), Harriett D. Foy (Lorraine/Ensemble), Eleasha Gamble (Wanda/Ensemble), Marva Hicks (Etta Mae/Ensemble), Monique L. Midgette (Kiswana/Ensemble), Tijuana T. Ricks (Cora Lee/Ensemble), Shelley Thomas (Lucielia/Ensemble); September 5–30, 2007

SLEUTH by Anthony Shaffer; Director, Kent Gash; Set, Edward E. Haynes, Jr.; Costumes, Elizabeth Novak; Lighting, Liz Lee; Fight Choreographer, Jason Armit; Dialects, Cynthia Barrett; PSM, Pat. A. Flora; Dramaturg, Jennifer Hebblethwaite; Casting, Jody Feldman; ASM, R. Lamar Williams; SM Apprentice, Ronnie L. Campbell; Assistant Director/Kenny Leon Directing Fellow, Brooks Brantly; Cast: Carl Cofield (Milo Tindle), David de Vries (Andrew Wyke); October 10–November 4, 2007

DEGAS' LITTLE DANCER by Wesley Middleton; Director, Rosemary Newcott; Choreographer, Lauri Stallings; Set, Kat Conley; Costumes, Anne Kennedy; Lighting, Liz Lee; Sound & Composer, Kendall Simpson; PSM, Colleen Janich; Dramaturg, Celise Kalke; Casting, Jody Feldman; ASM, Ronn K. Smith; SM Production Assistant, Liz Campbell; Cast: Tabitha Christopher (Closier/Museum Guard), Pamela Gold (Ms. Gannon/Mme. Von Goethem/Danielle), Chris Kayser (Edgar Degas), Noelle Kayser (Marie Gannon), Lena Mayfield (Dominique), Ronn K. Smith (Ballet Master/Auguste Degas); November 10–18, 2007

A CHRISTMAS CAROL by Charles Dickens, adapted by David H. Bell; Director, Rosemary Newcott; Set, D. Martyn Bookwalter; Costumes, Mariann Verheyen; Lighting, Diane Ferry Williams; Sound, Clay Benning; Musical Director, Michael Fauss; PSM, Pat A. Flora; Casting, Jody Feldman; Associate Lighting, Pete Shinn; ASM, R. Lamar Williams/Colleen Janich; Stage Management Apprentice, Mike Smith; Movement Consultant, Hylan Scott; Dialects, Matt Huff; Cast:

Taprena Augustine (Bess/Ensemble), Elizabeth Wells Berkes (Belle/Ensemble), Je Nie Fleming (Mrs. Cratchit), Crystal Fox (Christmas Past/Peg/Ensemble), Neal A. Ghant (Bob Cratchit), Bart Hansard (Fezziwig/Christmas Present/Ensemble), David Howard (Topper/Ensemble), Nia Imani (Melinda/Ensemble), Chris Kayser (Ebenezer Scrooge), Jahi Kearse (Dick Wilkins/Ensemble), J.C. Long (Peter/Ensemble), Tendal Mann (Tiny Tim/Ensemble), Daniel Thomas May (Marley/Ensemble), Bernardine Mitchell (Mrs. Dilber/Mrs. Fezziwig/Ensemble), Tessa Lene Palisoc (Want/Ensemble), Thomas Piper (Young Scrooge/Ensemble), Glenn Rainey (Ensemble), Brydan Rogers (Daniel/Turkey Boy/Ensemble), Morgan Saylor (Belinda/Ensemble), Brad Sherrill (Fred/Ensemble), Hanley Smith (Fan/Martha/Ensemble), James Washburn III (Wyatt/Ignorance/Ensemble), Minka Wiltz (Ensemble); November 30–December 24, 2007

DUKE ELLINGTON'S *SOPHISTICATED LADIES* Concept by Donald McKayle, based on the music of Duke Ellington; Musical, Dance/Vocal Arrangements, Lloyd Mayers; Vocal Arrangements, Malcolm Dodds; Original Musical Director, Mercer Ellington; Director/Additional Choreographer, Kent Gash; Choreographer, Byron Easley; Set, Emily Beck; Costumes, Austin K. Sanderson; Lighting, William H. Grant III; Sound, Clay Benning; Music Director/Additional Arrangements, William Foster McDaniel; PSM, lark hackshaw; Dramaturg, Celise Kalk7e; Casting, Jody Feldman & Alan Filderman; ASM, R. Lamar Williams; SM Apprentice, Ronnie L. Campbell; Cast: Eric B. Anthony, Tracee Beazer, Terry Burrell, Bryan Terrell Clark, DeWitt Fleming, Jr., Debra Walton, Laurie Williamson, Tommar Wilson; January 9–February 10, 2008

SEUSSICAL Music, book & concept by Stephen Flaherty, lyrics, book & concept by Lynn Ahrens, co-conceived by Eric Idle; based on the works of Dr. Seuss; Director, Rosemary Newcott; Choreographer, Hylan Scott; Set, Kat Conley; Costumes, Sydney Roberts; Lighting, Pete Shinn; Sound, Clay Benning; Music Director, Christopher Cannon; PSM, Colleen Janich; Dramaturg, Jade Lambert Smith; Casting, Jody Feldman; ASM, Liz Campbell; Cast: Rita Dolphin (Mrs. Mayor/Bird Girl), Jill Hames (Mayzie), Jamiah Hudson (JoJo), Jahi Kearse (Cat in the Hat), Wendy Melkonian (Gertrude), Ronvé O'Daniel (Lead Wickersham), Brandon O'Dell (Mr. Mayor/Wickersham), Alecia Robinson (Lead Bird Girl), Bree Shannon (Sour Kangaroo), Justin Tanner (Horton); February 23–March 23, 2008

DOUBT by John Patrick Shanley; Director, Susan V. Booth; Set, Todd Rosenthal; Costumes, Mariann Verheyen; Lighting, Deb Sullivan; Sound, Clay Benning; PSM, Pat A. Flora; Dramaturg, Jade Lambert Smith; Casting, Jody Feldman; SM Apprentice, Mike Smith; Directing Fellow, Brooks Brantly; Cast: Donna Biscoe (Mrs. Muller), Cara Mantella (Sister James), Pamela Nyberg (Sister Aloysius), Thomas Piper (Father Flynn); April 2–May 4, 2008

Hertz Stage

JACQUES BREL IS ALIVE AND WELL AND LIVING IN PARIS Production conception, English lyrics and additional material by Eric Blau and Mort Shuman, music by Jacques Brel; based on Jacques Brel's lyrics and commentary; Director, Susan V. Booth; Set, Leslie Taylor; Costumes, Mariann Verheyen; Lighting, Pete Shinn; Sound, Clay Benning; Music Director, Michael Fauss; Choreographer, Craig A. Meyer; PSM, lark hackshaw; Dramaturg, Michael Evenden; Casting, Jody Feldman & Harriet Bass; Assistant Director, Jason Najjoum; Cast: Courtenay Collins, Joseph Dellger, Lauren Kling, Craig A. Meyer; September 21–October 28, 2007

CURVY WIDOW by Bobby Goldman; Director, Scott Schwartz; Set and Costumes, David Woolard; Lighting, Michael Gilliam; Sound, Sten Severson & Mark Bennett; Projections, Michael Clark; Composer, Mark Bennett; Casting, Jay Binder; Associate Director, Nell Balaban; PSM, Andrea "Spook" Testani; Hair, Mark Rampmeyer; Makeup Consultant, Angelina Avallone; Projections, Paul Vershbow; Set Assistant, David Barber; Assistant to Ms. Shepherd, Jason Martin; Cast: Cybill Shepherd (The Curvy Widow); November 16–December 16, 2007

IN THE RED AND BROWN WATER by Tarell Alvin McCraney; Director, Tina Landau; Set, Mimi Lien; Costumes, Jessica Jahn; Lighting, Scott Zielinski; Sound, Mimi Epstein; PSM, Pat A. Flora; Dramaturg, Celise Kalke; Casting, Jody Feldman & Harriet Bass; SM Assistant, Mike Smith; Assistant Directors, Aaron Bean, Lauren E. Turner; Fights, Jason Armit; Cast: Will Cobbs (The Egungun), Rodrick Covington (Shango), Chinái J. Hardy (Mama Moja/The Woman Who Reminds You), Jon Michael Hill (Elegba), Andre Holland (Ogun), Daniel Thomas May (O Li Roon/The Man From State), Kianné Muschett (Oya), Carra Patterson (Shun), Heather Alicia Simms (Aunt Elegua), Sharisa Whatley (Nia); February 1–24, 2008

EURYDICE by Sarah Ruhl; Director, Richard Garner; Set, Kat Conley; Costumes, Miranda Hoffman; Lighting, Justin Townsend; Sound, Clay Benning; Composer, Kendall Simpson; Movement Consultant, Ivan Pulinkala; PSM, lark hackshaw; Dramaturg, Celise Kalke; Casting, Jody Feldman & Harriet Bass; SM Assistant, Ronnie L. Campbell; Cast: Justin Adams (Orpheus), Andrew Benator (A Nasty Interesting Man/Lord of the Underworld), Neal A. Ghant (Big Stone), Melinda Helfrich (Eurydice), Paul Hester (Little Stone), Chris Kayser (Father), Courtney Patterson (Loud Stone); March 14–April 13, 2008

American Repertory Theatre

Cambridge, Massachusetts

TWENTY-NINTH SEASON

Acting Artistic Director, Gideon Lester; Executive Director, Robert J. Orchard

A MARVELOUS PARTY Words and music by Noël Coward; devised by Mark Anders, David Ira Goldstein, Patricia Wilcox; Arrangements, Carl Danielsen; Director, Scott Edmiston; Music Director/Pianist, Will McGarrahan; Sets, Christine Jones; Costumes, Hilary Hacker; Lighting, Karen Perlow; Sound, David Remedios; Movement, Kelly Edwards; PSM, Christopher DeCamillis; Cast: Remo Airaldi, Thomas Derrah, Will LeBow, Karen MacDonald; Zero Arrow Theatre Club; July 13–August 5, 2007

DON JUAN GIOVANNI Based on the work of Molière and Mozart from the original production by Steven Epp, Felicity Jones, Dominique Serrand, and Paul Walsh; conception by Steven Epp and Dominique Serrand, text by Steven Epp; Director, Dominique Serrand; Music Adaptation, Bradley Greenwald; Music Director/Pianist, Barbara Brooks; Sets, Dominique Serrand; Costumes, Sonya Berlovitz; Lighting, Marcus Dilliard; Video, Dominique Serrand; Surtitles, Steven Epp; SM, Glenn D. Klapperich; ASM, Christopher DeCamillis; Cast: Christina Baldwin (Charlotte), Dieter Bierbrauer (Peter), Bryan Boyce (Don Giovanni), Steven Epp (Sganarelle), Bradley Greenwald (Leporello), Carrie Hennessey (Girl), Bryan Janssen (Commendatore), Jennifer Baldwin Peden (Elvire), Dominique Serrand (Don Juan), Momoko Tanno (Donna Anna); Loeb Drama Center; August 31–October 6, 2007

FIGARO Based on the work of Beaumarchais and Mozart, concept by Steven Epp and Dominique Serrand, text by Steven Epp; Director, Dominique Serrand; Music Adaptation, Bradley Greenwald; Music Director/Pianist, Barbara Brooks; Sets, Dominique Serrand; Costumes, Sonya Berlovitz; Lighting, Marcus Dilliard; Video Design, Dominique Serrand; Surtitles, Steven Epp; SM, Glenn D. Klapperich; ASM, Christopher DeCamillis; Cast: Christina Baldwin (Cherubino), Dieter Bierbrauer (Basilio), Bryan Boyce (Figaro), Steven Epp (Fig), Bradley Greenwald (Count Almaviva), Carrie Hennessey (Marcellina), Bryan Janssen (Bartolo), Jennifer Baldwin Peden (Countess), Dominique Serrand (Mr. Almaviva), Momoko Tanno (Susanna); Loeb Drama Center; August 31–October 6, 2007

THE VEILED MONOLOGUES Written and directed by Adelheid Roosen; Dramaturg, Dirkje Houtman; AD, Marjolein Polman; Set, Adelheid Roosen, Mijke de Jong; Video Editing, Titus Tiel Groenestege; Lighting, Geldof, Verhaart & Den Ottolander; Music Design, Seval Okyay, Serçan Engin; Voice Coach, Elizabeth Ingram/Shakespeare & Company; Translators, Discordia Translations, Maureen De Jong, Annet Kouwenhoven; International Production Leader, Julia Ackermans; Original Producer, Bos Theaterproductions; International Producer, Female Economy Foundation; Cast: Oya Capelle, Nazmiye Oral, Meral Polat, Serçan Engin; American Premiere; Loeb Drama Center; October 16–21, 2007

DONNIE DARKO Adapted and directed by Marcus Stern, based on a screenplay by Richard Kelly; Sets, Matt McAdon; Lighting, Scott Zielinski; Costumes, Clint Ramos; Sound, David Remedios, Marcus Stern; SM, Katherine Shea; Cast: Dan McCabe (Donnie Darko), Flora Diaz (Gretchen Ross), Paula Langton (Rose Darko), Will LeBow (Eddie Darko), Carolyn McCandlish (Samantha Darko), Angela Nahigian (Elizabeth Darko/Dorky Girl), Mara Sidmore (Dr. Lilian Thurman), Thomas Derrah (Jim Cunningham), Karen MacDonald (Kitty Farmer), Sarah Jorge Leon (Karen Pomeroy/Linda Connie), Remo Airaldi (Principal Cole), DeLance Minifee (Dr. Monnitoff/Larry/Ricky), Perry Jackson (Rabbit/Frank), Thomas Kelley (Seth Devlin), Katherine Lebrón (Joanie/Lanky Kid), Talisa Friedman (Cherita Chen), Greta Merchant (Roberta Sparrow), Gillian Gordan (Sparkle Motion Dancer), Lisa Woods (Sparkle Motion Dancer); World Premiere; Zero Arrow Theatre; October 27–November 18, 2007

NO CHILD… by Nilaja Sun; Director, Hal Brooks; Sets, J. Michael Griggs; Original Sets, Narelle Sissons; Costumes, Jessica Gaffney; Lighting, Mark Barton; Sound Design, Ron Russell; Cast: Nilaja Sun; Loeb Drama Center; November 23–December 23, 2007

COPENHAGEN by Michael Frayn; Director, Scott Zigler; Sets and Costumes, David Reynoso; Lighting, Kenneth Helvig; Sound Design, David Remedios; PSM, Amy James; Cast: Karen MacDonald (Margrethe Bohr), Will LeBow (Niels Bohr), John Kuntz (Werner Heisenberg); Loeb Drama Center; January 5–February 3, 2008

JULIUS CAESAR by William Shakespeare; Director, Arthur Nauzyciel; Sets, Riccardo Hernandez; Costumes, James Schuette; Lighting, Scott Zielinski; Sound Design, David Remedios; Dance, Damien Jalet; SM, Chris De Camillis; Cast: Jim True-Frost (Marcus Brutus), Sara Kathryn Bakker (Portia/Calpurnia), Jared Craig (Lucius, the boy), Thomas Derrah (Julius Caesar), Mark L. Montgomery (Cassius), Remo Airaldi (Casca), Daniel Le (Trebonius), Neil Patrick Stewart (Decius Brutus), Gardiner Comfort (Metellus Cimber), Perry Jackson (Cinna), James Waterston (Mark Antony), Thomas Kelly (Octavius), Will LeBow (Lepidus), Jeremy Geidt (Cicero), Kunal Prasad (Soothsayer); Jazz Trio: Blake Newman (Bass), Eric Hoftbauer (Guitar), Marianne Solivan (Singer); Loeb Drama Center; February 9–March 16, 2008

ELECTIONS & ERECTIONS: A Chronicle of Fear and Fun Created and performed by Pieter-Dirk Uys; Zero Arrow Theatre Club; April 3–May 4, 2008

CARDENIO by Stephen Greenblatt and Charles L. Mee, Director, Les Waters; Sets, Annie Smart; Costumes Christal Weatherly; Lights, James Ingalls; Sound David Remedios, Movement, Doug Elkins; SM, Chris De Camillis; Cast: Remo Airaldi (Rudi), Thomas Kelley (Will), Sarah Baskin (Camilla), Thomas Derrah (Melchiore), Nathan Keepers (Edmund), Will LeBow (Alfred), Karen MacDonald (Luisa), Maria Elena Ramirez (Doris), Leenya Rideout (Susanna), Mickey Solis (Anselmo), Elizabeth Wilson (Sally); World Premiere; Loeb Drama Center; May 10–June 8, 2008

Arden Theatre Company

Philadelphia, Pennsylvania

TWENTIETH SEASON

Producing Artistic Director, Terrance J. Nolen; Managing Director, Amy L. Murphy

ASSASSINS Music and lyrics by Stephen Sondheim, book by John Weidman; Director, Terrance J. Nolen; Set, David P. Gordon; Costumes, Alison Roberts; Lighting, John Stephen Hoey; Sound/Projections, Jorge Cousineau; Music, Eric Ebbenga; SM, Patricia G. Sabato; Cast: Erin Brueggemann, Jeffrey Coon, Ben Dibble, Scott Greer, Timothy Hill, Mary Martello, Christopher Patrick Mullen, Jay Pierce, Jim Poulos, James Sugg; Hass Stage; September 13–October 21, 2007

AN EMPTY PLATE IN THE CAFÉ DU GRAND BOEUF by Michael Hollinger; Director, Whit MacLaughlin; Set, Donald Eastman; Costumes, Rosemarie E. McKelvey; Lighting, Jerold R. Forsyth; Sound, Jorge Cousineau; AD, Rebecca Wright; Stage Managers, Patricia G. Sabato, Elana Wolff; Cast: James William Ijames, Mikaela Kafka, Mary McCool, Ian Merrill Peakes, Douglas Rees, Richard Ruiz; Arcadia Stage; October 11–December 9, 2007

WITTENBERG by David Davalos; Director, J.R. Sullivan; Set/Lighting, Michael Philippi; Costumes, Elizabeth Covey; Sound, Jorge Cousineau; Assistand Director, Matt Pfeiffer; SM, Patricia G. Sabato; Cast; Shawn Fagan, Scott Greer, Kate Udall, Greg Wood; World Premiere; Arcadia Stage; January 17–March 16, 2008

THE PIANO LESSON by August Wilson; Director, Walter Dallas; Set, Donald Eastman, Costumes, Alison Roberts; Lighting, Curtis V. Hodge; Sound, Jorge Cousineau; AD, Megan O'Brien; SM, Katharine M. Hanley; Cast; Kala Moses Baxter, Katrina Yvette Cooper, Chioma Dunkley, Kes Khemnu, Julian Rozzell, Jr., Harum Ulmer, Jr., Yaegel T. Welch, Brian Anthony Wilson; Musicians: David Ames, Andrew Nelson; Haas Stage; March 6–April 6, 2008

GO, DOG. GO! by Allison Gregory and Steven Dietz, music by Michael Koerner; based on the book by P.D. Eastman; Director, Matt Pfeiffer; Choreographer, Lisa Zinni; Set, Brian Sidney Bembridge; Costumes, Lisa Zinni; Lighting, James Leitner; Music Director, David Ames; SM, Stephanie Cook; Cast; Chris Faith, Doug Hara, Andrew Kane, Geneviève Perrier, Elyse McKay Taylor, Julianna Zinkel; Arcadia Stage; April 16–June 1, 2008

OUR TOWN by Thornton Wilder; Director, Terrence J. Nolen; Set, James Kronzer; Lighting, Justin Townsend; Costumes, Richard St. Clair; Sound, Troy Herion; SM, Thomas E. Shotkin; Assistant Director, Ed Robins; Associate Producer, Matthew Decker; Cast: Oberon K.A. Adjepong, Frederick Andersen, Bev Appleton, Carla Belver, Rebecca Blumhagen, David Corenswet, Chioma Dunkley, Sherri L. Edelen, Nathan Edmondson, Eric Hissom, Jordan Johnson, Kevyn Morrow, JoAnna Rhinehart, Peterson Townsend, Damien J. Wallace, Brian Anthony Wilson, Greg Wood; Townspeople: Krista Apple, Robert Bauer, Katrina Yvette Cooper. Juanita Frederick, Dylan Jackson, Andy Joos, Brian Kurtas, Harry Philibosian, Erin DeBlois Read, Chaz Rose, Wendy Staton; Hass Stage; May 22–June 22, 2008

Arena Stage

Washington, DC and Arlington, Virginia

FIFTY-SEVENTH SEASON

Artistic Director, Molly Smith; Executive Director, Stephen Richard

EMERGENCE-SEE! Written and performed by Daniel Beaty; Lighting, Jason Arnold; Sound, Timothy M. Thompson; SM, John Eric Scutchins; ASM, Kurt Hall; Kreeger Theater; July 5–22, 2007

33 VARIATIONS Written and directed by Moisés Kaufman; Co-production with Tectonic Theater Project; Set, Derek McLane; Costumes, Janice Pytel; Lighting, David Lander; Sound, André Pluess; Projections, Jeff Sugg; Choreographer, Peter Anastos; SM, Meghan Gauger; Cast: Don Amendolia (Anton Diabelli), Greg Keller (Mike Clark), Susan Kellermann (Dr. Gertie Ladenborger), Graeme Malcolm (Ludwig van Beethoven), Laura Odeh (Clara Brandt), Mary Beth Peil (Katherine Brandt), Erik Steele (Anton Schindler), Diane Walsh (Pianist); World Premiere; Kreeger Theater; August 24–September 30, 2007

WELL by Lisa Kron; Director, Kyle Donnelly; Set, Thomas Lynch; Costumes, Nan Cibula-Jenkins; Lighting, Nancy Schertler; Sound, Lindsay Jones; SM, Lloyd Davis, Jr.; Cast: Emily Ackerman (Lisa Kron), Nancy Robinette (Ann Kron), Scott Drummond (Howard Norris/Head Nurse), Donnetta Lavinia Grays (Lori Jones/Mrs. Price), Marc Damon Johnson (Jim Richardson/Nurse 2), Susan Lynskey (Joy/Dottie); Regional Premiere; Fichandler Stage; September 14–October 14, 2007

THE WOMEN OF BREWSTER PLACE Music, lyrics and book by Tim Acito, based on the novel by Gloria Naylor; Co-production with the Alliance Theatre; Director, Molly Smith; Set, Anne Patterson; Costumes, Paul Tazewell; Lighting, Michael Gilliam; Sound, Garth Hemphill; Music Director/Conductor, William Foster McDaniel; Projections, Adam Larsen; Choreographer, Kenneth L. Roberson; SM, Amber Dickerson; Cast: Cheryl Alexander (Sophie/Ensemble), Terry Burrell (Mrs. Browne/Ensemble), Suzzanne Douglas (Tee/Ensemble), Tina Fabrique (Mattie), Harriett D. Foy (Lorraine/Ensemble), Eleasha Gamble (Wanda/Ensemble), Marva Hicks (Etta Mae), Monique L. Midgette (Kiswana), Tijuana T. Ricks (Cora Lee), Shelley Thomas (Lucielia); World Premiere; Kreeger Theater; October 19–December 9, 2007

CHRISTMAS CAROL 1941 by James Magruder, adapted from Charles Dickens's A Christmas Carol; music by Henry Krieger, lyrics by Susan Birkenhead; Director, Molly Smith; Set, William Schmuck; Costumes, Vicki R. Davis; Lighting, John (Jock) Munro; Sound, Garth Hemphill; Music Director, George Fulginiti-Shakar; Choreographer, Parker Esse; SM, Susan R. White; Cast: Christopher Bloch (Albert Schroen/Mr. Bates), Clinton Brandhagen (Butch Schroen/Prime Strube), Mollie Clement (Carolyn/Ensemble), Daniel Eichner (Recruiting Officer 1/Fishmonger), James Gale (Elijah Strube), Tim Getman (Donald/Bartender), Tara Giordano (Hazel B/Fan), C.J. Harrison-Davies (Young Elijah/Delivery Boy), Gia Mora (Kay/Winged Victory), Connan Morrissey (Freedom/Mrs. Bates), Hugh Nees (Marley/Minister), Lawrence Redmond (Henry Schroen/Ensemble), Nancy Robinette (Margarette/Ensemble), Clay Steakley (Grant Yagel/Cornelius), Bayla Whitten (Sally Dunlavey/Grief); Standby children: Madeleine Carr, Julia Proctor; Fichandler Stage; November 16–December 30, 2007

ELLA book by Jeffrey Hatcher, conceived by Rob Ruggiero & Dyke Garrison; Director, Rob Ruggiero; Musical Director/Arrangements by Danny Holgate; Set, Michael Schweikardt; Costumes, Alejo Vietti; Lighting, John Lasiter; Sound, Michael Miceli; SM, Martha Knight; Cast: Tina Fabrique (Ella Fitzgerald), George Caldwell (Piano/Conductor), Elmer Brown (trumpet 12/28–1/27), Thaddeus Wilson (trumpet 1/29–2/24), Rodney Harper (drums), Clifton Kellem (bass), Harold Dixon (Norman Granz); Regional Premiere; Arena Stage in Crystal City; December 28, 2007–February 24, 2008

THE MYSTERY OF IRMA VEP by Charles Ludlam; Director, Rebecca Bayla Taichman; Set, Jim Noone; Costumes, David Zinn; Lighting, Dan Wagner; Sound, Bray Poor; Fights, David S. Leong; SM, Amber Dickerson; Cast: Brad Oscar (Multiple characters), J. Fred Shiffman (Multiple characters); Arena Stage in Crystal City; June 6–July 13, 2008

The Arthur Miller Festival

DEATH OF A SALESMAN by Arthur Miller; Director, Timothy Bond; Set, Loy Arcenas; Costumes, Laurie Churba Kohn; Lighting, Nancy Schertler; Composer, Michael G. Keck; Fight Choreographer, David S. Leong; Dialect Consultant, Robert Barry Fleming; SM, Susan R. White; Cast: Jamieson Baker (Second Waiter), Louis Cancelmi (Bernard), Rick Foucheux (Willy Loman), Tim Getman (Happy), Tara Giordano (Jenny/Letta), Jeremy S. Holm (Biff), Naomi Jacobson (The Woman), Virginia Kull (Miss Forsythe), Nancy Robinette (Linda), Stephen F. Schmidt (Howard Wagner), J. Fred Shiffman (Uncle Ben), Noble Shropshire (Charley), Cliff Williams III (Stanley); Arena Stage in Crystal City; March 14–May 18, 2008

A VIEW FROM THE BRIDGE by Arthur Miller; Director, Daniel Aukin; Set, Loy Arcenas; Costumes, Laurie Churba Kohn; Lighting, Nancy Schertler; Composer, Michael G. Keck; Fight Choreographer, David S. Leong; Dialect Consultant, Robert Barry Fleming; SM, Susan R. White; Cast: David Agranov (Rodolpho), Louis Cancelmi (Marco), Rick Foucheux (Louis), Tim Getman (Mike), Tara Giordano (2nd Submarine/Ensemble), Jeremy S. Holm (Tony/1st Submarine), Naomi Jacobson (Beatrice), Virginia Kull (Catherine), Nancy Robinette (Mrs. Lipari), Stephen F. Schmidt (1st Immigration Officer), J. Fred Shiffman (Mr. Lipari), Noble Shropshire Alfieri), Cliff Williams III (2nd Immigration Officer), Delaney Williams (Eddie); Arena Stage in Crystal City; March 21–May 17, 2008

Arizona Theatre Comapny

Phoenix and Tucson, Arizona

FORTY-FIRST SEASON

Artistic Director, David Ira Goldstein; Executive Director, Jessica L. Andrews; Producing Director, John Kingsbury; Managing Director, Kevin E. Moore

HERSHEY FELDER AS GEORGE GERSHWIN ALONE Book by Hershey Felder, music and lyrics by George and Ira Gershwin; Director, Joel Zwick; Set, Yael Pardess; Lighting, Michael T. Gilliam; Sound, Jon Gottlieb; Costumes, Kenneth Cole; SM, GiGi Garcia; Production Manager and Technical Director, Matt Marsden; Cast: Hershey Felder (George Gershwin/Playwright); Temple of Music and Art (Tucson), September 12–October 2, 2007; Herberger Theater Center (Phoenix), October 11–28, 2007

HERSHEY FELDER AS MONSIEUR CHOPIN Book by Hershey Felder, music of Fryderyk Chopin; Director, Joel Zwick; Set, Yael Pardess, Lighting, Richard Norwood; Projections, John Boesche; Production Manager and Technical Director, Matt Marsden; Production Consultant, Jeffrey Kallberg, Ph.D.; SM, GiGi Garcia; Cast: Hershey Felder (Fryderyk Chopin); Temple of Music and Art (Tucson), October 5–7, 2007; Herberger Theater Center (Phoenix), October 31–November 4, 2007

TOUCH THE NAMES Concept by Randal Myler and Chic Street Man, music and lyrics by Chic Street Man; Director, Randal Myler; Set, Vicki Smith; Lighting, Don Darnutzer; Costumes, Kish Finnegan; Sound, Brian Jerome Peterson; SM, Glenn Bruner; Cast: Elsie Ly Escobar, Ann Guilbert, Karen Tsen Lee, Stephen Mailer, Elizabeth Rainer, Kim Staunton, Chic Street Man, Ray Anthony Thomas, Charles Weldon; Temple of Music and Art (Tucson), October 16–November 4, 2007; Herberger Theater Center (Phoenix), November 8–25, 2007

THE PAJAMA GAME Book by George Abbott and Richard Bissell, music and lyrics by Richard Adler and Jerry Ross; Director, David Ira Goldstein; Choreographer, Patti Wilcox; Set, Bill Forrester; Costumes, Lindsay W. Davis; Lighting, Dennis Parichy; Sound, Abe Jacob; Musical Director, Christopher McGovern; Projections, Peter Beudert; SM, Glenn Bruner; Cast: Bob Sorenson (Hines), Joel Newsome (Prez), Jeff Guilfoyle (Joe), Tony DeBruno (Hasler), Michelle Aravena (Gladys), Kevyn Morrow (Sid Sorokin), Susan J. Jacks (Mabel),

Sean Patrick Doyle (First Helper), Brandon Tyler (Second Helper), Brandon Bieber (Charlie), Kelly McCormick (Babe Williams), Emily Mulligan-Ferry (Mae), Laura Beth Wells (Brenda), Elizabeth Oates (Poopsie), Robert Encila (Max), Tony DeBruno (Pop); Ensemble: Brandon Bieber, Sean Patrick Doyle, Robert Encila, Kathryn Fraggos, Jeff Guilfoyle, Sterling Masters, Elizabeth Oates, Carol Schuberg, Brandon Tyler; Temple of Music and Art (Tucson), November 24–December 15, 2007; Herberger Theater Center (Phoenix), December 31,2007–January 26, 2008

DR. JEKYLL AND MR. HYDE by Jeffrey Hatcher; Director, David Ira Goldstein; Set, Kent Dorsey; Costumes, Anna Oliver; Lighting, Dawn Chiang; Sound, Brian Jerome Peterson; Composer, Roberta Carlson; Fight Director, Ken Merckx; Dramaturg, Jennifer Bazzell; SM, Bret Torbeck; Cast: R. Hamilton Wright (Dr. Henry Jekyll), Ken Ruta (Edward Hyde/Gabriel Utterson), Stephen D'Ambrose (Edward Hyde/Sir Danvers Carew), Mark Anderson Phillips (Richard Enfield/O.F. Sanderson/Inspector/Edward Hyde/Dr. H.K. Lanyon), Carrie Paff (Police Doctor/Surgical Student/ Edward Hyde/Poole/Surgical Student/Police Doctor), Anna Bullard (Elizabeth Jelkes), Rebecca Angel (Orderly), Stephen Gaeto (Orderly); Temple of Music and Art (Tucson), January 12–February 2, 2008; Herberger Theater Center (Phoenix), February 7–24, 2008

TO KILL A MOCKINGBIRD Adapted by Christopher Sergel; Director, Samantha K. Wyer; Set, Hugh Landwehr; Costumes, Sam Fleming; Lighting, Dennis Parichy; Sound, John Story; Composer, Peter Ostroushko; Dialects, Dianne Winslow; Fight Choreographer, Brent Gibbs; SM, Bruno Ingram; Cast: Wendy Robie (Jean Louise Finch), Daria LeGrand (Scout), Julia Lema (Calpurnia), Bruce Nelson (Reverend Sykes), Maedell Dixon (Mrs. DuBose), Adam Moffitt (Jem) Christopher Moffitt (Charles Baker Harris/Dill), Roberto Guajardo (Mr. Radley/ Judge Taylor), John Rensenhouse (Atticus Finch), David Alexander Johnston (Walter Cunningham/Boo Radley), Mike Lawler (Sheriff Heck Tate), Scott Cordes (Bob Ewell), Cale Epps (Mr. Gilmer), James T. Alfred (Tom Robinson), Jessica Goldapple (Mayella Ewell), Tamika Lawrence (Helen Robinson), Lorin F. Akers, Mark Alderson, Victor Bowleg, Jonathan A.J. Northover, Desiree Thompson, Brittney Vega (Ensemble); Temple of Music and Art (Tucson), March 1–22, 2008; Herberger Theater Center (Phoenix), March 27–April 13, 2008

THE CLEAN HOUSE by Sarah Ruhl; Director, Jon Jory; Set, Neil Patel; Costumes, Lorraine Venberg; Lighting, Brian J. Lilienthal; Sound, Matt Callahan; Dialects, Gillian Lane-Plescia; Music Coach and Spanish Tutor, Ilse Apéstegui; Dramaturg, Amy Wegener; Assistant Lighting, T. Greg Squires; PSM, Glenn Bruner; Cast: Alexandra Tavares (Matilde), Felicity La Fortune (Lane), Kate Goehring (Virginia), Barnard Burak Sheredy (Charles), Rae C Wright (Ana); Ensemble: Charlotte Bernhardt, Julie Garrison; Temple of Music and Art (Tucson), April 5–26, 2008; Herberger Theater Center (Phoenix), May 1–18, 2008

Arkansas Repertory Theatre

Little Rock, Arkansas

THIRTY-SECOND SEASON

Producing Artistic Director, Robert Hupp; General Manager, Mike McCurdy

THE LEGACY PROJECT: It Happened in Little Rock by Rajendra Ramoon Maharaj; Director, Rajendra Ramoon Maharaj; Choreographer/Assitant Director, Michael Susko; Dramaturg, Sybil Roberts Williams; Set, E. Mike Nichols; Costumes, Leslie Bernstein; Properties, Lynda Kwallek; Lighting, Matthew Webb; Sound, M. Jason Pruzin; Music Director, Charles Creath; Video, Michael Myhrum; Production Manager, Rafael Colon Castanera; SM, Brian Westmoreland; Cast: Destan Owens (Reporter/Artist), Julian Rebolledo (Actor 1) Taïfa Harris (Actor 2), Nick Petrie (Actor 3), Mary-Pat Green (Actor 4), Aruthur W. Marks (Actor 5), Gia McGlone (Actor 6), J. Bernard Calloway (Actor 7), Shannon Lamb (Actor 8), Vanessa Lemonides (Actor 9), Steve Hudelson (Musician); September 14–30, 2007

BAREFOOT IN THE PARK by Neil Simon; Director Robert Hupp; Set, E. Mike Nichols; Lighting, Tony Mulanix; Sound, M. Jason Pruzin; Properties, Lynda Kwallek; Costumes, Stephanie Khoury; Production Manager, Rafael Colon Castanera; SM, Tara Kelly; Cast: Whitney Kirk (Corie Bratter), Christian Pedersen (Paul Bratter), Alanna Hamill Newton (Mrs. Banks), Robert Lydiard (Victor Velasco), Jason Thompson (Telephone Repair Man), Steve Marshall (Delivery Man); October 26–November 11, 2007

HELLO, DOLLY! Book by Michael Stewart, music and lyrics by Jerry Herman, based on the play *The Matchmaker* by Thornton Wilder; Director, Brad Mooy; Music Director, Eric K. Johnston; Choreographer, Ron Hutchins; Set, E. Mike Nichols; Lighting, Andrew Meyers; Sound, M. Jason Pruzin; Properties, Lynda Kwallek; Costumes, Rafael Colon Castanera; Production Manager, Rafael Colon Castanera; SM, Shawn Pace; ASM, Stephen Horton; Cast: Mary Robin Roth (Dolly Gallagher Levi), Jonathan Burgard (Ambrose Kemper), Ron Wisniski (Horace Vandergelder), Nina Ordman (Ermengarde), James Donegan (Cornelius Hackl), Jason Edward Cook (Barnaby Tucker), Amy Shure (Minnie Fay), Maria Couch (Irene Molloy), Michelle Tauber (Mrs. Rose/Ernestina Money), Tom Kagy (Rudolph/Judge); Ensemble: Kelsie Adkisson, Delaine Andrzejewski, Conly Basham, Tom Bruett, Andrew Buck, William James Daniels, Lacy Dunn, Megan Florence, Evie Hutton, Graham Kurtz, Jeremy Matthey, Lauren McCarty, Rommel O'Choa, Ano Okera, Ryan Overberg, Timothy Roller, Dave Schoonover, Ian Scott, Christopher Shin, Molly Winter Stewart; December 7, 2007–January 6, 2008.

DOUBT by John Patrick Shanley; Director, Cliff Fannin Baker; Set, Don Yanik; Costumes, Trish Clark; Lighting, Matthew Webb, Sound, M. Jason Pruzin; Production Manager, Rafael Colon Castanera; SM, Stephen Horton; Properties,

Lynda Kwallek; Cast: Scott Barrow (Father Flynn), JoAnn Johnson (Sister Aloysius), Charlotte Purser (Sister James), Verda Davenport (Mrs. Muller); February 8–24, 2008

SHERLOCK HOLMES: THE FINAL ADVENTURE by Steven Dietz, based on the original 1899 play by William Gillette and Arthur Conan Doyle; Director, Robert Hupp; Set, E. Mike Nichols; Costumes, Marianne Custer; Lighting, Nan Zhang; Sound, M. Jason Pruzin; Production Manager, Rafael Colon Castanera; SM, Erin Albrecht; Properties, Lynda Kwallek; Cast: Joe Graves (Sherlock Holmes), Sophia Bushong (Madge), Heidi Marie Ferren (Irene Adler), Michael Lopez (James Larabee), Colin McPhillamy (Doctor Watson), Jason O'Connell (King of Bohemia), Mark Waterman (Moriarty), Raven Peters (Sid/ Policeman); April 11–27, 2008

FIRE ON THE MOUNTAIN by Randal Myler and Dan Wheetman; Director, Randal Myler; Set, Vicki Smith; Costumes, Marcia Dixcy Jory; Lighting, Don Darnutzer; Sound, M. Jason Pruzin; Production Manager, Rafael Colon Castanera; Projections, Jeff Cady; Properties, Lynda Kwallek; Cast: "Mississippi" Charles Bevel, Al Tharp, Conner Frederick, James Leva, Jason Edwards, Margaret Bowman, Mike Reagan, Molly Andrews, Zan McLeod; May 30 – June 22, 2008

Asolo Repertory Theatre

Sarasota, Florida

FOURTY-NINTH SEASON

Producing Artistic Director, Michael Donald Edwards; Managing Director, Linda M. DiGabriele

A TALE OF TWO CITIES Music lyrics, and book by Jill Santoriello; Based on the novel by Charles Dickens; Director, Michael Donald Edwards; Music Director, Jerry Steichen; Musical Staging, Warren Carlyle; Sets, Tony Walton; Costumes, David Zinn; Lighting, Richard Pilbrow; Sound, Carl Casella & Domonic Sack; Hair, Tom Watson; Orchestrations, Edward B. Kessel; PSM, Kim Vernac; ASM, Jason A. Quinn; Music Supervisor Wendy Bobbitt Cavett; Music Coordinator, James Neglia; Dramaturg, Greg Leaming; New York Casting, Barry Moss, Bob Kale; Press, The Jacksina Company; General Management, Town Square Productions; Cast: James Barbour (Sydney Carton), Craig Bennett (Jerry Cruncher), Joe Cassidy (Ernest Defarge), Kevin Greene (Gabelle), Tim Hartman (Attorney General/Cronie), Michael Hayward-Jones (Mr. Jarvis Lorry), Alex Howley (Seamstress), Derek Keeling (Charles Darnay), Jay Lusteck (Judge/Turnkey), Bruce Merkle (The Boy), Katherine McGrath (Miss Pross), Les Minski (Marquis St. Evremonde), Catherine Missal (Little Lucie), Winston Oneil (Cronie Walter), Rob Richardson (Gaspard), Rebecca Robbins (Mrs. Cruncher), Lucie Manette (Jessica Rush), Alex Santoriello (Dr. Alexandre Manette), Wayne Schroder (C.J. Stryver), Owen Teague (Little Gaspard), Natalie Toro (Madame Therese Defarge), Nick Wyman (Mr. John Barsad); Ensemble: Shane Austin, Matt Brown, Juan Javier Cardenas, Richard Caldwell, Ryan Clark, Karis Danish, Janine DiVita, Kim Fanok, Ryan Fitts, Amy E. Gray, Marcus Denard Johnson, Heather Kopp, Julie Lachance, Jodie Langel, Troy Lewis, Jennifer Logue, Stephen Missal; Mertz Theatre; October 13–November 18, 2007

MISERY by Stephen King, adapted by Simon Moore; Director, Seth Barrish; Sets, Jeffrey W. Dean; Costumes, Nicole Bartet; Lighting, James D. Sale; Sound, Edward Cosla; Fight Director, Tiza Garland; SM, Marian Wallace; Cast: David Breitbarth (Paul Sheldon), Devora Millman (Annie Wilkes) Cook Theater; October 30–December 9, 2007

THE CONSTANT WIFE by W. Somerset Maugham; Director, Mark Rucker; Sets, Erik Flatmo; Costumes, Katherine Roth; Lighting, James D. Sale; Sound, Matthew Parker; SM, Juanita Munford; Vocal Coach, Patricia Delorey; Casting, Stuart Howard, Amy Schecter & Paul Hardt; Cast: Carolyn Michel (Mrs. Culver), Matt Brown (Bentley), Jessi Blue Gormezano (Martha Culver), Sameerah Luqmaan-Harris (Barbara Fawcett), Dana Green (Constance Middleton), Julie Lachance (Marie-Louise Durham), Bryan Torfeh (Dr. John Middleton), John G. Preston (Bernard Kersal), Douglas Jones (Mortimer Durham); Mertz Theatre; December 7, 2007–March 12, 2008

DOUBT by John Patrick Shanley; Director, Anne Kauffman; Sets, Kris Stone; Costumes, Emily Rebholz; Lighting, Mark Barton; Sound, Matthew Parker; SM, Juanita Munford; Vocal Coach, Patricia Delorey; Cast: Paul Molnar (Father Brendan Flynn), Randy Danson (Sister Aloysius Beauvier), Karis Danish (Sister James), Sameerah Luqmaan-Harris (Mrs. Muller); Mertz Theatre; December 14, 2007–May 1, 2008

THE PLAY'S THE THING by Ferenc Molnar, adapted by P.G. Wodehouse; Director, Greg Leaming; Sets, Nathan Heverin; Costumes, Andrea Huelse; Lighting, Dan Kotlowitz; Sound, Matthew Parker; SM, Marian Wallace; Cast: James Clarke (Mansky), Douglas Jones (Sandor Turai), Juan Javier Cardenas (Albert Adam), Bradford Wallace (Johann Dwornitschek), Dana Green (Ilona Szabo), Bryan Torfeh (Almady), Marcus Denard Johnson (Mell); Julie Lachance and Jennifer Logue (Hotel Staff), Mertz Theatre; December 21, 2007–March 13, 2008

THE BLONDE, THE BRUNETTE AND THE VENGEFUL REDHEAD by Robert Hewett; Director, Melissa Kievman; Set and Costumes, Clint Ramos; Lighting/Projections, Dan Scully; Sound, Matthew Parker; SM, Jon Merlyn; Cast: Sharon Scruggs; Asolo Theater; January 11–February 2, 2008

SMASH Adapted by Jeffrey Hatcher from the novel "An Unsocial Socialist" by George Bernard Shaw; Director, Lillian Groag; Set, Kate Edmunds; Costumes, Martha Hally; Lighting, Josh Bradford; Sound, Matthew Parker; Vocal Coach, Patricia Delorey; SM, Juanita Munford; Cast: Paul Molnar (Sidney Trefusis), Kris Danford (Henrietta Jansenius), James Clarke (Mr. Jansenius), Marcus Denard Johnson (Photographer), Jessi Blue Gormezano (Jane Carpenter), Jennifer Logue (Gertrude Lindsay), Carolyn Michel (Miss Wilson), David Breitbarth

(Chichester Erskine), Bradford Wallace (Lumpkin), Julie Lachance (Agatha Wylie), Matt Brown (Sir Charles Brandon); Mertz Theatre; February 15–May 3, 2008

EQUUS by Peter Shaffer; Director, Michael Donald Edwards; Sets and Lighting, Clint Ramos; Lighting, Lap-Chi Chu; Sound, Robby MacLean; Choreographer, Jimmy Hoskins; Vocal Coach, Patricia Delorey; SM, Marian Wallace; Cast: Juan Javier Cardenas (Alan Strang), Yashin Sheikh (Nugget/Horseman), Paul Whitworth (Martin Dysart), Sameerah Luqmaan-Harris (Nurse), Randy Danson (Hesther Salomon), Douglas Jones (Frank Strang), Devora Millman (Dora Strang), James Clarke (Harry Dalton), Jessi Blue Gormezano (Jill Mason); Horses: Shane Austin, Matt Brown, Marcus Denard Johnson, Troy Lewis, Jennifer Logue; Mertz Theatre; March 28–May 4, 2008

LADY by Craig Wright; Director, Hal Brooks; Set, Andromache Chalfant; Costumes, Nicole Bartet; Lighting, Joseph Oshry; Sound, Kevin Kennedy; Fight Director, Ron Keller; SM, Marian Wallace; Cast: David Breitbarth (Kenny), Douglas Jones (Dyson), James Clarke (Graham); Cook Theater; May 9–June 1, 2008

WORKING Based on the book by Studs Terkel; Adapted by Stephen Schwartz and Nina Faso; Music and lyrics by Stephen Schwartz, James Taylor, Craig Carnelia, Micki Grant, Mary Rodgers, Susan Birkenhead, Matt Landers, Lin-Manuel Miranda, Graciela Daniele; Director, Gordon Greenberg; Music Director, Mark Hartman; Choreography, Joshua Rhodes; Set, Beowulf Boritt; Costumes, Mattie Ullrich; Lighting, Jeff Croiter; Video, Aaron Rhyne and Beowulf Boritt; Sound, Matthew Parker; SM, Juanita Munford; Cast: Marie-France Arcilla, Darrin Baker, Colin Donnell, Danielle Lee Greaves, Nehal Joshi, Liz McCartney; Mertz Theatre; May 16–June 8, 2008

MENOPAUSE THE MUSICAL Book and lyrics by Jeanie Linders, music by various; Director, Kathryn Conte; Choreography, Patty Bender; Music Supervisor, Alan J. Plado; Local Music Director, Michael Sebastian; Sets, Bud Clark, Miranda Clark; Costumes, Stephen Horne; National Lighting, Yean-Yves Tessier; On-Site Lighting, Ryan Patridge; Sound, Matthew Parker; Wigs/Hair, Michelle Hart; SM, Roxanne Fay; Cast: Nadeen Halloway (Professional Woman), Christopher Callen (Soap Star), Suzanne H. Smart (Earth Mother), Sandy DeWoody (Iowa Housewife); Band: Michael Sebastian (keyboards), Jerome Butler (bass), Chris Bowen (percussion); Mertz Theatre; June 13–July 13, 2008

FSU/Asolo Conservatory Productions

MURDER BY POE Adapted by Jeffrey Hatcher from stories by Edgar Allen Poe; Director, Greg Leaming; Set/Lighting, Jim Florek; Costumes, David Covach; SM, Sarah Gleissner; Cast: Elisabeth Ahrens (Woman), Brent Bateman (Accent Actor/Old Man/The Minister), Heather Kelley Pluto the Cat/The Queen/Mrs. Clemm), DeMario McGrew (Cat), Steven O'Brien (Usher/Policeman 1), Kevin O'Callaghan (Heart), Dolph Paulsen (Inspector/William Wilson), Jason Peck (C. Auguste Dupin), Michelle Trachtenberg (Marie Roget/The Wife), David Yearta (Zoo Man/Policeman 2/The Prefect); Asolo Theater; October 31–November 18, 2007

SPEED THE PLOW by David Mamet; Director, Andrei Malaev-Babel; Set/Lighting, James Florek; Costumes, Amy J. Cianci; SM, Sarah Gleissner; Vocal Coach, Patricia Delorey; Movement, Margaret Eginton; Hair/Makeup, Michelle Hart; ASM, Sarah Gavitt; Cast: Jason Peck (Bobby Gould), Kevin O'Callaghan (Charlie Fox), Karen (Elisabeth Ahrens); Cook Theater, January 2–20, 2008

THE DUCHESS OF MALFI by John Webster; Director, Susanna Gellert; Set, James Florek; Lighting, Scott Zielinski; Costumes, Amy J. Cianci; Original Music, Ian Turner; SM, Sarah Gleisssner; Voice and Speech, Patricia Delorey; Fights, Paul Molnar; Movement, Margaret Eginton; Technical Director, Rick Cannon; Hair and Makeup, Michelle Hart; ASM, Kevin Stanfa; Cast: Elisabeth Ahrens (Duchess), Heather Kelley (Cariola), Michelle Trachtenberg (Julia), Jason Peck (Bosola), DeMario McGrew (Ferdinand), David Yearta (Cardinal), Dolph Paulsen (Antonio), Kevin O'Callaghan (Delio), Steve O'Brien (Silvio/Lord 1), Brent Bateman (Roderigo/Lord 2); Cook Theater; February 27–March 16, 2008

THE UNDERPANTS Adapted by Steve Martin from the original play by Carl Sternheim; Cast: Brent Bateman (Theo), Heather Kelley (Louise), Michelle Trachtenberg (Gertrude), Dolph Paulsen (Versati), David Yearta (Cohen), DeMario McGrew (Klinglehoff), Steve O'Brien (Kling); Cook Theater; April 16–May 4, 2008

Barrington Stage Company

Pittsfield, Massachusetts

THIRTEENTH SEASON

Artistic Director, Julianne Boyd

WEST SIDE STORY Music by Leonard Bernstein, lyrics by Stephen Sondheim, book by Arthur Laurents; Based on a conception of Jerome Robbins; Director, Julianne Boyd; Choreographer, Joshua Bergasse; Musical Director, Darren R. Cohen; Sets, Luke Hegel-Cantarella; Costumes, Anne Kenney; Lighting, Scott Pinkney; Sound, Randy Hansen and Matt Krauss; Casting, Patt McCorkle; SM, Renee Lutz; Cast: Julie Craig (Maria), Chris Peluso (Tony), Jacqueline Colmer (Anita), Freddy Ramirez (Bernardo), Justin Bohon (Riff), Beth Crandall (Anybodys), Gordon Stanley (Doc), Dale Radunz (Lt. Schrank/Glad Hand), Xavier Cano (Nibbles), Nicky Cooper (Teresita), Billy Fagen (Chino), Matt Gibson (Diesel), Melinda Hall (Minnie), Spencer Howard (Big Deal/Snowboy), Joey Calveri (Pepe), Jamie Markovich (Velma), Michael McGurk (Action), Michael Mindlin (Baby John), Kristin Piro (Consuela), John Raterman (A-Rab), Rebecca Riker (Francesco), Manuel Santos (Indio), Kiira Schmidt (Gaziela), Vanessa Van Vrancken (Rosalia); June 13–July 14, 2007

BLACK COMEDY by Peter Shaffer; Director, Lou Jacob; Set, Karl Eigsti; Costumes, Ilona Smogyi; Lighting, Scott Pinkney; Sound, Daniel A. Little; Casting, Pat McCorkle; SM, Renne Alexander; Cast: Brian Avers (Brindsley Miller), Nell Mooney (Carol Melkett), Beth Dixon (Miss Furnival), Gerry Bamman (Colonel Melkett), Mark H. Dold (Harold Gorringe), Gordon Stanley (Schuppanzigh), Ginifer King (Clea); July 19–August 4, 2007

UNCLE VANYA Translated by Paul Schmidt from the play by Anton Chekhov; Director, Julianne Boyd; Set, Karl Eigsti; Costumes, Elizabeth Flauto; Lighting, Scott Pinkney; Sound/Original Music, Matthew M. Nielson; Casting, Pat McCorkle; SM, Renee Lutz; Cast: Jack Gilpin (Vanya), Keira Naughton (Sonya), Heidi Armbruster (Yelena), Mark L. Montgomery (Astrov), Patricia Conolly (Marina), Kenneth Tigar (Professor), Robert Grossman (Telegin), Rob Holland (Hired Man/Watchman), Alaina Warren Zachary (Maria); August 9–26, 2007

THE WORLD GOES 'ROUND Music by John Kander, lyrics by Fred Ebb, conceived by Scott Ellis, Susan Stroman and David Thompson; Director, Julianne Boyd; Music Director, Brian Usifer; Choreography, Joshua Bergasse; Set, Ken Goldstein; Costumes, Elizabeth Flauto; Lighting, Stephen Arnold; Sound, Matthew M. Nielson; Cast: Kevin Duda, Angela Grovey, Bianca Marroquin, Andrea Rivette, Kurt Robbins; October 10–21, 2007

FULLY COMMITTED by Becky Mode; Director, Andrew Volkoff; Cast: Vince Gatton (Sam Peliczowski); November 7–18, 2007

LADY DAY AT EMERSON'S BAR & GRILL by Lanie Robertson; Cast: Gail Nelson (Billie Holliday), Danny Holgate (piano), David Jackson (bass); December 5–9, 2007

Barrington Stage Musical Theatre Lab at BSC Stage II

CALVIN BERGER Book, music and lyrics by Barry Wyner; Director/Choreographer, Stephen Terrell; Music Director, Justin Paul; Sets, Brian Prather; Costumes, Amela Baksic; Lighting, Scott Pinkney; Sound, Megan B. Henninger; Casting, Pat McCorkle; SM, Jamie Thoma; Cast: David Perlman (Calvin), Elizabeth Lundberg (Rosanna), Aaron Tveitt (Matt), Gillian Goldberg (Bret); June 26–July 14, 2007

FUNKED UP FAIRY TAILS Book, music and lyrics by Kirsten Childs; Director, Kevin Del Aguila; Music Director, Darren R. Cohen; Sets, Brian Prather; Costumes, Matthew Hemesath; Lighting, Jeff Davis; Sound, Daniel A. Little; SM, Jamie Thoma; Cast: Heath Calveri, Edwina Findley, Demond Green, Christy McIntosh, Rashidra Scott, Alysha Umphress; July 31–August 18, 2007

THE MYSTERIES OF HARRIS BURDICK Music by Chris Miller, lyrics by Nathan Tysen, book and direction by Joe Calarco; Based on the picture book by Chris Van Allsburg; Sets, Brian Prather; Costumes, Guy Lee Bailey; Lighting, Kat Fleishhacker and Garrett Herzig; Sound, Daniel A. Little; SM, Jamie Thoma; Cast: Donna Lynne Champlin, Charlie Bradie, Michael Winther, Caroline McMahon, Lynne Wintersteller, Matt Caplan; August 21–September 1, 2007

Barter Theatre

Abingdon, Virginia

SEVENTY-FIFTH SEASON

Producing Artistic Director, Richard Rose; Director of Production, Nicholas Piper; Director of Advancement, Jayne Duehring; Managing Director, Loren White

POW'R IN THE BLOOD by T. Cat Ford; Director, Susanne Boulle; Set, Cheri Prough DeVol; Costumes, Amanda Aldridge; Lighting, Cheri Prough DeVol; Sound, Bobby Beck; SM, Cindi A. Raebel; Cast: Amy Baldwin (Dorothy), Melissa Owens (Heather), Nicholas Piper (John), Ashley Campos (Ruby Mae), Rick McVey (Brother Brady), Mary Lucy Bivins (Ada), Chandler Davis (Dr. Chen); January 25–March 30, 2008

PETER PAN by J.M. Barrie, adapted by Richard Rose; Director, Richard Rose; Set, Charles Vess; Set Assistant, Ben Nicholson; Costumes, Amanda Aldridge; Wigs and Makeup, Heather Fleming; Lighting, Todd Wren; Sound, Bobby Beck; Fight Choreographer, Mike Ostroski; Dramaturges, Catherine Bush and Katy Brown; SM, Jessica Borda; ASM, Holley Housewright; Cast: Ben Mackel (Peter Pan), Gwen Edwards (Wendy/Jane), Michael Poisson (Mr. Darling/Captain Hook), Tricia Matthews (Mrs. Darling/Pirate), Stephanie Fieger (Liza/Tiger Lilly), Logan Fritz/Noah Schrayer (Michael), Nick Austin/Blake Jones (John), Robert Kitchens (Lost Boy), Christopher Salazar (Lost Boy), Wendy Piper (Lost Boy/Mermaid), Tom Angland (Lost Boy), Joshua Gibby (Lost Boy), Eugene Wolf (Smee), Sean Campos (Pirate/Indian), Frank Taylor Green (Running Deer/Pirate), Christopher Dwyer (Pirate), Seth Marstrand (Indian/Pirate/Crocodile), Mike Ostroski (Pirate/Indian), Buddy Woodward (Smee); February 5–April 13, 2008

BLACKBIRD by David Harrower; Director, Susanne Boulle; Set, Derek Smith; Costumes, Kelly Jenkins; Lighting, Heather Eisenhart; Sound, Bobby Beck; SM, Cindi A. Raebel; Cast: Ashley Campos (Una), Rick McVey (Ray), Samantha Walls (Visitor); February 21–April 13, 2008

SAINT JOAN by George Bernard Shaw; Director, Richard Rose; Set, Richard Rose; Set Assistant, Ben Nicholson; Costumes, Kimberly Stockton; Wigs and Makeup, Heather Fleming; Lighting, Richard Rose; Sound, Bobby Beck; Dramaturg, Catherine Bush; SM, Jessica Borda; ASM, Holley Housewright; Cast: Stephanie Fieger (Joan), Frank Taylor Green (Dunois), Mike Ostroski (Chaplin John de Stogumber), Ben Mackel (Dauphin, Charles VII), Michael Poisson (Archbishop of Rheims/The Executioner), Wendy Piper (Bertrand de Poulengey/Brother Martin Ladvenu), Christopher Salazar (Peter Cauchon/Bishop of Beauvais), Mary Lucy Bivins (Dunois' Page/Canon De Courcelles),

Sean Campos (Captain La Hire/English Soldier), Joshua Gibby (Steward/Soldier), Tricia Matthews (La Tremouille/ Canon d'Estivet), Chandler Davis (Warwick's Page/Soldier), Tom Angland (Robert de Baudricourt/The Inquisitor), Seth Marstrand (Gilles de Rais, Bluebeard/Soldier), Christopher Dwyer (Richard, Earl of Warwick); February 29–April 19, 2008

THE ROAD WHERE IT CURVES AWAY by Derek Davidson; Director, John Hardy; Set, Cheri Prough DeVol; Costumes, Heather Fleming; Lighting, Cheri Prough DeVol; Sound, Bobby Beck; SM, Cindi A. Raebel; Cast: Buddy Woodward (Loudon), Robert Kitchens (Garland), Gwen Edwards (Rachel), Nicholas Piper (Jimmy), Amy Baldwin (Opal), Melissa Owens (Joan), Rick McVey (Buddy), Ashley Campos (Mabel); March 11–April 12, 2008

MUCH ADO ABOUT NOTHING by William Shakespeare, adapted by Richard Rose; Director, Richard Rose; Set, Cheri Prough DeVol; Costumes, Kimberly Stockton; Lighting, Cheri Prough DeVol; Sound, Bobby Beck; SM, Jessica Borda; Cast: Amy Baldwin (Beatrice), Mike Ostroski (Benedick), Frank Taylor Green (Don Pedro), Sean Campos (Don John), Ben Mackel (Claudio), Ashley Campos (Hero), Tricia Matthews (Leonato), Wendy Piper (Dogberry), Gwen Edwards (Conrade), Tony Cedeño (Borachio); April 15–May 24, 2008

KEEP ON THE SUNNY SIDE by Douglas Pote; Director, Nicholas Piper; Set, Cheri Prough DeVol; Costumes, Amanda Aldridge; Lighting, Heather Eisenhart; Sound, Bobby Beck; SM, Cindi A. Raebel; ASM, Holley Housewright; Cast: Eugene Wolf (AP Carter), Jill Anderson (Sarah Carter), Joy Lynn White (Maybelle Carter), Kimberly Mays (Janette), Buddy Woodward (Musician #1), Peter Barent Lewis (Musician #2); April 24–May 24, 2008

DON'T CRY FOR ME MARGARET MITCHELL by Duke Ernsberger and Virginia Cate; Director, Katy Brown; Set, Gary Aday; Costumes, Amanda Aldridge; Lighting, Heather Eisenhart; Sound, Bobby Beck; Dramaturge, Catherine Bush; SM, Jessica Borda; Cast: Michael Poisson (David Selznick), Rick McVey (Victor Fleming), Ezra Colon (Ben Hecht), Mary Lucy Bivins (Miss Peabody, Hedda Hopper); May 15–August 16, 2008

EVITA Book and lyrics by Tim Rice; music by Andrew Lloyd Webber; Director, Evalyn Baron; Choreographer, Amanda Aldridge; Set, Daniel Ettinger; Costumes, Amanda Aldridge; Lighting, Lucas Krech; Sound, Bobby Beck; Musical Director, Tim Robertson; SM, Cindi A. Raebel; ASM, Holley Housewright; Cast: Hannah Ingram (Eva), Mike Ostroski (Peron), Peter Yonka (Che), Sean Campos (Magaldi), Gwen Edwards (Mistress); Ensemble: Tony Cedeño, Amy Baldwin, Ashley Campos, Frank Taylor Green, Ben Mackel, Wendy Piper, Eugene Wolf, Julia VanderVeen, Ryan Henderson, David McCall, Chandler Davis, Aria Binkley, Rachel Boyd, Cassandra Brooks, Annie Carr, Nicholas Doggett, Adam Gambrel, Clara Gambrel, Gretchen Gross, Rachel Locke, Laura Masters, Maria Masters, Bronwyn Redvers-Lee, Casey Shea, Tony Guerrero, Seth Marstrand; May 30–August 9, 2008

THE CURE FOR LOVE by Jay Berkow, inspired by an Alexander Dumas novel; Director, Nicholas Piper; Set, Daniel Ettinger; Costumes, Michele Macadaeg; Lighting, Lucas Krech; Sound, Bobby Beck; SM, Cindi A. Raebel; Cast: Amy Baldwin (Fernande), Evalyn Baron (The Baroness de Barthele), Ashley Campos (Clotilde de Barthele), Wendy Piper (Madame du Neuille), Eugene Wolf (The Count de Montigiroux), Sean Campos (Maurice de Barthele), Ryan Henderson (Fabien de Rieulle); June 13–August 10, 2008

TOMMY Music, book and lyrics by The Who; Director, Richard Rose; Choreographer, Amanda Aldridge; Set, Cheri Prough DeVol; Costumes, Kimberly Stockton; Lighting, Cheri Prough DeVol; Sound, Bobby Beck; Musical Director, Tim Robertson; Cast: Logan Fritz (Young Tommy), David McCall (Adult Tommy), Tricia Matthews (Mrs. Nora Walker, Tommy's Mother), Mike Ostroski (Captain Walker, Tommy's Father), Frank Taylor Green (Frank Hobbs, the lover), Ben Mackel (Cousin Kevin/Pinball Wizard), Tony Cedeño (Uncle Ernie), Hannah Ingram (The Acid Queen), Gwen Edwards (Sally Simpson); Dancers: Casey Shea, Tony Guerrero, Seth Marstrand, Chandler Davis, Julia VanderVeen, Philena Gilmer; Youth: Sarah Gregorczyk, Gabrielle Manning, Jessica Presnell, Aleia Warren, Nicholas Doggett (swing); June 25–August 10, 2008

SWEENEY TODD by Hugh Wheeler; music and lyrics by Stephen Sondheim; Director, Richard Rose; Set, Dale Jordan; Costumes, Amanda Aldridge; Lighting, Dale Jordan; Sound, Bobby Beck; SM, Cindi A. Raebel; ASM, Holley Housewright; Cast: Jill Anderson (Mrs. Lovett), Bob Cuccioli (Sweeney Todd), Mick Houlahan (Judge Turpin), Danny Vaccaro (Pirelli/Jonas Fogg), Charles Wahl (Tobias), Michael Hance (The Beadle), Sarah Solie (Beggar Woman), J. Casey Barrett (Anthony), Amanda Johnson (Johanna); August 16–September 13, 2008

COMIN' UP A STORM by Catherine Bush; Director, Katy Brown; Set, Cheri Prough DeVol; Costumes, Heather Fleming; Lighting, Cheri Prough DeVol; Sound, Bobby Beck; Dramaturg, Katy Brown; SM, Jessica Borda; Cast: Tricia Matthews (Faye Thacker), Nicholas Piper (Vernon Cobb), Wendy Piper (Evelyn Thacker), Amy Baldwin (Siobhan O'Malley), Tom Angland (Father Timothy Ryan), James Felton Graham (Elray Slaughter), Gwen Edwards (Sarah Pierce); August 27–November 8, 2008

BAT BOY Book by Keithe Farley and Brian Flemming; music and lyrics by Laurence O'Keefe; Director, Paul Russell; Choreographer, Wendy Piper; Set, Daniel Ettinger; Costumes, Kimberly Stockton; Lighting, Daniel Ettinger; Sound, Bobby Beck; Musical Director, Tim Robertson; SM, Cindi A. Raebel; ASM, Holley Housewright; Cast: Ben Mackel (Bat Boy), Cathy Whelan (Meredith Parker, wife/mother), Tom Anglund (Dr. Thomas Parker), Gwen Edwards (Shelley Parker), James Felton Graham (Sheriff Reynolds), Sean Campos (Rick Taylor/ Lorraine/Doctor/Mr. Dillon), Cheyenne Nelson (Ron Taylor/ Maggie/Clem/Mother), Amy Baldwin (Ruthie Taylor/Ned), Darrick Penny (Mrs. Taylor/Roy/Rev. Billy Hightower/

Institute Man), David McCall (Bud/Daisy/Pan/Doctor); September 6–November 9, 2008

BEAUTY AND THE BEAST by Linda Woolverton; music by Alan Menken; lyrics by Howard Ashman & Tim Rice; Director, Evalyn Baron; Choreographer, Amanda Aldridge; Set, Cheri Prough DeVol; Costumes, Amanda Aldridge; Lighting, Lucas Krech; Sound, Bobby Beck; Musical Director, Tim Robertson; SM, Cindi A. Raebel; ASM, Holley Housewright; Cast: Dan Folino (Beast), Hannah Ingram (Belle), Mike Ostroski (Gaston), Michael Poisson (Cogsworth), Cathy Whelan (Mrs. Potts), Sean Campos (Lumiere), Eugene Wolf (Maurice), Ezra Colon (Lefou), Ashley Campos (Babette), Cheyenne Nelson (Madame de la Grande Bouche); Ensemble: May Lucy Bivins, Frank Taylor Green, Ben Mackel, Rick McVey, Darrick Penny, Seth Marstrand; September 19–November 15, 2008

THE DESPERATE HOURS by Joseph Hayes; Director, Richard Rose; Set, Richard Finkelstein; Costumes, Kimberly Stockton; Lighting, Lucas Krech; Sound, Bobby Beck; Dramaturg, Catherine Bush; SM, Jessica Borda; Cast: Seth Marstrand (Tom Winston), Michael Poisson (Jesse Bard), Dan Folino (Harry Carson), Mary Lucy Bivins (Eleanor Hilliard), Logan Fritz or Kevin O'Brien (Ralphie Hilliard), Rick McVey (Dan Hilliard), Ashley Campos (Cindy Hilliard), Nicholas Piper (Glenn Griffin), Ezra Colon (Hank Griffin), Frank Taylor Green (Robish), Ryan Henderson (Chuck Wright), Eugene Wolf (Mr. Patterson/Lt. Fredericks), Hannah Ingram (Miss Swift); October 3–November 14, 2008

MIRACLE ON 34TH STREET Book and lyrics by Vern Stefanic, Music by Doug Smith; Director, Mary Lucy Bivins; Set, Daniel Ettinger; Costumes, Karen Brewster; Lighting, Tonry Lathroum; Sound, Bobby Beck; Dramaturg, Catherine Bush; SM, Cindi A. Raebel; ASM, Holley Housewright; Cast: Frank Taylor Green (Dr. Pierce), Rick McVey (Kris Kringle), Amy Baldwin (Doris), Mike Ostroski (Fred), Tom Anglund (Mr. Macy), Ezra Colon (Shellhammer), Nicholas Piper (Dr. Sawyer), Sean Campos (Finley), Ben Mackel (Mara), Michael Poisson (Judge Harper); Ensemble: Ashley Campos, Gwen Edwards, Tricia Matthews; November 21–December 28, 2008

ANOTHER NIGHT BEFORE CHRISTMAS... by Sean Grennan and Leah Okimoto; Director/Dramaturg, Richard Rose; Set, Mark DeVol; Costumes, Amanda Aldridge; Lighting, Heather Eisenhart; Sound, Bobby Beck; Co-Dramaturg, Catherine Bush; SM, Jessica Borda; Cast: Wendy Piper (Karol Elliott), Eugene Wolf (The Guy); November 26–December 28, 2008

Bay Street Theatre

Sag Harbor, New York

SIXTEENTH SEASON

Co-Artistic Directors, Sybil Christopher and Murphy Davis

THINGS BEING WHAT THEY ARE by Wendy Macleod; Director, Leonard Foglia; Cast; Brian d'Arcy James, Tom McGowan; East Coast Premiere, May 22–June 3, 2007

THE NIGHT SEASON by Rebecca Lenkiewicz; Director, Lonny Price; Cast; Rosie Benton, Katherine Helmond, David Patrick Kelly, Michael O'Keefe, Kellie Overbie, Ana Reeder, Richard Short; American Premiere, June 12–July 1, 2007

TURANDOT: THE RUMBLE FOR THE RING created Diane Paulus and Randy Weiner; book and lyrics by Randy Weiner; Director, Diane Paulus; Set, Scott Pask; Music Director, Arranger & Orchestrator, Roger Butterley; Fight Director, Rick Sordelet; Cast; Uzo Abuda, Matthew Scott Campbell, Ryan Dunn, Manoel Felciano, Mark Jacoby, Billy Kuehnle, Michael Lanning, Bryce Ryness, Don Stephenson, Teal Wicks, Ray Willis; July 10–August 5, 2007

THE LADY IN QUESTION by Charles Busch; Director, Christopher Ashley; Cast; Charles Candy Buckley (Augusta Von Elsner/Raina Aldric), Charles Busch (Gertrude Garnet), Barrett Foa (Karel), Julie Halston (Kitty), Larry Keith (Professor Mittelhoffer/Dr. Maximilian), Richard Kind (Baron Wilhelm Von Elsner), Matt McGrath (Lotte/Hugo), Perry Ojeda (Professor Erik Maxwell), Ana Reeder (Heidi Mittelhoffer); August 14–September 2, 2007

Berkeley Repertory Theatre

Berkeley, California

FORTIETH SEASON

Artistic Director, Tony Taccone; Managing Director, Susan Medak; Associate Artistic Director, Les Waters

HEARTBREAK HOUSE by George Bernard Shaw; Director, Les Waters; Set, Annie Smart; Costumes, Anna R. Oliver; Lighting, Alexander V. Nichols; Sound, Obadiah Eaves; Dramaturg, Madeleine Oldham; Dialect/Text Coach, Lynne Soffer; SM, Michael Suenkel; ASM, Karen Szpaller; Cast: Chris Ayles (Burglar), Stephen Caffrey (Hector Hushabye), David Chandler (Boss Mangan), Matt Gottlieb (Mazzini Dunn), Michelle Morain (Hesione Hushabye), Lynne Soffer (Nurse Guinness), Allison Jean White (Ellie Dunn), Susan Wilder (Ariadne Utterword), Michael Winters (Captain Shotover), Michael Ray Wisely (Randall Utterword); Roda Theatre; August 31–October 14, 2007

after the quake Adapted by Frank Galati, based on selections from the novel by Haruki Murakami; Director, Frank Galati;

Set, James Schuette; Costumes, Mara Blumenfeld; Lighting, James F. Ingalls; Sound/Original Compositions, Andre Pluess and Ben Sussman; SM, Malcolm Ewen; Cast: Madison Logan V. Phan (Sala), Paul YH. Juhn (Katagiri/Takatsuki), Gemma Megumi Fa-Kaji (Sala), Keong Sim (Narrator/Frog), Jennifer Shin (Sayoko/Nurse), Hanson Tse (Junpei), Jason McDermott (Cello), Jeff Wichmann (Koto); Thrust Stage; October 12–December 2, 2007

ARGONAUTIKA Written and directed by Mary Zimmerman, adapted from The Voyage of Jason and the Argonauts; Set, Daniel Ostling; Costumes, Ana Kuzmanic; Lighting, John Culbert; Sound and Original Compositions, Andre Pluess and Ben Sussman; Puppetry, Michael Montenegro; SM, Cynthia Cahill; Cast: Justin Blanchard (Hylas/Dymas), Allen Gilmore (Pelias & others), Sofia Jean Gomez (Athena), Casey Jackson (Pollux & others), Chris Kipiniak (Castor & others), Tessa Klein (Aphrodite & others), Ronete Levenson (Andromeda & others), Atley Loughridge (Medea), Andy Murray (Meleager), Søren Oliver (Hercules/Aietes), Jesse J. Perez (Idmon & others), Christa Scott-Reed (Hera), Paul Oakley Stovall (Amycus & others), Jake Suffian (Jason); West Coast Premiere; Roda Theatre; November 2–December 23, 2007

TAKING OVER Written and performed by Danny Hoch; Director, Tony Taccone; Set and Costumes, Annie Smart; Lighting/Video, Alexander V. Nichols; Sound, Robyn Bykofsky; Composers, Asa Taccone & Drew Campbell; Photography, Reesa Tansey; SM, Michael Suenkel; World Premiere; Thrust Stage; January 11–February 10, 2008

WISHFUL DRINKING Created and performed Carrie Fisher; Presented in association with Jonathan Reinis Productions; Director, Tony Taccone; Set, Lighting and Projection, Alexander V. Nichols; Costumes, Christina Wright; Sound, Heather Bradley; Piano Recording, Billy Philadelphia; SM, Nicole Dickerson; Roda Theatre; February 8–April 12, 2008

TRAGEDY: A TRAGEDY by Will Eno; Director, Les Waters; Set, Antje Ellermann; Costumes, Meg Neville; Lighting, Matt Frey; Sound, Cliff Caruthers; SM, Michael Suenkel; ASM, Karen Szpaller; Cast: David Cromwell (Frank in the Studio), Max Gordon Moore (Michael, Legal Advisor), Thomas Jay Ryan (John in the Field), Marguerite Stimpson (Constance at the Home), Danny Wolohan (The Witness); American Premiere; Thrust Stage; March 14–April 13, 2008

FIGARO Conceived by Steven Epp and Dominique Serrand, text by Steven Epp; Director, Dominique Serrand; Set/Video, Dominique Serrand; Costumes, Sonya Berlovitz; Lighting, Marcus Dilliard; Sound, Zach Humes; Music Adaptation, Bradley Greenwald; Music Director/Piano, Barbara Brooks; Subtitles, Steven Epp; SM, Glenn D. Klapperich; Cast: Christina Baldwin (Cherubino), Bryan Boyce (Figaro), Steven Epp (Fig), Bradley Greenwald (Count Almaviva), Carrie Hennessey (Marcellina), Bryan Janssen (Bartolo), Justin D. Madel (Basilio), Jennifer Baldwin Peden (Countess), Dominique Serrand (Mr. Almaviva), Momoko Tanno (Susanna), Julie Kurtz (Susanna Swing), Musicians: Alex Kelly, Justin Mackewich, Katrina Weeks, Sarah Jo Zaharako; West Coast Premiere; Roda Theatre; April 25–June 8, 2008

Berkshire Theatre Festival

Stockbridge, Massachusetts

SEVENTY-NINTH SEASON

Artistic Director, Kate Maguire; Administrative Producer, M. Edgar Rosenblum

Main Stage

LOVE! VALOUR! COMPASSION! by Terrence McNally; Director, Anders Cato; Sets, Hugh Landwehr, Costumes, Laurie Churba; Lighting, Jeff Davis; Resident Composer/Sound, Scott Killian; SM, Marjorie Gallant; Movement, Darrell Pucciarello; Casting, Alan Filderman Cast: David Adkins (James Jeckyll,/ John Jeckyll), Stephen DeRosa (Buzz Hauser), Jonathan Fried (Perry Sellars), Ricky Fromeyer (Ramon Fornos), Romain Frugé (Gregory Mitchell), James Lloyd Reynolds (Arthur Pape), Matthew Wilkas (Bobby Brahms); June 19–July 7, 2007

ONE FLEW OVER THE CUCKOO'S NEST by Dale Wasserman; Director, Eric Hill; Sets, Karl Eigsti, Costumes, Jessica Risser-Milne; Lighting, Matthew E. Adelson; Sound, J Hagenbuckle; Casting, Alan Filderman; SM, Jason Hindelang; Cast: Ron Bagden (Dr. Spivey), Sheldon Best (Aide Warren), Crystal Bock (Candy Starr), Austin Durant (Chief Bromden), Jonathan Epstein (Randle P. McMurphy), Linda Hamilton (Nurse Ratched), Randy Harrison (Billy Bibbit), Jerry Krasser (Scanlon), Stew Nantell (Ruckly), Tommy Schrider (Dale Harding), Robert Serrell (Martini), E. Gray Simons III (Cheswick), Anthony Mark Stockard (Aide Williams/Aide Turkle), Rebecca Leigh Webber (Various Roles); July 10–28, 2007

MORNING'S AT SEVEN by Paul Osborn; Director, Vivian Matalon; Sets, R. Michael Miller, Costumes, David Murin; Lighting, Ann G. Wrightson; Sound, Craig Kaufman; Wig Master, David Lawrence; Casting, Alan Filderman; SM, Marjorie Gallant; Cast: Kevin Carolan (Homer Bolton), David Green (David Crampton), Anita Gillette (Esther Crampton), Paul Hecht (Theodore Swanson), Jonathan Hogan (Carl Bolton), Lucy Martin (Cora Swanson), Joyce Van Patten (Aaronetta Gibbs), Debra Jo Rupp (Ida Bolton), Christianne Tisdale (Myrtle Brown); July 31–August 11, 2007

MRS. WARREN'S PROFESSION by George Bernard Shaw; Director, Anders Cato; Sets, Carl Sprague, Costumes, Olivera Gajic; Lighting, Dan Kotlowitz; Resident Composer/Sound, Scott Killian; Dramaturg, James Leverett; Dialects, David Alan Stern; Casting, Alan Filderman; Stage Managers, Jason Hindelang and Marjorie Gallant; Cast: Lisa Banes (Mrs. Kitty Warren), Xanthe Elbrick (Vivie Warren), Randy Harrison (Frank Gardner), Walter Hudson (Sir George Crofts), Mark

Nelson (Praed), Stephen Temperley (The Reverend Samuel Gardner); August 14–September 14, 2007

Unicorn Theatre

THE GLASS MENAGERIE by Tennessee Williams; Director, Eric Hill; Sets, Carl Sprague, Costumes, Olivera Gajic; Lighting, Matthew E. Adelson; Resident Composer/Sound, Scott Killian; Dialects, David Alan Stern; Casting, Alan Filderman; SM, Mary P. Costello; Cast: Kate Maguire (Amanda Wingfield), Aya Cash (Laura Wingfield), Tom Story (Tom Wingfield), Greg Keller (Jim O'Connor); Berkshire Theatre Festival; May 24–June 30, 2007

MY PAL GEORGE by Rick Cleveland; Director, Eric Simonson; Sets, Dave Brooks; Lighting, Erik Seidel; SM, Stephen Horton; Cast: Rick Cleveland; July 3–July 21, 2007

TWO-HEADED by Julie Jensen; Director, Marc Geller; Sets, Aaron P. Mastin, Costumes, Dennis Ballard; Lighting, Frank DenDanto III; Composer, Daniel T. Denver; Sound, Craig Kaufman; Casting, Alan Filderman; SM, Mary P. Costello; Cast: Corinna May (Lavinia), Diane Prusha (Hettie); July 25–August 18, 2007

EDUCATING RITA by Willy Russell; Director, Richard Corley; Sets, Joseph Varga, Costumes, Sarah Reever; Lighting, Holly Blomquist; Composer/Sound, Joe Cerqua; Dialects, David Alan Stern; Casting, Alan Filderman; SM, Stephen Horton; Cast: Jonathan Epstein (Frank), Tara Franklin (Rita); August 21–October 30, 2007

Family Programming

CINDERELLA Adapted by E. Gray Simons III from the Brothers Grimm fairytale; Director, Cristina Miles; Sets, Jonathan Wentz; Costumes, Samantha Fromm; Lighting, Jeffrey Small; Sound, Sean-Michael Galgano; SM, Sarah Rowland; Cast: Andrew Belcher (Uncle), Michael Brahce (Chorus 5/Father/Town Crier), Rebecca Chapman (Chorus 2/Bird/Shoemaker), Patrice Foster (Cinderella), Leah Henoch (Chorus 1/Bird/Dressmaker), Ashley Blair Isenhower (Younger Cousin – Lurlene), Gwen Lawson (Older Cousin – Lindie), Suzanne Lenz (Chorus 3/Nurse 1/Jeweler), Kara Manson (Chorus 6/Mother/Queen), Lee Matthews (Auntie), Bryan Pridgen (Prince), Caroline Pugliese (Chorus 4/Nurse 2/Old Gardner); June 27–July 28, 2007

AESOP'S NETWORK: Broadcasting Theatrical Fables by E. Gray Simons III; Director, Amanda Byron; Sets, Eliza S. Rankin; Costumes, Elizabeth Barrett Groth; Lighting, Patience Edwards; Sound, Adam W. Johnson; SM, Christine A. Sanders; Cast: Holly Bittinger (Reporter 3/Clown 1/Attorney 2), David Michael Brown (Villager 3/Ant 1/Wolf 1), Evan Charest (Reporter 4/Lion), Alison Clayton (P.T. Skeeter/Boy), Bess Allison Eckstein (Tortoise/Ladybug 2), Thomas J. Ferguson (Hare/Sheep 2), Christian Grunnah (Villager 2/Grasshopper), Sara Lynn Herman (Boy's Mother/Lightning Bug/Attorney 1), Brittany Marryott (Villager 1/Ant 2), Bess Rowen (Reporter 1/Ant 3), Allison Vanouse (Mouse/Ladybug 1/Wolf 2), Elizabeth Wagner (Anchor/Clown 2), Jenni Weisphal (Reporter 2/Sheep 1/Announcer); August 1–August 18, 2007

Caldwell Theatre Company

Boca Raton, Florida

THIRTY-THIRD SEASON - Inaugural Season in the new Count de Hoernle Theatre

Artistic & Managing Director, Michael Hall

DOUBT by John Patrick Shanley; Director, Michael Hall; Set, Tim Bennett; Costumes, Patricia Burdett; Lighting, Thomas Salzman; Sound, Sean Lawson; PSM, Justin Hossle; Cast: Terrell Hardcastle (Father Brendan Flynn), Pat Nesbit (Sister Aloysius Beauvier), Amy Montminy (Sister James), Pat Bowie (Mrs. Muller); December 2, 2007–January 6, 2008

SUITE SURRENDER by Michael McKeever; Director, Joe Warik; Set, Tim Bennett; Costumes, T. Michael Hall; Lighting, Thomas Salzman; Sound, Sean Lawson; PSM, Marci A. Glotzer; Cast: David Perez-Ribada (Otis), Tom Wahl (Francis), John Felix (Bernard S. Dunlap), Kay Brady (Mrs. Everett P. Osgood), Pat Nesbit (Dora del Rio), Elizabeth Dimon (Claudia McFadden), Michael McKeever (Mr. Pippet), SuEllen Estey (Athena Sinclair), Autumn Horne (Murphy Stevens); World Premiere; January 13–February 17, 2008

MARIE ANTOINETTE: The Color of Flesh by Joel Gross; Director, Michael Hall; Set, Tim Bennett; Costumes, T. Michael Hall; Lighting, Thomas Salzman; Sound, Sean Lawson; PSM, Justin Hossle; Cast: Janine Theriault (Elisabeth Louise Vigee Le Brun), Jason Griffith (Count Alexis de Ligne), Amanda Jones (Marie Antoinette, Queen of France), A.J. Dasher (Footman); February 24–March 30, 2008

TUESDAYS WITH MORRIE by Jeffrey Hatcher & Mitch Albom, based on the book by Mitch Albom; Director, Michael Hall; Set, Tim Bennett; Lighting, Thomas Salzman; Sound, Sean Lawson; PSM, Marci A. Glotzer; Cast: Jim Ballard (Mitch Albom), Peter Haig (Professor Morrie Schwartz); April 6–May 11, 2008

Casa Mañana

Fort Worth, Texas

FORTY-NINTH SEASON

President and Executive Producer, Denton Yockey

A FEW GOOD MEN by Aaron Sorkin; Director, Elliot Wasserman; Set, Claire DeVries; Costumes, Marty Van Kleek; Lighting, Jay Isham; Sound, Ryan Mansfield; Production Manager, Theresa Furphy; Cast: Lou Diamond Phillips (Colonel Nathan R. Jessep), Jensen Ackles (Lt. Daniel Kaffee), Lydia Mackay (Lt. Cmdr. Joanne Galloway), Ben Rauch (Lt. JG Sam Weinberg), Jerome Bethea (LCpl Harold W. Dawson),

Justin Arnold (Pvt. First Class Louden Downey), Vince Davis (Captain Isaac Whitaker), Sean McGuirk (Captain Matthew A. Markinson), Ayal Miodovnik (Lt. Jack Ross), David Ristuccia (Private First Class William T. Santiago), Jeff Schmidt (Lt. Jonathan James Kendrick), Rick L. Spivey (Corporal Jeffery Owen Howard), Derik Webb (Sergeant at Arms), Richard Zavaglia (Captain Julius Alexander Randolph); June 5–10, 2007

CINDERELLA Music by Rodgers, lyrics and book by Oscar Hammerstein II; Director, Mark Madama; Choreographer, Brandon Mason; Costumes, Craig Windham; Lighting, Jay Isham; Sound, Ryan Mansfield; Music Director, Eugene Gwozdz; Production Manager, Theresa Furphy; Cast: Kimberly Whalen (Cinderella), Christopher Deaton (Prince Christopher), Gina Biancardi (Queen), Brad Jackson (King), Deborah Brown (Fairy Godmother), Melissa Jobe (Stepmother), Alison Cimmet (Joy), Shannon K. McGrann (Portia), Brian Mathis (Chef), Greg Dulcie (Herald), Darrel Blackburn (Steward); July 10–15, 2007

THE WIZARD OF OZ Music and lyrics by Harold Arlen and E.Y. Harburg, adapted by John Kane from the book by Frank L. Baum and motion picture owned by Turner Entertainmet; Co-produced Tour; Director, Phillip Wm. McKinley; Choreography, Paula Lynn; Set, James Danford; Costumes, Kansas City Costume; Musical Director, Anthony Edwards; ASMs, Susan Forbes and Steve Henry; Orchestrations, Larry Wilcox; Arrangements, Peter Howard; Background Music, Herbert Stothart; Cast: Kate Manning (Dorothy), Jane Blass (The Wicked Witch), David Titus (The Lion), Jaymes Hodges (The Tinman), Eric Imhoff (The Scarecrow), Suzanne Ishee (Glinda), Gary Neal Johnson (The Wizard), David Coffee (Uncle Henry), Tory the dog (Toto); Ensemble: Diana Cammarata, Lou Castro, Kym Chambers, Michael Parrish Dudell, Michelle Dyer, Melissa Fleck, Matt Keirnan, Missy Morrison, Tom Pacio, Dante Puleio, Chuck Ragsdale, Alison Rose, Brad Siebeking, Tara Siesener, Amy Shure, Christopher Sloan, Kristen J. Smith, Matthew Winnegge, Jessica Wu; August 14–19, 2007

MAN OF LA MANCHA Book by Dale Wasserman, music by Mitch Leigh, lyrics by Joe Darion; Director, Elliot Wasserman; Choreographer, Brandon Mason; Lighting, Jay Isham; Sound, Ryan Mansfield; Wardrobe Supervisor, Tammy Spencer; Musical Director, Art Yelton; Technical Director, Paul Rubin; Production Manager, Theresa Furphy; ASM, Craig Windham; Cast: David McDonald (Cervantes/Quixote), Jacqueline Colmer (Aldonza/Dulcinea), Michael Lluberes (Sancho), Brian Mathis (Governor/Innkeeper), Jackson Ross Best, Jr. (Padre), Blake Davidson (Duke/Dr. Carrasco), D'Lytha Myers (Antonia), Dennis Yslas (Barber), Greg Dulcie (Pedro), Lois Sonnier Hart (Housekeeper), Margaret Shafer (Maria), Kia Dawn Fulton (Fermina), Christopher Deaton (Anselmo), Sydney Erik Wright (Jose), Jerome Bethea (Juan), Michael Newberry (Tenorio), Willy Welch (Guitar Player), Ben Giddings (Paco), Doug LoPachin (Captain Inquisition); Guards: Shance Ryan Brentham, Jeremy Inman, Timothy Riley; November 6–11, 2007

A CHRISTMAS CAROL by Charles Dickens; Cast: Michael Hayward-Jones (Scrooge), Brian Mathis (Ghost of Jacob Marley), Andy Baldwin (Ghost of Christmas Past), Keron Jackson (Ghost of Christmas Present), Paul Taylor (Cratchit), Wendy Welch (Mrs. Cratchit), Brad Jackson (Mr. Fezziwig), Amy Mills (Mrs. Fezziwig), Barry Busby (Young Scrooge); Ensemble: Michael Newberry, Lindsey Holloway, Marjorie Hayes, Lois Sonnier Hart, Kim Whalen, Barry Busby, Allison Rogers, Carolyn Willemis, Van Dijk, Parish Mechling, Cassie Chestnutt, Leslie Marie Collins, Merrill West, Lexi Windsor, Allyson Turner, Brandon Mason, Con O'Shea-Creal, Aaron Umsted, Yolanda Williams, Darrel Blackburn, Mark Frie, Sarah Comely, Doug LoPachin; December 21–29, 2007

STEEL MAGNOLIAS by Robert Harling; Director, Guy Stroman; Set, Aaron Bell; Costumes, LaLonnie Lehman; Lighting, Jay Isham; Sound, Ryan Mansfield; Production Manager, Theresa Furphy; Cast: Ruta Lee (Clairee Belcher), Sally Struthers (Truvy Jones), Margaret Colin (M'Lynn Eatenton), June Squibb (Ouiser Boudreaux), Jennifer Blood (Annelle Dupuy Desoto), Erinn Krakow (Shelby Eatenton Latcherie); February 12–17, 2008

Center Theatre Group

Los Angeles, California

FORTY-FIRST SEASON

Artistic Director, Michael Ritchie, Managing Director, Charles Dillingham

Mark Taper Forum Series*

THE HISTORY BOYS by Alan Bennett; Recreated from The National Theatre of Great Britain production; Produced by special arrangement with the original Broadway producers; Director, Paul Miller; Original Director, Nicholas Hytner; Set, Bob Crowley; Lighting, Mark Henderson; Sound, Colin Pink and Jon Gottlieb; Casting, Erika Sellin; Video, Austin Swister; Music, Richard Sisson; Production Manager, Andy Ward; Stage Managers, James T. McDermott, David S. Franklin and Susie Walsh; Cast: John Apicella (TV Director), Adam Armstrong (Lockwood), Ryder Bach (Boy), Alex Brightman (Posner), Charlotte Cornwell (Mrs. Lintott), H. Richard Greene (Headmaster), Cord Jackman (Rudge), Sean Marquette (Timms), Dakin Matthews (Hector), Andrew McClain (Boy), Seth Numrich (Dakin), Peter Paige (Irwin), Ammar Ramzi (Akthar), Demond Robertson (Crowther), Brett Ryback (Scripps), Edward Tournier (Boy), Elizabeth West (Make-Up Lady); November 7–December 9, 2007

SWEENEY TODD, The Demon Barber of Fleet Street Book by Hugh Wheeler, music and lyrics by Stephen Sondheim, adaptation by Christopher Bond; Director and Set, John Doyle; Original Broadway Director, Harold Prince; Lighting, Richard G. Jones; Sound, Dan Moses Schreier; Wigs/Hair, Paul Huntley; Makeup, Angelina Avallone; Telsey + Company; Music

Coordinator, John Miller; Resident Music Director, Andy Einhorn; Music Director, David Loud; Production Manager, Kai Brothers; PSM, Newton Cole; Associate Director, Adam John Hunter; Music Supervision/Orchestrations, Sarah Travis; Cast: Edmund Bagnell (Tobias), Keith Buterbaugh (Judge Turpin), Diana DiMarzio (Beggar Woman), Benjamin Eakeley (The Beadle), David Hess (Sweeney Todd), Judy Kaye (Mrs. Lovett), Benjamin Magnuson (Anthony), Steve McIntyre (Jonas Fogg); Standbys: Edwin Cahill (Anthony/Tobias/The Beadle/ Jonas Fogg), David Garry (Sweeney Todd/Judge Turpin/ The Beadle), Megan Loomis (Mrs. Lovett/Beggar Woman), Elisa Winter (Johanna/Jonas Fogg/Pirelli), Andy Einhorn (keyboard); March 11–April 6, 2008

*As the Mark Taper Forum was closed for renovations this season, these shows were presented in the Ahmanson Theatre

Ahmanson Theatre (National Touring Shows)

AVENUE Q Book by Jeff Whitty, music, lyrics and concept by Robert Lopez and Jeff Marx; Director, Jason Moore, Choreographer, Ken Roberson; Set, Anna Louizos; Costumes, Mirena Rada; Lighting, Howell Binkley; Sound, Acme Sound Partners; Animation, Robert Lopez; Incidental Music, Gary Adler; Musical Director, Andrew Graham; Music Coordinator, Michael Keller; Casting, Cindy Tolan; Technical Director, Brian Lynch; Associate Director, Evan Ensign; Tour Marketing/ Publicity, TMG – The Marketing Group; General Manager, John Corker; SM, Marian DeWitt; Associate Producers, Sonny Everett; Walter Grossman, Mort Swinsky; Music Supervision, Arrangements/Orchestrations, Stephen Oremus; Cast: Angela Ai (Christmas Eve), Christian Anderson (Nicky/Trekkie Monster/Bear/Others), Minglie Chen (Mrs. T./Bear/Others), Robert McClure (Princeton/Rod), Cole Porter (Brian), Carla Renata (Gary Coleman), Kelli Sawyer (Kate Monster/Lucy/ Others); Ensemble: Maggie Lakis, Seth Rettberg, and Danielle K. Thomas; September 6–October 14, 2007

THE COLOR PURPLE Book by Marsha Norman, music and lyrics by Brenda Russell, Allee Willis & Stephen Bray; Director, Gary Griffin; Choreographer, Donald Byrd; Set, John Lee Beatty; Costumes, Paul Tazewell; Lighting, Brian MacDevitt; Sound, Jon Weston; Casting, Telsey + Company; Hair, Charles G. LaPointe; Production Managers, Arthur Siccardi & Curtis Cowley; Production Supervisor, Kristen Harris; Tour Marketing and Press, C Major Marketing; General Management, NLA/Amy Jacobs; Music Director, Sheilah Walker; Dance Arrangements, Daryl Waters; Additional Arrangements, Joseph Joubert; Music Coordinator, Seymour Red Press; Orchestrations, Jonathan Tunick; Music Supervisor/ Incidental Music Arrangements, Kevin Stites; Cast: Diamond White (Young Nettie/Young Henrietta), Alex De Castro (Young Celie/Young Olivia/Older Henrietta), Bridgette Bentley (Church Soloist), Kimberly Ann Harris (Doris), Virginia Ann Woodruff (Darlene), Lynette Dupree (Jarene), Trent Armand Kendall (Preacher/Prison Guard), Quentin Earl Darrington (Pa/Chief), LaToya London (Nettie), Jeannette Bayardelle (Celie), Rufus Bonds, Jr. (Mister), Anthony Williams II (Young Harpo/Young Adam), Stu James (Harpo), Felicia P. Fields (Sofia), Stephanie St. James (Squeak), Michelle Williams (Shug Avery), Adam Wade (Ol' Mister), Lesly Terrell Donald (Buster, Bobby), Keith Byron Kirk (Grady), Tiffany Daniels (Daisy), Sumayah McRae (Older Olivia), Grasan Kingsberry (Older Adam); Ensemble: Bridgette Bentley, Reneé Monique Brown, Tiffany Daniels, Quentin Earl Darrington, Alex De Castro, Lesly Terrell Donald, Lynette Dupree, Rhett George, Kimberly Ann Harris, Dameka Hayes, Jenna Ford Jackson, Trent Armand Kendall, Grasan Kingsberry, Keith Byron Kirk, Sumayah McRae, Kristopher Tompson-Bolden, Anthony Wayne, Diamond White, Virginia Ann Woodruff; Swings: Shani M. Borden, Brian Harlan Brooks, Aliyah D. Flowers, André Garner, Mariama Whyte; December 13, 2007–March 9, 2008

MY FAIR LADY Book and lyrics by Alan Jay Lerner, music by Frederick Loewe, adapted from George Bernard Shaw's play and Gabriel Pascal's motion picture *Pygmalion;* Director, Trevor Nunn; Choreographer, Matthew Bourne; Set, Anthony Ward; Lighting, David Hersey; Sound, Paul Groothuis; Orchestrator, William David Brohn; Dance Arranger, Chris Walker; Musical Director/Conductor, James Lowe; Music Contractor, Seymour Red Press; PSM, Harold Goldfaden; Production Manager, Jerry Donaldson; Company Manager, Chris Danner; General Management, Gregory Vander Ploeg, Gentry & Associates; Casting, Tara Rubin; For the *My Fair Lady* U.S. tour: Set Associate, Matt Kinley; Sound Associate, Ed Clarke; Costume Associate, Christine Rowland; Lighting, Oliver Fenwick and Rob Halliday; Dance Staging, Fergus Logan; Musical Supervisor, Stephen Brooker; Redirector, Shaun Kerrison; Cast: Lisa O'Hare (Eliza Doolittle), Justin Bohon (Freddy Eynsford-Hill), Cathy Newman (Mrs. Eynsford-Hill/Angry Neighbor), Lisa Kassay (Clara Eynsford-Hill/Servant), Walter Charles (Colonel Hugh Pickering), Christopher Cazenove (Professor Henry Higgins), Tim Jerome (Alfred P. Doolittle), Bill Dietrich (Jamie/Charles/Mrs. Higgins' Chauffer), Lee Zarrett (Harry/Footman), Barbara Marineau (Mrs. Pearce), Marni Nixon (Mrs. Higgins), David Abeles (Costermonger/ Servant/Policeman), Harlan Bengel (Dustbin Lid Dancer/ Prince of Transylvania), Eric Briarley (Servant), Wilson Bridges (Dustbin Lid Dancer/Embassy Waltz Guest), Ronald L. Brown (Selsey Man/Costermonger/Lord Boxington), Debra Cardona (Servant/Queen of Transylvania), Dana Delisa (Servant/Eliza Doolittle alternate), Elizabeth Derosa (Embassy Waltz Guest/ Mrs. Higgins' Maid); Michael J. Farina (Hoxton Man/George/ Bartender/Zoltan Karpathy), Warren Freeman (Costermonger/ Embassy Waltz Guest), Jazmin Gorsline (Servant), Robin Haynes (Butler/Sir Reginald Tarrington), Marnee Hollis (Servant/Lady Boxington), Adam Laird (Costermonger/ Dustbin Lid Dancer), Georga Osborne (Mrs. Hopkins), Byron St. Cyr (Bystander/Costermonger/Dustbin Lid Dancer), Erin Willis (Flower Girl/Embassy Waltz Guest); Ensemble: Buddy Hammonds, Lauren Pastorek; Swings: Lainie Munro, Jesse Swimm, David Tankersley, Stephanie Van Duynhoven; April 9–27, 2008

A CHORUS LINE Book by James Kirkwood and Nicholas

Dante, music by Marvin Hamlisch, lyrics by Ed Kleban; Conceived and originally directed and choreographed by Michael Bennett; Originally co-choreographed by Bob Avian; Director, Bob Avian; Choreography re-staged by Baayork Lee; Set, Robin Wagner; Costumes, Theoni V. Aldredge; Lighting, Tharon Musser, adapted by Natasha Katz; Sound, Acme Sound Partners; Music Supervision, Patrick Vaccariello, Music Direction, John O'Neill, Orchestrations, Jonathan Tunick, Bill Byers, and Hershy Kay; Vocal Arrangements, Don Pippin; Cast: Clyde Alves (Mike), John Carroll (Larry), Emily Fletcher (Sheila), Stephanie Gibson (Judy), Michael Gruber (Zach), Venny Carranza (Roy), Natalie Elise Hall (Val), Derek Hanson (Don), Hollie Howard (Maggie), Jay Armstrong Johnson (Mark), Julie Kotarides (Vicki, Denis Lambert (Greg), Jessica Latshaw (Kristine), Ian Liberto (Bobby), Stephanie Martignetti (Tricia), Sterling Masters (Lois), Pilar Millhollen (Bebe), Colt Prattes (Al), Gabrielle Ruiz (Diana), Clifton Samuels (Tom), Kevin Santos (Paul), Nikki Snelson (Cassie), Brandon Tyler (Frank), Anthony Wayne (Richie), J.R. Whittington (Butch,), Jessica Wu (Connie), Swings: Colin Bradbury, Erica Mansfield, Rebecca Riker, Alex Ringler; May 21–July 6, 2008

Kirk Douglas Theatre

CLAY Written and performed by Matt Sax; Developed in collaboration with and directed by Eric Rosen; Set, Walt Spangler; Lighting, Howell Binkley; Sound/Orchestrations, Joshua Horvath; Additional Music, Jon Schmidt & Johnny Williams; SM, Elizabeth Atkinson; September 13–October 14, 2007

EN UN SOL AMARILLO (Memorias de un Temblor) [In A Yellow Sun (Memories of an Earthquake)] Written and directed by Pablo Brie; Set, Gonzalo Callejas; Costumes, Soledad Ardaya & Danuta Zarzyka; Lighting and Sound, Giampaolo Nalli & Danuta Zarzyka; Music Coordination, Lucas Achirico & Pablo Brie; Cast: Lucas Achirico, Daniel Aguirre, Gonzalo Callejas, Alice Guimaraes; October 26–November 25, 2007

BLOODY BLOODY ANDREW JACKSON Written and directed by Alex Timbers, music and lyrics by Michael Friedman; Choreography, Kelly Devine; Set, Robert Brill; Costumes, Emily Rebholz; Lighting, Jeff Croiter; Sound, Bart Fasbender; Music Direction/Orchestrations, Gabriel Kahane; Projections, Jake Pinholster; Casting, Bonnie Grisan; Dramaturg, Mike Sablone; Stage Managers, David S. Franklin, Elizabeth Atkinson & Michelle Blair, Cast: Anjali Bhimani (Rachel/Ensemble), Will Collyer (Male Soloist/Ensemble), Diane Davis (Elizabeth/Ensemble), Zack DeZon (Ensemble), Erin Felgar (Female Soloist,/Ensemble), Kristin Findley (Ensemble), Jimmy Fowlie (Ensemble), Patrick Gomez (Ensemble), Sebastian Gonzalez (Lyncoya/Ensemble), Will Greenberg (Clay/Ensemble), Greg Hildreth (Red Eagle/ Ensemble), Brian Hostenske (Van Buren/Ensemble), Adam O'Byrne (Calhoun/Ensemble), Matthew Rocheleau (John Quincy Adams/Ensemble), Ben Steinfeld (Monroe/Ensemble), Ian Unterman (Defense Attorney/Ensemble), Benjamin Walker (Andrew Jackson), Taylor Wilcox (Storyteller/Ensemble); World Premiere; January 13–February 17, 2008

NO CHILD... Written and performed by Nilaja Sun; Director, Hal Brooks; Set, Sibyl Wickersheimer; Original Set, Narelle Sissons; Costumes, Jessica Gaffney; Lighting, Mark Barton; Sound, Ron Russell; SM, James T. McDermott; March 6–April 13, 2008

TWO UNRELATED PLAYS - Keep Your Pantheon and **The Duck Variations** by David Mamet; Director, Neil Pepe; Set, Takeshi Kata; Costumes, Ilona Somogyi; Lighting, Christopher Akerlind; Sound, Cricket S. Myers; PSM, David S. Franklin; SM, Elizabeth Atkinson; Casting, Bonnie Grisan; Associate Producer, Kelley Kirkpatrick; Cast: The Duck Variations: Harold Gould (Emil Varec), Michael Lerner (George S. Aronovitz); Keep Your Pantheon: Jeffrey Addiss (Ensemble), Michael Cassidy (Philius), Steven Goldstein (Quintus Magnus), Vincent Guastaferro (Herald), Dominic Hoffman (Lupus Albus Secundus), J.J. Johnston (Titus), Rod McLachlan (Messenger, Ensemble), Ed O'Neill (Starbo), David Paymer (Pelargon), Jonathan Rossetti (Ensemble), Jack Wallace (Ramus); May 11–June 8, 2008

Cincinnati Playhouse in the Park

Cincinnati, Ohio

FORTY-EIGHTH SEASON

Producing Artistic Director, Edward Stern; Executive Director, Buzz Ward

DRACULA by Hamilton Deane & John L. Balderston; Director, Stephen Hollis; Set, Paul Shortt; Costumes, Wade Laboissonniere; Lighting, Kirk Bookman; Sound and Composer, David B. Smith; Fight Director, Drew Fracher; Casting, Rich Cole; Flying Effects, ZFX, Inc.; PSM, Jenifer Morrow; SM, Andrea L. Shell; Cast: Jeffrey Withers (Jonathan Harker), Elizabeth Helitzer (Miss Wells), Richert Easley (Dr. Seward), John Michalski (Abraham Van Helsing), Scott Schafer (R.M. Renfield), Larry Bull (Butterworth/Attendant), Julia Coffey (Lucy Seward), Kurt Rhoads (Count Dracula); September 4–October 5, 2007

OTHELLO by William Shakespeare; Director, Edward Stern; Set, Joseph P. Tilford; Costumes, Mattie Ullrich; Lighting, Thomas C. Hase; Composer, Douglas Lowry; Sound, Chuck Hatcher; Text Consultant, Philip Thompson; Fight Director, Drew Fracher; Casting, Rich Cole; SM, Suann Pollock; SM, Wendy J. Dorn; Cast: Scott Barrow (Roderigo), R. Ward Duffy (Iago), Joneal Joplin (Brabantio/Ludovico), Esau Pritchett (Othello), Anthony Marble (Cassio), Jeff Groh (Officer), Greg Thornton (Duke of Venice/Montano), Sarah Dandridge (Desdemona), Ryan Imhoff (Soldier), Carine Montbertrand (Emilia), Angela Lin (Bianca); September 22–October 21, 2007

ALTAR BOYZ Book by Kevin Del Aguila, music and lyrics by Gary Adler & Michael Patrick Walker, conceived by

Marc Kessler and Ken Davenport; Director, Stafford Arima; Choreographer, Christopher Gattelli; Set, Anna Louizos; Costumes, Alejo Vietti; Lighting, Ben Stanton; Sound, Eric Stahlhammer; Musical Director, Henry Palkes; Associate Choreographer, Lou Castro; Associate Seter, Todd Potter; PSM, Jenifer Morrow; First SM, Andrea L. Shell; Cast: Michael Kadin Craig (Matthew), Shua Potter (Mark), Adam Fleming (Luke), Mauricio Perez (Juan), Ravi Roth (Abraham); Band: Henry Palkes (keyboard #1), Adaron "Pops" Jackson (keyboard #2), James Jackson (percussion), Shaun Robinson (guitar); October 16–November 16, 2007

THE MUSICAL OF MUSICALS (The Musical!) Music by Eric Rockwell, lyrics by Joanne Bogart, book by Eric Rockwell & Joanne Bogart; Director and Choreographer, Pamela Hunt; Set, James Morgan; Costumes, John Carver Sullivan; Lighting, Mary Jo Dondlinger; Sound, David Gotwald; Musical Director, Rich Silverstein; Casting, Rich Cole; SM, Suann Pollock; Cast: Joanne Bogart (Abby et al.), Margaret-Ellen Jeffreys (June et. al), Brent Schindele (Big Willy et. al), Rich Silverstein (Jitter et al.); November 3–December 23, 2007

A CHRISTMAS CAROL by Charles Dickens, adapted by Howard Dallin; Director, Michael Evan Haney; Choreographer, Dee Anne Bryll; Set, James Leonard Joy; Costumes, David Murin; Lighting, Kirk Bookman; Sound/Composer, David B. Smith; Lighting Contractor, Susan Terrano; Costume Coordinator, Cindy Witherspoon; Music Director, Rebecca N. Childs; Casting, Rich Cole; PSM, Jenifer Morrow; Stage Manager, Andrea L. Shell; Cast: Bruce Cromer (Ebenezer Scrooge), Wayne Pyle (Mr. Cupp/Percy/Rich Father at Fezziwig's), Ron Simons (Mr. Sosser/Tailor at Fezziwig's/ Topper/Man with Shoe Shine), Andy Prosky (Bob Cratchit/ Schoolmaster Oxlip), Tony Roach (Fred), Gregory Procaccino (Jacob Marley/Old Joe), Dale Hodges (Ghost of Christmas Past/Rose/Mrs. Peake), Jack Bender (Boy Scrooge/Boy at Fezziwig's/Bootblack), Alexandra Roberts (Fan/Fezziwig Guest), Keith Jochim (Mr. Fezziwig/Ghost of Christmas Present), Amy Warner (Mrs. Fezziwig/Patience), Gregory J. Pendzick (Dick Wilkins), Amy Attaway (Mary at Fezziwig's), Todd Lawson (Young/Mature Scrooge/Ghost of Christmas Future), Shannon Koob (Belle/Catherine Margaret), Aaron Sharff (Poor Caroler/Constable at Fezziwig's/Undertaker), Regina Pugh (Mrs. Cratchit/Laundress), Eben Franckewitz (Peter Cratchit/Gregory/Apprentice at Fezziwig's), Katie Chase (Belinda Cratchit/Fezziwig Guest), Jo Ellen Pellman (Martha Cratchit/Fezziwig Guest), Asa Trent Franckewitz (Tiny Tim), Elizabeth Helitzer (Rich Caroler/Rich Wife at Fezziwig's), Ryan Imhoff (Poor Caroler/Poulterer/Accountant at Fezziwig's), Jonathan Richard Grunert (Rich Caroler/Man with Pipe/Baker at Fezziwig's), Methani Ryan (Matthew/ Rich Son at Fezziwig's/Ignorance), Emmye Kearney (Want/ Fezziwig Guest), Liz Holt (Mrs. Dilber/Fezziwig Guest), Christian M. Spaulding (Charles/Apprentice at Fezziwig's/ George), December 1–30, 2007

THE BLONDE, THE BRUNETTE AND THE VENGEFUL REDHEAD by Robert Hewett; Director, Mark Lamos; Set, Andrew Jackness; Costumes, Candice Donnelly; Lighting, Thomas C. Hase; Sound, David Stephen Baker; Composer, John Gromada; Video Designer, Peter Nigrini; Casting, Stephanie Klapper; Assistant Director, Jennifer Vellenga; Assistant Lighting, John Frautschy; Assistant Video, Benjamin Keightley; Dialects, Rocco Dal Vera; PSM, Jenifer Morrow; SM, Andrea Shell; Cast: Annalee Jefferies; Understudy: Amy Warner; January 15–February 15, 2008

CRIME AND PUNISHMENT by Marilyn Campbell & Curt Columbus, based on the novel by Fyodor Dostoevsky; Director, Michael Evan Haney; Set and Lighting, Kevin Rigdon; Costumes, Trish Rigdon; Sound, Fitz Patton; Casting, Rich Cole; SM, Wendy J. Dorn; Cast: Nick Cordileone (Raskolnikov), John Campion (Porfiry Petrovich), Deborah Knox (Sonia); February 2–March 2, 2008

DOUBT by John Patrick Shanley; Director, Wendy C. Goldberg; Set, Todd Rosenthal; Costumes, Gordon DeVinney; Lighting, Josh Epstein; Sound and Composer, Ryan Rumery; Casting, Rich Cole; Dialects, Rocco Dal Vera; PSM, Jenifer Morrow; SM, Suann Pollock; Cast: Ted Deasy (Father Flynn), Joy Hooper (Mrs. Muller), Caitlin O'Connell (Sister Aloysius), Makela Spielman (Sister James); March 4–April 4, 2008

A SLEEPING COUNTRY by Melanie Marnich; Director, Mark Rucker; Set, Rachel Hauck; Costumes, Katherine Roth; Lighting, Phil Monat; Sound Designer and Composer, Ryan Rumery; Casting, Rich Cole; Dialects, Rocco Dal Vera; Assistant Seter, Katy Monthei; Fight Director, K. Jenny Jones; SM, Wendy J. Dorn; Cast: Kate Levy (Isabella Orsini), Susan Louise O'Connor (Dr. Midge/Gondolier/Carlotta), Andy Paris (Greg/Franco/Carlo), Dana Slamp (Julia Fracassi); World Premiere; March 22–April 20, 2008

ELLA Book by Jeffrey Hatcher, conceived by Rob Ruggiero & Dyke Garrison; Director, Rob Ruggiero; Musical Director/ Arrangements, Danny Holgate; Set, Michael Schweikardt; Costumes, Alejo Vietti; Lighting, John Lasiter; Sound, Michael Miceli; PSM, Jenifer Morrow; SM, Suann Pollock; Cast: Tina Fabrique (Ella Fitzgerald), Harold Dixon (Norman Granz), George Caldwell (Piano/Conductor), Thaddeus Wilson (Trumpet), Rodney Harper (Drums) Clifton Kellem (Bass), Joilet F. Harris (Understudy); April 22–May 25, 2008

AROUND THE WORLD IN 80 DAYS Adapted by Mark Brown from the novel by Jules Verne; Director, Michael Evan Haney; Set, Joseph P. Tilford; Costumes, David Kay Mickelsen; Lighting, Betsy Adams; Sound, David Andrew Levy; Stage Managers, Wendy J. Dorn, Andrea L. Shell; Cast: Jay Russell (Actor #1), John Keating (Actor #2), Evan Zes (Actor #3), Lauren Elise McCord (Actor # 4), Daniel Freedom Stewart (Actor #5); May 10–June 8, 2008

City Theatre Company

Pittsburgh, Pennsylvania

THIRTY-THIRD SEASON

Artistic Director, Tracy Bridgen; Managing Director, Greg Quinlan

MOTHER TERESA IS DEAD by Eve Helen Edmundson; Director, Tracy Brigden; Set, Tony Ferrieri; Costumes, Angela M. Vesco; Lighting, Andrew David Ostrowski; Sound, Elizabeth Atkinson; PSM, Patti Kelly; First PA, Lauren C. Connolly; Second PA, Jamie Buczkowski; Dialects, Sheila McKenna; Cast: Kristin Griffith (Frances), Sam Redford (Mark), Nehal Joshi (Srinivas), Rebecca Harris (Jane); October 4–28, 2007

MURDERERS by Jeffrey Hatcher; Director, Michael Bush; Set, Tony Ferrieri; Costumes, Robert C.T. Steele; Lighting, Traci Klainer; Sound, Elizabeth Atkinson; Wigs, Elsen Associates, Inc.; PSM, Patti Kelly; Rehearsal SM, Jody Clair-West; First PA, Lauren C. Connolly; Second PA, Lissa Brennan; Cast: Daniel Krell (Gerald Halverson), Jennifer Harmon (Lucy Stickler), Sheila McKenna (Minka Lupino); November 8–December 22, 2007

SISTER'S CHRISTMAS CATECHISM by Maripat Donovan with Marc Silvia & Jane Morris; Director, Marc Silvia; Set, Tony Ferrieri; Costumes, Catherine Evans; PA, Jamie Buczkowski; Cast: Kimberly Richards (Sister); December 4–30, 2007

THE VAGINA MONOLOGUES by Eve Ensler; Director, Tracy Brigden; Set, Tony Ferrieri; Costumes, Angela M. Vesco; Lighting, Andrew David Ostrowski; Sound, Elizabeth Atkinson; PSM, Jody Clair-West; Cast: Erica Bradshaw, Holli Hamilton, Laurie Klatscher; January 10–February 17, 2008

THE 13TH OF PARIS by Mat Smart; Director, Melia Bensussen; Set, Judy Gailen; Costumes, Pei-Chi Su; Lighting, Andrew David Ostrowski; Sound, Joe Pino; Dramaturg, Carlyn Aquiline; Dialects, Don Wadsworth; Fight Choreographer, Catherine Moore; PSM, Patti Kelly; First PA, Lauren C. Connolly; Second PA, Ashley Martin; Cast: Edmond Genest (Jacques), Matthew Dellapina (Vincent), Bridget Connors (Chloe), Theo Allyn (Annie), Jenny Wales (Jessica), Gregory Johnstone (William); January 24–February 17, 2008

FLIGHT by Charlayne Woodard; Director, Liesel Tommy; Choreographer, Oronde Sharif; Set, Tony Ferrieri; Costumes, Pei-Chi Su; Lighting, Marcus Doshi; Sound, Elizabeth Atkinson; Composer, Karl Fredrik Lundeberg; Music Director, Thomas W. Douglas; Dialects, Don Wadsworth; PSM, Patti Kelly; First PA, Lauren C. Connolly; Second PA, Ashley Martin; Third PA, Regina Connolly; Cast: Avery Sommers (Oh Beah), DeWanda Wise (Mercy), Kevin Brown (Ezra), Taifa Harris (Alma), Joshua Elijah Reese (Nate), George Jones (Percussionist); March 13–April 6, 2008

LATE NIGHT CATECHISM by Vicki Quade and Maripat Donovan; Original Staging, Nancy Burkholder; Set, Tony Ferrieri; Cast: Kimberly Richards (Sister); March 27–April 20, 2008

BUST by Lauren Weedman; Director, Allison Narver; Set, Tony Ferrieri; Lighting, Allen Hahn; PSM, Jody Claire-West; Cast: Lauren Weedman; May 22–June 29, 2008

A MARRIAGE MINUET by David Wiltse; Director, Tracy Brigden; Choreographer, Peter Pucci; Set, Jeff Cowie; Costumes, Markas Henry; Lighting, Howell Binkley; Composer, Ryan Rumery; Sound, Elizabeth Atkinson; PSM, Patti Kelly; Cast: Tami Dixon (Girl), Deirde Madigan (Violet), Douglas Rees (Douglas), Ross Bickell (Rex), Helena Ruoti (Lily Zweig); May 1–25, 2008

Cleveland Playhouse

Cleveland, Ohio

NINETY-SECOND SEASON

Artistic Director, Michael Bloom; Managing Director, Kevin Moore

MAN OF LA MANCHA Book by Dale Wasserman, music by Mitch Leigh, lyrics, Joe Darion; Director, Amanda Dehnert; Musical Director, Bill Corcoran; Set, Kris Stone; Costumes, Ana Kuzmanic; Lighting, Lap-Chi Chu; Sound, James C. Swonger; SM, John Godbout; Fight/Movement Choreographer, Ron Wilson; Casting, Arnold J. Mungioli; Cast: Heidi Dean (Fermina), Brandon Ellis (Anselmo), Josh Foldy (Pedro/Captain), Jerome Lucas Harmann (Governor/Innkeeper), Philip Hernandez (Cervantes/Don Quixote), Elizabeth Inghram (Antonia), Jamie La Verdiere (Manservant/Sancho), Daniel C. Levine (Housekeeper), Chris McBurney (Padre), Will Pailen (Barber), Patrick Porter (Duke/Dr. Carrasco), Rachael Warren (Aldonza); Drury Theatre; September 14–October 7, 2007

SHERLOCK HOLMES: The Final Adventure by Steven Dietz, based on the original 1899 play by William Gillette and Arthur Conan Doyle; Director, Tim Ocel; Set, Rob Koharchik; Costumes, Pamela Scofield; Lighting, Peter West; Sound, Scotty Iseri; Composer, Andrew Hopson; Fight Choreographer, John Stead; Dialects, Eric Armstrong; Assistant Director, Melissa Rain Anderson; Stage Manger, Amanda M. Harland; Casting, Elissa Myers and Paul Fouquet; Cast: Nick Berg Barnes (Doctor Watson), Timothy Crowe (Professor Moriarty), Catherine Lynn Davis (Madge Larrabee), Krista Hoeppner (Irene Adler), Christian Kohn (Sherlock Holmes), Remi Sandri (King of Bohemia), Matthew Schneck (James Larrabee/Policeman), Jim Wisniewski (Sid Prince/Clergyman/Policeman/Swiss Man); Bolton Theatre; October 12–November 2, 2007

THE CHOSEN Adapted by Aaron Posner and Chaim Potok from the novel by Chaim Potok; Director, Seth Gordon; Set, Michael Raiford; Costumes, David Kay Mickelsen; Lighting, Michael Lincoln; Sound, James C. Swonger; Dialects, Charles

Kartali; Stage Mangers, John Godbout & Amanda M. Harland; Casting, Elissa Myers and Paul Fouquet and Lelia Shearer; Cast: Kenneth Albers (Reb Saunders), Andrew Pastides (Danny Saunders), Adam Richman (Reuven Malter), Jeremy Rishe (Young Reuven Malter), George Roth (David Malter); Drury Theatre; November 2–25, 2007

A CHRISTMAS STORY by Philip Grecian, based on the motion picture written by Jean Shepherd, Leigh Brown and Bob Clark; Director, Seth Gordon; Set, Michael Ganio; Costumes, David Kay Mickelsen; Lighting, Richard Winkler; Sound, James C. Swonger; Fight Choreographer, Larry Nehring; Stage Manger, John Godbout; Casting, Elissa Myers, Paul Fouquet, Lelia Shearer; Cast: Naomi Hill (Helen), Charles Kartali (The Old Man), Billy Lawrence (Ralphie), Christopher McHale (Ralph), Cameron McKendry (Scut Farkas), Carole Monferdini (Miss Shields), Kolin Morgenstern (Flick), Justin Montgomery Peck (Schwartz), Lily Richards (Esther Jane), Joey Stefanko (Randy), Elizabeth Ann Townsend (Mother); Bolton Theatre; November 29–December 23, 2007

HERSHEY FELDER AS GEORGE GERSHWIN ALONE Created and performed by Hershey Felder; Music and lyrics by George Gershwin and Ira Gershwin, book by Hershey Felder; Director, Joel Zwick; Set, Yael Pardess; Lighting, Michael T. Gilliam; Sound, Jon Gottlieb; Production Manger/Technical Director, Matt Marsden; Lighting Assistant, Tamora Wilson; SM, Gigi Garica; Drury Theatre; January 15–February 3, 2008

HERSHEY FELDER AS MONSIEUR CHOPIN Created and performed by Hershey Felder; Music by Fryderyk Chopin, book by Hershey Felder; Director, Joel Zwick; Set, Yael Pardess; Lighting, Richard Norwood; Projection Designer, John Boesche; Sound, Benjamin Furiga; Production Manager/Technical Director, Matt Marsden; Lighting Assistant, Tamora Wilson; Production Consultant, Jeffrey Kallberg, Ph. D.; SM, Gigi Garcia; Drury Theatre; February 7–10, 2008

GEE'S BEND by Elyzabeth Gregory Wilder; Director, Shirley Jo Finney; Set, Michael Vaughn Sims; Costumes, Myrna Colley-Lee; Lighting, Victor En Yu Tan; Sound, James C. Swonger; Musical Director, Edward E. Ridley, Jr.; Stage Manger, John Godbout; Casting, Elissa Myers, Paul Fouquet, Lelia Shearer, Chemin Sylvia Bernard; Cast: Shanesia Davis (Nella), Wendell B. Franklin (Macon), Erika LaVonn (Sadie), Wanda Christine (Alice/Asia); Baxter Stage; February 1–24, 2008

DOUBT by John Patrick Shanley; Director, Seth Gordon; Set, Russell Parkman; Costumes, Jeffrey Van Curtis; Lighting, Trad A Burns; Sound, James C. Swonger; Dialects, Charles Kartali; Stage Manger, Amanda Harland; Casting, Elissa Myers, Paul Fouquet, Lelia Shearer; Cast: Barbara Andres (Sister Aloysius Beauvier), Michael Frederic (Father Brendan Flynn), Jennifer Ruffner (Sister James), Cherene Snow (Mrs. Muller); Drury Theatre; February 29–March 23, 2008

PRIDE AND PREJUDICE by Jane Austen, originally adapted by James Maxwell, revised by Alan Stanford; Director, Peter Amster; Set, Robert Koharchik; Costumes, Gail Brassard; Lighting, Ann G. Wrightson; Sound, James C. Swonger; Dialects, Don Wadsworth; Composer, Andrew R. Hopson; SM, John Godbout; Casting, Claire Simon; Cast: Annabel Armour (Lady Catherine de Bourgh/Mrs. Reynolds), Cassandra Bissell (Mary Bennet/Miss Jenkinson), Jason Bradley (Mr. Fitzwilliam Darcy), Chaon Cross (Elizabeth Bennet), Judith Day (Mrs. Bennet), Tom Degnan (Mr. Charles Bingley), Amanda Duffy (Caroline Bingley), Roni Geva (Lydia Bennet), Mark Alan Gordon (Sir William Lucas), Michele Graff (Jane Bennet), Daniel Graham (Mr. Wickham), Nathan Gurr (Mr. Denny), Bill McGough (Mr. Bennet), Deric McNish (Captain Carter/Ensemble), Nigel Patterson (Mr. Collins), Annie Paul (Kitty Bennet/Miss Anne de Bourgh), Taylor Valentine (Colonel Fitzwilliam), Melynee Saunders Warren (Charlotte Lucas); Bolton Theatre; March 21–April 13, 2008

ALL HAIL HURRICANE GORDO by Carly Mensch; Director, Sean Daniels; Set, Paul Owen; Costumes, Lorraine Venberg; Lighting, Deb Sullivan; Sound, Matt Callahan; Fight Supervisor, Lee Cook; SM, Amanda Harland; Casting, Emily Ruddock; Cast: Patrick James Lynch (Gordo), Matthew Dellapina (Chaz), Tracee Chimo (India); William McNulty (Oscar); Drury Theatre; April 18–May 11, 2008

Delaware Theatre Company

Wilmington, Delaware

TWENTY-NINETH SEASON

Producing Director, Anne Marie Cammarato; Managing Director, Robert Jansen

THE DIARY OF ANNE FRANK by Frances Goodrich and Albert Hackett, newly adapted by Wendy Kesselman; Director, Meredith McDonough; Sets, Kevin Judge; Costumes, Emily Pepper; Lighting, Thom Weaver; Sound/Original Music, Fabian Obispo; Casting, Stephanie Klapper, Jennifer Pardilla; SM, Brian V. Klinger; Cast: Sara Kapner (Anne Frank), Joel Leffert (Otto Frank), Dori Legg (Edith Frank), Nikki Coble (Margot Frank), Maggie Kettering (Miep Gies), Henry Raphael Glovinsky (Peter Van Daan), Michael Boudewyns (Mr. Kraler), Geraldine Librandi (Mrs. Van Daan), Paul L. Nolan (Mr. Van Daan), John Morrison (Mr. Dussel), Dan Rich (First Man), David Sweeny (Second Man), Michael Collins (Additional Man 1), Joseph Finn (Additional Man 2), Michael Freebery (Additional Man 3), Ryan Henzes (Additional Man 4), Daniel Jones (Additional Man 5), Jeff Robleto (Additional Man 6), Ted Strowhouer (Additional Man 7); October 17–November 9, 2007

THE COMPLETE WORKS OF WILLIAM SHAKESPEARE (abridged) by Adam Long, Daniel Singer and Jess Winfield; Director, Steve Tague; Assistant Director, Kerry Barber; Sets, Stefanie Hansen; Costumes, Andrea Barrier; Lighting, Troy A. Martin-O'Shia; Sound, Christopher Colucci; Casting, Stephanie Klapper, Jennifer Pardilla; SM, Brian V. Klinger; Cast: Jeffery C. Hawkins (Jeffery), Joseph Midyett (Joseph), Jason O'Connell (Jason); December 5–December 23, 2007

ART by Yasmina Reza, translated by Christopher Hampton; Director, David Stradley; Sets, Beowulf Boritt; Costumes, Charlotte Cloe Fox Wind; Lighting, Joshua Schulman; Sound, Mark Valenzuela; Fight Director, Tim Gallagher; Casting, Stephanie Klapper, Jennifer Pardilla; SM, Rick Cunningham; Cast: Pete Pryor (Yvan), Stephen Patrick Martin (Marc), James Michael Reilly (Serge); January 23–February 10, 2008

MARY'S WEDDING by Stephen Massicotte; Director, Anne Marie Cammarato; Sets, Beowulf Boritt; Costumes, Andrea Barrier; Lighting, Tyler Micoleau; Composer and Sound, Fabian Obispo; Casting, Stephanie Klapper; SM, Brian V. Klinger; Cast: Stafford Clark-Price (Charlie), Erin Moon (Mary/Flowers); February 27–March 16, 2008

THE PIANO LESSON by August Wilson; Director, Kevin Ramsey; Sets, Ina Mayhew; Costumes, Janus Stefanowicz; Lighting, Troy A. Martin-O'Shia; Sound, Fabian Obispo; Fight Director, John Bellomo; Casting, Stephanie Klapper; SM, Brian V. Klinger; Cast: Tracey Conyer Lee (Berniece), Nathan Hinton (Aveery Brown), Cedric Turner (Wining Boy), Malik Yoba (Boy Willie), Roger Robinson (Doaker), Edward O'Blenis (Lymon), Joniece Abbott-Pratt (Grace), Lauryn Jones (Maretha); April 9–April 27, 2008

Denver Center Theatre Company

Denver, Colorado

TWENTY-NINTH SEASON

Artistic Director, Kent Thompson; Associate Artistic Director, Bruce K. Sevy; General Manager, Charles Varin; Production Manager, Edward Lapine

THIRD by Wendy Wasserstein; Director, Wendy C. Goldberg; Set, Lisa M. Orzolek; Costumes, Anne Kennedy; Lighting, Charles R. MacLeod; Sound, Craig Breitenbach; SM, Lyle Raper; ASM, Kurt Van Raden; Cast: Caitlin O'Connell (Laurie Jameson), Billy Wheelan (Woodson Bull III), Philip Pleasants (Jack Jameson), Mattie Hawkinson (Emily Imbrie), Patricia Randell (Nancy Gordon); September 14–October 20, 2007

YOU CAN'T TAKE IT WITH YOU by Moss Hart and George S. Kaufman; Director, Penny Metropulos; Set, William Bloodgood; Costumes, Deb Trout; Lighting, Don Darnutzer; Sound, Richard M. Scholwin; Dialects, Kathryn G. Maes; Dramaturg, Douglas Langworthy; Fight Director, Geoffrey Kent; SM, Christopher C. Ewing; ASM, Christi B. Spann; Cast: Jeanne Paulsen (Penelope Sycamore), Christine Rowan (Essie), Ailish Riggs (Reba), James Michael Reilly (Paul Sycamore), Larry Paulsen (Mr. DePinna), David Ivers (Ed), Richard Thieriot (Donal), Randy Moore (Grandpa Martin Vanderhof), Nisi Sturgis (Alice), Sam Gregory (William C. Henderson), Patrick Jones (Tony Kirby), Mike Hartman (Boris Kolenkhov), Jill Tanner (Gay Wellington), John Hutton (Mr. Kirby), Lauren Klein (Mrs. Kirby), Michael J. Fulvio, Michael Mallard, Robert Wells III (Three Men), Kathleen M. Brady (Grand Duchess Olga); September 21–October 20, 2007

THE DIARY OF ANNE FRANK by Frances Goodrich and Albert Hackett; adapted by Wendy Kesselman; Director, Paul Mason Barnes; Set, Robert Mark Morgan; Costumes, Susan Branch; Lighting, Charles R. MacLeod; Sound, Kimberly Fuhr; Fight Director, Geoffrey Kent; Dialects, Kathryn G. Maes, SM, Christi B. Spann; PA, D. Lynn Reiland; Cast: John Hutton (Mr. Frank), Aya Cash (Anne Frank), Deirdre Madigan (Mrs. Frank); Danielle Slavick (Margot Frank), Elgin Kelley (Miep), Bob Braswell (Peter Van Daan), Leslie O'Carroll (Mrs. Van Daan), Sam Gregory (Mr. Van Daan), Erik Sandvold (Mr. Kraler), Philip Pleasants (Mr. Dussel), Mark Rossman (Nazi Officer), Michael Mallard (2nd Man), Zach Evenson (3rd Man); November 9–December 15, 2007

PRIDE AND PREJUDICE by Jon Jory, based on the novel by Jane Austen, music by Gregg Coffin; Director Bruce K. Sevy; Choreographer, Robert Davidson; Set, Vicki Smith; Costumes, David Kay Mickelsen; Lighting, Rick Paulsen; Sound, Richard M. Scholwin; Vocal Coach, Michael Cobb; SM, Christopher C. Ewing; ASM, Kurt Van Raden; Cast: Larry Paulsen (Mr. Bennet), Jeanne Paulsen (Mrs. Bennet), Brenda Withers (Jane Bennet), Nisi Sturgis (Elizabeth Bennet), Kristen Sieh (Mary Bennet), Jennifer Le Blanc (Kitty Bennet), Lori Prince (Lydia Bennet), Steven Cole Hughes (Mr. Bingley), Ailish Riggs (Miss Bingley), David Ivers (Mr. Lucas/Mr. Gardiner/Collins), Jill Tanner (Mrs. Lucas/Lady Catherine de Bourgh/Housekeeper at Pemberly), Michael J. Fulvio, Richard Thieriot, Robert Wells III (Ensemble); November 16–December 15, 2007

IRVING BERLIN'S *WHITE CHRISTMAS* Music and lyrics by Irving Berlin, book by Paul Blake and David Ives; based upon the Paramount Pictures Film written for the screen by Norman Krasna, Norman Panama and Melvin Frank; Director, Kent Thompson; Choreographer, Patti Colombo; Set, Anna Louizos; Costumes, Carrie Robbins; Lighting, Tom Sturge; Sound, Philip G. Allen; Music Director/Conducter, Paulette Haupt; Associate Music Director/Conductor, Lee Stametz; AD, Christy Montour Larson; Set Supervisor, Lisa M. Orzolek; Supplemental Costumes, David Kay Michelsen; Associate Sound, Craig Breitenbach; Vocal Coach, Hillary Blair; SM, Richard Costabile; ASMs, Mister Erock & Mark D. Leslie; Cast: Andrew Samonsky (Bob Wallace), Benjie Randall (Phil Davis), Amy Bodnar (Betty Haynes), Kate Marilley (Judy Haynes), Mike Hartman (General Henry Waverly), Dorothy Stanley (Martha Watson), Desirée Samler or Chloe Nosan (Susan Waverly), Jeffrey Roark (Ralph Sheldrake), Michelle Dyer (Rita), Brandi Wooten (Rhoda), Randy Moore (Ezekiel Foster), Chris Mixon (Mike/Ed Sullivan Announcer/Snoring Man), Christine Rowan (Tessie/Mrs. Snoring Man), Denise Payne (Assistant Seamstress/Sheldrake Secretary/Ensemble), Antwayn Hopper (Jimmy), Elizabeth Clinard (Cigarette Girl), Alan Bennett (Train Conductor), Rod Roberts (Dance Captain), Elizabeth Polito (Seamstress/Passenger 4/Ensemble), Cameron Henderson (Regency Room Announcer, Passenger 2/Ensemble), Mark Roland (Passenger 1/Ensemble), Kolina Janneck (Passenger 3/Ensemble), Ensemble: Brian Barry, Lindsay Juneau, Peter Leskowicz, Tiffany Sudol, Tracy Rae

Wilson (Ensemble); Swings: Shane Hall, Tara Jeanne Vallee; November 23–December 30, 2007

OUR HOUSE Conceived and written by Theresa Rebeck, co-conceived and directed by Daniel Fish; Set, Andrew Lieberman; Costumes, Kaye Voyce; Lighting, Scott Zielinski; Sound, Richard M. Scholwin; Fight Director, Geoffrey Kent; SM, Christi B. Spann; ASM, Kurt Van Raden; Video, Jim Furrer, Diane Bullock; Cast: Danny Mastrogiorgio (Wes), Molly Ward (Jennifer), Rob Campbell (Merv), Kate Nowlin (Alice), Suzy Jane Hunt (Grigsby), Haynes Thigpen (Vincent), Jonathan Fried (Stu), Jennifer Le Blanc (Assistant); World Premiere; January 11–February 16, 2008

LYDIA by Octavio Solis; Director, Juliette Carrillo; Set, Antje Ellermann; Costumes, Christal Weatherly; Lighting, Charles R. MacLeod; Sound, Kimberly Fuhr; Music, Chris Webb; Fight Director, Geoffrey Kent; Dramaturg, Douglas Langworthy; AD, Dara Weinberg; SM, Lyle Raper; ASM, D. Lynn Reiland; Cast: Onahoua Rodriguez (Cece), Carlo Albán (Misha), René Millán (Rene), Catalina Maynard (Rosa), Ricardo Gutierrez (Claudio), Christian Barillas (Alvaro), Stephanie Beatriz (Lydia); World Premiere; January 18–March 1, 2008

PLAINSONG by Eric Schmiedl, based on the novel by Kent Haruf; Director, Kent Thompson; Set, Vicki Smith; Costumes, Susan E. Mickey; Lighting, Don Darnutzer; Sound, Craig Breitenbach; Composer, Gary Grundei; Fight Director, Geoffrey Kent; Vocal Coach/Dialects, Michael Cobb; Dramaturg, Allison Horsley; Assistant to the Director, D. Marie Long; SM, Christopher C. Ewing; ASM, Mister Erock; PA, Rick Noble; Cast: John Hutton (Tom Guthrie), Gabe Antonelli, Ian Frazier (Ike), Keean Johnson, Jeremy Singer (Bobby), Tiffany Ellen Solano (Victoria Roubideaux), Lauren Klein (Mama Roubideaux/Mrs. Stearns), Erik Sandvold (Lloyd Crowder/Monroe/Bailey/Mr. Frazier), Stephanie Cozart (Ella Guthrie), Kathleen McCall (Maggie Jones), Sam Gregory (Irving Curtis/Mr. Beckman/Hardin), Josh Clayton (Russell Beckman), Danielle Slavick (Sharlene/Alberta), Michael J. Fulvio (Murphy), Mike Hartman (Raymond McPheron), Philip Pleasants (Harold McPheron), Randy Moore (Mr. Jackson/Schramm/Dr. Martin), Leslie O'Carroll (Mrs. Beckman/Mrs. Barnes/Aunt Joann), David Ivers (Buster Wheelright/Bus Driver/Carl), Kendra Kohrt (Judy/Female Patient/Hospital Nurse/Randy), Jeremiah Miller (Dwayne); World Premiere; January 25–February 23, 2008

GEE'S BEND by Elyzabeth Gregory Wilder; Director, Kent Gash; Set, Lisa M. Orzolek; Costumes, Alvin B. Perry; Lighting, Liz Lee; Sound, Richard M. Scholwin; SM, Christi B. Spann; ASM, A. Phoebe Sacks; Cast: Nikki E. Walker (Sadie Pettway), Stephanie Berry (Alice Pettway/Asia), Daphne Gaines (Nella Pettway), Eric Ware (Macon Pettway); March 14–April 19, 2008

THE MERRY WIVES OF WINDSOR by William Shakespeare; Director, David Ivers; Set, Hugh Landwehr; Costumes, David Kay Mickelsen; Lighting, Charles R. MacLeod; Sound, Craig Breitenbach; Vocal Coach/Dialects, Philip Thompson; Dramaturg, Douglas Langworthy; SM, Christopher C. Ewing; ASM, Kurt Van Raden: PAs, Kyra Berkness & Katie Preissner; Cast: Brian Keith Russell (Sir John Falstaff), Mat Hostetler (Fenton), Randy Moore (Shallow), Jeffrey Evan Thomas (Slender), John Hutton (Ford), John Livingstone Rolle (Page), Ahman Woods (William Page), Philip Pleasants (Sir Hugh Evans), Michael Santo (Doctor Caius), Mike Hartman (Host of the Garter Inn), Richard Thomsen (Bardolph), Chris Kendall (Pistol), Jeffrey Roark (Nym), Mark Siegel (Robin), Rob Hille (Simple/Robert), Leigh Miller (Rugby), Kathleen McCall (Mistress Ford), Sharon Washington (Mistress Page), Kwana Martinez (Anne Page), Kathleen M. Brady (Mistress Quickly), Christian Haines (John); March 21–April 19, 2008

DOUBT by John Patrick Shanley; Director, Bruce K. Sevy; Set, Vicki Smith; Costumes, Bill Black; Lighting, Jane Spencer; Sound, Kimberly Fuhr; SM, Mister Erock; ASM, D. Lynn Reiland; Cast: Sam Gregory (Father Flynn), Jeanne Paulsen (Sister Aloysius), Nisi Sturgis (Sister James), Kim Staunton (Mrs. Muller); April 4–May 17, 2008

3 MO' DIVAS, A Musical Celebration of Class, Sass and Style Conceived, directed and choreographed by Marion J. Caffey; Set, Dale F. Jordan; Costumes, Toni-Leslie James; Lighting, Richard Winkler; Sound, Craig Breitenbach; Musical Director, Annastasia Victory; Orchestrator, Joseph Joubert; Stage Managers, Christopher C. Ewing & Lyle Raper; Production Assistant, Kyra Berkness; Cast: Laurice Lanier, Nova Payton, Jamet Pittman; May 9–June 29, 2008

The 5th Avenue Theatre Company

Seattle, Washington

NINETEENTH SEASON

Producing Artistic Director, David Armstrong; Managing Director, Marilynn Sheldon

LONE STAR LOVE Conceived by John L. Haber, book by Robert Horn & John L. Haber, music and lyrics by Jack Herrick; Director/Choreographer, Randy Skinner; Assistant Choreographer, Sara Brians; Set, Derek McLane; Costumes, Jane Greenwood; Lighting, Ken Billington & Paul Miller; Sound, Tom Morse; Music Director, Jack Herrick; Associate MD, Ken Lundie; Hair and Wigs, Tom Watson; Production Manager, Peter Fulbright; PSM, Rolt Smith; Casting, Barry Moss & Bob Kale; General Manager, Roger Alan Gindi; Producers, Edmund and Eleanor Burke, Bob Boyett,, Roger Berlind, Rusty Carter, Susan Carter, John Rando, Avenue A Productions, Peter Alkalay, Daisy Theatricals LLC, Michael Speyer, Bernard Abrams; Executive Producer, Mary Ann Anderson; Associate Producers, Frank Golden, Frederic B. Vogel & Linda Wright; Producing Artistic Director, Donna Trinkoff, AMAS Musical Theatre; Tour Direction, Avid Touring Group, LTD; Cast: Randy Quaid (Colonel John Falstaff), Robert Cuccioli (Frank Ford), Dee Hoty (Margaret Anne Page), Lauren Kennedy (Agnes Ford), Clarke Thorell (Fenton),

Ramona Keller (Miss Quickly), Drew McVety (Doctor Caius), Dan Sharkey (George Page), Kara Lindsay (Miss Anne Page), Nick Sullivan (Sheriff Bob Shallow), Brandon Williams (Abraham Slender), Jeremy Benton (Swing/Dance Captain), Stacey Harris (Consuela), Anne Horak (Swing), Amanda Lea Lavergne (Ruby), Tony Lawson (Swing), Ryan Murray (Chester), Monica Patton (Grace), Miguel A. Romero (Rugby), Kristie Dale Sanders (Standby), Chad Seib (Lucas), Chris Frank (Private Bardolph), Jack Herrick (Captain Pistol), Sam Bardfeld (Musician), Gary Bristol (Musician), Shannon Ford (Sticks), Emily Mikesell (Corporal Nym); September 8–30, 2007

INTO THE WOODS Music and lyrics by Stephen Sondheim, book by James Lapine; Director/Musical Staging, Mark Waldrop; Musical Director/Conductor, Ian Eisendrath; Set, Todd Edward Ivins; Lighting, Tom Sturge; Sound, Ken Travis; Costumes, Lynda L. Salsbury; Hair/Makeup, Mary Pyanowski; Associate Choreographer, Dannul Dailey; Casting, Bill Berry; PSM, Bret Torbeck; Associate MD, Faith Seetoo; ASMs, Jessica C. Bomball & Michael B. Paul; TD, Mark Schmidt; Production Supervisor, Andy Luft; Cast: Eric Ankrim (Jack), Logan Benedict (Rapunzel's Prince), Eric Brotherson (Milky White), Darla Cardwell (Lucinda), Dannul Dailey (Steward), Bob De Dea (Baker), Anne Eisendrath (Rapunzel), Lisa Estridge (Witch), Allen Fitzpatrick (Narrator/Mysterious Man), Allen Galli (Cinderella's Father), Pamela Hamill (Jack's Mother), Michael Hunsaker (Wolf/Cinderella's Prince), Leslie Law (Baker's Wife), Cheryl Massey-Peters (Grandmother), Krista Severeid (Florinda), Carol Swarbrick (Cinderella's Stepmother/ Giant), Billie Wildrick (Cinderella), Ireland Woods (Little Red Ridinghood), Stephanie Miller (Snow White), Laura Thornquist (Sleeping Beauty); Undertudy: Amelia Rose Brummel (Little Red); October 19–November 10, 2007

WHISTLE DOWN THE WIND Music and book by Andrew Lloyd Webber, lyrics by Jim Steinman, book by Patricia Knop, Gale Edwards; Director, Bill Kenwright; Choreographer, Henry Metcalfe; Music Director/Conductor, Jim Vukovich; Music Supervisor/Orchestrations/Arrangements, David Steadman; Set/Costumes, Paul Farnsworth; Lighting, Nick Richings; Sound, Ben Harrison; PSM, Allen McMullen; Stage Managers, Nancy Wernick & Nathan D. Frye; ASM, Randy Andre' Davis; Associate Choreographer, Jody Ripplinger; Music Coordinator, John Monaco; Production Manager, Larry Morley; Casting, Stuart Howard, Amy Schecter & Paul Hardt; General Management, Alan Wasser, Jim Brandeberry; Cast: Eric Kunze (The Man), Andrea Ross (Swallow), Dann Fink (Boone), Nadine Jacobson (Brat), Carole Denise Jones (Candy), Gerry McIntyre (Ed), Adam Shonkwiler (Earl), Matt Skrincosky (Amos), Greg Stone (Snake Preacher), Austin J. Zambito-Valente (Poor Baby), Kurt Zischke (Sheriff); Ensemble: Ryan Appleby, Renee Claire Bergeron, Al Bundonis, Elizabeth Earley, Raisa Ellingson, Olivia Ford, Alexis Hightower, Stephen Horst, James Jackson, Jr., Dana Kluczyk, Justine Magnusson, Rebecca Naomi Moyes, Jason Ostrowski, Thomas Rainey, Mickey Toogood; Children's Ensemble: Lauren Carlos, Brayden Daher, Natalie Dungey, Olivia Ford, Drea Gordon, Alexandria Gray, Mariah Lotz, Elijah J. Ostrow, Mary Rising, Sarah Safer, Jake Schwencke, Aaron Smith, Isabella Stachurski, Kaija Stern, Sam Tacher, Keaton Whittaker, Elijah Williams, Paris Williams; November 13–December 2, 2007

JERSEY BOYS Book by Marshall Brickman & Rick Elice, music by Bob Gaudio, lyrics by Bob Crewe; Director, Des McAnuff; Choreographer, Sergio Trujillo; Music Direction, Vocal Arrangements/Incidental Music, Ron Melrose; Set, Klara Zieglerova; Costumes, Jess Goldstein, Lighting, Howell Binkley; Sound, Steve Canyon Kennedy; Projections, Michael Clark; Wigs/Hair, Charles LaPointe; Fight Director, Steve Rankin; Production Supervisor, Richard Hester; SM, Lori Byars; ASM, Anna Belle Gilbert; Orchestrations, Steve Orich; Music Coordinator, John Miller; Conductor, Andrew Wilder; Technical Supervisor, Peter Fulbright; Casting, Tara Rubin; Company Manager, R. Doug Rodgers; PSM, Eric Insko; Dance Captain, Jennifer Evans; Fight Captain, Erik Bates; Executive Producer, Sally Campbell Morse; Tour Booking/Marketing, Broadway Booking Office NYC; Associate Choreographer, Kelly Devine; Dialects, Stephen Gabis; Producers, Dodger Theatricals, Joseph J. Grano, Jr., Kevin & Tamara Kinsella, The Pelican Group, Latitude Link and Rick Steiner; Associate Producer, Lauren Mitchell; Cast: Erich Bergen/Andrew Rannels (Bob Gaudio), Steve Gouveia (Nick Massi), Christopher Kale Jones (Frankie Valli), Deven May (Tommy DeVito), John Altieri/Jonathan Hadley (Bob Crewe/ others), Joseph Siravo (Gyp DeCarlo and others), Miles Aubrey (Norman Waxman and others), Erik Bates (Swing/Fight Captain), Holly Ann Butler (Church Lady/Angel/Lorraine/ others), Sarah Darling (Francine/others), Eric Gutman (Hank Majewski/others), Jamie Karen (Mary Delgado/others), Nathan Klau (Billy Dixon/others), Michelle Knight (Swing), Brandon Matthieus (Barry Belson/others), Zachary Prince (Frankie Valli alternate), Courter Simmons (Joey/others) Michael Pearce & Josh Weinstein (Thugs); Swings: Eric Bates, Christopher DeAngelis, Jennifer Evans, Taylor Sternberg; December 5, 2007–January 12, 2008

MAME Book by Jerome Lawrence & Robert E. Lee, music & lyrics by Jerry Herman; Director/Musical Staging, David Armstrong; Choreographer, Dannul Dailey; Musical Director/ Conductor, David Holcenberg; Set, Walt Spangler; Costumes, Gregg Barnes; Lighting, Tom Sturge; Sound, Ken Travis; Associate Costumes, Lynda L. Salsbury; Hair and Makeup, Mary Pyanowski; PSM, Jeffrey K. Hanson; Production Supervisor, Andy Luft; TD, Mark Schmidt; Casting, Bill Berry; Associate MD, Matt Goodrich; ASMs, Lori Amondson Flint & Amy Gornet; Assistant Choreographer, Tinka Gutrick Dailey; Assistant to the Director, Leslie Asplund; Music Coordinator, Ian Eisendrath; Music Preparation, Dane Anderson; Copyist, Paul Hansen; Orchestral Reductions, Daniel K. Perrin; Cast: Dee Hoty (Mame Dennis), Richard White (Beauregard Jackson Pickett Burnside), Carol Swarbrick (Vera Charles), Kat Ramsburg (Agnes Gooch), Nick Robinson (Young Patrick Dennis), Ben Gonio (Ito), Sean G. Griffin (Dwight Babcock), Matt Owen (Patrick Dennis), Timothy McCuen Piggee (M.

Lindsay Woolsey), Taryn Darr (Gloria Upson), Michael Winters (Uncle Jeff), Laura Kenny (Madame Branislowski), Cheryl Massey-Peters (Cousin Fan), Karen Skrinde (Sally Cato), Greg McCormick Allen (Ralph Devine/Messenger/Stage Manager/Gregor), Michael Ericson (Junior Babcock), Anders Ledell (Peter Dennis); Timothy Gleason (Doorman/Leading Man), John David Scott (Elevator Boy), Greg McCormick Allen (Messenger), Laura Kenny (Mother Burnside), Cheryl Massey-Peters (Mrs. Upson), Michael Winters (Mr. Upson), Heather Roberts (Pegeen Ryan), Ensemble: David Alewine, Jeffrey Alewine, Gabe Corey, Taryn Darr, Michael Ericson, Kristen Gaetz, Timothy Gleason, Brittany Jamieson, Nikki Long Womac, Cheryl Massey-Peters, Lauralyn McClelland, Trina Mills, Kasey Nusbickel, Jimmy Scheider, John David Scott, Pamela Turpen; Performance Interns: Nicholas Beach, Meaghan Foy, Krista Gibbon, Bryce Henry, Diana Huey, Lindsay Powers, Heather Roberts, Jenny Singer, Luke Vroman, Thaddeus Wilson; February 9–March 2, 2008

CABARET Book by Joe Masteroff, music by John Kander lyrics by Fred Ebb; Director, Bill Berry; Musical Director/Conductor, Ian Eisendrath; Choreographer, Bob Richard; Set/Lighting, Tom Sturge; Costumes, Thomas G. Marquez; Sound, Jeremy J. Lee; Makeup/Hair, Sharon Ridge; Orchestrations, Bruce Monroe; PSM, Bret Torbeck; Production Supervisors, Bob Bones & Andy Luft; TDs, Mark Schmidt & John Draginoff; ASMs, Stina Lotti, Gregg Rehrig; Associate MD, R.J. Tancioco; Company Manager, Kristina Wicke; Dialects, Kimberly Mohene Hill; Assistant Choreographer, Dannul Dailey; Assistant to the Director, Jayme McDaniel; Cast: Tari Kelly (Sally Bowles), Nick Garrison (Emcee), Louis Hobson (Cliff Bradshaw), Allen Fitzpatrick (Herr Schultz), Suzy Hunt (Fraulein Schneider), Tyson Forbes (Ernst Ludwig), Angie Louise (Fraulein Kost), Alexandra Ausman (Fritzi), Lisa Bartholomew-Given (Ensemble/Swing), Nicole Boote (Helga), Scott Brateng (Gunter), Ross Cornell (Ensemble/Swing), Dannul Dailey (Max), Jadd Davis (Otto), Kirsten E. Gerding (Mausie), Melody McArtor (Hilde), Carrie Madsen (Cabaret Performer), Ellyn Marie Marsh (Rosie), Brandon O'Neill (Helmut), Maya RS Perkins (Frenchie), Troy L. Wageman (Hanz), Aaron Young (Bobby); March 25–April 13, 2008

Florida Stage

Manalpan, Florida

TWENTIETH and TWENTY-FIRST SEASONS

Artistic Director, Louis Tyrrell; Managing Director, Nancy Barnett

A MARVELOUS PARTY: The Noel Coward Celebration Words and music by Noel Coward, devised by David Ira Goldstein, Carl Danielsen, Mark Anders, Patricia Wilcox & Anna Lauris; Musical Arrangements, Carl Danielsen; Director, David Ira Goldstein; Choreographer, Patricia Wilcox; Set, Bill Forrester; Costumes, David Kay Mickelsen; Lighting, Todd Hensley; Musical Director, Christopher McGovern; Casting, Rosen & Wojcik, Inc.; PSM, Suzanne Clement Jones; Cast: Mark Anders, Stefanie Morse, Jeffrey Rockwell (Ensemble), Christopher McGovern (Piano), Julie Jacobs (Percussion), Rupert Ziawinski (Bass); Southeastern Premiere; June 30–August 19, 2007

End Days by Deborah Zoe Laufer; Director, Louis Tyrrell; Set and Lighting, Richard Crowell; Costumes Erin Amico; Sound, Matt Kelly; PSM, James Danford; Cast: Scott Borish (Nelson Steinberg), Michaela Cronan (Rachel Stein), Elizabeth Dimon (Sylvia Stein), Terry Hardcastle (Jesus/Stephen Hawking), Jim Shankman (Arthur Stein), National New Play Network World Premiere; October 19–November 25, 2007

A MURDER, A MYSTERY & A MARRIAGE Book and lyrics by Aaron Posner, music by James Sugg; Director, Louis Tyrrell; Choregrapher, Karma Camp; Set and Costumes, Mark Pirolo; Lighting, John McFadden; Casting, Rosen & Wojcik, Inc; Musical Director, Tom Kenaston; PSM: Suzanne Clement Jones; Cast: Eric Scott Anthony (Hugh Gregory), Richard Henzel (David Gray/Sheriff Hiram P. Thwacker), Dan Leonard (John Gray), Bruce Linser (Stranger), David M. Lutken (Clem/Rev. Jonathon P. Hurley), Kiera O'Neil (Mary Gray), Lourelene Snedeker (Sally Gray), Tom Kenaston (Piano), Gary Mackey (Fiddle), Rupert Ziawinski (Bass), Southeastern Premiere; December 7, 2007–January 13, 2008

THE COUNT by Roger Hedden; Director, Louis Tyrrell; Set, Richard Crowell; Costumes, Nelson Fields; Lighting, Suzanne M. Jones; Sound, Matt Kelly; Casting, Rosen & Wojcik, Inc.; PSM, James Danford; Cast: Dan Leonard (The Count), Deborah Hazlett (Jane Gray), Richard Henzel/Bill Galarno (Lester Grabowski), Warren Kelley (Michael Grabowski), Lois Markle (Connie Grabowski), Michael Marotta (Monty Barclay), World Premiere; January 25–March 2, 2008

WARD 57 by Jessica Goldberg; Director, Michael Bigelow Dixon; Set, Victor Becker; Costumes, Marcia Dixcy Jory; Lighting, Jim Fulton; Sound, Matt Kelly; PSM, Suzanne Clement Jones; Cast: Buddy Haardt (Private Anthony Small), Brandon Morris (Captain Gray Whitrock), Aditi Kapil (Wendy Hoffman), Sid Solomon (Eric), Bonni Allen (Lydia Whitrock), World Premiere; March 19–April 27, 2008

ORDINARY NATION by Carter W. Lewis; Director, Louis Tyrrell; Set, Richard Crowell; Costumes, Erin Amico; Lighting, Michael Jon Burris; Sound, Matt Kelly; PSM, James Danford; Cast: Joe Kimble (Nation), Dan Leonard (GJ), Peter Thomasson (Gibb), Annie Fitzpatrick (Allison), Emily Zimmer (Frankie); Southeastern Premiere; May 9–June 15, 2008

Ford's Theatre

Washington, DC

FORTIETH SEASON*

Producing Director, Paul R. Tetreault; Associate Producers, Mark Ramont and Kristin Fox-Siegmund; Special Project

Director, James R. Riley; General Manager, Alfred Butler

A CHRISTMAS CAROL: A Ghost Story of Christmas Adapted by Michael Wilson, based on the production conceived for Ford's Theatre; Original staging recreated by Mark Ramont; Director, Matt August; Set, Court Watson; Costumes, Fabio Toblini; Lighting, Matthew Richards; Original Set, G.W. Mercier; Original Lighting, Pat Collins; Original Music, Mark Bennett; Sound, Ryan Rumery; Choreography, Karma Camp; Choral Director, George Fulginiti-Shakar; Original Sound, Michael Creason, Dialects, Leigh Wilson Smiley; Wigs/Hair, Cookie Jordan; PSM, Craig A. Horness; ASM, Brandon Prendergast; Cast: Michael Bunce (First Solicitor), Michael John Casey (Bob Cratchit), David Covington (Nephew Fred/Young Scrooge), Katie Culligan (Mrs. Fred's Sister), Elliot Dash (Fruit Vendor Bert/Ghost of Christmas Present), Andy English (Dick Wilkins/Topper), Carlos Gonzales (Clock Vendor/Ghost of Christmas Future), Michael Goodwin (Jacob Marley/Old Joe/Minister/Fezziwig Guest), Jewel Greenberg (Mrs. Fred/Beggar Woman), Bill Hensel (Mr. Fezziwig), Claudia Miller (Mrs. Dilber/Mrs. Fezziwig/Mother at Doll Stand), Caitlin O' Grady (Martha), Martin Rayner (Ebenezer Scrooge), Suzanne Richard (Doll Vendor/Ghost of Christmas Past), Kimberly Schraf (Mrs. Cratchit), Todd Scofield (Second Solicitor), Halsy Varady (Belle), Noah Foster/Benjamin Cook (Tiny Tim Cratchit/Boy Scrooge), Dominque Ross/Taylor Dawson (Schoolboy/Want), Adiin Walker/John Anderson (Peter Cratchit/Schoolboy), Brittany O'Grady (Fan/Daughter at Doll Stand), Nadia Ross/ Jamie Boyd (Belinda/Cratchit/Schoolboy), Jace Casey/Xavier Johnson (Child Beggar/Boy at Market/Ignorance); The Lansburgh Theatre; December 6–29, 2007

*Ford's Theatre was closed this season for renovations

Geva Theatre Center

Rochester, New York

THIRTY-FIFTH ANNIVERSARY SEASON

Artistic Director, Mark Cuddy; Managing Director, Greg Weber; Executive Director, Nan Hildebrandt

URINETOWN THE MUSICAL Book and lyrics by Greg Kotis, music and lyrics by Mark Hollman; Director, Mark Cuddy; Choreographer, Peggy Hickey; Sets/Costumes, G.W. Mercier; Lighting, Robert Wierzel; Sound, Lindsay Jones; Music Director, Don Kot; PSM, Kirsten Brannen; Cast: Melissa Rain Anderson (Josephine Strong), James Brennan (Officer Lockstock), Ray DeMattis (Caldwell B. Cladwell), Kurt Domoney (Billy Boy Bill/UGC Executive/Police Officer), Michael Brian Dunn (Mr. McQueen), Michael J. Farina (Officer Barrel), Michael Fitzpatrick (Senator Fipp), Ben Franklin (Tiny Tom/UGC Executive/Police Officer), Ellyn Marie Marsh (Little Becky Two-Shoes/Mrs. Millennium/ Police Officer), Adriana McPhee (Soupy Sue/Cladwell's Secretary), Karen Murphy (Penelope Pennywise), Jim Poulos (Bobby Strong), Carolann M. Sanita (Hope Cladwell), Tom Souhrada (Old Man Strong/Hot Blades Harry), Charles E. Wallace (Robby the Stockfish/Dr. Billeaux/Lockstock), Erin Webley (Little Sally); May 15–June 24, 2007

MENOPAUSE THE MUSICAL Book and lyrics by Jeanie Linders; Director, Kathryn Conte, Choreographer, Patty Bender; Set, Miranda Clark; Lighting, Jean-Yves Tessier; Sound, Gary Faller; Lighting, Ryan A. Partridge; National Music Supervisor, Alan J. Plado; PSM, Gary Wayne Demumbrum; Cast: Linda Boston (Professional Woman), Kimberly Vanbiesbrouck (Soap Star), Renee Lawless-Orsini (Earth Mother), Teri Adams (Iowa Housewife); July 6–August 26, 2007

SHERLOCK HOLMES: The Final Adventure by Steven Dietz; Director, Tim Ocel; Set, Rob Koharchik; Costumes, Pamela Scofield; Lighting, Peter West; Sound, Scotty Iseri; Composer, Andrew Hopson; Fight Choreographer, John Stead; SM, Kirsten Brannen; Cast: Nick Berg Barnes (Dr. Watson), Timothy Crowe (Prof. Moriarty), Catherine Lynne Davis (Madge Larrabee), Krista Hoeppner (Irene Adler), Christian Kohn (Sherlock Holmes), Remi Sandri (King of Bohemia), Matthew Schneck (James Larrabee), Jim Wisniewski (Sid Prince), Jim Wisneiwski (Clergyman/Policeman/Swiss Man), Erin Kate Howard (Standby); September 4–30, 2007

DOUBT by John Patrick Shanley; Director, Skip Greer; Set, Rob Koharchik; Costumes, Ann R. Emo; Lighting, Ken Smith; Sound, Dan Roach; Cast: Lia Aprile (Sister James), Judith Delgado (Sister Aloysius), Sean Patrick Reilly (Father Flynn), Nikki W. Walker (Mrs. Muller); October 9–November 4, 2007

A CHRISTMAS CAROL by Charles Dickens, adapted by Richard Hellesen, music and lyrics by David de Berry; Director, Emma Griffin; Choreographer, Meggins Kelley; Set, Ramsey Avery; Costumes, B. Modern; Lighting, Kendall Smith; Music Director, Don Kot; AD/SM, Kirsten Brannen; Cast: Michael Amato or Timothy Hight (Turkey Boy), Melissa Rain Anderson (Tailor's Wife/Mrs. Fezziwig/Belle), David Autovino (Topper/Clerk/Under Man), Trevor Bachman (Dick Wilkins/Peter Cratchit), Evan Baldwin or Maggie Nagar (Tiny Tim), Guy Bannerman (Ghost of Christmas Present/Subscription Gentleman), Mitchell Canfield (Man #2), Bret Carr (Ebenezer), Michael Centanni (Boy Scrooge), Robin Chadwick (Ebenezer Scrooge), Lorraine Cink (Belle/ Martha/Maid), Michael Fitzpatrick (Fezziwig/Subscription Gentleman/Belle's Husband), Emma Germano (Belinda Cratchit), Susan Haefner (First Miss Fezziwig/Fred's Wife/ The Laundress), Erin Kate Howard (Second Miss Fezziwig/ Fred's Sister in law/The Charwoman), Robert B. Kennedy (Bob Cratchit), Selene Klasner (Belinda Cratchit), Katie Germano or Teri Madonna (Girl), Brian Monahan (Fred), Colin Nims (Ebenezer The Child), Ross Pedersen (Man #2), John Pribyl (Ghost of Jacob Marley/Old Joe), Emily Putnam (Girl), Rebecca Rand or Allie Waxman (Beggar Child), Mhari Sandoval (Ghost of Christmas Past/Mrs. Cratchit), Scott Scaffidi (Man #1), Meredith Watson or Alizabeth York (Want), Emily Tyler or Annaleigh York (Fan), Henri Young or Regan

Young (Edward Cratchit); November 23–December 23, 2007

CABARET Book by Joe Masteroff, music by John Kander, lyrics by Fred Ebb; based on the play by John van Druten and stories by Christopher Isherwood; Director, Chris Coleman; Choreographer, Joel Ferrell; Set, G.W. Mercier; Costumes, Jeff Cone; Lighting, Daniel Ordower; Sound, William Pickens; Music Director, Don Kot; Fight Director, John Armour; SM, Kirsten Brannen; Cast: Romain Frugé (Clifford Bradshaw), Storm Large (Sally Bowles), Chrisse Roccaro (Fraulein Schneider), Richard Matthews (Herr Schultz), Wade McCollum (Emcee), Pilar Milhollen (Fraulein Kost/Kit Kat Girl/), Randy Rollison (Ernst Ludwig), Ensemble: Scott Sachs, Kristyn Smith, Tommy Berklund, Gretchen Burghart, Buddy Hammonds, Karen Hyland, Timothy Hughes, Emily Lockhart, Amy Palomino; Understudies/Swings: Mary Krickmire (Fraulein Schneider), Nick Perry, Stefanie Seamens; January 9–February 17, 2008

BAD DATES by Theresa Rebeck; Director, Mark Cuddy; Set, Jack Magaw; Costumes, Jennifer Caprio, Lighting, Ann G. Wrightson; Sound, Lindsay Jones; SM, Janine Wochna; Cast: Susannah Schulman (Haley Walker); February 26–March 30, 2008

THE PIANO LESSON by August Wilson; Director, Seret Scott; Set, Russell Metheny; Costumes, Karen Perry; Lighting, Michael Lincoln; Sound, Todd Reischman; SM, Janine Wochna; Cast: Carl Cofield (Boy Willie), Jessica Frances Dukes (Grace), Warner Miller (Lymon), Chuck Patterson (Doaker), Roslyn Ruff (Berniece), Glenn Turner (Wining Boy), Geoffrey D. Williams (Avery); April 15–May 11, 2008

PRIDE AND PREJUDICE by Jane Austen, adapted by Marge Betley and Mark Cuddy; Director, Mark Cuddy; Choreographer, Meggins Kelley; Set/Costumes, G.W. Mercier; Video, Peter Nigrini; Lighting, Robert Wierzel; Sound, Lindsay Jones; Composer, Gregg Coffin; SM, Kirsten Brannen; Cast: Keenan Bloom (Servant), Patti Lewis Browne (Lady Lucas/Mrs. Reynolds), Peggy Cosgrove (Mrs. Bennet), Jenna Cole (Aunt Gardiner), Ellen Herzman (Servant/Ensemble), Creighton James (Mr. Darcy), Shannon Koob (Caroline Bingley), Vanessa LaFortune (Charlotte Lucas), Jeff Leiske (Servant), Melanie Little (Mary Bennet), Samantha Mehnert (Georgiana Darcy), Carole Monferdini (Lady Catherine), Alyssa Rae (Jane Bennet), Randy Rollison (Mr. Collins), Liv Rooth (Lydia Bennet), Robert Rutland (William Lucas), Jessica Sabatini (Kitty Bennet), Remi Sandri (Col. Fitzwilliam), Michael Sheehan (Servant), David Christopher Wells (Mr. Wickham), Meghan Wolf (Elizabeth Bennet); May 21–June 22, 2008

Goodman Theatre

Chicago, Illinois

EIGHTY-THIRD SEASON

Artistic Director, Robert Falls; Managing Director, Roche Schulfer

PASSION PLAY: a cycle in three parts by Sarah Ruhl; Director, Mark Wing-Davey; Set, Allen Moyer; Costumes, Gabriel Berry; Lighting, James F. Ingalls; Sound, Cecil Averett; Dramaturg, Tanya Palmer; Projections, Ruppert Bohl; PSM, Joseph Drummond; SM, T. Paul Lynch; Casting, Adam Belcuore, Vince Liebhart; Voice/Dialects, Linda Gates; Fight Consultant, Nick Sandy; Cast: Brendan Averett (Carpenter 1/ Townsman), Joaquin Torres (John the Fisherman/Eric/J), Keith Kupferer (Carpenter 2/Townsman), Brian Sgambati (Pontius the fish gutter/Footsoldier/P), Alan Cox (Visiting Friar/ Visiting Englishman/Young Director), Polly Noonan (Village Idiot/Violet), Craig Spidle (Director), Nicole Wiesner (Mary 2), Kristen Bush (Mary 1), John Hoogenakker (Machinist/ German Officer/VA), T. Ryder Smith (Queen Elizabeth/ Hitler/Reagan); Ensemble/Understudies: Tiffany Bedwell, Jeremy Clark, Kyle Lemieux, Ron Rains, Jace Ryan; Albert Theatre; September 15–October 21, 2007

THE COOK by Eduardo Machado; Director, Henry Godinez; Set, Todd Rosenthal; Costumes, Ana Kuzmanic; Lighting, Robert Christen; Sound, Ray Nardelli and Andre Pluess; Original Music, Gustavo Leone; Dramaturg, Tom Creamer; PSM, Kimberly Osgood; Casting, Adam Belcuore; Cast: Karen Aldridge (Gladys), Edward F. Torres (Carlos), Monica Lopez (Elena/Rosa), Maricela Ochoa (Adria/Lourdes), Phillip James Brannon (Julio); Owen Theatre; October 20–November 18, 2007

A CHRISTMAS CAROL by Charles Dickens, adapted by Tom Creamer; 30th Anniversary Production; Director, William Brown; Set, Todd Rosenthal; Costumes, Heidi Sue McMath; Lighting, Robert Christen; Sound, Cecil Averett; Composer, Andrew Hansen; PSM, Alden Vasquez; SM, Jamie Wolfe; Casting, Adam Belcuore; Music Director, Andrew Hansen; Choreography, Susan Hart; Dance Captain, Steven Hinger; Cast: Larry Yando (Scrooge), Ron Rains (Bob Cratchitt), William J. Norris (Mr. Ortle), Ann Joseph (Miss Crumb), Steven Hinger (Fred), Bradley Mott (Poulterer/Mr. Fezziwig/ Ghost of Christmas Present), Eric Galvan (Singing Urchin/ Johnston), Matthew Gold (Servant Boy/Pratt), Sharon Sachs (Charwoman/Mrs. Fezziwig/Adelle), Martin Yurek (Ghost of Jacob Marley/Marley as a Young Man/Old Joe), Steve Haggard (Ghost of Christmas Past/Topper), Bret Tuomi (Schoolmaster), Robert Gerdisch (Scrooge as a Boy/Peter Cratchitt/ Ignorance), Lucy Godinez (Fan/Belinda Cratchitt), Brendan Marshall-Rashid (Scrooge as a Young Man/Tree Seller/Ghost of Christmas Future), Adam Poss (Dick Wilkins/Young Man), Katie Jeep (Belle/Catherine), Bret Tuomi (Chestnut Seller), Karen Janes Woditsch (Mrs. Cratchit), Laney Kraus-Taddeo (Emily Cratchitt/Want), Laura Coover (Martha Cratchitt/ Young Woman), Ryan Cowhey (Tiny Tim), Penelope Walker (Abby/Mrs. Dilber), Bethany Jorgensen (Philomena/Musician), Kevin Theis (Percy/Undertaker), Greg Hirte (Spencer/ Musician); Musicians: Justin Amolsch, Malcolm Ruhl; Albert Theatre; November 16–December 29, 2007

SHINING CITY by Conor McPherson; Presented in association with the Huntington Theatre Company; Director, Robert Falls; Set, Santo Loquasto; Costumes, Kaye Voyce; Lighting, Christopher Akerlind; Sound, Obadiah Eaves; PSM, Josephe Drummond; SM, T. Paul Lynch; Casting, Adam Belcuore; Voice and Dialects, Linda Gates; Cast: Jay Wittaker (Ian), John Judd (John), Nicole Wiesner (Neasa), Keith Gallagher (Laurence); Understudy: Robin Lewis-Bedz (Neasa); Albert Theatre; January 12–February 17, 2008

TALKING PICTURES by Horton Foote; Presented as part of the Horton Foote Festival; Director, Henry Wishcamper; Set, Tom Burch; Costumes, Birgit Rattenborg Wise; Lighting, Robert Christen; Sound, Richard Woodbury; PSM, Kimbery Osgood; Dramaturg, Jennifer Shook; Casting, Adam Belcuore; Vocal/Dialects, Christine Adaire; Cast: Lee Stark (Katie Bell Jackson), Kathleen Redmond (Vesta), Jenny McKnight (Myra), Jason Wells (Mr. Jackson), Judy Blue (Mrs. Jackson), Philip Earl Johnson (Willis), Gabriel Notarangelo (Estaquio), Bubba Weiler (Pete), Audrey Francis (Gladys), E. Vincent Teninty (Ashenback), Dan Waller (Gerard); Owen Theatre; January 26–March 2, 2008

BLIND DATE and **THE ACTOR** An evening of one-act plays by Horton Foote; Presented as part of the Horton Foote Festival; Directors, Steve Scott (Blind Date), Rick Snyder (The Actor); Set, Tom Burch; Costumes, Birgit Rattenborg Wise; Lighting, Robert Christen; Sound, Richard Woodbury; PSM for Blind Date, Kimberly Osgood; PSM for The Actor, Deya S. Friedman; Dramaturg, Jennifer Shook; Casting, Adam Belcuore; Vocal/Dialects, Christine Adaire: Cast: Blind Date: Jason Wells (Robert), Kathleen Romond (Sarah Nancy), Judy Blue (Dolores), Dan Hale (Felix); The Actor: Patrick Andrews (Horace), Lee Stark (Girl), Gabirel Notarangelo (1st Boy), Dan Hale (2nd Boy), Audrey Francis (Dorothy), Bubba Weiler (Jim), Jenny McKnight (Elizabeth), Philip Earl Johnson (Horace, Sr.); Owen Theatre; February 21–March 2, 2008

THE TRIP TO BOUNTIFUL by Horton Foote; Presented as part of the Horton Foote Festival; Director, Harris Yulin; Set, E. David Cosier; Costumes, Martin Pakledinaz; Lighting, John McKernon; Sound, Brett Jarvis; Composer, Loren Toolajian; PSM, Alden Vasquez; SM, Jamie Wolfe; Chicago Casting, Adam Belcuore; Cast: Lois Smith (Carrie Watts), Devon Abner (Ludie), Hallie Foote (Jessie Mae), Meghan Andrews (Thelma), Bradley Armacost (Ticket Agent #1/Houston Traveler), Danny Goldring (Ticket Agent #2/Houston Traveler); Frank Girardeau (Roy), James Demarse (Sheriff), Houston Travelers/Understudies: Taube Brahms, Erica Elam, Stephen Georgiou, Dean Hill, Ellen Karas, James Krag, Emily Mark, John Ruhaak, Mary Seibel, Kyle Warren; Albert Theatre; March 1–April 13, 2008

THE BALLAD OF EMMETT TILL by Ifa Bayeza; Director, Oz Scott; Set, Skip Mercier; Costumes, Myrna Colley-Lee; Lighting, Victor En Yu Tan; Sound, Richard Woodbury; Composer, Kathryn Bostic; Projections, John Boesche; Cast: Joseph Anthony Byrd (Emmett "Bo" Till), Deidreie Henry (Mamie Till), John Wesley (Moses Wright), Karen Aldridge (Lizabeth Wright), Samuel G. Roberson, Jr. (Simeon), Phillip James Brannon (Maurice), Morocco Omari (Wheeler Parker), Nambi E. Kelley (Ruthie May), Cliff Chamberlain (Roy Bryant), Kristina Johnson (Caroline Bryant), Chris Sullivan (J.W. Millam), Kirk Anderson (JJ. Breeland/Elmer Kimbrell), Brian McCaskill (Hon. Robert B. Smith); Albert Theatre; April 26–June 1, 2008

GAS FOR LESS by Brett Neveu; Director, Dexter Bullard; Set, Tom Burch; Costumes, Tif Bullard; Lighting, Keith Parham; Sound, Joseph Fosco; Cast: Robert Breuler (Art Pelenkovic), Ernest Perry, Jr. (Pat Munson), Rain Jairell (Anthony Pelenkovic), Nathan Allan Davis (Benji Colan Vera), Kareem Bandealy (Bilal Asif); Owen Theatre; May 24–June 22, 2008

AIN'T MISBEHAVIN' Music by Fats Waller, book and lyrics by Richard Maltby, Jr., lyrics by Andy Razaf and others; based on an idea by Murray Horowitz and Richard Maltby, Jr.; Director, Chuck Smith; Music Director, Malcolm Ruhl; Chroregraphy, Lisa Willingham-Johnson; Sets, Linda Buchanan; Costumes, Birgit Rattebog Wise; Lighting, Robert Christen; Sound, Josh Horvath and Ray Nardelli; Cast: Lina Kernan, E. Faye Butler, Parrish Collier, Alexis Rogers, John Steven Crowley; Musicians: Peter Benson (piano), Larry Bowen (trumpet), Y.L Douglas (drums), Anderson Edwards (bass), T.S. Galoway (trombone), Jarrard Harris & Stephen Leinheiser (saxes and clarinets), Malcolm Ruhl (Conductor/guitar); Albert Theatre; June 21–July 27, 2008

Goodspeed Musicals

East Haddam and Chester, Connecticut

FORTY-FOURTH SEASON

Executive Director, Michael P. Price; General Manager, Harriett Guin-Kittner

SINGIN' IN THE RAIN Songs by Nacio Herb Brown and Arthur Freed, based on the MGM film with screenplay by Betty Comden and Adolph Green and original choreography by Gene Kelly and Stanley Donen; Director, Ray Roderick; Choreographer, Rick Conant; Set, James Noone; Costumes, Angela Wendt; Lighting, Kirk Bookman; Music Director, Michael O'Flaherty; Assistant Music Director, F. Wade Russo; Orchestrations, Dan DeLange; Production Manager, R. Glen Grusmark; PSM, Bradley G. Spachman; Associate Producer, Bob Alwine; Line Producer, Donna Lynn Cooper Hilton; Cast: Scott Barnhardt (Cosmo Brown), James Dybas (Roscoe Dexter), David Elder (Don Lockwood), Sarah Jane Everman (Kathy Selden), Michael Hayward-Jones (R.F. Simpson), Stacey Logan (Lina Lamont); Ensemble: Jodie Adkins, Paul Aguirre, Jacob ben Widmar, Melinda Cowan, Tim Falter, Jenny Florkowski, Jillanne Galter, Danny Gardner, Daryl Getman, Chad Harlow, Drew Humphrey, Sarah Lin Johnson, Dorothy Stanley, Tara Jeanne Vallee; Swings: Kevin Leary, Kate Vallee; Goodspeed Opera House; April 20–July 6, 2007

HIGH BUTTON SHOES Music by Jule Styne, lyrics by Sammy Cahn, book by Stephen Longstreet; Director, Greg Ganakas; Choreographer, Linda Goodrich; Set, Howard Chrisman Jones; Costumes, Gregory Gale; Lighting, Kirk Bookman; Hair, Darlene Dannenfelser; Makeup, Justen M. Brosnan; Music Director, Michael O'Flaherty; Assistant Music Director, William J. Thomas; Orchestrations, Dan DeLange; Dance Arrangements, Sam Davis; Production Manager, R. Glen Grusmark; PSM, Bradley G. Spachman; Associate Producer, Bob Alwine; Line Producer, Donna Lynn Cooper Hilton; Cast: Jennifer Allen (Mrs. Sara Longstreet), Stephen Bienskie (Mr. Harrison Floy), Brian Hissong (Hubert Ogglethorpe), Ken Jennings (Mr. Pierre Pontdue), Russell Arden Koplin (Miss Fran Beck), William Perry (Mr. Henry Longstreet), Emmett Rahn-Oakes (Stephen Longstreet); Ensemble: Tommy Berklund, Keith Coughlin, Eric Giancola, Susan Grady, Sara Hart, David Hull, Cheryl McMahon, Hallie Metcalf, Mahri Relin, Dorothy Stanley, Jesse Swimm, Drew Taylor; Swings: Colby Lindeman, Dani Spieler; Replacements: Beth Glover (Mrs. Sara Longstreet, September 5–22); Goodspeed Opera House; July 13–September 22, 2007

HAPPY DAYS: A New Musical Music and lyrics by Paul Williams, book by Garry Marshall; Based on the Paramount Pictures television series *Happy Days,* created by Garry Marshall; Director, Gordon Greenberg; Choreographer, Michele Lynch; Set, Walt Spangler; Costumes, David C. Woolard; Lighting, Jeff Croiter; Sound,, Randy Hansen; Music Director, Shawn Gough; Music Supervisor, Arranger, Orchestrator, John McDaniel; PSM, Jess W. Speaker, III; Technical Director, Lily Twining; For Goodspeed Musicals: Michael P. Price (Executive Director), Michael O'Flaherty (Music Director), R. Glen Grusmark (Production Manager), Hattie Guin-Kittner (General Manager), Bob Alwine (Associate Producer), Donna Lynn Cooper Hilton (Line Producer); Producing assistance from Robert Boyett Theatricals LLC; Originally produced at the Falcon Theatre, Burbank, CA, produced and directed by Garry Marshall, Ronny Hallin, and Kathleen Ward Marshall; Cast: Natalie Bradshaw (Joanie), Todd Buonopane (Ralph), Michael J. Farina (Arnold), Cynthia Ferrer (Marion), Felicia Finley (Pinky), Patrick Garner (Howard), Rory O'Malley (Richie), Christopher Ruth (Potsie), Eric Schneider (Chachi), Joey Sorge (Fonzie); Ensemble: Julia Burrows (Lori Beth), Andrea Dora (Paula/Pinkette Lola), Lauren Parsons (Joy/Pinkette Sally), Tom Plotkin (Student/ Leopard Mac/Jumpy Malachi), Andrew Varela (Bully/Leopard Manny/Count Malachi); Norma Terris Theatre; August 9–September 2, 2007

1776 Music, lyrics and concept by Sherman Edwards, book by Peter Stone; Director, Rob Ruggiero; Choreographer, Ralph D. Perkins; Set, Michael Schweikardt; Costumes, Alejo Vietti; Lighting, John Lasiter; Music Director, Michael O'Flaherty; Assistant Music Director, William J. Thomas; Orchestrations, Dan DeLange; Production Manager, R. Glen Grusmark; PSM, Bradley G. Spachman; Associate Producer, Bob Alwine; Line Producer, Donna Lynn Cooper Hilton; Cast: Jack F. Agnew (Dr. Josiah Bartlett), Glenn Seven Allen (Edward Rutledge), Dean Bellais (George Read), Peter A. Carey (John Adams), Paul Carlin (Samuel Chase), Ronn Carroll (Ben Franklin), Michael P. Cartwright (Joseph Hewes), Kenneth Cavett (Col. Thomas McKean), Jerry Christakos (Rev. Jonathan Witherspoon), John M. Costa (Andrew McNair), Jay Goede (John Dickinson), Dennis Holland (Dr. Lyman Hall), Paul Jackel (Robert Livingston), Christopher Michael Kauffmann (Courier), Marc Kessler (James Wilson), John Newton (Stephen Hopkins), Jayne Paterson (Abigail Adams), Michael A. Pizzi (Lewis Morris), Trip Plymale (Caesar Rodney), Greg Roderick (Roger Sherman), Alan Rust (John Hancock), Charlie Tirrell (Charles Thomson), Marcellus Waller (Leather Apron/Painter), Edward Watts (Thomas Jefferson), Richard White (Richard Henry Lee), Teal Wicks (Martha Jefferson); Swings: Kristofer Holz, Erin Williams; Replacement: Rebecca Watson (Abigail Adams Oct. 31-Dec. 9); Goodspeed Opera House; September 28 –December 9, 2007

Guthrie Theatre

Minneapolis, Minnesota

FORTY-FIFTH SEASON

Director, Joe Dowling; Theater Manager, Jacques Brunswick

1776 Book by Peter Stone, music and lyrics by Sherman Edwards; Director, John Miller-Stephany; Choreographer, James Sewell; Set, James Youmans; Costumes, Matthew J. LeFebvre; Lighting, Donald Holder; Sound, Scott W. Edwards; Dramaturg, Jo Holcomb; Musical Director & Conductor, Andrew Cooke; Speech and Dialects, Kate Burke; Assistant Director, Sarah Gioia; SM, Martha Kulig; ASM, Jason Clusman; Cast: Michael Thomas Holmes (John Adams), Peter Michael Goetz (Benjamin Franklin), Tyson Forbes (Thomas Jefferson), Richard White (Richard Henry Lee), Norah Long (Abigail Adams), Robert O. Berdahl (Robert Livingston), Bob Beverage (Caesar Rodney), Raye Birk (Stephen Hopkins), Michael Booth (Rev. John Witherspoon), Mark Bradley (a Painter), Elizabeth Broadhurst (Martha Jefferson), Philip Callen (Dr. Lyman Hall), Sean Michael Dooley (Leather Apron), Wayne A. Evenson (Samuel Chase), Dan Foss (Roger Sherman), Bradley Greenwald (Edward Rutledge), Jon Andrew Hegge (Charles Thomson), Robb McKindles (Joseph Hewes), Lee Mark Nelson (John Dickinson), James Ramlet (Col. Thomas McKean), Mark Rosenwinkel (Andrew McNair), Brian Skellenger (Courier), Brian Sostek (James Wilson), Vern Sutton (Lewis Morris), Peter Thomson (John Hancock), Tony Vierling (Dr. Josiah Bartlett), Jon Whittier (George Read); Wurtele Thrust Stage; June 23–August 26, 2007

PRIVATE LIVES by Noël Coward; Director, Peter Rothstein; Set, John Arnone; Costumes, Devon Painter; Lighting, Marcus Dilliard; Sound, Reid Rejsa; Dramaturg, Jo Holcomb; Voice and Speech Coach, Lucinda Holshue; Movement, Marcela Lorca; Fight Director, Peter Moore; Assistant Director, Aaron Gabriel; SM, Michele Harms; ASM, Justin Hossle; Cast: Veanne

Cox (Amanda Prynne), Stephen Pelinski (Elyot Chase), Kris L. Nelson (Victor Prynne), Tracey Maloney (Sybil Chase), Sally Wingert (Louise, a maid); McGuire Proscenium Stage; July 21–September 2, 2007

JANE EYRE by Charlotte Brontë, adapted by Alan Stanford; Director, John Miller-Stephany; Set/Costumes, Patrick Clark; Lighting, Matthew Reinert; Sound, Scott W. Edwards; Composer, Andrew Cooke; Dramaturg, Carla Steen; Voice/Dialects, Lucinda Holshue; Movement, Marcela Lorca; Fight Director, Assistant Director, Suzy Messerole; Peter Moore; SM, Chris A. Code; ASM, Amy Monroe; Cast: Sam Stacia Rice (Jane Eyre), Margaret Daly (Jane Senior), Sean Haberle (Edward Rochester), Barbara Bryne (Mrs. Fairfax), Jessie Austrian (Blanche Ingram/Barbara), Jennifer Blagen (Miss Scatcherd/Diana Rivers), Caroline Cooney (Leah), Laura Esping (Miss Temple/Mary Rivers), Nathaniel Fuller (Mr. Brocklehurst/Mr. Wood), Peter Christian Hansen (St. John Rivers/Surgeon), Charity Jones (Mrs. Reed/Bertha), Barbara Kingsley (Lady Ingram/Hannah), Ron Menzel (Richard Mason), Peggy O'Connell (Grace Poole), John Skelley (Davie), Peter Thomson (Lord Ingram/Briggs); Wurtele Thrust Stage; September 8–November 10, 2007

THE HOME PLACE by Brian Friel; Director, Joe Dowling; Set, Frank Hallinan Flood; Costumes, Monica Frawley; Lighting, Matthew Reinert; Sound, Reid Rejsa; Dramaturg, Michael Lupu; Voice and Speech Coach, Cathal Quinn; Movement, Marcela Lorca; Assistant Director, Alex Torra; SM, Russell W. Johnson; ASM, Elizabeth R. MacNally; Cast: Simon Jones (Christopher Gore), Michael Bakkensen (David Gore), Richard S. Iglewski (Dr. Richard Gore), Sarah Agnew (Margaret O'Donnell), Matthew Amendt (Con Doherty), Virginia S. Burke (Mary Sweeney), Maggie Chestovich (Sally Cavanagh), Charles Keating (Clement O'Donnell), Steve Lewis (Perkins), Samuel Finnegan Pearson (Tommy Boyle) and James Ramlet (Johnny MacLoone); US Premiere; McGuire Proscenium Stage; September 22–November 25, 2007

PEN by David Marshall Grant; Director/Set, Rob Melrose; Costumes, Christine Richardson; Lighting, Frank Butler; Sound, C. Andrew Mayer; Dramaturg, Michael Lupu; SM, Michele Harms; ASM, Christopher Flores; Cast: Marc Halsey (Matt), Michelle Barber (Helen), Philip Callen (Jerry); Dowling Studio; November 3–November 25, 2007

A CHRISTMAS CAROL by Charles Dickens, adapted by Barbara Field; Director, Gary Gisselman; Set, Neil Patel; Costumes, Jess Goldstein; Lighting, Marcus Dilliard; Sound, Scott W. Edwards; Composer, Victor Zupanc; Dramaturg, Michael Lupu; Voice/Dialects, Elisa Carlson; Associate Director/Movement, Myron Johnson; Music Director, Anita Ruth; AD, Robert Goudy; Assistant Costumes, David Kay Mickelsen; SM, Martha Kulig; ASM, Jason Clusman; Cast: Raye Birk (Ebenezer Scrooge), Michael Booth (Bob Cratchit), Laura Esping (Mrs. Dilber/Dorothea), Nathaniel Fuller (Jacob Marley/Topper), Beth Gilleland (Mrs. Cratchit), Jon Andrew Hegge (Dick Wilkins/Ghost of Christmas Yet to Come), Whitney Hudson (Petunia Fezziwig), Kathleen Humphry (Jane), Charity Jones (Ghost of Christmas Past/Mrs. Fred), Hugh Kennedy (Cecil/Young Scrooge/Squeeze), Michael Kissin (Fiddler/Krookings), Kris L. Nelson (Forrest/Snarkers), Lee Mark Nelson (Fred), Stephen Pelinski (Ghost of Christmas Present), Randy Reyes (Albert Hall/Edwards/Joe), Courtney Roche (Marigold Fezziwig), Doug Sholz-Carlson (Mr. Grub/Mr. Squeeze/Blackings Foreman), John Skelley (Young Jacob Marley/Gasper), Elizabeth Stahlmann (Belle/Ella), Vern Sutton (Blakely/Mr. Fezziwig/Elliott), Suzanne Warmanen (Sophia); Wurtele Thrust Stage; November 20–December 29, 2007

PEER GYNT Translated and adapted by Robert Bly from the play by Henrik Ibsen, Director, Tim Carroll; Set/Costumes, Laura Hopkins; Lighting, Stan Pressner; Sound, Scott W. Edwards; Composer, Claire Van Kampen; Dramaturg, Carla Steen; Voice/Dialects, Lucinda Holshue; Movement, Marcela Lorca; AD, Benjamin McGovern; SM, Chris A. Code; ASM, Michele Harms; Cast: Mark Rylance (Peer Gynt), Matthew Amendt (Blacksmith's Friend/Cook), Richard S. Iglewski (Wedding Host/Troll King/Monsieur Airhead), Jim Lichtscheidl (Buglebrain/Button Moulder), Michelle O'Neill (Solveig's Mother/Kari), Jonas Goslow (Bridegroom/Lord Cotton), Isabell Monk O'Connor (Åsa), Tracey Maloney (Girl at Wedding/Troll Princess), Bill McCallum (Solveig's Father/Ship's Captain/Head of the Asylum), Tyson Forbes (Blacksmith/Voice of the Boyg/Hussein), Maha Chehlaoui (Anitra), Miriam Silverman (Solveig), Richard Ooms (Bridegroom's Father/Boarhead/Skinny Devil), Catherine Johnson Justice (Girl at Wedding/Ingrid), Phyllis Wright (Old Woman/Bridegroom's Mother); Wurtele Thrust Stage; January 12–March 2, 2008

THIRD by Wendy Wasserstein; Director, Casey Stangl; Set, John Arnone; Costumes, David Kay Mickelsen; Lighting, Marcus Dilliard; Sound, C. Andrew Mayer; Dramaturg, Jo Holcomb; Voice/Speech, Lucinda Holshue; Movement, Marcela Lorca; AD, Carin Bratlie; SM, Martha Kulig; ASM, Jason Clusman; Cast: Sally Wingert (Laurie Jameson), Tony Clarno (Woodson Bull III), Raye Birk (Jack Jameson), Emily Gunyou Halaas (Emily), Angela Timberman (Nancy Gordon); McGuire Proscenium Stage; February 16–March 30, 2008

NINE PARTS OF DESIRE by Heather Raffo; Director and Set, Joel Sass; Costumes, Amelia Cheever; Lighting, Marcus Dilliard; Sound, C. Andrew Mayer; Composer, Gregory Brosofske; Dramaturg, Carla Steen; Voice/Dialects, Lucinda Holshue; SM, Elizabeth R. MacNally; ASM, Christopher Flores; Cast: Kate Eifrig; Dowling Studio; March 1–March 23, 2008

A MIDSUMMER NIGHT'S DREAM by William Shakespeare; Director, Joe Dowling, Set, Frank Hallinan Flood; Costumes, Paul Tazewell; Lighting, Jane Cox; Sound, Scott W. Edwards; Fight Director, John Stead; Composer, Keith Thomas; Dramaturg, Michael Lupu; Voice/Dialects/Language Consultant, Andrew Wade; Movement, Marcela Lorca; ADD, Sarah Gioia; Co-Fight Director, Joel Harris; SM, Russell W. Johnson; ASM, Michele Harms; Cast: Jonas Goslow (Demetrius), William Sturdivant (Lysander), Kathryn Lawrey

(Hermia), Valeri Mudek (Helena), Nic Few (Oberon/Theseus), Emily Swallow (Titania/Hippolyta), Namir Smallwood (Puck), Erin Cherry (First Fairy), Sherwin F. Resurreccion (Fairy), Ian Holcomb (Fairy), Mike Rasmussen (Fairy), John Skelley (Fairy), Brandon Weinbrenner (Fairy), Richard S. Iglewski (Tom Snout), Jim Lichtscheidl (Peter Quince), Stephen Pelinski (Nick Bottom), Sally Wingert (Robin Starveling), Stephen Yoakam (Snug), Randy Reyes (Francis Flute), Nathaniel Fuller (Egeus); Wurtele Thrust Stage; April 12–June 22, 2008

Hartford Stage Company

Hartford, Connecticut

FORTY-THIRD SEASON

Artistic Director, Michael Wilson; Managing Director, Michael Stotts

OUR TOWN by Thornton Wilder; Director, Gregory Boyd; Set, Jeff Cowie; Costumes, Alejo Vietti; Lighting, Rui Rita; Original Music and Sound, John Gromada; PSM, Tree O' Halloran; Cast: Hal Holbrook (Stage Manager), Ross Bickell (Dr. Gibbs), Jacob Lombardi (Joe Crowell/Si Crowell), Bill Kux (Howie Newsome/Belligerent Man), Josie de Guzman (Mrs. Gibbs), Annalee Jefferies (Mrs. Webb), Donovan Patton (George Gibbs), Erin S. Courtney (Rebecca Gibbs), Jordan Cyr or Andrew Shipman (Wally Webb), Ginna Carter (Emily Webb), Nafe Katter (Professor Willard/Joe Stoddard), Frank Converse (Editor Webb), Charlotte Booker (Mrs. Soames), Noble Shropshire (Simon Stimson), Robert Hannon Davis (Constable Warren), Tom Libonate (Sam Craig), Justin Fuller, Michael Angelo Morlani (Baseball Players); Ensemble: Jessi Ehrlich, Rick Guliani, Joseph Kornfeld, Rob Pawlikowski, Denise Walker, Debra Walsh; August 30–October 7, 2007

CHICK: The Great Osram by David Grimm; Director, Michael Wilson; Set, Tony Straiges; Costumes, David C. Woolard; Lighting, Rui Rita; Original Music and Sound, John Gromada; PSM, Gregory R. Covert; Cast: Robert Sella (Chick), Enid Graham (Helen); October 13–November 11 2007

A CHRISTMAS CAROL by Charles Dickens; Director, Michael Wilson; Original Set, Tony Straiges; Costumes, Zack Brown; Lighting, Robert Wierzel; Original Music/Sound, John Gromada; PSM, Martin Lechner; Cast: Bill Raymond or Gustave Johnson (Ebenezer Scrooge), Bill Kux (Mrs. Dilber/ Jacob Marley), Robert Hannon Davis (Bob Cratchit/Mr. Fezziwig), Chris Connor (Fred/Young Scrooge), Colin Gold (Lamplighter/Male Swing), Nafe Katter (First Solicitor/ Undertaker), Gustave Johnson (Second Solicitor), Johanna Morrison (Bettye Pidgeon/Sprit of Christmas Past), Stephanie LaRiviere (Rich Lady), Helmar Augustus Cooper (Bert/Spirit of Christmas Present), Curtis Billings (Mr. Marvel), Kit Treece (Scrooge at Fourteen/Party Guest/Ghostly Apparition/Citizen of London), Natalie Brown (Mrs. Fezziwig/Old Jo/Ghostly Apparition/Citizen of London), Amanda Tudor (Nichola/ Ghostly Apparition/Citizen of London), Kaitlin Marrin (Wendy/Ghostly Apparition/Citizen of London), Virginia Welch (Fiddler), Michael Angelo Morlani (Dick Wikins/ Ghostly Apparition/Citizen of London), Matt Faucher (Party Guest/Mr. Topper/Ghostly Apparition/Citizen of London), Michelle Hendrick (Belle/Fred's wife), Rebecka Jones (Mrs. Cratchit), Maya Stojan (Martha Cratchit), Spirit of Christmas Furture (Himself), Danielle Barry (Female Swing), Zackary Cyr or Brendan Fitzgerald (Tim Cratchit), Joy Rachel Del Valle or Karmen Renee-Huerta (Spoiled Child/Fred's Party), Julia Beebe, Thomas Beebe, Kristen Fitzpatrick, Michael Foley Griffin, Ahmad Jordan, Miles Leland Wilson-Toliver (Schoolboys), Jordan Cyr or Andrew Shipman (Boy Scrooge/ Fred Party), Christina Nicholas or Leach Elizabeth Zavlick (Fan), Nora Holland or Summer Raign Martin (Claire), Stephanie Mailhot or Kaitlynn F. O'Brien (Belinda Cratchit), Traylon Butler-Neal or John Holland (Peter Cratchit), Lauren May Baker or Abbi Roce (Ignorance/Cider Child), Patrick Beebe or Andrew Holland (Want/Fruit Child), Michael (Micky) Vespa or Zachary Scott Zavalick (Turkey Boy), Connor Fitzgerald or Nicolas Mehlman (Urchin); November 23–December 29, 2007

ZERLINE'S TALE by Herman Broch, adapted by Jeremy Sams with John David Casey; Director, Michael Wilson; Set, Alexander Dodge; Costumes, Jane Greenwood; Lighting, Howell Binkley; Original Music/Sound, John Gromada; PSM, Linda Marvel; Cast: John David Casey (Man), Elizabeth Ashley (Zerline); January 12–February 10, 2008

THE BLUEST EYE by Lydia Diamond, based on the novel by Toni Morrison; Director, Eric Ting; Set, Scott Bradley; Costumes, Toni-Leslie James; Lighting, Russell H. Champa; Original Music/Sound, Michael Bodeen & Rob Milburn; Cast: Bobbi Barker (Claudia), Miche Braden (Mama/Woman/ Vocal and Music Arrangements), Leon Addison Brown (Cholly), Ellis Foster (Soaphead Church/Daddy), Oni Faida Lampley (Mrs. Breedlove/Woman), Adepero Oduye (Pecola), Ronica V. Reddick (Frieda/Darlene), Shelly Thomas (Maureen Pearl/White Girl/Woman); February 21–March 23, 2008

THE SCENE by Theresa Rebeck; Director, Jeremy B. Cohen; Set, Kris Stone; Lighting, Robert Wierzel; Costumes, Miranda Hoffman; Original Music and Sound, Lindsay Jones; Cast: Matthew Arkin (Charlie), Liam Craig (Lewis), Christy McIntosh (Clea), Henny Russell (Stella); April 3–May 4, 2008

THE MILK TRAIN DOESN'T STOP HERE ANYMORE by Tennessee Williams; Director, Michael Wilson; Sets, Jeff Cowie; Costumes, David Woolard; Lighting, Rui Rita; Original Music/Sound, John Gromada; PSM, Susie Cordon; Cast: Kevin Anderson (Christopher Flanders), Olympia Dukakis (Flora Goforth), Maggie Lacey (Blackie), Curtis Billings (Giulio), Amanda Tudor (Simonetta), Judith Roberts (Witch of Capri); May 15–June 15, 2008

Illinois Theatre Center

Park Forest, Illinois

THIRTY-SECOND SEASON

Producing Artistic Director, Etel Billig; Associate Director, Jonathan R. Billig; Technical Director, James Corey

THAT CHAMPIONSHIP SEASON by Jason Miller; Director, Etel Billig; Cast: Bernard Rice, Peter Robel, Mark Stegman, Tucker Curtis, Howie Johnson; September 21–October 7, 2007

THE LADY FROM HAVANA by Luis Santeiro; Director, Etel Billig; Cast: Madeleine Fallon, Rosy Gonzalez, Teri Lopez; October 26–November 11, 2007

TRIUMPH OF LOVE Book by James Magruder, music by Jeffrey Stock, lyrics by Susan Birkenhead; Director, Etel Billig; Musical Director, Jonathan R. Billig; Choreographer, Frank Roberts; Cast: Iris Lieberman, Bill Scharpen, Laura Grene, Riley Thomas, Laura Sturm, David Zizic, Frank Thomas; November 30–December 16, 2007

COLLECTED STORIES by Donald Margulies; Director, Bernard Rice; Cast: Judy Rossignuolo-Rice, Laura Lodewyck; January 11–27, 2008

NEAT by Charlayne Woodard; Director, Etel Billig; Cast: Inda Craig-Galvan; February 15–March 2, 2008

SUDDENLY LAST SUMMER by Tennessee Williams; Director, David Boettcher; Cast: Katrina Kuntz, Peter Robel, Etel Billig, Chris Blumer, Zachary Clark, Hayley L. Rice, Jeanne Scurek; March 21–April 6, 2008

SEE WHAT I WANNA SEE by Michael John LaChiusa; Director, David Perkovich; Musical Director, Jonathan R. Billig; Cast: Alan Ball, Marilynn Bogetich, Jeff Max, Lauren Creel, Matthew Sean Callahan; April 25–May 11, 2008

Indiana Repertory Theatre

Indianapolis, Indiana

THIRTY-SIXTH SEASON

Artistic Director, Janet Allen; Managing Director, Steven Stolen; Associate Artistic Director, Priscilla Lindsay; Associate Managing Director, Suzanne Sweeney; Playwright-in-Residence, James Still

OUR TOWN by Thornton Wilder; Director, Peter Amster; Sets, David Birn; Costumes, Ann Sheffield; Lighting, Shannon McKinney; Sound, Todd Mack Reischman; Music, Gregg Coffin; Dramaturg; Richard J. Roberts; SM, Nathan Garrison; ASM, Joel Markus; Casting, Claire Simon; Cast: Robert Elliott (Stage Manager), Sawyer Harvey (Joe Crowell, Jr./Si Crowell), Mark Goetzinger (Dr. Gibbs), Michael Shelton (Howie Newsome/Sam Craig), Priscilla Lindsay (Mrs. Gibbs), Manon Halliburton (Mrs. Webb), Tom Conner (George Gibbs), Katherine Shelton (Rebecca Gibbs), Bryce Miller (Wally Webb), Gwendolyn Whiteside (Emily Webb), Eddie Curry (Professor Willard), Charles Goad (Mr. Webb), Jolene Mentink Moffatt (Woman in Balcony/Mrs. Soames), Ryan Artzberger (Man in Auditorium/Simon Stimson), Kate Braun (Woman in Box), Jeff Keel (Constable Warren/Joe Stoddard); Mainstage; September 12–October 6, 2007

HAMLET by William Shakespeare; Director, Andrew Tsao; Sets, Robert M. Koharchik; Costumes, Joel Ebarb; Lighting, Ryan Koharchik; Sound, Todd Mack Reischman; Dramaturg, Richard J. Roberts; Fight Choreographer, Robert K. Johansen; SM, Joel Grynheim; Casting, Claire Simon Casting; Cast: Benjamin Harris (Horatio), Robert Neal (Claudius), Nick Carpenter (Laertes), Brian Noffke (Polonius/Gravedigger), Matthew Brumlow (Hamlet), Lynne Perkins (Gertrude), Kristen Lennox (Gertrude), Jessica Martin (Ophelia), Ben Tebbe (Rosencrantz), Collin Poynter (Guildenstern); Upperstage; September 30–November 3, 2007

A CHRISTMAS CAROL by Charles Dickens, adapted by Tom Haas; Director, Priscilla Lindsay; Sets, Russell Metheny; Costumes, Murell Horton; Lighting, Michael Lincoln; Composer, Andrew Hopson; Choreography, David Hochoy; Associate Lighting, Betsy Cooprider-Bernstein; Musical Director, Christopher Ludwa; Dramaturg, Richard J Roberts; SM, Nathan Garrison; ASM, Joel Markus; Young Actor Supervisor, Mary Ferguson; Casting, Claire Simon; Cast: Charles Goad (Ebenezer Scrooge), Robert K. Johansen (Bob Cratchit/Schoolmaster/Broker), Sam Misner (Fred/Young Marley/Undertaker), Jennifer Carpenter (Felicity/Postboy), Nikkeili DeMone (Portly Gentleman/Fezziwig/Topper/Old Joe), Kate Goetzinger (Sister of Mercy/Martha Cratchit), Constance Macy (Mrs. Cratchit/Roses Sister), Ben Ayres (Waiter/Willful Smackers/Nutley), Mark Goetzinger (Marley's Ghost/Christmas Present), Gerson Decanay (Christmas Past/Charwoman/Dance Captain), Jason Bradley (Young Scrooge/Lamplighter/Broker), Lynne Perkins (Mrs. Fezziwig/Plump Sister/Laundress/Choral Leader), Jennifer Johansen (Belle/Fred's Maid/Christmas Future), Eric VanTielen (Belle's Husband/Broker/Poulterer's Man), Aaron Huey or Bryce Miller (Waif/Henry Cratchit/Ignorance/Turkey Boy), Molly Will or Anna Garrison (Belinda Cratchit/Fan), Kevin Mull or McKeith Pearson II (Peter Cratchit/Adolescent Scrooge/Dick Wilkins), Sam Melnikove or Ciarra Krohne (Tiny Tim/Boy Scrooge), Reagan Smith or Keeley Miller (Betsy Cratchit/Want); Mainstage; November 3, 2007–December 24, 2008

TUESDAYS WITH MORRIE by Jeffrey Hatcher and Mitch Albom, based on the novel by Mitch Albom; Director, Risa Brainin; Sets, Nayna Ramey; Costumes, Linda Pisano; Lighting, Michael Klaers; Sound, Todd Mack Reischman; Dramaturg, Richard J. Roberts; SM, Amy Denkmann; Cast: Ryan Artzberger (Mitch), Jon Farris (Morrie); Upperstage; December 4, 2007–January 13, 2008

DOUBT by John Patrick Shanley; Director, James Still; Sets and Costumes, Ann Sheffield; Lighting, Lap-Chi Chu; Music

Consultant/English Horn, Roger Roe; Sound Associate, Michael Lamirand; Dramaturg, Richard J. Roberts; SM, Joel Grynheim; Casting, Claire Simon Casting; Cast: Lenny Von Dohlen (Father Flynn), Priscilla Lindsay (Sister Aloysius), Cora Vander Broek (Sister James), Dwandra Nickole (Mrs. Muller); Mainstage; January 16–February 9, 2008

THE POWER OF ONE Created by the IRT; Director, Richard J. Roberts; Sets, Fred Duer; Costumes, Christine Joern Martin; Lighting, Betsy Cooprider-Bernstein; Sound, Todd Mack Reischman; SM, Amy K. Denkmann; Cast: Milicent Wright (Harriet Tubman/Madame C.J. Walker/Rosa Parks); Upperstage; February 2–March 8, 2008

THE PIANO LESSON by August Wilson; Co-Produced with Geva Theatre Center; Director, Seret Scott; Sets, Russell Metheny; Costumes, Karen Perry; Lighting, Michael Lincoln; Assistant to Lighting, John Woody; Sound, Todd Mack Reischman; Fight Consultant, Robert K. Johansen; Dramaturg, Richard J. Roberts; SM, Nathan Garrison; Casting, Harriet Bass; Cast: Chuck Patterson (Doaker), Carl Cofield (Boy Willie), Warner Miller (Lymon), Roslyn Ruff (Berniece), Mackenzie Isaac (Maretha), Geoffrey D. Williams (Avery), Glenn Turner (Wining Boy), Jessica Frances Dukes (Grace); Mainstage; February 20–March 15, 2008

LOOKING OVER THE PRESIDENT'S SHOULDER by James Still; Director, Janet Allen; Sets, Robert M. Koharchik; Costumes, Martin Chapman-Bowman; Lighting, Ryan Koharchik; Sound, Todd Mack Reischman; Composer, Michael Keck; SM, Amy K. Denkmann; Cast: David Alan Anderson (Alonzo Fields); Mainstage; April 1–May 3, 2008

IRON KISSES by James Still; Director, David Bradley; Sets, Russell Metheny; Costumes, Kathleen Egan; Lighting, Lap-Chi Chu; Sound, Chris Colucci; Dramaturg, Richard J. Roberts; SM, Nathan Garrison; Cast: Ryan Artzberger (Billy), Constance Macy (Barbara); Upperstage; April 15–May 11, 2008

THE FANTASTICKS Book and lyrics by Tom Jones, music by Harvey Schmidt; Co-Produced with Syracuse Stage; Director and Choreographer, Peter Amster; Sets, Russell Metheny; Costumes, Maria Marrero; Lighting, Ann G. Wrightson; Music Director, David Nelson; Sound, Todd Mack Reischman; Dramaturg, Richard J. Roberts; SM, Nathan Garrison; Casting, Alan Filderman; Casting, Claire Simon Casting; Cast: Alexa Silvaggio (the Mute), David Studwell (El Gallo), Mackenzie Thomas (Luisa), Erik Van Tielen (Matt), Mark Goetzinger (Hucklebee), Charles Goad (Bellomy), William J. Norris (Henry), Robert K. Johansen (Mortimer), David Nelson (Piano); Mainstage; May 27–June 22, 2008

Intiman Theatre

Seattle, Washington

THIRTY-FIFTH SEASON

Artistic Director, Bartlett Sher; Managing Director, Laura Penn

THE LIGHT IN THE PIAZZA Music and lyrics by Adam Guettel, book by Craig Lucas, based on the novel by Elizabeth Spencer; Presented in association with Broadway Across America–Seattle and Seattle Theatre Group at the Paramount Theatre; Director, Bartlett Sher; Set, Michael Yeargan; Costumes, Catherine Zuber; Lighting, Christopher Akerlind; Sound, Acme Sound Partners; Orchestrations, Ted Sperling and Adam Guettel; Music Director, Kimberly Grigsby; Musical Staging, Jonathan Butterell; Casting, Janet Foster, C.S.A.; PSM, Wendiana Walker; SM, Anna Belle Gilbert; Cast: Christine Andreas (Margaret Johnson), Craig Bennett (Priest, Ensemble), Wendi Bergamini (Franca Naccarelli), Jane Brockman (Tour Guide, Ensemble), David Burnham (Fabrizio Naccarelli), Katie Rose Clarke (Clara Johnson), Betsy DiLellio (Ensemble), Diana DiMarzio (Signora Naccarelli), Laurent Giroux (Ensemble), Jonathan Hammond (Giuseppe Naccarelli), Leslie Henstock (Ensemble), Prudence Wright Holmes (Ensemble), David Ledingham (Signor Naccarelli), Adam Overett (Ensemble), John Procaccino (Roy Johnson), Andrew Ragone (Ensemble); April 17–29, 2007

THE SKIN OF OUR TEETH by Thornton Wilder; Director, Bartlett Sher; Set, Michael Yeargan; Costumes, Catherine Zuber; Lighting, Marcus Doshi; Composer and Sound, Peter John Still; Vocal Coach, Alyssa Keene; SM, Lisa Ann Chernoff; ASM, Tamesis Batiste; Cast: Kelly Balch (Gladys Antrobus), Laurence Ballard (Homer/Mr. Tremayne), Amy Conant (Miss E. Muse/Musician), Clayton Corzatte (Announcer/Judge Moses/Fred Bailey), Kristin Flanders (Sabina), Catherine E. Harris-White (Miss T. Muse/Musician), David Hunter Koch (Mr. Fitzpatrick/Professor/Musician), Ernest L. Pumphrey Jr. (Mammoth/Chair Pusher/Musician), Chelsey Rives (Doctor/Ivy), Gregory Scott Rocha (Telegraph Boy), Derek Schreck (Mammoth/Broadcast Official/Musician), Anne Scurria (Mrs. Antrobus), Howie Seago (Mr. Antrobus), Lucia Sher (Baby Dinosaur), J.D. Tracy (Henry Antrobus), Kate Wisniewski (Miss M. Muse/Fortune Teller/Musician); April 28–June 2, 2007

UNCLE VANYA by Anton Chekhov; adapted by Craig Lucas; Director, Bartlett Sher; Set, John McDermott; Costumes, Deb Trout; Lighting, Brian MacDevitt; Music, Adam Guettel; Sound, Joseph Swartz; SM, Claire E. Zawa; ASM, Ross Whippo; Cast: Carter J. Davis (Worker), Allen Fitzpatrick (Professor Serebriakov), Kristin Flanders (Sonya), Tim Hopper (Astrov), Lori Larsen (Maria), Samantha Mathis (Elena), Todd Jefferson Moore (Telegin), Mark Nelson (Vanya), Paula Nelson (Nanny); June 12–July 18, 2007

PRAYER FOR MY ENEMY by Craig Lucas; Produced in association with the Long Wharf Theatre; Director, Bartlett Sher; Set, John McDermott; Costumes, Catherine Zuber; Lighting, Stephen Strawbridge; Sound, Stephen LeGrand; New York Casting, James Calleri, C.S.A.; SM, Lisa Ann Chernoff; ASM, Tamesis Batiste; Cast: Kimberly King (Dolores Endler), James McMenamin (Tad Voelkl), John Procaccino (Austin), Chelsey Rives (Marianne), Cynthia Lauren Tewes (Karen), Daniel Zaitchik (Billy Noone); World Premiere; July 27–August 26, 2007

TO KILL A MOCKINGBIRD by Harper Lee, adapted by Christopher Sergel; Director, Fracaswell Hyman; Set, Alec Hammond.; Costumes, Elizabeth Hope Clancy; Lighting, Greg Sullivan; Composer and Music Coach, Grant Dermody; Sound, Joseph Swartz; Fight Director, Geoffrey Alm; Dialects, Judith Shahn; New York Casting, Janet Foster, C.S.A.; SM, Wendiana Walker; Assistant to the SM, Ross Whippo; Cast: David Bishins (Atticus Finch), Patti Cohenour (Maudie Atkinson), Peter Crook (Nathan Radley, Mr. Gilmer, Boo Radley), David Drummond (Heck Tate), Stephen Grenley (Judge Taylor, Walter Cunningham), William Hall Jr. (Reverend Sykes), Russell Hodgkinson (Bob Ewell), Josephine Howell (Calpurnia), Lori Larsen (Stephanie Crawford), Lino Marioni (Dill), Liz Morton (Mayella Ewell), Sean Phillips (Tom Robinson) Nick Robinson (Jem Finch), Walayn Sharples (Mrs. Dubose/Clerk), Keaton Whittaker (Scout Finch); September 14–November 10, 2007

BLACK NATIVITY by Langston Hughes; Director, Jacqueline Moscou; Choreographer, Kabby Mitchell III; Musical Director/Arrangements, Pastor Patrinell Wright; Featuring Pastor Patrinell Wright, the Reverend Dr. Samuel B. McKinney, gospel performances by the Total Experience Gospel Choir and the Black Nativity Choir; November 28–December 28, 2007

Kansas City Repertory Company

Kansas City, Missouri

FORTY-FOURTH SEASON

Managing Director, Bill Prenevost

Spencer Theatre

DOUBT by John Patrick Shanley; Director, Stephen Rothman; Set, David Potts; Costumes, David Murin; Lighting, James Moody; Sound/Composer, Joe Cerqua; PSM, Mary R. Honour; ASM, Byron F. Abens; Cast: Eric Thal (Father Flynn), Laurie Kennedy (Sister Aloysius), Gardner Reed (Sister James), Gina Daniels (Mrs. Muller); October 19–November 11, 2007

A CHRISTMAS CAROL by Charles Dickens, adapted by Barbara Field; Director, Linda Ade Brand; Choreographer, Jennifer Martin; Set, John Ezell; Costumes, Pheobe Boynton; Lighting, Shane Rowse; Sound, John Story; Musical Director, Mark Ferrell; PSM, Beth Ellen Spencer; ASM, Mary R. Honour; Cast: Gary Neal Johnson (Ebenezer Scrooge), Robert Gibby Brand (Charles Dickens), Dean Vivian (Bob Cratchit), Charles Fugate (Fred), Brad Shaw (Solicitor), Merle Moores (Solicitor/Grandma Fezziwig/Charwoman), Logan Ernstthal (Poulterer/Businessman), Angela Cristantello (Poulterer's Wife/Martha Cratchit), Caroline Adams (Belinda Cratchit), Katie Hall (Belinda Cratchit), Ashley Beth Burnett (Chestnut Vendor/Clovia Fezziwig), Holland Broce (Want), Brock Lorenzen (Ignorance), Ian Von Fange (Peter Cratchit), Toccarra Cash (Toy Vendor/Laundress), Samuel T. Gaines (Young Man), Jim Gall (Rat Catcher/Ghost of Christmas Present), Larry Greer (Marley), Kathleen Warfel (Ghost of Christmas Past), Dakota Hoar (Scrooge as a boy), Jessica Ims (Fan), Zach Harris (Simon), David Graham Jones (Scrooge as a young man), Cassandra Schwanke (Belle/Mrs. Fred), Kathryn Bartholomew (Aunt Fezziwig/Giggly Sister), Sarah LaBarr (Serious Sister), Kyle L. Mowry (Undertaker), Brad Shaw (Solicitor/Ghost of Christmas Future), Phil Fiorini (Dick Wilkins), Michael Linsley Rapport (Mr. Fezziwig/Businessman), Peggy Friesen (Mrs. Fezziwig/Harpist), Lyndsey Agron (Saphronella Fezziwig), Seth Golay (Albert Hall/Young man), Evan Absher (A Bobby), Mark Robbins (Old Joe), Jeanne Averill (Mrs. Cratchit), Zackary Hoar/Whittaker Hoar/Grant Lorenzen (Tiny Tim); Ensemble: Elizabeth Ernst, Kelsey Kallenberger, Teonna Wesley, Chris Fielder, James Michael Hicks, Kristin Astourian-Nixon; November 17–December 24, 2007

TO KILL A MOCKINGBIRD by Harper Lee, adapted by Christopher Sergel; Director, Samantha K. Wyer; Set, Hugh Landwehr; Costumes, Sam Fleming; Lighting, Dennis Parichy; Composer, Peter Ostroushko; Sound, John Story; PSM, Bruno Ingram; ASM, Beth Ellen Spencer; Cast: Wendy Robie (Jean Louise), Daria LeGrand (Scout), Julia Lema (Calpurnia), Walter Coppage (Reverend Sykes), Kathleen Warfel (Mrs. Dubose), Adam Moffitt (Jem), Christopher Moffitt (Dill), Roberto Guajardo (Mr. Radley/Judge Taylor), John Rensenhouse (Atticus Finch), Kyle L. Mowry (Walter Cunningham/Boo Radley), Bruce Roach (Sheriff Heck Tate), Scott Cordes (Bob Ewell), Nathan Darrow (Mr. Gilmer), James T. Alfred (Tom Robinson), Kathryn Bartholomew (Mayella Ewell), Antonia Butler-Johnson (Helen Robinson); Ensemble: Dan Hillaker, Frank Dodson, Dana Thompson; January 18–February 10, 2008

A MARVELOUS PARTY! words and music by Noel Coward, devised by David Ira Goldstein, Carl J. Danielsen, Mark Anders, and Patricia Wilcox, musical arrangements by Carl J. Danielsen; Director, David Ira Goldstein; Choreographer, Patricia Wilcox; Set, Bill Forrester; Costumes, David K. Mickelsen; Lighting, Todd Hensley; Sound, Brian Jerome Peterson; Music Director, Tom Kenaston; PSM, Mary R. Honour; ASM, Brooke Redler; Cast: Mark Anders (Company), Carl J. Danielsen (Company), Stefanie Morse (Company), Zack Albetta, Jeff Harshbarger, Tom Kenaston (Musicians); February 29–March 23, 2008

THE DRAWER BOY by Michael Healey; Director, Jeff Church; Set, Donald Eastman; Composer and Sound, Joe Cerqua; Sound, John Story; Costumes, Janice Pytel; Lighting, Mark Kent Varns; SM, Mary R. Honour; ASM, Brooke Redler; Cast: Gary Holcombe (Angus), Gary Neal Johnson (Morgan), David Graham Jones (Miles); May 9–June 1, 2008

Copaken Stage

BAD DATES by Theresa Rebeck; Director, Michael Evan Haney; Set, William Bloodgood; Costumes, Lindsay W. Davis; Lighting, Victor En Yu Tan; Sound, John Story; PSM, Beth Ellen Spencer; Assistant to the SM, Brooke Redler; Cast: Rebecca Dines (Haley); September 21–October 21, 2007

A JOHN DENVER HOLIDAY CONCERT by Randal Myler & Dan Wheetman; Artistic Director, Randal Myler; Musical Director, Dan Wheetman; Lighting, Don Darnutzer; Sound, Eric Stahlhammer; Projections, Jeffrey Cady; Production Supervisor, Michael B. Paul; Associate Director, Jerry Genochio; ASM, Victoria Franke; Costumes, Mary Traylor; Props, Nancy Wagner; Cast: Gail Bliss, Denny Brooks, Nova Devonie, David Jackson, David Miles Keenan, Dan Wheetman; November 24–December 2, 2007

GEE'S BEND by Elyzabeth Gregory Wilder; Director, Marion McClinton; Set, Timothy J. Jones; Costumes, Karen Perry; Lighting, Michelle Habeck; Sound, John Story; PSM, Beth Ellen Spencer; Cast: Nikkole Salter (Sadie), Starla Benford (Alice/Asia), Pascale Armand (Nella), Lloyd Goodman (Macon); March 28–April 27, 2008

Laguna Playhouse

Laguna Beach, California

EIGHTY-SEVENTH SEASON

Artistic Director, Andrew Barnicle; Managing Director, Karen Wood

MENOPAUSE THE MUSICAL Book and lyrics by Jeanie Linders, music by various; Director, Kathryn Conte; Choreography, Patty Bender; National Music Supervisor, Alan J. Plado; Set, Bud Clark; Sound, Gary Faller; Lighting, Jean-Yves Tessier; SM, Kimberly L. Simari; ASM, Vernon Willet; Production Manager, Jim Ryan; Cast: Fredena Williams (Professional Woman), Juliet Hicks (Soap Star), Roberta Wall (Earth Mother), Lisa Robinson (Iowa Housewife), Tanja Lynne Lee (understudy); Moulton Theater; July 10–September 2, 2007

ART by Yasmina Reza, translated by Christopher Hampton; Director, Andrew Barnicle; Set/Costumes, Dwight Richard Odle; Lighting, Paulie Jenkins; Sound, David Edwards; Casting, Wally Ziegler; PSM, Rebecca Michelle Green; SM, Vernon Willet; ASM, Victoria A. Gathe; Production Manager, Jim Ryan; Cast: John Herzog (Marc), Kyle Colerider-Krugh (Yvan), Steve Vinovich (Serge); Moulton Theater; September 11–October 14, 2007

HANK WILLIAMS: Lost Highway by Randal Myer and Mark Harelik; Director, Randal Myler; Music Director, Dan Wheetman; Set. Vicki M. Smith; Lighting, T. Greg Squires; Costumes, Robert Blackman; Sound, Eric Stahlhammer; PSM, Victoria A. Gathe; ASM, Mia D. Osherow; Production Manager, Jim Ryan; Cast: Van Zeiler (Hank Williams), Regan Southard (Audrey Williams), Margaret Bowman (Mamma Lilly), Mike Regan (Fred Ross aka Pap), "Mississippi" Charles Bevel (Tee-Tot); Moulton Theater; November 13–December 16, 2007

SISTER'S CHRISTMAS CATECHISM: The Mystery of the Magi's Gold Written by Maripat Donovan, Jane Morris, and Marc Silvia; Director, Marc Silvia: Cast: Maripat Donovan (Sister); December 17–23, 2007

TRANCED by Bob Clyman; Director, Jessica Kubzansky; Set, Narelle Sissons; Costumes, Julie Keen; Lighting, Jeremy Pivnick; Sound, David Edwards; SM, Rebecca Michelle Green; Casting, Wally Ziegler; ASM, Victoria A. Gathe; Production Manager, Jim Ryan; Cast: Erica Tazel (Azmera), Thomas Fiscella (Dr. Philip Malaad), Ashley West Leonard (Beth, a journalist), Andrew Borba (Logan, Director of African Affairs); World Premiere; Moulton Theater; January 1–February 3, 2008

RED HERRING by Michael Hollinger; Director, Andrew Barnicle; Set, Bruce Goodrich; Costumes, Julie Keen; Lighting, Paulie Jenkins; Sound, David Edwards; PSM, Vernon Willet; Casting, Wally Ziegler; Production Manager, Jim Ryan; ASM, Jennifer Ellen Butler; Cast: Traci L. Crouch (Lynn/Clerk), Brendan Ford (Frank/Priest/Major Hartwell), Kirsten Potter (Maggie Pelletier), DeeDee Rescher (Mrs. Kravitz/Mrs. McCarthy/Mrs. Van Nostrand), Brett Ryback (James/Woody/Harry/Bartender), Tom Shelton (Andrei Borchevsky/Peter/Dr. Kasden/Herbert); Moulton Theater; February 12–March 16, 2008

BROWNSTONE Written and directed by Catherine Butterfield; Set, Lauren Helpern; Lighting, Paulie Jenkins; Costumes, Julie Keen; Sound, David Edwards; PSM, Rebecca Michelle Green; Casting, Wally Ziegler; ASM, Victoria A. Gathe; Production Manager, Jim Ryan; Cast: Deborah Puette (Davia), Brian Rohan (Stephen), Kim Shively (Maureen), Dorthea Harahan (Deena), Laurie Naughton (Jessica), Gino Anthony Pesi (Jason); World Premiere; Moulton Theater; March 25–April 27, 2008

ALEXANDROS by Melinda Lopez; Director, David Ellenstein; Set, Marty Burnett; Lighting, Paulie Jenkins; Costumes, Julie Keen; Sound, David Edwards; SM, Rebecca Michelle Green; ASM, Jennifer Ellen Butler; Casting, Wally Ziegler; Production Manager, Jim Ryan; Cast: Saundra Santiago (Maritza), Katharine Luckinbill (Marty), Kevin Symons (Eric), Chaz Mena (Tio), Maria Cellario (Abuela); World Premiere; Moulton Theater; May 27–June 29, 2008

La Jolla Playhouse

La Jolla, California

THIRTY-EIGHTH SEASON

Artistic Director, Christopher Ashley; Managing Director, Stephen B. Libman; Associate Artistic Director, Shirley Fishman

CARMEN Book by Sarah Miles, music by John Ewbank, lyrics and vocal arrangements by AnnMarie Milazzo; Director, Franco Dragone; Choreography, Sarah Miles; Music Director/Arrangements, Jeffrey Klitz; Orchestrations, Doug Katsaros; Set, Klara Zieglerova; Costumes, Suzy Benzinger; Lighting, Christopher Akerlind; Sound, Francois Bergeron; Wigs, Mark Adam Rampmeyer; Associate Director, Terry Berliner;

Flamenco Dances, Omayra Amaya; Spanish Music Consultant, Roque Banos; PSM, Phyllis Schray; ASMs, Justin Mabardi aand Jenny Slattery; Production Manager, Peter J. Davis; Casting, Dave Clemmons; Cast: Neal Benari (Zuniga/Judge), Genson Blimline (Lilias), Jacqui Graziano (Frasquita), Shannon Lewis (Juanita), Caesar Samayoa (Garcia), Ryan Silverman (José), Shelley Thomas (Micaela), Janien Valentine (Carmen), Victor Wallace (Escamillo), Natalia Zisa (Mercedes); Ensemble: Genson Blimline, Iresol Cardona, Gabriel Croom, Maria Eberline, Jorge E. Maldonado, Michelle Marmolejo, Rocio Ponce, Marcos Santana, Carlos Sierra Lopez, Victor Wallace; Swings: Noemi Del Rio, Tony Falcon; Mandell Weiss Theatre; June 5–July 22, 2007

THE DECEPTION Adapted by Steven Epp and Dominique Serrand from "La Fausse Suivante" by Pierre Marivaux; Co-Produced by Theatre de la Jeune Lune; Director, Dominique Serrand; Sets, David Coggins; Costumes, Sonya Berlovitz; Lighting, Marcus Dilliard; Sound, Zachary Humes; Hair and Wigs, Mark Adam Rampmeyer; PSM, Benjamin McGovern; ASM, Jenifer Morrow; Production Manager, Linda S. Cooper; Cast: J.C. Cutler (Trivelin), Casey Greig (Lelio), Emily Gunyou Halaas (The Countess), Merritt Janson (Chevalier), Nathan Keepers (Arlequino); Ensemble: Dorian Christian Baucum, Michelle Diaz, Liz Elkins, Larry Herron, Brandon D. Taylor; Sheila and Hughes Potiker Theatre; July 17–August 19, 2007

after the quake Adapted and directed by Frank Galati from the novel by Haruki Murakami; Presented by Steppenwolf Theatre; Co-Produced with Berkeley Repertory Theatre; Set, James Schuette; Costumes, Mara Blumenfeld; Lighting, James F. Ingalls; Sound and Original Compositions, Andre Pluess and Ben Sussman; SM, Malcolm Ewen; Cast: Madison Logan V. Phan (Sala), Paul YH. Juhn (Katagiri/Takatsuki), Gemma Megumi Fa-Kaji (Sala), Keong Sim (Narrator/Frog), Jennifer Shin (Sayoko/Nurse), Hanson Tse (Junpei), Jason McDermott (Cello), Jeff Wichmann (Koto); Mandell Weiss Forum; July 24–August 26, 2007

THE ADDING MACHINE by Elmer Rice; Director, Daniel Aukin; Sets, Andrew Lieberman; Costumes, Maiko Matsushima; Lighting, Japhy Weideman; Sound, Colbert S. Davis IV; Original Music, Cassia Streb; Wigs and Hair, Mark Adam Rampmeyer; Fight Director, Steve Rankin; Dialects, Robert Barry Fleming; SM, Anjee Nero; ASM, Heather Toll; Production Manager, Linda S. Cooper; Casting, Telsey + Company; Cast: Walter Belenky (Joe/Mr. Two), Richard Crawford (Mr. Zero), Molly Fite (Judy/Mrs. One), Jan Leslie Harding (Mrs. Zero), Liz Jenkins (Mrs. Three), Joshua Everett Johnson (Shrdlu), Rufio Lerma (Young Man/Mr. One), Diana Ruppe (Daisy/Mrs. Two), Paul Morgan Stetler (Boss/Lt. Charles/Mr. Three), Peter Wylie (Policeman); Sheila and Hughes Potiker Theatre; September 11–October 7, 2007

MOST WANTED Music and lyrics by Mark Bennett, book and lyrics by Jessica Hagedorn; Director, Michael Greif; Music Director, Charlie Alterman; Choreography, Javier Velasco; Orchestrations, Dan Lipton; Sets, Steven C. Kemp; Costumes, Clint Ramos; Lighting, Tom Ontiveros; Sound, Philip G. Allen; Dramaturg, Shirley Fishman; SM, J. Philip Bassett; ASM, Heather Hogan; Production Manager, Peter J. Davis; Cast: Arthur Acuña (Lee Reyes/Apolo Serra), Merle Dandridge (Elizabeth Mitchell), Zandi De Jesus (Angie Reyes/others), Danny Gurwin (Chris Bradley/Javier Luna), Michael Grant Hall (Daddyo/DeWitt/others), Kathleen Halm (Soprano/others), Leah Hocking (Teresa Reyes/Apolonia Serra), Peter Kapetan (Daddyo/Marv Easton/others), Ken Page (Stormy Leather), David Nathan Perlow (Daddyo/Bartender/others), Daniel Torres (Danny Reyes); Madell Wiss Forum; October 2–14, 2007

CRY-BABY Book by Mark O'Donnell and Thomas Meehan, songs by David Javerbaum and Adam Schlesinger; based on the Universal Pictures film written and directed by John Waters; Director, Mark Brokaw; Choreography, Rob Ashford; Orchestrations, Christopher Jahnke; Dance Arrangements, David Chase; Sets, Scott Pask; Costumes, Catherine Zuber; Lighting, Howell Binkley; Sound, Peter Hylenski; Wigs and Hair, Tom Watson; Makeup, Randy Houston Mercer; Fight Director, Rick Sordelet; PSM, Mahlon Kruse; SM, Richard C. Rauscher; ASM, Jenny Slattery; Produciton Manager, Peter J. Davis; Casting, Telsey + Company; Cast: Chester Gregorry II (Dupree), Christopher J. Hanke (Baldwin), Harriet Harris (Mrs. Vernon-Williams), Carly Jibson (Pepper), Lacey Kohl (Wanda), Alli Mauzey (Lenora), Cristen Paige (Mona), Richard Poe (Judge Stone), James Snyder (Cry-Baby), Elizabeth Stanley (Allison); Ensemble: Cameron Adams, Ashley Amber, Nick Blaemire, Michael Buchanan, Eric L. Christian, Colin Cunliffe, Joanna Glushak, Stacy Todd Holt, Marty Lawson, Spencer Liff, Mayumi Miguel, Tory Ross, Eric Sciotto, Peter Matthew Smith, Allison Spratt, Charlie Sutton; Swings: Michael D. Jablonski, Courtney Laine Mazza; Mandell Weiss Theatre; November 6–December 16, 2007

THE SEVEN Book and lyrics by Will Power, music by Will Power, Will Hammond, Justin Ellington, adapted from Aeschylus' "Seven Against Thebes;" Developed and directed by Jo Bonney; Choreography, Bill T. Jones; Music Director, Daryl Waters; Set, Richard Hoover; Costumes, Emilio Sosa; Lighting, David Weiner; Sound, Darron L West; Projections, Robin Silvestri; Music Producer, Justin Ellington; SM, Wendy Ouellette; ASM, Anjee Nero; Associate Producer, Dana I. Harrel; Production Manager, Peter J. Davis; Casting, Jack Doulin; Cast: Uba Aduba, Shawtane Monroe Bowen, Jamyl Dobson, Dashiell Eaves, Edwin Lee Gibson, Benton Greene, Flaco Navaja, Chinasa Ogbuagu, Postell Pringle, Pearl Sun, Charles Turner, Bernard White; Sheila and Hughes Potiker Theatre; February 12–March 16, 2008

Maltz Jupiter Theatre

Jupiter, Florida

FIFTH SEASON

Artistic Director, Andrew Kato; Managing Director, Murray Green

SAME TIME, NEXT YEAR by Neil Simon; Director, J. Barry Lewis; Set, Steven Capone; Costumes, Gail Baldoni; Lighting, Kirk Bookman; Sound, Keith Kohrs; Wigs and Hair, Gerard James Kelly; PSM, Andrew John Tucker; Cast: Paul DeBoy (George), Henny Russell (Doris); November 6-18, 2007

THE BOY FRIEND Book, music and lyrics by Sandy Wilson; Director, Mark Martino; Choreographer, Denis Jones; Set, Dan Kuchar; Costumes, Jose M. Rivera; Lighting, Donald Thomas; Sound, Keith Kohrs; Music Director, Helen Gregory; SM, Emily Swiderski; ASM, Brandy DeMil; Cast: Natalie Hall (Polly), Susan Cella (Madame Dubonnet), Ann McNeely (Lady Brockhurst), Dick Decareau (Lord Brockhurst), Erin Maguire (Hortense), Michael Scott (Percival Brown), Julie Kotarides (Maisie), Krista Kurtzberg (Dulcie), Kerri Rose (Fay), Nancy Renee Braun (Nancy), Mike Frankey (Tony), Connor Gallagher (Bobby), Warren Curtis (Marcel), Jonathan Richard Sandler (Pierre); December 4–23, 2007

SMOKEY JOE'S CAFÉ Music and lyrics by Jerry Leiber and Mike Stoller; Director, Bill Castellino; Choreographer, Joshua Bergasse; Set, Cliff Simon; Lighting, Chris Landy; Sound, Keith Kohrs; Music Director, David Nehls; PSM, Andrew John Tucker; ASM, Tara Wiedenfeller; Cast: Jody Reynard (Ken), Dwayne Clark (Adrian), Steve Dorian (Michael), Philip Lamar Boykin (Fredrick), Eric LaJuan Summers (Victor), Jaygee Macapugay (Brenda), Gayle Turner (BJ), Marya Grandy (Pattie), Erica Sweany (DeLee); January 22–February 10, 2008

THE FULL MONTY Music and lyrics by David Yazbek, book by Terrence McNally; Director, Alan Souza; Choreographer, Ron De Jesus; Set, Michael Philippi; Costumes, M. Shan Jensen; Lighting, Don Thomas; Sound, Keith Kohrs; Music Director, Helen Gregory; PSM, Emily Swiderski; Cast: Mimi Hines (Jeanette), Heather Adair (Estelle), Mark Willis Borum (Ethan), Tony Barton (Teddy), Emily Crosby (Pam), Todd A. Horman (Dave), Tyson Jeannette (Horse), Bruce Linser (Reg), Gavin Lodge (Jerry), Philip Labes (Nathan), Wayne LeGette (Harold), Adam Overett (Malcolm), Sharon Owens (Susan), Rebecca Rich (Vicki), Michael Risco (u/s Nathan), Lucy Sorensen (Georgie), Matthew Steffens (Keno), Tonya Thompson (Joanie); February 26–March 16, 2008

MASTER CLASS by Terrence McNally; Director, Marcia Milgrom Dodge; Set, Michael Schweikardt; Costumes, Susan Branch; Lighting, Donald Thomas; Sound, Keith Kohrs; Music Director, Wilson Sutherland; PSM, Andrew John Tucker; Cast: Gordana Rasovich (Maria Callas), Wilson Southerland (Manny Weinstock), Kim Whalen (Sophie De Palma), Jared Slater (Stagehand), Carey Brown (Sharon Graham), Coke Stuart Morgan (Tony Candolino); April 1–13, 2008

McCarter Theatre Center

Princeton, New Jersey

FORTY-EIGHTH SEASON

Artistic Director, Emily Mann; Managing Director, Jeffrey Woodward; Producer Director, Mara Isaacs; Director of Production, David York

STICK FLY by Lydia R. Diamond; Director, Shirley Jo Finney; Set, Felix E. Cochren; Costumes, Karen Perry; Lighting, Victor En Yu Tan; Sound, Darron L West; Casting, Laura Stanczyk; PSM, Cheryl Mintz; SM, Alison Cote; Cast: Kevin T. Carroll (Kent LeVay), Javon Johnson (Flip LeVay), Monette Magrath (Kimber Davies), Julia Pace Mitchell (Cheryl Washington), John Wesley (Joseph LeVay), Michole Briana White (Taylor Bradley Scott); Berlind Theatre; September 7–October 14, 2007

TARTUFFE by Moliere, translated by Richard Wilbur; Director, Daniel Fish; Set, John Conklin; Costumes, Kaye Voyce; Lighting, Jane Cox; Video, Alexandra Eaton; Sound, Karin Graybash; Dramaturg, Janice Paran; Casting, Laura Stanczyk; PSM, Alison Cote; SM, Christine Whalen; Co-production with Yale Repertory Theatre; Cast: Michelle Beck (Mariane), Christopher Donahue (Cléante), Zach Grenier (Tartuffe), Andy Paterson (M. Loyal), Christina Rouner (Elmire), Michael Rudko (Orgon), Tom Story (Police Officer), Daniel Cameron Talbott (Val¨¨re), Nick Westrate (Damis), Sally Wingert (Dorine); Matthews Theatre; October 7–28, 2007

A CHRISTMAS CAROL by Charles Dickens, adapted by David Thompson; Director, Michael Unger; Choreographer, Rob Ashford; Set, Ming Cho Lee; Costumes, Jess Goldstein; Lighting, Stephen Strawbridge; Original music and lyrics, Michael Starobin; Casting, Laura Stanczyk; Supervising SM, Cheryl Mintz; ASM, Hannah Woodward; Cast: Lisa Altomare (Mrs. Dilber), Barnaby Carpenter (Bob Cratchit), Kevin Collins (Jacob Marley/Mr. Stocks), Kathy Fitzgerald (Mrs. Fezziwig/Mrs. Stocks/Laundress), Richard Gallagher (Young Scrooge/Mr. Bonds), Karron Graves (Fan/Mrs. Bonds), Janet Metz (Mrs. Cratchit), Ned Noyes (Fred/Undertaker), John O'Creagh (Mr. Fezziwig/Old Joe), Karen Pittman (Lily/Belle), Ronica Reddick (Christmas Present), James A. Stephens (Ebenezer Scrooge); Matthews Theatre; December 2–23, 2007

ME, MYSELF & I by Edward Albee; Director, Emily Mann; Set, Thomas Lynch; Costumes, Jennifer von Mayrhauser; Lighting, Kenneth Posner; Sound, Darron L West; Casting, Laura Stanczyk; PSMs, Cheryl Mintz and Alison Cote; Cast: Tyne Daly (Mother), Colin Donnell (otto), Michael Esper (OTTO), Brian Murray (Dr.), Charlotte Parry (Maureen), Stephen Payne (The Man); World Premiere; Berlind Theatre; January 15–February 17, 2008.

ARGONAUTIKA Written and directed by Mary Zimmerman; adapted from *The Voyage of Jason and the Argonauts;* Co-production with Berkeley Repertory Theatre, Shakespeare Theatre Company and Lookingglass Theatre Company; Set,

Daniel Ostling; Costumes, Ana Kuzmanic; Lighting, John Culbert; Original Music/Sound, Andre Pluess & Ben Sussman; Puppetry, Michael Montenegro; Casting, Laura Stanczyk, Amy Potozkin; PSM, Alison Cote; ASM, Lauren Kurinskas; Cast: Justin Blanchard (Hylas/Dymas), Allen Gilmore (Pelias/others) Sofia Jean Gomez (Athena), K.C. Jackson (Pollux/others), Chris Kipiniak (Castor/others), Tessa Klein (Aphrodite/others), Ronete Levenson (Andromeda/others), Atley Loughridge (Medea/others), Andy Murray (Meleager/others), Søren Oliver (Hercules/Aietes), Jesse J. Perez (Idmon/others), Jake Suffian (Jason), Lisa Tejero (Hera/others), Jason Vande Brake (Amycus/others); Matthews Theatre; March 16–April 6, 2008

A SEAGULL IN THE HAMPTONS Written and directed by Emily Mann, adapted from Chekhov's The Seagull; Set, Eugene Lee; Costumes, Jennifer von Mayrhauser; Lighting, Jane Cox; Composer, Baikida Carroll; Sound, Karin Graybash; Casting, Laura Stanczyk; PSM, Cheryl Mintz; SM, Alison Cote; Cast: Jacqueline Antaramian (Paula), Morena Baccarin (Nina), Laura Heisler (Milly), David Andrew Macdonald (Philip), Matthew Maher (Harold), Brian Murray (Nicholas), Daniel Oreskes (Lorenzo), Larry Pine (Ben), Stark Sands (Alex), Maria Tucci (Maria); World Premiere Adaptation; Berlind Theatre; May 2–June 8, 2008

Merrimack Repertory Theatre

Lowell, Massachusetts

TWENTY-NINTH SEASON

Artistic Director, Charles Towers; Executive Director, Tom Parrish

THE PURSUIT OF HAPPINESS by Richard Dresser; Director, Charles Towers; Set and Lighting, Pavel Dobrusky; Costumes, Deb Newhall; SM, Emily McMullen; Cast: Jim Frangione (Tucker), Allyn Burrows (Neil), Monique Fowler (Annie), John Wodja (Spud), Ameila McClain (Jodi); Regional Premiere; October 4–October 28, 2007

TUNNEY/SHAKESPREARE IN SIX ROUNDS by David E. Lane; Artistic Director, Charles Towers; Lighting, Jon Ambrosone; SM, Emily McMullen; Cast: Jack Wetheral (Gene Tunney); World Premiere; November 15–December 9, 2007

2 PIANOS 4 HANDS by Ted Dykstra and Richard Greenblatt; Director, Richard Greenblatt; Set and Lighting, Steve Lucas; Associate Lighting, Jason Golinsky; SM, Brady Poole; Cast: Tom Frey (Ted), Richard Carsey (Richard); January 3–January 27, 2008

THE MISSIONARY POSITION by Keith Reddin; Director, Tracy Brigden; Set, Gianni Downs; Lighting, Andy Ostrowski; Costumes, Robert C. T. Steele; Sound, Elizabeth Atkinson; SM, Emily McMullen; Cast: Tony Bingham (Roger), Tami Dixon (Julie), Jeffrey Carpenter (Neil), Rebecca Harris (Maria/Barbara/Pamela/Rebecca/Gretchen); Regional Premiere; February 7–March 2, 2008

A DELICATE BALANCE by Edward Albee; Director, Charles Towers; Set, Bill Clarke; Lighting, John Ambrosone; Costumes, Martha Hally; SM, Emily McMullen; Cast: Penny Fuller (Claire), Jack Davidson (Tobias), Jennifer Harmon (Agnes), Ross Bickel (Harry), Jill Tanner (Edna), Gloria Biegler (Julia); March 13–April 6, 2008

THE FOUR OF US by Itamar Moses; Director, Kyle Fabel; Set, Bill Clarke; Lighting, Brian Lilienthal; Costumes, Deb Newhall; SM, Emily McMullen; Cast: Jed Orlemann (David), Bhavesh Patel (Benjamin); Regional Premiere; April 17–May 11, 2008

Music Theatre of Wichita

Wichita, Kansas

THIRTY-SIXTH SEASON

Producing Artistic Director, Wayne Bryan

DISNEY'S HIGH SCHOOL MUSICAL – On Stage book by David Simpatico; songs by Matthew Gerrard, Robbie Nevil, Ray Cham, Greg Cham, Andrew Seeley, Randy Peterson, Kevin Quinn, Andy Dodd, Adam Watts, Bryan Louiselle, David N. Lawrence, Faye Greenberg & Jamie Houston; music adapted, arranged and produced by Bryan Louiselle; based on a Disney Channel original movie by Peter Barsocchini; Director/Choreographer, Roger Castellano; Sets, J Branson; Costumes, Debbie Roberts; Lighting, David Neville; Sound, David Muehl; Hair and Wigs, Brandalyn Fulton; Music Director, Brian Hamilton; AD/Assistant Choreographer, Lauren Masiello; Technical Director, Derek Olson; PSM, Suann Pollock; SM, Emily F. McMullen; Company Manager, Nancy Reeves; Production Manager, David Neville; Cast: Desi Oakley (Gabriella), Matthew Elliott (Troy), Sophia Drummond (Sharpay), Evan Kilgore (Ryan), Karen L. Robu (Ms. Darbus), Timothy W. Robu (Coach Bolton), Miles Mattal (Jack Scott), Elliot Metz (Chad), Maurice Sims (Zeke), Shina Ann Morris (Taylor), Emma Craig (Martha), Alex Johnson (Kelsi), Tom Wine (Mr. Tenny), Steve Landes (Adjudicator); Jocks: Daxton Lee Bloomquist, Cody Davis, Kyle Gallegos, Chance Victor Gates, Jacob Gutierrez, Jacob January, Logan Moore, Kevin Munhall, Javier Perez-Gomez; Brainiacs: Brylee Beiswanger, Sophie Menas, Krista Rawson, Sarah Shelton, Alexandra Taylor, Nicole M. Tucker, Reagan Wagner, Janet Wiggins, Alasyn Zimmerman; Thespians: Sally Auchterlonie, Riley Bruce, Maddy Campbell, Grace Cha, Sam Corridoni, Injoy Fountain, Cora Kilgour, Mark Meier, Kassiani Menas, Audra Miller, Julia Miller, Meredith Olney, Kyle Reid, Garrett Robinson, Sarah Schwindt, Lizz White, Michelle Wilke, Jenny Wine; Thespians/Mascots: Brady Rohling, Alex Roths; Thespian/Cheerleaders: Joey Yates, Nathan Dibben, Mason Holmes; Cheerleaders: Keli Carey, Anna Cooper, Whitney Cooper, Shaelynn French, Rebecca Gans, Maddie Richie, Kristina Sims, Alexis Paige Tedder; Skaters: Rebekah Baldridge, Emily Donell, Kaitlyn Felts, Erin Isherwood, William A. Johnson, Ryan Neville, Luke Svoboda; Drumline: Devon Alford, Alexandra Blasi,

Bailey Burcham, Liz Cannon, Kyle Cooper, Whitney Franklin, Stewart Grindel, Shavonte McClinton, Parker Messomore, Tommy Richardson, Jennifer Solis, Brandon Somerhalder; June 11–17, 2007; Encore presentation August 25–26, 2007

CATS Music by Andrew Lloyd Webber, based on "Old Possum's Book of Practical Cats" by T.S. Eliot; Director/Choreographer, Dana Solimando; Set, Peter Barbieri, Jr.; Costumes, Mela Hoyt-Heydon; Lighting, David Neville; Sound, David Muehl; Wigs/Makeup, Dana Solimando, Billy Johnstone, Brandalyn Fulton & Barbara Parafati; AD/Assistant Choreographer, Billy Johnstone; Musical Director, Thomas Wesley Douglas; TD, Derek Olson; PSM, Emily F. McMullen; SM, Suann Pollock; Company Manager, Nancy Reeves; Production Manager, David Neville; Cast: Garrett Long (Grizabella), Nicholas F. Saverine (Bustopher Jones/Asparagus/Growltiger), Annie Funke (Jennyanydots), E. Mani Cadet (Old Deuteronomy), Melinda Wakefield Alberty (Jellylorum/Griddlebone), Chaz Wolcott (Misoffelees), Johnny Stellard (Munkustrap), Billy Johnstone (Skimbleshanks), Roy Lightner (Mungojerrie), Sam Berman (Rumpleteazer), Alex Stoll (Rum Tum Tugger), Todd Walker (Alonzo), Tyler Foy (Bill Bailey), Kimberly Fauré (Bombalurina), Aaron Umsted (Carbucketty), Tiffany Ocvirk (Cassandra), David A. Caamano (Coricopat), Lisa Rohinsky (Demeter), Stephanie Martignetti (Etcetera/U/S Grizabella), Taurean Everett (Plato/Macavity), Ryan Koss (Pouncival/Genghis), Deanna Glover (Sillabub), Paige A. Williams (Tantomile), Olivia Policicchio (Victoria), Erin Kelly (Signing Interpreter); Ensmble: Emma Craig, Cody Davis, Christopher McKim, Kevin Munhall, Desi Oakley, Javier Perez-Gomez, Maurice Sims, Jenny Wine; June 27–July 1, 2007

IRVING BERLIN'S *WHITE CHRISTMAS* Music and lyrics by Irving Berlin, book by David Ives & Paul Blake; based on the Paramount Pictures film written for the screen by Norman Krasna, Norman Panama & Melvin Frank; Director, Wayne Bryan; Choreographer, Roger Castellano; Set, Bruce Brockman; Costumes, Debbie Roberts; Lighting, David Neville; Sound, David Muehl; Wigs/Makeup, Erin Kennedy Lunsford & Brandalyn Fulton; Musical Director, Thomas Wesley Douglas; TD, Derek Olson; PSM, Suann Pollock; SM, Emily F. McMullen; Company Manager, Nancy Reeves; Production Manager, David Neville; Cast: John Bisom (Bob Wallace), Kim Huber (Betty Haynes), John MacInnis (Phil Davis), Anne Horak (Judy Haynes), Charles Parker (General Waverly), Karen L. Robu (Martha Watson), Caitlin Belcik (Susan Waverly), Timothy W. Robu (Ralph Sheldrake), Lisa Rohinsky (Rita), Rhoda (Tiffany Ocvirk), Javier Perez-Gomez (Ezekiel), Roy Lightner (Mike), Aaron Umsted (Mr. Snoring Man/Ensemble), Annie Funke (Mrs. Snoring Man/Ensemble); Ensemble: Melinda Wakefield Alberty, Sam Berman, David A. Caamano, Cody Davis, Taurean Everett, Tyler Foy, Deanna Glover, Ryan Koss, Stephanie Martignetti, Shina Ann Morris, Kevin Munhall, Desi Oakley, Olivia Policicchio, Maurice Sims, Johnny Stellard, Todd Walker, Paige A. Williams, Chaz Wolcott; July 11–15, 2007

DAMN YANKEES Music and lyrics by Richard Adler & Jerry Ross, book by George Abbott & Douglass Wallop; based on the novel by Douglass Wallop "The Year the Yankees Lost the Pennant;" Director, Mark Madama; Choreographer, John MacInnis; Set, Gill Moralis for Fullerton Civic Light Opera; Costumes, George Mitchell; Lighting, David Neville; Sound, David Muehl; Hair/Wigs/Makeup, Brandalyn Fulton; Musical Director, Flint Hawes; TD, Derek Olson; PSM, Emily F. McMullen; SM, Suann Pollock; Company Manager, Nancy Reeves; Production Manager, David Neville; Cast: James Brennan (Applegate), JoAnn M. Hunter (Lola), Chris Peluos (Joe Hardy), Alma Cuervo (Meg Boyd), Timothy W. Robu (Van Buren), Charles Parker (Joe Boyd), Karen L. Robu (Gloria Thorpe), Betti O. (Sister), Patty Reeder (Doris), Ryan Koss (Smokey), Roy Lightner (Vernon), Javier Perez-Gomez (Rocky), David A. Caamano (Bouley), Cody Davis (Davis), Tyler Foy (Foy), Robert Hartwell (Hartwell), Max Kumangai-McGee (Sohovic), Kevin Munhall (Bryan), Maurice Sims (Martin), Johnny Stellard (Lowe), Alex Stoll (Linville), Aaron Umsted (Henry), Todd Walker (Del), Chaz Wolcott (Mickey), Mary Lou Phipps-Winfrey (Mrs. Welch), Cody Proctor (Lynch/Commissioner), Paige A. Williams (Miss Weston), Marilyn Heffner (Postmistress), Mike Whalen (Radio Announcer), Dwight Oxley (TV Announcer); Ensemble: Melinda Wakefield Alberty, Sam Berman, Ebony Blake, Annie Funke, Kimberly Fauré, Deanna Glover, Stephanie Martignetti, Shina Ann Morris, Tiffany Ocvirk, Olivia Policicchio, Lisa Rohinsky, Desi Oakley; Fans: Caroline Breit, Jordan Erskin, Hannah Grebe, Justin Kim, Stevie Mack, Gavin Myers, Faith Northcutt, Taryn Northcutt, Jace Shoenwald, Jacob Wasson; July 25–29, 2007

HAIRSPRAY Book by Mark O'Donnell & Thomas Meehan, music by Marc Shaiman, lyrics by Scott Wittman & Marc Shaiman; based on the New Line Cinema film written and directed by John Waters; Orchestrations, Harold Wheeler; Arrangements, Marc Shaiman; Director and Choreographer, Greg Graham; Set, J Branson; Costumes, Tiia E. Torchia; Hair, Wigs/Makeup, Erin Kennedy Lunsford; Musical Director, Thomas Wesley Douglas; TD, Derek Olson; PSM, Suann Pollock; SM, Emily F. McMullen; Company Manager, Nancy Reeves; Production Manager, David Neville; Cast: Blake Hammond (Edna Turnblad), Annie Funke (Tracy Turnblad), Ray DeMattis (Wilbur Turnblad), Todd DuBail (Corny Collins), Altamiecé Ballard (Motormouth Maybelle), Alex Stoll (Link Larken), Christi Moore-Leslie (Velma Von Tussle), Stephanie Martignetti (Amber Von Tussle), Audrie Neenan (Prudy/Matron/Gym Teacher), Robert Hartwell (Seaweed), Deanna Glover (Penny), Melinda Wakefield Alberty (Little Inez), Timothy W. Robu (Male Authority Roles), Ebony Blake (Dynamite/Cindy Watkins), Betti O. (Dynamite/Pearl), Paige A. Williams (Dynamite/Peaches), Aaron Umsted (Brad), Olivia Policicchio (Tammy), Johnny Stellard (Fender), Lisa Rohinsky (Brenda), Tyler Foy (Sketch), Desi Oakley (Shelley), Roy Lightner (I.Q.), Tiffany Ocvirk (Lou Ann), Max Kumangai-McGee (Duane), Taurean Everett (Gilbert), Shina Ann Morris (Lorraine), Maurice Sims (Thad), Todd Walker (Stooie), Ryan Koss (Flasher), David A. Caamano (Bum), Kimberly Fauré (Bag

Lady/TV Model), Chaz Wolcott (Paper Boy); August 8–12, 2007

Northlight Theatre

Skokie, Illinois

THIRTY-THIRD SEASON

Artistic Director, BJ Jones; Executive Director, Timothy J. Evans

THE MISER by Jean Baptiste Moliere; translation and adaptation by James Magruder; Director, Mark E. Lococo; Set, Tim Morrison; Costumes, Rachel Healy; Lighting, Diane Fairchild; Sound, Lindsay Jones; Dramaturg, Meghan McCarthy; SMs, Rita Vreeland, Danielle Boyke; PA, Corinne Kabat; Production Manager, Chris Fitzgerald; Company Manager/Assistant Production Manager, Victoria Martini; Cast: Patrick Clear (S Anselme/M Simon/D Claude), Lea Coco (Cliente), Bob Fairbrook (Maitre Jacques), Kate Fry (Elise), Dieterich Gray (La Fleche/La Merluche/Commissioner), Timothy Edward Kane (Valere), Mark Mysliwiec (Brindavoine), Erica Peregrine (Mariane), Gene Weygandt (Harpagon), Jacqueline Williams (Frosine); October 3–November 11, 2007

ELLA book by Jeffrey Hatcher, conceived by Rob Ruggiero and Dyke Garrison; Director, Rob Ruggiero; Set, Michael Schweikardt; Costumes, Alejo Vietti; Lighting, John Lasiter; Sound, Michael Miceli; Music Director, George Caldwell; Arrangements, Danny Holgate; Sound Assistant, Emery Roth; Wigs, Charles LaPointe; Dramaturg, Meghan McCarthy; AD, Nick Eilerman; SM, Kristi J. Martens; PA, Corinne Kabat; Production Manager, Chris Fitzgerald; Company Manager/APM, Victoria Martini; Cast: E. Faye Butler (Ella), Anderson Edwards (Piano/Conductor), Ron Haynes (Trumpet), Walter Kindred (Percussion), David Parkes (Norman), John Whitfield (Bass); November 28, 2007–January 11, 2008

GEE'S BEND by Elyzabeth Gregory Wilder; Director, Chuck Smith; Set, Richard and Jacqueline Penrod; Costumes, Frances Maggio; Lighting, Keith Parham; Associate Lighting, Seth Reinick; Sound, Josh Horvath & Ray Nardelli; Fight Consultant, David Woolley; Dramaturg, Meghan McCarthy; SM, Rita Vreeland; Production Assistant, Corinne Kabat; Production Manager, Chris Fitzgerald; Company Manager/APM, Victoria Martini; Cast: John Steven Crowley (Macon), Charlette Speigner (Sadie), Penelope Walker (Alice/Asia), Jacqueline Williams (Nella); January 30–March 9, 2008

BETTER LATE by Larry Gelbart and Craig Wright; Director, BJ Jones; Set, Jack Magaw; Costumes, Rachel Laritz; Lighting, JR Lederle; Sound, Michael Bodeen & Rob Milburn; Projections, Stephan Mazurek; Dramaturg, Meghan McCarthy; SM, Laura D. Glenn; Production Assistant, Corinne Kabat; Production Manager, Chris Fitzgerald; Company Manager/APM, Victoria Martini; Cast: Steve Key (Billy), Linda Kimbrough (Nora), John Mahoney (Lee), Mike Nussbaum (Julian); March 28–May 11, 2008

THE LADY WITH ALL THE ANSWERS by David Rambo; Director, BJ Jones; Set, Tom Burch; Costumes, Tatjana Radisic; Lighting, Todd Hensley; Sound, Kevin O'Donnell; Props, Daniel Pellant; Dramaturg, Meghan McCarthy; SM, Rose Marie Packer; PA, Corinne Kabat; Production Manager, Chris Fitzgerald; Company Manager/APM, Victoria Martini; Cast: Judith Ivey (Eppie Lederer); May 21–June 29, 2008

The Old Globe

San Diego, Californa

SEVENTY-THIRD SEASON

Executive Producer, Louis G. Spisto; Co-Artistic Directors, Jerry Patch and Darko Tresnjak; Artistic Director Emeritus, Jack O'Brien; Founding Director, Craig Noel

WHO'S AFRAID OF VIRGINIA WOOLF? by Edward Albee; Director, Richard Seer; Set, Alan Muraoka; Costumes, Charlotte Devaux; Lighting, Chris Rynne; Sound, Paul Peterson; SM, Leila Knox; Cast: Scott Ferrara (Nick), Monique Fowler (Martha), Nisi Sturgis (Honey), James Sutorius (George); Cassius Carter Centre Stage; May 19–June 24, 2007

HAMLET by William Shakespeare; Director, Darko Tresnjak; Set, Ralph Funicello; Costumes, Robert Morgan; Lighting, York Kennedy; Dramaturg, Scott Horstein; Sound and Original Music, Christopher Walker; Fight Director, Steve Rankin; SM, Mary K Klinger; ASMs, Moira Gleason, Diana Moser & Anjee Nero; Cast: Chris Bresky (Osric), Chip Brookes (Rosencrantz), Celeste Ciulla (Gertrude), Joy Farmer-Clary (Ophelia), Lucas Hall (Hamlet), Sam Henderson (Reynaldo/Player), Charles Janasz (Polonius), John Keabler (Voltimand/Player), Michael Kirby (Francisco/Player Queen), James Knight (Marcellus/Player King), Nathanial McIntyre (Guildenstern), Jonathan McMurtry (1st Player/Gravedigger), Ryan Quinn (Horatio), Corey Sorenson (Laertes), Bruce Turk (Claudius/Ghost), Sam Breslin Wright (Barnardo/Player); Lowell Davies Festival Theatre; June 16–September 30, 2007

THE TWO GENTLEMEN OF VERONA by William Shakespeare; Director, Matt August; Set, Ralph Funicello; Costumes, Fabio Tablini; Lighting, York Kennedy; Dramaturg, Scott Horstein; Sound and Original Music, Christopher Walker; Fight Director, Steve Rankin; SM, Mary K Klinger; ASMs, Moira Gleason, Diana Moser & Anjee Nero; Cast: Chris Bresky (Ensemble), Chip Brookes (Ensemble), Celeste Ciulla (Lucetta), Joy Farmer-Clary (Julia), Stephanie Fieger (Silvia), Kimberly Parker-Green (Ensemble), Tom Hammond (Duke of Milan), Rhett Henckel (Ensemble), Sam Henderson (Ensemble), Eric Hoffmann (Eglamour/Antonio), John Keabler (Ensemble), Michael Kirby (Thurio), Jonathan McMurtry (Launce), Aaron Misakian (Ensemble), Ryan Quinn (Valentine), Carolyn Ratteray (Ensemble), Summer Shirey (Ensemble),

Corey Sorenson (Proteus), Kate Turnbull (Duke's Whore/ Ensemble), Sam Breslin Wright (Speed); Lowell Davies Festival Theatre; June 16–September 30, 2007

MEASURE FOR MEASURE by William Shakespeare; Director, Paul Mullins; Set, Ralph Funicello; Costumes, Robert Morgan; Lighting, York Kennedy; Dramaturg, Scott Horstein; Sound and Original Music, Christopher Walker; Fight Director, Steve Rankin; SM, Mary K Klinger; ASMs, Moira Gleason, Diana Moser & Anjee Nero; Cast: Chris Bresky (Froth/Gentleman 3), Chip Brookes (Friar Thomas), Celeste Ciulla (Mistress Overdone), Stephanie Fieger (Isabella), Kimberly Parker-Green (Nun/Whore), Cara Greene (The Justice/Nun/Whore), Lucas Hall (Lucio), Tom Hammond (Duke Vincentio), Rhett Henckel (Claudio), Eric Hoffmann (Pompey), Charles Janasz (Escalus), John Keabler (Gentleman 1), Michael Kirby (Servent to Angelo), Jonathan McMurtry (Barnadine), Aaron Misakian (Gentleman 2), Carolyn Ratteray (Juliet), Summer Shirey (Francisca/Woman), Bruce Turk (Provost), Kate Turnbull (Mariana/Woman), Sam Breslin Wright (Elbow); Lowell Davies Festival Theatre; June 16–September 30, 2007

AVENUE Q Book by Jeff Whitty, music and lyrics by Robert Lopez and Jeff Marx, Director, Jason Moore; Choregrapher, Ken Roberson; Set, Anna Louizos; Costumes, Mirena Rada; Puppets, Rick Lyon; Lighting, Howell Binkley; Sound, Acme Sound Partners; Music Supervisor, Stephen Oremus; Music Director, Andrew Graham; Cast: Robert McClure (Princeton/ Rod), Cole Porter (Brian), Kelli Sawyer (Kate Monster/Lucy The Slut), Christian Anderson (Nicky/Trekkie Monster), Angela Ai (Christmas Eve), Carla Renata (Gary Coleman), Minglie Chen (Mrs. T./Bear), Jennie Kwan (Ensemble/ Swing), Maggie Lakis (Ensemble/Swing); West Coast Premiere; Spreckels Theatre; June 30–August 5, 2007

HAY FEVER by Noel Coward; Director, Robert Longbottom; Set, Andrew Jackness; Costumes, Gregg Barnes; Lighting, Chris Akerlind; Sound, Paul Peterson; SM, Tracy Skoczelas; Cast: Alan Campbell (Richard Greatham), Judith Lightfoot Clarke (Judith Bliss), Santino Fontana (Simon Bliss), Mikel Sarah Lambert (Clara), Bridget Moloney (Jackie Coryton), Brian Slaten (Sandy Tyrell), Sarah Grace Wilson (Sorel Bliss), John Windsor-Cunningham (David Bliss), Yvonne Woods (Myra Arundel); Old Globe Theatre; July 14–August 19, 2007

BELL, BOOK AND CANDLE by John Van Druten; Director, Darko Tresnjak; Set, Alexander Dodge, Costumes, Emily Pepper; Lighting, Matt Richards; Sound, Paul Peterson; SM, Lisa Porter; Cast: Melinda Page Hamilton (Gillian Holroyd), John Lavelle (Nicky Holroyd), Adrian La Tourelle (Shep Henderson), Gregor Paslawsky (Sidney Redlitch), Deborah Taylor (Miss Holroyd); Cassius Carter Centre Stage; August 4–September 9, 2007

A CATERED AFFAIR Book by Harvey Fierstein, music and lyrics by John Bucchino; Director, John Doyle; Music Director, Constantine Kitsopoulos; Orchestrator, Don Sebesky; Set, David Gallo; Costumes, Ann Hould-Ward; Lighting, Brian MacDevitt; Sound, Dan Moses Schreier; SM, Claudia Lynch; Cast: Matt Cavenaugh (Ralph Halloran), Harvey Fierstein (Uncle Winston), Philip Hoffman (Mr. Halloran/Sam), Katie Klaus (Alice/Army Sergeant), Leslie Kritzer (Janey Hurley), Heather MacRae (Delores/Caterer), Faith Prince (Aggie Hurley), Lori Wilner (Mrs. Halloran/Pasha), Tom Wopat (Tom Hurley), Kristine Zbornik (Myra/Dress Saleswoman); World Premiere; Old Globe Theatre; September 20–November 4, 2007

OSCAR AND THE PINK LADY by Eric-Emmanuel Schmitt; Director, Frank Dunlop; Set, Michael Vaughn Sims; Costumes, Jane Greenwood; Lighting, Trevor Norton; Sound, Lindsay Jones; SM, Monica Cuoco; Cast: Rosemary Harris (Granny Pink); American premiere; Cassius Carter Centre Stage; September 22–November 4, 2007

DR SEUSS' HOW THE GRINCH STOLE CHRISTMAS! Book and lyrics by Timothy Mason, music by Mel Marvin; Director, Jack O'Brien; Choreographer, John DeLuca; Set, John Lee Beatty; Costumes, Robert Morgan; Lighting, Pat Collins; Sound, Paul Peterson; Additional Choreography, Bob Richard; Musical Director and Conductor, Ron Colvard; Orchestrator, Anita Ruth; Vocal Arrangements and Incidental Music, Joshua Rosenblum; Dance Music Arranger, David Krane; Associate Director, Benjamin Endsley Klein; SM, Leila Knox; ASM, Tracy Skoczelas; Cast: Kevin Bailey (The Grinch), Eileen Bowman (Grandma Who), Ian Brininstool or Ari Lerner (Danny Who), James Royce Edwards (Young Max), A.J. Foggiano or Noah Leung (Boo Who), Melinda Gilb (Mama Who), Steve Gunderson (Papa Who), Gaby Greenwald or Skylar Starrs Siben (Cindy-Lou Who), Samantha Littleford or Bibi Valderrama (Annie Who), Alison Grace Norwood or Hannah Prater (Betty Lou Who), James Vasquez (Grandpa Who); Adult Ensemble: Amy Biedel, Randall Dodge, Ron Christopher Jones, Paul Morgavo, Anise Ritchie, Sarah Sumner; Children's Ensemble: Maddie Shea Baldwin, Charisma McKorn, Emily Mittleman, Dallas Perry, Kayla Solsbak, Kayla Stults, Celia Tedde, Ashely Twomey, Tommy Twomey, Jada Temple; Old Globe Theatre; November 25–December 30, 2007

IN THIS CORNER by Steven Drukman; Director, Ethan McSweeny; Set, Lee Savage; Costumes, Tracy Christensen; Lighting, Tyler Micoleau; Sound, Lindsay Jones; SM, Diana Moser; Cast: Katie Barrett (Nurse/Reporter/Girl/Anny/ Tutor/USO Girl), Rufus Collins (Max Schmeling), David Deblinger (Reporter/Jacobs), Dion Graham (Joe Louis), John Keabler (Boxer), T. Ryder Smith (Announcer/Hitler/Ref/ Officer), Al White (Blackburn/Pastor); World Premiere; Cassius Carter Centre Stage; January 6–February 10, 2008

SEA OF TRANQUILITY by Howard Korder; Director, Michael Bloom; Set, Scott Bradley; Costumes, David Kay Mickelsen; Lighting, Robert Vierzel; Sound, Paul Peterson; SM, Elizabeth Lohr; Cast: Carlos Akuna (Gilbert/Roman), Ashley Clements (Kat), Nike Doukas (Phyllis), Joy Farmer-Clary (Astarte), Sloan Grenz (Josh), Ted K ch (Ben), Jeffrey Kuhn (Randy), Rosina Reynolds (Ashley/Adele), Erika Rolfsrud (Nessa), Ned Schmidtke (Johannsen/Barry); Old Globe Theatre; January 12–February 10, 2008

THE AMERICAN PLAN by Richard Greenberg; Director, Kim Rubinstein; Set, Wilson Chin; Costumes, Emily Pepper; Lighting, Chris Rynne; Sound, Paul Peterson; SM, Leila Knox; Cast: Kate Arrington (Lily Adler), Sharon Hope (Olivia Shaw), Michael Kirby (Gil Harbison), Sandra Shipley (Eva Adler), Patrick Zeller (Nick Lockridge); West Coast Premiere; Cassius Carter Centre Stage; February 23–March 30, 2008

DANCING IN THE DARK Book by Douglas Carter Beane, music by Arthur Schwartz, lyrics by Howard Dietz; adapted from the screenplay, "The Band Wagon," by Betty Comden and Adolph Green; Director, Gary Griffin; Choreographer, Warren Carlyle; Set, John Lee Beatty; Costumes, David Woolard; Lighting, Ken Billington; Music Supervision and Arrangements, Eric Stern; Orchestrations, Larry Hochman; Music Director, Don York; SM, Dan Rosokoff; Cast: Scott Bakula (Tony Hunter), Mara Davi (Gabrielle Gerard), Adam Heller (Lester Martin), Benjamin Howes (Hal Meadows), Sebastian La Cause (Paul Byrd), Beth Leavel (Lily Martin), Patrick Page (Jeffrey Cordova); Ensemble: Robin Campbell, Rachel Coloff, Dylis Croman, Nicholas Dromard, Cara Kjellman, Adam Perry, Eric Santagata, Kiira Schmidt, Jacob ben Widmar, Branch Woodman, Ashley Yeater; World Premiere; Old Globe Theatre; March 4–April 20, 2008

THE GLASS MENAGERIE by Tennessee Williams; Director, Joe Calarco; Set, Michael Fagin; Costumes, Anne Kennedy; Lighting, Chris Lee; Sound, Lindsay Jones; SM, Diana Moser; Cast: Michele Federer (Laura Wingfield), Kevin Isola (Jim O'Connor), Michael Simpson (Tom Wingfield), Mare Winningham (Amanda Wingfield); Cassius Carter Centre Stage; April 12–May 18, 2008

Oregon Shakespeare Festival

Ashland, Oregon

SEVENTY-SECOND SEASON

Artistic Director, Libby Appel; Executive Director, Paul Nicholson

Angus Bowmer Theatre

AS YOU LIKE IT by William Shakespeare; Director, J.R. Sullivan; Set, William Bloodgood; Costumes, Joyce Kim Lee; Lighting, Robert Peterson; Composer, John Tanner, Dramaturg, Lue Morgan Douthit; Voice/Text Director, Louis Colaianni; Fight Choreographer, U. Jonathan Toppo, Choreographer, Suzanne Seiber; Music Assistant/Music Vocal Coach, Kay Hilton; SM, Gwen Turos; ASM, Mandy Younger; FAIR Assistant Director, Alex Torra; Cast: Jonathan Haugen (Duke Senior), Brad Whitmore (Duke Frederick), Miriam A. Laube (Rosalind), Julie Oda (Celia), Terri McMahon (Le Beau), David Kelly (Touchstone), Todd Bjurstrom (Charles), Jeff Cummings (Oliver), Rafael Untalan (Jacques), Danforth Comins (Orlando), Mark Murphey (Adam), Kersti Bryan (Secretary to Oliver), Robert Sicular (Jaques), Adam Yazbeck (Amiens), Jeffrey King (Corin), Sarah Rutan (Phebe), Juan Rivera LeBron (Silvius), Teri Watts (Audrey), Robert Negron (Sir Oliver Martext), Mark Peterson (William), Daniel L. Haley (Ensemble); February 16–October 28, 2007

THE CHERRY ORCHARD by Anton Chekhov; Adaptor and Director, Libby Appel; Set, Rachel Hauck; Costumes, Deborah M. Dryden; Lighting, James F. Ingalls; Composer/Sound, Todd Barton, Translator/Dramaturg, Allison Horsley; Voice/Text Director, Scott Kaiser; Fight Choreographer, U. Jonathan Toppo; Choreographer, Suzanne Seiber; Music Assistant, Kay Hilton; SM, Jeremy Eisen; Production Assistant, Emily Carr; Assistant Director, Alex Torra; Cast: Richard Howard (Leonid Andreyevich Gayev), Judith-Marie Bergan (Lyubov Andreyevna Ranevskaya), Christine Albright (Anya), Gwendolyn Mulamba (Vavara Mikailovna), Gregory Linington (Pyotr Sergeyevich Trofimov), Robynn Rodriguez (Charlotta Ivanovna), Anthony Heald (Boris Simyonov-Pischik), Richard Elmore (Firs), Christopher DuVal (Semyon Yepikhodov), Nancy Rodriguez (Avdotya Feyoderovna), U. Jonathan Toppo (Ensemble), Raphael Untalan (Ensemble), Adam Yazbeck (Ensemble); February 17–July 8, 2007

ON THE RAZZLE by Tom Stoppard; Director, Laird Williamson; Set, Michael Ganio; Csotumes, Robert Blackman; Lighting, Kendall Smith; Composer, Larry Delinger; Sound, Dennis M. Kambury; Dramaturg, David Copelin; Voice/Text Director, Louis Colaianni; Choreographer, Ken Roht; SM, Susan L. McMillan; Production Assistant, Mara Filler; Cast: Tony DeBruno (Zangler), Teri Watts (Marie), Shad Willingham (Sonders), Eileen DeSandre (Gertrud), Robert Vincent Frank (Ensemble), G. Valmont Thomas (Melchior), Tyrone Wilson (Hupfer), Rex Young (Weinberl), Tasso Feldman (Christopher), Emily Sophia Knapp (Philippine, Lisette), Suzanne Irving (Mme. Knorr), Terri McMahon (Frau Fischer), Michael Elich (Bodelheimer), Catherine E. Coulson (Fräulein Blumenblatt), John J. O'Hagan (Ensemble), James J. Peck (Ensemble), Jason Esquerra (Ensemble), John Michael Goodson (Ensemble), Alexander Barnes (A Ragamuffin); February 18–October 28, 2007

GEM OF THE OCEAN by August Wilson; Director, Timonthy Bond; Set, William Bloodgood; Costumes, Susan E. Mickey; Lighting, Robert Peterson; Composer, Michael Keck; Assistant Director, Larissa Paige Kokernot; Dramaturb, David Copelin; Voice/Text Director, Evamarii Johnson; Movement Director, Patdro Harris, Fight Choreographer, U. Jonathan Toppo; SM, Jill Rendall; Production Assistant, Erin E. Heare; Cast: Greta Oglesby (Aunt Ester), Josiah Phillis (Eli), Shona Tucker (Black Mary), Kevin Kenerly (Citizen Barlow), G. Valmont Thomas (Solly Two Kings), Bill Geisslinger (Rutherford Selig), Derrick Lee Weeden (Caesar); April 17–October 27, 2007

TARTUFFE by Molière, translated by Ranjit Bolt; Director, Peter Amster; Set, Richard L. Hay; Costumes, Mara Blumenfeld; Lighting, Chris Binder; Composer/Sound, Todd Barton; Dramaturg, David Copelin; Voice/Text Director, Bonnie Raphael; Movement Director, John Sipes; SM, D.

Christian Bolender; Production Assistant, Mara Filler; Assistant Director, Dara Weinberg; Cast: Richard Elmore (Orgon), Laura Morache (Mariane), Suzanne Irving (Elmire), Gregory Linington (Damis), Eileen DeSandre (Mme. Pernelle), Richard Howard (Cleante), Linda Alper (Dorine), Kevin Kenerly (Valere), Anthony Heald (Tartuffe), John Michael Goodson (Laurent), Richard Farrell (Monsieru Loyal), Rex Young (An Officer), Amanda Wilkins (Flipote), Jason Esquerra (Ensemble), Tasso Feldman (Ensemble); July 25–October 27, 2007

New Theatre

RABBIT HOLE by David Lindsay-Abaire; Director, James Edmondson; Set, Richard L. Hay; Costumes, Deborah Trout; Lighting, Darren McCroom; Composer, Irwin Appel; Dramaturg, David Copelin; Voice/Text Director, Scott Kaiser; SM, Amy Miranda Warner; Production Assistant, Erin E. Heare; Cast: Robin Goodrin Nordli (Becca), Tyler Layton (Izzy), Dee Maaske (Nat), Bill Geisslinger (Howie), Jerris Schaefer (Jason); February 22–June 22, 2007

TRACY'S TIGER based on a novella by William Saroyan, book, music and lyrics by Linda Alper, Douglas Langworthy, Penny Metropolis & Sterling Tinsley; Director, Penny Metropulos; Choreographer, Patdro Harris; Set, William Bloodgood; Costumes, Deborah M. Dryden; Lighting, Michael Chybowski; Composer/Music Director, Sterling Tinsley; Sound, Jeff Mockus; Orchestrator, Bruce Monroe; Dramaturg, Lue Morgan Douthit; Voice/Text Director, Evamarii Johnson; Assistant Music Director, Laurie Anne Hunter; SM, D. Christian Bolender; ASM, Melissa L. Wanke; FAIR Assistant Director, Matthew Ozawa; Cast: Jeremy Peter Johnson (Thomas Tracy), Laura Morache (Laura Luthy), René Millán (Tiger), David Kelly (Ringert/Officer Earl Huzinga), Brad Whitmore (Peberdy/Chief Bly), Michael J. Hume (Nimmo/Dr. Rudolph Pingitzer), Miriam A. Laube (Viola Luthy), Nell Geisslinger (Tigress), Richard Farrell (Otto Seyfang/Oliver Luthy/Art Pliley), Linda Alper (Mrs. Seyfant/Betty/Mabel Stark), Juan Rivera LeBron (Phoenix/Victor Tosca/Don Mambo), Sterling Tinsley (Piano), Bruce McKern (Bass), Ed Dunsavage (Guitar), Terry Longshore (Percussion); March 28–October 28, 2007

DISTRACTED by Lisa Loomer; Director, Liz Diamond; Set, Robert Brill; Video Design, Peter Flaherty; Costumes, Ilona Somogyi; Lighting, Christopher Akerlind; Sound, Jeremy J. Lee; Dramaturg, Lue Morgan Douthit; Voice/Text Director, Bonnie Raphael; Movement Director, John Sipes; SM, Jill Rendall; Production Assistant, Emily Carr; FAIR Assistant Director, Kristin Horton; Cast; Robynn Rodriguez (Mama), U. Jonathan Toppo (Dad), James Edson (Jesse), Caroline Shaffer (Dr. Zavala/ Carolyn/Waitress), Gwendolyn Mulamba (Mrs. Holly/Dr. Waller/Nurse), Thom Rivera (Daniel Broder/Dr. Jinks/Dr. Karnes), Judith-Marie Bergan (Sherry), Vilma Silva (Vera), Kjerstine Anderson (Natalie); July 3–October 28, 2007

Elizabethan Stage/Allen Pavilion

THE TEMPEST by William Shakespeare; Director, Libby Appel; Set, William Bloodgood; Costumes, Deborah M. Dryden; Lighting, Robert Peterson; Composer and Sound, Todd Barton; Assistant Director, Larissa Paige Kokernot; Dramaturg, Barry Kraft; Voice/Text Director, Rebecca Clark Carey; Movement and Fight Director, John Sipes; Assistant Fight Director, U. Jonathan Toppo; SM, Susan L. McMillan; ASM, Melissa L. Wanke; Cast: Derrick Lee Weeden (Prospero), Nell Geisslinger (Miranda), Dan Donohue (Caliban), Nancy Rodriguez (Ariel), Armando Durán (Alsonso), Tyrone Wilson (Sebastian), John Tufts (Ferdinand), Antonia (Greta Oglesby), James Edmondson (Gonzalo), John J. O'Hagan (Adrian), Michael J. Hume (Stephano), Christopher DuVal (Trinculo), James J. Peck (Boatswain), Orion Bradshaw (Ariel's Shadow), Robert Vincent Frank (Ariel's Shadow), Paul Michael Garcia (Ariel's Shadow), Jeremy Peter Johnson (Ariel's Shadow), Vanessa Nowitzky (Ariel's Shadow); June 5-October 6, 2007

THE TAMING OF THE SHREW by William Shakespeare; Director, Kate Buckley; Set, Richard L. Hay; Costumes, David Kay Mickelsen; Lighting, Robert Peterson; Composer and Sound, Todd Barton; Dramaturg, Kate McConnell; Voice/ Text Director, Rebecca Clark Carey; Movement and Fight Director, John Sipes; Assistant Fight Director, U. Jonathan Toppo; SM, Gwen Turos; ASM, Amy Miranda Warner; FAIR Assistant Director, Kristin Horton; Cast: Jeffrey King (Baptista), Vilma Silva (Katherina), Sarah Rutan (Bianca), Jeris Schaefer (Nicholas), Tony DeBruno (Vincentio), Danforth Comins (Lucentio), Jeff Cummings (Tranio), Mark Bedard (Biondello), Michael Elich (Petruchio), Robin Goodrin Nordli (Grumio), Tasso Feldman (Curtis/Ensemble), James Edmondson (Gremio), Shad Willingham (Hortensio), Tyler Layton (A Widow), Robert Vincent Frank (A Pedant/Ensemble), Catherine E. Coulson (Tailor), Dee Maaske (Haberdasher), Kjerstine Anderson, Orion Bradshaw, Emily Sophia Knapp, John R. Lewis (Ensemble); June 6–October 7, 2007

ROMEO AND JULIET by William Shakespeare; Director, Bill Rauch; Set, Christopher Acebo; Costumes, Shigeru Yaji; Lighting, Robert Peterson; Composer, Paul James Prendergast; Dramaturg, Kate McConnell; Voice/Text Director, Scott Kaiser; Movement and Fight Director, John Sipes; Assistant Fight Director, U. Jonathan Toppo, Choreographer, Jessica Wallenfels; SM, Jeremy Eisen; ASM, Mandy Younger; FAIR Assistant Director, Brian Sivesind; Assistant Director, Dara Weinberg; Cast: Robert Sicular (Lord Montague), Liisa Ivary (Lady Montague), John Tufts (Romeo), Juan Rivera LeBron (Benvolio), Adam Yazbeck (Balthasar): Todd Bjurstrom (Abram/ Friar John), Mark Murphey (Friar Laurence/Cornelius), Jonathan Haugen (Lord Capulet), Shona Tucker (Lady Capulet), Christine Albright (Juliet), Demetra Pittman (Nurse), René Millán (Tybalt), Julie Oda (Prudence), Mark Peterson (Samson), Josiah Phillips (Escalus), Dan Donohue (Mercutio), Rafael Untalan (Paris), Daniel L. Haley, Carlyn K. Blount, Kersti Bryan, Paul Michael Garcia, Richard Howard, Robert Negron, Vanessa Nowitzky (Ensemble), Edward Condon, Kay Hilton (Musicians); June 7–October 5, 2007

Paper Mill Playhouse

Millburn, New Jersey

FOUNDED IN 1934

Executive Director, Mark W. Jones, Artistic Director, Mark S. Hoebee

HAPPY DAYS: A New Musical Book by Garry Marshall, music and lyrics by Paul Williams; Director, Gordon Greenberg; Music Director, Shawn Gough; Choreographer, Michele Lynch; Set, Walt Spangler; Costumes, David C. Woolard; Lighting, Jeff Croiter; Sound, Randy Hansen; PSM, Brian Rardin; Casting, Jay Binder, Sara Schatz; Press, Shayne A. Miller; Cast: Rory O'Malley (Richie), Patrick Garner (Howard), Cynthia Ferrer (Joanie), Todd Buonopane (Ralph), Christopher Ruth (Potsie), Eric Schneider (Chachi), Michael J. Farina (Arnold), Julia Burrows (Lori Beth), Lauren Parsons (Louise), Andrea Dora (Paula), Scott Barnhardt (Scooter), Stephanie Gibson (Betty/Carhop/Pinkette Lola), Lisa Gajda (Joy/Carhop/Pinkette Sally), Tom Plotkin (Sheldon/Leopard Mac/Jumpy Malachi), Joey Sorge (Fonzie), Andrew Varela (Bully/Leopold Manny/Count Malachi), Felicia Finley (Pinky); Replacements 10/17–10/28: Kate Loprest (Joanie), Robb Sapp (Chachi); September 26–October 28, 2007

MEET ME IN ST. LOUIS Book by Hugh Wheeler, music and lyrics by Hugh Martin & Ralph Blane; Director, Mark Hoebee; Music Director, Tim Helm; Choreographer, Denis Jones; Set, Rob Bissinger; Costumes, Thom Heyer; Lighting, Charlie Morrison; Sound, Randy Hansen; PSM, Brian Meister; Casting, Alison Franck; Press, Shayne A. Miller; Cast: Sophie Rudin (Tootie Smith), Ed Romanoff (Postman), Roni Caggiano (Agnes Smith), Christian Del Croix (Lon Smith), Donna English (Anna Smith), Patti Mariano (Katie), JB Adams (Grandpa Prophater), Julia Osborne (Rose Smith), Brynn O'Malley (Esther Smith), Brian Hissong (John Truitt), Gregg Edelman (Alonso Smith), Allison Couture (Eve), Patrick Cummings (Warren Sheffield), Ed Romanoff (Motorman), Lucille Ballard (Erin Henry), Matt Condello (Peewee Drummond), Elliot Bradley (Sidney Purvis); Ensemble: Ashley Arcement, Tommy Berklund, Jessica Bircann, Alicia Charles, Leah Greenhaus, Wes Hart, Mary Jo McConnell, Kake Pfarr, Dani Spieler; November 7–December 16, 2007

THE MIRACLE WORKER by William Gibson; Director, Susan Fenichell; Set and Costumes, David Zinn; Lighting, Mary Louis Geiger; Sound, Randy Hansen; Hair/Wigs, Charles LaPointe; PSM, Jennifer Grutza; Animal Training, William Berloni; Casting, Alison Franck; Press, Shayne A. Miller; Cast: Stuart Zagnit (Doctor), John Hickok (Captain Keller), Emily Dorsch (Kate Keller), Meredith Lipson or Lily Maketansky (Helen Keller), Elijah Isiah Cook (Percy), Cherelle Cargill (Viney), Beth Dixon (Aunt Ev), Will Fowler (James Keller), Annika Boras (Anne Sullivan), Stuart Zagnit (Doctor Anagnos), Argyle (Belle); January 23–February 24, 2008

STEEL MAGNOLIAS by Robert Harling; Director, Karen Carpenter; Set, Randy Hanson; Costumes, David Murin; Lighting, Jeff Croiter; Sound, Randy Hansen; Hair/Wigs, Mark Adam Rampmeyer; PSM, Brian Meister; Casting, Alison Franck; Press, Shayne A. Miller; Cast: Charlotte Booker (Truvy), Kate Wetherhead (Annelle), Kelly Bishop (Clairee), Kelly Sullivan (Shelby), Monqiue Fowler (M'Lynn), Beth Fowler (Ouiser); March 5–April 6, 2008

KISS ME KATE Music and lyrics by Cole Porter, book by Sam and Bella Spewack; Director, James Brennan; Choreographer, Patti Colombo; Music Director, Tom Helm; Set, James Fouchard; Costumes, Gail Baldoni; Lighting, F. Mitchell Dana; Sound, Randy Hansen; Hair/Wigs, Mark Adam Rampmeyer; PSM, Richard Rauscher; Cast: Timothy J. Alex (Bill/Lucentio), Mike McGowan (Fred/Petruchio), Michele Ragusa (Lilli/Kate), Amanda Watkins (Lois/Bianca), Stephen Carrasco (Hortensio), Eugene Fleming (Paul), Herb Foster (Harry/Trevor), Wes Hart (Gremio), William Ryall (Second Man), Stacey Sargeant (Hattie), Bob Stoeckle (General Harrison Howell), Gordon Joseph Weiss (First Man); Ensemble: Megan Adams, Elliott Bradley, Desiree Davar, Katie Hagen, Cameron Henderson, Todd Horman, Tiffany Howard, Danielle Jordan, Kate Marilley, Rod Roberts, Eric Shorey, Elisa Van Duyne, Kyle Vaughn, Ryan Worsing; April 16–May 18, 2008

LITTLE SHOP OF HORRORS Book and lyrics by Howard Ashman, music by Alan Menken; based on the film by Roger Corman with screenplay by Charles Griffith; Director, Mark Waldrop; Choreographer, Vince Pesce; Music Director, Bruce Coyle; Set, Adam Koch; Costumes, Matthew Hemesath; Lighting, Ben Stanton; Sound, Randy Hansen; Hair and Wigs, Charles LaPointe, PSM, Brian Meister; Cast: Stephen Berger (Mushnik), Darin DePaul (Ensemble), Badia Farha (Crystal), Jenny Fellner (Audrey), Jared Gertner (Seymour), Montego Glover (Chiffon), Angela Grovey (Ronnette), Stacey Harris (Ensemble), Michael Latini (Ensemble), Michael James Leslie (Voice of Audrey 2), Asa Somers (Orin), Tally Sessions (Ensemble); June 4–July 6, 2008

People's Light & Theatre Company

Malvern, Pennsylvania

THIRTY-THIRD SEASON

Artistic Director, Abigail Adams; Managing Director, Grace E. Grillet

THEOPHILUS NORTH by Matthew Burnett, based on the novel by Thornton Wilder; Director, Abigail Adams; Set, James F. Pyne, Jr.; Costumes, Marla J. Jurglanis; Lighting, Dennis Parichy; SM, Charles T. Brastow; Dramaturg, Elizabeth Pool; Cast: John Wernke (Theophilus North); Ensemble: Julianna Zinkel, Alda Cortese, Lenny Haas, Tom Teti, Ahren Potratz, Mary Elizabeth Scallen; September 12–October 7, 2007

SIX CHARACTERS IN SEARCH OF AN AUTHOR by Luigi Pirandello, newly translated & adapted by Louis Lippa;

Director, Ken Marini; Set, Arthur R. Rotch; Costumes, Marla J. Jurglanis; Lighting, Dennis Parichy; Sound, Charles T. Brastow; Dramaturg, Elizabeth Pool; SM, Kate McSorley; Cast: Cathy Simpson (Stage Manager), Peter DeLaurier (The Director), Kevin Bergen (A Lead Actor), Melanye Finister (A Lead Actress), Elena Bossler (A Young Actress), Mark Del Guzzo (A Young Actor), Matt Mezzacappa (Assistant Stage Manager), Stephen Novelli (The Father), Kim Carson (The Stepdaughter), Ceal Phelan (The Mother), Evan Jonigkeit (The Son), Connor Murtagh (The Young Boy), Julia Giampietro (The Little Girl), Marcia Saunders (Madame Pace), Gregory Scott Miller/Ahren Potratz (Harry Andrews); October 10–November 11, 2007

TREASURE ISLAND: A Musical Panto by Kathryn Petersen, original music and lyrics by Michael Ogborn; Musical Direction/Additional Vocal Arrangements by David Ames; Director, David Bradley; Set, James F. Pyne, Jr.; Costumes, Rosemarie McKelvey; Lighting, Paul Hackenmueller; Stage Manager/Sound,, Charles T. Brastow; Fight & Movement Choreographer, Samantha Bellomo; Cast: Mark Lazar (Mother Hawkins), Erin Weaver (Jamie Hawkins), Pete Pryor (Captain Smilenot), Susan McKey (Evelyn Treelawnee), Tom Teti (Squire Treelawnee), Ian Bedford (Long John Silver), Ben Dibble (Dr. Livesee), Joilet Harris (Mama Kura), Maggie Fitzgerald (Polly the Parrot), Chris Faith (Ezekial Machete Scabbs), Matt Hultgren (Tinnitus Tom the Terrible), Justin Jain (Israel Chopped Hand), Jefferson Haynes (Hackin' Devil Dan); November 14, 2007–January 1, 2008

CRISPIN: The Cross of Lead by Russell Davis, based on the novel by Avi; Director, Andy Belser; Set, Randy Ward; Costumes, Marla J. Jurglanis; Lighting, John Ambrosone; Sound, John Nuhn; SM, Kate McSorley; Movement Conception, Stephanie Skura; Cast: Erin Brueggemann (Crispin), Christopher Patrick Mullen (Bear), Stephen Novelli (John Aycliffe), Julianna Zinkel (Goodwife Peregrine/One-Eyed Man/Ensemble), Kathleen Lisa Clarke (Widow Daventry/Ensemble), Michael Lopez (Father Quinel/John Ball/Ensemble), Nate Dryden (Priest/Ensemble), Josh Beckel (Cedric/Ensemble); January 17–February 24, 2008

THE GLASS MENAGERIE by Tennessee Williams; Director, Ken Marini; Set, James F. Pyne, Jr.; Costumes, Rosemarie E. McKelvey; Lighting, Gregory Scott Miller; Sound/Stage Manager, Charles T. Brastow; Dramaturg, Elizabeth Pool; Cast: Kevin Bergen (Tom Wingfield), Elizabeth Webster Duke (Laura Wingfield), Marcia Saunders (Amanda Wingfield), Darren Michael Hengst (Jim O'Connor); February 13–March 22, 2007

GETTING NEAR TO BABY by Y York, based on the novel by Audrey Couloumbis; Director, Abigail Adams; Set, Jim Kronzer; Costumes, Marla J. Jurglanis; Lighting, Dennis Parichy; Sound/Composer, Christopher Colucci; Dramaturgy, Elizabeth Pool; Dialects, Graham Smith; SM, Kate McSorley; Cast: Claire Inie-Richards (Willa Jo), Maggie Fitzgerald (Little Sister), Mary Elizabeth Scallen (Aunt Patty), Christopher Patrick Mullen (Uncle Hob), Katie Johantgen (Liz Fingers), Nathaniel Brastow (Isaac Fingers), Susan McKey (Lucy Wainwright), Meg Rose (Cynthia Wainwright); March 27–April 20, 2008

I HAVE BEFORE ME A REMARKABLE DOCUMENT GIVEN TO ME BY A YOUNG LADY FROM RWANDA by Sonja Linden; Director, David Bradley; Set, Arthur R. Rotch; Costumes, Abbie Wysor; Lighting, Dennis Parichy; Sound and SM, Charles T. Brastow; Cast: David Ingram (Simon), Miriam Hyman (Juliette); May 28–June 22, 2008

SHERLOCK HOLMES & THE CASE OF THE JERSEY LILY by Katie Forgette; Director, Steve Umberger; Set, James F. Pyne, Jr.; Costumes, Marla J. Jurglanis; Lighting, Dennis Parichy; Sound, Christopher Colucci; SM, Kate McSorley; Cast: Peter DeLaurier (Sherlock Holmes), Mark Lazar (Dr. Watson), Susan McKey (Mrs. Lillie Langtry), Jeb Kreager (Oscar Wilde), Alda Cortese (Kitty), Lenny Haas (John Smythe), Graham Smith (Professor Moriarty); June 18–July 13, 2008

Philadelphia Theatre Company

Philadelphia, Pennsylvania

THIRTY-FOURTH SEASON

Producing Artistic Director, Sara Garonzik; Managing Director, Diane Claussen

BEING ALIVE Music and lyrics by Stephen Sondheim, additional text by William Shakespeare; Conceived and directed by Billy Porter; Assistant Director, Matt Gould; Music Director, Ethan Popp; Vocal Director, Michael McElroy; Choreographer, AC Ciulla; Set, Allen Moyer; Costumes, Anita Yavich; Lighting, Kevin Adams; Sound, Robert J. Killenberger; SM, Victoria L. Hein; Cast: Bryan Terrell Clark, Chuck Cooper, Vanita Harbour, Patina Renea Miller, Jesse Nager, Leslie Odom Jr., Nandi Walker, Rema Webb; Suzanne Roberts Theater; October 24–December 2, 2007

M. BUTTERFLY by David Henry Hwang; Director, Joe Calarco; Choreographer, Chu Shan Zhu; Set, Michael Fagin; Lighting, Chris Lee; Costumes, Helen Huang; Sound, Matthew Nielson; Composer, Robert Maggio; SM, Victoria L. Hein; Cast: Jared Michael Delaney (Marc and others), Christopher Innvar (Rene Gallimard), Telly Leung (Song Liling), Wen Tao Li (Dancer), Yin Chun Li (Dancer), Doan Ly (Comrade Chin and others), Anne Marie Nest (Renee and others), Larry Peterson (Ambassador Toulon and others), Susan Wilder (Helga Gallimard); Philadelphia Premiere; Suzanne Roberts Theater; January 18–February 24, 2008

THIRD by Wendy Wasserstein; Director, Mary B. Robinson; Set, James Noone; Lighting, Russell Champa; Costumes, Karen Ann Ledger; Sound, Fitz Patton; Composer, Robert Maggio; SM, Victoria L. Hein; Cast: Jennifer Blood (Emily), Melanye Finister (Nancy), Will Fowler (Third), Ben Hammer (Jack), Lizbeth Mackay (Laurie); Philadelphia Premiere; Suzanne Roberts Theater; March 21–April 20, 2008

THE HAPPINESS LECTURE by Bill Irwin; Collaborator/ PSM, Nancy Harrington; Set, Kelly Hanson; Lighting, Nancy Schertler; Sound and Video, Jorge Cousineau; Costumes, Rebecca Lustic; SM, Victoria L. Hein; Cast: Bill Irwin, Ephrat "Bounce" Asherie, Nichole Canuso, Jennifer Childs, Aaron Cromie, Lee Ann Etzold, Makoto Hirano, Cori Olinghouse; Swing: Dawn Falato; World Premiere; Suzanne Roberts Theater; May 16–June 22, 2008

Playmakers Repertory Company

Chapel Hill, North Carolina

THIRTY-SECOND SEASON

Producing Artistic Director, Joseph Haj

Mainstage

ROMEO AND JULIET by William Shakespeare; Director, Davis McCallum; Sets, Scott Bradley; Costumes, Olivera Gajic; Lighting, Matt Richards; Composer, Ryan Rumery; Choreographer, Casey Sams, Fight Arranger, Craig Turner; Cast: Janie Brookshire (Juliet), Kathryn Hunter-Williams (Nurse/Lady/Montague), Joy Jones (Lady Capulet), Heaven Stephens (Capulet Servant/Party Guest), Lesley Shires (Prince's Officer/Party Guest), Flor De Liz Perez (Paris' Page/Party Guest), Matt Dickson (Romeo), Justin Adams (Mercutio), Wesley Schultz (Benvolio), David McClutchey (Tybalt), Marshall Spann (Paris), Ray Dooley (Friar Laurence), Jeffrey Blair Cornell (Capulet), David Adamson (Montague/Friar John), Prince T. Bowie (Prince of Verona), William Stutts, Jr. (Prince's Officer), David Friedlander (Gregory/Peter/Masker), Jason Powers (Capulet Fighter/Balthazar), Christopher Taylor (Abram/Valentine/Apothecary/Musician), Matthew Murphy (Samson/Capulet/Servant/Musician); September 26–October 14, 2007

CRIMES OF THE HEART by Beth Henley; Director, John Feltch; Sets/Costumes, Jan Chambers, Lighting, Mary Louise Geiger; Sound, Michèl Marrano; Cast: Janie Brookshire (Meg Magrath), Annie Meisels (Chick Boyle), Wesley Schultz (Doc Porter), Lesley Shires (Babe Botrelle), Marshall Spann (Barnette Lloyd), Regan Thompson (Lenny Magrath); October 24–November 11, 2007

THE LITTLE PRINCE Adapted by Rick Cummins and John Scoullar from the book by Antoine de Saint Exupéry; Director, Tom Quaintance; Sets and Costumes, McKay Coble; Lighting, Justin Townsend; Sound, Michèl Marrano; Cast: Lesley Shires (Little Prince), Kenneth P. Strong (Aviator), Matthew Murphy (Turkish Astronomer), Heaven Stephens (Rose/Wall of Roses), David Friedlander (King/Merchant), Joy Jones (Conceited Man/Snake/Wall of Roses), Flor De Liz Perez (Tippler/ Wall of Roses), William Stutts, Jr. (Businessman), Jason Powers (Lamplighter/Fox); November 28–December 16, 2007

DOUBT by John Patrick Shanley; Director, Drew Barr; Sets, Marion Williams; Costumes, Jan Chambers; Lighting, Justin Townsend; Sound, Michèl Marrano; Cast, Jeffrey Blair Cornell (Father Flynn), Julie Fishell (Sister Aloysius), Janie Brookshire (Sister James) Kathryn Hunter-Williams (Mrs. Muller); January 26–February 29, 2008 (in repertory with Topdog/Underdog)

TOPDOG/UNDERDOG by Suzan-Lori Parks; Director Raelle Myrick-Hodges; Sets, Marion Williams; Costumes, Jan Chambers; Lighting, Justin Townsend; Sound, Michèl Marrano; Cast: Brandon J. Dirden (Booth), Tyrone Mitchell Henderson (Lincoln); January 26–February 29, 2008 (in repertory with Doubt)

AMADEUS by Peter Shaffer; Director, Joseph Haj; Sets, McKay Coble; Costumes, Bill Black; Lighting, Marcus Doshi; Sound, Michèl Marrano; Cast: David Adamson (Kappellmeister Bonno), Janie Brookshire (Constanze), Jeffrey Blair Cornell (Baron von Swieten), Ray Dooley (Antonio Salieri), John Feltch (Joseph II, Emperor of Austria), David Friedlander (Venticello 1), Jeffrey Meanza (Venticello 2), Vince Nappo (Wolfgang Amadeus Mozart), Wesley Shultz (Salieri's Cook), Lesley Shires (Teresa Salieri), Marshall Spann (Salieri's Valet), Heaven Stephens (Katherina Cavalieri), Kenneth P. Strong (Johann von Strack), William Stutts, Jr. (Count Orsini-Rosenberg), Christopher Jason Taylor (Major-Domo); Servants and Citizens of Verona: Allison Altman, Prince T. Bowie, Matthew Murphy, Flor De Liz Perez, Jason Flowers; April 2–20, 2008

PRC [2] Second Stage

WHEN THE BULBUL STOPPED SINGING by Raja Shehadeh, adapted by David Grieg; Director, Ellen Hemphill; Set, Jan Chambers; Lighting, Ross Kolman; Sound, Jason Romney; Projection Artist, Michael Bagley; Cast: Joseph Haj (Raja Shehadeh); September 12–16, 2007

2.5 MINUTE RIDE Written and performed by Lisa Kron; Director, Mark Brokaw; Lighting, Kenneth Posner; Sound, Darron L West; Original Music, Dan Froot; January 9–13, 2008

WITNESS TO AN EXECUTION Written and performed by Mike Wiley; Commissioned by PlayMakers Repertory Company; Director, Kathryn Hunter-Williams; Set, Charles McClennahan; Lighting, Eric Ketchum; Projections, David Colagiovanni; Sound, Michel Marrano; World premiere April 23–27, 2008

Portland Stage Company

Portland, Maine

THIRTY-FORTH SEASON

Artistic Director, Anita Stewart; Managing Director, Camilla Barrantes

THE PIANO LESSON by August Wilson; Director, Ron OJ Parson; Set, Anita Stewart; Costumes, Jacqueline Firkins; Lighting, Bryon Winn; Sound, Gregg Carville; SM, Myles

C. Hatch; Cast: Tyla Abercrumbie (Berniece), Victor J. Cole (Wining Boy), Ronald Conner (Boy Willie), Allen Edge (Avery), Tamberla Perry (Grace), Patrick J. Sims (Lymon), A.C. Smith (Doaker), Nyanen Deng, Dorcas Thete (Maretha); September 25–October 21, 2007

INDOOR/OUTDOOR by Kenny Finkle; Director, Samuel Buggeln; Set, Tobin Ost; Costumes, Frank Champa; Lighting, Gregg Carville; Sound, Stephen Swift; SM, Marjorie Gallant; Cast: J.T. Arbogast (Shuman), Laura Jordan (Matilda), Susan Louise O'Connor (Samantha), Chapin Springer (Oscar); October 30–November 18, 2007

A CHRISTMAS CAROL based on the story by Charles Dickens; Director and Set, Anita Stewart; Costumes, Jacqueline Firkins & Susan Thomas; Lighting: Bryon Winn; Musical Director, Edward Reichert; Music, Peter John Still; SM, Myles C. Hatch; Cast: Maureen Butler (Mrs. Crachit), Mark Honan (Bob Crachit), Cristine McMurdo-Wallis (The Ghosts), Daniel Noel (Jacob Marley), Edward Reichert (Charles Dickens), Evan Thompson (Scrooge), Dustin Tucker (Nephew Fred), Sally Wood (Belle); November 30–December 24, 2007

FULLY COMMITTED by Becky Mode; Director, Lucy Smith Conroy; Set, Anita Stewart; Costumes, Susan Thomas; Lighting, Gregg Carville; Sound, Jill BC DuBoff; SM, Marjorie Gallant; Cast: Dustin Tucker (Sam); January 22–February 17, 2008

MUCH ADO ABOUT NOTHING by William Shakespeare; Director, Cecil MacKinnon; Set, Anita Stewart; Costumes, Anna-Alisa Belous; Lighting, Bryon Winn; Sound, Christopher Fitze; SM, Myles C. Hatch; Cast: Gerry Bamman (Leonato/ Dogberry), Ron Botting (Don Pedro/Sexton, Patricia Buckley (Margaret/Conrad), Ariel Francoeur (Hero), Robin Galloway (Beatrice), J. Paul Guimont (Borachio), Ephraim Lopez (Claudio), Tony Reilly (Antonio/Friar), Peter Allen Stone (Benedick), Jeffries Thaiss (Don John/Verges); February 26–March 23, 2008

MAGNETIC NORTH by William Donnelly; Director, Richard Hamburger; Set, Anita Stewart; Costumes, Ellen McCartney; Lighting, Bryon Winn; Composer, Hans Indigo Spencer; SM, Marjorie Gallant; Cast: Tom Butler (James), Jessica Dickey (Leigh), Quincy Dunn-Baker (Emmett), Danielle Skraastad (Mara); World Premiere; April 1–20, 2008

DOUBT by John Patrick Shanley; Director, Sally Wood; Set, Dan Bilodeau; Costumes, Susan Picinich; Lighting, Lynne Chase; Sound, Stephen Swift; SM, Myles C. Hatch; Cast: Tamela Aldridge (Mrs. Muller), Timothy Deenihan (Father Flynn), Cristine McMurdo-Wallis (Sister Aloysius), Kate Turnbull (Sister James); April 29–May 25, 2008

19TH ANNUAL LITTLE FESTIVAL OF THE UNEXPECTED Included: Out of Sterno by Deborah Zoe Laufer; Peer Gynt by Henrik Ibsen (Co-production with Figures of Speech Theater); The Passion of the Hausfrau by Bess Welden, Annette Jolles, & Nicole Chaison; I Don't Want to Talk About It by Kenny Finkle; May 13–17, 2008

The Repertory Theatre of St. Louis

St. Louis, Missouri

FORTY-FIRST SEASON

Artistic Director, Steven Woolf; Managing Director, Mark Bernstein

Mainstage

THE HISTORY BOYS by Alan Bennett; Director, Steven Woolf; Set, Adrian W. Jones; Costumes, Elizabeth Covey; Lighting, Marcus Doshi; Sound, Tori Meyer; Casting, Rich Cole; SM, Glenn Dunn; ASM, Champe Leary; Cast: Adam Farabee (Timms), Eric Gilde (Dakin), Charles Sydney Hirsh (Lockwood), Matt Leisy (Scripps), Jonathan Monk (Posner), Bhavesh Patel (Akthar), Steven Pierce (Crowther), Brian White (Rudge), Thomas Carson (Hector), Anderson Matthews (Headmaster), Bryant Richards (Irwin), Carolyn Swift (Mrs. Lintott), Michael Perkins (T.V. Director); September 5–September 30, 2007

DRACULA by Hamilton Deane and John L. Balderston, adapted from Bram Stoker's novel; Director, Stephen Hollis; Set, Paul Shortt; Costumes, Wade Laboissonniere; Lighting, Kirk Bookman; Original Music and Sound, David B. Smith; Fight Director, Drew Fracher; Casting, Rich Cole; Flying Effects, ZFX, Inc.; SM, T.R. Martin; ASM, Tony Dearing; Cast: Jeffrey Withers (Jonathan Harker), Elizabeth Helitzer (Miss Wells), Richert Easley (Dr. Seward), John Michalski (Abraham Van Helsing), Scott Schafer (R.M. Renfield), Larry Bull (Butterworth/Attendant), Julia Coffey (Lucy Seward), Kurt Rhoads (Count Dracula); October 10–November 4, 2007

KISS ME, KATE Book by Samuel and Bella Spewack, music and lyrics by Cole Porter; Director, Victoria Bussert; Choreographer, Ralph Perkins; Music Director, Dale Rieling; Set, John Ezell; Costumes, Dorothy Marshall Englis; Lighting, Peter Sargent; Sound, Tori Meyer; Casting, Rich Cole; SM, Glenn Dunn; ASM, Shannon B. Sturgis; Cast: Stacey Sargeant (Hattie), Darryl Reuben Hall (Paul), John Woodson (Ralph/ Harrison Howell), Jessica Leigh Brown (Lois Lane); David Larsen (Bill Calhoun), Diane Sutherland (Lilli Vanessi), Brian Sutherland (Fred Graham), Whit Reichert (Harry Trevor), Steve Isom (Man 1), Joneal Joplin (Man 2), Andrew Cao (Hortensio), Ben Nordstrom (Gremio); Ensemble: Tyler Adcock, Michael Baxter, Haven Eaves, Megan Kane, Amanda Kloots, Kelli Stryker; November 28–December 28, 2007

TUESDAYS WITH MORRIE by Jeffrey Hatcher and Mitch Albom; Director, Mark Cuddy; Set, Vicki Smith; Costumes, Christina Selian; Lighting, Don Darnutzer; Sound, Brian Jerome Peterson; Composer, Scott Killian; SM, T.R. Martin; ASM, Tony Dearing; Cast: Remi Sandri (Mitch), Bernie Passeltiner (Morrie); January 2–January 27, 2008

TWELVE ANGRY MEN by Reginald Rose; Director, Martin Platt; Set, Judy Gailen; Costumes, Claudia Stephens; Lighting,

Dan Kotlowitz; Casting, Rich Cole; SM, Glenn Dunn; ASM, Shannon B. Sturgis; Cast: Peter Van Wagner (Juror 1), Gary Wayne Barker (Juror 2), Greg Thornton (Juror 3), Richmond Hoxie (Juror 4), Rich Pisarkiewicz (Juror 5), James Anthony (Juror 6), R. Ward Duffy (Juror 7), Jeff Talbott (Juror 8), Dane Knell (Juror 9), Steve Brady (Juror 10), Jerry Vogel (Juror 11), Craig Wroe (Juror 12), Greg Johnston (Guard); February 6–March 2, 2008

ELLA Book by Jeffrey Hatcher, conceived by Rob Ruggiero and Dyke Garrison; Director, Rob Ruggiero; Musical Director/Arrangements, Danny Holgate; Set, Michael Schweikardt; Costumes, Alejo Vietti; Lighting, John Lasiter; Sound, Michael Miceli; Wigs, Charles LaPointe; SM, Glenn Dunn; ASM, Tony Dearing; Cast: Tina Fabrique (Ella Fitzgerald), George Caldwell (Jimmy/piano/Conductor), Thad Wilson (Donny/trumpet), Rodney Harper ("Sticks" Fletcher/drums), Clifton Kellem (Sam/bass), Harold Dixon (Norman Granz), Joilet Harris (Understudy Ella Fitzgerald); March 19–April 13, 2008

Studio Theatre

THE CLEAN HOUSE by Sarah Ruhl; Director, Susan Gregg; Set and Lighting, Michael Philippi; Costumes, Lou Bird; Sound, Tori Meyer; Movement, Millie Garvey; Casting, Rich Cole; SM, Champe Leary; Cast: Roni Geva (Matilde), Andrea Cirie (Lane), Carol Schultz (Virginia), John Rensenhouse (Charles), June Gable (Ana); October 24–November 11, 2007

THE VERTICAL HOUR by David Hare; Director, Jim O'Connor; Set and Costumes, Marie Anne Chiment; Lighting, Mark Wilson; Casting, Rich Cole; SM, Champe Leary; Cast: Anderson Matthews (Oliver Lucas), Gloria Biegler (Nadia Blye), Brian White (Dennis Dutton), Jeremiah Wiggins (Philip Lucas), Jamie Lynn Concepcion (Terri Scholes); January 16–February 3, 2008

RABBIT HOLE by David Lindsay-Abaire; Director, Jane Page; Set, Robert Mark Morgan; Costumes, Garth Dunbar; Lighting, John Wylie; Sound, Tori Meyer; Casting, Rich Cole; SM, Champe Leary; Cast: Ashley West (Izzy), Victoria Adams-Zischke (Becca), Timothy McCracken (Howie), Carolyn Swift (Nat), Adam King (Jason); March 12–March 30, 2008

Off-Ramp

ALTAR BOYZ Book by Kevin Del Aguila, music,lyrics and vocal arrangements by Gary Adler & Michael Patrick Walker; Conceived by Marc Kessler & Ken Davenport; Director, Stafford Arima; Choreographer, Christopher Gattelli; Set, Anna Louizos; Costumes, Alejo Vietti; Lighting, Ben Stanton; Sound, Tori Meyer; Musical Director, Henry Palkes; Associate Choreographer, Lou Castro; Set Associate, Todd Potter; Casting, David Petro;Orchestrations, Doug Katsaros & Lynne Shankel; Dance Music/Additional Arrangements, Lynne Shankel; SM, Shannon B. Sturgis; ASM, Mary Jane Probst; Cast: Michael Kadin Craig (Matthew), Shua Potter (Mark), Adam Fleming (Luke), Mauricio Perez (Juan), Ravi Roth (Abraham); September 19–October 7, 2007

BAD DATES by Theresa Rebeck; Director, Michael Evan Haney; Set, Narelle Sissons; Costumes, Elizabeth Eisloeffel; Lighting, John Wylie; SM, Shannon B. Sturgis; Cast: Annie Fitzpatrick (Haley); October 17–November 4, 2007

THE BOMB-ITTY OF ERRORS by Jordan Allen-Dutton, Jason Catalano, Gregory Qaiyum & Erik Weiner; music by Jeffrey Qaiyum; Director, Nick Corley; Set, Luke Hegel-Cantarella; Costumes, Maiko Matsushima; Lighting, Jeff Nellis; Sound, Tori Meyer; Casting, Stephanie Klapper & Associates; SM, Tony Dearing; ASM, Mary Jane Probst; Cast: Jason Babinsky (Dromio of Ephesus), Omar Evans (Dromio of Syracuse), Jake Mosser (Antipholus of Syracuse), Jason Veasey (Antipholus of Ephesus), DJ Spae a.k.a. Jordan Connors (DJ); November 14–December 9, 2007

The Imaginary Theatre Company

THE ANT AND THE GRASSHOPPER Book, music and lyrics by Brian Hohlfeld; Director, Jeffery Matthews; Set and Costumes, Lou Bird; Musical Director, Neal Richardson; SM, Sarah Allison; Director of Education, Marsha Coplon; Artistic Supervisor, Jeffery Matthews; Cast: Meghan Brown (Mother Ant), Jason Contini (Father Ant), Maria Tholl (Little Ant), Chauncy Thomas (Grasshopper); Touring Company; November 5, 2007–April 5, 2008

MYTH ADVENTURES by Kim Esop Wylie; Director, Kat Singleton; Set, Lou Bird; Costumes, Betsy Krausnick; SM, Sarah Allison; Director of Education, Marsha Coplon; Artistic Supervisor, Jeffery Matthews; Cast: Meghan Brown (Pandora), Jason Contini (Midas), Maria Tholl (Persephone), Chauncy Thomas (Zeus); Touring Company; November 5, 2007–April 5, 2008

San Jose Repertory Theatre

San Jose, California

TWENTY-SEVENTH SEASON

Senior Artistic Advisor, Timothy Near; Managing Director, Nick Nichols

ELLA by Jeffrey Hatcher, conceived by Rob Ruggiero and Dyke Garrison; Director, Rob Ruggiero; Musical Director/Arrangements, Danny Holgate; Set, Michael Schweikardt; Costumes, Alejo Vietti; Lighting, John Lasiter; Sound, Michael Miceli; PSM, Laxmi Kumaran; ASM, Jenessa Schwartz; Cast: Tina Fabrique (Ella Fitzgerald), George Caldwell (Jimmy/piano/Conductor), Brian Sledge (Donny/trumpet), Rodney Harper ("Sticks" Fletcher/drums), Clifton Kellem (Sam/bass), Harold Dixon (Norman Granz); June 23–July 22, 2007

THE TRIUMPH OF LOVE by Pierre Marivaux, translated by Frederick Kluck, adapted and directed by Lillian Groag; Co production with California Shakespeare Theater; Set, Kate Edmunds; Costumes, Raquel Barreto; Lighting, Russell Champa; Sound, Jeff Mockus; PSM, Laxmi Kumaran; ASM,

Peter Royston; Cast: Ron Campbell (Dimas), Catherine Castellanos (Corine/Hermidas), Dan Hiatt (Hermocrates), Domenique Lozano (Leontine), Stacy Ross (Leonide/Phocion), Danny Scheie (Arlecchino), Jud Williford (Agis); World Premiere Adaptation, September 22–October 21, 2007

THIS WONDERFUL LIFE by Steve Murray; Director, Kirsten Brandt; Set, Robin Roberts; Costumes, Brandin Baron; Lighting, David Lee Cuthbert; Sound, Jeff Mockus; PSM, Laxmi Kumaran; ASM, Melissa Berkson; Cast: Dan Hiatt (All Characters); Regional Premiere, November 24–December 23, 2007

TRANCED by Robert Clyman; Director, Barbara Damashek; Set, Kris Stone; Costumes, B Modern; Lighting, Daniel Ordower; Sound, Jeff Mockus; PSM, Laxmi Kumaran; ASM, Melissa Berkson; Cast: Kenya Brome (Azmera), James Carpenter (Logan), Thom Rivera (Philip), Stacy Ross (Beth); Regional Premiere, January 26–February 24, 2008

SOUVENIR by Stephen Temperley; Director, R. Hamilton Wright; Set, Edie Whitsett; Costumes, Marcia Dixcy Jory; Lighting, Rick Paulsen; Sound, Steve Schoenbeck; PSM, Laxmi Kumaran; ASM, Melissa Berkson; Cast: Mark Anders (Cosme McMoon), Patti Cohenour (Florence Foster Jenkins); Regional Premiere, March 22–April 20, 2008

DR. JEKYLL AND MR. HYDE by Jeffery Hatcher, based on the novella by Robert Louis Stevenson; Director, David Ira Goldstein; Co-Produced with Arizona Theatre Company; Set, Kent Dorsey; Costumes, Anna Oliver; Lighting, Dawn Chiang; Sound, Brian Jerome Peterson; Composer, Roberta Carlson; Fight Director, Ken Merckx; Cast: Hamilton Wright (Dr. Henry Jekyll), Ken Ruta (Edward Hyde/Gabriel Utterson), Stephen D'Ambrose (Edward Hyde/Sir Danvers Carew/Richard Enfield/O.F. Sanderson/Inspector) Mark Anderson Phillips (Edward Hyde/Dr. H. K. Lanyon/Police Doctor/Surgical Student), Carrie Paff (Edward Hyde/Poole/Surgical Student/Police Doctor), Anna Bullard (Elizabeth Jelkes), Alan Kaiser & Danielle Perata (Orderlies); World Premiere; May 10–June 8, 2008

Seattle Repertory Theatre

Seattle, Washington

FORTY-FIFTH SEASON

Artistic Director, David Esbjornson; Managing Director, Benjamin Moore

TWELFTH NIGHT by William Shakespeare; Director, David Esbjornson; Set, Michael Pavelka; Costumes, Frances Kenny; Lighting, Scott Zilinski; Composer, Wayne Barker; Sound, Ken Travis; Dialects, Deborah Hecht; Fight Choreographer, Geoff Alm; Casting, Jerry Beaver; SM, Jennifer Shenker, ASM, Stina Lotti; Cast: Barzin Akhavan (Orsinio), Jacob Blumer (Sebastian), Christine Marie Brown (Viola), Cheyenne Casebier (Olivia), Bradford Farwell (Valentine), Nick Garrison (Fabian), Charles Leggett (Sir Toby Belch), Andrew McGinn (Sir Andrew Aguecheek), Mari Nelson (Maria), David Pichette (Feste), MJ Sieber (Antonio), Frank X (Malvolio), Brandon Whitehead (Captain/Priest); September 13–October 20, 2007

MURDERERS by Jeffrey Hatcher; Director, Steven Dietz; Set, Carey Wong; Costumes, Susan E. Mickey; Lighting, Rick Paulsen; Sound, Eric Chapelle; SM, Cristine Anne Reynolds; Cast: Mark Anders (Gerald Halvorson), Sarah Rudinoff (Minka Lupino), Joan Porter Hollander (Lucy Stickler); October 4–November 4, 2007

THE COOK by Eduardo Machado; Director, Juliette Carrillo; Set, Mikikp Suzuki McAdams; Costumes, Elizabeth Hope Clancy; Lighting, Geoff Korf; Composer, Chris Webb; Cast: Al Espinosa (Carlos), Yetta Gottesman (Adria/Lourdes), Zabryna Guevara (Gladys), A.K. Murtadha (Julio), Jessica Pimental (Elena/Rosa); November 1–December 1, 2007

BIRDIE BLUE by Cheryl L. West; Director, Chuck Smith. Set, Carey Wong; Dramaturg, Christine Sumption; Costumes, Frances Kenny; Lighting, Greg Sullivan; Sound, Christopher Walker; Fight Choreographer, Geoffrey Alm; SM, Stina Lotti; Cast: Velma Austin (Birdie), Sean Blake (Bam/Sook/Little Pimp/Minerva), William Hall Jr. (Jackson); November 15–December 16, 2007

BACK HOME AGAIN: A John Denver Holiday Concert Co-written and musical direction by Dan Wheetman, co-written and directed by Randal Myler; Lighting, Don Darnutzer, Projections, Jeffrey Cady; Sound, Eric Stahlhammer; Production Supervisor, Michael B. Paul; Sound Mixer, Mike Paul; Cast: Gail Bliss (Vocalist), Denny Brooks, Nova Devoni, Dan Wheetman, David Miles Keenan (Musicians); December 5–December 24, 2007

THE BREACH by Catherine Filloux, Tarrell McCraney and Joe Sutton; Director, David Esbjornson; Sets, Dana Perreault; Costumes, Elizabeth Hope Clancy; Lighting, Jim Ingalls; Composer, Mark Bennett; Choreographer, Sonia Dawkins; Projections, LB Morse; Fight Choreographer, Geoff Alm; SM, Elisabeth Farwell; ASM, Amy Poisson; Cast: John Aylward (Mac), Michelove René Bain (Quan), Michael Braun (Lynch), Kelly Conway (Francis), Crystal Fox (Linda), William Hall, Jr. (Pere Leon), Nike Imoru (Water), Hubert Point-Du Jour (Severence), Michele Shay (Woman); January 10–February 9, 2008

BY THE WATERS OF BABYLON by Robert Schenkkan; Director, Richard Seyd; Set, Michael Ganio; Costumes, Frances Kenny; Lighting, York Kennedy; Sound, Christopher Walker; Choreographer, Olivier Wevers; Dialects, Judith Shahn; Projections, Peter Bjordahl; SM, JR Welden; Cast: Armando Duran (Arturo), Suzanne Bouchard (Catherine); January 31–March 2, 2008

THE IMAGINARY INVALID by Moliére, adapted by Constance Congdon; Director, David Schweizer; Set, Riccardo Hernandez; Costumes, David Woolard; Lighting, Alexander

V. Nichols, Sound, Matt Starritt; Composer, Eyving Kang; Choreographer, Wade Madsen; SM, Michael John Egan; ASM, Jessica Bomball; Cast: Ian Bell (Claude de Aria), Julie Briskman (Beline), Bradford Farwell (Monsieur de Bonnefoi), David Pichette (Dr. Purgeon), Alice Playten (Toinette), Rocco Sisto (Argan), Andrew William Smith (Cleante), Zoë Winters (Angelique), Brandon Whitehead (Monsieur Fleurant); February 21–March 22, 2008

HOW? HOW? WHY? WHY? WHY? by Kevin Kling; Director, David Esbjornson; Sound, Eric Chappelle; Lighting, Jessica Trundy; SM, Amy Poisson; Cast: Kevin Kling with Simone Perrin on Accordion; March 13–April 19, 2008

THE CURE AT TROY by Seamus Heaney; Director, Tina Landau; Set, Blythe Quinlan; Costumes, Anita Yavich; Lighting, Scott Zielinski; Sound, Josh Schmidt; SM, Elisabeth Farwell; ASM, Lori Amondson Flint; Cast: Guy Adkins (Chorus), Hans Altwies (Odysseus), Ben Gonio (Chorus), Jon Hill (Chorus), Boris McGiver (Philoctetes), Seth Numrich (Neoptolemus); April 3–May 3, 2008

Shakespeare Theatre Comapny

Washington, D.C.

TWENTY-SECOND SEASON

Artistic Director, Michael Kahn

THE TAMING OF THE SHREW by William Shakespeare; Director, Rebecca Bayla Taichman; Set, Narelle Sissons; Costumes, Miranda Hoffman; Lighting, Robert Wierzel; Sound, Daniel Baker & Ryan Rumery; Vocal Coach, Deena Burke; Choreographer, Seán Curran; Fight Director, Rick Sordelet; Assistant Fight Director, Drew Vidal; Assistant Director, Paul Takacs; Literary Associate, Akiva Fox; SM, Sarah Bierenbaum; ASM, Rebecca Berlin; Cast: Nicholas Hormann (Baptista Minola), Charlayne Woodard (Katherina), Christopher Innvar (Petruchio), Lisa Birnbaum (Bianca), Louis Butelli (Grumio), Aubrey K. Deeker (Hortensio), J. Fred Shiffman (Gremio), Michael Milligan (Lucentio), Bruce Nelson (Tranio), Todd Scofield (Biondello), Bill Hamlin (Vincentio/Tailor), Drew Eshelman (A Pedant of Mantua), Erika Rose (Curtis); Ensemble: Wyckham Avery, Andy English, Sean Michael Fraser, Nick Vienna; Lansburgh Theatre; September 25–November 25, 2007

EDWARD II by Christopher Marlowe; Director, Gale Edwards; Set, Lee Savage; Costumes, Murell Horton; Lighting, Mark McCullough; Sound, Phillip Scott Peglow; Voice/Text Coach, Ellen O'Brien; Choreographer, Daniel Pelzig; Fight Director, Rick Sordelet; Assistant Fight Director, Drew Vidal; Assistant Director, Alexander Burns; Directorial Assistant, Alan Paul; Literary Associate, Akiva Fox; Resident SM, M. William Shiner; SM, Jeremy B. Wilcox; Cast: Wallace Acton (Edward II), Vayu O'Donnell (Piers Gaveston), Deanne Lorette (Isabella), Andrew Long (Mortimer), Jay Whittaker (Edmund of Kent), Jonathan Earl Peck (Lancaster), David McCann (Warwick), James Denvil (Pembroke), Scott Jaeck (Archbishop of Canterbury), Danyon Davis (Spencer), Amy Kim Waschke (Margaret de Clare), Kurt Uy (Baldock), Terence Archie (Arundel), Michael Bunting (Young Prince Edward), Chris Crawford (Edward III), John Lescault (Bishop of Coventry/Abbott), James Konicek (Lightborn), David Emerson Toney (Spencer Senior), Craig Wallace (Rice ap Howell), Floyd King (Sir John Hainault), Robert Jason Jackson (Leicester), David Sabin (Mortimer Senior), Franchelle Stewart Dorn (Baroness), Christopher Marino (Matrevis), Blake DeLong (Gurney), Adriano Gatto (Beaumont), Jefferson A. Russell (Levune), JJ Area (James), Kenric Green (Captain to Mortimer); Ensemble: Abe Cruz, Austin Herzing, Anthony Jackson, Jair Kamperveen, Kaitlin Manning, Kaytie Morris, Kevin Pierson and Majed Sayess; Sidney Harman Hall; October 27, 2007–January 6, 2008

TAMBURLAINE by Christopher Marlowe, adapted and directed by Michael Kahn; Set, Lee Savage; Costumes, Jennifer Moeller; Lighting, Mark McCullough; Voice/Text Coach, Ellen O'Brien; Fight Director, Rick Sordelet; Assistant Fight Director, Drew Vidal; Resident Assistant Director, Stephen Fried; Directorial Assistant, Alan Paul; Literary Associate, Akiva Fox; Resident SM, M. William Shiner; SM, Benjamin Royer; Cast: Avery Books (Tamburlaine), Craig Wallace (Usumcasane), Terence Archie (Calyphas), Kurt Uy (Amyras), Abe Cruz (Celebinus/Ensemble), Floyd King (Mycetes/Christian Priest), Andrew Long (Cosroe), Scott Jaeck (Theridamas), David Emerson Toney (Meander/Sultan of Egypt/A Muslim Cleric), James Denvil (Menaphon/King of Jerusalem), Jonathan Earl Peck (Ortygius/Orcanes), John Lescault (Persian Lord/King of Fez/Governor of Babylon), Christopher Marino (Persian Lord/King of Argier/King of Soria), Vayu O'Donnell (Persian Lord), Jefferson A. Russell (Persian Lord/King of Morocco-Turkish General), Mia Tagano (Zenocrate), Robert Jason Jackson (Agydas/Egyptian General/Almeda), James Konicek (A Median Lord/Turkish Lord/Turkish General), Amy Kim Waschke (Anippe), David Sabin (Governor of Damascus), Kaytie Morris (Virgin of Damascus/Ensemble), Kaitlin Manning (Virgin of Damascus/Ensemble), Deanne Lorette (Virgin of Damascus/Ebea), David McCann (Bajazeth/Sigismund/Physician), Franchelle Stewart Dorn (Zabina), Jeremy Pryzby (Young Callapine), Jay Whittaker (Adult Callapine) Ensemble: JJ Area, Chris Crawford, Blake DeLong, Adriano Gatto, Kenric Green, Austin Herzing, Anthony Jackson, Jair Kamperveen, Kevin Pierson, Majed Sayess; Sidney Harman Hall; October 30, 2007–January 6, 2008

ARGONAUTIKA Written and directed by Mary Zimmerman, adapted from *The Voyage of Jason and the Argonauts*; Set, Daniel Ostling; Costumes, Ana Kuzmanic; Lighting, John Culbert; Sound, Andre Pluess and Ben Sussman; Pupperty, Michael Montenegro; Directorial Assistant, Alan Paul; SM, M. William Shiner; ASM, Benjamin Royer; Cast: Jake Suffian (Jason), Soren Oliver (Hercules/Aietes), Andy Murray (Meleager), Justin Blanchard (Hylas/Dymas), Allen Gilmore (Perlias), Jesse J. Perez (Idmon), Liza Tejero (Hera), Sofia Jean Gomez (Athena),

Tessa Klein (Aphrodite), Ronete Levenson (Andromeda), Atley Loughridge (Medea), Casey Jackson (Pollux), Chris Kipiniak (Casto), Jason Vande Brake (Amycus); Lansburgh Theatre; January 15–March 2, 2008

MAJOR BARBARA by George Bernard Shaw; Director, Ethan McSweeny; Set, James Noone; Costumes, Robert Perdziola; Lighting, Robert Wierzel; Sound, David Maddox; Resident Assistant Director, Stephen Fried; Literary Associate, Akiva Fox; SM, James Latus; ASM, Cary Louise Gillett; Cast: Helen Carey (Lady Britomart Undershaft), Tom Story (Stephen Undershaft), Vivienne Benesch (Major Barbara Undershaft), Leah Curney (Sarah Undershaft), Karl Kenzler (Adolphus Cusins), Kevin O'Donnell (Charles Lomax), Leo Erickson (Morrison), Ted van Griethuysen (Andrew Undershaft), Catherine Flye (Rummy Mitchens), James Ricks (Snobby Price), Tiffany Fillmroe (Jenny Hill), Floyd King (Peter Shirley), Andrew Long (Bill Walker), Jennifer Mendenhall (Mrs. Baines), Blake DeLong (Bilton/Ensemble); Ensemble: Adriano Gatto, Kenric Green, Austin Herzing, Kaitlin Manning, Kaytie Morris, Kevin Pierson; Sidney Harman Hall; February 19–March 23, 2008

ANTONY AND CLEOPATRA by William Shakespeare; Director, Michael Kahn; Cast: Andrew Long (Mark Antony), Suzanne Bertish (Cleopatra), Aubrey Deeker (Octavius Caesar), Ted van Griethuysen (Lepidus), Craig Wallace (Pompey), Dan Kremer (Enobarbus), Michael Sharon (Canidius), John Michael Marrs (Eros), Ethan Bowen (Scarus), Glen Pannell (Maecenas), Dean Nolen (Agrippa), Tom Hammond (Dolabella), Jan Knightley (Proculeius), Tyrone M. Henderson (Thidias), Ethan Bowen (Menas), Kaytie Morris (Octavia), Kurt Rhoads (Ventidius), Kim Martin Cotton (Charmian), Nancy Rodriguez (Iras), Robert Jason Jackson (Alexas), Peter Stray (Mardian), Kryetov Lindquis (Soothsayer); Ensemble: Adriano Gatto, Kenric Green, Richard Huffman, Jair Kamperveen, Craig Klein, Steve Lotterman, Kaitlin Manning, Kaytie Morris, Kevin Pierson, Cameron Pippitt, Armand Sindoni, James Svatko, Matt Volner, S. Matthew Wilburn, Brian Clarke, Blake DeLong, Catherine Frels; Sidney Harman Hall; April 26–July 6, 2008

JULIUS CAESAR by William Shakespeare; Director, David Muse; Set, James Noone; Costumes, Jennifer Moeller; Lighting, Mark McCullough; Original Music, Martin Desjardins; Sound, Daniel Baker; Voice and Text, Gary Logan and Ellen O'Brien; Assistant Director, David Paul; Literary Associate, Akiva Fox; Resident SM, M. William Shiner; SM, Jeremy B. Wilcox; Associate Casting, Merry Alderman; Production Assistant, Jeremiah Mullane; Cast: Dan Kremer (Julius Caesar), Tom Hammond (Brutus), Andrew Long (Mark Antony), Scott Parkinson (Cassius), Aubrey Deeker (Octavius Caesar), Nancy Rodriguez (Portia), Ted van Griethuysen (Lepidus/Cobbler), J. Garrett Brennan (Lucius), Robert Jason Jackson (Cicero), Kurt Rhoads (Cinna/Messala), Kim Martin-Cotton (Calphurnia), Tyrone M. Henderson (Thidias/Metellus Cimber), Glen Pannell (Decius Brutus), Craig Wallace (Caius Ligarius/Lucilius), Michael Sharon (Murellus), Ethan Bowen (Scarus), Kryztov Lindquist (Soothsayer), Peter Stray (Cinna the Poet), Dean Nolen (Casca), Jan Knightley (Pindarus); Ensemble: John Brennan, Brian Clarke, Blake DeLong, Catherine Frels, Adriano Gatto, Kenric Green, Richard Huffman, Jair Kamperveen, Craig Klein, Steve Lotterman, Kaitlin Manning, Kaytie Morris, Steve Nixon, Kevin Pierson, Cameron Pippitt, Armand Sindoni, James Svatko, Matt Volner, S. Matthew Wilburn (Ensemble); Sidney Harman Hall; April 27–July 6, 2008

THE IMAGINARY INVALID by Molière, adapted by Alan Drury; Director, Keith Baxter; Music Director/Composer, Barbara Irvine; Musical Staging, Gillian Lynne; Sets, Simon Higlett; Costumes, Robert Perdziola; Lighting, Peter West; Sound, Martin Desjardins; Text Consultant, Ellen O'Brien; Cast: René Auberjonois (Argan), Nancy Robinette (Toinette), Gia Mora (Angélique), Kaitlin O'Neal (Beline), Tony Roach (Cléante), Drew Eshelman (Bonnefoi/Mr. Purgon), Vince Eisenson (Valere), Levi Ben-Israeil (Thomas Diafoirus), Peter Land (Punchinello, David Manis (Mr. Fleurant/Sganarelle), Ian Pedersen, Kara Quick (Lucille), Todd Scofield (Gros-Rene), Anne Stone (Flora/Sabine/Aunt), John Robert Tillotson (Dr. Diafoirus/Gorgibus), Emily Whitworth (Louisson), Ian Pedersen (Little Boy); Ensemble: Leslie Sarah Cohen, Danielle Davy, Chris Dinolfo, Marissa Molnar; Lansburgh Theatre; June 10–July 27, 2008

South Coast Repertory

Costa Mesa, California

FORTY-FOURTH SEASON

Producing Artistic Director, David Emmes; Artistic Director, Martin Benson; Managing Director, Paula Tomei

A LITTLE NIGHT MUSIC Book by Hugh Wheeler, music and lyrics by Stephen Sondheim; suggested by a film by Ingmar Berman; originally produced and directed on Broadway by Harold Prince; Director, Stefan Novinski; Choreographer, Ken Roht; Set, Sibyl Wickersheimer; Costumes, Shigeru Yaji; Lighting, Christopher Akerlind; Sound, Drew Dalzell; Cast: Christopher Carothers (Mr. Lindquist), Misty Cotton (Petra), Karen Culliver (Mrs. Nordstrom), Katie Horwitch (Fredrika Armfeldt), Joe Farrell (Henrik Egerman), Mark Jacoby (Fredrik Egerman), Damon Kirsche (Count Carl-Magnus Malcolm), Ann Marie Lee (Mrs. Anderssen), Tracy Lore (Mrs. Segstrom), Branden McDonald (Frid), Kevin McMahon (Mr. Erlanson), Amanda Naughton (Countess Charlotte Malcolm), Teri Ralston (Madame Armfeldt), Carolann Sanita (Anne Egerman), Stephanie Zimbalist (Desirée Armfeldt); Segerstrom Stage; September 7–October 7, 2007

SHIPWRECKED! AN ENTERTAINMENT – The Amazing Adventures of Louis de Rougemont (As Told by Himself) by Donald Margulies; Director, Bart DeLorenzo; Set, Keithe Mitchell; Costumes, Candice Cain; Lighting, Rand Ryan; Sound and Original Music, Steven Cahill; Shadow Set, Christine Marie; Dramaturg, John Glore; Cast: Melody Butiu

(Player One), Michael Daniel Cassady (Player Two), Gregory Itzin (Louis de Rougemont); World Premiere, Julianne Argyros Stage, September 23–October 14, 2007

DOUBT by John Patrick Shanley; Director, Martin Benson; Set, Thomas Buderwitz; Costumes, Angela Balogh Calin; Lighting, Lonnie Rafael Alcaraz; Sound, Tom Cavnar; Cast: Linda Gehringer (Sister Aloysius Beauvier), Rebecca Mozo (Sister James), James Joseph O'Neil (Father Brendan Flynn), Kimberly Scott (Mrs. Muller); Segerstrom Stage, October 19–November 18, 2007

A CHRISTMAS CAROL by Charles Dickens, adapted by Jerry Patch; 28th Annual Production; Director, John-David Keller; Choreographer, Linda Kostalik; Set, Thomas Buderwitz; Costumes, Dwight Richard Odle; Lighting, Donna & Tom Ruzika; Sound, Drew Dalzell; Music Arrangement and Composer, Dennis McCarthy; Vocal Director, Dennis Castellano; Assistant Director, Hisa Takakuwa; Cast: Nathan Baesel (Fred/Gentleman), Daniel Blinkoff (Bob Cratchit), Jennifer Chu (Lena/Belle/Scavenger), Richard Doyle (Solicitor/Spirit of Christmas Past/Gentleman), Karen Hensel (Mrs. Fezziwig/Solicitor), John-David Keller (Mr. Fezziwig/ Gentleman), Art Koustik (Joe/Ensemble), Timothy Landfield (Spirit of Christmas Present), Hal Landon Jr. (Ebenezer Scrooge), Ann Marie Lee (Toy Lady/Sally/Scavenger), Jennifer Parsons (Mrs. Cratchit), Joe Quintero (Undertaker/ Young Ebenezer), Tom Shelton (Marley/Spirit of Christmas Yet-to-Come); Ensemble and Children: Sean Durrie, Jessie Kim, Branden McDonald, Bryan Vickery; Anita Abdi, Brenna Barker, Brianna Beach, Kamisha Brooks, Parker Cohn, Zachary Diamond, Gracie Gordon, Nickolas Johnston, Pranav Mutatker, Matthew Pancoe, Karoline Ribak, Jason Risdana, Lauren Speakman, Phillip Swanson, Jacob Waller, Renée Waller; Segerstrom Stage; November 24– December 24, 2007

LA POSADA MÁGICA (The Magical Journey) Written and directed by Octavio Solis, music by Marcos Loya; 14th Annual Production; Choreographer, Linda Kostalik; Set, Christopher Acebo; Costumes, Shigeru Yaji; Lighting, Lonnie Rafael Alcaraz; Musical Director, Marcos Loya; Cast: Denise Blasor (Consuelo/Widow), Danny Bolero (Papi/Jose Cruz), Sol Castillo (Refugio/Buzzard), David DeSantos (Eli/Bones/ Lauro), Gloria Garayua (Gracie), Marcos Loya (Musician/ Ensemble), Lorenzo Martinez (Musician/Ensemble), Miguel Najera (Horacio), Erica Ortega (Mariluz/Mom), Teresa Velarde (Caridad/Widow); Julianne Argyros Stage; December 7–23, 2007

A FEMININE ENDING by Sarah Treem; Produced in association with Portland Center Stage; Director, Timothy Douglas; Set, Tony Cisek; Costumes, Candice Cain; Lighting, Peter Maradudin; Sound, Colbert S. Davis IV; Composer, Vincent Olivieri; Assistant Director, Scott Bishop; Cast: Amy Aquino (Kim), Brooke Bloom (Amanda), Alan Blumenfeld (David), Peter Katona (Jack), Jedadiah Schultz (Billy); West Coast Premiere; Julianne Argyros Stage; January 6–27, 2008.

THE IMPORTANCE OF BEING EARNEST by Oscar Wilde; Director, Warner Shook; Set, Michael Olich; Costumes, Nephelie Andonyadis; Lighting, Lap-Chi Chu; Original Music and Music Direction, Michael Roth; Dialects, Philip D. Thompson; Cast: Christine Marie Brown (Gwendolen Fairfax), Kandis Chappell (Lady Bracknell), Richard Doyle (Rev. Canon Chasuble), Michael Gotch (Algernon Moncrieff), Elise Hunt (Cecily Cardew), John-David Keller (Merriman/Lane), Tommy Schrider (Jack Worthington), Bryan Vickery (Footman/ Ensemble) and Amelia White (Miss Prism); Segerstrom Stage; February 8–March 9, 2008

CULTURE CLASH IN AMERICA Created, written and performed by Culture Clash: Richard Montoya, Ric Salinas & Herbert Siguenza; Director, David Emmes; Set and Costume Consultant, Angela Balogh Calin, Lighting, Lonnie Rafael Alcaraz; Sound, B.C. Keller; Julianne Argyros Stage; March 16–April 6, 2008

WHAT THEY HAVE by Kate Robin; Director, Chris Fields; Set, Christopher Barreca; Costumes, Alex Jaeger; Lighting, Lap-Chi Chu; Original Music and Music Direction, Michael Roth; Dramaturg, Megan Monahan; Cast: Nancy Bell (Suzanne), Marin Hinkle (Connie), Matt Letscher (Jonas), Kevin Rahm (Matt); World Premiere; Segerstrom Stage; April 4–May 4, 2008

THE INJURED PARTY by Richard Greenberg; Director, Trip Cullman; Set, David Korins; Costumes, Candice Cain; Lighting, Ben Stanton; Original Music and Music Direction, John Gromada; Cast: T. Scott Cunningham (Lawrence), Cynthia Harris (Maxene), Marin Ireland (Becca), Caroline Lagerfelt (Bettina), Lorenzo Pisoni (Multiple Roles), Reg Rogers (Seth); World Premiere, Julianne Argyros Stage; April 20–May 11, 2008

2008 PACIFIC PLAYWRIGHTS FESTIVAL Included: *Sunlight* by Sharr White; Director, David Emmes; Workshop Production; Nicholas Studio, May 2–4, 2008; *By the Way, Meet Vera Stark* by Lynn Nottage; Director, Mark Rucker; Staged Reading; Segerstrom Stage; May 2, 2008; *Emilie – The Marquise du Châtelet Defends Her Life at the Petit Théâtre at Cirey Tonight* by Lauren Gunderson; Director, Kate Whoriskey; Staged Reading; Julianne Argyros Stage; May 2, 2008; *Goldfish* by John Kolvenbach; Director, Loretta Greco; Staged Reading; Segerstrom Stage; May 3, 2008; *You, Nero* by Amy Freed; Director, Sharon Ott; Staged Reading; Segerstrom Stage; May 4, 2008

TAKING STEPS by Alan Ayckbourn; Director, Art Manke; Set, Ralph Funicello; Costumes, Maggie Morgan; Lighting, Geoff Korf; Cast: Bill Brochtrup (Mark), Emily Eiden (Kitty), Louis Lotorto (Leslie), Kasey Mahaffy (Tristram), Rob Nagle (Roland) and Kristen Potter (Elizabeth); Segerstrom Stage; May 16–June 15, 2008

Theatre for Young Audiences

THE BFG (Big Friendly Giant) by Roald Dahl; adapted by David Wood; Director, Anne Justine D'Zmura; Set, Nephelie

Andonyadis; Costumes, Angela Balogh Calin; Lighting, Christina L. Munich; Sound, Tom Cavnar; Puppets, Aaron Cromie; Cast: Larry Bates, David DeSantos, Dawn-Lyen Gardner, Kate James, Louis Lotorto, Preston Maybank, Jennifer Parsons, Amy Tolsky; Julianne Argyros Stage; November 2–18, 2007

CHARLOTTE'S WEB by E.B. White, adapted by Joseph Robinette; Director, Shelley Butler; Set, Sibyl Wickersheimer; Costumes, Paloma Helena Young; Lighting, Sara Broadhead; Sound, Tom Cavnar; Cast: Guilford Adams, Diana Burbano, Sol Castillo, Jennifer Chang, Pamela Shaddock; Julianne Argyros Stage; Febraury 8–24, 2008

IMAGINE by Doug Cooney; Director, Stefan Novinski; Set, Donna Marget; Costumes, Angela Calin; Lighting, Tom Ruzika; Sound, Drew Dalzell; Music Director, Deborah Wicks La Puma; Choreography, Sara Wilber; Cast: Meaghan Boeing, Diana Burbano, Dawn-Lyen Gardner, Jamey Hood, James Michael Lambert, Brett Ryback; May 30–June 15, 2008

Steppenwolf Theatre Company

Chicago, Illinois

THIRTY-SECOND SEASON

Artistic Director, Martha Lavey; Artistic Director, David Hawkanson

THE CRUCIBLE by Arthur Miller; Director, Anna D. Shapiro; Set, Todd Rosenthal; Costumes, Virgil C. Johnson; Lighting, Don Holder; Sound, Michael Bodeen & Rob Milburn; Assistant Director, David Kersnar; SM, Michelle Medvin; ASM, Lauren V. Hickman; Cast: Alana Arenas, Ian Barford, Francis Guinan, Tim Hopper, Ora Jones, James Vincent Meredith, Sally Murphy, Austin Pendleton, Alan Wilder, Lucy Carapetyan, Maury Cooper, Justin James Farley, Chike Johnson, Leonard Kraft, Mildred Marie Langford, John Lister, Ginger Lee McDermott, Kelly O'Sullivan, Tim Edward Rhoze, Mary Seibel, Philip R. Smith, Rebecca Spence, Lee Stark; Downstairs Theatre; September 13–November 18, 2007

THE ELEPHANT MAN by Bernard Pomerance; Director, Sean Graney; Set, Marcus Stephens; Costumes, Alison Siple; Lighting, Keith Parham; Sound, Kevin O'Donnell; Dramaturg, Libby Ford; SM, Shelia Schmidt; Cast: Rom Barkhordar, Thomas J. Cox, Kurt Ehrmann, Kirsten Fitzgerald, Erik Hellman, Lily Mojekwu, Michael Patrick Thornton; Downstairs Theatre (Steppenwolf for Young Adults); October 20–November 4, 2007

365 DAYS/365 PLAYS–Week 52 by Suzan-Lori Parks; Directors, Jay Geneske, J.R. Lederle, Stephen Mazurek, Sam Porretta, Brant Russell, Galina Shevchenko, Jessica Thebus, Saverio Truglia & Dave Urlakis; Sound, Noelle Hoffman, Miles Polaski & Edward Reardon; Flash, Felix Jung; Coats, Mikalina Rabinsky; Project Producers, Brant Russell & Dave Urlakis; Cast: Francis Guinan, Ray Baker, Bonnie Bandurski, Seth Bockley, Jasmin Cardenas, Amy J. Carle, Lucas Crawford, Cary Cronholm, Adrienne Day, Julia Dossett, Eric Evenskaas, Libby Ford, James Ford, Ana Gagliardi, Rick Haefele, Jamie Hayes, Lindsey Hedge, Tom Horan, Luis Ibarra, Elizabeth Levy, Anthony Martinez, Elizabeth McKnight, Jessica Moran, David New, Nina O'Keefe, Leah Rose Orleans, Jill Paider, James Palmer, Miles Polaski, Sam Porretta, Edward Reardon, Jan Rose, Kathy Scambiatterra, Galina Shevchenko, Dave Urlakis, John Zinn; Online Multimedia; November 5–12, 2007

GOOD BOYS AND TRUE by Roberto Aguirre-Sacasa; Director, Pam MacKinnon; Set, Todd Rosenthal; Costumes, Nan Cibula-Jenkins; Lighting, Ann Wrightson; Original Music, Rob Milburn; Sound, Michael Bodeen; Dramaturg, Edward Sobel; SM, Christine D. Freeburg; ASM, Jonathan Templeton; Cast: Martha Lavey, Stephen Louis Grush, Nick Horst, Mark Minton, Kelly O'Sullivan, John Procaccino, Trevor Reusch, Tim Rock, Kelli Simpkins; Upstairs Theatre; December 12, 2007–February 16, 2008

HARRIET JACOBS by Lydia R. Diamond; Director, Hallie Gordon; Choreographer, Lisa Johnson-Willingham; Set, Collette Pollard; Costume, Ana Kuzmanic; Lighting, J.R. Lederle; Original Music, McKinley Johnson; Sound, Victoria Delorio; SM, Calyn P. Swain; Dramaturg, Jocelyn Prince; Cast: Christoph Horton Abiel, Kenn E. Head, Errón Jay, Nambi E. Kelley, Leslie Ann Sheppard, Genevieve VenJohnson, Sean Walton, Celeste Williams; Upstairs Theatre (Steppenwolf for Young Adults); February 8–March 2, 2008

CARTER'S WAY by Eric Simonson; Director, Eric Simonson; Set, Neil Patel; Costumes, Karin Kopischke; Lighting, Keith Parham; Original Music, Darrell Leonard; Sound, Barry G. Funderburg; Dramaturg, Edward Sobel; Assistant Director, Megan Schuchman; SM, Malcolm Ewen; ASM, Lauren V. Hickman; Cast: Robert Breuler, K. Todd Freeman, Ora Jones, James Vincent Meredith, Anne Adams, Scott Cummins, Calvin Dutton, Curtis M. Jackson, Keith Kupferer, Michael Pogue; Downstairs Theatre; February 28–April 27, 2008

DEAD MAN'S CELL PHONE by Sarah Ruhl; Director, Jessica Thebus; Set, Scott Bradley; Costumes, Linda Roethke; Lighting, James F. Ingalls; Original Music, Andre Pluess & Ben Sussman; SM, Christine D. Freeburg; ASM, Michelle Medvin; Cast: Molly Regan, Sarah Charipar, Marilyn Dodds Frank, Géraldine Dulex, Mary Beth Fisher, Coburn Goss, Marc Grapey, Polly Noonan, Ben Whiting; Upstairs Theatre; March 27–July 27, 2008

SUPERIOR DONUTS by Tracy Letts; Director, Tina Landau; Set, Loy Arcenas; Costumes, Ana Kuzmanic; Lighting, Christopher Akerlind; Original music/sound, Rob Milburn and Michael Bodeen; Dramaturg, Edward Sobel; SM, Laura Glenn; ASM, Lauren V. Hickman; Cast: Jon Hill, Yasen Peyankov, James Vincent Meredith; Downstairs Theatre; June 19–August 17, 2008

Steppenwolf Visiting Company Initiative

THE NUTCRACKER by Phillip C. Klapperich, Presented by The House Theatre of Chicago; Director/Choreographer, Tommy Rapley; Set, Collette Pollard; Costumes, Debbie Baer; Lighting, Ben Wilhelm; Sound, Scotty Iseri; Original Music, Kevin O'Donnell; Dramaturg, Kelly Kerwin; SM, Katie Beeks; ASM, Julia Dossett; Cast: Seth Bockley, Laura Grey, Joshua Holden, Fannie Hungerford, Maria McCullough, Ericka Ratcliffe, Geoff Rice, Michael Smith, Vanessa Stalling, Joey Steakley; Upstairs Theatre; November 13–December 29, 2007

WEDDING PLAY by Eric Rosen; Presented by About Face Theatre; Director, Eric Rosen; Cast: Kareem Bandealy, Lesley Bevan, Sean Cooper, Joe Dempsey, Craig Spidle, Benjamin Sprunger; Garage Theatre; October 24–December 2, 2007

SKETCHBOOK 2008 Included: *Bad News* Written and directed by Eric Ziegenhagen; Chicago Summer by Cassandra Sanders; Director, Scott Illingworth; *Cowboy Birthday Party* by Emily Schwartz; Director, Amanda Berg Wilson; *Count Orlock's Castle* by Gregory Moss; Director, Joel Moorman; Dated: *A Cautionary Tale For Facebook Users* by Ira Gamerman; Director, John Gawlik; *Fragment* conceived by and directed by Ann Boyd; Hackneyed by Greg Allen; Director, Jen Ellison; *Iâ#™S N UR B1UDStR33M C0ZIN FA60SIT0SIZ* by Sean Graney; Director; Michael Patrick Thorton; *The Lurker Radio Hour* by Drew Dir; Director, Karin Shook; *Parkersburg* by Laura Jacqmin; Director by Greg Allen; *Pie* by Mara Casey; Director, Marika Mashburn; *R UNHO ME TE DDY* by Jesse Weaver; Director, Cecilie Keenan; *Treadmills* by Itamar Moses, Director, Joanie Schultz; *Yellow* by Jose Rivera; Director, Adam Belcuore; Garage Theatre; May 15–June 15, 2008

Steppenwolf Traffic

I SING AMERICA by Various; Director, Jessica Thebus; Featuring Martha Lavey, John Mahoney, Yasen Peyankov, Cheryl Lynn Bruce, Daniel J. Bryant, Chicago Children's Choir, Josephine Lee and Penelope Walker; Millennium Park; September 6, 2007

AN EVENING WITH DAVID SEDARIS Featuring David Sedaris; Producer, Sylvia M. Ewing; SM, Michelle Medvin; Audio Engineer, Martha Wegner; Lighting Engineer, J.R .Lederle; Lighting Board Operator, Ernesto Gomez; Assistant Audio Engineer, Gregor Mortis; Master Electrician, Rich Bryant; Production Manager, Al Franklin; Assistant Production Manager, Johanna Cohan; Company Manager, Cat Tries; Sound, Katy Hite; Artistic Apprentice, Michael Vinson; Upstairs Theatre; January 8–13, 2008

THE POCKETBOOK MONOLOGUES by Sharon K. McGhee; Producer, Sylvia M. Ewing; SM, Michelle Medvin; Audio Engineer, Martha Wegner; Lighting Engineer, J.R .Lederle; Lighting Board Operator, Ernesto Gomez; Assistant Audio Engineer, Gregor Mortis; Master Electrician, Rich Bryant; Production Manager, Al Franklin; Assistant Production Manager, Johanna Cohan; Company Manager, Cat Tries; Sound Operator, Katy Hite; Artistic Apprentice, Michael Vinson; Cast: Ora Jones, Ramsey Carey, Kim Coles, Deborah Crable, Sharon K. McGhee, La Donna Tittle; Downstairs Theatre; January 14, 2008

A LEGACY OF JAZZ AND POETRY Producer, Sylvia M. Ewing; SM, Lauren V. Hickman; Company Manager, Cat Tries; Audio Engineer, Martha Wegener; Lighting Supervisor, J.R. Lederle; House Carpenter, Rick Haefele; Assistant Audio Engineer, Gregor Mortis; Master Electrician, Rich Bryant; Stage Carpenter, Dawn Przybylski; Artistic Apprentice, Michael Vinson; Featuring Jeff Baraka, Africa Brown, Maggie Brown, Duane Jones, Keith M. Kelley, Dexter Sims, Kwame Steve Cobb, Shawn Wallace; Downstairs Theatre; February 4, 2008

A CELEBRATION OF CHICAGO SKETCH COMEDY Producer, Sylvia M. Ewing; Featuring Inda Craig-Galvan, Kevin Douglas, Kate James, Justin Kaufmann, Sandy Marshall and Stephen Schmidt; Upstairs Theatre; April 14, 2008

TATSU AOKI'S MIYUMI PROJECT: East Meets the Rest Producer, Sylvia M. Ewing; Featuring Tatsu Aoki, Mwata Bowden, Jeff Chan, Jonathan Chen, Amy Homma, Cinatsu Nakano, Yoko Noge, Melody Takata, Joel Wanek, Francis Wong, Hide Yoshihashi and the Japanese American Service Committee's Tsukasa Taiko Youth; Downstairs Theatre; May 9, 2008

SONES DE MÉXICO ENSEMBLE: de corason "From the Heart" Producer, Sylvia M. Ewing; Featuring the Sones de México Ensemble; Downstairs Theatre; May 16, 2008

KUUMBA LYNX ENSEMBLE Producer, Sylvia M. Ewing; Featuring Urban Griots, Lil Bit and Baby Boo; Downstairs Theatre; May 22, 2008

TEACHER TALES: Stories from the Frontlines Producer, Sylvia M. Ewing; Featuring Dr. Robert Boone, Bill Ayers, Idris Goodwin, Amanda Klonsky, Toni Lightfoot, Billy Lombardo and Curie Youth Radio; Downstairs Theatre; June 1, 2008

Syracuse Stage

Syracuse, New York

THIRTY-FIFTH SEASON

Producing Artistic Director, Timothy Bond; Managing Director, Jeffrey Woodward

LES LIAISONS DANGEREUSES Written by Christopher Hampton from the novel by Choderlos de Laclos; Director, Robert Moss; Sets & Lighting, Steve Ten Eyck; Costumes, Tracy Dorman; Sound, Jonathan Herter; PSM, Stuart Plymesser; Casting, Alan Filderman; Fight Director/Movement Consultant, Anthony Salatino; Assistant Director/Drama League Directing Fellow, D. Wambui Richardson; Cast: Jessica Bues (Émilie), Kirstin Dahmer (Cécile), Rita Gardner (Madame de Rosamunde), Tom Garruto (Azolan), Susannah

Livingston (La Marquise de Merteuil), Lanie MacEwan (Madame de Volanges), Kelly Mares (Madame de Tourvel), Jared Michael Poulin (Various Servants), John G. Preston (Le Vicomte de Valmont), Matthew Stucky (Danceny); September 26–October 14, 2007

MISERY by Stephen King, adapted by Simon Moore; Director, Emma Griffin; Set, Felix E Cochren; Costumes, Jessica Trejos; Lights, Mark Barton; Sound, Jeremy J. Lee; Fight Consultant, Timothy Davis-Reed; SM, Adam Ganderson; Casting, Alan Filderman; Cast: Kate Buddeke (Annie Wilkes), John Sierros (Paul Sheldon); October 24–November 1, 2007

FIDDLER ON THE ROOF Book by Joseph Stein, music by Jerry Bock, lyrics by Sheldon Harnick; Director/Choreographer, Anthony Salatino; Musical Director, Dianne Adams McDowell; Sets, Troy Hourie; Costumes, Jessica Ford; Lights, Dawn Chiang; Sound, Jonathan Herter; Associate Music Director, Frederick Willard; PSM, Stuart Plymesser; Casting, Alan Filderman; Cast: Stephen Anthony (Perchik), Mary Ellen Ashley (Yente), Rachel Baker (Fruma-Sarah), Catherine Charlebois (Hodel), Justin Conte (Russian Dancer), Andrew Dain (Older Village Boy), Camille Francis (Shprintze), Alec Funiciello (Younger Village Boy), Amanda Funiciello (Shprintze), John Galas (Avram), Kara Gantos (Bielke), John Garry (Nachum), Mary Gutzi (Golde), Camissa Hill (Village Woman), Michael Howell (Motel), Nathan Hurwitz (Rabbi), Ian Joseph (Mordcha), Sarah Lester (Bielke), Arielle Lever (Chava), Craig MacDoanld (Constable/Ensemble), Chrissy Malon (Village Woman), Nadine Malouf (Tzeitel/Dream Grandmother), Gordon Maniskas (Sasha/Russian Dancer), Mason McDowell (Older Village Boy), Jason N Mesches (Mendel), Lauren Nolan (Village Woman), Sarah Olbrantz (Village Woman/Shandel), Frank J Paparone (Russian Dancer), Aidan Procopio (Younger Village Boy), Michael Rios (Fiddler/Russian Dancer/Jewish Boy), Nicholas F. Saverine (Lazar Wolf), Stephen Simowski (Yussel), Dominique Stasiulis (Fyedka/Russian Dancer), Brendon Stimson (Russian Dancer), Kathleen Wrinn (Village Woman), Stuart Zagnit (Tevye), Katja Zarolinski (Village Woman); November 28–December 30, 2007

THE LIEUTENANT OF INISHMORE by Martin McDonagh; Director, Robert Moss; Sets, Adam Stockhausen; Costumes, Camille Assaf; Lights, Matthew Richards; Sound, Jonathan Herter; Special Effects/Firearms Choreographer, Waldo Warshaw; Assistant Director, Dominic D'Angela; Dialects, Malcolm Ingram; SM, Ryan Raduechel; Casting, Alan Filderman; Cast: Don Amendolia (Donny), Molly Camp (Mairead), TJ Clark (Joey), Christian Conn (Padraic), Patrick Edgar (Davey), Sean Tarrant (Christy), Brent Vimtrup (James/Brendan); January 16–February 3, 2008

DOUBT by John Patrick Shanley; Director, M. Burke Walker; Sets, David Birn; Costumes, Katrin Naumann; Lights, Phil Monat; Sound, Jonathan Herter; Assistant Director, Susan A. Merwin; Casting, Alan Filderman; PSM, Stuart Plymesser; Cast: Rod Brogran (Father Flynn), Lucy Martin (Sister Aloysius), Laiona Michelle (Mrs. Muller), Devin Preston (Sister James); February 13–March 2, 2008

THE BOMB-ITTY OF ERRORS by Jordan Allen-Dutton, Jason Catalano, Gregory Qaiyum, Jeffrey Qaiyum, and Erik Weiner; Director; Andy Goldberg; Music, Jeffrey Qaiyum; DJ/Music Director, Kheedim Oh; Sets, Shoko Kambara; Costumes, Amelia Dombrowski; Lights, Aaron Spivey; Sound, Jonathan Herter; SM, Adam Ganderson; Casting, Alan Filderman; Cast: Jason Babinsky (Antipholus of Syracuse), James Barry (Antipholus of Ephesus), Darian Dauchan (Dromio of Syracuse), Griffin Matthews (Dromio of Ephesus); March 12–April 12, 2008

THE FANTASTICKS Book and lyrics, Tom Jones, music by Harvey Schmidt; Co-produced with Indiana Repertory Theatre; Director/Choreographer, Peter Amster; Music Director, David Nelson; Sets, Scott Bradley; Costumes, Maria Marrero; Lights, Ann Wrightson; Sound, Todd Mack Reischman; PSM, Stuart Plymesser; Dramaturg, Richard J. Roberts; Casting, Alan Filderman; Cast: Charles Goad (Bellomy), Mark Goetzinger (Hucklebee), Robert K. Johansen (Mortimer), Williams J. Norris (Henry-The Old Actor), Alexa Silvaggio (The Mute), David Studwell (El Gallo), Mackenzie Thomas (Luisa), Eric Van Tielen (Matt); April 23–May 17, 2008

Tennessee Repertory Company

Nashville, Tennessee

TWENTY-THIRD SEASON

Producing Artistic Director, Rene D. Copeland

THE CRUCIBLE by Arthur Miller; Director, Rene D. Copeland; Set, Gary C. Hoff; Costumes, Trish Clark; Lighting, Karen Palin; Technical Director, Jonathan Hammel; SM, David Wilkerson; Production Assistant, Lauren Shouse; Cast: David Alford (John Proctor), Chip Arnold (Deputy-Governor Danforth), Evelyn Blythe (Ann Putnam), Matthew Carlton (Thomas Putnam), Emmett Furrow (Judge Hathorne), Jenny Littleton (Elizabeth Proctor), Jessejames Locorriere (Ezekiel Cheever), Veronica Longo (Mercy Lewis), Michael Montgomery (Francis Nurse), Eric D. Pasto-Crosby (Reverend Hale), Delali Potakey (Tituba), Kahle Reardon (Abigail Williams), Brian Russell (Giles Corey), Tia Shearer (Mary Warren), Kevin Shell (Marshall Willard), Cassie Tesauro (Susanna Wallcott), Sally Welch (Rebecca Nurse), Sam Whited (Reverend Parris), Rachel Woods (Betty Parris); October 4–13, 2007

IT'S A WONDERFUL LIFE: a Live Radio Play adapted by Joe Landry from the film directed by Frank Capra; Director, David Alford; Set, Gary C. Hoff; Costumes, Trish Clark; Lighting, Karen Palin; Technical Director, Jonathan Hammel; SM, David Wilkerson; Production Assistant, Lauren Shouse; Cast: David Alford (Freddie "Fingers" Filmore), Matthew Carlton (Harry "Jazzbo" Heywood), Jenny Littleton (Lana Sherwood), Marin

Miller (Sally Applewhite), Todd Truly (Jake Laurents), Jeff Pettit & Frazier Smith (Interns); November 29–December 22, 2007

THE GOAT OR, WHO IS SYLVIA? by Edward Albee; Director, Rene D. Copeland; Set, Gary C. Hoff; Costumes, Trish Clark; Lighting, Phillip Franck; Technical Director, Jonathan Hammel; SM, David Wilkerson; Assistant Director, Lauren Shouse; Cast: Matthew Carlton (Martin), Ruth Cordell (Stevie), Henry Haggard (Ross), Andy Kanies (Billy); January 31–February 16, 2008

DOUBT by John Patrick Shanley; Director, Rene D. Copeland; Set, Gary C. Hoff; Costumes, Trish Clark; Lighting, Phillip Franck; Technical Director, Jonathan Hammel; Properties, Kate Foreman; SM, David Wilkerson; Assistant Director, Lauren Shouse; Cast: Rona Carter (Sister Aloysius), Jenny Littleton (Sister James), Jessejames Locorriere (Father Flynn), Delali Potakey (Mrs. Muller); March 13–29, 2008

THE UNDERPANTS adapted by Steve Martin from the original play by Carl Sternheim; Director, Lane Davies; Set, Gary C. Hoff; Costumes, Trish Clark; Lighting, Michael Barnett; Technical Director, Jonathan Hammel; SM, David Wilkerson; Production Assistant, Lauren Shouse; Cast: Lane Davies (The King), Marin Miller (Louise Maske), Marc Silver (Theo Maske), Patrick Waller (Frank Versati), Sam Whited (Klinglehoff), Martha Wilkinson (Gertrude Deuter), Bobby Wycoff (Benjamin Cohen); May 1–17, 2008

Theatre Under the Stars

Houston, Texas

FORTIETH ANNIVERSARY SEASON

Founder/Producing Artistic Director, Frank M. Young; Associate Artistic Director, Roy Hamlin; Company Manager, Nicole A. Young

WHISTLE DOWN THE WIND Music and book by Andrew Lloyd Webber, lyrics by Jim Steinman, book co-written by Patricia Knop and Gale Edwards; Producer/Director, Bill Kenwright; Music Director/Conductor, Jim Vucovich; Music Coordinator, John Monaco; Music Supervisor/Orchestrations/Arrangements, David Steadman; Choreographer, Henry Metcalfe; Set/Costumes, Paul Farnsworth; Lighting, Nick Richlings; Sound, Ben Harrison; Associate Choreographer, Jody Ripplinger; Production Manager, Larry Morley; PSM, Allen McMullen; Stage Managers, Nancy Wernick, Nathan D. Frye; ASM/Children's Coordinator, Randy Andre Davis; Technical Supervisor, Larry Morley; Casting, Stuart Howard, Amy Schecter, Paul Hardt; General Manager, Alan Wasser Associates; Press, David Greiss & AWA Touring Services; Cast: Al Bundois (Vault Preacher), Austin J. Zambito-Valente (Poor Baby), Andrea Ross (Swallow), Nadine Jacobson (Brat), Adam Shonkwiler (Earl), Greg Stone (Snake Preacher), Matt Skrincosky (Amos), Kurt Zischke (Sheriff), Dann Fink (Boone), Gerry McIntyre (Ed), James Jackson Jr. (Sam), Eric Kunze (The Man), Thomas Rainey (Frank), Carole Denise Jones (Candy), Mickey Toogood (Deputy); Ensemble: Ryan Appleby, Renee Claire Bergeron, Raisa Ellingson, Alexis Hightower, Stpehen Horst; Children: Olivia Ford, Dana Kluczyk, Justine Magnusson, Sarah Safer; Swings: Elizabeth Earley (Dance Captain), Jason Sotrowski; September 9–22, 2007

DREAMGIRLS Book and lyrics by Tom Eyen, music by Henry Krieger; Director, Robert Clater; Choreographer, Lesia Kaye; Set, Robin Wagner; Costumes, Theoni V. Aldredge; Lighting, Richard Winkler; Sound, Christopher K. Bond, Music Director/Conductor, Robert Strickland; Casting, David Petro; PSM, Roger Allan Raby; SM, Debs Ramser; Associate Musical Director, Darren Ledbetter; Wardrobe Supervisor, Ray Delle Robbins; Hair/Wigs, Bobbie Grizzle; Press, David Greiss; Cast: Aurelia Williams (Effie Melody White), Karla Mosely (Deena Jones), Brian Evaret Chandler (Curtis Taylor, Jr.), Ron Kellum (C.C. White), Milton Craig Nealy (Marty), Manoly Farrell (Michelle Morris/Ensemble), Crystal Joy (Lorrell Robinson), Eugene Fleming (James Thunder Early); Ensemble: Randy Aaron, Melvin Bell III, Chanté Carmel, N Darryl E. Calmese Jr., David La Duca, Nkrumah M. Gatling, William Hubert II, Logan Keslar, Ano Okera, Ian Paget, Cassandra Palacio, Will Perez, Kayla Repan, Briana Resa, Marc Spaulding, Teacake, Lyndsay Thomas, Marvin Thornton, Holland Vavra, Pearce Wegener; October 9–21, 2007

A WONDERFUL LIFE Book and lyrics by Sheldon Harnick, music by Joe Raposo; Director, Roy Hamlin; Choreographer, Paula Sloan; Set/Projections, Charlie Smith; Costumes, Gail Baldoni; Lighting, Richard Winkler; Sound, Christopher K. Bond; Co-Projections, William Cusick; Casting, Sherie L. Seff; Music Director/Conductor, Ed Goldschneider; Co-Conductor, Art Yelton; PSM, Roger Allan Raby; SM, Rebecca Skupin; Wardrobe Supervisor, Ray Delle Robbins; Hair/Wigs, Bobbie Grizzle; Press, David Greiss; Cast: George Dvorsky (George Bailey), Mary Illes (Mary Hatch Bailey), Erick Devine (Matthew/Bob Hepner/Mr. Martini/Tom Bailey/Carter), Michael Arnold (Ernie Bishop), Kevin Cooney (Uncle Billy), David Koch (Sam Wainwright), Hal Robinson (Henry Potter), Susan Shofner (Milly Bailey), Corby Sullivan (Harry Bailey), Michael Tapley (Bert), Patrick Richwood (Clarence); Ensemble: Gary Bankston, John Berno, Marybelle Chaney, Ven Daniel, Angela Kristin Dickens, Ashlee Fife, Nkrumah Gatling, Mitchell Greco, Mark Laskowski, Reid Lee, Philip Lehl, Pamela M. Moore, Theresa Nelson, Marc Oka, Briana Resa, Krissy Richmond, Jim Shaffer, Christina Stroup, Lee Jane Walker, Karl Warden, Paige Wheat ,Nirayl Wilcox; Children: Michael Bevan, Sam Burkett, Sarah Burkett, Chris Canal, Sydney Crofton, Jack Delac, Maureen Fenninger, Jessica Ferguson, Noelle Flores, Trey Harrington, Mark Jackson, Trey Stoker, Caroline Taylor, Emily Thompson, Charity Van Tassel, Samantha West; December 11–23, 2007

HELLO, DOLLY! Book by Michael Stewart, music and lyrics by Jerry Herman; Director, Lee Roy Reams; Choreographer, Randy Slovacek; Set, Michael Anania; Costumes Designer,

James Schutte; Lighting, Richard Winkler; Associate Lighting, Julie Duro; Sound, Christopher K. Bond; Casting, Sherie L. Self; Musical Director/Conductor, Jeff Rizzo; PSM, Roger Allan Raby; SM, Debs Ramser; Wardrobe Supervisor, Ray Delle Robbins; Hair/Wigs, Bobbie Grizzle; Press, David Greiss; Cast: Leslie Uggams (Dolly Gallagher Levi), Lewis J. Stadlen (Horace Vandergelder), Glory Crampton (Irene Molloy), Kevin Earley (Cornelius), Michael McGurk (Barnaby Tucker), Amy Shure (Minnie Fay), Ron Kellum (Ambrose Kemper), Katharine Randolph (Ermengarde Vandergelder), Jessica Sheridan (Ernestina Simple), Erick R. Walck (Rudolph Reisenweber); Ensemble: Melanie Allen, Brian Barry, Alan Bennett, Jennifer Blakeney Young, Nathaniel Braga, Byron Dement, Dominic Di Felice, Craig Foster, Adam Gibbs, Kevin P. Hill, Traci Hines, Darrel T. Joe, Tony Johnson, Laura Kaldis, Richard M. Keck, Dominique Kelley, Chris Klink, David La Duca, Alissa Ann Lavergne, Reid Lee, Sarah Moore, Christina Stroup, Mary Jo Todaro, Gia Valenti, Paige Wheat; February 26–March 9, 2008

THE 25TH ANNUAL PUTNAM COUNTY SPELLING BEE Music and Lyrics by William Finn, book by Rachel Sheinkin, conceived by Rebecca Feldman; Additional material written by Jay Reiss; Director, James Lapine; Associate Director, Darren Katz; Choreographer, Dan Knechtges; Set, Beowulf Boritt; Costumes, Jennifer Caprio; Lighting, Natasha Katz; Sound, Dan Moses Schreier; Music Director, Jodie Moore; Orchestrations, Michael Starobin; Vocal Arrangements, Carmel Dean; Music Coordinator, Michael Keller; PSM, Brian J. L'ecuyer; SM, Lori Lundquist; ASM, E. Cameron Holsinger; Press, David Greiss and TMG-The Marketing Group; Cast: Katie Boren (Marcy Park), Elsa Carmona (Logainne Schwartzandgrubenierre), Roberta Duchak (Rona Lisa Peretti), James Kall (Douglas Panch), Andrew Keenan-Bolger (Leaf Coneybear), Justin Keyes (Chip Tolentino), Kevin Smith Kirkwood (Mitch Mahoney), Vanessa Ray (Olive Ostrovsky), Eric Roediger (William Barfee); Swings: Jeffrey James Binney, Christine Bunuan, Robin Alexis Childress, Julius Thomas III; March 25–April 6, 2008

THE DROWSY CHAPERONE Book by Don McKellar, music and lyrics by Lisa Lambert and Greg Morrison; Director and Choreographer, Casey Nicholaw; Set, David Gallo; Costumes, Gregg Barnes; Lighting, Ken Billington and Brian Monahan; Sound, Acme Sound Partners; Casting, Telsey + Company; Hair, Josh Marquette; Makeup, Justen M. Brosnan; Orchestrations, Larry Blank; Dance/Incidental Arrangements, Glen Kelly; Music Supervisor/Vocal Arrangements, Phil Reno; Music Director, Robert Billig; Music Coordinator, John Miller; Production Supervisor, Brian Lynch/Theatretech; Assistant Director, Casey Hushion; Assistant Choreographer, Josh Rhodes; PSM, Eric Sprosty; SM, Allison Harma; ASM, Tom Jeffords; Tour Marketing and Publicity, TMG-The Marketing Group; Press, David Greiss; Cast: Cliff Bemis (Feldzieg), Andrea Chamberlain (Janet Van De Graff), Jonathan Crombie (Man in Chair), Robert Dorfman (Underling), Georgia Engel (Mrs Tottendale), Fran Jaye (Trix), Mark Ledbetter (Robert Martin), Marla Mindelle (Kitty), James Moye (Aldolpho), Nancy Opel (The Drowsy Chaperone), Paul Riopelle (Gangster #1), Peter Riopelle (Gangster #2), Richard Vida (George); Chuck Rea (Super/Ensemble), Ensemble: Kevin Crewell, Tiffany Haas, Jennifer Swiderski; Swings: Megan Nicole Arnoldy, Alicia Irving, Jody Madaras, Mason Roberts; May 20–June 1, 2008

Trinity Repertory Theatre

Providence, Rhode Island

FORTY-FOURTH SEASON

Artistic Director, Curt Columbus; Executive Director, Michael Gennaro; Production Director, Laura E. Smith; Associate Production Director, Mark Turek; Finance and Administration, Joan B. Glazer; External Relations, Richard Jaffe; Associate Marketing, April Rosenberger

ALL THE KING'S MEN by Adrian Hall, adapted from a novel by Robert Penn Warren; Director, Brian McEleney; Set, Michael McGarty; Costumes, William Lane; Lighting, John Ambrosone; Sound, Peter Sasha Hurowitz; Properties, S. Michael Getz; Musical Direction, David Tessier, Voice Coach, Thom Jones; PSM, Barbara Reo; SM, Lori Lundquist; Assistant Director, Jesse Geiger; Cast: Stephen Berenson (Tiny Duffy/Ellis Burden), Angela Brazil (Anne Stanton), Janice Duclos (Mrs. Patton), Mauro Hantman (Jack Burden), Charlie Hudson, III (Sugar-Boy/Tom Stark), Phyllis Kay (Sadie Burke), Barbara Meek (Slade/Lily Littlepaugh), Anne Scurria (Mother), Fred Sullivan, Jr. (Judge Irwin), Stephen Thorne (Adam Stanton), Joe Wilson, Jr. (Willie Stark), Kelby Akin (Dolph Pillsbury/Hugh Miller), Jill Knox (Lucy Stark), Alan McNaney (Editor/Dr. Bland/Announcer), Scott Raker (Alex/Sheriff/Theodore Murrell/Mr. Pettus), Jessa Sherman (Miss Dumonde), David Tessier (Musician/Old Man), Kevin Fallon (Byram T. White/Musician); Sarah and Joseph Dowling, Jr. Theater; September 14–October 21, 2007

A CHRISTMAS CAROL by Charles Dickens, adapted by Adrian Hall and Richard Cumming; Director, Fred Sullivan, Jr.; Musical Director, William Damkoehler; Set, William Lane; Costumes, Ron Cesario; Lighting, Richard Van Voris; Sound, Peter Sasha Hurowitz; Properties, S. Michael Getz; Choreographer, Stephen Buescher; Voice Coach, Thom Jones; PSM, Lori Lundquist; SM, Megan Schwarz; ASM, Jennifer Grutza, Emily Glinick; Brian McEleney or William Damkoehler (Ebenezer Scrooge), Kelby T. Akin or Joe Wilson, Jr. (Solicitor/Schoolmaster/Ghost of Christmas Present), Christopher Bonewitz or Jonathan Horvath (Will Davidge/Young Scrooge/Miner/Businessman), Sam Babbitt or Fred Sullivan, Jr. (Jacob Marley/Old Joe), Stephen Thorne or Mauro Hantman (Fred/Ghost of Christmas Past/Businessman); Joe Donovan or Alan McNaney (Young Marley/Ghost of Christmas Future), Tom Gleadow or Joe Mecca (Solicitor/Fezziwig/Miner/Cook/Businessman), Tony Estrella or Richard Donelly (Bob Cratchit), Jeanine Kane or Phyllis Kay (Mrs. Cratchit), Charlie Hudson III or Haas Regen (Topper/

Undertaker's Man), Jill Knox or Rachael Warren (Wretched Beggar Woman/Belle), Janice Duclos or Cynthia Strickland (Mrs. Partlet), Cynthia Strickland or Kimiye Corwin (Maid), Georgia Cohen or Elizabeth Larson (Mrs. Fezziwig/Sister-in-Law/Caroline), Elizabeth Larson or Piper Goodeve (Mother Goose), Kimiye Corwin or Angela Brazil (Fan), Piper Goodeve or Angela Brazil (Lucy/Mrs. Dilber), Austin Adams, Cameron Connaughton, Robert Capron, or Ian Wams (Boy Caroler/ Ignorance/Boy in Street); Brooke Conneally, Haley Leech, Meghan Hackett, or Sakari Monteiro (Belinda); Dustin Isom, Dylan Dupont, Christopher Lysik or Nicholas Corey (Peter); Ariel Dorsey, Kimiye Corwin, or Patti Laliberte (Martha); Katherine Kerwin, Stephanie Petrone, Kimberly Dalton, or Dominique DeSimone (Wretched Child/Want); Teddy McNulty, Max Theroux, Eric Halvarson or Jeremy Roth-Rose (Scrooge as a Young Boy/Tiny Tim); Musicians: Rachel Malone/Chris Turner/David Tessier or Kevin Fallon/Steve Jobe/Chris Lussier; Elizabeth and Malcolm Chace Theater; November 16–December 30, 2007

MEMORY HOUSE by Kathleen Tolan; Director, Curt Columbus; Set, Eugene Lee; Costumes, Marilyn Salvatore; Sound, Peter Sasha Hurowitz; Dramaturge, Craig Watson; Properties, S. Michael Getz; Voice Coach, Thom Jones; PSM, Lloyd Davis, Jr.; Cast: Anne Scurria (Maggie), Susannah Flood (Katia); Sarah and Joseph Dowling, Jr. Theater; November 30, 2007–January 6, 2008

RICHARD III by William Shakespeare; Director, Kevin Moriarty; Set, Michael McGarty; Costumes, William Lane; Lighting, Tyler Micoleau; Sound Ryan Rumery; Fight Choreographer Craig Handel; Voice Coach, Thom Jones; PSM, Buzz Cohen: ASM, Christina Lowe; Cast: Kelby T. Akin (Sir Richard Ratcliffe), Stephen Berenson (The Duke of Clarence), Christopher Bonewitz (Lord Grey), Angela Brazil (Lady Anne), Johnny Lee Davenport (King Edward IV/Lord Mayor of London), Mauro Hantman (Lord Hastings), Jonathan Horvath (Lord Rivers), Charlie Hudson III (Crown Prince Edward/Lord Cardinal Bourchier/Earl of Richmond), Phyllis Kay (Queen Elizabeth), Brian McEleney (Richard, Duke of Gloucester, later King Richard III), Barbara Meek (Duchess of York), Scott Raker (Sir William Catesby), Timothy John Smith (King Henry VI/Lord Stanley), Fred Sullivan, Jr. (The Duke of Buckingham), Noah Tuleja (Marquess of Dorset); Children: Cameron Connaughton (Prince Edward), Christopher Lysik (Prince Edward), Teddy McNulty (The Duke of York), Max Theroux (The Duke of York); Elizabeth and Malcolm Chace Theater; January 25–March 2, 2008

SOME THINGS ARE PRIVATE by Deborah Salem Smith and Laura Kepley; Director, Laura Kepley; Set, Wilson Chin; Costumes, William Lane; Lighting, Brian J. Lilienthal; Sound, Peter Sasha Hurowitz; Projection, Jamie Jewett; Voice Coach, Thom Jones; PSM, Barbara Reo; Cast: Richard Donelly (Narrator #1/Security Guard/Fashion Icon/Governor of Virginia), Janice Duclos (Narrator #2/Museum Employee/AP Photo Editor/Critic/A Woman), Anne Scurria (Sally Mann), Stephen Thorne (Thomas Kramer), Rachael Warren (Narrator #3/Julia/Museumgoer/Playboy Interviewer/A Mother/ Daughter); Sarah and Joseph Dowling, Jr. Theater; February 15–March 23, 2008

BLITHE SPIRIT by Noel Coward; Director, Curt Columbus; Set, James Schuette; Costumes, William Lane; Lighting, John Ambrosone; Sound, Peter Sasha Hurowitz; Voice Coach, Thom Jones; PSM, Jennifer Grutza; ASM, Robin Grady; Production Director, Laura E. Smith; Cast: Angela Brazil (Ruth), William Damkoehler (Dr. Bradman), Phyllis Kay (Elvira), Barbara Meek (Madame Arcati), Cynthia Strickland (Mrs. Bradman), Fred Sullivan, Jr. (Charles), Anna Van Valin (Edith); Elizabeth and Malcolm Chace Theater; March 28–April 27, 2008

PARIS BY NIGHT Book and lyrics by Curt Columbus, music by Andre Pluess and Amy Warren; Director, Birgitta Victorson; Musical Director, Michael Rice; Set, Eugene Lee; Costumes, William Lane; Lighting, Deb Sullivan; Sound, Peter Sasha Hurowitz; Properties, S. Michael Getz; Choreographer, Greg Webster; Voice Coach, Thom Jones; PSM, Lori Lundquist; ASM, Emily Glinick; Assistant Director, Mia Rovegno; Cast: Stephen Berenson (Harry), Janice Duclos (Henriette), James Royce Edwards (Buck), Lynette Freeman-Maiga (Chorus), Charise Greene (Chorus), Mauro Hantman (Frank), Michael Propster (Chorus), Jude Sandy (Chorus), Timothy John Smith (Le Mec), Adam Suritz (Chorus), Erin Tchoukaleff (Chorus), Stephen Thorne (Patrick), Rachael Warren (Marie), Joe Wilson, Jr. (Sam); Sarah and Joseph Dowling, Jr. Theater; April 25–June 1, 2008

Tri-State Actors Theatre

Sussex, New Jersey

TWENTIETH SEASON

Artistic Director, Paul Meacham; Managing Director, Patricia Meacham

TWELFTH NIGHT by William Shakespeare; Director, Paul Meacham; Original Music, Vince di Mura; Choreographer, Lisa Brailoff; Scenic Artist, Jacqueline Perry; Costumes, Patricia Meacham; Sound, Steven Silvia; SM, Lara Terrell; Technical Director, Brian Coposky; Cast: Andrew Danish (Orsino), Craig Dudley (Sir Toby Belch), Jason Shane (Curio), Janeslle Sosa (Maria), Ben Schaub (Valentine), Bill Edwards (Sir Andrew Aguecheek), Celia Montgomery (Viola), Clark Gookin (Feste), Ted Odell (Sea Captain), Katie Tame (Olivia), Freeman Borden (Sebastian), Kevin Shinnick (Malvolio), Daniel Mian (Antonio/ Pirate), Ted Odell (Priest); April 18–May 6, 2007

GREATER TUNA by Jaston Williams, Joe Sears, & Ed Howard; Director, Paul Meacham; Scenic Artist, Jackie Perry; Costumes, Patricia Meacham & Nicole Lee Silva; Lighting, Lara Terrell; SM, Kevin M.S. Brophy; Cast: Bill Edwards (Arlis Struvie/Didi Snavely/Harold Dean Lattimer/Petey Fisk/Jody Bumiller/ Stanley Bumiller/Charlene Bumiller/Chad Hartford/Phinas Blye/Vera Carp), Scotty Watson (Thurston Wheelis/Elmer

Watkins/Bertha Bumiller/Yippy/Leonard Childers/Pearl Burras/R.R. Snavely/Rev. Spikes/Sheriff Givens/Hank Bumiller); June 7–24, 2007

THE PRICE by Arthur Miller; Director/Set, Paul Meacham; Costumes, Patricia Meacham; Sound/Props, Steven Silvia; Scenic Artist, Jacqueline Perry; SM, Lara Terrell; Cast: Randall McCann (Victor Franz), Tara Bowles (Esther Franz), P. Brendan Mulvey (Gregory Solomon), Paul Falzone (Walter Franz); October 25–November 11, 2007

A CHRISTMAS CAROL by Charles Dickens, adapted by Christopher Schario; Director, Paul Meacham; Scenic Artist, Jacqueline Perry; Costumes, Patrica Meacham; Sound, Steven Silvia; SM, Lara Terrell; Cast: Paul Meacham (Scrooge), Philip Mutz (Young Scrooge/Tiny Tim/Christmas Yet to Come/ Turkey Boy), Bill Edwards (Bob Cratchit/Marley's Ghose/Old Joe/Dick Wilkins), Clark Gookin (Fred/Fezziwig/Christmas Present/Peter Cratchit), Jenelle Sosa (Gentlewoman/Fan/ Mrs. Fezziwig/Belle/Martha/Laundress), Sarah Koestner (Gentlewoman/Christmas Past/Mrs. Cratchit/Charwoman); December 12–30, 2007

Woolly Mammoth Theatre Comapny

Washington, DC

TWENTY-EIGHTH SEASON

Artistic Director, Howard Shalwitz; Managing Director, Jeffery Herrmann

DEAD MAN'S CELL PHONE by Sarah Ruhl; Director, Rebecca Bayla Taichman; Set, Neil Patel; Costumes, Kate Turner-Walker; Lighting, Colin K. Bills; Sound, Martin Desjardins; Cast: Rick Foucheux, Polly Noonan, Jennifer Mendenhall, Naomi Jacobson, Bruce Nelson, Sarah Marshall; World Premiere; Mainstage; June 4–July 14, 2007 (last show of the Twenty-Seventh Season)

THE UNMENTIONABLES by Bruce Norris; Director, Pam MacKinnon; Set, James Kronzer; Costumes, Helen Q. Huang; Lighting, Colin K. Bills; Sound, Matthew Nielson; Cast: Kofi Owusu, Naomi Jacobson, Charles H. Hyman, Dawn Ursula, John Livingston Rolle, Marni Penning, Tim Getman, James J. Johnson, James Foster Jr.; Mainstage; August 27–September 30, 2007

CURRENT NOBODY by Melissa James Gibson; Director, Daniel Aukin; Set, Tony Cisek; Costumes, Helen Q. Huang; Lighting, Colin K. Bills; Sound, Ryan Rumery; Projection Design, Jake Pinholster; Cast: Jesse Lenat, Michael Willis, Christina Kirk, Deb Gottesman, Casie Platt, Jessica Dunton, Kathryn Falcone; Mainstage; World Premiere; October 29–November 25, 2007

NOW WHAT? Written and performed by Josh Lefkowitz; Melton Rehearsal Hall; October 31–December 9, 2007

ONE-MAN STAR WARS TRILOGY Written and performed by Charles Ross; Director, T.J. Dawe; Mainstage; December 11–30, 2007

NO CHILD… Written & peformed by Nilaja Sun; adapted by Daniel Ettinger; Director, Hal Brooks; Set, Narelle Sissons, Costumes, Jessica Gaffney; Lighting, Mark Barton; Sound, Ron Russell; Mainstage; January 21–February 17, 2008

The K of D, an urban legend by Laura Schellhardt; Director, John Vreeke; Set and Costumes, Marie-Noelle Daigneault; Lighting, Andrew Griffin; Sound, Matt Otto; Properties, Jennifer Sheetz; World Premiere; Melton Rehearsal Hall; January 16–February 10, 2008

STUNNING by David Adjmi; Director, Anne Kauffman; Set, Daniel Conway; Costumes, Helen Q. Huang; Lighting, Colin K. Bills; Sound, Ryan Rumery; Cast: Laura Heisler, Quincy Tyler Bernstine, Michael Gabriel Goodfriend, Clinton Brandhagen, Gabriela Fernandez-Coffey, Abby Wood; World Premiere; Mainstage; March 10–April 6, 2008

MEASURE FOR PLEASURE by David Grimm; Director, Howard Shalwitz; Set, Robin Stapley; Costumes, Helen Q. Huang; Lighting, Colin K. Bills; Sound, Ryan Rumery; Cast: Jennifer Mendenhall, Doug Brown, Kimberly Gilbert, Joel Reuben Ganz, Andrew Honeycutt, Kimberly Schraf; Mainstage; May 26–June 29, 2008

Yale Repertory Theatre

New Haven, Connecticut

FOURTY-SECOND SEASON

James Bundy, Artistic Director; Victoria Nolan, Managing Director; Jennifer Kiger, Associate Artistic Director

RICHARD II by William Shakespeare; Director, Evan Yionoulis; Original Music, Mike Yionoulis; Set, Brenda Davis; Costumes, Melissa E. Trn; Lighting, Ji-Youn Chang; Sound, Sarah Pickett; Production Dramaturgs, Lydia Garcia, Rebecca Phillips; Vocal and Text Coach, Keely Eastley; Fight Director, Rick Sordelet; Casting, Tara Rubin; SM, James Mountcastle; Cast: Jeffrey Carlson (King Richard II), Alvin Epstein (John of Gaunt/Gardener), Billy Eugene Jones (Henry Bolingbroke), Christopher Grant (Thomas Mowbray/Sir Piers of Exton), Caroline Stefanie Clay (Duchess of Gloucester/Duchess of York), Brent Langdon (Duke of Surrey/Earl of Salisbury), Allen E. Read (Duke of Aumerle), Brian Robert Burns (Bolingbroke's Herald/Harry Percy), Joseph Parks (Sir Henry Green/Stable Groom), Christopher McFarland (Sir John Bushy/Prisoner Keeper), Alex Knox (Sir William Bagot/ Exton's Man), George Bartenieff (Edmund of Langley), Caitlin Clouthier (Queen Isabelle), Jonathan Fried (Henry Percy), Joe Tapper (Lord Ross), Edward O'Blenis (Lord Willoughby), Michael Leibenluft (York's Servant/Gardener's Man), Dan Moran (Lord Berkeley/Sir Stephen Scroop/Abbot of Westminster), Christopher McHale (Bishop of Carlisle),

Kristjiana Gong (Lady-in-Waiting), Josh Odsess-Rubin (Gardener's Man); September 21–October 13, 2007

TROUBLE IN MIND by Alice Childress; Director, Irene Lewis; Sets, Michael Locher; Costumes, Paul Carey; Lighting, Melissa Mizell; Sound, David Budries; Dialect and Vocal Coach, Beth McGuire; Dramaturgs, Miriam Felton-Dansky, Catherine Sheehy; Casting, Janet Foster, Tara Rubin; SM, Lisa-Marie Shuster; Cast: E. Faye Butler (Wiletta Mayer), Laurence O'Dwyer (Henry), Don Guillory (John Nevins), Starla Benford (Millie Davis), Thomas Jefferson Byrd (Sheldon Forrester), Natalia Payne (Judy Sears), Kevin O'Rourke (Al Manners), Garrett Neergaard (Eddie Fenton), Daren Kelly (Bill O'Wray), Aaron M. Larkin (Stagehand), Slate Holmgren (Stagehand); October 26–November 17, 2007

TARTUFFE, or the Imposter by Molière, translated into English verse by Richard Wilbur; Produced in association with McCarter Theatre Center; Director, Daniel Fish; Sets, John Conklin; Costumes, Kaye Voyce; Lighting, Jane Cox; Sound, Karin Graybash; Video Design, Alexandra Eaton; Vocal Coach, Ralph Zito; Dramaturgs, Janice Paran, Joseph P. Cermatori, Jennifer Shaw; Casting, Laura Stanczyk; Stage Managers, Alison Cote, James Mountcastle; Cast: Beth Dixon (Mme. Pernelle), Michael Rudko (Orgon), Christina Rouner (Elmire), Nick Westrate (Damis), Michelle Beck (Mariane), Daniel Talbott (Valère), Christopher Donahue (Cléante), Zach Grenier (Tartuffe), Sally Wingert (Dorine), Andy Paterson (M. Loyal), Tom Story (Police Officer); December 3–December 22, 2007

Alliance Theatre: *Tina Fabrique, Shelley Thomas, Marva Hicks in the world premiere of* The Women of Brewster Place *(photo by Greg Mooney)*

THE EVILDOERS by David Adjmi; Director, Rebecca Bayla Taichman; Sets, Riccardo Hernandez; Costumes, Susan Hilferty; Lighting, Stephen Strawbridge; Sound, Bray Poor; Fight Director, Rick Sordelet; Company Voice Work, Walton Wilson; Dramaturg, Michael Walkup; Casting, Tara Rubin; SM, Joanne E. McInerney; Cast: Samantha Soule (Judy), Stephen Barker Turner (Jerry), Johanna Day (Carol), Matt McGrath (Martin); World Premiere; January 18–February 9, 2008

A WOMAN OF NO IMPORTANCE by Oscar Wilde; Director, James Bundy; Sets, Lauren Rockman; Costumes, Anya Klepikov; Lighting, Ola Bråten; Sound, Jana Hoglund; Dialects, Stephen Gabis; Dramaturgs, Amy Boratko, Jennifer L. Shaw; Casting, Tara Rubin; SM, Sarah Hodges; Cast: Judith-Marie Bergan (Lady Caroline Pontefract), Erica Sullivan (Miss Hester Worsley), Anthony Newfield (Sir John Pontefract), Patricia Kilgarriff (Lady Hunstanton), Bryce Pinkham (Gerald Arbuthnot), René Augesen (Mrs. Allonby), Felicity Jones (Lady Stutfield), Michael Rudko (Mr. Kelvil), Geordie Johnson (Lord Illingworth), John Doherty (Lord Alfred Rufford), Will Connolly (Francis), Kate Forbes (Mrs. Arbuthnot), Terence Rigby (Archdeacon Daubeny), Liz Wisan (Alice), John Little (Farquhar); March 21–April 21, 2008

BOLEROS FOR THE DISENCHANTED by José Rivera; Director, Henry Godinez; Composer, Gustavo Leone; Sets, Linda Buchanan; Costumes, Yuri Cataldo; Lighting, Joseph Appelt; Sound, Veronika Vorel; Vocal Coach, Walton Wilson; Dramaturg, Kristina Corcoran Williams; Casting, Tara Rubin, SM, Danielle Federico; Cast: Sona Tatoyan (Flora/Eva), Adriana Sevan (Dona Milla/Flora), Gary Perez (Don Fermin/Eusebio), Felix Solis (Manuelo/Priest), Lucia Brawley (Petra/Monica), Joe Minoso (Eusebio/Oskar); World Premiere; April 25–May 17, 2008

Woolly Mammoth Theatre Company: *Naomi Jacobson, Polly Noonan and Sarah Marshall in* Dead Man's Cell Phone *(photo by Stan Barouh)*

Theatrical Awards

2007–2008

2008 Theatre World Award Winners

de'Adre Aziza of Passing Strange

Cassie Beck of The Drunken City

Daniel Breaker of Passing Strange

Ben Daniels of Les Liaisons Dangereuses

Deanna Dunagan of August: Osage County

Hoon Lee of Yellow Face

Alli Mauzey of Cry-Baby

Jenna Russell of Sunday in the Park with George

Mark Rylance of Boeing-Boeing

Loretta Ables Sayre of South Pacific

Jimmi Simpson of The Farnsworth Invention

Paulo Szot of South Pacific

64th Annual Theatre World Awards

Tuesday, June 10, 2008 at The Helen Hayes Theatre

Originally dubbed *Promising Personalities* in 1944 by co-founders Daniel Blum, Norman MacDonald, and John Willis to coincide with the first release of *Theatre World*, the now sixty-four-year-old definitive pictorial and statistical record of the American theatre, the Theatre World Awards, as they are now known, are the oldest awards given for debut performances in New York City, as well as one of the oldest honors bestowed on New York actors.

Administered by the Theatre World Awards Board of Directors, a committee of current New York drama critics chooses six actors and six actresses for the Theatre World Award who have distinguished themselves in Broadway and Off-Broadway productions during the past theatre season. Occasionally, Special Theatre World Awards are also bestowed on performers, casts, or organizations that have made a particularly lasting impression on the New York theatre scene.

The Theatre World Award "Janus" statuette is an original bronze sculpture in primitive-modern style created by internationally recognized artist Harry Marinsky. It is adapted from the Roman myth of Janus, god of entrances, exits, and all beginnings, with one face appraising the past and the other anticipating the future. The awards were cast and in the Del Chiaro Foundry in Pietrasanta, Italy, and at Sculpture House Casting, New York.

The Theatre World Awards are voted on by the following committee of New York drama critics: Peter Filichia (*Theatermania.com*), Harry Haun (*Playbill*), Matthew Murray (*TalkinBroadway.com*), Frank Scheck (*New York Post*), Michael Sommers (*Newhouse Papers)*, Doug Watt (Critic Emeritus, *New York Daily News*), and Linda Winer (*Newsday*).

Theatre World Awards Board of Directors: Leigh Giroux, President; Kati Meister, Vice President; Erin Oestreich, Secretary; Scott Denny, Treasurer; Tom Lynch; Barry Keating

Ceremony Highlights

Written and Hosted by Peter Filichia; Executive Producers, Scott Denny, Kati Meister, Erin Oestreich; Director, Barry Keating; Music Director/Accompanist, Henry Aronson; Production Manager/Program Design, Mary Botosan; Associate Director, Press, Jim Baldassare; PSM, Donald Fried; *Xanadu* PSM, Arturo E. Porazzi; *Xanadu* Company Manager, Jolie Gabler; Lighting Associate, Ryan O'Gara; Sound Associate, Emile Lafargue; Design Associate, Anita Easterling; Staff Photographers: Bruce Glikas, Jack Williams, Aubrey Ruben, Michael Viade, Walter McBride; Volunteer Coordinator/Reservations, Betsy Krouner; Assistant to the Director, Carey McCray; Assistant Stage Managers, Christina Lowe and Vikki DeMeo; Video Photographers, Richard Ridge and Bradshaw Smith; Presented on the set of the Broadway production of *Xanadu* designed by David Gallo, lighting by Howell Binkley, and sound by T. Richard Fitzgerald and Carl Casella

Presenters

Alec Baldwin – *Loot* (1986); Jonathan Cake – *Medea* (2003); John Cullum – *On a Clear Day You Can See Forever* (1966); Griffin Dunne – *Search and Destroy* (1992); Alexander Gemignani – *Assassins* (2004); Laura Linney – *Sight Unseen* (1992); Andrea Martin – *My Favorite Year* (1993); Lin-Manuel Miranda – *In the Heights* (2007); Rosie Perez – *References to Salvador Dali Make Me Hot* (2001); Alice Playten – *Henry, Sweet Henry* (1968); B.D. Wong – *M. Butterfly* (1988)

Performances

Carol Lawrence – *West Side Story* (1958): "West Side Story Medley" (music by Leonard Bernstein, lyrics by Stephen Sondheim); Tyler Maynard – *Altar Boyz* (2005): "Epiphany" from *Altar Boyz* (by Gary Adler and Michael Patrick Walker); Alice Playten – *Henry, Sweet Henry* (1968): "L'Amour" (music by Alice Playten); Karen Akers – *Nine* (1982): "I've Been Here" from *The Glorious Ones* (lyrics by Lynn Ahrens, music by Stephen Flaherty)

2008 Theatre World Award "Janus" Wranglers: Kelsey Fowler and Alison Horowitz, from the company of *Sunday in the Park With George*

Staff for the Helen Hayes Theatre: Owned and operated by Little Theatre Group LLC: Martin Markinson and Donald Tick; General Manager, Susan S. Myerberg; Associate General Manager, Sharon Fallon; House Management, Alan R. Markinson, Tom Santopietro; Head Usher, John Biancamano; Stage Door, Robert Seymour

Staff for Xanadu: Production Manager, Juniper Street Productions; Head Carpenter, Doug Purcell; Head Electrician, Joseph Beck; Head Props, Roger Keller; Sound Mixer, Emile Lafargue; Deck Sound, Bot Etter; Follow Spot, Joseph Redmond; Fly Person, Ann Cavanaugh

Volunteer Staff: Patrick Burns, Amelie Cherubin-Grillo, Kelly Childress, Nikki Curmaci, Alece DeLuca, Luciana Faulhaber, Sharon Hunter, Arielle Kaufman, John Krieger, Andy Lebon, Kelsey Maples, John MacDonald, Haytham Noor, Joanna Parson, C.J. Schwartz, Stephen Wilde, Frank York

Extraordinary Thanks for Financial Support: Alec Baldwin, Susan Stroman, Ben Hodges

Very Special Thanks for Financial Support: Blythe Danner, Christopher Goutman, Peter & Marsue MacNicol, Dylan Baker, Linda Hart, The Producing Office, Jamie deRoy, Laurence Guittard

Special Thanks for Financial Support: Howard Atlee-Heinlen, Richard Backus, Warren Berlinger, Helen Carey Raudenbush, Dixie Carter, Brent Carver, Tisa Chang, Barbara Cook, Patricia Crowley, David Cryer, Stephanie D'Abruzzo, Bambi Linn

Winner de'Adre Aziza meets the press and kisses our newest Theatre World cover, featuring her Passing Strange *cast mates.*

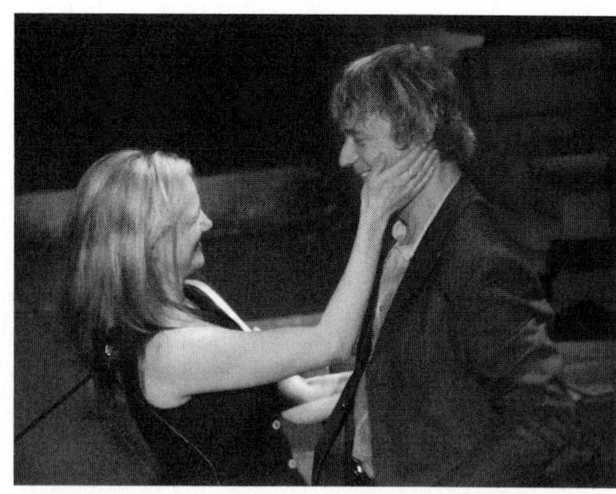

Laura Linney presents to her Les Liaisons Dangereuses *cast mate, Ben Daniels.*

Winner Cassie Beck

Alice Playten (Henry, Sweet Henry, *1968) presents to Paulo Szot*

Winner Hoon Lee

"Janus" presenter Kelsey Fowler shares a special moment with presenter Alec Baldwin (Loot, 1986)

Karen Akers (Nine, 1982) ends the show with a moving performance of "I Was Here" from The Glorious Ones

Winner Deanna Dunagan

Carol Lawrence (West Side Story, *1958) opens the show with a medley of songs from* West Side Story

DeJesus, Leslie Denniston, Patricia Elliott, Brian D. Farrell, Bette-Lee Fox, Bonnie Franklin, David Fritz, Gail Gerber, Anita Gillette, Marlene J. Gould, Faye Grant, Jane Harmon, Rosemary Harris, Murray Horwitz, Jayne Houdyshell, Katharine Houghton Grant, Ernestine Jackson, Jonathan Kagan, Laurie Kennedy, Gavin Lee, Elisa Loti Stein, Raymond and Suzy Lowry, Spiro Malas, Daisy Maryles, Mary Stuart Masterson, Scott McClintock, John McMartin, Lin-Manuel Miranda, Brian Stokes Mitchell, James Naughton, Charles Nolte, Christopher Noth, Estelle Parsons, Linda Platzer, Charles Repole, Clifford P. Robertson, Greg Rossi, Elaine Joyce Simon, Spring Sirkin, Sheila A. Smith, Marianne Tatum, Eli Wallach, Jennifer Warren, Caroline Winston

Presenter Andrea Martin (My Favorite Year, *1993) presents the award and a Magnolia Bakery cupcake to Alli Mauzey*

Acknowledgements: Raj Atencio, Barlow Hartman Public Relations, Miriam Berman, Hillary Blanken, Boneau/Bryan-Brown, Broadway Beat, Allison Graham, Giani Filidi and Sardi's, Brian Ferdman and Theatremania.com, Jolie Gabler, Summer Grindle, Richard Hillman, Hello Entertainment (David Garfinkle and Adam Silberman), Jessica Johnson, Michael Messina, Barry Monush, PRG (Darren DeVerna, Fred Gallo, Jere Harris), Connie Leahy, Stella Morelli & Leslie Strong, The Publicity Office, Richard Ridge, Philip Rinaldi and Barbara Carroll, Sam Rudy, Pete Sanders, Dana Saltzman at Sony BMG, Sculpture House Casting, Inc (Michael Perrotta), Susanne Tighe, Cascina Ristorante (Emilio Barletta, Pino Manica, Gianni Onofri and Karen Carzo), New York Plaza Florists (Alex and Bill Anastasakis)

Theatre Awards After-Party generously provided by Cascina Ristorante, 647 9th Avenue (between West 45th & 46th); Floral Arrangements provided by New York Plaza Florists, 1166 Avenue of the Americas; Supplemental sound equipment generously provided by Jeremiah Harris, Production Resource Group; Custom Lighting Pattern generously donated by Apollo Design Technology, Inc.

Winner Loretta Ables Sayre

Gift Bag Promotions supplied by Applause Theatre and Cinema Books/Hal Leonard Publications, The Araca Group, Dodger Properties, Lincoln Center Theater, MonaVie, Roundabout Theatre Company, Sony BMG- Broadway Masterworks, and Theatremania.com

The Theatre World Awards, Inc. is a 501 (c)(3) nonprofit organization, and our annual presentation is made possible by the generous contributions of previous winners and friends. For more information please visit the website at www.theatreworldawards.org.

Tax-deductible contributions can be sent via PayPay® to info@theatreworldawards.org, or checks and money orders sent to:

Theatre World Awards, Inc.
Box 246 Radio City Station
New York, NY 10101-0246

Previous Theatre World Award Recipients

1944-45: Betty Comden (*On the Town*), Richard Davis (*Kiss Them For Me*), Richard Hart (*Dark of the Moon*), Judy Holliday (*Kiss Them for Me*), Charles Lang, Bambi Linn (*Carousel*), John Lund (*The Hasty Heart*), Donald Murphy (*Signature* and *Common Ground*), Nancy Noland (*Common Ground*), Margaret Phillips (*The Late George Apley*), John Raitt (*Carousel*)

1945-46: Barbara Bel Geddes (*Deep Are the Roots*), Marlon Brando (*Truckline Café* and *Candida*), Bill Callahan (*Call Me Mister*), Wendell Corey (*The Wind is Ninety*), Paul Douglas (*Born Yesterday*), Mary James (*Apple of His Eye*), Burt Lancaster (*A Sound of Hunting*), Patricia Marshall (*The Day Before Spring*), Beatrice Pearson (*The Mermaids Singing*)

1946-47: Keith Andes (*The Chocolate Soldier*), Marion Bell (*Brigadoon*), Peter Cookson (*Message for Margaret*), Ann Crowley (*Carousel*), Ellen Hanley (*Barefoot Boy With Cheek*), John Jordan (*The Wanhope Building*), George Keane (*Brigadoon*), Dorothea MacFarland (*Oklahoma!*), James Mitchell (*Brigadoon*), Patricia Neal (*Another Part of the Forest*), David Wayne (*Finian's Rainbow*)

1947-48: Valerie Bettis (*Inside U.S.A.*), Edward Bryce (*The Cradle Will Rock*), Whitfield Connor (*Macbeth*), Mark Dawson (*High Button Shoes*), June Lockhart (*For Love or Money*), Estelle Loring (*Inside U.S.A.*), Peggy Maley (*Joy to the World*), Ralph Meeker (*Mister Roberts*), Meg Mundy (*The Happy Journey to Trenton and Camden* and *The Respectful Prostitute*), Douglass Watson (*Antony and Cleopatra*), James Whitmore (*Command Decision*), Patrice Wymore (*Hold It!*)

1948-49: Tod Andrews (*Summer and Smoke*), Doe Avedon (*The Young and Fair*), Jean Carson (*Bravo!*), Carol Channing (*Lend an Ear*), Richard Derr (*The Traitor*), Julie Harris (*Sundown Beach*), Mary McCarty (*Sleepy Hollow*), Allyn Ann McLerie (*Where's Charley?*), Cameron Mitchell (*Death of a Salesman*), Gene Nelson (*Lend an Ear*), Byron Palmer (*Where's Charley?*), Bob Scheerer (*Lend an Ear*)

1949-50: Nancy Andrews (*Touch and Go*), Phil Arthur (*With a Silk Thread*), Barbara Brady (*The Velvet Glove*), Lydia Clarke (*Detective Story*), Priscilla Gillette (*Regina*), Don Hanmer (*The Man*), Marcia Henderson (*Peter Pan*), Charlton Heston (*Design for a Stained Glass Window*), Rick Jason (*Now I Lay Me Down to Sleep*), Grace Kelly (*The Father*), Charles Nolte (*Design for a Stained Glass Window*), Roger Price (*Tickets, Please!*)

1950-51: Barbara Ashley (*Out of This World*), Isabel Bigley (*Guys and Dolls*), Martin Brooks (*Burning Bright*), Richard Burton (*The Lady's Not For Burning*), Pat Crowley (*Southern Exposure*), James Daly (*Major Barbara* and *Mary Rose*), Cloris Leachman (*A Story for a Sunday Evening*), Russell Nype (*Call Me Madam*), Jack Palance (*Darkness at Noon*), William Smithers (*Romeo and Juliet*), Maureen Stapleton (*The Rose Tattoo*), Marcia Van Dyke (*Marcia Van Dyke*), Eli Wallach (*The Rose Tattoo*)

1951-52: Tony Bavaar (*Paint Your Wagon*), Patricia Benoit (*Glad Tidings*), Peter Conlow (*Courtin' Time*), Virginia de Luce (*New Faces of 1952*), Ronny Graham (*New Faces of 1952*), Audrey Hepburn (*Gigi*), Diana Herbert (*The Number*), Conrad Janis (*The Brass Ring*), Dick Kallman (*Seventeen*), Charles Proctor (*Twilight Walk*), Eric Sinclair (*Much Ado About Nothing*), Kim Stanley (*The Chase*), Marian Winters (*I Am a Camera*), Helen Wood (*Seventeen*)

1952-53: Edie Adams (*Wonderful Town*), Rosemary Harris (*The Climate of Eden*), Eileen Heckart (*Picnic*), Peter Kelley (*Two's Company*), John Kerr (*Bernardine*), Richard Kiley (*Misalliance*), Gloria Marlowe (*In Any Language*), Penelope Munday (*The Climate of Eden*), Paul Newman (*Picnic*), Sheree North (*Hazel Flagg*), Geraldine Page (*Mid-Summer*), John Stewart (*Bernardine*), Ray Stricklyn (*The Climate of Eden*), Gwen Verdon (*Can-Can*)

1953-54: Orson Bean (*John Murray Anderson's Almanac*), Harry Belafonte (*John Murray Anderson's Almanac*), James Dean (*The Immoralist*), Joan Diener (*Kismet*), Ben Gazzara (*End as a Man*), Carol Haney (*The Pajama Game*), Jonathan Lucas (*The Golden Apple*), Kay Medford (*Lullaby*), Scott Merrill (*The Threepenny Opera*), Elizabeth Montgomery (*Late Love*), Leo Penn (*The Girl on the Via Flaminia*), Eva Marie Saint (*The Trip to Bountiful*)

1954-55: Julie Andrews (*The Boy Friend*), Jacqueline Brookes (*The Cretan Woman*), Shirl Conway (*Plain and Fancy*), Barbara Cook (*Plain and Fancy*), David Daniels (*Plain and Fancy*), Mary Fickett (*Tea and Sympathy*), Page Johnson (*In April Once*), Loretta Leversee (*Home is the Hero*), Jack Lord (*The Traveling Lady*), Dennis Patrick (*The Wayward Saint*), Anthony Perkins (*Tea and Sympathy*), Christopher Plummer (*The Dark is Light Enough*)

1955-56: Diane Cilento (*Tiger at the Gates*), Dick Davalos (*A View From the Bridge*), Anthony Franciosa (*A Hatful of Rain*), Andy Griffith (*No Time for Sergeants*), Laurence Harvey (*Island of Goats*), David Hedison (*A Month in the Country*), Earle Hyman (*Mister Johnson*), Susan Johnson (*The Most Happy Fella*), John Michael King (*My Fair Lady*), Jayne Mansfield (*Will Success Spoil Rock Hunter?*), Sarah Marshall (*The Ponder Heart*), Gaby Rodgers (*Mister Johnson*), Susan Strasberg (*The Diary of Anne Frank*), Fritz Weaver (*The Chalk Garden*)

1956-57: Peggy Cass (*Auntie Mame*), Sydney Chaplin (*Bells Are Ringing*), Sylvia Daneel (*The Tunnel of Love*), Bradford Dillman (*Long Day's Journey Into Night*), Peter Donat (*The First Gentleman*), George Grizzard (*The Happiest Millionaire*), Carol Lynley (*The Potting Shed*), Peter Palmer (Li'l Abner), Jason Robards (*Long Day's Journey Into Night*), Cliff Robertson (*Orpheus Descending*), Pippa Scott (*Child of Fortune*), Inga Swenson (*The First Gentleman*)

1957-58: Anne Bancroft (*Two for the Seesaw*), Warren Berlinger (*Blue Denim*), Colleen Dewhurst (*Children of Darkness*), Richard Easton (*The Country Wife*), Tim Everett (*The Dark at the Top of the Stairs*), Eddie Hodges (*The Music Man*), Joan Hovis (*Love Me Little*), Carol Lawrence (*West Side Story*), Jacqueline McKeever (*Oh, Captain!*), Wynne Miller (*Li'l Abner*), Robert Morse (*Say, Darling*), George C. Scott (*Richard III*)

1958-59: Lou Antonio (*The Buffalo Skinner*), Ina Balin (*A Majority of One*), Richard Cross (*Maria Golovin*), Tammy Grimes (*Look After Lulu*), Larry Hagman (*God and Kate Murphy*), Dolores Hart (*The Pleasure of His Company*), Roger Mollien (French Theatre National Populaire), France Nuyen (*The World of Suzie Wong*), Susan Oliver (*Patate*), Ben Piazza (*Kataki*), Paul Roebling (*A Desert Incident*), William Shatner (*The World of Suzie Wong*), Pat Suzuki (*Flower Drum Song*), Rip Torn (*Sweet Bird of Youth*)

1959-60: Warren Beatty (*A Loss of Roses*), Eileen Brennan (*Little Mary Sunshine*), Carol Burnett (*Once Upon a Mattress*), Patty Duke (*The Miracle Worker*), Jane Fonda (*There Was a Little Girl*), Anita Gillette (*Russell Patterson's Sketchbook*), Elisa Loti (*Come Share My House*), Donald Madden (*Julius Caesar*), George Maharis (*The Zoo Story*), John McMartin (*Little Mary Sunshine*), Lauri Peters (*The Sound of Music*), Dick Van Dyke (*The Boys Against the Girls*)

1960-61: Joyce Bulifant (*Whisper to Me*), Dennis Cooney (*Every Other Evil*), Sandy Dennis (*Face of a Hero*), Nancy Dussault (*Do Re Mi*), Robert Goulet (*Camelot*), Joan Hackett (*Call Me By My Rightful Name*), June Harding (*Cry of the Raindrop*), Ron Husmann (*Tenderloin*), James MacArthur (*Invitation to a March*), Bruce Yarnell (*The Happiest Girl in the World*)

1961-62: Elizabeth Ashley (*Take Her, She's Mine*), Keith Baxter (*A Man for All Seasons*), Peter Fonda (*Blood, Sweat and Stanley Poole*), Don Galloway (*Bring Me a Warm Body*), Sean Garrison (*Half-Past Wednesday*), Barbara Harris (*Oh, Dad, Poor Dad, Mamma's Hung You in the Closet and I'm Feeling So Sad*), James Earl Jones (*Moon on a Rainbow Shawl*), Janet Margolin (*Daughter of Silence*), Karen Morrow (*Sing, Muse!*), Robert Redford (*Sunday in New York*), John Stride (*Romeo and Juliet*), Brenda Vaccaro (*Everybody Loves Opal*)

1962-63: Alan Arkin (*Enter Laughing*), Stuart Damon (*The Boys from Syracuse*), Melinda Dillon (*Who's Afraid of Virginia Woolf?*), Robert Drivas (*Mrs. Dally Has a Lover*), Bob Gentry (*Angels of Anadarko*), Dorothy Loudon (*Nowhere to Go But Up*), Brandon Maggart (*Put It in Writing*), Julienne Marie (*The Boys from Syracuse*), Liza Minnelli (*Best Foot Forward*), Estelle Parsons (*Mrs. Dally Has a Lover*), Diana Sands (*Tiger Tiger Burning Bright*), Swen Swenson (*Little Me*)

1963-64: Alan Alda (*Fair Game for Lover*), Gloria Bleezarde (*Never Live Over a Pretzel Factory*), Imelda De Martin (*The Amorous Flea*), Claude Giraud (*Phédre*), Ketty Lester (*Cabin in the Sky*), Barbara Loden (*After the Fall*), Lawrence Pressman (*Never Live Over a Pretzel Factory*), Gilbert Price (*Jerico-Jim Crow*), Philip Proctor (*The Amorous Flea*), John Tracy (*Telemachus Clay*), Jennifer West (*Dutchman*)

1964-65: Carolyn Coates (*The Trojan Women*), Joyce Jillson (*The Roar of the Greasepaint – The Smell of the Crowd*), Linda Lavin (*Wet Paint*), Luba Lisa (*I Had a Ball*), Michael O'Sullivan (*Tartuffe*), Joanna Pettet (*Poor Richard*), Beah Richards (*The Amen Corner*), Jaime Sanchez (*Conerico Was Here to Stay* and *The Toilet*), Victor Spinetti (*Oh, What a Lovely War*), Nicolas Surovy (*Helen*), Robert Walker (*I Knock at the Door* and *Pictures in the Hallway*), Clarence Williams III (*Slow Dancing on the Killing Ground*)

1965-66: Zoe Caldwell (*Slapstick Tragedy*), David Carradine (*The Royal Hunt of the Sun*), John Cullum (*On a Clear Day You Can See Forever*), John Davidson (*Oklahoma!*), Faye Dunaway (*Hogan's Ghost*), Gloria Foster (*Medea*), Robert Hooks (*Where's Daddy?* and *Day of Absence*), Jerry Lanning (*Mame*), Richard Mulligan (*Mating Dance* and *Hogan's Ghost*), April Shawhan (*3 Bags Full*), Sandra Smith (*Any Wednesday*), Leslie Ann Warren (*Drat! The Cat!*)

1966-67: Bonnie Bedelia (*My Sweet Charlie*), Richard Benjamin (*The Star-Spangled Girl*), Dustin Hoffman (*Eh?*), Terry Kiser (*Fortune and Men's Eyes*), Reva Rose (*You're A Good Man, Charlie Brown*), Robert Salvio (*Hamp*), Sheila Smith (*Mame*), Connie Stevens (*The Star-Spangled Girl*), Pamela Tiffin (*Dinner at Eight*), Leslie Uggams (*Hallelujah, Baby*), Jon Voight (*That Summer – That Fall*), Christopher Walken (*The Rose Tattoo*)

1967-68: David Birney (*Summertree*), Pamela Burrell (*Arms and the Man*), Jordan Christopher (*Black Comedy*), Jack Crowder – aka Thalmus Rasulala (*Hello, Dolly!*), Sandy Duncan (*Ceremony of Innocence*), Julie Gregg (*The Happy Time*), Stephen Joyce (*Stephen D.*), Bernadette Peters (*George M*), Alice Playten (*Henry, Sweet Henry*), Michael Rupert (*The Happy Time*), Brenda Smiley (*Scuba Duba*), Russ Thacker (*Your Own Thing*)

1968-69: Jane Alexander (*The Great White Hope*), David Cryer (*Come Summer*), Blythe Danner (*The Miser*), Ed Evanko (*Canterbury Tales*), Ken Howard (*1776*), Lauren Jones (*Does a Tiger Wear a Necktie?*), Ron Leibman (*We Bombed in New Haven*), Marian Mercer (*Promises, Promises*), Jill O'Hara (*Promises, Promises*), Ron O'Neal (*No Place to Be Somebody*), Al Pacino (*Does a Tiger Wear a Necktie?*), Marlene Warfield (*The Great White Hope*)

1969-70: Susan Browning (*Company*), Donny Burks (*Billy Noname*), Catherine Burns (*Dear Janet Rosenberg, Dear Mr. Kooning*), Len Cariou (*Henry V* and *Applause*), Bonnie Franklin (*Applause*), David Holliday (*Coco*), Katharine Houghton (*A Scent of Flowers*), Melba Moore (*Purlie*), David Rounds (*Child's Play*), Lewis J. Stadlen (*Minnie's Boys*), Kristoffer Tabori (*How Much, How Much*), Fredricka Weber (*The Last Sweet Days of Isaac*)

1970-71: Clifton Davis (*Do It Again*), Michael Douglas (*Pinkville*), Julie Garfield (*Uncle Vanya*), Martha Henry (*The Playboy of the Western World, Scenes From American Life,* and *Antigone*), James Naughton (*Long Days Journey Into Night*), Tricia O'Neil (*Two by Two*), Kipp Osborne (*Butterflies Are Free*), Roger Rathburn (*No, No, Nanette*), Ayn Ruymen (*The Gingerbread Lady*), Jennifer Salt (*Father's Day*), Joan Van Ark (*School for Wives*), Walter Willison (*Two by Two*)

1971-72: Jonelle Allen (*Two Gentlemen of Verona*), Maureen Anderman (*Moonchildren*), William Atherton (*Suggs*), Richard

Backus (*Promenade, All!*), Adrienne Barbeau (*Grease*), Cara Duff-MacCormick (*Moonchildren*), Robert Foxworth (*The Crucible*), Elaine Joyce (*Sugar*), Jess Richards (*On The Town*), Ben Vereen (*Jesus Christ Superstar*), Beatrice Winde (*Ain't Supposed to Die a Natural Death*), James Woods (*Moonchildren*)

1972-73: D'Jamin Bartlett (*A Little Night Music*), Patricia Elliott (*A Little Night Music*), James Farentino (*A Streetcar Named Desire*), Brian Farrell (*The Last of Mrs. Lincoln*), Victor Garber (*Ghosts*), Kelly Garrett (*Mother Earth*), Mari Gorman (*The Hot l Baltimore*), Laurence Guittard (*A Little Night Music*), Trish Hawkins (*The Hot l Baltimore*), Monte Markham (*Irene*), John Rubinstein (*Pippin*), Jennifer Warren (*6 Rms Riv Vu*), Alexander H. Cohen (Special Award)

1973-74: Mark Baker (*Candide*), Maureen Brennan (*Candide*), Ralph Carter (*Raisin*), Thom Christopher (*Noel Coward in Two Keys*), John Driver (*Over Here*), Conchata Ferrell (*The Sea Horse*), Ernestine Jackson (*Raisin*), Michael Moriarty (*Find Your Way Home*), Joe Morton (*Raisin*), Ann Reinking (*Over Here*), Janie Sell (*Over Here*), Mary Woronov (*Boom Boom Room*), Sammy Cahn (Special Award)

1974-75: Peter Burnell (*In Praise of Love*), Zan Charisse (*Gypsy*), Lola Falana (*Dr. Jazz*), Peter Firth (*Equus*), Dorian Harewood (*Don't Call Back*), Joel Higgins (*Shenandoah*), Marcia McClain (*Where's Charley?*), Linda Miller (*Black Picture Show*), Marti Rolph (*Good News*), John Sheridan (*Gypsy*), Scott Stevensen (*Good News*), Donna Theodore (*Shenandoah*), Equity Library Theatre (Special Award)

1975-76: Danny Aiello (*Lamppost Reunion*), Christine Andreas (*My Fair Lady*), Dixie Carter (*Jesse and the Bandit Queen*), Tovah Feldshuh (*Yentl*), Chip Garnett (*Bubblin' Brown Sugar*), Richard Kelton (*Who's Afraid of Virginia Woolf?*), Vivian Reed (*Bubblin' Brown Sugar*), Charles Repole (*Very Good Eddie*), Virginia Seidel (*Very Good Eddie*), Daniel Seltzer (*Knock Knock*), John V. Shea (*Yentl*), Meryl Streep (*27 Wagons Full of Cotton*), *A Chorus Line* (Special Award)

1976-77: Trazana Beverley (*for colored girls…*), Michael Cristofer (*The Cherry Orchard*), Joe Fields (*The Basic Training of Pavlo Hummel*), Joanna Gleason (*I Love My Wife*), Cecilia Hart (*Dirty Linen*), John Heard (*G.R. Point*), Gloria Hodes (*The Club*), Juliette Koka (*Piaf…A Remembrance*), Andrea McArdle (*Annie*), Ken Page (*Guys and Dolls*), Jonathan Pryce (*Comedians*), Chick Vennera (*Jockeys*), Eva LeGallienne (Special Award)

1977-78: Vasili Bogazianos (*P.S. Your Cat Is Dead*), Nell Carter (*Ain't Misbehavin'*), Carlin Glynn (*The Best Little Whorehouse in Texas*), Christopher Goutman (*The Promise*), William Hurt (*Ulysses in Traction, Lulu,* and *The Fifth of July*), Judy Kaye (*On the 20th Century*), Florence Lacy (*Hello, Dolly!*), Armelia McQueen (*Ain't Misbehavin'*), Gordana Rashovich (*Fefu and Her Friends*), Bo Rucker (*Native Son*), Richard Seer (*Da*), Colin Stinton (*The Water Engine*), Joseph Papp (Special Award)

1978-79: Philip Anglim (*The Elephant Man*), Lucie Arnaz (*They're Playing Our Song*), Gregory Hines (*Eubie!*), Ken Jennings (*Sweeney Todd*), Michael Jeter (*G.R. Point*), Laurie Kennedy (*Man and Superman*), Susan Kingsley (*Getting Out*), Christine Lahti (*The Woods*), Edward James Olmos (*Zoot Suit*), Kathleen Quinlan (*Taken in Marriage*), Sarah Rice (*Sweeney Todd*), Max Wright (*Once in a Lifetime*), Marshall W. Mason (Special Award)

1979-80: Maxwell Caulfield (*Class Enemy*), Leslie Denniston (*Happy New Year*), Boyd Gaines (*A Month in the Country*), Richard Gere (*Bent*), Harry Groener (*Oklahoma!*), Stephen James (*The 1940's Radio Hour*), Susan Kellermann (*Last Licks*), Dinah Manoff (*I Ought to Be in Pictures*), Lonny Price (*Class Enemy*), Marianne Tatum (*Barnum*), Anne Twomey (*Nuts*), Dianne Wiest (*The Art of Dining*), Mickey Rooney (Special Award)

1980-81: Brian Backer (*The Floating Light Bulb*), Lisa Banes (*Look Back in Anger*), Meg Bussert (*The Music Man*), Michael Allen Davis (*Broadway Follies*), Giancarlo Esposito (*Zooman and the Sign*), Daniel Gerroll (*Slab Boys*), Phyllis Hyman (*Sophisticated Ladies*), Cynthia Nixon (*The Philadelphia Story*), Amanda Plummer (*A Taste of Honey*), Adam Redfield (*A Life*), Wanda Richert (*42nd Street*), Rex Smith (*The Pirates of Penzance*), Elizabeth Taylor (Special Award)

1981-82: Karen Akers (*Nine*), Laurie Beechman (*Joseph and the Amazing Technicolor Dreamcoat*), Danny Glover (*Master Harold… and the Boys*), David Alan Grier (*The First*), Jennifer Holliday (*Dreamgirls*), Anthony Heald (*Misalliance*), Lizbeth Mackay (*Crimes of the Heart*), Peter MacNicol (*Crimes of the Heart*), Elizabeth McGovern (*My Sister in This House*), Ann Morrison (*Merrily We Roll Along*), Michael O'Keefe (*Mass Appeal*), James Widdoes (*Is There Life After High School?*), Manhattan Theatre Club (Special Award)

1982-83: Karen Allen (*Monday After the Miracle*), Suzanne Bertish (*Skirmishes*), Matthew Broderick (*Brighton Beach Memoirs*), Kate Burton (*Winners*), Joanne Camp (*Geniuses*), Harvey Fierstein (*Torch Song Trilogy*), Peter Gallagher (*A Doll's Life*), John Malkovich (*True West*), Anne Pitoniak (*'Night Mother*), James Russo (*Extremities*), Brian Tarantina (*Angels Fall*), Linda Thorson (*Streaming*), Natalia Makarova (*On Your Toes* Special Award)

1983-84: Martine Allard (*The Tap Dance Kid*), Joan Allen (*And a Nightingale Sang*), Kathy Whitton Baker (*Fool For Love*), Mark Capri (*On Approval*), Laura Dean (*Doonesbury*), Stephen Geoffreys (*The Human Comedy*), Todd Graff (*Baby*), Glenne Headly (*The Philanthropist*), J.J. Johnston (*American Buffalo*), Bonnie Koloc (*The Human Comedy*), Calvin Levels (*Open Admissions*), Robert Westenberg (*Zorba*), Ron Moody (Special Award)

1984-85: Kevin Anderson (*Orphans*), Richard Chaves (*Tracers*), Patti Cohenour (*La Boheme* and *Big River*), Charles S. Dutton (*Ma Rainey's Black Bottom*), Nancy Giles (*Mayor*), Whoopi Goldberg (*Whoopi Goldberg*), Leilani Jones (*Grind*), John Mahoney (*Orphans*), Laurie Metcalf (*Balm in Gilead*), Barry

Miller (*Biloxi Blues*), John Turturro (*Danny and the Deep Blue Sea*), Amelia White (*The Accrington Pals*), Lucille Lortel (Special Award)

1985-86: Suzy Amis (*Fresh Horses*), Alec Baldwin (*Loot*), Aled Davies (*Orchards*), Faye Grant (*Singin' in the Rain*), Julie Hagerty (*House of Blue Leaves*), Ed Harris (*Precious Sons*), Mark Jacoby (*Sweet Charity*), Donna Kane (*Dames at Sea*), Cleo Laine (*The Mystery of Edwin Drood*), Howard McGillin (*The Mystery of Edwin Drood*), Marisa Tomei (*Daughters*), Joe Urla (*Principia Scriptoriae*), Ensemble Studio Theatre (Special Award)

1986-87: Annette Bening (*Coastal Disturbances*), Timothy Daly (*Coastal Disturbances*), Lindsay Duncan (*Les Liaisons Dangereuses*), Frank Ferrante (*Groucho: A Life in Revue*), Robert Lindsay (*Me and My Girl*), Amy Madigan (*The Lucky Spot*), Michael Maguire (*Les Misérables*), Demi Moore (*The Early Girl*), Molly Ringwald (*Lily Dale*), Frances Ruffelle (*Les Misérables*), Courtney B. Vance (*Fences*), Colm Wilkinson (*Les Misérables*), Robert DeNiro (Special Award)

1987-88: Yvonne Bryceland (*The Road to Mecca*), Philip Casnoff (*Chess*), Danielle Ferland (*Into the Woods*), Melissa Gilbert (*A Shayna Maidel*), Linda Hart (*Anything Goes*), Linzi Hateley (*Carrie*), Brian Kerwin (*Emily*), Brian Mitchell (*Mail*), Mary Murfitt (*Oil City Symphony*), Aidan Quinn *A Streetcar Named Desire*), Eric Roberts (*Burn This*), B.D. Wong (*M. Butterfly*), Tisa Chang and Martin E. Segal (Special Awards)

1988-89: Dylan Baker (*Eastern Standard*), Joan Cusack (*Road* and *Brilliant Traces*), Loren Dean (*Amulets Against the Dragon Forces*), Peter Frechette (*Eastern Standard*), Sally Mayes (*Welcome to the Club*), Sharon McNight (*Starmites*), Jennie Moreau (*Eleemosynary*), Paul Provenza (*Only Kidding*), Kyra Sedgwick (*Ah, Wilderness!*), Howard Spiegel (*Only Kidding*), Eric Stoltz (*Our Town*), Joanne Whalley-Kilmer (*What the Butler Saw*); Pauline Collins (*Shirley Valentine* – Special Award), Mikhail Baryshnikov (Special Award)

1989-90: Denise Burse (*Ground People*), Erma Campbell (*Ground People*), Rocky Carroll (*The Piano Lesson*), Megan Gallagher (*A Few Good Men*), Tommy Hollis (*The Piano Lesson*), Robert Lambert (*Gypsy*), Kathleen Rowe McAllen (*Aspects of Love*), Michael McKean (*Accomplice*), Crista Moore (*Gypsy*), Mary-Louise Parker (*Prelude to a Kiss*), Daniel von Bargen (*Mastergate*), Jason Workman (*Jason Workman*), Stewart Granger and Kathleen Turner (Special Awards)

1990-91: Jane Adams (*I Hate Hamlet*), Gillian Anderson (*Absent Friends*), Adam Arkin (*I Hate Hamlet*), Brenda Blethyn (*Absent Friends*), Marcus Chong (*Stand-up Tragedy*), Paul Hipp (*Buddy*), LaChanze (*Once on This Island*), Kenny Neal (*Mule Bone*), Kevin Ramsey (*Oh, Kay!*), Francis Ruivivar (*Shogun*), Lea Salonga (*Miss Saigon*), Chandra Wilson (*The Good Times Are Killing Me*); Tracey Ullman (*The Big Love* and *Taming of the Shrew*), Ellen Stewart (Special Award)

1991-92: Talia Balsam (*Jake's Women*), Lindsay Crouse (*The Homecoming*), Griffin Dunne (*Search and Destroy*), Laurence Fishburne (*Two Trains Running*), Mel Harris (*Empty Hearts*), Jonathan Kaplan (*Falsettos* and *Rags*), Jessica Lange (*A Streetcar Named Desire*), Laura Linney (*Sight Unseen*), Spiro Malas (*The Most Happy Fella*), Mark Rosenthal (*Marvin's Room*), Helen Shaver (*Jake's Women*), Al White (*Two Trains Running*), *Dancing at Lughnasa* cast (Special Award), Plays for Living (Special Award)

1992-93: Brent Carver (*Kiss of the Spider Woman*), Michael Cerveris (*The Who's Tommy*), Marcia Gay Harden (*Angels in America: Millennium Approaches*), Stephanie Lawrence (*Blood Brothers*), Andrea Martin (*My Favorite Year*), Liam Neeson (*Anna Christie*), Stephen Rea (*Someone Who'll Watch Over Me*), Natasha Richardson (*Anna Christie*), Martin Short (*The Goodbye Girl*), Dina Spybey (*Five Women Wearing the Same Dress*), Stephen Spinella (*Angels in America: Millennium Approaches*), Jennifer Tilly (*One Shoe Off*), John Leguizamo (Special Award), Rosetta LeNoire (Special Award)

1993-94: Marcus D'Amico (*An Inspector Calls*), Jarrod Emick (*Damn Yankees*), Arabella Field (*Snowing at Delphi* and *4 Dogs and a Bone*), Aden Gillett (*An Inspector Calls*), Sherry Glaser (*Family Secrets*), Michael Hayden (*Carousel*), Margaret Illman (*The Red Shoes*), Audra Ann McDonald (*Carousel*), Burke Moses (*Beauty and the Beast*), Anna Deavere Smith (*Twilight: Los Angeles, 1992*), Jere Shea (*Passion*), Harriet Walter (*3Birds Alighting on a Field*)

1994-95: Gretha Boston (*Show Boat*), Billy Crudup (*Arcadia*), Ralph Fiennes (*Hamlet*), Beverly D'Angelo (*Simpatico*), Calista Flockhart (*The Glass Menagerie*), Kevin Kilner (*The Glass Menagerie*), Anthony LaPaglia (*The Rose Tattoo*), Julie Johnson (*Das Barbecü*), Helen Mirren (*A Month in the Country*), Jude Law (*Indiscretions*), Rufus Sewell (*Translations*), Vanessa Williams (*Kiss of the Spider Woman*), Brooke Shields (Special Award)

1995-96: Jordan Baker (*Suddenly Last Summer*), Joohee Choi (*The King and I*), Karen Kay Cody (*Master Class*), Viola Davis (*Seven Guitars*), Kate Forbes (*The School for Scandal*), Michael McGrath (*Swinging on a Star*), Alfred Molina (*Molly Sweeney*), Timothy Olyphant (*The Monogamist*), Adam Pascal (*Rent*), Lou Diamond Phillips (*The King and I*), Daphne Rubin-Vega (*Rent*), Brett Tabisel (*Big*), *An Ideal Husband* cast (Special Award)

1996-97: Terry Beaver (*The Last Night of Ballyhoo*), Helen Carey (*London Assurance*), Kristin Chenoweth (*Steel Pier*), Jason Danieley (*Candide*), Linda Eder (*Jekyll & Hyde*), Allison Janney (*Present Laughter*), Daniel McDonald (*Steel Pier*), Janet McTeer (*A Doll's House*), Mark Ruffalo (*This Is Our Youth*), Fiona Shaw (*The Waste Land*), Antony Sher (*Stanley*), Alan Tudyk (*Bunny Bunny*), *Skylight* cast (Special Award)

1997-98: Max Casella (*The Lion King*), Margaret Colin (*Jackie*), Ruaidhri Conroy (*The Cripple of Inishmaan*), Alan Cumming (*Cabaret*), Lea Delaria (*On the Town*), Edie Falco (*Side Man*), Enid Graham (*Honour*), Anna Kendrick (*High Society*), Ednita Nazario (*The Capeman*), Douglas Sills (*The Scarlet Pimpernel*), Steven Sutcliffe (*Ragtime*), Sam Trammel (*Ah, Wilderness!*), Eddie Izzard (Special Award), *Beauty Queen of Leenane* cast (Special Award)

1998-99: Jillian Armenante (*The Cider House Rules*), James Black (*Not About Nightingales*), Brendan Coyle (*The Weir*), Anna Friel (*Closer*), Rupert Graves (*Closer*), Lynda Graváttt (*The Old Settler*), Nicole Kidman (*The Blue Room*), Ciáran Hinds (*Closer*), Ute Lemper (*Chicago*), Clarke Peters (*The Iceman Cometh*), Toby Stephens (*Ring Round the Moon*), Sandra Oh (*Stop Kiss*), Jerry Herman (Special Award)

1999-2000: Craig Bierko (*The Music Man*), Everett Bradley (*Swing!*), Gabriel Byrne (*A Moon for the Misbegotten*), Ann Hampton Callaway (*Swing!*), Toni Collette (*The Wild Party*), Henry Czerny (*Arms and the Man*), Stephen Dillane (*The Real Thing*), Jennifer Ehle (*The Real Thing*), Philip Seymour Hoffman (*True West*), Hayley Mills (*Suite in Two Keys*), Cigdem Onat (*The Time of the Cuckoo*), Claudia Shear (*Dirty Blonde*), Barry Humphries (Special Award)

2000-2001: Juliette Binoche (*Betrayal*), Macaulay Culkin (*Madame Melville*), Janie Dee (*Comic Potential*), Raúl Esparza (*The Rocky Horror Show*), Kathleen Freeman (*The Full Monty*), Deven May (*Bat Boy*), Reba McEntire (*Annie Get Your Gun*), Chris Noth (*The Best Man*), Joshua Park (*The Adventures of Tom Sawyer*), Rosie Perez (*References to Salvador Dali Make Me Hot*), Joely Richardson (*Madame Melville*), John Ritter (*The Dinner Party*), Seán Campion and Conleth Hill (*Stones in His Pocket* – Special Awards)

2001-2002: Justin Bohon (*Oklahoma!*), Simon Callow (*The Mystery of Charles Dickens*), Mos Def (*Topdog/Underdog*), Emma Fielding (*Private Lives*), Adam Godley (*Private Lives*), Martin Jarvis (*By Jeeves*), Spencer Kayden (*Urinetown*), Gretchen Mol (*The Shape of Things*), Anna Paquin (*The Glory of Living*), Louise Pitre (*Mamma Mia!*), David Warner (*Major Barbara*), Rachel Weisz (*The Shape of Things*)

2002-2003: Antonio Banderas (*Nine*), Tammy Blanchard (*Gypsy*), Thomas Jefferson Byrd (*Ma Rainey's Black Bottom*), Jonathan Cake (*Medea*), Victoria Hamilton (*A Day in the Death of Joe Egg*), Clare Higgins (*Vincent in Brixton*), Jackie Hoffman (*Hairspray*), Mary Stuart Masterson (*Nine*), John Selya (*Movin' Out*), Daniel Sunjata (*Take Me Out*), Jochum ten Haaf (*Vincent in Brixton*), Marissa Jaret Winokur (*Hairspray*), Peter Filichia (Special Award), Ben Hodges (Special Award)

2003-2004: Shannon Cochran (*Bug*), Stephanie D'Abruzzo (*Avenue Q*), Mitchel David Federan (*The Boy From Oz*), Alexander Gemignani (*Assassins*), Hugh Jackman (*The Boy From Oz*), Isabel Keating (*The Boy From Oz*), Sanaa Lathan (*A Raisin in the Sun*), Jefferson Mays (*I Am My Own Wife*), Euan Morton (*Taboo*), Anika Noni Rose (*Caroline, or Change*), John Tartaglia (*Avenue Q*), Jennifer Westfeldt (*Wonderful Town*), Sarah Jones (*Bridge and Tunnel* Special Award)

2004-2005: Christina Applegate (*Sweet Charity*), Ashlie Atkinson (*Fat Pig*), Hank Azaria (*Spamalot*), Gordon Clapp (*Glengarry Glen Ross*), Conor Donovan (*Privilege*), Dan Fogler (*The 25th Annual Putnam County Spelling Bee*), Heather Goldenhersh (*Doubt*), Carla Gugino (*After the Fall*), Jenn Harris (*Modern Orthodox*), Cheyenne Jackson (*All Shook Up*), Celia Keenan-Bolger (*The 25th Annual Putnam County Spelling Bee*), Tyler Maynard (*Altar Boyz*)

2005-2006: Harry Connick , Jr. (*The Pajama Game*), Felicia P. Fields (*The Color Purple*), Maria Friedman (*The Woman in White*), Richard Griffiths (*The History Boys*), Mamie Gummer (*Mr. Marmalade*), Jayne Houdyshell (*Well*), Bob Martin (*The Drowsy Chaperone*), Ian McDiarmid (*Faith Healer*), Nellie McKay (*The Threepenny Opera*), David Wilmot (*The Lieutenant of Inishmore*), Elisabeth Withers-Mendes (*The Color Purple*), John Lloyd Young (*Jersey Boys*)

2006–2007: Eve Best (*A Moon for the Misbegotten*), Mary Birdsong (*Martin Short: Fame Becomes Me*), Erin Davie (*Grey Gardens*), Xanthe Elbrick (*Coram Boy*), Fantasia (*The Color Purple*), Johnny Galecki (*The Little Dog Laughed*), Jonathan Groff (*Spring Awakening*), Gavin Lee (*Mary Poppins*), Lin-Manuel Miranda (*In the Heights*), Bill Nighy (*The Vertical Hour*), Stark Sands (*Journey's End*), Nilaja Sun (*No Child...*)

1955 Theatre World Award winner Julie Andrews receives her award from 1954 winner Eva Marie Saint

Major New York Awards

AMERICAN THEATRE WING'S ANTOINETTE PERRY "TONY" AWARDS

Sunday, June 15, 2008 at Radio City Music Hall; Host: Whoopi Goldberg. The 62nd annual Tony Awards are presented in recognition of distinguished achievement in the Broadway theater; presented by a joint venture of the Broadway League (Charlotte St. Martin, Executive Director; Nina Lannan, Chair) and the American Theatre Wing (Sondra Gilman, Chairman; Douglas B. Leeds, President; Howard Sherman, Executive Director); Managing Producer for Tony Award Productions, Elizabeth I. McCann; Coordinating Producer, Joey Parnes; Executive Producer for telecast, Ricky Kirshner, Glenn Weiss.

BEST PLAY *August: Osage County* by Tracy Letts; Producers: Jeffrey Richards, Jean Doumanian, Steve Traxler, Jerry Frankel, Ostar Productions, Jennifer Manocherian, The Weinstein Company, Debra Black/Daryl Roth, Ronald & Marc Frankel/ Barbara Freitag, Rick Steiner/Staton Bell Group, The Steppenwolf Theatre Company

Nominees: *Rock 'n' Roll* by Tom Stoppard; Producers: Bob Boyett & Sonia Friedman Productions, Ostar Productions, Roger Berlind, Tulchin/Bartner, Douglas G. Smith, Dancap Productions, Jam Theatricals, The Weinstein Company, Lincoln Center Theater, The Royal Court Theatre London; *The Seafarer* by Conor McPherson; Producers: Ostar Productions, Bob Boyett, Roy Furman, Lawrence Horowitz, Jam Theatricals, Bill Rollnick/Nancy Ellison Rollnick, James D'Orta, Thomas S. Murphy, Ralph Guild/Jon Avnet, Philip Geier/Keough Partners, Eric Falkenstein/Max OnStage, The National Theatre of Great Britain; *The 39 Steps* by Patrick Barlow; Producers: Roundabout Theatre Company, Todd Haimes, Harold Wolpert, Julia C. Levy, Bob Boyett, Harriet Newman Leve/ Ron Nicynski, Stewart F. Lane/Bonnie Comley, Manocherian Golden Prods., Olympus Theatricals/Douglas Denoff, Marek J. Cantor/Pat Addiss, Huntington Theatre Company/Nicholas Martin/Michael Maso, Edward Snape for Fiery Angel Ltd.

BEST MUSICAL *In the Heights* Producers: Kevin McCollum, Jeffrey Seller, Jill Furman, Sander Jacobs, Goodman/Grossman, Peter Fine, Everett/Skipper

Nominees: *Cry-Baby* Producers: Adam Epstein, Allan S. Gordon, Élan V. McAllister, Brian Grazer, James P. MacGilvray, Universal Pictures Stage Productions, Anne Caruso, Adam S. Gordon, Latitude Link, The Pelican Group, Philip Morgaman, Andrew Farber/Richard Mishaan; *Passing Strange* Producers: The Shubert Organization, Elizabeth Ireland McCann LLC, Bill Kenwright, Chase Mishkin, Barbara & Buddy Freitag, Broadway Across America, Emily Fisher Landau, Peter May, Boyett Ostar, Larry Hirschhorn, Janet Pailet/Steve Klein, Elie Hirschfeld/Jed Bernstein, Spring Sirkin/Ruth Hendel, Vasi Laurence/Pat Flicker Addiss, Wendy Federman/Jackie Barlia Florin, Joey Parnes, The Public Theater, The Berkeley Repertory Theatre; *Xanadu* Producers: Robert Ahrens, Dan Vickery, Tara Smith/B. Swibel, Sarah Murchison/Dale Smith

BEST BOOK OF A MUSICAL *Passing Strange* by Stew

Nominees: *Cry-Baby* by Mark O'Donnell and Thomas Meehan; *In the Heights* by Quiara Alegría Hudes; *Xanadu* by Douglas Carter Beane

BEST ORIGINAL SCORE *In the Heights* Music & Lyrics: Lin-Manuel Miranda

Nominees: *Cry-Baby* Music & Lyrics: David Javerbaum & Adam Schlesinger; *The Little Mermaid* Music: Alan Menken Lyrics: Howard Ashman and Glenn Slater; *Passing Strange* Music: Stew and Heidi Rodewald Lyrics: Stew

BEST REVIVAL OF A PLAY *Boeing-Boeing* Producers: Sonia Friedman Productions, Bob Boyett, Act Productions, Matthew Byam Shaw, Robert G. Bartner, The Weinstein Company, Susan Gallin/Mary Lu Roffe, Broadway Across America, Tulchin/ Jenkins/DSM, The Araca Group

Nominees: *The Homecoming* Producers: Jeffrey Richards, Jerry Frankel, Jam Theatricals, Ergo Entertainment, Barbara & Buddy Freitag, Michael Gardner, Herbert Goldsmith Productions, Terry E. Schnuck, Harold Thau, Michael Filerman/Lynne Peyser, Ronald Frankel/David Jaroslawicz, Love Bunny Entertainment; *Les Liaisons Dangereuses* Producers: Roundabout Theatre Company, Todd Haimes, Harold Wolpert, Julia C. Levy; *Macbeth* Producers: Duncan C. Weldon & Paul Elliott, Jeffrey Archer, Bill Ballard, Terri & Timothy Childs, Rodger Hess, David Mirvish, Adriana Mnuchin, Emanuel Azenberg, BAM, The Chichester Festival Theatre

BEST REVIVAL OF MUSICAL *South Pacific* Producers: Lincoln Center Theater, André Bishop, Bernard Gersten, Bob Boyett

Nominees: *Grease* Producers: Paul Nicholas and David Ian, Nederlander Presentations Inc., Terry Allen Kramer, Robert Stigwood; *Gypsy* Producers: Roger Berlind, The Routh-Frankel-Baruch-Viertel Group, Roy Furman, Debra Black, Ted Hartley, Roger Horchow, David Ian, Scott Rudin, Jack Viertel; *Sunday in the Park with George* Producers: Roundabout Theatre Company, Todd Haimes, Harold Wolpert, Julia C. Levy, Bob Boyett, Debra Black, Jam Theatricals, Stephanie P. McClelland, Stewart F. Lane/Bonnie Comley, Barbara Manocherian/ Jennifer Manocherian, Ostar Productions, The Menier Chocolate Factory/David Babani

BEST PERFORMANCE BY A LEADING ACTOR IN A PLAY Mark Rylance, *Boeing-Boeing*

Nominees: Ben Daniels, *Les Liaisons Dangereuses*; Laurence Fishburne, *Thurgood*; Rufus Sewell, *Rock 'n' Roll*; Patrick Stewart, *Macbeth*

BEST PERFORMANCE BY A LEADING ACTRESS IN A PLAY Deanna Dunagan, *August: Osage County*

Nominees: Eve Best, *The Homecoming*; Kate Fleetwood, *Macbeth*; S. Epatha Merkerson, *Come Back, Little Sheba*; Amy Morton, *August: Osage County*

BEST PERFORMANCE BY A LEADING ACTOR IN A MUSICAL Paulo Szot, *South Pacific*

Nominees: Daniel Evans, *Sunday in the Park with George*; Lin-Manuel Miranda, *In the Heights*; Stew, *Passing Strange*; Tom Wopat, *A Catered Affair*

BEST PERFORMANCE BY A LEADING ACTRESS IN A MUSICAL Patti LuPone, *Gypsy*

Nominees: Kerry Butler, *Xanadu*; Kelli O'Hara, *South Pacific*; Faith Prince, *A Catered Affair*; Jenna Russell, *Sunday in the Park with George*

BEST PERFORMANCE BY A FEATURED ACTOR IN A PLAY Jim Norton, *The Seafarer*

Nominees: Bobby Cannavale, *Mauritius*; Raúl Esparza, *The Homecoming*; Conleth Hill, *The Seafarer*; David Pittu, *Is He Dead?*

BEST PERFORMANCE BY A FEATURED ACTRESS IN A PLAY Rondi Reed, *August: Osage County*

Nominees: Sinead Cusack, *Rock 'n' Roll*; Mary McCormack, *Boeing-Boeing*; Laurie Metcalf, *November*; Martha Plimpton, *Top Girls*

BEST PERFORMANCE BY A FEATURED ACTOR IN A MUSICAL Boyd Gaines, *Gypsy*

Nominees: Daniel Breaker, *Passing Strange*; Danny Burstein, *South Pacific*; Robin De Jesús, *In the Heights*; Christopher Fitzgerald, *Young Frankenstein*;

BEST PERFORMANCE BY A FEATURED ACTRESS IN A MUSICAL Laura Benanti, *Gypsy*

Nominees: de'Adre Aziza, *Passing Strange*; Andrea Martin, *Young Frankenstein*; Olga Merediz, *In the Heights*; Loretta Ables Sayre, *South Pacific*

BEST DIRECTION OF A PLAY Anna D. Shapiro, *August: Osage County*

Nominees: Maria Aitken, *The 39 Steps*; Conor McPherson, *The Seafarer*; Matthew Warchus, *Boeing-Boeing*

BEST DIRECTION OF A MUSICAL Bartlett Sher, *South Pacific*

Nominees: Sam Buntrock, *Sunday in the Park with George*; Thomas Kail, *In the Heights*; Arthur Laurents, *Gypsy*

BEST SCENIC DESIGN OF A PLAY Todd Rosenthal, *August: Osage County*

Nominees: Peter McKintosh, *The 39 Steps*; Scott Pask, *Les Liaisons Dangereuses*; Anthony Ward, *Macbeth*

BEST SCENIC DESIGN OF A MUSICAL Michael Yeargan, *South Pacific*

Nominees: David Farley and Timothy Bird & The Knifedge Creative Network, *Sunday in the Park with George*; Anna Louizos, *In the Heights*; Robin Wagner, *Young Frankenstein*

BEST COSTUME DESIGN OF A PLAY Katrina Lindsay, *Les Liaisons Dangereuses*

Nominees: Gregory Gale, *Cyrano de Bergerac*; Rob Howell, *Boeing-Boeing*; Peter McKintosh, *The 39 Steps*

BEST COSTUME DESIGN OF A MUSICAL Catherine Zuber, *South Pacific*

Nominees: David Farley, *Sunday in the Park with George*; Martin Pakledinaz, *Gypsy*; Paul Tazewell, *In the Heights*

BEST LIGHTING DESIGN OF A PLAY Kevin Adams, *The 39 Steps*

Nominees: Howard Harrison, *Macbeth*; Donald Holder, *Les Liaisons Dangereuses*; Ann G. Wrightson, *August: Osage County*

BEST LIGHTING DESIGN OF A MUSICAL Donald Holder, *South Pacific*

Nominees: Ken Billington, *Sunday in the Park with George*; Howell Binkley, *In the Heights*; Natasha Katz, *The Little Mermaid*

BEST SOUND DESIGN OF A PLAY (new) Mic Pool, *The 39 Steps*

Nominees: Simon Baker, *Boeing-Boeing*; Adam Cork, *Macbeth*; Ian Dickson, *Rock 'n' Roll*

BEST SOUND DESIGN OF A MUSICAL (new) Scott Lehrer, *South Pacific*

Nominees: Acme Sound Partners, *In the Heights*; Sebastian Frost, *Sunday in the Park with George*; Dan Moses Schreier, *Gypsy*

BEST CHOREOGRAPHY Andy Blankenbuehler, *In the Heights*

Nominees: Rob Ashford, *Cry-Baby*; Christopher Gattelli, *South Pacific*; Dan Knechtges, *Xanadu*

BEST ORCHESTRATIONS Alex Lacamoire & Bill Sherman, *In the Heights*

Nominees: Jason Carr, *Sunday in the Park with George*; Stew & Heidi Rodewald, *Passing Strange*; Jonathan Tunick, *A Catered Affair*

REGIONAL THEATRE TONY AWARD Chicago Shakespeare Theater (Barbara Gaines, Artistic Director; Criss Henderson, Executive Director)

SPECIAL TONY AWARD Robert Russell Bennett (1894-1981) in recognition of his historic contribution to American musical theatre in the field of orchestrations

SPECIAL TONY FOR LIFETIME ACHIEVEMENT IN THE THEATRE Stephen Sondheim

DRAMA DESK AWARDS

Sunday, May 18, 2008 at LaGuardia Concert Hall-Lincoln Center; 53rd annual; Hosts: The cast of *[title of show]*: Jeff Bowen, Hunter Bell, Susan Blackwell, and Heidi Blickenstaff. Presented for outstanding achievement in the 2007–2008 season for Broadway, Off-Broadway, and Off-Off Broadway productions, voted on by an association of New York drama reporters, editors and critics: Barbara Siegel - Chairperson (TalkinBroadway.com, TheaterMania.com), Dan Bacalzo (TheaterMania.com), Robert Cashill (*New York Theater News*, *Live Design*), Celia Ipiotis (Eye on the Arts), Gerard Raymond (*Back Stage*, *The Advocate*) and Richard Ridge (Broadway Beat TV); Executive Producer, Robert R. Blume; President, William Wolf.

NEW PLAY: *August: Osage County* by Tracy Letts

NEW MUSICAL: *Passing Strange* by Stew and Heidi Rodewald

REVIVAL OF A PLAY: *Boeing-Boeing* by Marc Camoletti

REVIVAL OF A MUSICAL: *South Pacific* by Richard Rodgers, Oscar Hammerstein II, and Josh Logan

REVUE: *Forbidden Broadway: Rude Awakening*

ACTOR IN A PLAY: Mark Rylance, *Boeing-Boeing*

ACTRESS IN A PLAY: Deanna Dunagan, *August: Osage County*

FEATURED ACTOR IN A PLAY: Conleth Hill, *The Seafarer*

FEATURED ACTRESS IN A PLAY: Linda Lavin, *The New Century*

ACTOR IN A MUSICAL: Paolo Szot, *South Pacific*

ACTRESS IN A MUSICAL: Patti LuPone, *Gypsy*

FEATURED ACTOR IN A MUSICAL: Boyd Gaines, *Gypsy*

FEATURED ACTRESS IN A MUSICAL: Laura Benanti, *Gypsy*

DIRECTOR OF A PLAY: Anna D. Shapiro, *August: Osage County*

DIRECTOR OF A MUSICAL: Bartlett Sher, *South Pacific*

CHOREOGRAPHY: Rob Ashford, *Cry-Baby*

MUSIC: Stew and Heidi Rodewald, *Passing Strange*

LYRICS: Stew, *Passing Strange*

BOOK OF A MUSICAL: Douglas Carter Beane, *Xanadu*

ORCHESTRATIONS: Jason Carr, *Sunday in the Park with George*

SET DESIGN OF A PLAY: Scott Pask, *Les Liaisons Dangereuses*

SET DESIGN OF A MUSICAL: Michael Yeargan, *South Pacific*

COSTUME DESIGN: Katrina Lindsay, *Les Liaisons Dangereuses*

LIGHTING DESIGN: Kevin Adams, *The 39 Steps*

SOUND DESIGN: Scott Lehrer, *South Pacific*

UNIQUE THEATRICAL EXPERIENCE: *The 39 Steps*

SOLO PERFORMANCE: Laurence Fishburne, *Thurgood*

OUTSTANDING ENSEMBLE PERFORMANCES: *The Homecoming* (Broadway), *The Dining Room* (Off-Broadway)

SPECIAL AWARDS: Edward Albee, James Earl Jones, 59E59 Theaters, Playwrights Horizons

VILLAGE VOICE OBIE AWARDS

Monday, May 19, 2008 at the Skirball Center; 53rd annual; Hosts: Elizabeth Marvel and Bill Camp. Presented for outstanding achievement in Off- and Off-Off-Broadway theatre; Judges: Michael Feingold (Chair, *Village Voice* chief theatre critic), Alexis Soloski (*Village Voice* theatre critic), Mark Blankenship (*Variety* theatre critic), Jeremy Gerard (*Bloomberg News* editor and critic), Robert O'Hara (playwright-director), Neil Patel (set designer), Helen Shaw (*Time Out New York/ New York Sun* theatre critic); Secretary to the committee: Clint Allen; Producer/Director, Eileen Phelan; Publicist, Gail Parenteau.

PERFORMANCE: LisaGay Hamilton, *The Ohio State Murders;* Kate Mulgrew, *Iphigenia 2.0*; Francis Jue, *Yellow Face;* Rebecca Wisocky, *Amazons and Their Men;* Joel Hatch, *Adding Machine;* Heidi Schreck, *Drum the Waves of Horikawa;* Veanne Cox & Sean McNall, Sustained Excellence of Performance

DIRECTION: Krzysztof Warlinkowski, *Krum;* David Cromer, *Adding Machine*

PLAYWRITING: Horton Foote, *Dividing the Estate;* David Henry Hwang, *Yellow Face*

DESIGN: Takeshi Kata (Set) & Keith Parham (Lighting), *Adding Machine;* Peter Ksander (Set), *Untitled Mars (This Title May Change);* Ben Katchor (Drawings), John Findlay & Jeff Sugg (Set & Projections), and Russell H. Champa (Lighting), *The Slug Bearers of Kayrol Island;* Jane Greenwood, Sustained Excellence of Costume Design; David Zinn, Sustained Excellence of Costume and Set Design

SPECIAL CITATIONS: Nature Theatre of Oklahoma's Production of *No Dice;* David Greenspan for *The Argument*

BEST NEW THEATER PIECE ($1,000): Stew, Heidi Rodewald, Annie Dorsen for *Passing Strange*

ROSS WETZSTEON MEMORIAL AWARD ($2,000): Cherry Lane Theatre Mentor Project

LIFETIME ACHIEVEMENT: Adrienne Kennedy

OBIE GRANTS ($5,000): Keen Company and Theater of a Two-Headed Calf

OUTER CRITICS CIRCLE AWARDS

Thursday, May 22, 2008 at Sardi's Restaurant; 58th annual. Presented for outstanding achievement in the 2007–2008 season. Winners are voted on by theatre critics of out-of-town periodicals and media.

BROADWAY PLAY: *August: Osage County*

BROADWAY MUSICAL: (tie) *Xanadu* and *Young Frankenstein*

OFF-BROADWAY PLAY: *Dividing the Estate*

OFF-BROADWAY MUSICAL: *Adding Machine*

NEW SCORE: (tie) *Adding Machine* and *Next to Normal*

REVIVAL OF A PLAY: *The Homecoming*

REVIVAL OF A MUSICAL: *South Pacific*

DIRECTOR OF A PLAY: Anna D. Shapiro, *August: Osage County*

DIRECTOR OF A MUSICAL: Bartlett Sher, *South Pacific*

CHOREOGRAPHY: Rob Ashford, *Cry-Baby*

ACTOR IN A PLAY: Kevin Kline, *Cyrano de Bergerac*

ACTRESS IN A PLAY: Deanna Dunagan, *August: Osage County*

FEATURED ACTOR IN A PLAY: James Earl Jones, *Cat on a Hot Tim Roof*

FEATURED ACTRESS IN A PLAY: Laurie Metcalf, *November*

ACTOR IN A MUSICAL: Paulo Szot, *South Pacific*

ACTRESS IN A MUSICAL: Patti LuPone, *Gypsy*

FEATURED ACTOR IN A MUSICAL: Danny Burstein, *South Pacific*

FEATURED ACTRESS IN A MUSICAL: Laura Benanti, *Gypsy*

SCENIC DESIGN: David Farley & Timothy Bird, *Sunday in the Park with George*

COSTUME DESIGN: Katrina Lindsay, *Les Liaisons Dangereuses*

LIGHTING DESIGN: Ken Billington, *Sunday in the Park with George*

SOLO PERFORMANCE: Laurence Fishburne, *Thurgood*

JOHN GASSNER PLAYWRITING AWARD: Liz Flahive, *From Up Here*

LUCILLE LORTEL AWARDS

Monday, May 5, 2008 at Union Square Theatre; 23rd Annual; Host: Julie White. Presented by the League of Off-Broadway Theatres and Producers for outstanding achievement Off-Broadway. 2007–2008 Awards Administration Committee: Terry Byrne, Denise Cooper, Margaret Cotter, Maria Di Dia, Carol Fishman, George Forbes, Harry McFadden, Tom Smedes, Leslie Smith; Nominating Committee: Arnold Aronson, Roni Claypool, John Clinton Eisner, Barrack Evans, Kurt Everhart, Peter Filichia, David Finkle, Liz Frankel, Melanie Herman, Linda Herring, Walt Kiskaddon, Renee Lasher, Russell Lehrer, Adam Moore, Niclas Nagler, Victor Pappas, Barbara Pasternack, David Savran, Barbara Toy.

PLAY: *Betrayed* by George Packer; Produced by Culture Project

MUSICAL: *Adding Machine* Music by Joshua Schmidt, libretto by Jason Loewith and Joshua Schmidt; Produced by Scott Morfee, Tom Wirtshafter, Margaret Cotter

SOLO SHOW: *Dai (enough)* Written and performed by Iris Bar; Produced by Bernie Kukoff, Jonathan Pollard, Jon Cutler, in association with Highbrow Entertainment

REVIVAL: *Ohio State Murders* by Adrienne Kennedy; Produced by Theatre for a New Audience

DIRECTOR: David Cromer, *Adding Machine*

CHOREOGRAPHER: Peter Pucci, *Queens Boulevard (the musical)*

LEAD ACTOR: Joel Hatch, *Adding Machine*

LEAD ACTRESS: Elizabeth Franz, *The Piano Teacher*

FEATURED ACTOR: Francis Jue, *Yellow Face*

FEATURED ACTRESS: Mare Winningham, *10 Million Miles*

SCENIC DESIGN: Jim Findlay and Jeff Sugg, *The Slug Bearers of Kayrol Island (or the Friends of Dr. Rushower)*

COSTUME DESIGN: Michael Bottari & Ronald Case, and Jessica Jahn, *Die Mommie Die!*

LIGHTING DESIGN: Keith Parham, *Adding Machine*

SOUND DESIGN: Jorge Cousineau, *Opus*

BODY OF WORK: Primary Stages

EDITH OLIVIER AWARD FOR SUSTAINED EXCELLENCE: Theodore Mann

UNIQUE THEATRICAL EXPERIENCE: *Horizon* by Rinde Eckert, New York Theatre Workshop

NEW YORK DRAMA CRITICS' CIRCLE AWARDS

Monday, May 19, 2008 at the Algonquin Hotel; 73rd Annual. Presented by the members of the press in the New York area. 2008 New York Drama Critics' Circle Committee: Adam Feldman – President (*Time Out New York*), Eric Grode – Vice President (*The New York Sun*), Joe Dziemianowicz – Treasurer (*The Daily News*), Hilton Als (*New Yorker*), Clive Barnes (*The*

New York Post), Melissa Rose Bernardo (*Entertainment Weekly*), David Cote (*Time Out New York*), Michael Feingold (*The Village Voice*), Robert Feldberg (*The Bergen Record*), Elysa Gardner (*USA Today*), John Heilpern (*The New York Observer*), Michael Kuchwara (The Associated Press), Jacques le Sourd (*Gannett Newspapers*), Jeremy McCarter (*New York*), David Rooney (*Variety*), Frank Scheck (*New York Post*), David Sheward (*Back Stage*), John Simon (*Bloomberg News*), Michael Sommers (*The Star-Ledger/Newhouse* Newspapers), Linda Winer (*Newsday*), Terry Teachout (*The Wall Street Journal*), Richard Zoglin (*Time*)

BEST PLAY: *August: Osage County* by Tracy Letts

BEST MUSICAL: *Passing Strange* Book and lyrics by Stew, music by Stew and Heidi Rodewald

DRAMA LEAGUE AWARDS

Friday, May 16, 2008; Broadway Ballroom at The Marriott Marquis; 74th annual. Presented for distinguished achievement in the New York theater; winners are selected by members of the League.

DISTINGUISHED PRODUCTION OF A PLAY: *August: Osage County*

DISTINGUISHED PRODUCTION OF A MUSICAL: *A Catered Affair*

DISTINGUISHED REVIVAL OF A PLAY: *Macbeth*

DISTINGUISHED REVIVAL OF A MUSICAL: *South Pacific*

DISTINGUISHED PERFORMANCE: Patti LuPone, *Gypsy*

JULIA HANSEN AWARD FOR EXCELLENCE IN DIRECTING: Bartlett Sher

DISTINGUISHED ACHIEVEMENT IN MUSICAL THEATRE: Paul Gemignani

UNIQUE CONTRIBUTION TO THEATER: Ellen Stewart and La MaMa ETC

PULITZER PRIZE AWARD WINNERS FOR DRAMA

Established in 1917; Administered by the Pulitzer Prize Board, Columbia University; Lee C. Bollinger, President. Winner is chosen by a jury, composed of three to four critics, one academic and one playwright, however the board has final authority over choice. Presented for an outstanding drama or musical presented in New York or regional theater. The award goes to the playwright but production of the play as well as the script, is taken into account.

2008 WINNER: *August: Osage County* by Tracy Letts

Regional and Other Theatrical Awards

AMERICAN THEATRE CRITICS ASSOCIATION AWARDS

STEINBERG NEW PLAY AWARD AND CITATIONS March 29, 2008; Humana Festival at Actors Theatre Louisville; founded in 1977. The Harold and Mimi Steinberg/ATCA Awards honor new plays that had their world premieres in the previous year in professional productions outside New York City. The principal citation comes with a $25,000 prize and others are awarded a $7,500 prize. 2008 Citations: *33 Variations* by Moises Kaufman (principal – Arena Stage); *End Days* by Deborah Zoe Laufer (Florida Stage); *Dead Man's Cell Phone* by Sarah Ruhl (Woolly Mammoth Theatre Company)

M. ELIZABETH OSBORN AWARD March 29, 2008; Humana Festival at Actors Theatre Louisville; established in 1993. Presented in memory of TCG and American Theatre play editor M. Elizabeth Osborn to an emerging playwright whose plays have not received a major production. Recipients are awarded a $1,000 prize and recognition in *The Best Plays Theater Yearbook* edited by Jeffrey Eric Jenkins. 2008 Winner: Elyzabeth Gregory Wilder for her career and the play *Gee's Bend* (Alabama Shakespeare Festival)

BARRYMORE AWARDS

October 1, 2007; Crystal Teal Room; 13th Annual; Hosts: Chris Faith and Greg Wood. Presented by the Theatre Alliance of Greater Philadelphia for excellence in theatre in the greater Philadelphia area for the 2006-2007 season.

PRODUCTION OF A PLAY: *Of Mice and Men* (Walnut Street Theatre)

PRODUCTION OF A MUSICAL: *Caroline, or Change* (Arden Theatre Company)

DIRECTION OF A PLAY: Mark Clements, *Of Mice and Men* (Walnut Street Theatre)

DIRECTION OF A MUSICAL: Charles Abbott, *42nd Street* (Walnut Street Theatre)

MUSICAL DIRECTION: Mat Wright & Aaron Cromie, *The Fantasticks* (Mum Puppettheatre)

LEADING ACTOR IN A PLAY: John Campion, *The Life of Galileo* (The Wilma Theater)

LEADING ACTRESS IN A PLAY: Susan Riley Stevens, *Bad Dates* (Act II Playhouse)

LEADING ACTOR IN A MUSICAL: Rob McClure, *The Bomb-itty of Errors* (11th Hour Theatre Company)

LEADING ACTRESS IN A MUSICAL: Joliet F. Harris, *Caroline, or Change* (Arden Theatre Company)

SUPPORTING ACTOR IN A PLAY: Harry Philibosian, *Glengarry Glen Ross* (Theatre Exile)

SUPPORTING ACTRESS IN A PLAY: Charlotte Northeast, *Skin in Flames* (InterAct Theatre Company)

SUPPORTING ACTOR IN A MUSICAL: Dave Jadico, *The Fantasticks* (Mum Puppettheatre)

SUPPORTING ACTRESS IN A MUSICAL: Dee Hoty, *Stormy Weather: Imagining Lena Horne* (Prince Music Theater)

SET DESIGN: Jorge Cousineau, *The Four of Us* (1812 Productions)

LIGHTING DESIGN: Shelly Hicklin, *Of Mice and Men* (Walnut Street Theatre)

COSTUME DESIGN: Rosemarie E. McKelvey, *Caroline, or Change* (Arden Theatre Company)

SOUND DESIGN: Jorge Cousineau, *The Giver* (People's Light & Theatre Company)

MUSIC: Hal Goldberg, *Nerds://A Musical Software Satire* (Philadelphia Theatre CompanY)

CHOREOGRAPHY/MOVEMENT: Karen Getz, *Hair* (Prince Music Theater)

NEW PLAY: *Nerds://A Musical Software Satire*, book and lyrics by Jordan Allen-Dutton & Erik Weiner, music by Hal Goldberg (Philadelphia Theatre Company)

ENSEMBLE IN A PLAY: *Glengarry Glen Ross* (Theatre Exile)

ENSEMBLE IN A MUSICAL: *The Bomb-itty of Errors* (11th Hour Theatre Company)

F. OTTO HAAS AWARD FOR EMERGING PHILADELPHIA THEATRE ARTIST: Matt Saunders

EXCELLENCE IN THEATRE EDUCATION/COMMUNITY SERVICE: Adapt-A-School (Walnut Street Theatre)

LIFETIME ACHIEVEMENT HONOREE: Carole Haas Gravagno

TED & STEVIE WOLF AWARD FOR NEW APPROACHES TO COLLABORATIONS: Brat Producitons & the rock bands: Toothless George, Allison Polans, Danny Mackane, Devin Greenwood & Franzschubert (Three Chord Fiction)

SUZANNE ROBERTS THEATRE ALLIANCE COLLEGE SCHOLARSHIP AWARD: Caitlin Reed

JOSEPH CAIRNS JR. AND ERNESTINE BACON CAIRNS MEMORIAL SCHOLARSHIP: Shoshana Katz

CARBONELL AWARDS

Monday, April 7, 2008; Broward Center for the Performing Arts – Amaturo Theatre; 32nd annual. Presented for outstanding achievement in South Florida theatre during the 2007 calendar year. Mistress of Ceremonies: Christine Andreas; Special Guests: The Off-Broadway Cast of *Forbidden Broadway*; Produced and directed by Dan Barnett.

Regional Awards

THE GEORGE ABBOTT AWARD FOR OUTSTANDING ACHIEVEMENT IN THE ARTS: Jack Zink, Carbonell Awards Executive Director & critic for the *Palm Beach Post*

THE HOWARD KLEINBERG AWARD: Theatre League of South Florida

THE RUTH FOREMAN AWARD: Michael Hall, Artistic Director of the Caldwell Theatre Company

THE BILL HINDMAN AWARD: Rafael de Acha, Co-Founder of the New Theatre, Coral Gables

FRED DIEKMANN EMERGING ARTIST AWARD: no award given

NEW WORK: *Melt* by Michael McKeever (New Theatre, Coral Gables)

ENSEMBLE: *Glengarry Glen Ross* (Mosaic Theatre)

PRODUCTION OF A PLAY: *The Lieutenant of Inishmore* (GableStage)

DIRECTOR OF A PLAY: Joseph Adler, *The Lieutenant of Inishmore* (GableStage)

ACTOR IN A PLAY: Paul Tei, *Talk Radio* (Mosaic Theatre)

ACTRESS IN A PLAY: Lela Elam, *In the Continuum* (GableStage)

SUPPORTING ACTOR IN A PLAY: Paul Tei, *Glengarry Glen Ross* (Mosaic Theatre)

SUPPORTING ACTRESS IN A PLAY: Kim Morgan, *The Lieutenant of Inishmore* (GableStage)

PRODUCTION OF A MUSICAL: *Man of La Mancha* (Maltz Jupiter Theatre)

DIRECTOR OF A MUSICAL: Peter Flynn, *La Cage aux Folles* and *Man of La Mancha* (Maltz Jupiter Theatre)

ACTOR IN A MUSICAL: Gary Marachek, *La Cage aux Folles* (Actors' Playhouse at the Miracle Theatre)

ACTRESS IN A MUSICAL: Irene Adjan, *Funny Girl* (New Vista Theatre Company)

SUPPORTING ACTOR IN A MUSICAL: Jim Ballard, *Urinetown, the Musical* (Actors' Playhouse at the Miracle Theatre)

SUPPORTING ACTRESS IN A MUSICAL: Rachel Jones, *Urinetown, the Musical* (Actors' Playhouse at the Miracle Theatre)

MUSICAL DIRECTION: David Nagy, *Urinetown, the Musical* (Actors' Playhouse at the Miracle Theatre)

CHOREOGRAPHY: Denis Jones, *The Boy Friend* (Maltz Jupiter Theatre)

SCENIC DESIGN: Dan Kuchar, *The Boy Friend* (Maltz Jupiter Theatre)

LIGHTING DESIGN: Donald Edmund Thomas, *Man of La Mancha* (Maltz Jupiter Theatre)

COSTUME DESIGN: Jose M. Rivera, *The Boy Friend* (Maltz Jupiter Theatre)

SOUND DESIGN: Matt Corey, *Talk Radio* (Mosaic Theatre)

Stock/Roadshow Awards

PRODUCTION: *Monty Python's Spamalot*

DIRECTOR: Mike Nichols, *Monty Python's Spamalot*

CHOREOGRAPHY: Graciela Daniele, *Chita Rivera – The Dancer's Life*

ACTOR: Michael Siberry, *Monty Python's Spamalot*

ACTRESS: Rachel York, *Camelot*

SUPPORTING ACTOR: Tim Jerome, *My Fair Lady*

SUPPORTING ACTRESS: Sally Ann Howes, *My Fair Lady*

SCENIC DESIGN: Anthony Ward, *My Fair Lady*

LIGHTING DESIGN: Hugh Vanstone, *Monty Python's Spamalot*

COSTUME DESIGN: Anthony Ward, *My Fair Lady*

CRAIG NOEL AWARDS

January 21, 2008; 6th annual. Presented by the San Diego Theatre Critics Circle for outstanding achievement in the greater San Diego theatre in the 2007 calendar year.

NEW MUSICAL: *A Catered Affair* (Old Globe Theatre)

RESIDENT MUSICAL: (tie) *West Side Story* (Moonlight Stage Productions); *Ragtime* (Starlight Theatre)

LYRICS: David Javerbaum and Adam Schlesinger, *Cry-Baby* (La Jolla Playhouse)

SCORE FOR A MUSICAL: John Bucchino (music and lyrics), *A Catered Affair* (Old Globe Theatre)

DIRECTION OF A MUSICAL: John Doyle, *A Catered Affair* (Old Globe Theatre)

MUSIC DIRECTION: (tie) Justin Gray, *Buddy: The Buddy Holly Story* (Welk Resort Theatre); Don Le Master, *The Full Monty* (San Diego Musical Theatre)

LEAD PERFORMANCE IN A MUSICAL, FEMALE: (tie) Deborah Gilmour Smyth, *Ragtime* (Starlight Musical Theatre); Faith Prince, *A Catered Affair* (The Old Globe)

LEAD PERFORMANCE IN A MUSICAL, MALE: Tom Wopat, *A Catered Affair* (Old Globe Theatre)

FEATURED PERFORMANCE IN A MUSICAL, FEMALE: Alli Mauzey, *Cry-Baby* (La Jolla Playhouse)

FEATURED PERFORMANCE IN A MUSICAL, MALE: Robert Barry Fleming, *Ain't Misbehavin'* (San Diego Repertory Theatre)

CHOREOGRAPHY: (tie) Robin Christ and Kathy Meyer, *Sailor's Song* (New Village Arts); Rob Ashford, *Cry-Baby* (La Jolla Playhouse)

ORIGINAL MUSIC FOR A PLAY: Andre Pluess and Ben Sussman, *after the quake* (La Jolla Playhouse)

DIRECTION OF A PLAY: Kristianne Kurner, *Sailor's Song* (New Village Arts)

SOUND DESIGN: Paul Peterson, *Bell, Book and Candle* (Old Globe Theatre)

COSTUME DESIGN: (tie) Jessica John, *Sailor's Song* (New Village Arts); Karen Perry, *Two Trains Running* (Old Globe Theatre)

LIGHTING DESIGN: Brian MacDevitt, *A Catered Affair* (Old Globe Theatre)

SET DESIGN: Nick Fouch, *Yellowman* (Cygnet Theatre), *Sailor's Song* (New Village Arts), *Devil Dog Six* (Moxie Theatre)

ENSEMBLE: *Sailor's Song* (New Village Arts)

LEAD PERFORMANCE IN A PLAY, FEMALE: (tie) Monique Gaffney, *Yellowman* (Cygnet Theatre); Rosina Reynolds, *Wit* (North Coast Repertory)

LEAD PERFORMANCE IN A PLAY, MALE: (tie) Chuck Cooper, *Two Trains Running* (Old Globe Theatre); James Sutorius, *Who's Afraid of Virginia Woolf?* (Old Globe Theatre); Matthew Weeden, *Torch Song Trilogy* (Diversionary Theatre)

FEATURED PERFORMANCE IN A PLAY, FEMALE: Sandy Campbell, *Communication Doors* (Cygnet Theatre)

FEATURED PERFORMANCE IN A PLAY, MALE: (tie) Joshua Everett Johnson, *The Adding Machine* (La Jolla Playhouse); Luke Marinkovich, *Victoria Martin: Math Team Queen* (Moxie Theatre); Jonathan McMurty, body of work at Old Globe Shakespeare Festival 2007

SOLO PERFORMANCE: (tie) Ron Choularton, *St. Nicholas* (Cygnet Theatre); Adriana Sevan, *Taking Flight* (San Diego Repertory Theatre)

TOURING PRODUCTION: *Jersey Boys* (Broadway San Diego)

NEW PLAY: (tie) *The Four of Us* by Itamar Moses (Old Globe Theatre); *Devil Dog Six* by Mary Fengar Gail (Moxie Theatre)

DRAMATIC PRODUCTION: *Yellowman* by Dael Orlandersmith (Cygnet Theatre)

SPECIAL AWARD: Floyd Gaffney

LIFETIME ACHIEVEMENT AWARD: Jack O'Brien

JACK O'BRIEN EXCELLENCE IN DIRECTING: Esther Emery

CREATIVE SPIRIT AWARDS

February 4, 2008; 12th Annual. Presented by Daryl Roth; Dedicated to nurturing and supporting a gifted theatre artists and provide them with support as they develop new work in an artistic residency. 2008 Winner: Brett C. Leonard (Playwright - LAByrinth Theater Company)

DRAMATIST GUILD AWARDS

Established in 2000, these awards are presented by the Dramatists Guild of America to outstanding writers at the Dramatists Guild Annual Benefit and Awards Gala. 2008 Winners: Elizabeth Hull-Kate Warriner Award (for a play or musical dealing with controversial subjects involving political, religious or social mores): Tracy Letts for *August: Osage County;* Frederick Loewe Award (for dramatic musical composition or contribution to the musical theatre): Lin-Manuel Miranda for *In The Heights;* Wendy Wasserstein Prize (to an accomplished and promising female writer): Laura Jacqmin for *And when we awoke there was light and light;* Lifetime Achievement Award: Joseph Stein

THE EQUITY AWARDS

ST. CLAIR BAYFIELD AWARD Established in 1973 in memory of Equity member St. Clair Bayfield, the Award honors the best performance by an actor in a Shakespearean play in the New York metropolitan area. 2007 Winner: Jay O. Sanders ("Bottom" in *A Midsummer Night's Dream* at the Public Theater)

JOE A. CALLAWAY AWARD Established by Equity member Joe A. Callaway in 1989 to encourage participation in the classics and non-profit theatre. 2007 Winners: Lauren Ambrose ("Juliet" in *Romeo and Juliet* at the Public Theater); Byron Jennings ("Bastien André" in *Is He Dead?* at the Lyceum Theatre)

CLARENCE DERWENT AWARDS 64th annual; Given to a female and male performer in a supporting role by Actors Equity Association, based on work in New York that demonstrates promise. 2008 Winners: Zoe Kazan, *100 Saints You Should Know, Things We Want,* and *Come Back, Little Sheba;* Michael Esper, *Crazy Mary*

LUCY JORDAN AWARD Established in 1992 to honor the legacy of Lucy Finney Jordan, a former ballerina and chorus "gypsy" who, for many years, was the "face" of Actors' Equity in the Western Region as the Union's Outside Field Rep. The award is given to those who demonstrate a lifetime commitment to the theatre and especially, helping other theatre artists. 2007 Winner: Rick Star of Hollywood Sheet Music

ROSETTA LENOIRE AWARD Established in 1988, the award was named in honor of the actress Rosetta LeNoire, who was also the first recipient, not only because of her body of work in the theatre - and her work with the then titled Actors' Equity Association's Ethnic Minorities Committee - but also for founding the AMAS Repertory Theatre Company. 2007 Winner: Willie Boston

PAUL ROBESON AWARD Established in 1974 to recognize a person who best exemplified the principles by which Mr. Robeson lived. 2007 Winner: Mercedes Ellington

RICHARD SEFF AWARD Established in 2003, this annual award is given to a male and female character actor who is 50 years old or older and who has been a member of the Actors' Equity for 25 years or longer, for the best performance in a featured or unfeatured supporting role in a Broadway or Off Broadway production. 2007 Winners: Mary Louise Wilson ("Edith Bouvier Beale" in *Grey Gardens)*; David Margulies ("Rabbi Stephen Wise Raymond" in *All That I Will Ever Be* at the New York Theatre Workshop)

ARIZONA THEATRE SERVICE AWARD The Arizona Theatre Service Award is given by Equity members in Arizona, to recognize individuals who have contributed to the health and visibility of live theatre in their state. 2007 Winner: Shelley Cohn

ROGER STURTEVANT MUSICAL THEATRE AWARD 4th Annual; established in 2005 in memory of Roger Sturtevant, a beloved box office treasurer and part-time casting director. This award is presented to Equity Membership Candidates who have demonstrated outstanding abilities in the musical theatre field. 2008 Winners: Chelsea Cree Groen; Ricardo Rust

PATRICK QUINN AWARD 1st Annual; Established in memory of beloved actor, humanitarian and former AEA President, Patrick Quinn who passed away in September, 2006; presented to a person who has worked tirelessly for the betterment of actors. 2007 Winner: Jeanna Belkin, AEA Councilor

FRED EBB AWARD

November 26th, 2007; The American Airlines Theatre Penthouse Lounge; 3rd Annual. The Fred Ebb Award recognizes excellence in musical theatre songwriting, by a lyricist, composer, or songwriting team that has not yet achieved significant commercial success. 2007 Winner: Peter Mills

ELLIOT NORTON AWARDS

Monday, May 12, 2008; Harvard University's Sanders Theatre; 26th annual; Guest of Honor: Andrea Martin. Presented for outstanding contribution to the theater in Boston for the 2007–2008 season; voted by a Boston Theater Critics Association selection committee comprising of Terry Byrne, Carolyn Clay, Iris Fanger, Louise Kennedy, Joyce Kullhawik, Robert Nesti, Ed Siegel and Caldwell Titcomb.

OUTSTANDING VISITING PRODUCTION: *My Fair Lady* (Broadway Across America)

OUTSTANDING SOLO PERFORMANCE: Nilaja Sun, *No Child...* (American Repertory Company)

OUTSTANDING MUSICAL PERFORMANCE: Lisa O'Hare, *My Fair Lady* (Broadway Across America)

OUTSTANDING NEW SCRIPT: *Radio Free Emerson* by Paul Grellong (Sandra Feinstein-Gamm Theatre)

OUTSTANDING DIRECTOR, LARGE COMPANY: David Wheeler, *No Man's Land* (American Repertory Thetre)

OUTSTANDING DIRECTOR, MIDSIZED COMPANY: Paul Daigneault, *Parade, Some Men,* and *Zanna Don't!* (SpeakEasy Stage Company)

OUTSTANDING DIRECTOR, SMALL/FRINGE COMPANY: Jason Southerland and Nancy Curran Willis, *Angels in America* (Boston Theatre Works)

OUTSTANDING ACTOR, LARGE COMPANY: Max Wright, *No Man's Land* (American Repertory Theatre)

OUTSTANDING ACTOR, SMALL/MIDSIZED COMPANY: Maurice E Parent, *Angels in America* (Boston Theatre Works), *The Wild Party* (New Repertory Theatre), and *Some Men* (SpeakEasy Stage Company)

OUTSTANDING ACTRESS: LARGE COMPANY: Nancy E. Carroll, *Brendan* and *Present Laughter* (Huntington Theatre Company)

OUTSTANDING ACTRESS: SMALL/MIDSIZED COMPANY: Rachel Harker, *A Streetcar Named Desire* (New Repertory Theatre), *A Pinter Duet* (Downtown @ New Rep), and *The Cutting* (Stoneham Theatre)

OUTSTANDING PRODUCTION BY A FRINGE COMPANY: *The Kentucky Cycle* (Zeitgeist Stage Company/Way Theatre Artists)

OUTSTANDING PRODUCTION BY A SMALL COMPANY: *Angels in America* (Boston Theatre Works)

OUTSTANDING PRODUCTION BY A MIDSIZE COMPANY: *The Clean House* (New Repertory Theatre)

OUTSTANDING PRODUCTION BY A LARGE COMPANY: *Present Laughter* (Huntington Theatre Company)

OUTSTANDING MUSICAL PRODUCTION: *A Marvelous Party: The Noel Coward Celebration* (American Repertory Theatre)

OUTSTANDING DESIGN, LARGE COMPANY: Alexander Dodge (sets), *Brendan* and *Present Laughter* (Huntington Theatre Company)

OUTSTANDING DESIGN, SMALL/MIDSIZE COMPANY: Cristina Todesco (set), Deb Sullivan (lighting), Jamie Whoolery (projections), *The Clean House* (New Repertory Theatre)

OUTSTANDING CHROREOGRAPHY: Patti Colombo, *Seven Brides for Seven Brothers* (North Shore Music Theatre)

NORTON PRIZE FOR SUSTAINED EXCELLENCE: Nicholas J. Martin

GEORGE JEAN NATHAN AWARD

For dramatic criticism; 2006–2007 winner: H. Scott McMillin, awarded posthumously for his book *The Musical as Drama*

HELEN HAYES AWARDS

Monday, April 28, 2008; The Warner Theatre and JW Marriott Hotel; 24th annual. Presented by the Washington Theatre Awards Society in recognition of excellence in Washington, D.C professional theatre in the 2007–2008 season; Honorary Producers, Ina and Fenner Milton; Show Director, Jerry Whiddon; Produced by Daniel MacLean Wagner; Musical Director, Glenn Pearson and George Fulginiti-Shakar.

Resident Productions

PLAY: *Macbeth* (Synetic Theater)

MUSICAL: *Reefer Madness: The Musical* (The Studio Theatre 2ndStage)

LEAD ACTOR, MUSICAL: Marc Kudisch, *The Witches of Eastwick* (Signature Theatre)

LEAD ACTRESS, MUSICAL: Heidi Blickenstaff, *Meet John Doe* (Ford's Theatre)

LEAD ACTOR, PLAY: J. Fred Shiffman, *Souvenir* (Studio Theatre)

LEAD ACTRESS, PLAY: Nancy Robinette, *Souvenir* (Studio Theatre)

SUPPORTING ACTOR, MUSICAL: Erik Liberman, *Merrily We Roll Along* (Signature Theatre)

SUPPORTING ACTRESS, MUSICAL: (tie) E. Faye Butler, *Saving Aimee* (Signature Theatre); Karlah Hamilton, *The Witches of Eastwick* (Signature Theatre)

SUPPORTING ACTOR, PLAY: (tie) Daniel Escobar, *She Stoops to Comedy* (Woolly Mammoth Theatre); Philip Fletcher, *Macbeth* (Synetic Theatre)

SUPPORTING ACTRESS, PLAY: Kate Eastwood Norris, *She Stoops to Comedy* (Woolly Mammoth Theatre)

DIRECTOR OF A PLAY: Paata Tsikurishvili, *Macbeth* (Synetic Theater)

DIRECTOR OF A MUSICAL: (tie) Keith Alan Baker/Ryan Christie/Matthew Gardnier, *Reefer Madness: The Musical* (Studio Theatre 2ndStage); Eric Schaeffer, *Meet John Doe* (Ford's Theatre)

SET DESIGN, PLAY OR MUSICAL: Neil Patel, *Dead Man's Cell Phone* (Woolly Mammoth Theatre)

COSTUME DESIGN, PLAY OR MUSICAL: Reggie Ray, *Souvenir* (Studio Theatre)

LIGHTING DESIGN, PLAY OR MUSICAL: Colin K. Bills, *Dead Man's Cell Phone* (Woolly Mammoth Theatre)

SOUND DESIGN, PLAY OR MUSICAL: Irakli Kavsadze, *Macbeth* (Synetic Theatre)

MUSICAL DIRECTION, PLAY OR MUSICAL: (tie) Jon Kalbfleisch, *Merrily We Roll Along* (Signature Theatre); Christopher Youstra, *Titanic, the Musical* (Toby's Dinner Theatre)

CHOREOGRAPHY: Irina Tsikurishvili, *Macbeth* (Synetic Theater)

ENSEMBLE: *Hamlet…the rest is silence* (Synetic Theater)

CHARLES MACARTHUR AWARD FOR OUTSTANDING NEW PLAY OR MUSICAL: Sarah Ruhl, *Dead Man's Cell Phone* (Woolly Mammoth Theatre)

Non-Resident Productions

PRODUCTION: *Avenue Q* (National Theatre)

LEAD ACTRESS: Cherry Jones, *Doubt* (National Theatre)

LEAD ACTOR: Bill Irwin, *Who's Afraid of Virginia Woolf?* (Kennedy Center)

SUPPORTING PERFORMER: Caroline Stefanie Clay, *Doubt* (National Theatre)

IRNE AWARDS

Monday, April 14, 2008; Boston Center for the Arts. Founded in 1997 by Beverly Creasey and Larry Stark. Presented by The Independent Reviewers of New England for extraordinary theatre in the Boston area during the 2007 calendar year.

Small Theatre

BEST NEW PLAY: *Surviving the Nian* by Melissa Li and Abe Rybeck (Theatre Offensive)

BEST MUSICAL: *Man of LaMancha* (Lyric Stage)

BEST PLAY: *A Streetcar Named Desire* (New Repertory Theatre)

SET DESIGN: Janie E. Howland, *Man of LaMancha* (Lyric Stage), *To Kill a Mockingbird* (Wheelock Family Theatre), *A Streetcar Named Desire* (New Repertory Theatre)

LIGHTING: Scott Clyve, *Man of LaMancha* (Lyric Stage)

COSTUMES: Stacey Stephens, *My Fair Lady* (Fiddlehead Theatre), *Parade* (SpeakEasy Stage)

SOUND: Haddon Kime, *The Kentucky Cycle* (Zeitgeist Stage Company and Way Theatre Artists)

CHOREOGRAPHY: Linda Sughrue, *Cabaret* (Metro Stage Co.)

SOLO PERFORMANCE: Kathy St. George, *And Now, Ladies and Gentleman, Miss Judy Garland* (Backyard Productions)

ENSEMBLE: *The Wild Party* (New Rep)

SUPPORTING ACTRESS, DRAMA: Elise Manning, *Kindertransport* (West End Theater)

SUPPORTING ACTOR, DRAMA: Bates Wilder, *A Streetcar Named Desire* (New Rep)

ACTRESS, DRAMA: Rachel Harker, *A Streetcar Named Desire* (New Rep)

ACTOR, DRAMA: Derek S. Nelson, *Much Ado About Nothing* (Wellesley Summer Theatre)

SUPPORTING ACTRESS, MUSICAL: Sarah Corey, *The Wild Party* (New Rep)

SUPPORTING ACTOR, MUSICAL: Robert Saoud, *Man of LaMancha* (Lyric Stage)

ACTRESS, MUSICAL: Caroline DeLima, *Man of LaMancha* (Lyric Stage)

ACTOR, MUSICAL: Brendan McNabb, *My Fair Lady* (Fiddlehead) and *Parade* (SpeakEasy)

MUSIC DIRECTOR: Jonathan Goldberg, *Man of LaMancha* (Lyric Stage)

DIRECTOR, MUSICAL: Spiro Veloudos, *Man of LaMancha* (Lyric Stage)

DIRECTOR, PLAY: Rick Lombardo, *A Streetcar Named Desire* (New Rep)

VISITING PRODUCTION: *George M Cohan Tonight!* (Stoneham Theatre)

Large Theatre

BEST NEW PLAY: *Brendan* by Ronan Noone (Huntington Theatre Company)

BEST MUSICAL: *Seven Brides for Seven Brothers* (North Shore Music Theatre)

BEST PLAY: *No Man's Land* (American Repertory Theatre)

SET DESIGN: Alexander Dodge, *Present Laughter* (Huntington Theatre Company)

LIGHTING: Christopher Akerlind, *Britannicus* (A.R.T.), and *The Light in the Piazza* (Broadway Across America)

COSTUMES: Mariann Verheyen, *Present Laughter* (Huntington Theatre Company)

SOUND: Mic Pool, *The 39 Steps* (Huntington Theatre Company)

CHOREOGRAPHY: Patti Colombo, *Seven Brides for Seven Borthers* (North Shore Music Theatre)

SOLO PERFORMANCE: Nilaja Sun, *No Child…* (A.R.T.)

ENSEMBLE: *Present Laughter* (Huntington Theatre Company)

SUPPORTING ACTRESS, DRAMA: Caroline Stefanie Clay, *Doubt* (Broadway Across America)

SUPPORTING ACTOR, DRAMA: Arnie Burton & Cliff Saunders, *The 39 Steps* (Huntington Theatre Company)

ACTRESS, DRAMA: Cherry Jones, *Doubt* (Broadway Across America)

ACTOR, DRAMA: Max Wright, *No Man's Land* (A.R.T.)

SUPPORTING ACTRESS, MUSICAL: Lauren Molina, *Sweeney Todd* (Broadway Across America)

SUPPORTING ACTOR, MUSICAL: Ben Magnuson, *Sweeney Todd* (Broadway Across America)

ACTRESS, MUSICAL: Judy Kaye, *Sweeney Todd* (Broadway Across America)

ACTOR, MUSICAL: Jeffry Denman, *Crazy for You* (North Shore Music Theatre) and *Irving Berlin's White Christmas* (Citi Performing Arts Center)

MUSIC DIRECTOR: David Lord, *Sweeney Todd* (Broadway Across America)

DIRECTOR, MUSICAL: Scott Schwartz, *Seven Brides for Seven Brothers* (North Shore Music Theatre)

DIRECTOR, PLAY: David Wheeler, *No Man's Land* (A.R.T.)

VISITING PRODUCTION: *Sweeney Todd* (Broadway Across America)

JOSEPH JEFFERSON AWARDS

Equity Wing Awards

October 29, 2007 at the North Shore Center for Performing Arts, Skokie, Illinois; 39th Annual. Presented for achievement in Chicago Equity theater from August 1, 2006–July 31, 2007; given by the Jefferson Awards Committee.

NEW WORK, PLAY: *August: Osage County* by Tracy Letts (Steppenwolf Theatre Company)

NEW WORK, MUSICAL: *The Snow Queen* by Michael Smith and Frank Galati (Victory Gardens Theater)

NEW ADAPTATION: Mary Zimmerman, *Argonautika: The Voyage of Jason and the Argonauts* (Lookingglass Theatre Company)

PRODUCTION OF A PLAY: *August: Osage County,* produced by Steppenwolf Theatre Company

PRODUCTION OF A MUSICAL: *Ragtime,* produced by Porchlight Music Theatre Chicago

PRODUCTION OF A REVUE: *The All Night Strut,* produced by Marriott Theatre

DIRECTOR OF A PLAY: Anna D. Shapiro, *August: Osage County* (Steppenwolf)

DIRECTOR OF MUSICAL: L. Walter Stearns, *Ragtime* (Porchlight Music Theatre)

DIRECTOR OF A REVUE: Marc Robin, *The All Night Strut* (Marriott Theatre)

ACTOR IN A PRINCIPAL ROLE, PLAY: Ben Carlson, *Hamlet* (Chicago Shakespeare Theater)

ACTRESS IN A PRINCIPAL ROLE, PLAY: Deanna Dunagan, *August: Osage County* (Steppenwolf)

ACTOR IN A SUPPORTING ROLE, PLAY: Maury Cooper, *The Price* (Shattered Globe Theatre)

ACTRESS IN A SUPPORTING ROLE, PLAY: Penny Slusher, *Another Part of the Forest* (Writers Theatre)

ACTOR IN A PRINCIPAL ROLE, MUSICAL: David Hess, *Shenandoah* (Marriott Theatre)

ACTRESS IN A PRINCIPAL ROLE, MUSICAL: Ernestine Jackson, *Raisin* (Court Theatre)

ACTOR IN A SUPPORTING ROLE, MUSICAL: Aaron Graham, *Ragtime* (Porchlight Music Theatre)

ACTRESS IN A SUPPORTING ROLE, MUSICAL: Sara R. Sevigny, *Assassins* (Porchlight Music Theatre)

ACTRESS IN A REVUE: Molly Andrews, *Fire on the Mountain* (Northlight Theatre)

ACTOR IN A REVUE: "Mississippi" Charles Bevel, *Fire on the Mountain* (Northlight Theatre)

ENSEMBLE: *August: Osage County* (Steppenwolf Theatre Company)

SCENIC DESIGN: Todd Rosenthal, *August: Osage County* (Steppenwolf)

COSTUME DESIGN: Mara Blumenfeld, *Mirror of the Invisible World* (Goodman Theatre)

LIGHTING DESIGN: John Culbert, *Mirror of the Invisible World* (Goodman Theatre)

SOUND DESIGN: Richard Woodbury, *King Lear* (Goodman Theatre)

CHOREOGRAPHY: Marc Robin, Beverly Durand, Mark Stuart Eckstein, Sylvia Hernandez-DiStasi and Sasha Vargas, *The All Night Strut* (Marriott Theatre)

ORIGINAL INCIDENTAL MUSIC: Michael Bodeen, *Mirror of the Invisible World* (Goodman Theatre)

MUSICAL DIRECTION: Eugene Dizon, *Ragtime* (Porchlight Music Theatre)

CAMEO PERFORMANCE: Douglas Vickers, *The Best Man* (Remy Bumppo Theatre Company)

SOLO PERFORMANCE: Lance Stuart Baker, *Thom Pain* (Theatre Wit) and Matt Sax, *Clay* (Lookingglass Theatre Company and About Face Theatre)

OTHER: Michael Montenegro, Puppet Design, *The Puppetmaster of Lodz* (Writers Theatre)

Non-Equity Wing Awards

June 11, 2007 at the Park West; 33rd Annual. Formerly called the Citations, the Non-Equity Awards are for outstanding achievement in professional productions played from April 1, 2006–March 31, 2007 which played at Chicago theaters not operating under union contracts; given by the Jefferson Awards Committee

PRODUCTION, PLAY: (tie) *Blues for an Alabama Sky,* produced by Eclipse Theatre Company; *The Sparrow,* produced by The House Theatre of Chicago

PRODUCTION, MUSICAL: (tie) *Fiorello,* produced by TimeLine Theatre Company; *Side Show,* produced by Bohemian Theatre Ensemble

ENSEMBLE: (tie) *Marathon '33* (Strawdog Theatre Company); *The Sparrow* (The House Theatre of Chicago)

DIRECTOR OF A PLAY: (tie) Nathan Allen, *The Sparrow* (The House Theatre of Chicago); Steven Fedoruk, *Blues for an Alabama Sky* (Eclipse Theatre Company)

DIRECTOR OF A MUSICAL OR REVUE: (tie) Nick Bowling, *Fiorello* (TimeLine Theatre Company); Stephen M. Genovese, *Side Show* (Bohemian Theatre Ensemble)

NEW WORK, PLAY: (tie) Chris Matthews, Jake Minton, Nathan Allen, *The Sparrow* (The House Theatre of Chicago); David Alan Moore, *In Times of War* (Stage Left Theatre)

NEW ADAPTATION: Frances Limoncelli, *Gaudy Night* (Lifeline Theatre)

ACTRESS IN A PRINCIPAL ROLE, PLAY: (tie) Deborah Hearst, *Fat Pig,* Profiles Theatre; Michelle Courvais, *Boy Gets Girl* (Eclipse Theatre Company)

ACTOR IN A PRINCIPAL ROLE, PLAY: Peter Oyloe, *Equus* (Actors Workshop Theatre)

ACTRESS IN A SUPPORTING ROLE, PLAY: (tie) Charlette Speigner, *Blues for an Alabama Sky* (Eclipse Theatre Company); Danica Ivancevic, *Faith Healer* (Uma Productions); Lindsay Weisberg, *One Fine Day* (Stage Left Theatre)

ACTOR IN A SUPPORTING ROLE, PLAY: Alfred Kemp, *Blues for an Alabama Sky* (Eclipse Theatre Company)

ACTRESS IN A PRINCIPAL ROLE, MUSICAL OR REVUE: (tie) Andrea Prestinario and Vanessa Panerosa, *Side Show* (Bohemian Theatre Ensemble); Cat Davis, *Mack and Mabel* (Circle Theatre)

ACTOR IN A PRINCIPAL ROLE, MUSICAL: Michael Mahler, *My Favorite Year* (Bailiwick Repertory)

ACTRESS IN A SUPPORTING ROLE, MUSICAL OR REVUE: Danielle Brothers, *Flora the Red Menace* (Theo Ubique Theatre Company/Michael James)

ACTOR IN A SUPPORTING ROLE MUSICAL OR REVUE: (tie) Eric Lindahl, *Side Show* (Bohemian Theatre Ensemble); Terry Hamilton, *Fiorello!* (TimeLine Theatre Company)

SCENIC DESIGN: Courtney O'Neill, *Mud* (The Hypocrites)

COSTUME DESIGN: Jesus Perez, *Mack and Mabel* (Circle Theatre)

LIGHTING DESIGN: Jared Moore, *Angels in America, Part Two: Perestroika* (The Hypocrites and Bailiwick Repertory)

SOUND DESIGN: Michael Griggs and Mikhail Fiksel, *Angels in America, Part Two: Perestroika* (The Hypocrites and Bailiwick Repertory)

CHOREOGRAPHY: Tommy Rapley, *The Sparrow* (The House Theatre of Chicago)

ORIGINAL INCIDENTAL MUSIC: Kevin O'Donnell, *The Sparrow* (The House Theatre of Chicago)

MUSICAL DIRECTION: Doug Peck, *Fiorello!* (TimeLine Theatre Company)

FIGHT CHOREOGRAPHY: Matt Hawkins, *Hatfield and McCoy* (The House Theatre of Chicago)

OBJECT DESIGN: *The Golden Truffle* (Redmoon Theater)

PROJECTIONS DESIGN: Lucas Merino, *The Sparrow* (The House Theatre of Chicago)

PUPPET DESIGN: Kass Copeland, *Once Upon a Time (or the Secret Language of Birds)* (Redmoon Theatre)

KENNEDY CENTER

HONORS 30th annual; December 2, 2007 (broadcast on CBS December 26, 2007). Presented for distinguished achievement by individuals who have made significant contributions to American culture through the arts. 2007 Recipients: Leon Fleisher, Steve Martin, Diana Ross, Martin Scorsese, Brian Wilson

MARK TWAIN PRIZE 10th annual; October 11, 2007 (broadcast on PBS November 12, 2007). Presented for American humor. 2007 Recipient: Billy Crystal

KEVIN KLINE AWARDS

March 31, 2008; Loretto-Hilton Center; 3rd Annual; Host: Lara Teeter. Presented for outstanding achievement in professional theatre in the Greater St. Louis area for the 2007 calendar year; Produced by The Professional Theatre Awards Council (Steve Isom, Executive Director); Winners selected by a floating pool of 45 judges

PRODUCTION OF A PLAY: *Standing on My Knees* (The Orange Girls)

DIRECTOR OF A PLAY: Doug Finlayson, *Kindertransport* (New Jewish Theatre)

PRODUCTION OF A MUSICAL: *The Full Monty* (Stages St. Louis)

DIRECTOR OF A MUSICAL: (tie) Michael Hamilton, *The Full Monty* (Stages St. Louis); Bobby Miller, *I Love You, You're Perfect, Now Change* (Playhouse at West Port Plaza)

MUSICAL DIRECTION: Henry Palkes, *Altar Boyz* (Repertory Theatre of St. Louis)

CHOREOGRAPHY: Christopher Gattelli, *Altar Boyz* (Repertory Theatre of St. Louis)

COSTUMES: Dorothy Marshall Englis, *A Little Night Music* (Stages St. Louis)

LIGHTING: Glenn Dunn, *Remnant* (Mustard Seed Theatre)

SET: Dunsi Dai, *Remnant* (Mustard Seed Theatre)

SOUND: David B. Smith, *Dracula* (Repertory Theatre of St. Louis)

NEW PLAY OR MUSICAL: *Demons...and Other Blunt Objects* by Dan Rubin (HotCity Theatre)

ENSEMBLE IN A PLAY: (tie) *Kindertransport* (New Jewish Theatre); *Women's Minyan* (New Jewish Theatre)

ENSEMBLE IN A MUSICAL: *Crazy for You* (Stages St. Louis)

LEAD ACTOR IN A MUSICAL: David Elder, *Crazy for You* (Stages St. Louis)

LEAD ACTOR IN A PLAY: Jason Babinsky, *The Bomb-itty of Errors* (Repertory Theatre of St. Louis)

LEAD ACTRESS IN A MUSICAL: Julie Tolivar, *Crazy for You* (Stages St. Louis)

LEAD ACTRESS IN A PLAY: Lavonne Byers, *A Delicate Balance* (St. Louis Actors' Studio)

SUPPORTING ACTOR IN A MUSICAL: Keith Tyrone, *The Full Monty* (Stages St. Louis)

SUPPORTING ACTOR IN A PLAY: John Kinney, *What's Wrong with This Picture?* (New Jewish Theatre)

SUPPORTING ACTRESS IN A MUSICAL: Jennifer Cody, *Hello Dolly* (The Muny)

SUPPORTING ACTRESS IN A PLAY: Teresa Doggett, *Enchanted April* (Act, Inc.)

PRODUCTION FOR YOUNG AUDIENCES: *Snoopy!!!* (Stages St. Louis

ED KLEBAN AWARDS

June 4, 2008; American Society of Composers, Authors and Publishers; 18th Annual. Presented by New Dramatists in honor of Edward Kleban; award is given annually to both a librettist and a lyricist ($100,000 to each recipient payable over two years). 2008 Winners: David Lindsay-Abaire (lyricist); tie: Laura Harrington and Bill Solly/Donald Ward (librettists)

GLAAD MEDIA AWARDS

March 19, 2008; Marriott Marquis; 19th annual. Presented by the Gay and Lesbian Alliance Against Defamation for fair, accurate and inclusive representations of gay individuals in the media as a means of eliminating homophobia and discrimination based on gender identity and sexual orientation. 2008 Winners in the Theatre Categories: New York Theater – Broadway & Off-Broadway: *The Beebo Brinker Chronicles* by Kate Moira Ryan and Linda S. Chapman; New York Theater – Off-Off-Broadway: *BASH'd: A Gay Rap Opera* by Chris Craddock, Nathan Cuckow, and Aaron Macri; Los Angeles Theater: *Avenue Q,* book by Jeff Whitty, music and lyrics by Robert Lopez and Jeff Marx; Special Recognition: Theatre Rhinoceros, San Francisco

JONATHAN LARSON PERFORMING ARTS FOUNDATION AWARDS

February 14, 2008; 21 Club; created in 1996. Jonathan Larson's dream was to infuse musical theatre with a contemporary, joyful urban vitality. After 12 years of struggle as a classic "starving artist," his dream came true with the phenomenal success of Rent. To celebrate his creative spirit and honor his memory, Jonathan's family and friends created the Jonathan Larson Performing Arts Foundation. 2008 Recipients: Individual Artist Awards: Gaby Alter, Susan DiLallo, Joel New, Jason Rhyne, Jeff Thomson and Jordan Mann; Organization Award: Pittsburgh's City Theatre

LOS ANGELES DRAMA CRITICS CIRCLE

March 17, 2008 at El Portal Theatre; 39th Annual; Host: Jason Graae. Presented for excellence in theatre in the Los Angeles and Orange County during the 2007 calendar year.

PLAY: *In Arabia We'd All Be Kings* by Stephen Adly Guirgis (Elephant Theatre Company in association with VS. Theatre Company)

MUSICAL: *13* by Jason Robert Brown (Center Theatre Group – Mark Taper Forum)

REVIVAL: *The Hasty Heart* by John Patrick (Pacific Resident Theatre Company)

DIRECTION: Dan Bonnell, *Anatol* (Pacific Resident Theatre); Nick DeGruccio, *Zanna Don't!* (West Coast Ensemble at the Lyric-Hyperion Theatre); Michael Michetti, *dark play or stories for boys* (The Theatre at Boston Court)

WRITING: Jeff Goode, *Love Loves a Pornographer* (Circle X at Inside the Ford); Stephen Adly Guirgis, *In Arabia We'd All Be Kings*

ADAPTATION: Matt Walker, *Alice In One-Hit Wonderland* (Troubadour Theatre Company at Flacon Theatre)

MUSICAL DIRECTION: David O, *13* (Center Theatre Group – Mark Taper Forum); Gerald Sternbach, *On Your Toes* (Reprise! Broadway's Best at UCLA Freud Playhouse)

MUSICAL SCORE: Jason Robert Brown, *13* (Center Theatre Group – Mark Taper Forum)

CHOREOGRAPHY: Lee Martino, *On Your Toes* (Reprise! Broadway's Best at UCLA Freud Playhouse); Janet Miller, *Winter Wonderettes* (El Portal Forum Theatre)

LEAD PERFORMANCE: Danny Calvert, *Zanna, Don't!* (West Coast Ensemble at the Lyric-Hyperion Theatre); Matt Letscher, *Anatol* (Pacific Resident Theatre); Alan Mandell, *Trying* (Colony Theatre); Rebecca Marcotte, *Loyal Women* (Theatre Banshee); Laurie Metcalf, *The Quality of Life* (Geffen Playhouse-Audrey Skirball Kenis Theater); Gabriel Olds, *Tryst* (Black Dahlia Theatre)

ENSEMBLE PERFORMANCE: *13* (Center Theatre Group – Mark Taper Forum); *Zanna, Don't!* (West Coast Ensemble)

SCENIC DESIGN: Joel Daavid, *In Arabia We'd All Be Kings* (Elephant Theatre Company in association with VS. Theatre Company)

LIGHTING DESIGN: Joel Daavid, *In Arabia We'd All Be Kings* (Elephant Theatre Company in association with VS. Theatre Company)

COSTUME DESIGN: Shon LeBlanc, *The Milk Train Doesn't Stop Here Anymore* (Fountain Theatre)

SOUND DESIGN: Lindsay Jones, *Bug* (Lost Angels Theatre Company at Coast Playhouse)

PUPPET DESIGN: Rick Lyon, *Avenue Q* (Center Theatre Group – Ahmanson Theatre)

MARGARET HARFORD AWARD (for Sustained Excellence in Theatre): Musical Theatre West

POLLY WARFIELD AWARD (for outstanding single season by a small to mid-sized theatre): Theatre Banshee

TED SCHMITT AWARD (for outstanding world premiere play in Los Angeles): Jane Anderson, *The Quality of Life*

ANGSTROM AWARD (for career achievement in lighting design): Leigh Allen

JOEL HIRSCHHORN AWARD (for outstanding achievement in musical theatre): Jason Graae

SPECIAL AWARD: Jon Maher for outstanding achievement as an ASL interpreter

NATIONAL ARTS CLUB

JOSEPH KESSELRING FELLOWSHIP AND HONORS

Founded in 1978 in honor of National Arts Club member Joseph Otto Kesselring, a New York born actor, author, producer, and playwright who died in 1967. A monetary award is presented to a playwright whose dramatic work has demonstrated the highest possible merit and promise and who has not received prominent national notice or acclaim. In addition to a cash prize, the first prize winner also receives a staged reading of a work of his or her choice. The Club redefined the award in 2007 to consist of the Kesselring Fellowship, and created a new category called the Kesselring Honors. 2007 Winner: Jordan Harrison; Kesselring Honors: Will Eno, Rinne Groff, Marcus Gardley

GOLD MEDAL Founded in 1898 by Charles de Kay. Presented by the National Arts Club Theatre/Drama Committee. 2008 Winner: Lin-Manuel Miranda, *In the Heights*

NEW DRAMATISTS LIFETIME ACHIEVEMENT AWARD

May 15, 2008; Marriott Marquis Hotel; 59th Annual. Presented to an individual who has made an outstanding artistic contribution to the American theater. 2008 Winner: Harvey Fierstein

MUSICAL THEATER HALL OF FAME

Established at New York University on November 10, 1993.

Harold Arlen, Irving Berlin, Leonard Bernstein, Eubie Blake, Abe Burrows, George M. Cohan, Betty Comden, Dorothy Fields, George Gershwin, Ira Gershwin, Adolph Green, Oscar Hammerstein II, E.Y. Harburg, Larry Hart, Jerome Kern, Burton Lane, Alan Jay Lerner, Frank Loesser, Frederick Loewe, Mary Martin, Ethel Merman, Cole Porter, Jerome Robbins, Richard Rodgers, Harold Rome

NEW YORK INNOVATIVE THEATRE AWARDS

3rd Annual; September 24, 2007 at the Fashion Institute of Technology's Haft Auditorium. Presented annually to honor individuals and organizations who have achieved artistic excellence in the Off-Off-Broadway theatre. The New York IT Awards committee recognizes the unique and essential role Off-Off-Broadway plays in contributing to American and global culture, and believes that publicly recognizing excellence in independent theatre will expand audience awareness and appreciation of the full New York theatre experience. Staff: Jason Bowcutt, Executive Director; Shay Gines, Executive Director; Nick Micozzi, Executive Director; Awards Committee: Paul Adams (Artistic Director, Emerging Artists Theatre), Dan Bacalzo (Managing Editor, TheatreMania), Christopher Borg (Actor, Director), Jason Bowcutt (Executive Director, New York IT Awards), Tim Errickson (Artistic Director, Boomerang Theatre Co.), Thecla Farrell (Outreach Coordinator, Castillo Theatre Co.), Constance Congdon (Playwright), Shay Gines, (Executive Director, New York IT Awards), Ben Hodges (Executive Producer, Theatre World Awards, Inc.), Leonard Jacobs (National Theatre Editor, Back Stage), Ron Lasko (Public Relations, Spin Cycle), Blake Lawrence, Bob Lee, Nick Micozzi (Executive Director, New York IT Awards), Risa Shoup, (Programming Director, Chashama), Nicky Paraiso (Curator for Performance, La MaMa ETC), Jeff Riebe (The January Initiative), Akia Squiterri (Artistic Director, Rising Sun Performance Company).

OUTSTANDING ACTOR IN A FEATURED ROLE: Joe Plummer, *As You Like It* (poortom Productions)

OUTSTANDING ACTRESS IN A FEATURED ROLE: Boo Killebrew, *6969* (CollaborationTown)

OUTSTANDING SOLO PERFORMANCE: Mike Houston, *The Ledge,* (eavesdrop)

OUTSTANDING ORIGINAL SHORT SCRIPT: Daniel Reitz, *Rules of the Universe,* (Rising Phoenix Repertory)

OUTSTANDING ORIGINAL FULL-LENGTH SCRIPT: Saviana Stanescu, *Waxing West* (East Coast Artists)

OUTSTANDING ORIGINAL MUSIC: Leanne Darling, *The Landlord* (Toy Box Theatre Company)

OUTSTANDING CHOREOGRAPHY/MOVEMENT: Dan Safer, *Dancing vs. the Rat Experiment* (La MaMa ETC in association with Witness Relocation)

OUTSTANDING SOUND DESIGN: Ryan Maeker and Tim Schellenbaum, *Dancing vs. the Rat Experiment* (La MaMa ETC in association with Witness Relocation)

OUTSTANDING COSTUME DESIGN: David Withrow, *Bug Boy Blues* (The Looking Glass Theatre)

OUTSTANDING LIGHTING DESIGN: Peter Hoerburger, *The Present Perfect* (The Operating Theater)

OUTSTANDING SET DESIGN: George Allison, *Picasso at the Lapin Agile* (T. Schreiber Studio)

OUTSTANDING ACTRESS IN A LEAD ROLE: Susan Louise O'Connor, *the silent concerto* (Packawallop Productions)

OUTSTANDING ACTOR IN A LEAD ROLE: Max Rosenak, *6969* (CollaborationTown)

OUTSTANDING DIRECTOR: Daniel Talbott, *Rules of the Universe* (Rising Phoenix Repertory

OUTSTANDING ENSEMBLE: *6969* (CollaborationTown, A Theatre Company, Inc.): Boo Killebrew, Julia Lowrie Henderson, Ryan Purcell, Max Rosenak, Phillip Taratula, Daniel Walker Stowell

OUTSTANDING PERFORMANCE ART PRODUCTION: *Dancing vs The Rat Experiment* (La MaMa ETC in association with Witness Relocation)

OUTSTANDING PRODUCTION OF A MUSICAL: *Urinetown, the Musical* (The Gallery Players)

OUTSTANDING PRODUCTION OF A PLAY: *Buoffon Glass Menajoree* (Ten Directions)

2007 Honorary Awards

ARTISTIC ACHIEVEMENT AWARD for significant artistic contribution to the Off-Off-Broadway community: Doric Wilson

STEWARDSHIP AWARD for significant contribution to the Off-Off-Broadway community through service, support and leadership: Alliance of Resident Theatres/New York

THE CAFFE CINO FELLOWSHIP AWARD for consistent production of outstanding work (includes a grant of $1,000 to be used toward an Off-Off-Broadway production): Rising Phoenix Repertory

OTTO RENÉ CASTILLO AWARDS

June 9, 2008 at the All Stars Project; 10th annual; Presented for Political Theatre. The Otto Award is named for the Guatemalan poet and revolutionary Otto Rene Castillo. 2008 Winners: Claque Theatre, Human Nature Dance Theatre, Pillsbury House Theatre, Projekt Theater Studio, Zero No Zero Theatre Company; Aimé Césaire Lifetime Achievement Award: Woodie King, Jr.

RICHARD RODGERS AWARDS

For staged readings of musicals in nonprofit theaters, administered by the American Academy of Arts and Letters. 2008 Winners: Alive at Ten by Kirsten A. Guenther and Ryan Scott Oliver; Kingdom by Aaron Jafferis and Ian Williams; See Rock City & Other Destinations by Brad Alexander and Adam Mathias

ROBERT WHITEHEAD AWARD

For outstanding achievement in commercial theatre producing, bestowed on a graduate of the fourteen-week Commercial Theatre Institute Program who has demonstrated a quality of production exemplified by the late producer, Robert Whitehead. 2008 Award: Nick Scandalios

SUSAN SMITH BLACKBURN PRIZE

March 30, 2008; Houston, Texas; 30th annual. Presented to women who have written works of outstanding quality for the English-speaking theater. 2008 Winner: Judith Thompson, *Palace of the End;* Special Commendations: Lisa McGee, *Girls and Dolls;* Polly Stenham, *That Face;* Jenny Schwartz, *God's Ear;* Finalists: Linda Brogan, *Black Crows;* Julie Marie Myatt, *Boats on a River;* Victoria Stewart, *Hardball;* Lydia Diamond, *Stick Fly;* Bryony Lavery, *Stockholm;* Linda McLean, *Strangers, Babies*

THE THEATER HALL OF FAME

January 28, 2008; The Gershwin Theatre; 37th Annual; Host: Tommy Tune. The Theater of Hall of Fame was created in 1971 to honor those who have made outstanding contributions to the American theater in a career spanning at least twenty-five years, with at least five major credits. 2008 Inductees: John Cullum, Mel Gussow, Harvey Fierstein, Dana Ivey, Jack O'Brien; Peter Shaffer; Lois Smith; Joseph Stein

FOUNDERS AWARD Established in 1993 in honor of Earl Blackwell, for outstanding contribution to the theater. 2008 Winner: Roy Somlyo

MARGO JONES CITIZEN OF THEATER MEDAL Presented annually to a citizen of the theater who has made a lifetime commitment to theater and has demonstrated an understanding and affirmation of the craft of playwriting. 2007 Winners: David Emmes and Martin Benson

WILLIAM INGE THEATRE FESTIVAL AWARD

Saturday, April 26, 2008; 27th annual. Given for distinguished achievement in American theater. 2008 Honoree: Christopher Durang; 16th Annual Otis Guernsey New Voices in Playwrighting Award: Adam Bock

Longest-Running Shows

Broadway

★ Production is still running as of May 31, 2008; count includes performances up to and including that date.

The Phantom of the Opera★
8,463 performances
Opened January 26, 1988

Cats
7,485 performances
Opened October 7, 1982
Closed September 10, 2000

Les Misérables
6,680 performances
Opened March 12, 1987
Closed May 18, 2003

A Chorus Line
6,137 performances
Opened July 25, 1975
Closed April 28, 1990

Oh! Calcutta (revival)
5,959 performances
Opened September 24, 1976
Closed August 6, 1989

Beauty and the Beast
5,464 performances
Opened April 18, 1994
Closed July 29, 2007

Rent★
5,009 performances
Opened April 29, 1996

Chicago★ (revival)
4,786 performances
Opened November 19, 1996

The Lion King★
4,371 performances
Opened November 13, 1997

Miss Saigon
4,097 performances
Opened April 11, 1991
Closed January 28, 2001

42nd Street
3,486 performances
Opened August 25, 1980
Closed January 8, 1989

Grease
3,388 performances
Opened February 14, 1972
Closed April 13, 1980

Fiddler on the Roof
3,242 performances
Opened September 22, 1964
Closed July 2, 1972

Life With Father
3,224 performances
Opened November 8, 1939
Closed July 12, 1947

Tobacco Road
3,182 performances
Opened December 4, 1933
Closed May 31, 1941

Hello, Dolly!
2,844 performances
Opened January 16, 1964
Closed December 27, 1970

Mamma Mia!★
2,734 performances
Opened October 12, 2001

My Fair Lady
2,717 performances
Opened March 15, 1956
Closed September 29, 1962

The Producers
2,502 performances
Opened April 19, 2001
Closed April 22, 2007

Hairspray★
2.393 performances
Opened August 15, 2002

Cabaret (1998 revival)
2,378 performances
Opened March 19, 1998
Closed January 4, 2004

Annie
2,377 performances
Opened April 21, 1977
Closed January 22, 1983

Man of La Mancha
2,328 performances
Opened November 22, 1965
Closed June 26, 1971

Abie's Irish Rose
2,327 performances
Opened May 23, 1922
Closed October 21, 1927

Oklahoma!
2,212 performances
Opened March 31, 1943
Closed May 29, 1948

Smokey Joe's Café
2,036 performances
Opened March 2, 1995
Closed January 16, 2000

Avenue Q★
1,996 performances
Opened July 31, 2003

Pippin
1,944 performances
Opened October 23, 1972
Closed June 12, 1977

South Pacific
1,925 performances
Opened April 7, 1949
Closed January 16, 1954

The Magic Show
1,920 performances
Opened May 28, 1974
Closed December 31, 1978

Wicked★
1,893 performances
Opened October 30, 2003

Aida
1,852 performances
Opened March 23, 2000
Closed September 5, 2004

Gemini
1,819 performances
Opened May 21, 1977
Closed September 6, 1981

Deathtrap
1,793 performances
Opened February 26, 1978
Closed June 13, 1982

Harvey
1,775 performances
Opened November 1, 1944
Closed January 15, 1949

Dancin'
1,774 performances
Opened March 27, 1978
Closed June 27, 1982

La Cage Aux Folles
1,761 performances
Opened August 21, 1983
Closed November 15, 1987

Hair
1,750 performances
Opened April 29, 1968
Closed July 1, 1972

The Wiz
1,672 performances
Opened January 5, 1975
Closed January 29, 1979

Born Yesterday
1,642 performances
Opened February 4, 1946
Closed December 31, 1949

The Best Little Whorehouse in Texas
1,639 performances
Opened June 19, 1978
Closed March 27, 1982

Crazy for You
1,622 performances
Opened February 19, 1992
Closed January 7, 1996

Ain't Misbehavin'
1,604 performances
Opened May 9, 1978
Closed February 21, 1982

Mary, Mary
1,572 performances
Opened March 8, 1961
Closed December 12, 1964

Evita
1,567 performances
Opened September 25, 1979
Closed June 26, 1983

The Voice of the Turtle
1,557 performances
Opened December 8, 1943
Closed January 3, 1948

Jekyll & Hyde
1,543 performances
Opened April 28, 1997
Closed January 7, 2001

Barefoot in the Park
1,530 performances
Opened October 23, 1963
Closed June 25, 1967

Brighton Beach Memoirs
1,530 performances
Opened March 27, 1983
Closed May 11, 1986

42nd Street (revival)
1,524 performances
Opened May 2, 2001
Closed January 2, 2005

Dreamgirls
1,522 performances
Opened December 20, 1981
Closed August 11, 1985

Mame
1,508 performances
Opened May 24, 1966
Closed January 3, 1970

Grease (1994 revival)
1,505 performances
Opened May 11, 1994
Closed January 25, 1998

Same Time, Next Year
1,453 performances
Opened March 14, 1975
Closed September 3, 1978

Arsenic and Old Lace
1,444 performances
Opened January 10, 1941
Closed June 17, 1944

The Sound of Music
1,443 performances
Opened November 16, 1959
Closed June 15, 1963

Me and My Girl
1,420 performances
Opened August 10, 1986
Closed December 31, 1989

How to Succeed in Business Without Really Trying
1,417 performances
Opened October 14, 1961
Closed March 6, 1965

Hellzapoppin'
1,404 performances
Opened September 22, 1938
Closed December 17, 1941

The Music Man
1,375 performances
Opened December 19, 1957
Closed April 15, 1961

Funny Girl
1,348 performances
Opened March 26, 1964
Closed July 15, 1967

Mummenschanz
1,326 performances
Opened March 30, 1977
Closed April 20, 1980

Monty Python's Spamalot*
1,317 performances
Opened March 17, 2005

Movin' Out
1,303 performances
Opened October 24, 2002
Closed December 11, 2005

Angel Street
1,295 performances
Opened December 5, 1941
Closed December 30, 1944

Lightnin'
1,291 performances
Opened August 26, 1918
Closed August 27, 1921

Promises, Promises
1,281 performances
Opened December 1, 1968
Closed January 1, 1972

The King and I
1,246 performances
Opened March 29, 1951
Closed March 20, 1954

Cactus Flower
1,234 performances
Opened December 8, 1965
Closed November 23, 1968

Sleuth
1,222 performances
Opened November 12, 1970
Closed October 13, 1973

Torch Song Trilogy
1,222 performances
Opened June 10, 1982
Closed May 19, 1985

1776
1,217 performances
Opened March 16, 1969
Closed February 13, 1972

Equus
1,209 performances
Opened October 24, 1974
Closed October 7, 1977

Sugar Babies
1,208 performances
Opened October 8, 1979
Closed August 28, 1982

Guys and Dolls
1,200 performances
Opened November 24, 1950
Closed November 28, 1953

Amadeus
1,181 performances
Opened December 17, 1980
Closed October 16, 1983

Cabaret
1,165 performances
Opened November 20, 1966
Closed September 6, 1969

Mister Roberts
1,157 performances
Opened February 18, 1948
Closed January 6, 1951

Annie Get Your Gun
1,147 performances
Opened May 16, 1946
Closed February 12, 1949

Guys and Dolls (1992 revival)
1,144 performances
Opened April 14, 1992
Closed January 8, 1995

The Seven Year Itch
1,141 performances
Opened November 20, 1952
Closed August 13, 1955

The 25th Annual Putnam County Spelling Bee
1,136 performances
Opened May 2, 2005
Closed January 20, 2008

Bring in 'da Noise, Bring in 'da Funk
1,130 performances
Opened April 25, 1996
Closed January 19, 1999

Butterflies Are Free
1,128 performances
Opened October 21, 1969
Closed July 2, 1972

Pins and Needles
1,108 performances
Opened November 27, 1937
Closed June 22, 1940

Plaza Suite
1,097 performances
Opened February 14, 1968
Closed October 3, 1970

Fosse
1,093 performances
Opened January 14, 1999
Closed August 25, 2001

They're Playing Our Song
1,082 performances
Opened February 11, 1979
Closed September 6, 1981

Grand Hotel (musical)
1,077 performances
Opened November 12, 1989
Closed April 25, 1992

Kiss Me, Kate
1,070 performances
Opened December 30, 1948
Closed July 25, 1951

Don't Bother Me, I Can't Cope
1,065 performances
Opened April 19, 1972
Closed October 27, 1974

The Pajama Game
1,063 performances
Opened May 13, 1954
Closed November 24, 1956

Jersey Boys*
1,050 performances
Opened November 6, 2006

Shenandoah
1,050 performances
Opened January 7, 1975
Closed August 7, 1977

Annie Get Your Gun (1999 revival)
1,046 performances
Opened March 4, 1999
Closed September 1, 2001

The Teahouse of the August Moon
1,027 performances
Opened October 15, 1953
Closed March 24, 1956

Damn Yankees
1,019 performances
Opened May 5, 1955
Closed October 12, 1957

Contact
1,010 performances
Opened March 30, 2000
Closed September 1, 2002

Never Too Late
1,007 performances
Opened November 26, 1962
Closed April 24, 1965

Big River
1,005 performances
Opened April 25, 1985
Closed September 20, 1987

The Will Rogers Follies
983 performances
Opened May 1, 1991
Closed September 5, 1993

Any Wednesday
982 performances
Opened February 18, 1964
Closed June 26, 1966

Sunset Boulevard
977 performances
Opened November 17, 1994
Closed March 22, 1997

Urinetown
965 performances
Opened September 20, 2001
Closed January 18, 2004

A Funny Thing Happened on the Way to the Forum
964 performances
Opened May 8, 1962
Closed August 29, 1964

The Odd Couple
964 performances
Opened March 10, 1965
Closed July 2, 1967

Anna Lucasta
957 performances
Opened August 30, 1944
Closed November 30, 1946

Kiss and Tell
956 performances
Opened March 17, 1943
Closed June 23, 1945

Show Boat (1994 revival)
949 performances
Opened October 2, 1994
Closed January 5, 1997

Dracula (1977 revival)
925 performances
Opened October 20, 1977
Closed January 6, 1980

Bells Are Ringing
924 performances
Opened November 29, 1956
Closed March 7, 1959

The Moon Is Blue
924 performances
Opened March 8, 1951
Closed May 30, 1953

Beatlemania
920 performances
Opened May 31, 1977
Closed October 17, 1979

Proof
917 performances
Opened October 24, 2000
Closed January 5, 2003

The Elephant Man
916 performances
Opened April 19, 1979
Closed June 28, 1981

The Color Purple
910 performances
Opened December 1, 2005
Closed February 24, 2008

Kiss of the Spider Woman
906 performances
Opened May 3, 1993
Closed July 1, 1995

Thoroughly Modern Millie
904 performances
Opened April 18, 2002
Closed June 20, 2004

Luv
901 performances
Opened November 11, 1964
Closed January 7, 1967

The Who's Tommy
900 performances
Opened April 22, 1993
Closed June 17, 1995

Chicago
898 performances
Opened June 3, 1975
Closed August 27, 1977

Applause
896 performances
Opened March 30, 1970
Closed July 27, 1972

Can-Can
892 performances
Opened May 7, 1953
Closed June 25, 1955

Carousel
890 performances
Opened April 19, 1945
Closed May 24, 1947

I'm Not Rappaport
890 performances
Opened November 19, 1985
Closed January 17, 1988

Hats Off to Ice
889 performances
Opened June 22, 1944
Closed April 2, 1946

Fanny
888 performances
Opened November 4, 1954
Closed December 16, 1956

Children of a Lesser God
887 performances
Opened March 30, 1980
Closed May 16, 1982

Follow the Girls
882 performances
Opened April 8, 1944
Closed May 18, 1946

Kiss Me, Kate (revival)
881 performances
Opened November 18, 1999
Closed December 30, 2001

City of Angels
878 performances
Opened December 11, 1989
Closed January 19, 1992

Camelot
873 performances
Opened December 3, 1960
Closed January 5, 1963

I Love My Wife
872 performances
Opened April 17, 1977
Closed May 20, 1979

The Bat
867 performances
Opened August 23, 1920
Unknown closing date

My Sister Eileen
864 performances
Opened December 26, 1940
Closed January 16, 1943

No, No, Nanette (revival)
861 performances
Opened January 19, 1971
Closed February 3, 1973

Ragtime
861 performances
Opened January 18, 1998
Closed January 16, 2000

Song of Norway
860 performances
Opened August 21, 1944
Closed September 7, 1946

Chapter Two
857 performances
Opened December 4, 1977
Closed December 9, 1979

A Streetcar Named Desire
855 performances
Opened December 3, 1947
Closed December 17, 1949

Barnum
854 performances
Opened April 30, 1980
Closed May 16, 1982

Comedy in Music
849 performances
Opened October 2, 1953
Closed January 21, 1956

Raisin
847 performances
Opened October 18, 1973
Closed December 7, 1975

Blood Brothers
839 performances
Opened April 25, 1993
Closed April 30, 1995

You Can't Take It With You
837 performances
Opened December 14, 1936
Unknown closing date

La Plume de Ma Tante
835 performances
Opened November 11, 1958
Closed December 17, 1960

Three Men on a Horse
835 performances
Opened January 30, 1935
Closed January 9, 1937

The Subject Was Roses
832 performances
Opened May 25, 1964
Closed May 21, 1966

Black and Blue
824 performances
Opened January 26, 1989
Closed January 20, 1991

The King and I (1996 revival)
807 performances
Opened April 11, 1996
Closed February 22, 1998

Inherit the Wind
806 performances
Opened April 21, 1955
Closed June 22, 1957

Anything Goes (1987 revival)
804 performances
Opened October 19, 1987
Closed September 3, 1989

Titanic
804 performances
Opened April 23, 1997
Closed March 21, 1999

No Time for Sergeants
796 performances
Opened October 20, 1955
Closed September 14, 1957

Fiorello!
795 performances
Opened November 23, 1959
Closed October 28, 1961

Where's Charley?
792 performances
Opened October 11, 1948
Closed September 9, 1950

The Ladder
789 performances
Opened October 22, 1926
Unknown closing date

Fiddler on the Roof (2004 revival)
781 performances
Opened February 26, 2004
Closed January 8, 2006

Forty Carats
780 performances
Opened December 26, 1968
Closed November 7, 1970

Lost in Yonkers
780 performances
Opened February 21, 1991
Closed January 3, 1993

The Prisoner of Second Avenue
780 performances
Opened November 11, 1971
Closed September 29, 1973

M. Butterfly
777 performances
Opened March 20, 1988
Closed January 27, 1990

The Tale of the Allergist's Wife
777 performances
Opened November 2, 2000
Closed September 15, 2002

Oliver!
774 performances
Opened January 6, 1963
Closed November 14, 1964

The Pirates of Penzance (1981 revival)
772 performances
Opened January 8, 1981
Closed November 28, 1982

The Full Monty
770 performances
Opened October 26, 2000
Closed September 1, 2002

Woman of the Year
770 performances
Opened March 29, 1981
Closed March 13, 1983

My One and Only
767 performances
Opened May 1, 1983
Closed March 3, 1985

Sophisticated Ladies
767 performances
Opened March 1, 1981
Closed January 2, 1983

Bubbling Brown Sugar
766 performances
Opened March 2, 1976
Closed December 31, 1977

Into the Woods
765 performances
Opened November 5, 1987
Closed September 3, 1989

State of the Union
765 performances
Opened November 14, 1945
Closed September 13, 1947

Starlight Express
761 performances
Opened March 15, 1987
Closed January 8, 1989

The First Year
760 performances
Opened October 20, 1920
Unknown closing date

Broadway Bound
756 performances
Opened December 4, 1986
Closed September 25, 1988

You Know I Can't Hear You When the Water's Running
755 performances
Opened March 13, 1967
Closed January 4, 1969

Two for the Seesaw
750 performances
Opened January 16, 1958
Closed October 31, 1959

Joseph and the Amazing Technicolor Dreamcoat
747 performances
Opened January 27, 1982
Closed September 4, 1983

Death of a Salesman
742 performances
Opened February 10, 1949
Closed November 18, 1950

for colored girls who have considered suicide/when the rainbow is enuf
742 performances
Opened September 15, 1976
Closed July 16, 1978

Sons o' Fun
742 performances
Opened December 1, 1941
Closed August 29, 1943

Candide (1974 revival)
740 performances
Opened March 10, 1974
Closed January 4, 1976

Gentlemen Prefer Blondes
740 performances
Opened December 8, 1949
Closed September 15, 1951

The Man Who Came to Dinner
739 performances
Opened October 16, 1939
Closed July 12, 1941

Nine
739 performances
Opened May 9, 1982
Closed February 4, 1984

Call Me Mister
734 performances
Opened April 18, 1946
Closed January 10, 1948

Victor/Victoria
734 performances
Opened October 25, 1995
Closed July 27, 1997

West Side Story
732 performances
Opened September 26, 1957
Closed June 27, 1959

High Button Shoes
727 performances
Opened October 9, 1947
Closed July 2, 1949

Finian's Rainbow
725 performances
Opened January 10, 1947
Closed October 2, 1948

Claudia
722 performances
Opened February 12, 1941
Closed January 9, 1943

The Gold Diggers
720 performances
Opened September 30, 1919
Unknown closing date

Jesus Christ Superstar
720 performances
Opened October 12, 1971
Closed June 30, 1973

Carnival!
719 performances
Opened April 13, 1961
Closed January 5, 1963

The Diary of Anne Frank
717 performances
Opened October 5, 1955
Closed June 22, 1955

A Funny Thing Happened on the Way to the Forum (revival)
715 performances
Opened April 18, 1996
Closed January 4, 1998

I Remember Mama
714 performances
Opened October 19, 1944
Closed June 29, 1946

Tea and Sympathy
712 performances
Opened September 30, 1953
Closed June 18, 1955

Junior Miss
710 performances
Opened November 18, 1941
Closed July 24, 1943

Footloose
708 performances
Opened October 22, 1998
Closed July 2, 2000

Last of the Red Hot Lovers
706 performances
Opened December 28, 1969
Closed September 4, 1971

The Secret Garden
706 performances
Opened April 25, 1991
Closed January 3, 1993

Company
705 performances
Opened April 26, 1970
Closed January 1, 1972

Seventh Heaven
704 performances
Opened October 30, 1922
Unknown closing date

Gypsy
702 performances
Opened May 21, 1959
Closed March 25, 1961

The Miracle Worker
700 performances
Opened October 19, 1959
Closed July 1, 1961

That Championship Season
700 performances
Opened September 14, 1972
Closed April 21, 1974

The Music Man (2000 revival)
698 performances
Opened April 27, 2000
Closed December 30, 2001

Da
697 performances
Opened May 1, 1978
Closed January 1, 1980

Cat on a Hot Tin Roof
694 performances
Opened March 24, 1955
Closed November 17, 1956

Li'l Abner
693 performances
Opened November 15, 1956
Closed July 12, 1958

The Children's Hour
691 performances
Opened November 20, 1934
Unknown closing date

Purlie
688 performances
Opened March 15, 1970
Closed November 6, 1971

Dead End
687 performances
Opened October 28, 1935
Closed June 12, 1937

The Lion and the Mouse
686 performances
Opened November 20, 1905
Unknown closing date

White Cargo
686 performances
Opened November 5, 1923
Unknown closing date

Dear Ruth
683 performances
Opened December 13, 1944
Closed July 27, 1946

East Is West
680 performances
Opened December 25, 1918
Unknown closing date

Come Blow Your Horn
677 performances
Opened February 22, 1961
Closed October 6, 1962

The Most Happy Fella
676 performances
Opened May 3, 1956
Closed December 14, 1957

The Drowsy Chaperone
672 performances
Opened May 1, 2006
Closed December 30, 2007

Defending the Caveman
671 performances
Opened March 26, 1995
Closed June 22, 1997

The Doughgirls
671 performances
Opened Dec. 30, 1942
Closed July 29, 1944

A Chorus Line* (revival)
670 performances
Opened October 5, 2006

The Impossible Years
670 performances
Opened October 13, 1965
Closed May 27, 1967

Irene
670 performances
Opened November 18, 1919
Unknown closing date

Boy Meets Girl
669 performances
Opened November 27, 1935
Unknown closing date

The Tap Dance Kid
669 performances
Opened December 21, 1983
Closed August 11, 1985

Beyond the Fringe
667 performances
Opened October 27, 1962
Closed May 30, 1964

Who's Afraid of Virginia Woolf?
664 performances
Opened October 13, 1962
Closed May 16, 1964

Blithe Spirit
657 performances
Opened November 5, 1941
Closed June 5, 1943

A Trip to Chinatown
657 performances
Opened November 9, 1891
Unknown closing date

The Women
657 performances
Opened December 26, 1936
Unknown closing date

Bloomer Girl
654 performances
Opened October 5, 1944
Closed April 27, 1946

The Fifth Season
654 performances
Opened January 23, 1953
Closed October 23, 1954

Rain
648 performances
Opened September 1, 1924
Unknown closing date

Witness for the Prosecution
645 performances
Opened December 16, 1954
Closed June 30, 1956

Call Me Madam
644 performances
Opened October 12, 1950
Closed May 3, 1952

Mary Poppins*
643 performances
Opened November 16, 2006

Janie
642 performances
Opened September 10, 1942
Closed January 16, 1944

The Green Pastures
640 performances
Opened February 26, 1930
Closed August 29, 1931

Auntie Mame
639 performances
Opened October 31, 1956
Closed June 28, 1958

A Man for All Seasons
637 performances
Opened November 22, 1961
Closed June 1, 1963

Jerome Robbins' Broadway
634 performances
Opened February 26, 1989
Closed September 1, 1990

The Fourposter
632 performances
Opened October 24, 1951
Closed May 2, 1953

The Music Master
627 performances
Opened September 26, 1904
Unknown closing date

Two Gentlemen of Verona (musical)
627 performances
Opened December 1, 1971
Closed May 20, 1973

The Tenth Man
623 performances
Opened November 5, 1959
Closed May 13, 1961

The Heidi Chronicles
621 performances
Opened March 9, 1989
Closed September 1, 1990

Is Zat So?
618 performances
Opened January 5, 1925
Closed July 1926

Anniversary Waltz
615 performances
Opened April 7, 1954
Closed September 24, 1955

The Happy Time (play)
614 performances
Opened January 24, 1950
Closed July 14, 1951

Separate Rooms
613 performances
Opened March 23, 1940
Closed September 6, 1941

Affairs of State
610 performances
Opened September 25, 1950
Closed March 8, 1952

Oh! Calcutta!
610 performances
Opened June 17, 1969
Closed August 12, 1972

Star and Garter
609 performances
Opened June 24, 1942
Closed December 4, 1943

The Mystery of Edwin Drood
608 performances
Opened December 2, 1985
Closed May 16, 1987

The Student Prince
608 performances
Opened December 2, 1924
Unknown closing date

Sweet Charity
608 performances
Opened January 29, 1966
Closed July 15, 1967

Bye Bye Birdie
607 performances
Opened April 14, 1960
Closed October 7, 1961

Riverdance on Broadway
605 performances
Opened March 16, 2000
Closed August 26, 2001

Irene (revival)
604 performances
Opened March 13, 1973
Closed September 8, 1974

Sunday in the Park With George
604 performances
Opened May 2, 1984
Closed October 13, 1985

Adonis
603 performances
Opened circa. 1884
Unknown closing date

Broadway
603 performances
Opened September 16, 1926
Unknown closing date

Peg o' My Heart
603 performances
Opened December 20, 1912
Unknown closing date

Master Class
601 performances
Opened November 5, 1995
Closed June 29, 1997

Street Scene (play)
601 performances
Opened January 10, 1929
Unknown closing date

Flower Drum Song
600 performances
Opened December 1, 1958
Closed May 7, 1960

Kiki
600 performances
Opened November 29, 1921
Unknown closing date

A Little Night Music
600 performances
Opened February 25, 1973
Closed August 3, 1974

Art
600 performances
Opened March 1, 1998
Closed August 8, 1999

Agnes of God
599 performances
Opened March 30, 1982
Closed September 4, 1983

Don't Drink the Water
598 performances
Opened November 17, 1966
Closed April 20, 1968

Wish You Were Here
598 performances
Opened June 25, 1952
Closed November 28, 1958

Sarafina!
597 performances
Opened January 28, 1988
Closed July 2, 1989

A Society Circus
596 performances
Opened December 13, 1905
Closed November 24, 1906

Spring Awakening*
593 performances
Opened December 10, 2006

Absurd Person Singular
592 performances
Opened October 8, 1974
Closed March 6, 1976

A Day in Hollywood/A Night in the Ukraine
588 performances
Opened May 1, 1980
Closed September 27, 1981

The Me Nobody Knows
586 performances
Opened December 18, 1970
Closed November 21, 1971

The Two Mrs. Carrolls
585 performances
Opened August 3, 1943
Closed February 3, 1945

Kismet (musical)
583 performances
Opened December 3, 1953
Closed April 23, 1955

Gypsy (1989 revival)
582 performances
Opened November 16, 1989
Closed July 28, 1991

Brigadoon
581 performances
Opened March 13, 1947
Closed July 31, 1948

Detective Story
581 performances
Opened March 23, 1949
Closed August 12, 1950

No Strings
580 performances
Opened March 14, 1962
Closed August 3, 1963

Brother Rat
577 performances
Opened December 16, 1936
Unknown closing date

Blossom Time
576 performances
Opened September 29, 1921
Unknown closing date

Pump Boys and Dinettes
573 performances
Opened February 4, 1982
Closed June 18, 1983

Show Boat
572 performances
Opened December 27, 1927
Closed May 4, 1929

The Show-Off
571 performances
Opened February 5, 1924
Unknown closing date

Sally
570 performances
Opened December 21, 1920
Closed April 22, 1922

Jelly's Last Jam
569 performances
Opened April 26, 1992
Closed September 5, 1993

Golden Boy (musical)
568 performances
Opened October 20, 1964
Closed March 5, 1966

One Touch of Venus
567 performances
Opened October 7, 1943
Closed February 10, 1945

The Real Thing
566 performances
Opened January 5, 1984
Closed May 12, 1985

Happy Birthday
564 performances
Opened October 31, 1946
Closed March 13, 1948

Look Homeward, Angel
564 performances
Opened November 28, 1957
Closed April 4, 1959

Morning's at Seven (revival)
564 performances
Opened April 10, 1980
Closed August 16, 1981

The Glass Menagerie
561 performances
Opened March 31, 1945
Closed August 3, 1946

I Do! I Do!
560 performances
Opened December 5, 1966
Closed June 15, 1968

Wonderful Town
559 performances
Opened February 25, 1953
Closed July 3, 1954

The Last Night of Ballyhoo
557 performances
Opened February 27, 1997
Closed June 28, 1998

Rose Marie
557 performances
Opened September 2, 1924
Unknown closing date

Strictly Dishonorable
557 performances
Opened Sept. 18, 1929
Unknown closing date

Sweeney Todd, the Demon Barber of Fleet Street
557 performances
Opened March 1, 1979
Closed June 29, 1980

The Great White Hope
556 performances
Opened October 3, 1968
Closed January 31, 1970

A Majority of One
556 performances
Opened February 16, 1959
Closed June 25, 1960

The Sisters Rosensweig
556 performances
Opened March 18, 1993
Closed July 16, 1994

Sunrise at Campobello
556 performances
Opened January 30, 1958
Closed May 30, 1959

Toys in the Attic
556 performances
Opened February 25, 1960
Closed April 8, 1961

Jamaica
555 performances
Opened October 31, 1957
Closed April 11, 1959

Stop the World—I Want to Get Off
555 performances
Opened October 3, 1962
Closed February 1, 1964

Florodora
553 performances
Opened November 10, 1900
Closed January 25, 1902

Noises Off
553 performances
Opened December 11, 1983
Closed April 6, 1985

Ziegfeld Follies (1943)
553 performances
Opened April 1, 1943
Closed July 22, 1944

Dial "M" for Murder
552 performances
Opened October 29, 1952
Closed February 27, 1954

Good News
551 performances
Opened September 6, 1927
Unknown closing date

Peter Pan (revival)
551 performances
Opened September 6, 1979
Closed January 4, 1981

How to Succeed in Business without Really Trying (revival)
548 performances
Opened March 23, 1995
Closed July 14, 1996

Let's Face It
547 performances
Opened October 29, 1941
Closed March 20, 1943

Milk and Honey
543 performances
Opened October 10, 1961
Closed January 26, 1963

Within the Law
541 performances
Opened September 11, 1912
Unknown closing date

Pal Joey (revival)
540 performances
Opened January 3, 1952
Closed April 18, 1953

The Sound of Music (revival)
540 performances
Opened March 12, 1998
Closed June 20, 1999

What Makes Sammy Run?
540 performances
Opened February 27, 1964
Closed June 12, 1965

The Sunshine Boys
538 performances
Opened December 20, 1972
Closed April 21, 1974

What a Life
538 performances
Opened April 13, 1938
Closed July 8, 1939

Crimes of the Heart
535 performances
Opened November 4, 1981
Closed February 13, 1983

Damn Yankees (revival)
533 performances
Opened March 3, 1994
Closed August 6, 1995

The Unsinkable Molly Brown
532 performances
Opened November 3, 1960
Closed February 10, 1962

The Red Mill (revival)
531 performances
Opened October 16, 1945
Closed January 18, 1947

Rumors
531 performances
Opened November 17, 1988
Closed February 24, 1990

A Raisin in the Sun
530 performances
Opened March 11, 1959
Closed June 25, 1960

Godspell
527 performances
Opened June 22, 1976
Closed September 4, 1977

Fences
526 performances
Opened March 26, 1987
Closed June 26, 1988

The Solid Gold Cadillac
526 performances
Opened November 5, 1953
Closed February 12, 1955

Biloxi Blues
524 performances
Opened March 28, 1985
Closed June 28, 1986

Irma La Douce
524 performances
Opened September 29, 1960
Closed December 31, 1961

The Boomerang
522 performances
Opened August 10, 1915
Unknown closing date

Follies
521 performances
Opened April 4, 1971
Closed July 1, 1972

Rosalinda
521 performances
Opened October 28, 1942
Closed January 22, 1944

The Best Man
520 performances
Opened March 31, 1960
Closed July 8, 1961

Chauve-Souris
520 performances
Opened February 4, 1922
Unknown closing date

Blackbirds of 1928
518 performances
Opened May 9, 1928
Unknown closing date

Dirty Rotten Scoundrels
627 performances
Opened March 3, 2005
Closed September 3, 2006

Doubt
525 performances
Opened March 9, 2005
Closed July 2, 2006

The Gin Game
517 performances
Opened October 6, 1977
Closed December 31, 1978

Side Man
517 performances
Opened June 25, 1988
Closed October 31, 1999

Sunny
517 performances
Opened September 22, 1925
Closed December 11, 1926

Victoria Regina
517 performances
Opened December 26, 1935
Unknown closing date

Fifth of July
511 performances
Opened November 5, 1980
Closed January 24, 1982

Half a Sixpence
511 performances
Opened April 25, 1965
Closed July 16, 1966

The Vagabond King
511 performances
Opened September 21, 1925
Closed December 4, 1926

The New Moon
509 performances
Opened September 19, 1928
Closed December 14, 1929

The World of Suzie Wong
508 performances
Opened October 14, 1958
Closed January 2, 1960

The Rothschilds
507 performances
Opened October 19, 1970
Closed January 1, 1972

On Your Toes (revival)
505 performances
Opened March 6, 1983
Closed May 20, 1984

Sugar
505 performances
Opened April 9, 1972
Closed June 23, 1973

The Light in the Piazza
504 performances
Opened March 17, 2005
Closed July 2, 2006

Shuffle Along
504 performances
Opened May 23, 1921
Closed July 15, 1922

Up in Central Park
504 performances
Opened January 27, 1945
Closed January 13, 1946

Carmen Jones
503 performances
Opened December 2, 1943
Closed February 10, 1945

Saturday Night Fever
502 performances
Opened October 21, 1999
Closed December 30, 2000

The Member of the Wedding
501 performances
Opened January 5, 1950
Closed March 17, 1951

Panama Hattie
501 performances
Opened October 30, 1940
Closed January 13, 1942

Personal Appearance
501 performances
Opened October 17, 1934
Unknown closing date

Bird in Hand
500 performances
Opened April 4, 1929
Unknown closing date

Room Service
500 performances
Opened May 19, 1937
Unknown closing date

Sailor, Beware!
500 performances
Opened September 28, 1933
Unknown closing date

Tomorrow the World
500 performances
Opened April 14, 1943
Closed June 17, 1944

Off-Broadway

The Fantasticks
17,162 performances
Opened May 3, 1960
Closed January 13, 2002

Perfect Crime*
8,618 performances
Opened April 5, 1987

Blue Man Group*
8,589 performances
Opened November 17, 1991

Stomp*
6,009 performances
Opened February 27, 1994

Tony 'n' Tina's Wedding*
5,702 performances
Opened May 1, 1987

I Love You, You're Perfect, Now Change*
4,937 performances
Opened August 1, 1996

Nunsense
3,672 performances
Opened December 12, 1985
Closed October 16, 1994

Naked Boys Singing*
2,690 performances
Opened July 22, 1999

The Threepenny Opera
2,611 performances
Opened September 20, 1955
Closed December 17, 1961

De La Guarda
2,475 performances
Opened June 16, 1998
Closed September 12, 2004

Forbidden Broadway 1982–87
2,332 performances
Opened January 15, 1982
Closed August 30, 1987

Little Shop of Horrors
2,209 performances
Opened July 27, 1982
Closed November 1, 1987

Godspell
2,124 performances
Opened May 17, 1971
Closed June 13, 1976

Vampire Lesbians of Sodom
2,024 performances
Opened June 19, 1985
Closed May 27, 1990

Jacques Brel is Alive and Well and Living in Paris
1,847 performances
Opened January 22, 1968
Closed July 2, 1972

Forever Plaid
1,811 performances
Opened May 20, 1990
Closed June 12, 1994

Vanities
1,785 performances
Opened March 22, 1976
Closed August 3, 1980

The Donkey Show
1,717 performances
Opened August 18, 1999
Closed July 16, 2005

Menopause the Musical
1,712 performances
Opened April 4, 2002
Closed May 14, 2006

You're A Good Man, Charlie Brown
1,597 performances
Opened March 7, 1967
Closed February 14, 1971

The Blacks
1,408 performances
Opened May 4, 1961
Closed September 27, 1964

The Vagina Monologues
1,381 performances
Opened October 3, 1999
Closed January 26, 2003

One Mo' Time
1,372 performances
Opened October 22, 1979
Closed 1982–83 season

Grandma Sylvia's Funeral
1,360 performances
Opened October 9, 1994
Closed June 20, 1998

Altar Boyz*
1,358 performances
Opened March 1, 2005

Let My People Come
1,327 performances
Opened January 8, 1974
Closed July 5, 1976

Late Nite Catechism
1,268 performances
Opened October 4, 1995
Closed May 18, 2003

Driving Miss Daisy
1,195 performances
Opened April 15, 1987
Closed June 3, 1990

The Hot L Baltimore
1,166 performances
Opened September 8, 1973
Closed January 4, 1976

I'm Getting My Act Together and Taking It on the Road
1,165 performances
Opened May 16, 1987
Closed March 15, 1981

Little Mary Sunshine
1,143 performances
Opened November 18, 1959
Closed September 2, 1962

Steel Magnolias
1,126 performances
Opened November 17, 1987
Closed February 25, 1990

El Grande de Coca-Cola
1,114 performances
Opened February 13, 1973
Closed April 13, 1975

The Proposition
1,109 performances
Opened March 24, 1971
Closed April 14, 1974

Our Sinatra
1,096 performances
Opened December 8, 1999
Closed July 28, 2002

Beau Jest
1,069 performances
Opened October 10, 1991
Closed May 1, 1994

Jewtopia
1,052 performances
Opened October 21, 2004
Closed April 29, 2007

Tamara
1,036 performances
Opened November 9, 1989
Closed July 15, 1990

One Flew Over the Cuckoo's Nest (revival)
1,025 performances
Opened March 23, 1971
Closed September 16, 1973

Slava's Snow Show
1,004 Performances
Opened September 8, 2004
Closed January 14, 2007

The Boys in the Band
1,000 performances
Opened April 14, 1968
Closed September 29, 1985

Fool For Love
1,000 performances
Opened November 27, 1983
Closed September 29, 1985

Forbidden Broadway: 20th Anniversary Celebration
994 performances
Opened March 20, 2002
Closed July 4, 2004

Other People's Money
990 performances
Opened February 7, 1989
Closed July 4, 1991

Cloud 9
971 performances
Opened May 18, 1981
Closed September 4, 1983

Secrets Every Smart Traveler Should Know
953 performances
Opened October 30, 1997
Closed February 21, 2000

Sister Mary Ignatius Explains it All for You & The Actor's Nightmare
947 performances
Opened October 21, 1981
Closed January 29, 1984

Your Own Thing
933 performances
Opened January 13, 1968
Closed April 5, 1970

Curley McDimple
931 performances
Opened November 22, 1967
Closed January 25, 1970

Leave It to Jane (revival)
928 performances
Opened May 29, 1959
Closed 1961–62 season

The Mad Show
871 performances
Opened January 9, 1966
Closed September 10, 1967

Hedwig and the Angry Inch
857 performances
Opened February 14, 1998
Closed April 9, 2000

Forbidden Broadway Strikes Back
850 performances
Opened October 17, 1996
Closed September 20, 1998

When Pigs Fly
840 performances
Opened August 14, 1996
Closed August 15, 1998

Scrambled Feet
831 performances
Opened June 11, 1979
Closed June 7, 1981

The Effect of Gamma Rays on Man-in-the-Moon Marigolds
819 performances
Opened April 7, 1970
Closed June 1, 1973

Forbidden Broadway SVU
816 performances
Opened December 16, 2004
Closed April 15, 2007

Over the River and Through the Woods
800 performances
Opened October 5, 1998
Closed September 3, 2000

A View From the Bridge (revival)
780 performances
Opened November 9, 1965
Closed December 11, 1966

The Boy Friend (revival)
763 performances
Opened January 25, 1958
Closed 1961–62 season

True West
762 performances
Opened December 23, 1980
Closed January 11, 1981

Forbidden Broadway Cleans Up Its Act!
754 performances
Opened November 17, 1998
Closed August 30, 2000

Isn't It Romantic
733 performances
Opened December 15, 1983
Closed September 1, 1985

Dime a Dozen
728 performances
Opened June 13, 1962
Closed 1963–64 season

The Pocket Watch
725 performances
Opened November 14, 1966
Closed June 18, 1967

The Connection
722 performances
Opened June 9, 1959
Closed June 4, 1961

The Passion of Dracula
714 performances
Opened September 28, 1977
Closed July 14, 1979

Love, Janis
713 performances
Opened April 22, 2001
Closed January 5, 2003

Adaptation & Next
707 performances
Opened February 10, 1969
Closed October 18, 1970

Oh! Calcutta!
704 performances
Opened June 17, 1969
Closed August 12, 1972

Scuba Duba
692 performances
Opened November 11, 1967
Closed June 8, 1969

The Foreigner
686 performances
Opened November 2, 1984
Closed June 8, 1986

The Knack
685 performances
Opened January 14, 1964
Closed January 9, 1966

Fully Committed
675 performances
Opened December 14, 1999
Closed May 27, 2001

The Club
674 performances
Opened October 14, 1976
Closed May 21, 1978

The Balcony
672 performances
Opened March 3, 1960
Closed December 21, 1961

Penn & Teller
666 performances
Opened July 30, 1985
Closed January 19, 1992

Dinner With Friends
654 performances
Opened November 4, 1999
Closed May 27, 2000

My Mother's Italian, My Father's Jewish & I'm in Therapy*
651 performances
Opened December 8, 2006

The Gazillion Bubble Show*
637 Performances
Opened February 15, 2007

America Hurrah
634 performances
Opened November 7, 1966
Closed May 5, 1968

Cookin'
632 Performances
Opened July 7, 2004
Closed August 7, 2005

The Fantasticks (revival)
628 performances
Opened August 23, 2006
Closed February 24, 2008

Oil City Symphony
626 performances
Opened November 5, 1987
Closed May 7, 1989

The Countess
618 performances
Opened September 28, 1999
Closed December 30, 2000

The Exonerated
608 performances
Opened October 10, 2002
Closed March 7, 2004

The Dining Room
607 performances
Opened February 11, 1982
Closed July 17, 1983

Hogan's Goat
607 performances
Opened March 6, 1965
Closed April 23, 1967

Drumstruck
607 performances
Opened June 16, 2005
Closed November 16, 2006

Beehive
600 performances
Opened March 30, 1986
Closed August 23, 1987

Criss Angel Mindfreak
600 performances
Opened November 20, 2001
Closed January 5, 2003

The Trojan Women
600 performances
Opened December 23, 1963
Closed May 30, 1965

The Syringa Tree
586 performances
Opened September 14, 2000
Closed June 2, 2002

Musical of Musicals the Musical!
(Company and Commercial runs)
583 Performances
Opened December 16, 2003; Closed January 25, 2004
Reopened June 10, 2004; Closed October 3, 2004
Reopened February 10 2005; Closed November 13, 2005

Krapp's Last Tape & The Zoo Story
582 performances
Opened August 29, 1960
Closed May 21, 1961

Three Tall Women
582 performances
Opened April 13, 1994
Closed August 26, 1995

The Dumbwaiter & The Collection
578 performances
Opened January 21, 1962
Closed April 12, 1964

Forbidden Broadway 1990
576 performances
Opened January 23, 1990
Closed June 9, 1991

Dames at Sea
575 performances
Opened April 22, 1969
Closed May 10, 1970

The Crucible (revival)
571 performances
Opened 1957
Closed 1958

The Iceman Cometh (revival)
565 performances
Opened May 8, 1956
Closed February 23, 1958

Forbidden Broadway 2001: A Spoof Odyssey
552 performances
Opened December 6, 2000
Closed February 6, 2002

The Hostage (revival)
545 performances
Opened October 16, 1972
Closed October 8, 1973

Wit
545 performances
Opened October 6, 1998
Closed April 9, 2000

What's a Nice Country Like You Doing in a State Like This?
543 performances
Opened July 31, 1985
Closed February 9, 1987

Forbidden Broadway 1988
534 performances
Opened September 15, 1988
Closed December 24, 1989

Gross Indecency: The Three Trials of Oscar Wilde
534 performances
Opened September 5, 1997
Closed September 13, 1998

Frankie and Johnny in the Claire de Lune
533 performances
Opened December 4, 1987
Closed March 12, 1989

Six Characters in Search of an Author (revival)
529 performances
Opened March 8, 1963
Closed June 28, 1964

All in the Timing
526 performances
Opened November 24, 1993
Closed February 13, 1994

Oleanna
513 performances
Opened October 3, 1992
Closed January 16, 1994

Making Porn
511 performances
Opened June 12, 1996
Closed September 14, 1997

Mary Beth Hurt, Lizbeth Mackay, Mia Dillon in Crimes of the Heart *(1981) (photo by Gerry Goodstein)*

The Dirtiest Show in Town
509 performances
Opened June 26, 1970
Closed September 17, 1971

Happy Ending & Day of Absence
504 performances
Opened June 13, 1965
Closed January 29, 1967

Greater Tuna
501 performances
Opened October 21, 1982
Closed December 31, 1983

A Shayna Maidel
501 performances
Opened October 29, 1987
Closed January 8, 1989

The Boys From Syracuse (revival)
500 performances
Opened April 15, 1963
Closed June 28, 1964

Carol Bruce

Lonny Chapman

Michael DelMedico

Alice Ghostley

Robert Goulet

George Grizzard

Charlton Heston

Deborah Kerr

Lois Nettleton

Suzanne Pleshette

Robert Symonds

Richard Widmark

Obituaries

Michael Abbott, 81, New York City-born actor and theatre, film, and television producer, died Jan. 24, 2008, in New York City, of cancer. Broadway credits as an actor include *Traitor,* and as a producer, *Late Love* with Arlene Francis, *A Very Special Baby, Rashomon,* and *The Incomparable Max*. His Off-Broadway credits include *Stalag 17* in 1951, which he was in preparation to mount on Broadway at the time of his death. He was a member of the Bucks County Playhouse acting company, and appeared on television in *Martin Kane, Philco-Goodyear Playhouse,* and in many *Milton Berle Texaco* shows. He also produced *From Here and There* in London. His numerous television credits include *The Prince and the Pauper, The Bridge of San Luis Rey, A Tale of Two Cities, The Moon and Sixpence, Something Special, At This Very Moment,* and *Hedda Hopper's Hollywood*. He studied at the American Academy of Dramatic Arts. He is survived by his sister, Helene Fields.

Judy Arnold, 68, Baltimore, MD-born theatre producer, died Nov. 10, 2007, in Encino, CA, of a heart attack. Her Broadway credits include *Bombay Dreams* and *Six Dance Lessons in Six Weeks* (which originated at the Geffen Playhouse). Her many Los Angeles production credits include *Give 'Em Hell, Harry* with Jason Alexander, *We Interrupt This Program* with Jennifer Aniston, Lisa Kudrow, Garry Marshall, Laraine Newman and Julia Sweeney, and *The Disputation,* at the Tiffany Theatre. She also produced *I Remember You* with Tony Danza at the Falcon Theatre and *Equinox* at the Odyssey Theatre. She was a graduate of UCLA and worked after her graduation with the Los Angeles Junior Programs, selecting and producing children's theater. Her survivors include her sons, Jonathan, and actor Evan Arnold. Her husband, prominent first director Newt Arnold, died in 2002.

Stephen Balint (Istvan Balint), 64, Hungarian-born theatre actor/director/writer, and founder of the Squat Theater, died Oct. 11, 2007, in Budapest, Hungary, of pneumonia, following a long illness. His experimental theater collective was founded in Hungary but immigrated to New York following persecution by Hungarian authorities in the 1970s. Taking root in the Chelsea Hotel before establishing a home on W. 23rd St, his Squat credits include *Pig, Child, Fire,* and Andy Warhol's *Last Love*. He wrote and appeared in photographer Robert Frank's film *Hunter* (1989). He returned to Hungary in 1991 following the communist regime collapse there. He published a book of prose with drawings by the artist Gabor Rosko, in 2005. He is survived by his daughter, performer Eszter Balint, of New York, Gaspar, of Budapest, and one grandchild.

Mary Barclay (Mary Biddulph), 91, British-born theatre, television, and film actress, died Feb. 18, 2008, in Guernsey, England, following complications of a stroke seven years ago. Her Broadway credits include *Ti-Cog* and *Witness for the Prosecution*. Her numerous film and television appearances include *A Touch of Class*, opposite Glenda Jackson and George Segal, *Crossroads, The Revolutionary, Sex and the Other Woman, Dixon of Dock Green,* and *The Headless Ghost*. She attended the Guildhall School of Music and Drama and Cambridge University.

Robert Guy Barrows, 81, Colorado-born writer/teacher, died Jan. 31, in Pueblo, CO, of complications of surgery for intestinal cancer. He was arrested twelve times during his staging of Beat poet Michael McClure's *The Beard*, leading to a landmark California Supreme Court ruling that the lewd-conduct law did not apply to live stage performances. His television credits as a writer include *Mission: Impossible, The Virginian, Daniel Boone,* and *The Fugitive*. He taught at New York University from 1957–1962, and was on the faculty of UCLA from 1964–1970. He taught at the Art Center College of Design in Pasadena and Loyola Marymount in the early 1980s. He also produced low-budget independent films. He earned a bachelor's degree in English literature from the University of Colorado in Boulder, CO, and a master's degree from UCLA. He was a veteran of WW II, serving with the Army's 10th Mountain Division in Italy. He is survived by his wife, Jeri Wacaster, six children, one stepchild, two grandchildren, a brother, and a sister.

Maurice Bejart (Maurice Jean Berger), 80, French-born choreographer/performer/artistic director, died Nov. 22, 2007, in Lausanne, Switzerland, of heart and kidney failure. His Broadway credits as a choreographer include *Nureyev* (1977) and *Béjart: Ballet of the Twentieth Century* (1979 and 1988). His other credits include Stravinsky's *Rite of Spring* (considered his signature work), in his first production with Belgium's Monnaie Theater, Ravel's *Bolero*, Beethoven's *Ode to Joy*, Berlioz's *Romeo and Juliet*, and Oscar Wilde's *Salome*. He wrote *Thank You, Gianni, With Love*, for Gianni Versace. He formed Ballet of the Twentieth Century in 1960, and later founded the Bejart Ballet Lausanne, which is still in existence.

June Bingham Birge, 88, New York-born writer, died Aug. 21, 2007, in Riverdale, Bronx, of cancer. Her Off-Broadway credits include *Asylum: The Strange Case of Mary Lincoln*, and the regional theatre production *Triangles*. Her nonfiction book credits include *Courage to Change: An Introduction to the Life and Thought of Reinhold Niebuhr* (Scribner, 1961), *U Thant: The Search for Peace* (Knopf, 1966), and *The Pursuit of Health* with Norman Tamarkin, (Walker, 1985). She is survived by her second husband, Robert B. Birge, whom she married in 1987, three children from her marriage to Mr. Bingham, Sherrell Downes, known as Sherry, of Brookline, MA, Timothy, of Emmaus, PA, and Claudia Meyers of Santa Fe, NM, a stepson, Robert R. Birge of Storrs, CT, ten grandchildren, two step-grandchildren, and fourteen great-grandchildren. A daughter from her first marriage to Congressman Jonathan Brewster Bingham, the Rev. June Mitchell Esselstyn, known as Micki, died in 1999.

Sherry Britton (Edith Zack), 89, New Jersey-born actress/Burlesque queen, died April 1, 2008, in New York City, of natural causes. Her Broadway credits include *Peer Gynt* and *Drink to Me Only*. She hosted *Best of Burlesque* at Carnegie Hall and her national tour credits include Adelaide in *Guys and Dolls*. When Burlesque was effectively banned from the stage during Mayor Fiorello LaGuardia's tenure in the 1940s, she performed in thirty-nine plays, including fourteen musicals, and sang in nightclubs and made numerous television appearances. She entertained troupes during WW II, and was named an honorary brigadier general by President Franklin D. Roosevelt. A graduate of Fordham University, she is survived by her half-sister, Emily Gendelman, of Brooklyn, NY, and cousin, Melaine Britton.

Kirk Browning, 86, New York City-born theatre and television producer, died Feb. 10, 2008, at his home in Manhattan, NY, of a heart attack. He directed 185 telecasts from Lincoln Center's opera, theatre, dance, and orchestra halls, premiering the first *Live from Lincoln Center* in 1976. He worked his way from filing music scores at NBC's music library, to directing telecasts of the NBC Symphony Orchestra, to directing *Live from Lincoln Center*, which would earn him 10 Emmy Awards. His other television direction credits include Gian Carlo Menotti's *Amahl and the Night Visitors*, Hallmark Hall of Fame music and drama specials from 1951–1958, *Great Performances* and *Live from the Met* on PBS, *Pavarotti in Concert at Madison Square Garden*, as well as numerous Broadway productions. His *Goya* with Plácido Domingo, and *Turandot*, won individual achievement Emmys. He is survived by his wife, the former Barbara Gum, son, David, of Somers, NY, and another son, Sean, of Nantucket, MA.

Carol Bruce (Shirley Levy), 87, New York-born actress, died Oct. 9, 2007, in Woodland Hills, CA, of chronic obstructive pulmonary disease. She made her Broadway debut in 1940 in *Louisiana Purchase*, followed by *New Priorities of 1943, Showboat* (1946 and 1948), *Along Fifth Avenue, A Family Affair, Do I Hear a Waltz?* and *Henry Sweet Henry*. Best known for her television role as Mama Carlson on *WKRP in Cincinnati* from 1979–1982, she made guest appearances in over 25 other television shows, including *The Golden Girls, Doogie Howser, M.D., Diff'rent Strokes, The Twilight Zone,* and *Party of Five*. Her film credits include *The Woman is Mine, Behind the Eight Ball, Keep 'Em Flying, American Gigolo,* and *Planes, Trains, and Automobiles*. Beginning her professional career as saleswoman at Namm's department store in Brooklyn by day, she eventually performed at nightclubs including Café Pierre, as well as the Waldorf-Astoria and the Plaza hotels in the 1930s. Survivors include her sister, Marilyn Berk, daughter, Julie Nathanson Coryell, two grandsons, and two great-grandsons.

Leo Burmester, 63, Kentucky-born actor, died June 28, 2007, in New York City, of complications from a tick bite combined with a compromised immune system from leukemia. He made his Off-Broadway debut in 1978 in Marsha Norman's *Getting Out* and his Broadway debut in 1979 in James McLure's one-act *Lone Star,* playing roles that he had created in both shows at his hometown theatre, Actors Theatre of Louisville, where his early career started. He is best known on the Broadway stage for playing Thénardier in original production of *Les Misérables.* Other Broadway appearances included *Buried Child, Ah, Wilderness, Raggedy Ann, Big River, The Civil War, Thou Shalt Not,* and *Urban Cowboy.* His last New York stage performance was playing the role of Hucklebee in the Off-Broadway revival of *The Fantasticks.* His film credits include *Sweet Liberty, The Abyss, Passion Fish, Lone Star, City by the Sea, The Last Temptation of Christ, Big Business,* and *Broadcast News.* A graduate of Western Kentucky University, he also held a Masters from the University of Denver. He is survived by his wife, Lora Lee Echobelli, and two children, Daniel and Colette.

Bart Burns (George Joseph Burns), 89, New York City-born actor, died July 11, 2007, at his home in West Hills, CA, of natural causes. His Broadway credits include *Mister Roberts, Barefoot in Athens,* and *One Bright Day*. On television he played Pat Chambers on the 1950 *Mike Hammer* series, and made hundreds of other television appearances, including those on *Gunsmoke* and *The Rockford Files.* His film appearances include *Frances, Seven Days in May,* and *Legal Eagles.* He was a veteran of WW II as a marine captain in the Pacific, where he was wounded twice, and won a Silver Star for his duties on Iwo Jima. He is survived by his wife, Fern, three sons, Brendan, Timothy, and Sean, daughter Siobhan Burns Walden, and a granddaughter.

Iris Burton (Iris Burstein), 77, New York City-born actress/dancer/agent, died April 5, 2008, at the Motion Picture and Television Country House, in Los Angeles, CA, of pneumonia. Her Broadway credits include *Music in My House,* followed by *Pardon Our French,* and her film credits include *Top Banana* and *The Ten Commandments,* before embarking on a long career as a talent agent for children and young adults, founding her own agency in 1977. She also appeared on the Milton Berle television show in her early years. Her eventual client list included all of the Phoenix children (including River and Joaquin), Fred Savage of *The Wonder Years,* Henry Thomas of *E.T.,* Mary-Kate and Ashley Olson, and many more. Her survivors include son, Tony-winning actor, Barry Miller (for Best Supporting Actor for *Biloxi Blues*).

Lonny Chapman, 87, Oklahoma-born actor, who grew up in Joplin, MO, and longtime artistic director of the Group Theatre (now the Lonny Chapman Group Repertory Theatre) in Los Angeles, died Oct. 12, 2007, at the Sherman Village Healthcare Center, in North Hollywood, CA, of heart disease. He made his Broadway debut in 1949 in *The Closing Door,* followed by *Come Back, Little Sheba, The Chase, The Whistler's Grandmother, The Ladies of the Corridor, The Traveling Lady, The Time of Your Life, General Seeger,* and *Marathon '33.* He directed *Nature of the Crime* Off-Broadway in 1970. Under Chapman's direction, the Group Theatre produced over 350 productions and at least 45 premieres, including an adaptation of Arthur Schnitzler's *La Ronde,* which was titled *Round Dance.* During the 1960s, he appeared in more than 80 summer productions and performed in 30 more at a theater in Fishkill, NY. He also appeared in more than 25 films, including *Baby Doll, The Birds,* and *Reindeer Games.* He was a veteran of WW II, having served several years in the South Pacific. His television appearances included several on *McCloud.* He is survived by his wife, Erma Dean, and son, Wyley Dean Chapman.

Alvin Colt, 91, Kentucky-born costume designer, died May 4, 2008, in Manhattan, NY, of natural causes. A Tony-winner for his design for *Pipe Dream* in 1955, he also received Tony nominations for *Phoenix '55, The Lark, Li'l Abner, The Sleeping Prince,* and *Greenwillow*. He made his Broadway debut in 1944 in *On the Town*, followed by *Around the World, Barefoot Boy With Cheek, Music in My Heart, Clutterbuck, Guys and Dolls* (1950, 1955), *Top Banana, The Frogs of Spring, Madam, Will You Walk, The Golden Apple, Fanny, Finian's Rainbow, Six Characters in Search of an Author, Copper and Brass, Rumple, Blue Denim, Say, Darling, First Impressions, Destry Rides Again, Christine, Wildcat, 13 Daughters, The Aspern Papers, The Beauty Part, Here's Love, The Seagull, The Crucible, Something More!, The Paisley Convertible, The Imaginary Invalid, A Touch of the Poet, Tonight at 8:30p.m., Henry, Sweet Henry, Golden Rainbow, The Goodbye People, Sugar, Lorelei, Broadway Follies, Parade of Stars Playing the Palace, Jerome Robbins' Broadway, Accomplice, Comedy Tonight, Sacrilege, The Herbal Bed, Waiting in the Wings,* and *If you ever leave me… I'm going with you.* He was a Drama Desk Award nominee three times for his work Off-Broadway on *Forbidden Broadway* (on which he worked for the past 15 years), and his other Off-Broadway credits include *Corialanus, The Carefree Tree, Miss Julie/The Stronger, A Month in the Country, The Littlest Revue, Diary of a Scoundrel, Livin' the Life, Mary Stuart, The Infernal Machine, Abe Lincoln in Illinois*, and *Mr. President*. He was inducted into the Theater Hall of Fame in 2002. An exhibition of his work, entitled "Costumes and Characters: The Designs of Alvin Colt," that displayed some of the more than 3,000 design sketches he had donated to the Museum of the City of New York, went on display in 2007. His companion of 47 years, actor Richard Tone, died in 2004.

Shirl Conway, 90, New York-born actress, died May 7, 2008, in Shelton, WA. Her Broadway credits include the role of Ruth Winters in *Plain and Fancy*, for which she won a 1955 Theatre World Award. Her other Broadway credits include *Gentleman Prefer Blondes*. Perhaps best known for her role on *The Nurses*, which ran from 1962–1965 on television, she received an Emmy nomination for her work on that show. Her other numerous television appearances include *Route 66, The Defenders, The Naked City, Joe & Mabel,* and Sid Caesar's *Caesar's Hour.* Her national tours include *Auntie Mame* in the U.S. and Canada. Having relocated to western Washington state in 1972, she founded the Harstine Island Theater Club there, where she wrote, directed, produced, and starred in productions well into her eighties.

Michael Evans (John Michael Evans), 87, British-born actor, died Sept. 4, 2007, at a Woodland Hills assisted living facility, of natural causes. His Broadway credits include *Ring Round the Moon, Gigi, Mary, Mary,* and *The Kingfisher*. National tours include that of *My Fair Lady*. His numerous film roles include those in *Bye Bye Birdie*, in addition to over 40 others. From 1980-1995, he appeared on *The Young and the Restless* on television. He graduated from Winchester College in England, and was a veteran of the Royal Air Force during WW II. He is survived by his sons, Nick and Christopher, of Westport, CA, and two sisters, Rosemarie and Bridget.

Anthony De Santis, 93, Chicago-area theatre owner and operator, died June 6, 2007, in Chicago, IL, following a long battle with cancer. Having built the Drury Lane Theatre empire in Chicago, in addition to the Drury Lane Theater that he opened in 1949, he eventually opened five Drury Lane Theaters: the North, South, East, Water Tower, and Oakbrook Terrace. Stars from Debbie Reynolds to Phyllis Diller played his theatres in their heyday. He is survived by his wife, Lucille, daughter, Diane Van Lente, brother, Dante, and four other grandchildren.

Michael Del Medico, 81, actor, died Oct. 7, 2007, in Chicago, IL. With Broadway credits including *Inherit the Wind*, and *The Disenchanted*, he eventually relocated to Chicago, where he had many regional theatre credits. He played several roles in the 1969 Indie film *Children's Games*, and was a veteran of the Korean War.

Ivan Dixon (Ivan Nathaniel Dixon III), 76, Harlem, NY-born actor/director, died March 16, 2008, in Charlotte, NC, of complications from kidney disease. Best known for his stint as Sgt. James Kinchloe on the 1960s sitcom *Hogan's Heroes*, his Broadway credits include *The Cave Dwellers* and *A Raisin in the Sun*. His numerous film and television credits include the 1964 film *Nothing But a Man* and 1973's *The Spook Who Sat by the Door*, which he also directed. He received a 1967 Emmy nomination for the title role in *The Final War of Olly Winter*. He directed numerous television projects, including episodes of *The Waltons, The Rockford Files, Magnum P.I., Quincy,* and *In the Heat of the Night*. He was a graduate of North Carolina Central University. He is survived by his wife, the former Berlie Ray, daughter Doris Nomathande Dixon, of Charlotte, NC, and son, Alan, of Oakland, CA.

Denny Martin Flinn, 59, performer/director, died Aug. 24, in Woodland Hills, of complications from cancer. Broadway credits include *Sugar*, followed by *Pal Joey*. Off-Broadway credits include *Six* and *Groucho*, which he wrote and directed. National tours include *Fiddler on the Roof* and *A Chorus Line*. He choreographed for the soap operas *Search for Tomorrow* and *Another World*, and for the feature films *The Deceivers* and *Ghost*. His author credits include *What They Did for Love*, the story of the making of the Broadway musical *A Chorus Line*, and the mystery novels *San Francisco Kills* and *Killer Finish*. He co-wrote the screenplay for *Star Trek VI: The Undiscovered Country*, and wrote two radio plays for the BBC: *Don Quixote*, which won a British Writer's Guild nomination, and an adaptation of Meyer's *The Seven-Per-Cent Solution*. He authored the *Star Trek* novel *The Fearful Summons* and *Musical! A Grand Tour–the Rise, Glory and Fall of an American Institution*, which won the ASCAP/Deems Taylor award. Other books include *How Not To Write a Screenplay* and *How Not To Audition, The Great American Book Musical: A Manifesto, A Monograph, A Manual;* and *Ready For My Close-Up, Great Movie Speeches*. He is survived by his wife, Barbara, and two children, Brook and Dylan.

Karen Fraction, 49, Michigan-born actress, died Oct. 30, 2007, in Key Largo, FL. Her Broadway credits include *The Tap Dance Kid, Cabaret* (1987), and *Oh, Kay!* Her numerous television and film credits include *My Brother and Me, Walker, Texas Ranger,* and *Swamp Thing.*

Chris Gampel (Morison Gampel), 87, Canadian actor, died May 14, 2008. His Broadway credits include *Captain Brassbound's Conversion, The Royal Family, King Richard II, Flight Into Egypt, Saint Joan, Compulsion, The Firstborn,* and *The Girl Who Came to Supper.* His numerous film appearances include *Death Wish, Annie Hall, The Wrong Man,* and television appearances including those on *Route 66, Philco Television Playhouse, Studio One, U.S. Steel Hour, Playwrights 56, Armstrong Circle Theatre,* and *Hallmark Hall of Fame.*

George W. George (George Warren Goldberg), 87, New York City-born theatre and film producer, died Nov. 7, 2007, in Manhattan, NY, of complications from Parkinson's disease. His Broadway credits as a producer include *Dylan* (Tony nomination), *Any Wednesday, Ben Franklin in Paris, The Great Indoors, Happily Never After, Murderous Angels, Night Watch, Via Galactica,* and *Bedroom Farce* (Tony nomination). Off-Broadway credits include *Alfred Kinsey: A Love Story.* He produced the landmark film *My Dinner With André*, a critically hailed film directed by Louis Malle, and starring Louis Malle and Wallace Shawn, that went to earn millions and be studied in classrooms. He also produced the films *The Nevadan* and *Smoke Signal*, as well as television programs such as *Bonanza* and *Peter Gunn.* He was a veteran of WW II. His first marriage, to Jacqueline Richards, ended in divorce. His second wife and collaborator, Judith Ross George, whom he married in 1956, died last year. He is survived by his daughter, Jennifer George, brother, Thomas, of Princeton, NJ, three children from his first marriage, Linda Tai, Laurie, and Larry, all of Los Angeles, CA, and three grandchildren.

Alice Ghostley, 81, Missouri-born actress, who grew up in Henryetta, OK, died Sept. 21, 2007, at her home in Studio City, CA, of colon cancer, following a series of strokes. A Tony Award winner for her Best Featured Actress in a Play in 1965 for *The Sign in Sidney Brustein's Window*, she made her Broadway debut in1952 in Leonard Sillman's *New Faces of 1952*, followed by *Sandhog, All in One, Shangri-La, Maybe Tuesday, A Thurber Carnival, The Beauty Part* (with Bert Lahr, Tony nomination), and *Annie* (as Miss Hannigan, which she played from 1978–1983). Best known for her supporting television roles as Bernice Clifton on *Designing Women* from 1986–1993 (a role which earned her an Emmy nomination in 1992), and Esmerelda on *Bewitched* from 1966–1972, she also appeared in the 1957 television production of Rodgers and Hammerstein's *Cinderella*, starring Julie Andrews. She made scores of television appearances in the '60s, '70s, and '80s, including those on *Mayberry R.F.D, Love: American Style,* and *Evening Shade.* Her film roles include *The Graduate, Gator, Grease,* and *To Kill a Mockingbird.* She accepted (though not won), the Academy Award for her friend, Maggie Smith, who had won Best Actress for her role in *The Prime of Miss Jean Brodie.* Her husband, actor Felice Orlandi, died in 2003. She is survived by her sister, Gladys.

Robert Goulet (Robert Gerard Goulet), 73, Massachusetts-born actor/singer, who grew up in Quebec, Canada, died Oct. 30, 2007, while awaiting a lung transplant at Cedars-Sinai Medical Center in Los Angeles, CA. A 1961 Theatre World Award winner for his role as Sir Lancelot in *Camelot*, he also received a Tony Award as Best Actor in a Musical for his role as Jacques Bonnard in Kander and Ebb's *The Happy Time.* His other Broadway credits include the revival of *Camelot* in 1963, *Moon Over Buffalo*, and *La Cage Aux Folles* (2004). His national tours include *South Pacific, Man of La Mancha,* and *On a Clear Day You Can See Forever*, among many others. Beginning his career singing with the Edmonton Symphony at age 16, he then worked as a disc jockey and then won a scholarship to the Royal Conservatory of Music in Toronto, Canada. He eventually recorded more than 60 albums, winning a 1962 Grammy Award for one of his first. He would become a staple of Las Vegas, NV, showrooms, winning 1982's Las Vegas Entertainer of the Year Award. He appeared on a multitude of variety and television programs such as *The Ed Sullivan Show, The Patty Duke Show, The Bell Telephone Hour,* and starred in the 1966 series *Blue Light.* Many times he played or parodied himself on television programs, including well-known episodes of *Alice* and *The Simpsons*, and a Sports Emmy Award-winning commercial spot on ESPN. His film roles include *Honeymoon Hotel, I'd Rather Be Rich, Atlantic City, Gay Purr-ee, Scrooged, Beetlejuice, Naked Gun 2 ½: the Smell of Fear, Mr. Wrong,* and *Toy Story 2.* He is survived by his third wife and business manager, Vera Novak; sons, Christopher and Michael (from his second marriage to actress Carol Lawrence), and daughter, Nicolette (from his first marriage to Louise Longmore.)

George Grizzard, 79, North Carolina-born actor, died Oct. 2, 2007, in New York, NY, of complications of lung cancer. A Theatre World Award winner for his role in 1957's *The Happiest Millionaire*, he won a 1996 Tony Award for Best Actor in a play (as well as a Drama Desk Award nomination), for his role in *A Delicate Balance.* His other Broadway credits include *The Desperate Hours, The Disenchanted* (Tony nomination), *Face of a Hero, Mary, Mary, Big Fish, Little Fish* (Tony nomination), *Who's Afraid of Virginia Woolf?, The Glass Menagerie, You Know I Can't Hear You When the Water's Running, Noël Coward's Sweet Potato, The Gingham Dog, Inquest, The Country Girl, The Creation of the World and Other Business, Crown Matrimonial, The Royal Family, California Suite, Man and Superman, Judgment at Nuremberg,* and *Seascape.* Off-Broadway credits include *The School for Scandal, The Tavern, The Beach House, Another Antigone, Love Letters, Beautiful Child,* and *Regrets Only.* His regional credits include *Volpone, St. Joan, Henry V,* and *Hamlet* at the Guthrie Theatre. His film roles include *Advise and Consent, Happy Birthday, Wanda June, Comes a Horseman,* and *Small Time Crooks.* His numerous television roles include many on *Law & Order,* and he received an Emmy nomination for his role as John Adams in *The Adams Chronicles.* He is survived by his life partner, William Tynan.

David Groh (David Lawrence Groh), 68, Brooklyn-born actor, died Feb. 12, 2008, in Los Angeles, CA, of kidney cancer. Best known for his role of Joe Gerard, wife to Rhoda Morgenstern, on the hit television show *Rhoda* from 1974–1977, his Broadway credits include *Chapter Two* and *Twilight of the Golds*. Off-Broadway, he appeared in *Be Happy for Me*, and *Road Show*, and his numerous television guest appearances include those on *Law & Order, Baywatch, Girlfriends, The X-Files, Melrose Place, Murder, She Wrote,* and *L.A. Law*. His film credits include *Get Shorty* and *Victory at Entebbe*. A Phi Beta Kappa graduate from Brown University, he was a veteran of the US Army. He is survived by his wife, Kristin Andersen, son, Spencer, mother, Mildred Groh, of Los Angeles, and sister, Marilyn Mamann, of the San Fernando Valley.

Larry Leon Hamlin, 58, North Carolina-born founder and executive director of National Black Theater Festival, died June 6, 2007, at his home in Pfafftown, NC, following a long illness. Creator of the festival in 1989 that occurs every two years, in order to bring together black theater companies from the South to talk about artistic and management challenges, has now grown to include 40 productions and an audience of 60,000. Artists who have been involved with the festival include Ruby Dee, Sidney Poitier, Denzel Washington, Oprah Winfrey, and August Wilson. He also formed the North Carolina Black Repertory Company, which is still active. He is survived by his wife, Sylvia Sprinkle-Hamlin, mother, Annie Hamlin Johnson, two sisters, Sherrie Darlene Hamlin and Linda Maxine Moore, son, Larente Leon Hamlin, and two grandchildren.

Bill Hart, 70, Missouri-born theatre director/dramaturg/actor/writer, died Jan. 20, 2008, in New York, NY, of pancreatic cancer. His Broadway credits include *Cuba and His Teddy Bear* (with Robert DeNiro). First moving professionally in New York among the Andy Warhol crowd, he then moved into working with Theater Genesis, which started at St. Mark's Church in-the-Bowery in 1964. He eventually became the director of the Razor Gallery in SoHo, and advocated graffiti art. He served as The Public Theater's literary manager in the 1980s, where he developed Larry Kramer's *Normal Heart*, among other projects. He also worked on Sam Shepard plays including *Tooth of Crime, States of Shock, A Lie of the Mind,* and *Simpatico*. He also worked on plays with John Malkovich and Nikky Paraiso. He is survived by his life partner, Rafael Pazmino.

Charlton Heston (John Charles Carter), 84, Illinois-born actor, who grew up in St. Helen, MI, died April 5, 2008, in Beverly Hills, CA. He had been diagnosed with Alzheimer's disease in 2002. A 1950 Theatre World Award winner for his role in *Design for a Stained Glass Window*, his other Broadway credits include *Antony and Cleopatra, Leaf and Bough, Mister Roberts,* and *The Tumbler*. His regional credits at the Ahmanson Theater in Los Angeles include *Long Day's Journey Into Night* and *Macbeth*. Best known for his roles as religious and science fiction scions, all played with a rough hewn ruggedness, he won his only Academy Award for 1959's *Ben-Hur*. His film roles, numbering over 100, include *Dark City, The Greatest Show on Earth, The Agony and the Ecstasy, The Wreck of the Mary Deare, Planet of the Apes, Beneath the Planet of the Apes, The President's Lady, The Buccaneer, Major Dundee, Will Penny, Diamond Head, The War Lord, All About People, Counterpoint, Number One, Julius Caesar, The Omega Man, Soylent Green, Earthquake, The Three Musketeers, The Four Musketeers, The Hawaiians, Airport '75, The Greatest Story Ever Told, 55 Days at Peking, Khartoum, El Cid, Touch of Evil,* and Tim Burton's 2001 remake of *The Planet of the Apes*. Early in his career he spent several seasons at the Thomas Wolfe Memorial Theatre in Asheville, NC. His numerous television appearances include *Robert Montgomery Presents, Philco Playhouse, Jane Eyre, Chiefs,* and *The Colbys*. He served as president of the Screen Actors Guild from 1966–1971, and in 1981, President Reagan appointed him co-chairman of the President's task force on the Arts and Humanities. In 1997, he was the recipient of the Kennedy Center honors, and he received the Presidential Medal of Freedom in 2003. In 1998, he was elected president of the National Rifle Association, a position to which he was elected an unprecedented four terms. He was a veteran of the US Air Force, and published *An Actor's Life: Journals 1956–1976* (Dutton 1976). He is survived by his wife, Lydia, son, Fraser, and daughter, Holly Ann, and three grandchildren.

Peter Howard (Howard Weiss), 80, Miami-born composer/arranger/conductor, died April 18, 2008, of pneumonia, at the Lillian Booth Actors' Home in Englewood, NJ. His numerous Broadway credits in any number of those capacities include *My Fair Lady, Oh Captain! Say, Darling, A Party with Betty Comden and Adolph Green, A Desert Incident, The Sound of Music, Carnival!, Subways Are for Sleeping, I Can Get It for You Wholesale, Here's Love, Hello, Dolly!* (1964, 1978, 1995), *The Roar of the Greasepaint–The Smell of the Crowd, How Now, Dow Jones, Her First Roman, 1776, La Strada, Minnie's Boys, Ari, Tricks, Chicago* (1975, 1996), *Annie, The Grand Tour, Barnum, Dance a Little Closer, Baby, The Tap Dance Kid, Harrigan 'n Har, Jerome Kern Goes to Hollywood, Into the Light, Stepping Out, Crazy For You, Comedy Tonight, Swinging on a Star, Chicago* (1969, 1997), and *Minnelli on Minnelli*. He was a graduate of Columbia University, and arranged music for the 1984 film, *Indiana Jones and the Temple of Doom*, in addition to other film credits including *Sugar*. His television work includes *Peter Pan*, starring Mary Martin. Recently, he had toured with a one-man show, *Peter Howard's Broadway*, about his career experiences. He is survived by his son, Jason, of Hackensack, NJ, and a granddaughter.

William Hutt, 87, Toronto -born actor and founding member of the Stratford Festival of Canada in Ontario, died June 28, 2007, in a Stratford hospital, of leukemia. His Broadway credits include *Tamburlaine the Great, Saint Joan,* and *Tiny Alice*. Off-Broadway credits include *Mary Stuart*, and *The Makropoulos Secret*. He appeared in *Much Ado About Nothing* at City Center, and also in New York in *The Miser*. Spending 39 seasons with the festival, his many roles there include those in *King Lear, Titus Andronicus, The Merry Wives of Windsor, As You Like It, The Tempest, The Importance of Being Earnest, Long Day's Journey Into*

Night (which was filmed for Canadian television and aired by PBS). He was awarded a military medal for his service in Canadian Forces in WW II, and was a graduate of the University of Toronto. No immediate survivors.

Bella Jarrett, 81, Georgia-born actress, died Oct. 19, 2007, at her home in Greenwich Village, Manhattan, New York, where she had lived for 40 years. Her Broadway credits include *Pequod, Welcome to Andromedia/Variety Obit, Breaking and Entering, The Trojan Women, The Good Natur'd Man, Phaedra, The Waltz of the Toreadors, Once in a Lifetime,* and *Lolita*. Off-Broadway, she made numerous appearances in regional theatre companies across the United States, including the Alley Theatre, Atlanta Alliance Theatre, Arena Stage, Huntington Theatre, and many performances as a principal performer at Indiana Repertory Theatre, including those in *Sister Mary Ignatius Explains It All for You, 'Night Mother, A Long Day's Journey Into Night*, and for her work at the Indiana Repertory, she was named Indianapolis's Best Actress of 1989, and received an Outlook Oration Award. Her film roles included those in *Arthur, The Cotton Club, The Lonely Guy, Hellfighters,* and *Jane Austen in Manhattan*, as well as television appearances that include those on *All My Children, Another World,* and *One Life to Live*. She was a graduate of Wesleyan College in Macon, GA, and also published four romance novels from 1979–1982 under the pseudonym Belle Thorne. She is survived by her nephews, John Brodie, of San Diego, CA, and Wick Jarrett, of Adairsville, GA.

Herbert Kenwith, 90, New Jersey-born theatre and television director/producer, died Jan. 30, 2008, of cancer. His Broadway credits include acting and stage managing *I Remember Mama*, as well as producing *Me and Molly*. He directed and produced six of the McCarter Theater's seasons. Best known for his television directing and producing work, his credits in that medium include *Diff'rent Strokes, Gimme a Break!, The Brady Brides, Bosom Buddies, Too Close for Comfort, Good Times, Sanford and Son, The Young and the Restless, The Partridge Family, Love, American Style, Star Trek,* and *The Jonathan Winters Show.* Survivors include his niece, Lori Low-Schwartz, and nephews, Arnold Winick, Richard Flexner, and Gary Low.

Deborah Kerr (Deborah Jane Kerr-Trimmer), 86, Scottish-born actress, died Oct. 16, 2007, in Suffolk, England, and had been suffering from Parkinson's disease in recent years. Her Broadway credits include *Tea and Sympathy* (Tony nomination; she also played the role in the film version), followed by *Seascape*. She won a Sarah Siddons Award for her performance in *Tea and Sympathy* in Chicago, IL. Best known for her many film roles, she was nominated six times for the Academy Award, finally being awarded an honorary Oscar in 1994. Her numerous credits in that medium include her nominated performances in *Edward, My Son, From Here to Eternity, The King and I, Heaven Knows, Mr. Allison, Separate Tables,* and *The Sundowners*, in addition to *An Affair to Remember, The Night of the Iguana, Beloved Infidel, Black Narcissus* (New York Film Critics Circle Best Actress Award), *Major Barbara, The Hucksters, Quo Vadis, Julius Caesar, King Solomon's Mines, The Prisoner of Zenda, Young Bess, The Arrangement,* and *The Assam Garden*. She is survived by her husband, writer Peter Viertel, daughters, Melanie and Francesca, stepdaughter, Christine Viertel, and three grandchildren.

Oni Faida Lampley (Vera Lampley), 49, Oklahoma-born actress, died April 28, 2008, in New York, NY, of cancer. Her Broadway acting credits include *Mule Bone* and *The Ride Down Mt. Morgan*, and her Off-Broadway credits include *The Dark Kalamazoo* (writer, and produced by the Drama Dept., of which she was a founding member), *Mud, River, Stone, Zooman and the Sign,* and *The Destiny of Me*. She was also a Usual Suspect at New York Theatre Workshop. She received the 1991 Charles MacArthur Award for Outstanding New Play and the Helen Hayes Award for *Mixed Babies*, produced by the Washington Stage Guild. She received a second MacArthur nomination for *The Dark Kalamazoo*, and was nominated for a 2001 Charlotte Cushman Award for Outstanding Leading Actress in a Play, as well as a Barrymore Award for her role in *The Dark Kalamazoo*, which garnered the Best Music Barrymore Award. She was nominated for an Outstanding Supporting Actress Helen Hayes Award for her role in *Rebel Armies Deep Into Chad*. She also received a DeComte du Nouy Award for *Mixed Babies*. For her play *Tough Titty*, which surrounded her struggle with breast cancer, she received the Helen Merrill Award, was the recipient of the Boomerang Fund Grant, and was a Susan Smith Blackburn finalist. She was a graduate of Oberlin College, and received a graduate acting degree from New York University. Her film roles include those in *Lone Star* and *Brother to Brother*. Her numerous television appearances include *Law & Order, The Sopranos, Third Watch*, and *Oz*. She had recently left the production of *The Bluest Eye* at the Long Wharf Theatre to treat her cancer. She is survived by her husband, Tommy Abney, and sons, Olu and Ade.

Robert Lantz, 93, Berlin-born talent agent/representative, died Oct. 18, 2007, in New York, NY, of heart failure. With clients ranging from Bette Davis to Lillian Hellman, from Leonard Bernstein to Chief Justice William Rehnquist, he operated an independent office in an age where talent representation increasingly followed a corporate model. His other notable clients included Carson McCullers, Richard Burton, Yul Brynner, Montgomery Clift, Alan Jan Lerner, Liv Ullman, Richard Avedon, and Elizabeth Taylor. He operated on a hand shake—not on contracts—and took only 10% of his clients' earnings, rather than the traditional 15%. His wife, Sherlee, and son, Anthony, survive him.

Floria Lasky (Floria Vivan Lasky), 84, Bronx, NY-born entertainment lawyer and one of the first successful female entertainment attorneys, died Sept. 21, 2007, in Manhattan, NY, of cancer. At her firm, Fitelson, Lasky, Aslan, & Couture, where she practiced for 62 years, she represented over the years Jerome Robbins, Elia Kazan, Tennessee Williams, Burl Ives, David Merrick, Gypsy Rose Lee, Jule Styne, and Frederick Loewe. She graduated first in her class at New York University Law School in 1945. Her survivors include her sister, Joyce Lasky Reed, of Washington, daughters, Emily

Altman, of Manhattan, Dara Altman, of Washington, and two grandchildren.

John Philip Law, 70, Hollywood-born actor, died May 13, 2008 at his home in Los Angeles, CA. With Broadway credits including *The Changeling* and *Tartuffe*, he is best known for his film roles including those in *Barbarella* and *The Russians Are Coming, the Russians Are Coming, The Red Baron, The Hawaiians,* and *Hurry Sundown*.

Ira Levin, 78, New York City-born writer, died Nov. 12, 2007, at his home in New York City, of a heart attack. Best known for his novels *Rosemary's Baby, The Stepford Wives,* and *The Boys from Brazil*, he also penned Broadway plays including *No Time for Sergeants, Deathtrap* (Best Play Tony Award nomination), *Interlock, Critic's Choice, General Seeger, Drat! The Cat!, Dr. Cook's Garden, Veronica's Room,* and *Break a Leg*. He also wrote television scripts, including *Clock, Lights Out,* and *U.S. Steel Hour*. He was a veteran of the US Army. His other novels include *A Kiss Before Dying*, which received the Edgar Award from the Mystery Writers of America for best first novel of 1953. He is survived by his sons, Adam, Jared, and Nicolas, and three grandchildren.

Marcel Marceau (Marcel Manel), 84, French-born world-renowned mime, died Sept. 22, 2007, in Cahors, France. His Broadway credits include *Marcel Marceau* and *Marcel Marceau on Broadway*. Off-Broadway, he appeared in *An Evening of Pantomime*. Working in the Resistance in Paris during WW II, he aided Jewish children from being discovered by the Gestapo and the French police, before joining the allied French Army in 1944. He gave his first public performance in 1945 for an audience of primarily American soldiers. Following the war he attended the School of Dramatic Art in the Sarah Bernhardt Theater in Paris, and eventually formed his own company, traveling throughout Europe and the United States, including venues such as the Olympia Theater in Paris, and in Hollywood, all of which brought him great acclaim. Performing an average of 200 shows a year since 1946, his acts included "Creation," "Youth, Maturity, Old Age, and Death," and "The Tribunal." He was deemed a "national treasure" in Japan, and was named a Chevalier de la Légion d'Honneur for cultural affairs in 1970 by the French government. His film roles include those in *Barbarella* and Mel Brooks's *Silent Movie*, in which he actually spoke the word, "No," and he was an accomplished painter and children's book author. He is survived by his sons, Michel and Baptiste, from his first marriage, to Huguette Mallet, which ended in divorce, and two daughters, Camille and Aurélia, by his third wife, Anne Sicco, which also ended in divorce. A second marriage, to Ella Jaroszewicz, ended in divorce as well.

Donald Murphy, 90, died May 19, 2008. A 1945 Theatre World Award winner for his role in *Signature*, his Broadway credits include *Janie, Try and Get It, For Keeps, Common Ground, Wonderful Journey, Dear Barbarians,* and *The Time of the Cuckoo*. His film and television credits include *Frankenstein's Daughter, Swamp Girl, Get Smart, Perry Mason, One Step Beyond, Bat Masterson, The Life and Legend of Wyatt Earp, Whirlybirds, On the Threshold of Space, Shack Out on 101, The Millionaire,* and *The Bamboo Prison*.

Beverly McKinsey (Beverlee Magruder), 72, Oklahoma-born actress, died May 2, 2008, in Los Angeles, CA, of complications of a kidney transplant. Her Broadway credits include *Mert & Phil* with Estelle Parsons. and the London production of *Who's Afraid of Virginia Woolf?* with Uta Hagen and Arthur Hill. Best known for her role as Iris Carrington on *Another World* from 1970–1979, and Alexandra Spaulding from 1984–1992 on *Guiding Light*, she also played Myrna Slaughter on *General Hospital* in 1994, and appeared on *Mannix, Hawaii Five-O,* and *McMillan & Wife*. She graduated from the University of Oklahoma. Her first marriage, to Mark McKinsey, ended in divorce, as did her second, to Angus Duncan. She survived her third husband, Berkeley Harris, who died in 1984. Survivors include her son, *General Hospital* director Scott McKinsey, and a grandson.

Allan Melvin, 84, Kansas City, KA-born actor, died Jan. 17, 2008, in Brentwood, CA, of cancer. One of the most familiar faces on television in roles like Sgt. Hacker on *Gomer Pyle, U.S.M.C.*, Sam the Butcher (Alice's boyfriend) on *The Brady Bunch*, and Barney Hefner on *All in the Family*. His sole Broadway credit was *Stalag 17*. He also appeared on *Route 66, Perry Mason, Lost in Space, The Andy Griffith Show,* and *With Six You Get Eggroll*. His many voiceover roles include *The Smurfs, Scooby Doo, The Flintstones,* and *Hong Kong Phooey*.

Anna Minot, 89, Boston, MA-born actress, died June 2, 2007, in Reno, NV. Her Broadway credits include *The Strings, My Lord, Are False, The Russian People, The Iceman Cometh, An Enemy of the People, Ivanov,* and *The Visitor*. Her Off-Broadway credits include *Steel Magnolias* and *Getting Out*. She also appeared in numerous productions at The Pearl Theatre Company, and stage managed and performed in readings at New Dramatists. Also known for her role as Martha Wilson on *As the World Turns* from 1966–1970, she appeared in the films *Condition Red, The Rosary Murders,* and *A World Apart*. She was a graduate of Vassar College. Her first marriage was to actor Arthur Franz, and her second to actor Joseph Warren. Her son, Michael Franz, and two granddaughters, survive her.

Barry Morse (Herbert Morse), 89, London, England-born actor, died Feb. 2, 2008, in London, England. His Broadway credits include *Hide and Seek, Staircase,* and *Hadrian VII*. Best known for his role as Lt. Philip Gerard in the 1960s television series *The Fugitive*, his creation of a radio show on the Canadian Broadcasting Corporation entitled *A Touch of Greasepaint*, about the history of acting, ran for 10 years. His other television appearances include *The Martian Chronicles, The Winds of War,* and *Anne of Greene Gable: The Continuing Story*. He served as artistic director of the Shaw Festival in Niagara-on-the-Lake. His wife of 60 years, Sydney Sturgess, died in 1999, and his daughter, actress Melanie Morse MacQuarrie, died in 2005. He is survived by four grandchildren and several great-grandchildren.

Carl Mueller, 76, St. Louis, MO-born theatre professor/translator, died Jan. 27, 2008, of a stroke, at the UCLA Medical Center in Los Angeles, CA. He was a professor in the critical studies program of the UCLA theatre department from 1966–1994, but achieved most notoriety for his translations, especially of German plays. Fifteen volumes of his translations, from German, Swedish, Italian, and ancient Greek are still in print. He graduated from Northwestern University and was a veteran of WW II. He is survived by his brother, Don, of Colorado Springs, CO, and sister, Shari Mueller, of Virginia.

Tom Murphy (Tom Jordan Murphy), 39, Rhodesian-born actor, died Oct. 6, 2007, in Dublin, Ireland, of Hodgkin's lymphoma. Best known for his performance in 1998 for *The Beauty Queen of Leenane* (for which he won the Tony Award for Best Supporting Actor, as well as a special "Cast" Theatre World Award) his other stage credits include those at the Court Theatre in London, the Gate, the Abbey Theaters, and the Dublin Theatre Festival. His film performances include those in *Intermission, Michael Collins, The General, Man About Dog*, and *Adam and Paul*. He is survived by his brother, Michael, and two sisters, Mary and Sheila.

Lois Nettleton, 80, Illinois-born actress, died Jan. 18, 2008, in Los Angeles, CA, of lung cancer. A Tony Award nominee as Best Featured Actress in a Play and Drama Desk Award nominee as Outstanding Actress in a Play for her role in *They Knew What They Wanted*, her other Broadway credits include *The Biggest Thief in Town, Darkness at Noon, God and Kate Murphy, Silent Night, Lonely Night, The Wayward Stork, A Streetcar Named Desire, Strangers,* and *Cat on a Hot Tin Roof.* Best known for over a hundred roles on television and film, she won two Daytime Emmy Awards for her roles in *The American Woman: Profiles in Courage* and for an episode of *Insight*. She also received three Emmy nominations for her work on *The Golden Girls, In the Heat of the Night,* and the television movie *Fear on Trial*. Her film roles include *A Face in the Crowd, A Period of Adjustment, Come Fly With Me, Mail Order Bride, The Bamboo Saucer, The Good Guys and the Bad Guys, Dirty Dingus Magee, The Honkers, Echoes of a Summer, Soggy Bottom, USA, Deadly Blessing, Butterfly,* and *The Best Little Whorehouse in Texas*. In 1948 she was Miss Chicago, and a semifinalist in the Miss America pageant.

Danny Newman, 88, Chicago, IL-born publicist/author, died Dec. 1, 2007, in Lincolnwood, IL, of pulmonary fibrosis. As longtime director of press and public relations for Lyric Opera of Chicago, he is best known for his 1977 publication *Subscribe Now!* that instructed how to build audiences through selling subscriptions. The publication has been printed in ten editions, and used in 31 countries. He was a veteran of WW II. He is survived by his wife, Alyce Katz Newman, and two stepsons, P. André of Chicago, IL, and Leonard Katz of Lincolnwood, IL. He received honorary degrees from DePaul and Roosevelt Universities, and published a memoir, *Tales of a Theatrical Guru*, in 2006.

Lee Nagrin, 78, Seattle. WA-born performance artist, died June 12, 2007, in Manhattan, NY, of colon cancer. Most notable as director and performer with Meredith Monk's theatre company, she appeared there between 1971–1981 in productions of *Vessel, Education of a Girl Child, Ping Chong and Monk, Quarry, Recent Ruins, Paris/Chacon/Venice/Milan,* and *Ellis Island*. She formed her own company, the Sky Fish Ensemble in 1979, and she exhibited such pieces as *Behind the Lid, Sky Fish, Bird/Devil, Whorl*, many produced by the Women's Interart Center. Early in her career she worked in New York, as well as the Seattle Repertory Playhouse. Her *Bird/Bear* won a 1986 Best New American Play Obie Award. She directed *Pathways*, by choreographer Margaret Beals in Boston in 1997, which was included by *The Boston Globe* as one of its Best Theater Works of the Year. She performed in the Karen Malpede plays *Blue Heaven,* and *Beekeeper's Daughter*. Her film roles include *The Blob*. Her survivors include her companion, Bruce Hutchinson.

Suzanne Pleshette, 70, New York City-born actress, died Jan. 19, 2008, in Los Angeles, CA, of respiratory failure, at her home in Los Angeles. She had undergone treatment for lung cancer in 2006. Best known for her role as Emily Hartley in the hit sitcom *The Bob Newhart Show*, from 1972–1978, it was a memorable role that brought her two Emmy nominations. Her numerous other film and television appearances brought her two more Emmy nominations and two Golden Globe nominations. Her Broadway credits include *Compulsion, The Cold Wind and the Warm, Golden Fleecing, The Miracle Worker,* and *Special Occasions*. Her film appearances include those in *The Geisha Boy, Rome Adventure, A Distant Trumpet, The Birds, The Shaggy D.A., Mister Buddwing, Nevada Smith, Fate Is the Hunter, The Adventures of Bullwhip Griffin, The Ugly Daschund, Blackbeard's Ghost, A Rage to Live, Youngblood Hawke, If It's Tuesday, It Must Be Belgium, The Power, Support Your Local Gunfighter,* and *Oh God, Book 2*. Her many television credits include many appearances on *The Tonight Show with Johnny Carson, Harbourmaster, Have Gun, Will, Travel, Dr. Kildare* (Emmy nomination), *The Boys Are Back, Bridges to Cross, Good Morning, Miami, Suzanne Pleshette is Maggie Briggs, Nightingales, Battling for Baby,* and *The Queen of Mean*, in which she famously played millionaire hotelier Leona Helmsley, which brought her final Emmy nomination. Her last role was playing the estranged mother of Megan Mullally character (Karen Walker) on *Will & Grace* from 2002–2004. Her most memorable small screen performance, however, is most likely her appearance in the final episode of Bob Newhart's second television sitcom, *Newhart*, in which she appeared as her former character, Emily, in bed with Newhart, implying the whole ten-year run of the subsequent *Newhart* series had been a nightmare. Her brief first marriage was to actor Troy Donahue. She survived her second husband, Texas oilman Tim Galligher, as she did her third husband, Tom Poston (who had been her friend for many years, as well as fellow *The Bob Newhart Show* costar).

Joseph Pevney, 96, New York City-born actor, died May 18, 2008, in Palm Desert, CA. Getting his start in vaudeville houses, his eventual Broadway credits include *Battle Hymn, Johnny Johnson, The World We Make, Horse Fever, Native Son, Lily of the Valley, Let Freedom Sing, Counselor at Law, Home of the Brave,* and *Swan Song*. His numerous film appearances include *Tammy and the Bachelor, Body and Soul, Man of a Thousand Faces,* and *The Plunderers*. His television appearances include *Star Trek* (three notable episodes), *Bonanza,* and *The Paper Chase.*

Kate Phillips (Mary Katherine Linaker), 94, actress/writer, died April 18, in Keene, NH. Her Broadway credits include *The Prince Consort, London Assurance,* and *We Can't Be As Bad As All That*, before achieving fame as the co-writer of the cult classic film *The Blob*, which made Steve McQueen a star. Her film roles as an actress include *The Girl from Mandalay, Kitty Foyle, Drums Along the Mohawk, Blood and Sand,* and five Charlie Chan movies. She was a graduate of New York University, and served in the Red Cross, as a hostess for U.S.O. Clubs. She also wrote for Voice of America. She is survived by her son, Bill, of El Cerito, CA, daughter, Regina Paquette, of Keene, and four grandchildren.

Sydney Pollack (Sydney Irwin Pollack), 73, Indiana-born and raised Academy Award-winning actor/director/producer/writer, died May 26, 2008, at his home in Los Angeles, CA, of cancer. One of the most prolific and well-respected film directors and producers of the 1970s and 1980s, his Broadway credits as an actor include *The Dark is Light Enough* and *A Stone for Danny Fisher*. He studied in New York for two years under Sanford Meisner, becoming his assistant for five years subsequent to his study at the Neighborhood Playhouse School of Theater. His television credits as an actor include *Playhouse 90's For Whom the Bell Tolls*. His television credits as a director include *Shotgun Slade, Ben Casey, Naked City, The Fugitive,* and a 1966 Emmy Award-winning turn as director of *Bob Hope Presents the Chrysler Theater*. His numerous and oft lauded film credits as a director, include *The Slender Thread, They Shoot Horses, Don't They?* (Academy Award nomination), *Jeremiah Johnson, This Property Is Condemned, The Swimmer, Castle Keep, The Yakuza, Bobby Deerfield, The Electric Horseman, The Way We Were, Three Days of the Condor, Absence of Malice, Tootsie* (Academy Award nomination), *Sketches of Frank Gehry, Out of Africa* (1986 Academy Awards as Best Director and Best Picture), *Havana, The Firm, Sabrina, Random Hearts, The Interpreter,* and most recently, *Michael Clayton*. Many of his films were produced under his own production company, Mirage, which he set up with fellow director/producer Anthony Minghella, who died last year. An accomplished screen actor, he played notable roles (and sometimes himself), in Woody Allen's *Husbands and Wives, Michael Clayton, Tootsie,* and on television most recently in HBO's *Entourage*. He often worked with the cream of the crop of Hollywood stars, such as Dustin Hoffman, Robert Redford, Meryl Streep, Natalie Wood, Nicole Kidman, Jane Fonda, Jessica Lange, Robert Mitchum, George Clooney, and Al Pacino. He was a veteran of the US Army, and served several times as executive director of Actors Studio West, chairman of American Cinematheque, and as an activist for artists' rights. Survivors include his wife of 50 years, Claire Griswold, and daughters Rachel and Rebecca. Their son, Steven, died in a plane crash in Santa Monica, CA, in 1993.

Joan Potter, 82, Nova Scotia-born actress/teacher, died March 14, 2008, following an extended illness. Her Broadway credits include *A Far Country* and *The Three Sisters*. Her television credits include *Philco Television Playhouse's The Rainmaker, Studio One,* and *The Nurses*. She was a noted and influential teacher for over 30 years at the Conservatory of Theater Arts and Film at Purchase College, and taught at Southern Methodist University for several years in the 1970s. She is survived by her brother, Robert W. Potter, of Plymouth, MN, and many relatives.

Hanon Reznikov (Hanon Reznik) 57, Brooklyn, NY-born actor/director/producer, died May 3, 2008, in Manhattan, NY, of pneumonia, following a stroke in early April. Following viewing a performance by The Living Theater in 1968, he then became a member of the company, which had been founded by Julian Beck and Judith Malina, in 1947. He later assumed the position, with Judith Malina, of co-artistic director, upon Julian Beck's death in 1985. He and Ms. Malina married two years later. Many of the works performed by The Living Theater were those of Mr. Reznikov's, among which were *Utopia, The Zero Method, Anarchia, And Then The Heavens Closed, Body of God, Capital Changes, Clearing The Streets, Code Orange Cantata, A Dream Of Water,* and *Enigma*. In 2007, a permanent home for The Living Theater opened on the Lower East Side. His survivors include Ms. Malina, two stepchildren, Isha Apell and Garrick Beck, and brother, James Reznik, of California.

Percy Rodrigues, 89, Montreal, Canada-born actor died Sept. 6, 2007, at his home in Indio, CA, of kidney failure. Best known for his television and film roles, including several memorable voiceovers, his Broadway credits include *Toys in the Attic* and *Blues for Mister Charlie*. He was one of the first black actors to portray characters, especially prominent ones, on television, including a neurosurgeon on *Peyton Place*, and a commodore on *Star Trek*, in addition to roles on *Ben Casey, The Fugitive, Mission Impossible, Medical Center, Benson, Sanford,* and *Roots: The Next Generation*. His films include *Come Back, Charleston Blue, Deadly Blessing*, and as the narrator for the famous radio and television ads for the 1975 film, *Jaws*. Survivors include his wife, Karen Cook-Rodgrigues, daughter, Hollis, and son Gerald, both of Canada, four grandchildren, and two great-grandchildren, by his first wife, Alameda, who preceded him in death.

Lawrence Roman, 86, Jersey City-born playwright/screenwriter, died May 18, 2008, at the Motion Picture & Television Country House and Hospital in Woodland Hills, CA, of kidney failure. Best known for his Broadway plays *Under the Yum-Yum Tree, P.S. I Love You,* and *Alone Together*, he also penned the teleplays *The Ernest Green Story* (Peabody Award), and *Anatomy of an Illness*. Other small screen credits include *Vice Squad*. His screenplay credits include that of *Under the Yum-Yum Tree, Paper Lion, McQ, A Kiss Before Dying,* and *A Warm December*. He was a graduate of UCLA and a veteran of

WW II. He is survived by his wife of 62 years, Evelyn, son, Steve, and a granddaughter.

Roy Scheider, 75, New Jersey-born actor, died Feb. 10, 2008, of a staph infection, at the University of Arkansas for Medical Sciences Hospital, which specializes in treatment of multiple myeloma, which he had been undergoing treatment for in recent years. Following several years of classical theatre in regional productions, his Broadway credits include *The Chinese Prime Minister, Tartuffe,* and *Betrayal* (Drama League Award). Other New York credits include *Romeo and Juliet*. Perhaps best known for his role as Martin Brody, the police chief in *Jaws*, he received Academy Award nominations as Best Actor for *All That Jazz* (1979), and as Best Supporting Actor for *The French Connection*. His other film roles include *Curse of the Living Corpse, Sorceror, The Wages of Fear, Klute, The Outside Man, The Seven Ups, Sheila Levene is Dead and Living in New York, Marathon Man, Jaws 2, Still of the Night, Blue Thunder, Romeo Is Bleeding, 52 Pick-Up, 2010, The Russia House, The Peackeeper, The Rainmaker,* and *Naked Lunch*. His television series roles included those on *Sea Quest DSV* and *Third Watch*. He was a veteran of the US Air Force, and a graduate of Marshall College, in Lancaster, PA. With Kathy Engle, he helped to found Hayground School in Bridgehampton, NY. He is survived by his wife, documentary filmmaker Brenda King, daughters, Maximillia Scheider and Molly Mae Scheider, son, Christian Verrier Scheider, brother, Glenn Scheider, of Summit, NJ, and two grandchildren. A first marriage to film editor, Cynthia Bebout Scheider, ended in divorce.

Paul Scofield (David Paul Scofield), 86, British-born actor, died March 19, 2008, at his home in southern England, of leukemia. A Best Actor Tony Award winner for his role as Sir Thomas More in *A Man for All Seasons*, he also won an Academy Award for his film reprisal of the role. He toured in England and made many stage appearances there, including a notable performance onstage in *Amadeus*. He was an Emmy Award winner for his role in *Male of the Species* (1969), and also appeared on television in *The Attic: The Hiding of Anne Frank*. He received three British Academy of Film and Television Arts nominations for his roles in *That Lady, A Man for All Seasons,* and *The Crucible*. Other film roles include those in *The Train, Scorpio, Henry V, A Delicate Balance,* and *Hamlet*. He was also nominated for a Best Supporting Actor Academy Award for his role in *Quiz Show*. In 2001, he was named a Companion of Honor, one of Britain's top honors. He is survived by his wife and children.

David Shaw (Samuel David Shamforoff), 90, Brooklyn, NY-born playwright/screenwriter, died July 27, 2007, in Beverly Hills, CA, of natural causes. A Tony Award winner (along with Herbert and Dorothy Fields and Sidney Sheldon), for *Redhead*, his other Broadway credits as a writer include *They Should Have Stood in Bed,* and *Tovarich*. Early in his career he worked as a writer for radio and television, and his credits include *The Defenders, Playhouse 90, Studio One,* and *The Philco Television Playhouse*. His screenplays include *If It's Tuesday, This Must Be Belgium*. He was a veteran of the Army Air Corp in WW II. He survived his first wife, Vivian Rosenthal, and is survived by his second wife, actress Maxine Stuart, two daughters, Ellen Agress, of Manhattan, and Liz Baron, of Dallas, TX, stepdaughter, Chris Ann Maxwell, of Beverly Hills, CA, and four grandchildren.

Robert Sidney, 98, New York City-born dancer/choreographer/director, died March 26, 2008, at Cedars-Sinai Medical Center in Los Angeles, CA. Best known for his Broadway show *This Is the Army* in 1942, his other Broadway credits include *On Your Toes, Keep Off the Grass, The Boys from Syracuse, Three to Make Ready, Along Fifth Avenue, Dance Me a Song,* and *Bing Crosby on Broadway*. His numerous film credits as a choreographer include *The Loves of Carmen, Susan Slept Here,* and *Party Girl*. He was a veteran of the U.S. Army in WW II, helped found the Professional Dancers Society (an affiliate of the Actors Fund), and penned a memoir entitled *With Malice Toward Some, Tales from Dancing With the Army*, in 2003. Survivors include many nieces and nephews.

Allan Stevenson, 89, actor, died Oct. 24, 2007, when he was struck by a hit-and-run driver in New York City. His Broadway credits include *A Family Affair, Anne of the Thousand Days, Angels Kiss Me, Small War on Murray Hill,* and *Do Re Mi*. His film roles include those in *Age of Innocence,* and *Murder By Phone*. His television roles include those on *Studio One, Kraft Television Theater,* and *Hallmark Hall of Fame*.

Robert Symonds, (Robert Barry Symonds), 80, Oklahoma-born actor, died Aug. 23, 2007, at Cedars-Sinai Medical Center in Los Angeles, CA, of complications of prostate cancer. His Broadway credits include *Danton's Death, The Country Wife, The Caucasian Chalk Circle, The Alchemist, The East Wind, Galileo, The Little Foxes, Saint Joan, Cyrano de Bergerac, A Cry of Players, In the Matter of J. Robert Oppenheimer, The Time of Your Life, Camino Real, The Good Woman of Setzuan, Mary Stuart, Narrow Road to the Deep North, Twelfth Night, The Crucible, Man of La Mancha, Enemies, The Plough and the Stars, The Merchant of Venice, A Streetcar Named Desire* (both 1973 productions), and *The Poison Tree*. Off-Broadway credits include *Bananas, The Inner Journey, The Year Boston Won the Pennant, The Increased Difficulty of Concentration, The Disintegration of James Cherry, Landscape/Silence, Amphitryon,* and *In Celebration*. He accrued many regional theatre credits, and his Los Angeles stage credits include *Park Your Car in Harvard Yard*. As a member of the Actors Worskshop in San Francisco early in his career, he performed works by Bertolt Brecht, Harold Pinter, and Samuel Beckett. He was an associate director of the Repertory Theatre of Lincoln Center between 1965 and 1972, and worked as an actor there for more than 10 years during the 1960s and 1970s, with credits including *The Miser*. His television credits include *Dynasty* and *MASH, The Adams Chronicles,* and *The Blue and the Gray* miniseries. His film credits include *And Justice for All, The Exorcist, Micki & Maude, Primary Colors, Rumplestiltskin,* and *The Ice Pirates*. Since 1982 he and his wife, actress Priscilla Pointer, spent part of every year in Paris, performing in plays in English with the Dear Conjunction Company. He was a veteran of the U.S. Army in WW II. He is survived by his wife, actress Priscilla Pointer, children, Vicki Morrison, Barry Symonds, and Rebecca Woolridge, stepchildren, actress Amy Irving, and

David and Katie Irving, six granddaughters, and five step-grandchildren.

Amy Sullivan, 54, Newark-born director of the Eugene O'Neill Center, died June 10, 2007, in Old Lyme, CT. She eventually became the executive director of the Center in 2003 until January 2007, and under her tenure the budget and development both substantially increased. She also directed the renovations of Eugene O'Neill's Monte Cristo Cottage in New London, CT, which is now a National Historic Landmark. She was a graduate of Upsala College, and worked for several Broadway producers before becoming director of development of the O'Neill Center in 1993, where *In the Heights*, the current Broadway hit, debuted. While at the Center she also restarted the Cabaret Conference, for budding cabaret performances, and created the National Theater Institute, a training program for theater students. She is survived by her husband, Bruce Josephy, mother, Catherine Zizza Sullivan, and son, Dan.

Isa Thomas, 75, actress, died April 6, 2008, in New York, NY, of a heart attack. Her Broadway credits include *Lost in Yonkers, Any Given Day,* and *Waiting in the Wings*. Her Off-Broadway credits include *States of Shock* and *Richard III*, and regional credits include *Day Trips* at Hartford Stage and the McCarter Theatre. Her film and television credits include *Flash of Green, Iron Jawed Angels, Law & Order,* and *Another World*. The doyenne of the Asolo Repertory Theatre in Sarasota, FL, where she appeared in more than 125 roles over 36 seasons, her roles there include Eleanor in *The Lion in Winter,* Agnes in *A Delicate Balance*, Fanny in *The Royal Family*, Penelope in *You Can't Take It With You*, Amanda in *The Glass Menagerie*, Serafina in *The Rose Tattoo*, Juno in *Juno and the Paycock*, Fonisa in *The Gin Game*, Lady Bracknell and *The Importance of Being Earnest*. Her regional directing credits include *The Crucible, Da, Cat on a Hot Tin Roof, The Last Night of Ballyhoo, On Golden Pond,* and *Children of a Lesser God*. She is survived by her daughter, Koren, of New York, and twin sons, Jason and Derek, of Sarasota.

Miyoshi Umeki, 78, Japanese-born actress/singer, died Aug. 28, 2007, in Licking, MO, of complications from cancer. The first Asian performer (Best Supporting Actress) to win an Academy Award for her performance in *Sayonara*, her Broadway role as Mei-Li in *Flower Drum Song* in 1959 garnered a Tony Award nomination for Best Actress in a Musical. Beginning her career as a nightclub singer in Japan, she landed several recording contracts there, as well as in the U.S., and had television credits including *Arthur Godfrey and Friends*. Her other film credits include *Cry for Happy, The Horizontal Lieutenant,* and *A Girl Named Tamiko*. Her television credits include *The Donna Reed Show, Dr. Kildare, Rawhide, Mister Ed,* and is best known for her role as Ms. Livingston in *The Courtship of Eddie's Father*, which debuted in 1969. Following the end of its run in 1972, she retired from show business to focus on being a wife and mother. Her roles in *Sayonara, Flower Drum Song,* and *The Courtship of Eddie's Father* brought her Golden Globe nominations. She is survived by her son, Michael Hood, of Licking, MO, and two grandchildren. Her first marriage ended in divorce, and her second husband, television director Randall Hood, died in 1976.

Henrietta Valor (Henrietta Embick), 62, Pennsylvania-born actress, died Oct. 23, 2007, in Studio City, CA, of complications of Alzheimer's disease. Her Broadway credits include *Half a Sixpence, Applause, Jacque Brel is Alive and Well and Living in Paris,* and *Annie.* Her Off-Broadway credits include *Fashion, A Bistro on the CNR,* and *One Two Three Four Five*. Her regional credits include *Fashion* at the Alex Theatre in Glendale, CA, and *Lettice and Lovage* at the Pasadena Playhouse. She was a graduate of Northwestern University and in the early 1960s she toured with the USO, performing in Europe, Africa, and Asia. Survivors include her husband, John Towey.

Thommie Walsh, 57, New York-born actor/dancer/choreographer/director, died at his mother's home in Auburn, NY, of complications of lymphoma. A 1976 Special Theatre World Award winner for his creation of the role of Bobby in *A Chorus Line* (along with the ensemble), he received two Tony Awards for collaborations with Tommy Tune: *A Day in Hollywood/A Night in the Ukraine* (1980), and *My One and Only* (1983), for which he also received a Drama Desk Award for Best Choreography, as well as a Best Director Tony nomination. He also received a Tony nomination for *Nine*, and his other Broadway credits in any number of capacities, are *Seesaw, Rachael Lily Rosenbloom and Don't You Ever Forget It, The Best Little Whorehouse in Texas* (1978, 1982), *The 1940s Radio Hour, Do Black Patent Leather Shoes Really Reflect Up?* and *My Favorite Year*. His Off-Broadway credits include *Little Stiff*, and he co-authored *On the Line: The Creation of 'A Chorus Line,'* (with Bayork Lee and Robert Viagas) (William Morrow, 1990), about the origins of the show. He is survived by his mother, Ellie Walsh, and sister, Barbara Walsh.

Richard Widmark, 93, Minnesota-born actor, died March 24, 2008, in Roxbury, CT, of complications from a fractured vertebrae. His Broadway credits include *Kiss and Tell, Get Away Old Man, Trio, Kiss Them for Me,* and *Dunnigan's Daughter*, before embarking on a prolific film career. His credits in that medium include *Kiss of Death, The Street With No Name, Road House, Slattery's Hurricane, The Cobweb, The Alamo, Yellow Sky, Down to the Sea in Ships, Night and the City, Panic in the Streets, No Way Out, The Halls of Montezuma, The Frogmen, Don't Bother to Knock, Pickup on South Street, Hell and High Water, Garden of Evil, Broken Lance, Saint Joan, Time Limit, The Alamo, The Secret Ways, Judgment at Nuremberg, How the West Was Won, Cheyenne Autumn, The Bedford Incident, Madigan, Death of a Gunfighter, Murder on the Orient Express, To the Devil a Daughter, Twilight's Last Gleaming, The Domino Principle,* and *The Swarm*. He formed his own production company and his film producing credits include *Time Limit, The Secret Ways*, and *The Bedford Incident*. He received a 1970 Emmy nomination for his role in *Vanished*, and his other television credits include *Once Upon a Texas Train* and *A Gathering of Old Men*. He was a graduate of Lake Forest College. He survived his first wife of 55 years, Jean Hazelwood, and his second wife, Ms. Blanchard, and daughter Anne Heath Widmark, of Santa Fe, NM, survive him.

Index

JOHN WILLIS (EDITOR IN CHIEF EMERITUS) was editor in chief of both *Theatre World* and its companion series *Screen World* for forty-three years. *Theatre World* and *Screen World* are the oldest definitive pictorial and statistical records of each American theatrical and foreign and domestic film season, and are referenced daily by industry professionals, students, and historians worldwide.

Mr. Willis has also served as editor of *Dance World, Opera World, A Pictorial History of the American Theatre 1860–1985*, and *A Pictorial History of the Silent Screen*. Previously, he served as assistant to *Theatre World* founder Daniel Blum on *Great Stars of the American Stage, Great Stars of Film, A Pictorial History of the Talkies, A Pictorial History of Television*, and *A Pictorial Treasury of Opera in America*.

For over forty years he presided over the presentation of the annual Theatre World Awards, incorporated in 1997 as a 501 (c)(3) nonprofit organization. Begun in 1945 and presented by past winners, they are the oldest awards given to actors for a Broadway or Off-Broadway debut role.

On behalf of *Theatre World*, Mr. Willis received a 2001 Tony Honor for Excellence in the Theatre, the 2003 Broadway Theater Institute Lifetime Achievement Award, a 1994 special Drama Desk Award, and in 1993, the first Outstanding Special Lucille Lortel Award. On behalf of *Screen World*, he received the prestigious 1998 National Board of Review Wiliam K. Everson Award for Film History. He has also received a Professional Excellence Award from his alma mater, Milligan College.

He has served on the nominating committees of the Tony Awards and the New York University Musical Hall of Fame, and has served on the national board of directors for the Clarence Brown Theatre at the University of Tennessee in Knoxville, TN, as well as the past board of directors of the National Board of Review. In addition, Mr. Willis is retired from the New York City public school system.

In 1993, the auditorium in which he had performed as a high school student was renovated and christened the John Willis Performing Arts Center at Morristown-Hamblen High School East, in Morristown, TN. And in 2007, a classroom in the new Milligan College theatre complex was be named in his honor.

BEN HODGES (EDITOR IN CHIEF) served as an editorial assistant for seven years on *Theatre World*, becoming the associate editor to John Willis in 1998 and editor in chief in 2007. Also an assistant for seven years to John Willis for the prestigious Theatre World Awards given for Broadway and Off-Broadway debut performances, Ben was elected to the Theatre World Awards board of directors in 2002, serving as executive producer for the annual ceremony from 2002-2007. In 2003 he was presented with a Special Theatre World Award in recognition of his ongoing stewardship of the event. He has also served as the executive producer for the LAMBDA Literary Foundation "Lammy" Awards, given for excellence in LGBT publishing.

In 2001, Ben became the director of development and then served as executive director for Fat Chance Productions Inc. and the Ground Floor Theatre, a New York-based nonprofit theatre and film production company. *Prey for Rock and Roll* was developed by Fat Chance from their stage production into a critically acclaimed feature film starring Gina Gershon and *The Sopranos* Emmy winner Drea de Matteo.

In 2003, frustrated with the increasingly daunting economic prospects involved in producing theatre on a small scale in New York, Ben organized NOOBA, the New Off-Off-Broadway Association, an advocacy group dedicated to representing the concerns of expressly Off-Off-Broadway producers in the public forum and in negotiations with other local professional arts organizations; their chief objective the reformation of the Actors' Equity Basic Showcase Code.

In 2005 Ben founded and served for two years as executive director of The Learning Theatre Inc., a 501(c)(3) nonprofit organization incorporating theatre into the development and lives of learning disabled and autistic children. He currently serves on its board of directors.

Ben has appeared on nationwide radio on *The Joey Reynolds Show, The Michael Dresser Show*, and on television on New York 1 and *Philly Live* in Philadelphia, PA. Reviews and articles on Ben, his projects, or publications have appeared in *The New York Times, The New Yorker, GQ, Elle, Genre, Back Stage, Time Out New York, Playbill, Next, New York Blade, Library Journal, The Advocate, Chicago Free Press, Philadelphia Gay News, Houston Voice, Stage Directions, Between the Lines, The Flint Journal*, and *Citizen Tribune*, as well as the web sites CurtainUp.com and in Peter Filichia's Diary on Theatermania.com.

Ben holds a BFA in Theatre Acting and Directing from Otterbein College in Westerville, Ohio, is an alumnus of the Commercial Theater Institute, and is a candidate for a 2012 Juris Doctor degree from Seton Hall University School of Law in Newark, New Jersey. He lives in New York City. For more information or to schedule speaking engagements, please e-mail inquiries to info@applausepub.com

SCOTT DENNY (ASSOCIATE EDITOR) Scott Denny is and actor and singer and has worked professionally for over twenty years. Originally from Terre Haute, Indiana, he attended Western Kentucky University in Bowling Green, Kentucky and holds a degree in performing arts. His professional theatrical credits include Richard Henry Lee in the national tour of *1776,* Uncle Wes in the Las Vegas and national touring production of *Footloose,* and the assistant company manager and swing performer on the first national tour of Susan Stroman's production of *The Music Man.* Regionally he has appeared in *Evita, The Wizard of Oz,* and *The King and I* at Houston's Theatre Under the Stars, regional premieres of *Silver Dollar* and *Paper Moon* at Stage One in Wichita, Kansas. His summer stock and dinner theatre credits include *Me and My Girl, Gypsy, She Loves Me, The Best Little Whorehouse in Texas*, among several others. In New York he has appeared Off-Off-Broadway in *Election Day, Like You Like It, Vanity Fair,* and in several readings and workshops. His screen credits include the independent films *Red Hook* and *Redefining Normal.* Scott served as assistant editor on *Theatre World* Volume 60, and as associate editor on Volume 61 and 62. In the fall of 2006 Scott was elected to the board of directors of the Theatre World Awards where he now serves as the Treasurer. He served as an associate producer for the 2006 Theatre World Awards, and as co-producer of the 2007 and 2008 Awards. Scott also works for a cruise travel agency in Fort Myers, Florida, specializing in incentive groups.

ALLISON GRAHAM (ASSOCIATE EDITOR) Allison Graham (Associate Editor) is from Columbus, Ohio. She graduated magna cum laude from Otterbein College in 2004, where she studied music and dance. In New York, Allison sings as a member of St. Bartholomew's Choir and St. John the Divine's "Nightwatch" program.